FORD

FORD/MERCURY MID-SIZE CARS
1971-85 REPAIR MANUAL

CHILTON'S

President, Chilton Enterprises	David S. Loewith
Senior Vice President	Ronald A. Hoxter
Publisher & Editor-In-Chief	Kerry A. Freeman, S.A.E.
Executive Editors	Dean F. Morgantini, S.A.E., W. Calvin Settle, Jr., S.A.E.
Managing Editor	Nick D'Andrea
Special Products Manager	Ken Grabowski, A.S.E., S.A.E.
Senior Editors	Jacques Gordon, Michael L. Grady, Debra McCall, Kevin M. G. Maher, Richard J. Rivele, S.A.E., Richard T. Smith, Jim Taylor, Ron Webb
Project Managers	Martin J. Gunther, Will Kessler, A.S.E., Richard Schwartz
Production Manager	Andrea Steiger
Product Systems Manager	Robert Maxey
Director of Manufacturing	Mike D'Imperio
Editor	Gordon Louiscious Tobias, S.A.E.

CHILTON BOOK COMPANY

ONE OF THE **DIVERSIFIED PUBLISHING COMPANIES,**
A PART OF **CAPITAL CITIES/ABC,INC.**

Manufactured in USA
© 1995 Chilton Book Company
Chilton Way, Radnor, PA 19089
ISBN 0-8019-8667-2
Library of Congress Catalog Card No. 94-069443
1234567890 4321098765

Contents

Contents

SAFETY NOTICE

Proper service and repair procedures are vital to the safe, reliable operation of all motor vehicles, as well as the personal safety of those performing repairs. This manual outlines procedures for servicing and repairing vehicles using safe, effective methods. The procedures contain many NOTES, CAUTIONS, and WARNINGS which should be followed along with standard procedures to eliminate the possibility of personal injury or improper service which could damage the vehicle or compromise its safety.

It is important to note that the repair procedures and techniques, tools and parts for servicing motor vehicles, as well as the skill and experience of the individual performing the work vary widely. It is not possible to anticipate all of the conceivable ways or conditions under which vehicles may be serviced, or to provide cautions as to all of the possible hazards that may result. Standard and accepted safety precautions and equipment should be used when handling toxic or flammable fluids, and safety goggles or other protection should be used during cutting, grinding, chiseling, prying, or any other process that can cause material removal or projectiles.

Some procedures require the use of tools specially designed for a specific purpose. Before substituting another tool or procedure, you must be completely satisfied that neither your personal safety, nor the performance of the vehicle will be endangered.

Although information in this manual is based on industry sources and is complete as possible at the time of publication, the possibility exists that some car manufacturers made later changes which could not be included here. While striving for total accuracy, Chilton Book Company cannot assume responsibility for any errors, changes or omissions that may occur in the compilation of this data.

PART NUMBERS

Part numbers listed in this reference are not recommendation by Chilton for any product by brand name. They are references that can be used with interchange manuals and aftermarket supplier catalogs to locate each brand supplier's discrete part number.

SPECIAL TOOLS

Special tools are recommended by the vehicle manufacturer to perform their specific job. Use has been kept to a minimum, but where absolutely necessary, they are referred to in the text by the part number of the tool manufacturer. These tools can be purchased, under the appropriate part number, from your local dealer or regional distributor, or an equivalent tool can be purchased locally from a tool supplier or parts outlet. Before substituting any tool for the one recommended, read the SAFETY NOTICE at the top of this page.

ACKNOWLEDGMENTS

The Chilton Book Company expresses appreciation to Ford Motor Company for their generous assistance.

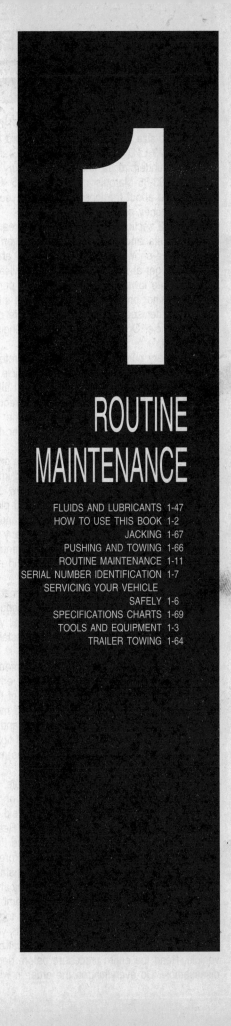

1
ROUTINE MAINTENANCE

HOW TO USE THIS BOOK

Chilton's Total Car Care Manual for 1971-85 Ford and Mercury mid-size vehicles includes the Ford Elite, 1983-85 LTD, 1977-79 LTD II, Ranchero, Torino, Gran Torino and the 1977-85 Thunderbird as well as the Mercury Montego, 1972-85 Cougar, 1983-85 Marquis and the 1980-85 XR-7. It is intended to teach you about the inner workings of your vehicle and save you money on its upkeep.

The first 2 sections will be used most frequently, since they contain maintenance and tune-up information and procedures. Studies have shown that a properly tuned and maintained engine can get at least 10% better gas mileage (which translates into lower operating costs) and periodic maintenance will catch minor problems before they turn into major repair bills. The other sections deal with the more complex systems of your vehicle. Operating systems from engine through brakes are covered.

A secondary purpose of this book is a reference guide for owners who want to understand their vehicle and/or their mechanics better. In this case, no tools at all are required. Knowing just what a particular repair job requires in parts and labor time will allow you to evaluate whether or not you're getting a fair price quote and help decipher itemized bills from a repair shop.

Before attempting any repairs or service on your vehicle, read through the entire procedure outlined in the appropriate sections. This will give you the overall view of what tools and supplies will be required. Read ahead and plan ahead. Each operation should be approached logically and all procedures thoroughly understood before attempting any work. Special tools that may be required can often be rented from local automotive jobbers or places specializing in renting tools and equipment.

All sections contain adjustments, maintenance, removal and installation procedures, and overhaul procedures. When overhaul is not considered practical, we tell you how to remove the failed part and then how to install the new or rebuilt replacement.

Two basic mechanic's rules should be mentioned here. First, whenever the LEFT side of the vehicle or engine is referred to, it is meant to specify the DRIVER'S side of the vehicle. Conversely, the RIGHT side of the vehicle means the PASSENGER'S side. Second, all screws and bolts are removed by turning counterclockwise, and tightened by turning clockwise (left loosen, right tighten,) unless mentioned otherwise.

Safety is always the MOST important rule. Constantly be aware of the dangers involved in working on or around any vehicle and take proper precautions to avoid the risk of personal injury or damage to the vehicle. Read the topic in this section, Servicing Your Vehicle Safely, and the SAFETY NOTICE on the acknowledgment page before attempting any service procedures. Pay attention to the instructions provided. There are 3 common mistakes in mechanical work:

1. Incorrect order of assembly, disassembly or adjustment. When taking something apart or putting it together, doing things in the wrong order usually just costs you extra time; besides, damage can occur to an individual component or the vehicle. Read the entire procedure before beginning disassembly. Do everything in the order in which the instructions say, even if you can't immediately see a reason for it. When you're taking apart something that is very intricate (for example a carburetor), you might want to draw a picture of how it looks when assembled in order to make sure you get everything back in its proper position. We will supply exploded views whenever possible, but sometimes the job requires more attention to detail than an illustration provides. When making adjustments (especially tune-up adjustments), do them in order. One adjustment often affects another.

2. Overtorquing (or undertorquing) nuts and bolts. While it is more common for overtorquing to cause damage, undertorquing can cause a fastener to vibrate loose causing serious damage, especially when dealing with aluminum parts. Pay attention to torque specifications and utilize a torque wrench in assembly. If a torque figure is not available, remember that if you are using the right tool to do the job, you will probably not have to strain yourself to get a fastener tight enough. The pitch of most threads is so slight that the tension you put on the wrench will be multiplied many times in actual force on what you are tightening. A good example of how critical torque is can be seen in the case of spark plug installation, especially where you are putting the plug into an aluminum cylinder head. Too little torque can fail to crush the gasket, causing leakage of combustion gases and consequent overheating of the plug and engine parts. Too much torque can damage the threads or distort the plug, which changes the spark gap at the electrode. Since more and more manufacturers are using aluminum in their engine and chassis parts to save weight, a torque wrench should be in any serious do-it-yourselfers tool box.

There are many commercial chemical products available for ensuring that fasteners won't come loose, even if they are not torqued just right (a very common brand is Loctite®). If you're worried about getting something together tight enough to hold, but loose enough to avoid mechanical damage during assembly, these products may offer substantial insurance. Read the label on the package and make sure the product is compatible with the materials, fluids, etc. involved before choosing one.

3. Crossthreading. This occurs when a part such as a bolt is screwed into a nut or casting at the wrong angle and forced, causing the threads to become damaged. Crossthreading is more likely to occur if access is difficult. It helps to clean and lubricate fasteners, and to start threading the part to be installed, using your fingers. If you encounter resistance, unscrew the part and start over again at a different angle until it can be inserted and turned several times without much effort. Keep in mind that many parts, especially spark plugs, use tapered threads so that gentle turning will automatically bring the part you're threading to the proper angle if you don't force it, or resist a change in angle. Don't put a wrench on the part until it's been turned in a couple of times by hand. If you suddenly encounter resistance and the part has not seated fully, don't force it. Pull it back out and make sure it's clean and threaded properly.

Always take your time and be patient; once you have some experience, working on your vehicle may become an enjoyable hobby.

TOOLS AND EQUIPMENT

▶ **See Figures 1, 2, 3, 4, 5, 6, 7, 8, 9, 10, 11, 12, 13 and 14**

Naturally, without the proper tools and equipment it is impossible to properly service your vehicle. It would be impossible to catalog each tool that you would need to perform each or every operation in this book. It would also be unwise for the amateur to rush out and buy an expensive set of tools on the theory that he may need one or more of them at sometime. The best approach is to proceed slowly, gathering together a good quality set of tools that are used most frequently. Don't be misled by the low cost of bargain tools. It is far better to spend a little more for better quality. Forged wrenches, 6 or 12-point sockets and fine tooth ratchets are by far preferable to their less expensive counterparts. As any good mechanic can tell you, there are few worse experiences than trying to work on any vehicle with bad tools. Your monetary savings will be far outweighed by frustration and mangled knuckles.

Certain tools, plus a basic ability to handle them, are required to get started. A basic mechanics tool set, a torque wrench and a Torx® bits set. Torx® bits are hexlobular drivers which fit both inside and outside on special Torx® head fasteners used in various places on modern vehicles. Begin accumulating those tools that are used most frequently; those associated with routine maintenance and tune-up. In addition to the normal assortment of screwdrivers and pliers you should have the following tools for routine maintenance jobs:

1. SAE/Metric wrenches, sockets and combination open end/box end wrenches in sizes from 1/8 in. (3mm) to 3/4 in. (19mm) and a spark plug socket (13/16 in. or 5/8 in.). If possible, buy various length socket drive extensions. The metric sockets available in the U.S. will all fit the ratchet handles and extensions which you may already have (1/4 in., 3/8 in., and 1/2 in. drive).
2. Jackstands for support.
3. Oil filter wrench.
4. Oil filter spout for pouring oil.
5. Grease gun for chassis lubrication.
6. Hydrometer for checking the battery.
7. A container for draining oil.
8. Many rags (paper or cloth) for wiping up the inevitable mess.

In addition to the above items there are several others that are not absolutely necessary, but are handy to have around. These include a hydraulic floor jack, oil-dry, a transmission funnel and the usual supply of lubricants, antifreeze and fluids. This is a basic list for routine maintenance, but only your personal needs and desires can accurately determine your list of necessary tools.

The second list of tools is for tune-ups. While the tools involved here are slightly more sophisticated, they need not be outrageously expensive. There are several inexpensive tach/dwell meters on the market that are every bit as good for the average mechanic as an expensive professional model. Just be sure that it works on 4, 6 and 8 cylinder engines. A basic list of tune-up equipment could include:

9. Tach/dwell meter.
10. Spark plug wrench.
11. Timing light. A DC light that works from the vehicle's battery is best, although an AC light that plugs into 110V house current will suffice at some sacrifice in brightness.
12. Wire spark plug gauge/adjusting tools.

Here again, be guided by your own needs. While not absolutely necessary, an ohmmeter can be useful in determining whether or not a spark plug wire is within its resistance specification

In addition to these basic tools, there are several other tools and gauges you may find useful. These include:

13. A compression gauge. The screw-in type is slower to use, but eliminates the possibility of a faulty reading due to escaping pressure.
14. A manifold vacuum gauge.
15. A test light.
16. An induction meter. This is used for determining whether or not there is current in a wire. These are handy for use if a wire is broken somewhere in a wiring harness.

As a final note, you will probably find a torque wrench necessary for all but the most basic work. The beam type models are perfectly adequate, although click (breakaway) types are more precise. The breakaway torque wrenches are more expensive. Keep in mind all torque wrenches should be recalibrated periodically.

The torque specification for each fastener will be given in the procedure in any case that a specific torque value is required. If no torque specifications are given, use the following values as a guide, based upon fastener size:

Bolts marked 6T
6mm bolt/nut — 5-7 ft. lbs. (7-9 Nm)
8mm bolt/nut — 12-17 ft. lbs. (16-23 Nm)
10mm bolt/nut — 23-34 ft. lbs. (31-46 Nm)
12mm bolt/nut — 41-59 ft. lbs. (55-66 Nm)
14mm bolt/nut — 56-76 ft. lbs. (76-103 Nm)

Bolts marked 8T
6mm bolt/nut — 6-9 ft. lbs. (8-12 Nm)
8mm bolt/nut — 13-20 ft. lbs. (18-27 Nm)
10mm bolt/nut — 27-40 ft. lbs. (37-54 Nm)
12mm bolt/nut — 46-69 ft. lbs. (62-93 Nm)
14mm bolt/nut — 75-101 ft. lbs. (102-137 Nm)

Special Tools

Normally, the use of special factory tools is avoided for repair procedures, since these are not readily available for the do-it-yourself mechanic. When it is possible to perform the job with more commonly available tools, it will be pointed out. However, occasionally a special tool was designed to perform a specific function and should be used. Before substituting another tool, you should be convinced that neither your safety nor the performance of the vehicle will be compromised. Where possible, an illustration of the special tool will be provided so that an equivalent tool may be used.

Some special tools are available commercially from major tool manufacturers. Others can be purchased through your Ford/Mercury dealer or local parts supplier.

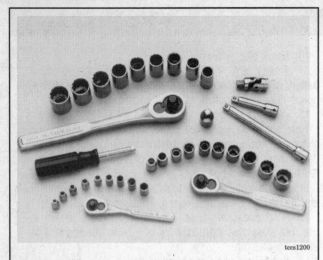

Fig. 1 All but the most basic procedures will require an assortment of ratchets and sockets

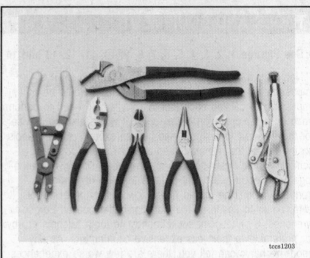

Fig. 4 An assortment of pliers will be handy, especially for old rusted parts and stripped bolt heads.

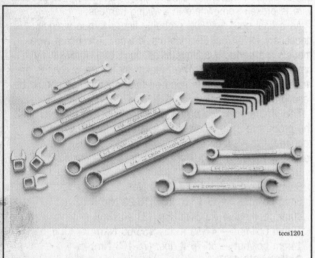

Fig. 2 In addition to ratchets, a good set of wrenches and hex keys will be necessary

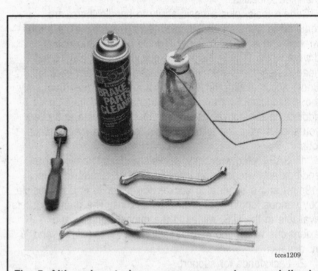

Fig. 5 Although not always necessary, using specialized brake tools will save time.

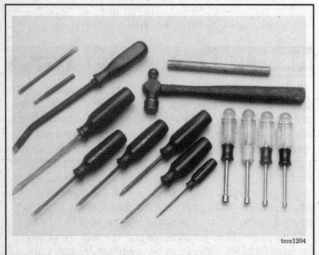

Fig. 3 Various screwdrivers, a hammer, chisels and prytools are necessary to have in your toolbox

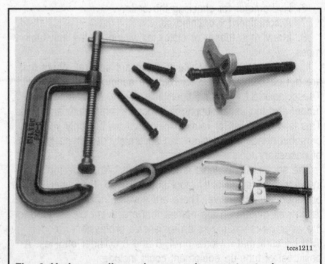

Fig. 6 Various pullers, clamps and separator tools are useful for the repair of many components.

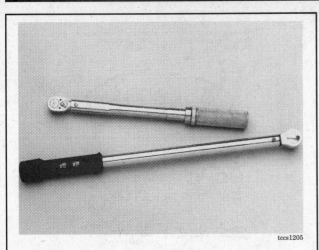

Fig. 7 Many repairs will require the use of a torque wrench to assure the components are properly tightened.

Fig. 8 A few inexpensive lubrication tools will make regular service easier.

Fig. 9 A hydraulic floor jack and a set of jackstands are essential for safely lifting and supporting the vehicle.

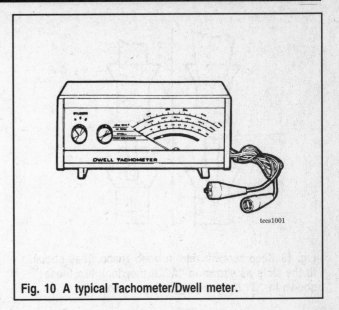

Fig. 10 A typical Tachometer/Dwell meter.

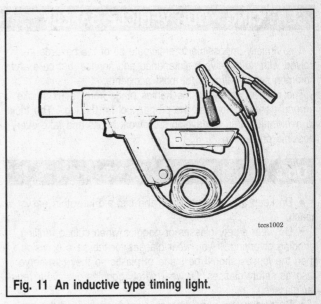

Fig. 11 An inductive type timing light.

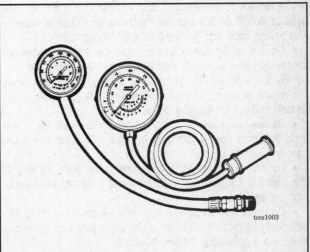

Fig. 12 A compression gauge and a combination vacuum/pressure test gauge.

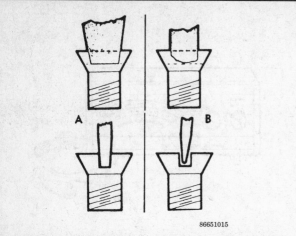

Fig. 13 Keep screwdrivers in good shape. They should fit the slots as shown in "A". If they look like those shown in "B" they need grinding or replacing

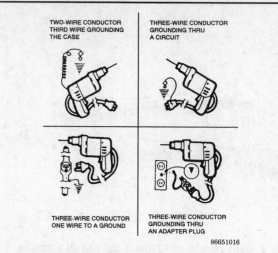

Fig. 14 When using electric tools, make sure they are properly grounded

SERVICING YOUR VEHICLE SAFELY

It is virtually impossible to anticipate all of the hazards involved with automotive maintenance and service, but care and common sense will prevent most accidents.

The rules of safety for mechanics range from "don't smoke around gasoline" to "use the proper tool for the job." The trick to avoid injuries is to develop safe work habits and take every possible precaution.

Do's

• Do keep a fire extinguisher and first aid kit within easy reach.

• Do wear safety glasses or goggles when cutting, drilling, grinding or prying. If you wear glasses for the sake of vision, then the lenses should be made of plastic so they can serve also as safety glasses. Or wear safety goggles over your regular glasses.

• Do shield your eyes whenever you work around the battery. Batteries contain sulfuric acid. In case of contact with the eyes or skin, flush the area with water or a mixture of water and baking soda and get medical attention immediately.

• Do use safety stands for any under-car service. Jacks are for raising vehicles; safety stands are for making sure the vehicle stays raised until you want it to come down. Whenever the vehicle is raised, block the wheels remaining on the ground and set the parking brake.

• Do use adequate ventilation when working with any chemicals. Asbestos dust resulting from brake lining wear can cause cancer.

• Do disconnect the negative battery cable when working on the electrical system. The ignition system produces extremely high voltage.

• Do follow manufacturer's directions whenever working with potentially hazardous materials. Both brake fluid and some antifreeze are poisonous if taken internally.

• Do properly maintain your tools. Loose hammerheads, mushroomed punches and chisels, frayed or poorly grounded electrical cords, excessively worn screwdrivers, spread wrenches (open end) and cracked sockets can cause accidents.

• Do use the proper size and type of tool for the job being performed.

• Do when possible, pull on a wrench handle rather than push on it, and adjust your stance to prevent a fall.

• Do be sure that adjustable wrenches are tightly adjusted on the nut or bolt and pulled so that the face is on the side of the fixed jaw.

• Do select a wrench or socket that fits the nut or bolt. The wrench or socket should sit straight, not cocked.

• Do strike squarely with a hammer to avoid glancing blows.

• Do set the parking brake and block the drive wheels if the procedure requires that the engine is running.

Don'ts

• Don't run an engine in a garage or anywhere else without proper ventilation EVER! Carbon monoxide is poisonous. It is absorbed by the body 400 times faster than oxygen. It takes a long time to leave the body and you can build up a deadly supply of it in you system by simply breathing in a little every day. You may not realize you are slowly poisoning yourself. Always use power vents, windows, fans or open the garage doors.

• Don't work around moving parts while wearing a necktie or other loose clothing. Short sleeves are much safer than long, loose sleeves. Hard-toed shoes with neoprene soles protect your toes and give a better grip on slippery surfaces. Jewelry such as watches, fancy belt buckles, beads or body adornment of any kind is not safe to wear when working around a car. Long hair should be kept under a hat or cap.

• Don't use pockets as toolboxes. A fall or bump can drive a screwdriver deep into you body. Even a wiping cloth hanging from the back pocket can wrap around a spinning shaft or fan.

• Don't smoke when working around gasoline, cleaning solvent or other flammable material.

• Don't smoke when working around the battery. When the battery is being charged, it gives off explosive hydrogen gas.

• Don't use gasoline to wash your hands. There are many excellent soaps available.

• Don't service the air conditioning system unless you are equipped with the necessary tools, training and certification.

The refrigerants, R-12, if available, are extremely cold and when exposed to the air, will instantly freeze any surface they come in contact with, including eyes. Although the refrigerant is normally nontoxic, R-12 becomes a deadly poisonous gas in the presence of an open flame. One good whiff of the vapors from burning refrigerant can be fatal.

SERIAL NUMBER IDENTIFICATION

Vehicle

1971-80 MODELS

▶ See Figures 15 and 16

The official vehicle identification number for title and registration purposes is an eleven digit number stamped on a metal tag, which is fastened to the top of the instrument panel. The tag is located on the driver's side, visible through the windshield. The first digit in the vehicle identification number is the model year of the car (0-1970, 4-1974, etc.). The second digit is the assembly plant code for the plant in which the vehicle was built. the third and fourth digits are the body serial code designations (2-dr sedan, 4-dr sedan). The fifth digit is the engine code which identifies the type of engine originally installed in the vehicle (see the Engine Codes chart). The last six digits are the consecutive unit numbers which start at 100,001 for the first car of a model year built at each assembly plant.

1981-85 MODELS

▶ See Figure 17

Beginning in 1981, the serial number contained seventeen digits or letters. The first three give the world manufacturer code; the fourth is the type of restraint system; the fifth will remain the letter P the sixth and seventh is the car line, series and body type; the eighth is the engine type; the ninth is a

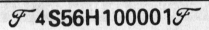

F 4S56H100001F
(VEHICLE IDENTIFICATION NUMBER)
Vehicle identification plate, 1972 and later

86671001

Fig. 16 Vehicle identification plate — 1972-80

check digit; the tenth is the model year; the eleventh is the assembly plant; the remaining number are the production sequence.

Vehicle Certification Label

▶ See Figures 18, 19, 20 and 21

The vehicle certification label is attached to the left door lock pillar on 2-door models and on the rear face of the driver's door on 4-door models. The top half of the label contains the name of the vehicle manufacturer, date of manufacture and the

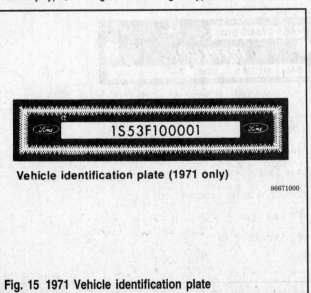

1S53F100001

Vehicle identification plate (1971 only)

86671000

Fig. 15 1971 Vehicle identification plate

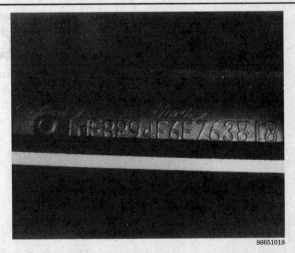

86651018

Fig. 17 The Vehicle Identification Number (VIN) plate is visible through the windshield

manufacturer's certification statement. On 1973 and later models, the top half of the label also contains the gross vehicle weight rating and the front and rear gross vehicle axle ratings. The gross vehicle weight rating is useful in determining the load carrying capacity of your car. Merely subtract the curb weight from the posted gross weight and what is left over is how much you can haul around. The bottom half of the vehicle certification label contains the vehicle identification number (as previously described), the body type code, the exterior pant color code, the interior trim color and material code, the rear axle code, the transmission code (see Transmission Codes chart) and the district and special order codes.

The vehicle certification label is constructed of special material to guard against its alteration. If it is tampered with or removed, it will be destroyed or the word VOID will appear.

Engine Identification Number

The engine identification number is found on the vehicle identification plate which is attached to the top left (driver's)

86671500

Fig. 18 The vehicle certification label can be found on the door pillar or door, depending on the model

side of the instrument panel. On the 1971-80 the fifth digit of the vehicle identification number represents the engine identification code. On the 1981-85 models the eighth digit of the vehicle identification number represents the engine identification code.

Transmission

The transmission identification code can be found on the vehicle identification number, and on the vehicle certification label (located on the driver's side door) on the earlier models. On 1971-76 models, the 12th digit in the vehicle certification label is the transmission code. On 1977-78 models, the 10th digit in the vehicle identification number is the transmission code. On 1979 models, the 13th digit in the vehicle identification number is the transmission code. On 1980 models, the 15th digit in the vehicle identification number is the transmission code. On 1981-85 models, the 12th digit in the vehicle identification number is the transmission code.

Rear Drive Axle Identification

A metal tag stamped with the model designation and gear ratio is usually secured to one of the rear cover-to-housing bolts. The axle identification code number can also be found on the vehicle identification number or the vehicle certification label, depending on the year and model. On 1971-77 vehicles, the 11th digit in the vehicle identification number will usually be the rear axle code. On some of the models, the number may be located on the vehicle certification label. On 1977-78 vehicles, the 11th digit in the vehicle identification number will be the rear axle code. On 1979 vehicles, the 12th digit in the vehicle identification number will be the rear axle code. On 1980 vehicles, the 14th digit in the vehicle identification number will be the rear axle code. On 1981-85 vehicles, the 11th digit in the vehicle identification number will be the rear axle code.

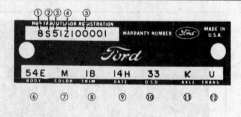

1	MODEL YEAR CODE	7	COLOR CODE
2	ASSEMBLY PLANT CODE	8	TRIM CODE
3	BODY SERIAL CODE	9	DATE CODE
4	ENGINE CODE	10	DISTRICT OR DISTRICT AND SPEC. EQUIP. CODE
5	CONSECUTIVE UNIT NO.	11	REAR AXLE CODE
6	BODY TYPE CODE	12	TRANSMISSION CODE

8667119a

Fig. 19 Vehicle certification label — 1971-72 models

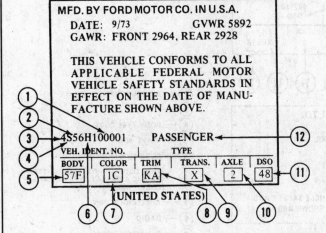

ℱ 4S56H100001ℱ

(VEHICLE IDENTIFICATION NUMBER)

MFD. BY FORD MOTOR CO. IN U.S.A.

DATE: 9/73   GVWR 5892
GAWR: FRONT 2964, REAR 2928

THIS VEHICLE CONFORMS TO ALL
APPLICABLE FEDERAL MOTOR
VEHICLE SAFETY STANDARDS IN
EFFECT ON THE DATE OF MANU-
FACTURE SHOWN ABOVE.

4S56H100001   PASSENGER
VEH. IDENT. NO.   TYPE

BODY	COLOR	TRIM	TRANS.	AXLE	DSO
57F	1C	KA	X	2	48

(UNITED STATES)

① CONSECUTIVE UNIT NO.
② BODY SERIAL CODE
③ MODEL YEAR CODE
④ ASSEMBLY PLANT CODE
⑤ ENGINE CODE
⑥ BODY TYPE CODE
⑦ COLOR CODE
⑧ VEHICLE TYPE
⑨ DISTRICT – SPECIAL EQUIPMENT
⑩ REAR AXLE CODE
⑪ TRANSMISSION CODE
⑫ TRIM CODE

MFD. BY FORD MOTOR CO. IN U.S.A.

DATE: 09/73   GVWR 5892
GAWR: FRONT 2964   REAR 2928

THIS VEHICLE MANUFACTURED FOR
EXPORT ONLY ON DATE
SHOWN ABOVE.

4 S 56 H 100002   PASSENGER
VEH. IDENT. NO.   TYPE

BODY	COLOR	TRIM	TRANS.	AXLE	DSO
57F	1C	DA	X	2	90

(EXPORT)

MFD. BY FORD MOTOR CO.
OF CANADA LTD.

THIS VEHICLE CONFORMS TO
ALL APPLICABLE FEDERAL MOTOR
VEHICLE SAFETY STANDARDS IN
EFFECT ON THE DATE OF
MANUFACTURE SHOWN ABOVE

VEH. IDENT. NO. | TYPE

BODY	COLOR	TRIM	TRANS.	AXLE	DSO

MADE IN CANADA

(CANADA)

8667119b

Fig. 20 Vehicle certification label — 1973-80 models

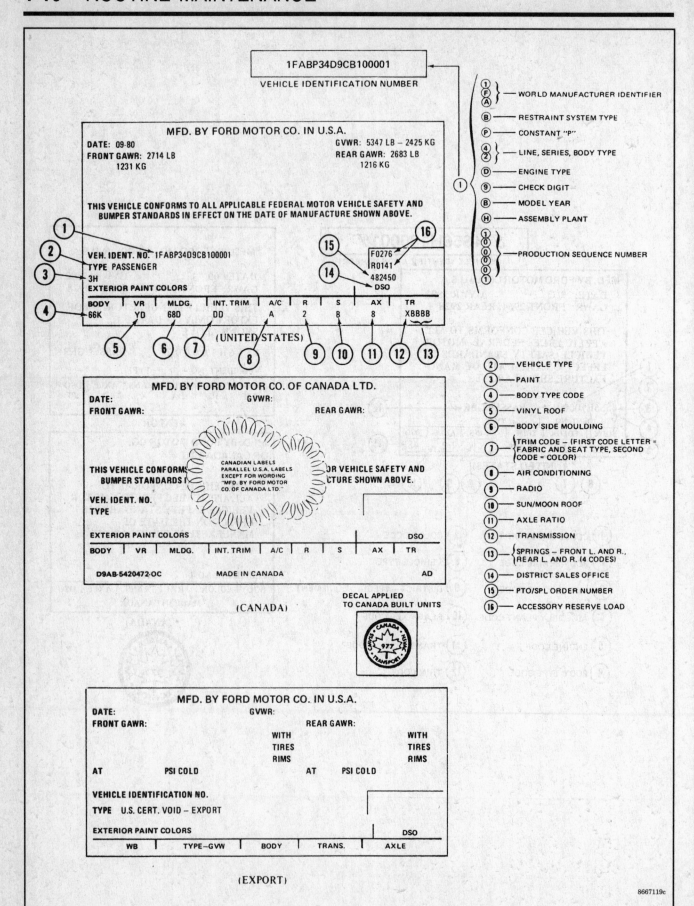

Fig. 21 Vehicle certification label — 1981-85 models

ROUTINE MAINTENANCE

▶ **See Figures 22, 23, 24 and 25**

Proper maintenance is the key to long and trouble-free vehicle life. As a conscientious owner and driver, set aside a Saturday morning, say once a month, to check or replace items which could cause major problems later. Keep your own personal log to jot down which services you performed, how much the parts cost you, the date, and the exact odometer reading at the time. Keep all receipts for such items as engine oil and filters, so that they may be referred to in case of

related problems or to determine operating expenses. As a do-it-yourselfer, these receipts are the only proof you have that the required maintenance was performed. In the event of a warranty problem, these receipts will be invaluable.

The literature provided with your vehicle when it was originally delivered includes the factory recommended maintenance schedule. If you no longer have this literature, replacement copies are usually available from the dealer. A maintenance schedule is provided later in this section, in case you do not have the factory literature.

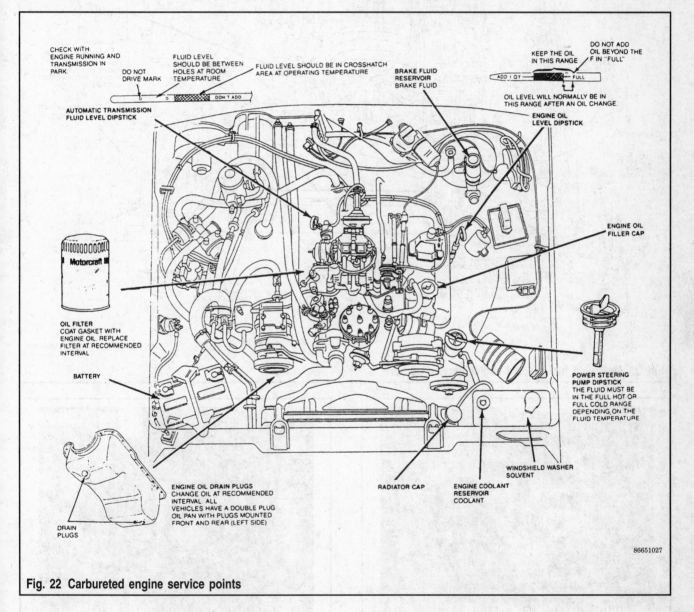

Fig. 22 Carbureted engine service points

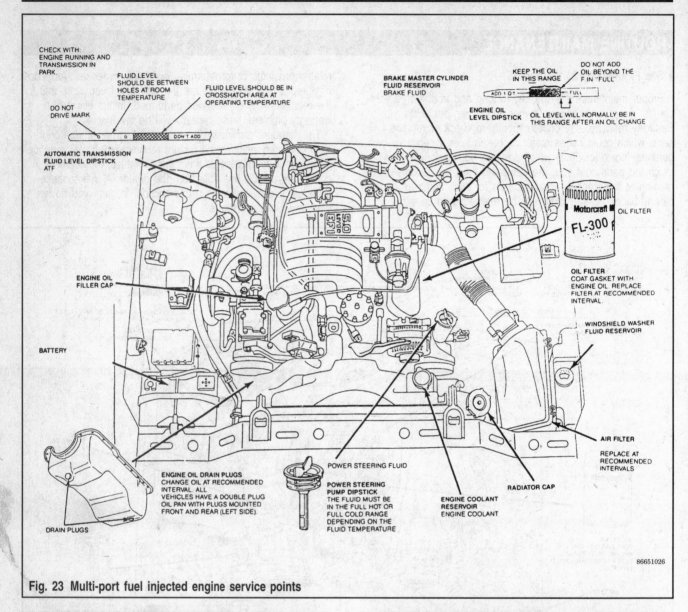

CHECK WITH:
ENGINE RUNNING AND
TRANSMISSION IN
PARK.

FLUID LEVEL
SHOULD BE BETWEEN
HOLES AT ROOM
TEMPERATURE

FLUID LEVEL SHOULD BE IN
CROSSHATCH AREA AT
OPERATING TEMPERATURE

DO NOT
DRIVE MARK

BRAKE MASTER CYLINDER
FLUID RESERVOIR
BRAKE FLUID

KEEP THE OIL
IN THIS RANGE

DO NOT ADD
OIL BEYOND THE
F IN "FULL"

ENGINE OIL
LEVEL DIPSTICK

OIL LEVEL WILL NORMALLY BE IN
THIS RANGE AFTER AN OIL CHANGE

AUTOMATIC TRANSMISSION
FLUID LEVEL DIPSTICK
ATF

Motorcraft OIL FILTER
FL-300

OIL FILTER
COAT GASKET WITH
ENGINE OIL. REPLACE
FILTER AT RECOMMENDED
INTERVAL.

ENGINE OIL
FILLER CAP

WINDSHIELD WASHER
FLUID RESERVOIR

BATTERY

AIR FILTER

REPLACE AT
RECOMMENDED
INTERVALS

ENGINE OIL DRAIN PLUGS
CHANGE OIL AT RECOMMENDED
INTERVAL. ALL
VEHICLES HAVE A DOUBLE PLUG
OIL PAN WITH PLUGS MOUNTED
FRONT AND REAR (LEFT SIDE).

POWER STEERING FLUID

POWER STEERING
PUMP DIPSTICK
THE FLUID MUST BE
IN THE FULL HOT OR
FULL COLD RANGE
DEPENDING ON THE
FLUID TEMPERATURE

ENGINE COOLANT
RESERVOIR
ENGINE COOLANT

RADIATOR CAP

DRAIN PLUGS

86651026

Fig. 23 Multi-port fuel injected engine service points

86651202

Fig. 24 Don't forget to properly mark any harnesses or hoses before disconnecting them

86671501

Fig. 25 Whenever you are underneath your car, always look for leaks or broken parts

Air Cleaner

All engines are equipped with a dry type, replaceable air filter element. The element should be replaced at the recommended intervals shown on the Maintenance Interval Chart. If your vehicle is operated under severely dusty conditions or severe operating conditions, more frequent changes are necessary. Inspect the element at least twice a year. Early spring and at the beginning of fall are good times for the inspection. Remove the element and check for holes in the filter. Check the cleaner housing for signs of dirt or dust that has leaked through the filter element. Place a light on the inside of the element and look through the filter at the light. If no glow of light can be seen through the element material, replace the filter. If holes in the filter are apparent or signs of dirt leakage through the filter are noticed, replace the filter.

➡**When servicing the air filter element make sure that the air cleaner cover is properly installed.**

REMOVAL & INSTALLATION

Air Filter Element
▶ **See Figures 26, 27, 28, 29, 30, 31 and 32**

1. Identify and tag all hoses at the assembly. Disconnect all hoses, ducts and vacuum tubes from the air cleaner assembly.

2. Remove the top cover wing nut or clips and grommet (if equipped). Remove the side bracket retaining bolts (if equipped).

3. Remove the cover and the element, wipe clean all inside surfaces of the air cleaner housing and cover.

4. If necessary, remove the air cleaner assembly from the top of the carburetor or intake assembly.

5. Check the condition of the mounting gasket (cleaner base to carburetor). Replace the mounting gasket if it is worn or broken.

To install:

6. Install a new mounting gasket if needed. Place and position the new air filter in the housing.

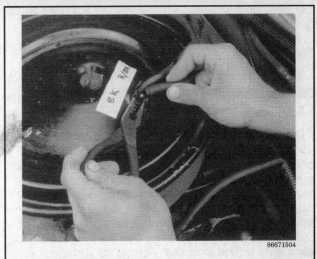
Fig. 27 If equipped with any vacuum hose attached to the cover, tag and remove them

Fig. 28 Remove the air filter element from the housing

Fig. 26 Remove the wing nut, or clips if equipped

Fig. 29 Lift the air cleaner assembly away from the carburetor to disconnect the vacuum lines from the clip

7. Position the cleaner assembly, element and cover on the carburetor or intake assembly.

8. Reconnect all hoses, duct and vacuum hoses removed. Tighten the wing nut finger-tight or secure the clips, if equipped.

Crankcase Ventilation Filter

▶ See Figures 33, 34 and 35

Replace or inspect the air cleaner mounted crankcase ventilation filter (on models equipped) at the same time the air cleaner filter element is serviced. To replace the filter, simply remove the air cleaner top cover and pull the filter from its housing. Push a new filter into the housing and install the air cleaner cover. If the filter and plastic holder need replacement, remove the clip securing the breather hose to the air cleaner housing, and remove the assembly from the air cleaner. Installation is the reverse of removal. Refer to the illustrations as necessary.

Fuel Filter

REMOVAL & INSTALLATION

❈❈CAUTION

Never smoke when working around or near gasoline! Make sure that there is no igniting source near your work area!

Carbureted Engines

EXCEPT VARIABLE VENTURI CARBURETORS

▶ See Figures 36 and 37

1. Disconnect the negative battery cable.
2. Remove the air cleaner assembly.
3. Locate the filter in the engine compartment. If connected to a rubber hose, loosen the hose clamps with a pair of pliers, then slide the clamp down the hose, away from the filter.

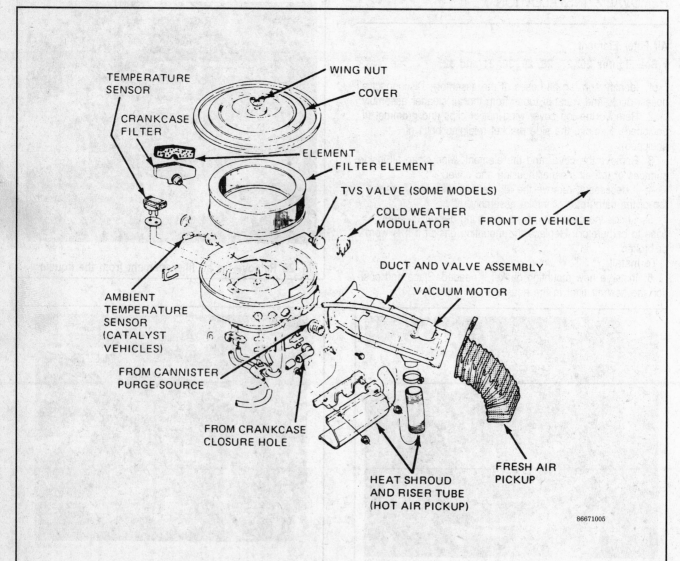

Fig. 30 Carbureted air cleaner assembly — 1971-85

TEMPERATURE SENSOR
CRANKCASE FILTER
WING NUT
COVER
ELEMENT
FILTER ELEMENT
TVS VALVE (SOME MODELS)
COLD WEATHER MODULATOR
FRONT OF VEHICLE
AMBIENT TEMPERATURE SENSOR (CATALYST VEHICLES)
DUCT AND VALVE ASSEMBLY
VACUUM MOTOR
FROM CANNISTER PURGE SOURCE
FROM CRANKCASE CLOSURE HOLE
HEAT SHROUD AND RISER TUBE (HOT AIR PICKUP)
FRESH AIR PICKUP

86671005

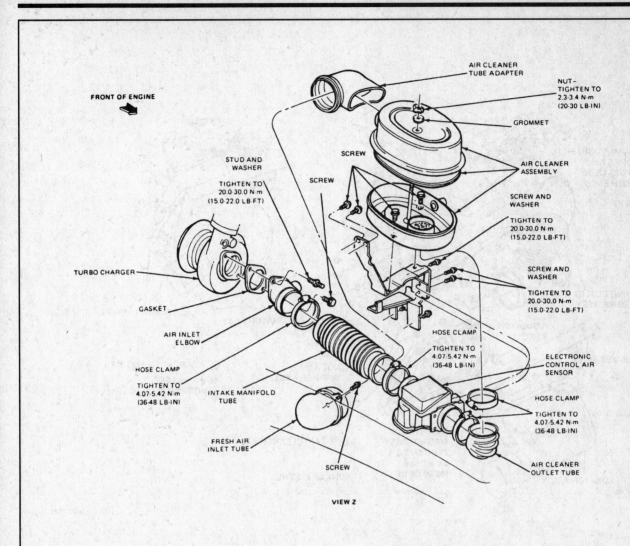

FRONT OF ENGINE

AIR CLEANER TUBE ADAPTER

NUT– TIGHTEN TO 2.3-3.4 N·m (20-30 LB·IN)

GROMMET

SCREW

AIR CLEANER ASSEMBLY

STUD AND WASHER TIGHTEN TO 20.0-30.0 N·m (15.0-22.0 LB·FT)

SCREW

SCREW AND WASHER TIGHTEN TO 20.0-30.0 N·m (15.0-22.0 LB·FT)

TURBO CHARGER

SCREW AND WASHER TIGHTEN TO 20.0-30.0 N·m (15.0-22.0 LB·FT)

GASKET

AIR INLET ELBOW

HOSE CLAMP TIGHTEN TO 4.07-5.42 N·m (36-48 LB·IN)

ELECTRONIC CONTROL AIR SENSOR

HOSE CLAMP TIGHTEN TO 4.07-5.42 N·m (36-48 LB·IN)

INTAKE MANIFOLD TUBE

HOSE CLAMP TIGHTEN TO 4.07-5.42 N·m (36-48 LB·IN)

FRESH AIR INLET TUBE

SCREW

AIR CLEANER OUTLET TUBE

VIEW Z

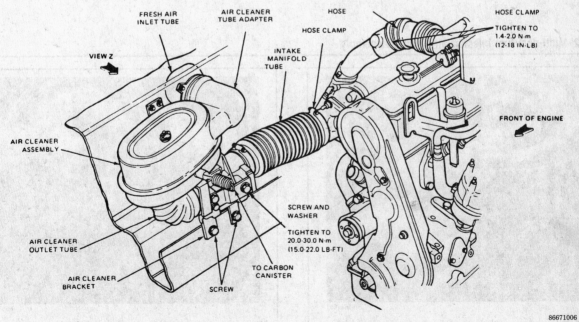

FRESH AIR INLET TUBE

AIR CLEANER TUBE ADAPTER

HOSE

HOSE CLAMP

HOSE CLAMP TIGHTEN TO 1.4-2.0 N·m (12-18 IN·LB)

VIEW Z

INTAKE MANIFOLD TUBE

FRONT OF ENGINE

AIR CLEANER ASSEMBLY

AIR CLEANER OUTLET TUBE

AIR CLEANER BRACKET

SCREW

SCREW AND WASHER TIGHTEN TO 20.0-30.0 N·m (15.0-22.0 LB·FT)

TO CARBON CANISTER

86671006

Fig. 31 Air cleaner assembly — 4-cylinder turbo models

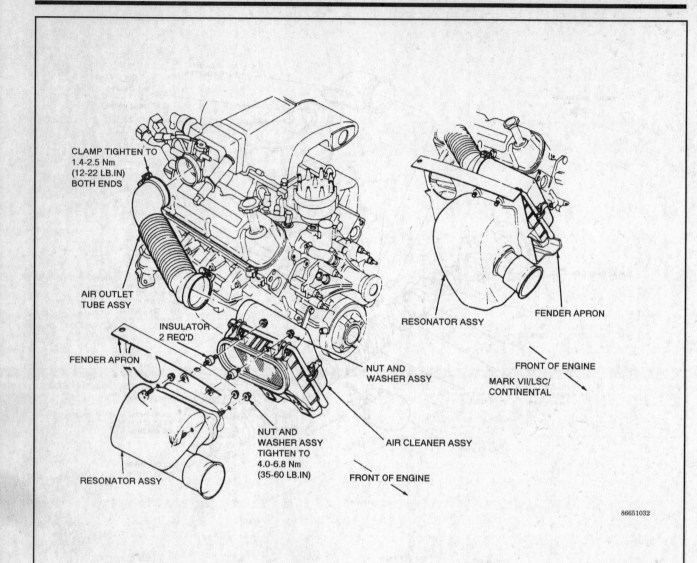

CLAMP TIGHTEN TO
1.4-2.5 Nm
(12-22 LB.IN)
BOTH ENDS

AIR OUTLET
TUBE ASSY

INSULATOR
2 REQ'D

FENDER APRON

RESONATOR ASSY

NUT AND
WASHER ASSY
TIGHTEN TO
4.0-6.8 Nm
(35-60 LB.IN)

NUT AND
WASHER ASSY

AIR CLEANER ASSY

FRONT OF ENGINE

RESONATOR ASSY

FENDER APRON

FRONT OF ENGINE

MARK VII/LSC/
CONTINENTAL

86651032

Fig. 32 Multi-port fuel injected air cleaner assembly

86651207

Fig. 33 Remove the clip securing the breather hose to the air cleaner housing

86651208

Fig. 34 The ventilation filter can now be removed from the air cleaner housing

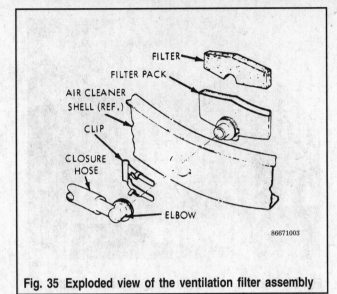

Fig. 35 Exploded view of the ventilation filter assembly

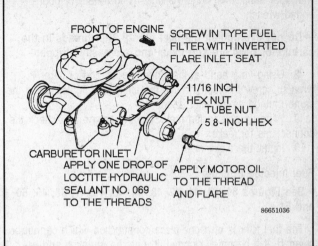

Fig. 36 Filter used on carburetors equipped with a steel fuel line

4. If the filter is connected to a steel line, position an appropriate open-ended or flare type wrench on the filter hex nut to hold the filter in position. Now, remove the steel line from the filter using another open-ended or flare wrench.

5. Use an appropriate flare type or open-ended wrench to remove the filter from the carburetor.

To install:

6. If equipped with a rubber hose, install the new length of hose to the fuel line. Use a new clamp to secure it.

7. Place one drop of Loctite® Hydraulic Sealant No. 069, or equivalent, on the filter threads.

8. Insert the filter in the mounting hole, and turn the filter by hand. When hand-tight, use a suitable wrench to tighten it completely.

9. If installing a rubber hose, slide the hose onto the filter and secure with a new clamp.

10. If equipped with a steel line, apply a thin layer of motor oil to the threads of the steel line. Insert the line into the filter and tighten fitting by hand. When hand-tight, use a flare or open-ended wrench and tighten until just snug.

11. Install the air cleaner.

12. Connect the negative battery cable.

13. Start the engine and check for fuel leaks.

VARIABLE VENTURI CARBURETORS

▶ See Figure 38

→ Model 2700 VV and 7200 VV carburetors use a replaceable filter located behind the carburetor inlet fitting.

✳✳CAUTION

The engine should be cool before beginning this procedure. Otherwise your hands may get burned while attempting the removal and installation.

1. Disconnect the negative battery cable.
2. Remove the air cleaner assembly.

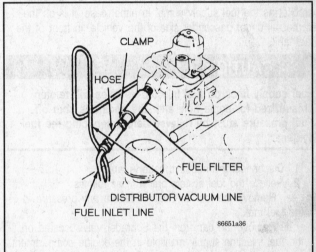

Fig. 37 Filter used on carburetors equipped with a length of rubber hose between the fuel line and filter

3. Wrap a rag around the fitting, and use a open-ended or flare wrench on the inlet fitting to unscrew the fuel line from the inlet fitting.

✳✳CAUTION

Because of pressure build up in the fuel line, it is possible for gasoline to spray out when unscrewing the line! Wear protective glasses to protect your eyes, and loosen the fitting slowly!

4. Move the fuel line out of the way and unscrew the inlet fitting from the carburetor.

5. Pull out the filter. The spring behind the filter may come out with it.

To install:

6. Install the spring and a new filter. Some kits come with a new spring, use it.

7. Coat the threads of the inlet fitting with a non-hardening, gasoline-proof sealer, then screw it into place by hand. Tighten

with your hand, then tighten snugly using a flare or open-ended wrench.

➡**Do not overtighten the inlet fitting! The threads in the carburetor bowl are soft metal and are easily stripped!**

8. Using your hand at first, then a open-end or flare wrench, screw the fuel line into the fitting and tighten using the same method as the inlet fitting.

9. Wipe up any spilled fuel. Start the engine and check the connections for leaks.

10. Install the air cleaner.

Fuel Injected Engines

▶ **See Figures 39, 40, 41, 42, 43, 44, 45, 46, 47, 48, 49, 50 and 51**

The fuel filter is of a one-piece construction which cannot be cleaned. If it becomes clogged, it must be removed and replaced. When replacing the fuel filter use the filter type which is specified for the engine being serviced.

The inline filter can be mounted by itself, or on the same bracket as the fuel supply pump. In either case, it is on the frame rail under passenger side of the vehicle, in front of the fuel tank.

✳✳CAUTION

Fuel supply lines on fuel injected vehicles will remain pressurized for some time after the engine is shut off. Fuel pressure must be relieved before servicing the fuel system.

1. Disconnect the negative battery cable.
2. Relieve the fuel system pressure as follows:
   a. Remove the fuel tank cap to relieve any pressure in the fuel tank.
   b. Remove the cap from the Schrader valve located on the fuel injection supply manifold in the engine compartment.
   c. Attach fuel pressure gauge T80L-9974-A or equivalent, to the Schrader valve and drain the fuel through the drain tube into a suitable container.

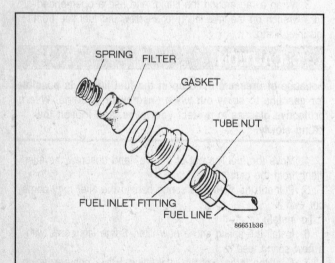

Fig. 38 Inline fuel filter for 2700 and 7200 VV type carburetors

86651210

Fig. 39 Whenever you see a warning label, read it

d. After the fuel system pressure is relieved, remove the fuel pressure gauge and install the cap on the Schrader valve.

3. Raise and safely support the vehicle on jackstands.
4. Disconnect the fittings from both ends of the fuel filter as follows:
   a. Inspect the visible portion of the fitting for dirt accumulation. Clean the fitting before disassembly.
   b. Some adhesion between the seals in the fitting and the filter will occur with time. To separate, twist the fitting on the filter, then push and pull the fitting until it moves freely on the filter.
   c. Remove the hairpin clip from the fitting by first bending and breaking the shipping tab. Next, spread the 2 clip legs by hand about ⅛ in. (3.1mm) each to disengage the body, then push the legs into the fitting. Lightly pull the triangular end of the clip and work it clear of the filter and fitting.

➡**Do not use hand tools to complete this operation. Damage to the fittings may result.**

d. Grasp the fitting and pull in an axial direction to remove the fitting from the filter. Be careful on 90° elbow connectors, as excessive side loading could break the connector body.

e. After disassembly, inspect the inside of the fitting for any internal parts such as O-rings and/or spacers that may have been dislodged from the fitting. Replace any damaged connector(s).

5. If equipped, remove the filter retainer bolts and remove the filter and retainer from the mounting bracket. Remove the filter from the retainer. Note that the direction of the flow arrow on the fuel filter. Remove the rubber insulator rings, if installed. Inspect the rings for cracks or wear, and replace if needed.

To install:

6. Install the fuel filter with the flow arrow facing the proper direction as before, then tighten the filter retaining clamp(s).

7. If the original filter was equipped with rubber insulator rings, install the rubber insulator rings on the new filter. Install the filter into the retainer with the flow arrow pointing in the correct direction. Install the retainer on the bracket and tighten the mounting bolts to 27-44 inch lbs. (3-5 Nm).

Fig. 40 Underneath the passenger side; fuel pump and filter are visible — but some models have only a filter in this location as the pump is in the tank.

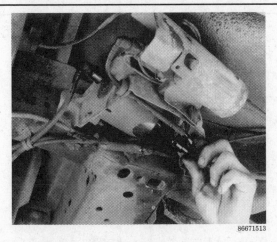

Fig. 41 Unfasten the fuel line from the fuel tank to the filter by removing the hairpin clip. Place a container under the filter to capture any excess fuel spillage

Fig. 42 An example of a hairpin clip

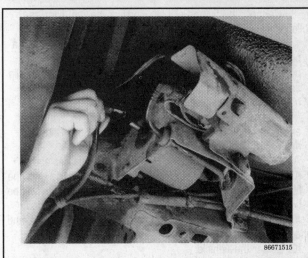

Fig. 43 Remove the fuel line from the fuel filter to the engine using the same method

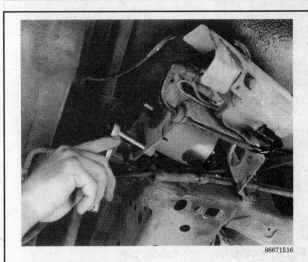

Fig. 44 Loosen and remove the bolts securing the fuel filter mounting bracket

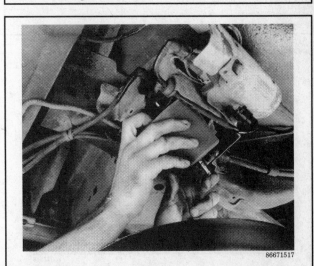

Fig. 45 Remove the fuel filter and bracket from the vehicle. Capture any remaining fuel in a container

8. Connect the fittings at both ends of the fuel filter as follows:

a. Install a new connector if damage was found. Insert a new clip into any 2 adjacent openings with the triangular portion pointing away from the fitting opening. Install the clip until the legs of the clip are locked on the outside of the body. Piloting with an index finger is necessary.

b. Before installing the fitting on the filter, wipe the filter end with a clean cloth. Inspect the inside of the fitting to make sure it is free of dirt and/or obstructions.

c. Apply a light coating of engine oil to the filter end. Align the fitting and filter axially and push the fitting onto the filter end. When the fitting is engaged, a definite click will be heard. Pull on the fitting to make sure it is fully engaged.

9. Connect the negative battery cable. Start the engine and check for fuel leaks.

10. Lower the vehicle.

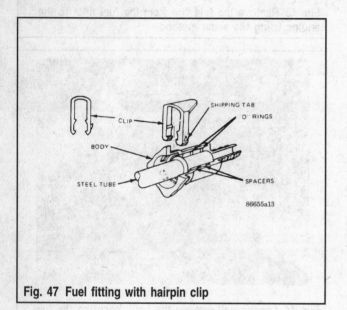

Fig. 47 Fuel fitting with hairpin clip

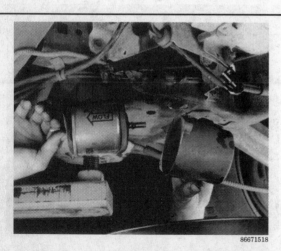

Fig. 46 Remove the filter from the bracket noting the directional flow arrow on the filter — be sure to install the new filter facing the same way

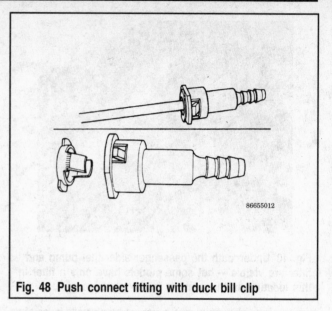

Fig. 48 Push connect fitting with duck bill clip

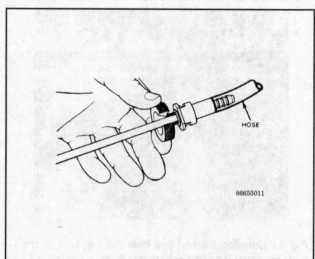

Fig. 49 Use a disassembly tool to remove the push connect fuel line

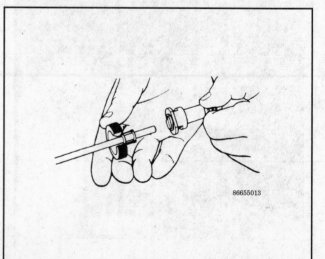

Fig. 50 With tool inserted into the fitting, the lines can be separated

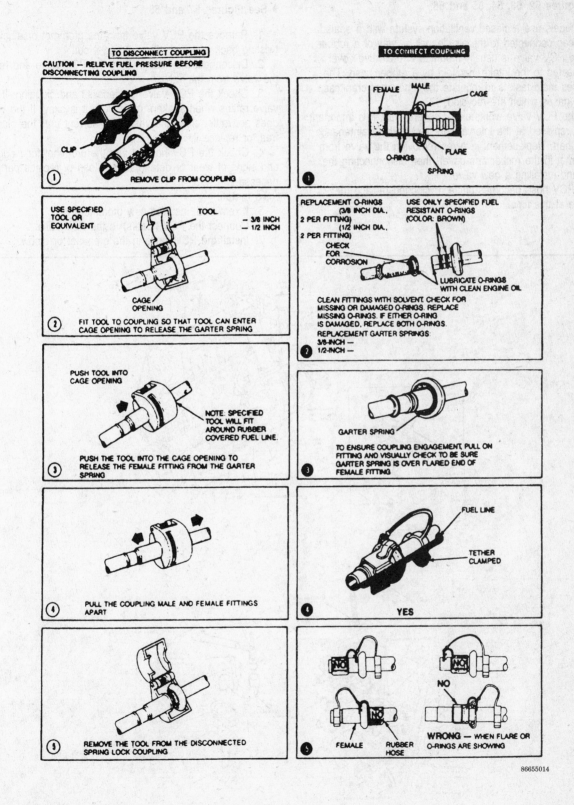

Fig. 51 Spring lock coupling removal chart

86655014

PCV Valve

▶ **See Figures 52, 53, 54, 55 and 56**

Most models use a closed ventilation system with a sealed breather cap connected to the air cleaner by way of a rubber hose. The PCV valve is usually mounted in the valve cover and connected to the intake manifold by a rubber hose. The PCV valves main task is to regulate the amount of crankcase (blow-by) gases which are recycled.

Since the PCV valve works under severe load, it is important that it be replaced at the interval specified in the Maintenance Interval Chart. Replacement involves removing the valve from the grommet in the rocker arm cover, then disconnecting the hose(s) and installing a new valve.

If The PCV hose becomes brittle or clogged replace the PCV hose at this time.

REMOVAL & INSTALLATION

▶ **See Figures 57 and 58**

1. Remove the PCV valve from the grommet or elbow, by twisting back and forth, then pulling it out.
2. Disconnect the hose(s) from the PCV valve and remove the valve from the vehicle.
3. Check the PCV valve for deposits and clogging. If the valve rattles when shaken, most likely it is okay. If the valve does not rattle, clean the valve with solvent until the plunger is free, or replace it.
4. Check the PCV hose(s) and the grommet for clogging and signs of wear or deterioration. Clean or replace parts, as necessary.
   To install:
5. If removed, install a new grommet.
6. Connect the PCV hose(s) to the PCV valve.
7. Install the PCV valve in the grommet or elbow.

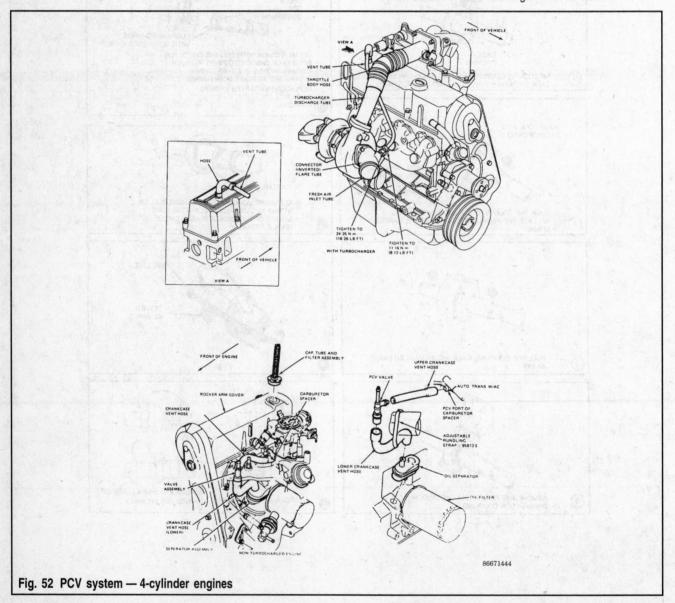

Fig. 52 PCV system — 4-cylinder engines

86671444

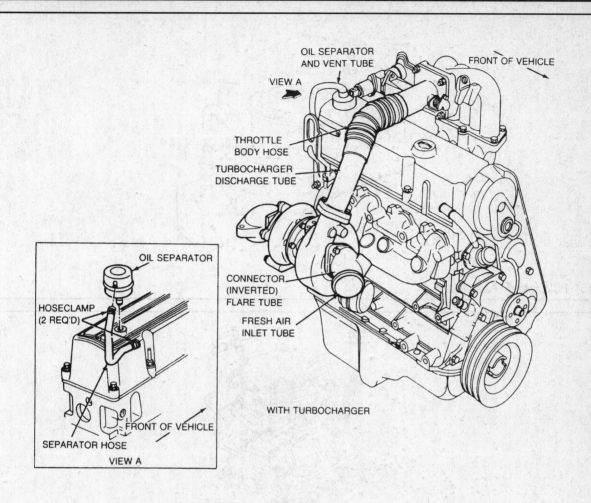

VIEW A

OIL SEPARATOR
AND VENT TUBE

FRONT OF VEHICLE

THROTTLE
BODY HOSE

TURBOCHARGER
DISCHARGE TUBE

CONNECTOR
(INVERTED)
FLARE TUBE

FRESH AIR
INLET TUBE

WITH TURBOCHARGER

OIL SEPARATOR

HOSECLAMP
(2 REQ'D)

FRONT OF VEHICLE

SEPARATOR HOSE

VIEW A

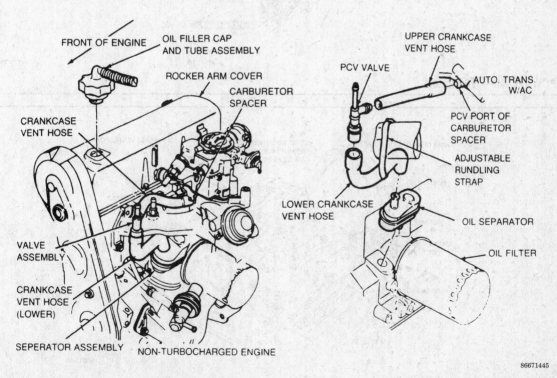

FRONT OF ENGINE

OIL FILLER CAP
AND TUBE ASSEMBLY

ROCKER ARM COVER

CARBURETOR
SPACER

CRANKCASE
VENT HOSE

VALVE
ASSEMBLY

CRANKCASE
VENT HOSE
(LOWER)

SEPERATOR ASSEMBLY

NON-TURBOCHARGED ENGINE

PCV VALVE

UPPER CRANKCASE
VENT HOSE

AUTO. TRANS.
W/AC

PCV PORT OF
CARBURETOR
SPACER

ADJUSTABLE
RUNDLING
STRAP

LOWER CRANKCASE
VENT HOSE

OIL SEPARATOR

OIL FILTER

86671445

Fig. 53 PCV system — 4-cylinder tubo engines

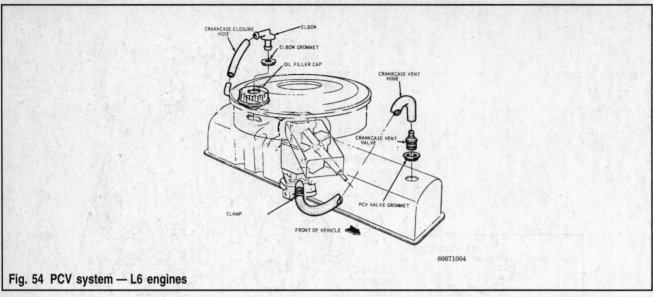

Fig. 54 PCV system — L6 engines

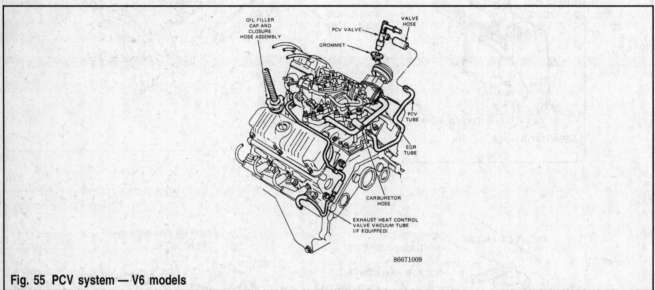

Fig. 55 PCV system — V6 models

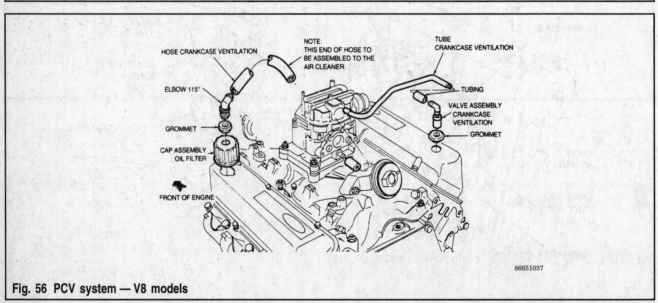

Fig. 56 PCV system — V8 models

Fig. 57 Twist the PCV valve back and forth and pull it from the grommet

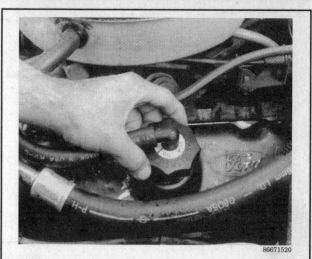

Fig. 59 The crankcase filler cap should be checked regularly

Fig. 58 Not all PCV valves look alike. Some have multiple ends

Crankcase Filler Cap

▶ See Figure 59

At the recommended intervals in the maintenance interval chart, the oil filler cap must be cleaned. Disconnect the positive crankcase ventilation hose from the cap and lift the cap from the rocker cover. Soak the cap in kerosene or mineral spirits to clean the internal element of sludge and any blow-by material. After agitating the cap in the solution, shake the cap dry. Reinstall the cap and connect the hose.

Evaporative Emissions Canister

▶ See Figure 60

The vapor, or carbon canister is located in the right front fender of the engine compartment and is part of the evapora-

tive emission control system. This system prevents the emission of harmful fuel vapors into the atmosphere. The canister contains activated charcoal which absorbs the fuel vapors from the fuel tank and carburetor float bowl (if equipped.) The fuel vapors are stored in the canister until the engine is started. Then the vapors are drawn into the engine for burning through a vacuum operated purge valve or solenoid purge valve.

SERVICING

▶ See Figure 61

Servicing the evaporative canister is only necessary if it becomes clogged or contains liquid fuel. If replacement is necessary, the canister must be replaced as a unit; it cannot be disassembled. For more detailed information on the evaporative emission control system, refer to Section 4.

Exhaust Control Valve (Heat Riser)

▶ See Figures 62 and 63

Some models are equipped with exhaust control valves, or heat risers near the headpipe in the exhaust manifold. These valves aid initial warm-up in cold weather, by restricting exhaust gas flow slightly. The heat generated by this restriction is transferred to the intake manifold where it results in improved fuel vaporization.

The operation of the exhaust control valve should be checked every 6 months or 6000 miles (9661 km). Make sure that the thermostatic spring is hooked on the stop pin and that the tension holds the valve shut. Rotate the counter weight by hand and make sure that it moves freely through about 90° degrees of rotation. A valve which is operating properly will open when light finger pressure is applied (cold engine). Lubricate the shaft bushing with a mixture of penetrating oil and graphite. Operate the valve manually a few times to work in the lubricant.

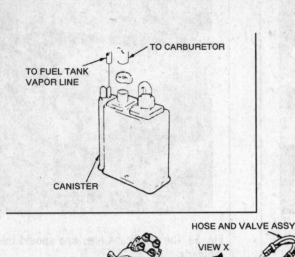

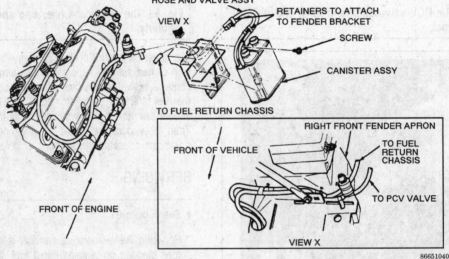

Fig. 60 Evaporative emissions system

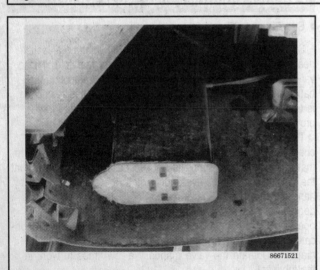

Fig. 61 The canister can be found on most mid-sized Ford cars behind the right front fender

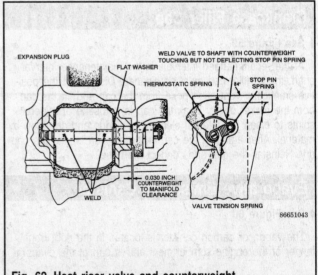

Fig. 62 Heat riser valve and counterweight

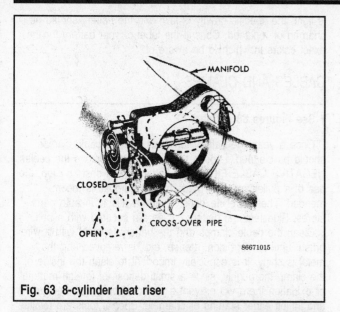

Fig. 63 8-cylinder heat riser

Battery

❄❄CAUTION

Batteries normally produce explosive gases which can cause personal injury. Do not allow flames, sparks or lighted tobacco to come near the battery. When charging or working near a battery, always shield your face and protect your eyes. Always provide ventilation when working on a battery.

GENERAL MAINTENANCE

▶ **See Figures 64, 65 and 66**

Corrosion of the battery terminals and cable clamps interferes with both the flow of power out of the battery and the charge flowing back into the battery from the charging system. This can result in a "no start" condition. If the battery becomes completely discharged, battery life may be shortened. In some cases, a totally discharged battery may not readily accept a charge.

To reduce the need for service and to extend battery life, keep the top of the battery, the battery terminals, and the cable clamps clean and free of corrosion. Make sure the cable clamps are tightly fastened to the battery terminals. If corrosion is found, disconnect the cables and clean the clamps and terminals with a wire brush. Neutralize the corrosion with a solution of baking soda and water. After installing the cables, apply a light coating of petroleum jelly to the cable clamps and terminals to help prevent corrosion.

FLUID LEVEL

➡**Maintenance free batteries are sealed units, and therefore cannot have their fluid levels checked or adjusted.**

Check the battery electrolyte level every month, or more often in hot weather or during periods of extended car opera-

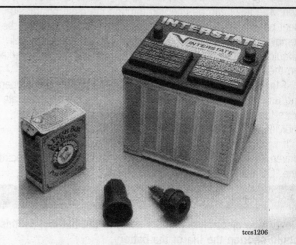

Fig. 64 Battery care may be accomplished with household items like baking soda, and/or special tools like terminal cleaners

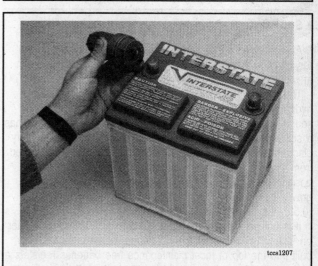

Fig. 65 The underside of the battery post tool contains a brush to clean the post terminals

Fig. 66 Place the tool over the terminal and twist to clean the post

tion. The level can be checked through the case on translucent polypropylene batteries; the cell caps or covers must be removed on other models. The electrolyte level in each cell should be kept filled to the split ring inside, or the line marked on the outside of the case.

If the level is low, add only distilled water through the opening until the level is correct. Each cell is completely separate from the others, so each must be checked and filled individually.

If water is added in freezing weather, the car should be driven several miles to allow the water to mix with the electrolyte. Otherwise, the battery could freeze.

❋❋WARNING

Never add electrolyte (battery acid) to the battery, as this could shorten the life of the battery.

SPECIFIC GRAVITY

▶ See Figure 67

At least once a year, check the specific gravity of the battery. It should be between 1.20 in. Hg and 1.26 in. Hg when at room temperature.

The specific gravity can be checked with the use of an hydrometer, an inexpensive instrument available from many sources, including automotive parts stores. The hydrometer has a squeeze bulb at one end and a nozzle at the other. Battery electrolyte is sucked into the hydrometer until the float is lifted from its seat. The specific gravity is then read by noting the position of the float. Generally, if after charging, the specific gravity between any two cells varies more than 50 points (0.50), the battery is bad and should be replaced.

It is not possible to check the specific gravity in this manner on sealed (maintenance free) batteries. Instead, the indicator built into the top of most maintenance free batteries registers a colored display on the condition of the battery. If the indicator is dark, the battery can be assumed to be OK. If the indicator

is light, the specific gravity is low, and the battery should be charged or replaced. Consult the label of your battery for the exact colors in which to be aware of.

CABLES AND CLAMPS

▶ See Figures 68, 69 and 70

Once a year, the battery terminals and the cable clamps should be cleaned. Loosen the clamps and remove the cables, NEGATIVE CABLE FIRST. On batteries with posts on top, the use of a puller specially made for the purpose is recommended. These are inexpensive, and available in auto parts stores. Side terminal battery cables are secured with a bolt.

Clean the cable clamps and the battery terminal with a wire brush, until all corrosion, grease, etc., is removed and the metal is shiny. It is especially important to clean the inside of the clamp thoroughly, since a small deposit of foreign material or oxidation there will prevent a sound electrical connection and inhibit either starting or charging. Special tools are available for cleaning these parts, one type for conventional batteries and another type for side terminal batteries.

Before installing the cables, loosen the battery hold-down clamp or strap, remove the battery and check the battery tray. Clean the tray of any debris, and check it for soundness. The battery tray can be cleaned with a solution of baking soda and water. Use 2 teaspoons of baking soda to every 1 cup of water. Rust should be wire brushed away, and the metal given a coat of anti-rust paint. Install the battery and tighten the hold-down clamp or strap securely. Be careful not to overtighten, which could crack the battery case.

After the clamps and terminals are clean, reinstall the cables, negative cable last; do not hammer on the clamps to install. Tighten the clamps securely, but do not distort them. Give the clamps and terminals a thin external coat of grease/petroleum jelly or equivalent after installation, to retard corrosion.

Check the cables at the same time that the terminals are cleaned. If the cable insulation is cracked or broken, or if the

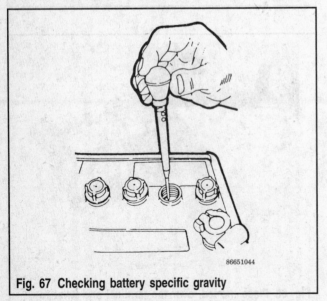

86651044

Fig. 67 Checking battery specific gravity

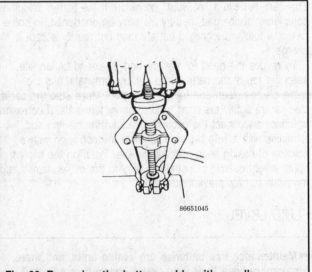

86651045

Fig. 68 Removing the battery cable with a puller

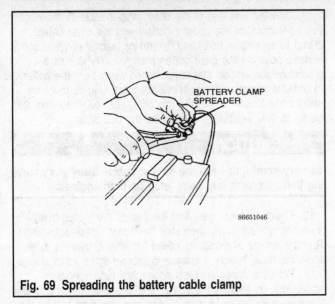

Fig. 69 Spreading the battery cable clamp

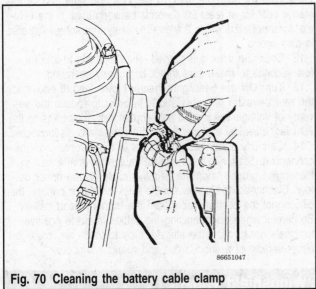

Fig. 70 Cleaning the battery cable clamp

ends are frayed, the cable should be replaced with a new cable of the same length and gauge.

❋❋CAUTION

Battery electrolyte contains sulfuric acid. If you should splash any on your skin or in your eyes, flush the affected area with plenty of clear water. If it lands in your eyes, get medical help immediately.

CHARGING

❋❋CAUTION

Keep flame or sparks away from the battery. The battery emits explosive hydrogen gas, especially when being charged. Battery electrolyte contains sulfuric acid. If elec-

trolyte accidently comes in contact with your skin or eyes, flush with plenty of clear water. If it lands in your eyes, get medical help immediately.

A cold battery will not readily accept a charge, therefore allow the battery to warm up to approximately 41°F (5°C) before charging. This may take 4 to 8 hours at room temperature, depending on initial temperature and battery size.

A completely discharged battery may be slow to accept a charge initially and in some cases may not accept a charge at all. If the battery is in this condition, it should be replaced.

If it has been determined that the battery has begun to accept a charge, it can be charged either using the manual (constant current) setting on the charger or the automatic (adjusting current) setting, if the charger is so equipped.

If the charger is equipped with an automatic setting, the charging rate can be maintained at a safe level. A completely discharged battery will require approximately 2-4 hours to charge to a serviceable state. For a full state of charge, the charge can be completed by a low current rate of 3-5 amps for several hours.

To charge the battery using the manual setting, initially set the charging rate for 30-40 amps and maintain this setting for approximately 30 minutes or as long as there is no excessive gassing or displacement of electrolyte. If there is excessive gassing, reduce the charge rate to a level where the gassing stops. This is especially important with maintenance free batteries as the excessive gassing results in the non-replaceable loss of electrolyte, shortening battery life.

The total charge required will vary with battery size and initial state of charge. As a rule, to bring a discharged battery to a serviceable state of charge, current-time input should equal the battery amp-hour capacity. For example, a 45 amp-hour battery will require a 15 amp charge for 3 hours or a 9 amp charge for 5 hours. To achieve a full state of charge, the charge can be completed by a low constant current of 3-5 amps for several hours.

JUMP STARTING A DEAD BATTERY

▶ See Figure 71

Whenever a vehicle must be jump started, precautions must be followed in order to prevent the possibility of personal injury. Remember that batteries contain a small amount of explosive hydrogen gas which is a by product of battery charging. Sparks should always be avoided when working around batteries, especially when attaching jumper cables. To minimize the possibility of accidental sparks, follow the procedure carefully.

❋❋WARNING

NEVER hook the batteries up in a series circuit or the entire electrical system may go up in smoke, especially the starter!

Always follow these precautions:
• Be sure that both batteries are of the same voltage. All vehicles covered by this manual and most vehicles on the road today utilize a 12 volt charging system.
• Be sure that both batteries are of the same polarity (have the same grounded terminal; in most cases NEGATIVE).

• Be sure that the vehicles are not touching or a short circuit could occur.

• On serviceable batteries, be sure the vent cap holes are not obstructed.

• Do not smoke or allow sparks anywhere near the batteries.

• In cold weather, make sure the battery electrolyte is not frozen. This can occur more readily in a battery that has been in a state of discharge.

• Do not allow electrolyte to contact your skin or clothing.

1. Make sure that the voltages of the 2 batteries are the same. Most batteries and charging systems are of the 12 volt variety.

2. Pull the jumping vehicle (with the good battery) into a position so the jumper cables can reach the dead battery and that vehicle's engine. Make sure that the vehicles DO NOT touch.

3. Place the transmissions of both vehicles in NEUTRAL or PARK, as applicable, then firmly set their parking brakes.

➡If necessary for safety reasons, both vehicle's hazard lights may be operated throughout the entire procedure without significantly increasing the difficulty of jump starting the dead battery.

4. Turn all lights and accessories OFF on both vehicles. Make sure the ignition switches on both vehicles are turned to the OFF position.

5. Cover the battery cell caps with a rag, but do not cover the terminals.

6. Make sure the terminals on both batteries are clean and free of corrosion or proper electrical connection will be impeded. If necessary, clean the battery terminals before proceeding.

7. Identify the positive (+) and negative (-) terminals on both batteries.

8. Connect the first jumper cable to the positive (+) terminal of the dead battery, then connect the other end of that cable to the positive (+) terminal of the booster (good) battery.

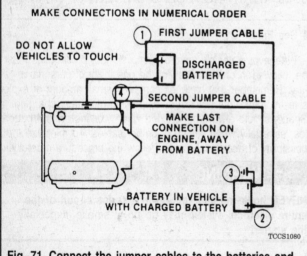

MAKE CONNECTIONS IN NUMERICAL ORDER

DO NOT ALLOW VEHICLES TO TOUCH

① FIRST JUMPER CABLE

DISCHARGED BATTERY

SECOND JUMPER CABLE

MAKE LAST CONNECTION ON ENGINE, AWAY FROM BATTERY

BATTERY IN VEHICLE WITH CHARGED BATTERY

TCCS1080

Fig. 71 Connect the jumper cables to the batteries and engine in the order shown

9. Connect one end of the other jumper cable to the negative (-) terminal of the booster battery and the other cable clamp to an engine bolt head, alternator bracket or other solid, metallic point on the dead battery's engine. Try to pick a ground on the engine that is positioned away from the battery, in order to minimize the possibility of the 2 clamps touching should one loosen during the procedure. DO NOT connect this clamp to the negative (-) terminal of the bad battery.

✳✳CAUTION

Be very careful to keep the jumper cables away from moving parts (cooling fan, belts, etc.) on both engines.

10. Check to make sure that the cables are routed away from any moving parts, then start the donor vehicle's engine. Run the engine at moderate speed for several minutes to allow the dead battery a chance to receive some initial charge.

11. With the donor vehicle's engine still running slightly above idle, try to start the vehicle with the dead battery. Crank the engine for no more than 10 seconds at a time and let the starter cool for at least 20 seconds between tries. If the vehicle does not start within 3 tries, it is likely that something else is also wrong.

12. Once the vehicle is started, allow it to run at idle for a few seconds to make sure that it is properly operating.

13. Turn ON the headlights, heater blower and, if equipped, the rear defroster of both vehicles in order to reduce the severity of voltage spikes and subsequent risk of damage to the vehicles' electrical systems when the cables are disconnected.

14. Carefully disconnect the cables in the reverse order of connection. Start with the negative cable that is attached to the engine ground, then the negative cable on the donor battery. Disconnect the positive cable from the donor battery, then disconnect the positive cable from the formerly dead battery. Be careful when disconnecting the cables from the positive terminals not to allow the alligator clips to touch any metal on either vehicle or a short circuit and sparks will occur.

Windshield Wipers

For maximum effectiveness and longest element lift, the windshield and wiper blades should be kept clean. Dirt, tree sap, road tar and so on will cause streaking, smearing and blade deterioration if left on the glass. It is advisable to wash the windshield carefully with a commercial glass cleaner at least once a month. Wipe off the rubber blades with the wet rag afterwards. Do not attempt to move the wipers by hand; damage to the motor and drive mechanism will result.

If the blades are found to be cracked, broken or torn, they should be replaced immediately. Replacement intervals will vary with usage, although ozone deterioration usually limits blade life to about one year. If the wiper pattern is smeared or streaked, or if the blade chatters across the glass, the elements should be replaced. It is easiest and most sensible to replace the elements in pairs.

There are basically three different types of refills, which differ in their method of replacement.

ARM & BLADE REPLACEMENT

♦ **See Figure 72**

Original Equipment Type

1. Lift wiper arm up as much as possible.
2. Insert a small prytool in the slot at the middle of the blade. Push down on the spring lock and pull the blade assembly from the wiper arm pin.
3. Using a small prytool, and twist it slowly until the element clears 1 side of the jaws. Slide the element out of the jaws.

To install:

4. Slide the element into the jaws, starting with the second set from either end of the blade assembly. Slide the element into all the jaws to the element stop.
5. Insert the element into 1 side of the end jaws and with a rocking motion, push the element upward until it snaps in.
6. Push the blade assembly on the wiper arm pin so the spring lock engages the pin. Make sure the blade assembly is securely attached to the pin.

Aftermarket Types

There are several different types of refills, and your vehicle could have any kind, since aftermarket blades and arms may not use exactly the same type refill as the original equipment.

The Anco® type uses a release button that is pushed down to allow the refill to slide out of the yoke jaws. The new refill slides back into the frame and locks in place.

Some Trico® refills are removed by locating where the metal backing strip or the refill is wider. Insert a small prytool between the frame and metal backing strip. Press down to release the refill from the retaining tab.

Other types of Trico® refills have two metal tabs which are unlocked by squeezing them together. The rubber filler can then be withdrawn from the frame jaws. A new refill is installed by inserting the refill into the front frame jaws and sliding it rearward to engage the remaining frame jaws. There are usually four jaws; be certain when installing, that the refill is engaged in all of them. At the end of its travel, the tabs will lock into place on the front jaws of the wiper blade frame.

Another type of refill is made from polycarbonate. The refill has a simple locking device at one end which flexes downward out of the groove into which the jaws of the holder fit, allowing easy release. By sliding the new refill through all the jaws and pushing through the slight resistance when it reaches the end of its travel, the refill will lock into position.

To replace the Tridon® refill, it is necessary to remove the wiper arm or blade. This refill has a plastic backing strip with a notch about 1 in. (25mm) from the end. Hold the blade (frame) on a hard surface so the frame is tightly bowed. Grip the tip of the backing strip and pull up while twisting counterclockwise. The backing strip will snap out of the retaining tab. Do this for the remaining tabs until the refill is free of the arm. The length of these refills is molded into the end and they should be replaced with identical types.

Regardless of the type of refill used, make sure that all of the frame jaws are engaged as the refill is pushed into place and locked. If the metal blade holder and frame are allowed to touch the glass during wiper operation, the glass will be scratched.

Belts

INSPECTION

♦ **See Figures 73 and 74**

Once a year or at 12,000 mile (19,000 km) intervals, the tension and condition of the drive belts should be checked. If your vehicle is equipped a serpentine drive belt, this interval may be extended to every other year or 30,000 miles (48,000 km). Loose accessory drive belts can lead to poor engine cooling and diminish alternator, power steering pump, air conditioning compressor or Thermactor® air pump output. A belt that is too tight places a severe strain on the component bearings.

Replace any belts that are glazed, worn or stretched.

➡**On serpentine belts, rib cracking is not a reason for concern and the belt is still perfectly functional until "chunking" occurs. Belt "chunking" is where the rubber material actually breaks away between the cracks. The belt should be replaced if this condition exists.**

On vehicles with matched belts, replace both belts. New belts should be initially tensioned to 80 lbs. (36 kg) using a belt tension gauge. If a belt tension gauge is unavailable, adjust the belt until the deflection does not exceed ¼ in. (6mm). After a new belt has been installed, run the engine for 10 minutes, then check the tension, and adjust if necessary. Any belt that has been operating for a minimum of 10 minutes is considered a used belt. In the first 10 minutes, the belt should stretch to its maximum extent. Belt tension for a used belt should be maintained at 60 lbs. (27 kg).

V-BELT ADJUSTMENT

✳✳CAUTION

On models equipped with an electric cooling fan, disconnect the negative battery cable or fan motor wiring harness connector before replacing or adjusting drive belts. The fan may come on, under certain circumstances, even though the ignition is OFF.

Alternator Drive Belt

♦ **See Figure 75**

1. Position a ruler perpendicular to the drive belt at its longest run. Test the tightness of the belt by pressing it firmly with your thumb. The deflection should not exceed ¼in. (6mm).
2. If the deflection exceeds ¼ in. (6mm), loosen the alternator mounting and adjusting arm bolts.
3. On 1971-72 V8 and 6 cylinder models, use a prytool to move the alternator toward or away from the engine until the proper tension is reached.

➡**Apply tension to the front of the alternator only. Positioning the prytool against the rear end housing will damage the alternator.**

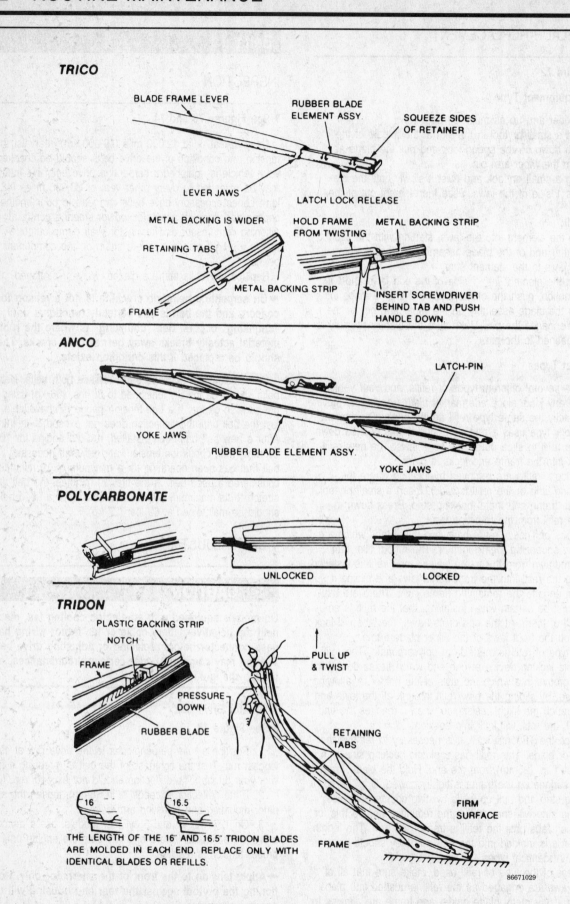

Fig. 72 Wiper blade insert replacement

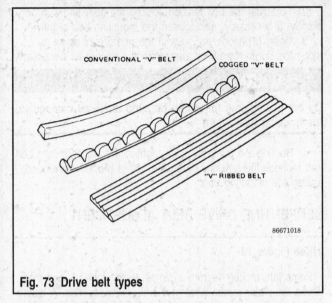

Fig. 73 Drive belt types

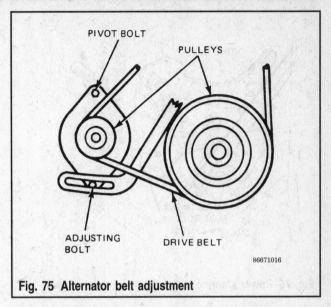

Fig. 75 Alternator belt adjustment

4. On 1973 and later V8 models, place a 1 in. (25mm) open-end or equivalent wrench on the adjusting arm bolt and pull on the wrench until the proper tension is achieved.

5. Holding the alternator in place, tighten the adjusting arm bolt. Inspect the belt tension. When the belt is properly tensioned, tighten the alternator mounting bolt.

Power Steering Drive Belt

▶ See Figure 76

ALL 6-CYLINDER AND 1971-72 V8 MODELS

1. Holding a ruler perpendicular to the drive belt at its longest run, test the tightness of the belt by pressing it firmly with your thumb. The deflection should not exceed 1/4in. (6mm).

2. To adjust the belt tension, loosen the adjusting and mounting bolts on the front face of the steering pump cover plate (hub side).

3. Using a prytool on the pump hub, move the power steering pump toward or away from the engine until the proper

tension is reached. Do not pry against the reservoir as it is relatively soft and easily deformed.

4. Hold the pump in place, tighten the adjusting arm bolt and then inspect the belt tension. When the belt is properly tensioned tighten the mounting bolts.

1973 AND LATER V8 MODELS

1. Position a ruler perpendicular to the drive belt at its longest run. Test the tightness of the belt by pressing it firmly with your thumb. The deflection should be about 1/4in. (6mm).

2. To adjust the belt tension, loosen the three bolts in the three elongated adjusting slots at the power steering pump attaching bracket.

3. Turn the steering pump drive belt adjusting nut as required until the proper deflection is obtained. Turning the adjusting nut clockwise will increase tension and decrease deflection; counterclockwise will decrease tension and increase deflection.

4. Without disturbing the pump, tighten the three attaching bolts.

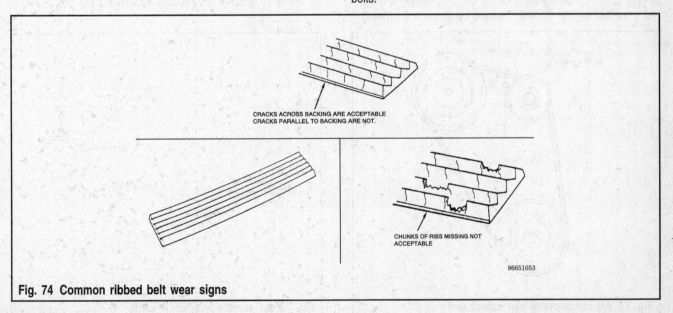

Fig. 74 Common ribbed belt wear signs

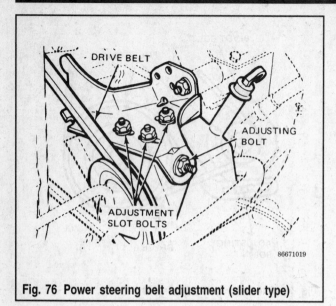

Fig. 76 Power steering belt adjustment (slider type)

Air Conditioning Compressor Drive Belt
▶ See Figure 77

1. Position a ruler perpendicular to the drive belt at its longest run. Test the tightness of the belt by pressing it firmly with your thumb. The deflection should not exceed ¼in. (6mm).

2. If the engine is equipped with an idler pulley, loosen the idler pulley adjusting boot, insert a prytool between the pulley and the engine (or in the idler pulley adjusting slot), and adjust the tension accordingly. If the engine is not equipped with an idler pulley, the alternator must be moved to adjust, as outlined under Alternator Drive Belt.

3. When the proper tension is reached, tighten the idler pulley adjusting bolt (if so equipped) or the alternator adjusting and mounting bolts.

Thermactor® Air Pump Drive Belt
▶ See Figure 78

1. Position a ruler perpendicular to the drive belt at its longest run. Test the tightness of the belt by pressing it firmly with your thumb. The deflection should be about ¼ in. (6mm).

2. To adjust the belt tension, loosen the adjusting arm bolt slightly. If necessary, also loosen the mounting belt slightly.

3. Using a prytool, pry against the pump rear cover to move the pump toward or away from the engine as necessary.

✳✳WARNING

Do not pry against the pump housing itself, as damage to the housing may result.

4. Holding the pump in place, tighten the adjusting arm bolt and recheck the tension. When the belt is properly tensioned, tighten the mounting bolt.

SERPENTINE DRIVE BELT ADJUSTMENT

▶ See Figure 79

Some late models feature a single, wide, ribbed V-belt that drives the water pump, alternator and power steering. A spring loaded tensioner eliminates the need for periodic adjustments. The drive belt should not require tension adjustment for the life of the belt. Automatic tensioners do not have to be removed to remove a drive belt. To remove a drive belt, rotate the tensioner away from the drive belt by using a ½ in. breaker bar.

➡**Check to make sure that the V-ribbed belt is located properly in all drive pulleys before applying tensioner pressure.**

REMOVAL & INSTALLATION

All V-belts
▶ See Figures 80, 81, 82, 83 and 84

1. Using the appropriate tools, loosen the necessary hardware enough to allow the belt driven accessary to move forward.

2. Remove the belt from the pulley(s). Inspect each pulley for bends or grooves which could shorten the life of a V-belt. If

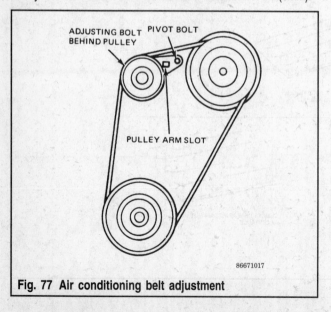

Fig. 77 Air conditioning belt adjustment

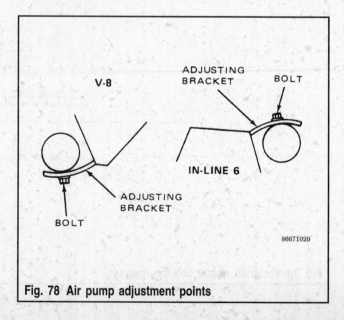

Fig. 78 Air pump adjustment points

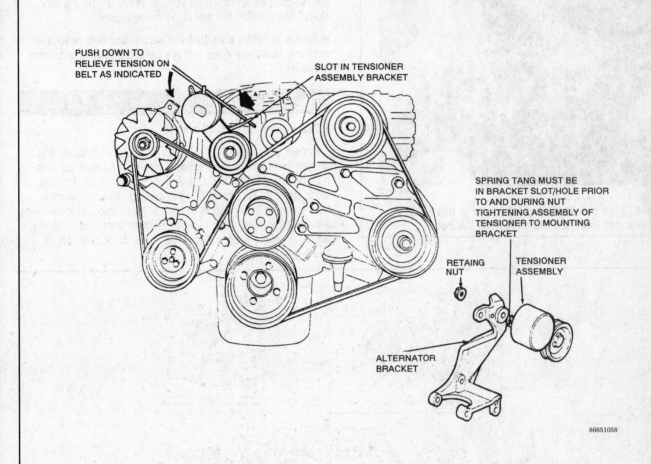

Fig. 79 Serpentine belt and tensioner assembly

small enough, a groove can be filed. Otherwise replace the pulley(s).

3. If replacing other belts, remove the remaining belts using the same procedure.

To install:

4. Position the belt on to the pulley(s).

5. Using a suitable prytool, apply pressure against the belt driven accessary, until the desired tension or deflection is obtained. Refer to the previous Section for more details.

6. Once tight, start the engine and allow it to run for 10 minutes. Then shut off the engine and check the tension again. Adjust if needed.

Serpentine Belt

▶ See Figures 85 and 86

To remove a serpentine belt, simply rotate the tensioner away from the drive belt using a 1/2 in. breaker bar. As the tensioner loosens, remove the belt from its position. Continue removing the belt from all the pulleys until it can be removed from the engine compartment.

Fig. 80 With the accessory loosened, the belt can be removed

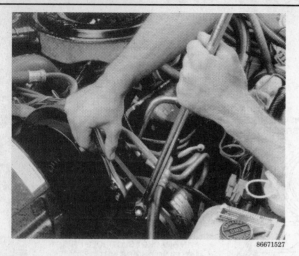

Fig. 81 Use a suitable prytool, or as in this case, a breaker bar to adjust the tension of the belt

To install, position the serpentine belt on or around the necessary pulleys. If you have forgotten the order in which the belt should run, consult the belt routing label found in most engine compartments. When you are ready, rotate the tensioner and position the belt on to the tensioner.

➡ Check to make sure that the serpentine belt is located properly in all the drive pulleys before applying tensioner pressure

Tires and Wheels

▶ See Figures 87, 88, 89 and 90

Inspect your tires often for signs of improper inflation and uneven wear, which may indicate a need for balancing, rotation, or wheel alignment. Check the tires frequently for cuts, stone bruises, abrasions, blisters, and for objects that may have become imbedded in the tread. More frequent inspections are recommended when rapid or extreme temperature changes occur, or where road surfaces are rough or occasionally littered with debris.

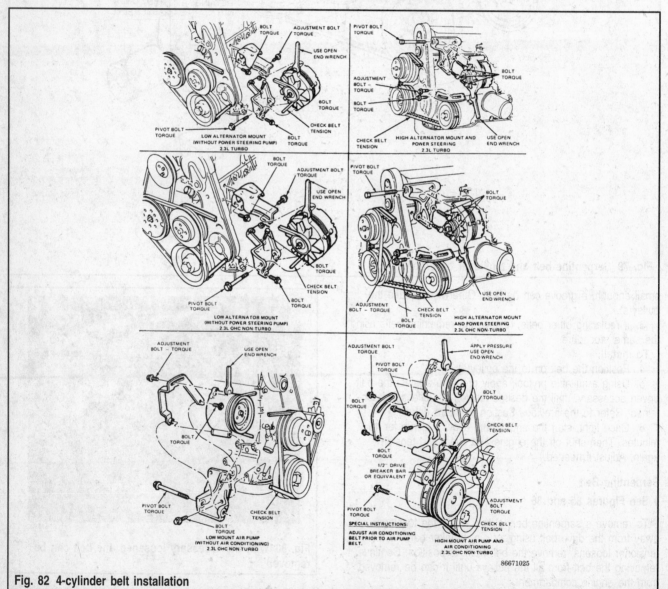

Fig. 82 4-cylinder belt installation

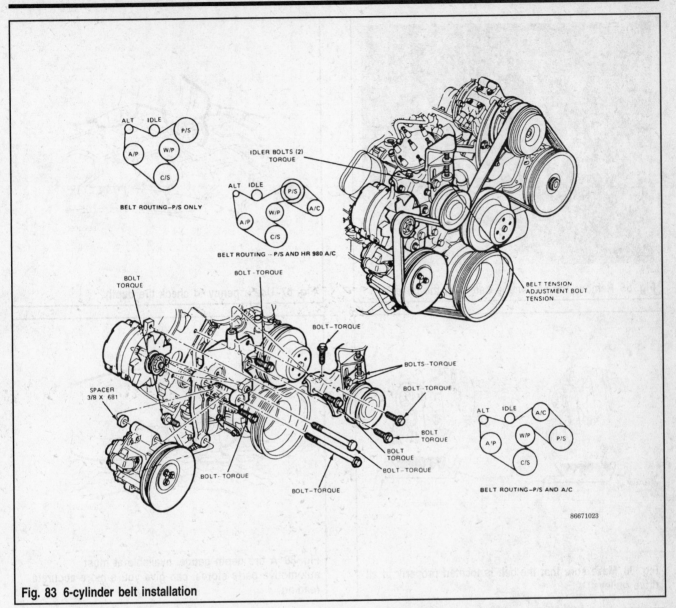

Fig. 83 6-cylinder belt installation

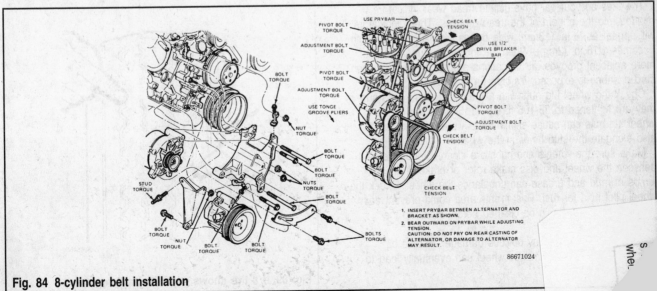

Fig. 84 8-cylinder belt installation

Fig. 85 Remove the serpentine belt from the pulleys

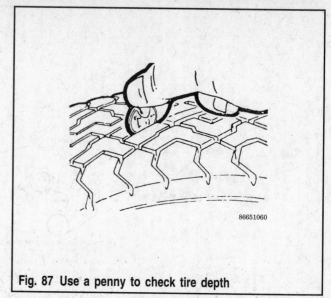

Fig. 87 Use a penny to check tire depth

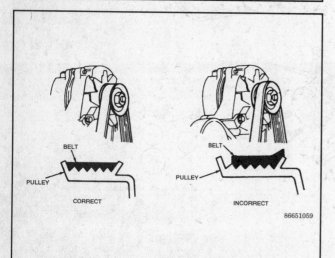

Fig. 86 Make sure that the belt is located properly in all drive pulleys

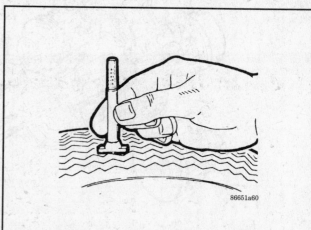

Fig. 88 A tire depth gauge, available at most automotive parts stores, can give you a more accurate reading

The tires on your car have built-in tread wear indicators molded into the bottom of the tread grooves. These indicators will appear as ½ in. (13mm) wide bands when the tread depth becomes 1/16 in. (2mm). When the indicators appear in 2 or more adjacent grooves, at 3 locations around the tire, or when cord or fabric is exposed, it's time for new tires.

Check the wheel lug nuts with a torque wrench. Make sure they are tightened to 85-105 ft. lbs. (115-142 Nm). Loose wheel lug nuts can cause shimmy and vibration, and could also elongate the stud holes in the wheels.

Make sure the wheels and hubs are clean. Stones wedged between the wheel and disc brake rotor or brake drum, or lumps of mud and grease can unbalance the wheel. Check the wheel pilot hole for rust. Rust in this area could prevent easy wheel removal, it should be cleaned before installing the wheel.

Check the wheel for any obvious damage. Wobble or shimmy caused by a damaged wheel can eventually lead to bearing failure.

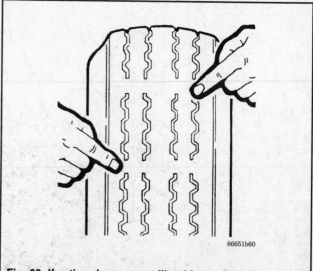

Fig. 89 If a tire shows gaps like this, replace it

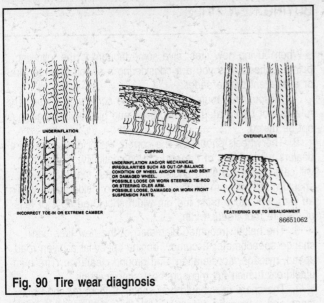

Fig. 90 Tire wear diagnosis

TIRE ROTATION

▶ See Figure 91

Front and rear tires perform different jobs and can often wear differently. To obtain even tire wear and maximum tire life, the tires should be rotated at approximately 7,500 miles (13,000 km) and then each 15,000 miles (24,000 km) thereafter. Rotate the tires according to one of the diagrams in the figure. Note that if the vehicle is equipped with a temporary spare, this tire should not be included in the tire rotation.

TIRE DESIGN

▶ See Figure 92

✳✳CAUTION

Do not mix tires of different construction (radial, bias ply or bias belted) on the same vehicle. Vehicle handling will be seriously affected with the possibility of loss of control.

All tires have identification marks pertaining to size, tire pressure and load range molded into the sidewall of the tire. The Department of Transportation grades all tires for tread wear, traction and temperature resistance. This Uniform Quality Grading System information is also molded into the sidewall.

The tread wear grade is expressed as a number. The number is derived from a test conducted under controlled conditions on a government test course. If a tire is graded 150, it means that the tire wore 1½ times as well on the test course as a tire graded 100.

The traction and temperature grades are expressed as the letters A, B or C; A being the best and C being the minimum standard that all tires must meet. The traction grade represents the tire's ability to stop on wet pavement, in a test conducted under controlled conditions on a government test course. The temperature grade represents the tire's resistance to the generation of heat and its ability to dissipate heat, once again during a government test conducted under controlled conditions.

TIRE INFLATION

At least once a month, check the inflation pressure on all tires, including the spare. Use an accurate tire pressure gauge. Do not trust the gauges on service station air pumps, as they are not always accurate. The inflation specifications are listed on the tire pressure decal which is located on the right door pillar. Check and adjust inflation pressures only when the tires are cold, as pressures can increase as much as 6 psi (41 kPa) due to heat.

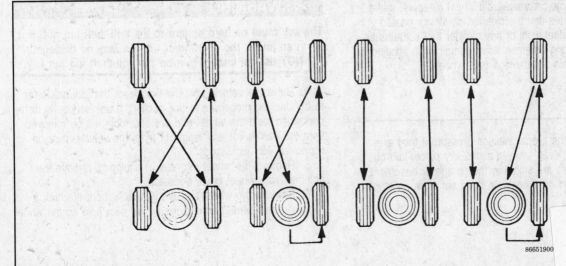

Fig. 91 Tire rotation patterns

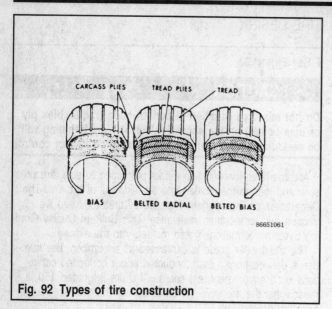

CARCASS PLIES   TREAD PLIES   TREAD

BIAS   BELTED RADIAL   BELTED BIAS

86651061

Fig. 92 Types of tire construction

Inflation pressures that are higher than recommended can cause a hard ride, tire bruising, carcass damage and rapid tread wear at the center of the tire. Inflation pressures that are lower than recommended can cause tire squeal, hard steering, rim dents, high temperatures and rapid wear on the outer edges of the tires. Unequal tire pressures can compromise handling and cause uneven braking.

As previously stated, radial tires have a highly flexible sidewall and this accounts for the characteristic sidewall bulge that makes the tire appear underinflated. This is normal for a radial tire, so you should not attempt to reduce this bulge by overinflating the tire.

CARE OF ALUMINUM WHEELS

Aluminum wheels are standard on certain models and optional on others. These wheels are coated to preserve their appearance.

To clean the aluminum wheels, use a mild soap and water solution and rinse thoroughly with clean water. If you want to use one of the commercially available wheel cleaners, make sure the label indicates that the cleaner is safe for coated wheels. Never use steel wool or any cleaner that contains an abrasive, or use strong detergents that contain high alkaline or caustic agents, as this will damage your wheels.

STORAGE

Store the tires at the proper inflation pressure if they are mounted on wheels. Keep them in a cool dry place, laid on their sides. If the tires are stored in the garage or basement, do not let them stand on a concrete floor; set them on strips of wood.

BUYING NEW TIRES

When buying new tires, give some thought to the following points, especially is you are considering a switch to larger tires or a different profile series:

1. All four tires must be of the same construction type. This rule cannot be violated. Radial, bias, and bias-belted tires must not be mixed.

2. The wheels should be the correct width for the tire. Tire dealers have charts of tire and rim compatibility. A mismatch will cause poor handling and rapid tire wear. the tread width should match the rim width (inside bead to inside bead) within an inch. For radial tires, the rim width should be 80% or less of the tire (not tread) width.

3. The height (mounted diameter) of the new tires can change speedometer accuracy, engine speed at a given road speed, mileage, acceleration, and ground clearance. Tire manufacturers furnish full measurement specifications.

4. The spare tire should be usable, at least for short distance and low speed operation, with the new tires.

5. There shouldn't be any body interference when loaded, on bumps, or in turns.

REMOVAL & INSTALLATION

▶ **See Figure 93**

1. If equipped with a conventional wheel cover, remove the cover by inserting the end of the lug wrench and prying against the wheel cover flange.

2. If equipped with optional anti-theft wire wheel covers, pry the center ornament cover from the wheel cover using the key wrench. Use the key wrench to remove the lock bolt, then pry the wheel cover from the wheel.

3. Loosen, but do not remove the wheel lug nuts. If equipped with anti-theft lug nuts, insert the key into the slot of the lug nut, then position the lug wrench or socket on the key. Apply pressure on the key to keep it from slipping and loosen the lug nut.

✳✳WARNING

The key must be held square to the anti-theft lug nut. If it is on an angle, the key and/or lug nut may be damaged. DO NOT use an impact gun on the anti-theft lug nut key.

4. Raise the vehicle until the tire clears the ground. Refer to the Jacking procedure in this section. If any service is to be performed, or if the wheel and tire assembly will be removed from the vehicle for any length of time, the vehicle must be supported with jackstands.

5. Remove the wheel lug nuts. If equipped, remove the anti-theft wire wheel cover pedestal.

6. Remove the wheel and tire assembly from the hub. If corrosion has formed around the center pilot hole so the wheel

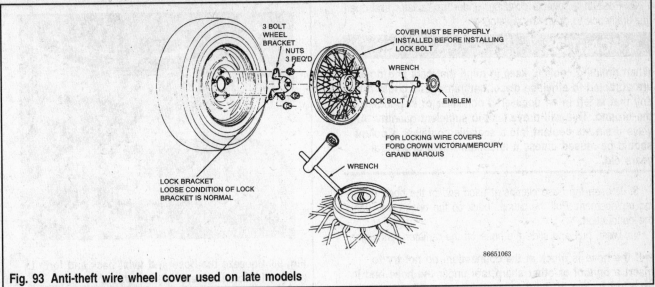

Fig. 93 Anti-theft wire wheel cover used on late models

cannot be removed by hand, use a suitable wheel puller to remove the wheel.

✳✳WARNING

Do not apply heat to a frozen wheel in an effort to remove it, as the heat will damage the wheel bearings.

To install:

7. Clean all dirt and corrosion from the hub mounting surface and center pilot hole of the wheel. Apply a thin coat of disc brake caliper slide grease or equivalent, to the axle pilot flange to reduce corrosion.

8. Install the wheel and tire assembly on the hub. Install the anti-theft wire wheel cover pedestal, if equipped.

9. Install the lug nuts. Tighten them alternately and evenly to draw the wheel against the hub.

10. Lower the vehicle.

11. Tighten the wheel lug nuts to 85-105 ft. lbs. (115-142 Nm) using a star-shaped pattern.

12. If equipped, install the wheel cover by hand, being careful to line up the tire valve stem with the hole in the wheel cover. Make sure the wheel cover is securely attached to the wheel.

13. If equipped with anti-theft wire wheel covers, install the lockbolt and tighten with the key. Install the center ornament cover.

Hoses

✳✳CAUTION

On models equipped with an electric cooling fan, disconnect the negative battery cable, or fan motor wiring harness connector before replacing any radiator/heater hose. The fan may come on, under certain circumstances, even though the ignition is OFF.

INSPECTION

Inspect the condition of the radiator and heater hoses periodically. Early spring and at the beginning of the fall or winter, when you are performing other maintenance, are good times. Make sure the engine and cooling system are cold. Visually inspect for cracking, rotting or collapsed hoses, and replace as necessary. Run your hand along the length of the hose. If a weak or swollen spot is noted when squeezing the hose wall, replace the hose.

REMOVAL & INSTALLATION

▶ See Figures 94, 95 and 96

1. Remove the radiator cap and/or the cap from the overflow tank.

✳✳CAUTION

Never remove the radiator cap while the engine is running or personal injury from scalding hot coolant or steam may result. If possible, wait until the engine has cooled to remove the radiator cap. If this is not possible, wrap a thick cloth around the radiator cap and turn it slowly to the first stop. Step back while the pressure is released from the cooling system. When you are sure all the pressure has been released, press down on the cap, with the cloth, and turn remove it.

2. Position a suitable container under the radiator and open the draincock to drain the radiator.

✳✳CAUTION

When draining coolant, keep in mind that cats and dogs are attracted to ethylene glycol antifreeze, and could drink any that is left in an uncovered container or in puddles on the ground. This will prove fatal in sufficient quantity. Always drain the coolant into a sealable container. Coolant should be reused unless it is contaminated or several years old.

3. Loosen the hose clamps at each end of the hose requiring replacement. Pull the clamps back on the hose away from the connection.

4. Twist, pull and slide the hose off the radiator connection.

→If the hose is stuck at the connection, do not try to insert a prytool or other sharp tool under the hose end in an effort to free it. Hose connections are easily damaged. If the hose is not to be reused, slice the end of the hose with a single edge razor blade, perpendicular to the end of the hose. The hose can then be peeled from the connection.

5. Clean both hose mounting connections. Inspect the condition of the hose clamps and replace them, if necessary.

To install:

6. Coat the connection surfaces with a water resistant sealer.

7. Slide the hose clamps over the replacement hose and slide the hose ends over the connections into position.

8. Position the hose clamps at least 1/8 in. (3mm) from each end of the hose. Make sure they are located beyond the raised bead of the connector, and centered in the clamping area of the connection.

9. If the clamps are the screw type, tighten them to 22-31 inch lbs. (2-3 Nm). Do not overtighten.

10. Close the radiator draincock and fill the cooling system.

11. Start the engine and allow it to reach normal operating temperature. Check for leaks.

Fig. 96 Squeeze the hose and twist back and forth to remove it. Some are easier than others

Fig. 95 Loosen the clamp around the hose

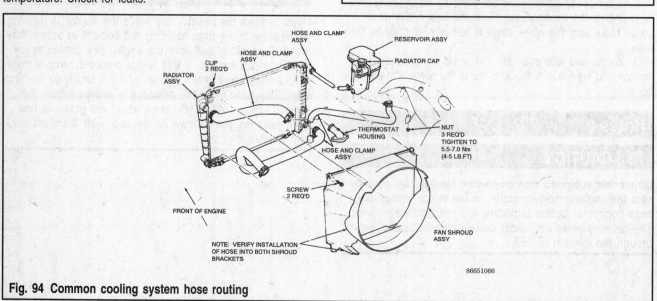

Fig. 94 Common cooling system hose routing

Air Conditioning

➡R-12 refrigerant is a chlorofluorocarbon which, when released into the atmosphere, contributes to the depletion of the ozone layer in the upper atmosphere. Ozone filters out harmful radiation from the sun. Consult the laws in your area before attempting to service the air conditioning system. In some states it is illegal to perform repairs involving refrigerant unless the work is done by a certified technician.

SAFETY WARNINGS

• When exposed to air, liquid R-12 refrigerant will instantly freeze anything it comes in contact with. Be extremely careful not let any liquid refrigerant come in contact with your skin and especially your eyes. Always wear safety goggles when servicing any part of the refrigerant system.

• Never weld, solder, steam clean, use a blow torch, bake paint or use any excessive amount of heat on or in the immediate area of any part of the refrigerant system. Any excessive heat could cause an explosion.

• Although normally non-toxic, refrigerant gas becomes highly poisonous in the presence of an open flame. One good whiff of the vapor formed by burning refrigerant can be fatal. Keep all forms of fire (including cigarettes) well clear of the air conditioning system.

• Avoid contact with a charged refrigeration system. If a heavy tool comes into contact with a section of copper tubing or a heat exchanger, it can easily cause the relatively soft material to rupture.

• When it is necessary to apply force to a fitting which contains refrigerant; use a wrench on both parts of the fitting involved. This will avoid putting torque on the refrigerant tubing. It is advisable, when possible, to use flare type wrenches when tightening these flare nut fittings.

• Do not attempt to discharge the system by merely loosening a fitting, or opening the service valves. Discharge using only approved recovery/recycling equipment. Wear protective gloves when connecting or disconnecting service gauge hoses.

• Discharge the system only into a container made for the recovery/recycling of used refrigerant.

• Never start a system without first verifying that both service valves are backseated, if equipped, and that all fittings throughout the system are snugly connected.

SYSTEM INSPECTION

Visually inspect the air conditioning system for refrigerant leaks, damaged compressor clutch, compressor drive belt tension and condition, plugged evaporator drain tube, blocked condenser fins, disconnected or broken wires, blown fuses, corroded connections and poor insulation.

A refrigerant leak will usually appear as an oily residue at the leakage point in the system. The oily residue soon picks up dust or dirt particles from the surrounding air and appears greasy. Through time, this will build up and appear to be a heavy dirt impregnated grease. Most leaks are caused by damaged or missing O-ring seals at the component connections, damaged charging valve cores or missing service gauge port caps.

The evaporator drain tube expels the condensation that accumulates on the bottom of the evaporator housing, into the engine compartment. If the tube is obstructed, air conditioning performance can be restricted and condensation buildup can spill over onto the vehicle floor.

Any obstruction of or damage to the condenser configuration will restrict the air flow which is essential to its efficient operation. It is therefore a good rule to keep the condenser clean and in proper physical shape.

Move the refrigerant hoses and look for signs of cracks, rotted hoses or loose connections.

SYSTEM PERFORMANCE CHECK

▶ See Figures 97, 98 and 99

1. Connect a manifold gauge set to the air conditioning system as explained in this section.
2. Start the engine and turn the air conditioner **ON**.
3. As soon as the system is stabilized, record the high and low pressures shown on the manifold gauges. The low side should cycle between approximately 25-45 psi (172-310 kPa). As low pressure drops, high pressure should rise. When the compressor clutch is disengaged, the low side should rise and the high side should drop.
4. Determine the clutch cycle rate per minute. Clutch on time + clutch off time = 1 cycle.

➡When the ambient temperature is above 80°F (26°C), the clutch may not cycle.

5. Record the following:
   • Clutch **OFF** time in seconds
   • Clutch **ON** time in seconds
   • Center dash register discharge temperature
   • Ambient temperatures
6. Plot a vertical line for recorded ambient temperature from the scale at the bottom of each chart to the top of each chart in the figures.
7. Plot a horizontal line for each of the other test readings from the scale at the left-hand side of the appropriate chart.
8. If the point where the 2 lines cross on each of the charts falls within the dark band, the system is operating properly. If the lines cross outside the dark band on one or more of the charts, there is a malfunction. To determine the cause of the malfunction, refer to the chart in the figure.

GAUGE SETS

▶ See Figures 100 and 101

Most of the service work performed in air conditioning requires the use of a set of two gauges, one for the high pressure side of the system and the other for the low pressure side of the system.

The low side gauge records both pressure and vacuum. Vacuum readings are calibrated from 0 to 30 inches Hg (0-99 kPa) and the pressure graduations read from 0 to no less than 60 psi (0-414 kPa). The high side gauge measures pressure from 0 to at least 600 psi (4140 kPa).

IMPORTANT — TEST REQUIREMENTS

The following test conditions must be established to obtain accurate pressure readings:

- Run engine at 1500 rpm for 10 minutes.
- Operate A/C system on max A/C (recirculating air).
- Run blower at max speed.
- Stabilize in car temperature @ 70°F to 80°F (21°C to 22°C).

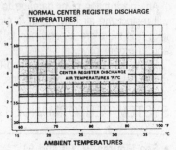

NORMAL CENTER REGISTER DISCHARGE TEMPERATURES

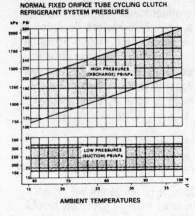

NORMAL FIXED ORIFICE TUBE CYCLING CLUTCH REFRIGERANT SYSTEM PRESSURES

86651068

Fig. 97 Normal air conditioning system pressure/temperature relationships

IMPORTANT — TEST REQUIREMENTS

The following test conditions must be established to obtain accurate clutch cycle rate and cycle time readings:

- Run engine at 1500 rpm for 10 minutes.
- Operate A/C system on max A/C (recirculating air).
- Run blower at max speed.
- Stabilize in car temperature @ 70°F to 80°F (21°C to 22°C).

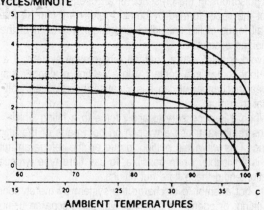

NORMAL CLUTCH CYCLE RATE PER MINUTE CYCLES/MINUTE

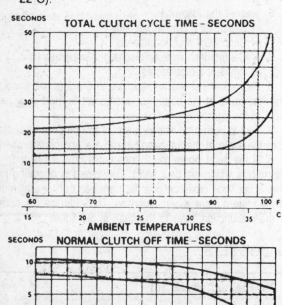

TOTAL CLUTCH CYCLE TIME – SECONDS

NORMAL CLUTCH OFF TIME – SECONDS

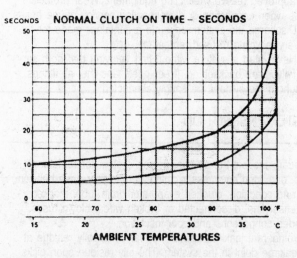

NORMAL CLUTCH ON TIME – SECONDS

86651069

Fig. 98 Normal compressor clutch cycle rates and times

NOTE: System test requirements must be met to obtain accurate test readings for evaluation. Refer to the normal refrigerant system pressure/temperature and the normal clutch cycle rate and times charts.

HIGH (DISCHARGE) PRESSURE	LOW (SUCTION) PRESSURE	CLUTCH CYCLE TIME			COMPONENT — CAUSES
		RATE	ON	OFF	
HIGH	HIGH	CONTINUOUS RUN			CONDENSER — Inadequate Airflow
HIGH	NORMAL TO HIGH				ENGINE OVERHEATING
NORMAL TO HIGH	NORMAL				AIR IN REFRIGERANT REFRIGERANT OVERCHARGE (a) HUMIDITY OR AMBIENT TEMP VERY HIGH (b)
NORMAL	HIGH				FIXED ORIFICE TUBE — Missing O-Rings Leaking/Missing
NORMAL	NORMAL	SLOW OR NO CYCLE	LONG OR CONTINUOUS	NORMAL OR NO CYCLE	MOISTURE IN REFRIGERANT SYSTEM EXCESSIVE REFRIGERANT OIL
NORMAL	LOW	SLOW	LONG	LONG	CLUTCH CYCLING SWITCH — Low Cut Out
NORMAL TO LOW	HIGH	CONTINUOUS RUN			Compressor — Low Performance
NORMAL TO LOW	NORMAL TO HIGH				A/C SUCTION LINE — Partially Restricted or Plugged (c)
NORMAL TO LOW	NORMAL	FAST	SHORT	NORMAL	EVAPORATOR — Low or Restricted Airflow
			SHORT TO VERY SHORT	NORMAL TO LONG	CONDENSER, FIXED ORIFICE TUBE, OR A/C LIQUID LINE — Partially Restricted or Plugged
			SHORT TO VERY SHORT	SHORT TO VERY SHORT	LOW REFRIGERANT CHARGE
			SHORT TO VERY SHORT	LONG	EVAPORATOR CORE — Partially Restricted or Plugged
NORMAL TO LOW	LOW	CONTINUOUS RUN			A/C SUCTION LINE — Partially Restricted or Plugged (d)
ERRATIC OPERATION OR COMPRESSOR NOT RUNNING		—	—	—	CLUTCH CYCLING SWITCH — Dirty Contacts or Sticking Open POOR CONNECTION AT A/C CLUTCH CONNECTOR OR CLUTCH CYCLING SWITCH CONNECTOR A/C ELECTRICAL CIRCUIT ERRATIC — See A/C Electrical Circuit Wiring Diagram

ADDITIONAL POSSIBLE CAUSE COMPONENTS ASSOCIATED WITH INADEQUATE COMPRESSOR OPERATION

- COMPRESSOR DRIVE BELT — Loose • COMPRESSOR CLUTCH — Slipping
- CLUTCH COIL Open — Shorted, or Loose Mounting
- CONTROL ASSEMBLY SWITCH — Dirty Contacts or Sticking Open
- CLUTCH WIRING CIRCUIT — High Resistance, Open or Blown Fuse
- COMPRESSOR OPERATION INTERRUPTED BY ENGINE COMPUTER

ADDITIONAL POSSIBLE CAUSE COMPONENTS ASSOCIATED WITH A DAMAGED COMPRESSOR

- CLUTCH CYCLING SWITCH — Sticking Closed or Compressor Clutch Seized
- SUCTION ACCUMULATOR DRIER — Refrigerant Oil Bleed Hole Plugged
- REFRIGERANT LEAKS

(a) Compressor may make noise on initial run This is slugging condition caused by excessive liquid refrigerant
(b) Compressor clutch may not cycle in ambient temperatures above 80°F depending on humidity conditions
(c) Low pressure reading will be normal to high if pressure is taken at accumulator and if restriction is downstream of service access valve
(d) Low pressure reading will be low if pressure is taken near the compressor and restriction is upstream of service access valve

86651070

Fig. 99 Air conditioning system pressure and clutch cycle timing evaluation

Both gauges are threaded into a manifold that contains two hand shut-off valves. The manifold valves are designed so they have no direct effect on gauge readings, but serve only to meter the flow of refrigerant through the manifold. During all testing and hook-up operations, the valves are kept in the closed position to avoid disturbing the refrigeration system.

Connect the manifold gauge set as follows:

1. Turn both manifold valves fully to the right, to close the high and low pressure hoses to the center manifold and hose.

2. Remove the caps from the high and low pressure service gauge port valves. The high pressure service gauge port valve is located between the compressor and the condenser on the high pressure discharge line. The low pressure service gauge port valve is located between the suction accumulator/drier and the compressor on the low pressure suction line, or is located directly on the suction accumulator/drier.

3. Connect the high and low pressure hoses to the respective high and low pressure service gauge port valves.

➡If the manifold gauge set hoses do not have valve depressing pins in them, install fitting adapters T71P-19703-S/R or equivalent on the low and high pressure hoses. High side adapter set D81L-19703-A or Motorcraft® tool YT-354/355 or equivalent, must be used to connect the manifold gauge set to the high pressure service gauge port valve.

DISCHARGING THE SYSTEM

Discharging the refrigerant from the air conditioning system should be performed by a qualified facility equipped with recovery/recycling equipment meeting Society of Automotive Engineers (SAE) Standard J 1991 standards.

EVACUATING

1. Connect a manifold gauge set as explained in this section.

2. Leak test the system, as explained in this section.

3. Properly discharge the refrigerant from the system into a recovery/recycling machine.

4. Make sure both manifold gauge valves are closed (turned all the way to the right).

5. Make sure the center hose connection at the manifold gauge set is tight. Connect the center hose to a suitable vacuum pump.

6. Open the manifold gauge set valves and start the vacuum pump.

7. Run the vacuum pump until the low pressure gauge reads at least 25 in. Hg (82.5 kPa) or as close to 30 in. Hg (99 kPa) as possible. Continue to operate the vacuum pump for 15 minutes. If a part of the system has been replaced, operate the vacuum pump for 20-30 minutes.

8. When evacuation is completed, close the manifold gauge set valves and turn the vacuum pump off.

9. Observe the low pressure gauge for 5 minutes to make sure vacuum is held. If vacuum is held, the system can be charged. If vacuum is not held for 5 minutes, the system might have a leak. Repair the leak and evacuate the system again.

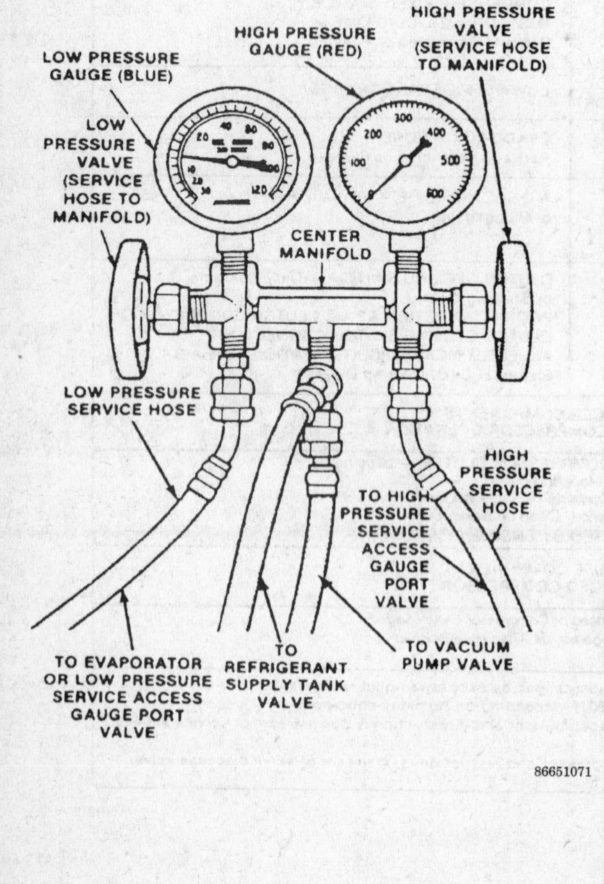

Fig. 100 Air conditioning manifold gauge set

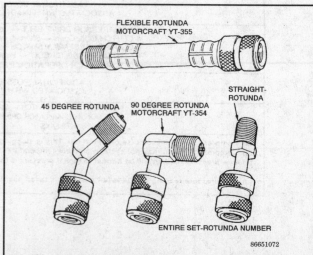

Fig. 101 Fitting adaptors must be used to connect the gauge sets on some systems

CHARGING

➡Charging the air conditioning system should be performed by a qualified facility equipped with recovery/recycling equipment meeting Society of Automotive Engineers (SAE) Standard J 1991.

1. Evacuate The A/C system.
2. Make sure the manifold gauge set valves are still closed to the center hose, then disconnect the vacuum pump.
3. Connect the center hose to a refrigerant charging container.
4. Loosen the center hose at the manifold gauge set and open the refrigerant charging cylinder valve. Allow only enough refrigerant to escape to purge the air and moisture from the center hose, then tighten the center hose connection at the manifold gauge set.
5. Disconnect the wire harness connector from the clutch cycling pressure switch and install a jumper wire across the 2 terminals of the connector.
6. Open the manifold gauge set low side valve to let refrigerant enter the system. Keep the refrigerant container in an upright position if the vehicle's low pressure service gauge port is not on the suction accumulator/drier.
7. When no more refrigerant is being drawn into the system, start the engine and move the control panel lever to the **AC** position and the blower switch to **HI** to draw the remaining refrigerant into the system.
8. Continue adding refrigerant to the system until the required weight of refrigerant is in the system.
9. Close the manifold gauge set low pressure valve and the refrigerant supply valve.
10. Remove the jumper wire from the clutch cycling pressure switch connector and engage the connector to the pressure switch.
11. Operate the system until pressures stabilize to verify normal operation and system pressures.
12. In high ambient temperatures, it may be necessary to operate a high volume fan positioned to blow air through the radiator and condenser to aid in cooling the engine and prevent excessive refrigerant system pressures.

13. When charging is completed and system operating pressures are normal, disconnect the manifold gauge set from the vehicle. Install the protective caps on the service gauge port valves.

LEAK TESTING

▶ **See Figure 102**

➡**This procedure requires the use of electronic leak detector tool 055-00014, 055-00015 or equivalent.**

Turn the control switch on the electronic leak detector to the **ON** position. The detector will automatically calibrate itself. Move the detector probe at approximately 1 in. per second in the suspected leak area. When escaping refrigerant gas is located, the ticking/beeping signal from the detector will increase in ticks/beeps per second. If the gas is relatively concentrated, the signal will be increasingly shrill. Follow the instructions included with the detector for further operating information.

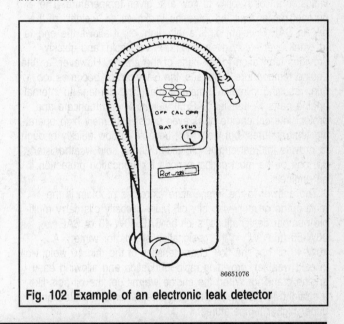

86651076

Fig. 102 Example of an electronic leak detector

FLUIDS AND LUBRICANTS

Fluid Disposal

Used fluids such as engine oil, transmission fluid, antifreeze and brake fluid are hazardous wastes and must be disposed of properly. Before draining any fluids, consult with the local authorities; in many areas, waste oil, etc. is being accepted as a part of recycling programs. A number of service stations and auto parts stores are also accepting waste fluids for recycling.

Be sure of the recycling center's policies before draining any fluids, as many will not accept different fluids that have been mixed together.

Fuel and Engine Oil Recommendations

FUEL

Depending on the year produced, your car may be equipped with a catalytic converter as a part of its emission control system, necessitating the use of unleaded gasoline. Using leaded fuel will damage the catalytic converter, resulting in poor vehicle performance and excessive exhaust emissions.

If the engine in your car is designed to function on unleaded fuel, use gasoline with a minimum octane rating of 87, which in most areas means regular unleaded gasoline. Always use a high quality fuel containing detergent additives, to keep fuel injectors and intake valves clean.

If the engine occasionally knocks lightly under acceleration, or when going up a hill, do not be concerned. However, if the engine knocks heavily under all driving conditions, or knocks lightly at cruising speeds, try switching to another brand or higher grade of gasoline. If knocking persists, the cause should be investigated or serious engine damage could result.

OIL

▶ See Figures 103 and 104

Always use a high quality detergent motor oil. To determine an oil's quality and viscosity, look for the American Petroleum Institute (API) symbol on the oil container label. Always use an oil with an API classification "SG" or higher.

For maximum fuel economy, look for an oil that carries the words "Energy Conserving II" in the API symbol. This means that the oil contains friction reducing additives that help reduce the amount of fuel burned to overcome engine friction.

The Society of Automotive Engineers (SAE) viscosity rating indicates an oil's ability to flow at a given temperature. The number designation indicates the thickness or "weight" of the oil. An SAE 5 weight oil is a thin, light oil; it allows the engine to crank over easily even when it is very cold, and quickly provides lubrication for all parts of the engine. However, as the engine temperature increases, the 5 weight oil becomes too thin, resulting in metal-to-metal contact and damage to internal engine parts. A heavier SAE 50 weight oil can lubricate and protect internal engine parts even under extremely high operating temperatures, but would not be able to flow quickly enough to provide internal engine protection during cold weather start-up, one of the most critical periods for lubrication protection in an engine.

The answer to the temperature extremes problem is the multi-grade or multi-viscosity oil. Multi-viscosity oils carry multiple number designations, such as SAE 10W-40 or SAE 20W-50 (the "W" in the designation stands for winter). A 10W-40 oil has the flow characteristics of the thin 10 weight oil in cold weather, providing rapid lubrication and allowing easy engine cranking. When the engine warms up, the oil acts like a straight 40 weight oil, providing internal engine protection under higher temperatures.

Ford Motor Company recommends using either SAE 5W-30 or SAE 10W-30 oil. SAE 5W-30 should be used if you anticipate the ambient temperature in which you'll be driving to fall below 0°F (-18°C) but not go higher than 100°F (38°C) during the period before your next oil change. SAE 10W-30 should be used if you anticipate the temperature in which you'll be driving to be between 0°F (-18°C) and 100°F (38°C) and above, during the period before your next oil change.

Engine

OIL LEVEL CHECK

▶ See Figures 105, 106, 107 and 108

Check the engine oil level every time you fill the gas tank. Make sure the oil level is between the FULL and ADD marks on the engine oil level dipstick. The engine and oil must be

Fig. 103 An example of the API Symbol

Oil Viscosity—Temperature Chart

When Outside Temperature is Consistently	Use SAE Viscosity Number
SINGLE GRADE OILS	
−10°F to 32°F	10W
10°F to 60°F	20W-20
32°F to 90°F	30
Above 60°F	40
MULTIGRADE OILS	
Below 32°F	5W-30*
−10°F to 90°F	10W-30
Above—10°F	10W-40
Above 10°F	20W-40
Above 20°F	20W-50

*When sustained high-speed operation is anticipated, use the next higher grade.

86671204

Fig. 104 Choose your oil based on anticipated outdoor temperatures for the next few months

warm and the vehicle parked on level ground to get an accurate reading. Also, allow a few minutes after turning off the engine for the oil to drain back into the pan before checking, or an inaccurate reading will result. Check the engine oil level as follows:

1. Open the hood and locate the engine oil dipstick.
2. If the engine is hot, you may want to wrap a rag around the dipstick handle before removing it.
3. Remove the dipstick and wipe it with a clean, lint-free rag, then reinsert it into the dipstick tube. Make sure it is inserted all the way or an inaccurate reading will result.
4. Pull out the dipstick and note the oil level. The correct should be between the ADD and FULL marks.
5. If the oil level is below the ADD mark, remove the oil filler cap from the rocker arm cover and add fresh oil to bring the level within the proper range. Do not overfill; approximately 1 quart of oil is required to raise the oil level from the ADD mark to the FULL mark.

➡Using a funnel when adding oil helps prevent spillage.

Fig. 105 The engine oil level dipstick usually has a bright colored handle

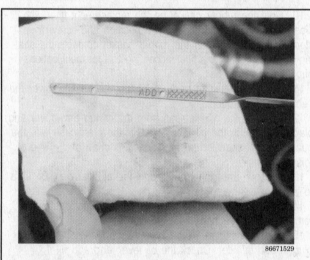

Fig. 106 If the oil level is correct, oil should be visible in the hash-marked area on the dipstick

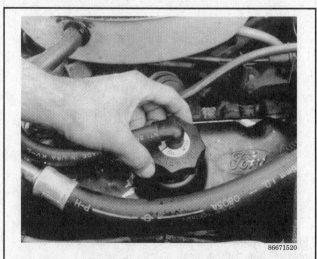

Fig. 107 If oil needs to be added, remove the oil filler cap, but try not to disconnect the breather line

Fig. 108 Use a funnel to help prevent spilling oil over the engine

6. Wait a few minutes for the oil to drain into the pan and recheck the oil level. Add more oil only if required.

7. Install the oil filler cap. Install the dipstick, making sure it is fully inserted into the dipstick tube. Close the hood.

OIL AND FILTER CHANGE

▶ See Figures 109, 110, 111, 112, 113 and 114

The engine oil and oil filter should be changed at the recommended intervals on the Maintenance Intervals chart. The oil should be changed more frequently if the vehicle is being operated in very dusty areas. Before draining the oil, make sure the engine is at operating temperature. Hot oil will hold more impurities in suspension and will flow better, allowing the removal of more oil and dirt.

Change the oil and filter as follows:

1. Apply the parking brake and block the drive wheels.
2. Run the engine until it reaches the normal operating temperature, then turn the engine OFF.
3. Raise and safely support the front of the car on jackstands. Refer to the Jacking portion in this section.
4. Slide a drain pan under the oil pan drain plug. Vehicles equipped with 5.0L or 5.8L engines, have 2 oil drain plugs on the oil pan; both must be removed.

✷✷CAUTION

The EPA warns that prolonged contact with used engine oil may cause a number of skin disorders, including cancer! You should make every effort to minimize your exposure to used engine oil. Protective gloves should be worn when changing the oil. Wash your hands and any other exposed skin areas as soon as possible after exposure to used engine oil. Soap and water, or waterless hand cleaner should be used.

5. Wipe the drain plug and the surrounding area clean. Loosen the drain plug with a socket or box wrench, and then remove it by hand, using a rag to shield your fingers from the

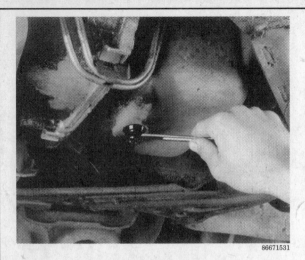

Fig. 109 Using a suitable wrench, loosen and remove the drain plug(s)

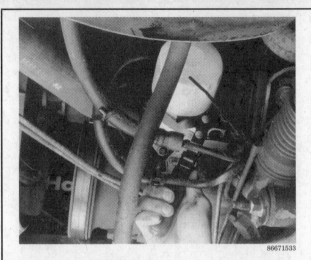

Fig. 111 Remove the oil filter. A filter wrench makes this much easier

10. Coat the rubber gasket on the replacement filter with clean engine oil. Place the filter in position and screw it on clockwise by hand. After the rubber gasket contacts the sealing surface, tighten the filter according to the specifications supplied with the filter.

11. Pull the drain pan from under the vehicle and lower the vehicle to the ground.

12. Remove the oil filler cap from the rocker arm cover and place a funnel in the oil filler hole. Fill the crankcase with the quantity of oil specified in the Capacities chart at the end of this section.

13. Remove the funnel and install the oil filler cap. Be sure to wipe away any spilled oil.

14. Start the engine and let it run until normal operating temperature is reached.

15. Turn the engine **OFF**. Check for oil leaks at the drain plug(s) and oil filter. Check the oil level, and add oil if necessary.

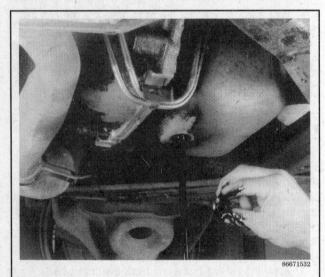

Fig. 110 Allow the oil to drain into a suitable container

heat. Push in on the plug as you turn it out, so that no oil escapes until the plug is completely removed.

6. Allow the oil to drain into the pan. Be careful; if the engine is at operating temperature, the oil is hot enough to burn you.

7. Clean and install the drain plug, making sure that the gasket is still on the plug. If the gasket is missing or damaged, install a new one. Tighten the drain plugs on 5.0L and 5.8L engines to 15-25 ft. lbs. (20-34 Nm). Tighten the drain plug on all other engines to 8-12 ft. lbs. (11-16 Nm).

8. Slide the drain pan under the oil filter. Slip an oil filter wrench onto the filter and turn it counterclockwise to loosen it. Wrap a rag around the filter and unscrew it the rest of the way. Be careful of oil running down the side of the filter.

9. Make sure the old oil filter gasket is not stuck on the cylinder block or oil filter adapter. Thoroughly clean the sealing surface and mounting threads on the cylinder block or adapter.

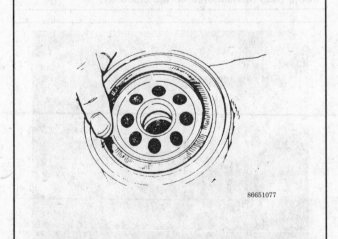

Fig. 112 Apply a thin layer of clean motor oil to the new oil filter rubber seal

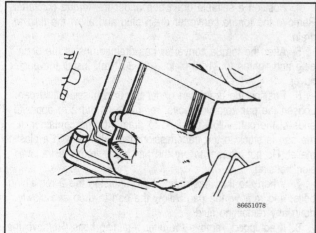

Fig. 113 Install the oil filter by hand. Never tighten it with a filter wrench

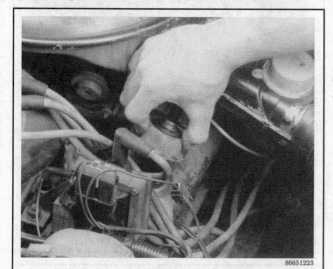

Fig. 114 Don't forget to add the oil

Automatic Transmission

FLUID RECOMMENDATIONS

Depending on the production date of the transmission, Motorcraft MERCON® or DEXRON® type automatic transmission fluid is required. To determine which type of fluid your transmission requires, inspect the base of your transmission dipstick. The recommended fluid will be stamped on the bottom of the dipstick.

LEVEL CHECK

▶ **See Figures 115, 116 and 117**

The automatic transmission fluid level should be checked when the fluid is at an operating temperature of 150-170°F

(66-77°C). This fluid temperature can be reached by driving the car for 15-20 miles (24-32 km) of city type driving with an ambient air temperature of 50°F (10°C) or higher. When the fluid is checked at this temperature, the fluid level should be within the cross-hatched area on the dipstick.

Check the transmission fluid level as follows:

1. Make sure the vehicle is parked on a level surface. Place the transmission selector lever in **P** and start the engine.

2. Apply the foot brake and move the transmission selector lever to each position, pausing for a moment while the transmission is in each position.

3. Place the transmission selector lever in **P** and apply the parking brake. Leave the engine running.

4. Clean any dirt from the transmission fluid dipstick cap.

5. Remove the dipstick from the tube. You may want to wrap a rag around the dipstick handle; it will be hot. Wipe the fluid from the dipstick using a clean lint-free rag and reinsert the dipstick into the tube. Make sure the dipstick is fully seated.

6. Pull the dipstick from the tube and check the fluid level. It should be within the cross-hatched area on the dipstick.

➡**In order to obtain an accurate reading, if the vehicle has been operated for an extended period at high speed, in city traffic, in hot weather, or has been pulling a trailer, allow the fluid to cool for at least ½ hour after the vehicle is shut off.**

7. If the fluid level is okay, reinstall the dipstick in the tube, making sure it is fully seated.

8. If the fluid level is low, add only enough fluid through the dipstick tube to bring the fluid to the correct level. Use a funnel to prevent spilling the fluid over the engine.

✳✳WARNING

Do not overfill the transmission. Overfilling can result in foaming, fluid loss through the vent, or possible transmission malfunction. If the transmission is overfilled, the excess fluid must be drained by removing the pan.

9. When the transmission fluid level is correct, reinstall the dipstick in the tube, making sure it is fully seated.

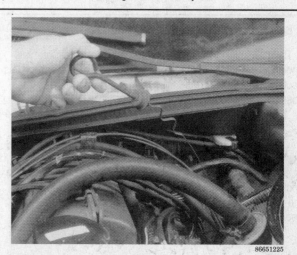

Fig. 115 Remove the transmission dipstick. Do not get it confused with the oil dipstick

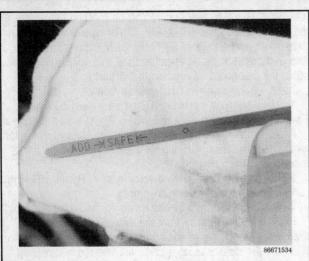

Fig. 116 If the transmission fluid level is correct, it should be between the add and safe marks

Fig. 117 Use a funnel to prevent spilling the fluid over the engine

DRAIN AND REFILL

▶ **See Figures 118, 119, 120, 121 and 122**

The transmission fluid should be changed at the intervals specified in the Maintenance Intervals chart at the end of this section. Anytime the transmission pan is removed, the transmission filter should be replaced.

1. Raise and safely support the vehicle on jackstands. Refer to the Jacking Procedure in this section.

2. Remove the torque converter dust cover from the transmission housing.

3. If equipped with a torque converter drain plug, install a socket and breaker bar on the crankshaft damper bolt. Turn the crankshaft until the torque converter drain plug can be seen.

4. Position a suitable drain pan under the torque converter. Remove the torque converter drain plug and allow the fluid to drain.

5. After the torque converter has drained, install the drain plug and tighten to 21-23 ft. lbs. (28-30 Nm). Install the dust cover.

6. Position the drain pan under the transmission fluid pan. Loosen the pan retaining bolts, removing all but 2 at opposite ends of the pan. Allow the fluid to drain into the container. If the pan is stuck to the transmission, tap it lightly with a plastic mallet. Do not attempt to pry the pan away from the transmission housing.

7. When the fluid has drained off, unfasten the 2 remaining bolts, and remove the pan. Allow the pan to drop and slowly drain any remaining fluid.

8. If equipped, remove the filter retaining bolts. Remove the filter, grommet or gasket.

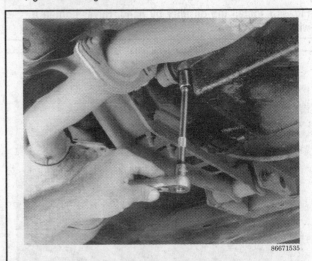

Fig. 118 Loosen all the pan retaining bolts. Remove all the bolts except 2 at opposite ends of the pan

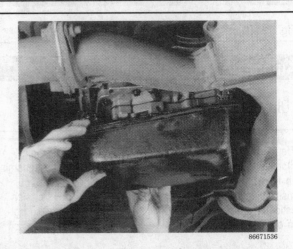

Fig. 119 Allow any excess fluid remaining in the pan to drain out, then unfasten the remaining bolts and remove the pan

Fig. 120 With the pan removed, the screen is plainly visible

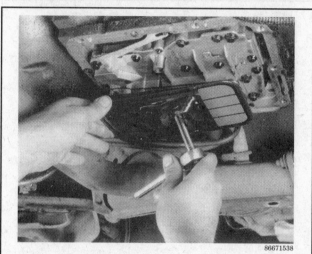

Fig. 121 If the filter is secured with bolt(s), remove them

Fig. 122 Remove the filter by pulling it straight down. Don't forget to remove the gasket or grommet

9. Remove the magnet from the transmission fluid pan, if equipped. Thoroughly clean the pan and magnet. Clean all old pan gasket material from the transmission housing.

➡The magnet is installed to collect any metal shavings from the transmission fluid. A small amount of shavings clinging to the magnet are not cause for concern; they are caused by normal wear of internal components during transmission operation. However, you should consult a reputable transmission shop if any large pieces of metal are found on the magnet, especially if the transmission is not operating properly.

To install:
10. If equipped with automatic overdrive transmission, install a new filter on the transmission valve body, using a new gasket. Install the retaining bolts and tighten to 80-120 inch lbs. (9-14 Nm).
11. Place the magnet, if equipped, in the fluid pan in its original location. Install a new gasket on the fluid pan.
12. Install the fluid pan with the retaining bolts. Tighten the retaining bolts, evenly, to 107-119 inch lbs. (12-14 Nm).
13. Lower the vehicle.
14. Fill the transmission with the proper quantity of fluid. Refer to the Capacities chart at the end of this section. Check the fluid level according to the procedure described earlier.

Manual Transmission

FLUID RECOMMENDATIONS

It is recommended that an SAE 80W-90 weight gear oil be used in the manual transmission.

LEVEL CHECK

➡Manual transmission have no provision for a dipstick to check fluid level.

To check the transmission fluid level, proceed as follows:
1. Raise and support the entire vehicle safely on jackstands.
2. Locate the fluid filler plug on the right side of the transmission.
3. Loosen and remove the fluid filler plug. Upon removing the plug, if gear oil drips out, the level is satisfactory. If upon removing the plug, gear oil does not drip out, additional fluid will have to be added.
4. To add fluid, pour gear oil into the transmission hole and install the plug. Wait several minutes and check the level. continue adding gear oil until it begins to drip out.

DRAIN AND REFILL

The gear oil should be changed at the intervals specified in the Maintenance Intervals chart at the end of this section.
With the entire vehicle raised and supported on jackstands, remove the transmission plug at the base of the transmission and allow the fluid to drain into a drain pan. Once the fluid

has drained completely, install the plug. If equipped with a 3-speed transmission, fill the transmission with 3.5 qts of gear oil. If equipped with a 4-speed transmission, fill the transmission with 4.0 qts of gear oil. Always check the fluid levels before lowering the vehicle, and adjust as needed.

Rear Drive Axle

FLUID RECOMMENDATIONS

SAE 90 weight hypoid gear oil is required. If equipped with Traction-Lok differential, the addition of friction modifier additive C8AZ-19B546-A or equivalent, is also required when draining and refilling.

LEVEL CHECK

▶ See Figure 123

Checking the differential fluid level is generally unnecessary unless a leak is suspected.

1. Raise and safely support the entire vehicle on jackstands. Refer to the Jacking procedure in this section.
2. Remove the oil fill plug from the differential housing. The hex drive on a ⅜ in. drive ratchet, breaker bar or extension works well on most applications.
3. Insert a finger into the fill hole; be careful as the threads may be sharp. The oil level should be about ¼ in. (6mm) below the bottom of the fill hole.
4. If the oil level feels low, add oil through the fill hole. Most hypoid gear oils come in squeeze bottles equipped with small fill nozzles, designed for this purpose.
5. When the oil level is correct, install the oil fill plug and tighten to 15-30 ft. lbs. (20-41 Nm).

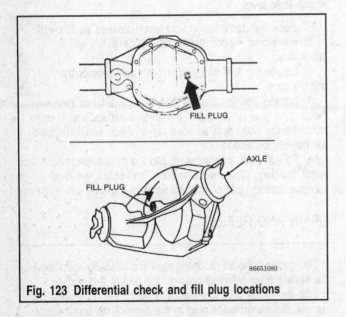

Fig. 123 Differential check and fill plug locations

DRAIN AND REFILL

▶ See Figures 124, 125, 126, 127 and 128

The differential should be drained and refilled every 100,000 miles (161,000 km) or if the axle has been submerged in water.

1. Raise and safely support the vehicle on jackstands. Refer to the Jacking procedure in this section.
2. Clean all dirt from the area of the differential cover.
3. Position a drain pan under the differential.
4. Loosen and remove all the cover retaining bolts except 2. Allow the fluid to drain from the differential.
5. Remove the remaining bolts, then remove the differential cover. Cover the differential carrier with a clean rag to prevent axle contamination, then clean all the old sealant from the machined surface of the differential housing.
6. Make sure the machined surfaces of the cover and differential are clean and free of oil. Apply a ¼ in. (6mm) wide

Fig. 124 With the vehicle safely supported, check the differential case for any signs of leaking

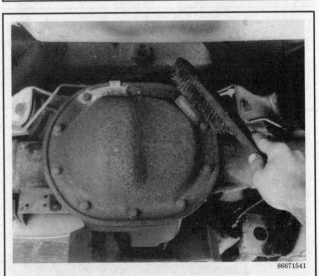

Fig. 125 Clean the cover using a wire brush

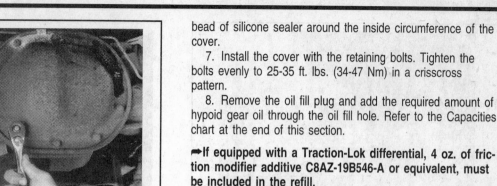

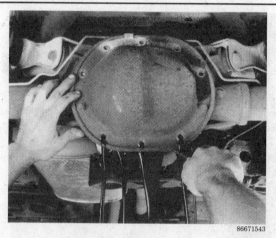

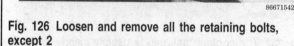

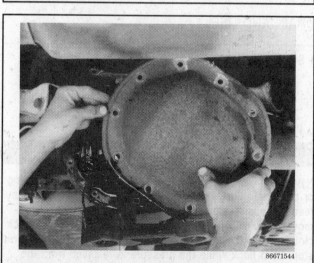

Fig. 126 Loosen and remove all the retaining bolts, except 2

Fig. 127 If necessary, carefully pry the cover away from the differential and allow the fluid to drain. Notice the 2 bolts still in place

Fig. 128 When the fluid has drained, unfasten the remaining bolts and remove the cover

bead of silicone sealer around the inside circumference of the cover.

7. Install the cover with the retaining bolts. Tighten the bolts evenly to 25-35 ft. lbs. (34-47 Nm) in a crisscross pattern.

8. Remove the oil fill plug and add the required amount of hypoid gear oil through the oil fill hole. Refer to the Capacities chart at the end of this section.

➡If equipped with a Traction-Lok differential, 4 oz. of friction modifier additive C8AZ-19B546-A or equivalent, must be included in the refill.

9. Install the oil fill plug and tighten to 15-30 ft. lbs. (20-41 Nm). Lower the vehicle.

10. Road test the vehicle to warm the fluid. Check for leaks.

Cooling System

Check the cooling system at the interval specified in the Maintenance Interval chart at the end of this section.

Hose clamps should be tightened, and soft or cracked hoses replaced. Damp spots, or accumulations of rust or dye near hoses, water pump or other areas, indicate areas of possible leakage. Check the radiator cap for a worn or cracked gasket. If the cap doesn't seal properly, fluid will be lost and the engine will overheat. A worn cap should be replaced with a new one.

Periodically clean any debris such as leaves, paper, insects, etc. from the radiator fins. Pick the large pieces off by hand. The smaller pieces can be washed away with water pressure from a hose.

Carefully straighten any bent radiator fins with a pair of needle nose pliers. Be careful the fins are very soft.

FLUID RECOMMENDATIONS

The recommended fluid is a 50/50 mixture of antifreeze and water for year round use. Use a good quality antifreeze with water pump lubricants, rust inhibitors and other corrosion inhibitors along with acid neutralizers. Use only antifreeze that is safe for use with an aluminum radiator.

LEVEL CHECK

▶ See Figures 129, 130, 131, 132 and 133

The coolant level should be checked at least once a month. With the engine cold, the coolant level should be at or above the FULL COLD mark on the coolant reservoir.

Check the appearance of the coolant. If it is dirty or rusty, it should be replaced in order to protect the cooling system from corrosion damage.

Check the coolant concentration using an antifreeze tester. The protection level should be at least -20°F (-30°C) to maintain the proper freeze and boil over protection and for maximum anti-rust corrosion protection.

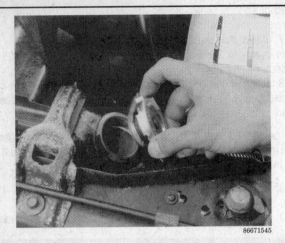

Fig. 129 If the vehicle is not equipped with a reservoir tank, check the fluid level by removing the radiator cap. Do this ONLY when the radiator is cool

Fig. 130 If the engine is equipped with a coolant tank, coolant level is checked at the reservoir. Do not confuse it with the washer reservoir next to it

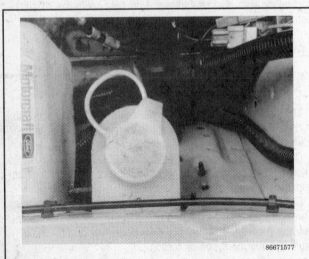

Fig. 131 An example of a washer fluid tank next to a coolant reservoir

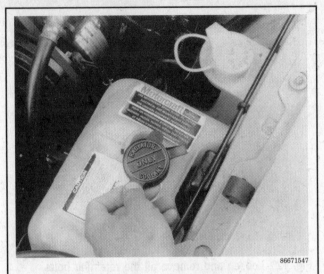

Fig. 132 The coolant tank cap is usually clearly marked

Fig. 133 If necessary, add at the water/coolant mixture to the reservoir tank

DRAIN AND REFILL

▶ See Figures 134 and 135

1. Raise and safely support the vehicle on jackstands, as necessary. Refer to the Jacking procedure in this section.
2. Position a suitable drain pan under the radiator draincock. Remove the radiator cap.

✳✳CAUTION

Never remove the radiator cap while the engine is running or personal injury from scalding hot coolant or steam may result. If possible, wait until the engine has cooled to remove the radiator cap. If this is not possible, wrap a thick cloth around the radiator cap and turn it slowly to the first stop. Step back while the pressure is released from the cooling system. When it is certain all the pressure has been released, press down on the cap with the cloth, then remove it.

3. Open the radiator draincock and allow the coolant to drain into the pan.

➡ The cylinder block drain plugs, located on the sides of the engine block, must be removed to completely drain the system.

✳✳CAUTION

When draining coolant, keep in mind that cats and dogs are attracted to ethylene glycol antifreeze, and could drink any that is left in an uncovered container or in puddles on the ground. This will prove fatal in sufficient quantity. Always drain the coolant into a sealable container.

4. After the coolant has drained, close the radiator draincock and install the cylinder block drain plugs, if removed. Flush the system, if necessary.

5. Fill the cooling system with a 50/50 mixture of water and ethylene glycol. Fill to the level of the radiator filler neck seat.

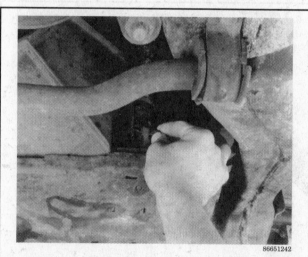

86651242

Fig. 134 Turn the draincock counterclockwise to drain the radiator

86651243

Fig. 135 Use a funnel to add water/coolant mixture to the radiator

6. Install the radiator cap to the first notch to keep spillage to a minimum.

7. Place the heater temperature selector in the maximum heat position.

8. Start the engine and let it idle until the upper radiator hose is warm. This indicates that the thermostat is open and coolant is flowing through the entire system.

9. Stop the engine. Fill the reservoir to the correct level with the coolant mixture. Install the pressure cap securely.

FLUSHING AND CLEANING THE SYSTEM

To remove rust, sludge and any other foreign matter from the cooling system, it should be flushed whenever the coolant is replaced. Flushing the system restores cooling efficiency and helps avoid engine overheating.

In some cases, where a cleaning solvent is not enough to clean the system, it will be necessary to pressure flush the system. In this case, the thermostat should be removed prior to flushing. Various types of pressure flushing equipment are available; consult your auto parts store.

Radiator and Engine

The easiest way to flush the system is to use a can of liquid cooling system flush, available at most auto parts stores. Proceed as follows:

1. After draining the cooling system, close the draincock(s) and add water and the radiator flush to the cooling system.

2. Run the engine until the upper radiator hose gets hot, then drain the system.

3. Repeat the process using fresh water until the drained water is clear and free of scale.

➡ These are general radiator flushing instructions. Always follow the directions on the radiator flush container label. Make sure the flush is safe for use with an aluminum radiator.

4. Disconnect the coolant reservoir from the system and flush it with clean water. Reconnect the reservoir to the system.

5. Refill the cooling system, as described earlier.

Heater Core

Regardless of the type of engine cooling system flush used, the heater core must be flushed separately to prevent engine cooling system particles from clogging the heater core tubes and reducing coolant flow through the heater core. Flush the heater core as follows:

1. Disconnect the heater core outlet hose from the water pump fitting on 5.0L or 5.8L engines, or from the return fitting on all other engines. Install a female garden hose end fitting adapter in the end of the outlet heater hose and secure with a hose clamp.

2. Connect the female garden hose end of the outlet heater hose to the male end of a water supply garden hose.

3. Disconnect the heater core inlet heater hose from the engine block on 5.0L or 5.8L engines, or the intake manifold fitting on all other engines. Allow the hose to drain into a suitable container.

4. If a water valve is installed in the heater core inlet heater hose, make sure the valve is open (no vacuum).

5. Turn the water supply valve on and off several times so the surge action will help to dislodge larger stubborn particles from the heater core tubes. Allow full water pressure to flow for about 5 minutes.

6. If a water valve is installed in the heater core inlet hose, apply vacuum to the valve vacuum motor, using a vacuum pump, to make sure the valve is operating properly. When the valve is closed there should be no water leakage. Replace the valve, if required.

7. Remove the hose clamp and female garden hose end adapter from the end of the outlet heater hose and reconnect the hose to the water pump fitting or heater return fitting, as required.

8. Connect the inlet heater hose to the engine block fitting or intake manifold fitting, as required.

9. Fill the cooling system, as described earlier. Check the heating system for proper operation.

Master Cylinder

FLUID RECOMMENDATIONS

The brake master cylinder requires brake fluid that meets or exceeds DOT 3 standards.

LEVEL CHECK

▶ See Figures 136, 137 and 138

Wipe away any accumulated dirt or grease from the reservoir. Disengage the clamp securing the reservoir cap. Lift the cap up slowly and check the fluid. Add fluid if it is not up to the fill lines marked on the reservoir. Avoid spilling brake fluid on any painted surface as it will harm the finish.

Power Steering Pump

FLUID RECOMMENDATIONS

Ford power steering fluid part number E6AZ-19582-AA or equivalent should be used.

LEVEL CHECK

▶ See Figures 139, 140, 141 and 142

1. Run the engine until the fluid reaches a normal operating temperature of 165-175°F (74-79°C).

2. Turn the steering wheel all the way to the left and right, several times.

3. Shut the engine OFF.

4. Wipe away any accumulated dirt or grease, then remove the dipstick from the power steering fluid reservoir. Wipe the dipstick with a clean cloth, reinsert it fully into the reservoir, then remove it. The fluid level should be within the FULL HOT

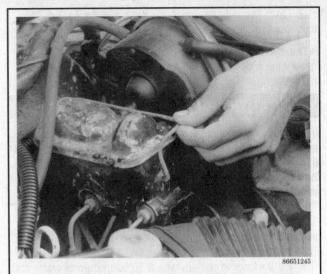

Fig. 136 Disengage the fluid reservoir retaining clamp

Fig. 137 With the cap removed, the fluid level can be checked

Fig. 138 If necessary, add fluid to the reservoir

range on the dipstick if the fluid is at normal operating temperature, within the FULL COLD range if it is not.

5. If the fluid level is low, add the specified fluid. Be careful not to overfill it.

Chassis Greasing

▶ See Figure 143

Lubrication of steering and suspension parts requires the use of a pressure-type grease gun, in order to force the lubricant through the grease fitting. A premium long life chassis grease should be used.

There are grease fittings located on the inner and outer tie rod ends, pitman arm and lower ball joints on all vehicles. In addition, some vehicles are equipped with grease fittings on the upper ball joints. These should be lubricated as indicated in the Maintenance Interval chart at the end of this section.

Wipe away any dirt or accumulated grease from the fitting. Attach the grease gun to the fitting and pump lubricant into the

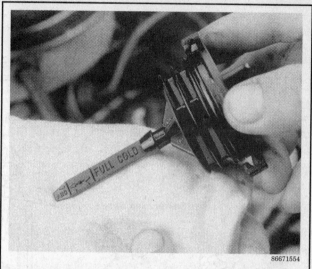

86671554

Fig. 141 While this side shows fluid level when COLD

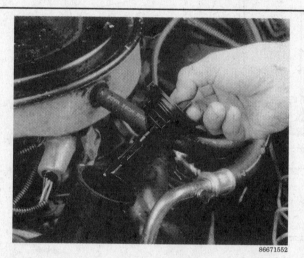

86671552

Fig. 139 The power steering fluid reservoir cap has a level indicator like the engine oil dipstick

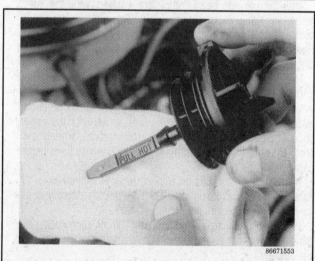

86671553

Fig. 140 The dipstick indicates the level based on fluid temperature. This side shows the HOT level. . .

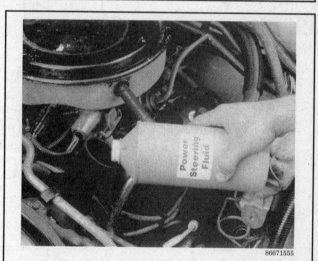

86671555

Fig. 142 Add fluid to the power steering reservoir if necessary

joint. Be careful not to pump in so much lubricant that the joint boot splits.

Use a brush to apply grease to the steering stop pads, (if equipped) located on the lower control arms.

In addition to the steering and suspension components, the cable guides, levers and linkage of the parking brake should be lubricated periodically, using multi-purpose spray grease.

Body Maintenance

Regular body maintenance will preserve your car's appearance. A great looking car instills pride of ownership and helps resale value. All the maintenance records in the world mean little to a prospective buyer if the car appears ill-kept.

EXTERIOR

Your car should be washed frequently. Never try to wipe dirt from the car with a dry cloth, as this will only tend to rub the

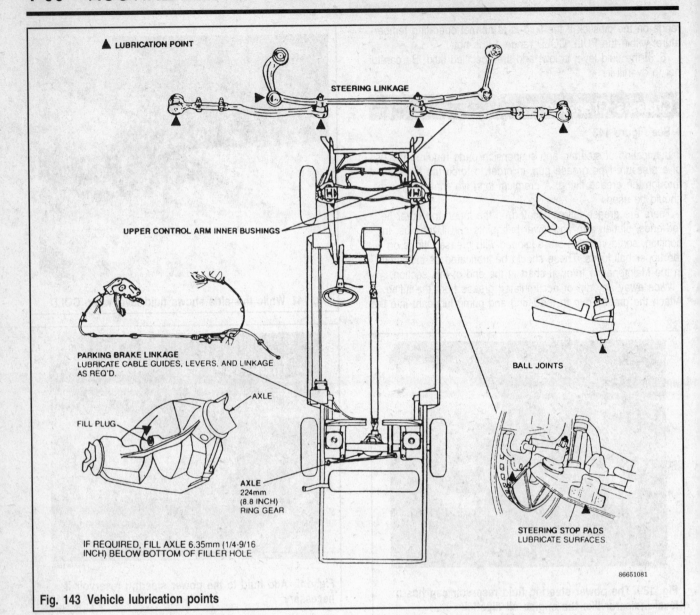

Fig. 143 Vehicle lubrication points

dust and dirt into the surface, scratching the finish. Wash the car with a clean sponge or cloth, using a mild soap and cold water solution. There are many types of car wash cleaning concentrates on the market; these can be found at your local auto parts store.

Wash one section of the car at a time, starting at the top, and rinse frequently with cold water. Never wash your car with hot water, in direct sunlight, or if the sheet metal is hot.

➡ **Rinsing the car is a good time to check for water leaks at the doors, trunk and hood. If a leak is found, it can be cured by repair or replacement of the weather-strips, or adjustment of the body part.**

If you live in an area where the roads are frequently salted for snow and ice removal, the underside of the car should be flushed frequently with clean water, especially after driving on salt covered roads. Pay particular attention to cleaning out underbody members and drain holes where dirt and other foreign material have collected.

After the car has been completely washed, wipe the surfaces dry with a clean lint-free cloth. This will prevent water spotting, which results if the car is merely allowed to air dry. However, the car must be absolutely clean before it is wiped dry, to prevent scratching the paint.

The paint and bright metal on your car should be polished and/or waxed periodically to remove harmful deposits and provide added protection. There are many specialized products available at your local auto parts store to care for the appearance of painted metal surfaces, plastic, chrome, wheels and tires. Be sure to follow the manufacturer's instructions before using them.

Touch-up paint should be applied to any chipped or scratched areas. Consult your Ford or Lincoln-Mercury dealer for the correct color match.

There are drain holes on the underside of each rocker panel, quarter panel and door. These should be cleared periodically.

INTERIOR

The interior of your car should be vacuumed thoroughly on a regular basis. Clean the carpeting, seats, trim panels, instrument panel and headliner. There are many specialized products available at your local auto parts store for cleaning and preserving interior components; be sure to follow the manufacturer's instructions before using them.

Check all weather-stripping. Replace any pieces that are cracked or broken and no longer usable; use weatherstrip cement to attach any pieces that are usable but loose. Apply silicone lubricant to the weather-stripping to preserve it and to prevent squeaks.

Lubricate all hinges, pivots and latches with multi-purpose spray grease. Apply lock lubricant to all lock cylinders.

Front Wheel Bearings

REMOVAL, PACKING AND INSTALLATION

▶ See Figures 144, 145, 146, 147, 148, 149, 150, 151, 152, 153, 154, 155, 156 and 157

1. Raise and support the vehicle safely on jackstands. See the procedure on jacking in this section.
2. Remove the wheel and tire assembly. If equipped with disc brakes, remove the disc brake caliper. Suspend the caliper with a length of wire; do not let it hang from the brake hose.
3. Pry off the dust cap. Remove and discard the cotter pin.
4. Remove the nut retainer.
5. Loosen, then remove the retaining nut.
6. Remove the outer wheel bearing from the hub.
7. Remove the brake disc and wheel hub assembly.
8. Remove the inner grease seal using a small prytool. Remove the inner wheel bearing.
9. Clean the wheel bearings with solvent and inspect them for pits, scratches and excessive wear. Wipe all the old grease from the hub and inspect the bearing races (cups). If either bearings or races are damaged, the bearing races must be removed and the bearings and races replaced as an assembly.
10. If the bearings are to be replaced, drive out the races (cups) from the hub using a brass drift, or pull them from the hub using a puller.
11. Make sure the spindle, hub and bearing assemblies are clean prior to installation.

To install:
12. If the bearing races (cups) were removed, install new ones using a suitable bearing race installer. Pack the bearings with high-temperature wheel bearing grease using a bearing packer. If a packer is not available, work as much grease as possible between the rollers and cages using your hands.
13. Coat the inner surface of the hub and bearing races (cups) with grease.
14. Install the inner bearing in the hub. Using a seal installer or an appropriate sized socket, install a new grease seal into the hub. Lubricate the lip of the seal with grease.
15. Install the hub/disc assembly on the spindle, being careful not to damage the oil seal.

Fig. 144 Clean the front wheel bearing dust cap with a wire brush

Fig. 145 Remove the dust cover

Fig. 146 With the cap removed, inspect the hardware for grime or other foreign matter

Fig. 147 Remove and discard the cotter pin

Fig. 150 With the nut removed, the washer can come out. Note the locating tang on the washer

Fig. 148 Remove the nut retainer

Fig. 151 Remove the outer wheel bearing

Fig. 149 Loosen and remove the retaining nut

Fig. 152 Grasp the rotor with both hands and remove it from the vehicle

Fig. 153 Front outer wheel bearing and hardware

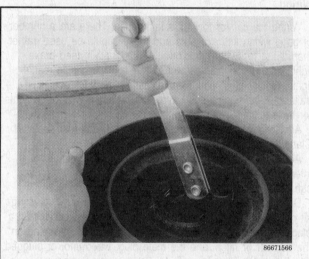

Fig. 154 Remove the inner seal using a seal remover or suitable prytool

Fig. 155 Inner bearing seal removed from the rotor

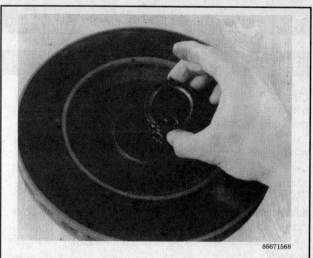

Fig. 156 With the seal removed, the inner bearing can be lifted out

Fig. 157 To install the seal, a seal/race tool can be used as well as a socket. Tap lightly to seat the seal in the hub

16. Install the outer bearing, washer and spindle nut. Install the caliper and the wheel and tire assembly. Adjust the bearings as follows:

a. Loosen the adjusting nut 3 turns and rock the wheel in and out a few times to release the brake pads from the rotor.

b. While rotating the wheel and hub assembly in a counterclockwise direction, tighten the adjusting nut to 17-25 ft. lbs. (23-34 Nm).

c. Back off the adjusting nut ½ turn, then retighten to 10-28 inch lbs. (1.1-3.2 Nm).

d. Install the nut retainer and a new cotter pin. Replace the grease cap.

17. Lower the vehicle. Before driving the vehicle, pump the brake pedal several times to restore normal brake pedal travel.

TRAILER TOWING

General Recommendations

Because trailer towing puts extra strain on your car and is more demanding of you as a driver, the following precautions must be observed:

- Do not overload your vehicle. Stay within the recommended load limits.
- Prepare your vehicle carefully for towing. Use the proper equipment and make sure it is correctly installed.
- Drive with extra care when towing. Your car will handle quite differently when towing a trailer. Take time to familiarize yourself with various driving maneuvers.
- Your vehicle must be serviced more frequently when used for towing.

NECESSARY EQUIPMENT

Your Ford vehicle could have been ordered with an optional trailer towing package. It will be much easier to tow with your car if it was ordered with this package, or if your car has been equipped with the individual upgrades that comprise the trailer towing package.

The actual trailer towing package equipment varies somewhat from model year to model year, but generally includes: heavy duty (72 amp hour) battery, trailer towing suspension and wiring harness, extra engine cooling capacity, auxiliary power steering and transmission oil coolers, heavy-duty flasher system, conventional spare tire, heavy-duty U-joints, dual exhaust system, lower (higher numerically) rear axle ratio with Traction-Lok differential carrier.

Trailer Hitches

The type of trailer hitch you use can be determined by the weight of the trailer you wish to tow. If the total trailer (loaded) weight is 2000 lbs. (3221 km) or less, you can use a Class I hitch. However, since this type of hitch places the tongue load of the trailer on the vehicle's rear wheels, the trailer load must be distributed so that only 10-15% of the total trailer weight is on the tongue.

Using a Class III hitch along with the optional trailer towing package equipment will allow you to tow a trailer weighing up to 5000 lbs. (2250 kg) with a 6 cylinder engine, 6000 lbs. (2700 kg) with a V8 engine. With this type of hitch, the tongue load of the trailer is evenly distributed between the front and rear wheels of the tow vehicle and the trailer wheels.

If your car is equipped with a rear air suspension system, proceed as follows when hooking up a trailer using a load equalizing hitch:

1. Park the unloaded vehicle on level ground. Turn the ignition ON and leave all doors closed. Allow 1-2 minutes for the vehicle to level automatically.
2. Turn the air suspension switch, located on the right side of the trunk OFF.
3. Measure the height of a reference point on the front and rear bumpers at the center of the vehicle.
4. Attach the trailer to the vehicle and adjust the hitch equalizer(s) so the front bumper height is 0-½ in. below the unloaded height.
5. After adjustment, the rear bumper should not be higher than that recorded in Step 3.

Regardless of the type of hitch used, be sure to follow the hitch and trailer manufacturers instructions for installation and use.

Always connect safety chains between the trailer and your car. The chains should be crossed under the trailer tongue and attached to your car's frame or hook retainers. Never attach the safety chains to the bumper. Always make sure there is enough slack in the chains to allow corners to be turned.

Wiring

Wiring the car for towing is fairly easy. There are a number of good wiring kits available and these should be used, rather than trying to design your own. All trailers will need brake lights and turn signals as well as tail lights and side marker lights. Most states require extra marker lights for oversized trailers. Also, most states have recently required back-up lights for trailers.

Additionally, some Class I, most Class II and just about all Class III trailers will have electric brakes.

Add to this number an accessories wire, to operate trailer internal equipment or to charge the trailer's battery, and you can have as many as seven wires in the harness.

Determine the equipment on your trailer and buy the wiring kit necessary. The kit will contain all the wires needed, plus a plug adapter set which included the female plug, mounted on the bumper or hitch, and the male plug, wired into, or plugged into the trailer harness.

When installing the kit, follow the manufacturer's instructions. The color coding of the wires is standard throughout the industry.

One point to note: some domestic vehicles, and most imported vehicles, have separate turn signals. On most domestic vehicles, the brake lights and rear turn signals operate with the same bulb. For those vehicles with separate turn signals, you can purchase an isolation unit so that the brake lights won't blink whenever the turn signals are operated, or, you can go to your local electronics supply house and buy four diodes to wire in series with the brake and turn signal bulbs. Diodes will isolate the brake and turn signals. The choice is yours. The isolation units are simple and quick to install, but far more expensive than the diodes. The diodes, however, require more work to install properly, since they require the cutting of each bulb's wire and soldering in place of the diode.

One, final point, the best kits are those with a spring loaded cover on the vehicle mounted socket. This cover prevents dirt and moisture from corroding the terminals. Never let the vehicle socket hang loosely; always mount it securely to the bumper or hitch.

Cooling

ENGINE

One of the most common, if not THE most common, problem associated with trailer towing is engine overheating.

If your car is equipped with the optional trailer towing package, it already has a heavy duty radiator and you shouldn't have any overheating problems. If your car is not equipped with the trailer towing package, check with your Ford or Lincoln-Mercury dealer, or a with a reputable radiator shop to see what can be done to increase your car's cooling system capacity.

Aftermarket engine oil coolers are helpful for prolonging engine oil life and reducing overall engine temperatures. Both of these factors increase engine life.While not absolutely necessary in towing Class I and some Class II trailers, they are recommended for heavier Class II and all Class III towing.

Engine oil cooler systems consist of an adapter, screwed on in place of the oil filter, a remote filter mounting and a multi-tube, finned heat exchanger, which is mounted in front of the radiator or air conditioning condenser.

TRANSMISSION

The increased load of a trailer causes an increase in the temperature of the automatic transmission fluid. Heat is the worst enemy of an automatic transmission. As the temperature of the fluid increases, the life of the fluid decreases. It is essential, therefore, that you install an automatic transmission cooler.

The cooler, which consists of a multi-tube, finned heat exchanger, is usually installed in front of the radiator or air conditioning condenser, and installed inline with the transmission cooler tank inlet line. Follow the cooler manufacturer's installation instructions.

Select a cooler of at least adequate capacity, based upon the combined gross weights of the car and trailer.

Cooler manufacturers recommend that you use an aftermarket cooler in addition to, and not instead of, the present cooling tank in your car's radiator. If you do want to use a cooler in place of the radiator cooling tank, get a cooler at least two sizes larger than normally necessary.

One note: the transmission cooler can sometimes cause slow or harsh shifting in the transmission during cold weather, until the fluid has a chance to come up to normal operating temperature. Some coolers can be purchased with or retrofitted with a temperature bypass valve which will allow fluid flow through the cooler only when the fluid has reached operating temperature, or above.

Trailer and Tongue Weight Limits

▶ **See Figures 158 and 159**

If your car is equipped with a 6 cylinder engine and you are using a Class I hitch, the loaded trailer weight must not exceed 2000 lbs. (900 kg). If you are using a Class III hitch, the loaded trailer weight must not exceed 5000 lbs. (2250 kg). If your car is equipped with an 8 cylinder engine and you are using a Class III hitch, the loaded trailer weight must not exceed 6000 lbs. (2700 kg).

Make sure that only 10-15% of the trailer's weight is on the tongue, with the tongue weight not exceeding 10% of the maximum weight your car's engine can safely tow.

The load you add to your vehicle must never exceed its Gross Vehicle Weight Rating (GVWR). The GVWR can be found on the Vehicle Certification Label, located on the left front door lock panel. To figure the total weight of the load, add the weights of the following: driver and passengers, luggage and anything else carried in the vehicle, the loaded trailer's tongue weight, and any equipment added to the vehicle.

If you cannot easily determine these weights, you can take your car to a place equipped for weighing vehicles, such as a shipping company or truck inspection station. Weigh your car without the driver, passengers, luggage or trailer. Then weigh the car with the driver, passenger, luggage and trailer attached. The total weight of the load is the difference between the two weights.

After determining the weight of the load, you must make sure the load weight plus the vehicle weight does not exceed the GVWR. You must also make sure that the weight carried over each axle does not exceed the Gross Axle Weight Rating (GAWR), which is also found on the Vehicle Certification Label.

If your vehicle exceeds the GVWR, remove part of the load until the loaded vehicle weight is within the limit. If the GAWR is exceeded on either axle, shift the load or remove part of it from the vehicle.

Driving with a Trailer

Your car will feel quite different when towing a trailer. Before towing on a long trip, take some time to drive your car locally with the trailer to familiarize yourself with its handling, especially if you have never towed before.

Towing a trailer (even if equipped with trailer brakes) requires greater stopping distances. Try to anticipate stops and allow extra room between your car and the vehicle in front of you. Sudden braking can jackknife the trailer or cause the car to skid. To avoid overheating the brakes when going down a steep grade, place the gearshift in a lower gear.

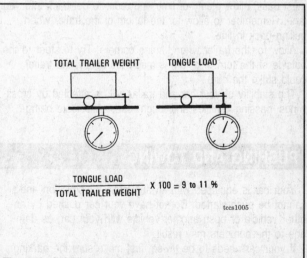

Fig. 158 Calculate the proper tongue weight for your trailer

Recommended Equipment Checklist

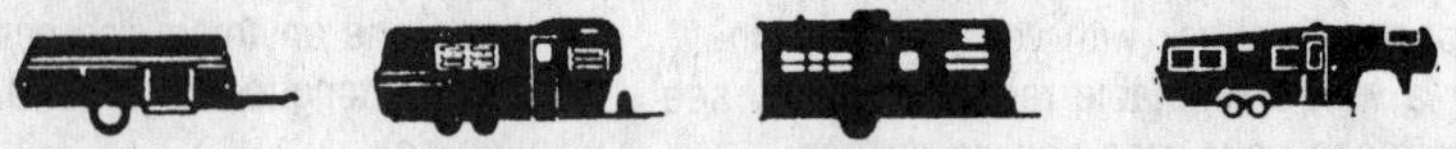

Equipment	Class I Trailers Under 2,000 pounds	Class II Trailers 2,000-3,500 pounds	Class III Trailers 3,500-6,000 pounds	Class IV Trailers 6,000 pounds and up
Hitch	Frame or Equalizing	Equalizing	Equalizing	Fifth wheel Pick-up truck only
Tongue Load Limit**	Up to 200 pounds	200-350 pounds	350-600 pounds	600 pounds and up
Trailer Brakes	Not Required	Required	Required	Required
Safety Chain	3/16" diameter links	1/4" diameter links	5/16" diameter links	—
Fender Mounted Mirrors	Useful, but not necessary	Recommended	Recommended	Recommended
Turn Signal Flasher	Standard	Constant Rate or heavy duty	Constant Rate or heavy duty	Constant Rate or heavy duty
Coolant Recovery System	Recommended	Required	Required	Required
Transmission Oil Cooler	Recommended	Recommended	Recommended	Recommended
Engine Oil Cooler	Recommended	Recommended	Recommended	Recommended
Air Adjustable Shock Absorbers	Recommended	Recommended	Recommended	Recommended
Flex or Clutch Fan	Recommended	Recommended	Recommended	Recommended
Tires	***	***	***	***

NOTE: The information in this chart is a guide. Check the manufacturer's recommendations for your car if in doubt

*Local laws may require specific equipment such as trailer brakes or fender mounted mirrors. Check your local laws. Hitch weight is usually 10-15% of trailer gross weight and should be measured with trailer loaded.

**Most manufacturer's do not recommend towing trailers of over 1,000 pounds with compacts. Some intermediates cannot tow Class III trailers.

***Check manufacturer's recommendations for your specific car - trailer combination

—Does not apply

86651094

Fig. 159 Recommended equipment chart

Acceleration will be reduced when towing a trailer. If you must pass, allow plenty of time and room to get back into your lane. Remember to allow for the length of the trailer when pulling back in line.

Allow for the trailer when turning corners. Try to steer to the outside of the turn. If a turn is made too tightly, the trailer could strike the curb.

The stability of your car and trailer will be affected by crosswinds, passing vehicles and rough roads. Anticipate being passed by large vehicles, such as tractor trailers, so you won't be surprised.

If the car and trailer begins to sway, grip the steering wheel firmly and hold the vehicle straight ahead. Reduce your speed gradually, without using the brakes. The car and trailer should stabilize quickly if there aren't any extreme corrections made to braking, throttle or steering.

The art of backing up when towing a trailer can only be learned through much practice. Do not wait until backing up is absolutely necessary, to learn how to do it.

PUSHING AND TOWING

Your car is equipped with an automatic transmission and cannot be push-started. Do not have your car pushed by another vehicle or push another vehicle with your car, as damage to the bumpers may result.

If your car needs to be towed, first make sure the parking brake is released and place the gearshift in **N**. Optimally it should be towed from the rear, with the rear wheels off the ground. When towed in this manner, the steering wheel must be clamped with the front wheels in the straight-ahead position, using a steering wheel clamping device designed for towing service use. Do not rely on the steering column lock to lock the wheels in the straight-ahead position.

If it is necessary to tow the car from the front, with the rear wheels on the ground, the transmission and differential must be working properly. When towed in this manner, do not exceed 35 mph or go farther than 50 miles, or transmission damage may result.

If the transmission or differential is inoperable, or the speed and distance requirement stated above cannot be maintained, use a dolly under the rear wheels.

JACKING

The service jack that comes with your car should ONLY be used for changing a flat tire. It should NEVER be used to raise the car for any other purpose.

Hydraulic, screw or scissors jacks of adequate lifting capacity are satisfactory for raising the vehicle; jackstands should then be used to support it. Drive-on trestles or ramps are also a handy and safe way to both raise and support the car.

Service Jack

▶ See Figures 160 and 161

1. Place the gearshift lever in **P** and apply the parking brake. Block the wheel diagonally opposite the wheel to be removed.
2. Insert the bottom of the jack post into the base. Pull up on the small lever near the jack handle socket. Insert the jack hook into the slot in the bumper, making sure it fits snugly.
3. Position the jack so the bottom of the post is slightly angled in toward the vehicle.
4. Put the jack handle into the jack handle socket. Push up and down on the handle until the vehicle is raised.
5. Remove and install the wheel and tire assembly, as described earlier in this section.
6. To lower the vehicle, place the small lever near the jack handle socket in the down position. Move the handle up and down to lower the vehicle, keeping a firm grasp on the jack handle.
7. If equipped, turn the air suspension switch **ON**.

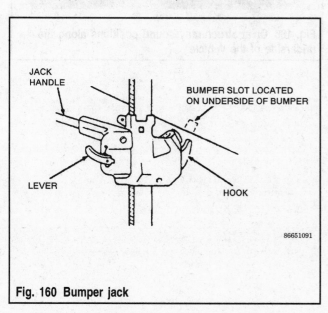

Fig. 160 Bumper jack

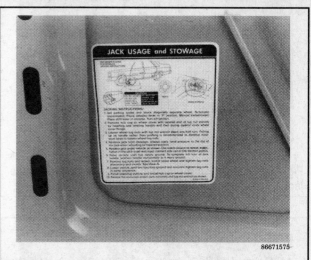

Fig. 161 An instruction label is usually fitted to the underside of the trunk lid

Floor Jack

▶ See Figures 162, 163, 164, 165 and 166

When using a floor jack, either side of the front of the vehicle can be raised by positioning the jack on the lower control arm, at the spindle connection. However, it is usually easier to raise the front of the vehicle at the front crossmember.

At the rear of the vehicle, the jack can be positioned under the rear axle housing tubes, between the suspension arm brackets and the differential housing.

Before raising the vehicle, always make sure the gearshift lever is in the **P** position and the parking brake is applied. Block the wheels at the opposite end of the vehicle. If your car is equipped with air suspension, always turn the air suspension switch **OFF** before raising the vehicle.

After the vehicle has been raised, it must be supported with jackstands, especially if you will be working under it. Never use cinder blocks or stacks of wood to support the car, even if you're only going to be under it for a few minutes. Jackstands can be positioned under the frame rails, under the rear axle tubes, and/or under the front lower control arms, at the spindle connections.

Fig. 162 When raising the front of the vehicle, place the jack on the frame, center between the tires

Fig. 165 Or along the frame of the car. . .

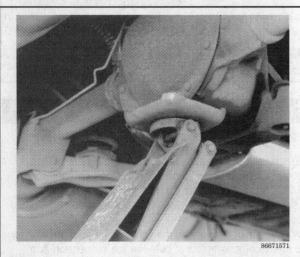

Fig. 163 To raise the rear, position the jack in the center of the differential

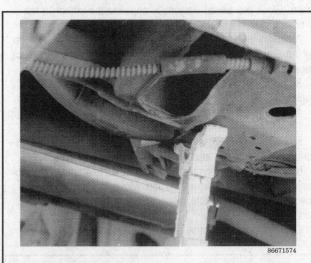

Fig. 166 Or at structurally sound positions along the underside of the vehicle

Fig. 164 When using jackstands, position them under the jacking points of the vehicle. . .

Maintenance Interval Chart

Operation	Thousand Miles									See Chapter
	'71	'72	'73	'74	'75	'76	'77–'79	'80–'82	'83–'85	
ENGINE										
Air cleaner replacement—exc. V8	12	12	—	—	—	—	—	30	30	1
Air cleaner replacement—V8	24	12	12	24	20	20	30	30	30	1
Air intake temperature control system check	12	12	12	12	15	15	20	22.5	22.5	4
Carburetor idle speed and mixture, fast idle, throttle solenoid adj	12	12	12	24	15	15	22.5	30	30	2
Cooling system check	12	12	12	12	15	15	12	12	12	1
Coolant replacement; system draining and flushing	24	24	24	24	40	40	45	52.5	52.5	1
Crankcase breather cap cleaning	6	6	12	12	20	20	30	52.5	52.5	1
Crankcase breather filter replacement (in air cleaner)	6	6	8	24	20	20	30	52.5	52.5	1
Distributor breaker points inspection	12	12	12	6	—	—	—	—	—	2
Distributor breaker points replacement	12	12	24	24	—	—	—	—	—	2
Distributor cap and rotor inspection	12	12	24	①	15	15	22.5	22.5	22.5	2
Drive belts adjustment	12	12	12	12	15	15	22.5	30	30	1
Evaporative control system check; inspect carbon canister	12	12	12	24	20	20	30	52.5	52.5	1
Exhaust control valve (heat riser) lubrication and inspection	6	6	8	6	15	15	15	15	15	1
Exhaust gas recirculation system (EGR) check	—	—	12	12	15	15	15	15	15	4
Fuel filter replacement	12	12	12	6	15	10	10	12	12	1
Ignition timing adjustment	12	12	12	②	⑤	⑤	⑤	⑤	⑤	2
Intake manifold bold torque check (V8 only)	12	12	24	12	15	15	15	15	15	3
Oil change (Turbo—every 5,000 miles)	6	6	4	6	5	5	7.5	7.5	7.5	1
Oil filter replacement (Turbo—each oil change)	6	6	8	12	10	10	15	15	15	1
PCV system valve replacement, system cleaning	12	12	12	24	20	20	22.5	52.5	52.5	4
Spark plug replacement; plug wire check	12	12	12	③	15	15	22.5	30	30	2
Thermactor air injection system check	—	—	—	24	15	15	22.5	22.5	22.5	4
CHASSIS										
Automatic transmission band adjustment	④	④	④	④	④	④	④	④	④	6
Automatic transmission fluid level check	6	6	8	12	15	15	15	15	15	1
Brake system inspection, lining replacement	30	30	24	24	25	30	30	30	30	9
Brake master cylinder reservoir fluid level check	6	6	8	12	15	30	30	30	30	1
Clutch pedal free-play adjustment	6	—	—	—	—	—	—	—	—	6
Front suspension ball joints and steering linkage lubrication	36	36	36	36	30	30	30	30	30	1
Front wheel bearings cleaning, adjusting and repacking	30	30	24	24	25	30	30	30	30	9

Maintenance Interval Chart (Cont.)

Operation	Thousand Miles									See Chapter
	'71	'72	'73	'74	'75	'76	'77–'79	'80–'82	'83–'85	
Manual transmission fluid level check	6	—	—	—	—	—	—	15	15	1
Power steering pump reservoir fluid level check	6	6	4	6	15	15	15	15	15	1
Rear axle fluid level check	6	6	8	12	15	15	15	15	15	1
Steering arm stop lubrication; steering linkage inspection	12	12	12	12	15	15	15	15	15	1

① Conventional ignition—24; electronic ignition—18
② Conventional ignition—12; electronic ignition—18
③ Conventional ignition—12; electronic ignition—18
④ Normal service—12,000 mi. only; severe (fleet) service—6,000/18,000/30,000 mi. intervals
⑤ Periodic adjustment unnecessary

86671201

Capacities

| Year | Engine No. Cyl Displacement (cu in.) | Engine Crankcase (Add 1 qt for new filter) | Transmission (pts to refill after draining) | | | Drive Axle (pts) | Gasoline Tank (gals) | Cooling System (qts) | |
| | | | Manual | | Automatic (Total Capacity) | | | W/heater | W A/C |
			3 spd	4/5 spd					
'71	6-250	3.5	3.5	—	18	4	20[3]	11	11
	8-302	4	3.5	—	18	4	20[3]	15	15.5
	8-351	4	3.5	4	22	5	20[3]	15.5	16.5
	8-429	6[2]	—	4	26	5	20[3]	19.5	19.5
'72–'73	6-250	3.5	3.5	—	18	4	22.5[3]	11.5	11.5
	8-302	4	3.5	—	18	4	22.5[3]	15	15
	8-351	4	—	4	20.5[4]	4	22.5[3]	15.5	16
	8-400	4	—	—	26	4	22.5[3]	17.5	17.5
	8-429	4	—	—	26	5	22.5	19	19
'74	6-250	4	—	—	[5]	4	26.5[6]	11.5	—
	8-302	4	3.5	—	[5]	4	26.5[6]	15.7	15.7
	8-351	4	—	—	[7]	4	26.5[6]	[8]	[8]
	8-400	4	—	—	25	5	26.5[6]	17.7	18.3
	8-460	6	—	—	25	5	26.5[6]	18.9	19.5
'75	8-351	4[11]	—	—	[9]	4	26.5[6]	[10]	[10]
	8-400	4[11]	—	—	[9]	5	26.5[6]	17.1	17.5
	8-460	4	—	—	[9]	5	26.5[6]	19.2	19.2
'76	8-351	4	—	—	[9]	5	26.5[6]	[10]	[10]
	8-400	4	—	—	[9]	5	26.5[6]	17.1	17.5[13]
	8-460	4[1]	—	—	24.4	5	26.5[6]	19.2	19.2[14]
'77–'78	8-302	4	—	—	22	4	26.0[6]	14.8	15.1
	8-351	4	—	—	[17]	5	26.0[6][12]	[15]	[15]
	8-400	4	—	—	[18]	5	26.0[6]	17.0[16]	17.0[16]
'78–'80	Versailles 8-302	4	—	—	20.5[17]	5.0	19.2	14.6	14.6
	8-351W	4	—	—	20.5	5.0	19.2	15.7	15.7
'78–'79	LTD II, Thunderbird, Cougar, Cougar XR-7 8-302	4	—	—	[18]	5.0	21.0[19]	14.3	14.6
	8-351W	4	—	—	[18]	5.0	21.0[19]	15.5	16.0
	8-351M	4	—	—	[18]	5.0	21.0[19]	16.5	16.5
	8-400	4	—	—	[18]	5.0	21.0[19]	16.5	16.5
'80–'81	Cougar XR-7, Thunderbird 6-200	4	—	—	16	3.5	17.5	13.0	13.2
	8-255	4	—	—	20[20]	3.5	17.5	13.2	13.3
	8-302	4	—	—	20[20]	3.5	17.5	12.7	12.8
'81	Cougar 4-140	4	—	2.8	16	3.5	14.7	8.6	8.6
	6-200	4	—	—	16	3.5	16.0	8.1	8.1
	8-255	4	—	—	19	3.5	16.0	13.4	13.5

86671202

Capacities (Cont.)

Year	Engine No. Cyl Displacement (cu in.)	Engine Crankcase (Add 1 qt for new filter)	Transmission (pts to refill after draining)		Automatic (Total Capacity)	Drive Axle (pts)	Gasoline Tank (gals)	Cooling System (qts)	
			Manual					W/heater	W A/C
			3 spd	4/5 spd					
'82	Cougar XR-7, Thunderbird, Lincoln Continental 6-200	4	—	—	22	3.25	21	8.4	8.4
	6-232	4	—	—	24	3.25	21 ㉑	8.3	8.6
	8-255	4	—	—	24	3.25	21	14.9	15
	8-302	4	—	—	24	3.25	22.6	13.3	13.4
'82	Cougar 4-140	4	—	—	16	㉓	16.0 ㉓	10.2	10.2
	6-200	4	—	—	22	3.25	16.0 ㉓	8.4	8.4
	6-232	4	—	—	22	3.25	16.0 ㉓	8.3	8.3
'83–'85	LTD/Marquis 4-140	4	—	2.8	16	3.25 ㉔	16	8.6	9.4
	4-140P	4	—	—	16	3.25 ㉔	24	8.6	9.4
	6-200	4	—	—	22	3.25 ㉔	16	8.4	8.5
	6-232	4	—	—	22 ⑳	3.25 ㉔	16	10.7	10.8
'83–'85	Thunderbird, Cougar Continental 4-140 Turbo	4.5 ㉕	—	4.75	—	3.25 ㉔	18	8.4	8.7
	6-232	4	—	—	22 ⑳	3.25 ㉔	21	10.4	10.7
	8-302	4	—	—	22 ⑳	3.25 ㉔	20.7 ㉖	13.3	13.4

T-Turbocharged
P-Propane
① 460 police is 4
② 429 4 bbl—4 qts
429 CJ, SCJ—6 qts
add 1 qt if equipped with oil cooler
③ Less 2 gals—station wagon, Ranchero
④ 26 pts for 351 CJ
⑤ C4—18 or 20 pts: FMX—22 pts
⑥ Station wagon—21.2 gallons
⑦ 351 2V with C4—20 pts; 351 2V with FMX—22 pts; 351 2V with C6—25 pts; 351 4V with C6—21 pts
⑧ 351W 2v—16.4 qts w/heater; 16.8 w/AC
351C 2v—15.9 qts w/heater; 16.5 w/AC
351C 4v—15.9 qts w/heater; 16.9 w/AC
⑨ C4—20 pts; FMX—22 pts: C6—25 pts
⑩ 351 Windsor—15.9 qts w/heater; 16.2 w/AC
351 Modified—17.1 qts w/heater; 17.5 w/AC; 18.0 police

⑪ Add only ½ qt of oil for new service filter
⑫ T-bird w/351 for Calif.—22.0
⑬ Police or heavy trailer tow—18.0
⑭ Police or heavy trailer tow—19.7
⑮ 351W—15.9 w/heater; 16.2 w/AC
351M—17.0 w/heater or w/AC; 17.5 police and taxi
⑯ 17.5 police
⑰ 1979 and later; 20 pts
⑱ C4: 20 pts. C6: 25 pts. FMX: 22 pts.
⑲ 1979 optional tank; 27.5 gals.
⑳ AOD transmission—24 pts.
㉑ Continental: 20 gals std: 22.6 gals optional
㉒ 6.75 in. axle—2.5 pts; 7.5 in. axle—3.5 pts.
㉓ 20 gals optional
㉔ Traction-Lok; 3.55 pts.
㉕ Turbo: 4.5 qts, add ½ qt with filter
㉖ 22.3 gal Continental

86671203

VEHICLE IDENTIFICATION CHART

	Engine Code						Model Year	
Code	Liters	Cu. In. (cc)	Cyl.	Fuel Sys.	Eng. Mfg.		Code	Year
A	2.3	140	4	1 BBL, 2 BBL	Ford		1	71
W(T)	2.3	140	4	EFI	Ford		2	72
T	3.3	200	6	1 BBL	Ford		3	73
3	3.8	232	6	2 BBL, EFI	Ford		4	74
L	4.1	250	6	1 BBL	Ford		5	75
D	4.2	255	8	2 BBL, VV	Ford		6	76
F	5.0	302	8	2 BBL, 4 BBL, VV, EFI	Ford		7	77
H	5.8	351	6	2 BBL	Ford		8	78
Q	5.8	351	8	VV	Ford		A	79
S	6.6	400	8	2 BBL	Ford		B	80
P	7.0	429	8	4 BBL	Ford		C	81
N	7.0	429	8	4 BBL	Ford		D	82
A	7.5	460	8	4 BBL	Ford		E	83
C	7.5	460	8	4 BBL	Ford		F	84
							G	85

86671c00

Engine Identification Codes

Engine	Year	Code
4-140 Non-Turbo	1981–85	A
4-140 Turbo	1984–85	W(T)
6-200	1981–83	B
6-232	1982–85	3
6-250	1971–74	L
8-255	1980–82	D
8-302	1971–85	F
8-351C	1971–74	H
8-351C 4bbl	1971	M
8-351M	1975–79	Q
8-351W	1973–79	H
8-400	1972–78	S
8-429	1972–73	N
8-429CJ	1971	C
8-429CJ-RA	1971	J
8-460	1974–75	A
8-460PI	1973–76	C

C: Cleveland
M: Modified Cleveland
W: Windsor
CJ: Cobra Jet
RA: Ram Air
PI: Police Interceptor

86671c02

Transmission Codes

Type	Year	Code
3 Speed Manual	1971–74	1
4 Speed Manual	1980–83	6
4 Speed Manual	1980–83	4
4 Speed Manual	1983–85	7
5 Speed Manual	1984–85	2
C3 Automatic	1983–85	V
C4 Automatic	1971–80	W
C5 Automatic	1982–85	C
AOD Auto Overdrive	1980–85	T
CW Automatic	1974–75	Y
FMX Automatic	1971–80	X
C6 Automatic	1971–80	U
C6 Auto Special	1971–79	Z

86671c01

Rear Axle Codes

Ratio	Year	Code
2.26	1979–80	G
2.47	1978, 82–83	B(C)
2.50	1978	1(J)
2.73	1979–85	8(H)(M)
2.75	1971–78	2(K)
3.00	1971–78	6(O)
3.07	1971, 74–75	B, 5(E)
3.08	1979–85	Y(Z)
3.25	1971–77	9(R)
3.27	1983–85	5(E)
3.42	1982–85	4(D)
3.45	1982–85	F(R)
3.55	1984–85	2(K)
3.63	1983	A
3.73	1984–85	(W)
3.85	1983	J

NOTE: *Figures in Parentheses Indicate locking differential.*

86671c03

2

ENGINE PERFORMANCE AND TUNE-UP

TUNE-UP PROCEDURES

In order to extract the full measure of performance and economy from your engine it is essential that it be properly tuned at regular intervals. A regular tune-up will keep your vehicle's engine running smoothly and will help prevent the annoying minor breakdowns and poor performance associated with an untuned engine.

A complete tune-up should be performed on older vehicles every 12,000 miles (19,000 km) or twelve months, whichever comes first. On newer model cars, tune-up service should be performed at 30,000 miles (48,000 km) or 24 months. Items that should be inspected or replaced include spark plugs, air filter and emission control components. This interval should be halved if the vehicle is operated under severe conditions, such as trailer towing, prolonged idling, continual stop and start driving, or if starting or running problems are noticed. It is assumed that the routine maintenance described in Section 1 has been kept up, as this will have a decided effect on the results of a tune-up. All of the applicable steps of a tune-up should be followed in order, as the result is a cumulative one.

➡**If the specifications on the tune-up sticker in the engine compartment disagree with the tune-up specifications chart in this section, the figures on the sticker must be used. The sticker often reflects changes made during the production run.**

Spark Plugs

▶ **See Figure 1**

A typical spark plug consists of a metal shell surrounding a ceramic insulator. A metal electrode extends downward through the center of the insulator and protrudes a small distance. Located at the end of the plug and attached to the side of the outer metal shell is the side electrode. The side electrode bends in at a 90° angle so that its tip is even with, and parallel to, the tip of the center electrode. The distance between these two electrodes (measured in thousandths of an inch or hundredths of a millimeter) is called the spark plug gap. The spark plug in no way produce a spark but merely provides a gap across which the current can arc. The coil produces 20,000-40,000 volts which travels to the distributor then through the spark plug wires to each individual spark plug. The current passes along the center electrode and jumps the gap to the side electrode, and, in do doing, ignites the air/fuel mixture in the combustion chamber.

HEAT RANGE

▶ **See Figure 2**

Spark plug heat range is a measure of a plug's ability to dissipate heat. The longer the insulator (or the farther it extends into the engine), the hotter the plug will operate; the shorter the insulator the cooler it will operate. A plug that absorbs little heat and remains too cool will quickly accumulate

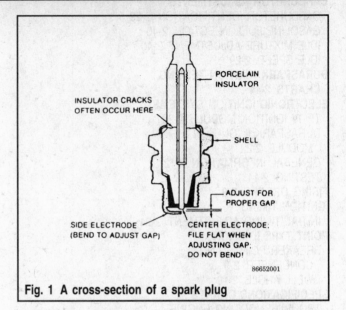

Fig. 1 A cross-section of a spark plug

deposits of oil and carbon since it is not hot enough to burn them off. This leads to plug fouling and consequently to misfiring. A plug that absorbs too much heat will have no deposits, but, due to the excessive heat, the electrodes will burn away quickly and in some instances, pre-ignition may result. Preignition takes place when plug tips get so hot that they glow sufficiently to ignite the fuel/air mixture before the actual spark occurs. This early ignition will usually cause a pinging during low speeds and heavy loads.

The general rule of thumb for choosing the correct heat range when picking a spark plug is: if most of your driving is long distance, high speed travel, use a colder plug; if most of your driving is stop and go, use a hotter plug. Original equipment plugs are compromise plugs, but most people never have occasion to change their plugs from the factory recommended heat range.

REMOVAL & INSTALLATION

▶ **See Figures 3, 4, 5, 6, 7, 8, 9 and 10**

A set of spark plugs usually requires replacement after about 20,000-30,000 miles (32,000-48,000 km), depending on your style of driving (for more information, please refer to the Maintenance Interval Chart in Section 1). In normal operation, plug gap increases about 0.001 in. (0.025mm) for every 1000-2500 miles (1600-4000 km). As the gap increases, the plug's voltage requirement also increases. It requires a greater voltage to jump the wider gap and about two to three times as much voltage to fire a plug at high speeds than at idle.

When you're removing spark plugs, you should work on one at a time. Don't start by removing the plug wires all at once, because unless you number them, they may become mixed up. Take a minute before you begin and number the wires with tape. The best location for numbering is near where the

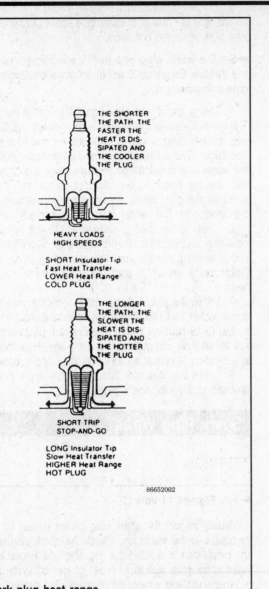

THE SHORTER
THE PATH THE
FASTER THE
HEAT IS DIS-
SIPATED AND
THE COOLER
THE PLUG

HEAVY LOADS
HIGH SPEEDS

SHORT Insulator Tip
Fast Heat Transfer
LOWER Heat Range
COLD PLUG

THE LONGER
THE PATH, THE
SLOWER THE
HEAT IS DIS-
SIPATED AND
THE HOTTER
THE PLUG

SHORT TRIP
STOP-AND-GO

LONG Insulator Tip
Slow Heat Transfer
HIGHER Heat Range
HOT PLUG

86652002

Fig. 2 Spark plug heat range

Fig. 3 A variety of tools and gauges are needed for spark plug service

Fig. 4 Remove the spark plug wire boot using a twisting motion

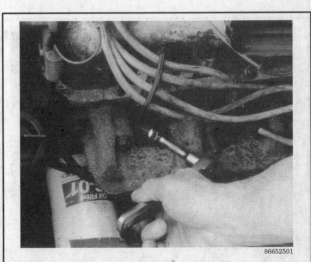

Fig. 5 Using a suitable socket and ratchet, loosen the spark plug

wires come out of the distributor cap. Refer to the engine "Firing Order" illustrations if necessary.

➡On models equipped with electronic ignition, apply a small amount of silicone dielectric compound (D7AZ-19A331-A or the equivalent) to the inside of the terminal boots whenever an ignition wire is disconnected from the plug, or coil/distributor cap connection.

1. Twist the spark plug boot and remove the boot and wire from the plug. Do not pull on the wire itself as this may ruin the wire. A special tool is available for this job if necessary.

2. If possible, use a brush or rag to clean the area around the spark plug. Make sure that all the dirt is removed so that no debris can enter the cylinder after the plug is removed.

3. Remove the spark plug using the proper sized socket and rachet. Most vehicles use either a $5/8$ in. or $13/16$ in. size socket depending on the engine. Turn the socket counterclockwise to remove. Be sure to hold the socket straight on the plug to avoid breakage, or rounding off the hex.

4. Once the plug is out, check it against the plugs shown in the section on spark plug condition to determine overall

Fig. 6 Remove the spark plug from the engine

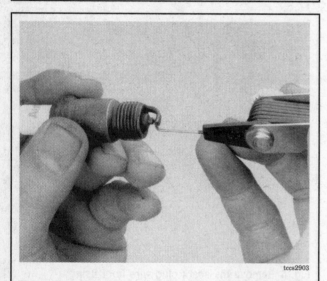

Fig. 7 Checking the spark plug gap with a feeler gauge

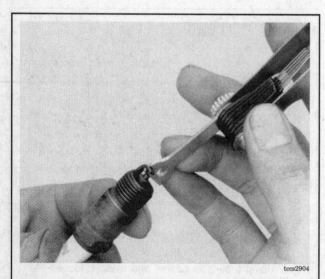

Fig. 8 Adjusting the spark plug gap

engine fitness. This is crucial since spark plug condition is a vital sign of engine condition.

➡ **Set the spark plug gap to the specification as shown on the Vehicle Emission Control Information Decal in the engine compartment.**

5. Use a round wire feeler gauge to check the plug gap. The correct size gauge should pass through the electrode gap with a slight drag. If you're in doubt, try one size smaller and one larger. The smaller gauge should go through easily while the larger one shouldn't go through at all. If the gap is incorrect, use the electrode bending tool on the end of the gauge to adjust the gap. When adjusting the gap, always bend the side electrode. The center electrode is non-adjustable.

6. Apply a thin coat of anti-sieze® to the threads of the new plug and install it. Turn the plug in clockwise by hand until it is snug. Always start the spark plug threads by hand. Never use a wrench to start the spark plug in the cylinder head.

7. When the plug is finger-tight, tighten it with a correct sized socket and rachet. Torque specifications should be 7-15 ft. lbs. (9-19 Nm) on 14mm thread spark plugs and 15-20 (19-26 Nm) on 18mm thread spark plugs. Note that the torque specification is critical on all spark plug applications.

8. Install the plug wire firmly over the spark plug. Then, proceed to the next spark plug.

Spark Plug Wires

TESTING

◆ **See Figures 11 and 12**

Visually inspect the spark plug cables (wires) for burns, cuts, or breaks in the insulation. Check the spark plug boots and the nipples on the distributor cap and coil. Replace any damaged spark plug wire in all types of ignition systems.

When installing a new set of spark plug cables (wires), replace the cables one at a time so there will be no confusion Start by replacing the longest cable first. Install the boot firmly over the spark plug. Route the cable exactly the same as the original. Insert the nipple firmly into the tower on the distributor cap. Repeat the process for each cable.

Whenever a spark plug wire is removed on a vehicle equipped with an Electronic Ignition System (EIS), silicone dielectric compound (grease) should be applied to the boot before it is reconnected. Using a small clean tool, coat the entire interior surface of the boot with Ford Silicone grease (D7AZ 19A331-A or equivalent).

➡ **Use an oscilloscope for testing and diagnosis. Do not puncture wires or use adapters as that can cause misfiring.**

Duraspark Type Plug Wires

The spark plug wires used with the Duraspark type ignition system are $5/16$ in. (8mm) in diameter to contain the higher output voltage. There are two types of wires used in this system, and some engines may have both types installed. It is important to properly identify the type of wire used for each cylinder before replacements are made.

Tracking Arc
High voltage arcs between a fouling deposit on the insulator tip and spark plug shell. This ignites the fuel/air mixture at some point along the insulator tip, retarding the ignition timing which causes a power and fuel loss.

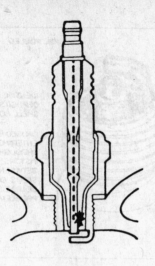

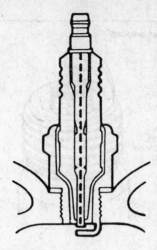

Wide Gap
Spark plug electrodes are worn so that the high voltage charge cannot arc across the electrodes. Improper gapping of electrodes on new or "cleaned" spark plugs could cause a similar condition. Fuel remains unburned and a power loss results.

Flashover
A damaged spark plug boot, along with dirt and moisture, could permit the high voltage charge to short over the insulator to the spark plug shell or the engine. AC's buttress insulator design helps prevent high voltage flashover.

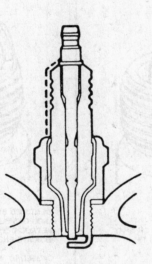

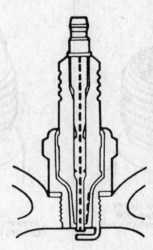

Fouled Spark Plug
Deposits that have formed on the insulator tip may become conductive and provide a "shunt" path to the shell. This prevents the high voltage from arcing between the electrodes. A power and fuel loss is the result.

Bridged Electrodes
Fouling deposits between the electrodes "ground out" the high voltage needed to fire the spark plug. The arc between the electrodes does not occur and the fuel air mixture is not ignited. This causes a power loss and exhausting of raw fuel.

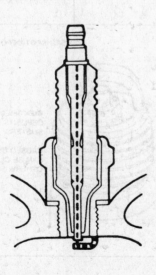

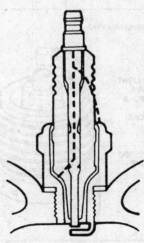

Cracked Insulator
A crack in the spark plug insulator could cause the high voltage charge to "ground out." Here, the spark does not jump the electrode gap and the fuel air mixture is not ignited. This causes a power loss and raw fuel is exhausted.

tccs2001

Fig. 9 Spark plug condition chart

GAP BRIDGED

IDENTIFIED BY DEPOSIT BUILD—UP CLOSING GAP BETWEEN ELECTRODES.

CAUSED BY OIL OR CARBON FOULING, REPLACE PLUG, OR, IF DEPOSITS ARE NOT EXCESSIVE THE PLUG CAN BE CLEANED.

OIL FOULED

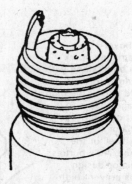

IDENTIFIED BY WET BLACK DEPOSITS ON THE INSULATOR SHELL BORE ELECTRODES.

CAUSED BY EXCESSIVE OIL ENTERING COMBUSTION CHAMBER THROUGH WORN RINGS AND PISTONS, EXCESSIVE CLEARANCE BETWEEN VALVE GUIDES AND STEMS, OR WORN OR LOOSE BEARINGS. CORRECT OIL PROBLEM. REPLACE THE PLUG.

CARBON FOULED

IDENTIFIED BY BLACK, DRY FLUFFY CARBON DEPOSITS ON INSULATOR TIPS, EXPOSED SHELL SURFACES AND ELECTRODES.

CAUSED BY TOO COLD A PLUG, WEAK IGNITION, DIRTY AIR CLEANER, DEFECTIVE FUEL PUMP, TOO RICH A FUEL MIXTURE, IMPROPERLY OPERATING HEAT RISER OR EXCESSIVE IDLING. CAN BE CLEANED.

NORMAL

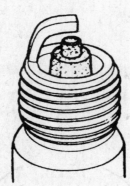

IDENTIFIED BY LIGHT TAN OR GRAY DEPOSITS ON THE FIRING TIP.

PRE-IGNITION

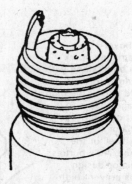

IDENTIFIED BY MELTED ELECTRODES AND POSSIBLY BLISTERED INSULATOR. METALIC DEPOSITS ON INSULATOR INDICATE ENGINE DAMAGE.

CAUSED BY WRONG TYPE OF FUEL, INCORRECT IGNITION TIMING OR ADVANCE, TOO HOT A PLUG, BURNT VALVES OR ENGINE OVERHEATING. REPLACE THE PLUG.

OVERHEATING

IDENTIFIED BY A WHITE OR LIGHT GRAY INSULATOR WITH SMALL BLACK OR GRAY BROWN SPOTS AND WITH BLUISH-BURNT APPEARANCE OF ELECTRODES.

CAUSED BY ENGINE OVER-HEATING, WRONG TYPE OF FUEL, LOOSE SPARK PLUGS, TOO HOT A PLUG, LOW FUEL PUMP PRESSURE OR INCORRECT IGNITION TIMING. REPLACE THE PLUG.

FUSED SPOT DEPOSIT

IDENTIFIED BY MELTED OR SPOTTY DEPOSITS RESEMBLING BUBBLES OR BUSTERS.

CAUSED BY SUDDEN ACCELERATION. CAN BE CLEANED IF NOT EXCESSIVE, OTHERWISE REPLACE PLUG.

tccs2002

Fig. 10 Spark plug electrode/insulator condition chart

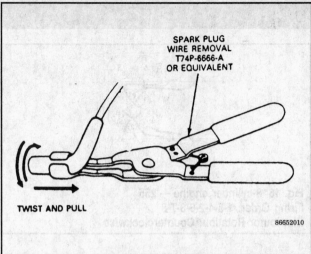

Fig. 11 Using a spark plug wire removal tool will help prevent damage to the cables

Both types are blue in color and have silicone jacketing. The insulation material underneath the jacketing on some plug wires is a silicone layer separated by glass braid. The plug cable not incorporating the silicone layer is used where engine temperatures are cooler and are identified with the letter SE with black printing. The plug cables with the silicone insulation are used where high engine temperatures are present. These cables are identified with the letters SS with white printing.

Each spark plug cable, if original, is marked with the cylinder number, model year and date of cable manufacture (quarter and year). Service replacement wires will not have cylinder numbers, or manufacture date.

➡**On any vehicle equipped with a catalytic converter, never allow the engine to run for more than 30 seconds with a spark plug wire disconnected. Unburned fuel in the cylinder may ignite in the converter as it is exhausted and damage the converter.**

REMOVAL & INSTALLATION

When removing spark plug wires, mark and tag the individual wires. Grasp, then slowly, twist the insulator back and forth on the spark plug to free the insulator. Do not pull on the wire directly as it may become separated from the connector inside the insulator. Special tools are available which can help ease plug wire removal, and prevent damage to a cable.

When installing a new set of spark plug wires, replace the wires one at a time so there will be no confusion. Start by replacing the longest wire first. Route the wire exactly the same as the original.

1. Disconnect the negative battery cable.
2. Grasp the wire by the rubber boot. Twist and pull the boot and wire from the spark plug. Never pull on the plug wire directly.
3. Remove the necessary wire retainer clips and separators, then remove the spark plug wire.
   To install:
4. Apply a small amount of silicone dielectric compound D7AZ-19A331-A or equivalent, to the entire inside surface of the spark plug wire boots. This is extremely important on the Duraspark wires.
5. Install the wire to the proper distributor cap or ignition coil terminal, making sure the boot is firmly seated.
6. Route the wire through the necessary retainer clips and separators.
7. Connect the spark plug wire to the spark plug.
8. Connect the negative battery cable.

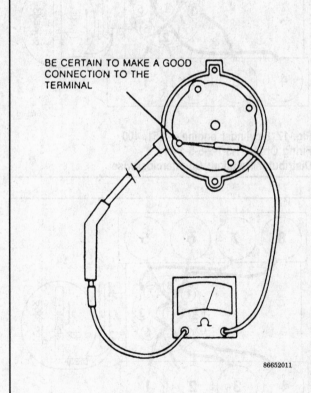

Fig. 12 Testing spark plug wire resistance with an ohmmeter

FIRING ORDERS

➡To avoid confusion, remove and tag the spark plug wires one at a time.

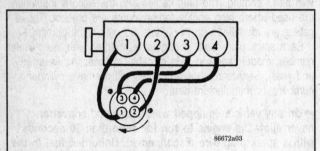

Fig. 13 4-cylinder engine — 140
Firing Order: 1-3-4-2
Distributor Rotation: Clockwise

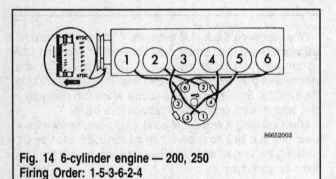

Fig. 14 6-cylinder engine — 200, 250
Firing Order: 1-5-3-6-2-4
Distributor Rotation: Clockwise

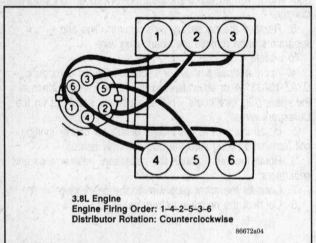

3.8L Engine
Engine Firing Order: 1-4-2-5-3-6
Distributor Rotation: Counterclockwise

Fig. 15 6-cylinder engine — 232
Firing Order: 1-4-2-5-3-6
Distributor Rotation: Counterclockwise

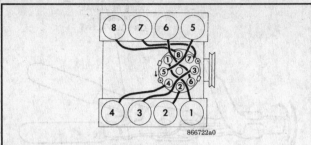

Fig. 16 8-cylinder engine — 255
Firing Order: 1-5-4-2-6-3-7-8
Distributor Rotation: Counterclockwise

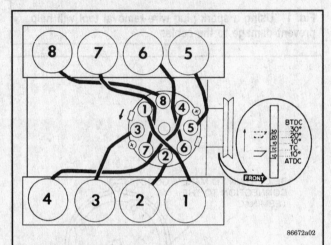

Fig. 17 8-cylinder engine — 351, 400
Firing Order: 1-3-7-2-6-5-4-8
Distributor Rotation: Counterclockwise

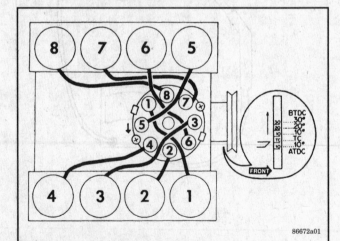

Fig. 18 8-cylinder engine — 302, 429, 460
Firing Order: 1-5-4-2-6-3-7-8
Distributor Rotation: Counterclockwise

POINT TYPE IGNITION

Breaker Points and Condenser

▶ See Figures 19 and 20

All 1971-1973, and some 1974 Ford full sized cars used a breaker point type ignition system.

The points function as a circuit breaker for the primary circuit of the ignition system. The ignition coil must boost the 12 volts of electrical current supplied by the battery to as much as 25,000 volts in order to properly fire the spark plugs. To do this, the coil depends on the points and the condenser to make a clean break in the primary circuit.

The coil has both primary and secondary circuits. When the ignition is turned **ON**, the battery supplies voltage through the coil to the points. The points are connected to ground, completing the primary circuit. As the current passes through the coil, a magnetic field is created in the iron center core of the coil. As the cam in the distributor turns, the points open and the primary circuit collapses. The magnetic field in the primary circuit of the coil cuts through the secondary circuit winding around the iron core. Because of the scientific phenomenon called "electromagnetic induction," the battery voltage is increased to a level sufficient to fire the spark plugs.

When the points open, the electrical charge in the primary circuit jumps the gap created between the two open contacts of the points. If this electrical charge is not transferred elsewhere, the metal contacts of the points would melt and the gap would start to change rapidly. Without the proper gap, the points will be unable to break the primary circuit, and the end result will be the secondary circuit will not have enough voltage to fire the spark plugs.

The function of the condenser is to absorb excessive voltage from the points when they open and prevent the points from becoming pitted or burned.

It is interesting to note that the cycle must be completed by the ignition system every time a spark plug fires. In a V8 engine, all of the spark plugs fire once for every two revolutions of the crankshaft. That means that in one revolution, four spark plugs fire. So when the engine is at an idle speed of 800 rpm, the points are opening and closing 3,200 times a minute.

There are two ways to inspect the breaker point gap: it can be checked with a feeler gauge, or a dwell meter. In either way, when you set the points, you are basically adjusting the amount of time that the points remain open. The time is measured in degrees of distributor rotation. When you measure the gap between the breaker points with a feeler gauge, you are setting the maximum level at which the points will open when the rubbing block on the points is on a high point of the distributor cam. When you adjust the points with a dwell meter, you are adjusting the number of degrees that the points will remain closed as a high point of the distributor cam approaches the rubbing block of the points.

➡ **When you replace a set of points, ALWAYS replace the condenser at the same time.**

When you change the point gap or dwell, you will also have to check the ignition timing. If the point gap or dwell is changed, the ignition timing must be checked and adjusted as needed.

INSPECTION

▶ See Figure 21

1. Disconnect the negative battery cable.
2. Disconnect the high tension wire from the top of the distributor and the coil.
3. Remove the distributor cap by prying off the spring clips on the sides of the cap.
4. Remove the rotor from the distributor shaft by pulling it straight up. Examine the condition of the rotor. If it is cracked or the metal tip is excessively worn, it should be replaced.

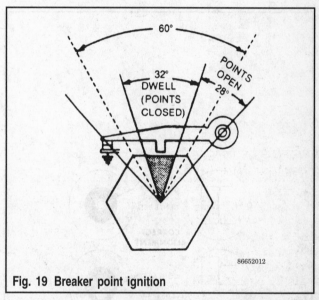

Fig. 19 Breaker point ignition

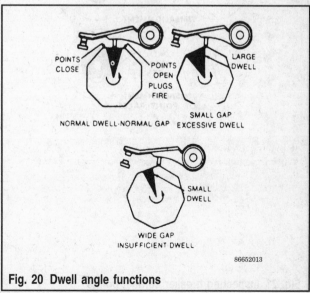

Fig. 20 Dwell angle functions

5. Pry open the contacts of the points with a small prytool and check the condition of the contacts. If they are excessively worn, burned or pitted, they should be replaced.

6. Inspect the condition of the condenser. If the wire insulation is cracked or burnt, replace the unit.

7. If the points and condenser are in good condition, adjust them, and install the rotor and the distributor cap. If the points need to be replaced, follow the replacement procedure given below.

REPLACEMENT

▶ **See Figures 22, 23, 24, 25, 26, 27 and 28**

1. Disconnect the negative battery cable.

2. Remove the coil high tension wire from the top of the distributor cap. Remove the cap from the distributor and place it out of the way. Remove the rotor from the distributor shaft.

3. Loosen the screw that holds the condenser lead to the body of the breaker points, then disconnect the lead.

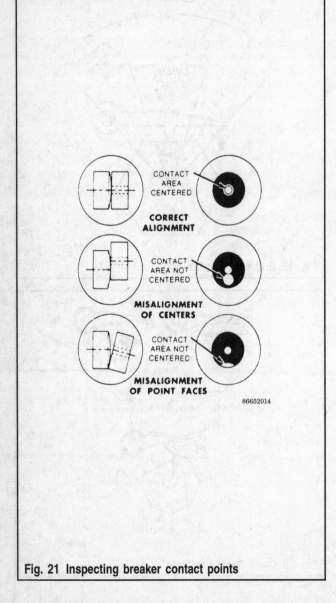

Fig. 21 Inspecting breaker contact points

4. Remove the screw that holds and grounds the condenser to the distributor body. Remove the condenser from the distributor and discard it.

5. Unfasten the points assembly attaching screws and adjustment lockscrews. A screwdriver with a magnetic tip will come in handy here so you don't drop a screw into the distributor and have to remove the entire assembly to retrieve it.

6. Remove the points. Wipe off the cam and apply new cam lubricant. Discard the old point set.

To install:

7. Position the new set of points with the locating peg in the hole on the breaker plate, and install the screws that hold the assembly onto the plate. Do not tighten them all the way.

8. Attach the new condenser to the plate with the ground screw.

9. Attach the condenser lead to the points.

10. Apply a small amount of cam lubricant to the shaft where the rubbing block of the points touches.

11. Attach the negative battery cable.

Dwell Angle

ADJUSTMENT

Using a Feeler Gauge
▶ **See Figure 26**

1. If the contact points of the assembly are not parallel, bend the stationary contact so they make contact across the entire surface of the contacts. Bend only the stationary bracket part of the point assembly, not the movable contact.

2. Turn the engine until the rubbing block of the point is on one of the high points of the distributor cam. You can do this by either turning the ignition switch to the **START** position and releasing it quickly (bumping the engine) or by using a wrench on the crankshaft pulley bolt and rotating the crankshaft. Be sure to remove the wrench before starting the engine!

3. Place the correct size feeler gauge between the contacts. Make sure the feeler gauge is parallel with the contact

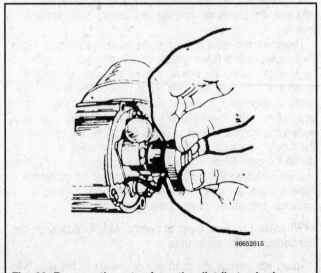

Fig. 22 Remove the rotor from the distributor body

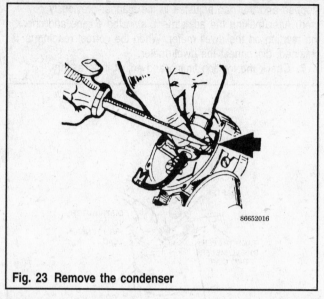

Fig. 23 Remove the condenser

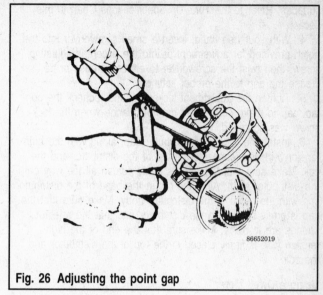

Fig. 26 Adjusting the point gap

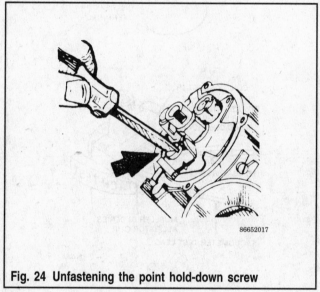

Fig. 24 Unfastening the point hold-down screw

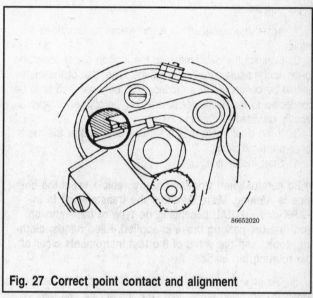

Fig. 27 Correct point contact and alignment

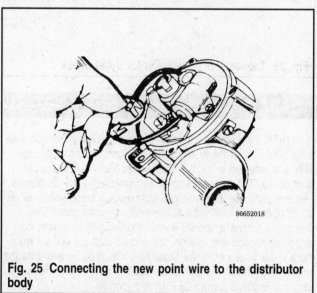

Fig. 25 Connecting the new point wire to the distributor body

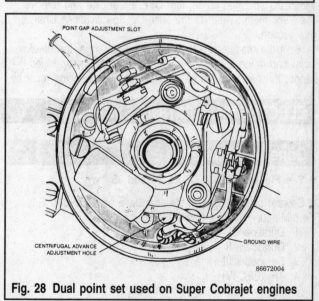

Fig. 28 Dual point set used on Super Cobrajet engines

surfaces. Refer to the Tune-Up Specifications Chart in this section.

4. With your free hand, insert a small screwdriver into the notch provided for adjustment or into the eccentric adjusting screw, then twist the screwdriver to either increase or decrease the gap to the proper setting.

5. Tighten the adjustment lockscrew and recheck the contact gap to make sure that it did not change when the lockscrew was tightened.

6. Install the rotor and distributor cap, along with the high tension wire that connects the top of the distributor and the coil. Make sure that the rotor is firmly seated all the way onto the distributor shaft. Align the tab in the base of the distributor cap with the notch in the distributor body. Make sure that the cap is firmly seated on the distributor and that the retainer springs are in place. Make sure that the end of the high tension wire is firmly placed in the top of the distributor and the coil.

Using a Dwell Meter

▶ See Figure 29

1. Adjust the points with a feeler gauge as described earlier.

2. Connect the dwell meter to the ignition circuit according to the tool manufacturer's instructions. One lead of the meter should be connected to a ground, and the other lead is to be connected to the distributor post (-) on the coil. An adapter is usually provided for this purpose.

3. If the dwell meter has a set line on it, adjust the meter to zero the indicator.

4. Start the engine.

➡Be careful when working on any vehicle while the engine is running. Make sure that the transmission is in PARK or NEUTRAL depending on type of transmission, and that the parking brake is applied. Keep hands, clothing, tools, and the wires of the test instruments clear of the rotating fan blades.

5. Observe the reading on the dwell meter. If the reading is within the specified range, turn OFF the engine and remove the dwell meter. Refer to the Tune-Up Specifications Chart in this section.

6. If the reading is above the specified range, the breaker point gap is too small. If the reading is below the specified range, the gap is too large. In either case, the engine must be stopped and the gap adjusted in the manner previously covered. After making the adjustment, start the engine and check the reading on the dwell meter. When the correct reading is obtained, disconnect the dwell meter.

7. Check the ignition timing and adjust if necessary.

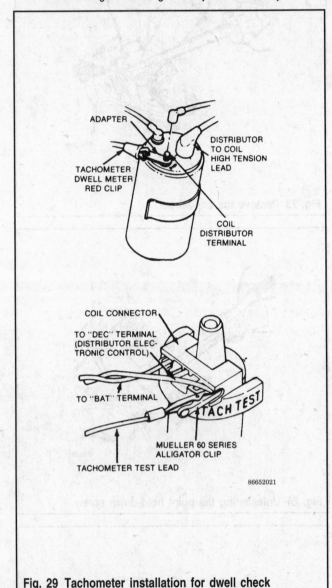

Fig. 29 Tachometer installation for dwell check

ELECTRONIC IGNITION SYSTEMS

General Information

▶ See Figures 30, 31, 32, 33, 34 and 35

Several different ignition systems have been used in Ford/Mercury vehicles from 1971-85:

1. Duraspark I
2. Duraspark II
3. Duraspark III
4. TFI (EEC-IV)

In 1974, Ford/Mercury began to use breakerless ignition systems. The first of these electronic ignition systems was originally just referred to as the breakerless ignition system, but later, in 1977, it became known as Duraspark. The Duraspark I system, and the next version, Duraspark II were nearly identical in operation, and virtually identical in appearance. The Duraspark I uses a special control module which senses current flow through the ignition coil and adjusts the coil for maximum spark intensity. If the Duraspark I module senses that the ignition is ON, but the distributor shaft is not turning, the current to the coil is turned OFF by the module.

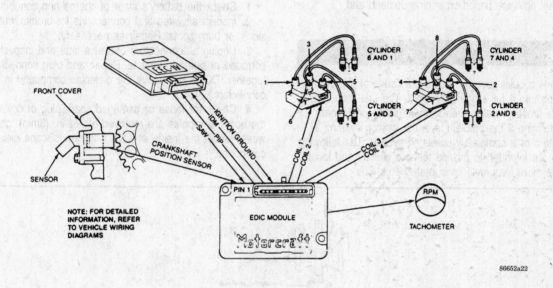

Fig. 30 Electronic ignition system components

The Duraspark II system does not have this feature. The coil is energized for the full amount of time that the ignition switch is **ON**. Keep this in mind when servicing the Duraspark II system, as the ignition system could inadvertently fire while performing ignition system services (such as distributor cap removal) while the ignition is **ON**. All Duraspark II systems are easily identified by having a two-piece, flat topped distributor cap.

➡**Duraspark I was discontinued after the 1981 model year.**

In 1980, the new Duraspark III system was introduced. This version is based on the previous systems, but the input signal is controlled by the EEC system, rather than as function of engine timing and distributor armature position. The distributor, rotor, cap, and control module are unique to this system; the spark plugs and plug wires are the same as those used with the Duraspark II system. Although the Duraspark II and III control modules are similar in appearance, they cannot be interchanged.

Some 1978 and later engines use a special Duraspark Dual Mode ignition control module. This module is equipped with an altitude sensor, and an economy modulator. This module, when combined with the additional switches and sensor, varies the base engine timing according to altitude and engine load conditions. Duraspark Dual Mode ignition control modules can be identified by the three wiring harnesses emerging from the control module.

Some 1981 and later Duraspark II systems used with the 5.0L engine are quipped with a Universal Ignition Module (UIM) which includes a run/retard function. The operation of the module is basically the same as the Duraspark Dual Mode module.

The (EEC-IV) distributor has a diecast base which incorporates an externally mounted TFI-IV ignition module, and contains a Hall Effect vane switch stator assembly and provision for fixed octane adjustment. No distributor calibration is required and initial timing adjustment is normally not required. The primary function of the EEC-IV Universal Distributor system is to direct a high secondary voltage to the spark plugs. In addition, the distributor supplies crankshaft position and frequency information to a computer using a Profile Ignition Pickup (PIP). The Hall Effect switch in the distributor consists of a sensor device on one side and a magnet on the other side. A rotary cup which has windows and tabs rotates and passes through the space between the device and the magnet. When a window is between the sides of the switch the magnetic path is not completed and the switch is off, sending no signal. When a tab passes between the switch the magnetic path is completed, and the Hall Effect device is turned on and a signal is sent. The voltage pulse (signal) is used by is EEC-IV system for sensing crankshaft position and computing the desired spark advance based on engine demand and calibration.

Testing

Many times a quick test can locate the cause of a problem without going into a full system checkout. The first step is to verify that a problem exists, then to make some preliminary tests to determine if the problem is in the ignition system, a related system or a completely unrelated system. The following procedures are intended to provide tests to identify and locate some of the more frequently encountered problems.

Intermittent faults may be the result of corroded terminals, cracked or broken wires, voltage leakage, heat related failures, etc.. Verify the conditions of the ignition system and engine when the malfunction occurs. Examples include, hot or cold engine, acceleration or deceleration, etc.

PRELIMINARY CHECKS

1. Check the battery's state of charge and connections.
2. Inspect all wires and connections for breaks, cuts, abrasions, or burn spots. Repair as necessary.
3. Unplug all connectors one at a time and inspect for corroded or burned contacts. Repair and plug connectors back together. DO NOT remove the dielectric compound in the connectors.
4. Check for loose or damaged spark plug or coil wires. If the boots or nipples are removed on $5/16$ in. (8mm) ignition wires, recoat the inside of each with new silicone dielectric compound.

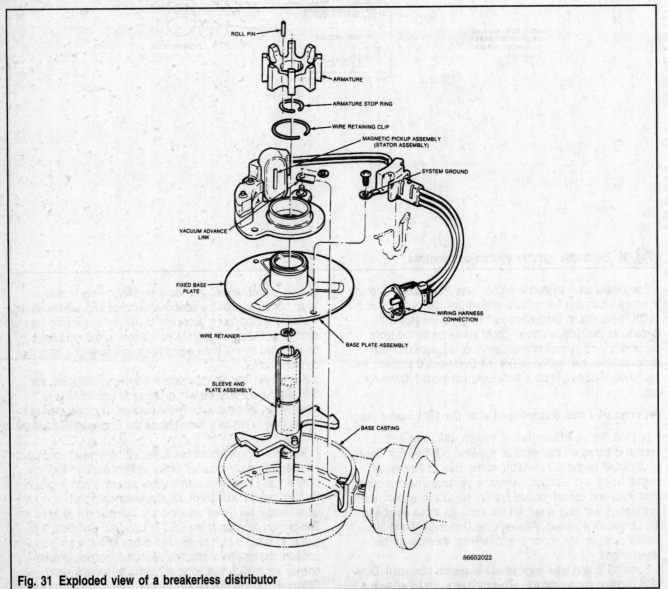

ROLL PIN
ARMATURE
ARMATURE STOP RING
WIRE RETAINING CLIP
MAGNETIC PICKUP ASSEMBLY (STATOR ASSEMBLY)
SYSTEM GROUND
VACUUM ADVANCE LINK
FIXED BASE PLATE
WIRING HARNESS CONNECTION
WIRE RETAINER
BASE PLATE ASSEMBLY
SLEEVE AND PLATE ASSEMBLY
BASE CASTING

86652022

Fig. 31 Exploded view of a breakerless distributor

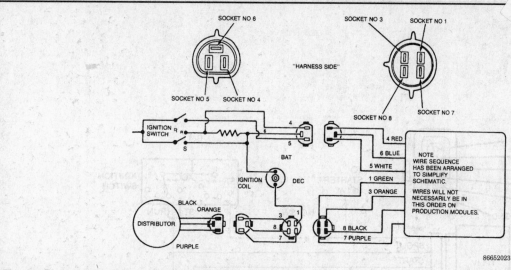

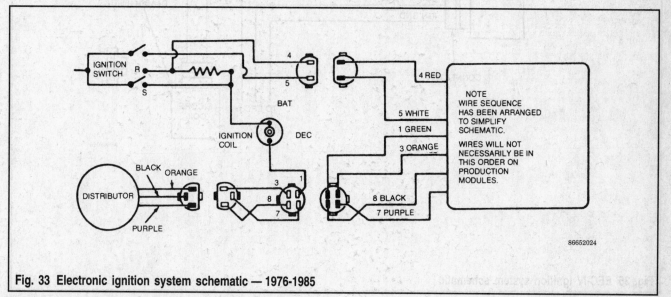

Fig. 32 Electronic ignition system schematic — 1971-1975

Fig. 33 Electronic ignition system schematic — 1976-1985

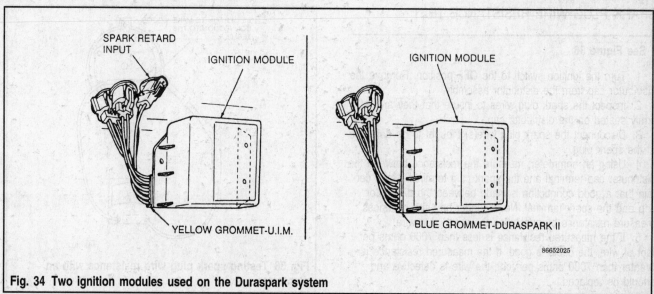

Fig. 34 Two ignition modules used on the Duraspark system

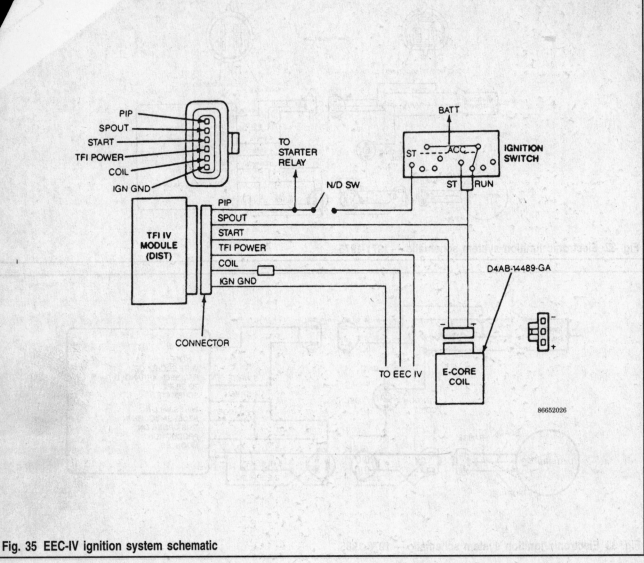

Fig. 35 EEC-IV ignition system schematic

SPARK PLUG WIRE RESISTANCE TEST

▶ **See Figure 36**

1. Turn the ignition switch to the **OFF** position. Remove the distributor cap from the distributor assembly.

2. Inspect the spark plug wires to insure that they are firmly seated on the distributor cap.

3. Disconnect the spark plug wire(s) thought to be defective at the spark plug.

4. Using an ohmmeter, measure the resistance between the distributor cap terminal and the spark plug terminal. Make certain that a good connection is made between the distributor cap and the spark terminal. Never, under any circumstances, measure resistance by puncturing the spark plug wire.

5. If the measured resistance is less than 7000 ohms per foot of wire, the cable is good. If the measured resistance is greater than 7000 ohms per foot, the wire is defective and should be replaced.

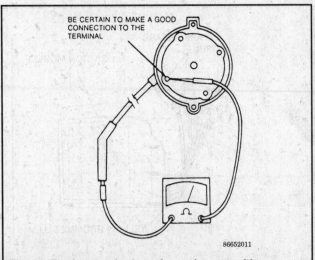

Fig. 36 Testing spark plug wire resistance with an ohmmeter

DURASPARK II CHECKS

➡Additional testing and diagnostic flow charts can be found at the end of this section.

Ignition Coil

PRIMARY RESISTANCE TEST

▶ See Figure 37

1. Turn the ignition switch to the **OFF** position. Unplug the ignition coil connector, clean and inspect for dirt or corrosion.
2. Measure the resistance between the BAT and TACH terminals (positive and negative terminals of the coil) with an ohmmeter. Resistance should measure 0.8-1.6 ohms.
3. Replace the ignition coil if resistance is not within specifications.

SECONDARY RESISTANCE TEST

▶ See Figure 38

1. Turn the ignition switch to the **OFF** position. Unplug and inspect the ignition coil connector and coil wire.
2. Measure the secondary resistance from the BAT terminal to the high voltage terminal with an ohmmeter. The resistance specification should measure 7700-10500 ohms.
3. Replace the ignition coil if resistance is not within specifications.

System Troubleshooting

The following procedures can be used to determine whether the ignition system is working or not. If these procedures fail to locate and correct the problem, full troubleshooting procedures should be performed by a qualified service technician.

SPECIAL TOOLS

▶ See Figure 39

To perform the following tests, two special tools are needed: an ignition test jumper, and a modified spark plug. The modified spark plug is basically a spark plug with the side electrode removed. Ford makes a special tool called a spark tester for this purpose, which besides not having a side electrode is equipped with a spring clip so that it can be grounded to engine metal. It is recommended that the spark tester be used as there is less chance of being shocked.

➡After completing the following tests (that involve using a straight pin) apply a small amount of silicone sealer to the pin holes in the wires.

Run Mode Spark Test

STEP 1

▶ See Figures 40 and 41

➡The wire colors given here are the main color of the wires, not the dots or stripe marks.

1. Remove the distributor cap and rotor from the distributor.
2. With the ignition **OFF**, turn the engine over by hand until one of the teeth on the distributor armature aligns with the magnet in the pick-up.
3. Remove the primary wire from the distributor cap. Install the modified spark plug in the primary wire terminal and using insulated pliers, hold the spark plug base against the engine block.
4. Turn the ignition to **RUN** (not **START**) and tap the distributor body with your hand. There should be a spark at the modified spark plug or at the primary wire terminal.
5. If a good spark is evident, the primary circuit is OK, perform Start Mode Spark Test. If there is no spark, proceed to Step 2.

STEP 2

1. Unplug the module connector(s) which contain(s) the green and black module leads.
2. In the harness side of the connector(s), install the special test jumper between the leads which connect the green and black leads of the module pig tails. Use a paper clip(s) on the connector socket holes to make a connection. Do not allow the clips to ground.
3. Turn the ignition switch to **RUN** (not **START**) and close the test jumper switch. Leave closed for about one second, then open. Repeat several times. There should be a spark each time the switch is opened.

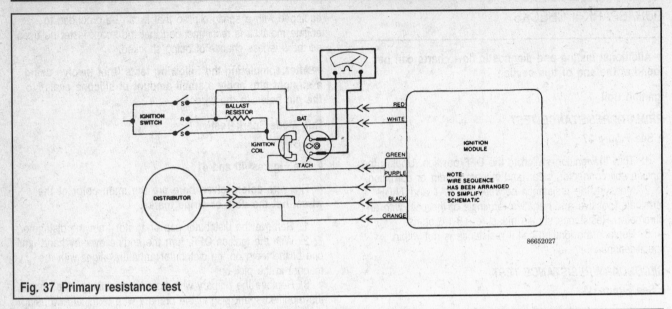

Fig. 37 Primary resistance test

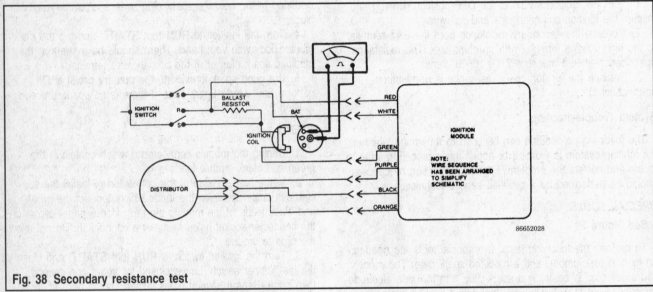

Fig. 38 Secondary resistance test

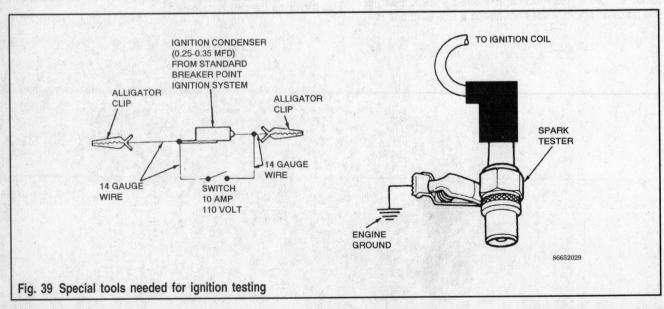

Fig. 39 Special tools needed for ignition testing

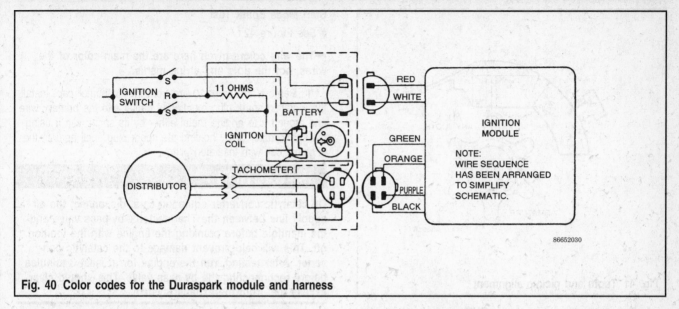

Fig. 40 Color codes for the Duraspark module and harness

4. If there is NO spark, the problem is probably in the primary circuit through the ignition switch, proceed to Step 3. If there IS a spark, the primary circuit wiring and primary are probably OK. The problem is probably in the distributor pick-up, the module red wire, or the module. Proceed to Step 6.

STEP 3

1. Disconnect the test jumper lead from the black lead and connect it to a good ground. Turn the test jumper switch on and off several times as in Step 2.

2. If there is NO spark, the problem is probably in the green lead, the primary, or the primary feed circuit. Perform Step 5.

3. If there IS spark, the problem is probably in the black lead or the distributor ground connections. Perform Step 4.

STEP 4

1. Connect an ohmmeter between the black lead and ground. With the meter on its lowest scale, there should be NO measurable resistance in the circuit. If there is resistance, check the distributor ground connections and the black lead from the module. Repair as necessary, remove the ohmmeter, plug in all connections and repeat Step 1.

2. If there is NO resistance, the primary ground wiring is OK. Perform Step 6.

STEP 5

1. Disconnect the test jumper from the green lead and ground and connect it between the TACH-TEST terminal of the primary and a good ground on the engine.

2. With the ignition switch in the **RUN** position, turn the jumper switch on. Hold it on for about one second then turn it off as in Step 2. Repeat several times. There should be a spark each time the switch is turned **OFF**. If there is NO spark, the problem is probably in the primary circuit running through the ignition switch to the primary BAT terminal, or in the primary itself. Check the primary resistance (test given in this section), and check the primary for internal shorts or opens. Check the primary feed circuit for opens, shorts or high resistance. Repair as necessary, fasten all connectors and re-

peat Step 1. If there IS spark, then the primary and its feed circuit are OK. The problem could be in the green lead between the primary and the module. Check for an open or short, repair as necessary, plug in all connectors and repeat Step 1.

STEP 6

To perform this step, an analog voltmeter which is not combined with a dwell meter is needed. The slight needle oscillations (0.5V) you'll be looking for may not be detectable on the combined voltmeter/dwell meter unit.

1. Connect a voltmeter between the orange and purple leads on the harness side of the module connectors.

✳✳CAUTION

On catalytic converter equipped cars, disconnect the air supply line between the Thermactor® by-pass valve and the manifold before cranking the engine with the ignition off. This will help prevent damage to the catalytic converter. After testing, run the engine for at least 3 minutes before reconnecting the by-pass valve. This should clear excess fuel from the exhaust system.

2. Set the voltmeter on its lowest scale and crank the engine. The meter needle should oscillate slightly (about 0.5V). If the meter does not oscillate, check the circuit through the magnetic pick-up in the distributor for open shorts, shorts to ground and resistance. Resistance between the orange and purple leads should be 400-1000 ohms. Resistance between each lead and ground should be more than 70,000 ohms. Repair as necessary, fasten all connectors and repeat Step 1.

3. If the meter oscillates, the problem is probably in the power feed to the module (red wire) or in the module itself. Proceed to Step 7.

STEP 7

▶ See Figure 42

1. Remove all meters and jumpers, then plug in all connectors.

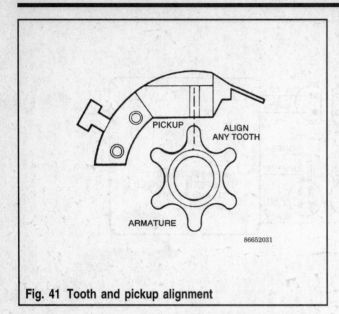

Fig. 41 Tooth and pickup alignment

2. Turn the ignition switch to the **RUN** position and measure voltage between the battery positive terminal and engine ground. It should be 12 volts.

3. Next, measure voltage between the red lead of the module and engine ground. To make this measurement, it will be necessary to pierce the red wire with a straight pin and connect the voltmeter to the straight pin and to ground.

➡**DO NOT ALLOW THE STRAIGHT PIN TO GROUND ITSELF!**

4. The two readings should be within one volt of each other. If not within one volt, the problem is in the power feed to the red lead. Check for shorts, opens, or high resistance and correct as necessary. After repairs, repeat Step 1.

If the readings are within one volt, the problem is probably in the module. Replace with a good module and repeat Step 1. If this corrects the problem reconnect the old module and repeat Step 1. If the problem returns, replace the module.

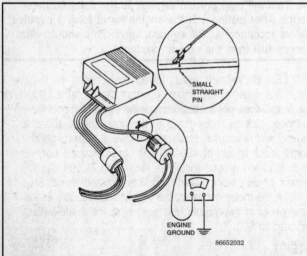

Fig. 42 Pierce the wire with a straight pin to connect the tester

Start Mode Spark Test
▶ **See Figure 42**

➡The wire colors given here are the main color of the wires, not the dots and stripe marks.

1. Remove the primary wire from the distributor cap. Install the modified spark plug mentioned earlier into the primary wire and ground it to engine metal either by its spring clip if using the spark tester or by holding the spark plug shell against the engine block with insulated pliers.

✳✳CAUTION

On catalytic converter equipped cars, disconnect the air supply line between the Thermactor® by-pass valve and the manifold before cranking the engine with the ignition off. This will help prevent damage to the catalytic converter. After testing, run the engine for at least 3 minutes before reconnecting the by-pass valve. This should clear excess fuel from the exhaust system.

2. Have an assistant crank the engine using the ignition switch and check for spark. If there IS a good spark, the problem is most probably in the distributor cap, rotor, ignition cables or spark plugs. If there is NO spark, proceed to Step 3.

3. Measure the battery voltage and record the reading. Next, measure the voltage at the white wire of the module while cranking the engine. To make this measurement, it will be necessary to pierce the white wire with a straight pin and connect the voltmeter to the straight pin and to ground. The battery voltage and the voltage at the white wire should be within one volt of each other. If the readings are not within one volt of each other, check and repair the feed through the ignition switch to the white wire. Recheck for spark (Step 1). If the readings are within one volt of each other, or if there is still NO spark after the power feed to white wire is repaired, proceed to Step 4.

➡**DO NOT ALLOW THE STRAIGHT PIN TO GROUND ITSELF!**

4. Measure the primary BAT terminal voltage while cranking the engine. The reading should be within one volt of battery voltage. If the readings are not within one volt of each other, check and repair the feed through the ignition switch to the primary. If the readings are within one volt of each other, the problem is probably in the ignition module. Substitute another module and repeat test for spark (Step 1).

Ballast Resistor

The ballast resistor wire is usually red with light green stripes. To check the resistor wire you must disconnect it at the primary BAT connections and at the connector at the end of the wiring harness. The connector at the end of the wiring harness is a rectangular connector with eight terminals. Connect an ohmmeter to each end of the wire and set the meter to the high scale. The resistance of the wire should be between 1.05-1.15 ohms. Any other reading merits replacement of the resistor wire with one of the correct service resistor wires.

THICK FILM IGNITION (TFI-IV) SYSTEM CHECKS

▶ See Figures 43 and 44

➡Additional testing and diagnostic flow charts can be found at the end of this section.

Before proceeding with any tests, refer to the preliminary checks, spark plug wire resistance test procedure and special tool paragraphs of the General and Dura-Spark Troubleshooting sections. In addition to preliminary checks mentioned, inspect to be sure the TFI module is securely attached to the distributor.

The TFI-IV ignition system features a universal distributor using no centrifugal or vacuum advance and a provision for a fixed octane adjustment.

Most testing for this system should be done by an authorized factory technician or ASE certified trained technician, specializing in this area.

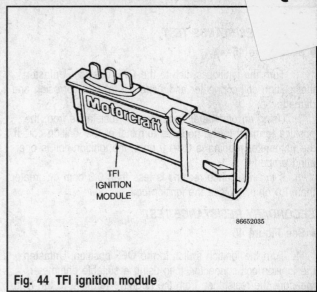

Fig. 44 TFI ignition module

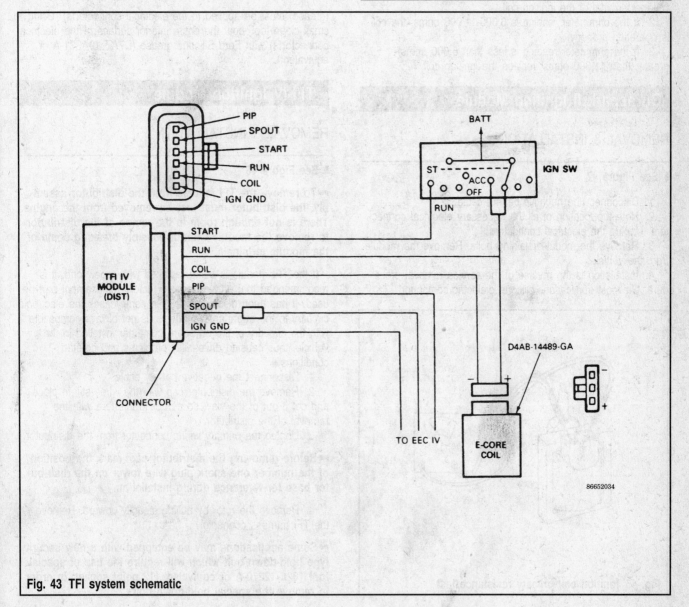

Fig. 43 TFI system schematic

Ignition Coil

PRIMARY RESISTANCE TEST

▶ See Figure 45

1. Turn the ignition switch to the **OFF** position. Unfasten the ignition coil connector and inspect it for dirt, corrosion and damage.
2. Using an ohmmeter, measure the resistance from the positive terminal to the negative terminal of the ignition coil. If the ohmmeter reading is 0.3-1.0 ohm, the ignition coil is operating properly.
3. If the resistance reading is less than 0.3 ohm or greater than 1.0 ohm, replace the ignition coil.

SECONDARY RESISTANCE TEST

▶ See Figure 46

1. Turn the ignition switch to the. **OFF** position. Unfasten the ignition coil connector, then using a suitable ohmmeter, measure the resistance from the negative terminal to the high voltage terminal of the ignition coil.
2. If the ohmmeter reading is 6,000-11,000 ohms, the coil is operating properly.
3. If the ohmmeter reading is less than 6,000 ohms or greater than 11,500 ohms, replace the ignition coil.

Duraspark II Ignition Module

REMOVAL & INSTALLATION

▶ See Figure 47

1. Disconnect the negative battery cable.
2. Note the location of all the necessary electrical connectors. Unplug the electrical connectors.
3. Remove the module retaining bolts. Remove the module from the vehicle.
4. Installation is the reverse of the service removal procedure. On most applications silicone dielectric compound

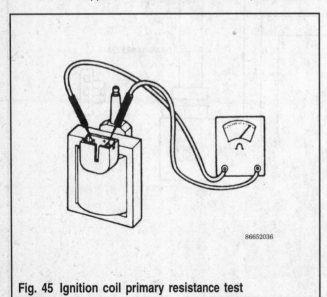

Fig. 45 Ignition coil primary resistance test

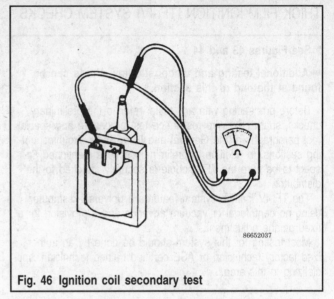

Fig. 46 Ignition coil secondary test

(grease) must be applied to the electrical connector(s). Using a small clean tool, coat the entire interior surface of the electrical connector(s) with Ford Silicone grease (D7AZ 19A331-A or equivalent).

TFI-IV Ignition Module

REMOVAL & INSTALLATION

▶ See Figure 48

➡ To remove the TFI module from the distributor assembly, the distributor must first be removed from the engine. There is not enough room in the region of the distributor to remove the module without possibly breaking some of the module terminals.

If the TFI module is being replaced with a new one, it is recommended that only a genuine factory replacement part be used. It has been discovered that in some cases the electronic circuitry in the aftermarket modules, is not always compatible with the circuitry of the on board computer installed in the vehicle, thus causing driveability problems and no-start conditions.

1. Disconnect the negative battery cable.
2. Remove the distributor cap with the wires still in place and set it out of the way, so as not to interfere with the removal of the distributor.
3. Unplug the primary wiring connector from the distributor.

➡ Before removing the distributor cap, mark the position of the number one spark plug wire tower on the distributor base for reference during installation.

4. Remove the rotor by pulling steadily upward. Remove the TFI harness connector.

➡ Some applications may be equipped with a new security type hold-down bolt which will require the use of special tool T82L-12270-A or equivalent (12 point socket) in order to remove the special hold-down bolts.

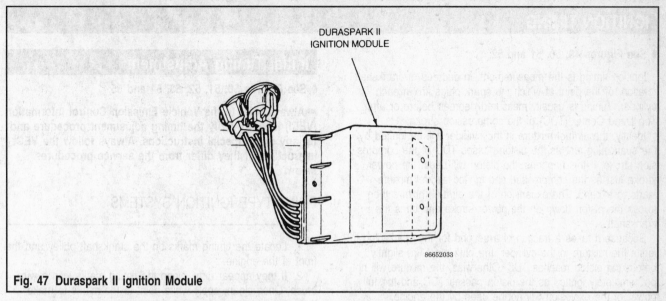

Fig. 47 Duraspark II ignition Module

5. Remove the distributor hold-down bolts and or clamps. Remove the distributor by lifting it straight out of the engine being careful not to disturb the intermediate shaft.

6. Place the distributor into a suitable vise. Remove the 2 module retaining screws.

7. Pull the right hand side of the TFI module down the distributor mounting flange and back up to disengage the module terminals from the connectors at the distributor base. The module may now be pulled toward the flange and away from the distributor.

✳✳WARNING

Do not attempt to remove module from the mounting surface prior to sliding the entire module toward the distributor flange. If the correct procedure is not followed, the pins will break at the distributor and module connector.

To install:

8. Coat the metal base of the TFI module with a thin layer of silicone dielectric compound. Place the module on the base of the distributor.

9. Carefully position the TFI module assembly toward the distributor bowl and engage the 3 distributor connector pins securely.

10. Install the 2 TFI module retaining screws starting with the upper right hand screw and tighten them to 16-35 inch lbs. (2-4 Nm).

11. Reinstall the distributor on the engine and tighten the hold-down bolts to 17-25 ft. lbs. (2-3 Nm). Reinstall the distributor cap and wires.

12. Install the TFI wiring harness connector. Reset the initial timing and make all necessary adjustments.

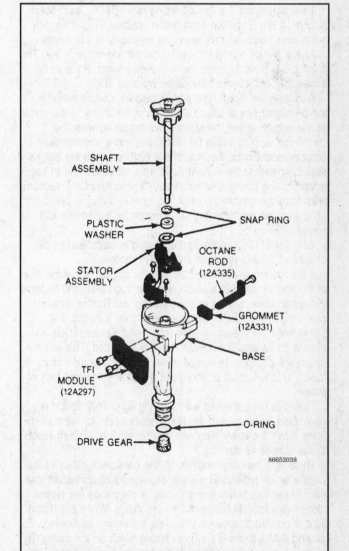

Fig. 48 Exploded view of a distributor with a TFI module

IGNITION TIMING

▶ **See Figures 49, 50, 51 and 52**

Ignition timing is the measurement, in degrees of crankshaft rotation, of the point at which the spark plugs fire in each cylinder. Timing is usually measured degrees before or after Top Dead Center (TDC) of the compression stroke.

Ideally, the air/fuel mixture in the cylinder will be ignited by the spark plug just as the piston passes TDC of the compression stroke. If this happens, the piston will begin the power stroke just as the compressed and ignited air/fuel mixture starts to expand. The expansion of the air/fuel mixture then forces the piston down on the power stroke and turns the crankshaft.

Because it takes a fraction of a second for the spark plug to ignite the mixture in the cylinder, the plug must fire slightly before the piston reaches TDC. Otherwise, the mixture will not be completely ignited as the piston passes TDC and the full power of the explosion will not be used by the engine.

If the setting for the ignition timing is 5° BTDC, each spark plug must fire 5° before each piston reaches TDC. This only holds true, however, only when the engine is at idle speed.

As the engine speed increases, the pistons move faster. The spark plugs have to ignite the fuel even sooner if it is to be completely ignited when the piston reaches TDC.

With both the Point Type and Duraspark ignition systems, the distributor has a means to advance the timing of the spark as the engine speed increases. This is accomplished by centrifugal weights within the distributor and a vacuum diaphragm mounted on the side of the distributor. As the engine speed increases, the vacuum level also increases and in turn advances the timing. It is necessary to disconnect the vacuum lines from the diaphragm when the ignition timing is being set. Otherwise the timing marks will advance as the engine idle speed increases.

With the TFI-IV system, ignition timing is calculated at all phases of vehicle operation by the TFI module.

If the ignition is advanced too far, the ignition and expansion of the fuel in the cylinder will occur too soon and tend to force the piston down while it is still traveling up. This causes engine ping. If the ignition spark is set too far retarded, the piston will have already passed Top Dead Center (TDC) and started on its way down when the fuel is ignited. This will cause the piston to be forced down for only a portion of its travel. This will result in poor engine performance and lack of power.

Timing is best checked with a timing light. This device is connected in series with the No. 1 spark plug. As the current flows down the spark plug wire, the timing light to flash reacts to the current by flashing.

There is a series of notches on the crankshaft pulley of the engine which represents a scale of degrees of crankshaft rotation. These are called timing marks. A pointer on the engine block helps identify the marks on the pulley. When the timing light is pointed at these marks while the engine is running, the pulsing light will identify a given timing notch on the pulley. By adjusting the position of the distributor, the timing of the vehicle, and their corresponding notches on the crankshaft pulley will change accordingly.

Initial Timing Adjustment

▶ **See Figures 50, 51, 52, 53, 54 and 55**

➡**Always refer to the Vehicle Emission Control Information (VECI) label to verify the timing adjustment procedure and for any other special instructions. Always follow the VECI instructions if they differ from the service procedures below.**

POINT TYPE IGNITION SYSTEMS

1. Locate the timing marks on the crankshaft pulley and the front of the engine.
2. If they appear dirty, clean the timing marks with a wire brush. Once clean, apply white paint to the marks to make them more visible.
3. Attach a dwell meter/tachometer to the engine.
4. Attach a timing light according to the tool manufacturer's instructions.
5. Unfasten the distributor vacuum line at the distributor and plug the vacuum line. A small bolt, center punch, golf-tee, or similar object is satisfactory for a plug.
6. Check to make sure that all of the wires, whether disconnected or attached to the timing light or tachometer, clear the fan and belts.
7. Start the engine and allow it to reach normal operating temperature.
8. Adjust the idle to the correct setting, if needed.
9. Aim the timing light at the timing marks and depress the trigger on the light. If the marks on the pulley and the engine are aligned when the light flashes, the timing is correct. Turn **OFF** the engine, then remove the tachometer and the timing light. If the marks are not in alignment, proceed with the following steps.
10. Loosen the distributor lockbolt (a special distributor wrench is available) just enough so that the distributor can be turned with effort.
11. With the timing light aimed at the pulley and the marks on the engine, turn the distributor in the direction of rotor rotation to retard the spark, and in the opposite direction of rotor rotation to the advance spark. Align the marks on the pulley and the engine using the flashes of the timing light.
12. When the marks are aligned, tighten the distributor lockbolt and recheck the timing to make sure that the distributor did not move when you tightened the lockbolt.
13. After timing has been set, tighten the distributor hold-down bolt to 17-25 ft. lbs. (23-34 Nm).

DURASPARK SYSTEMS

1. Locate the timing marks and pointer on the crankshaft pulley and the timing cover. Clean the marks so they will be visible with a timing light. Apply chalk or bright-colored paint, if necessary.
2. Place the transmission in **P** or **N**. The air conditioning and heater controls should be in the **OFF** position.

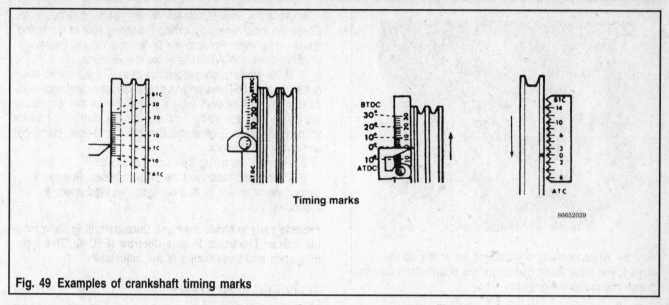

Fig. 49 Examples of crankshaft timing marks

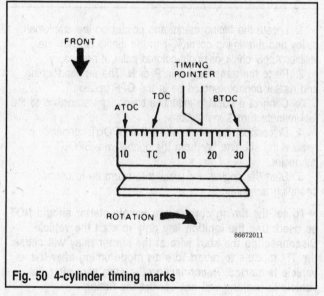

Fig. 50 4-cylinder timing marks

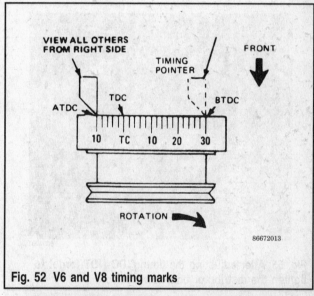

Fig. 52 V6 and V8 timing marks

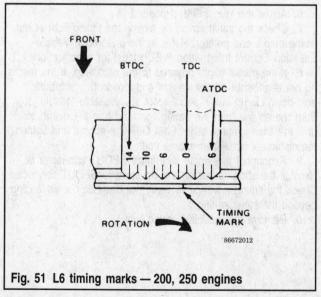

Fig. 51 L6 timing marks — 200, 250 engines

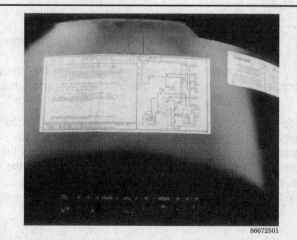

Fig. 53 The Vehicle Emission Control Information (VECI) label can be found on the fan shroud on most mid sized vehicles

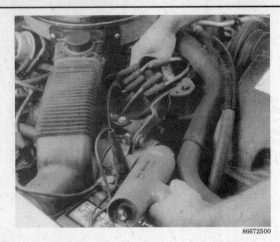

86672500

Fig. 54 While pointing the timing light at the timing marks, the other hand can rotate the distributor body to reach the correct alignment

86652701

Fig. 55 After adjusting the timing, DO NOT forget to tighten the distributor hold-down bolt

3. Disconnect the vacuum hose(s) from the distributor vacuum advance and plug the hoses.

4. Connect a suitable inductive timing light and a tachometer according to the tool manufacturer's instructions.

5. If equipped with a barometric pressure switch, disconnect it from the ignition module and place a jumper wire across the pins at the ignition module connector (yellow and black wires).

➡To set timing correctly, a remote starter should NOT be used. Use the ignition key only to start the vehicle. Disconnecting the start wire at the starter relay will cause the Duraspark module to revert to start mode timing after the vehicle is started. Reconnecting the start wire after the vehicle is running will not correct the timing.

6. Allow the engine to reach normal operating temperature. Check the initial timing by aiming the timing light at the timing marks and pointer. Refer to the underhood Vehicle Emission Control Information (VECI) label for specifications.

7. If the marks align, proceed to Step 9. If the marks do not align, shut OFF the engine and loosen the distributor hold-down clamp bolt (special tools are available for this job). Start the engine, aim the timing light and turn the distributor until the timing marks align. Tighten the distributor hold-down clamp bolt and check the timing again.

8. Remove the timing light and tachometer.

9. Unplug and reconnect the vacuum hoses. Remove the jumper wire from the ignition connector and reconnect, if applicable.

➡Some early vehicles may use Duraspark III ignition module with an Electronic Engine Controls (EEC-III). This type of system and base timing is not adjustable.

TFI-IV EEC-IV SYSTEMS

1. Locate the timing marks and pointer on the crankshaft pulley and the timing cover. Clean the marks so they are visible. Apply chalk or bright-colored paint, if necessary.

2. Place the transmission in P or N. The air conditioning and heater controls should be in the OFF position.

3. Connect a suitable inductive timing light according to the tool manufacturer's instructions.

4. Disconnect the single wire inline SPOUT connector or remove the shorting bar from the double wire SPOUT connector.

5. Start the engine and allow it to warm up to normal operating temperature.

➡To set the timing correctly, a remote starter should NOT be used. Use the ignition key only to start the vehicle. Disconnecting the start wire at the starter relay will cause the TFI module to revert to start mode timing after the vehicle is started. Reconnecting the start wire after the vehicle is running will not correct the timing.

6. Adjust the idle speed, if needed.

7. Check the initial timing by aiming the timing light at the timing marks and pointer. Refer to the underhood Vehicle Emission Control Information (VECI) label for specifications.

8. If the marks align, proceed to the next step. If the marks do not align, shut off the engine and loosen the distributor hold-down clamp bolt (special tools are available for this job). Start the engine, aim the timing light and turn the distributor until the timing marks align. Shut OFF the engine and tighten the distributor hold-down clamp bolt.

9. Reconnect the single wire inline SPOUT connector or reinstall the shorting bar on the double wire SPOUT connector. Check the timing advance to verify the distributor is advancing beyond the initial setting.

10. Remove the inductive timing light.

VALVE LASH

All engines covered by this manual are equipped with hydraulic valve lifters. Valve systems with hydraulic valve lifters operate with zero clearance in the valve train, and because of this, the rocker arms are usually nonadjustable. With the exception of the 2.3L 4-cylinder engine, the only means by which valve system clearances can be altered is by installing 0.060 in. (1.5mm) over or undersize pushrods; but, because of the hydraulic lifter's natural ability to compensate for slack in the valve train, all components of the valve system should be checked for wear if there is excessive play in the system.

If equipped with a V6, L6 or V8 engine, when a valve is in the closed position, the lifter rests on the base circle of the camshaft lobe, with the pushrod its lowest position. To remove this additional clearance from the valve train, the valve lifter expands to maintain zero clearance. When a rocker arm is loosened or removed from the engine, the lifter expands to its fullest travel. When the rocker arm is reinstalled on the engine, the proper valve setting is obtained by tightening the rocker arm to a specified limit. But with the lifter fully expanded, if the camshaft lobe is on a high point it will require excessive torque to compress the lifter and obtain the proper setting. Because of this, when any component of the valve system has been removed in an engine of this type, a preliminary valve adjustment procedure must be followed to ensure that when the rocker arm is reinstalled on the engine and tightened, the camshaft lobe for that cylinder is in the low position.

The 2.3L 4-cylinder engine uses neither pushrods or rocker arms. Instead, because this engine is an overhead cam design, the camshaft is placed at the top of the engine, directly above the valve /lifter assembly. The valve lifters function exactly as lifters in a pushrod equipped engine, although no provisions are made for valve clearance adjustments. If there is excessive valve clearance, most likely this would be an indication of a worn part(s). In this event, check the cam follower, valve height and lash adjuster.

Adjustment

4-CYLINDER ENGINES

▶ **See Figure 56**

The 2.3L engine is an overhead cam engine with hydraulic lash adjusters. These units are placed at the fulcrum point of the cam followers (rocker arms). Their action are similar to hydraulic tappets used in pushrod engines and are serviced in the same manner.

The valve arrangement in a 2.3L engine, looking from the front to rear of the vehicle is exhaust valve, then intake valve. This order applies to all four cylinders.

1. Position the camshaft so that the base circle of the lobe is facing the cam follower of the valve to be checked.
2. Using the appropriate tool (T74P-6565 or equivalent), slowly apply pressure to the cam follower until the lash adjuster is completely collapsed. Hold the follower in this position and insert the proper size feeler gauge between the base circle of the cam and the follower.

3. If the clearance is excessive, remove the cam follower and inspect for damage.
4. If the cam follower appears to be intact and not excessively worn, measure the valve spring assembled height to be sure the valve is not sticking.
5. If the valve spring assembled height is correct, check the dimensions of the camshaft.
6. If the camshaft dimensions are within specifications, remove, clean and test the lash adjuster.
7. Reinstall the lash adjuster and check the clearance. Replace any damaged or worn parts, as necessary.

6-CYLINDER ENGINES

➡**This procedure applies only when cylinder head components have been removed. Because of their hydraulic lifter assemblies, routine adjustments are not necessary.**

1. Crank the engine until the TDC mark on the crankshaft pulley is aligned with the timing pointer on the cylinder front cover.
2. Scribe a mark on the pulley in relation to the pointer. This we will call A.
3. Scribe two more marks on the damper, each equally spaced from the first mark. These marks we will call B and C.
4. With the engine on TDC of the compression stroke, (mark A aligned with the pointer) back off the rocker arm adjusting nut until there is end-play in the pushrod. Tighten the adjusting nut until all clearance is removed. Tighten the adjusting nut an additional ¾ turn. To check that all the excess clearance is removed, turn the pushrod with your fingers. When the pushrod can no longer be turned, all the clearance has been removed.
5. Repeat this procedure for each valve, turning the crankshaft ⅓ turn to the next mark each time and following the engine firing order of 1-5-3-6-4-2.

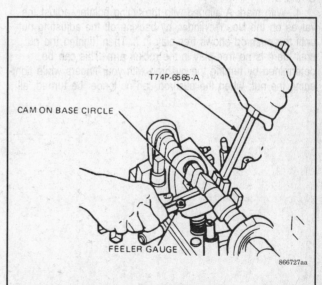

Fig. 56 Checking the hydraulic valve lash — 2.3L engine

8-CYLINDER ENGINES

→**This procedure applies only when cylinder head components have been removed. Because of their hydraulic lifter assemblies, routine adjustments are not necessary.**

Identifying Type of Rocker Arm

The 8-cylinder engines covered in this manual use 2 different type rocker arms. Before proceeding with any cylinder head work or valve adjustment, it is important to identify the type of rocker arms installed.

→**The early 5.0L engine were equipped with adjustable rocker arms. However, due to production differences, some of these early 5.0L engines may be equipped with positive stop rocker arm mounting studs.**

To identify the type of rocker arm installed, proceed as follows:

1. Remove the rocker arm cover from the cylinder head. Refer to section 3 for details.
2. Examine the studs used to secure the rocker arms.
3. If the shank portion of the stud exposed above the cylinder head is the same diameter as the threaded portion to which the rocker arm retaining nut attaches, this is an adjustable type rocker arm.
4. If the shank of the stud is of greater diameter than the threaded portion, this identifies the stud as a positive stop rocker arm stud.
5. Refer to the appropriate procedure below.

Adjustable Rocker Arms

1. Crank the engine until the No. 1 cylinder is at TDC of the compression stroke and the timing pointer is aligned with the mark on the crankshaft pulley.
2. Scribe a mark on the pulley at this point. This we will call A.
3. Scribe three more marks on the damper, dividing the damper into 4 quarters. These additional marks we will call B, C and D.
4. With mark A aligned with the timing pointer, adjust the valves on the No. 1 cylinder, by backing off the adjusting nut until the pushrod shows free-play in it. Then, tighten the nut until there is no free-play in the rocker arm. This can be determined by turning the pushrod with your fingers while tightening the nut; when the pushrod can no longer be turned, all

clearance has been removed. After the clearance has been removed, tighten the nut an additional ¾ of a turn.
5. Repeat this procedure for each valve, turning the crankshaft ¼ turn to the next mark each time and following the engine firing order of 1-5-4-2-6-3-7-8.

Positive Stop Type Rocker Arms

1. Crank the engine until the No. 1 cylinder is at TDC of the compression stroke and the timing pointer is aligned with the mark on the crankshaft pulley.
2. Scribe a mark on the pulley at this point. This point we will call A.
3. Scribe two additional marks on the pulley. These points we will call B and C.
4. With the timing pointer aligned with mark A on the pulley, tighten the following valves to the specified torque:
   4.2L, 5.0L, 7.0L, and 7.5L Engines
   - Intake Valve on Cylinder No. 1, 7 and 8,
   - Exhaust Valve on Cylinder No. 1, 5, and 4
   5.8L and 6.6L Engines
   - Intake Valve on Cylinder No. 1, 4, and 8
   - Exhaust Valve on Cylinder No. 1, 3, and 7
5. Rotate the crankshaft 180° to point B and tighten the following valves:
   4.2L, 5.0L, 7.0L, and 7.5L Engines
   - Intake Valve on Cylinder No. 5 and 4
   - Exhaust Valve on Cylinder No. 2 and 6
   5.8L and 6.6L Engines
   - Intake Valve on Cylinder No. 3 and 7
   - Exhaust Valve on Cylinder No. 2 and 6
6. Rotate the crankshaft 270° to point C and tighten the following valves:
   4.2L, 5.0L, 7.0L, and 7.5L Engines
   - Cylinder Intake Valve No. 2, 3, and 6
   - Cylinder Exhaust Valve No. 7, 3 and 8
   5.8L and 6.6L Engines
   - Cylinder Intake Valve No. 2, 5, and 6
   - Cylinder Exhaust Valve No. 4, 5, and 8
7. Tighten the rocker arms on 4.2L , 5.0L and 5.8L engines until the nut contacts the rocker shoulder, then tighten to 18-20 ft. lbs. (24-27 Nm).
8. Tighten the rocker arms on 6.6L engines until the nut contacts the rocker shoulder then tighten to 18-25 ft. lbs. (24;34 Nm).
9. Tighten the rocker arms on 7.0L and 7.5L engines until the nut contacts the rocker shoulder then tighten to 18-22 ft. lbs. (24-30 Nm).

CARBURETOR ADJUSTMENTS

→**Always refer to the Vehicle Emission Control Information (VECI) label to verify the adjustment procedure and any other special instructions.Always follow the VECI label instructions if they differ from the service procedures.**

This section contains only carburetor adjustments as they normally apply to engine tune-up. Descriptions of the carburetor and complete adjustment procedures can be found in Section 5.

When the engine in your car is running, air/fuel mixture from the carburetor is drawn into the engine by a partial vacuum. The vacuum is created by the downward movement of the pistons on the intake stroke of the 4-stroke cycle of the engine. The amount of air/fuel mixture which enters the engine is controlled by the throttle plate(s) in the bottom of the carburetor. When the engine is not running the throttle plate(s) is (are) closed blocking off the bottom of the carburetor from the inside of the engine. The throttle plates are connected, through the throttle linkage, to the accelerator in the passenger compartment of the car. After you start the engine and put the transmission in gear, you depress the accelerator to start the car moving. What you actually are doing when you depress the accelerator is opening the throttle plate(s) in the carburetor to admit more of the air/fuel mixture to the engine. The farther you open the throttle plates in the carburetor, the higher the engine speed becomes.

As previously stated, when the engine is not running, the throttle plates in the carburetor are closed. When the engine is idling, it is necessary to open the throttle plate slightly. To prevent having to keep your foot on the accelerator when the engine is idling, an idle speed adjustment screw is incorporated into the carburetor. The idle speed adjusting screw contacts a lever (the throttle lever) on the outside of the carburetor, and when turned clockwise, the throttle plate on the carburetor is opened, raising the idle speed of the engine.

In addition to the idle adjusting screw, most engines have a throttle solenoid positioner. Ford has found it necessary to raise the idle speed on the these engines to obtain a smooth engine idle. When the key is turned **OFF**, the current to the spark plugs is cut off and the engine normally stops running. However, if an engine has a high operating temperature and a high idle speed, it is possible for the temperature of the cylinder, instead of the spark plug, to ignite the air/fuel mixture. When this happens, the engine continues to run after the key is turned **OFF**. To solve this problem, a throttle solenoid was added to the carburetor. The solenoid is a cylinder with an adjustable plunger and an electrical lead. When the ignition key is turned to **ON**, the solenoid plunger extends to contact the carburetor throttle lever and raise the idle speed of the engine. when the ignition key is turned **OFF**, the solenoid is de-energized and the solenoid plunger falls back from the throttle lever. This allows the throttle lever to fall back and rest on the curb idle adjusting screw. which closes the throttle plates far enough so that the engine will not run on.

Since it is difficult for the engine to draw the air/fuel mixture from the carburetor with the small amount of throttle plate opening that is present when the engine is idling, an idle mixture passage is provided in the carburetor. This passage delivers an air/fuel mixture to the engine from a hole which is located in the bottom of the carburetor below the throttle plates. This idle mixture passage contains an adjustment screw which restricts the amount of air/fuel entering the engine at idle. The procedures given in this section will tell how to set the idle mixture adjusting screw(s).

→**When the electric solenoid is disengaged, the carburetor idle speed adjusting screw must make contact with the throttle lever to prevent the throttle plates from jamming in the throttle bore when the engine is turned OFF.**

Carburetor Identification

◗ **See Figures 57, 58, 59, 60 and 61**

To help identify which carburetor may be installed on your vehicle, refer to the diagrams to in this section.

Idle Speed

1971-73 MODEL YEARS

◗ **See Figures 62, 63, 64 and 65**

1. With the engine **OFF**, turn the idle fuel mixture screw and limiter cap to the full counterclockwise position.
2. Turn the idle speed adjusting screw(s) out until the throttle plate(s) seats in the throttle bore(s).
3. Make certain that the solenoid plunger is not interfering with the throttle lever.
4. Turn the idle speed adjusting screw in until it contacts the stop on the throttle shaft and lever assembly, then turn the screw inward 1½ turns.
5. Start the engine and allow it to warm it up.
6. Check, and if necessary, adjust the ignition timing.
7. Put the transmission in **N** (manual) or **D** (automatic). Set the parking brake. Block the wheels.
8. Check that the choke plate is in the full open position; turn the headlights on high beam.
9. Install a tachometer according to the tool manufacturer's instructions.
10. If possible leave the air cleaner on while making the adjustments.
11. Loosen the solenoid locknut and turn the solenoid in or out to adjust the idle speed.
12. Disconnect the solenoid lead wire.
13. Adjust the carburetor throttle stop screw to obtain 500 rpm.
14. Connect the lead wire and open the throttle slightly by hand.
15. Turn the mixture adjusting screw(s) inward to obtain the smoothest possible idle with the air cleaner installed.

Carburetor Identification

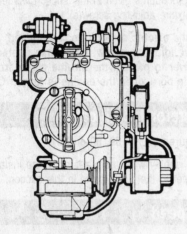

TOP VIEW

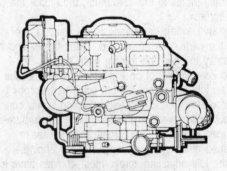

**TYPICAL CARTER
YFA-1V CARBURETOR,
NON-FEEDBACK**

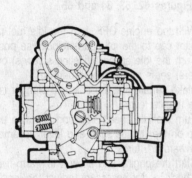

CENTER VIEW

LEFT SIDE VIEW

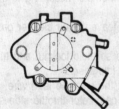

BOTTOM VIEW

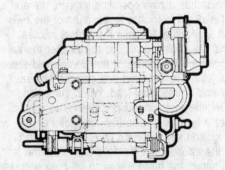

RIGHT SIDE VIEW

86652050

Fig. 57 YFA-1V carburetor — non-feedback type

Carburetor Identification

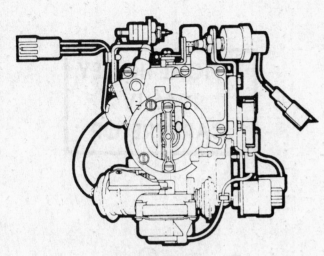

TOP VIEW

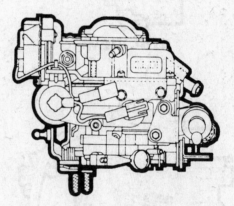

**TYPICAL CARTER
YFA-1V CARBURETOR
WITH FEEDBACK**

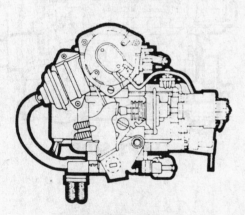

CENTER VIEW

RIGHT SIDE VIEW

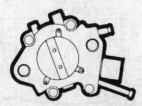

BOTTOM VIEW

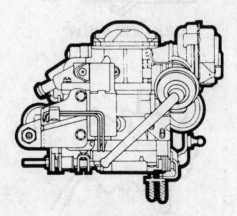

LEFT SIDE VIEW

86652051

Fig. 58 YFA-1V carburetor — feedback type

Carburetor Identification

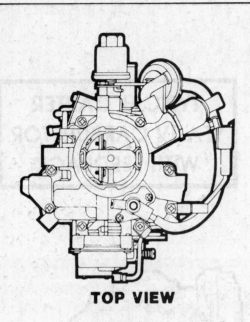

TOP VIEW

**TYPICAL HOLLEY
1946-1V
CARBURETOR**

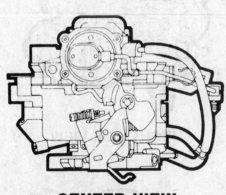

CENTER VIEW

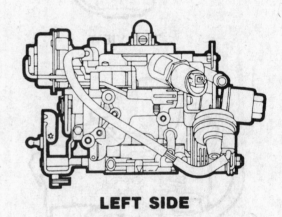

LEFT SIDE

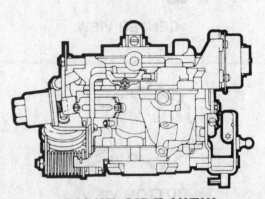

BOTTOM VIEW

RIGHT SIDE VIEW

86652052

Fig. 59 1946-1V carburetor

Carburetor Identification

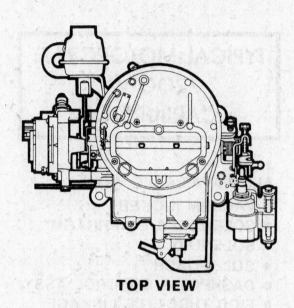

TOP VIEW

TYPICAL MOTORCRAFT 2150-2V & 2150A-2V CARBURETOR

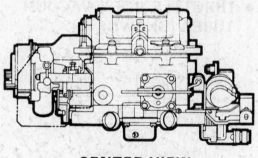

CENTER VIEW

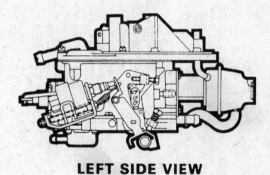

LEFT SIDE VIEW

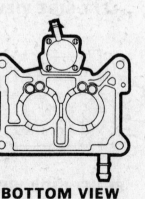

BOTTOM VIEW

RIGHT SIDE VIEW

86652053

Fig. 60 2150-2V & 2150A-2V carburetor

Carburetor Identification

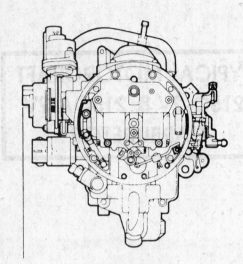

TOP VIEW

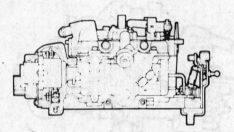

CENTER VIEW

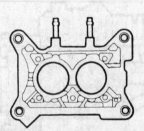

BOTTOM VIEW

TYPICAL MOTORCRAFT 7200-VV CARBURETOR

ALSO AVAILABLE WITH:
- VACUUM KICKER
- SOLENOID & DIAPHRAGM
- SOLENOID
- SOL-A-DASH
- DASHPOT & CONTROL ASSY.
- FIOD THROTTLE LINKAGE
- THROTTLE POSITION SENSOR
- THROTTLE BODY VACUUM TUBES (SHOWN)

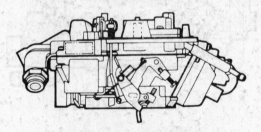

LEFT SIDE VIEW

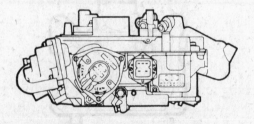

RIGHT SIDE VIEW

86652054

Fig. 61 7200 VV carburetor

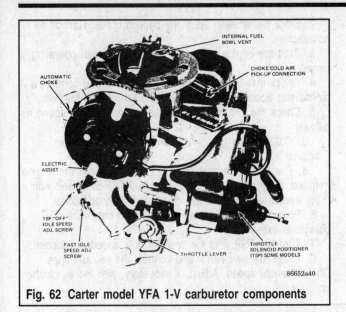

Fig. 62 Carter model YFA 1-V carburetor components

86652a40

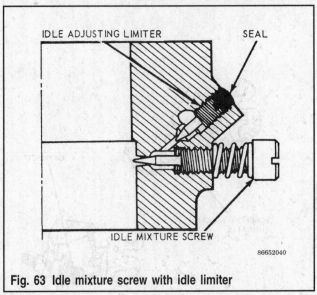

Fig. 63 Idle mixture screw with idle limiter

86652040

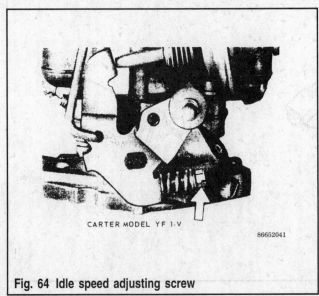

Fig. 64 Idle speed adjusting screw

86652041

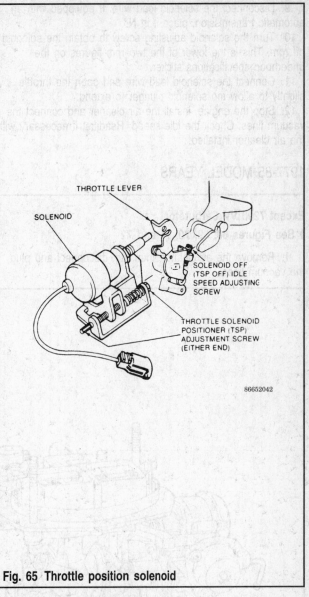

Fig. 65 Throttle position solenoid

86652042

1974-76 MODEL YEARS

▶ **See Figures 66 and 67**

➡ **The procedures and adjustments for the 5200 carburetor can also be used on the 6500 carburetor.**

1. Remove the air cleaner and tag then plug the vacuum lines.
2. Set the parking brake and block the wheels.
3. Connect a tachometer according to the tool manufacturer's instructions.
4. Run the engine to obtain normal operating temperatures.
5. Check, and if necessary, reset the ignition timing.
6. Make certain that the choke plate is fully open.
7. If equipped with a manual transmission, place it in **N**. If equipped with an automatic transmission, place it in **D**
8. Turn the solenoid adjusting screw in or out to adjust the idle speed. The idle speed is the higher of the two rpm figures on the underhood specification sticker.

9. Disconnect the solenoid lead wire. If equipped with an automatic transmission, place it in **N**.

10. Turn the solenoid adjusting screw to obtain the solenoid off rpm. This is the lower of the two rpm figures on the underhood specifications sticker.

11. Connect the solenoid lead wire and open the throttle slightly to allow the solenoid plunger to extend.

12. Stop the engine, install the air cleaner and connect the vacuum lines. Check the idle speed. Readjust if necessary with the air cleaner installed.

1977-85 MODEL YEARS

Except 7200 VV Carburetor
▶ **See Figures 68, 69, 70, 71 and 72**

1. Remove the air cleaner, then tag, disconnect and plug the vacuum lines.

2. Block the wheels, apply the parking brake. Turn off all accessories.

3. Start the engine and allow it to reach normal operating temperature.

4. Check that the choke plate is fully open and connect a tachometer according to the tool manufacturer's instructions.

5. Check the Throttle Stop Positioner-off (TSP-off) speed as follows:

   a. Collapse the plunger by forcing the throttle lever against it.

   b. Place the transmission in **N** or **P** and check the engine speed. If necessary, adjust to specified TSP-off speed with the throttle adjusting screw. See the underhood sticker.

6. Place the transmission in **N** or **D** and check the TSP plunger is extended.

7. Turn the TSP until the specified idle speed is obtained.

8. Install the air cleaner and connect the vacuum lines. Check the idle speed. Adjust, if necessary, with the air cleaner on.

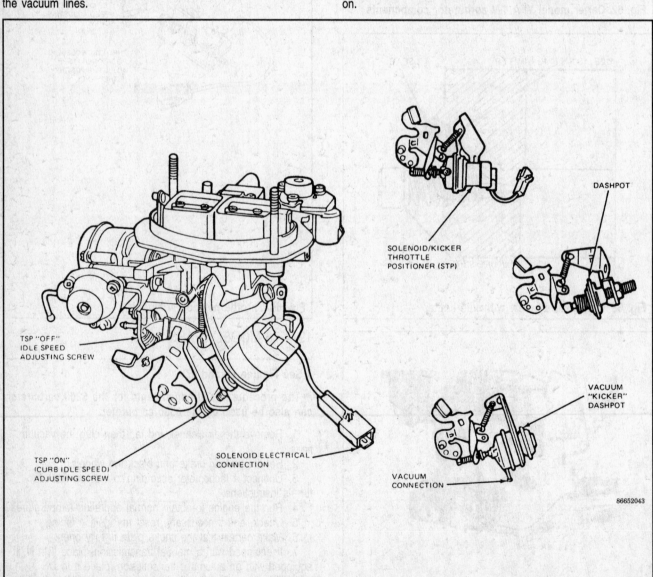

Fig. 66 5200/6500 2-V carburetor with adjustment positions

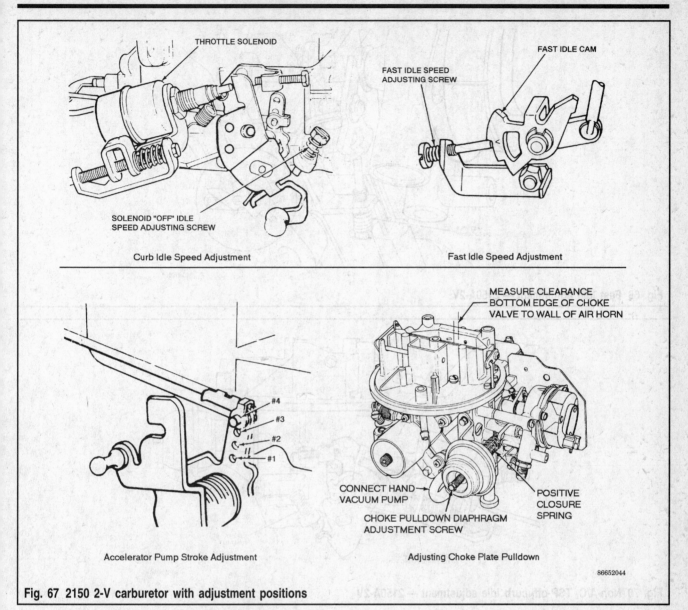

Fig. 67 2150 2-V carburetor with adjustment positions

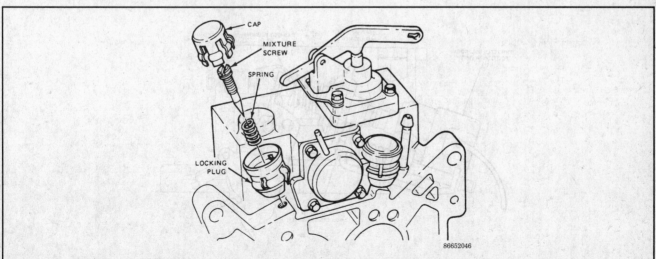

Fig. 68 On later model 2150 carburetors, the metal plug cap must be carefully removed before any adjustments are made.

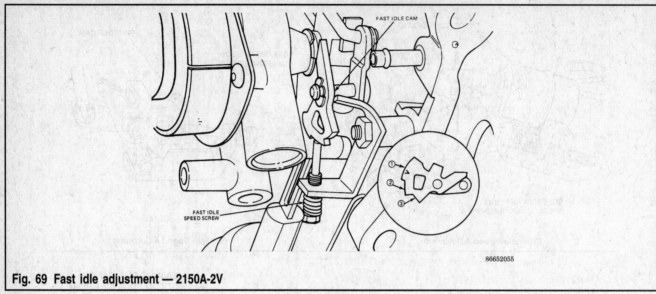

Fig. 69 Fast idle adjustment — 2150A-2V

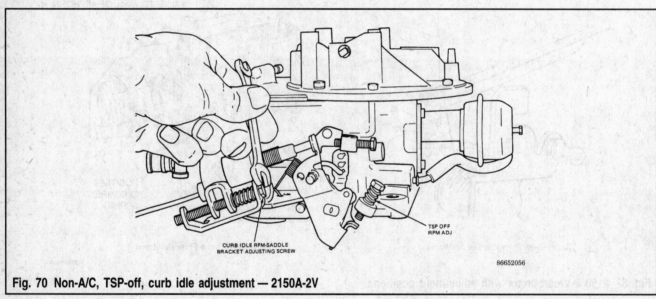

Fig. 70 Non-A/C, TSP-off, curb idle adjustment — 2150A-2V

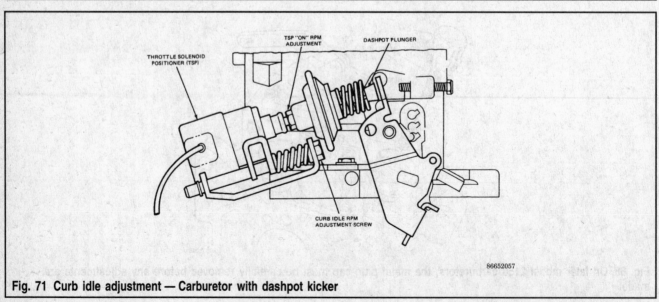

Fig. 71 Curb idle adjustment — Carburetor with dashpot kicker

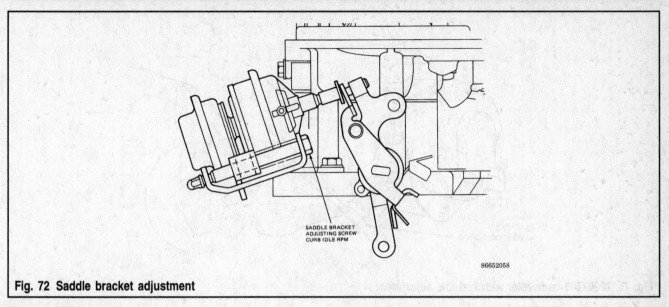

Fig. 72 Saddle bracket adjustment

86652058

7200 VV Carburetor

▶ See Figures 73, 74 and 75

➡The procedures and adjustments for the 7200 carburetor can also be used on the 700 carburetor.

1. Place the transmission in **N** or **P**. Apply the parking brake and block the wheels. If equipped with an automatic brake release, disconnect the vacuum hose and plug it.

2. Bring the engine to normal operating temperature. Place the air conditioner/heater selector to the **OFF** position.

3. Disconnect the vacuum hose at the EGR valve and plug.

4. Place the fast idle adjustment on the second step of the fast idle cam. Check and/or adjust fast idle rpm if needed. Refer to the emission calibration label.

5. Rev the engine momentarily and repeat Step 4. Remove the plug from the EGR vacuum hose and reconnect.

6. Disconnect and plug the vacuum hose at the throttle kicker and place the transmission in the idle setting position specified on the emission calibration label. If adjustment is required, turn the curb idle speed screw and set the idle to the speed specified on the emission calibration label.

7. Put the transmission in **N** or **P**, increase the engine speed momentarily and recheck.

8. Apply a slight pressure on top of the nylon nut located on the accelerator pump to take up the linkage clearance. Turn the nut on the accelerator pump rod clockwise until a clearance of 0.005-0.015 in. (0.12-0.38mm) is obtained between the top of the accelerator pump and the pump lever.

9. Turn the accelerator pump rod 1 turn counterclockwise to set the lever lash preload. Remove the plug from the throttle kicker vacuum hose and reconnect.

10. Disconnect and plug the vacuum hose at the Vacuum Operated Throttle Modulator (VOTM) kicker. Connect an external vacuum source providing a minimum of 10 in. Hg. (33.7 kPa) to the VOTM kicker. Check and adjust the VOTM kicker speed if needed.

11. If adjustment is required, turn the saddle bracket adjusting screw. Remove the external vacuum source and reconnect VOTM kicker hose.

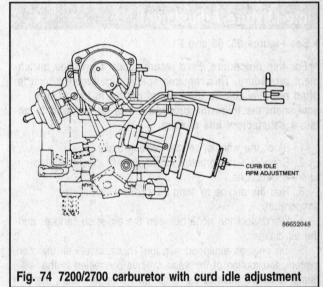

86652048

Fig. 74 7200/2700 carburetor with curd idle adjustment

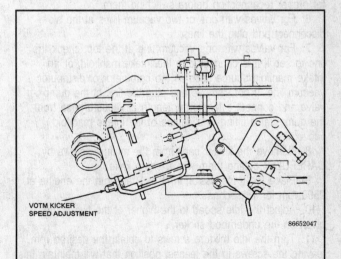

86652047

Fig. 73 7200/2700 VV carburetor with kicker speed adjustment

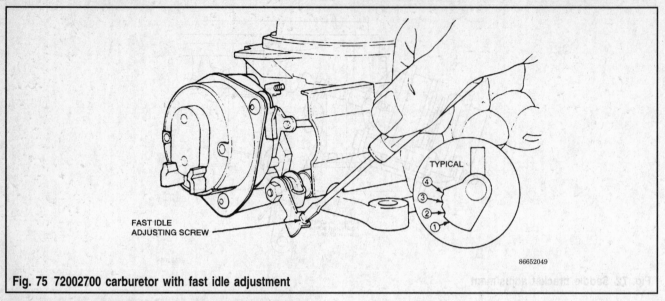

FAST IDLE
ADJUSTING SCREW

TYPICAL

86652049

Fig. 75 72002700 carburetor with fast idle adjustment

Idle Mixture Adjustment

▶ See Figures 66, 68 and 74

➡For this procedure, Ford recommends a propane enrichment procedure. This requires special equipment which is often not available to the general public. In lieu of this equipment the following procedure may be followed to obtain a satisfactory idle mixture.

1. Block the wheels, set the parking brake.
2. Connect a tachometer according to the tool manufacturer's instructions.
3. Run the engine to bring it to normal operating temperature.
4. Disconnect the hose between the emission canister and the air cleaner.
5. On engines equipped with the Thermactor® air injection system, the routing of the vacuum lines connected to the dump valve will have to be temporarily changed. Mark them for proper reconnection before switching them.
6. For valves with one or two vacuum lines at the side, disconnect and plug the lines.
7. For valves with one vacuum line at the top, check the line to see if it is connected to the intake manifold, or an intake manifold source such as the carburetor or distributor vacuum line. If not, remove and plug the line at the dump valve and connect a temporary length of vacuum hose from the dump valve fitting to a source of the intake manifold vacuum.
8. Remove the limiter caps from the mixture screws by CAREFULLY cutting them with a sharp knife.
9. Place the transmission in N or P and run the engine at 2500 rpm for 15 seconds.
10. Adjust the idle speed to the higher of the two figures given on the underhood sticker.
11. Turn the idle mixture screws to obtain the desired rpm, leaving the screws in the leanest position that will maintain this rpm.
12. Repeat steps 9-11 until further adjustment of the mixture screws does not increase the rpm.

13. Turn the screws in until the lower of the two idle speed figures is reached. Turn the screws in ¼ turn increments to insure a balance.
14. Turn the engine OFF and remove the tachometer. Reinstall all equipment.

➡Rough idle, that cannot be corrected by normal service procedures on 1977 and later models, may be caused by a leakage between the EGR valve body and diaphragm. To determine if this is the cause:

Tighten the EGR bolts to 15 ft. lbs. (20 Nm). Connect a vacuum gauge to the intake manifold. Lift up on the diaphragm to exert a sideways pressure on the diaphragm housing. If the idle changes or the reading on the vacuum gauge varies, replace the EGR valve.

Gasoline Fuel Injection

CENTRAL FUEL INJECTION (CFI)

▶ See Figure 76

Fuel injected engines have the idle speed and idle mixture controlled by the TFI-IV/EEC-IV system and no normal service adjustments are necessary.

➡If a change in idle speed occurs, most likely it is a result of a problem elsewhere in the system. Refer to Section 5 for more details.

Adjustments

FAST IDLE

▶ See Figure 77

1. Block the wheels, set the parking brake.
2. Connect a tachometer according to the tool manufacturer's instructions.
3. Run the engine to bring it to normal operating temperature, then shut OFF

4. Disconnect the EGR valve and plug the connection. Unfasten the hose between the emission canister and the air cleaner.

5. Disconnect and plug the vacuum hose at the fast idle pulldown motor. Set the lever to the high step on the fast idle cam stem,

6. Connect a tachometer according to the tool manufacturer's instructions.

7. Start the engine and record the fast idle speed. If needed adjust the fast idle speed by turning the fast idle speed adjusting screw at the base of the assembly.

➡**Any fast idle adjustment must be made within 60 seconds of starting the vehicle.**

8. Turn the engine **OFF** and remove the tachometer. Reinstall all equipment.

CURB IDLE

▶ **See Figure 78**

1. Block the wheels, set the parking brake.
2. Connect a tachometer according to the tool manufacturer's instructions.
3. Run the engine to bring it to normal operating temperature, then shut **OFF**
4. Connect a tachometer according to the tool manufacturer's instructions.
5. Start the engine and run at 2000 rpm for at least 60 seconds. Allow the idle to stabilize for 30 seconds.
6. Place the transmission in **R** and record the curb idle speed.

7. If the curb idle speed needs adjustment, loosen the saddle bracket locking screw, and adjust the curb idle by turning the adjust screw.

8. When the curb idle speed has been adjusted, secure the adjusting screw by tighten the locking screw on the saddle bracket.

9. Turn the engine **OFF** and remove the tachometer. Reinstall all equipment.

MULTIPORT FUEL INJECTION

Fuel injected engines have the idle speed and idle mixture controlled by the TFI-IV/EEC-IV system and no normal service adjustments are necessary.

➡**If a change in idle speed occurs, most likely it is a result of a problem elsewhere in the system. Refer to Section 5 for more details.**

Turbocharged Fuel Injection

A turbocharged option is available on the 2.3L 4-cylinder engine. Like the non-turbo 2.3L engine, this model uses a multiport fuel injection system to deliver fuel to the engine. Idle mixture and speed in addition to turbo boost control are monitored and adjusted by the EEC-IV module. No routine service or adjustments are needed.

➡**If a change in idle speed occurs, most likely it is a result of a problem elsewhere in the system. Refer to Section 5 for more details.**

Carburetor Identification

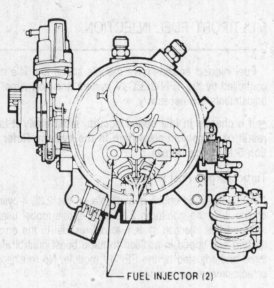

FUEL INJECTOR (2)

TOP VIEW

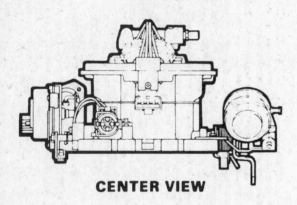

CENTER VIEW

BOTTOM VIEW

TYPICAL MOTORCRAFT ELECTRONIC FUEL INJECTION

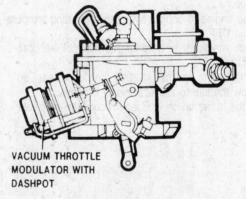

VACUUM THROTTLE
MODULATOR WITH
DASHPOT

LEFT SIDE VIEW

FUEL PRESSURE
REGULATOR

HIGH CAM PULLDOWN
VACUUM MOTOR

THROTTLE POSITION
SENSOR

ALL ELECTRIC
BIMETAL

RIGHT SIDE VIEW

86652059

Fig. 76 Early fuel injection system

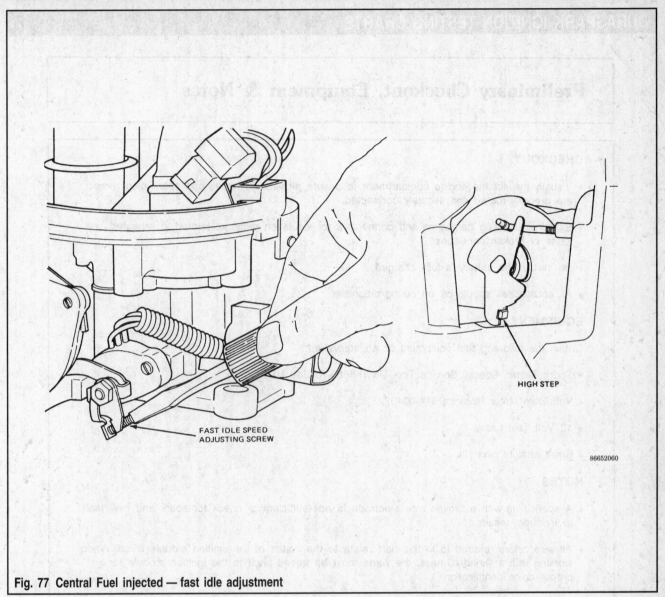

HIGH STEP

FAST IDLE SPEED
ADJUSTING SCREW

86652060

Fig. 77 Central Fuel injected — fast idle adjustment

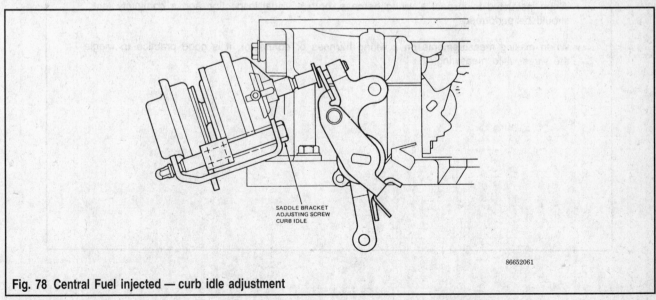

SADDLE BRACKET
ADJUSTING SCREW
CURB IDLE

86652061

Fig. 78 Central Fuel injected — curb idle adjustment

DURASPARK IGNITION TESTING CHARTS

Preliminary Checkout, Equipment & Notes

CHECKOUT

- Visually inspect the engine compartment to ensure all vacuum hoses and spark plug wires are properly routed and securely connected.

- Examine all wiring harnesses and connectors for insulation damage, burned, overheated, loose or broken conditions.

- Be certain the battery is fully charged.

- All accessories should be off during diagnosis.

EQUIPMENT

Obtain the following test equipment or an equivalent:

- Spark Tester, Special Service Tool D81P-6666-A. See **NOTE**.

- Volt/Ohm Meter Rotunda 014-00407.

- 12 Volt Test Lamp.

- Small straight pins (2).

NOTES

- A spark plug with a broken side electrode **is not** sufficient to check for spark and may lead to incorrect results.

- All wire colors referred to in this part relate to the colors of the ignition module wires. When working with a wiring harness, the wires must be traced back to the ignition module for proper color identification.

- When instructed to inspect a wiring harness, both a visual inspection and a continuity test should be performed.

- When making measurements on a wiring harness or connector, it is good practice to wiggle the wires while measuring.

86652100

Start Circuits

DS II   **Test 1**

TEST STEP	RESULT ▶	ACTION TO TAKE
1. Connect spark tester between ignition coil wire and engine ground. 2. Crank engine using ignition switch. **3. Were sparks present?**	Yes ▶ No ▶	GO to Test 2. MEASURE resistance of ignition coil wire. REPLACE if greater than 7,000 ohms per foot. INSPECT ignition coil for damage, carbon tracking. CRANK engine to verify distributor rotation. GO to Test 5.

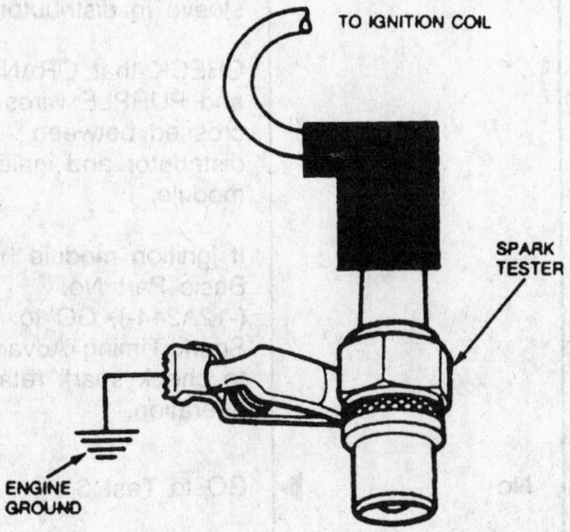

TO IGNITION COIL

SPARK TESTER

ENGINE GROUND

86652101

Run Circuits	DS II	Test 2

TEST STEP	RESULT ▶	ACTION TO TAKE
1. Turn ignition switch from OFF to RUN to OFF position several times. 2. Spark should occur each time switch goes from RUN to OFF position. 3. Remove spark tester, reconnect coil wire to distributor cap. 4. **Were sparks present?**	Yes ▶	INSPECT distributor cap, adapter, rotor for cracks, carbon tracking. CHECK for roll pin securing armature to sleeve in distributor. CHECK that ORANGE and PURPLE wires not crossed between distributor and ignition module. If ignition module has Basic Part No. (-12A244-), GO to Spark Timing Advance to check spark retard operation.
	No ▶	GO to Test 3.

86652102

Module Voltage		DS II	Test 3

TEST STEP	RESULT ▶	ACTION TO TAKE
• Turn ignition switch off. 1. Carefully insert small straight pin in RED module wire. ⌐ CAUTION ¬ **Do not allow straight pin to contact electrical ground.** 2. Attach negative (–) VOM lead to distributor base. 3. Measure battery voltage. 4. Measure voltage at straight pin with ignition switch in RUN position. 5. Turn ignition switch to OFF position. 6. Remove straight pin. 7. **Is voltage 90 percent of battery voltage or greater?**	Yes ▶ No ▶	GO to Test 4. REFER to vehicle wiring diagram. INSPECT wiring harness between module and ignition switch. Damaged or worn ignition switch.

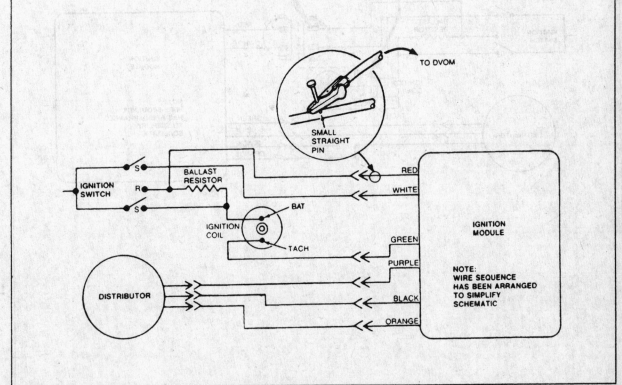

86652103

Ballast Resistor			DS II	Test 4

TEST STEP	RESULT ▶	ACTION TO TAKE
1. Separate and inspect ignition module two wire connector with RED and WHITE wires. 2. Disconnect and inspect ignition coil connector. 3. Measure ballast resistor between BAT terminal of ignition coil connector and wiring harness connector mating with RED module wire. 4. Reconnect all connectors. 5. **Was the resistance 0.8 to 1.6 ohms?**	Yes ▶ No ▶	REPLACE ignition module. REPLACE ballast resistor.

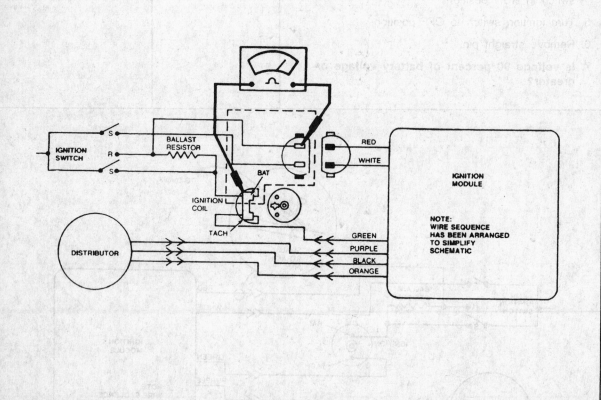

Supply Voltage Circuits	DS II	Test 5

TEST STEP	RESULT ▶	ACTION TO TAKE
1. Remove SPARK TESTER, reconnect coil wire to distributor cap. 2. If starter relay has I terminal, disconnect cable from starter relay to starter motor. 3. If starter relay does not have I terminal, disconnect wire to S terminal of starter relay. 4. Carefully insert small straight pins in RED and WHITE module wires. ┆ CAUTION ┆ **Do not allow straight pins to contact electrical ground.** 5. Measure battery voltage. 6. Following table below, measure voltage at points listed with ignition switch in position shown. NOTE: Attach negative (–) VOM lead to distributor base. Wiggle wires in wiring harness when measuring.	Yes ▶ No ▶	Test result OK. GO to Test 6. REFER to vehicle wiring diagram. INSPECT wiring harness and connector(s) in faulty circuit(s). Damaged or worn ignition switch. Radio interference capacitor on ignition coil.

Wire/ Terminal	Circuit	Ignition Switch Test Position
Red	Run	Run
White	Start	Start
'Bat' Terminal Ignition Coil	Ballast Resistor Bypass	Start

7. Turn ignition switch to OFF position.

8. Remove straight pins.

9. Reconnect any cables/wires removed from starter relay.

10. **Is voltage 90 percent of battery voltage or greater?**

86652105

Supply Voltage Circuits — Continued

DS II   **Test 5**

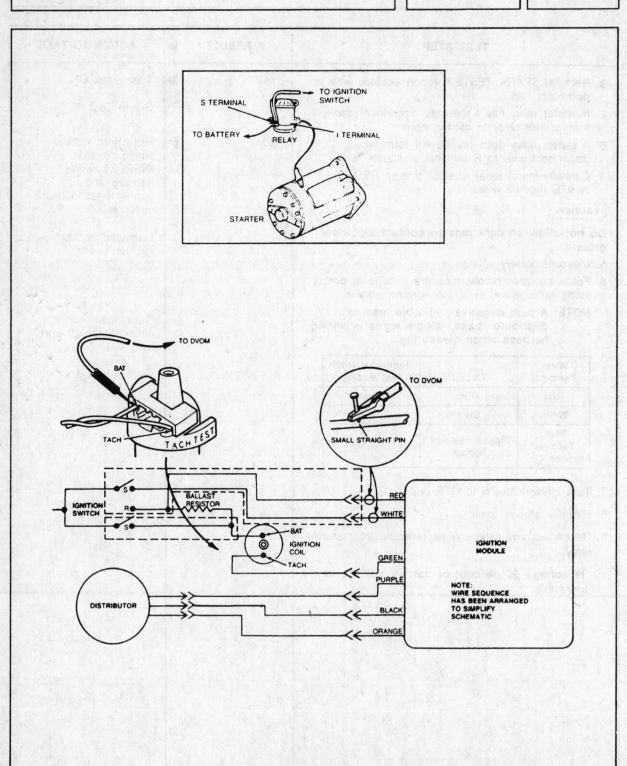

Ignition Coil Supply Voltage	DS II	Test 6

TEST STEP	RESULT ▶	ACTION TO TAKE
1. Attach negative (−) lead of VOM to distributor base. 2. Turn ignition switch to RUN position. 3. Measure voltage at BAT terminal of ignition coil. 4. Turn ignition switch to OFF position. 5. **Was the voltage 6 to 8 volts?**	Yes ▶ No ▶	GO to Test 7. GO to Test 12.

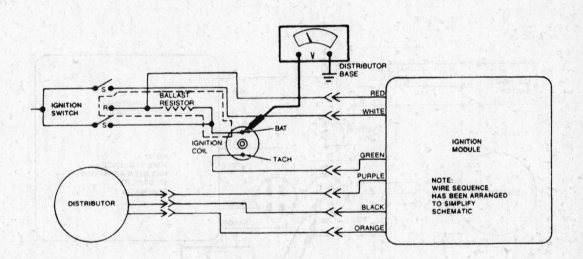

Distributor Stator Assembly and Wiring Harness	DS II	Test 7

TEST STEP	RESULT ▶	ACTION TO TAKE
1. Separate ignition module four wire connector. Inspect for dirt, corrosion, and damage. 2. Measure stator assembly and wiring harness resistance between wiring harness terminals mating with ORANGE and PURPLE module wires. **NOTE: Wiggle wires in wiring harness when measuring.** 3. **Was the resistance 400 to 1,300 ohms?**	Yes ▶ No ▶	Test result OK. GO to Test 8. GO to Test 11.

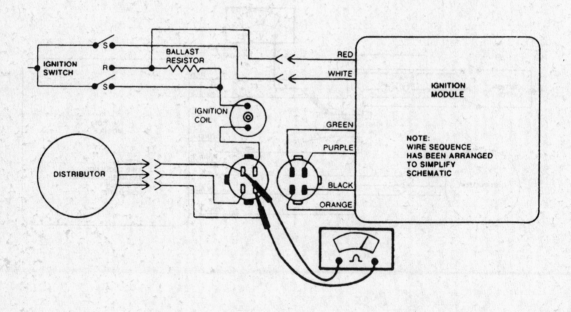

Ignition Module to Distributor Stator Assembly Wiring Harness

| DS II | Test 8 |

TEST STEP	RESULT ▶	ACTION TO TAKE
1. Attach one VOM lead to distributor base. 2. Alternately measure resistance between wiring harness terminals mating with ORANGE and PURPLE module wires and ground. 3. Reconnect four wire connector. 4. **Was the resistance greater than 70,000 ohms?**	Yes ▶ No ▶	TEST result OK. GO to Test 9. INSPECT wiring harness between module connector and distributor, including distributor grommet.

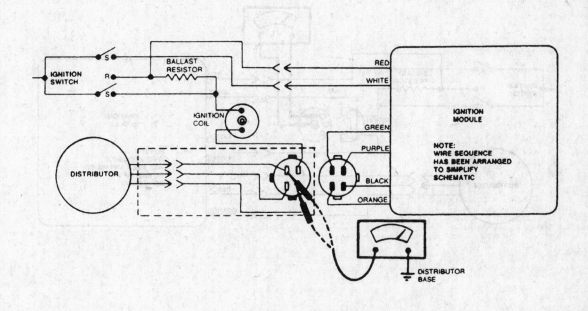

Ignition Coil Secondary Resistance		DS II	Test 9

TEST STEP	RESULT ▶	ACTION TO TAKE
1. Disconnect and inspect ignition coil connector and coil wire. 2. Measure secondary resistance from BAT terminal to high voltage terminal. 3. Reconnect ignition coil wire. 4. **Was the resistance 7,700 to 10,500 ohms?**	Yes ▶ No ▶	Test result OK. GO to Test 10. REPLACE ignition coil.

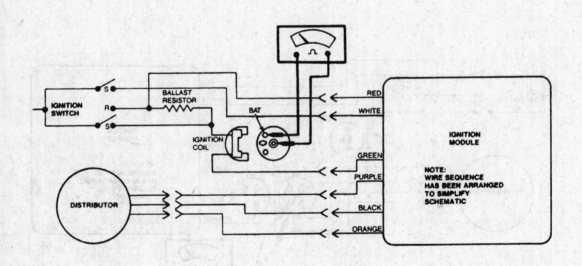

86652110

Module to Coil Wire		DS II	Test 10

TEST STEP	RESULT ▶	ACTION TO TAKE
1. Separate and inspect ignition module four wire connector and ignition coil connector from coil. 2. Connect one lead of VOM to distributor base. 3. Measure resistance between TACH terminal of ignition coil connector and ground. 4. Reconnect ignition module and coil connectors. 5. **Was the resistance greater than 100 ohms?**	Yes ▶ No ▶	REPLACE ignition module. INSPECT wiring harness between ignition module and coil.

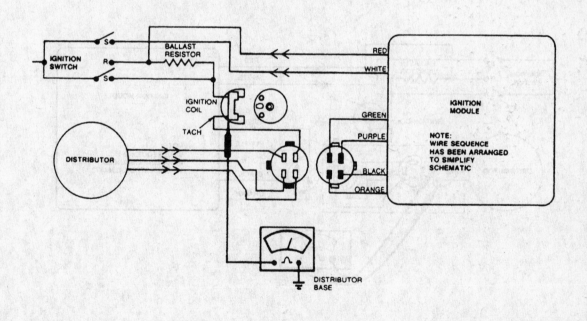

Distributor Stator Assembly	DS II	Test 11

TEST STEP	RESULT ▶	ACTION TO TAKE
1. Separate distributor connector from harness. Inspect for dirt, corrosion, and damage. 2. Measure stator assembly resistance across ORANGE and PURPLE wires at distributor connector. 3. Reconnect distributor and module connectors. 4. **Was resistance 400 to 1,300 ohms?**	Yes ▶	Test result OK. INSPECT wiring harness between distributor and ignition module.
	No ▶	REPLACE stator assembly.

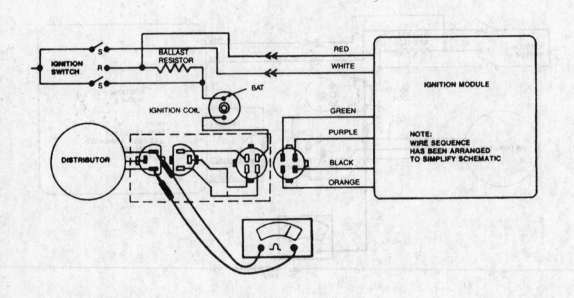

Ignition Coil Primary Resistance

DS II   Test 12

TEST STEP	RESULT ▶	ACTION TO TAKE
1. Disconnect ignition coil connector. 2. Measure primary resistance from BAT to TACH terminal. 3. Reconnect ignition coil connector. **4. Was resistance 0.8 to 1.6 ohms?**	Yes ▶ No ▶	Test result OK. GO to Test 13. REPLACE ignition coil.

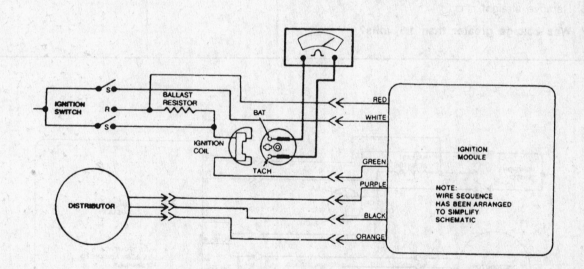

IGNITION SWITCH
S
R
S
BALLAST RESISTOR
IGNITION COIL
BAT
TACH
DISTRIBUTOR
RED
WHITE
GREEN
PURPLE
BLACK
ORANGE
IGNITION MODULE
NOTE:
WIRE SEQUENCE HAS BEEN ARRANGED TO SIMPLIFY SCHEMATIC

Primary Circuit Continuity		DS II	Test 13

TEST STEP	RESULT ▶	ACTION TO TAKE
1. Carefully insert small straight pin in module GREEN wire. ┌ CAUTION ┐ **Do not allow straight pin to contact electrical ground.** 2. Attach negative (–) VOM lead to distributor base. 3. Turn ignition switch to RUN position. 4. Measure voltage at GREEN module wire. 5. Turn ignition switch to OFF position. 6. Remove straight pin. 7. **Was voltage greater than 1.5 volts?**	Yes ▶ No ▶	GO to Test 14. INSPECT wiring harness and connectors between ignition module and coil.

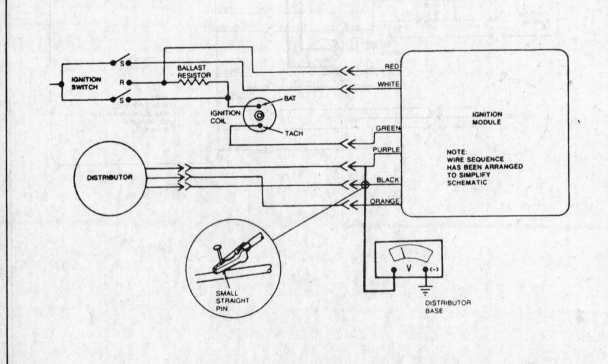

86652114

Ground Circuit Continuity

DS II Test 14

TEST STEP	RESULT ▶	ACTION TO TAKE
1. Carefully insert small straight pin in module BLACK wire. ┌ CAUTION ┐ **Do not allow straight pin to contact electrical ground.** 2. Attach negative (–) VOM lead to distributor base. 3. Turn ignition switch to RUN position. 4. Measure voltage at BLACK wire. 5. Turn ignition switch to OFF position. 6. Remove straight pin. 7. **Was voltage greater than 0.5 volts?**	Yes ▶ No ▶	GO to Test 15. REPLACE ignition module.

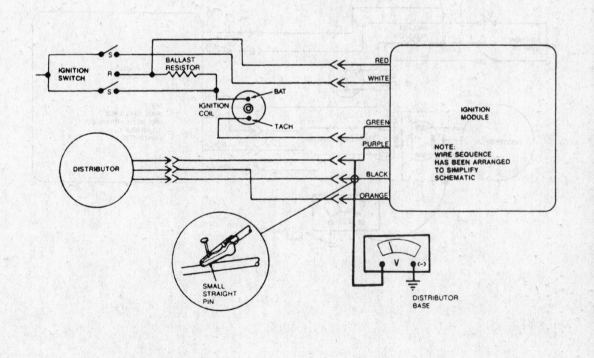

86652115

Distributor Ground Circuit Continuity		DS II	Test 15

TEST STEP	RESULT ▶	ACTION TO TAKE
1. Separate distributor connector from harness. Inspect for dirt, corrosion, and damage. 2. Attach one lead of VOM to distributor base. 3. Measure resistance by attaching other VOM lead to BLACK wire in distributor connector. **NOTE: Wiggle distributor grommet when measuring.** 4. Reconnect distributor connector. 5. **Was resistance less than 1 ohm?**	Yes ▶ No ▶	Test result OK. INSPECT wiring harness and connectors between distributor and ignition module. INSPECT ground screw in distributor.

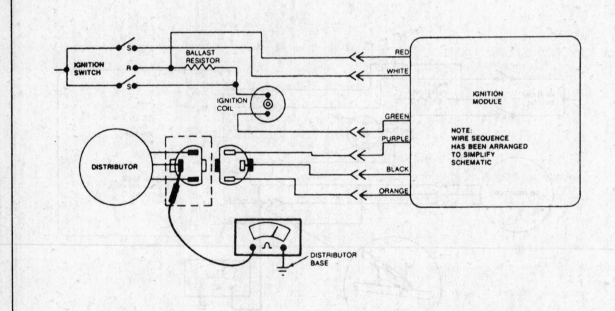

Spark Timing Advance — Non-EEC

TEST STEP	RESULT ▶	ACTION TO TAKE
STEP 1 • Disconnect and plug distributor vacuum hose(s). • Connect timing light and tachometer.	▶	GO to Step 2.
STEP 2 **If Ignition Module (-12A244-) is used:** • Disconnect two wire connector (YELLOW and BLACK wires). • Jumper pins in module connector. • If (-12A244-) Ignition Module not used, skip this Step.	▶	GO to Step 3.
STEP 3 • Start and warm-up engine. • Check that engine speed is at or below timing rpm.* • **Is engine speed at or below timing rpm*?**	Yes ▶ No ▶	OK. GO to Step 4. RESET rpm below timing rpm. GO to Step 4.

* Refer to Vehicle Emission Control Information Decal.

86652117

Spark Timing Advance — Non-EEC

TEST STEP	RESULT	►	ACTION TO TAKE
STEP 4			
• **Positive-Buy timing?**	Yes	►	GO to Step 5.
	No	►	GO to Step 6.
STEP 5			
• Check initial timing.	Yes	►	GO to Step 7.
NOTE: Record reading for later use.	No	►	RESET timing. REMOVE or deface positive buy label.
• **Is timing within ± 4 degrees of required?***			GO to Step 7.
STEP 6			
• Check initial timing.	Yes	►	GO to Step 7.
NOTE: Record reading for later use.	No	►	RESET timing.
• **Is timing within ± 2 degrees of required?***			GO to Step 7.

* Refer to Vehicle Emission Control Information Decal.

86652118

Spark Timing Advance — Non-EEC

TEST STEP	RESULT	▶	ACTION TO TAKE
STEP 7			
• Basic Part No. (-12A244-) on ignition module?	Yes	▶	REMOVE jumper in two wire connector.
			RECONNECT two wire connector.
			GO to Step 8.
	No	▶	GO to Step 11.
STEP 8			
• Check initial timing at timing rpm.	Yes	▶	DISCONNECT two wire connector (YELLOW and BLACK wires) at ignition module.
• **Is timing the same as Step 5 or 6?**			
			GO to Step 9.
			NOTE: Engine may die when connector is separated due to excessive spark retard. If this happens spark retard operation is OK. RECONNECT two wire connector, GO to Step 11.
	No	▶	return to Step 2.
STEP 9			
• Check initial timing at timing rpm.	Yes	▶	Retard operation OK.
• **Is timing retarded from Step 8?**			REMOVE vacuum gauge and RECONNECT vacuum hose (if used).
			GO to Step 11.
	No	▶	GO to Step 10.

86652119

Spark Timing Advance — Non-EEC

TEST STEP	RESULT	▶	ACTION TO TAKE
STEP 10 • Substitute new ignition module. • Connect two wire (RED and WHITE wires) and four wire connectors. • Jumper pins in two wire (YELLOW and BLACK wires) connector. • Check initial timing at timing rpm. • **Is timing the same as Step 5 or 6?**	Yes No	▶ ▶	RETURN to Step 8. **NOTE: If ignition module substitution appears to correct problem, RECONNECT original module and REPEAT this Step to verify service.** REPEAT Step 10.
STEP 11 • Increase engine speed to 2,500 rpm. • Check spark timing. • Return to idle rpm. **NOTE: Refer to the Service Performance Manual for total advance at 2,500 rpm/vacuum advance disconnected under the correct engine calibration for specification.** • **Is timing within specification?**	Yes No	▶ ▶	GO to Step 12. REPLACE distributor. REPEAT this Step.
STEP 12 • Check initial timing at timing rpm. • **Is timing the same as Step 5 or 6?**	Yes No	▶ ▶	Distributor mechanical advance mechanism OK. GO to Step 13. REPLACE distributor. RETURN to Step 11.

86652120

Spark Timing Advance — Non-EEC

TEST STEP	RESULT ▶		ACTION TO TAKE
STEP 13			
• Install distributor vacuum **advance** hose without spark delay valve if used. • Increase engine speed to 2,500 rpm, hold for 60 seconds. • Check spark timing. • Return to idle rpm. • **Is timing within specification?**	Yes	▶	Distributor vacuum advance mechanism OK. CHECK operation of spark-delay valve if used. GO to Step 17.
	No	▶	GO to Step 14.
STEP 14			
• Install vacuum gauge in vacuum advance hose, using tee connector. • Increase engine speed to 2,500 rpm, hold for 60 seconds. • Check for presence of vacuum. • Return to idle rpm. • **Was a minimum of 51 kPa (15 in-Hg) vacuum obtained?**	Yes	▶	INSPECT diaphragm for vacuum leaks and stator assembly for sticking/binding. SERVICE/REPLACE as necessary. RETURN to Step 13.
	No	▶	GO to Step 15.
STEP 15			
• Check engine for vacuum lockout devices. (Refer to Vehicle Emission Control Information Decal) • **Does engine have lockout devices?**	Yes	▶	GO to Step 16.
	No	▶	SERVICE vacuum source. RETURN to Step 13.

86652121

Spark Timing Advance — Non-EEC

TEST STEP	RESULT ▶	ACTION TO TAKE
STEP 16		
• Disconnect and plug distributor vacuum advance hose.	Yes ▶	SERVICE vacuum source.
• Attach vacuum hose between distributor vacuum advance diaphragm connection and manifold vacuum.		DISCONNECT manifold vacuum.
• Increase engine speed to 2,500 rpm.		REMOVE vacuum gauge and tee.
• Check spark timing.		RETURN to Step 13.
• Return to idle rpm.		
	No ▶	INSPECT diaphragm for leaks and stator assembly for sticking/binding. SERVICE/REPLACE as necessary.
• **Is timing within specification?**		DISCONNECT manifold vacuum.
		RECONNECT normal vacuum source.
		RETURN to Step 13.
STEP 17		
• **Does distributor have dual diaphragm?**	Yes ▶	GO to Step 18.
	No ▶	Spark timing systems OK.

Spark Timing Advance — Non-EEC

TEST STEP	RESULT ▶	ACTION TO TAKE
STEP 18 • Disconnect and plug vacuum hose to vacuum advance connection on diaphragm. • Connect vacuum hose to retard connection on diaphragm. • Check spark timing at idle rpm. • **Is timing retarded from Step 5 or 6?**	Yes ▶ No ▶	Spark timing systems OK. RECONNECT vacuum hose to vacuum advance connection. GO to Step 19.
STEP 19 • Install vacuum gauge in vacuum hose to retard connection on diaphragm. • Check for presence of vacuum at idle rpm. • **Is a minimum of 15 kPa (15 in-Hg) vacuum obtained?**	Yes ▶ No ▶	REPLACE distributor diaphragm assembly. RETURN to Step 18. SERVICE vacuum source. RETURN to Step 18.

86652123

THICK FILM IGNITION (TFI) TESTING CHARTS

Preliminary Checkout, Equipment & Notes

CHECKOUT

- Visually inspect the engine compartment to ensure all vacuum hoses and spark plug wires are properly routed and securely connected.

- Examine all wiring harnesses and connectors for insulation damage, and burned, overheated, loose or broken conditions.

- Check that the TFI module is securely fastened to the distributor base.

- Be certain the battery is fully charged.

- All accessories should be off during diagnosis.

EQUIPMENT

Obtain the following test equipment or an equivalent:

- Spark Tester, Special Service Tool D81P-6666-A. See **NOTES.**

- Volt/Ohm Meter Rotunda 014-00407 or 007-00001.

- 12 Volt Test Lamp.

- Small straight pin.

- Remote Starter Switch.

- TFI Ignition Tester, Rotunda 105-00002.

- E-core Ignition Coil E73F-12029-AB.

- Ignition coil secondary wire E43E-12A012-AB.

NOTES

- A spark plug with a broken side electrode is not sufficient to check for spark and may lead to incorrect results.

- When instructed to inspect a wiring harness, both a visual inspection and a continuity test should be performed.

- When making measurements on a wiring harness or connector, it is good practice to wiggle the wires while measuring.

- References to pin-in-line connector apply to a shorting bar type connector used to set base timing.

86652124

Functional Schematic

The TFI-IV system electrical schematic is shown below.

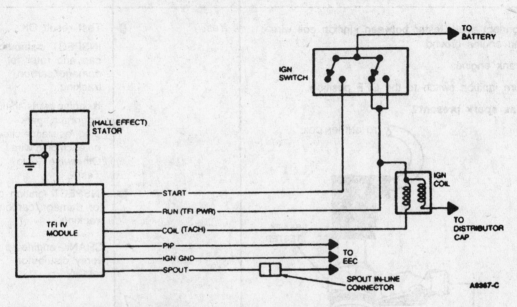

The TFI-IV with CCD system electrical schematic is shown below.

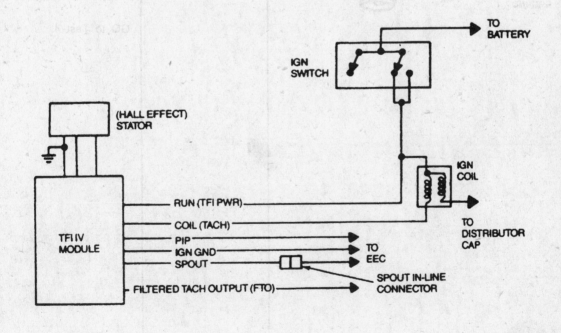

86652125

Ignition Coil Secondary Voltage (Crank Mode)	TFI-IV And TFI With CCD	Test 1

TEST STEP	RESULT ▶	ACTION TO TAKE
1. Connect spark tester between ignition coil wire and engine ground. 2. Crank engine. 3. Turn ignition switch to the OFF position. **4. Was spark present?** TO IGNITION COIL SPARK TESTER ENGINE GROUND	Yes ▶ No ▶	Test result OK. INSPECT distributor cap and rotor for damage/carbon tracking. If engine starts, then perform a spark plug resistance check on each plug wire. Otherwise GO to Test 2. INSPECT ignition coil for damage/carbon tracking. CRANK engine to verify distributor rotation. GO to Test 4.

86652126

Ignition Coil Secondary Voltage (Run Mode)	TFI-IV And TFI With CCD	Test 2

TEST STEP	RESULT ▶	ACTION TO TAKE
1. Place the transmission shift lever in the PARK (A/T) or NEUTRAL (M/T) position and set the parking brake. **CAUTION** **Failure to perform this step may result in the vehicle moving when the starter is subsequently engaged during the test.** 2. Disconnect wire at S terminal of starter relay. 3. Attach remote starter switch. 4. Turn ignition switch to the RUN position. 5. Crank the engine using remote starter switch. 6. Turn ignition switch to the OFF position. 7. Remove remote starter switch. 8. Reconnect wire to S terminal of starter relay. 9. **Was spark present?**	Yes ▶ No ▶	Test result OK. Problem is not in the ignition system. GO to Test 3.

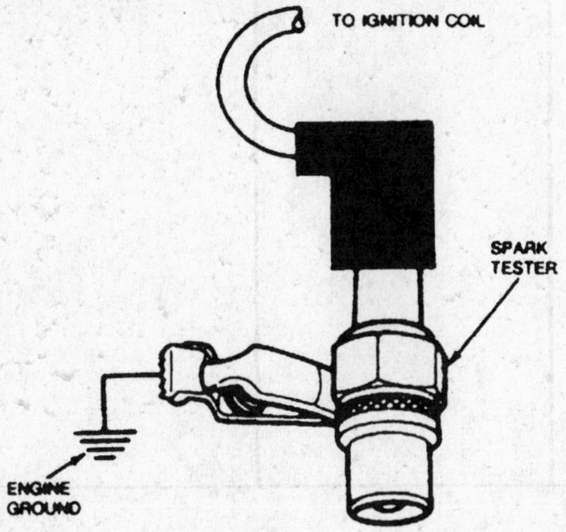

TO IGNITION COIL

SPARK TESTER

ENGINE GROUND

86652127

Wiring Harness	TFI-IV And TFI With CCD	Test 3

TEST STEP	RESULT ▶	ACTION TO TAKE
1. Separate wiring harness connector from ignition module. Inspect for dirt, corrosion, and damage. **NOTE: Push connector tabs to separate.**	Yes ▶	REPLACE TFI module.
2. Verify that the wire to the S terminal of starter relay is disconnected.	No ▶	INSPECT for faults in wiring harness and connectors.
3. Attach negative (–) VOM lead to distributor base.		
4. Measure battery voltage.		
5. Following the appropriate table below, measure connector terminal voltage by attaching VOM to small straight pin inserted into connector terminal and turning ignition switch to position shown.		Damaged or worn ignition switch.

`CAUTION`

Do not allow straight pin to contact electrical ground.

TFI without CCD		
Connector Terminal	**Wire/Circuit**	**Ignition Switch Test Position**
#3	Run Circuit	Run and Start
#4	Start Circuit	Start

TFI with CCD		
Connector Terminal	**Wire/Circuit**	**Ignition Switch Test Position**
#3	Run Circuit	Run and Start

6. Turn ignition switch to OFF position.
7. Remove straight pin.
8. Reconnect wire to S terminal of starter relay.
9. **Was the value at least 90 percent of battery voltage in each case?**

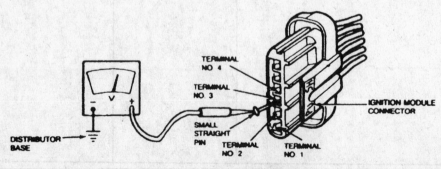

Stator — TFI	TFI-IV And TFI With CCD	Test 4

TEST STEP	RESULT ▶	ACTION TO TAKE
1. Place the transmission shift lever in the PARK (A/T) or NEUTRAL (M/T) position and set the parking brake. [CAUTION] **Failure to perform this step may result in the vehicle moving when the starter is subsequently engaged during the test.** 2. Disconnect the harness connector from the TFI module and connect the TFI tester. 3. Connect the red lead from the tester to the positive (+) side of the battery. 4. Disconnect the wire at the S terminal of the starter relay, and attach remote starter switch. 5. Crank the engine using the remote starter switch and note the status of the two LED lamps. 6. Remove the tester and remote starter switch. 7. Reconnect the wire to the starter relay and the connector to the TFI. 8. **Did the PIP light blink?**	Yes ▶ No ▶	GO to Test 6. REMOVE distributor cap and VERIFY rotation. If OK, GO to Test 5.

86652129

Stator — TFI-IV	TFI-IV And TFI With CCD	Test 5

TEST STEP	RESULT ▶	ACTION TO TAKE
1. Remove the distributor from the engine and the TFI module from the distributor.	Yes ▶	Replace stator.
2. Measure resistance between TFI module terminals as shown below.	No ▶	Replace TFI.

Measure Between These Terminals	Resistance Should Be
GND — PIP In	Greater than 500 Ohms
PIP PWR — PIP IN	Less than 2K Ohms
PIP PWR — TFI PWR	Less than 200 Ohms
GND — IGN GND	Less than 2 Ohms
PIP In — PIP	Less than 200 Ohms

3. Are all these readings as specified?

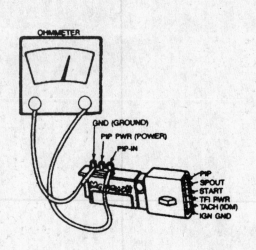

TFI Module	TFI-IV And TFI-IV With CCD	Test 6

TEST STEP	RESULT ▶	ACTION TO TAKE
1. Use status of Tach light from Test 4. 2. **Did the Tach light blink?**	Yes ▶ No ▶	GO to Test 7. REPLACE TFI module and CHECK for spark using the method described in Test 1. If spark was not present REPLACE the coil also.

86652131

Ignition Coil and Secondary Wire	TFI-IV And TFI With CCD	Test 7

TEST STEP	RESULT ▶	ACTION TO TAKE
1. Disconnect ignition coil connector. Inspect for dirt, corrosion and damage. 2. Connect the ignition coil connector to a known good ignition coil. 3. Connect one end of a known good secondary wire to the spark tester. Connect the other end to the known good ignition coil. ⌐ CAUTION ⌐ **DO NOT HOLD THE COIL while performing this test. Dangerous voltages may be present on the metal laminations as well as the high voltage tower.** 4. Crank engine. 5. Turn ignition switch to OFF position. 6. **Was spark present?**	Yes ▶	MEASURE resistance of the ignition coil wire (from vehicle). REPLACE if greater than 7,000 ohms per foot. If OK, REPLACE ignition coil.
	No ▶	RECONNECT coil connector to the vehicle coil and spark tester to vehicle secondary wire and GO to Test 8.

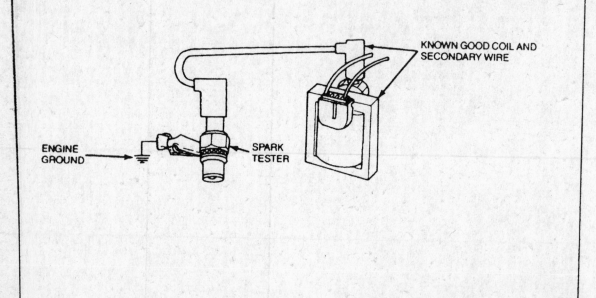

KNOWN GOOD COIL AND SECONDARY WIRE

ENGINE GROUND

SPARK TESTER

86652132

EEC-IV — TFI-IV	TFI-IV And TFI-IV With CCD	Test 8

TEST STEP	RESULT ▶	ACTION TO TAKE
1. Disconnect pin-in-line connector near the distributor. 2. Crank engine. 3. Turn ignition switch to OFF position. 4. **Was spark present?** 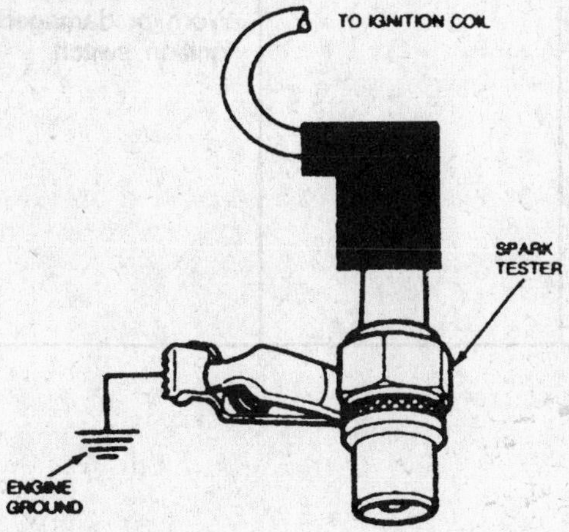	Yes ▶	CHECK PIP and Ignition ground wires for continuity. SERVICE as necessary.
	No ▶	GO to Test 9.

TO IGNITION COIL

SPARK TESTER

ENGINE GROUND

86652133

Ignition Coil Supply Voltage	TFI-IV And TFI-IV With CCD	Test 9

TEST STEP	RESULT ▶	ACTION TO TAKE
1. Attach negative (−) VOM lead to distributor base. 2. Measure battery voltage. 3. Turn ignition switch to RUN position. 4. Measure voltage at POSITIVE (+) terminal of ignition coil. 5. Turn ignition switch to OFF position. 6. Was the value 90 percent of battery voltage or more?	Yes ▶ No ▶	GO to Test 10. INSPECT and SERVICE wiring between ignition coil and ignition switch. Worn or damaged ignition switch.

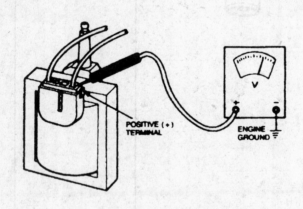

POSITIVE (+) TERMINAL   ENGINE GROUND

86652134

Wiring Harness	TFI-IV	Test 10

TEST STEP	RESULT ▶	ACTION TO TAKE
1. Separate wiring harness connector from ignition module. Inspect for dirt, corrosion, and damage. **NOTE: Push connector tabs to separate.** 2. Disconnect the wire at S terminal of starter relay. 3. Attach negative (−) VOM lead to distributor base. 4. Measure battery voltage. 5. Following the appropriate table below, measure connector terminal voltage by attaching VOM to small straight pin inserted into connector terminal and turning ignition switch to position shown.	Yes ▶	INSPECT for faults in wiring between the coil and TFI module terminal No. 2 or any additional wiring or components connected to that circuit.
`CAUTION` **Do not allow straight pin to contact electrical ground.**	No ▶	INSPECT for faults in wiring harness and connectors.

TFI without CCD		
Connector Terminal	Wire/Circuit	Ignition Switch Test Position
# 3	Run Circuit	Run and Start
# 4	Start Circuit	Start

TFI with CCD		
Connector Terminal	Wire/Circuit	Ignition Switch Test Position
# 3	Run Circuit	Run and Start

Damaged or worn ignition switch.

6. Turn ignition switch to OFF position.

7. Remove straight pin.

8. Reconnect wire to S terminal of starter relay.

9. **Was the value at least 90 percent of battery voltage in each case?**

86652135

Spark Timing Advance — EEC

Test 1

TEST STEP	RESULT ▶	ACTION TO TAKE
1. Key in OFF position. 2. Disconnect the pin in-line connector near the TFI module (SPOUT). 3. Attach the negative (–) VOM lead to the distributor base. 4. Start the engine and measure the battery voltage at idle. 5. Measure the voltage on the TFI module side of the pin in-line connector. 6. **Is the result between 30 percent and 60 percent of battery voltage?**	Yes ▶ No ▶	TFI is OK. GO to Test 2.

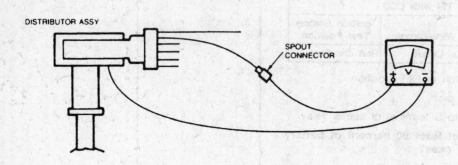

DISTRIBUTOR ASSY

SPOUT CONNECTOR

Spark Timing Advance — EEC

Test 2

TEST STEP	RESULT ▶	ACTION TO TAKE
1. Separate wiring harness connector from ignition module. Inspect for dirt, corrosion and damage. **NOTE: PUSH connector tabs to separate.** 2. Using small straight pin inserted into connector terminal 5, measure resistance between the terminal and the TFI module side of the pin in-line connector. 3. **Is the result less than 5 ohms?**	Yes ▶ No ▶	REPLACE the TFI module. SERVICE the wiring between the pin in-line connector and the TFI connector.

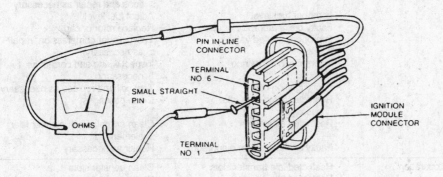

86652137

Troubleshooting Engine Performance

Problem	Cause	Solution
Hard starting (engine cranks normally)	• Binding linkage, choke valve or choke piston	• Repair as necessary
	• Restricted choke vacuum diaphragm	• Clean passages
	• Improper fuel level	• Adjust float level
	• Dirty, worn or faulty needle valve and seat	• Repair as necessary
	• Float sticking	• Repair as necessary
	• Faulty fuel pump	• Replace fuel pump
	• Incorrect choke cover adjustment	• Adjust choke cover
	• Inadequate choke unloader adjustment	• Adjust choke unloader
	• Faulty ignition coil	• Test and replace as necessary
	• Improper spark plug gap	• Adjust gap
	• Incorrect ignition timing	• Adjust timing
	• Incorrect valve timing	• Check valve timing; repair as necessary
Rough idle or stalling	• Incorrect curb or fast idle speed	• Adjust curb or fast idle speed
	• Incorrect ignition timing	• Adjust timing to specification
	• Improper feedback system operation	• Refer to Chapter 4
	• Improper fast idle cam adjustment	• Adjust fast idle cam
	• Faulty EGR valve operation	• Test EGR system and replace as necessary
	• Faulty PCV valve air flow	• Test PCV valve and replace as necessary
	• Choke binding	• Locate and eliminate binding condition
	• Faulty TAC vacuum motor or valve	• Repair as necessary
	• Air leak into manifold vacuum	• Inspect manifold vacuum connections and repair as necessary
	• Improper fuel level	• Adjust fuel level
	• Faulty distributor rotor or cap	• Replace rotor or cap
	• Improperly seated valves	• Test cylinder compression, repair as necessary
	• Incorrect ignition wiring	• Inspect wiring and correct as necessary
	• Faulty ignition coil	• Test coil and replace as necessary
	• Restricted air vent or idle passages	• Clean passages
	• Restricted air cleaner	• Clean or replace air cleaner filler element
	• Faulty choke vacuum diaphragm	• Repair as necessary
Faulty low-speed operation	• Restricted idle transfer slots	• Clean transfer slots
	• Restricted idle air vents and passages	• Clean air vents and passages
	• Restricted air cleaner	• Clean or replace air cleaner filter element
	• Improper fuel level	• Adjust fuel level
	• Faulty spark plugs	• Clean or replace spark plugs
	• Dirty, corroded, or loose ignition secondary circuit wire connections	• Clean or tighten secondary circuit wire connections
	• Improper feedback system operation	• Refer to Chapter 4
	• Faulty ignition coil high voltage wire	• Replace ignition coil high voltage wire
	• Faulty distributor cap	• Replace cap
Faulty acceleration	• Improper accelerator pump stroke	• Adjust accelerator pump stroke
	• Incorrect ignition timing	• Adjust timing
	• Inoperative pump discharge check ball or needle	• Clean or replace as necessary
	• Worn or damaged pump diaphragm or piston	• Replace diaphragm or piston

86652200

Troubleshooting Engine Performance (cont.)

Problem	Cause	Solution
Faulty acceleration (cont.)	• Leaking carburetor main body cover gasket	• Replace gasket
	• Engine cold and choke set too lean	• Adjust choke cover
	• Improper metering rod adjustment (BBD Model carburetor)	• Adjust metering rod
	• Faulty spark plug(s)	• Clean or replace spark plug(s)
	• Improperly seated valves	• Test cylinder compression, repair as necessary
	• Faulty ignition coil	• Test coil and replace as necessary
	• Improper feedback system operation	• Refer to Chapter 4
Faulty high speed operation	• Incorrect ignition timing	• Adjust timing
	• Faulty distributor centrifugal advance mechanism	• Check centrifugal advance mechanism and repair as necessary
	• Faulty distributor vacuum advance mechanism	• Check vacuum advance mechanism and repair as necessary
	• Low fuel pump volume	• Replace fuel pump
	• Wrong spark plug air gap or wrong plug	• Adjust air gap or install correct plug
	• Faulty choke operation	• Adjust choke cover
	• Partially restricted exhaust manifold, exhaust pipe, catalytic converter, muffler, or tailpipe	• Eliminate restriction
	• Restricted vacuum passages	• Clean passages
	• Improper size or restricted main jet	• Clean or replace as necessary
	• Restricted air cleaner	• Clean or replace filter element as necessary
	• Faulty distributor rotor or cap	• Replace rotor or cap
	• Faulty ignition coil	• Test coil and replace as necessary
	• Improperly seated valve(s)	• Test cylinder compression, repair as necessary
	• Faulty valve spring(s)	• Inspect and test valve spring tension, replace as necessary
	• Incorrect valve timing	• Check valve timing and repair as necessary
	• Intake manifold restricted	• Remove restriction or replace manifold
	• Worn distributor shaft	• Replace shaft
	• Improper feedback system operation	• Refer to Chapter 4
Misfire at all speeds	• Faulty spark plug(s)	• Clean or replace spark plug(s)
	• Faulty spark plug wire(s)	• Replace as necessary
	• Faulty distributor cap or rotor	• Replace cap or rotor
	• Faulty ignition coil	• Test coil and replace as necessary
	• Primary ignition circuit shorted or open intermittently	• Troubleshoot primary circuit and repair as necessary
	• Improperly seated valve(s)	• Test cylinder compression, repair as necessary
	• Faulty hydraulic tappet(s)	• Clean or replace tappet(s)
	• Improper feedback system operation	• Refer to Chapter 4
	• Faulty valve spring(s)	• Inspect and test valve spring tension, repair as necessary
	• Worn camshaft lobes	• Replace camshaft
	• Air leak into manifold	• Check manifold vacuum and repair as necessary
	• Improper carburetor adjustment	• Adjust carburetor
	• Fuel pump volume or pressure low	• Replace fuel pump
	• Blown cylinder head gasket	• Replace gasket
	• Intake or exhaust manifold passage(s) restricted	• Pass chain through passage(s) and repair as necessary
	• Incorrect trigger wheel installed in distributor	• Install correct trigger wheel

86652201

Troubleshooting Engine Performance (cont.)

Problem	Cause	Solution
Power not up to normal	• Incorrect ignition timing	• Adjust timing
	• Faulty distributor rotor	• Replace rotor
	• Trigger wheel loose on shaft	• Reposition or replace trigger wheel
	• Incorrect spark plug gap	• Adjust gap
	• Faulty fuel pump	• Replace fuel pump
	• Incorrect valve timing	• Check valve timing and repair as necessary
	• Faulty ignition coil	• Test coil and replace as necessary
	• Faulty ignition wires	• Test wires and replace as necessary
	• Improperly seated valves	• Test cylinder compression and repair as necessary
	• Blown cylinder head gasket	• Replace gasket
	• Leaking piston rings	• Test compression and repair as necessary
	• Worn distributor shaft	• Replace shaft
	• Improper feedback system operation	• Refer to Chapter 4
Intake backfire	• Improper ignition timing	• Adjust timing
	• Faulty accelerator pump discharge	• Repair as necessary
	• Defective EGR CTO valve	• Replace EGR CTO valve
	• Defective TAC vacuum motor or valve	• Repair as necessary
	• Lean air/fuel mixture	• Check float level or manifold vacuum for air leak. Remove sediment from bowl
Exhaust backfire	• Air leak into manifold vacuum	• Check manifold vacuum and repair as necessary
	• Faulty air injection diverter valve	• Test diverter valve and replace as necessary
	• Exhaust leak	• Locate and eliminate leak
Ping or spark knock	• Incorrect ignition timing	• Adjust timing
	• Distributor centrifugal or vacuum advance malfunction	• Inspect advance mechanism and repair as necessary
	• Excessive combustion chamber deposits	• Remove with combustion chamber cleaner
	• Air leak into manifold vacuum	• Check manifold vacuum and repair as necessary
	• Excessively high compression	• Test compression and repair as necessary
	• Fuel octane rating excessively low	• Try alternate fuel source
	• Sharp edges in combustion chamber	• Grind smooth
	• EGR valve not functioning properly	• Test EGR system and replace as necessary
Surging (at cruising to top speeds)	• Low carburetor fuel level	• Adjust fuel level
	• Low fuel pump pressure or volume	• Replace fuel pump
	• Metering rod(s) not adjusted properly (BBD Model Carburetor)	• Adjust metering rod
	• Improper PCV valve air flow	• Test PCV valve and replace as necessary
	• Air leak into manifold vacuum	• Check manifold vacuum and repair as necessary
	• Incorrect spark advance	• Test and replace as necessary
	• Restricted main jet(s)	• Clean main jet(s)
	• Undersize main jet(s)	• Replace main jet(s)
	• Restricted air vents	• Clean air vents
	• Restricted fuel filter	• Replace fuel filter
	• Restricted air cleaner	• Clean or replace air cleaner filter element
	• EGR valve not functioning properly	• Test EGR system and replace as necessary
	• Improper feedback system operation	• Refer to Chapter 4

86652202

Tune-Up Specifications

Year	Engine No. Cyl Displacement (cu. in.)	hp	Spark Plugs Orig. Type	Spark Plugs Gap (in.)	Distributor Point Dwell ° (deg)	Distributor Point Gap (in.)	Ignition Timing (deg) ▲ Man Trans	Ignition Timing (deg) ▲ Auto Trans	Intake Valve Opens ■(deg)	Fuel Pump Pressure (psi)	Idle Speed (rpm) ▲● Man Trans	Idle Speed (rpm) ▲● Auto Trans
'71	6-250	145	BRF-82	.034	36	.027/ .025	6B	6B	10	4–6	750	600
	8-302	210	BRF-42	.034	27	.021	6B	6B	16	4–6	800/500	575 (600/500)
	8-351C	240	ARF-42	.034	27	.021	6B	6B	12	5–7	700/500	600
	8-351W	240	BRF-42	.034	27	.021	6B	6B	12	5–7	700/500	575 (600/500)
	8-351C	285	AFR-32	.034	27/29	.021/ .017	6B	6B	18	5–7	800/500	600
	8-429	360	BRF-42	.034	27/29	.021/ .017	4B	4B	16	5–7	700	600 (600/500)
	8-429CJ	370	ARF-42	.034	25	.020	10B	10B	32	4½–6½	700	650 (650/500)
	8-429SCJ	385	ARF-42	.034	28	.020	10B	10B	40½	4½–6½	650/500	700/500
'72	6-250	95	BRF-82	.034	37	.027	6B	6B	10(16)	4½–6½	750/500	600/500
	8-302	140	BRF-42	.034	28	.017	6B	6B	16	5½–6½	800/500	575 (600/500)
	8-351C	165	ARF-42	.034	28	.017	6B	6B	12	5½–6½	800/500	575/500 (625/500)
	8-351W	165	BRF-42	.034	28	.017	—	6B	12	5½–6½	—	575 (600/500)
	8-400	168	ARF-42	.034	28	.017	—	6B	17	4½–5½	—	625/500
	8-429	205	ARF-42	.034	28	.017	—	10B	8	5½–6½	—	600/500
'73	6-250	95	BRF-82	.034	37	.027/ .025	6B	6B	16	4½–6½	750/500	600/500
	8-302	140	BRF-42	.034	28	.017	6B	6B	16	5½–6½	800/500	575 (600/500)
	8-351C	165	ARF-42	.034	28	.017	—	6B	12	5½–6½	—	625/500
	8-351W	165	BRF-42	.034	28	.017	—	6B	12	5½–6½	—	575 (600/500)
	8-400	168	ARF-42	.034	28	.017	—	6B	17	5½–6½	—	625–500
	8-429	205	ARF-42	.034	28	.017	—	10B	8	5½–6½	—	600/500
	8-460PI	269	ARF-42	.035	28	.017	—	10B	18	5½–6½	—	600
'74	6-260	91	BRF-82	.044	37 ⑩	.027	6B	6B	26	5½–6½	800/500	625/500
	8-302	140	BRF-42	.044	28 ⑩	.017	10B	6B	16 ⑦	5½–6½	800/500	625/500
	8-351W	162	BRF-42	.044	28 ⑩	.017	—	6B	15	5½–6½	—	600/500
	8-351C	163	ARF-42	.044	28 ⑩	.017	—	14B	11.5	5½–6½	—	600/500
	8-400	170	ARF-42	.044	Electronic		—	12B ⑥	17	5½–6½	—	625/500
	8-460	195, 220 260	ARF-42	.054	Electronic		—	14B	8	5½–6½	—	650/500
'75	8-351W	153, 154	ARF-42	.044	Electronic		—	6B	15	5½–6½	—	600/500
	8-351M	148, 150	ARF-42	.044	Electronic		—	6B	19½	5½–6½	—	700/500
	8-400	144, 158	ARF-42	.044	Electronic		—	6B	17	5½–6½	—	625/500
	8-460	216, 217	ARF-52	.044	Electronic		—	14B	8	5½–6½	—	650/500
	8-460PI	226	ARF-52	.044	Electronic		—	14B	18	5½–7	—	700/500
'76	8-351W	All	ARF-42/52 ⑧	.054	Electronic		—	⑧	15	5½–6½	—	650
	8-351M	All	ARF-42/52 ⑧	.044	Electronic		—	⑧	19½	5½–6½	—	650 (650/675 ⑧)
	8-400	All	ARF-42/52 ⑧	.044	Electronic		—	⑧	17	5½–6½	—	650(625)
	8-460	All	ARF-52	.044	Electronic		—	8/14B ⑧ ⑨ @ 650	8	5½–6½	—	650
	8-460PI	226	ARF-52	.044	Electronic		—	14B ⑨ @ 650	18	5½–7	—	650
'77	8-302	All	ARF-52 ④	.050	Electronic		—	8B ⑬	16	5½–6½	—	650
	8-351W	All	ARF-52 ④	.050	Electronic		—	4B	23	4–6	—	650

86672x10

Tune-Up Specifications (Cont.)

Year	No. Cyl Displacement (cu. in.)	hp	Spark Plugs Orig. Type	Gap (in.)	Distributor Point Dwell (deg)	Point Gap (in.)	Ignition Timing (deg) ▲ Man Trans	Auto Trans	Intake Valve Opens ■(deg)	Fuel Pump Pressure (psi)	Idle Speed (rpm) ▲● Man Trans	Auto Trans
	8-351M	All	ARF-52 ④	.050	Electronic		—	8B ⑭	19½	6½–7½	—	650
'77	8-400	All	ARF-54 ④	.050	Electronic		—	8B	17	7–8	—	650
'78	8-302	All	ARF-52 ⑮	.050	Electronic		—	14B	16	5½–6½	—	650
	8-351M	All	ARF-52 ⑮	.050	Electronic		—	14B	23	4–6	—	650
	8-351W	All	ARF-52 ⑮	.050	Electronic		—	14B ⑯	19½	6½–7½	—	650
	8-400	All	ARF-5 ⑮	.050	Electronic		—	13B ⑯	17	6½–7½	—	650
'79	8-302	All	ASF-52	.050	Electronic		—	8B	16	5½–6½	—	600
	8-351M	All	ASF-52	.050	Electronic		—	12B ⑪	17 ⑫	7–8	—	600
	8-351W	All	ASF-52	.050	Electronic		—	15B	23	6½–8	—	600
'80	8-255	All	ASF-42	.050	Electronic		—	8B	16	5½–6	—	550
	8-255 Calif.	All	ASF-42	.050	Electronic		—	EEC	16	5½–6½	—	EEC
	8-302	All	ASF-52	.050	Electronic		—	8B	16	5½–6½	—	550
	8-302 Calif.	All	ASF-52	.050	Electronic		—	EEC	16	5½–6½	—	EEC
'81	4-140	All	AWSF-42	.034	Electronic		6B	6B	22	5½–6½	700	700
	6-200	All	BSF-92	.050	Electronic		10B	10B	20	6–8	900	900
	8-255	All	ASF-52	.050	Electronic		—	10B	16	6–8	—	800
	8-302	All	ASF-52	.050	Electronic		—	8B	16	6–8	—	800
'82–'85	4-140	All	AWSF-42 ⑱	.034	Electronic		—	⑧	22	6–8	850 ⑧	750 ⑧
	6-200	All	BSF-92	.050	Electronic		—	⑧	20	6–8	—	700 ⑧
	6-232	All	AGSF-52 ⑲	.044	Electronic		—	⑧	13	6–8 ⑳	—	500 ⑰⑧
	8-255	All	ASF-52	.050	Electronic		—	⑧	16	6–8	—	700 ⑧
	8-302	All	ASF-52 ⑧	.050 ㉑	Electronic		—	⑧	16	6–8 ㉓	—	500 ⑧

NOTE: The underhood specifications sticker often reflects tune-up specification changes made in production. Sticker figures must be used if they disagree with those in this chart.

* Where two dwell or point gap figures are separated by a slash, the first figure is for engines equipped with dual diaphragm distributors and the second figure is for engines equipped with single diaphragm distributors

▲ See text for procedure

● In all cases where two idle speed figures are separated by a slash, the first is for idle speed with solenoid energized and automatic transmission in Drive, while the second is for idle speed with solenoid disconnected and automatic transmission in Neutral. Figures in parentheses are for California

■ All figures are in degrees Before Top Dead Center

① For air conditioned vehicles, adjust idle speed to 600 rpm with A/C on

② For air conditioned vehicles, adjust idle speed to 800 rpm with A/C on

③ Figure is .020 for manual transmission with dual point distributor

④ ARF-52-6 for Calif. engines, gap is .060 in.

⑤ Figure is 32°–35° on manual transmission model with dual point distributor with both point sets combined

⑥ At 500 rpm

⑦ 20° BTC for 302 automatic

⑧ Depends on emission equipment; check underhood specifications sticker

⑨ In Drive

⑩ Electronic ignition used on all engines assembled after May, 1974

⑪ 14B in Calif.

⑫ Calif. 19.5

⑬ Versailles: 12B

⑭ California: 9B

⑮ California: ARF-52-6; gap .060

⑯ California: 16B

⑰ California: T'bird & XR-7 — 700 w/TSP on
    Cougar — 650 w/TSP off
    Continental — 700 w/TSP on

⑱ Turbo models: AWSF-32C

⑲ CFI (injected) models: AWSF-54

⑳ CFI (injected) 40–45

㉑ .044, 83 and later

㉒ Injected models—39

B Before Top Dead Center

C Cleveland

M Modified Cleveland

CJ Cobra Jet

HO High Output

N.A. Not available

SCJ Super Cobra Jet

W Windsor

EEC: Electrical Engine Control; Adjustment is not possible.

—Not applicable

86672x12

3

ENGINE
AND
ENGINE
OVERHAUL

BASIC ELECTRICITY

Understanding Basic Electricity

For any electrical system to operate, it must make a complete circuit. This simply means that the power flow from the battery must make a full circle. When an electrical component is operating, power flows from the battery to the components, passes through the component (load) causing it to function, and returns to the battery through the ground path of the circuit. This ground may be either another wire or the actual metal part of the vehicle depending upon how the component is designed.

Perhaps the easiest way to visualize this is to think of connecting a light bulb with two wires attached to it to the battery. If one of the two wires was attached to the negative (-) post of the battery and the other wire to the positive (+) post, the light bulb would light and the circuit would be complete. Electricity could follow a path from the battery to the bulb and back to the battery. It's not hard to see that with longer wires on our light bulb, it could be mounted anywhere on the vehicle. Further, one wire could be fitted with a switch so that the light could be turned on and off at will. Various other items could be added to our primitive circuit to make the light flash, become brighter or dimmer under certain conditions, or advise the user that it's burned out.

Some automotive components are grounded through their mounting points. The electrical current runs through the chassis of the vehicle and returns to the battery through the ground (-) cable; if you look, you'll see that the battery ground cable connects between the battery and the body of the vehicle.

Every complete circuit must include a "load" (something to use the electricity coming from the source). If you were to connect a wire between the two terminals of the battery (DON'T do this) without the light bulb, the battery would attempt to deliver its entire power supply from one pole to another almost instantly. This is a short circuit. The electricity is taking a short cut to get to ground and is not being used by any load in the circuit. This sudden and uncontrolled electrical flow can cause great damage to other components in the circuit and can develop a tremendous amount of heat. A short in an automotive wiring harness can develop sufficient heat to melt the insulation on all the surrounding wires and reduce a multiple wire cable to one mass of plastic and copper. Two common causes of shorts are broken insulation (thereby exposing the wire to contact surrounding metal surfaces or other wires) or a failed switch (the pins inside the switch come apart and touch).

Some electrical components which require a large amount of current to operate also have a relay in their circuit. Since these circuits carry a large amount of current (amperage or amps), the thickness of the wire in the circuit (wire gauge) is also greater. If this large wire were connected from the load to the control switch on the dash, the switch would have to carry the high amperage load and the dash would be twice as large to accommodate wiring harnesses as thick as your wrist. To prevent these problems, a relay is used. The large wires in the circuit are connected from the battery to one side of the relay and from the opposite side of the relay to the load. The relay is normally open, preventing current from passing through the circuit. An additional, smaller wire is connected from the relay to the control switch for the circuit. When the control switch is turned on, it grounds the smaller wire to the relay and completes its circuit. The main switch inside the relay closes, sending power to the component without routing the main power through the inside of the vehicle. Some common circuits which may use relays are the horn, headlights, starter and rear window defogger systems.

It is possible for larger surges of current to pass through the electrical system of your vehicle. If this surge of current were to reach the load in the circuit, it could burn it out or severely damage it. To prevent this, fuses, circuit breakers and/or fusible links are connected into the supply wires of the electrical system. These items are nothing more than a built-in weak spot in the system. It's much easier to go to a known location (the fusebox) to see why a circuit is inoperative than to dissect 15 feet of wiring under the dashboard, looking for a cause.

When an electrical current of excessive power passes through the fuse, the fuse blows and breaks the circuit, preventing the passage of current and protecting the components. .

A circuit breaker is basically a self repairing fuse. It will open the circuit in the same fashion as a fuse, but when either the short is removed or the surge subsides, the circuit breaker resets itself and does not need replacement.

A fuse link (fusible link or main link) is a wire that acts as a fuse. One of these is normally connected between the starter relay and the main wiring harness under the hood. Since the starter is the highest electrical draw on the vehicle, an internal short during starting could direct about 130 amps into the wrong place(s). Consider the damage potential of introducing this current into a system whose wiring is rated at 15 amps and you'll understand the need for protection. Since this link is very early in the electrical path, it's the first place to look if nothing on the vehicle works, but the battery seems to be charged and is properly connected.

Electrical problems generally fall into one of three areas:
- The component that is not functioning, is not receiving current.
- The component is receiving power, but is not using it or is using it incorrectly (component failure).
- The component is improperly grounded.

Some circuits can be checked with a test light and a jumper wire. The test light is a device that looks like a pointed screwdriver with a wire on one end and a bulb in its handle. A jumper wire is simply a piece of wire with an alligator clip at each end. If a component is not working, you must follow a systematic plan to determine which of the three condition(s) is the cause.

1. Turn on the switch that controls the item not working.

➡**Some items only work when the ignition switch is turned ON.**

2. Disconnect the power supply from the component.

3. Attach the ground wire from the test light to a good metal ground.

4. Touch the end probe of the test light to the power wire; if there is current in the wire, the light in the test light will come on. You have now established that current is getting to the component.

5. Turn the ignition or dash switch **OFF** and reconnect the wire to the component.

If the test light did not go on, then the problem is between the battery and the component. This includes all the switches, fuses, relays and the battery itself. The next place to look is the fusebox; check carefully either by eye or by using the test light across the fuse clips. The easiest way to check is to simply replace the fuse. If the fuse is blown, and upon replacement, immediately blows again, there is a short between the fuse and the component. This is generally (not always) a sign of an internal short in the component. Disconnect the power wire at the component again and replace the fuse; if the fuse holds, the component is the problem.

If all the fuses are good and the component is not receiving power, find the switch for the circuit. Bypass the switch with the jumper wire. This is done by connecting one end of the jumper to the power wire coming into the switch and the other end to the wire leaving the switch. If the component comes to life, the switch has failed.

✳✳WARNING

Never substitute a jumper wire for the component. The circuit needs the electrical load of the component. If you bypass it, you will cause a short circuit.

Checking the ground for any circuit can mean tracing wires to the body, cleaning connections or tightening mounting bolts for the component itself. If the jumper wire can be connected to the case of the component or the ground connector, you can ground the other end to a piece of clean, solid metal on the vehicle. Again, if the component starts working, you've found the problem.

A systematic search through the fuse, connectors, switches and the component itself will almost always yield an answer. Loose and/or corroded connectors, particularly in ground circuits, are becoming a larger problem in modern vehicles. The computers and on-board electronic (solid state) systems are highly sensitive to improper grounds and will change their function drastically if a change in the ground occurs.

Remember that for any electrical circuit to work, ALL the connections must be clean and tight.

Battery, Starting and Charging Systems

BASIC OPERATING PRINCIPLES

Battery

The battery is the first link in the chain of mechanisms which work together to provide cranking of the automobile engine. In most modern vehicles, the battery is a lead/acid electrochemical device consisting of six 2V subsections (cells) connected in series so the unit is capable of producing approximately 12V of electrical pressure. Each subsection consists of a series of positive and negative plates held a short distance apart in a solution of sulfuric acid and water.

The two types of plates are dissimilar metals. This causes a chemical reaction which produces current flow from the battery when its positive and negative terminals are connected to an electrical component such as a lamp or motor. The continued transfer of electrons would eventually convert the sulfuric acid to water, and make the two plates identical in chemical composition. As electrical energy is removed from the battery, its voltage output tends to drop. Thus, measuring battery voltage and battery electrolyte composition are two ways of checking the ability of the battery to supply power. During the starting of the engine, electrical energy is removed from the battery. However, if the charging circuit is in good condition and the operating conditions are normal, the power removed from the battery will be replaced by the alternator which will force electrons back through the battery, reversing the normal flow, and restoring the battery to its original chemical state.

Starting System

The battery and starting motor are linked by very heavy electrical cables designed to minimize resistance to the flow of current. Generally, the major power supply cable that leaves the battery goes directly to the starter, while other electrical system needs are supplied by smaller cables. During starter operation, power flows from the battery to the starter and is grounded through the vehicle's frame and the battery's negative ground strap.

The starting motor is a specially designed, direct current electric motor capable of producing a great amount of power for its size. One thing that allows the motor to produce a great deal of power is its tremendous rotating speed. It drives the engine through a tiny pinion gear (attached to the starter's armature), which drives the very large flywheel ring gear at a greatly reduced speed. Another factor allowing it to produce so much power is that only intermittent operation is required of it. Thus, little allowance for air circulation is required, and the windings can be built into a very small space.

The starter solenoid is a magnetic device which is actuated by a small current supplied by the starter circuit of the ignition switch. This magnetic action moves a plunger which mechanically engages the starter and closes the heavy switch connecting it to the battery. The starting circuit consists of the starting switch contained within the ignition switch, a transaxle neutral safety switch, and the wiring necessary to connect these in series with the starter solenoid or relay.

The pinion, a small gear, is mounted to a one way drive clutch. This clutch is splined to the starter armature shaft. When the ignition switch is moved to the **START** position, the solenoid plunger slides the pinion toward the flywheel ring gear via a collar and spring. If the teeth on the pinion and flywheel match properly, the pinion will engage the flywheel immediately. If the gear teeth butt one another, the spring will still be compressed and will force the gears to mesh as soon as the starter turns far enough to allow them to do so. As the solenoid plunger reaches the end of its travel, it closes the contacts that connect the battery and starter and then the engine is cranked.

As soon as the engine starts, the flywheel ring gear begins turning fast enough to drive the pinion at an extremely high rate of speed. At this point, the one-way clutch begins allowing the pinion to spin faster than the starter shaft so that the starter will not operate at excessive speed. When the ignition switch is released from the starter position, the solenoid is de-energized, and a spring pulls the gear out of mesh interrupting the current flow to the starter.

Some starters employ a separate relay, mounted away from the starter, to switch the motor and solenoid current on and off. The relay replaces the solenoid electrical switch, but does not eliminate the need for a solenoid mounted on the starter used to mechanically engage the starter drive gears.

Charging System

The automobile charging system provides the electrical power for the operation of the vehicle's ignition system, starting system and all electrical accessories. The battery serves as an electrical storage tank, storing (in chemical form) the energy originally produced by the engine driven alternator. The system also provides a means of regulating output to protect the battery from being overcharged and to avoid excessive voltage to the accessories.

The chemical reaction taking place in the battery is reversible, so that when the alternator is producing a voltage (electrical pressure) greater than that produced by the battery, electricity is forced into the battery, and the battery is returned to its fully charged state.

Most automobiles today use alternators in place of generators. They are more efficient, and can be rotated at higher speeds, and have fewer brush problems. In an alternator, the field rotates while all the current produced passes only through the stator winding. The brushes bear against continuous slip rings. This causes the current produced to periodically reverse the direction of its flow. Diodes (electrical one way valves) block the flow of current from traveling in the wrong direction. A series of diodes is wired together to permit the alternating flow of the stator to be rectified back to 12 volts DC for use by the vehicles's electrical system.

The voltage regulating function is performed by a regulator. The regulator is often built into the alternator; this system is termed an integrated or internal regulator.

ENGINE ELECTRICAL

Ignition Coil

REMOVAL & INSTALLATION

▶ **See Figures 1, 2 and 3**

1. Disconnect the negative battery cable.
2. Unplug or unfasten all the wires from the coil (note the location of all electrical connectors for correct installation. Remove the high tension wire from the top of the coil).
3. Remove the condenser connector from the coil, if equipped.
4. Unbolt and remove the coil assembly.
5. Installation is the reverse of removal. Make sure that the coil wire is fully inserted into the terminal.

Fig. 2 Be careful not to break the locktab when unplugging the connector

Ignition Module

REMOVAL & INSTALLATION

Duraspark Type Modules
▶ **See Figure 4**

➡ Refer to Section 2 for testing procedures.

1. Disconnect the negative battery cable.
2. Remove the fasteners that attach the module to the fender or firewall.
3. Pull apart the wire harness connectors. When unplugging the connectors, pull them apart with a firm, straight pull. NEVER PRY THEM APART! This may damage the wire harness or connector.

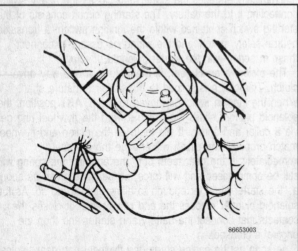

Fig. 1 Unplugging the electrical connector from an early type ignition coil

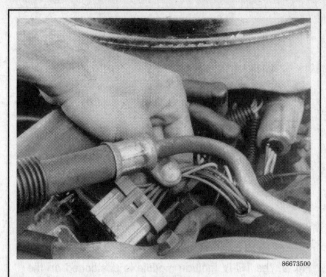

Fig. 3 A closeup of the coil harness

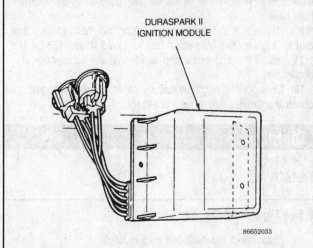

DURASPARK II
IGNITION MODULE

Fig. 4 Duraspark II module. Other Duraspark modules are similar

To install:

4. Before connecting the wire harness(s), coat the mating ends with silicone dielectric grease to waterproof the connection. Press the connectors together firmly to overcome any vacuum lock caused by the grease.

5. Secure the module to the fender or firewall, using the retaining hardware removed earlier.

6. Connect the negative battery cable.

7. Start the engine to check that the module functions correctly.

➡**If the locking tabs weaken or break, secure the connection with electrical tape or tie straps.**

TFI-IV Module

➡**On some models, it is not necessary to remove the distributor to access the TFI module.**

▶ **See Figures 5, 6, 7, 8 and 9**

1. Disconnect the negative battery cable.

2. Except on vehicles equipped with Multi-Port Fuel Injection (MPFI), remove the air cleaner assembly for additional access.

3. Mark the position of the distributor flange on the intake manifold.

4. Loosen the distributor hold-down bolt, and turn the distributor until the module retaining screws are accessible. If you choose to remove the distributor from the vehicle, remove the hold-down bolt and bracket.

➡**If you are removing the distributor, be sure to make matchmarks to assure proper alignment upon installation.**

5. Unplug the connector from the module. If removing the distributor from the vehicle, lift it out now and place on a clean table. Remove its retaining screws.

Fig. 5 Clearly mark each spark plug wire at the distributor cap

Fig. 6 Remove the distributor cap. Unfasten the spark plug wires if this makes the job easier

Fig. 7 If removing the distributor, mark the rotor cap, distributor body and engine block

Fig. 8 With the distributor removed, the TFI is clearly visible and can be disassembled

6. Slide the module assembly down towards the distributor flange to disengage the module terminals from the distributor base.

✳✳WARNING

Do not attempt to remove module from the mounting surface prior to sliding the entire module toward the distributor flange. If the correct procedure is not followed, the pins will break at the distributor and module connector.

To install:

7. Coat the metal base of the TFI module with a thin layer of silicone dielectric compound. Place the module on the base of the distributor.

8. Carefully slide the TFI module assembly up towards the distributor bowl to engage the module connector pins.

9. Install the TFI module retaining screws, starting with the upper right hand screw and tighten them to 16-35 inch lbs. (2-4 Nm). Engage the module electrical connector. If the dis-

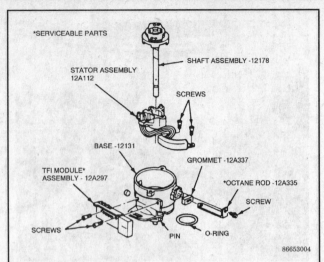

Fig. 9 The TFI-IV ignition module is positioned on the side of the distributor

tributor was removed from the engine, position in the mounting hole now.

10. Reposition the distributor, aligning the matchmark made earlier. Tighten the hold-down bolt to 17-25 ft. lbs. (23-34 Nm).

11. Install the distributor cap and install the air cleaner, if applicable.

12. Connect the negative battery cable. Start the engine and check the timing. Adjust as necessary.

Distributor

REMOVAL

▶ **See Figures 10, 11, 12, 13 and 14**

1. Disconnect the negative battery cable.

2. Remove the air cleaner and/or the Thermactor® (air) pump to permit access to the distributor. If necessary, disconnect the Thermactor® air filter and lines as well. Tag the lines prior to removal.

3. Remove the distributor cap, then position the cap and ignition wires to the side.

4. Mark and tag any vacuum lines attached to the distributor. Also mark and tag any wire harness connectors. Once these parts are clearly marked, they may be unplugged or removed.

5. Rotate the crankshaft until the No. 1 cylinder is at Top Dead Center (TDC) of the compression stroke.

6. With No. 1 cylinder at TDC, the alignment marks on the crankshaft pulley and pointer should align correctly. Mark the rotor and the location of the rotor in relation to the distributor body.

7. Scribe or paint an alignment mark on the distributor body, and a similar mark on the engine block showing the position of the distributor body to the engine block. These marks are used for reference when installing the distributor.

8. Remove the distributor hold-down bolt and clamp.

9. Lift the distributor up and out until the shaft clears the mounting hole

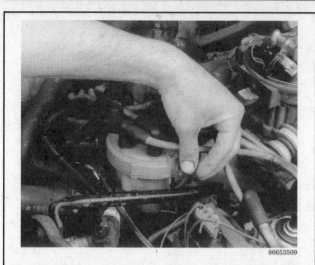

Fig. 10 Remove the retaining clips, or screws from the distributor cap

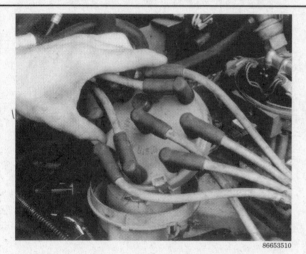

Fig. 11 Position the distributor cap aside with the spark plug wires attached

Fig. 12 Unplug any vacuum or wire connectors, in this case, the ignition module harness

Fig. 13 Mark both the rotor cap and distributor body for ease of reinstallation

Fig. 14 Remove the rotor cap and replace if needed

INSTALLATION

Engine Not Rotated

1. Rotate the distributor shaft so the mark on the blade of the rotor is aligned with the paint mark on the distributor body base made during removal.

2. Lower the distributor into the engine block hole aligning the mark on the distributor body with the mark on the engine block. If installed correctly, the rotor should be pointing at the No. 1 mark on the distributor base.

3. Install the distributor retaining bolt. Tighten the bolt so the distributor can just be moved.

4. Install the distributor cap and connect all wiring. Tighten the distributor cap to 18-23 inch lbs. (2-3 Nm), if retained with screws, or engage the clips to the cap.

5. Start vehicle and set initial timing according to the procedures in Section 2.

6. After the timing has been set, tighten the distributor hold-down bolt to 17-25 ft. lbs. (23-34 Nm).

Engine Rotated

If the crankshaft was rotated while the distributor was re-moved, the engine must be brought to Top Dead Center (TDC) on the compression stroke of the No. 1 cylinder.

1. Remove the No. 1 spark plug. Place a finger over the hole and rotate the crankshaft slowly in the direction of normal rotation, until engine compression is felt. When engine compression is felt at the spark plug hole (indicating that the piston is approaching TDC), continue to turn the crankshaft until the timing mark on the pulley is aligned with the pointer on the engine.

➡**Another method of determining TDC is to remove the valve cover over cylinder No. 1 and rotate the crankshaft until both valves are equally spaced. As the timing mark approaches the pointer, one valve will be closing as an-other valves begins to open. At the point where they are equally opened, the timing mark should align with the pointer. If you are using this method, replace the valve cover gasket when reinstalling the valve cover.**

2. Begin lowering the distributor into the mounting hole, making sure it is not binding on the side of the hole as it is lowered in.

3. If the distributor is seated properly, the distributor base will be flush with the engine block base, and the rotor should be pointing at the No. 1 mark on the distributor base.

4. Install the distributor hold-down bolt and tighten so the distributor can just be moved.

5. Install the distributor cap and connect all wiring har-nesses and vacuum lines. Tighten the distributor cap to 18-23 inch lbs. (2-3 Nm), if secured with screws, otherwise engage the clips to the cap.

6. Start the vehicle and set the initial timing according to the procedures in Section 2.

7. After timing has been set, tighten the distributor hold-down bolt to 17-25 ft. lbs. (23-34 Nm).

Alternator

▶ See Figures 15, 16, 17, 18, 19, 20 and 21

The alternator charging system consists of the alternator, voltage regulator, warning light, battery, and fuse link wire.

A failure of any component of the charging system can cause the entire system to stop functioning. Because of this, the charging system can be very difficult to troubleshoot when problems occur.

When the ignition key is turned **ON**, current flows from the battery, through the charging system indicator light on the in-strument panel, to the voltage regulator, and to the alternator. Since the alternator is not producing any current, the alternator warning light comes on. When the engine is started, the alter-nator begins to produce current and turns the alternator light off. As the alternator begins to generate power, the output is divided between the battery to charge the cells, and the elec-trical components of the vehicle A voltage regulator is wired into the alternator to prevent it from receiving too much power which could cause serious damage to electrical components in the vehicle. Conversely, if the voltage regulator does not allow the alternator to receive enough current, the battery will not be fully charged and will eventually go dead.

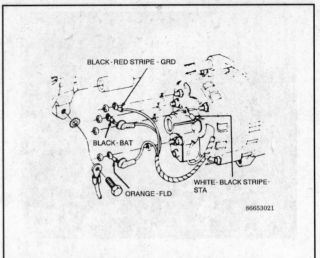

Fig. 15 Alternator harness connections, 65 ampere Autolite model — 1971-72 models

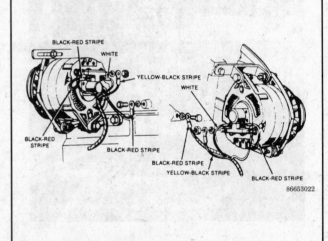

Fig. 16 1971-72 alternator harness connections — Leece Neville 65 ampere model

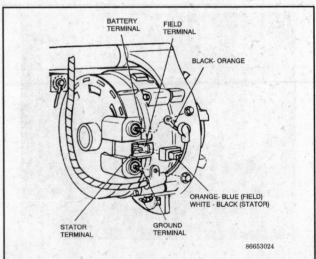

Fig. 17 Motorcraft side terminal alternator — 1972 and later

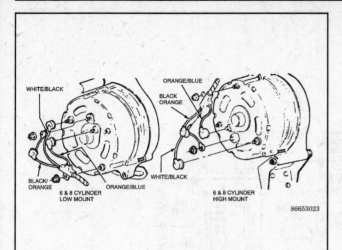

Fig. 18 Motorcraft rear terminal alternator — 1973 and later

The battery is connected to the alternator at all times, whether the ignition key is turned on or not. If the battery were shorted to ground, the alternator would also be shorted. This could damage the alternator. To prevent this, a fuse link is installed in the wiring between the battery and the alternator on all 1971 and later models. If the battery is shorted, the fuse link is melted, protecting the alternator.

ALTERNATOR PRECAUTIONS

Several precautions must be observed with alternators to avoid damaging the unit. They are as follows:
- If the battery is removed for any reason, make sure that it is reconnected with the correct polarity. Reversing the battery connections may result in damage to the one-way rectifiers.
- When utilizing a booster battery as a starting aid, always connect it as follows: positive to positive, and negative (booster battery) to a good ground on the engine of the car being started.

- Never use a fast charger as a booster to start cars with alternating current (AC) circuits.
- When charging the battery with a fast charger, always disconnect the car battery cables.
- Never attempt to polarize an alternator.
- Avoid long soldering times when replacing diodes or transistors. Prolonged heat is damaging to alternators.
- Do not use test lamps of more than 12 volts for checking diode continuity.
- Do not short across or ground any of the terminals on the alternator.
- The polarity of the battery, alternator, and regulator must be matched and considered before making any electrical connections within the system.
- Never separate the alternator on an open circuit. Make sure that all connections within the circuit are clean and tight.
- Disconnect the battery terminals when performing any service on the electrical system. This will eliminate the possibility of accidental reversal of polarity.
- Disconnect the battery ground cable if arc welding is to be done on any part of the car.

TESTING

Testing of the charging system requires the use of a Sun VAT 40 (or equivalent) charging system tester. Since this is usually not readily available, it is recommended that alternator testing be performed by a reputable repair facility equipped with this equipment.

REMOVAL & INSTALLATION

▶ **See Figures 22, 23, 24, 25, 26, 27, 28 and 29**

1. Disconnect the negative battery cable.
2. Unplug all electrical connections (mark wire locations for correct installation) from the alternator assembly.
3. Loosen the alternator adjusting bolt(s) and remove the drive belt.

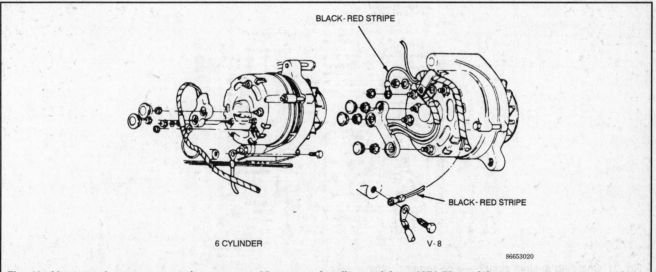

Fig. 19 Alternator harness connections, except 65 ampere Autolite models — 1971-72 models

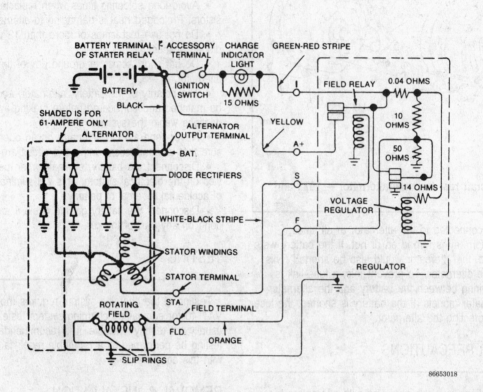

Fig. 20 Charging system circuit — rear terminal type

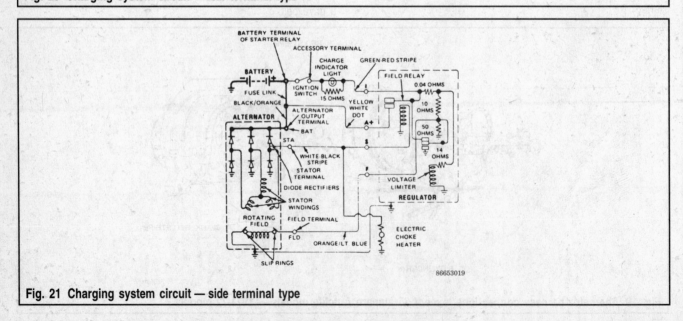

Fig. 21 Charging system circuit — side terminal type

4. Remove the alternator mounting bolts and spacer (if equipped), and remove the alternator assembly.

To install:

5. Position the alternator assembly to the brackets and install the attaching bolts and spacer (if equipped).

6. Fasten all electrical connections to the alternator assembly.

7. Position the drive belt on the alternator pulley. Adjust the belt tension. Refer to the necessary service procedures in Section 1.

8. Connect the negative battery cable.

Voltage Regulator

Voltage regulators used through 1978 were either electro-mechanical or transistorized. To determine whether your regulator is an adjustable type, locate the regulator and note in what manner the cover is secured. If the cover is secured using metal rivets, this is a non-adjustable regulator. If the cover is secured using screws, it is adjustable.

Fig. 24 If equipped, remove the protective rubber cap over the wiring

Fig. 22 After the adjusting bolt is loosened . . .

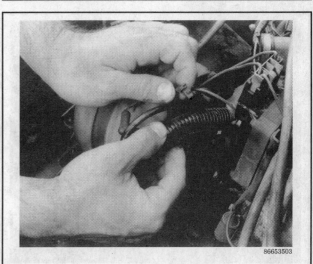

Fig. 25 Unclip the wire harness from the back of the alternator, if necessary

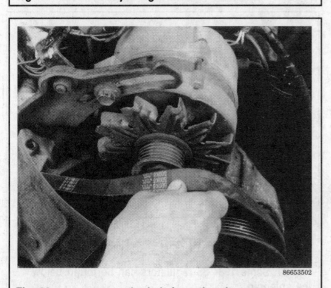

Fig. 23 . . . remove the belt from the alternator

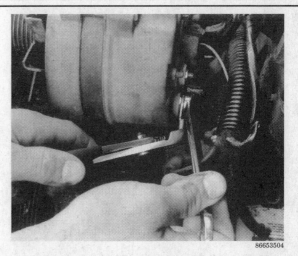

Fig. 26 After tagging, loosen and remove the wires from the alternator

Fig. 27 Remove the adjusting bolt

Fig. 28 Remove the lower pivot bolt . . .

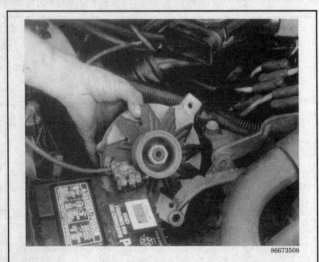

Fig. 29 Then lift the alternator out of the engine compartment

Solid state regulators used on 1979 and later models are not adjustable.

REMOVAL & INSTALLATION

▶ See Figures 30 and 31

1. Disconnect the negative battery terminal. On models with the regulator mounted behind the battery, it is necessary to remove the battery.
2. Remove the regulator mounting screws or bolts.
3. Disconnect the regulator from the wiring harness.
To install:
4. Position the regulator on the mounting plate. If equipped, the radio suppression condenser mounts under one of the mounting screws; the ground lead under the other mounting screw. Tighten the screws until snug.
5. If the battery was moved to gain access to the regulator, install it.

Fig. 30 The regulator is usually mounted on the inner fender — solid state type shown

Fig. 31 Some 1984-85 regulators can be found below the solenoid

6. Connect the negative battery cable. Start the engine, and test the system for proper operation.

VOLTAGE ADJUSTMENT

Leece-Neville Electro-Mechanical Unit

▶ See Figure 32

1. Run the engine for 10-15 minutes to allow the regulator to reach operating temperature. Connect a voltmeter across the battery posts. Turn off all electrical equipment. Check the voltage at the battery. It should be 13.9-14.1 volts. If necessary, adjust the voltage.

2. Remove the regulator cover. Voltage may be adjusted by increasing or decreasing the voltage limiter contact gap. Loosen the lockscrew and move the contact gap adjusting arms.

➡Voltage will drop about ½ volt when the regulator cover is installed and should be compensated for in the adjustment.

3. Start the engine and check the voltage. Readjust as necessary.

Transistorized Regulator

▶ See Figure 33

1. Run the engine to normal operating temperature, then shut it **OFF**.

2. Remove the regulator cover.

3. Using a plastic strip as a screwdriver, turn the adjusting screw clockwise to increase the voltage setting, counterclockwise to decrease the setting.

4. Install the regulator cover.

5. Start the engine and check the voltage reading. Readjust if necessary.

Starter

▶ See Figures 34 and 35

All except the 7.0L and 7.5L V8 engines, use a positive engagement type starter. This medium duty unit uses a remote starter relay to open and close the circuit to the battery.

The starter installed in 7.0L and 7.5L V8 models is a solenoid actuated starter. This heavy duty unit uses an outboard solenoid mounted on top of the starter which has an internal electric switch to open and close the circuit to the battery.

REMOVAL & INSTALLATION

▶ See Figures 36, 37 and 38

1. Disconnect the negative battery cable.

2. Raise the front of the car and install jackstands beneath the frame. Firmly apply the parking brake and place blocks in back of the rear wheels.

3. Unfasten the heavy starter cable at the starter and any other electrical connections. On solenoid actuated starters label and disconnect the wires from the solenoid.

➡Do not pull on the wire when removing, or damage to the connector could result.

4. Turn the front wheels fully to the right. On most models, it will be necessary to remove the two bolts retaining the steering idler arm to the frame to gain access to the starter, and/or remove any support braces if in the way.

5. Remove the starter mounting bolts and remove the starter.

6. Reverse the above procedure to install. Finger-start all bolts and tighten the mounting bolts evenly to 15-20 ft. lbs (20-27 Nm) and the idler arm retaining bolts to 28-35 ft. lbs. (38-47 Nm), if removed. Make sure that the nut securing the heavy cable to the starter is snugged down tightly.

Starter Relay

▶ See Figure 39

REMOVAL & INSTALLATION

1. Disconnect the negative battery cable.

2. Unfasten the positive battery cable from the battery terminal. If equipped with dual batteries, unfasten the connecting cable at both ends.

3. Remove the nut securing the positive battery cable at the relay. Use a back-up wrench on the inside nut on the relay to hold terminal connection steady while removing the outer nut.

4. Remove the positive cable and any other wiring under that cable.

5. Tag and remove the connectors from the front of the relay.

6. Remove the nut and disconnect the cable from the starter side of the relay.

7. Remove the relay attaching bolts and remove the relay.

8. Installation is the reverse of removal.

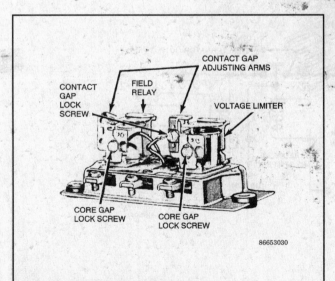

CONTACT GAP ADJUSTING ARMS

FIELD RELAY

CONTACT GAP LOCK SCREW

VOLTAGE LIMITER

CORE GAP LOCK SCREW

CORE GAP LOCK SCREW

86653030

Fig. 32 Leece Neville regulator adjustments

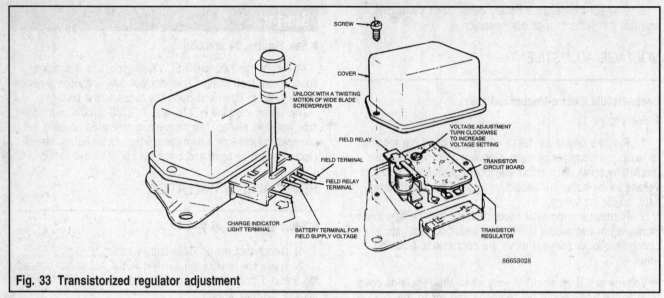

Fig. 33 Transistorized regulator adjustment

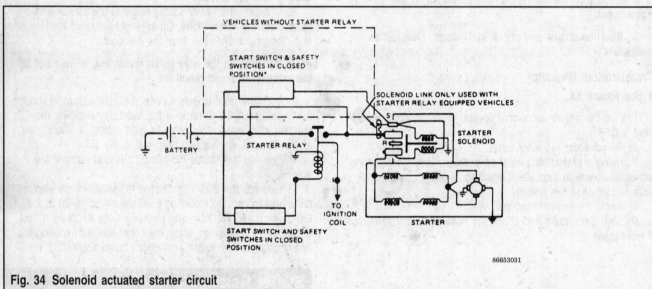

Fig. 34 Solenoid actuated starter circuit

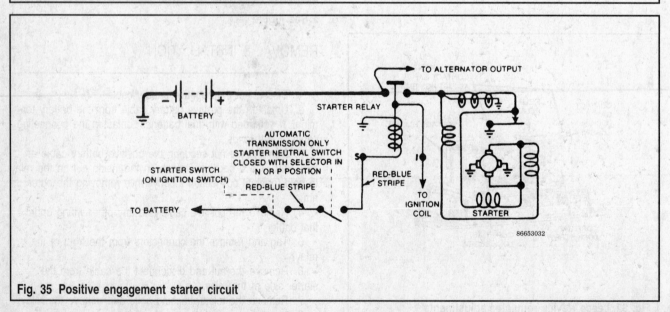

Fig. 35 Positive engagement starter circuit

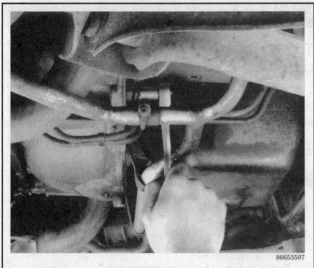

Fig. 36 Remove the bolts securing the starter

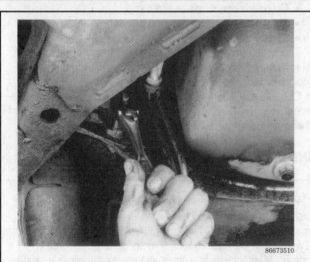

Fig. 37 some of these bolts can be located in tight areas

Fig. 38 Lower the starter and remove it from the engine

Fig. 39 Starter relay located on inside fender wall

Battery

REMOVAL & INSTALLATION

1. Disconnect the negative battery cable.
2. Remove the positive battery cable. If the cable insulation on both the positive and negative cables are the same color, tag the cables before removing.
3. Remove the hold-down screws from the battery box, if equipped.
4. Remove the battery from the vehicle.

To install:

5. Before installing the battery in the vehicle, make sure that the battery terminals are clean and free from corrosion. Use a battery terminal cleaner on the terminals and on the inside of the battery cable ends. If a cleaner is not available, use a heavy sandpaper to remove the corrosion. A mixture of baking soda and water will neutralize any exposed/ leaking acid.

6. Place the battery in the vehicle. Install the cables on the terminals. Tighten the nuts on the cable ends. Smear a light coating of grease on the cable ends and the tops of the terminals. This will prevent buildup of oxidation on the terminals and the cable ends. Install and tighten the nuts of the battery box. Refer to Section 1 for additional service procedures and illustrations.

ENGINE MECHANICAL

Design

A number of different engines have been offered since 1971. All of the engines use conventional cast iron, water cooled blocks. The cylinder heads on most are of the overhead valve design, while the valves are actuated by pushrods and hydraulic valve lifters. The engines fall into several basic families.

A 2.3L inline 4-cylinder engine with an optional turbocharger. Unlike other engines used in the mid-sized Ford vehicle, this engine is an overhead camshaft design, where no pushrods or rocker arms are used. The camshaft rests on top of the valve/spring/lifter assembly. The hydraulic lifter assembly is still utilized. With the optional turbo unit installed, horsepower is increased by as much as 30% while fuel economy is maintained at a respectable level.

Two different varieties of 6-cylinder engine were available on these vehicles. The 3.8L V-patterned design, and two versions of a straight L6 engine in the 3.3L and the 4.1L.

The final and largest category includes a series of V8 engines. They include; the 4.2L, 5.0L, 5.8L, 6.6L, 7.0L and 7.5L engines. The 5.0L was the standard engine from 1971 through 1972 and then again from 1978 through 1980. In 1981, the 4.2L cubic inch V8 became the standard engine, replacing the 5.0L. The 4.2L featured weight reductions by about sixty pounds (from the 5.0L) and had been designed to be adaptable to a variety of fuel metering systems. In 1981, the 5.0L and 5.8L (and a high output version of the 5.8L, for police and towing) were offered as options. The 5.8L Cleveland (C) was used on 1972-74 models. The 5.8L Modified (M), which is a modified Cleveland design, was used starting in 1975. The 6.6L V8 was available from 1971-78 models. This engine is based on the smaller 5.0L-5.8L(W) series, but enjoys a higher volumetric efficiency quotient due to its larger valves and better breathing semi-hemispherical combustion chambers.

The largest engines used in the mid-sized Ford include the 7.0L and 7.5L. The 7.0L V8 was installed in 1971-73 models. The 7.5L V8 may be found in mid-sized Fords starting in 1974. It was last used in 1978. This group of engines are based on the smaller 5.0L and 5.8L Windsor (W) design. Identifying features of these powerplants are their great bulk and the tunnelport shaped configuration of the intake manifold.

Engine Overhaul Tips

Most engine overhaul procedures are fairly standard. In addition to specific parts replacement procedures and complete specifications for your individual engine, this section also is a guide to engine rebuilding procedures. Examples of standard rebuilding practices are shown and should be used along with specific details concerning your particular engine.

Competent and accurate machine shop services will ensure maximum performance, reliability and engine life

In most instances it is more profitable for the do-it-yourself mechanic to remove, clean and inspect the component, buy the necessary parts and deliver these to a shop for actual machine work.

TOOLS

The tools required for an engine overhaul or parts replacement will depend on the depth of your involvement. With a few exceptions, they will be the tools found in a mechanic's tool kit (see Section 1). More in-depth work will require any or all of the following:
- A dial indicator (reading in thousandths) mounted on a universal base
- Micrometers and telescope gauges
- Jaw and screw-type pullers
- Scraper
- Valve spring compressor
- Ring groove cleaner
- Piston ring expander and compressor
- Ridge reamer
- Cylinder hone or glaze breaker
- Plastigauge®
- Engine stand

The use of most of these tools is illustrated in this section. Many can be rented for a one-time use from a local parts jobber or tool supply house specializing in automotive work.

Occasionally, the use of special tools is called for. See the information on Special Tools and Safety Notice in the front of this book before substituting another tool.

INSPECTION TECHNIQUES

Procedures and specifications are given in this section for inspecting, cleaning and assessing the wear limits of most major components. Other procedures such as Magnaflux® and Zyglo® can be used to locate material flaws and stress cracks. Magnaflux® is a magnetic process applicable only to ferrous materials. The Zyglo® process coats the material with a fluorescent dye penetrant and can be used on any material. Checks for suspected surface cracks can be more readily made using spot check dye. The dye is sprayed onto the suspected area, wiped off and area sprayed with a developer. Cracks will show up brightly.

OVERHAUL TIPS

Aluminum has become extremely popular for use in engines, due to its low weight. Observe the following precautions when handling aluminum parts:

Never hot tank aluminum parts (the caustic hot-tank solution will eat the aluminum).

Remove all aluminum parts (identification tag, etc.) from engine parts prior to hot-tanking.

Always coat threads lightly with engine oil or anti-seize compounds before installation, to prevent seizure.

Never over-tighten bolts or spark plugs, especially in aluminum threads. Stripped threads can usually be repaired using any of several commercial repair kits (Heli-Coil®, Microdot®, Keenserts®, etc.)

When assembling the engine, any parts that will be in frictional contact must be prelubed to provide lubrication at initial start-up.

When semi-permanent (locked, but removable) installation of bolts or nuts is desired, threads should be cleaned and coated with Loctite® or other similar, commercial non-hardening sealant.

To determine whether a particular engine or component is constructed of aluminium, use a magnet. If the magnet attaches to the item, it is not made of aluminium, but a metal with a high iron content. If the magnet does not attach to the item, it is most likely made of aluminium.

REPAIRING DAMAGED THREADS

▶ **See Figures 40, 41, 42, 43 and 44**

Several methods of repairing damaged threads are available. Heli-Coil®, Keenserts® and Microdot® are among the most widely used. All involve basically the same principle — drilling out the stripped threads, tapping the hole and installing a prewound insert — making welding, plugging and oversize fasteners unnecessary.

Two types of thread repair inserts are usually supplied: a standard type for most Inch Coarse, Inch Fine, Metric Coarse and Metric Fine thread sizes and a spark plug type to fit most spark plug port sizes. Consult the individual manufacturer's catalog to determine exact applications. Typical thread repair kits will contain a selection of prewound threaded inserts, a tap (corresponding to the outside diameter threads of the insert) and an installation tool. Spark plug inserts usually differ because they require a tap equipped with pilot threads and combined reamer/tap section. Most manufacturers also supply blister-packed thread repair inserts separately in addition to a master kit containing a variety of taps and inserts plus installation tools.

Before repairing a threaded hole, remove any snapped, broken or damaged bolts or studs. Penetrating oil can be used to free frozen threads; the offending item can be removed with locking pliers or with a screw or stud extractor. After the hole is clear, the thread can be repaired, as shown in the figures.

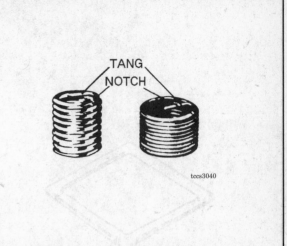

Fig. 41 Standard thread repair insert (left), and spark plug thread insert

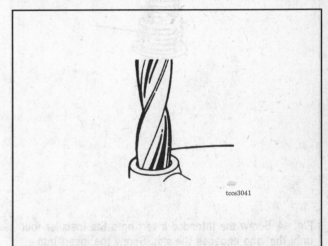

Fig. 42 Drill out the damaged threads with the specified drill. Drill completely through the hole or to the bottom of a blind hole

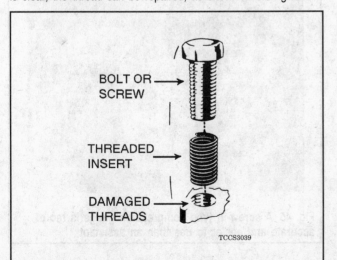

Fig. 40 Damaged bolt hole threads can be replaced with thread repair inserts

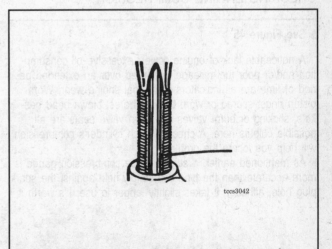

Fig. 43 With the tap supplied, tap the hole to receive the thread insert. Keep the tap well oiled and back it out frequently to avoid clogging the threads

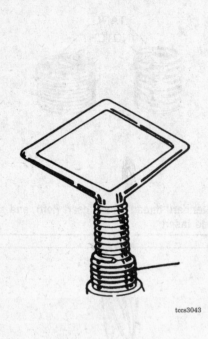

tccs3043

Fig. 44 Screw the threaded insert onto the installer tool until the tang engages the slot. Screw the insert into the tapped hole until it is 1/4 or 1/2 turn below the top surface. After installation, break off the tang with a hammer and punch

CHECKING ENGINE COMPRESSION

▶ See Figure 45

A noticeable lack of engine power, excessive oil consumption and/or poor fuel mileage measured over an extended period of time are all indicators of internal engine wear. Worn piston rings, scored or worn cylinder bores, blown head gaskets, sticking or burnt valves and worn valve seats are all possible culprits here. A check of each cylinder's compression will help you locate the problems.

As mentioned earlier, a screw-in type compression gauge is more accurate than the type you simply hold against the spark plug hole, although it takes slightly longer to use. It's worth it

to obtain a more accurate reading. Check engine compression as follows:

1. Make sure the engine oil level is correct and the battery is properly charged. Warm up the engine to normal operating temperature.

2. Turn the ignition switch **OFF**. Remove all spark plugs.

3. Screw the compression gauge into the No. 1 cylinder spark plug hole until the fitting is snug.

➡**Be careful not to crossthread the plug hole.**

4. Install an auxiliary starter switch in the starter circuit.

5. Ask an assistant to depress the accelerator pedal fully. Then, while you read the compression gauge, crank the engine at least 5 compression strokes using the auxiliary starter switch (ignition switch in **OFF** position). Note the approximate number of compression strokes required to obtain the highest reading.

6. Repeat the compression test on each cylinder, cranking the engine approximately the same number of compression strokes.

7. Compare your lowest and highest compression readings with those in the figure. Compression pressures are considered within specification if the lowest reading cylinder is within 75% of the highest.

8. If a cylinder is unusually low, pour a tablespoon of clean 20W-50 engine oil into the cylinder through the spark plug hole and repeat the compression test. If the compression comes up after adding the oil, it appears that the cylinder's piston rings or bore are damaged or worn. If the pressure remains low, the valves may not be seating properly (a valve job is needed), or the head gasket may be blown near that cylinder. If compression in any two adjacent cylinders is low, and if the addition of oil doesn't help the compression, there is probably leakage past the head gasket. Oil and coolant water in the combustion chamber can result from this problem. There may be evidence of water droplets on the engine dipstick when a head gasket has blown.

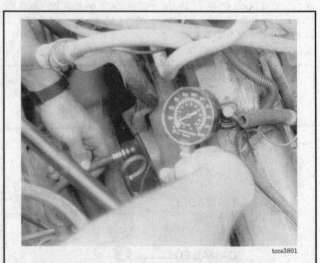

tccs3801

Fig. 45 A screw-in type compression gauge is more accurate and easier to use than an assistant

General Engine Specifications

Year	Engine No. Cyl Displacement (cu. in.)	Carb Type	■ Advertised Horsepower (@ rpm)	■ Advertised Torque @ rpm (ft. lbs.)	Bore and Stroke (in.)	Advertised Compression Ratio	Oil Pressure (psi) (@ 2000 rpm)
'71	6-250	1 bbl	145 @ 4000	232 @ 1600	3.682 x 3.910	9.0:1	35—60
	8-302	2 bbl	210 @ 4600	296 @ 2600	4.000 x 3.000	9.0:1	35—60
	8-351 C	2 bbl	240 @ 4600	355 @ 2600	4.000 x 3.500	9.5:1	35—60
	8-351 C	4 bbl	285 @ 5400	370 @ 3400	4.000 x 3.500	10.7:1	35—60
	8-429	4 bbl	360 @ 4600	480 @ 2800	4.362 x 3.590	10.5:1	35—75
	8-429 CJ	4 bbl	370 @ 5400	450 @ 3400	4.362 x 3.590	11.3:1	35—75
	8-429 SCJ	4 bbl	375 @ 5600	450 @ 3400	4.362 x 3.590	11.3:1	35—75
'72	6-250	1 bbl	99 @ 3600	184 @ 1600	3.680 x 3.910	8.0:1	35—60
	8-302	2 bbl	141 @ 4000	242 @ 2000	4.000 x 3.000	8.5:1	35—60
	8-351	2 bbl	164 @ 4000	276 @ 2000	4.000 x 3.500	8.6:1	35—85
	8-351 CJ	4 bbl	248 @ 5400	290 @ 3800	4.000 x 3.500	8.6:1	35—85
	8-400	2 bbl	168 @ 4200	297 @ 2200	4.000 x 4.000	8.4:1	35—85
	8-429	4 bbl	205 @ 4400	322 @ 2600	4.326 x 3.590	8.5:1	35—75
'73	6-250	1 bbl	92 @ 3200	197 @ 1600	3.680 x 3.910	8.0:1	35—60
	8-302	2 bbl	135, 137 @ 4200	228, 230 @ 2200	4.000 x 3.000	8.0:1	35—60
	8-351 W	2 bbl	156 @ 3800	260 @ 2400	4.000 x 3.500	8.0:1	50—70
	8-351 W	2 bbl	154, 159 @ 4000	246, 250 @ 2400	4.000 x 3.500	8.0:1	50—70
	8-351 CJ	4 bbl	246 @ 5400	312 @ 3600	4.000 x 3.500	8.0:1	50—70
	8-400	2 bbl	163, 168 @ 3800	300, 310 @ 2000	4.000 x 4.000	8.0:1	50—70
	8-429	4 bbl	197, 201 @ 4400	320, 322 @ 2600	4.362 x 3.590	8.0:1	35—75
	8-460 PI	4 bbl	274 @ 4600	392 @ 2800	4.362 x 3.850	8.8:1	50—75
'74	6-250	1 bbl	91 @ 3200	190 @ 1600	3.680 x 3.190	8.0:1	35—65
	8-302	2 bbl	140 @ 3800	230 @ 2600	4.000 x 3.000	8.0:1	35—55
	8-351 W	2 bbl	162 @ 4000	275 @ 2200	4.000 x 3.500	8.0:1	50—70
	8-351 C	2 bbl	163 @ 4200	278 @ 2000	4.000 x 3.500	8.0:1	50—70
	8-351 CJ	4 bbl	255 @ 5600	290 @ 3400	4.000 x 3.500	7.9:1	50—70
	8-400	2 bbl	170 @ 3400	330 @ 2000	4.000 x 4.000	8.0:1	50—70
	8-460	4 bbl	195 @ 3800	355 @ 2600	4.362 x 3.850	8.0:1	35—75
	8-460	4 bbl	200 @ 4000	355 @ 2600	4.362 x 3.850	8.0:1	35—75
	8-460 PI	4 bbl	260 @ 4400	380 @ 2700	4.362 x 3.850	8.8:1	50—75
'75–'76	8-351 W 49	2 bbl	154 @ 3800	268 @ 2200	4.000 x 3.500	8.2:1	40—65
	8-351 W Cal.	2 bbl	153 @ 3400	270 @ 2400	4.000 x 3.500	8.2:1	40—65
	8-351 M 49	2 bbl	148 @ 3800	243 @ 2400	4.000 x 3.500	8.0:1	50—75
	8-351 M Cal.	2 bbl	150 @ 3800	244 @ 2800	4.000 x 3.500	8.0:1	50—75
	8-400 49	2 bbl	158 @ 3800	276 @ 2000	4.000 x 4.000	8.0:1	50—75
	8-400 Cal.	2 bbl	144 @ 3600	255 @ 2200	4.000 x 4.000	8.0:1	50—75

86673x08

General Engine Specifications (Cont.)

Year	Engine No. Cyl Displacement (cu. in.)	Carb Type	■ Advertised Horsepower (@ rpm)	■ Advertised Torque @ rpm (ft. lbs.)	Bore and Stroke (in.)	Advertised Compression Ratio	Oil Pressure (psi) (@ 2000 rpm)
'75–'76	8-460 49	4 bbl	216 @ 4000	366 @ 2600	4.362 x 3.850	8.0:1	40–65
	8-460 Cal.	4 bbl	217 @ 4000	365 @ 2600	4.362 x 3.850	8.0:1	40–65
	8-460 PI	4 bbl	266 @ 4000	374 @ 2600	4.263 x 3.850	8.0:1	40–65
'77–'78	8-302	2 bbl	130 @ 2400	243 @ 1800	3.000 x 3.000	8.4:1	40–60
	8-351 W	2 bbl	149 @ 3200	291 @ 1600	4.000 x 3.500	8.3:1	40–60
	8-351 M	2 bbl	161 @ 3600	285 @ 1800	4.000 x 3.500	8.0:1	50–75
	8-400	2 bbl	173 @ 3800	326 @ 1600	4.000 x 4.000	8.0:1	50–75
'79	8-302	2 bbl	140 @ 3600	250 @ 1800	4.000 x 3.000	8.4:1	40–65
	8-302 Cal.	vv	134 @ 3600	243 @ 2300	4.000 x 3.000	8.1:1	40–65
	8-351 M	2 bbl	152 @ 3600	270 @ 2200	4.000 x 3.500	8.0:1	51–75
	8-351 W	2 bbl	135 @ 3200	286 @ 1400	4.000 x 3.500	8.3:1	40–65
'80	8-255	2 bbl	119 @ 3800	194 @ 2200	3.680 x 3.000	8.8:1	40–60
	8-255 Cal.	vv	119 @ 3800	194 @ 2200	3.680 x 3.000	8.8:1	40–60
	8-302	2 bbl	134 @ 3600	232 @ 1600	4.000 x 3.000	8.4:1	40–60
	8-302	vv	131 @ 3600	231 @ 1400	4.000 x 3.000	8.4:1	40–60
'81–'82	4-140	2 bbl	88 @ 4600	118 @ 2600	3.781 x 3.126	9.0:1	40–60
	6-200	1 bbl	88 @ 3200	154 @ 1400	3.683 x 3.126	8.6:1	30–50
	6-232	2 bbl	112 @ 4000	175 @ 2600	3.814 x 3.388	8.8:1	40–60
	8-255	2 bbl	115 @ 3400	205 @ 2200	3.680 x 3.000	8.2:1	40–60
	8-255	vv	120 @ 3400	205 @ 2600	3.680 x 3.000	8.2:1	40–60
	8-302	2 bbl	160 @ 4200	247 @ 2400	4.000 x 3.000	8.4:1	40–60
	8-302	vv	130 @ 3400	235 @ 1800	4.000 x 3.000	8.4:1	40–50
'83	4-140	1bbl	86 @ 4600	117 @ 2600	3.781 x 3.126	9.0:1	40–60
	6-200	1 bbl	87 @ 3800	154 @ 1400	3.680 x 3.130	8.6:1	30–50
	6-232	2 bbl	112 @ 4000	175 @ 2600	3.810 x 3.390	8.7:1	40–60
	8-302	CFI	130 @ 3200	240 @ 2000	4.000 x 3.000	8.4:1	40–60
'84–'85	4-140	1 bbl	88 @ 4600	118 @ 2800	3.781 x 3.126	9.0:1	40–60
	4-140	EFI	145 @ 3800	180 @ 3600	3.781 x 3.126	8.0:1	40–60
	6-232	CFI	120 @ 3600	205 @ 1600	3.810 x 3.390	8.6:1	40–60
	6-232	2 bbl	112 @ 4000	175 @ 2600	3.810 x 3.390	8.6:1	40–60
	8-302	2 bbl	155 @ 3600	265 @ 2000	4.000 x 3.000	8.4:1	40–60
	8-302	CFI	140 @ 3200 ①	250 @ 1600 ①	4.000 x 3.000	8.4:1	40–60

■Beginning 1972 horsepower and torque are SAE net figures. They are measured at the rear of the transmission with all accessories installed and operating.
W: Windsor
C: Cleveland
M: Modified Cleveland
PI: Police interceptor
49: 49 states only
Cal: California only
VV: Variable Venturi
① H.O.: 165 @ 3800 245 @ 2000

Valve Specifications

Year	Engine No. Cyl. Displacement (cu. in.)	Seat Angle (deg)	Face Angle (deg)	Spring Test Pressure (lbs. @ in.)	Spring Intalled Height (in.)	Stem to Guide Clearance (in.)		Stem Diameter (in.)	
						Intake	Exhaust	Intake	Exhaust
'71	6-250	45	44	150 @ 1.22	1¹⁹⁄₃₂	.0008–.0025	.0010–.0027	.3104	.3102
	8-302	45	44	180 @ 1.23	1²¹⁄₃₂	.0010–.0027	.0015–.0032	.3420	.3415
	8-351 ①	45	44	215 @ 1.34	1²⁵⁄₃₂	.0010–.0027	.0015–.0032	.3420	.3415
	8-351 ②	45	44	210 @ 1.42	1¹³⁄₁₆	.0010–.0027	.0015–.0032	.3420	.3415
	8-351 ③	45	44	285 @ 1.31	1¹³⁄₁₆	.0010–.0027	.0015–.0032	.3420	.3415
	8-429	45	45	229 @ 1.33	1¹³⁄₁₆	.0010–.0027	.0010–.0027	.3420	.3420
'72–'76	6-250	45	44	150 @ 1.22	1¹⁹⁄₃₂	.0008–.0025	.0010–.0027	.3104	.3102
	8-302	45	44	200 @ 1.23	1¹¹⁄₁₆	.0010–.0027	.0015–.0032	.3420	.3415
	8-351 ①	45	44	200 @ 1.34	1²⁵⁄₃₂	.0010–.0027	.0015–.0032	.3420	.3415
	8-351 ②	45	44	210 @ 1.42	1¹³⁄₁₆	.0010–.0027	.0015–.0032	.3420	.3415
	8-351 ③	45	44	285 @ 1.23	1¹³⁄₁₆	.0010–.0027	.0015–.0032	.3420	.3415
	8-400	45	44	226 @ 1.39	1¹³⁄₁₆	.0010–.0027	.0015–.0032	.3420	.3515
	8-429	45	45	229 @ 1.33	1¹³⁄₁₆	.0010–.0027	.0010–.0027	.3420	.3420
'77–'78	6-250	45	44	150 @ 1.22	1¹⁹⁄₃₂	.0008–.0025	.0010–.0027	.3104	.3102
	8-302	45	44	200 @ 1.22	1⁹⁄₁₆	.0010–.0027	.0015–.0032	.3420	.3415
	8-351 ①	45	44	200 @ 1.34	1²⁵⁄₃₂	.0010–.0027	.0015–.0032	.3420	.3415
	8-351 ②	45	44	282 @ 1.32	1¹³⁄₁₆	.0010–.0027	.0015–.0032	.3420	.3415
	8-351 ③	45	44	285 @ 1.32	1¹³⁄₁₆	.0010–.0027	.0015–.0032	.3420	.3415
	8-400	45	44	226 @ 1.39	1¹³⁄₁₆	.0010–.0027	.0015–.0032	.3420	.3415
	8-460	45	44	253 @ 1.33	1¹³⁄₁₆	.0010–.0027	.0010–.0027	.3420	.3420
'79	8-302	45	44	④	⑤	.0010–.0027	.0015–.0032	.3420	.3415
	8-351 M	45	44	228 @ 1.39	1¹³⁄₁₆	.0010–.0027	.0015–.0032	.3420	.3415
	8-351 W	45	44	⑥	⑦	.0010–.0027	.0015–.0032	.3420	.3415
'80	8-255	45	44	⑦	⑧	.0010–.0027	.0015–.0032	.3420	.3415
	8-302	45	44	⑦	⑧	.0010–.0027	.0015–.0032	.3420	.3415
'81	4-140	45	44	⑨	1⁹⁄₁₆	.0010–.0027	.0015–.0032	.3420	.3415
	6-200	45	44	55 @ 1.59	1¹⁹⁄₃₂	.0008–.0025	.0010–.0027	.3104	.3102
	8-255	45	44	⑦	⑧	.0010–.0027	.0015–.0032	.3420	.3415
	8-302	45	44	⑦	⑧	.0010–.0027	.0015–.0032	.3420	.3415
'82–'85	4-140	45	44	75 @ 1.56	1⁹⁄₁₆	.0010–.0027	.0015–.0032	.3420	.3415
	6-200	45	44	55 @ 1.59	1¹⁹⁄₃₂	.0008–.0025	.0010–.0027	.3104	.3102
	6-232	⑨	⑩	202 @ 1.27	1¾	.0010–.0027	.0015–.0032	.3420	.3415
	8-255	⑨	⑩	⑪	⑧	.0010–.0027	.0015–.0032	.3420	.3415
	8-302	45	45	⑦	⑧	.0010–.0027	.0015–.0032	.3420	.3415

① Windsor heads
② Cleveland or modified Cleveland 2 bbl
③ Cleveland or modified Cleveland 4 bbl
④ Int.: 200 @ 1.31
  Exh.: 200 @ 1.20
⑤ Int.: 1¹¹⁄₁₆
  Exh.: 1⅝
⑥ Int.: 200 @ 1.34
  Exh.: 200 @ 1.20
⑦ Int.: 204 @ 1.36
  Exh.: 200 @ 1.20
⑧ Int.: 1¹¹⁄₁₆
  Exh.: 1¹⁹⁄₃₂
⑨ 44°30'–45°
⑩ 45°30'–45°45'
⑪ Int.: 192 @ 1.40
  Exh.: 191 @ 1.23

86673x11

Crankshaft and Connecting Rod Specifications

All measurements are given in inches

| Year | Engine No. Cyl. Displacement (cu. in.) | Crankshaft | | | | Connecting Rod | | |
		Main Brg. Journal Dia	Main Brg. Oil Clearance	Shaft End-Play	Thrust on No.	Journal Diameter	Oil Clearance	Side Clearance
'81–'85	4-140	2.3982–2.3990	.0008–.0015 ⑧	.004–.008	3	2.0464–2.0472	.0008–.0015 ⑨	.0035–.0105
'81–'82	6-200	2.2482–2.2490	.0008–.0015 ⑧	.004–.008	5	2.1232–2.1240	.0008–.0015 ⑨	.0035–.0105
'82–'85	6-232	2.5185–2.5195	.0005–.0023 ⑩	.004–.008	3	2.1228–2.1236	.0008–.0026	.010–.020
'71–'77	6-250	2.3982–2.3990	.0005–.0022	.004–.008	5	2.1232–2.1240	.0008–.00024	.003–.010
'81–'82	8-255	2.2482–2.2490	.0005–.0015 ③⑪	.004–.008	3	2.1228–2.1236	.0008–.0015 ⑫	.010–.020
'71–'85	8-302	2.2482–2.2490	.0005–.0024 ⑤④	.004–.008	3	2.1228–2.1236	.0008–.0026	.010–.020
'73–'79	8-351W	2.9994–3.0002	.0013–.0030 ②	.004–.008	3	2.3103–2.3111	.0008–.0026 ⑦①	.010–.020
'71–'79	8-351C or M	2.7484–2.7492 ⑥	.0009–.0026 ⑦	.004–.008	3	2.3103–2.3111	.0008–.0026 ⑦①	.010–.020
'72–'78	8-400	2.9994–3.0002	.0011–.0028	.004–.008	3	2.3103–2.3111	.0011–.0026 ①	.010–.020
'71–'76	8-429, 460	2.9994–3.0002	.0010–.0020 ③	.004–.008	3	2.4992–2.5000	.0008–.0028	.010–.020

① .008–.0015 in. in 1974–77
② .008–.0025 in. in 1974–77
③ No. 1: .0010–.0015
④ .0005–.0015 in. in 1974–77
⑤ 302: .0001–.0005 No. 1 bearing only
⑥ 8-351C given; 8-351M: 2.9994–3.0002
⑦ 351C or M 4-bbl: .0011–.0015
⑧ .0008–.0026 allowed
⑨ .0008–.0024 allowed
⑩ Horiz.: .0009–.0027
⑪ 1982: .0005–.0024
⑫ 1982: .0007–.0020

86673x15

Camshaft Specifications

(All measurements in inches)

| Engine | Journal Diameter | | | | | Bearing Clearance | Lobe Lift | | Endplay |
	1	2	3	4	5		Intake	Exhaust	
4-140 (2.3L)	1.7713–1.7720	1.7713–1.7720	1.7713–1.7720	1.7713–1.7720	—	.001–.003	.2437 ①	.2437 ①	.001–.007
6-200 (3.3L)	1.8095–1.8105	1.8095–1.8105	1.8095–1.8105	1.8095–1.8105	—	.001–.003	.245	.245	.001–.007
6-232 (3.8L)	2.0505–2.0515	2.0505–2.0515	2.0505–2.0515	2.0505–2.0515	—	.001–.003	.240	.241	②
6-250 (4.1L)	1.8095–1.8105	1.8095–1.8105	1.8095–1.8105	1.8095–1.8105	—	.001–.003	.245	.245	.001–.007
8-255 (4.2L)	2.0805–2.0815	2.0655–2.0665	2.0505–2.0515	2.0355–2.0365	2.0205–2.0215	.001–.003	.2375	.2375	.001–.007
8-302 (5.0L)	2.0805–2.0815	2.0655–2.0665	2.0505–2.0515	2.0355–2.0365	2.0205–2.0215	.001–.003	.2375 ③	.2474 ③	.001–.003
8-351W (5.8L)	2.0805–2.0815	2.0655–2.0665	2.0505–2.0515	2.0355–2.0365	2.0205–2.0215	.001–.003	.260 ④	.260 ④	.001–.007
8-351M (5.8L) 8-400 (6.6L)	2.1238–2.1248	2.0655–2.0665	2.0505–2.0515	2.0355–2.0365	2.0205–2.0215	.001–.003	.235 .247	.235 .250	.001–.003
8-460 (7.5L)	2.1238–2.1248	2.1238–2.1248	2.1238–2.1248	2.1238–2.1248	2.1238–2.1248	.001–.003	.253 ④	.278 ④	.001–.006

① '84 and later: .2381
② Endplay controlled by button and spring on camshaft end.
③ HO engine: Intake—.2600; Exhaust—.2780
④ HO engine: Intake—.2780; Exhaust—.2830

86673x16

Ring Gap (inches)

Year	Engine	Top Compression	Bottom Compression	Oil [1] Control
1971–73	250	.010–.020	.010–.020	.015–.055
1974–82	200, 250	.008–.016	.008–.016	.015–.055
1971	302, 351	.010–.020	.010–.020	.015–.069
1971	429	.010–.020	.010–.020	.010–.035
1972–78	400	.010–.020	.010–.020	.015–.069
1972–85	Except 200, 250, 400	.010–.020	.010–.020	.015–.055 [2]

[1] Steel Rails
[2] 1972–73 351 C is .015–.069

86673x17

Ring Side Clearance (Inches)

Year	Engine	Top Compression	Bottom Compression	Oil Control
1971–85	All engines	.002–.004	.002–.004	Snug

86673x18

Piston Clearance (Inches)

Year	Engine	Piston-to-Bore Clearance
1971–82	200, 250	0.0013–0.0021
1971–85	255, 302, 351W	0.0018–0.0026
1971–85	140, 351C, 351M, 400 429, 460	0.0014–0.0022 [1]
1971	429 CJ and SCJ	0.0042–0.0050
1981–85	232	.0014–.0028

[1] 79–82 Turbo .0034–.0042
  83–85 Turbo .0030–.0038

86673x19

Torque Specifications
(All Readings in ft. lbs.)

Year	Engine No. Cyl Displacement (cu in.)	Cylinder Head Bolts*	Rod Bearing Bolts	Main Bearing Bolts	Crankshaft Pulley Bolt	Flywheel-to-Crankshaft Bolts	Manifold	
							Intake	Exhaust
'71–'73	6-250	70–75	21–26	60–70	85–100	75–85	—	13–18
	8-302	65–72	19–24	60–70	70–90	75–85	23–25	12–16
	8-351	95–100	40–45	95–105 ②	70–90	75–85	23–25 (5/16) 28–32 (3/8) 6–9 (1/4)	12–22
	8-400	95–105 ③	40–45	④	70–90	75–85	21–25 (5/16) 27–33 (3/8) 6–9 (1/4)	12–16
	8-429, 460	130–140	40–45	95–105 ①	70–90	75–85	25–30	28–33
'74–'79	6-250	70–75	21–26	60–70	85–100	75–85	—	13–18
	8-302	65–72	19–24	60–70	35–50	75–85	19–27	12–16
	8-351W	105–112	40–45	95–105	35–50	75–85	19–27	18–24
'74–'79	8-351C or M	95–105 ③	40–45	④	70–90	75–85	⑤	12–22
	8-400	95–105 ③	40–45	④	70–90	75–85	⑤	12–16
	8-460	130–140	40–45	95–105	35–50	75–85	22–32	28–33
'80–85	4-140	80–90 ⑨	30–36	80–90	100–120	54–64	14–21	16–23
	6-200	70–75	21–26	60–70	85–100	75–85	—	18–24
	6-232	65–81 ⑥	30–36 ⑥	62–81 ⑥	85–100	75–85	17–19	15–22
	8-255	65–75	19–24	60–70	70–90	75–85	18–20 ⑦	18–24
	8-302	65–75	19–24	60–70	70–90	75–85	23–25 ⑦	18–24

① 7/16 in. bolts—70–80 ft. lbs.
② 3/8 in. bolts—34–45 ft. lbs.
③ Three steps—55, 75, then maximum figure
④ 1/2 in.—13 bolts, 95–105, 3/8 in.—16 bolts, 35–45
⑤ 5/16 in. bolt, 21–25, 3/8 in. bolt, 22–32; 1/4 in. bolt, 6–9
⑥ Tighten to listed torque, loosen 2 complete turns, retighten to listed torque. Fasteners must be oil-coated
⑦ Torque cold, then retorque hot
⑧ Tighten in two steps: 50–60 then 80–90
* Tighten cylinder head bolts in three steps

86673x14

Standard Torque Specifications and Fastener Markings

In the absence of specific torques, the following chart can be used as a guide to the maximum safe torque of a particular size/grade of fastener.
- There is no torque difference for fine or coarse threads.
- Torque values are based on clean, dry threads. Reduce the value by 10% if threads are oiled prior to assembly.
- The torque required for aluminum components or fasteners is considerably less.

U.S. Bolts

SAE Grade Number	1 or 2			5			6 or 7		
Number of lines always 2 less than the grade number.									
Bolt Size (Inches)—(Thread)	Maximum Torque			Maximum Torque			Maximum Torque		
	Ft./Lbs.	Kgm	Nm	Ft./Lbs.	Kgm	Nm	Ft./Lbs.	Kgm	Nm
¼ — 20	5	0.7	6.8	8	1.1	10.8	10	1.4	13.5
— 28	6	0.8	8.1	10	1.4	13.6			
⁵/₁₆ — 18	11	1.5	14.9	17	2.3	23.0	19	2.6	25.8
— 24	13	1.8	17.6	19	2.6	25.7			
⅜ — 16	18	2.5	24.4	31	4.3	42.0	34	4.7	46.0
— 24	20	2.75	27.1	35	4.8	47.5			
⁷/₁₆ — 14	28	3.8	37.0	49	6.8	66.4	55	7.6	74.5
— 20	30	4.2	40.7	55	7.6	74.5			
½ — 13	39	5.4	52.8	75	10.4	101.7	85	11.75	115.2
— 20	41	5.7	55.6	85	11.7	115.2			
⁹/₁₆ — 12	51	7.0	69.2	110	15.2	149.1	120	16.6	162.7
— 18	55	7.6	74.5	120	16.6	162.7			
⅝ — 11	83	11.5	112.5	150	20.7	203.3	167	23.0	226.5
— 18	95	13.1	128.8	170	23.5	230.5			
¾ — 10	105	14.5	142.3	270	37.3	366.0	280	38.7	379.6
— 16	115	15.9	155.9	295	40.8	400.0			
⅞ — 9	160	22.1	216.9	395	54.6	535.5	440	60.9	596.5
— 14	175	24.2	237.2	435	60.1	589.7			
1 — 8	236	32.5	318.6	590	81.6	799.9	660	91.3	894.8
— 14	250	34.6	338.9	660	91.3	849.8			

Metric Bolts

Relative Strength Marking	4.6, 4.8			8.8		
Bolt Markings						
Bolt Size Thread Size x Pitch (mm)	Maximum Torque			Maximum Torque		
	Ft./Lbs.	Kgm	Nm	Ft./Lbs.	Kgm	Nm
6 x 1.0	2–3	.2–.4	3–4	3–6	.4–.8	5–8
8 x 1.25	6–8	.8–1	8–12	9–14	1.2–1.9	13–19
10 x 1.25	12–17	1.5–2.3	16–23	20–29	2.7–4.0	27–39
12 x 1.25	21–32	2.9–4.4	29–43	35–53	4.8–7.3	47–72
14 x 1.5	35–52	4.8–7.1	48–70	57–85	7.8–11.7	77–110
16 x 1.5	51–77	7.0–10.6	67–100	90–120	12.4–16.5	130–160
18 x 1.5	74–110	10.2–15.1	100–150	130–170	17.9–23.4	180–230
20 x 1.5	110–140	15.1–19.3	150–190	190–240	26.2–46.9	160–320
22 x 1.5	150–190	22.0–26.2	200–260	250–320	34.5–44.1	340–430
24 x 1.5	190–240	26.2–46.9	260–320	310–410	42.7–56.5	420–550

86673x20

Engine

REMOVAL & INSTALLATION

▶ See Figures 46, 47, 48, 49, 50, 51, 52 and 53

➡Label all wiring, vacuum hoses, fuel lines, etc. before disconnecting them; thereby making installation much easier.

The following procedure can be used on all years and models. Slight variations may occur due to extra connections, etc., but the basic procedure covers all years and models. Use this as a guide — read the entire service procedure before starting the repair.

1. Disconnect the negative battery cable. Once disconnected, it is recommended that the positive battery cable be disconnected as well.
2. Drain the crankcase and the cooling system into separate containers, and dispose of the fluids properly.

✳✳CAUTION

When draining coolant, keep in mind that cats and dogs are attracted to ethylene glycol antifreeze, and could drink any that is left in an uncovered container or in puddles on the ground. This will prove fatal in sufficient quantity. Always drain the coolant into a sealable container. Coolant should be reused unless it is contaminated or several years old.

3. Relieve the fuel system pressure, if fuel injected, then disconnect the fuel lines; refer to Section 5.
4. If the A/C compressor cannot be position out of the way without the compressor lines being removed, then discharge the air conditioning system into an approved recovery/recycling machine.
5. Mark the position of the hood on the hinges and remove the hood.
6. Unfasten the air cleaner by loosening the wing nut and/or the clips around the cover. On automatic transmission

Fig. 46 Use a marker to scribe the hood hinge position

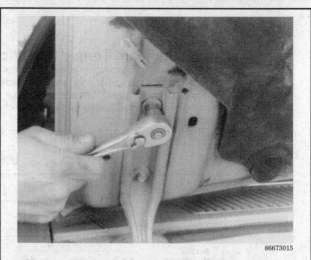

Fig. 47 Have an assistant secure the hood before removing hinge bolts

Fig. 48 With the hood removed, it is easier to work on the engine

equipped vehicles, disconnect and plug the fluid cooler lines at the radiator.

7. Remove the cooling fan, shroud and radiator, by loosening the upper and lower hose clamps and working the hoses off the radiator. Remove the shroud bolts, then lift the shroud out of the engine compartment. Finally, loosen and remove any remaining hardware securing the radiator, and pull the radiator out of the engine compartment.
8. Remove the air inlet tube. Unclamp the fuel lines from the fuel pump, if carbureted.
9. Tag, then disconnect the accelerator, cruise control cables and the throttle valve cable.
10. Tag any vacuum, breather or wire harnesses on top of or around the engine.
11. Unfasten the alternator harness from the fender apron and junction block. Unbolt the retaining hardware, and remove the alternator from the engine. Unbolt the air conditioning compressor from the engine and place aside. In some cases the compressor lines are not long enough. In this case, you must disconnect the air conditioning hoses from the compressor.

Fig. 49 After removing the hardware, remove the fan shroud

Fig. 50 With the hoses disconnected and the mounting bolts removed, the radiator can be removed from the engine compartment

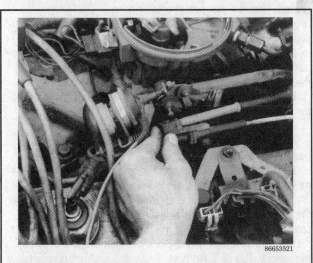

Fig. 51 Label the cables when disconnecting them from the throttle linkage

Fig. 52 Disconnect and tag the vacuum hoses

12. Unfasten the Electronic Variable Orifice (EVO) sensor connector from the power steering pump, if equipped. Also disconnect the body ground strap from the firewall.

13. Raise and safely support the vehicle on jackstands.

14. Disconnect the exhaust system from the exhaust manifolds and support the exhaust section with wire hung from the crossmember.

15. Remove the retaining nut from the transmission line bracket and remove the bolts retaining the engine to the transmission braces.

16. Remove the starter and dust seal. Remove the bolts retaining the power steering pump to the engine block and position aside.

17. On cars equipped with manual transmissions, remove the clutch retracting spring. Disconnect the clutch equalizer shaft and arm bracket at the underbody rail and remove the arm bracket and shaft from the vehicle.

18. Remove the plug from the engine block to access the converter retaining nuts. Rotate the crankshaft until each of the nuts is accessible and remove the nuts.

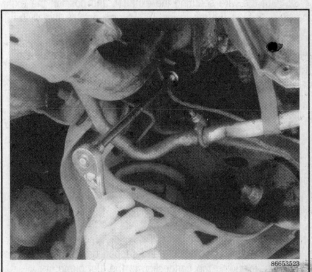

Fig. 53 Unbolt the pipes from the exhaust manifold

19. Remove the transmission-to-engine retaining bolts, including the flywheel or converter housing upper bolts. Remove the engine mount through-bolts.

20. Lower the vehicle. Support the transmission with a floor jack and remove the bolt retaining the right and left engine mounts to the lower underbody bracket.

21. Install an engine lifting bracket to the left cylinder head on the front and the right cylinder head on the rear. Connect suitable engine lifting equipment to the lifting brackets.

22. Raise the engine slowly, then carefully separate the engine from the transmission.

23. Carefully lift the engine out of the engine compartment and install it on an engine stand. Remove the engine lifting equipment.

To install:

24. Install the engine lifting brackets to the cylinder head. Connect the engine lifting equipment to the brackets and remove the engine from the stand.

25. Carefully lower the engine into the engine compartment. Make sure the studs on the converter align with the holes in the flexplate on automatic transmissions.

26. Fully engage the engine to the transmission and slowly lower the engine onto the left and right engine mounts. Remove the engine lifting equipment and brackets. Install the bolts securing the left and right engine mounts to the frame.

27. Raise and safely support the vehicle. Install the 6 engine-to-transmission bolts and tighten to 30-44 ft. lbs. (40-60 Nm).

28. Install the engine mount through-bolts and tighten to 15-22 ft. lbs. (20-30 Nm). Install the converter retaining nuts and tighten to 22-25 ft. lbs. (20-30 Nm). Install the plug into the access hole in the engine block.

29. Position the power steering pump on the engine block and install the retaining nuts. Tighten to 15-22 ft. lbs. (20-30 Nm). Install the starter.

30. Position the engine-to-transmission braces and install the bolt. Tighten the bolts to 18-31 ft. lbs. (25-43 Nm).

31. Position the transmission line bracket to the brace stud and install the retaining nut. Tighten to 15-22 ft. lbs. (20-30 Nm).

32. Cut the wire securing the exhaust, and position the exhaust system to the manifolds. Use a new gasket. Install the nuts and tighten to 20-30 ft. lbs. (27-41 Nm).

➡**Make sure the exhaust system does not interfere with the crossmember. Adjust as necessary.**

33. Lower the vehicle and connect the EVO sensor, if equipped.

34. Connect the heater hoses and fasten the vacuum supply hose to the throttle body adapter vacuum port.

35. Connect the power supply to the power distribution box and starter relay. Plug in and secure the remaining electrical connectors and vacuum hoses to their respective connections.

36. Connect the alternator harness from the fender apron and junction block.

37. Connect and if necessary, adjust the throttle valve, accelerator and cruise control cables.

38. Install the wiper module and support bracket. Secure the fuel lines, including the connection to the fuel pump. if carbureted.

39. Install the radiator, cooling fan and shroud. Install the air inlet tube.

40. Fill the crankcase with the proper type and quantity of engine oil. Fill the cooling system.

41. If the A/C lines were unfastened, connect the these lines to the compressor.

42. Install the hood, aligning the marks that were made during removal. Connect the battery cables.

43. Start the engine and adjust the timing and idle, if necessary. Check the levels of the coolant oil and transmission fluids. Check for leaks

44. Road test the vehicle.

45. Have the A/C system charged by a certified professional using an approved recovery/recycling machine.

Engine Mounts

REMOVAL & INSTALLATION

▶ **See Figure 54**

Front

1. Disconnect the negative battery cable, then the positive battery cable. Drain the cooling system into a container. Relieve the fuel system pressure if fuel injected.

2. If the A/C compressor must be positioned out of the way, and the compressor lines have to be removed to accomplish this, then discharge the air conditioning system into a recovery/recycling machine.

✳✳CAUTION

When draining coolant, keep in mind that cats and dogs are attracted to ethylene glycol antifreeze, and could drink any that is left in an uncovered container or in puddles on the ground. This will prove fatal in sufficient quantity. Always drain the coolant into a sealable container. Coolant should be reused unless it is contaminated or several years old.

3. Remove the air inlet tube and the cooling fan and shroud. Remove the upper radiator hose.

4. Disconnect the fuel lines. Remove the wiper module and support bracket.

5. If necessary, disconnect the air conditioning compressor outlet hose at the compressor and remove the bolt retaining the hose assembly to the right coil bracket.

6. Mark and tag the throttle cables, including the accelerator and cruise control cable.

7. Disconnect the heater outlet hose.

8. Disconnect the heater outlet hose to the right cylinder head and position aside.

9. Raise and safely support the vehicle on jackstands. Remove the engine mount through-bolts.

10. Disconnect the exhaust pipes from the manifolds. Lower the exhaust and hang the pipes with wire from the crossmember.

11. Position a jack and a block of wood under the oil pan, rearward of the oil drain hole. Raise the engine approximately 4 in. (10cm).

12. Install a block of wood under the oil pan and lower the engine onto the wood block. Remove the 3 retaining bolts

each from the right and left engine mounts and remove the mounts.

To install:

13. Position the mounts on the engine block, install the 3 retaining bolts and tighten to 45-60 ft. lbs. (60-81 Nm). Raise the engine and remove the wood block.

14. Lower the engine onto the mounts.

15. Install the engine mount through-bolts and tighten to 15-22 ft. lbs. (20-30 Nm).

16. Cut the wire securing the exhaust, and position the exhaust manifolds. Install a new gasket between the sections. Tighten the nuts to 20-30 ft. lbs. (27-41 Nm). Make sure the exhaust system clears the No. 3 crossmember; adjust as necessary.

17. Position the heater outlet hose. Install the upper stud and tighten the upper stud and lower bolt to 15-22 ft. lbs. (20-30 Nm). Install the ground strap onto the stud and tighten the nut to 15-22 ft. lbs. (20-30 Nm). Connect the heater outlet hose.

18. Connect and if necessary, adjust the throttle cables, including the accelerator and cruise cable.

19. Connect the air conditioning compressor outlet hose to the compressor and install the bolt retaining the hose assembly to the right coil bracket.

20. Install the upper radiator hose and connect the fuel lines. Install the wiper module and retaining bracket.

21. Install the cooling fan and shroud. Install the air inlet tube.

22. Fill the cooling system. Connect the battery cables, start the engine and check for leaks. Consult a professional who can evacuate and charge the air conditioning system.

Rear

▶ **See Figures 55 and 56**

1. Disconnect the negative battery cable. Raise and safely support the vehicle.

2. Support the transmission with a jack and wood block. Remove the nuts attaching the rear mount to the crossmember.

3. Remove the bolts attaching the mount to the transmission.

4. Raise the transmission with the jack and remove the mount.

To install:

5. Position the mount on the transmission. Install the 2 retaining bolts and tighten to 50-70 ft. lbs. (68-95 Nm).

6. Lower the transmission. Install the rear mount-to-crossmember retaining nuts and tighten to 35-50 ft. lbs. (48-68 Nm).

7. Lower the vehicle and connect the negative battery cable.

Valve/Rocker Arm Cover

REMOVAL & INSTALLATION

4-Cylinder Engines

▶ **See Figure 57**

1. Remove the air cleaner assembly and mounting brackets, if mounted on the valve cover.

2. Label (for identification) then remove all wires and vacuum hoses interfering with valve cover removal. Disconnect the PCV hose at the valve cover elbow. Remove the accelerator control cable bracket if necessary.

➡**4-cylinder turbocharged models require removal of the air intake tube and air throttle body.**

3. Remove the valve cover retaining bolts. The front bolts equipped with rubber sealing washers must be installed in the same location to prevent oil leakage.

4. Unfasten any bolts and clamps securing hot water pipes to the valve cover. Reposition the pipes and any wiring harnesses to permit removal of the valve cover.

5. Remove the valve cover. Clean all old gasket material from the valve cover and cylinder head gasket surfaces.

6. Installation is the reverse of removal. Be sure to use a new valve cover gasket. Coat the gasket contact surfaces of the valve cover and the Up side of the valve cover gasket with oil resistant sealing compound. When installing the valve cover gasket, make sure all the gasket locating tangs are engaged in the cover notches provided. Tighten the bolts to 6-8 ft. lbs (8-10 Nm).

L6 Engines

1. Remove the air cleaner and heat chamber air inlet hose, if equipped.

2. Remove the automatic choke tube, if equipped, and the fresh air tube from the valve cover.

3. If equipped with a PCV valve, remove it from the valve cover.

4. Remove the Thermactor® bypass valve and air supply hoses, as needed.

5. Disconnect and mark the spark plug wires. Remove the wire bracket if necessary.

6. Remove any other components if additional access is required. Remove the valve cover retaining bolts and the valve cover.

7. Installation is the reverse of removal. Tighten the bolts in two steps. First, tighten the bolts to 3-5 ft. lbs. (4-6 Nm) and, two minutes later, tighten them to the same specification.

➡**Always use new gasket(s) when installing the valve covers. Install the gasket(s) according to the manufacturer instructions.**

V6 and V8 Engines

▶ **See Figures 58, 59, 60 and 61**

➡**When disconnecting wires and vacuum lines, label them for reinstallation identification.**

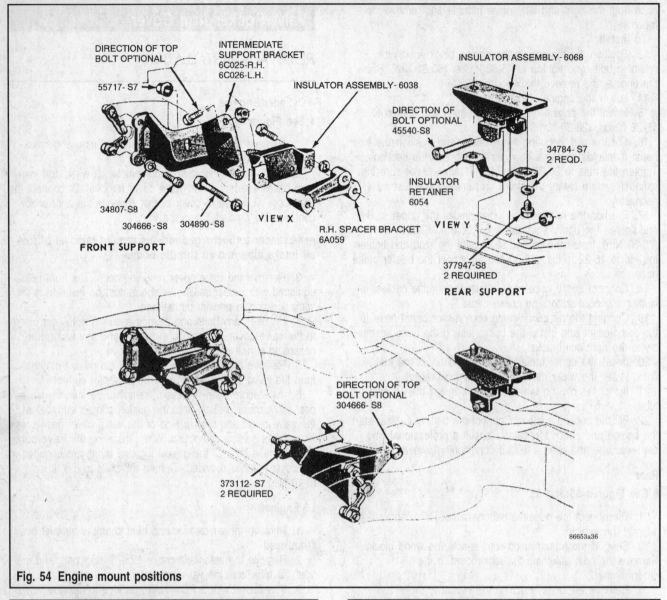

Fig. 54 Engine mount positions

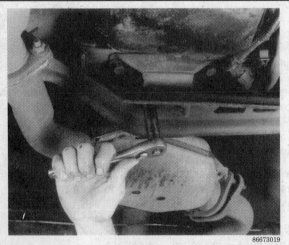

Fig. 55 Use a rachet and socket to remove the retaining hardware securing the rear mount

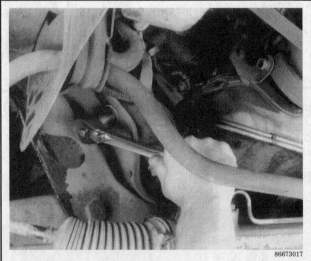

Fig. 56 Remove the nut securing the side engine mount

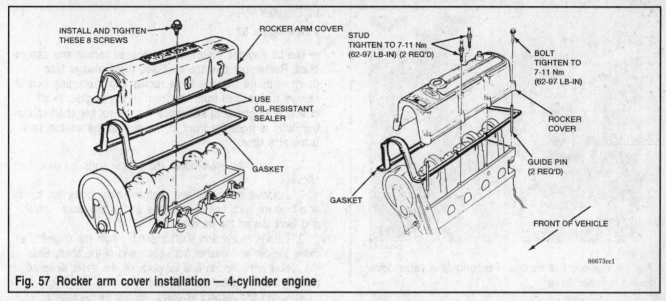

Fig. 57 Rocker arm cover installation — 4-cylinder engine

1. Remove the air cleaner assembly, except if equipped with Multi-Port Fuel Injection (MPFI).

2. If equipped with MPFI, remove the upper intake manifold assembly.

3. On the right side:

a. Disconnect the automatic choke heat chamber hose from the inlet tube near the right valve cover.

b. Remove the automatic choke heat tube if equipped and remove the PCV valve and hose from the valve cover. Disconnect the EGR valve hoses.

c. Remove the Thermactor® bypass valve and air supply hoses as necessary to gain clearance.

d. Disconnect the spark plug wires from the plugs. Twist then pull on the boots only, never on the wire. Position the wires and mounting bracket out of the way.

e. Remove the valve cover mounting bolts, then the valve cover. A plastic-faced hammer may be needed to loosen the cover from the gasket.

4. On the left side:

a. Remove the spark plug wires and bracket.

Fig. 58 If equipped, remove the PCV valve from the valve cover

b. Remove the wiring harness and any vacuum hose(s) from the bracket.

c. Remove the valve cover mounting bolts and valve cover. A plastic-faced hammer may be needed to loosen the cover from the gasket.

5. Clean all old gasket material from the valve cover and cylinder head mounting surfaces.

6. Installation is the reverse of removal procedure. Tighten all retaining bolts to 10-13 ft. lbs. (14-18 Nm). Use oil resistant sealing compound and a new valve cover gasket. Follow the gasket manufacturer instruction when installing the gasket. When positioning the valve cover gasket, make sure all the gasket tangs are engaged into the cover notches provided.

Rocker Arm Shaft/Rocker Arms

REMOVAL & INSTALLATION

4-Cylinder Engines

➡**A special tool is required to compress the lash adjuster.**

1. Remove the valve cover and related parts as described above.

2. Rotate the camshaft so that the base circle of the cam is against the cam follower you intend to remove.

3. Remove the retaining spring from the cam follower, if so equipped.

4. Using special tool T74P-6565-B or a valve spring compressor tool, collapse the lash adjuster and/or depress the valve spring, as necessary, and slide the cam follower over the lash adjuster and out from under the camshaft.

5. Install the cam follower in the reverse order of removal. Make sure that the lash adjuster is collapsed and released before rotating the camshaft.

6. Clean the mounting surfaces and install the valve cover with a new gasket, as described above.

7. Install the air cleaner assembly, PCV valve and any other parts which were moved.

Fig. 59 Remove the hardware securing the valve cover to the cylinder head

Fig. 60 When removing the valve cover be careful not to loose any of the retaining hardware

Fig. 61 Lift the valve cover off the cylinder head. Clean both mating surfaces

L6 Engines

▶ See Figure 62

➡The L6 engines utilize shaft-mounted rocker arm assemblies. Remember that the oil holes must always face downward and that the large rocker shaft retaining bolt is always the second from the front of the engine. In all cases, the tightening sequence for the rocker shaft retaining bolts is from the front to the rear of the engine, two turns at a time.

1. Remove the valve cover and related parts, as described above.
2. Remove the rocker arm shaft mounting bolts, two turns at a time for each bolt. Start at the end of the rocker shaft and work toward the middle.
3. Lift the rocker arm shaft assembly from the engine. Remove the pin and washer from each end of the shaft. Slide the rocker arms, spring and supports off the shaft. Keep all parts in order or label them by position.
4. Clean and inspect all parts, replace as necessary.
5. Assemble the rocker shaft parts in reverse order of removal. Be sure the oil holes in the shaft are pointed downward. install the rocker shaft assembly on the engine and tighten the mounting bolts two turns at a time, in sequence, from the front to the rear. After the supports fully contact the cylinder head, tighten the mounting bolts in the same sequence to 30-35 ft. lbs. (39-45 Nm).

➡**Lubricate all parts with motor oil before installation.**

6. Clean the mounting surfaces and install the valve cover with a new gasket, as described above.
7. Install the air cleaner assembly, PCV valve and any other parts which were moved.

V6 and V8 Engines

▶ See Figures 63, 64, 65, 65, 66, 67 and 68

1. Disconnect the negative battery cable.
2. Remove the rocker arm cover. A plastic-faced hammer may be needed to loosen the cover from the gasket.

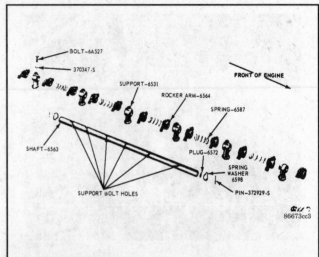

Fig. 62 Rocker arm arm shaft assembly — 4-cylinder engine

3. Remove the rocker arm stud nut or bolt, fulcrum seat and rocker arm. Inspect all the parts, and replace if necessary. Also inspect the pushrod.

To install:

4. Lubricate all parts with heavy SF oil before installation. When installing, rotate the crankshaft until the lifter is on the base of the cam circle (all the way down) and assemble the rocker arm. Tighten the nut or bolt to 17-23 ft. lbs. (23-30 Nm) and on later models 18-25 ft. lbs. (23-33 Nm).

Rocker Studs

REMOVAL & INSTALLATION

Rocker arm studs which are broken or have damaged threads may be replaced with standard studs. Studs which are loose in the cylinder head must be replaced with oversize studs which are available from most automotive parts stores.

Fig. 65 When lifting arm assemblies, grasp both the arm and the hardware to prevent parts from falling into the head

Fig. 63 Loosen and remove the retaining bolt securing the rocker arm

Fig. 66 With the rocker arms off, the pushrods can be removed and inspected

Fig. 64 Lift the rocker arm out. If removing more than one rocker arm, label them for correct reassembly

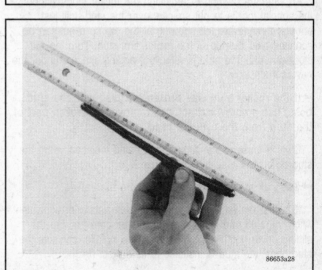

Fig. 67 Use a straightedge to check the pushrods for bends

Fig. 68 Use a torque wrench to tighten the rocker arm bolts

Refer to a local machine shop if necessary. The amount of oversize and diameter of the studs are as follows:
- 0.006 in. (0.152mm) oversize: 0.3774-0.3781 in. (9.586-9.604mm)
- 0.010 in. (0.254mm) oversize: 0.3814-0.3821 in. (9.688-9.705mm)
- 0.015 in. (0.381mm) oversize: 0.3864-0.3871 in. (9.815-9.832mm)

A tool kit for replacing the rocker studs is available and contains a stud remover and two oversize reamers: one for 0.006 in. (0.152mm) and one for 0.015 in. (0.381mm) oversize studs. For 0.010 in. (0.254mm) oversize studs, use reamer tool T66P-6A527-B. To press the replacement studs into the cylinder head, use the stud replacer tool T69P-6049-D. Use the smaller reamer tool first when boring the hole for oversize studs.

1. Remove the valve/rocker cover(s). Position the sleeve of the rocker arm stud remover over the stud with the bearing end down.

An alternate method of removing the rocker studs without the special tool is to put spacers over the stud until just enough threads are left showing at the top so a nut can be screwed onto the top of the rocker arm stud. Turn the nut clockwise until the stud is removed, adding spacers under the nut as necessary.

➡If the rocker stud was broken off flush with the stud boss, use a screw extractor to remove the broken part of the stud from the cylinder head.

2. If a loose rocker arm stud is being replaced, ream the stud bore for the selected oversize stud.

➡Keep all metal particles away from the valves.

3. Coat the end of the stud with Lubriplate® or equivalent. Align the stud and installer with the stud bore and tap the sliding driver until it bottoms. When the installer contacts the stud boss, the stud is installed to its correct height.

Thermostat

REMOVAL & INSTALLATION

▶ See Figures 69, 70, 71, 72, 73, 74, 75, 76 and 77

❋❋CAUTION

When draining coolant, keep in mind that cats and dogs are attracted to ethylene glycol antifreeze, and could drink any that is left in an uncovered container or in puddles on the ground. This will prove fatal in sufficient quantity. Always drain the coolant into a sealable container. Coolant should be reused unless it is contaminated or several years old.

1. Raise and support the vehicle safely on jackstands.
2. From the driver's side portion of the radiator, open the draincock and drain the radiator so the coolant level is below the coolant outlet elbow which houses the thermostat. If the radiator has been replaced, the replacement unit may not have a draincock. In this case the lower radiator hose will have to be loosened and removed to allow for the coolant to drain out.

➡On some models it may be necessary to remove the distributor in order to gain access to the thermostat housing mounting bolts.

3. Remove the outlet elbow retaining bolts and position the elbow clear of the intake manifold or cylinder head to provide access to the thermostat.

➡Remember the direction the thermostat was facing when removed to ensure that it is installed in the correct manner

4. Remove the thermostat and the gasket. Clean any gasket material from both mating surfaces. Always replace the gasket.

To install:

5. Coat the new gasket with water resistant sealer. Install the thermostat in the block on the 5.8L and 6.6L engines, then

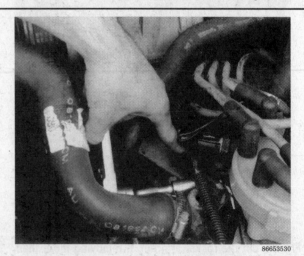

Fig. 69 Loosen and remove the bolts and/or stud which secure the thermostat housing to the engine

Fig. 70 Before removing any hardware, determine how the thermostat housing is secured. For example, this housing is secured from the top of the engine

Fig. 71 Note the thermostat position in the housing

Fig. 72 This thermostat is a locking type. To remove, twist the thermostat counterclockwise

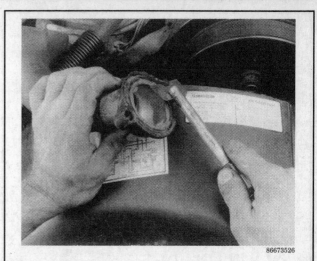

Fig. 73 Always clean off any remaining gasket material before reinstallation

install the gasket. On all other engines, position the gasket on the engine, and install the thermostat in the coolant elbow.

6. Install the outlet elbow then the retaining bolts on the engine. Tighten the bolts evenly in steps to 12-15 ft. lbs. (16-20 Nm).

7. Refill the radiator and overflow tank, if equipped.

8. Lower the vehicle. Start the engine and bleed the cooling system, if necessary. Refer to the service procedure as needed. Recheck the coolant level.

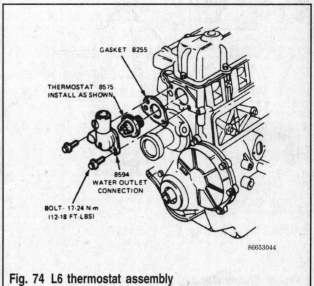

Fig. 74 L6 thermostat assembly

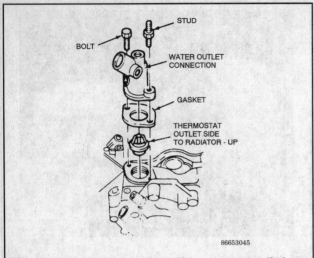

Fig. 75 Thermostat assembly used on some 8-cylinder engines

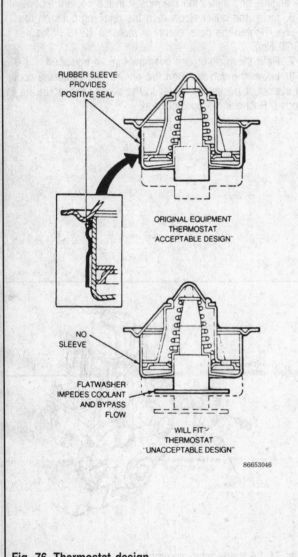

Fig. 76 Thermostat design

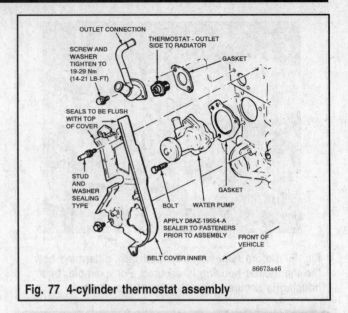

Fig. 77 4-cylinder thermostat assembly

Intake Manifold

REMOVAL & INSTALLATION

4-Cylinder Engines

WITH CARBURETOR

▶ See Figure 78

➡ The following procedure applies only to carburetor-equipped versions of the 4-cylinder engine. Fuel injected models utilize a two-piece intake manifold which requires a different removal and installation procedures.

1. Disconnect the negative battery cable.
2. Drain the cooling system.

✳✳CAUTION

When draining coolant, keep in mind that cats and dogs are attracted to ethylene glycol antifreeze, and could drink any that is left in an uncovered container or in puddles on the ground. This will prove fatal in sufficient quantity. Always drain the coolant into a sealable container. Coolant should be reused unless it is contaminated or several years old.

3. Remove the air cleaner and disconnect the throttle linkage from the carburetor.
4. Disconnect the fuel and vacuum lines from the carburetor.
5. Remove the oil dipstick and dipstick tube retaining bolt.
6. Disconnect the heat tube at the EGR valve.
7. Disconnect and remove PCV hoses at the intake manifold and the engine block.
8. Remove the distributor cap screws and distributor cap.
9. Remove the carburetor, if necessary.
10. Starting from each end and working towards the middle, remove the intake manifold attaching bolts and remove the manifold.

To install:

11. Clean all old gasket material from the manifold and cylinder head.

12. Position the intake manifold against the cylinder head and install intake manifold attaching bolts. Tighten the bolts in the proper sequence (see illustration) in two steps. First tighten them to 11-12½ ft. lbs. (14-16 Nm) and then to 14-21 ft. lbs. (18-27 Nm).

13. Install the carburetor with a new gasket, if it was removed.

14. Position the distributor cap and tighten its retaining screws.

15. Connect PCV hoses at the intake manifold and engine block.

16. Connect the heat tube at the EGR valve.

17. Install the oil dipstick and dipstick tube retaining bolt.

18. Connect the fuel and vacuum lines to the carburetor.

19. Connect the throttle linkage to the carburetor.

20. Install the air cleaner and fill the cooling system.

21. Connect the negative battery cable.

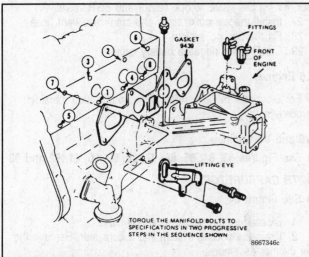

Fig. 78 Intake manifold installation and torque sequence — 4-cylinder carbureted engine

WITH FUEL INJECTION

▶ See Figures 79, 80, 81 and 82

1. Disconnect the negative battery cable.
2. Drain the cooling system.

✳✳CAUTION

When draining coolant, keep in mind that cats and dogs are attracted to ethylene glycol antifreeze, and could drink any that is left in an uncovered container or in puddles on the ground. This will prove fatal in sufficient quantity. Always drain the coolant into a sealable container. Coolant should be reused unless it is contaminated or several years old.

3. Unfasten electrical connectors at the throttle position sensor, air bypass valve, knock sensor and EGR valve.

4. Disconnect the upper intake manifold vacuum fitting connections.

5. Disconnect the throttle linkage, speed control, if so equipped, and kickdown cable. Unbolt the accelerator cable from its bracket, and position it out of the way.

6. Disconnect the air intake hose and crankcase vent hose.

7. Disconnect the PCV system by disconnecting the hose from its fitting on the underside of the upper intake manifold.

8. Disconnect the EGR tube from the EGR valve.

9. Remove the upper intake mounting bolts and the upper intake manifold assembly.

10. Disconnect the Push Connect Fittings at the fuel supply manifold supply and return lines.

11. Unfasten the electrical connectors from all four fuel injectors and move the harness aside.

12. Remove the two fuel supply manifold retaining bolts, and the fuel supply manifold/injectors assembly. If necessary, the fuel injectors can be removed from the fuel supply manifold by gently twisting and pulling.

13. Remove the four bottom retaining bolts from the lower manifold.

14. Remove the four upper retaining bolts and the lower intake manifold assembly.

To install:

15. Remove and discard the gasket between the cylinder head and lower manifold assembly. Clean and inspect the mating surfaces, and install a new gasket.

16. Position the lower manifold assembly and install the four upper retaining bolts finger-tight. The front two bolts may also secure an engine lifting bracket.

17. Install the four lower bolts and, using the appropriate sequence, tighten all of the bolts to the following specifications:
    1984-85: 12-15 ft. lbs. (16-19 Nm)

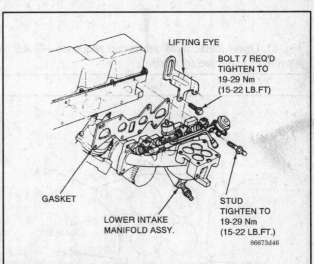

Fig. 79 Lower intake manifold installation — fuel injected 4-cylinder engine

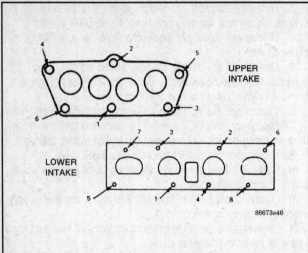

Fig. 80 Intake manifold torque sequences — 1984 4-cylinder fuel injected engine

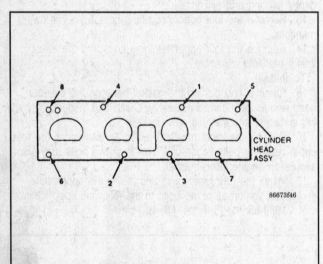

Fig. 81 Lower intake manifold torque sequence — 1985 4-cylinder fuel injected engine

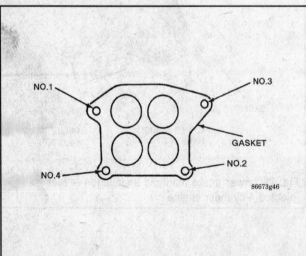

Fig. 82 Upper intake manifold torque sequence — 1985 4-cylinder fuel injected engine

18. Install the fuel supply manifold and injectors with two retaining bolts, and tighten to 12-15 ft. lbs. (16-19 Nm).

19. Fasten the four electrical connectors to the injectors.

20. Remove and discard the gasket between the lower and upper manifold assemblies. Clean and inspect the mating surfaces. If scraping is necessary, be careful not to damage either gasket surface, or to allow material to fall into the lower manifold. Install a new gasket on the lower manifold assembly.

21. Install the upper intake manifold on the lower intake manifold. On 1984 engines, tighten the six attaching bolts, beginning with the two center ones, to 15-22 ft. lbs. (19-29 Nm). On 1985 engines, tighten the four attaching bolts in a crisscross pattern to 15-22 ft. lbs. (19-29 Nm).

22. Connect the EGR tube to the EGR valve.

23. Connect the PCV system hose to the fitting on the underside of the upper intake manifold.

24. Connect the upper intake manifold vacuum fitting connections.

25. Install the accelerator cable and bracket assembly. Install the throttle linkage and speed control, if applicable.

26. Fasten electrical connectors at the throttle position sensor, air bypass valve, knock sensor and EGR valve.

27. Install the air intake hose and crankcase vent hose.

28. Fill the cooling system.

29. Connect the negative battery cable.

L6 Engines

For 6-cylinder models, refer to the combination manifold procedure.

V6 and V8 Engines

▶ See Figures 83, 84, 85, 86, 87, 88, 89, 90, 91, 92 and 93

WITH CARBURETOR

▶ See Figure 94

1. Disconnect the negative battery cable.

2. Drain the cooling system into a container. Remove the air cleaner assembly.

✲✲CAUTION

When draining coolant, keep in mind that cats and dogs are attracted to ethylene glycol antifreeze, and could drink any that is left in an uncovered container or in puddles on the ground. This will prove fatal in sufficient quantity. Always drain the coolant into a sealable container. Coolant should be reused unless it is contaminated or several years old.

3. Disconnect the upper radiator hose and water pump bypass hose from the thermostat housing and/or intake manifold. Unplug the temperature sending unit wire connector. Remove the heater hose from the choke housing bracket and disconnect the hose from the intake manifold.

4. Unfasten the automatic choke heat chamber air inlet tube and electric wiring connector from the carburetor. Remove the crankcase ventilation hose, vacuum hoses and EGR hose and coolant lines (if equipped). Label the various hoses and wiring for reinstallation identification.

Fig. 83 Label as many wires and vacuum lines as possible before removing

Fig. 86 If equipped with threaded fuel lines, use flare nut wrenches to loosen any fuel lines.

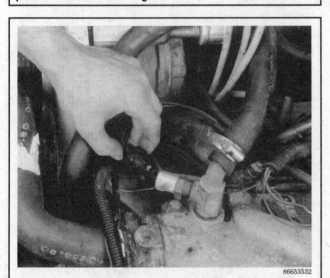

Fig. 84 Unplug the wire connectors and vacuum lines

Fig. 87 On some late model vehicles, the fuel line is connected with a hairpin clip. This must be removed

Fig. 85 Disconnect the throttle controls from the carburetor

Fig. 88 With the clip removed, slide the fuel line off

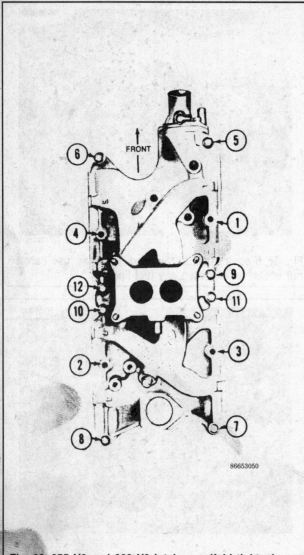

Fig. 89 255 V6 and 302 V8 intake manifold tightening sequence

86653050

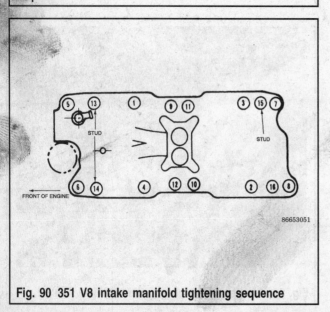

Fig. 90 351 V8 intake manifold tightening sequence

86653051

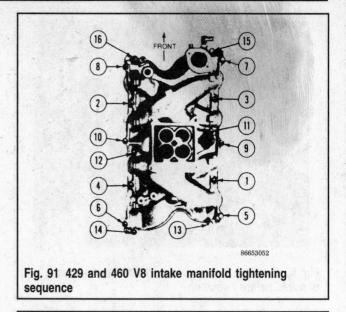

Fig. 91 429 and 460 V8 intake manifold tightening sequence

86653052

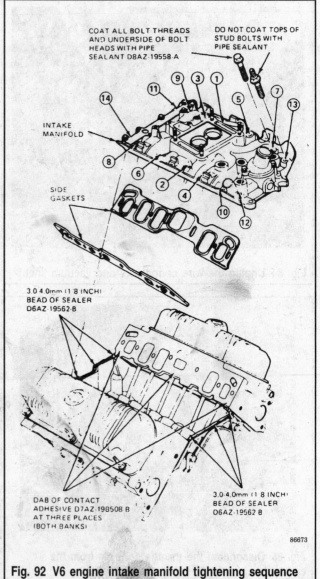

COAT ALL BOLT THREADS AND UNDERSIDE OF BOLT HEADS WITH PIPE SEALANT D8AZ-19558-A

DO NOT COAT TOPS OF STUD BOLTS WITH PIPE SEALANT

INTAKE MANIFOLD

SIDE GASKETS

3.0-4.0mm (1 8 INCH) BEAD OF SEALER D6AZ-19562-B

DAB OF CONTACT ADHESIVE D7AZ-19B508-B AT THREE PLACES (BOTH BANKS)

3.0-4.0mm (1 8 INCH) BEAD OF SEALER D6AZ-19562-B

Fig. 92 V6 engine intake manifold tightening sequence

86673

10. Remove the intake manifold mounting bolts. Lift off the intake manifold and carburetor out of the vehicle as an assembly.

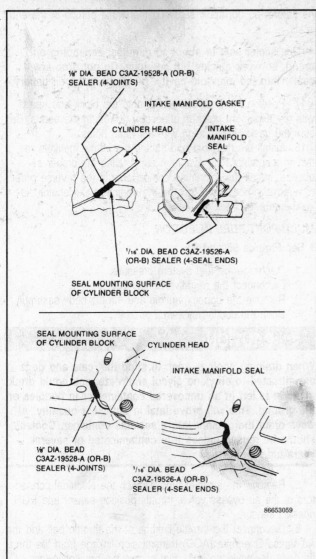

Fig. 93 RTV application areas for all V6 and V8 cylinder head gaskets

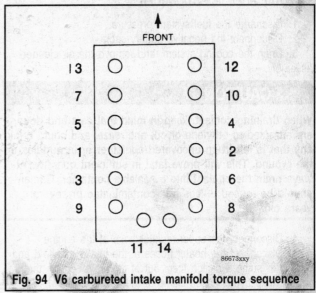

Fig. 94 V6 carbureted intake manifold torque sequence

To install:

11. Clean all gasket material from the mating surfaces.

12. Apply a ⅛ in. (3mm) bead of RTV sealant at each end of the engine where the intake manifold seats. Install the new intake gaskets, and place the manifold on top.

➡ **Make sure the intake gaskets interlock with the end seals. Use silicone rubber sealer (RTV) on the end seals.**

13. After installing the intake manifold, run a finger along the manifold ends to spread the RTV sealer and to make sure the end seals have not slipped out of place.

14. Tighten the manifold mounting bolts to the required specifications in the proper sequence. Refer to the diagram in this section.

15. Install the A/C brackets and compressor, if removed.

16. Install the distributor and secure with the hold-down bolt.

17. Install the carburetor and automatic transmission linkage attached to the carburetor or intake manifold, if equipped with an automatic transmission. Fasten the speed control servo and bracket, if equipped.

18. Connect the fuel line and any remaining vacuum hoses or wiring at the carburetor, solenoids, sensors, or intake manifold.

19. Connect the Thermactor® air supply hose at the check valve. Install the air bypass valve on its bracket.

20. Plug in the automatic choke heat chamber air inlet tube and electric wiring connector at the carburetor.

21. Install the crankcase ventilation hose, vacuum hoses and EGR hose and coolant lines (if equipped).

22. Connect the upper radiator hose and water pump bypass hose at the thermostat housing and/or intake manifold.

23. Fasten the temperature sending unit wire connector.

24. Install the heater hose on the choke housing bracket and connect the hose at the intake manifold.

25. Fill the cooling system and bleed if necessary.

26. Connect the negative battery cable.

27. Install the air cleaner assembly.

5. Remove the valve covers, rocker arm assemblies and the pushrods. Keep the pushrods in order so that they can be installed in their original positions.

6. Disconnect the Thermactor® air supply hose at the check valve. Loosen the hose clamp at the check valve bracket and remove the air bypass valve from the bracket and position to one side.

7. Remove the carburetor and automatic transmission linkage attached to the carburetor or intake manifold, if equipped with an automatic transmission. Remove the speed control servo and bracket, if equipped. Disconnect the fuel line and any remaining vacuum hoses or wiring from the carburetor, solenoids, sensors, or intake manifold.

8. Remove the distributor hold-down bolt and remove the distributor. (See Distributor Removal and Installation).

9. If your car is equipped with air conditioning and the compressor or mounting brackets interfere with manifold removal, remove the brackets and compressor and position them out of the way. Do not disconnect any compressor lines.

28. Connect the negative battery cable. Start the engine and check for leaks.

29. Check the ignition timing and idle. Adjust if necessary.

CENTRAL FUEL INJECTION (CFI)

1. Discharge the fuel system pressure.
2. Disconnect the negative battery cable.
3. Drain the cooling system, and remove the air cleaner assembly.

✳✳CAUTION

When draining coolant, keep in mind that cats and dogs are attracted to ethylene glycol antifreeze, and could drink any that is left in an uncovered container or in puddles on the ground. This will prove fatal in sufficient quantity. Always drain the coolant into a sealable container. Coolant should be reused unless it is contaminated or several years old.

4. Disconnect the upper radiator hose at the engine.

5. Disconnect the heater hoses at the intake manifold and the water pump. Position them out of the way. Loosen the water pump bypass hose clamp at the intake manifold.

6. Remove the PCV valve and hose at the right valve cover. Disconnect all of the vacuum lines at the rear of the intake manifold and tag them for proper reinstallation.

7. Disconnect the wires at the spark plugs, and remove the wires from the brackets on the valve cover. Disconnect the high tension wire from the coil and remove the distributor cap and wires as an assembly.

8. Detach all of the distributor vacuum lines at the fuel charging unit/throttle body and vacuum control valve and tag them for proper installation. Remove the distributor and vacuum lines as an assembly.

9. Disconnect the accelerator linkage. Remove the speed control linkage bracket, if equipped.

10. Disconnect the fuel line at the fuel charging unit/throttle body.

11. Unfasten the wiring harness at the coil battery terminal, engine temperature sending unit, oil pressure sending until, and other connections as necessary. Disconnect the wiring harness from the clips at the left valve cover and position the harness out of the way.

12. Remove the coil and bracket assembly.

13. Remove the intake manifold attaching bolts, then lift the manifold and fuel charging unit/throttle body assembly out of the engine compartment. It may be necessary to pry the manifold away from the cylinder heads. Do not damage the gasket sealing surfaces.

To install:

14. Clean the mating surfaces of the intake manifold. Apply a ⅛ in. (3mm) bead of silicone RTV sealant at the points shown in the diagram.

➡Do not apply sealer to the waffle portions of the seals as the sealer will rupture the end seal material.

15. Position the new seals on the block and press the seal locating extensions into the holes in the mating surfaces.

16. Apply a ¹⁄₁₆ in. (1.6mm) bead of sealer to the outer end of each manifold seal for the full length of the seal (4 places).

As before, do not apply sealer to the waffle portion of the end seals.

➡This sealer sets in about 15 minutes, depending on brand, so work quickly but carefully. Do not drop any sealer into the manifold cavity. It may plug the oil gallery.

17. Position the manifold gasket onto the block and heads with the alignment notches under the dowels in the heads. Be sure the gasket holes align with the head holes.

18. Install the manifold and tighten the intake manifold retaining mounting bolts evenly in steps using the proper sequence. Install the remaining components in the reverse order of removal procedure. Start the the engine, make engine adjustments and check for leaks.

MULTI-PORT FUEL INJECTION

▶ See Figures 95 and 96

1. Discharge the fuel system pressure.
2. Disconnect the negative battery cable.
3. Remove the upper manifold and throttle body assembly.
4. Drain the cooling system.

✳✳CAUTION

When draining coolant, keep in mind that cats and dogs are attracted to ethylene glycol antifreeze, and could drink any that is left in an uncovered container or in puddles on the ground. This will prove fatal in sufficient quantity. Always drain the coolant into a sealable container. Coolant should be reused unless it is contaminated or several years old.

5. Remove the air inlet tube. Detach the electrical connectors at the air bypass valve, throttle position sensor and EGR position sensor.

6. Disconnect the throttle linkage at the throttle ball and the Automatic Overdrive (AOD) transmission linkage from the throttle body. Remove the bolts that secure the bracket to the intake manifold and position the bracket and cables out of the way.

7. Remove the distributor assembly, cap and wires.

8. Detach the electrical connectors at the engine, coolant temperature sensor and sending unit, at the air charge temperature sensor and at the knock sensor.

9. Disconnect the injector wiring harness from the main harness assembly. Remove the ground wire from the intake manifold stud. The ground wire must be installed at the same position it was removed from.

10. Disconnect the PCV system by disconnecting the hose from the fitting at the rear of the upper manifold.

11. Disconnect the fuel supply and return lines from the fuel rails.

12. Remove the two canister purge lines from the fittings at the throttle body.

13. Disconnect the EGR tube from the EGR valve by loosening the flange nut.

14. Remove the bolt from the upper intake support bracket to upper manifold. Remove the upper manifold retaining bolts and remove the upper intake manifold and throttle body as an assembly.

15. Remove the upper radiator hose from the thermostat housing. Remove the bypass hose. Remove the heater outlet hose at the intake manifold.

16. Remove the intake manifold mounting bolts and studs. Pay attention to the location of the bolts and studs for reinstallation. Remove the lower intake manifold assembly.

To install:

17. Clean and inspect all mounting surfaces of the upper and lower intake manifolds.

18. Apply a 1/16 in. (1.6mm) bead of RTV sealer to the ends of the manifold seal (the junction point of the seals and gaskets). Install the end seals and intake gaskets on the cylinder heads. The gaskets must interlock with the seal tabs.

19. Install locator bolts at opposite ends of each head and carefully lower the intake manifold into position. Install and tighten the mounting bolts evenly in steps using the proper sequence. Tighten to 23-25 ft. lbs. (31-34 Nm). Install the remaining components in the reverse order of removal procedure. Start the the engine, bleed the cooling system and check for leaks.

Combination Manifold

REMOVAL & INSTALLATION

▶ See Figure 97

➡ The combination manifold is equipped only on the L6 engines

1. Disconnect the negative battery cable.

2. Remove the air cleaner. Remove the carburetor linkage and kick down linkage from the engine.

3. Disconnect the fuel line from the carburetor and all vacuum lines from the manifolds. Tag vacuum lines before removing.

4. Unfasten the alternator wire connector, then remove the alternator mounting bolts and remove the alternator from the engine.

5. Disconnect the muffler inlet pipe from the manifold.

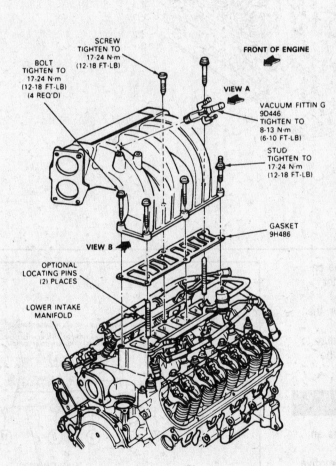
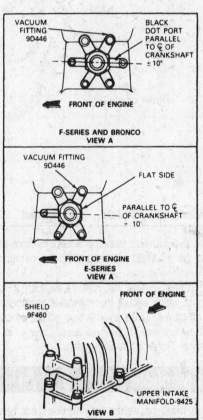

Fig. 95 Fuel injected engine, upper intake manifold assembly

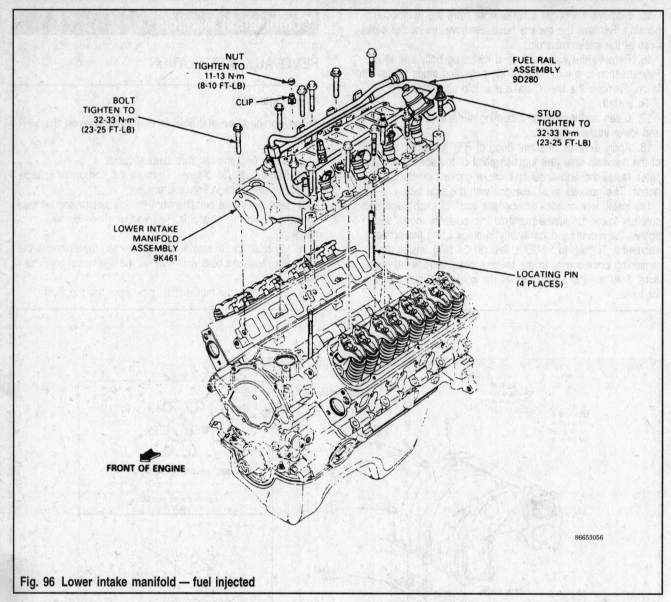

Fig. 96 Lower intake manifold — fuel injected

6. Remove the manifold retaining nuts/bolts from the engine. Remove the manifold assembly, with the carburetor attached.

7. To separate the manifolds, remove the carburetor, then remove the nuts which secure the manifolds together.

8. Clean all gasket areas and reverse above procedure to install using new gaskets. Tighten to specifications, in the proper sequence. Refer to the illustration.

Exhaust Manifold

→Although in most cases the engine does not have an exhaust manifold gasket installed by the factory, aftermarket gaskets are usually available from automotive parts stores. For 6-cylinder models, refer to the combination manifold procedure.

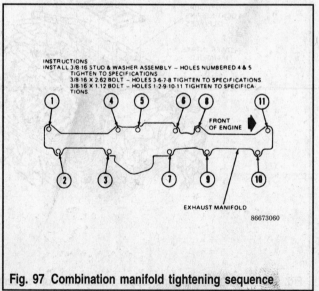

Fig. 97 Combination manifold tightening sequence

REMOVAL & INSTALLATION

4-Cylinder Engines

▶ See Figure 98

1. Remove the air cleaner.
2. Remove the heat shroud from the exhaust manifold. On turbocharged models, remove the turbocharger.
3. Place a block of wood under the exhaust pipe and disconnect the exhaust pipe from the exhaust manifold.
4. Remove the exhaust manifold attaching nuts and remove the manifold.

To Install:

5. Install a light coat of graphite grease on the exhaust manifold mating surface and position the manifold on the cylinder head.
6. Install the exhaust manifold attaching nuts and tighten them in the sequence shown in the illustration to 12 15 ft. lbs. (16-19 Nm).
7. Connect the exhaust pipe to the exhaust manifold and remove the wood support from under the pipe.
8. Install the air cleaner.

L6 Engines

Refer to the combination manifold procedure for details on the removal and installation of the exhaust manifold.

V6 and V8 Engines

▶ See Figures 99, 100, 101, 102, 103, 104, 105 and 106

1. Disconnect the negative battery cable.
2. If removing the right side exhaust manifold, remove the air cleaner and mounting hardware, as well as the heat stove, if equipped.
3. On 5.8L and 6.6L engines: if the left exhaust manifold is being removed, first drain the engine oil and remove the oil filter. On 4.2L and 5.0L engines, dipstick and tube moving or removal may be required. Remove any speed control brackets that interfere.

❋❋CAUTION

The EPA warns that prolonged contact with used engine oil may cause a number of skin disorders, including cancer! You should make every effort to minimize your exposure to used engine oil. Protective gloves should be worn when changing the oil. Wash your hands and any other exposed skin areas as soon as possible after exposure to used engine oil. Soap and water, or waterless hand cleaner should be used.

4. Disconnect the exhaust pipes from the manifolds.

➡On certain vehicles with automatic transmission and column shift, it may be necessary to disconnect the selector lever cross-shaft for clearance.

5. Disconnect the spark plug wires and remove the spark plugs and heat shields. Disconnect the EGR sensor (models so equipped), and heat control valve vacuum line (models so equipped).

➡On some engines the spark plug wire heat shields are removed with the manifold. Transmission dipstick tube and Thermactor® air tube removal may be required on certain models. Air tube removal is possible by cutting the tube clamp at the converter.

6. Remove the exhaust manifold attaching bolts and washers, and remove the manifold(s).

To install:

7. Inspect the manifold(s) for damaged gasket surfaces, cracks, or other defects.
8. Clean the mating surfaces of the manifold(s), cylinder head and muffler inlet pipe(s).
9. Install the manifold(s) in the reverse order of removal. Tighten the mounting bolts evenly (in steps). Refer to the torque specifications chart in this section. Start with the centermost bolt and work outward in both directions.

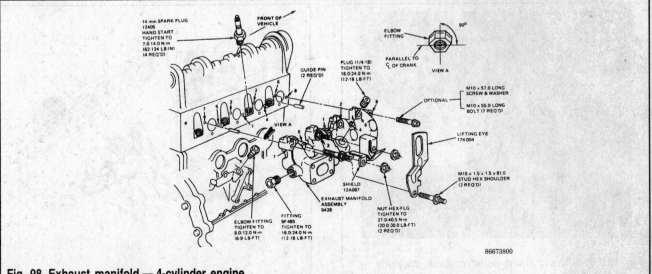

Fig. 98 Exhaust manifold — 4-cylinder engine

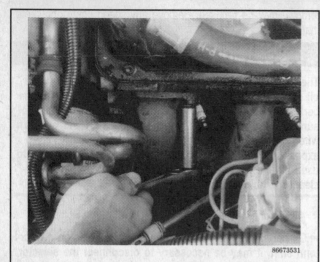

Fig. 99 Loosen and remove the exhaust manifold retaining nuts

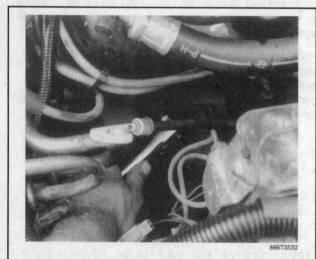

Fig. 100 On some engines, the oil dipstick may have to be moved out of the way or removed temporarily

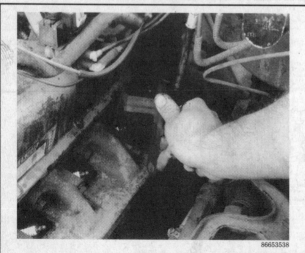

Fig. 101 With the retaining bolts removed, carefully move the dipstick tube out of the way

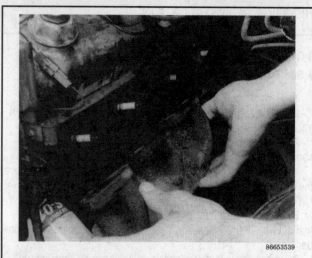

Fig. 102 Slide the exhaust manifold off the studs, and lift it out of the vehicle

Fig. 103 Clean all gasket material from the manifold and the cylinder head

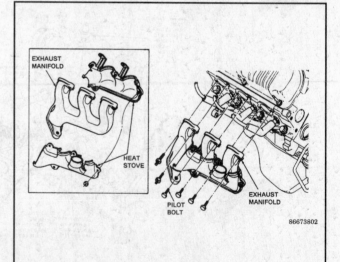

Fig. 104 Right side exhaust manifold — V6 engine

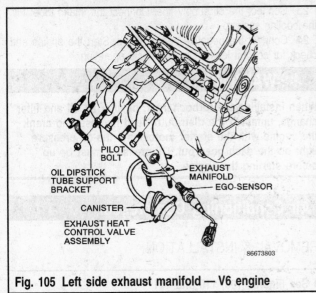

Fig. 105 Left side exhaust manifold — V6 engine

Turbocharger

REMOVAL & INSTALLATION

▶ See Figures 107 and 108

➡Before starting removal/service procedures, clean the area around the turbocharger with a non-caustic solution. Cover the openings of component connections to prevent the entry of dirt and foreign materials. Exercise care when handling the turbocharger not to nick, bend or in any way damage the compressor wheel blades.

1. Disconnect the negative battery cable.

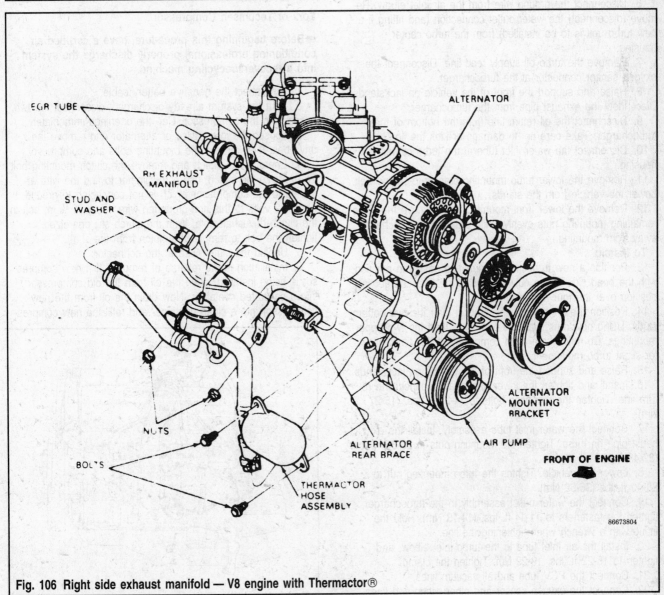

Fig. 106 Right side exhaust manifold — V8 engine with Thermactor®

2. Drain the cooling system.

✳✳CAUTION

When draining coolant, keep in mind that cats and dogs are attracted to ethylene glycol antifreeze, and could drink any that is left in an uncovered container or in puddles on the ground. This will prove fatal in sufficient quantity. Always drain the coolant into a sealable container. Coolant should be reused unless it is contaminated or several years old.

3. Loosen the upper clamp on the turbocharger inlet hose. Remove the two bolts mounting the throttle body discharge tube to the turbo.

4. Label for identification and location all vacuum hoses and tubes to the turbo and disconnect them.

5. Disconnect the PCV tube from the turbo air inlet elbow. Remove the throttle body discharge tube and hose as an assembly.

6. Disconnect the ground wire from the air inlet elbow. Remove (disconnect) the water outlet connection (and fitting if a new turbo unit is to be installed) from the turbo center housing.

7. Remove the turbo oil supply feed line. Disconnect the oxygen sensor connector at the turbocharger.

8. Raise and support the front of the vehicle on jackstands. Disconnect the exhaust pipe from the turbocharger.

9. Disconnect the oil return line from the bottom of the turbocharger. Take care not to damage or kink the line.

10. Disconnect the water inlet tube at the turbo center housing.

11. Remove the lower turbo mounting bracket-to-engine bolt. Lower the vehicle from the stands.

12. Remove the lower front mounting nut. Remove the three remaining mounting nuts evenly while sliding the turbocharger away from mounting.

To Install:

13. Position a new turbocharger mounting gasket in position with the bead side facing outward. Install the turbocharger in position over the four mounting studs.

14. Position the lower mounting bracket over the two bottom studs. Using new nuts, start the two lower then the two upper mountings. Do not tighten them completely at this time; allow for slight turbo movement.

15. Raise and support the front of the vehicle on jackstands.

16. Install and tighten the lower gasket and connect the return line. Tighten the mounting bolts to 14-21 ft. lbs. (18-27 Nm).

17. Connect the water inlet tube assembly. Install the exhaust pipe on turbo. Tighten the mounting nuts to 25-35 ft. lbs. (32-45 Nm).

18. Lower the vehicle. Tighten the turbo mounting nut to 28-40 ft. lbs (36-52 Nm).

19. Connect the water outlet assembly to the turbocharger, tighten the fasteners to 11-14 ft. lbs. (14-18 Nm). Hold the fitting with a wrench when tightening the line.

20. Install the air inlet tube to the turbo inlet elbow, and tighten to 15-22 ft. lbs. 19-29 Nm. Tighten the clamp.

21. Connect the PCV tube and all vacuum lines.

22. Connect the oxygen sensor and other wiring and lines.

23. Connect the oil supply line. Connect the intake tube. Fill the cooling system.

24. Connect the negative battery cable. Start the engine and check for coolant leaks. Check vehicle operation.

✳✳WARNING

When installing the turbocharger, or after an oil and filter change, unfasten the distributor feed harness and crank the engine with the starter motor until the oil pressure light on the dash goes out. Oil pressure must be up before starting the engine.

Air Conditioning Compressor

REMOVAL & INSTALLATION

▶ See Figures 109, 110 and 111

York or Tecumseh Compressor

➡Before beginning this procedure, have a certified air conditioning professional properly discharge the system into a recovery/recycling machine.

1. Disconnect the negative battery cable.

2. With the system already discharged, disconnect the two hoses from the compressor. Cap the openings immediately.

3. Loosen the idler pulley or alternator and remove the drive belt, then remove the mounting bolts and compressor.

4. Energize the clutch and remove the clutch mounting bolt. To energize the clutch, use a multimeter to find the wire attached to the compressor which is not connected to ground. Apply 12 volts to this non-grounded wire. Install a ⅝ in. bolt in the clutch driveshaft hole. With the clutch still energized, tighten the bolt to remove the clutch from the shaft.

5. Unplug the clutch wire at the connector.

6. Installation is the reverse of removal. If a new compressor is being installed, drain the oil from the old compressor into a calibrated container. Now drain the oil from the new compressor into a clean container and refill the new compres-

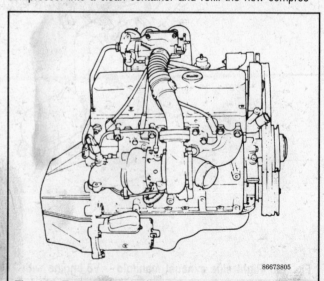

Fig. 107 Turbocharger placement — 2.3L engine

86673805

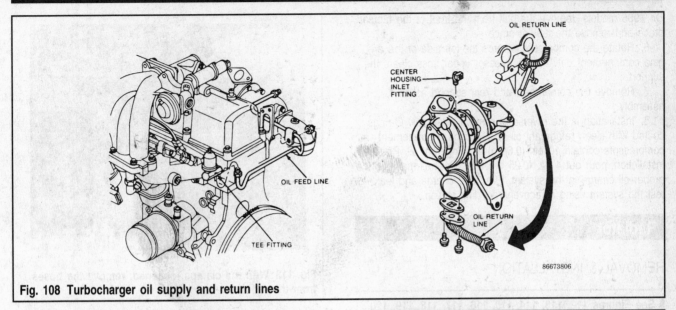

Fig. 108 Turbocharger oil supply and return lines

sor with the same amount of oil that was in the old one. Install the clutch and bolt finger-tight. Install the compressor on the mounting bracket and install those bolts finger-tight as well. Connect the clutch wire and energize the clutch. Tighten the clutch bolt to 23 ft. lbs. (31 Nm). Tighten the compressor mounting bolts to 30 ft. lbs. (41 Nm). Evacuate, charge and leak test the system using a recovery/recycling station. See Section 1 for procedures.

FS-6 Axial Compressor

➡Before beginning this procedure, have a certified air conditioning professional properly discharge the system into a recovery/recycling machine.

1. Disconnect the negative battery cable.
2. Disconnect the two refrigerant lines from the compressor. Cap the openings immediately.
3. Remove the compressor belt
4. Unplug the clutch wire at the connector.
5. Remove the two nuts from the rear support bracket. Remove the three bolts from the front bosses on the bracket.

Fig. 110 With the necessary belts removed, loosen and remove the bolts which secure the compressor to the bracket

Fig. 109 Unfasten the compressor wire harness

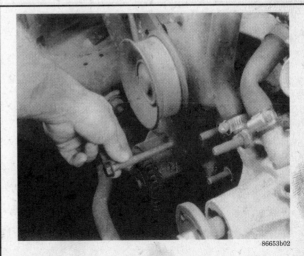

Fig. 111 Some bolts may be hidden near the bottom of the bracket

On 1985 models, remove the bolt from the front of the tubular brace and remove the tubular brace.

6. Rotate the compressor towards the left side of the engine compartment until the compressor upper boss clears the support.

7. Remove the compressor and rear support as an assembly.

8. Installation is the reverse of removal. Use new O-rings coated with clean refrigerant oil at all fittings. Replacement compressors contain 10 oz. (0.64 g) of refrigerant oil. Prior to installation, pour out 4 oz. (0.25 g) of oil. This will maintain the proper oil charge in the system. Evacuate, charge and leak test the system using a recovery/recycling station..

Radiator

REMOVAL & INSTALLATION

▶ See Figures 112, 113, 114, 115, 116, 117, 118, 119, 120 and 121

1. Drain the cooling system into a container.

❊❊CAUTION

When draining coolant, keep in mind that cats and dogs are attracted to ethylene glycol antifreeze, and could drink any that is left in an uncovered container or in puddles on the ground. This will prove fatal in sufficient quantity. Always drain the coolant into a sealable container. Coolant should be reused unless it is contaminated or several years old.

2. Disconnect the upper, lower and overflow hoses at the radiator.

3. If necessary, remove the retaining hardware securing the air filter intake hose, then remove the intake hose and place aside.

4. On automatic transmission equipped cars, disconnect and plug the fluid cooler lines at the radiator.

Fig. 113 With the clamps loosened, remove the hoses from the radiator

Fig. 114 Use a flare wrench to loosen the automatic transmission cooler lines

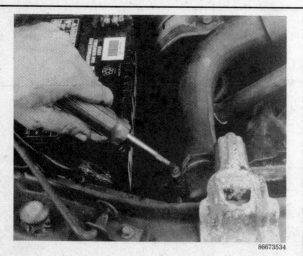

Fig. 112 Loosen the clamps to the upper and lower radiator hoses

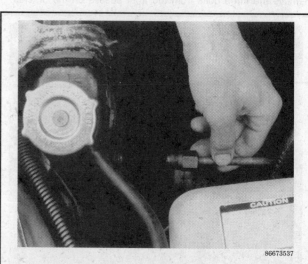

Fig. 115 Carefully move or reposition the line back away from the radiator

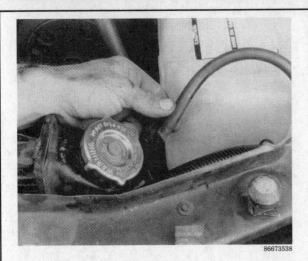

Fig. 116 If equipped with a reservoir tank, disconnect the overflow line at the radiator

Fig. 118 Slide the retaining clips off

5. If equipped with a radiator shroud, remove the shroud mounting bolts and position the radiator shroud out of the way.

6. If equipped with side mounting bolts, remove them at this time.

7. If equipped with top mount brackets, remove the retaining bolts securing the brackets. Check and make sure all retaining hardware has been removed.

8. If the air conditioner condenser is attached to the radiator, remove the retaining bolts and position the condenser out of the way. DO NOT disconnect the refrigerant lines.

9. Lift out the radiator. Be careful not to dent or bend any of the cooling fins on the radiator body.

To install:

10. If a new radiator is to be installed, transfer the petcock from the old radiator to the new one. On cars equipped with automatic transmissions, transfer the fluid cooler line fittings from the old radiator to the new unit.

11. Position the radiator into the vehicle and install, but do not tighten, the radiator support bolts.

12. On cars equipped with automatic transmissions, connect the fluid cooler lines. Then, tighten the radiator support bolts.

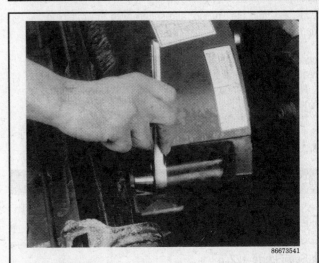

Fig. 119 Remove the bolts securing the fan shroud to the radiator

Fig. 117 Loosen the bolts securing the radiator retaining brackets

Fig. 120 Once the retaining bolts are removed, lift the fan shroud out of the engine compartment

Fig. 121 Lift the radiator out, being careful not to bend any of the cooling fins

13. Position the shroud, and secure with the retaining hardware.

14. Connect the radiator hoses. If the hoses are in poor condition, replace them. Close the radiator petcock, if not already done. Fill the cooling system.

15. Start the engine and bring it to operating temperature. Check for leaks.

16. On cars equipped with automatic transmissions, check the cooler lines for leaks and interference. Check the transmission fluid level.

Belt Driven Cooling Fan

REMOVAL & INSTALLATION

▶ See Figure 122

1. Remove the fan shroud attaching screws.

2. Loosen the fan belt(s). Remove bolts and washers attaching the fan drive clutch to the water pump hub. Remove the fan drive clutch and fan as an assembly, along with the shroud.

3. Remove the attaching bolts and washers to separate the fan assembly from the fan drive clutch.

To install:

4. Position the fan assembly on the drive clutch. Install the bolts and washers and tighten to 12-18 ft. lbs. (16-23 Nm).

5. Position the fan drive clutch, fan assembly and fan shroud, and fasten to the water pump hub. Install and tighten the clutch attaching bolts to 12-18 ft. lbs. (16-23 Nm) for 1979-83 engines, or to 15-22 ft. lbs. (19-29 Nm) for 1984-85 engines.

6. Install the fan belt(s) and adjust to the proper tension.

7. Install the fan shroud and adjust for equal fan-to-shroud clearance. Install and tighten the fan shroud screws.

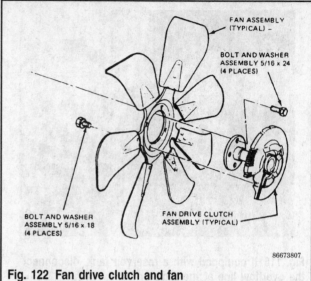

Fig. 122 Fan drive clutch and fan

Electric Cooling Fan

REMOVAL & INSTALLATION

▶ See Figure 123

Various models, are equipped with a bracket-mounted electric cooling fan that replaces the conventional water pump mounted fan.

Operation of the fan motor is dependent on engine coolant temperature and air conditioner compressor clutch engagement. The fan will run only when the coolant temperature is approximately 180°F (82°C) or higher, or when the compressor clutch is engaged. The fan, motor and mount can be removed as an assembly after unfastening the wiring harnesses and mounting bolts.

✱✱CAUTION

The cooling fan is automatic and may come on at any time without warning even if the ignition is switched OFF. To avoid possible injury, always disconnect the negative battery cable when working near the electric cooling fan.

1. Disconnect the negative battery cable.

2. Remove the fan wiring harness from the clip.

3. Unplug the harness at the fan motor connector.

4. Remove the mounting bracket attaching screws and remove the fan assembly from the vehicle.

5. Remove the retaining clip from the end of the motor shaft and remove the fan.

6. Installation is the reverse of removal procedure.

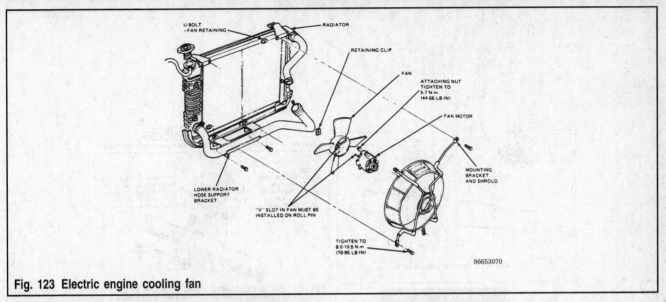

Fig. 123 Electric engine cooling fan

Air Conditioning Condenser

REMOVAL & INSTALLATION

1971-78 Models

▶ See Figure 124

1. Have a certified professional discharge the air conditioning system system using a recovery/recycling machine.
2. Disconnect the negative battery cable.
3. With the A/C system properly discharged, disconnect the refrigerant lines at the condenser and cap all openings immediately.
4. Remove the upper radiator mounts and tilt the radiator rearward, toward the engine.
5. Remove the four condenser mounting screws and lift out the condenser.
6. Installation is the reverse of removal. Always use new O-rings coated with clean refrigerant oil at the pipe fittings.
7. Evacuate, charge and leak test the system using an approved recovery/recycling station

1979-81 Models

▶ See Figure 124

1. Have a certified professional discharge the air conditioning system using a recovery/recycling machine.
2. Disconnect the negative battery cable.
3. Remove the 6 attaching screws and remove the grille.
4. Move the ambient cut-off switch away from the front of the radiator and condenser.
5. Remove the battery.
6. Disconnect the refrigerant lines at the condenser and cap all openings immediately.

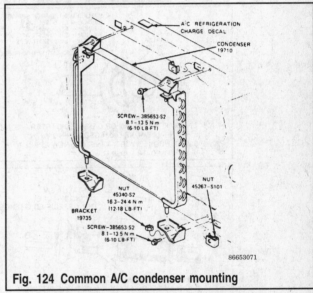

Fig. 124 Common A/C condenser mounting

7. Remove the bolts securing the condenser to the supports and remove the condenser.
8. Installation is the reverse of removal. Always use new O-rings coated with clean refrigerant oil at the pipe fittings.
9. Evacuate, charge and leak test the system using an approved recovery/recycling station. See Section 1 for details.

1982-1985 Models

▶ See Figure 125

➡Whenever the condenser assembly is replaced, it will be necessary to replace the suction accumulator/drier as well.

1. Have a certified professional discharge the air conditioning system using an approved recovery/recycling machine
2. Disconnect the negative battery cable.
3. Remove the battery from the vehicle.

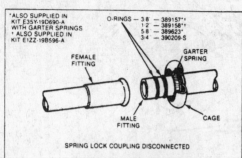

*ALSO SUPPLIED IN
KIT E35Y-19D690-A
WITH GARTER SPRINGS
† ALSO SUPPLIED IN
KIT E1ZZ-19B596-A

O-RINGS — 3/8 — 389157*†
1/2 — 389158*†
5/8 — 389623*
3/4 — 390209-S

FEMALE FITTING
GARTER SPRING
MALE FITTING
CAGE

SPRING LOCK COUPLING DISCONNECTED

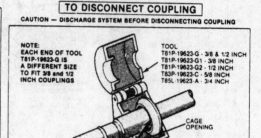

TO DISCONNECT COUPLING

CAUTION — DISCHARGE SYSTEM BEFORE DISCONNECTING COUPLING

NOTE:
EACH END OF TOOL
T81P-19623-G IS
A DIFFERENT SIZE
TO FIT 3/8 and 1/2
INCH COUPLINGS

TOOL
T81P-19623-G - 3/8 & 1/2 INCH
T81P-19623-G1 - 3/8 INCH
T81P-19623-G2 - 1/2 INCH
T83P-19623-C - 5/8 INCH
T85L-19623-A - 3/4 INCH

CAGE OPENING

① FIT TOOL TO COUPLING SO THAT TOOL CAN ENTER CAGE OPENING TO RELEASE THE GARTER SPRING.

TO CONNECT COUPLING

GARTER SPRING

REPLACEMENT GARTER SPRINGS
3/8 INCH — E1ZZ-19E576-A*
1/2 INCH — E1ZZ-19E576-B*
5/8 INCH — E35Y-19E576-A*
3/4 INCH — E69Z-19E576-A
*ALSO AVAILABLE IN
E35Y-19D690-A KIT WITH O-RINGS

① CHECK FOR MISSING OR DAMAGED GARTER SPRING — REMOVE DAMAGED SPRING WITH SMALL HOOKED WIRE — INSTALL NEW SPRING IF DAMAGED OR MISSING.

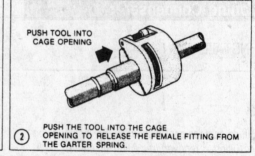

PUSH TOOL INTO CAGE OPENING

② PUSH THE TOOL INTO THE CAGE OPENING TO RELEASE THE FEMALE FITTING FROM THE GARTER SPRING.

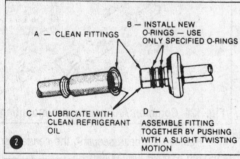

A — CLEAN FITTINGS

B — INSTALL NEW O-RINGS — USE ONLY SPECIFIED O-RINGS

C — LUBRICATE WITH CLEAN REFRIGERANT OIL

D — ASSEMBLE FITTING TOGETHER BY PUSHING WITH A SLIGHT TWISTING MOTION

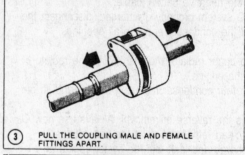

③ PULL THE COUPLING MALE AND FEMALE FITTINGS APART.

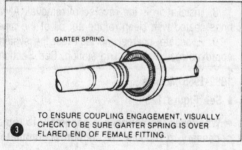

GARTER SPRING

③ TO ENSURE COUPLING ENGAGEMENT, VISUALLY CHECK TO BE SURE GARTER SPRING IS OVER FLARED END OF FEMALE FITTING.

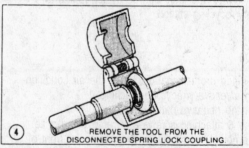

④ REMOVE THE TOOL FROM THE DISCONNECTED SPRING LOCK COUPLING.

86653072

Fig. 125 1982-85 A/C coupling connecting and disconnecting procedures

4. Disconnect the refrigerant lines at the condenser and cap all openings immediately.

➡The fittings spring-lock couplings require the use of tool T81P-19623-G or equivalent. The larger opening end of this tool is for ½ in. discharge lines; the smaller end for ⅜ in. liquid lines. To operate the tool, close the tool and push the tool into the open side of the cage. This expands the garter spring and release the female fitting. If the tool is not inserted straight, the garter spring will cock and will not release. After the garter spring is released, pull the fittings apart.

5. Remove the 4 bolts securing the condenser to the supports and remove the condenser.

6. Installation is the reverse of removal. Always use new O-rings coated with clean refrigerant oil at the pipe fittings. Check to ensure that the garter spring is in the cage of the male fitting, make sure the fittings are clean. Push the male and female fittings together until the garter springs snaps into place over the female fitting. Refer to the illustration in this section. Evacuate, charge and leak test the system using an approved recovery/recycling station. See Section 1.

Water Pump

REMOVAL & INSTALLATION

▶ **See Figures 126, 127, 128, 129, 130, 131, 132, 133 and 134**

1. Disconnect the negative battery cable.
2. Raise and safely support the vehicle on jackstands.
3. Drain the cooling system into a container.

✳✳CAUTION

When draining coolant, keep in mind that cats and dogs are attracted to ethylene glycol antifreeze, and could drink any that is left in an uncovered container or in puddles on the ground. This will prove fatal in sufficient quantity. Always drain the coolant into a sealable container. Coolant should be reused unless it is contaminated or several years old.

➡In some cases, it is easier to remove the fan shroud and/or the radiator

4. On vehicles equipped with belt driven radiator fans, loosen and remove the bolts securing the fan to the water pump pulley. With the bolts removed, lift the fan out of the engine compartment and place aside.

5. On 4-cylinder engines, remove the cam belt outer cover.

6. If the car is equipped with an electric fan, remove the fan as an assembly for working clearance. Loosen the water pump pulley bolts.

7. Remove any accessory belts. This could include power steering, air conditioning, Thermactor® and alternator. Because some vehicles use standard V-belts, while others use serpentine belts, or a combination of the two types, mark the belt for

Fig. 126 Loosen and remove the fan retaining bolts. With the belt installed, you should be able to loosen the bolts without too much effort

Fig. 127 Remove the fan blade and clutch assembly from the vehicle

ease of reinstallation. Belts may be loosened by unfastening the adjusting bolts or belt tensioners.

8. Remove the water pump pulley from the pump shaft. Since the bolts were removed earlier, the pulley should come off without any problem.

9. If the radiator is installed in the vehicle, disconnect the lower and upper radiator hose, along with the heater hose and bypass hose from the water pump.

10. On cars equipped with a water pump mounted alternator, loosen the alternator mounting bolts, and remove the alternator adjusting arm bracket from the water pump. If interference is encountered, remove the air pump pulley and pivot bolts. Remove the air pump adjusting bracket. Swing the upper bracket aside. Detach the air conditioner compressor and lay it aside. Do not disconnect any of the air conditioning lines. Remove any accessory mounting brackets from the water pump.

11. Remove the water pump retaining bolts and remove the pump from the engine. In many cases, a plastic-faced hammer

Fig. 128 With the belt(s) removed, pull the water pump pulley off

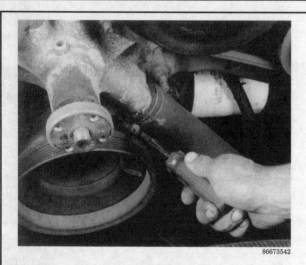

Fig. 129 Loosen and remove the hoses attached to the water pump

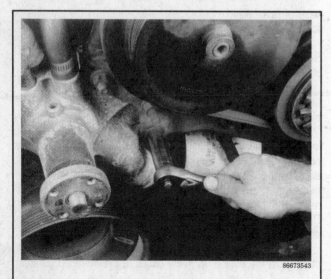

Fig. 130 Loosen the retaining bolts or studs

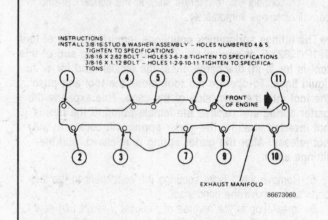

INSTRUCTIONS
INSTALL 3/8-16 STUD & WASHER ASSEMBLY – HOLES NUMBERED 4 & 5.
TIGHTEN TO SPECIFICATIONS
3/8-16 X 2.62 BOLT – HOLES 3-6-7-8 TIGHTEN TO SPECIFICATIONS
3/8-16 X 1.12 BOLT – HOLES 1-2-9-10-11 TIGHTEN TO SPECIFICATIONS

FRONT OF ENGINE

EXHAUST MANIFOLD

Fig. 131 Remove the retaining hardware. Remember the location of each bolt and stud. These pieces are not interchangeable

Fig. 132 Do not be surprised if excess coolant spills from one or more of the mounting holes

may be used to tap the water pump housing lightly to free the pump from the gasket.

➡Some engines originally used a one-piece gasket for the cylinder front cover and the water pump. Trim away the old gasket at the edge of the cylinder cover and replace with a new service gasket.

To install:

12. Clean any gasket material from the pump mounting surface on the engine block. If using the original water pump, clean any gasket material from it as well. On engines equipped with a water pump backing plate, remove the plate and clean the gasket mounting surfaces. Install a new gasket to the backing plate using sealant only if recommended by the gasket and/or water pump manufacturer.

13. If replacing the water pump, and the original was equipped with a threaded heater hose fitting, remove the heater hose fitting from the original pump, and coat the fitting threads with sealer. Install it on the new pump being careful not to crossthread during the installation.

Fig. 133 With the water pump retaining bolts removed, the pump can be lifted out of the engine compartment

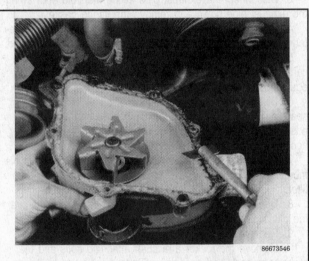

Fig. 134 If you are reinstalling the original water pump, remove any old gasket material and use a new gasket

14. If recommended by the gasket or water pump manufacturer, coat both sides of the new gasket with a sealer, then install to the water pump, aligning the holes on the gasket with the holes on the pump. Install the pump to the engine block, reversing the procedure. Tighten the attaching bolts diagonally, in rotation, to the following:
- 12-15 ft. lbs. (16-20 Nm) for 3.3L, 4.1L, 4.2L, 5.0L, 5.8L engines
- 12-15 lbs. (16-20 Nm) for 2.3L, 3.8L and 7.0L, 7.5L engines
- 20-25 ft. lbs. (27-34 Nm) for 6.6L engines

15. Connect the lower and upper radiator hose, as well as the heater hose, and water pump bypass hose at the water pump.

16. Install the cam belt cover, if removed from the 4-cylinder engine.

17. Install all accessory brackets attaching to the water pump. Install the pump pulley on the pump shaft. Fill the cooling system.

18. Lower the vehicle. Start the engine and check for leaks. Finally, when the engine is cool, check the fluid level and add coolant if needed.

Cylinder Head

REMOVAL & INSTALLATION

➡On cars with air conditioning, remove the mounting bolts and the drive belt, and position the compressor out of the way. Remove the compressor upper mounting bracket from the cylinder head.

✳✳CAUTION

If the compressor refrigerant lines do not have enough slack to permit repositioning of the compressor without first disconnecting the refrigerant lines, the air conditioning system will have to be evacuated using a recovery/recycling machine.

4-Cylinder Engines
▶ See Figure 135

➡Set the engine at TDC position for No. 1 piston, if possible, prior to head removal.

1. Drain the cooling system.

✳✳CAUTION

When draining coolant, keep in mind that cats and dogs are attracted to ethylene glycol antifreeze, and could drink any that is left in an uncovered container or in puddles on the ground. This will prove fatal in sufficient quantity. Always drain the coolant into a sealable container. Coolant should be reused unless it is contaminated or several years old.

2. Remove the air cleaner assembly from carburetor-equipped engines. Disconnect the negative battery cable.

3. Remove the valve cover. Note the location of the valve cover attaching screws that have rubber grommets.

4. Remove the intake and exhaust manifolds from the head. See the procedures for intake manifold, exhaust manifold and, if applicable, turbocharger removal.

5. Remove the camshaft drive belt cover. Note the location of the belt cover attaching screws that have rubber grommets.

6. Loosen the drive belt tensioner and remove the belt.

7. Remove the water outlet elbow from the cylinder head with the hose attached.

8. Remove the cylinder head attaching bolts.

9. Remove the cylinder head from the engine.

10. Clean all gasket material and carbon from the top of the cylinder block and pistons and from the bottom of the cylinder head.

11. Position a new cylinder head gasket on the engine. Rotate the camshaft so that the head locating pin is at the five o'clock position to avoid damage to the valves and pistons.

➡If you encounter difficulty in positioning the cylinder head on the engine block, it may be necessary to install guide studs in the block to correctly align the head and the block. To fabricate guide studs, obtain two new cylinder head bolts and cut their heads off with a hacksaw. Loosely install the bolts in the holes in the engine block which correspond with cylinder head bolt holes Nos. 3 and 4, as identified in the cylinder head bolt tightening sequence illustration. Then, install the head gasket and cylinder head over the bolts. Install the cylinder head attaching bolts, replacing the studs with the original head bolts.

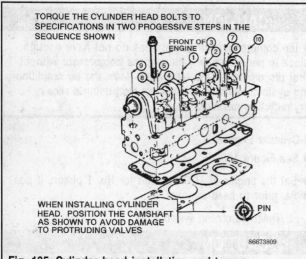

Fig. 135 Cylinder head installation and torque sequence — 4-cylinder engine

12. Using a torque wrench, tighten the cylinder head bolts in two steps. First tighten them to 50-60 ft. lbs. (65-78 Nm), then tighten them to 80-90 ft. lbs. (104-117 Nm).

13. Install the camshaft drive belt.

14. Install the camshaft drive belt cover and its attaching bolts. Make sure the rubber grommets are installed on the bolts. Tighten the bolts to 6-13 ft. lbs. (8-17 Nm).

15. Install the water outlet elbow and a new gasket on the engine and tighten the attaching bolts to 12-15 ft. lbs. (16-20 Nm).

16. Install the intake and exhaust manifolds. See the procedures for intake and exhaust manifold installation.

17. Install the valve cover and, if removed, the air cleaner assembly.

18. Connect the negative battery cable and fill the cooling system.

L6 Engines

▶ See Figures 136 and 137

✸✸CAUTION

When draining coolant, keep in mind that cats and dogs are attracted to ethylene glycol antifreeze, and could drink any that is left in an uncovered container or in puddles on the ground. This will prove fatal in sufficient quantity. Always drain the coolant into a sealable container. Coolant should be reused unless it is contaminated or several years old.

1. Drain the cooling system, remove the air cleaner assembly and disconnect the negative battery cable.

2. If equipped with air conditioning, remove the mounting bolts and the drive belt, and position the compressor out of the way of the cylinder head. Remove the compressor upper mounting bracket from the cylinder head.

➡If the compressor refrigerant lines do not have enough slack to permit repositioning of the compressor without first disconnecting the refrigerant lines, the air conditioning system will have to be discharged and evacuated using a recovery/recycling machine. Under no circumstances should an untrained person attempt to disconnect the air conditioning refrigerant lines.

3. Disconnect the exhaust pipe at the manifold end, swing the exhaust pipe down and remove the flange gasket.

4. Disconnect the fuel and vacuum lines from the carburetor. Disconnect the intake manifold line at the intake manifold.

5. Disconnect the accelerator and retracting spring at the carburetor. Disconnect the transmission kickdown linkage, if equipped.

6. Disconnect the carburetor spacer outlet line at the spacer. Disconnect the radiator upper hose and the heater hose at the water outlet elbow. Disconnect the radiator lower hose and the heater hose at the water pump.

7. Disconnect the distributor vacuum control line at the distributor. Disconnect the gas filter line on the inlet side of the filter.

8. Disconnect and label the spark plug wires and remove the plugs. Disconnect the temperature sending unit wire.

9. Remove the rocker arm (valve) cover.

10. Remove the rocker arm shaft attaching bolts and the rocker arm and shaft assembly. Remove the valve pushrods, keeping them in order for installation in their original positions.

11. Remove the remaining cylinder head bolts and lift off the cylinder head. Do not pry under the cylinder head as damage to the mating surfaces can easily occur. To help in installation of the cylinder head, you can use a pair of 6 in. x ⁷/₁₆-14 bolts with their heads cut off and the upper portion slightly tapered and slotted (for installation and removal with a screwdriver). These will reduce the possibility of damage during head replacement.

12. Clean the cylinder head and block surfaces. Be sure of flatness and no surface damage.

13. Apply cylinder head gasket sealer to both sides of the new gasket and slide the gasket down over the two guide studs in the cylinder block.

✸✸WARNING

Apply gasket sealer only to steel shim head gaskets. Steel/asbestos composite head gaskets are to be installed without any sealer.

14. Carefully lower the cylinder head over the guide studs. Place the exhaust pipe flange on the manifold studs, using a new gasket.

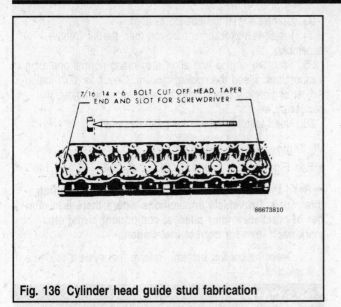

Fig. 136 Cylinder head guide stud fabrication

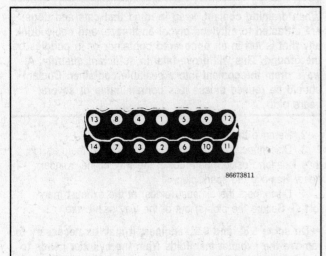

Fig. 137 Cylinder head torque sequence — 6-cylinder engine

15. Coat the threads of the end bolts for the right side of the cylinder head with a small amount of water-resistant sealer. Install, but do not tighten, two head bolts at opposite ends to hold the head gasket in place. Remove the guide studs and install the remaining bolts.

16. Cylinder head torquing should proceed in three steps and in the prescribed order. Tighten them first to 50-55 ft. lbs. (65-71 Nm), then give them a second tightening to 60-65 ft. lbs. (78-84 Nm). The final step is to 70-75 ft. lbs. (91-97 Nm), at which they should remain undisturbed.

17. Lubricate both ends of the pushrods and install them in their original locations.

18. Apply lubricant to the rocker arm pads and the valve stem tips and position the rocker arm shaft assembly on the head. Be sure the oil holes in the shaft are in a down position.

19. Tighten all the rocker shaft retaining bolts to 30-35 ft. lbs. (39-45 Nm), and check that there are no tight valve adjustments.

20. Connect the exhaust pipe.

21. Reconnect the heater and radiator hoses.

22. Position the distributor vacuum line, the carburetor gas line and the intake manifold vacuum line on the engine. Fasten them to their respective connections.

23. Connect the accelerator rod and retracting spring. Connect the choke control cable and adjust the choke. Connect the transmission kickdown linkage.

24. Reconnect the vacuum line at the distributor. Connect the fuel inlet line at the fuel filter and the intake manifold vacuum line at the vacuum pump.

25. Lightly lubricate the spark plug threads and install them. Connect spark plug wires and be sure the wires are all the way down in their sockets. Connect the coolant temperature sending unit wire.

26. If equipped with air conditioning, install the compressor and mounting bracket. Install the drive belt and adjust to proper tension.

27. Connect the negative battery cable.

28. Fill the cooling system. Run the engine to stabilize all engine part temperatures.

29. Adjust engine idle speed and idle fuel air adjustment.

30. Coat one side of a new rocker arm cover gasket with oil-resistant sealer. Lay the treated side of the gasket on the cover and install the cover. Be sure the gasket seals evenly all around the cylinder head.

31. Install the air cleaner assembly.

V6 Engines
▶ See Figure 138

1. Disconnect the negative battery cable.

2. Drain coolant into a container. Remove the air cleaner assembly.

3. Unfasten the negative battery cable from the cylinder head.

> ※※**CAUTION**
>
> **When draining coolant, keep in mind that cats and dogs are attracted to ethylene glycol antifreeze, and could drink any that is left in an uncovered container or in puddles on the ground. This will prove fatal in sufficient quantity. Always drain the coolant into a sealable container. Coolant should be reused unless it is contaminated or several years old.**

4. Disconnect the exhaust pipe at the manifold. Use wire to position exhaust system out of the way.

5. Unfasten the accelerator retracting spring, choke control cable and accelerator rod at the carburetor.

6. Disconnect the fuel line and distributor control vacuum line at the carburetor.

7. Remove the coolant tubes from the carburetor spacer. Disconnect the coolant and heater hoses.

8. Disconnect the distributor control vacuum line at the distributor and fuel inlet line at the filter. Remove all the lines as an assembly.

9. On an engine equipped with positive crankcase ventilation, disconnect the emission exhaust tube.

10. Disconnect and mark the spark plug wires at the plugs and the small wire from the temperature sending unit. On an engine equipped with a Thermactor® exhaust emission control system, disconnect the air pump hose at the air manifold assembly. Unscrew the tube nuts and remove the air manifold.

Disconnect the anti-backfire valve air and vacuum lines at the intake manifold. On a car equipped with power brakes, disconnect the brake booster vacuum line at the intake manifold.

11. Remove the rocker arm cover.

12. Loosen the rocker arm nut so that the rocker arm can be rotated to one side. Remove the pushrods and keep them in sequence.

13. Remove one cylinder head bolt from each end of the engine and install two 7/16 in. guide studs.

➡Guide studs can be purchased from an automotive tool supplier, or made by cutting the head off of several old head bolts.

14. Remove the remaining cylinder head bolts, then remove the cylinder head.

To install:

15. Prior to installation, clean the head and block surfaces of old gasket material.

16. Apply sealer to both sides of the head gasket. Position the gasket over the guide studs or dowel pins.

➡Apply gasket sealer only to steel shim head gaskets. Steel/asbestos composite head gaskets are to be installed without any sealer.

17. Install a new sealing gasket to the exhaust pipe flange.

18. Lift the cylinder head over the guide studs and slide it carefully into place while guiding the exhaust manifold studs into the exhaust pipe flange.

19. Coat cylinder head attaching bolts with water resistant sealer and install (but do not tighten), the head bolts.

20. Tighten the head, according to the illustrated sequence in three progressive steps. Tighten the bolts to 50-55 ft. lbs. (68-74 Nm), then 60-65 ft. lbs. (81-88 Nm) and finally to 75 ft. lbs. (102 Nm).

21. Lubricate both ends of the pushrods with oil and insert them in their original bores.

22. Lubricate the valve stem tips and rocker arm pads with oil.

23. Position the rocker arms and tighten the nuts enough to hold the pushrods in position.

24. Perform a preliminary cold valve lash adjustment. Refer to the procedure in Section 2.

25. Install exhaust pipe-to-manifold nuts and lockwashers. Tighten to 17-22 ft. lbs. (23-30 Nm)

26. Connect the radiator and heater hoses. Fasten the coolant tubes at the carburetor spacer.

27. Connect the distributor vacuum line and the carburetor fuel line. Connect battery cable at the cylinder head.

28. On engines equipped with positive crankcase ventilation, clean the components thoroughly and install.

29. On engines equipped with a Thermactor® exhaust emission control system, install the air manifold assembly on the cylinder head, the air pump outlet hose to the air manifold, and the anti-backfire valve, air and vacuum lines to the intake manifold.

30. Connect the accelerator rod pull-back spring. Fasten the choke control cable and the accelerator rod at the carburetor.

31. Attach the distributor control vacuum line at distributor. Connect carburetor fuel line at fuel filter.

32. Fasten the temperature sending unit wire at the sending unit. Connect spark plug wires.

33. Completely fill the cooling system.

34. Install valve/rocker arm cover, then the air cleaner assembly.

35. Start the engine and allow it to reach normal operating temperature. Bleed the cooling system. Check for fluid leaks. Adjust engine idle speed. check valve lash and adjust, if necessary.

36. Road test the vehicle for proper operation.

V8 Engines

▶ See Figures 139, 140, 141, 142, 143, 144, 145 and 146

➡Read the complete service procedure before starting this repair. On vehicle applications where there is a number of brackets and/or pulleys, component parts, etc., mark each item for correct installation.

1. Drain the cooling system. Relieve fuel system pressure if fuel injected.

✳✳CAUTION

When draining coolant, keep in mind that cats and dogs are attracted to ethylene glycol antifreeze, and could drink any that is left in an uncovered container or in puddles on the ground. This will prove fatal in sufficient quantity. Always drain the coolant into a sealable container. Coolant should be reused unless it is contaminated or several years old.

2. Remove the intake manifold.

3. Disconnect the spark plug wires, marking them as to their location Position them out of the way of the cylinder head. Remove the spark plugs.

4. Disconnect the exhaust (pipes) at the exhaust manifold(s). Secure the pipe(s) out of the way using wire.

➡On some 5.8L and 6.6L engines, it may be necessary to remove the exhaust manifolds from the cylinder heads to gain access to the lower head bolts.

5. Disconnect the negative battery cable at the cylinder head (if applicable).

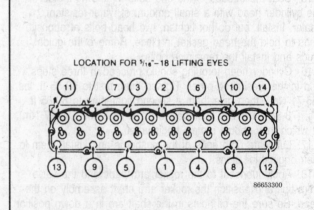

Fig. 138 Cylinder head bolt torque sequence — 6-cylinder engine

6. On cars with air conditioning, position the compressor out of the way of the cylinder head. Remove the compressor upper mounting bracket from the cylinder head.

7. In order to remove the left cylinder head on cars equipped with power steering, it may be necessary to remove the steering pump and bracket. Remove the drive belt, then secure the steering pump out of the way.

8. In order to remove the left cylinder head on a car equipped with Thermactor® exhaust emission control system, disconnect the hose from the air manifold on the left cylinder head.

9. In order to remove the right cylinder head, it may be necessary to remove the alternator mounting bracket bolt and spacer, the ignition coil, and the air cleaner inlet duct from the right cylinder head.

10. If the right cylinder head is to be removed on a car equipped with a Thermactor® exhaust emission control system, remove the Thermactor® air pump and its mounting bracket. Disconnect the hose from the air manifold on the right cylinder head.

11. On 7.0L engines, unbolt the rocker arm shafts from front to back, two turns at a time, and remove the rocker shaft and arm assembly. On all other V8 engines, loosen the rocker arm stud nuts or mounting bolts enough to rotate the rocker arms to one side in order to facilitate the removal of the pushrods. On all V8 engines, remove the pushrods in sequence and number them, so that they may be installed in their original positions.

12. Remove the cylinder head attaching bolts, noting their positions. Lift the cylinder head off the block. Remove and discard the old cylinder head gasket.

To install:

13. Prior to installation, clean all surfaces of old gasket material. These include the cylinder head, intake manifold, rocker arm (valve) cover, and the cylinder block contact surfaces.

14. Position the new cylinder head gasket over the cylinder dowels on the block. Coat the head bolts with water resistant sealer. Position new gaskets on the muffler inlet pipes at the exhaust manifold flange.

15. Position the cylinder head to the block, and install the head bolts, each in its original position. On all engines on

Fig. 140 Loosen and remove the cylinder head(s) retaining bolts using a long breaker bar

Fig. 141 Loosen and remove the bolts on the side of the cylinder head, above the exhaust manifold

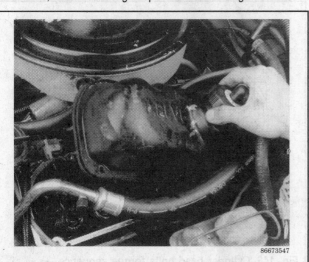

Fig. 139 Loosen and remove the valve/rocker arm cover(s)

Fig. 142 Lift the head up. The head may need to be tapped with a plastic faced hammer to loosen the gasket

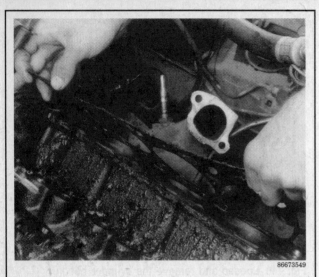

Fig. 143 Peel the old gasket off

Fig. 144 Clean both the cylinder head and engine block of old gasket material

20. On 7.0L engines, the intake manifold and rocker arm and shaft assemblies must now be installed. When tightening down the rocker arm shaft assembly, check the following;
   • The oil holes face downward.
   • The identification notch on the front right and the rear left face downward.
   • The crankshaft damper has the XX mark aligned with the pointer.
21. Tighten the rocker arms bolts front to rear, two turns at a time, to avoid bending any pushrods.
22. On all engines except the 7.0L, apply white lithium grease to the fulcrum seats and sockets. Turn the rocker arms to their proper positions and tighten the nuts or mounting bolts enough to hold the rocker arms in position. Make sure that the lower ends of the pushrods have remained properly seated in the valve lifters.
23. On all engines except the 7.0L, perform a preliminary valve lash adjustment. See Section 2.

Fig. 145 When installing the head(s), tighten each bolt to the correct specification using a torque wrench

which the exhaust manifold has been removed from the head to facilitate removal, it is necessary to properly guide the exhaust manifold studs into the muffler inlet pipe flange when installing the head.

16. Following the cylinder head tightening sequence. Tighten the cylinder head bolts in three stages. First, tighten the bolts to 50 ft. lbs. (68 Nm), then to 60 ft. lbs. (81 Nm), and finally to 70 ft. lbs. (95 Nm). When complete, tighten the exhaust manifold-to-cylinder head attaching bolts.

17. Tighten the nuts on the exhaust manifold studs at the muffler inlet flanges to 18 ft. lbs. (24 Nm).

18. Clean and inspect the pushrods one at a time. Clean the oil passage within each pushrod with a suitable solvent and blow the passage out with compressed air. Check the ends of the pushrods for nicks, grooves, roughness, or excessive wear. Visually inspect the pushrods for straightness, and replace any bent ones. Do not attempt to straighten pushrods.

19. Install the pushrods in their original positions. Apply Lubriplate® or a similar product to the valve stem tips and to the pushrod guides in the cylinder head.

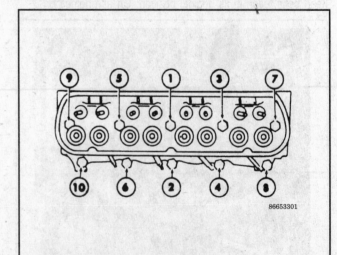

Fig. 146 Cylinder head bolts torque sequence — 8-cylinder engine

24. Position a new valve cover gasket, and install. Follow the gasket manufacture's instructions when installing. Tighten the bolts evenly to 10-23 ft. lbs. (10-18 Nm)

25. Install the intake manifold and carburetor or CFI unit.

26. Adjust all drive belts which were removed.

27. Refill the cooling system.

28. Connect the battery ground cable at the cylinder head (if applicable).

29. Install the spark plugs and connect the spark plug wires.

30. Check all fluid levels. Start the engine and check for leaks. Bleed the cooling system if needed.

31. With the engine running, check and adjust the carburetor idle speed and mixture.

32. With the engine running, listen for abnormal valve noises or irregular idle. Road test the vehicle for proper operation.

OVERHAUL

▶ See Figure 147

1. Remove the cylinder head(s) from the engine. Place the head(s) on a workbench and remove the manifolds, if still connected. Remove all the rocker arm retaining parts, keeping the parts in order.

2. Turn the cylinder head over so that the mounting surface is facing up and support it evenly on wood blocks.

3. Use a gasket scraper and remove all of the old gasket material stuck to the head mounting surface. Use a wire brush to clean away the carbon on the valve and head combustion chambers.

❊❊CAUTION

When scraping or decarbonizing the cylinder head, take care not to damage or nick the gasket mounting surface.

4. Number the valve heads with a permanent felt-tip marker for cylinder location.

5. Use an electric drill and rotary wire brush to clean the intake and exhaust valve ports, combustion chamber and valve seats. In some cases, the carbon will need to be chipped

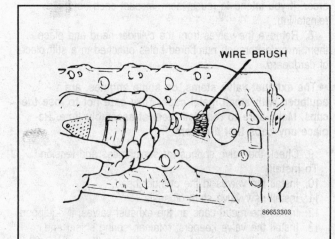

WIRE BRUSH

86653303

Fig. 147 Use an electric drill with a wire brush attachment to clean the carbon from the cylinder head

away. Use a blunt pointed drift for carbon chipping. Be careful around the valve seat areas.

➡**When using a wire brush to clean carbon on the valve ports, valves etc., be sure that the deposits are actually removed, rather than burnished.**

6. Wash and clean all valve springs, keepers, retaining caps etc., in solvent.

7. Clean the head with a brush and some solvent. Wipe dry.

8. Check the head for cracks. Cracks in the cylinder head usually start around an exhaust valve seat because it is the hottest part of the combustion chamber. If a crack is suspected but cannot be detected visually, have the area checked with dye penetrant or other method by the machine shop.

RESURFACING

▶ See Figure 148

Resurfacing should only be performed by a reputable machine shop. To determine whether resurfacing is necessary, perform the following.

Place a straightedge across the gasket surface of the cylinder head. Using a feeler gauge, determine the clearance at the center of the straightedge. If warpage exceeds 0.003 in. (0.08mm) in a 6 in. (152mm) span, or 0.006 in. (0.152mm) over the total length, the cylinder head must be resurfaced.

➡**If warpage exceeds the manufacturer's maximum tolerance for material removal, the cylinder head must be replaced.**

When milling the cylinder heads of V-type engines, the intake manifold mounting position is altered, and must be corrected by milling the manifold flange a proportionate amount. Do not plane or grind more than 0.010 in. (0.25mm) from the original cylinder head gasket surface. This service should be performed by a machine shop.

Valves and Springs

REMOVAL & INSTALLATION

▶ See Figures 149, 150, 151, 152, 153, 154 and 155

1. Remove the cylinder head from the vehicle, and place it on a clean, well lighted surface.

2. Block the head on its side, or install a pair of head-holding brackets made especially for valve removal.

3. Place a socket slightly larger than the valve stem and keepers over the valve stem and gently hit the socket with a plastic-faced hammer to break loose any varnish buildup.

4. Remove the valve keepers, retainer, spring shield and valve spring using a valve spring compressor (the locking C-clamp type is the best for this job).

5. Put the valve and spring parts in a separate container numbered for the cylinder. DO NOT mix parts from different valve assemblies.

6. Remove and discard the valve stem oil seals. A new seal will be used when assembling the valves.

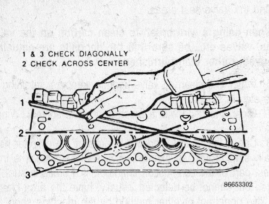

Fig. 148 Use a straight edge to check the cylinder head surface

Fig. 151 Loosen and remove the cylinder head(s) retaining bolts using a long breaker bar

Fig. 149 Compress the spring and remove the keepers with a magnet

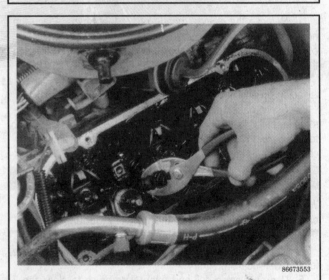

Fig. 152 Remove and discard the oil seal

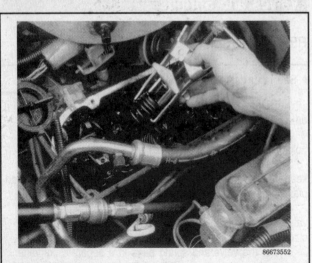

Fig. 150 With the keepers removed, lift the compressed spring out of the cylinder head

7. Remove the lifters one at a time and number them in order. If you intend to reuse them, inspect each before reinstalling.

8. Remove the valves from the cylinder head and place them in order through numbered holes punched in a stiff piece of cardboard.

➡The exhaust valve stems, on some engines, are equipped with small metal caps. Take care not to lose the caps. Make sure to reinstall them at assembly time. Replace any caps that are worn.

9. Check the valve springs for straightness and tension.
To install:
10. Install the valves in the cylinder head.
11. Install new valve stem oil seals.
12. Install the metal caps an the exhaust valves, if equipped.
13. Install the valve keepers, retainer, spring shield and valve spring using a valve spring compressor (the locking C-clamp type is the best for the procedure).
14. Check the valve spring installed height.

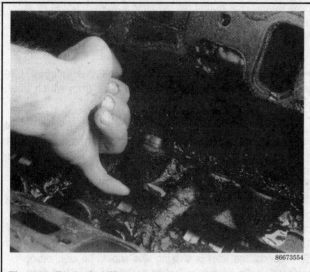

Fig. 153 Push the lifter up . . .

Fig. 154 . . . and out. Number each in order. Inspect for squareness if reinstalling

15. Measure the distance between the spring mounting pad and the lower edge of the spring retainer. Compare the measurement to the specifications found in the Valve Specifications chart. If the installed height is incorrect, add shims between the spring mounting pad and the spring. Use only shims designed for this purpose. These are available at most automotive parts stores.

VALVE SPRING INSPECTION

▶ See Figure 156

Place the valve spring on a flat surface next to a carpenter's square. Measure the height of the spring, and rotate the spring against the edge of the square to measure distortion. If the spring height varies (by comparison) by more than 1/16 in. (1.6mm) or if the distortion exceeds 1/16 in. (1.6mm), replace the spring.

Have the valve springs tested for spring pressure at the installed and compressed (installed height minus valve lift)

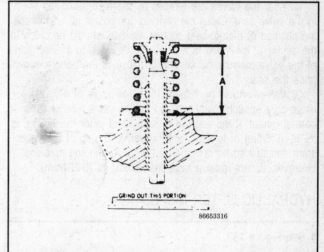

Fig. 155 Measure the installed valve spring height using a steel ruler

height using a valve spring tester. Springs should be within one pound, plus or minus each other. Replace springs as necessary.

VALVE REFACING

▶ See Figures 157 and 158

➡Because of exact tolerances required of valve surfaces, and the specialized tools, which are not readily available at most automotive stores, needed to perform valve refacing, it is recommended that you consult a professional machine shop when it comes to valve refacing

1. If necessary, have the valves and valve seats refaced. The valve seats should be a true 45° angle. Remove only enough material to clean up any pits or grooves. Be sure the valve seat is not too wide or narrow. Use a 60° grinding wheel to remove any material from the bottom of the seat and a 30° grinding wheel to remove material from the top of the seat.

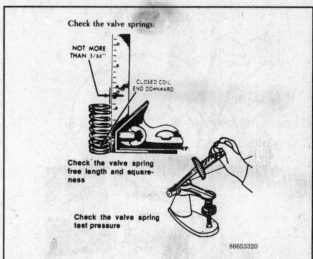

Fig. 156 Check the valve spring squareness and spring pressure

2. After the valves are refaced by machine, hand lap them to the valve seat. Clean the grinding compound off and check the position of face-to-seat contact. Contact should be close to the center of the valve face. If contact is close to the top edge of the valve, narrow the seat; if too close to the bottom edge, raise the seat.

3. Valves should be refaced to a true angle of 44°. Remove only enough metal to clean up the valve face or to correct runout. If the edge of a valve head, after machining, is 1/32 in. (0.8mm) or less replace the valve. The tip of the valve stem should also be dressed on the valve grinding machine. However, do not remove more than 0.010 in. (0.254mm).

HYDRAULIC LIFTER INSPECTION

▶ **See Figure 159**

Remove the lifter(s) from their bore(s) and remove any gum and/or varnish with a safe solvent. Check the lifters for concave wear. If the bottom of the lifter is worn concave or flat, replace the lifter. Lifters are built with a convex bottom. Any flatness would indicate wear. If a worn lifter is detected, carefully inspect the camshaft.

➡**When removing lifters, mark them cylinder location. Lifters must be reinstalled in the same bore from which they were removed.**

To test lifter leak down, submerge the lifter in a container of kerosene. Chuck a used pushrod that will not be reused or its equivalent into a drill press. Position the container of kerosene so the pushrod acts on the lifter plunger. Pump the lifter with the drill press until resistance increases. Pump several more times to bleed any air from the lifter. Apply very firm, constant pressure to the lifter and observe the rate which fluid bleeds out of the lifter. If the lifter bleeds down very quickly (less than 15 seconds), the lifter should be replaced. If the time exceeds 60 seconds, the lifter is sticking and should be cleaned or replaced. If the lifter is operating properly (leak down time 15-60 seconds) and is not worn, lubricate and reinstall it in the engine.

It is always better to replace a lifter than trying to clean it. Replace the complete set of lifters instead of one or two when performing this repair.

Oil Pan

REMOVAL & INSTALLATION

▶ **See Figures 160, 161, 162 and 163**

4-Cylinder Engines
▶ **See Figure 160**

✳✳CAUTION

The EPA warns that prolonged contact with used engine oil may cause a number of skin disorders, including cancer! You should make every effort to minimize your exposure to used engine oil. Protective gloves should be worn when changing the oil. Wash your hands and any other exposed skin areas as soon as possible after exposure to used engine oil. Soap and water, or waterless hand cleaner should be used. Recycle used engine oil, check local laws.

1. Disconnect the negative battery cable.
2. Drain the crankcase and cooling system.
3. Remove the right and left engine support bolts and nuts or through-bolts. Disconnect the hydraulic damper if so equipped. Disconnect the hydraulic damper if so equipped. Disconnect the upper and lower radiator hoses.
4. Using a jack, raise the engine as far as it will go. Place blocks of wood between the mounts and the chassis brackets. Remove the jack.
5. Remove the steering gear retaining nuts and bolts. Remove the bolt retaining the steering flex coupling to the steering gear. Position the steering gear forward and down.
6. Remove the shake brace and starter.
7. Remove the engine rear support-to-crossmember nuts.

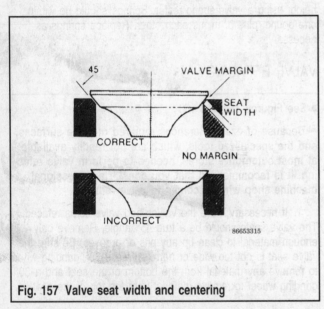

Fig. 157 Valve seat width and centering

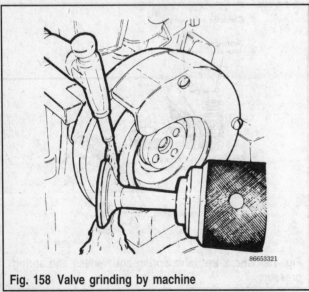

Fig. 158 Valve grinding by machine

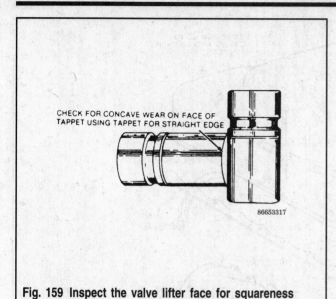

CHECK FOR CONCAVE WEAR ON FACE OF TAPPET USING TAPPET FOR STRAIGHT EDGE

86653317

Fig. 159 Inspect the valve lifter face for squareness

8. Position a jack under the transmission and take up its weight.

9. Remove the oil pan retaining bolts. Remove the oil pan. It may be necessary to turn the crankshaft when removing the pan to avoid interference.

To Install:

10. Position the new oil pan gasket and end seal on the cylinder block with gasket cement.

11. Position the oil pan on the cylinder block and install its retaining bolts.

12. Lower the jack under the transmission and install the crossmember nuts.

13. Replace the oil filter.

14. Position the flex coupling on the steering gear and install the retaining bolt.

15. Install the steering gear.

16. Install the shake brace. Install the starter.

17. Raise the engine enough to remove the wood blocks. Lower the engine and remove the jack. Install the engine support bolts and nuts. Connect the radiator hoses.

18. Lower the vehicle and fill the crankcase with oil and the cooling system with coolant.

19. Connect the battery.

20. Start the engine and check for leaks.

L6 Engines

1. Disconnect the two oil cooler lines at the radiator, if so equipped.

2. Remove the two radiator top support bolts. Remove or position the fan shroud back over the fan.

3. Remove the oil level dipstick. Drain the crankcase.

4. Remove the four bolts and nuts attaching the sway bar to the chassis and allow the sway bar to hang down.

5. Remove the K-brace.

6. Lower the front steering rack and pinion, or the center link and linkage, if necessary for clearance.

7. Remove the starter.

8. Remove the two nuts attaching the engine mounts to the support brackets.

9. Loosen the two rear insulator-to-crossmember attaching bolts.

10. Raise the engine and place a 1¼ in. (3.175mm) spacer between the engine support insulator and the chassis brackets.

11. Position a jack under the transmission and raise it slightly.

12. Remove the oil pan attaching bolts and lower pan to the crossmember.

13. Remove the oil pump intermediate driveshaft, pick-up tube and screen assembly, and lower these components into the pan.

14. Position the transmission cooler lines out of the way, if applicable, and remove the oil pan, rotating the crankshaft if required.

To install:

15. Clean and inspect the oil pan and gasket surface at the cylinder block.

16. The oil pan has a two-piece gasket. Coat the block surface and the oil pan gasket surfaces with oil resistant sealer, and position the gaskets on the cylinder block.

17. Position the oil pan seals in the cylinder front cover and rear bearing cap.

18. Insert the gasket tabs under the front and rear seals.

19. Place the oil pan on the front crossmember and install the oil pump, intermediate driveshaft, pick-up tube and screw assembly.

20. Position the oil pan on the cylinder block and install the attaching bolts. Tighten to 7-9 ft. lbs. (9-12 Nm).

21. Position the transmission cooler lines, if equipped.

22. Lower the jack from under the transmission.

23. Raise the engine to remove the spacers and lower the engine on the chassis.

24. Tighten the two nuts attaching the rear support insulator to the crossmember.

25. Install the two engine support-to-chassis through-bolts and nuts.

26. Install the starter motor and the sway bar. If moved, also install the steering rack and pinion, or the center link and linkage.

27. Install the K-brace, and fill the crankcase with oil. Replace the oil level dipstick.

28. Connect the oil cooler lines to the radiator, if applicable, and install the upper radiator support and fan shroud.

29. Lower the vehicle, start the engine and check for leaks.

V6 Engines

▶ **See Figures 161 and 162**

1. Disconnect the negative battery cable. Remove the air cleaner assembly including the air intake duct.

2. Drain the cooling system.

❋❋CAUTION

When draining coolant, keep in mind that cats and dogs are attracted to ethylene glycol antifreeze, and could drink any that is left in an uncovered container or in puddles on the ground. This will prove fatal in sufficient quantity. Always drain the coolant into a sealable container. Coolant should be reused unless it is contaminated or several years old.

3. Remove the fan shroud attaching bolts and position the shroud back over the fan.

4. Remove the oil level dipstick.

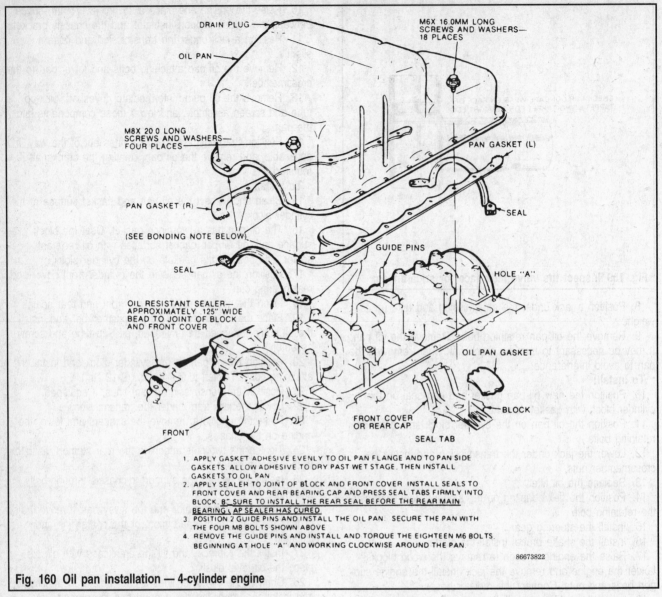

DRAIN PLUG

OIL PAN

M6X 16.0MM LONG
SCREWS AND WASHERS—
18 PLACES

M8X 20 0 LONG
SCREWS AND WASHERS—
FOUR PLACES

PAN GASKET (L)

PAN GASKET (R)

SEAL

(SEE BONDING NOTE BELOW)

SEAL

GUIDE PINS

HOLE "A"

OIL RESISTANT SEALER—
APPROXIMATELY .125" WIDE
BEAD TO JOINT OF BLOCK
AND FRONT COVER

OIL PAN GASKET

BLOCK

FRONT COVER
OR REAR CAP

SEAL TAB

FRONT

1. APPLY GASKET ADHESIVE EVENLY TO OIL PAN FLANGE AND TO PAN SIDE
GASKETS. ALLOW ADHESIVE TO DRY PAST WET STAGE, THEN INSTALL
GASKETS TO OIL PAN
2. APPLY SEALER TO JOINT OF BLOCK AND FRONT COVER. INSTALL SEALS TO
FRONT COVER AND REAR BEARING CAP AND PRESS SEAL TABS FIRMLY INTO
BLOCK. BE SURE TO INSTALL THE REAR SEAL BEFORE THE REAR MAIN
BEARING CAP SEALER HAS CURED
3. POSITION 2 GUIDE PINS AND INSTALL THE OIL PAN. SECURE THE PAN WITH
THE FOUR M8 BOLTS SHOWN ABOVE
4. REMOVE THE GUIDE PINS AND INSTALL AND TORQUE THE EIGHTEEN M6 BOLTS.
BEGINNING AT HOLE "A" AND WORKING CLOCKWISE AROUND THE PAN

86673822

Fig. 160 Oil pan installation — 4-cylinder engine

5. If equipped, remove the screws attaching the vacuum solenoids to the dash panel. Lay the solenoids on the engine without unfastening the vacuum hoses or electrical connectors.

6. Remove the exhaust manifold to exhaust pipe attaching nuts. Disconnect the radiator hoses from the radiator.

7. Drain the crankcase.

8. Remove the oil filter.

9. Remove the bolts attaching the shift linkage bracket to the transmission bellhousing. Remove the starter motor for more clearance, if necessary.

10. Disconnect the transmission cooler lines at the radiator. Remove power steering hose retaining clamp from frame.

11. Remove the converter cover.

12. Remove the nut and washer assembly attaching the front engine insulator to the chassis.

13. Raise the engine 2-3 in. (51-76mm) and insert wood blocks between the engine mounts and the vehicle frame.

14. Remove the oil pan attaching bolts and work the oil pan loose.

15. Lower the oil pan onto the crossmember. Remove the oil pick-up tube attaching bolts and the tube support bracket at-taching nut. Lower the pick-up tube/screen assembly into the pan and remove the oil pan.

16. Remove the oil pan seal from the main bearing cap.

To install:

17. Clean and inspect the gasket surfaces on the cylinder block, oil pan and oil pick-up tube.

18. Apply an 8mm bead of RTV sealer to all matching surfaces of the oil pan and the engine front cover.

19. Place the oil pick-up tube/screen assembly into the pan. Raise and support the oil pan.

20. Attach the oil pick-up tube/screen with a new gasket. Install and tighten the tube attaching bolts (15-22 ft. lbs.) and the support bracket nut (30-40 ft. lbs.).

21. Install the oil pan and pan bolts. Tighten the bolts to 80-106 inch lbs. (9-12 Nm).

22. Remove the wood blocks between the engine mounts and the vehicle frame and lower the engine onto the mounts.

23. Install the nut and washer assembly attaching the front engine insulator to the chassis.

24. Install the converter cover.

25. Connect the transmission cooler lines at the radiator.

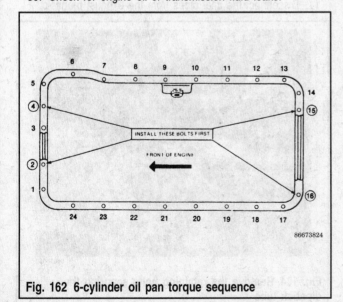

Fig. 161 Oil pan installation — 6-cylinder engine

26. Install the power steering hose retaining clamp to the frame.

27. Install the starter motor, if removed .

28. Install the bolts attaching the shift linkage bracket to the transmission bellhousing.

29. Install the oil filter.

30. Fill the crankcase with oil.

31. Install the exhaust manifold to exhaust pipe attaching nuts.

32. Connect the radiator hoses at the radiator.

33. Install the vacuum solenoids to the dash panel, if applicable.

34. Install the oil level dipstick and check the oil level.

35. Install the fan shroud.

36. Install the air cleaner assembly including the air intake duct.

37. Fill the cooling system.

38. Start the engine and check the fluid level in the transmission.

39. Check for engine oil or transmission fluid leaks.

Fig. 162 6-cylinder oil pan torque sequence

1971-78 V8 Engines

5.0L AND 5.8L ENGINES

1. Disconnect the negative battery cable. Remove the oil dipstick and drain the engine oil.

2. Remove the bolts attaching the fan shroud to the radiator and position the shroud over the fan.

3. Remove the nuts and lockwashers attaching the front engine supports to the chassis bracket.

4. If equipped with an automatic transmission, disconnect the oil cooler line at the left side of the radiator.

5. Raise the engine and place wood blocks under the engine supports.

6. Drain the crankcase oil.

✳✳CAUTION

The EPA warns that prolonged contact with used engine oil may cause a number of skin disorders, including cancer! You should make every effort to minimize your exposure to used engine oil. Protective gloves should be worn when changing the oil. Wash your hands and any other exposed skin areas as soon as possible after exposure to used engine oil. Soap and water, or waterless hand cleaner should be used.

7. Remove the oil pan attaching bolts and lower the oil pan onto the crossmember.

8. Remove the two bolts attaching the oil pump pickup tube to the oil pump. Remove the nut attaching the oil pump pickup tube to the number 3 main bearing cap stud. Lower the pickup tube and screen into the oil pan.

9. Remove the oil pan from the vehicle.

10. Clean any old gasket material from the oil pan and engine block mounting surface.

To install:

11. Clean the oil pump inlet tube and remove any gasket material. Inspect the gasket sealing surface for damages and distortion due to overtightening of the bolts. Repair and straighten as required.

12. Position a new oil pan gasket and seal to the cylinder block.

13. Position the oil pump pickup tube and screen to the oil pump, and install the lower attaching bolt and gasket loosely. Install the nut attaching the pump to number 3 main bearing cap stud.

14. Place the oil pan on the crossmember. Install the upper pickup tube bolt. Tighten the pickup tube bolts.

15. Position the oil pan to the cylinder block and install the attaching bolts. Tighten to 10-12 ft. lbs. (13-16 Nm) evenly in steps using a diagonal pattern.

All Other V8 Engines Through 1978

EXCEPT 5.0L AND 5.8L ENGINES

▶ See Figure 163

1. Remove the shroud from the radiator and position it rearward over the fan.

2. Disconnect the negative battery cable.

3. Raise and safely support the car on jackstands.

4. Drain the oil into a container. Loosen and position the transmission cooler lines out of the way, if equipped with an automatic transmission.

5. Remove the sway bar attaching bolts and move the sway bar forward on the struts.

✳✳CAUTION

The EPA warns that prolonged contact with used engine oil may cause a number of skin disorders, including cancer! You should make every effort to minimize your exposure to used engine oil. Protective gloves should be worn when changing the oil. Wash your hands and any other exposed skin areas as soon as possible after exposure to used engine oil. Soap and water, or waterless hand cleaner should be used.

6. Remove the nuts and lockwashers from the engine front support-to-intermediate support bracket.

7. Install a block of wood on a jack and position the jack under the leading edge of the oil pan.

8. Raise the engine approximately 1¼ in. (32mm) and insert a 1 in. (25mm) block between the insulator and crossmember. Remove the floor jack.

9. On 5.8L, 6.6L and 7.5L engines, remove the starter. On 7.5L engines through 1977, remove the oil filter.

10. Remove the oil pan attaching screws and lower the pan to the frame crossmember.

11. Turn the crankshaft to obtain enough clearance between the crankshaft counterweight and the rear of the pan.

12. Remove the oil pump attaching bolts.

13. Position the tube and the screen out of the way and remove the pan.

14. With the oil pan removed, clean any gasket material from the pan and engine mounting surface.

To install:

15. Clean the gasket mounting surfaces thoroughly. Coat the surfaces on the block and pan with oil resistant sealer. Position the pan side gaskets on the engine block.

16. Install the front cover oil seal on the cover, with the tabs over the pan side gaskets. Install the rear main cap seal with the tabs over the pan side gaskets.

17. Install the pan mounting bolts. Tighten the bolts on each side from the center outwards to 9-11 ft. lbs. (12-15 Nm) for ⁵⁄₁₆ in. bolts, 7-9 ft. lbs. (9-12 Nm) for ¼ in. bolts.

18. Complete the installation by reversing the removal steps.

1979-85 V8 Engines

▶ See Figures 164, 165, 166, 167 and 168

1. Disconnect the negative battery cable.

2. Remove the air cleaner and disconnect the accelerator and kickdown rods at the carburetor.

3. Remove the accelerator mounting bracket bolts and remove the bracket.

4. Remove the fan shroud attaching bolts and position the shroud up and over the fan.

5. Disconnect the windshield wiper motor wiring from the harness and remove the wiper motor.

6. Disconnect the windshield washer hose.

7. Unfasten the wiper motor mounting cover.

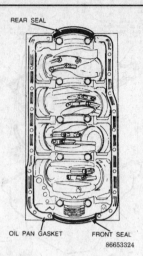

Fig. 163 Some engines use rubber end seals in addition the the oil pan gasket

8. Remove the dipstick and remove the dipstick retaining bolt from the exhaust manifold.

✳✳CAUTION

The EPA warns that prolonged contact with used engine oil may cause a number of skin disorders, including cancer! You should make every effort to minimize your exposure to used engine oil. Protective gloves should be worn when changing the oil. Wash your hands and any other exposed skin areas as soon as possible after exposure to used engine oil. Soap and water, or waterless hand cleaner should be used.

9. Raise the car and safely support on jackstands. Drain the crankcase oil.

➡Engines with dual oil pans must be drained by removing BOTH drain plugs.

10. Disconnect the fuel line at the fuel pump.

11. Disconnect the inlet pipes from the exhaust manifold.

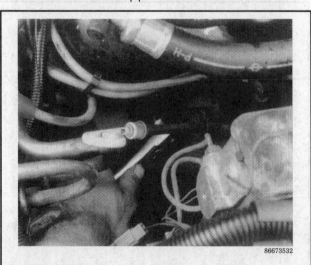

Fig. 164 Remove the retaining bolts securing the dipstick tube

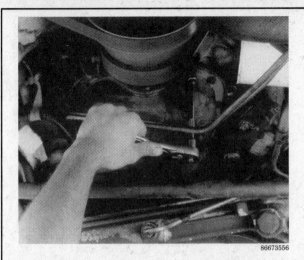

Fig. 165 Loosen and remove all but two oil pan retaining bolts

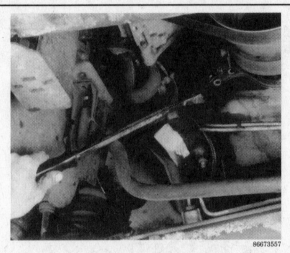

Fig. 166 If necessary use a prytool to carefully separate the oil pan from the engine block

12. Remove the dipstick tube from the oil pan.

13. Loosen the rear engine mount attaching nuts. Remove the engine mount through-bolts.

14. Remove the shift selector crossover bolts and remove the crossover.

15. Disconnect the transmission kickdown rod.

16. Remove the torque converter cover.

17. Remove the brake line retainer from the front crossmember.

18. Place a jack under the engine and raise it as far as it will go without component damage.

19. Place a small block of wood between each engine mount and the chassis brackets to support the engine. Slowly lower, then remove the jack.

20. Remove the oil pan attaching bolts and lower the oil pan.

21. Remove the three oil pump attaching bolts from the cylinder block and allow the pump to fall into the pan.

22. Remove the oil pan from the car.

23. Clean any gasket material from the oil pan and engine block mounting surface.

To install:

24. Inspect the oil pan for damage. Thoroughly clean the oil pump pickup tube and screen assembly.

25. Install the front cover oil seal on the cover, with the tabs over the pan side gaskets. Install the rear main cap seal with the tabs over the pan side gaskets.

26. Position the pan under the car and install the oil pump.

27. Install the pan mounting bolts, tightening them on each side from the center outwards to 9-11 ft. lbs. (12-15 Nm) for $5/16$ in. bolts, 7-9 ft. lbs. (9-12 Nm) for $1/4$ in. bolts.

28. Connect the engine mounts.

29. Install the brake line retainer at the front crossmember.

30. Install the torque converter cover.

31. Connect the transmission kickdown rod.

32. Install the shift selector crossover bolts and install the crossover.

33. Install the engine mount through-bolts. Tighten the rear engine mount attaching nuts.

34. Install the dipstick tube.

35. Connect the inlet pipes at the exhaust manifold.

36. Connect the fuel line at the fuel pump.

37. Lower the car.

38. Fill the crankcase with oil.

39. Install the dipstick and install the dipstick retaining bolt from the exhaust manifold.

40. Install the wiper motor mounting cover.

41. Connect the windshield washer hose.

42. Install the wiper motor. Connect the windshield wiper motor wiring at the harness.

43. Install the fan shroud.

44. Install the accelerator mounting bracket.

45. Connect the accelerator and kickdown rods at the carburetor.

46. Install the air cleaner.

47. Start the engine and check for oil leaks.

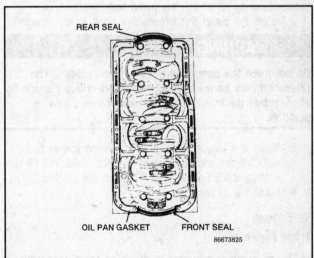

Fig. 167 Oil pan gasket and seal installation — V8 models

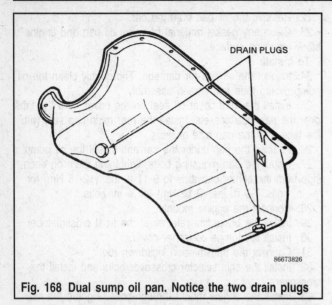

Fig. 168 Dual sump oil pan. Notice the two drain plugs

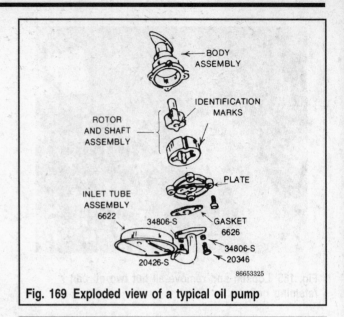

Fig. 169 Exploded view of a typical oil pump

Oil Pump

REMOVAL & INSTALLATION

All Engines Except V6
▶ See Figures 169 and 170

1. Remove the oil pan.
2. Remove the oil pump inlet tube and screen assembly.
3. Remove the oil pump attaching bolts and remove the oil pump gasket and the intermediate shaft.
4. Prime the oil pump by filling the inlet and outlet ports with engine oil and rotating the pump shaft to distribute it.
5. Position the intermediate driveshaft into the distributor socket.
6. Position a new gasket on the pump body and insert the intermediate driveshaft into the pump body.
7. Install the pump and intermediate shaft as an assembly.

❊❊WARNING

Do not force the pump if it does not seat readily. The driveshaft may be misaligned with the distributor shaft. To align, rotate the intermediate driveshaft into a new position.

8. Install and torque the oil pump attaching screws to:
   • 4-Cylinder and L6 Engines — 12-15 ft. lbs. (16-19 Nm)
   • V6 and V8 Engine — 22-32 ft. lbs. (29-42 Nm)
9. Install the oil pan.

V6 Engines
▶ See Figure 171

➡The oil pump is mounted in the front cover assembly. Oil pan removal is only necessary for pick-up tube/screen replacement or service.

1. Raise and safely support the vehicle on jackstands.
2. Remove the oil filter.
3. Remove the cover/filter mount assembly.

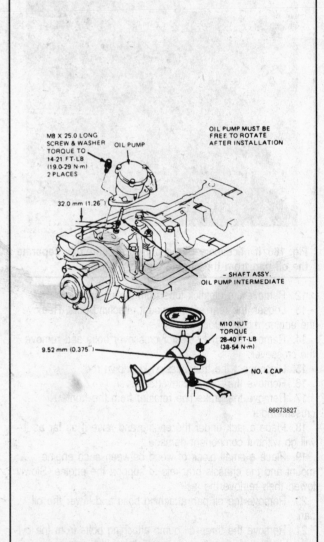

Fig. 170 Oil pump installation — 4-cylinder engine; location similar for others

4. Lift the two pump gears from their mounting pocket in the front cover.

5. Clean all gasket mounting surfaces.

6. Inspect the mounting pocket for wear. If excessive wear is present, complete timing cover assembly replacement is necessary.

7. Inspect the cover/filter mounting gasket-to-timing cover surface for flatness. Place a straightedge across the flat and check the clearance with a feeler gauge. If the measured clearance exceeds 0.004 in. (0.102mm), replace the cover/filter mount.

8. Replace the pump gears if wear is excessive.

9. Remove the plug from the end of the pressure relief valve passage using a small drill and slide hammer. Use caution when drilling.

10. Remove the spring and valve from the bore. Clean all dirt, gum and metal chips from the bore and valve. Inspect all parts for wear. Replace as necessary.

11. Install the valve and spring after lubricating them with engine oil. Install a new plug flush with the machined surface.

12. Install the pump gears and fill the pocket with petroleum jelly. Install the cover/filter mount using a new mounting gasket. Tighten the mounting bolts to 18-22 ft. lbs. (23-29 Nm). Install the oil filter and add oil, as necessary, to maintain the correct level.

Crankshaft Pulley (Vibration Damper)

REMOVAL & INSTALLATION

▶ See Figures 172, 173, 174, 175 and 176

1. Remove the fan shroud, as required. If necessary, drain the cooling system and remove the radiator. Remove drive belts from the pulley.

❄❄CAUTION

When draining coolant, keep in mind that cats and dogs are attracted to ethylene glycol antifreeze, and could drink any that is left in an uncovered container or in puddles on the ground. This will prove fatal in sufficient quantity. Always drain the coolant into a sealable container. Coolant should be reused unless it is contaminated or several years old.

2. On those engines with a separate pulley, remove the retaining bolts and separate the pulley from the vibration damper.

3. Remove the vibration damper/pulley retaining bolt from the crankshaft end.

4. Using a puller, remove the damper/pulley from the crankshaft.

5. Upon installation, align the key slot of the pulley hub to the crankshaft key. Complete the assembly in the reverse order of removal. Tighten the retaining bolts to specifications. Refer to the Torque Specification chart in this section.

Timing Belt Cover and Seal

➡The only engine to utilize a timing belt is the 4-cylinder engine.

REMOVAL & INSTALLATION

➡Replacement of the seal is recommended any time the front cover is removed. It is possible to replace the front cover seal with the cover installed.

1. Remove the seal from the cover with the cover on the engine, using a special seal removal tool (Ford part no. T74P-6700-B or equivalent).
   To install:
2. Using a special seal installer tool (Ford part no. T74P-6150-A or equivalent), press the seal into place.

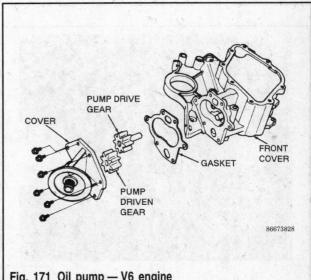

Fig. 171 Oil pump — V6 engine

Fig. 172 Remove the main crankshaft pulley bolts

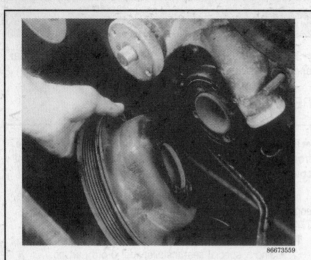

Fig. 173 With the retaining bolts unfastened, remove the pulley

Fig. 174 Loosen and remove the crankshaft main bolt. Use a long breaker bar to loosen the crankshaft bolt

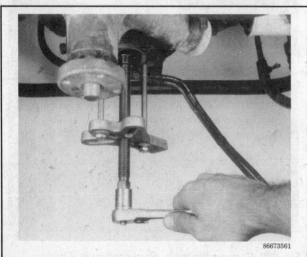

Fig. 175 Use a puller assembly to press the damper away from the crankshaft

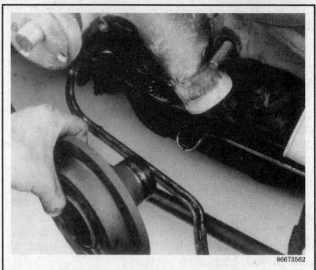

Fig. 176 Remove the damper when complete

Timing Chain Cover and Seal

REMOVAL & INSTALLATION

L6 Engines

➡Replacement of the cover seal is recommended any time the front cover is removed.

1. Disconnect the negative battery cable.
2. Drain the cooling system and disconnect the radiator upper hose at the coolant outlet elbow. Remove the two upper radiator retaining bolts.

❋❋CAUTION

When draining coolant, keep in mind that cats and dogs are attracted to ethylene glycol antifreeze, and could drink any that is left in an uncovered container or in puddles on the ground. This will prove fatal in sufficient quantity. Always drain the coolant into a sealable container. Coolant should be reused unless it is contaminated or several years old.

3. Raise the vehicle and safely support on jackstands. Drain the crankcase oil.

❋❋CAUTION

The EPA warns that prolonged contact with used engine oil may cause a number of skin disorders, including cancer! You should make every effort to minimize your exposure to used engine oil. Protective gloves should be worn when changing the oil. Wash your hands and any other exposed skin areas as soon as possible after exposure to used engine oil. Soap and water, or waterless hand cleaner should be used.

4. Remove the splash shield and the automatic transmission oil cooling lines, if so equipped, then remove the radiator.
5. Loosen and remove the fan belt, fan and pulley.

6. Use a gear puller to remove the crankshaft pulley damper.

7. Remove the cylinder front cover retaining bolts and gently pry the cover away from the block. Remove the gasket.

8. Drive out the old seal with a pin punch from the rear of the cover. Clean out the recess in the cover.

To install:

9. Coat the new seal with grease and drive it into the cover until fully seated. Check the seal to make sure that the spring around the seal is in the proper position.

10. Clean the cylinder front cover and the gasket surface of the cylinder block. Apply an oil resistant sealer to the new front cover gasket and install the gasket onto the cover.

11. Position the front cover assembly over the end of the crankshaft and against the cylinder block. Start, but do not tighten, the cover and pan attaching bolts. Slide a front cover alignment tool (Ford part no. T68P-6019-A or equivalent) over the crank stub and into the seal bore of the cover. Tighten all front cover attaching bolts to 12-18 ft. lbs. (16-24 Nm) and all oil pan bolts to 10-15 ft. lbs. (13-20 Nm). Tightening the oil pan bolts first.

➡**Trim away the exposed portion of the old oil pan gasket flush with the front of the engine block. Cut and position the required portion of a new gasket to the oil pan and apply sealer to both sides.**

12. Lubricate the hub of the crankshaft damper/pulley with Lubriplate® to prevent damage to the seal during installation or on initial starting of the engine.

13. Install and assemble the remaining components in the reverse order of removal.

14. Start the engine and check for leaks.

V6 and V8 Engines

➡**Replacement of the cover seal is recommended any time the front cover is removed.**

Refer to the section on Timing Chain Removal for information on cover removal and replacement.

➡**On V6 engines, the seal may be removed after the crankshaft pulley is removed. The cover does not have to be removed.**

With the cover removed from the vehicle, drive the old seal from the rear of the cover with a pin punch. Clean out the recess in the cover. Coat the new seal with grease and work it into the cover until it is fully seated. Check the seal after installation to be sure the spring is properly positioned in the seal.

Timing Belt

The correct installation and adjustment of the camshaft drive belt is critical if the engine is to run properly. When any given piston is on the intake stroke, the corresponding intake valve must be open to admit air/fuel mixture into the cylinder. When the same piston is on the compression and power strokes, both valves in that cylinder must be closed. When the piston is on the exhaust stroke, the exhaust valve for that cylinder must be open. If the opening and closing of the valves is not coordi-

nated with the movements of the pistons, the engine will run very poorly, if at all.

The camshaft drive belt also turns the engine auxiliary shaft. The distributor is driven by the engine auxiliary shaft. Since the distributor controls ignition timing, the auxiliary shaft must be coordinated with the camshaft and crankshaft, since both valves in any given cylinder must be closed and the piston in that cylinder near the top of the compression stroke when the spark plug fires.

Due to this complex interrelationship between the camshaft, the crankshaft and the auxiliary shaft, the cogged pulleys on each component must be aligned when the camshaft drive belt is installed. In order to prevent an unanticipated breakdown, and possible engine damage, it is recommended that the camshaft drive belt be replaced every 60,000 miles (97,000 km).

TROUBLESHOOTING

Should the camshaft drive belt jump timing by a tooth or two, the engine could still run; but very poorly. To visually check for correct timing of the crankshaft, auxiliary shaft and the camshaft, follow this procedure:

➡**There is an access plug provided in the cam drive belt cover, so that the camshaft timing can be checked without removing the cover.**

1. Remove the access plug.
2. Turn the crankshaft until the timing marks on the crankshaft indicate TDC.
3. Make sure that the timing mark on the camshaft drive sprocket is aligned with the pointer on the inner belt cover. Also, the rotor of the distributor must align with the No. 1 cylinder firing position.

❉❉WARNING

Never turn the crankshaft of any overhead cam engine in the opposite direction of normal rotation. Backward rotation of the crankshaft may cause the timing belt to slip and alter the timing.

REMOVAL & INSTALLATION

▶ **See Figures 177 and 178**

1. Set the engine to TDC as described in the troubleshooting section. The crankshaft and camshaft timing marks should align with their respective pointers and the distributor rotor should point to the No. 1 plug tower.

2. Loosen the adjustment bolts on the alternator and other belt-driven accessories, and remove the drive belts. To provide clearance for removing the belt outer cover and camshaft belt, remove the fan (if applicable) and pulley from the water pump hub.

3. Reposition the fuel vapor tube running to the evaporator canister, if necessary, to provide clearance for cover removal.

4. Remove the belt outer cover attaching bolt.

5. Remove the belt outer cover.

6. Remove the distributor cap from the distributor and position it out of the way.

7. Loosen the belt tensioner adjustment and pivot bolts. Lever the tensioner away from the belt and retighten the adjustment bolt to hold it away.

8. Remove the crankshaft bolt and pulley. Remove the belt guide behind the pulley.

9. Remove the camshaft drive belt.

To install:

10. Install the new belt over the crankshaft sprocket first, then counterclockwise over the auxiliary shaft sprocket and the camshaft sprocket. Adjust the belt fore and aft so that it is centered on the sprockets.

11. Loosen the tensioner adjustment bolt, allowing it to spring back against the belt.

12. Rotate the crankshaft two complete turns in the normal rotational direction to remove any belt slack. Turn the crankshaft until the timing check marks are lined up. If the timing has slipped, remove the belt and repeat the procedure.

13. Tighten the tensioner adjustment bolt to 14-21 ft. lbs. (18-27 Nm), and the pivot bolt to 28-40 ft. lbs. (36-52 Nm).

14. Install the distributor cap.

15. Install the belt guide, belt outer cover and crankshaft pulley. Install the water pump pulley and, if applicable, the cooling fan.

16. Install the drive belts and accessories and adjust the drive belt tension. Reposition the fuel vapor tube, if necessary.

17. Start the engine and check the ignition timing.

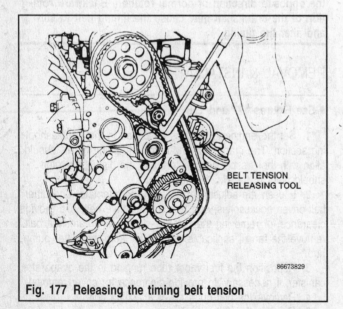

Fig. 177 Releasing the timing belt tension

Timing Chain

REMOVAL & INSTALLATION

L6 Engines

▶ See Figure 179

1. Drain the cooling system and crankcase.

✳✳CAUTION

When draining coolant, keep in mind that cats and dogs are attracted to ethylene glycol antifreeze, and could drink any that is left in an uncovered container or in puddles on the ground. This will prove fatal in sufficient quantity. Always drain the coolant into a sealable container. Coolant should be reused unless it is contaminated or several years old.

2. Disconnect the upper radiator hose from the intake manifold and the lower hose from the water pump. On cars with automatic transmission, disconnect the fluid cooler lines from the radiator.

3. Remove the radiator, fan and pulley, and engine drive belts. On models with air conditioning, remove the condenser retaining bolts and position the condenser forward. Do not disconnect the refrigerant lines.

4. Remove the cylinder front cover retaining bolts and front oil pan bolts, and gently pry the cover away from the block.

5. Remove the crankshaft pulley bolt and use a puller to remove the vibration damper.

6. With a socket wrench of the proper size on the crankshaft pulley bolt, gently rotate the crankshaft in a clockwise direction until all slack is removed from the left side of the timing chain. Scribe a mark on the engine block parallel to the present position on the left side of the chain. Next, turn the crankshaft in a counterclockwise direction to remove all the slack from the right side of the chain. Force the left side of the chain outward with your fingers and measure the distance between the reference point and the present position of the chain. If the distance exceeds ½ in. (13mm), replace the chain and sprockets.

7. Crank the engine until the timing marks are aligned as shown in the illustration. Remove the bolt, slide the sprocket and chain forward and remove them as an assembly.

To install:

8. Position the sprockets and chain on the engine, making sure that the timing marks are aligned, dot-to-dot.

9. Install the front cover, applying oil resistant sealer to the new gasket. Trim away the exposed portion of the old oil pan gasket flush with the front of the engine block. Cut and position the required portion of a new gasket to the oil pan, applying sealer to both sides of it.

10. Install the cylinder front cover retaining bolts and front oil pan bolts, and tighten them to 6-9 ft. lbs. (8-12 Nm).

11. Install the vibration damper or pulley on the crankshaft and torque the bolt to 85-100 ft. lbs. (110-130 Nm).

12. Install the fan, pulley and belts. Adjust the belt tension.

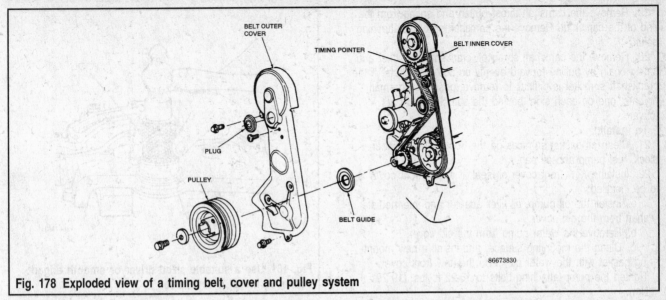

Fig. 178 Exploded view of a timing belt, cover and pulley system

13. Install the radiator and connect the radiator hoses and transmission cooling lines, if applicable. If equipped with air conditioning, install the condenser.

14. Fill the crankcase and cooling system. Start the engine and check for leaks.

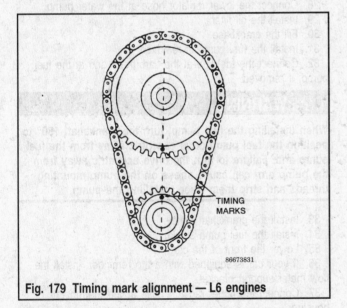

Fig. 179 Timing mark alignment — L6 engines

V6 Engines

▶ See Figures 180 and 181

1. Disconnect the negative battery cable from the battery. Drain the cooling system.

❋❋CAUTION

When draining coolant, keep in mind that cats and dogs are attracted to ethylene glycol antifreeze, and could drink any that is left in an uncovered container or in puddles on the ground. This will prove fatal in sufficient quantity. Always drain the coolant into a sealable container. Coolant should be reused unless it is contaminated or several years old.

2. Remove the air cleaner and air duct assemblies.

3. Remove the radiator fan shroud and position it back over the water pump. Remove the fan clutch assembly and shroud.

4. Remove the drive belt(s). If equipped with power steering, remove the pump with the hoses attached and position it out of the way. Be sure to keep the pump upright to prevent fluid leakage.

5. If your car is equipped with air conditioning, remove the front compressor mounting bracket. It is not necessary to remove the compressor.

6. Disconnect the coolant bypass hose and the heater hose at the water pump.

7. Disconnect the upper radiator hose at the thermostat housing.

8. Remove the distributor.

9. If your car is equipped with a trip reminder, remove the flow meter support bracket and allow the meter to be supported by the hoses.

10. Raise the front of the car and support on jackstands.

11. Remove the crankshaft pulley using a suitable puller. Remove the fuel pump shield.

12. If carburetor equipped, disconnect the fuel line from the carburetor at the fuel pump, then remove the mounting bolts and the fuel pump. Position pump out of the way with the tank line still attached.

13. Drain the engine oil and remove the oil filter.

14. Disconnect the lower radiator hose at the water pump.

15. Remove the oil pan mounting bolts and lower the oil pan.

➡The front cover cannot be removed unless the oil pan is lowered.

16. Lower the car from the jackstands.

17. Remove the front cover mounting bolts. It is not necessary to separate the water pump.

➡A front cover mounting bolt is located behind the oil filter adapter. If this bolt is not removed and the cover is pried upon, breakage will occur.

18. Remove the timing indicator. Remove the front cover and water pump as an assembly.

19. Remove the camshaft thrust button and spring from the end of the camshaft. Remove the camshaft sprocket attaching bolts.

20. Remove the camshaft sprocket, crankshaft sprocket and timing chain by pulling forward evenly on both sprockets. If the crankshaft sprocket is difficult to remove, position two small prybars, one on each side, behind the sprocket and pry forward.

To install:

21. Clean all gasket surfaces on the front cover, cylinder block, fuel pump and oil pan.

22. Install a new front cover oil seal. If a new front cover is to be installed:

    a. Install the oil pump, oil filter adapter and intermediate shaft from the old cover.

    b. Remove the water pump from the old cover.

    c. Clean the mounting surface, and install a new mounting gasket with the water pump on the new front cover. Tighten the pump attaching bolts to 15-22 ft. lbs. (19-29 Nm).

23. Rotate the crankshaft, if necessary, to bring No. 1 piston to TDC with the crankshaft keyway at the 12 o'clock position.

24. Lubricate the timing chain with motor oil. Install the chain over the two sprockets making sure that the marks on both sprockets are positioned across from each other. Install the sprockets and chain on the cam and crankshaft. Install the camshaft mounting bolts. Tighten the bolts to 15-22 ft. lbs. (19-29 Nm)

25. Install the camshaft thrust button and spring. Lubricate the thrust button with polyethylene grease before installation.

❊❊WARNING

The thrust button and spring must be bottomed in the camshaft seat and must not be allowed to fall out during front cover installation.

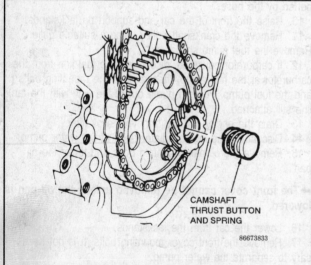

Fig. 180 Camshaft thrust button and spring

CAMSHAFT THRUST BUTTON AND SPRING

86673833

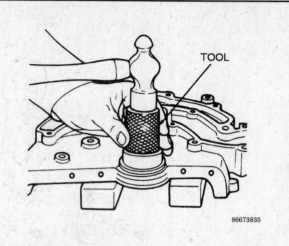

TOOL

86673835

Fig. 181 Use a suitable sized driver or smooth edged socket to install a cover seal

26. Position a new cover gasket on the front of the engine and install the cover and water pump assemblies. Install the timing indicator. Torque the front cover bolts to 15-22 ft. lbs. (19-29 Nm).

27. Install the oil pan.

28. Connect the lower radiator hose at the water pump.

29. Install the oil filter.

30. Fill the crankcase.

31. Install the fuel pump, if removed.

32. Connect the fuel line at the carburetor and at the fuel pump, if removed.

❊❊WARNING

When installing the fuel pump, turn the crankshaft 180° to position the fuel pump drive eccentric away from the fuel pump arm. Failure to turn the drive eccentric away from the pump arm can cause stress on the pump mounting threads and strip them when installing the pump.

33. Install the crankshaft pulley.

34. Install the fuel pump shield.

35. Lower the front of the car.

36. If your car is equipped with a trip reminder, install the flow meter support bracket.

37. Connect the upper radiator hose at the thermostat housing.

38. Install the distributor.

39. Connect the coolant bypass hose and the heater hose at the water pump.

40. If your car is equipped with air conditioning, install the front compressor mounting bracket.

41. If equipped with power steering, install the pump. Be sure to keep the pump upright to prevent fluid leakage.

42. Install the drive belt(s) and adjust to the proper tension.

43. Install the fan clutch assembly.

44. Install the radiator fan shroud.

45. Install the air cleaner and air duct assemblies.

46. Connect the negative battery cable at the battery.

47. Fill the cooling system.

V8 Engines

EXCEPT 7.5L ENGINES

▶ See Figures 182, 183, 184, 185, 186, 187, 188, 189, 190, 191, 192, 193, 194 and 195

1. Disconnect the negative battery cable, and drain the cooling system.

❈❈CAUTION

When draining coolant, keep in mind that cats and dogs are attracted to ethylene glycol antifreeze, and could drink any that is left in an uncovered container or in puddles on the ground. This will prove fatal in sufficient quantity. Always drain the coolant into a sealable container. Coolant should be reused unless it is contaminated or several years old.

2. Remove the air cleaner assembly, if mounted above the intake manifold.
3. Disconnect the radiator hoses and transmission cooler lines, if so equipped, and remove the radiator.
4. Disconnect the heater hose at the water pump. Slide the water pump bypass hose clamp toward the pump.
5. Loosen the alternator mounting bolts at the alternator. Remove the alternator support bolt at the water pump. Remove the Thermactor pump on all engines so equipped. If equipped with power steering or air conditioning, unbolt the component, remove the belt, and lay the pump or compressor aside with the lines attached.
6. Remove the fan, spacer, pulley, and drive belt.
7. Drain the crankcase and remove the engine oil dipstick.
8. Remove the pulley from the crankshaft pulley adapter. Remove the capscrew and washer from the front end of the crankshaft. Remove the crankshaft pulley adapter with a puller.
9. On carburetor equipped engines, disconnect the fuel outlet line at the fuel pump, then remove the fuel pump retaining bolts and lay the pump to the side.
10. Remove the front cover attaching bolts.
11. Remove the crankshaft oil slinger, if so equipped.

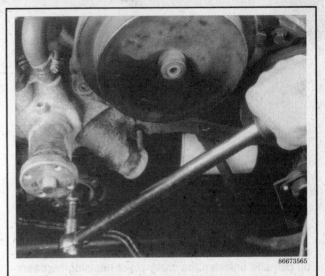

Fig. 183 Remove the crankshaft damper

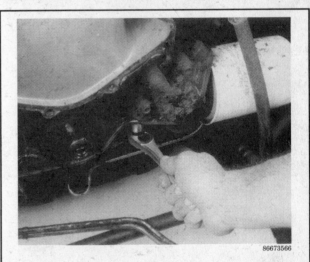

Fig. 184 Begin to remove the retaining hardware for the chain cover

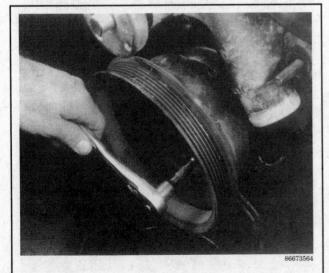

Fig. 182 Remove the crankshaft pulley

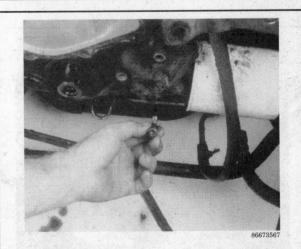

Fig. 185 Some of the hardware is standard nuts and bolts while some is hex-headed, requiring specific tools to loosen and remove

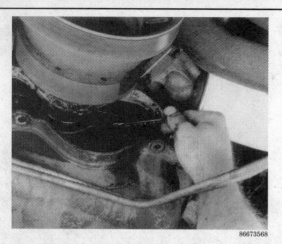

Fig. 186 With the oil pan hardware removed, lower the oil pan and unfasten the chain cover retaining hardware accessible from the bottom of the engine block

Fig. 187 Slowly separate the chain cover from the engine block

Fig. 188 With the chain cover removed, the timing chain is clearly visible

Fig. 189 You may wish to highlight the timing marks using a dab of paint

12. Check timing chain deflection, using the procedure outlined in Step 6 of the 6-200 engine Timing Chain Removal.

13. Rotate the engine until the sprocket timing marks are aligned as shown in the valve timing illustration.

14. Remove the camshaft sprocket bolt or capscrew, washers, and fuel pump eccentric or spacer. Slide the cam sprocket with the chain forward and off as an assembly.

15. If removing the crankshaft gear, use a gear puller to separate the gear from the crankshaft and keyway.

To install:

16. If both the camshaft and crankshaft sprockets were removed, position the sprockets and chain on the camshaft and crankshaft with both timing marks facing dot-to-dot on a centerline. If only one sprocket was removed, you will have to carefully align the chain and removed sprocket in relation to the installed sprocket. In most cases, it is easier to remove the sprocket and align all the dots and install. Position the fuel pump eccentric or spacer, washers and sprocket attaching bolt or capscrew. Torque the sprocket attaching bolt or capscrew to 40-45 ft. lbs. (52-58 Nm).

17. Install the crankshaft front oil slinger, if applicable.

Fig. 190 Remove the camshaft sprocket bolts

Fig. 191 Slide the camshaft sprocket off and disengage the chain from the crankshaft sprocket

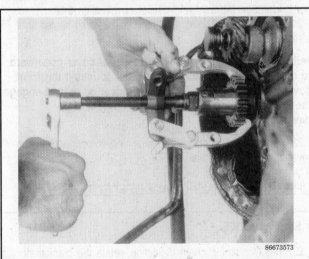

Fig. 192 To remove the crankshaft gear, use a gear puller to slide the piece off the shaft and keyway

Fig. 193 With the gear removed, inspect the teeth for wear

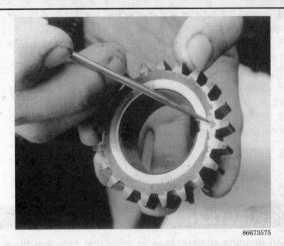

Fig. 194 When installing the the gear, align the point on the gear with the shaft keyway. Also have the point facing away from the engine block

18. Clean the front cover and mating surfaces of old gasket material. Install a new oil seal in the cover. Use a seal driver tool, if available.

19. Coat a new cover gasket with sealer and position it on the block.

➡Trim away the exposed portion of the oil pan gasket flush with the cylinder block. Cut and position the required portion of a new gasket to the oil pan, applying sealer to both sides of it.

20. Install the front cover, using a crankshaft-to-cover alignment tool. Coat the threads of the attaching bolts with sealer. Torque the attaching bolts to 12-18 ft. lbs. (16-23 Nm).

21. If removed, install the fuel pump and connect the fuel pump outlet tube.

22. Install the crankshaft pulley adapter and torque the attaching bolt. Install the crankshaft pulley.

23. Install the water pump pulley, drive belt, spacer and fan.

24. Install the alternator support bolt at the water pump. Tighten the alternator mounting bolts. Adjust the drive belt tension. Install the Thermactor pump if so equipped.

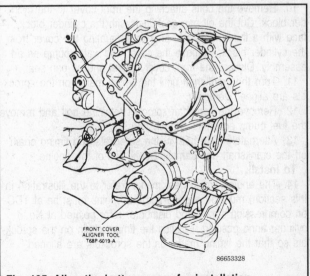

Fig. 195 Align the bottom cover for installation

25. Install the radiator and connect all coolant and heater hoses.

26. Install the engine oil dipstick. Refill the cooling system and the crankcase.

27. Connect the negative battery cable.

28. Start the engine and operate it at fast idle. Check for leaks.

29. Install the air cleaner assembly, if removed. Adjust the ignition timing and make all final adjustments.

7.5L ENGINES

1. Disconnect the negative battery cable.
2. Drain the cooling system.

✷✷CAUTION

When draining coolant, keep in mind that cats and dogs are attracted to ethylene glycol antifreeze, and could drink any that is left in an uncovered container or in puddles on the ground. This will prove fatal in sufficient quantity. Always drain the coolant into a sealable container. Coolant should be reused unless it is contaminated or several years old.

3. Remove the radiator shroud and fan.

4. Disconnect the upper and lower radiator hoses, and the automatic transmission oil cooler lines from the radiator.

5. Remove the radiator upper support and remove the radiator.

6. Loosen the alternator attaching bolts and air conditioning compressor idler pulley and remove the drive belts with the water pump pulley. Remove the bolts attaching the compressor support to the water pump and remove the bracket (support), if so equipped.

7. Remove the crankshaft pulley from the vibration damper. Remove the bolt and washer attaching the crankshaft damper and remove the damper with a puller. Remove the woodruff key from the crankshaft.

8. Loosen the bypass hose at the water pump, and disconnect the heater return tube at the water pump.

9. Disconnect and plug the fuel inlet and outlet lines at the fuel pump, and remove the fuel pump.

10. Remove the bolts attaching the front cover to the cylinder block. Cut the oil pan seal flush with the cylinder block face with a thin knife blade prior to separating the cover from the cylinder block. Remove the cover and water pump as an assembly. Discard the front cover gasket and oil pan seal.

11. Turn the crankshaft until the timing marks on the sprockets are aligned vertically.

12. Remove the camshaft sprocket retaining bolt and remove the fuel pump eccentric and washers.

13. Alternately slide both of the sprockets and timing chain off the crankshaft and camshaft until free of the engine.

To install:

14. The engine timing gear marks (refer to the illustration in this section) must be aligned and the engine must be at TDC on compression stroke and distributor rotor pointed at No. 1 cylinder firing position. Position the timing chain on the sprockets so that the timing marks on the sprockets are aligned vertically. Alternately slide the sprockets and chain onto the crankshaft and camshaft sprockets.

15. Install the fuel pump eccentric washers and attaching bolt on the camshaft sprocket. Tighten to 40-45 ft. lbs. (54-61 Nm).

16. Transfer the water pump if a new cover is going to be installed. Clean all of the gasket sealing surfaces on both the front cover and the cylinder block.

17. Coat the gasket surface of the oil pan with sealer. Cut and position the required sections of a new seal on the oil pan. Apply sealer to the corners.

18. Drive out the old front cover oil seal with a pin punch. Clean out the seal recess in the cover. Coat a new seal with Lubriplate® or equivalent grease. Install the seal, making sure the seal spring remains in the proper position. A front cover seal tool, Ford part no. T72J-117 or equivalent, makes installation easier.

19. Coat the gasket surfaces of the cylinder block and cover with sealer and position the new gasket on the block.

20. Position the front cover on the cylinder block. Use care not to damage the seal and gasket or mis-align them.

21. Coat the front cover attaching screws with sealer and install them.

➡️**It may be necessary to force the front cover downward to compress the oil pan seal in order to install the front cover attaching bolts. Use a screwdriver or drift to engage the cover screw holes through the cover and pry downward.**

22. Assemble and install the remaining components in the reverse order of removal.

CHECKING TIMING CHAIN DEFLECTION

▶ **See Figure 196**

To measure timing chain deflection, rotate the crankshaft clockwise to take up any slack on the left side of the chain. Choose a reference point and measure the distance from this point to the chain. Rotate the crankshaft in the opposite direction to take up slack on the right side of the chain. Force the left (slack) side of the chain out and measure the distance from the chain to the reference point chosen earlier. The difference between the two measurements is the deflection. The timing chain should be replaced if the deflection measurement exceeded the specified limit of ½ in. (13mm).

Camshaft

REMOVAL & INSTALLATION

4-Cylinder Engines

▶ **See Figure 197**

➡️**The following procedure covers camshaft removal and installation with the cylinder head on or off the engine. If the cylinder head has been removed start at Step 9.**

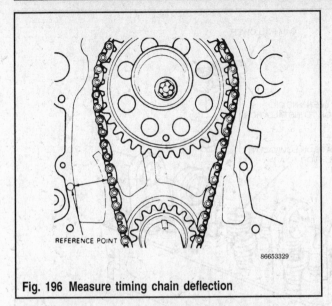

REFERENCE POINT

86653329

Fig. 196 Measure timing chain deflection

1. Remove the air cleaner assembly and disconnect the negative battery cable. Drain the cooling system.

✳✳CAUTION

When draining coolant, keep in mind that cats and dogs are attracted to the ethylene glycol antifreeze, and could drink any that is left in an uncovered container or in puddles on the ground. This will prove fatal in sufficient quantity. Always drain the coolant into a sealable container. Coolant should be reused unless it is contaminated or several years old.

2. Remove the spark plug wires from the plugs, disconnect the retainer from the valve cover and position the wires out of the way. Disconnect the rubber vacuum lines as necessary.

3. Remove all drive belts. Remove the alternator mounting bracket-to-cylinder head mounting bolts, and position the bracket and alternator out of the way.

4. Disconnect and remove the upper radiator hose. Disconnect the radiator shroud.

5. Remove the fan blades and water pump pulley and fan shroud. Remove the valve cover and timing belt outer cover.

6. Align the engine timing marks at TDC. Remove the timing belt.

7. Raise the front of the car and support it on jackstands. Remove the front motor mount bolts. Disconnect the lower radiator hose from the radiator. Disconnect and plug the automatic transmission cooler lines, if so equipped.

8. Position a piece of wood on a floor jack and raise the engine carefully as far as it will go. Place blocks of wood between the engine mounts and crossmember pedestals.

9. Remove the cam followers (rocker arms) as described earlier in this section.

10. Remove the camshaft sprocket and belt guide using a suitable puller. Remove the front oil seal with a sheet metal screw and slide hammer or special seal remover tool.

11. Remove the camshaft retainer located on the rear mounting stand, by unfastening the two bolts or screws.

12. Remove the camshaft by carefully withdrawing it toward the front of the engine. Caution should be used to prevent damage to the cam bearings, lobes and journals.

To install:

13. Check the camshaft journals and lobes for wear. Inspect the cam bearings. If they are worn, the cylinder head must be removed for new bearings to be installed by a machine shop.

14. Install the camshaft. Caution should be used to prevent damage to the cam bearings, lobes and journals. Coat the camshaft with heavy SG engine oil or a suitable prelube before sliding it into the cylinder head.

15. Install the camshaft retainer located on the rear mounting stand.

16. Install a new front oil seal.

17. Install the camshaft sprocket and belt guide. Apply a coat of sealer or Teflon® tape to the camshaft sprocket bolt before installation.

18. Install the cam followers as described earlier in this section.

✳✳WARNING

After any procedure requiring removal of the rocker arms, each lash adjuster must be fully collapsed after assembly, then released. This must be done before the camshaft is turned.

19. Remove the blocks of wood between the engine mounts and crossmember pedestals, and lower the engine onto the mounts.

20. Lower the front of the car.

21. Install the front motor mount bolts.

22. Connect the lower radiator hose at the radiator.

23. Connect the automatic transmission cooler lines, if applicable.

24. Align the engine timing marks at TDC.

25. Install the timing belt.

26. Install the timing belt outer cover and valve cover.

27. Install the fan blades and water pump pulley and fan shroud.

28. Connect and install the upper radiator hose.

29. Install the alternator and mounting bracket on the cylinder head.

30. Install all drive belts.

31. Install the spark plug wires on the plugs.

32. Connect the plug wires to the retainer on the valve cover.

33. Connect the rubber vacuum lines as necessary.

34. Fill the cooling system.

35. Install the air cleaner assembly.

36. Connect the negative battery cable.

L6 Engines

1. Remove the cylinder head. Refer to Cylinder Head Removal & Installation procedures, in this section.

2. Remove the cylinder front cover, timing chain and sprockets as outlined previously.

3. Disconnect and remove the radiator, condenser and grille. Remove the gravel deflector.

4. Using a magnet, remove the valve lifters and keep them in order so that they can be installed in their original positions.

5. Remove the camshaft thrust plate and remove the camshaft by pulling it from the front of the engine. Use care not to damage the camshaft lobes or journals while removing the cam from the engine.

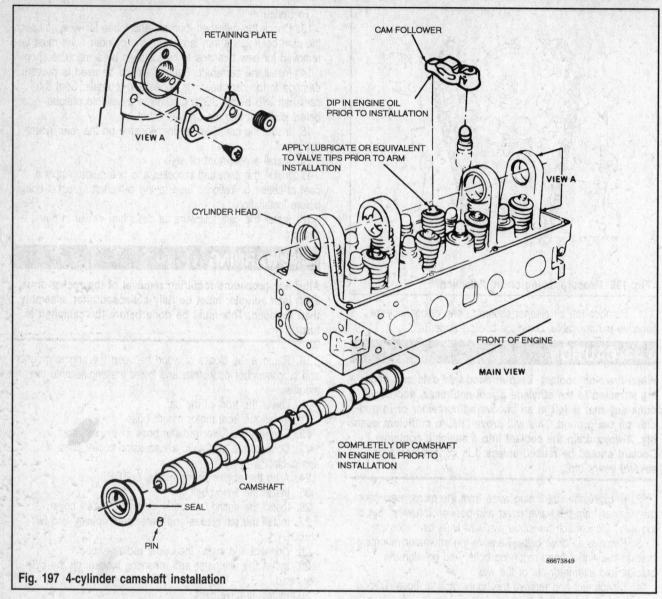

RETAINING PLATE

CAM FOLLOWER

DIP IN ENGINE OIL
PRIOR TO INSTALLATION

VIEW A

APPLY LUBRICATE OR EQUIVALENT
TO VALVE TIPS PRIOR TO ARM
INSTALLATION

VIEW A

CYLINDER HEAD

FRONT OF ENGINE

MAIN VIEW

COMPLETELY DIP CAMSHAFT
IN ENGINE OIL PRIOR TO
INSTALLATION

CAMSHAFT

SEAL

PIN

86673849

Fig. 197 4-cylinder camshaft installation

6. Before installing the camshaft, coat the lobes with engine assembly lubricant and the journals and all valve parts with heavy oil. Clean the oil passage at the rear of the cylinder block with compressed air.

V6 and V8 Engines

▶ See Figures 198, 199 and 200

1. Remove or reposition the radiator, A/C condenser, if so equipped, and grille components, as necessary, to provide clearance for camshaft removal.

2. Remove the cylinder front cover and timing chain as previously described in this section.

3. Remove the crankcase ventilation valve and tubes from the valve rocker covers. Remove the EGR cooler, if so equipped.

4. Remove the valve covers. On some engines, it may be necessary to remove the intake manifold and other related parts.

5. Loosen the rocker arm fulcrum bolts and rotate the rocker arms to the side.

6. Remove the valve pushrods and identify them, so that they can be installed in their original positions.

7. Remove the valve lifters and place them in a rack, so that they can be installed in their original bores.

8. Remove the camshaft thrust plate or button and spring, and carefully remove the camshaft by pulling toward the front of the engine. Be careful not to damage the camshaft bearings.

To install:

9. Before installing, oil the camshaft journals with heavy SG engine oil and apply Lubriplate® or equivalent to the lobes. Carefully slide the camshaft through the bearings.

10. Install the camshaft thrust plate with the groove towards the cylinder block.

11. Lubricate the lifters with heavy SG engine oil or suitable prelube and install in their original bores.

12. Apply Lubriplate® or equivalent to the valve stem tips and each end of the pushrods. Install the pushrods in their original positions.

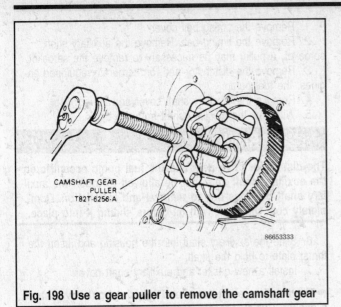

Fig. 198 Use a gear puller to remove the camshaft gear

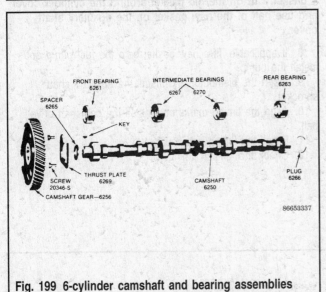

Fig. 199 6-cylinder camshaft and bearing assemblies

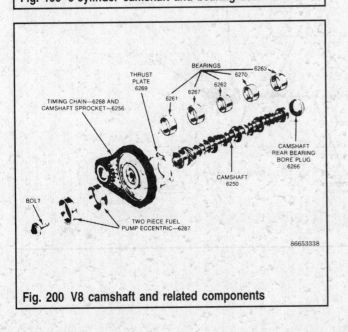

Fig. 200 V8 camshaft and related components

13. Lubricate the rocker arms and fulcrum seats with heavy SG engine oil and position the rocker arms over the push rods.

14. Install all other parts previously removed.

15. Fill the crankcase and cooling system and adjust the timing.

INSPECTION

▶ **See Figure 201**

Clean the camshaft using a safe solvent, and clean all oil grooves. Visually inspect the cam lobes and bearing journals for excessive wear. If a lobe is questionable, check all lobes and journals with a micrometer.

Measure the lobes from nose to base (measurement A) and again from side to side (measurement B). The lift is determined by subtracting the second measurement from the first. If all exhaust lobes and all intake lobes are not identical, the camshaft must be reground or replaced. Measure the bearing journals and compare to specifications. If a journal is worn there is a good chance that the cam bearings are worn too, requiring replacement.

If the lobes and journals appear intact, place the front and rear cam journals in V-blocks and rest a dial indicator on the center journal. Rotate the camshaft to check for straightness; if deviation exceeds 0.001 in. (0.025mm), replace the camshaft.

BEARING REPLACEMENT

▶ **See Figure 202**

➡**This procedure must be performed with the engine removed from the vehicle.**

1. Remove the camshaft, flywheel and crankshaft, following the appropriate procedures. Push the pistons to the top of the cylinder.

2. Remove the camshaft rear bearing bore plug. Remove the camshaft bearings with Tool T65L-6250-A or equivalent.

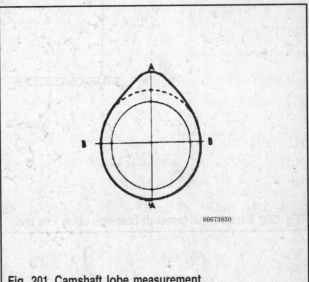

Fig. 201 Camshaft lobe measurement

3. Select the proper sized expanding collet and back-up nut and assemble on the mandrel. With the expanding collet collapsed, install the collet assembly in the camshaft bearing and tighten the back-up nut on the expanding mandrel until the collet fits the camshaft bearing.

4. Assemble the puller screw and extension (if necessary) and install on the expanding mandrel. Wrap a cloth around the threads of the puller screw to protect the front bearing or journal. Tighten the pulling nut against the thrust bearing and pulling plate to remove the camshaft bearing. Be sure to hold a wrench on the end of the puller screw to prevent it from turning.

5. To remove the front bearing, install the puller from the rear of the cylinder block.

To install:

6. Position the new bearings at the bearing bores, and press them in place with tool T65L-6250-A or equivalent. Be sure to center the pulling plate and puller screw to avoid damage to the bearing. Failure to use the correct expanding collet can cause severe bearing damage. Align the oil holes in the bearings with the oil holes in the cylinder block before pressing bearings into place.

7. Install the camshaft rear bearing bore plug.

8. Install the camshaft, crankshaft, flywheel and related parts, following the appropriate procedures.

9. Install the engine in the car, following procedures described earlier in this section.

Auxiliary Shaft

REMOVAL & INSTALLATION

▶ See Figure 203

➡This procedure applies to the 4-cylinder engine only.

1. Remove the timing belt cover.

2. Remove the timing belt. Remove the auxiliary shaft sprocket. A puller may be necessary to remove the sprocket.

3. Remove the distributor and, on carburetor-equipped engines, the fuel pump.

4. Remove the auxiliary shaft cover and thrust plate.

5. Withdraw the auxiliary shaft from the block.

❈❈WARNING

The distributor drive gear and the fuel pump eccentric on the auxiliary shaft must not be allowed to touch the auxiliary shaft bearings during removal and installation. Completely coat the shaft with oil before sliding it into place.

6. Slide the auxiliary shaft into the housing and insert the thrust plate to hold the shaft.

7. Install a new gasket and auxiliary shaft cover.

➡The auxiliary shaft cover and cylinder front cover share a gasket. Cut off the old gasket around the cylinder cover and use half of the new gasket on the auxiliary shaft cover.

8. If applicable, fit a new gasket onto the fuel pump and install the pump.

9. Insert the distributor and install the auxiliary shaft sprocket.

10. Align the timing marks and install the camshaft drive belt.

11. Install the timing belt cover.

12. Check the ignition timing.

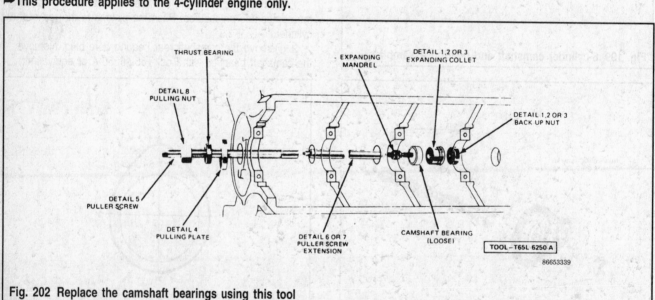

Fig. 202 Replace the camshaft bearings using this tool

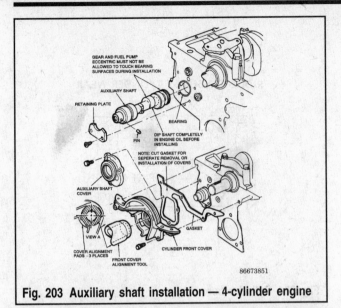

Fig. 203 Auxiliary shaft installation — 4-cylinder engine

Pistons and Connecting Rods

REMOVAL & INSTALLATION

▶ **See Figures 204, 205, 206, 207, 208, 209, 210, 211 and 212**

4-Cylinder Engines

1. Disconnect the negative battery cable.
2. Remove the engine from the car, as previously covered in this section.
3. Remove the cylinder head(s), oil pan and front cover (if necessary).
4. Using a ridge reamer, remove the ridge at the top of each cylinder bore, before removing the pistons and connecting rods. (Refer to the following section on Ridge Removal.)
5. Check the edges of the connecting rod and bearing cap for numbers or matchmarks. If none are present, mark the rod and cap numerically and in sequence from the front to back of the engine. The numbers or marks not only tell from which cylinder the piston came, but also ensures that the rod caps are installed in the correct matching position.
6. Turn the crankshaft until the connecting rod is at the bottom of its travel. Remove the two attaching nuts and the bearing cap. Take two pieces of rubber tubing and cover the rod bolts to prevent crankshaft or cylinder scoring. Use a wooden hammer handle to help push the piston and rod up and out of the cylinder. install the rod cap in its proper position. Remove all pistons and connecting rods, in this manner. Inspect the cylinder walls and deglaze or hone as necessary.

To install:

7. Before installing the piston/connecting rod assembly, be sure to clean all gasket mating surfaces. Oil the pistons, piston rings and the cylinder walls with light engine oil.
8. Be sure to install the pistons in the cylinders from which they were removed. The connecting rod and bearing caps are numbered. The numbers on the connecting rod and bearing cap must be on the same side when installed in the cylinder bore.

9. Make sure the ring gaps are properly spaced around the circumference of the piston. Make sure rubber hose lengths are fitted to the rod bolts. Fit a piston ring compressor around the piston and slide the piston and connecting rod assembly down into the cylinder bore, pushing it in with the wooden hammer handle. Push the piston down until it is only slightly below the top of the cylinder bore. Guide the connecting rods onto the crankshaft bearing journals carefully, using the rubber hose lengths, to avoid damaging the crankshaft.
10. Check the bearing clearance of all the rod bearings, fitting them to the crankshaft bearing journals.
11. After the bearings have been fitted, apply a light coating of engine oil to the journals and bearings.
12. Turn the crankshaft until the appropriate bearing journal is at the bottom of its stroke, then push the piston assembly all the way down until the connecting rod bearing seats on the crankshaft journal. Be careful not to allow the bearing cap screws to strike the crankshaft bearing journals and damage them.
13. After the piston and connecting rod assemblies have been installed, check the connecting rod side clearance on each crankshaft journal.
14. Prime and install the oil pump and the oil pump intake tube, then install the oil pan.
15. Reassemble the rest of the engine in the reverse order of disassembly.

6-Cylinder Engines

1. Disconnect the negative battery cable.
2. Drain the cooling system and the crankcase oil.

✷✷CAUTION

When draining coolant, keep in mind that cats and dogs are attracted to the ethylene glycol antifreeze, and could drink any that is left in an uncovered container or in puddles on the ground. This will prove fatal in sufficient quantity. Always drain the coolant into a sealable container. Coolant should be reused unless it is contaminated or several years old.

3. Remove the cylinder head.
4. Remove the oil pan, the oil pump inlet tube and the oil pump.
5. Turn the crankshaft until the piston to be removed is at the bottom of its travel and place a cloth on the piston head to collect any filings. Using a ridge reaming tool, remove any ridge of carbon or any other deposit from the upper cylinder walls where piston travel ends. Do not cut into the piston ring travel area more than $1/32$ in. (0.8mm) while removing the ridge.
6. Mark all of the connecting rod caps so that they can be reinstalled in the original positions from which they are removed and remove the connecting rod bearing cap. Also identify the piston assemblies as they, too, must be reinstalled in the same cylinder from which removed.
7. With the bearing caps removed, the connecting rod bearing bolts are potentially damaging to the cylinder walls during removal. To guard against cylinder wall damage, install 4 in. (101mm) or 5 in. (127mm) lengths of $3/8$ in. (9.5mm) rubber tubing onto the connecting rod bolts. These will also protect the crankshaft journal from scratches when the connecting rod is installed, and will serve as a guide for the rod.

8. Squirt some clean engine oil into each cylinder before removing the pistons. Using a wooden hammer handle, push the connecting rod and piston assembly out of the top of the cylinder (pushing from the bottom of the rod). Be careful to avoid damaging both the crank journal and the cylinder wall when removing the rod and piston assembly.

To install:

9. Before installing the piston/connecting rod assembly, be sure to clean all gasket mating surfaces, oil the pistons, piston rings and the cylinder walls with light engine oil.

10. Be sure to install the pistons in the cylinders from which they were removed. The connecting rod and bearing caps are numbered from 1-6 beginning at the front of the engine. The numbers on the connecting rod and bearing cap must be on the same side when installed in the cylinder bore. If a connecting rod is ever transposed from one engine or cylinder to another, new bearings should be fitted and the connecting rod should be numbered to correspond with the new cylinder number. The notch on the piston head goes toward the front of the engine.

11. Make sure the ring gaps are properly spaced around the circumference of the piston. Make sure rubber hose lengths are fitted to the rod bolts. Fit a piston ring compressor around the piston and slide the piston and connecting rod assembly down into the cylinder bore, pushing it in with the wooden hammer handle. Push the piston down until it is only slightly below the top of the cylinder bore. Guide the connecting rods onto the crankshaft bearing journals carefully, using the rubber hose lengths, to avoid damaging the crankshaft.

12. Check the bearing clearance of all the rod bearings, fitting them to the crankshaft bearing journals.

13. After the bearings have been fitted, apply a light coating of engine oil to the journals and bearings.

14. Turn the crankshaft until the appropriate bearing journal is at the bottom of its stroke, then push the piston assembly all the way down until the connecting rod bearing seats on the crankshaft journal. Be careful not to allow the bearing cap screws to strike the crankshaft bearing journals and damage them.

15. After the piston and connecting rod assemblies have been installed, check the connecting rod side clearance on each crankshaft journal.

16. Prime and install the oil pump and the oil pump intake tube, then install the oil pan.

17. Reassemble the rest of the engine in the reverse order of disassembly.

8-Cylinder Engines

1. Disconnect the negative battery cable.
2. Drain the cooling system and the crankcase oil.

❊❊CAUTION

When draining coolant, keep in mind that cats and dogs are attracted to ethylene glycol antifreeze, and could drink any that is left in an uncovered container or in puddles on the ground. This will prove fatal in sufficient quantity. Always drain the coolant into a sealable container. Coolant should be reused unless it is contaminated or several years old.

3. Remove the intake manifold.

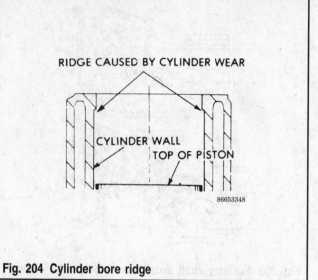

Fig. 204 Cylinder bore ridge

Fig. 205 Remove the ridge from the cylinder bore using a ridge reamer

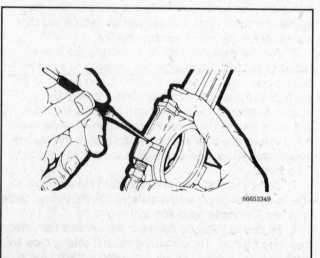

Fig. 206 Mark the connecting rod and cap for proper installation

Fig. 207 Use sections of rubber vacuum hose to protect the crankshaft journals and cylinder walls

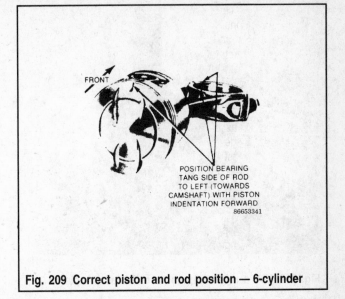
POSITION BEARING TANG SIDE OF ROD TO LEFT (TOWARDS CAMSHAFT) WITH PISTON INDENTATION FORWARD
86653341
Fig. 209 Correct piston and rod position — 6-cylinder

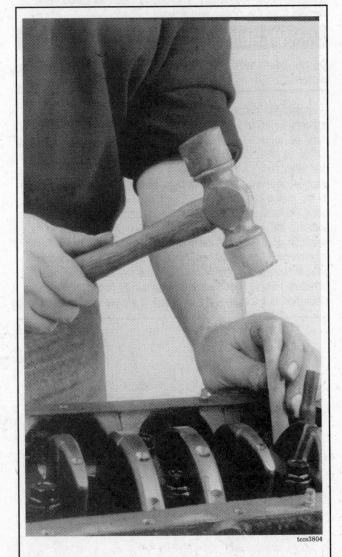
Fig. 208 Push the piston out with a hammer and wooden dowel

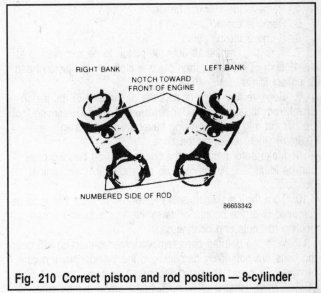
RIGHT BANK   LEFT BANK
NOTCH TOWARD FRONT OF ENGINE
NUMBERED SIDE OF ROD
86653342
Fig. 210 Correct piston and rod position — 8-cylinder

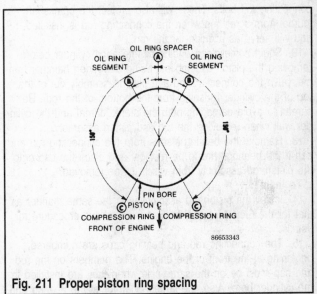
OIL RING SPACER
OIL RING SEGMENT   OIL RING SEGMENT
PIN BORE
PISTON
COMPRESSION RING   COMPRESSION RING
FRONT OF ENGINE
86653343
Fig. 211 Proper piston ring spacing

Fig. 212 Use a ring compressor to install the piston

4. Remove the cylinder heads.

5. Remove the oil pan.

6. Remove the oil pump.

7. Turn the crankshaft until the piston to be removed is at the bottom of its travel, then place a cloth on the piston head to collect filings.

8. Remove any ridge of deposits at the end of the piston travel from the upper cylinder bore, using a ridge reaming tool. Do not cut into the piston ring travel area more than $1/32$ in. (0.8mm) when removing the ridge.

9. Make sure that all of the connecting rod bearing caps can be identified, so they will be reinstalled in their original positions.

10. Turn the crankshaft until the connecting rod that is to be removed is at the bottom of its stroke and remove the connecting rod nuts and bearing cap.

11. With the bearing caps removed, the connecting rod bearing bolts are potentially damaging to the cylinder walls during removal. To guard against cylinder wall damage, install 4-5 in. (102-127mm) lengths of $3/8$ in. (0.8mm) rubber tubing onto the connecting rod bolts. These will also protect the crankshaft journal from scratches when the connecting rod is installed, and will serve as a guide for the rod.

12. Squirt some clean engine oil into each cylinder before removing the piston assemblies. Using a wooden hammer handle, push the connecting rod and piston assembly out of the top of the cylinder (pushing from the bottom of the rod). Be careful to avoid damaging both the crank journal and the cylinder wall when removing the rod and piston assembly.

13. Remove the bearing inserts from the connecting rod and cap if the bearings are to be replace, and place the cap onto the piston/rod assembly from which it was removed.

To install:

14. Install the piston/rod assemblies in the same manner as that for the 6-cylinder engine. See the previous procedure for details.

15. The connecting rod and bearing caps are numbered, beginning at the front of the engine. The numbers on the rod and cap must be on the same side when they are installed in the cylinder bore. Also, the largest chamfer at the bearing end of the rod should be positioned toward the crank pin thrust face of the crankshaft and the notch in the head of the piston faces toward the front of the engine.

16. See the appropriate component procedures in this section to assemble the engine.

INSPECTION

◆ See Figures 213 and 214

All of the Ford engines covered in this guide utilize pressed-in wrist pins, which can only be removed by an arbor press. The piston/connecting rod assemblies should be taken to an engine specialist or qualified machinist for wrist pin removal and installation.

A piston ring expander is necessary for removing the piston rings without damaging them; any other method will result in the rings being bent, scratched or distorted, or the piston itself being damaged. When the rings are removed, clean the ring grooves using an appropriate ring groove cleaning tool, using care not to cut too deeply. Thoroughly clean all carbon and varnish from the piston with solvent.

✳✳WARNING

Do not use a wire brush or caustic solvent (acids, etc.) on pistons.

Inspect the pistons for scuffing, scoring, cracks, pitting, or excessive ring groove wear. If these are evident, the piston must be replaced.

The piston should also be checked in relation to the cylinder diameter. Using a telescoping gauge and micrometer, or dial gauge, measure the cylinder bore diameter perpendicular (90°) to the piston pin, $2\frac{1}{2}$ in. (63.5mm) below the cylinder block deck (surface where the block mates with the heads). Then, with the micrometer, measure the piston, perpendicular to its wrist pin on the skirt. The difference between the two measurements is the piston clearance. If the clearance is within specification or slightly below (after the cylinders have been bored or hones), finish honing is all that is necessary. If the clearance is excessive, try to obtain a slightly larger piston to

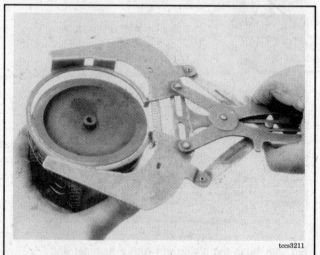

Fig. 213 Remove the old ring from the piston using a ring expander

Fig. 214 Cleaning the piston ring grooves

bring clearance to within specifications. If this is not possible, obtain the first oversize piston and hone (or if necessary, bore) the cylinder to size. Generally, if the cylinder bore is tapered 0.005 in. (0.127mm) or more, or is out-of-round 0.003 in. (0.076mm) or more, it is advisable to rebore for the smallest possible oversize piston and rings.

After measuring, mark the pistons with a felt tip pen for reference when assembling.

➡**Cylinder honing and/or boring should be performed by a reputable, professional mechanic with the proper equipment. In some cases, clean-up honing can be done with the cylinder block in the car, but most excessive honing and all cylinder boring must be done with the block stripped and removed from the vehicle.**

Measuring Pistons
▶ **See Figures 215, 216 and 217**

Check used piston-to-cylinder bore clearance as follows:
1. Measure the cylinder bore diameter with a telescope gauge.
2. Measure the piston diameter. When measuring the pistons for size or taper, measurements must be made with the piston pin removed.
3. Subtract the piston diameter from the cylinder bore diameter to determine piston-to-bore clearance.
4. Compare the piston-to-bore clearances obtained with those clearances recommended in the chart. Determine if the piston-to-bore clearance is in the acceptable range.
5. When measuring taper, the largest reading must be at the bottom of the skirt.

Selecting New Pistons

1. If the used piston is not acceptable, check the service piston size and determine if a new piston can be selected. Service pistons are available in standard, high limit and standard oversize.
2. If the cylinder bore must be reconditioned, measure the new piston diameter, then hone the cylinder bore to obtain the preferred clearance.

3. Mark the piston to identify the cylinder for which it was fitted.

Cylinder Honing
▶ **See Figures 218, 219 and 220**

1. When cylinders are being honed, follow the manufacturer's recommendations for the use of the hone.
2. Occasionally, during the honing operation, the cylinder bore should be thoroughly cleaned and the selected piston checked for correct fit.
3. When finish-honing a cylinder bore, the hone should be moved up and down at a sufficient speed to obtain a very fine uniform surface finish in a cross-hatch pattern of approximately 45-65° included angle. The finish marks should be clean but not sharp, free from imbedded particles and torn or folded metal.
4. Permanently mark the piston for the cylinder to which it has been fitted and proceed to hone the remaining cylinders.

✳✳WARNING

Handle the pistons with care. Do not attempt to force the pistons through the cylinders until the cylinders have been honed to the correct size. Pistons can be distorted through careless handling.

Thoroughly clean the bores with hot water and detergent. Scrub well with a stiff bristle brush and rinse thoroughly with hot water. It is extremely essential that a good cleaning operation be performed. If any of the abrasive material is allowed to remain in the cylinder bores, it will rapidly wear the new rings and cylinder bores. The bores should be swabbed several times with light engine oil and a clean cloth and then wiped with a clean dry cloth. CYLINDERS SHOULD NOT BE CLEANED WITH KEROSENE OR GASOLINE! Clean the remainder of the cylinder block to remove the excess material spread during the honing operation.

Piston Ring End-Gap
▶ **See Figure 221**

Piston ring end-gap should be checked while the rings are removed from the pistons. Incorrect end-gap indicates that the wrong size rings are being used; ring breakage could occur.

Compress the piston rings to be used in a cylinder, one at a time, into that cylinder. Squirt clean oil into the cylinder, so that the rings and the top 2 in. (51mm) of cylinder wall are coated. Using an inverted piston, press the rings approximately 1 in. (25mm) below the deck of the block. Measure the ring end-gap with the feeler gauge, and compare to the ring gap specification in this section. Carefully pull the ring out of the cylinder and file the ends squarely with a fine file to obtain the proper clearance.

Piston Ring Side Clearance
▶ **See Figure 222**

Check the pistons to see that the ring grooves and oil return holes have been properly cleaned. Slide a piston ring into its groove, and check the side clearance with a feeler gauge. Make sure you insert the gauge between the ring and its lower land (lower edge of the groove), because any wear that occurs

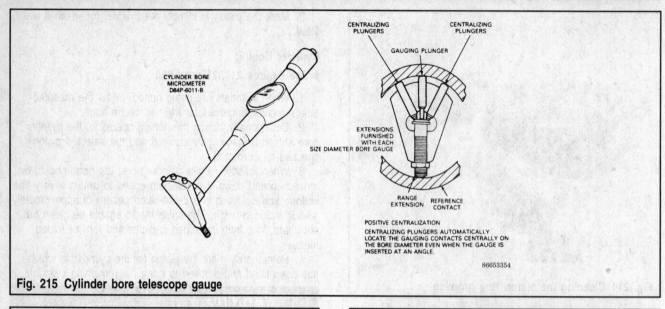

Fig. 215 Cylinder bore telescope gauge

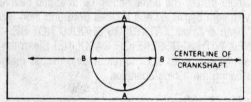

A - At Right angle to center line of engine
B - Parallel to center line of engine

Top Measurement Make 12 70mm (1 2 inch) below top of block deck

Bottom Measurement Make within 12 70mm (1 2 inch) above top of piston - when piston is at its lowest travel (B D C)

Bore Service Limit Equals the average of ''A'' and ''B'' when measured at the center of the piston travel

Taper Equals difference between ''A'' top and ''A'' bottom

Out-of-Round Equals difference between ''A'' and ''B'' when measured at the center of piston travel

Refer to Specification tables at end of each engine section

Fig. 216 Cylinder bore measurement

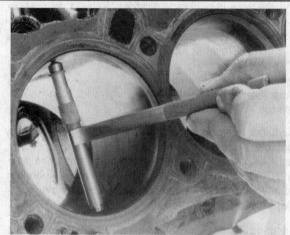

Fig. 217 Measuring the cylinder bore with a telescopic gauge

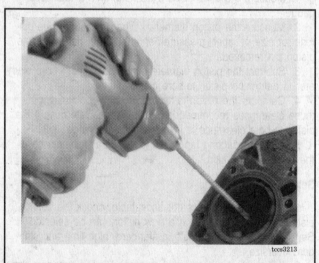

Fig. 218 Remove any cylinder glazing with a flexible hone and a power drill

Fig. 219 A properly cross-hatched cylinder bore

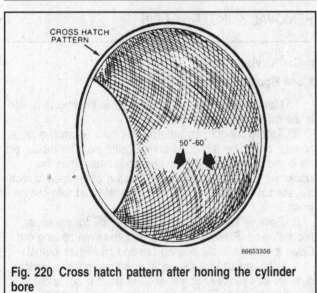

Fig. 220 Cross hatch pattern after honing the cylinder bore

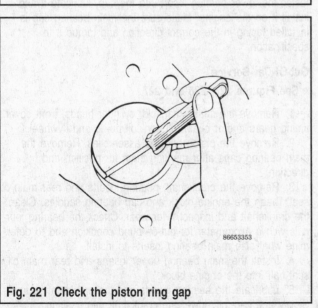

Fig. 221 Check the piston ring gap

forms a step at the inner portion of the lower land. If the piston grooves have worn to the extent that relatively high steps exist on the lower land, the piston should be replaced, because these will interfere with the operation of the new rings and ring clearance will be excessive. Piston rings are not furnished in oversize widths to compensate for ring groove wear.

Install the rings on the piston, lowest ring first, using a piston ring expander. There is a high risk of breaking or distorting the rings, or scratching the piston, if the rings are installed by hand or other means.

Position the rings on the piston. Spacing of the various piston ring gaps is crucial to proper oil retention and even cylinder wear. When installing new rings, refer to the installation diagram furnished with the new parts.

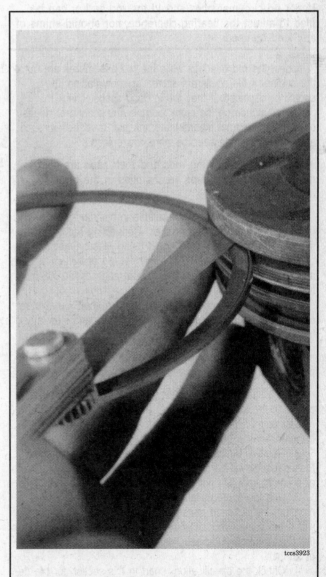

Fig. 222 Check the piston ring side clearance

Connecting Rod Bearings

INSPECTION

Connecting rod bearings for the engines covered in this guide consist of two halves or shells which are interchangeable in the rod and cap. When the shells are placed in position, the ends extend slightly beyond the rod and cap surfaces. When the rod bolts are tightened the shells will be clamped tightly in place to insure positive seating and to prevent turning. A tang holds the shells in place.

If a rod bearing becomes noisy or is worn so that its clearance on the crank journal is sloppy, a new bearing of the correct undersize must be selected and installed since there is a provision for adjustment.

✲✲WARNING

Under no circumstances should the rod end or cap be filed to adjust the bearing clearance, nor should shims of any kind be used.

Inspect the rod bearings while the rod assemblies are out of the engine. If the shells are scored or show flaking, they should be replaced. If they are in good shape, check for proper clearance on the crank journal. Any scoring or ridges on the crank journal means the crankshaft must be reground and fitted with undersized bearings, or replaced.

➡**Make sure connecting rods and their caps are kept together, and that the caps are installed in the proper direction.**

Replacement bearings are available in standard size, and in undersizes for reground crankshaft. Connecting rod-to-crankshaft bearing clearance is checked using Plastigauge® or equivalent gauging material at either the top or bottom of each crank journal. The Plastigauge® has a range of 0-0.003 in. (0-0.076mm).

1. Remove the rod cap with the bearing shell. Completely clean the bearing shell and the crank journal, and blow any oil from the oil hole in the crankshaft.

➡**The journal surfaces and bearing shells must be completely free of oil. Plastigauge® is soluble in oil.**

Place a strip of Plastigauge® lengthwise along the bottom center of the lower bearing shell, then install the cap with shell and tighten the bolt or nuts to specification. DO NOT TURN the crankshaft with the Plastigauge® installed in the bearing.

2. Remove the bearing cap with the shell. The flattened Plastigauge® will be found sticking to either the bearing shell or crank journal. Do not remove it yet.

3. Use the printed scale on the Plastigauge® envelope to measure the flattened material at its widest point. The number within the scale which most closely corresponds to the width of the Plastigauge® indicated bearing clearance in thousandths of an inch.

4. Check the specifications chart in this section for the desired clearance. It is advisable to install a new bearing if clearance exceeds 0.003 in. (0.076mm). However, if the bearing is

in good condition and is not being checked because of bearing noise, bearing replacement is not necessary.

5. If you are installing new bearings, try a standard size first, then each undersize in order until one is found that is within the specified limits. Each under size has its size stamped on it.

6. When the proper size shell is found, clean off the Plastigauge® material from the shell, oil the bearing thoroughly, reinstall the cap with its shell and tighten the rod bolt nuts to specification.

➡**With the proper bearing selected and the nuts tightened, it should be possible to move the connecting rod back and forth freely on the crank journal as allowed by the specified connecting rod end clearance. If the rod cannot be moved, either the rod bearing is too far undersize or the rod is misaligned.**

Crankshaft and Main Bearings

REMOVAL & INSTALLATION

In-Car Service
▶ **See Figures 223 and 224**

1. Main bearings may be replaced while the engine is still in the car by rolling them out and in.

2. Special roll-out pins are available from automotive parts houses, or can be fabricated from a cotter pin. The roll-out pin fits in the oil hole of the main bearing journal. When the crankshaft is rotated opposite the direction of the bearing lock tab, the pin engages the end of the bearing and rolls out the insert.

3. Remove the main bearing cap and roll out the upper bearing insert. Remove the insert from the main bearing cap. Clean the inside of the bearing cap and crankshaft journal.

4. Lubricate and roll the upper insert into position, making sure the lock tab is anchored and the insert is not cocked. Install the lower bearing insert into the cap, lubricate it and install it on the engine. Make sure the main bearing cap is installed facing in the correct direction and torque it to specification.

Out-Of-Car Service
▶ **See Figures 225, 226 and 227**

1. Remove the intake manifold, cylinder heads, front cover, timing gears and/or chain, oil pan, oil pump and flywheel.

2. Remove the piston and rod assemblies. Remove the main bearing caps after marking them for position and direction.

3. Remove the crankshaft, bearing inserts and rear main oil seal. Clean the engine block and cap bearing saddles. Clean the crankshaft and inspect it for wear. Check the bearing journals with a micrometer for out-of-round condition and to determine what size main bearing inserts to install.

4. Install the main bearing upper inserts and rear main oil seal half into the engine block.

5. Lubricate the bearing inserts and the crankshaft journals. Slowly and carefully lower the crankshaft into position.

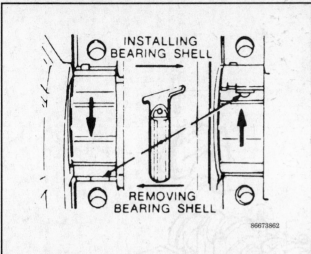

Fig. 223 Remove or install the upper bearing insert using a roll-out pin

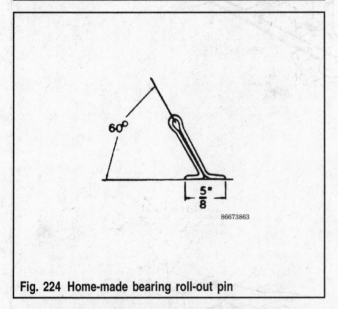

Fig. 224 Home-made bearing roll-out pin

6. Install the bearing inserts and rear main seal into the bearing caps. Install the caps working from the middle out. Torque the cap bolts to specification in stages, rotating the crankshaft after each torque stage. Note the illustration for thrust bearing alignment.

7. Remove the bearing caps, one at a time, and check the oil clearance with a gauging material, such as Plastigauge® or equivalent gauging material. Install if clearance is within specifications.

8. Check the crankshaft end-play. (This procedure is described below.) If it is within specifications, install the connecting rod and piston assemblies with new rod bearing inserts. Check the connecting rod bearing oil clearance and side-play. (This procedure is also described below.) If they are correct, assemble the rest of the engine.

➡If a journal is damaged on the crankshaft, repair is possible by having the crankshaft machined to a standard undersize. In most cases, however, since the engine must

be removed from the car and disassembled, some thought should be given to replacing the damaged crankshaft with a reground shaft kit. A reground crankshaft kit contains the necessary main and rod bearings for installation. The shaft has been ground and polished to undersize specifications, and will usually hold up well if installed correctly.

CHECKING MAIN BEARING CLEARANCES

◆ See Figures 228 and 229

1. Place a piece of Plastigauge® or equivalent gauging material, on the bearing surface across full width of bearing cap and about ¼ in. (6mm) off center.

2. Install cap and tighten bolts to specifications. Do not turn crankshaft while Plastigauge® is in place.

3. Remove the cap. Using Plastigauge® scale, check width of Plastigauge® at widest point to get the minimum clearance. Check at narrowest point to get maximum clearance. Difference between readings is taper of journal.

4. If clearance exceeds specified limits, try a 0.001 in. (0.0254mm) or 0.002 in. (0.051mm) undersize bearing in combination with the standard bearing. Bearing clearance must be within specified limits. If standard and 0.002 in. (0.051mm) undersize bearing does not bring clearance within desired limits, refinish crankshaft journal, then install undersize bearings.

CLEANING & INSPECTION

➡Handle the crankshaft carefully to avoid damage to the finished surfaces.

1. Clean the crankshaft with solvent, and blow out all oil passages with compressed air. On the 3.9L engine, clean the oil seal contact surface at the rear of the crankshaft with solvent to remove any corrosion, sludge or varnish deposits.

2. Use crocus cloth to remove any sharp edges, burrs or other imperfections which might damage the oil seal during installation or cause premature seal wear.

➡Do not use crocus cloth to polish the seal surfaces. A finely polished surface may produce poor sealing or cause premature seal wear.

3. Inspect the main and connecting rod journals for cracks, scratches, grooves or scores.

4. Measure the diameter of each journal at four places (at least) to determine out-of-round, taper or undersize condition.

5. Inspect the pilot bearing (manual transmissions,) when used, for roughness, evidence of overheating or loss of lubricant. Replace if any of these conditions are found.

COMPLETING THE REBUILDING PROCESS

Fill the oil pump with oil, to prevent cavitating (sucking air) on initial engine start up. Install the oil pump and the pickup tube on the engine. Coat the oil pan gasket as necessary, and

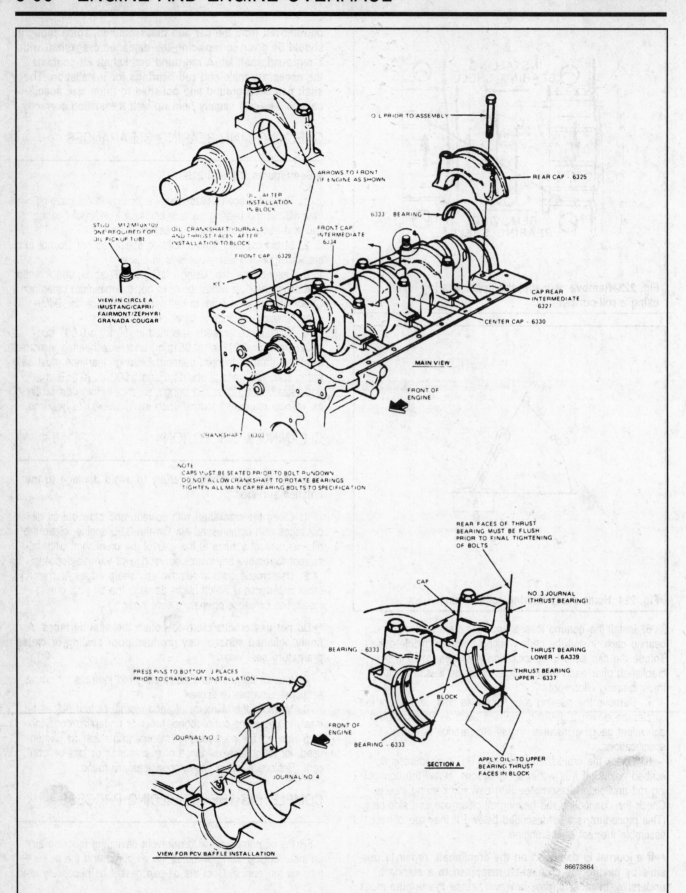

Fig. 225 Crankshaft and main bearing installation — 4-cylinder engine

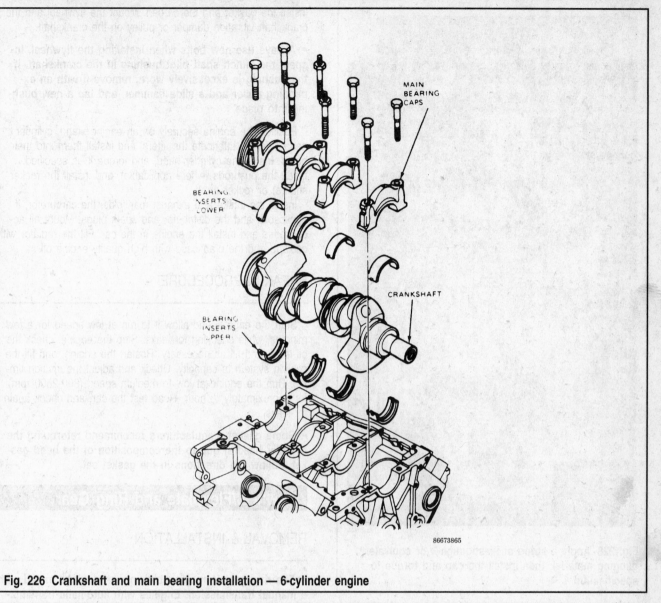

Fig. 226 Crankshaft and main bearing installation — 6-cylinder engine

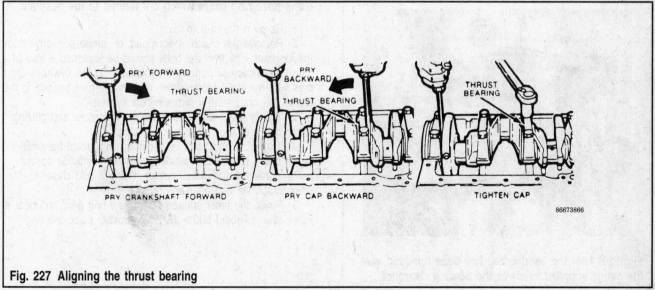

Fig. 227 Aligning the thrust bearing

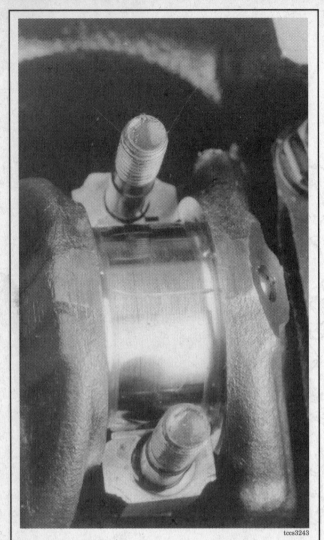

tccs3243

Fig. 228 Apply a stripe of Plastigauge® or equivalent gauging material, then install the cap and torque to specification

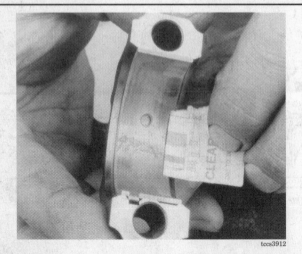

tccs3912

Fig. 229 After the bearing cap has been removed, use the gauge supplied to check the bearing clearance

install the gasket and the oil pan. Mount the flywheel and the crankshaft vibration damper or pulley on the crankshaft.

➡️**Always use new bolts when installing the flywheel. Inspect the clutch shaft pilot bushing in the crankshaft. If the bushing is excessively worn, remove it with an expanding puller and a slide hammer, and tap a new bushing into place.**

Position the engine securely on an engine stand, cylinder head side up. Lubricate the lifters, and install them into their bores. Install the cylinder head, and torque it as specified. Insert the pushrods (where applicable), and install the rocker shaft(s) or rocker arms.

Install the intake and exhaust manifolds, the carburetor, if applicable, and the distributor and spark plugs. Mount all accessories and install the engine in the car. Fill the radiator with coolant, and the crankcase with high quality engine oil.

BREAK-IN PROCEDURE

Start the engine, and allow it to run at low speed for a few minutes, while checking for leaks. Stop the engine, check the oil level, and fill as necessary. Restart the engine, and fill the cooling system to capacity. Check and adjust the ignition timing. Run the engine at low to medium speed (800-2500 rpm) for approximately ½ hour. Road test the car, and check again for leaks.

➡️**Some gasket manufacturers recommend retorquing the cylinder head(s) due to the composition of the head gasket. Follow the directions in the gasket set.**

Flywheel/Flexplate and Ring Gear

REMOVAL & INSTALLATION

➡️**The ring gear is replaceable only on engines mated with a manual transmission. Engines with automatic transmissions have ring gears which are welded to the flexplate.**

1. Remove the transmission.
2. Remove the clutch, if equipped, or torque converter from the flywheel. The flywheel bolts should be loosened a little at a time in a crisscross pattern to avoid warping the flywheel. On cars with manual transmissions, replace the pilot bearing in the end of the crankshaft if removing the flywheel.
3. The flywheel should be checked for cracks and glazing. It can be resurfaced by a machine shop.
4. If the ring gear is to be replaced on manual transmissions, drill a hole in the gear between two teeth. Be careful not to contact the flywheel surface. Using a cold chisel at this point, crack the ring gear and remove it.
5. Polish the inner surface of the new ring gear and heat it in an oven to about 600°F (316°C). Quickly place the ring

gear on the flywheel and tap it into place, making sure that it is fully seated.

✳✳WARNING

Never heat the ring gear past 800°F (426°C), or the tempering will be destroyed.

6. Position the flywheel on the end of the crankshaft. Tighten the bolts a little at a time, in a crisscross pattern, to the tighten figure shown in the Torque Specifications chart.

7. Install the clutch or tighten converter.

8. Install the transmission. Refer to the necessary service procedures.

Rear Main Bearing Oil Seal

REMOVAL & INSTALLATION

➡Refer to the build dates listed below to determine if the engine is equipped with a split-type or one-piece rear main oil seal. Engines manufactured after the dates indicated have a one-piece oil seal, while those built prior to the indicated dates are equipped with a split-type seal.

4-140 — 9/28/81
6-232 — 4/1/83
8-302 — 12/1/82

Split-Type Seal

▶ See Figure 230

➡The rear oil seal installed in these engines is a rubber type (split-lip) seal.

1. Remove the oil pan and, if required, the oil pump.

2. Loosen all the main bearing caps, allowing the crankshaft to lower slightly.

✳✳WARNING

The crankshaft should not be allowed to drop more than 1/32 in. (0.8mm).

3. Remove the rear main bearing cap and remove the seal from the cap and block. Be very careful not to scratch the sealing surface. Remove the old seal retaining pin from the cap, if equipped. It is not used with the replacement seal.

4. Carefully clean the seal grooves in the cap and block with solvent.

5. Soak the new seal halves in clean engine oil.

6. Install the upper half of the seal in the block with the undercut side of the seal toward the front of the engine. Slide the seal around the crankshaft journal until 3/8 in. (9.5mm) protrudes beyond the base of the block.

7. Tighten all the main bearing caps (except the rear main bearing) to specifications.

8. Install the lower seal into the rear cap, with the undercut side facing the front of the engine. Allow 3/8 in. (9.5mm) of the seal to protrude above the surface, at the opposite end from the block seal.

9. Squeeze a 1/16 in. (1.6mm) bead of silicone sealant onto the areas shown.

10. Install the rear cap and torque to specification.

11. Install the oil pump, if applicable, and the oil pan. Fill the crankcase with oil, start the engine, and check for leaks.

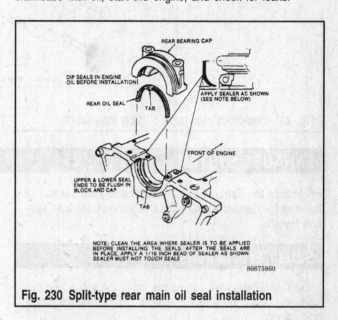

Fig. 230 Split-type rear main oil seal installation

One-Piece Seal

▶ See Figure 231

1. Remove the transmission, clutch, and flywheel or driveplate, after referring to the appropriate section for instructions.

2. Punch two holes in the crankshaft rear oil seal on opposite sides of the crankshaft, just above the bearing cap to the cylinder block split line. Install a sheet metal screw in each of the holes or use a small slide hammer, and pry the crankshaft rear main oil seal from the block.

✳✳WARNING

Use extreme caution not to scratch the crankshaft oil seal surface.

3. Clean the oil seal recess in the cylinder block and main bearing cap.

4. Coat the seal and all of the seal mounting surfaces with oil and install the seal in the recess, driving it into place with an oil seal installation tool or a large socket.

5. Install the driveplate or flywheel, clutch and transmission in the reverse order of removal.

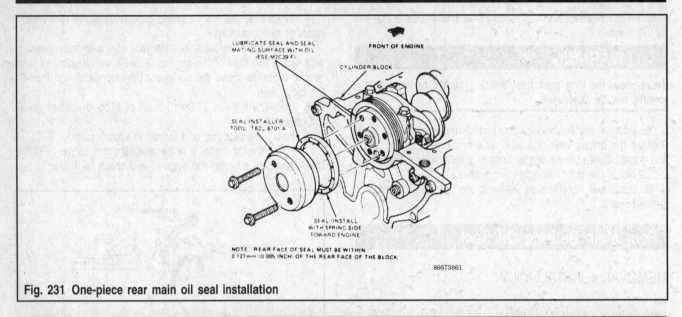

LUBRICATE SEAL AND SEAL
MATING SURFACE WITH OIL
(ESE M2C39 F)

FRONT OF ENGINE

CYLINDER BLOCK

SEAL INSTALLER
TOOL T82L 6701 A

SEAL INSTALL
WITH SPRING SIDE
TOWARD ENGINE

NOTE REAR FACE OF SEAL MUST BE WITHIN
0 127mm (0 005 INCH) OF THE REAR FACE OF THE BLOCK

86673861

Fig. 231 One-piece rear main oil seal installation

EXHAUST SYSTEM

➡Refer to the Exhaust System Exploded View section at the end for detailed descriptions of various exhaust system layouts

Safety Precautions

Exhaust system work can be the most dangerous type of work you can do on your car. Always observe the following precautions:

• Support the car securely. Not only will you often be working directly under it, but you'll frequently be using a lot of force, (heavy hammer blows, to dislodge rusted parts.) This can cause a car that's improperly supported to shift and possibly fall.

• Wear goggles. Exhaust system parts are always rusty. Metal chips can be dislodged, even when you're only turning rusted bolts. Attempting to pry pipes apart with a chisel makes the chips fly even more frequently.

• If you're using a cutting torch, keep it a great distance from the fuel tank or lines. Feel the temperature of the fuel pipes on the tank frequently. Even slight heat can expand and/or vaporize fuel, resulting in accumulated vapor, or even a liquid leak, near your torch.

• Watch where your hammer blows fall and make sure you hit squarely. You could easily tap a brake or fuel line when you hit an exhaust system part with a glancing blow. Inspect all lines and hoses in the area where you've been working.

❋❋CAUTION

Be very careful when working on or near the catalytic converter! External temperatures can reach 1500°F (816°C) and more, causing severe burns. Removal or installation should be performed only on a cold exhaust system.

Special Tools

A number of special exhaust system tools can be rented from auto supply houses or local stores that rent special equipment. A common one is a tail pipe expander, designed to enable you to join pipes of identical diameter.

It may also be quite helpful to use solvents designed to loosen rusted bolts or flanges. Soaking rusted parts the night before you do the job can speed the work of freeing rusted parts considerably. Remember that these solvents are often flammable. Apply only to parts after they are cool!

Muffler

REMOVAL & INSTALLATION

▶ See Figure 232

➡The following applies to exhaust systems using clamped joints. Some models, use welded joints at the muffler. These joints will, of course, have to be cut.

❋❋CAUTION

To protect your eyes wear safety goggles at ALL times.

1. Raise and safely support the rear end on jackstands placed under the frame. Allow the rear axle to lower to the full length of its travel.
2. Remove the U-bolt clamping the inlet pipe to the muffler, if equipped. These may have to be cut if they excessively rusted.
3. Unbolt the rear support bracket from the muffler. Some models use a multiple bracket system. In this case remove all necessary brackets in order to free the muffler assemble.
4. Unbolt the intermediate support bracket(s) from the muffler.

5. Remove the muffler outlet clamp and remove the muffler. If the muffler will not move, try turning the unit from side to side. If it still will not come off, the unit will have to be cut.

6. When the muffler is removed, clean the section of exhaust pipe where the section will be joined to it. The cleaner it is, the easier it will be to fit the section.

7. Installation is the reverse of removal. Always use new clamps. Always install all parts loosely until they are aligned and all clearances are satisfied. Tighten the support bracket bolts to 14 ft. lbs. (19 Nm); the flange nuts to 30 ft. lbs. (41 Nm).

Front Exhaust Pipe

REMOVAL & INSTALLATION

▶ See Figure 233

1. Raise and safely support the front end on jackstands.
2. On cars equipped with an exhaust shield, remove the shield(s).
3. Support the muffler sections.
4. Remove the muffler inlet clamp.
5. Unbolt the front pipe from the catalytic converter, if equipped.
6. Remove the heat shield brackets.
7. Separate the front pipe from the muffler slip joint connection. It may be necessary to remove the rear hanger connections for clearance purposes.
8. Unbolt the pipe ends from the exhaust manifolds.
9. Installation is the reverse of removal. Always use new clamps. Always replace the pipe ends-to-manifold packings. Always install all parts loosely and align the system so that clearances between the system components and surrounding parts are adequate. Tighten the support bracket bolts to 14 ft. lbs. (19 Nm); the clamp nuts to 35 ft. lbs. (46 Nm); the flange nuts to 30 ft. lbs. (39 Nm).

Catalytic Converter

REMOVAL & INSTALLATION

1. Raise and safely support the car on jackstands.
2. Remove the heat shield(s).
3. Support the inlet pipe with a length of wire at the crossmember.
4. Remove the discard the inlet pipe-to-converter flange bolts.
5. Remove the heat shield brackets.
6. Remove the converter-to-manifold flange nuts.

7. Slide the inlet pipes rearward until the converter can be removed.

8. Installation is the reverse of removal. Always use new clamps. Always replace the pipe ends-to-manifold packings. Always install all parts loosely and align the system, making sure that all clearances between the system parts and surrounding components are adequate. Tighten the flange nuts to 30 ft. lbs. (41 Nm); the manifold nuts to 35 ft. lbs. (47 Nm).

Exhaust System Exploded Views

▶ See Figures 234, 235, 236, 237, 238, 239, 240 and 241

Fig. 232 A properly installed muffler will fit within the confines of the vehicle and not rattle against the body

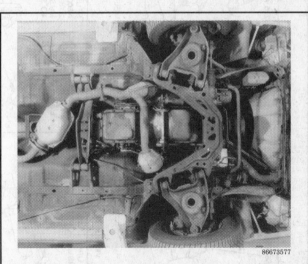

Fig. 233 On this vehicle, the front pipe is the Y-shaped pipe attached to the exhaust manifolds

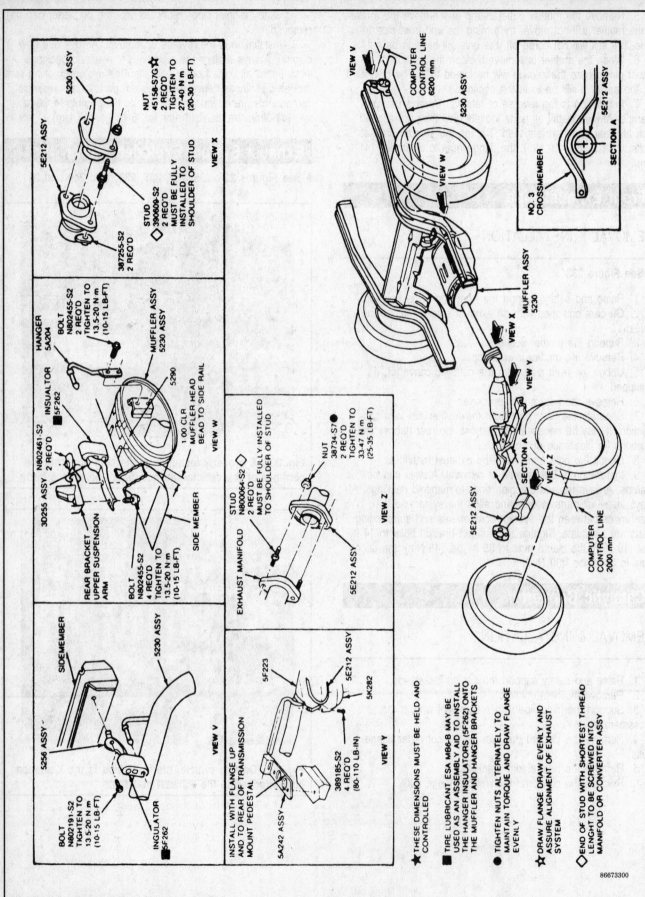

Fig. 234 Exhaust system — 2.3L engine

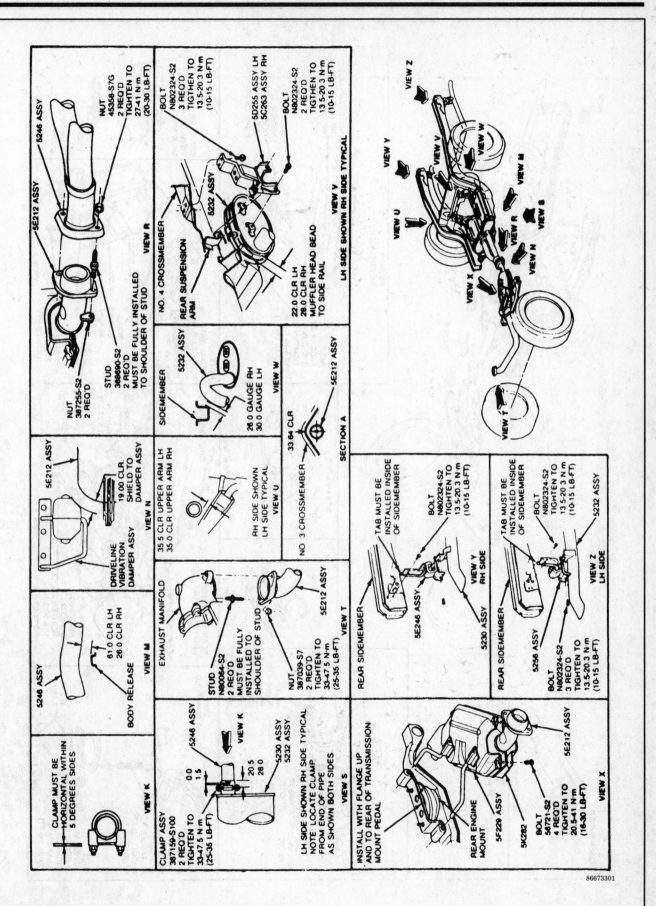

Fig. 235 Turbo exhaust system — 2.3L engine

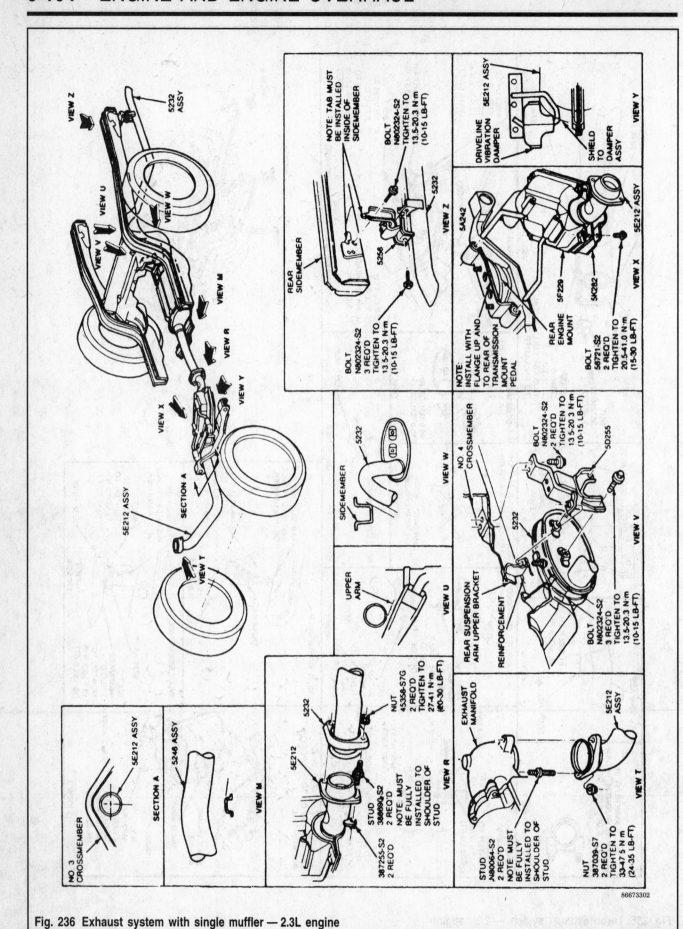

Fig. 236 Exhaust system with single muffler — 2.3L engine

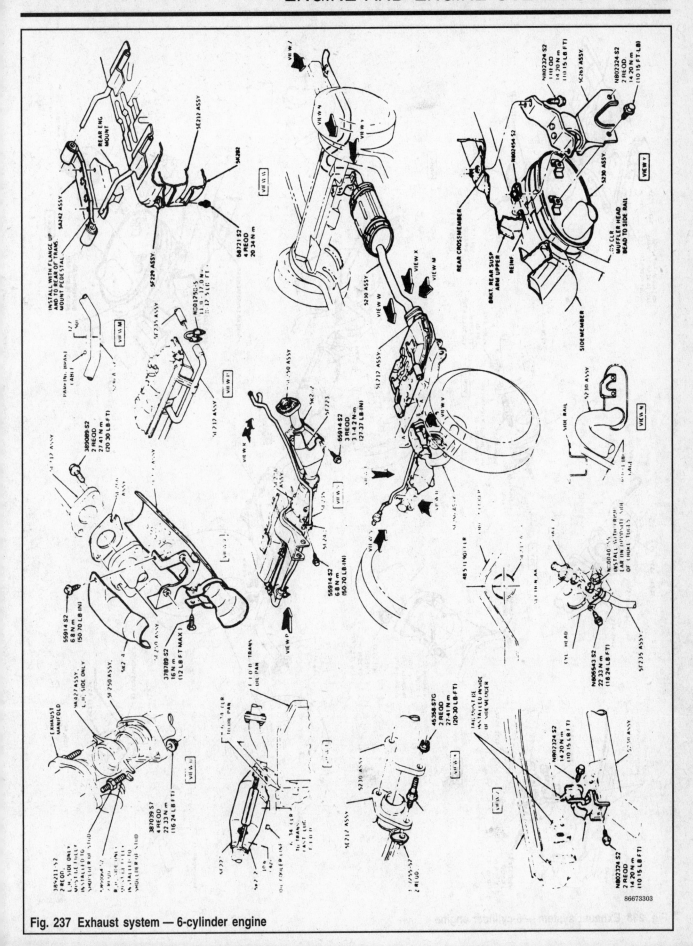

Fig. 237 Exhaust system — 6-cylinder engine

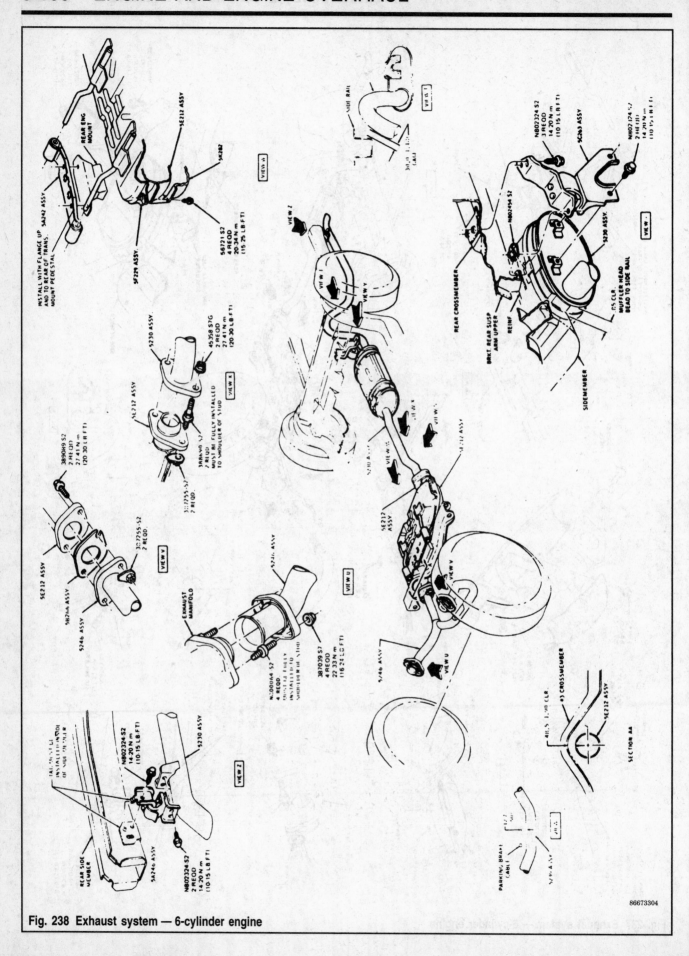

Fig. 238 Exhaust system — 6-cylinder engine

86673304

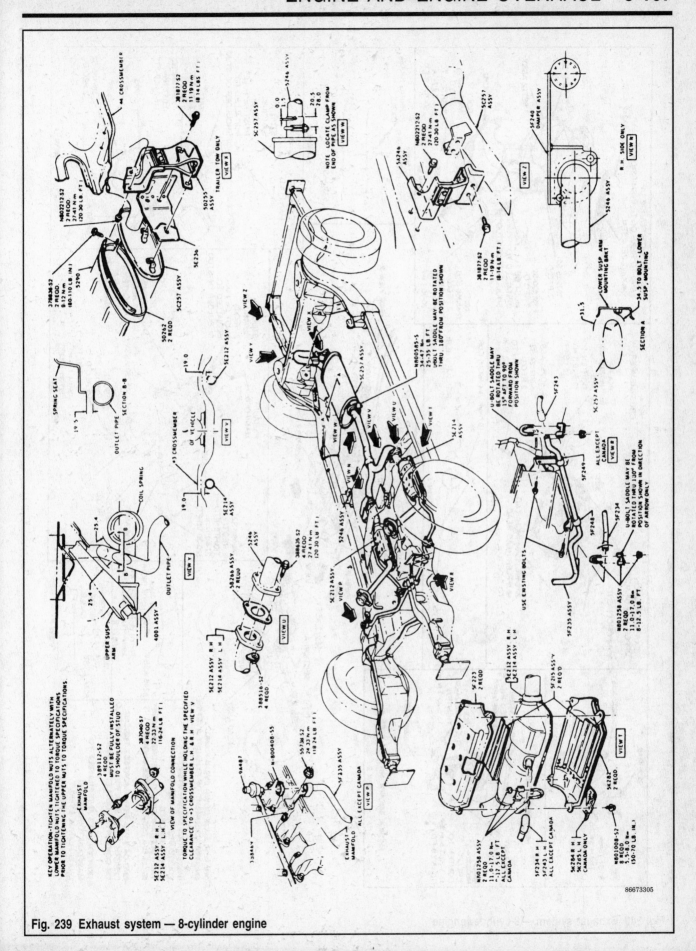

Fig. 239 Exhaust system — 8-cylinder engine

86673305

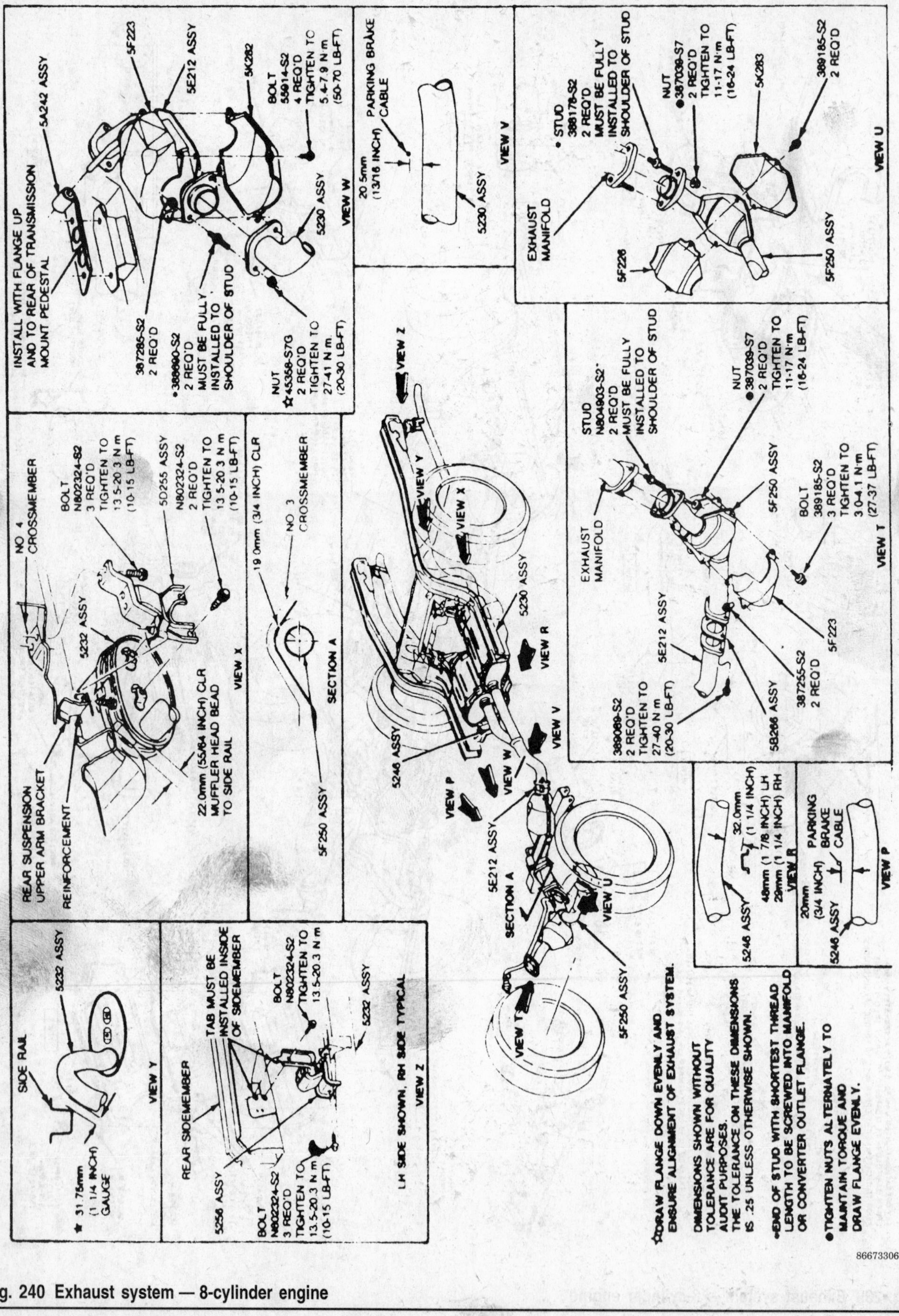

Fig. 240 Exhaust system — 8-cylinder engine

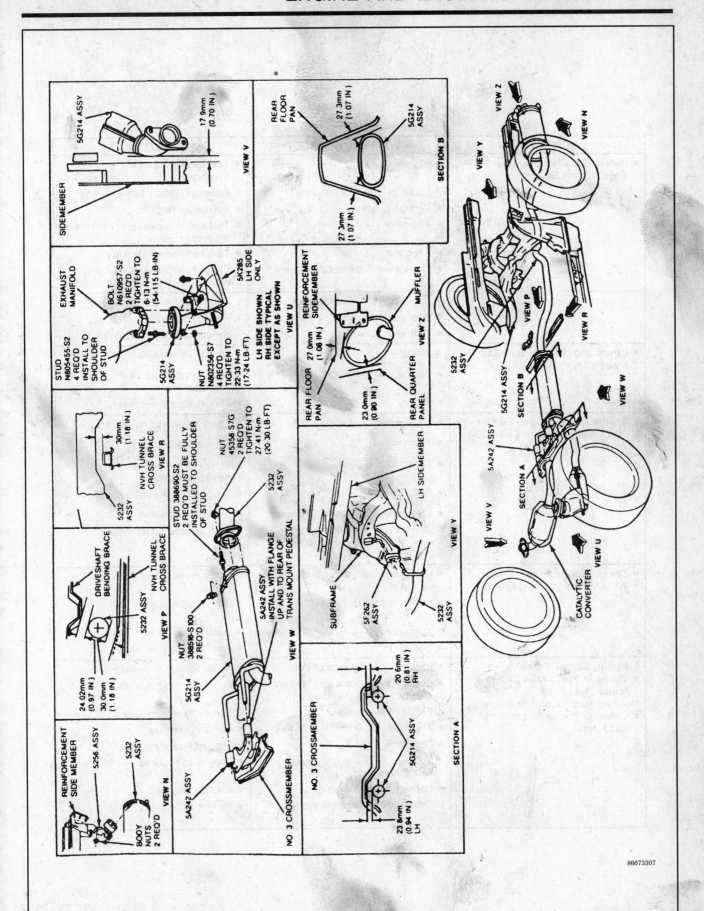

Fig. 241 Exhaust system — 8-cylinder engine

CHARGING SYSTEM DIAGNOSIS

CONDITION	POSSIBLE SOURCE	ACTION
• Battery Does Not Stay Charged — Engine Starts OK	• Battery.	• Test battery, replace if necessary
	• Loose or worn alternator belt.	• Adjust or replace belt
	• Wiring or cables.	• Service as required
	• Alternator.	• Test and/or replace components as required
	• Regulator.	• Test, replace if necessary
	• Other vehicle electrical systems.	• Check other systems for current draw. Service as required
• Alternator Noisy	• Loose or worn alternator belt.	• Adjust tension or replace belt
	• Bent pulley flanges.	• Replace pulley
	• Alternator.	• Service or replace alternator
• Lamps and/or Fuses Burn Out Frequently	• Wiring.	• Service as required
	• Alternator/Regulator.	• Test, service, replace if necessary
	• Battery.	• Test, replace if necessary
• Charge Indicator Lamp Flickers After Engine Starts or Comes On While Vehicle Is Being Driven	• Loose or worn alternator belt.	• Adjust tension or replace
	• Alternator.	• Service or replace
	• Field circuit ground.	• Service or replace worn or damaged wiring.
	• Regulator.	• Test, replace if necessary
	• Lamp circuit wiring and connector.	• Service as required.
	• Operation at low engine speed (idle) with heavy electrical load — IAR alternator only.	• Test, replace if neccessary.
• Charge Indicator Lamp Flickers While Vehicle Is Being Driven	• Loose or worn alternator belt.	• Adjust tension or replace belt
	• Loose or improper wiring connections.	• Service as required
	• Alternator.	• Service or replace
	• Regulator.	• Test, replace if necessary
Electronic Cluster Voltmeter • Voltmeter Bars Above Or Below Normal Area Non-Electronic Cluster Voltmeter • Voltmeter Pointer Reads in the Read Area	• Loose or worn alternator belt.	• Adjust tension or replace belt
	• Damaged or worn wiring (battery to alternator for ground or open).	• Service or replace wiring.
	• Field circuit ground.	• Service or replace wiring.
	• Alternator.	• Service or replace
	• Regulator.	• Test, replace if necessary
	• Voltmeter indicator gauge wiring and connections.	• Service as required
	• Damaged or worn gauge.	• Replace gauge
	• Other vehicle electrical system malfunction.	• Service as required.

86673x21

Troubleshooting Basic Starting System Problems

Problem	Cause	Solution
Starter motor rotates engine slowly	• Battery charge low or battery defective	• Charge or replace battery
	• Defective circuit between battery and starter motor	• Clean and tighten, or replace cables
	• Low load current	• Bench-test starter motor. Inspect for worn brushes and weak brush springs.
	• High load current	• Bench-test starter motor. Check engine for friction, drag or coolant in cylinders. Check ring gear-to-pinion gear clearance.
Starter motor will not rotate engine	• Battery charge low or battery defective	• Charge or replace battery
	• Faulty solenoid	• Check solenoid ground. Repair or replace as necessary.
	• Damage drive pinion gear or ring gear	• Replace damaged gear(s)
	• Starter motor engagement weak	• Bench-test starter motor
	• Starter motor rotates slowly with high load current	• Inspect drive yoke pull-down and point gap, check for worn end bushings, check ring gear clearance
	• Engine seized	• Repair engine
Starter motor drive will not engage (solenoid known to be good)	• Defective contact point assembly	• Repair or replace contact point assembly
	• Inadequate contact point assembly ground	• Repair connection at ground screw
	• Defective hold-in coil	• Replace field winding assembly
Starter motor drive will not disengage	• Starter motor loose on flywheel housing	• Tighten mounting bolts
	• Worn drive end busing	• Replace bushing
	• Damaged ring gear teeth	• Replace ring gear or driveplate
	• Drive yoke return spring broken or missing	• Replace spring
Starter motor drive disengages prematurely	• Weak drive assembly thrust spring	• Replace drive mechanism
	• Hold-in coil defective	• Replace field winding assembly
Low load current	• Worn brushes	• Replace brushes
	• Weak brush springs	• Replace springs

86673311

Troubleshooting Engine Mechanical Problems

Problem	Cause	Solution
External oil leaks	• Fuel pump gasket broken or improperly seated	• Replace gasket
	• Cylinder head cover RTV sealant broken or improperly seated	• Replace sealant; inspect cylinder head cover sealant flange and cylinder head sealant surface for distortion and cracks
	• Oil filler cap leaking or missing	• Replace cap
External oil leaks	• Oil filter gasket broken or improperly seated	• Replace oil filter
	• Oil pan side gasket broken, improperly seated or opening in RTV sealant	• Replace gasket or repair opening in sealant; inspect oil pan gasket flange for distortion
	• Oil pan front oil seal broken or improperly seated	• Replace seal; inspect timing case cover and oil pan seal flange for distortion
	• Oil pan rear oil seal broken or improperly seated	• Replace seal; inspect oil pan rear oil seal flange; inspect rear main bearing cap for cracks, plugged oil return channels, or distortion in seal groove
	• Timing case cover oil seal broken or improperly seated	• Replace seal
	• Excess oil pressure because of restricted PCV valve	• Replace PCV valve
	• Oil pan drain plug loose or has stripped threads	• Repair as necessary and tighten
	• Rear oil gallery plug loose	• Use appropriate sealant on gallery plug and tighten
	• Rear camshaft plug loose or improperly seated	• Seat camshaft plug or replace and seal, as necessary
	• Distributor base gasket damaged	• Replace gasket
Excessive oil consumption	• Oil level too high	• Drain oil to specified level
	• Oil with wrong viscosity being used	• Replace with specified oil
	• PCV valve stuck closed	• Replace PCV valve
	• Valve stem oil deflectors (or seals) are damaged, missing, or incorrect type	• Replace valve stem oil deflectors
	• Valve stems or valve guides worn	• Measure stem-to-guide clearance and repair as necessary
	• Poorly fitted or missing valve cover baffles	• Replace valve cover
	• Piston rings broken or missing	• Replace broken or missing rings
	• Scuffed piston	• Replace piston
	• Incorrect piston ring gap	• Measure ring gap, repair as necessary
	• Piston rings sticking or excessively loose in grooves	• Measure ring side clearance, repair as necessary
	• Compression rings installed upside down	• Repair as necessary
	• Cylinder walls worn, scored, or glazed	• Repair as necessary

Troubleshooting Engine Mechanical Problems (cont.)

Problem	Cause	Solution
	• Piston ring gaps not properly staggered	• Repair as necessary
	• Excessive main or connecting rod bearing clearance	• Measure bearing clearance, repair as necessary
No oil pressure	• Low oil level	• Add oil to correct level
	• Oil pressure gauge, warning lamp or sending unit inaccurate	• Replace oil pressure gauge or warning lamp
	• Oil pump malfunction	• Replace oil pump
	• Oil pressure relief valve sticking	• Remove and inspect oil pressure relief valve assembly
	• Oil passages on pressure side of pump obstructed	• Inspect oil passages for obstruction
	• Oil pickup screen or tube obstructed	• Inspect oil pickup for obstruction
	• Loose oil inlet tube	• Tighten or seal inlet tube
Low oil pressure	• Low oil level	• Add oil to correct level
	• Inaccurate gauge, warning lamp or sending unit	• Replace oil pressure gauge or warning lamp
	• Oil excessively thin because of dilution, poor quality, or improper grade	• Drain and refill crankcase with recommended oil
	• Excessive oil temperature	• Correct cause of overheating engine
	• Oil pressure relief spring weak or sticking	• Remove and inspect oil pressure relief valve assembly
	• Oil inlet tube and screen assembly has restriction or air leak	• Remove and inspect oil inlet tube and screen assembly. (Fill inlet tube with lacquer thinner to locate leaks.)
	• Excessive oil pump clearance	• Measure clearances
	• Excessive main, rod, or camshaft bearing clearance	• Measure bearing clearances, repair as necessary
High oil pressure	• Improper oil viscosity	• Drain and refill crankcase with correct viscosity oil
	• Oil pressure gauge or sending unit inaccurate	• Replace oil pressure gauge
	• Oil pressure relief valve sticking closed	• Remove and inspect oil pressure relief valve assembly
Main bearing noise	• Insufficient oil supply	• Inspect for low oil level and low oil pressure
	• Main bearing clearance excessive	• Measure main bearing clearance, repair as necessary
	• Bearing insert missing	• Replace missing insert
	• Crankshaft end play excessive	• Measure end play, repair as necessary
	• Improperly tightened main bearing cap bolts	• Tighten bolts with specified torque
	• Loose flywheel or drive plate	• Tighten flywheel or drive plate attaching bolts
	• Loose or damaged vibration damper	• Repair as necessary

Troubleshooting Engine Mechanical Problems (cont.)

Problem	Cause	Solution
Connecting rod bearing noise	· Insufficient oil supply	· Inspect for low oil level and low oil pressure
	· Carbon build-up on piston	· Remove carbon from piston crown
	· Bearing clearance excessive or bearing missing	· Measure clearance, repair as necessary
	· Crankshaft connecting rod journal out-of-round	· Measure journal dimensions, repair or replace as necessary
	· Misaligned connecting rod or cap	· Repair as necessary
	· Connecting rod bolts tightened improperly	· Tighten bolts with specified torque
Piston noise	· Piston-to-cylinder wall clearance excessive (scuffed piston)	· Measure clearance and examine piston
	· Cylinder walls excessively tapered or out-of-round	· Measure cylinder wall dimensions, rebore cylinder
	· Piston ring broken	· Replace all rings on piston
	· Loose or seized piston pin	· Measure piston-to-pin clearance, repair as necessary
	· Connecting rods misaligned	· Measure rod alignment, straighten or replace
	· Piston ring side clearance excessively loose or tight	· Measure ring side clearance, repair as necessary
	· Carbon build-up on piston is excessive	· Remove carbon from piston
Valve actuating component noise	· Insufficient oil supply	· Check for: (a) Low oil level (b) Low oil pressure (c) Plugged push rods (d) Wrong hydraulic tappets (e) Restricted oil gallery (f) Excessive tappet to bore clearance
	· Push rods worn or bent	· Replace worn or bent push rods
	· Rocker arms or pivots worn	· Replace worn rocker arms or pivots
	· Foreign objects or chips in hydraulic tappets	· Clean tappets
	· Excessive tappet leak-down	· Replace valve tappet
	· Tappet face worn	· Replace tappet; inspect corresponding cam lobe for wear
	· Broken or cocked valve springs	· Properly seat cocked springs; replace broken springs
	· Stem-to-guide clearance excessive	· Measure stem-to-guide clearance, repair as required
	· Valve bent	· Replace valve
	· Loose rocker arms	· Tighten bolts with specified torque
	· Valve seat runout excessive	· Regrind valve seat/valves
	· Missing valve lock	· Install valve lock
	· Push rod rubbing or contacting cylinder head	· Remove cylinder head and remove obstruction in head
	· Excessive engine oil (four-cylinder engine)	· Correct oil level

Troubleshooting the Cooling System

Problem	Cause	Solution
High temperature gauge indication—overheating	• Coolant level low	• Replenish coolant
	• Fan belt loose	• Adjust fan belt tension
	• Radiator hose(s) collapsed	• Replace hose(s)
	• Radiator airflow blocked	• Remove restriction (bug screen, fog lamps, etc.)
	• Faulty radiator cap	• Replace radiator cap
	• Ignition timing incorrect	• Adjust ignition timing
	• Idle speed low	• Adjust idle speed
	• Air trapped in cooling system	• Purge air
	• Heavy traffic driving	• Operate at fast idle in neutral intermittently to cool engine
	• Incorrect cooling system component(s) installed	• Install proper component(s)
	• Faulty thermostat	• Replace thermostat
	• Water pump shaft broken or impeller loose	• Replace water pump
	• Radiator tubes clogged	• Flush radiator
	• Cooling system clogged	• Flush system
	• Casting flash in cooling passages	• Repair or replace as necessary. Flash may be visible by removing cooling system components or removing core plugs.
	• Brakes dragging	• Repair brakes
	• Excessive engine friction	• Repair engine
	• Antifreeze concentration over 68%	• Lower antifreeze concentration percentage
	• Missing air seals	• Replace air seals
	• Faulty gauge or sending unit	• Repair or replace faulty component
	• Loss of coolant flow caused by leakage or foaming	• Repair or replace leaking component, replace coolant
	• Viscous fan drive failed	• Replace unit
Low temperature indication—undercooling	• Thermostat stuck open	• Replace thermostat
	• Faulty gauge or sending unit	• Repair or replace faulty component
Coolant loss—boilover	• Overfilled cooling system	• Reduce coolant level to proper specification
	• Quick shutdown after hard (hot) run	• Allow engine to run at fast idle prior to shutdown
	• Air in system resulting in occasional "burping" of coolant	• Purge system
	• Insufficient antifreeze allowing coolant boiling point to be too low	• Add antifreeze to raise boiling point
	• Antifreeze deteriorated because of age or contamination	• Replace coolant
	• Leaks due to loose hose clamps, loose nuts, bolts, drain plugs, faulty hoses, or defective radiator	• Pressure test system to locate source of leak(s) then repair as necessary

86673315

Troubleshooting the Cooling System (cont.)

Problem	Cause	Solution
Coolant loss—boilover	· Faulty head gasket · Cracked head, manifold, or block · Faulty radiator cap	· Replace head gasket · Replace as necessary · Replace cap
Coolant entry into crankcase or cylinder(s)	· Faulty head gasket · Crack in head, manifold or block	· Replace head gasket · Replace as necessary
Coolant recovery system inoperative	· Coolant level low · Leak in system · Pressure cap not tight or seal missing, or leaking · Pressure cap defective · Overflow tube clogged or leaking · Recovery bottle vent restricted	· Replenish coolant to FULL mark · Pressure test to isolate leak and repair as necessary · Repair as necessary · Replace cap · Repair as necessary · Remove restriction
Noise	· Fan contacting shroud · Loose water pump impeller · Glazed fan belt · Loose fan belt · Rough surface on drive pulley · Water pump bearing worn · Belt alignment	· Reposition shroud and inspect engine mounts · Replace pump · Apply silicone or replace belt · Adjust fan belt tension · Replace pulley · Remove belt to isolate. Replace pump. · Check pulley alignment. Repair as necessary.
No coolant flow through heater core	· Restricted return inlet in water pump · Heater hose collapsed or restricted · Restricted heater core · Restricted outlet in thermostat housing · Intake manifold bypass hole in cylinder head restricted · Faulty heater control valve · Intake manifold coolant passage restricted	· Remove restriction · Remove restriction or replace hose · Remove restriction or replace core · Remove flash or restriction · Remove restriction · Replace valve · Remove restriction or replace intake manifold

NOTE: *Immediately after shutdown, the engine enters a condition known as heat soak. This is caused by the cooling system being inoperative while engine temperature is still high. If coolant temperature rises above boiling point, expansion and pressure may push some coolant out of the radiator overflow tube. If this does not occur frequently it is considered normal.*

86673316

Troubleshooting the Serpentine Drive Belt

Problem	Cause	Solution
Tension sheeting fabric failure (woven fabric on outside circumference of belt has cracked or separated from body of belt)	• Grooved or backside idler pulley diameters are less than minimum recommended • Tension sheeting contacting (rubbing) stationary object • Excessive heat causing woven fabric to age • Tension sheeting splice has fractured	• Replace pulley(s) not conforming to specification • Correct rubbing condition • Replace belt • Replace belt
Noise (objectional squeal, squeak, or rumble is heard or felt while drive belt is in operation)	• Belt slippage • Bearing noise • Belt misalignment • Belt-to-pulley mismatch • Driven component inducing vibration • System resonant frequency inducing vibration	• Adjust belt • Locate and repair • Align belt/pulley(s) • Install correct belt • Locate defective driven component and repair • Vary belt tension within specifications. Replace belt.
Rib chunking (one or more ribs has separated from belt body)	• Foreign objects imbedded in pulley grooves • Installation damage • Drive loads in excess of design specifications • Insufficient internal belt adhesion	• Remove foreign objects from pulley grooves • Replace belt • Adjust belt tension • Replace belt
Rib or belt wear (belt ribs contact bottom of pulley grooves)	• Pulley(s) misaligned • Mismatch of belt and pulley groove widths • Abrasive environment • Rusted pulley(s) • Sharp or jagged pulley groove tips • Rubber deteriorated	• Align pulley(s) • Replace belt • Replace belt • Clean rust from pulley(s) • Replace pulley • Replace belt
Longitudinal belt cracking (cracks between two ribs)	• Belt has mistracked from pulley groove • Pulley groove tip has worn away rubber-to-tensile member	• Replace belt • Replace belt
Belt slips	• Belt slipping because of insufficient tension • Belt or pulley subjected to substance (belt dressing, oil, ethylene glycol) that has reduced friction • Driven component bearing failure • Belt glazed and hardened from heat and excessive slippage	• Adjust tension • Replace belt and clean pulleys • Replace faulty component bearing • Replace belt
"Groove jumping" (belt does not maintain correct position on pulley, or turns over and/or runs off pulleys)	• Insufficient belt tension • Pulley(s) not within design tolerance • Foreign object(s) in grooves	• Adjust belt tension • Replace pulley(s) • Remove foreign objects from grooves

Troubleshooting the Serpentine Drive Belt (cont.)

Problem	Cause	Solution
"Groove jumping" (belt does not maintain correct position on pulley, or turns over and/or runs off pulleys)	• Excessive belt speed • Pulley misalignment • Belt-to-pulley profile mismatched • Belt cordline is distorted	• Avoid excessive engine acceleration • Align pulley(s) • Install correct belt • Replace belt
Belt broken (Note: identify and correct problem before replacement belt is installed)	• Excessive tension • Tensile members damaged during belt installation • Belt turnover • Severe pulley misalignment • Bracket, pulley, or bearing failure	• Replace belt and adjust tension to specification • Replace belt • Replace belt • Align pulley(s) • Replace defective component and belt
Cord edge failure (tensile member exposed at edges of belt or separated from belt body)	• Excessive tension • Drive pulley misalignment • Belt contacting stationary object • Pulley irregularities • Improper pulley construction • Insufficient adhesion between tensile member and rubber matrix	• Adjust belt tension • Align pulley • Correct as necessary • Replace pulley • Replace pulley • Replace belt and adjust tension to specifications
Sporadic rib cracking (multiple cracks in belt ribs at random intervals)	• Ribbed pulley(s) diameter less than minimum specification • Backside bend flat pulley(s) diameter less than minimum • Excessive heat condition causing rubber to harden • Excessive belt thickness • Belt overcured • Excessive tension	• Replace pulley(s) • Replace pulley(s) • Correct heat condition as necessary • Replace belt • Replace belt • Adjust belt tension

86673318

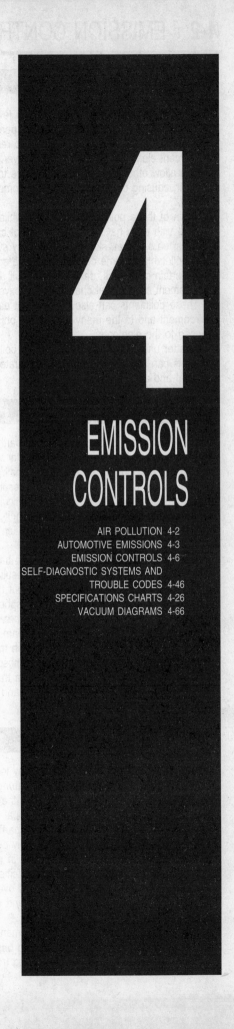

4

EMISSION CONTROLS

AIR POLLUTION

The earth's atmosphere, at or near sea level, consists approximately of 78 percent nitrogen, 21 percent oxygen and 1 percent other gases. If it were possible to remain in this state, 100 percent clean air would result. However, many varied sources allow other gases and particulates to mix with the clean air, causing our atmosphere to become unclean or polluted.

Certain of these pollutants are visible while others are invisible, with each having the capability of causing distress to the eyes, ears, throat, skin and respiratory system. Should these pollutants become concentrated in a specific area and under certain conditions, death could result due to the displacement or chemical change of the oxygen content in the air. These pollutants can also cause great damage to the environment and to the many man made objects that are exposed to the elements.

To better understand the causes of air pollution, the pollutants can be categorized into 3 separate types, natural, industrial and automotive.

Natural Pollutants

Natural pollution has been present on earth since before man appeared and continues to be a factor when discussing air pollution, although it causes only a small percentage of the overall pollution problem. It is the direct result of decaying organic matter, wind born smoke and particulates from such natural events as plain and forest fires (ignited by heat or lightning), volcanic ash, sand and dust which can spread over a large area of the countryside.

Such a phenomenon of natural pollution has been seen in the form of volcanic eruptions, with the resulting plume of smoke, steam and volcanic ash blotting out the sun's rays as it spreads and rises higher into the atmosphere. As it travels into the atmosphere the upper air currents catch and carry the smoke and ash, while condensing the steam back into water vapor. As the water vapor, smoke and ash travel on their journey, the smoke dissipates into the atmosphere while the ash and moisture settle back to earth in a trail hundreds of miles long. In some cases, lives are lost and millions of dollars of property damage result.

Industrial Pollutants

Industrial pollution is caused primarily by industrial processes, the burning of coal, oil and natural gas, which in turn produce smoke and fumes. Because the burning fuels contain large amounts of sulfur, the principal ingredients of smoke and fumes are sulfur dioxide and particulate matter. This type of pollutant occurs most severely during still, damp and cool weather, such as at night. Even in its less severe form, this pollutant is not confined to just cities. Because of air movements, the pollutants move for miles over the surrounding countryside, leaving in its path a barren and unhealthy environment for all living things.

Working with Federal, State and Local mandated regulations and by carefully monitoring emissions, big business has greatly reduced the amount of pollutant introduced from its industrial sources, striving to obtain an acceptable level. Because of the mandated industrial emission clean up, many land areas and streams in and around the cities that were formerly barren of vegetation and life, have now begun to move back in the direction of nature's intended balance.

Automotive Pollutants

The third major source of air pollution is automotive emissions. The emissions from the internal combustion engines were not an appreciable problem years ago because of the small number of registered vehicles and the nation's small highway system. However, during the early 1950's, the trend of the American people was to move from the cities to the surrounding suburbs. This caused an immediate problem in transportation because the majority of suburbs were not afforded mass transit conveniences. This lack of transportation created an attractive market for the automobile manufacturers, which resulted in a dramatic increase in the number of vehicles produced and sold, along with a marked increase in highway construction between cities and the suburbs. Multi-vehicle families emerged with a growing emphasis placed on an individual vehicle per family member. As the increase in vehicle ownership and usage occurred, so did pollutant levels in and around the cities, as suburbanites drove daily to their businesses and employment, returning at the end of the day to their homes in the suburbs.

It was noted that a smoke and fog type haze was being formed and at times, remained in suspension over the cities, taking time to dissipate. At first this "smog," derived from the words "smoke" and "fog" was thought to result from industrial pollution but it was determined that automobile emissions shared the blame. It was discovered that when normal automobile emissions were exposed to sunlight for a period of time, complex chemical reactions would take place.

It is now known that smog is a photo chemical layer which develops when certain oxides of nitrogen (NOx) and unburned hydrocarbons (HC) from automobile emissions are exposed to sunlight. Pollution was more severe when smog would become stagnant over an area in which a warm layer of air settled over the top of the cooler air mass, trapping and holding the cooler mass at ground level. The trapped cooler air would keep the emissions from being dispersed and diluted through normal air flows. This type of air stagnation was given the name "Temperature Inversion."

TEMPERATURE INVERSION

In normal weather situations, surface air is warmed by heat radiating from the earth's surface and the sun's rays. This causes it to rise upward, into the atmosphere. Upon rising it will cool through a convection type heat exchange with the cooler upper air. As warm air rises, the surface pollutants are carried upward and dissipated into the atmosphere.

When a temperature inversion occurs, we find the higher air is no longer cooler, but is warmer than the surface air, causing the cooler surface air to become trapped. This warm air blanket can extend from above ground level to a few hundred or even a few thousand feet into the air. As the surface air is trapped, so are the pollutants, causing a severe smog condition. Should this stagnant air mass extend to a few thousand feet high, enough air movement with the inversion takes place to allow the smog layer to rise above ground level but the pollutants still cannot dissipate. This inversion can remain for days over an area, with the smog level only rising or lowering from ground level to a few hundred feet high. Meanwhile, the pollutant levels increase, causing eye irritation, respiratory problems, reduced visibility, plant damage and in some cases, even disease.

This inversion phenomenon was first noted in the Los Angeles, California area. The city lies in terrain resembling a basin and with certain weather conditions, a cold air mass is held in the basin while a warmer air mass covers it like a lid.

Because this type of condition was first documented as prevalent in the Los Angeles area, this type of trapped pollution was named Los Angeles Smog, although it occurs in other areas where a large concentration of automobiles are used and the air remains stagnant for any length of time.

HEAT TRANSFER

Consider the internal combustion engine as a machine in which raw materials must be placed so a finished product comes out. As in any machine operation, a certain amount of wasted material is formed. When we relate this to the internal combustion engine, we find that through the input of air and fuel, we obtain power during the combustion process to drive the vehicle. The by-product or waste of this power is, in part, heat and exhaust gases with which we must dispose.

The heat from the combustion process can rise to over 4000°F (2204°C). The dissipation of this heat is controlled by a ram air effect, the use of cooling fans to cause air flow and a liquid coolant solution surrounding the combustion area to transfer the heat of combustion through the cylinder walls and into the coolant. The coolant is then directed to a thin-finned, multi-tubed radiator, from which the excess heat is transferred to the atmosphere by 1 of the 3 heat transfer methods, conduction, convection or radiation.

The cooling of the combustion area is an important part in the control of exhaust emissions. To understand the behavior of the combustion and transfer of its heat, consider the air/fuel charge. It is ignited and the flame front burns progressively across the combustion chamber until the burning charge reaches the cylinder walls. Some of the fuel in contact with the walls is not hot enough to burn, thereby snuffing out or quenching the combustion process. This leaves unburned fuel in the combustion chamber. This unburned fuel is then forced out of the cylinder and into the exhaust system, along with the exhaust gases.

Many attempts have been made to minimize the amount of unburned fuel in the combustion chambers due to quenching, by increasing the coolant temperature and lessening the contact area of the coolant around the combustion area. However, design limitations within the combustion chambers prevent the complete burning of the air/fuel charge, so a certain amount of the unburned fuel is still expelled into the exhaust system, regardless of modifications to the engine.

AUTOMOTIVE EMISSIONS

Before emission controls were mandated on internal combustion engines, other sources of engine pollutants were discovered along with the exhaust emissions. It was determined that engine combustion exhaust produced approximately 60 percent of the total emission pollutants, fuel evaporation from the fuel tank and carburetor vents produced 20 percent, with the final 20 percent being produced through the crankcase as a by-product of the combustion process.

Exhaust Gases

The exhaust gases emitted into the atmosphere are a combination of burned and unburned fuel. To understand the exhaust emission and its composition, we must review some basic chemistry.

When the air/fuel mixture is introduced into the engine, we are mixing air, composed of nitrogen (78 percent), oxygen (21 percent) and other gases (1 percent) with the fuel, which is 100 percent hydrocarbons (HC), in a semi-controlled ratio. As the combustion process is accomplished, power is produced to move the vehicle while the heat of combustion is transferred to the cooling system. The exhaust gases are then composed of nitrogen, a diatomic gas (N_2), the same as was introduced in the engine, carbon dioxide (CO_2), the same gas that is used in beverage carbonation, and water vapor (H_2O). The nitrogen (N_2), for the most part, passes through the engine unchanged, while the oxygen (O_2) reacts (burns) with the hydrocarbons (HC) and produces the carbon dioxide (CO_2) and the water vapors (H_2O). If this chemical process would be the only process to take place, the exhaust emissions would be harmless. However, during the combustion process, other compounds are formed which are considered dangerous. These pollutants are hydrocarbons (HC), carbon monoxide (CO), oxides of nitrogen (NOx) oxides of sulfur (SOx) and engine particulates.

HYDROCARBONS

Hydrocarbons (HC) are essentially fuel which was not burned during the combustion process or which has escaped into the atmosphere through fuel evaporation. The main sources of incomplete combustion are rich air/fuel mixtures, low engine temperatures and improper spark timing. The main sources of hydrocarbon emission through fuel evaporation on most vehicles used to be the vehicle's fuel tank and carburetor float bowl.

To reduce combustion hydrocarbon emission, engine modifications were made to minimize dead space and surface area in the combustion chamber. In addition, the air/fuel mixture was made more lean through the improved control which feedback carburetion and fuel injection offers and by the addition of external controls to aid in further combustion of the hydrocarbons outside the engine. Two such methods were the addition of air injection systems, to inject fresh air into the exhaust manifolds and the installation of catalytic converters, units that are able to burn traces of hydrocarbons without affecting the internal combustion process or fuel economy.

To control hydrocarbon emissions through fuel evaporation, modifications were made to the fuel tank to allow storage of the fuel vapors during periods of engine shut-down. Modifications were also made to the air intake system so that at specific times during engine operation, these vapors may be purged and burned by blending them with the air/fuel mixture.

CARBON MONOXIDE

Carbon monoxide is formed when not enough oxygen is present during the combustion process to convert carbon (C) to carbon dioxide (CO_2). An increase in the carbon monoxide (CO) emission is normally accompanied by an increase in the hydrocarbon (HC) emission because of the lack of oxygen to completely burn all of the fuel mixture.

Carbon monoxide (CO) also increases the rate at which the photo chemical smog is formed by speeding up the conversion of nitric oxide (NO) to nitrogen dioxide (NO_2). To accomplish this, carbon monoxide (CO) combines with oxygen (O_2) and nitric oxide (NO) to produce carbon dioxide (CO_2) and nitrogen dioxide (NO_2). ($CO + O_2 + NO = CO_2 + NO_2$).

The dangers of carbon monoxide, which is an odorless and colorless toxic gas are many. When carbon monoxide is inhaled into the lungs and passed into the blood stream, oxygen is replaced by the carbon monoxide in the red blood cells, causing a reduction in the amount of oxygen supplied to the many parts of the body. This lack of oxygen causes headaches, lack of coordination, reduced mental alertness and, should the carbon monoxide concentration be high enough, death could result.

NITROGEN

Normally, nitrogen is an inert gas. When heated to approximately 2500°F (1371°C) through the combustion process, this gas becomes active and causes an increase in the nitric oxide (NO) emission.

Oxides of nitrogen (NOx) are composed of approximately 97-98 percent nitric oxide (NO). Nitric oxide is a colorless gas but when it is passed into the atmosphere, it combines with oxygen and forms nitrogen dioxide (NO_2). The nitrogen dioxide then combines with chemically active hydrocarbons (HC) and when in the presence of sunlight, causes the formation of photo-chemical smog.

Ozone

To further complicate matters, some of the nitrogen dioxide (NO_2) is broken apart by the sunlight to form nitric oxide and oxygen. ($NO_2 + sunlight = NO + O$). This single atom of oxygen then combines with diatomic (meaning 2 atoms) oxygen (O_2) to form ozone (O_3). Ozone is one of the smells associated with smog. It has a pungent and offensive odor, irritates the eyes and lung tissues, affects the growth of plant life and causes rapid deterioration of rubber products. Ozone

can be formed by sunlight as well as electrical discharge into the air.

The most common discharge area on the automobile engine is the secondary ignition electrical system, especially when inferior quality spark plug cables are used. As the surge of high voltage is routed through the secondary cable, the circuit builds up an electrical field around the wire, which acts upon the oxygen in the surrounding air to form the ozone. The faint glow along the cable with the engine running that may be visible on a dark night, is called the "corona discharge." It is the result of the electrical field passing from a high along the cable, to a low in the surrounding air, which forms the ozone gas. The combination of corona and ozone has been a major cause of cable deterioration. Recently, different and better quality insulating materials have lengthened the life of the electrical cables.

Although ozone at ground level can be harmful, ozone is beneficial to the earth's inhabitants. By having a concentrated ozone layer called the "ozonosphere," between 10 and 20 miles (16-32 km) up in the atmosphere, much of the ultra violet radiation from the sun's rays are absorbed and screened. If this ozone layer were not present, much of the earth's surface would be burned, dried and unfit for human life.

OXIDES OF SULFUR

Oxides of sulfur (SOx) were initially ignored in the exhaust system emissions, since the sulfur content of gasoline as a fuel is less than $\frac{1}{10}$ of 1 percent. Because of this small amount, it was felt that it contributed very little to the overall pollution problem. However, because of the difficulty in solving the sulfur emissions in industrial pollutions and the introduction of catalytic converter to the automobile exhaust systems, a change was mandated. The automobile exhaust system, when equipped with a catalytic converter, changes the sulfur dioxide (SO_2) into the sulfur trioxide (SO_3).

When this combines with water vapors (H_2O), a sulfuric acid mist (H_2SO_4) is formed and is a very difficult pollutant to handle since it is extremely corrosive. This sulfuric acid mist that is formed, is the same mist that rises from the vents of an automobile battery when an active chemical reaction takes place within the battery cells.

When a large concentration of vehicles equipped with catalytic converters are operating in an area, this acid mist may rise and be distributed over a large ground area causing land, plant, crop, paint and building damage.

PARTICULATE MATTER

A certain amount of particulate matter is present in the burning of any fuel, with carbon constituting the largest percentage of the particulates. In gasoline, the remaining particulates are the burned remains of the various other compounds used in its manufacture. When a gasoline engine is in good internal condition, the particulate emissions are low but as the engine wears internally, the particulate emissions increase. By visually inspecting the tail pipe emissions, a determination can be made as to where an engine defect may exist. An engine with light gray or blue smoke emitting from the tail pipe normally indicates an increase in the oil consumption through burning due to internal engine wear. Black smoke would indicate a defective fuel delivery system, causing the engine to operate in a rich mode. Regardless of the color of the smoke, the internal part of the engine or the fuel delivery system should be repaired to prevent excess particulate emissions.

Diesel and turbine engines emit a darkened plume of smoke from the exhaust system because of the type of fuel used. Emission control regulations are mandated for this type of emission and more stringent measures are being used to prevent excess emission of the particulate matter. Electronic components are being introduced to control the injection of the fuel at precisely the proper time of piston travel, to achieve the optimum in fuel ignition and fuel usage. Other particulate after-burning components are being tested to achieve a cleaner emission.

Good grades of engine lubricating oils should be used, which meet the manufacturers specification. Cut-rate oils can contribute to the particulate emission problem because of their low flash or ignition temperature point. Such oils burn prematurely during the combustion process causing emission of particulate matter.

The cooling system is an important factor in the reduction of particulate matter. The optimum combustion will occur, with the cooling system operating at a temperature specified by the manufacturer. The cooling system must be maintained in the same manner as the engine oiling system, as each system is required to perform properly in order for the engine to operate efficiently for a long time.

Crankcase Emissions

Crankcase emissions are made up of water, acids, unburned fuel, oil fumes and particulates. These emissions are classified as hydrocarbons (HC) and are formed by the small amount of unburned, compressed air/fuel mixture entering the crankcase from the combustion area (between the cylinder walls and piston rings) during the compression and power strokes. The head of the compression and combustion help to form the remaining crankcase emissions.

Since the first engines, crankcase emissions were allowed into the atmosphere through a road draft tube, mounted on the lower side of the engine block. Fresh air came in through an open oil filler cap or breather. The air passed through the crankcase mixing with blow-by gases. The motion of the vehicle and the air blowing past the open end of the road draft tube caused a low pressure area (vacuum) at the end of the tube. Crankcase emissions were simply drawn out of the road draft tube into the air.

To control the crankcase emission, the road draft tube was deleted. A hose and/or tubing was routed from the crankcase to the intake manifold so the blow-by emission could be burned with the air/fuel mixture. However, it was found that

intake manifold vacuum, used to draw the crankcase emissions into the manifold, would vary in strength at the wrong time and not allow the proper emission flow. A regulating valve was needed to control the flow of air through the crankcase.

Testing, showed the removal of the blow-by gases from the crankcase as quickly as possible, was most important to the longevity of the engine. Should large accumulations of blow-by gases remain and condense, dilution of the engine oil would occur to form water, soots, resins, acids and lead salts, resulting in the formation of sludge and varnishes. This condensation of the blow-by gases occurs more frequently on vehicles used in numerous starting and stopping conditions, excessive idling and when the engine is not allowed to attain normal operating temperature through short runs.

Evaporative Emissions

Gasoline fuel is a major source of pollution, before and after it is burned in the automobile engine. From the time the fuel is refined, stored, pumped and transported, again stored until it is pumped into the fuel tank of the vehicle, the gasoline gives off unburned hydrocarbons (HC) into the atmosphere. Through the redesign of storage areas and venting systems, the pollution factor was diminished, but not eliminated, from the refinery standpoint. However, the automobile still remained the primary source of vaporized, unburned hydrocarbon (HC) emissions.

Fuel pumped from an underground storage tank is cool but when exposed to a warmer ambient temperature, will expand. Before controls were mandated, an owner might fill the fuel tank with fuel from an underground storage tank and park the vehicle for some time in warm area, such as a parking lot. As the fuel would warm, it would expand and should no provisions or area be provided for the expansion, the fuel would spill out of the filler neck and onto the ground, causing hydrocarbon (HC) pollution and creating a severe fire hazard. To correct this condition, the vehicle manufacturers added overflow plumbing and/or gasoline tanks with built in expansion areas or domes.

However, this did not control the fuel vapor emission from the fuel tank. It was determined that most of the fuel evaporation occurred when the vehicle was stationary and the engine not operating. Most vehicles carry 5-25 gallons (19-95 liters) of gasoline. Should a large concentration of vehicles be parked in one area, such as a large parking lot, excessive fuel vapor emissions would take place, increasing as the temperature increases.

To prevent the vapor emission from escaping into the atmosphere, the fuel systems were designed to trap the vapors while the vehicle is stationary, by sealing the system from the atmosphere. A storage system is used to collect and hold the fuel vapors from the carburetor (if equipped) and the fuel tank when the engine is not operating. When the engine is started, the storage system is then purged of the fuel vapors, which are drawn into the engine and burned with the air/fuel mixture.

EMISSION CONTROLS

➡Your vehicles should be equipped with a Vehicle Emission Control Information (VECI) label which is located in the engine compartment. The label contains updated emission control specifications, vacuum hose routing charts and changes specifically applicable to your vehicle. Refer to this label if the specifications disagree with this manual. All hoses must be connected and routed as shown in the chart.

Emission Control Equipment

1971-1973 MODELS

Emission controls between 1971 and 1973 are fairly simple compared to later systems. The controls listed are common to, but not necessarily found on, all models: air pump, closed Positive Crankcase Ventilation (PCV), calibrated carburetor and distributor, dual vacuum advance on the distributor, deceleration valve (6-cylinder), heated air cleaner, vapor control system canister storage, fresh air intake tube to the air cleaners, electronic distributor modulator, various vacuum check valves and Exhaust Gas Recirculation (EGR).

1974 MODELS

Late 1973 and 1974 models use an Exhaust Gas Recirculation (EGR) system to control oxides of nitrogen. On V8 engines, exhaust gases travel through the exhaust gas crossover passage in the intake manifold. A portion of these gases is diverted into a spacer which is mounted under the carburetor. The EGR control valve, which is attached to the rear of the spacer, consists of a vacuum diaphragm with an attached plunger which normally blocks off exhaust gases from entering the intake manifold. The EGR valve is controlled by a vacuum line from the carburetor which passes through a ported vacuum switch. The EGR ported vacuum switch provides vacuum to the EGR valve at coolant temperatures above 125°F (52°C). The vacuum diaphragm then opens the EGR valve permitting exhaust gases to flow through the carburetor spacer and enter the intake manifold where they combine with the fuel mixture and enter the combustion chambers. The exhaust gases are relatively oxygen-free and tend to dilute the combustion charge. This lowers peak combustion temperature thereby reducing oxides of nitrogen.

All models with a 5.8L Cleveland (C), 6.6L, or 7.5L engines use the new Delay Vacuum Bypass (DVB) park control system. This system provides two paths by which carburetor vacuum can reach the distributor vacuum advance. The system consists of a spark delay valve, a check valve, a solenoid vacuum valve, and an ambient temperature switch. When the ambient temperature is below 49°F (9°C), the temperature switch contacts are open and the vacuum solenoid is open (de-energized). Under these conditions, vacuum will flow from the carburetor, through the open solenoid, and to the distributor. Since the spark delay valve resists the flow of carburetor vacuum, the vacuum will always flow through the

solenoid when it is open (this is the path of least resistance). When the ambient temperature rises above 60°F (16°C), the contacts in the temperature switch (which is located in the door post) close. This passes ignition switch current to the solenoid, energizing the solenoid. This blocks one of the two vacuum paths. All distributor vacuum must now flow through the spark delay valve. When carburetor vacuum rises above a certain level on acceleration, a rubber valve in the spark delay valve blocks vacuum from passing through the valve for 5-30 seconds.

After this time delay has elapsed, normal vacuum is supplied to the distributor. When the vacuum solenoid is closed at temperatures above 60°F (16°C) the vacuum line from the solenoid to the distributor is vented to the atmosphere. To prevent the vacuum that is passing through the spark delay valve from escaping through the solenoid into the atmosphere, a one-way check valve is installed in the vacuum line from the solenoid to the distributor.

In order to meet 1974 California emission control standards, all 1974 Ford cars sold in that state are equipped with a Thermactor® (air injection) system to control hydrocarbons and carbon monoxide. The EGR system is retained to control oxides of nitrogen.

1975 MODELS

All mid-size Ford Motor Co. cars are equipped with catalytic converters. Some California models are equipped with two converters, while models sold in the 49 states have only one unit.

Catalytic converters change noxious emission of hydrocarbons (HC) and carbon monoxide (CO) into harmless carbon dioxide and water. The units are installed in the exhaust system ahead of the mufflers and are designed, if the engine is properly tuned, to last 100,000 miles (80,400 km) or more before replacement.

In addition to the converters, most 1975 Ford and Mercury cars are equipped with the Thermactor® air pump (air injection system) previously mentioned. the air injection system, which afterburns the uncombusted fuel mixture in the exhaust ports, is needed with the converters to prevent an overly rich mixture from reaching the converter, and to help supply oxygen to aid in converter reaction.

Other emission control equipment for 1975 includes a carry-over of the Positive Crankcase Ventilation (PCV) system, the Fuel Evaporative Control (FEC) system, and Exhaust Gas Recirculation (EGR) system.

Emission control related improvements for 1975 include standard solid state (breakerless) Ignition, induction hardened exhaust valve seats, exhaust manifold redesign, vacuum operated heat riser valves, and improved carburetors with more precise fuel metering control and a mechanical high speed bleed system.

All cars equipped with the 7.0L engine use a Cold Start Spark Advance (CSSA) system in 1975 to aid in cold start driveability. Basically, the system will allow full vacuum advance to the distributor until the coolant temperature reaches 125°F (52°C).

1976 MODELS

For 1976, the complexity of emission control equipment was reduced on Ford products. The average number of emission control components was reduced from 25 to 11 on most cars. All 1976 models have catalytic converters. In addition, a new proportional exhaust gas recirculation system has been introduced. Exhaust backpressure regulates the EGR valve spark port vacuum signal to modulate the recirculation of gases, matching EGR flow to engine load.

1977-79 MODELS

Most emission controls are carry-over from 1976. One exception, however, is the (Electronic Engine Control) EEC-II system. It is installed on all Mercury vehicles with the optional 5.8L engine.

The system is based on EEC-I control assembly used on earlier Ford products, but certain components have been changed to improve performance and reliability, and to reduce complexity and cost. EEC-II controls spark timing, EGR, and air/fuel ratio (mixture). A solid state module incorporating a digital microprocessor and other integrated circuits interprets information sent by seven sensors, calculates spark advance, EGR flow rate and fuel flow trim, and sends electrical signals to control the ignition module, EGR valve actuator, and an electric stepper motor in the carburetor. EEC-II also controls purging of vapors in the storage canister to prevent overly rich mixtures, high altitude fuel mixture adjustments, Thermactor® (air pump) air flow, and cold engine (fast idle) functions. Because the throttle idle position, ignition timing and mixture are controlled electronically, these functions cannot be adjusted in the conventional manner.

1980 MODELS

The major change in the emission control system for 1980 is in the EEC. The new system, EEC-III, performs the same functions as EEC-II but uses a new electronic control module. The EEC system computes information and makes any necessary changes about 30 times a second, controlling the air/fuel mixture, EGR, ignition timing and the air flow to the exhaust emission system.

1981-85 MODELS

The application of EEC-III is continued and EEC-IV and TFI-IV are introduced. Components include an oxygen sensor, a variable mixture carburetor, a three-way oxidation/reduction catalytic converter, an air pump, and a computer module.

Electronic Engine Control Systems

➡Because of the complicated nature of the EEC systems, special tools and procedures are often necessary for testing and troubleshooting.

EEC-I

▶ See Figure 1

Ford's EEC-I system was first introduced in the 1970's. Designed to precisely control ignition timing, Exhaust Gas Recirculation (EGR) and Thermactor® (air pump) flow, the system consists of an Electronic Control Assembly (ECA), seven monitoring sensors, a Duraspark ignition module and coil, a special distributor assembly, and EGR system designed to operate on air pressure.

The ECA is a solid state microcomputer, consisting of a processor assembly and a calibration assembly. The processor continuously receives inputs from the seven sensors, which it converts to usable information for the calculating section of the computer. It also performs ignition timing, Thermactor® and EGR flow calculations, processes the information and sends out signals to the ignition module and control solenoids to adjust the timing and flow of the systems accordingly. The calibration assembly contains the memory and programming for the processor.

Processor inputs come from sensors monitoring manifold pressure, barometric pressure, engine coolant temperature, inlet air temperature, crankshaft position, throttle position, and EGR valve position.

The manifold absolute pressure sensor determines changes in intake manifold pressure (barometric pressure minus manifold vacuum) which result from changes in engine load and speed, or in atmospheric pressure. Its signal is used by the ECA to set part throttle spark advance and EGR flow rate.

Barometric pressure is monitored by a sensor mounted on the firewall. Measurements taken are converted into usable electrical signal. The ECA uses this reference for altitude de-pendent EGR flow requirements.

Engine coolant temperature is measured at the rear of the intake manifold by a sensor consisting of a brass housing containing a thermistor (resistance decreases as temperature rises). When reference voltage (about 9 volts, supplied by the processor to all sensors) is applied to the sensor, the resis-tance can be measured by the resulting voltage drop. Resis-tance is then interpreted as coolant temperature by the ECA. EGR flow is cut off by the ECA when a predetermined temper-ature value is reached. The ECA will also advance initial igni-tion timing to increase idle speed if the coolant overheats due to prolonged idle. A faster idle speed increases coolant and radiator air flow.

Inlet air temperature is measured by a sensor mounted in the air cleaner. It functions in the same way as the coolant sensor. The ECA uses its signal for proper spark advance and Thermactor® flow. At high inlet temperatures, above 90°F (32°C) the ECA modifies timing advance to prevent spark knock.

The crankshaft is fitted with a four-lobed powdered metal pulse ring, positioned 10° BTDC. Its position is constantly monitored by the crankshaft position sensor. Signals are sent to the ECA describing both the position of the crankshaft at any given moment, and the frequency of the pulses (engine rpm). These signals are used to determine optimum ignition timing advance. If either the sensor or wiring is broken, the ECA will not receive a signal, and thus will be unable to send

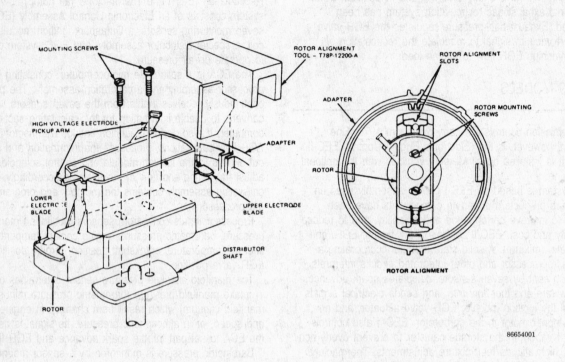

MOUNTING SCREWS

ROTOR ALIGNMENT
TOOL - T78P-12200-A

ADAPTER

HIGH VOLTAGE ELECTRODE
PICKUP ARM

ADAPTER

LOWER
ELECTRODE
BLADE

UPPER ELECTRODE
BLADE

DISTRIBUTOR
SHAFT

ROTOR

ROTOR ALIGNMENT
SLOTS

ROTOR MOUNTING
SCREWS

ADAPTER

ROTOR

ROTOR ALIGNMENT

86654001

Fig. 1 EEC rotor alignment through 1979

any signal to the ignition module. This would prevent the engine from starting.

The throttle position sensor is a rheostat connected to the throttle plate shaft. Changes in throttle plate angle change the resistance value of the reference voltage supplied by the processor. Signals are interpreted in one of three ways by the ECA.
- Closed throttle (idle or deceleration)
- Part throttle (cruise)
- Full throttle (maximum acceleration)

A position sensor is built into the EGR valve. The ECA uses its signal to determine EGR valve position. The valve and position sensor are replaced as a unit, should one fail.

✳✳CAUTION

Because of the complicated nature of this system, special diagnostic tools are necessary for troubleshooting. Any troubleshooting without these tools must be limited to mechanical checks of connectors and wiring.

The distributor is locked in place during engine manufacture; no rotational adjustment is possible for initial ignition timing, since all timing is controlled by the ECA. There are no mechanical advance mechanisms or adjustments under the rotor, thus there is no need to remove it except for replacement.

EEC-II

▶ **See Figure 2**

The second generation EEC system was introduced on mid-sized Fords and Mercury in 1979. It was based on the EEC-I system used on the full sized vehicles, but some changes were made to reduce complexity and cost, increase the number of controlled functions, and improve reliability and performance.

In general, the EEC-II system operates in the same manner as EEC-I. An Electronic Control Assembly (ECA) monitors reports from six sensors, and adjust the EGR flow, ignition timing, Thermactor® (air pump) air flow, and carburetor air/fuel mixture in response to the incoming signals. Although there are only six sensors, seven conditions are monitored. The sensors are:

- Engine coolant temperature
- Throttle position
- Crankshaft position
- Exhaust gas oxygen
- Barometric and manifold absolute pressure
- EGR valve position

These sensors function in the same manner as the EEC-I sensors, and are described in the EEC-I section. Note that inlet air temperature is not monitored in the EEC-II system, and that the barometric and manifold pressure sensors have been combined into one unit. One more change from the previous system is in the location of the crankshaft sensor: it is mounted on the front of the engine, behind the vibration damper and crankshaft pulley.

The biggest difference between EEC-I and EEC-II is that the newer system is capable of continually monitoring and adjusting the carburetor air/fuel ratio. Monitoring is performed by the oxygen sensor installed in the right exhaust manifold; adjustment is made via an electric stepper motor installed on the model 7200 VV carburetor.

The stepper motor has four separate armature windings, which can be sequentially energized by the ECA. As the motor varies the position of the carburetor metering valve, the amount of control vacuum exposed to the fuel bowl is correspondingly altered. Increased vacuum reduces pressure in the fuel bowl, causing a leaner air/fuel mixture, and vice versa. During engine starting and immediately after, the ECA sets the motor at a point dependent on its initial position. Thereafter, the motor position is changed in response to the ECA calculations of the six input signals.

EEC-II is also capable of controlling purging of vapors from the evaporative emission control storage canister. A canister purge solenoid, a combination solenoid and valve, is located in the line between the intake manifold purge fitting and the carbon canister. It controls the flow of vapors from the canister to

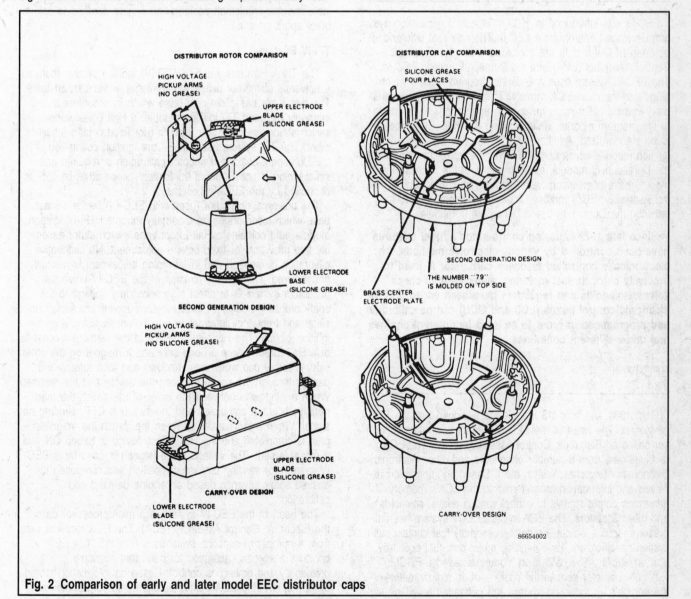

DISTRIBUTOR ROTOR COMPARISON

HIGH VOLTAGE PICKUP ARMS (NO GREASE)

UPPER ELECTRODE BLADE (SILICONE GREASE)

LOWER ELECTRODE BASE (SILICONE GREASE)

SECOND GENERATION DESIGN

HIGH VOLTAGE PICKUP ARMS (NO SILICONE GREASE)

UPPER ELECTRODE BLADE (SILICONE GREASE)

CARRY-OVER DESIGN

LOWER ELECTRODE BLADE (SILICONE GREASE)

DISTRIBUTOR CAP COMPARISON

SILICONE GREASE FOUR PLACES

SECOND GENERATION DESIGN

THE NUMBER "79" IS MOLDED ON TOP SIDE

BRASS CENTER ELECTRODE PLATE

CARRY-OVER DESIGN

86654002

Fig. 2 Comparison of early and later model EEC distributor caps

the intake manifold, opening and closing in response to signals from the ECA.

✳✳WARNING

As is the case with EEC-I, diagnosis and repair of the system requires special tools and equipment.

The distributor is locked in place during engine manufacture; no rotational adjustment is possible for initial ignition timing, since all timing is controlled by the ECA. There are no mechanical advance mechanisms or adjustments under the ignition rotor, and thus there is no need to remove it except for replacement.

Air/fuel mixture is entirely controlled by the ECA; no adjustments are possible.

EEC-III

EEC-III was introduced in 1980. It is a third generation system developed entirely from EEC-II. The only real differences between EEC-II and III are contained within the Electronic Control Assembly (ECA) and the Duraspark ignition module. The EEC-III system uses a separate program module which plugs into the main ECA module. This change allows various programming calibrations for specific applications to be made to the program module, while allowing the main ECA module to be standardized. Additionally, EEC-III uses a Duraspark III ignition module, which contains fewer electronic functions than the Duraspark II module; other functions of the Duraspark II module have been incorporated into the main Electronic Control Assembly (ECA) module. There is no interchangeability between the Duraspark II and Duraspark III modules.

➡**Since late 1979 emission controls and air/fuel mixtures have been controlled by various electronic methods. An electronically controlled feedback carburetor is used to precisely calibrate fuel metering, many vacuum check valves, solenoids and regulators have been added and the electronic control boxes (ECU and MCU) can be calibrated and programmed in order to be used by different engines and under different conditions.**

EEC-IV

Most 1984 and later US models are equipped with the EEC-IV system. The heart of the EEC-IV system is a microprocessor called an Electronic Control Assembly (ECA). The ECA receives data from a number of sensors and other electronic components (switches, relays, etc..). Based on information received and information programmed in the ECA's memory, it generates output signals to control various relays, solenoids and other actuators. The ECA in the EEC-IV system has calibration modules located inside the assembly that contain calibration specifications for optimizing emissions, fuel economy and driveability. The calibration module is called a PROM.

A potentiometer senses the position of an airflow meter in the engine's air induction system and generates a voltage signal that varies with the amount of air drawn into the engine. A sensor is the area of the airflow meter measures the temperature of the incoming air and transmits a corresponding electrical signal. Another temperature sensor inserted in the engine coolant tells if the engine is cold or warmed-up and a switch that senses throttle plate position produces electrical signals that tell the control unit when the throttle is closed or wide open.

A special probe (oxygen sensor) in the exhaust manifold measures the amount of oxygen in the exhaust gas, which is a indication of combustion efficiency, and sends a signal to the control unit. The sixth signal, crankshaft position information, is transmitted by a sensor integral with the new design distributor.

The EEC-IV microcomputer circuit process the input signals and produces output control signals to the fuel injectors to regulate fuel discharge to the injectors. The EEC-IV distributor incorporates a Hall Effect vane switch stator assembly and an integrally mounted thick film module. When the Hall Effect device is tuned on and a pulse is produced, the EEC-IV electronics computes crankshaft position and engine demand to calibrate spark advance.

TFI-IV System

The Thick Film Integrated-IV (TFI-IV) ignition system features a universal distributor using no centrifugal or vacuum advance. The distributor has a die cast base which incorporates an integrally mounted TFI ignition module, a Hall Effect vane switch stator assembly and provision for fixed octane adjustment. The TFI system uses an E-Core ignition coil in lieu of the Duraspark coil. No distributor calibration is required and initial timing is not a normal adjustment, since advance etc.. is controlled by the EEC-IV system.

The universal distributor (used with EEC-IV) has a diecast base which incorporates an externally mounted TFI-IV ignition module, and contains a Hall Effect vane switch stator assembly and provision for fixed octane adjustment. No distributor calibration is required and initial timing adjustment is normally not required. The primary function of the EEC-IV universal distributor system is to direct high secondary voltage to the spark plugs. In addition, the distributor supplies crankshaft position and frequency information to a computer using a profile ignition pickup. The Hall Effect switch in the distributor consists of a Hall Effect device on one side and a magnet on the other side. A rotary cup which has windows and tabs rotates and passes through the space between the device and the magnet. When a window is between the sides of the switch the magnetic path is not completed and the switch is **OFF**, sending no signal. When a tab passes between the switch the magnetic path is completed and the Hall Effect device is turned **ON** and a signal is sent. The voltage pulse (signal) is used by is EEC-IV system for sensing crankshaft position and computing the desired spark advance based on engine demand and calibration.

The heart of the EEC-IV system is a microprocessor called the Electronic Control Assembly (ECA). The ECA receives data from a number of sensors, switches and relays. The ECA contains a specific calibration for peak fuel economy, driveability and emissions control. Based on information stored in its memory, the ECA generates signals to control the various engine functions.

The ECA calibration module is located inside the ECA assembly. On all cars, the ECA is located on the left of the firewall, behind the kick panel.

Positive Crankcase Ventilation System

▶ **See Figures 3, 4 and 5**

All models are equipped with a Positive Crankcase Ventilation (PCV) system to control crankcase blow-by vapors. The system consists of a PCV valve and oil separator mounted on top of the valve cover, a non-ventilated oil filter cap, and a pair of hoses supplying filtered intake air to the valve cover and delivering the crankcase vapors from the valve cover to the intake manifold (6-cylinder) or carburetor (V8). The system functions as follows:

When the engine is running, a small portion of the gases which are formed in the combustion chamber leak by the piston rings and enter the crankcase. Since these gases are under pressure, they tend to escape from the crankcase and enter the atmosphere. If these gases are allowed to remain in the crankcase for any period of time, they contaminate the engine oil and cause sludge to build up in the crankcase. If the gases are allowed to escape into the atmosphere, they pollute the air, with unburned hydrocarbons.

The job of the crankcase emission control equipment is to recycle these gases back into the engine combustion chamber where they are reburned.

As the engine is running, clean, filtered air is drawn through the air filter and into the crankcase. As the air passes through the crankcase, it picks up the combustion gases and carries them out of the crankcase, through the oil separator, through the PCV valve, and into the induction system. As they enter the intake manifold, they are drawn into the combustion chamber where they are reburned.

The most critical component in the system is the PCV valve. This valve controls the amount of gases which are recycled into the combustion chamber. At low engine speeds, the valve is partially closed, limiting the flow of the gases into the intake manifold. As engine speed increases, the valve opens to admit greater quantities of the gases into the intake manifold. If the

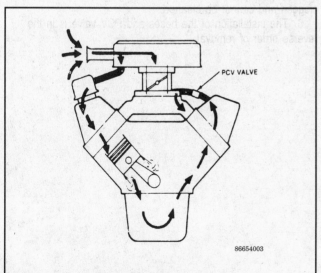

Fig. 3 PCV circulation through the engine

valve should become blocked or plugged, the gases will be prevented from escaping from the crankcase by the normal route. Since these gases are under pressure, they will find their own way out of the crankcase. This alternate route is usually a weak oil seal or gasket in the engine. As the gas escapes by the gasket, it also creates an oil leak. Besides causing oil leaks, a clogged PCV valve also allows these gases to remain in the crankcase for an extended period of time, promoting the formation of sludge in the engine.

TESTING

▶ **See Figure 6**

With a Tachometer

1. See if any deposits are present in the carburetor passages, the oil filler cap or the hoses. Clean these are required.
2. Connect a tachometer, as instructed by its manufacturer, to the engine.
3. With engine idling, do one of the following:
   a. Remove the PCV valve hose from the crankcase or the oil filter connections.
   b. On cars with the PCV valve located in a grommet on the valve cover, remove both the valve and the grommet.

➡ **If the valve and the hoses are not clogged up, a hissing sound should be present.**

4. Check the tachometer reading. Place a finger over the valve or hose opening (a suction should be felt).
5. Check the tachometer again. The engine speed should have dropped at least 50 rpm. It should return to normal when the finger is removed from the opening.
6. If the engine does not change speed or if the change is less than 50 rpm, the hose is clogged or the valve is defective. Check the hose first. If the hose is not clogged, replace, do not attempt to repair, the PCV valve.
7. Test the new valve in the above manner, to make sure that it is operating properly.

Without a Tachometer

With the engine running, pull the PCV valve and hose from the valve rocker cover rubber grommet. Block off the end of the valve with your finger. A strong vacuum should be felt. Shake the valve; a clicking noise indicates it is free. Replace the valve if it is suspected of being blocked.

REMOVAL & INSTALLATION

1. Pull the PCV valve and hose from the rubber grommet in the rocker arm cover or from the oil filler cap.
2. Remove the PCV valve from the hose. Inspect the inside of the PCV valve. If the valve is gummy it can be cleaned in a suitable, safe solvent. However, replacing a clogged, gummed up PCV valve with a new one is suggested.
3. Soak the rubber ventilation hose(s) in a low volatility petroleum base solvent to loosen the deposits. Pass a suitable cleaning brush through them and blow out with compressed air or let air-dry.

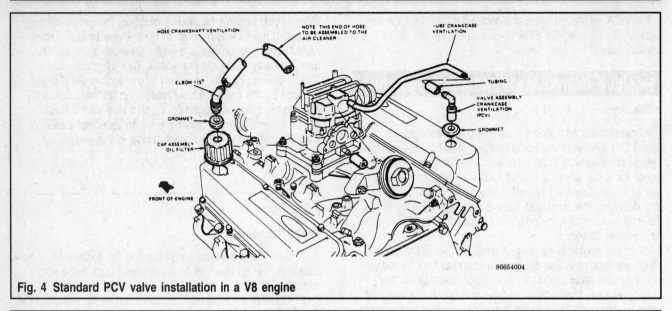

Fig. 4 Standard PCV valve installation in a V8 engine

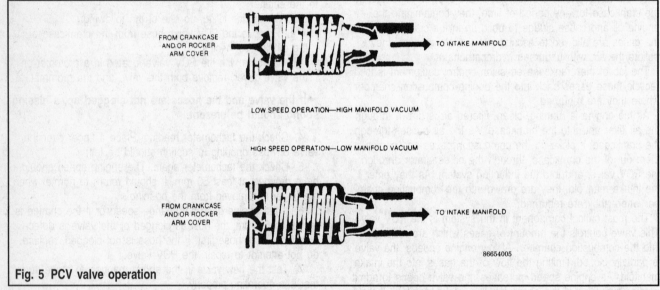

FROM CRANKCASE
AND/OR ROCKER
ARM COVER

TO INTAKE MANIFOLD

LOW SPEED OPERATION—HIGH MANIFOLD VACUUM

HIGH SPEED OPERATION—LOW MANIFOLD VACUUM

FROM CRANKCASE
AND/OR ROCKER
ARM COVER

TO INTAKE MANIFOLD

86654005

Fig. 5 PCV valve operation

4. Thoroughly wash the crankcase breather cap (if equipped) in solvent and shake dry. Do not dry with compressed air; damage to the filtering material may result.

5. Replace any hard or cracked hoses or ones that are clogged and cannot be cleaned.

6. The installation of the hoses and PCV valve is in the reverse order of removal.

TEST STEP	RESULT ▶	ACTION TO TAKE
PCV1 STUCK PCV VALVE CHECK		
• Remove PCV valve from rocker cover grommet (for 5.0L cars, the PCV valve is located on top of block by firewall). • Shake the PCV valve. • **Does PCV valve rattle when shaken?**	Yes ▶ No ▶	REINSTALL PCV valve. GO to PCV2 . PCV valve is sticking. REPLACE PCV valve.
PCV2 PCV SYSTEM CHECK		
• Start engine and bring to normal operating temperature. **For 2.3L HSC** — Remove the corrugated hose from the oil separator nipple. — Place a stiff piece of paper over the nipple end. Wait one minute. **For all others:** — Disconnect hose from remote air cleaner or air outlet tube (tube connecting mass air meter and throttle body). — Place a stiff piece of paper over the hose end. Wait one minute. — **Does vacuum hold the paper in place?**	Yes ▶ No ▶	System is OK. RECONNECT hose. GO to other possible causes of vehicle symptoms. System is plugged or Evaporative Emission Valve is leaking (if equipped). GO to PCV3 .
PCV3 EVAPORATIVE EMISSION SYSTEM CHECK		
• Disconnect evaporative hose (if equipped), cap the connector, and retest. • Place a stiff piece of paper over the hose/nipple, as in PCV2 . Wait one minute. • **Does vacuum hold the paper in place?**	Yes ▶ No ▶	GO to Evaporative Emission System, CHECK for vacuum leaks/obstruction in the system: oil cap, PCV valve, hoses, cut grommets (oil separator on 2.3L, HSC, and rocker cover for bolt torque/gasket leak. SERVICE as necessary.

86674eee

Fig. 6 PCV diagnostic chart

Fuel Evaporative Control System

▶ See Figures 7, 8, 9, 10, 11, 12, 13 and 14

All models sold nationwide are equipped with a fuel evaporative control system to prevent the evaporation of unburned gasoline. The 1971 system consists of a sealed fuel tank filler cap, an expansion area at the top of the gas tank, a combination vapor separator and expansion tank assembly, a 3-way vapor control valve, a carbon canister located in the engine compartment which stores these vapors, and the hoses which connect this equipment.

The 1972 and later system consists of a special vacuum/pressure relief filler cap, and expansion area at the top of the fuel tank, a foam-filled vapor separator mounted on top of the fuel tank, a carbon canister which stores fuel vapors and hoses which connect this equipment.

On carbureted systems, the carburetor fuel bowl vapors are retained within the fuel bowl until the engine is started, at which point they are internally vented into the engine for burning. The system functions as follows:

Changes in atmospheric temperature cause the gasoline in fuel tanks to expand or contract. If this expansion and consequent vaporization takes place in a conventional fuel tank, the fuel vapors escape through the filler cap or vent hose and pollute the atmosphere. The fuel evaporative emission control system prevents this by routing the gasoline vapors to the engine where they are burned.

As the gasoline in the fuel tank of a parked car begins to expand due to heat, the vapor that forms moves to the top of the fuel tank. The fuel tanks on all cars are enlarged so that there is an area representing 10-20% of the total fuel tank volume above the level of the fuel tank filler tube where these gases may collect. The vapors then travel upward into the vapor separator which prevents liquid gasoline from escaping from the fuel tank. The fuel vapor then travels through the vapor separator outlet hose, through the 3-way vapor control valve (1971 only), and to the charcoal canister in the engine compartment. The vapor enters the canister, where it is absorbed and stored by the charcoal filter until engine operating conditions permit its consumption. Once the proper operating conditions are reached, fresh air is drawn through the canister filter and then the fresh air removes the vapors from the charcoal and carries them into the engine to be burned during the normal air/fuel combustion process.

When the engine is started, vacuum created from the engine air intake draws fresh air into the canister. As the fresh air passes through the charcoal in the canister, it picks up the hydrocarbons that were deposited there by the fuel vapors. This mixture of hydrocarbons and fresh air is then carried through a hose in the air cleaner. It combines with the incoming air/fuel mixture and enters the combustion chambers of the engine where it is burned.

On all systems, there still remains the problem of allowing air into the tank to replace the gasoline displaced during normal use and the problem of relieving excess pressure from the fuel tank should it reach a dangerous level. On 1971 systems, the 3-way control valve accomplishes this. On 1971 and later systems, the special filler cap performs this task. Under normal circumstances, the filler cap functions as a check valve, allowing air to enter the tank replacing the consumed fuel. At the same time it prevents vapors from escaping from the cap. In case of severe pressure within the tank, the filler cap valve opens, venting the pollutants to the atmosphere.

DIAGNOSIS & TESTING

Canister Purge Regulator Valve

1. Disconnect the hoses at the purge regulator valve. Disconnect the electrical lead.
2. Connect a vacuum pump to the vacuum source port.
3. Apply 5 in. Hg (17 kPa) to the port. The valve should hold the vacuum. If not, replace it.

Canister Purge Valve

▶ See Figure 15

1. Apply vacuum to port **A**. The valve should hold vacuum. If not, replace it.
2. Apply vacuum to port **B**. Valves E5VE-AA, E4VE-AA and E77E-AA should show a slight vacuum leak-down. All other

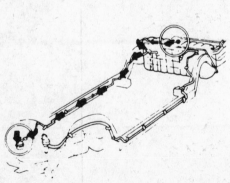

86654007

Fig. 7 Fuel tank vapor line routing in vehicle

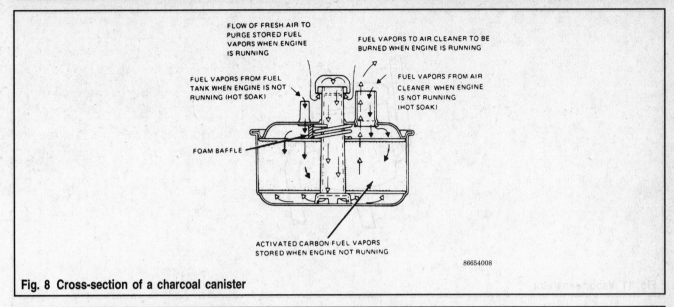

Fig. 8 Cross-section of a charcoal canister

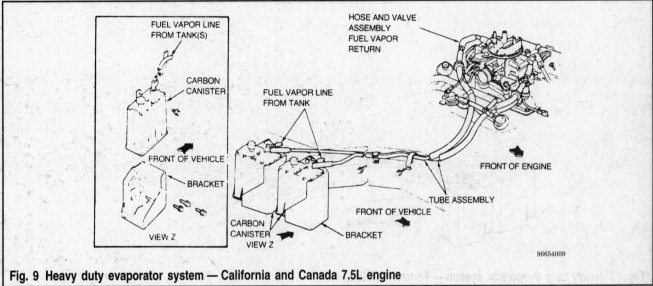

Fig. 9 Heavy duty evaporator system — California and Canada 7.5L engine

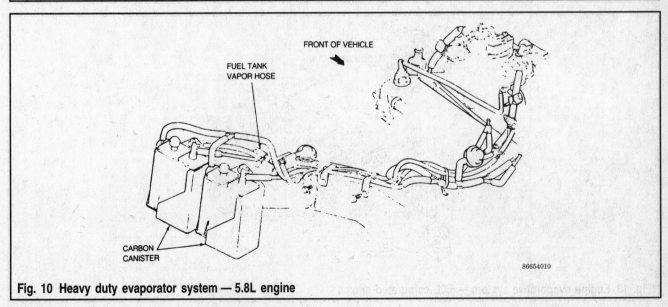

Fig. 10 Heavy duty evaporator system — 5.8L engine

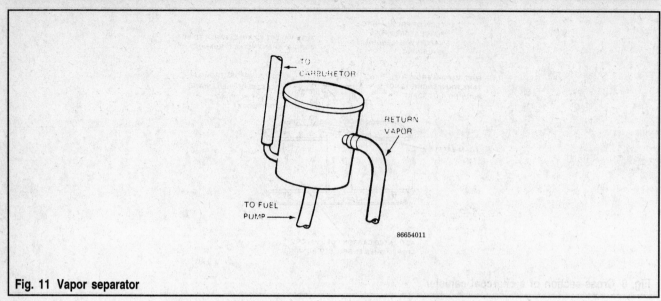

Fig. 11 Vapor separator

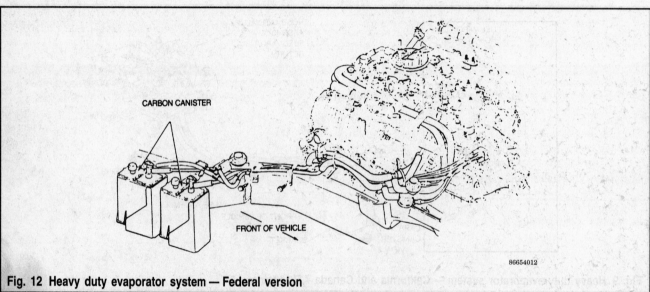

Fig. 12 Heavy duty evaporator system — Federal version

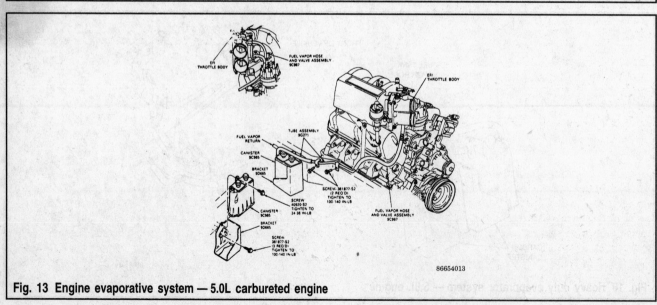

Fig. 13 Engine evaporative system — 5.0L carbureted engine

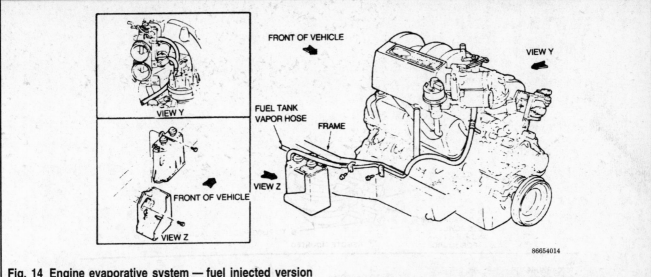

Fig. 14 Engine evaporative system — fuel injected version

valves should hold vacuum. If the valve doesn't operate properly, replace it.

3. Apply 16 in. Hg (53 kPa) to port **A** and apply vacuum to port **B**. Air should pass. On valves E5VE-AA, E4VE-AA and E77E-AA, the flow should be greater than that noted in Step 2.

➡**Never apply vacuum to port C. Doing so will damage the valve.**

4. If the valve fails to perform properly in any of these tests, replace it.

REMOVAL & INSTALLATION

Vent Valve

The only service performed on the evaporative control system is the replacement of the charcoal (carbon) canister at the intervals listed in the maintenance schedule in Section 1. The procedure is as follows.

1. Working under the vehicle, disconnect two hoses from the control valve. Remove the vent valve cover.

2. Remove the attaching bolts and remove the valve from the crossmember at the rear of the gas tank.

To install:

3. Position the valve to the crossmember and install two attaching bolts.

4. Connect the two hoses to the valve assembly. Install the cover.

Canister

Loosen and remove the canister mounting bolts from the mounting bracket. Disconnect the purge hose from the air cleaner and the feed hose from the fuel tank. Discard the old canister and install a new unit. Make sure that the hoses are connected properly.

Thermactor® System

▶ **See Figures 16, 17 and 18**

The Thermactor® emission control system makes use of a belt driven air pump to inject fresh air into the hot exhaust stream through the engine exhaust ports. The result is the extending burning of those fumes which were not completely ignited in the combustion chamber, and the subsequent reduction of some of the hydrocarbon and carbon monoxide content of the exhaust emissions into harmless carbon dioxide and water.

The Thermactor® system is composed of the following components:
- Air supply pump (belt driven)
- Air bypass valve
- Check valves
- Air manifold (internal or external)
- Air supply tubes (on external manifold only)

Air for the Thermactor® system is cleaned by means of a centrifugal filter fan mounted on the air pump driveshaft. The air filter does not require a replaceable element.

To prevent excessive pressure, the air pump is equipped with a pressure relief valve which uses a replaceable plastic plug to control the pressure setting.

The Thermactor® air pump has sealed bearings which are lubricated for the life of the unit, and preset rotor vane and bearing clearances, which do not require an periodic adjustments.

The air supply from the pump is controlled by the air bypass valve, sometimes called a dump valve. During deceleration, the air bypass valve opens, momentarily diverting the air supply through a silencer and into the atmosphere, thus preventing backfires within the exhaust system.

A check valve is incorporated in the air inlet side of the air manifolds. Its purpose is to prevent exhaust gases from backing up into the Thermactor® system. This valve is especially important in the event of drive belt failure, and during deceleration, when the air bypass valve is dumping the air supply.

The air manifolds and air supply tubes channel the air from the Thermactor® air pump into the exhaust ports of each

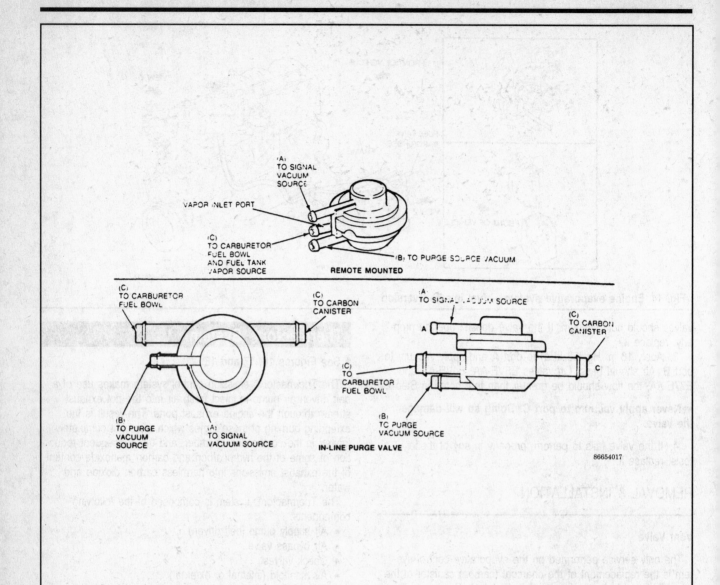

Fig. 15 Canister purge valve

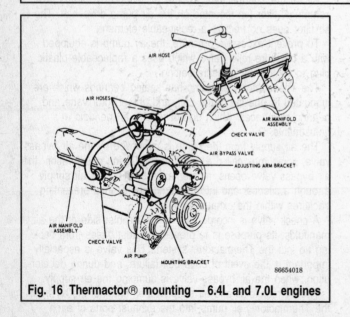

Fig. 16 Thermactor® mounting — 6.4L and 7.0L engines

Fig. 17 Thermactor® mounting — all 8-cylinder engines except 6.4L and 7.0L

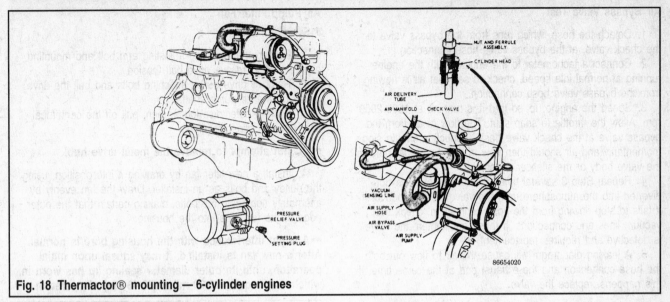

Fig. 18 Thermactor® mounting — 6-cylinder engines

cylinder, thus completing the cycle of the Thermactor® system.

SYSTEM CHECKS

Before performing an extensive diagnosis of the emission control systems, verify that all specifications on the Vehicle Emissions Control Information (VECI) label are met, because the following systems or components may cause symptoms that appear to be emission related.
- Improper vacuum connections
- Vacuum leaks
- Ignition timing
- Plugs, wires, cap and rotor
- Carburetor float level
- Carburetor main metering jets
- Choke operation

Belt Tension and Air Leaks

✳✳WARNING

Do not hammer on, pry or bend the pump housing while tightening the drive belt or testing the pump.

1. Before proceeding with the tests, check the pump drive belt tension to see if it is within specifications
2. Turn the pump by hand. If it has seized, the belt will slip, producing noise. Disregard any chirping, squealing, or rolling sounds from inside the pump; these are normal when it is turned by hand.
3. Check the hoses and connections for leaks. Hissing or a blast of air is indicative of a leak. Soapy water, applied lightly around the areas in question, is a good method of detecting leaks.

Air Output Test

1. Disconnect the air supply hose at the anti-backfire valve.

2. Connect a pressure gauge, using a suitable adaptor, to the air supply hose.

➡**If there are two hoses plug the second one.**

3. With the engine at normal operating temperature, increase the idle speed and watch the vacuum gauge.
4. The air flow from the pump should be steady and fall between 2-6 psi (13-41 kPa). If it is unsteady or falls below this, the pump is defective and must be replaced.

Pump Noise Diagnosis

The air pump is normally noisy; as engine speed increases, the noise of the pump will rise in pitch. The rolling sound the pump bearings make is normal; however, if this sound becomes louder than the road noise at certain speeds, the pump is defective and will have to be replaced.

A continual hissing sound from the air pump pressure relief valve at idle, indicates a defective valve. Replace the relief valve.

If the pump rear bearing fails, a continual knocking sound will be heard. since the rear bearing is not separately replaceable, the pump will the to be replaced as an assembly.

Check Valve Test

1. Before starting the test, check all of the hoses and connections for leaks.
2. Detach the air supply hose(s) from the check valve.
3. Insert a suitable probe into the check valve and depress the plate. Release it; the plate should return to its original position against the valve seat. If binding is evident, replace the valve.
4. If two valves are used, repeat step 3 on the remaining valve.
5. With the engine running at normal operating temperature, gradually increase it speed to 1500 rpm. Check for exhaust gas leakage. If any is present, replace the valve assembly.

➡**Vibration and flutter of the check valve at idle speed is a normal condition and does not mean that the valve should be replaced.**

Air Bypass Valve Test

1. Detach the hose, which runs from the bypass valve to the check valve, at the bypass valve hose connection.

2. Connect a tachometer to the engine. With the engine running at normal idle speed, check to see that air is flowing from the bypass valve hose connection.

3. Speed the engine up, so that it is running at 1500-2000 rpm. Allow the throttle to snap shut. The flow of air from the bypass valve at the check valve hose connection should stop momentarily and air should then flow from the exhaust port on the valve body or the silencer assembly.

4. Repeat Step 3 several times. If the flow of air is not diverted into the atmosphere from the valve exhaust port of if it fails to stop flowing from the hose connection, check the vacuum lines and connections. If these are tighten, the valve is defective and requires replacement.

5. A leaking diaphragm will cause the air to flow out both the hose connection and the exhaust port at the same time. If this happens, replace the valve.

REMOVAL & INSTALLATION

Air Pump

▶ See Figure 19

1. Disconnect the air outlet hose at the air pump.
2. Loosen the pump belt tension adjuster.
3. Disengage the drive belt.
4. Remove the mounting bolt and air pump.

To install:

5. Position the air pump on the mounting bracket and install the mounting bolts.

6. Place drive belt in pulleys and attach the adjusting arm to the air pump.

7. Tighten the mounting bolts and adjust the drive belt tension. Use a suitable belt tension gauge to check the tension.

8. Connect the air outlet hose to the air pump.

Air Pump Filter Fan

▶ See Figure 20

1. Loosen the air pump adjusting arm bolt and mounting bracket bolt to relieve drive belt tension.

2. Remove drive pulley attaching bolts and pull the drive pulley off the air pump shaft.

3. Pry the outer disc loose; then, pull off the centrifugal filter fan with slip-joint pliers.

➡ **Do not attempt to remove the metal drive hub!**

4. Install a new filter fan by drawing it into position, using the pulley and bolts as an installer. Draw the fan evenly by alternately tightening the bolts, making certain that the outer edge of the fan slips into the housing.

➡ **A slight interference with the housing bore is normal. After a new fan is installed, it may squeal upon initial operation, until its outer diameter sealing lip has worn in, which may require 20-30 miles (32-48 km) of operation.**

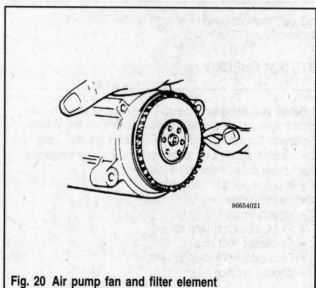

86654021

Fig. 20 Air pump fan and filter element

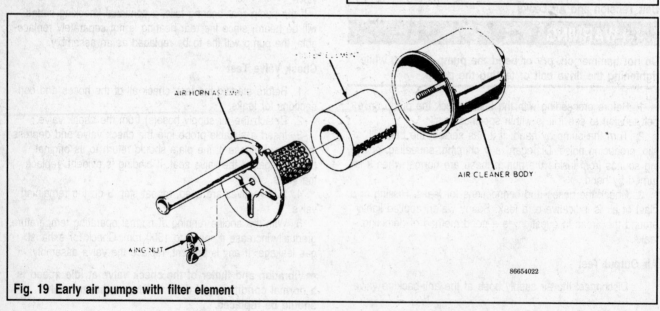

86654022

Fig. 19 Early air pumps with filter element

Check Valve

▶ **See Figures 21, 22, 23 and 24**

1. Apply a light coat of penetrating oil to the fitting prior to removal.

2. Disconnect the air supply hose at the valve. Use a crowfoot wrench or other suitable tool.

➡**The valve has a standard, right hand pipe thread.**

3. Clean the threads on the air manifold adaptor or air supply tube with a wire brush. Do not blow compressed air through the check valve in either direction.

4. Install the check valve and tighten.

5. Connect the air supply hose.

Air Bypass Valve

1. Disconnect the air and vacuum hoses at the air bypass valve body.

2. Position the air bypass valve, and connect the respective hoses.

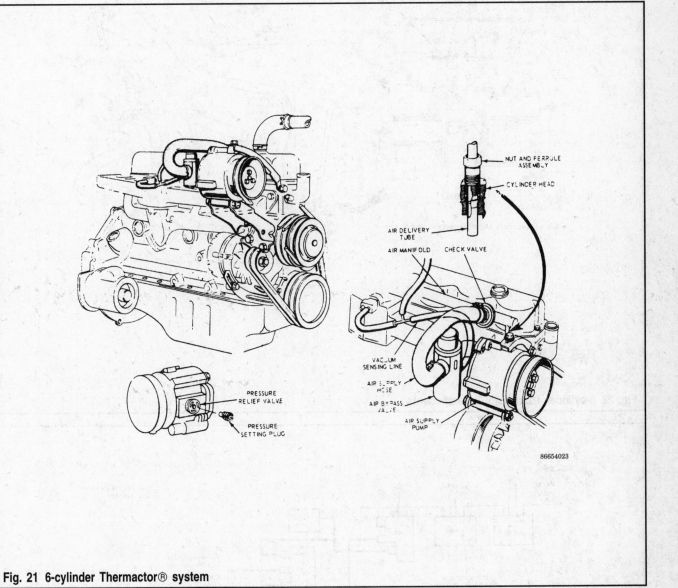

Fig. 21 6-cylinder Thermactor® system

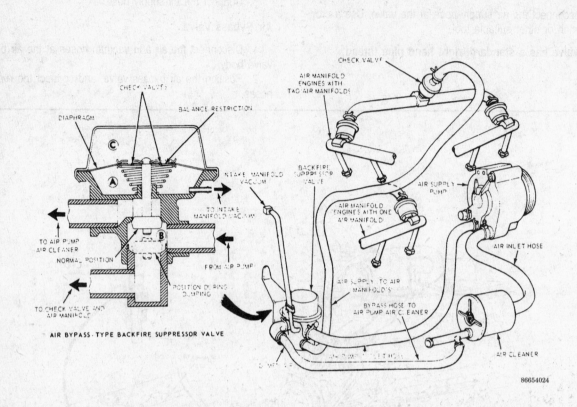

86654024

Fig. 22 6-cylinder Thermactor® components

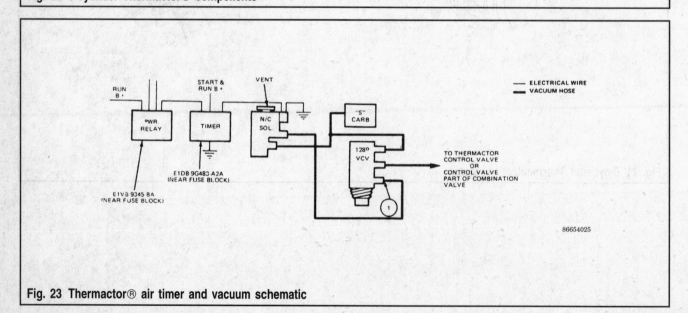

86654025

Fig. 23 Thermactor® air timer and vacuum schematic

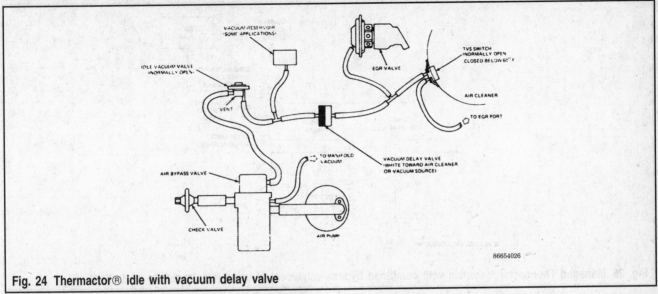

Fig. 24 Thermactor® idle with vacuum delay valve

Managed Thermactor® Air System

▶ **See Figures 25, 26, 27 and 28**

The Managed Thermactor® Air (MTA) system is used to inject fresh air into the exhaust manifolds or catalytic converters via an air control valve. Under some operating conditions, the air can be dumped back into the atmosphere via an air bypass valve. On some applications the two valves are combined into one unit. The air bypass valve can be either the normally closed type, when the valves are separate, or the normally open type, when the valves are combined.

TESTING

Normally Closed Air Bypass Valve

1. Disconnect the air supply hose at the valve.
2. Run the engine to normal operating temperature.

3. Disconnect the vacuum line and make sure vacuum is present. If no vacuum is present, remove or bypass any restrictors or delay valves in the vacuum line.
4. Run the engine at 1500 rpm with the vacuum line connected. Air pump supply air should be heard and felt at the valve outlet.
5. With the engine still at 1500 rpm, disconnect the vacuum line. Air at the outlet should shut off or dramatically decrease. Air pump supply air should now be felt or heard at the silencer ports.
6. If the valve doesn't pass each of these tests, replace it.

Normally Open Air Bypass Valve

1. Disconnect the air supply hose at the valve.
2. Run the engine to normal operating temperature.
3. Disconnect the vacuum lines from the valve.
4. Run the engine at 1500 rpm with the vacuum lines disconnected. Air pump supply air should be heard and felt at the valve outlet.

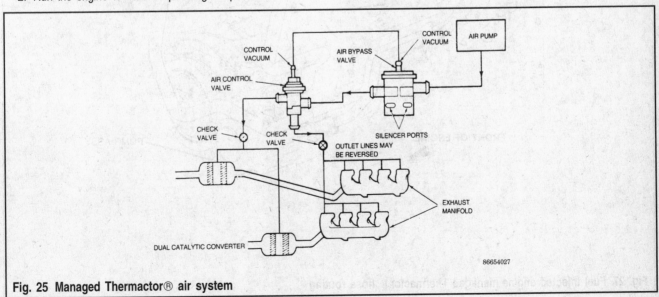

Fig. 25 Managed Thermactor® air system

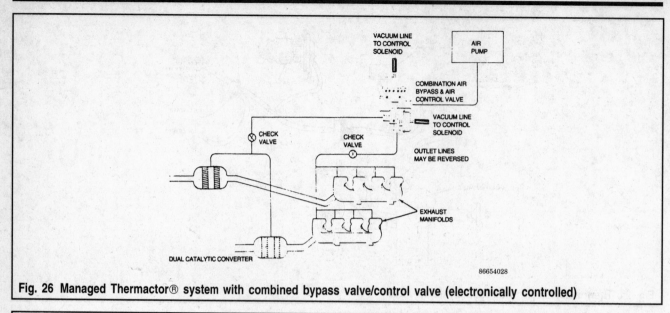

Fig. 26 Managed Thermactor® system with combined bypass valve/control valve (electronically controlled)

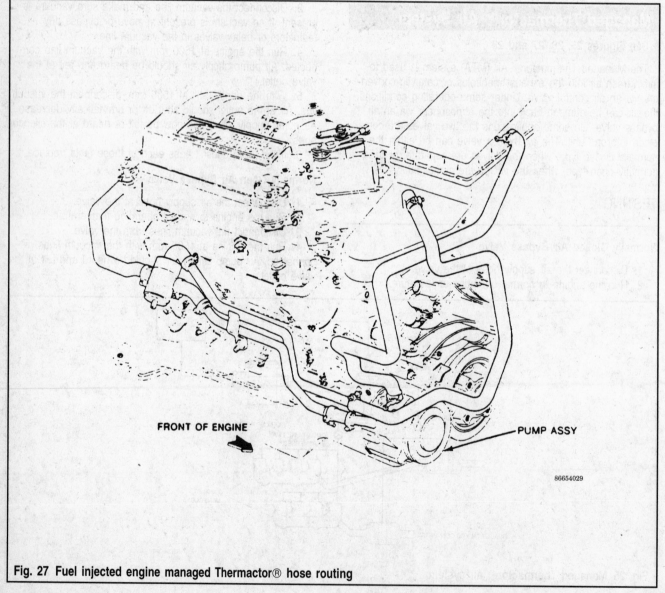

Fig. 27 Fuel injected engine managed Thermactor® hose routing

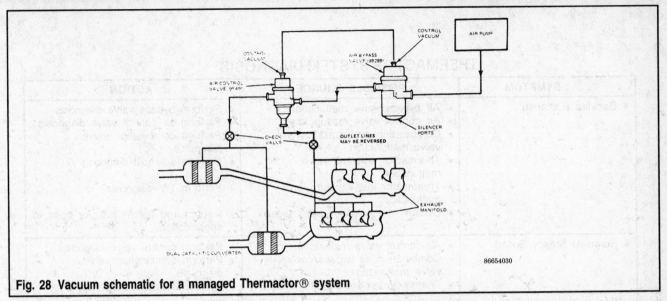

Fig. 28 Vacuum schematic for a managed Thermactor® system

86654030

5. Shut **OFF** the engine. Using a spare length of vacuum hose, connect the vacuum nipple of the valve to direct manifold vacuum.

6. Run the engine at 1500 rpm. Air at the outlet should shut off or dramatically decrease. Pump supply air should now be felt or heard at the silencer ports.

7. With the engine still in this mode, cap the vacuum vent. Accelerate the engine to 2000 rpm and suddenly release the throttle. A momentary interruption of pump supply air should be felt at the valve outlet.

8. If the valve doesn't pass each of these tests, replace it. Reconnect all lines.

Air Control Valve

1. Run the engine to normal operating temperature, then increase the speed to 1500 rpm.

2. Disconnect the air supply hose at the valve inlet and verify that there is airflow present.

3. Reconnect the air supply hose.

4. Disconnect the vacuum hose from the valve.

5. With the engine running at 1500 rpm, airflow should be felt and heard at the outlet on the side of the valve, with no airflow heard or felt at the outlet opposite the vacuum nipple.

6. Shut **OFF** the engine.

7. Using a spare piece of vacuum hose, connect direct manifold vacuum to the valve's vacuum fitting. Airflow should be heard and felt at the outlet opposite the vacuum nipple, and no airflow should be present at the other outlet.

8. If the valve is not functioning properly, replace it.

Air Supply Pump Functional Check

1. Check and, if necessary, adjust the belt tension. Press at the mid-point of the belt's longest straight run. You should be able to depress the belt about 1/2 in. (13mm) at most.

2. Run the engine to normal operating temperature and let it idle.

3. Disconnect the air supply hose from the bypass control valve. If the pump is operating properly, airflow should be felt at the pump outlet. The flow should increase as you increase the engine speed. The pump is not serviceable and should be replaced if it is not functioning properly.

THERMACTOR SYSTEM DIAGNOSIS

SYMPTOM	POSSIBLE SOURCE	ACTION
• Backfire (Exhaust)	• Air bypass valve malfunction • Air control valve malfunction • Combination air bypass/control valve malfunction • Thermactor solenoid valve malfunction • Thermactor idle vacuum valve malfunction • Exhaust manifolds or pipes loose	• Perform bypass valve diagnosis • Perform air control valve diagnosis • Perform combination valve diagnosis • Perform solenoid diagnosis • Perform TIV diagnosis • Inspect and tighten nuts or bolts to specification.
• Surge at Steady Speed	• Air control valve malfunction • Combination air bypass/control valve malfunction • Thermactor solenoid malfunction	• Perform control valve diagnosis • Perform combination valve diagnosis • Perform solenoid diagnosis
• Engine Noise - (Hiss) • Engine Noise - (Rap, Roar)	• Thermactor hose leaks or disconnects • Thermactor hose or valves leak exhaust	• Visual inspection of hoses and connections • Visual inspection of hoses and valves. Perform air check valve diagnosis
• Poor Fuel Economy	• Air control valve malfunction • Combination air bypass/control valve malfunction • Thermactor solenoid valve malfunction • Disconnected vacuum or electrical connections for thermactor components	• Perform air control valve diagnosis • Perform combination valve diagnosis • Perform solenoid diagnosis • Visual inspection
• Exhaust Smoke - (White)	• Disconnected vacuum or electrical connections for thermactor components • Air bypass valve malfunction • Air control valve malfunction • Combination air bypass/control valve malfunction • Thermactor solenoid valve malfunction	• Visual inspection • Perform bypass valve diagnosis • Perform air control valve diagnosis • Perform combination valve diagnosis • Perform solenoid diagnosis
• State Emission Test Failure	• Disconnected vacuum or electrical connections for thermactor components • Air bypass valve malfunction • Air control valve malfunction • Combination air bypass/control valve malfunction • Thermactor solenoid valve malfunction	• Visual inspection • Perform bypass valve diagnosis • Perform air control valve diagnosis • Perform combination valve diagnosis • Perform solenoid diagnosis
• Rolling Idle	• Thermactor solenoid valve malfunction • Disconnected vacuum or electrical connections for thermactor components • Air bypass valve malfunction • Air control valve malfunction • Combination air bypass/control valve malfunction	• Perform solenoid diagnosis • Visual inspection • Perform bypass valve diagnosis • Perform air control valve diagnosis • Perform combination valve diagnosis

86674ee1

THERMACTOR SYSTEM NOISE DIAGNOSIS

CAUTION

Do not use a pry bar to move the air pump for belt adjustment.

NOTE: The thermactor system is not completely noiseless. Under normal conditions, noise rises in pitch as engine speed increases. To determine if noise is the fault of the air injection system, disconnect the belt drive (only after verifying that belt tension is correct), and operate the engine. If the noise disappears, proceed with the following diagnosis.

Diagnosis

SYMPTOM	POSSIBLE SOURCE	ACTION
• Excessive Belt Noise	• Loose belt.	• Tighten to specification using Tool T75L-9480-A or equivalent to hold belt tension and Belt Tension Gauge T63L-8620-A or equivalent. **CAUTION: Do not use a pry bar to move air pump.**
	• Seized pump.	• Replace pump.
	• Loose pulley.	• Replace pulley and/or pump if damaged. Tighten bolts to 13.6-17.0 N·m (120-150 lb-in).
	• Loose or broken mounting brackets or bolts.	• Replace parts as required and tighten bolts to specification.
• Excessive Mechanical Noise, Chirps, Squeaks, Clicks or Ticks	• Overtightened mounting bolt.	• Tighten to 34 N·m (25 lb-ft).
	• Overtightened drive belt.	• Same as loose belt.
	• Excessive flash on the air pump adjusting arm boss.	• Remove flash from the boss.
	• Distorted adjusting arm.	• Replace adjusting arm.
	• Pump or pulley mounting fasteners loose.	• Tighten fasteners to specifications.

86674ee2

THERMACTOR SYSTEM DIAGNOSIS

SYMPTOM	POSSIBLE SOURCE	ACTION
• Excessive Thermactor System Noise (Putt-Putt, Whirling or Hissing)	• Leak in hose.	• Locate source of leak using soap solution and replace hoses as necessary.
	• Loose, pinched or kinked hose.	• Reassemble, straighten or replace hose and clamps as required.
	• Hose touching other engine parts.	• Adjust hose to prevent contact with other engine parts.
	• Bypass valve inoperative.	• Test the valve.
	• Check valve inoperative.	• Test the valve.
	• Restricted or bent pump outlet fitting.	• Inspect fitting and remove any flash blocking the air passage way. Replace bent fittings.
	• Air dumping through bypass valve (at idle only).	• On many vehicles, the thermactor system has been designed to dump air at idle to prevent overheating the catalyst. This condition is normal. Determine that the noise persists at higher speeds before proceeding.
	• Air dump through bypass valve (decel and cruise).	• On many vehicles, the thermactor air is dumped in the air cleaner or in remote silencer. Make sure hoses are connected and not cracked.
	• Air pump resonator leaking or blocked.	• Check resonator for hole or restricted inlet/outlet tubes.
• Excessive Pump Noise - (Chirps, Squeaks and Ticks)	• Worn or damaged pump.	• Check the thermactor system for wear or damage and make necessary corrections.
• Engine noise - (Rap or Roar)	• Hose disconnected.	• Audible and visual inspection to assure all hoses are connected.
• State Emissions Test Failure	• Restricted hose.	• Inspect hoses for crimped and/or kinked hoses.
	• Plugged pulse air silencer.	• Remove inlet hose and inspect silencer inlet for dirt and foreign material. Clean or replace silencer as appropriate.
	• Pulse air valve malfunction, leaking or restricted.	• Perform pulse air check valve diagnosis.
	• Pulse air control valve malfunction.	• Perform pulse air control valve diagnosis.

86674ee3

Improved Combustion (IMCO) System

All models (regardless of other exhaust emission control equipment) are equipped with the Improved Combustion (IMCO) system. The IMCO system controls emissions arising from the incomplete combustion of the air/fuel mixture in the cylinders. The IMCO system incorporates a number of modifications to the distributor spark control system, the fuel system, and the internal design of the engine.

Internal engine modifications include the following: elimination of surface irregularities and crevices as well as a low surface area-to-volume ratio in the combustion chambers, a high velocity intake manifold combined with short exhaust ports, selective valve timing and a higher temperature capacity and cooling system.

Modifications to the fuel system include the following: recalibrated carburetors to achieve a leaner air/fuel mixture, more precise calibration of the choke mechanism, the installation of idle mixture limiter caps and a heated air intake system.

Modifications to the distributor spark control system include the following: a modified centrifugal advance curve, the use of dual diaphragm distributors in most applications, a ported vacuum switch, a deceleration valve and a spark delay valve.

Heated Air Intake System

▶ **See Figures 29 and 30**

The heated air intake portion of the air cleaner consists of a thermostat or bimetal switch along with a vacuum motor and a spring loaded temperature control door in the snorkel of the air cleaner. The temperature control door is located between the end of the air cleaner snorkel which draws in air from the engine compartment and the duct that carries heated air up from the exhaust manifold. When underhood temperature is below 90°F (32°C), the temperature control door blocks off underhood air from entering the air cleaner and allows only heated air from the exhaust manifold to be drawn into the air cleaner. When underhood temperature rises above 130°F (54°C), the temperature control door blocks off heated air from the exhaust manifold and allows underhood air to be drawn into the air cleaner.

By controlling the temperature of the engine intake air this way, exhaust emissions are lowered and fuel economy is improved. In addition, throttle plate icing is reduced, and cold weather driveability is improved from the necessary leaner mixtures.

TESTING

Duct and Valve Assembly

1. Either start with a cold engine or remove the air cleaner from the engine for at least half an hour. While cooling the air cleaner, leave the engine compartment hood open.
2. Tape a thermometer, of known accuracy, to the inside of the air cleaner so that it is near the temperature sensor unit. Install the air cleaner on the engine but do not fasten its securing nut.

3. Start the engine. With the engine cold and the outside temperature less than 90°F (32°C), the door should be in the HEAT ON position (closed to outside air).
4. Operate the throttle lever rapidly to ½-¾ of its opening and release it. The air door should open to allow outside air to enter and then close again.
5. Allow the engine to warm-up to normal temperature. Watch the door. when it opens to the outside air, remove the cover from the air cleaner. the temperature should be over 90°F (32°C) and no more than 130°F (54°C). Keep in mind that 105°F (41°C) is about normal. If the door noes not work within these temperature ranges, or fails to work at all, check for linkage or door binding.

If binding is not present and the air door is not working, proceed with the vacuum tests given below. If these indicate no faults in the vacuum motor and the door is not working, the temperature sensor is defective and must be replaced.

Vacuum Motor

Be sure that the vacuum hose that runs between the temperature switch and the vacuum motor is not pinched by the retaining clip under the air cleaner. This could prevent the air door from closing.

1. Check all vacuum lines and fittings for leaks. Correct any leaks. If none are found, proceed with the test.
2. Remove the hose which runs from the sensor to the vacuum motor. Run a hose directly from the manifold vacuum source to the vacuum motor.
3. If the motor closes the air door, it is functioning properly and the temperature sensor is defective.
4. If the motor does not close the door and no binding is present in its operation, the vacuum motor is defective and must be replaced.

➡**If an alternate vacuum source is applied to the motor, insert a vacuum gauge in the line by using a T-fitting. Apply at least 9 in. Hg (30 kPa) of vacuum in order to operate the motor.**

REMOVAL & INSTALLATION

Duct and Valve Assembly

TEMPERATURE OPERATED

1. Remove the hex-head cap screws which secure the air intake duct and valve assembly to the air cleaner.
2. Remove the air intake duct and valve assembly from the engine.
3. If the duct and valve assembly was removed because of a suspected temperature malfunction, check the operation of the thermostat and valve plate assembly. Refer to the Duct and Valve Assembly test for the proper procedure.
4. If inspection reveals that the valve plate is sticking or the thermostat is malfunctioning, remove the thermostat and valve plates as follows:
   a. Detach the valve plate tension spring from the plate using long-nosed pliers.
   b. Loosen the thermostat locknut and unscrew the thermostat from the mounting bracket.
   c. Grasp the valve plate and withdraw it from the duct.

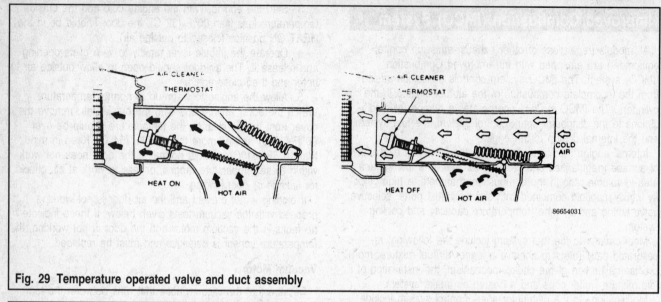

Fig. 29 Temperature operated valve and duct assembly

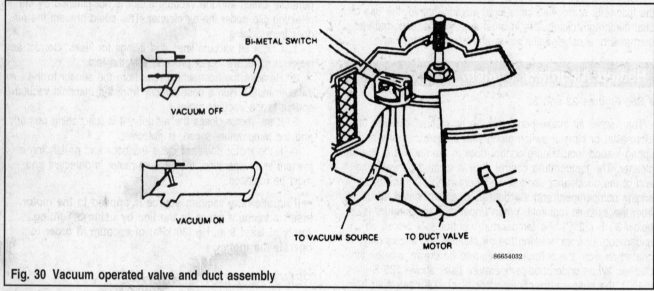

Fig. 30 Vacuum operated valve and duct assembly

5. Install the air intake duct and valve assembly on the shroud tube.

6. Connect the air intake duct and valve assembly to the air cleaner and tighten the hexhead retaining cap screws.

7. If it was necessary to disassemble the thermostat, air duct and valve, assemble the unit as follows:

   a. Install the valve plate. Install the locknut on the thermostat, and screw the thermostat into the mounting bracket. Install the valve plate tension spring on the valve plate and duct.

   b. Check the operation of the thermostat and air duct assembly. Refer to the Duct and Valve Assembly test for the proper procedure. Tighten the locknut.

   c. Install the vacuum override motor (if applicable) and check for proper operation.

VACUUM OPERATED

1. Disconnect the vacuum hose at the vacuum motor.

2. Remove the hex head cap screws which secure the air intake duct and ealve assembly to the air cleaner.

3. Remove the duct and valve assembly from the engine.

4. Position the duct and valve assembly to the air cleaner and heat stove tube. Install the attaching cap screws.

5. Connect the vacuum line at the vacuum motor.

Dual Diaphragm Distributors

Dual diaphragm distributors are installed in most models. They appear in many different engine/transmission/equipment combinations.

The dual diaphragm is a two-chambered housing which is mounted on the side of the distributor. The outer side of the housing is a distributor vacuum advance mechanism, connected to the carburetor by a vacuum hose. The purpose of the vacuum advance is to advance ignition timing according to the conditions under which the engine is operating. This device has been used on automobiles for many years not and its chief advantage is economical engine operation. The second side of the dual diaphragm is the side that has been added to help control engine exhaust emissions at idle and during deceleration.

The inner side of the dual diaphragm is connected by a vacuum hose to the intake manifold. When the engine is idling or decelerating, intake manifold vacuum is high and carburetor vacuum is low. Under these conditions, intake manifold vacuum, applied to the inner side of the dual diaphragm, retards ignition timing to promote more complete combustion of the air fuel mixture in the engine combustion chambers.

DIAPHRAGM TESTING

1. Connect a timing light to the engine. Check the ignition timing.

➡ **Before proceeding with the tests, disconnect any spark control devices, distributor vacuum valves, etc. If these are left connected, inaccurate result may be obtained.**

2. Remove the retard hose from the distributor and plug it. Increase the engine speed. The timing should advance. If it fails to do so, then the vacuum unit is faulty and must be replaced.

3. Check the timing with the engine at normal idle speed. Unplug the retard hose and connect it to the vacuum unit. The timing should instantly be retarded. If this does not occur, the retard diaphragm has a leak and the vacuum unit must be replaced.

REMOVAL & INSTALLATION

1. Remove the distributor cap and rotor.
2. Disconnect the vacuum lines.
3. Remove the clip that secure the diaphragm arm to the distributor advance plate.
4. Remove the screws that attach the diaphragm to the distributor (outside of the distributor).
5. Carefully remove the unit by tilting it downward to disengage the diaphragm arm from the plate.
6. Installation is the reverse of removal. Consult the instructions that come with the new diaphragm as to the calibration of the unit.

Distributor Vacuum Control Valve

▶ **See Figures 31 and 32**

The distributor vacuum control valve is a temperature sensitive valve which screws into the water jacket of the engine. Three vacuum lines are attached to the vacuum control valve: one which runs from the carburetor to the control valve, one which runs from the control valve to the distributor vacuum advance (outer) chamber, and one which runs from the intake manifold to the distributor vacuum control valve.

During normal engine operation, vacuum from the carburetor passes through the top nipple on the distributor control valve, through the valve body to the second nipple on the valve, and out the second nipple on the valve to the distributor vacuum advance chamber. When the engine is idling however, carbure-

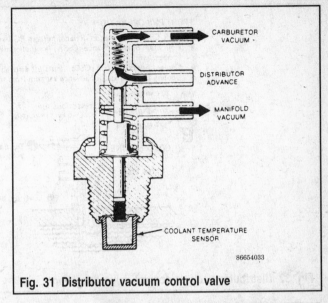

Fig. 31 Distributor vacuum control valve

tor vacuum is very low, so that there is little, if any vacuum in the passageways described above.

If the engine should begin to overheat while idling, a check ball inside the distributor vacuum control which normally blocks off the third nipple of the valve (intake manifold vacuum) moves upward to block off the first nipple (carburetor vacuum). This applies intake manifold vacuum (third nipple) to the distributor vacuum advance chamber (second nipple). Since intake manifold vacuum is very high while the engine is idling, ignition timing is advanced by the application of intake manifold vacuum to the distributor vacuum advance chamber. This raises the engine idle speed and helps to cool the engine.

TESTING

1. Block the wheels so the vehicle does not move.
2. Check the routing and connection of all vacuum hoses.
3. Attach a tachometer to the engine.
4. Bring the engine up to the normal operating temperature. The engine must not be overheated.
5. Note the engine rpm, with the transmission is in NEUTRAL, and the throttle in the curb idle position.
6. Disconnect the vacuum hose from the intake manifold at the temperature sensing valve. Plug or clamp the hose.
7. Note the idle rpm with the hose disconnected. If there is no change in rpm, the valve is good. If there is a drop of 100 or more rpm, the valve should be replaced. Replace the vacuum line.
8. Check to make sure that the all season cooling mixture meets specifications, and that the correct radiator cap is in place and functioning.
9. Block the radiator air flow to induce a higher-than-normal temperature condition.
10. Continue to operate until the engine temperature or heat indicator shows above normal.

If the engine speed by this time has increased 100 or more rpm, the temperature sensing valve is satisfactory. If not, it should be replaced.

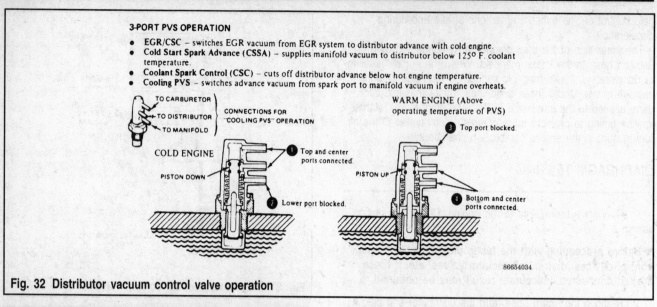

3-PORT PVS OPERATION
- **EGR/CSC** – switches EGR vacuum from EGR system to distributor advance with cold engine.
- **Cold Start Spark Advance (CSSA)** – supplies manifold vacuum to distributor below 125° F. coolant temperature.
- **Coolant Spark Control (CSC)** – cuts off distributor advance below hot engine temperature.
- **Cooling PVS** – switches advance vacuum from spark port to manifold vacuum if engine overheats.

TO CARBURETOR
TO DISTRIBUTOR
TO MANIFOLD

CONNECTIONS FOR "COOLING PVS" OPERATION

COLD ENGINE
PISTON DOWN
① Top and center ports connected.
② Lower port blocked.

WARM ENGINE (Above operating temperature of PVS)
PISTON UP
③ Top port blocked.
④ Bottom and center ports connected.

86654034

Fig. 32 Distributor vacuum control valve operation

Deceleration Valve

Some 1971-72 engines with dual diaphragm distributors are equipped with a distributor vacuum advance control valve (deceleration valve) which is used to further aid in controlling ignition timing. The deceleration valve is installed in the vacuum line which runs from the outer (advance) diaphragm to the carburetor; the normal vacuum supply for the distributor. During deceleration, the intake manifold vacuum rises causing the deceleration valve to close off any carburetor vacuum source, and connecting the intake manifold vacuum to the distributor advance diaphragm. The resulting increase in vacuum pressure provides maximum ignition timing advance, thus providing more complete fuel combustion, and decreasing exhaust system backfiring.

ADJUSTING

1. Connect a tachometer to the engine according to the manufacture's instructions. Bring the engine to the normal operating temperature.
2. Check the idle speed and set it to specifications with the headlights on high beam, as necessary.
3. Turn OFF the headlights and note the idle rpm.
4. Remove the plastic cover from the valve. Slowly turn the adjusting screw counterclockwise without pressing in. After 5 turns, no more than 6 turns, the idle speed should suddenly increase to about 1000 rpm. If the speed does not increase after six turns, push inward on the valve spring retainer and release. Speed should now increase.
5. Slowly turn the adjusting screw clockwise until the idle speed drops to the speed noted in Step 3. Make one more turn clockwise.
6. Increase the engine speed to 2000 rpm, hold for 5 seconds, and release the throttle. The engine speed should return idle speed within 4 seconds. If idle is not resumed in 4 seconds, back off the dashpot adjustment and repeat the check. If the idle is not resumed in 3 seconds with the dashpot back off, turn the deceleration valve adjustment screw

an addition quarter turn clockwise and repeat the check. Repeat the quarter turn adjustment and idle return checks until the engine returns to idle within the required time.
7. If it takes more than one complete turn from Step 5 to meet the idle return time specifications, replace the valve.

Spark Delay Valve

▶ **See Figure 33**

The spark delay valve is a plastic, spring-loaded, color coded valve which is installed in the vacuum line to the distributor advance diaphragm on many models. Under heavy throttle applications, the valve will close, blocking normal carburetor vacuum to the distributor. After the designated period of closed time, the valve opens, restoring the carburetor vacuum to the distributor.

TESTING

➡**If the distributor vacuum line contains a cut-off solenoid, it must be open during this test.**

1. Detach the vacuum line from the distributor at the spark delay valve end. Connect a vacuum gauge to the line, in its place.
2. Block the wheels so the vehicle can not move.
3. Connect a tachometer to the engine. Start the engine and rapidly increase its speed to 2000 rpm with the transmission in NEUTRAL or PARK.
4. As soon as the engine speed is increased, the vacuum gauge reading should drop to zero.
5. Hold the engine speed at a steady 2000 rpm. It should take longer than two seconds for the gauge to register 6 in. Hg. (20 kPa). If it takes less than two seconds, the valve is defective and must be replaced.
6. If it takes longer than the number of seconds specified for the gauge to reach 6 in. Hg. (20 kPa), disconnect the vacuum gauge from the spark delay valve. Disconnect the hose which runs from the spark delay valve to the carburetor at the valve end. Connect the vacuum gauge to this hose.

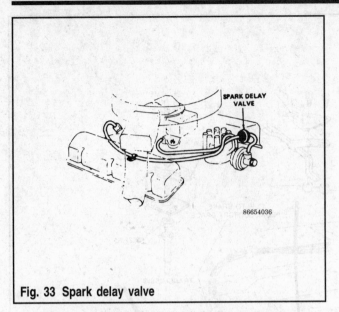

Fig. 33 Spark delay valve

7. Start the engine and increase its speed to 2000 rpm. The gauge should indicate 10-16 in. Hg. (33-53 kPa). If it does not, there is a blockage in the carburetor vacuum port or else the hose itself is plugged or broken. If the gauge reading is within specification, the valve is defective.

8. Reconnect all vacuum lines and remove the tachometer, once testing is completed.

REMOVAL & INSTALLATION

1. Locate the spark delay valve in the distributor vacuum line and disconnect it from the line.

2. Install a new spark delay valve in the line, making sure that the black end of the valve is connected to the line from the carburetor and the color coded end is connected to the line from the spark delay valve to the distributor.

Distributor Modulator (Dist-O-Vac) System

▶ **See Figures 34 and 35**

All 1971 models equipped with automatic transmission and the 5.0L, or 6.4L engines, along with 1971 models equipped with automatic transmission and the 6.4L 2, or 7.0L engines are equipped with a Dist-O-Vac spark control system.

The three components of the Dist-O-Vac system are the speed sensor, the thermal switch, and the electronic control module. The electronic control module consists of two sub assemblies: the electronic control amplifier and the three-way solenoid valve.

The speed sensor, a small unit mounted in the speedometer cable, contains a rotating magnet and a stationary winding which is insulated from the ground. The magnet, which rotates with the speedometer cable, generates a small voltage which increases directly with speed. This voltage is directed to the electronic control amplifier.

The thermal switch consists of a bimetallic element switch which is mounted in the right door pillar and senses the temperature, of the air. The switch is closed at 58°F (14°C) or

lower, and open at temperatures above 58°F (14°C). This switch is also connected to the electronic control amplifier.

Within the electronic control module case, there is a printed circuit board and an electronic amplifier. The speed sensor and thermal switch are connected to this assembly. The thermal switch is the dominant circuit. When the temperature of the outside air is 58°F (14°C) or lower, the circuit is closed, so that regardless of speed, the electronic control amplifier will not trigger the three-way solenoid valve. At temperatures above 58°F (14°C), however, the thermal switch circuit is open, allowing the circuit from the speed sensor to take over and control the action of the solenoid valve.

The three-way solenoid valve is located within the electronic control module and below the printed circuit board of the amplifier. It is vented to the atmosphere at the top, and connected at the bottom of the carburetor spark port (small hose) and the primary (advance) side of the dual-diaphragm distributor (large hose). The large hose is also channeled through the temperature sensing valve. The small hose is equipped with an air bleed to provide a positive airflow in the direction of the carburetor. The air bleed purges the hose of vacuum, thus

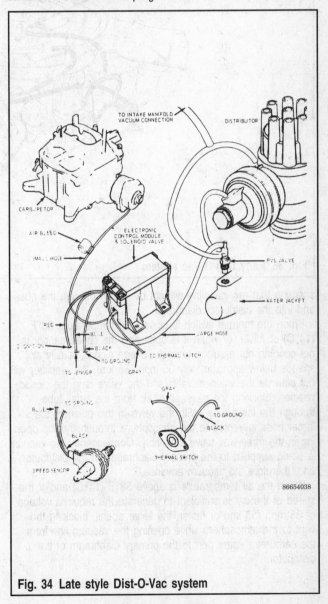

Fig. 34 Late style Dist-O-Vac system

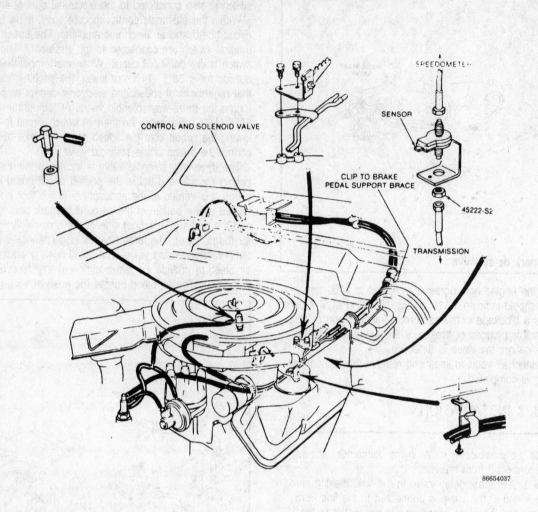

CONTROL AND SOLENOID VALVE

SPEEDOMETER

SENSOR

CLIP TO BRAKE
PEDAL SUPPORT BRACE

45222-S2

TRANSMISSION

86654037

Fig. 35 Early Dist-O-Vac system

assuring that raw gasoline will not be drawn through the hose and into the distributor diaphragm.

When the thermal switch is closed, air temperature 58°F (14°C) or lower, or when it is open and the speed sensor is not sending out a strong enough voltage signal, usually at speeds below approximately 35 mph (56 km), the amplifier will not activate the solenoid valve and the valve is in the closed position, blocking the passage of air from the small tube through the large tube. With the valve in this position, the larger hose is vented to the atmosphere through the top opening in the three-way valve assembly. Consequently, no vacuum is being supplied to the primary diaphragm on the distributor, and, therefore, no vacuum advance.

When the air temperature is above 58°F (14°C) and/or the speed of the car is sufficient to generate the required voltage of 35 mph (56 km) or faster, the valve opens, blocking the vent to the atmosphere while opening the vacuum line from the carburetor spark port to the primary diaphragm of the distributor.

Electronic Spark Control

♦ **See Figures 36 and 37**

All 1972 Fords manufactured for sale in California equipped with a 5.8L Cleveland (C) or 6.6L V8, and all 1972 Fords equipped with the 7.0L police interceptor engine, use the electronic spark control system.

Electronic Spark Control (ESC) is a system which blocks off carburetor vacuum to the distributor vacuum advance mechanism under certain temperature and speed conditions. The electronic spark control system consists of four components: a temperature sensor, a speed sensor, an amplifier, and a distributor modulator vacuum valve. The system serves to prevent ignition timing advance (by blocking off carburetor vacuum from the distributor vacuum advance mechanism) until the car reaches a speed of 35 mph (56 km) when the ambient temperature is over 65°F (18°C).

The temperature sensor, which is mounted on the front face of the left door pillar, monitors the outside air temperature and relays this information to the amplifier. The amplifier, which is

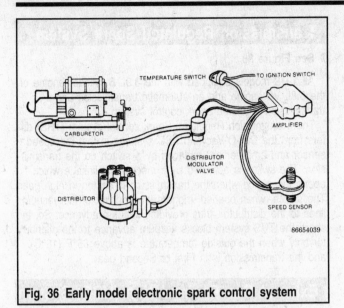

Fig. 36 Early model electronic spark control system

The speed sensor is a miniature generator which is connected to the speedometer cable of the car. As the speedometer cable turns, the inside of the speed sensor turns with the speedometer cable. As the speed of the car increases, a rotating magnet in the speed sensor induces an electronic current in the stationary winding in the speed sensor. This current is sent to the amplifier. As the speed of the vehicle increases, the amount of current sent to the amplifier by the speed sensor increases proportionately. When the car reaches a speed of 35 mph (56 kmph), the amplifier signals the distributor modulator vacuum valve to open, allowing carburetor vacuum to be sent to the distributor vacuum advance chamber. This permits the ignition timing to advance.

It should be noted that this system operates only when the ambient temperature is 65°F (18°C) or above, and then only when the speed of the car is below 35 mph (56 kmph).

TESTING

1. Raise the car until the rear wheels are clear of the ground by at least 4 in. (102mm). Support the rear of the car with jackstands.

✳✳CAUTION

The car must be firmly supported during this test. If one of the rear drive wheels should come in contact with the ground while it is turning, it will move forward very rapidly and unexpectedly. As an extra precaution, chock the front wheels and do not stand in front of the vehicle while the wheels are turning!

2. Disconnect the vacuum hose from the distributor vacuum advance chamber. This is the outer hose.
3. Connect the hose to a vacuum gauge.
4. Pour hot water on the temperature sensing switch to make sure that it is above 65°F (18°C).
5. Start the engine and apply the foot brake. Depress the clutch and shift the transmission into high gear, if equipped with a manual transmission. If equipped with an automatic transmission, shift into DRIVE and push on the gas pedal.

located under the instrument panel, controls the distributor modulator vacuum valve. The modulator valve, which is attached to the ignition coil mounting bracket, is connected into the carburetor vacuum line to the distributor, and is normally open. If the temperature of the outside air is below 48°F (9°C), the contacts in the temperature sensor are open and no signal is sent to the amplifier. Since no signal is sent to the amplifier, the amplifier does not send a signal to the distributor modulator valve, and the vacuum passage from the carburetor to the distributor vacuum advance remains open. When the outside temperature rises to 65°F (18°C) or above, the contacts in the temperature sensor close, and a signal is sent to the amplifier. The amplifier relays the message to the distributor modulator, which closes to block the vacuum passage to the distributor, preventing ignition timing advance.

When the ambient temperature is 65°F (18°C) or above, ignition timing advance is prevented until the amplifier receives a signal from the speed sensor that the speed of the vehicle has reached 35 mph (56 kmph), and the distributor modulator vacuum valve can be opened to permit ignition timing advance.

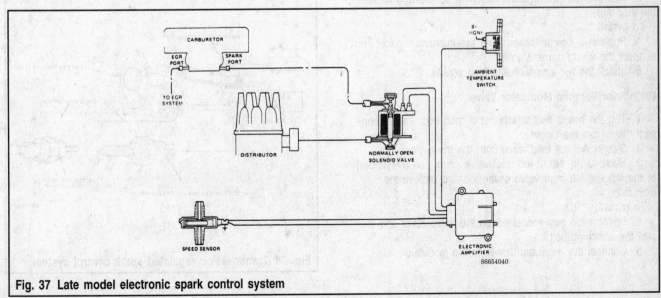

Fig. 37 Late model electronic spark control system

6. Have an assistant observe the vacuum gauge while you raise the speed of the engine until the speedometer reads 35 mph (56 kmph), at which time the vacuum gauge should show a reading.

7. If the vacuum gauge shows a reading below 35 mph (56 kmph), a component in the electronic spark control system is defective. If the vacuum gauge does not show a reading, even above 35 mph (56 kmph), there is either a defective component in the electronic spark control system, or there is a broken or clogged vacuum passage between the carburetor and the distributor.

REMOVAL & INSTALLATION

Temperature Sensor

1. Open the right door and remove the two screws which attach the temperature sensor to the right door pillar.
2. Disconnect the lead wires from the temperature sensor.
3. Remove the sensor.

To install:

4. Connect the lead wires to the new sensor.
5. Position the sensor on the door pillar and install the attaching screws.

Speed Sensor

1. Disconnect the lead wires from the sensor.
2. Disconnect the speed sensor from the speedometer cable.

To install:

3. Position the O-rings on both ends of the new speed sensor.
4. Connect both ends of the speedometer cable to the speed sensor.
5. Connect the lead wires to the speed sensor.

Amplifier

1. Locate the amplifier under the instrument panel, near the glove compartment.
2. Disconnect the wiring harness from the amplifier.
3. Remove the two amplifier attaching screws and remove the amplifier.

To install:

4. Position a new amplifier under the instrument panel and connect the wiring harness to it.
5. Install the two amplifier attaching screws

Distributor Vacuum Modulator Valve

1. Tag the hoses that attach to the modulator and disconnect them from the amplifier.
2. Disconnect the lead wires from the modulator.
3. Remove the No. 2 left front valve cover bolt (6-cylinder) or the inboard left front valve cover bolt and remove the modulator.

To install:

4. Position the new modulator on the valve cover and install the attaching bolt.
5. Connect the wires and hoses to the modulator.

Transmission Regulated Spark System

▶ **See Figure 38**

All 1972 models equipped with the 3.9L 6-cylinder engine or the 5.8L V8 engine and an automatic transmission use a transmission regulated spark control system.

The Transmission Regulated Spark control system (TRS) differs from the Dist-O-Vac and ESC systems in that the speed sensor and amplifier are replaced by a switch on the transmission. The switch is activated by a mechanical linkage which opens the switch when the transmission is shifted in high gear. The switch, when opened, triggers the opening of the vacuum lines to the distributor, thus providing vacuum advance. So, in short, the TRS system blocks vacuum advance to the distributor only when the outside temperature is above 65°F (18°C) and the transmission is in First or Second gear.

Exhaust Gas Recirculation (EGR) System

▶ **See Figures 39, 40, 41, 42, 43 and 44**

ELECTRONIC SYSTEM

The Electronic Exhaust Gas Recirculation (EEGR) system is found in all vehicles in which EGR flow is controlled according to computer commands by means of an EGR Valve Position (EVP) sensor attached to the valve.

The EEGR valve is operated by a vacuum signal from the dual EGR solenoid valves, or the electronic vacuum regulator which actuates the valve diaphragm.

As supply vacuum overcomes the spring load, the diaphragm is actuated lifting the pintle off of its seat allowing the exhaust gas to flow. The amount of flow is directly proportional to the pintle position. The EVP sensor sends an electrical signal alerting the EEC of its position.

The EEGR valve is not serviceable. If defective, it must be replaced. The EVP sensor may be serviced separately of the EEGR valve.

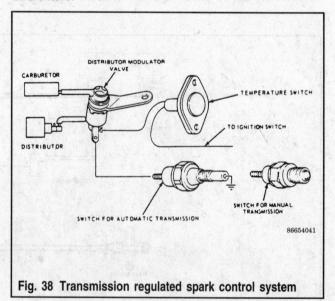

Fig. 38 Transmission regulated spark control system

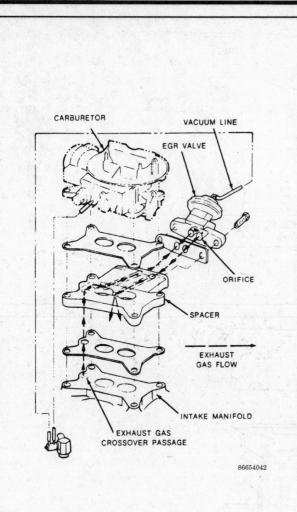

Fig. 39 EGR valve attached to the carburetor spacer plate

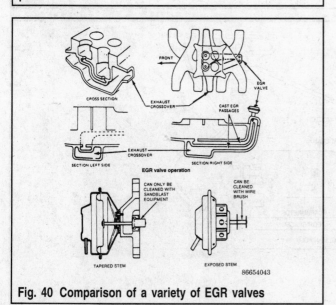

Fig. 40 Comparison of a variety of EGR valves

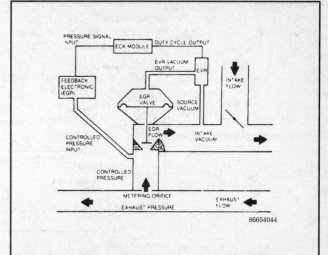

Fig. 41 Vacuum schematic of a pressure feedback electronic EGR system

INTEGRAL BACKPRESSURE (IBP) EGR SYSTEM

The Integral Backpressure (IBP) EGR system combines inputs of EGR port vacuum and backpressure into one unit. The valve requires both inputs for proper operation. The valve won't operate on vacuum alone.

Ported EGR

The ported EGR valve is a component of the IBP system. This valve is operated by engine vacuum alone. A vacuum signal from the carburetor activates the EGR valve diaphragm. As the vacuum signal increase it gradually opens the valve pintle allowing exhaust gases to flow. The amount of flow is directly proportional to the pintle position.

TESTING

1. Allow the engine to warm-up, so that the coolant temperature has reached at least 125°F (52°C).

2. Disconnect the vacuum hose which runs from the temperature cut-in valve to the EGR valve at the EGR valve end. Connect a vacuum gauge to this hose with a T-fitting.

3. Increase engine speed. Do not exceed half throttle or 3000 rpm. The gauge should indicate a vacuum. If no vacuum is present, check the following:

   a. The carburetor: look for a clogged vacuum port.

   b. The vacuum hoses: including the vacuum hoses to the transmission modulator.

   c. The temperature cut-in valve: if no vacuum is present at its outlet with the engine temperature above 125°F (52°C) and vacuum available from the carburetor, the valve is defective.

4. If all the preceding tests are positive, check the EGR valve itself.

5. Connect an outside vacuum source and a vacuum gauge to the valve.

6. Apply vacuum to the EGR valve. The valve should open at 3-10 in. Hg (10-33 kPa), as the engine idle speed slows down. As the idle speed decreases, the idle quality becomes rougher, causing the idle speed to decrease.

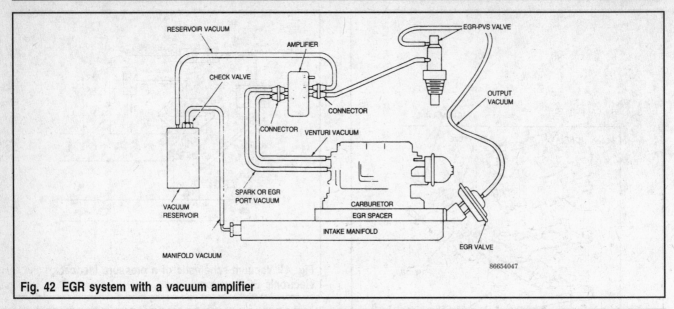

Fig. 42 EGR system with a vacuum amplifier

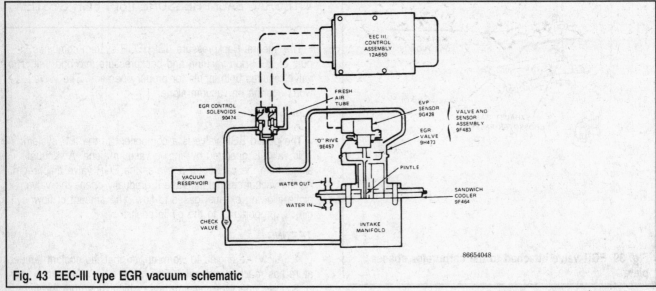

Fig. 43 EEC-III type EGR vacuum schematic

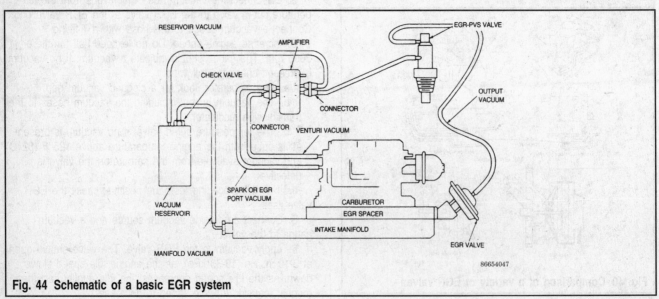

Fig. 44 Schematic of a basic EGR system

7. If this does not happen, that is the EGR valve remains closed or the idle speed does not decrease, the EGR valve is defective and must be replaced.

8. If the valve stem moves but the idle remains the same, the valve orifice is clogged and must be cleaned.

➡If an outside vacuum source is not available, disconnect the hose which runs between the EGR valve and the temperature cut-in valve, then plug the hose connections on the cut-in valve. Connect the EGR valve hose to a source of intake manifold vacuum and watch the idle. The results should be the same as in steps 6 and 7, above.

Temperature Cut-In Valve

TESTING

1. Remove the temperature cut-in valve from the engine.

2. Connect an outside source of vacuum to the top port on the valve. Leave the bottom port vented to the atmosphere.

3. Use ice or an aerosol spray to cool the valve below 60°F (16°C).

4. Apply 20 in. Hg (66 kPa) vacuum to the valve. The valve should hold a minimum of 19 in. Hg (63 kPa) vacuum for 5 minutes without leaking down.

5. Leave the vacuum source connected to the valve and place it, along with a high temperature thermometer, into a nonmetallic, heat resistance container full of water.

6. Heat the water. The vacuum in the valve should drop to zero once the temperature of the water reaches about 125°F (52°C).

7. Replace the valve if it fails either of the tests.

REMOVAL & INSTALLATION

▶ See Figures 45, 46, 47, 48 and 49

Ported Type Valve

1. Disconnect the vacuum line from the EGR valve.

2. Remove the mounting bolts and remove the EGR valve.

3. Installation is the reverse of removal. Remove all old gasket material. Use a new gasket during installation.

Fig. 45 Unfasten the wire harness attached to the EGR valve

86674500

Electronic Type Valve

1. Disconnect the negative battery cable.

2. Disconnect the vacuum line from the EGR valve.

3. Remove the mounting bolts and remove the EGR valve.

4. Remove the EVP sensor from the EGR valve.

5. Installation is the reverse of removal. Remove all old gasket material. Use a new gasket during installation.

CLEANING

▶ See Figure 50

Remove the EGR valve for cleaning. Do not strike hard on or pry the valve diaphragm housing or supports apart, as this may damage the valve operating mechanism and/or change the valve calibration. Check the orifice hole in the EGR valve body for deposits. A small hand drill of no more than 0.060 in. diameter may be used to clean the hole if plugged. Extreme care must be taken to avoid enlarging the hole or damaging the surface of the orifice plate.

Valves Which Cannot be Disassembled

Valves which are RIVETED or otherwise permanently assembled should be replaced if highly contaminated. these valves cannot be disassembled and cleaned.

Valves Which Can be Disassembled

These type of valves can be identified by the fact that they are secured using nuts and bolts or screws. Separate the diaphragm section from the main mounting body. Clean the valve plates, stem, and the mounting plate, using a small power-driven rotary type wire brush. Take care not to damage the parts. Remove deposits between stem and valve disc by using a steel blade or shim approximately 0.028 in. (0.7mm) thick in a sawing motion around the stem shoulder at both sides of the disc.

➡The poppet must wobble and move axially before reassembly.

Clean the cavity and passages in the main body of the valve with a power-driven rotary wire brush. If the orifice plate has a hole less than 0.450 in. (11.4mm) it must be removed. Remove all loosened debris using compressed air. Reassemble the diaphragm section on the main body using a new gasket. Tighten the attaching screws evenly. Clean the orifice plate and the counterbore in the valve body. Reinstall the orifice plate using a small amount of contact cement to retain the plate in place during assembly of the valve to the carburetor spacer. Apply cement to only outer edges of the orifice plate to avoid restriction of the orifice.

EGR Supply Passages and Carburetor Spacer Cleaning

Remove the carburetor and carburetor spacer on engines so equipped. Clean the supply tube with a small power-driven rotary type wire brush or blast cleaning equipment. Clean the exhaust gas passages in the spacer using a suitable wire brush and/or scraper. The machined holes in the spacer can be cleaned by using a suitable round wire brush. Hard encrusted material should be probed loose first, then brushed out.

Fig. 46 Remove the vacuum line(s) from the valve. If there is more than one mark each for installation

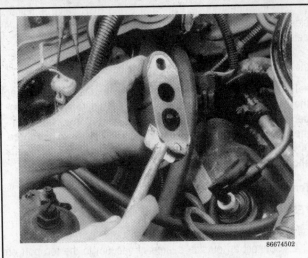

Fig. 49 Remove any gasket material from both mounting surfaces

Fig. 47 Loosen and remove the retaining bolts

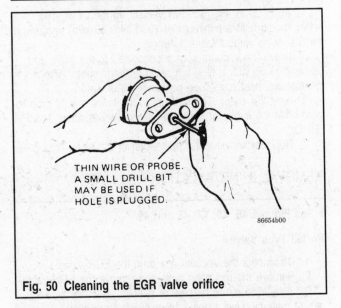

THIN WIRE OR PROBE. A SMALL DRILL BIT MAY BE USED IF HOLE IS PLUGGED.

Fig. 50 Cleaning the EGR valve orifice

EGR Exhaust Gas Channel Cleaning

Clean the exhaust gas channel, where applicable, in the intake manifold, using a suitable carbon scraper. Clean the exhaust gas entry port in the intake manifold by hand passing a suitable drill bit through the holes to auger out the deposits. Do not use a wire brush. The manifold riser bore(s) should be suitably plugged during the above action to prevent any of the residue from entering the induction system.

Fig. 48 Remove the EGR valve, if necessary tap lightly with your palm to loosen

"EGR SYSTEM DIAGNOSIS"

	TEST STEP	RESULT	▶	ACTION TO TAKE
EEGR1	CHECK SYSTEM INTEGRITY			
	• Check vacuum hoses and connections for looseness, pinching, leakage, splitting, blockage, and proper routing. • Inspect EGR valve for loose attaching bolts or damaged flange gasket. • **Does system appear to be in good condition and vacuum hoses properly routed?**	Yes No	▶ ▶	GO to EEGR2. SERVICE EGR system as required. RE-EVALUATE symptom.
EEGR2	CHECK EGR VACUUM AT IDLE			
	• Run engine until normal operating temperature is reached. • With engine running at idle, disconnect EGR vacuum supply at the EGR valve and check for a vacuum signal. NOTE: **The EVR solenoid has a constant internal leak. You may notice a small vacuum signal. This signal should be less than 3.4 kPa (1.0 in-Hg) at idle.** • **Is EGR vacuum signal less than 3.4 kPa (1.0 in-Hg) at idle?**	Yes No	▶ ▶	GO to EEGR3. RECONNECT EGR vacuum hose. INSPECT EVR solenoid for leakage. RUN EEC-IV Quick Test
EEGR3	CHECK EGR VALVE FUNCTION			
	• Install a tachometer • Disconnect the Idle Air Bypass Valve (9F715) electrical connector. • Remove and plug the vacuum supply hose from the EGR valve nipple. • Start engine, idle with transmission in NEUTRAL and observe idle speed. If necessary, adjust idle speed • Slowly apply 5-10 inches of vacuum to the EGR valve nipple using a hand vacuum pump • **Does idle speed drop more than 100 rpm with vacuum applied and return to normal (± 25 rpm) after the vacuum is removed?**	Yes No	▶ ▶	The EGR valve is OK. UNPLUG and RECONNECT the EGR valve vacuum supply hose. RECONNECT the idle air bypass valve connector. INSPECT the EGR valve for blockage or contamination. CLEAN the valve INSPECT valve for vacuum leakage. REPLACE if necessary.

86674ee5

Delay Vacuum Bypass (DVB) System

All 1973 models equipped with 5.8L, 6.6L, 7.0L or 7.5L engines manufactured before March 15, 1973 are equipped with the Delay Vacuum Bypass (DVB) spark control system. This system provides two paths by which carburetor vacuum can reach the distributor vacuum advance. The system consists of a spark delay valve, a check valve, a solenoid vacuum valve, and an ambient temperature switch. When the ambient temperature is below 49°F (9°C), the temperature switch contacts are open and the vacuum solenoid is open (de-energized). Under these conditions, vacuum will flow from the carburetor, through the open solenoid, and to the distributor. Since the spark delay valve resists the flow of carburetor vacuum, the vacuum will always flow through the solenoid when it is open (this is the path of least resistance).

When the ambient temperature rises above 60°F (16°C), the contacts in the temperature switch (which is located in the door post) close. This passes ignition switch current to the solenoid, energizing it. Once energized, the solenoid blocks one of the two vacuum paths. All distributor vacuum must now flow through the spark delay valve.

When carburetor vacuum rises above a certain level on acceleration, a rubber valve in the spark delay valve blocks vacuum from passing through the valve for from 5 to 30 seconds. After this time delay has elapsed, normal vacuum is supplied to the distributor. When the vacuum solenoid is closed, temperatures above 60°F (16°C) are vented to atmosphere. To prevent the vacuum that is passing through the spark delay valve from escaping through the solenoid into the atmosphere, a one-way check valve is installed in the vacuum line from the solenoid to the distributor.

Cold Temperature Actuated Vacuum (CTAV) System

This system is installed on 1973 models manufactured after March 15, 1973 and on many 1974 models to control distributor spark advance. It is basically a refinement of the spark control systems with the temperature switch relocated in the air cleaner and a latching relay added to maintain a strong vacuum signal to the distributor, whether it be EGR port or spark port carburetor vacuum, and to keep the system from intermittently switching vacuum signals when the intake air is 49-60°F (9-16°C).

When the temperature switch closes at 60°F (16°C), the latching relay (normally off) is energized and stays on until the ignition switch is turned **OFF**. The latching relay then overrides the temperature switch and forces the solenoid valve to keep the spark port vacuum system closed and open the EGR port vacuum system. This prevents full vacuum advance, once the engine is warmed-up, thereby lowering emissions.

EGR/Coolant Spark Control System

The Exhaust Gas Recirculation/Coolant Spark Control (EGR/CSC) system is used on most 1974 and later models. It regulates both distributor spark advance and the EGR valve operation according to coolant temperature by sequentially switching vacuum signals.

The major EGR/CSC system components are:
- 95°F (35°C) EGR/PVS valve
- Spark Delay Valve (SDV)
- Vacuum check valve

When the engine coolant temperature is below 82°F (28°C), the EGR/Ported Vacuum Switch (PVS) valve admits carburetor EGR port vacuum (occurring at about 2500 rpm) directly to the distributor advance diaphragm, through the one-way check valve. At the same time, the EGR/PVS valve shuts off carburetor EGR vacuum to the EGR valve and transmission diaphragm.

When engine coolant temperature is 95°F (35°C) and above, the EGR/PVS valve is actuated and directs carburetor EGR vacuum to the EGR valve and transmission instead of the distributor. At temperatures between 82-95°F (28-35°C), the EGR-PVS valve may be open, closed, or in mid-position.

The Spark Delay Valve (SDV) delays vacuum to the distributor advance diaphragm by restricting the vacuum signal through the SDV valve from a predetermined time. During normal acceleration, little or no vacuum is admitted to the distributor advance diaphragm until acceleration is completed, because of (1) the time delay of the SDV valve and (2) the re-routing of EGR port vacuum if the engine coolant temperature is 95°F (35°C) or higher.

The check valve blocks off vacuum signal from the SDV to the EGR/PVS so that carburetor spark vacuum will not be dissipated when the EGR/PVS is actuated above 95°F (35°C).

The 235°F (113°C) PVS is not part of the EGR/PVS system, but is connected to the distributor vacuum advance to prevent engine overheating while idling (as on previous models). At idle speed, no vacuum is generated at either the carburetor spark port or EGR port and engine timing is fully retarded. When engine coolant temperature reaches 235°F (113°C), however, the valve is actuated to admit intake manifold vacuum to the distributor advance diaphragm. This advances the engine timing and speeds up the engine. The increase in coolant flow and fan speed lowers engine temperature.

EGR Venturi Vacuum Amplifier System

TESTING

The amplifiers have built-in calibrations and no external adjustments are required. If the amplifier tests reveal it is malfunctioning, replace the amplifier. All connections are located on one side of the amplifier. A vacuum connector and hose assembly is used to assure that proper connections are made at the amplifier. The amplifier is retained with a sheetmetal screw.

1. Operate the engine until normal operating temperatures are reached.

2. Before the vacuum amplifier is checked, inspect all other basic components of the EGR system (EGR valve, EGR/PVS valve, hoses, routing, etc.).

3. Check vacuum amplifier connections for proper routing and installation. If necessary, refer to the typical vacuum amplifier schematic.

4. Remove hose at EGR valve.

5. Connect a vacuum gauge to EGR hose. The gauge must read in increments of at most 1 in. Hg (3 kPa) graduations.

6. Remove hose at carburetor venturi (leave off).

7. With engine at curb idle speed, vacuum gauge reading should be within 0.3 in. Hg (1 kPa) of the specified bias valve as shown in amplifier specifications for other than zero bias. Zero bias may read from 0-0.5 in. Hg. (0-16 kPa). If out of specification, replace amplifier.

8. Depress accelerator and release after engine has reached 1500-2000 rpm. After engine has returned to idle, the vacuum must return to bias noted in step 7. If bias has changed, replace amplifier. Also, if vacuum shows a marked increase, greater than 1 in. Hg (3 kPa) during acceleration period, the amplifier should be replaced.

9. Hook up venturi hose at carburetor with engine at curb idle rpm. If a sizeable increase in output vacuum is observed (more than 0.5 in. Hg/2 kPa above step 7), check idle speed. High idle speed could increase output vacuum due to venturi vacuum increase. See engine decal for correct idle specifications.

10. Check amplifier reservoir and connections as follows: Disconnect external reservoir hose to amplifier and AP or plug. Depress accelerator rapidly to 1500-2000 rpm. The vacuum should increase to 4 in. Hg (13 kPa) or more. If out of specification, replace the amplifier.

Cold Start Spark Advance System

▶ **See Figure 51**

All 1975-78 models using the 7.5L engine are equipped with the Cold Start Spark Advance (CSSA) system. It is a modification of the existing spark control system to aid in cold start driveability. The system uses a coolant temperature sensing vacuum switch located on the thermostat housing. When the engine is cold, below 125°F (52°C), it permits full manifold vacuum to the distributor advance diaphragm. After the engine warms up, normal spark control (retard) resumes.

Vacuum Operated Heat Control Valve

▶ **See Figure 52**

To further aid cold start driveability during engine warm-up, most 1975 and later engines use a Vacuum Operated Heat Valve (VOHV) located between the exhaust manifold and the exhaust inlet (header) pipe.

When the engine is first started, the valve is closed, blocking exhaust gases from exiting from one bank of cylinders. These gases are then diverted back through the intake manifold crossover passage under the carburetor. The result is quick heat to the carburetor and choke.

The VOHV is controlled by a ported vacuum switch which uses manifold vacuum to keep the vacuum motor on the valve closed until the coolant reaches a predetermined warm-up valve. When the engine is warmed-up, the PVS shuts off vacuum to the VOHV, and a strong return spring opens the VOHV butterfly.

TESTING

Riser

Testing the vacuum operated heat riser valve is a matter of making sure it opens and closes freely. You can move it by hand to see if it works, on a cool engine. When the engine is cold, the valve should be closed, and disconnecting the hose should allow it to open (engine idling). On a cold engine, there should be vacuum at the vacuum actuator. On a warm engine the vacuum should be shut off.

Dual Signal Spark Advance System

▶ **See Figure 53**

The Dual Signal Spark Spark Advance (DSSA) system is used on many engines. It incorporates a Spark Delay Valve (SDV) and a one-way check valve to provide improved spark and EGR function during mild acceleration.

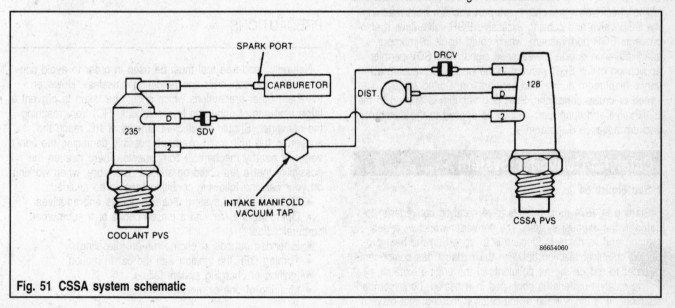

Fig. 51 CSSA system schematic

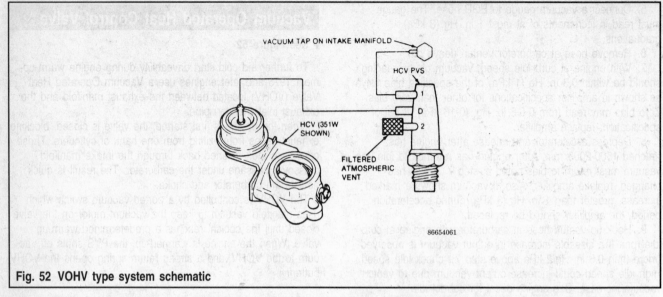

Fig. 52 VOHV type system schematic

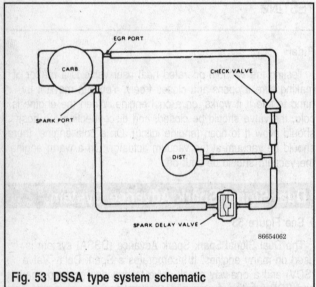

Fig. 53 DSSA type system schematic

The check valve prevents spark port vacuum from reaching the EGR valve and causing excessive EGR valve flow. It also prevents EGR port vacuum, which could result in improper spark advance due to a weakened signal. The SDV permits application of full EGR vacuum to the distributor vacuum advance diaphragm during mild acceleration. During steady speed or cruise conditions, EGR port vacuum is applied to the EGR valve and spark port vacuum is applied to the distributor vacuum advance diaphragm.

Catalytic Converter System

▶ See Figure 54

Starting in 1974 most models have catalytic converter(s) located in the exhaust system. The converter works as a gas reactor, and its catalytic function is to speed up the heat producing chemical reaction between the exhaust gas components in order to reduce the air pollutants in the engine exhaust.

The catalyst material is contained in a sealed, honeycombed chamber. It is the surface of the catalyst material that plays a major role in the heat-producing chemical reaction. There are basically three types of catalytic converters:

1. The Conventional Oxidation Catalyst (COC); used to oxidize hydrocarbons (HC) and carbon monoxide (CO).

2. The Three-Way Catalyst (TWC); not only works on HC and CO but also reduces nitrogen oxides (NOx).

3. The Light Off Catalyst (LOC); arranged in series with the main catalytic converter, is designed to handle the exhaust emissions during engine warm-up when the main converter has not reached the proper temperature for maximum efficiency.

In order to provide the oxygen necessary to obtain the converter's maximum efficiency a secondary air source is provided by the air pump (Thermactor®). The system is protected by several devices that block out the secondary air when the engine is laboring under any abnormal hot or cold operating situation.

The catalytic converter is expected to function without service for at least 50,000 miles (80,400 km). Use of leaded fuel would quickly cause catalyst failure and an expensive repair bill.

PRECAUTIONS

Naturally, lead-free fuel must be used in order to avoid contaminating the converter and rendering it useless. However, there are other precautions which should be taken to prevent a large amounts of unburned Hydrocarbons (HC) from reaching the converter. Should a sufficient amount of HC reach the converter, the unit could overheat, possibly damaging the converter or nearby mechanical components. There is even the possibility that a fire could be started. Therefore, when working on your car, the following conditions should be avoided:

• The use of fuel system cleaning agents and additives.
• Operating the car with a closed choke or a submerged carburetor float.
• Extended periods of engine run-on (dieseling).
• Turning **OFF** the ignition with the car in motion.
• Ignition or charging system failure.
• Misfiring of one or more spark plugs.

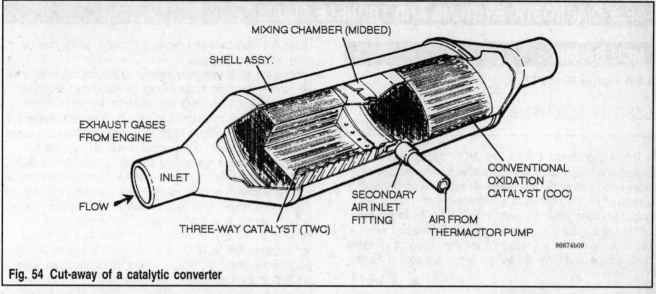

Fig. 54 Cut-away of a catalytic converter

- Disconnecting a spark plug wire while testing for a bad wire or plug, or poor compression in one cylinder.
- Pushing or tow-starting the car, especially when hot.
- Pumping the gas pedal when attempting to start a hot engine.

Bypass Air Idle Speed Control

The air bypass solenoid is used to control the engine idle speed and is operated by the EEC module.

The valve allows air to pass around the throttle plates to control:
- Cold engine fast idle
- Cold starting
- Dashpot operation
- Over-temperature idle boost
- Engine load correction

This valve is not serviceable. Therefore if defective the entire valve must be replaced.

Oxygen Sensor

▶ See Figure 55

REMOVAL & INSTALLATION

The oxygen sensor is located in the exhaust headpipe. To replace it, unplug the connector and unscrew the sensor using either a flare end wrench, long socket with a slot in it(to allow the wire to remain undamaged during removal and installation) or one of the specialty tools made for removing this sensor. Replacement senors will be packaged with anti-sieze compound for the threads. If not, or if you are reinstalling the old unit, the threads MUST be coated with anti-sieze compound! Tighten the sensor to 12 ft. lbs. (16 Nm).

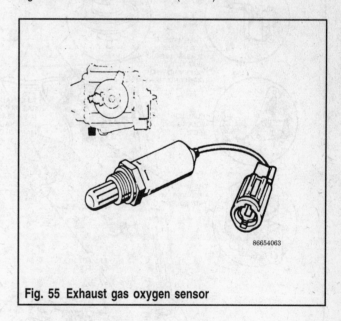

Fig. 55 Exhaust gas oxygen sensor

SELF-DIAGNOSTIC SYSTEMS AND TROUBLE CODES

MCU System

▶ See Figures 56 and 57

GENERAL DESCRIPTION

The Microprocessor Control Unit (MCU) system was the first to incorporate both a special test connector and the Self-Test Automatic Readout (STAR) hand-held scan tool for diagnostics. The MCU module is devoted to monitoring both input and output functions within the system. This ability forms the core of the self-diagnostic system. If a problem is detected within a circuit, the controller will recognize the fault, assign it an identification code, and store the code in a memory section. Fault

codes are represented by two-digit numbers, which may be retrieved during diagnosis.

While the MCU system is capable of recognizing many internal problems, certain faults will not be recognized. Because the computer system reads only electrical signals, it cannot sense or react to mechanical or vacuum faults affecting engine operation. Some of these faults may affect another component which will set a code. For example, the MCU monitors the output signal to the fuel control solenoid or feedback carburetor, but cannot detect a defective choke diaphragm. As long as the output driver responds correctly, the computer will read the system as functioning correctly. However, the improper choke pull-off may result in a rich mixture. This would, in turn, be detected by the oxygen sensor and noticed as a constantly rich signal by the MCU. Once the signal falls outside the pre-programmed limits, the engine control assembly would notice the fault and set an identification code.

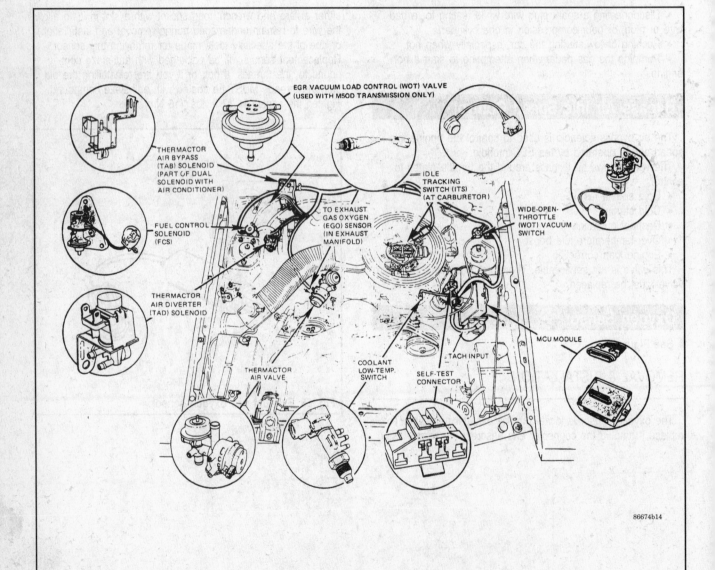

Fig. 56 MCU system component locations — 4-cylinder engine

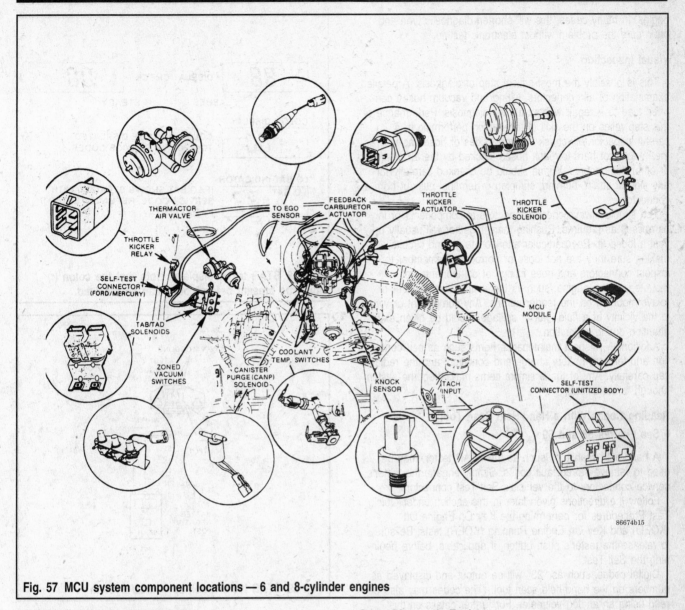

THERMACTOR
AIR VALVE

THROTTLE
KICKER
RELAY

SELF-TEST
CONNECTOR
(FORD/MERCURY)

TAB/TAD
SOLENOIDS

ZONED
VACUUM
SWITCHES

TO EGO
SENSOR

FEEDBACK
CARBURETOR
ACTUATOR

THROTTLE
KICKER
ACTUATOR

THROTTLE
KICKER
SOLENOID

MCU
MODULE

SELF-TEST
CONNECTOR (UNITIZED BODY)

COOLANT
TEMP. SWITCHES

CANISTER
PURGE (CANP)
SOLENOID

KNOCK
SENSOR

TACH
INPUT

86674b15

Fig. 57 MCU system component locations — 6 and 8-cylinder engines

TOOLS AND EQUIPMENT

Hand-Held Scan Tools

Although stored codes may be read through an analog voltmeter, the use of a hand-held scan tool such as Ford's Self-Test Automatic Readout (STAR) tester, or equivalent, is highly recommended. There are many manufacturers of such tools, but you must be certain that the tool is appropriate for the intended use.

The STAR tester is designed to communicate directly with the MCU system and interpret electrical signals. The scan tool allows any stored faults to be read from the engine controller memory. Use of the scan tool provides additional data during troubleshooting, but does not eliminate the need for diagnostic work. The scan tool makes information collection easier, but the data must still be correctly interpreted by an operator familiar with the system.

Other Diagnostic Tools

An analog (needle type) voltmeter with a voltage scale of 0-20 volts DC may be used to read stored fault codes if the STAR tester is not available. The codes are transmitted as visible needle sweeps on the face of the instrument.

Other necessary tools for testing/troubleshooting include a timing light, a vacuum gauge (for some applications), and a jumper wire. A quality tachometer, preferably with an inductive (clip-on) pickup and a range of 0-3000 rpm, will also be required to verify test rpm on 4-140 engines during Self-Test procedures.

DIAGNOSIS AND TESTING

Diagnosis of a driveability problem requires attention to detail and following the diagnostic procedures in the correct order. Resist the temptation to begin extensive testing before completing the preliminary diagnostic steps. The preliminary or visual inspection must be completed in detail before diagnosis begins. In many cases, this will shorten diagnostic time and often cure the problem without electronic testing.

Visual Inspection

This is possibly the most critical step of diagnosis. A detailed examination of all connectors, wiring and vacuum hoses can often lead to a repair without further diagnosis. Performance of this step relies on the skill of the person performing it; a careful inspector will check the undersides of hoses as well as the integrity of hard-to-reach hoses blocked by the air cleaner or other components. Wiring should be checked carefully for any sign of strain, burning, crimping or terminal pull-out from a connector.

You should always check connectors at components or in harnesses as required. Pushing them together will usually reveal a loose fit. Pay particular attention to ground circuits, making sure they are not loose or corroded. Remember to inspect connectors and hose fittings at components not mounted on the engine, such as the evaporative canister or relays mounted on the fender aprons. Any component or wiring in the vicinity of a fluid leak or spillage should be given extra attention during inspection.

Additionally, inspect maintenance items such as belt condition and tension, battery charge and condition, and the radiator cap carefully. Any of these simple items may affect the system enough to set a fault.

Reading Codes With a Hand-Held Scan Tool

▶ See Figures 58 and 59

A hand-held scan tool, such as the STAR tester, may be used to retrieve stored fault codes. Simply engage the tester's service connectors to the vehicle's Self-Test connectors.

Follow the directions given later in this section under Quick Test Procedures for performing the Key On Engine Off (KOEO) and Key On Engine Running (KOER) tests. Be sure to release the tester's push button, if applicable, before beginning the Self-Test.

Digital codes, such as "23" will be output and displayed as numbers on the hand-held scan tool. (The codes may also be read using an analog voltmeter. For further details on this alternative method, please refer to the following portion of this section.)

Reading Codes With an Analog Voltmeter

▶ See Figures 60 and 61

In the absence of a scan tool, an analog voltmeter may be used to retrieve stored fault codes. Set the meter range to read 0-15 volts DC. Connect the positive (+) lead of the meter to the positive battery terminal and connect the negative (-) lead of the meter to the self-test output pin of the diagnostic connector.

Follow the directions for performing the KOEO and KOER tests. To activate the tests, use a jumper wire to connect the signal return pin on the diagnostic connector to the self-test input connector. The self-test input line is the separate wire and connector that is located with or near the diagnostic connector.

The codes will be transmitted as groups of needle sweeps, whose cadence corresponds to the codes' numerical represen-

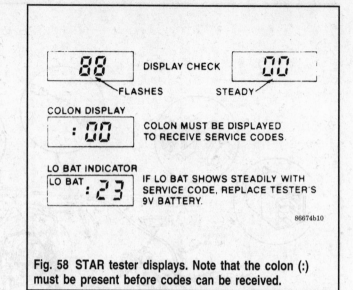

Fig. 58 STAR tester displays. Note that the colon (:) must be present before codes can be received.

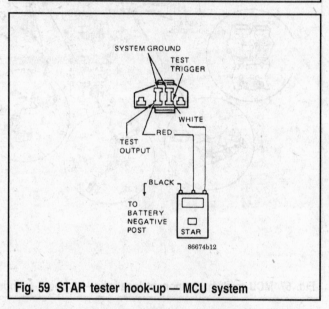

Fig. 59 STAR tester hook-up — MCU system

tation. Please refer to the accompanying illustration for details on counting the needle sweeps in order to determine the transmitted code.

SELF-TESTING (GENERATING STORED CODES)

▶ See Figures 62 and 63

Quick Test Procedures

The MCU system may be interrogated for stored codes using the Quick Test Procedures. These Quick Test procedures include: Key On Engine Off (KOEO) and Key On Engine Running (KOER). These diagnostic procedures must be performed correctly if the system is to run the internal Self-Test checks and provide accurate fault codes.

If the vehicle passes both sections of the Quick Test, the MCU system is all right and the vehicle's problem exists elsewhere. Once the Quick Test has been performed and all fault

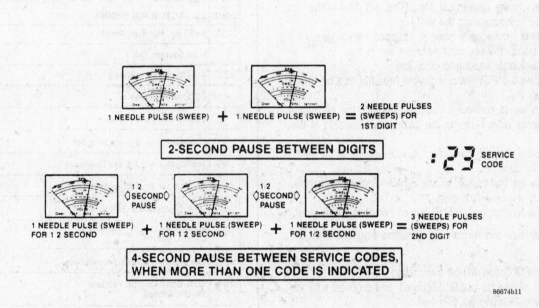

1 NEEDLE PULSE (SWEEP) + 1 NEEDLE PULSE (SWEEP) = 2 NEEDLE PULSES (SWEEPS) FOR 1ST DIGIT

2-SECOND PAUSE BETWEEN DIGITS

:23 SERVICE CODE

1 NEEDLE PULSE (SWEEP) FOR 1 2 SECOND + 1 2 SECOND PAUSE + 1 NEEDLE PULSE (SWEEP) FOR 1 2 SECOND + 1 2 SECOND PAUSE + 1 NEEDLE PULSE (SWEEP) FOR 1/2 SECOND = 3 NEEDLE PULSES (SWEEPS) FOR 2ND DIGIT

4-SECOND PAUSE BETWEEN SERVICE CODES, WHEN MORE THAN ONE CODE IS INDICATED

86674b11

Fig. 60 Code display patterns on an analog voltmeter

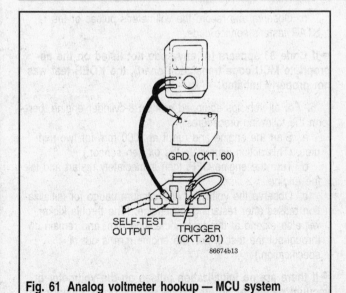

GRD. (CKT. 60)

SELF-TEST OUTPUT

TRIGGER (CKT. 201)

86674b13

Fig. 61 Analog voltmeter hookup — MCU system

codes recorded, refer to the code charts found later in this section.

✳✳CAUTION

To prevent injury and/or property damage, always block the drive wheels, firmly apply the parking brake, place the transmission in PARK or NEUTRAL and turn all electrical loads off before performing the Quick Test procedures.

KEY ON ENGINE OFF (KOEO)

➡Unless instructed otherwise, do not disconnect any sensor with the key ON or a service code may be stored.

1. Verify that the vacuum hoses are connected to the air cleaner. The air cleaner must be installed during these tests.

2. Start the engine and use an analog voltmeter to verify that there is power to the choke. Let the engine idle until it reaches normal operating temperature and the throttle is off fast idle. Turn the engine OFF.

3. Connect the scan tool or analog voltmeter to the self-test connectors, as shown. When using a voltmeter, connect a jumper wire from the Self-Test Trigger to the ground terminal of the Self-Test connector. When using a STAR tester, make certain the test button is unlatched or up.

4. On 4-cylinder engines with a vacuum purge valve, disconnect (but do not plug) the hose from the canister control valve that runs to the carbon canister. (This will disable the canister purge system during the test.)

5. On 6 and 8-cylinder engines if equipped with a vacuum delay valve, uncap the restrictor near the tee in the Thermactor® diverter vacuum control line.

   a. Remove the PCV valve from the breather cap on the valve cover.

   b. Use a tee to connect a vacuum gauge to the canister purge solenoid valve hose on the carbon canister side of the hose.

6. Make sure that the carburetor throttle linkage is off the high step of its cam.

7. Activate the test button on the STAR tester, if applicable. This will ready the Self-Test mode.

8. Turn the ignition switch **ON**, but do not start the engine.

➡**Do not depress the throttle on gasoline engines during the test.**

9. The KOEO codes will be transmitted.

10. Record all service codes displayed, and proceed with the Key On Engine Running (KOER) test.

➡**For a translation of potential MCU service codes, please refer to the charts later in this section.**

KEY ON ENGINE RUNNING (KOER)

➡**Unless instructed otherwise, do not disconnect any sensor with the key ON or a service code may be stored.**

1. On vehicles equipped with a 4-cylinder engine and a 5-speed transmission, locate and tape the hole on top of the wide-open-throttle vacuum valve. (Be sure to remove the tape after this test is completed.)

2. Verify that the engine is still at normal operating temperature.

3. Activate or latch the self-test button on the scan tool, if applicable.

4. For all vehicles **except** those equipped with an 8-cylinder engine, perform the following procedures. (For those vehicles equipped with an 8-cylinder engine, proceed to Step 5.)

   a. Start the engine and, within 20 seconds, increase the engine speed to 3000 rpm.

   b. Hold the rpm steady until a service code is received on the voltmeter or STAR tester. (The Self-Test sequence may run 10-40 seconds.) Return the engine to idle as soon as service code output begins.

➡**If, within the first seven seconds of starting the engine, the voltmeter does not pulse (sweep), or pulses more than two times, check the engine's TACH lead for continuity. Likewise, if the STAR tester's code does not change, or displays a code other than "20" or "30" check the TACH lead.**

VOLTMETER OR STAR TESTER SERVICE CODE INFORMATION	
CODE	**2.3L, 4-CYLINDER ENGINE**
:00	Self-Test, Not Functional
:11	MCU System, OK
:33	RUN Test, Not Initiated
:41	EGO, Always Lean
:42	EGO, Always Rich
:44	Thermactor Air System Problem
:45	Thermactor Air, Always Upstream
:46	Thermactor Air, Not Bypassing
:51	LOW-Temperature Switch, Open
:53	Wide-Open-Throttle Vacuum Switch, Open
:62	Idle Tracking Switch, Inoperative
:63	Wide-Open-Throttle Vacuum Switch, Closed

86674b17

Fig. 62 MCU system service codes — 4-cylinder engine

   c. Observe and record the voltmeter's pulses or the STAR tester's service code.

➡**If Code 33 appears (or any code not listed on the appropriate MCU code translation chart), the KOER test was not properly initiated.**

5. For all vehicles equipped with an 8-cylinder engine, perform the following procedures:

   a. Start the engine and run it at 2000 rpm for two minutes. (This action warms up the oxygen sensor.)

   b. Turn the engine **OFF**, then immediately restart and idle the engine.

   c. Observe the voltmeter and vacuum gauge for initialization pulses after restarting the engine. (The throttle kicker will also extend at this time, increasing rpm, and remain on throughout the test. If not, the engine rpm is out of specification.)

➡**If there are no initialization pulses on the voltmeter or vacuum gauge, or an erroneous service code appears on the STAR tester, there is no Self-Test output.**

VOLTMETER OR STAR TESTER SERVICE CODE INFORMATION	
CODE	
:00	Self-Test, Not Functional
:11	MCU System, OK
:12	Idle Speed, Incorrect
:25	Knock Sensor System, Inoperative
:41	EGO, Always Lean
:42	EGO, Always Rich
:44	Thermactor Air System Problem
:45	Thermactor Air, Always Upstream
:46	Thermactor Air, Not Bypassing
:51	Hi/Lo Vacuum Switch(es), Open
:53	Dual Temperature Switch, Open
:54	MID-Temperature Switch, Open
:55	MID-Vacuum Switch, Open
:61	Hi/Lo Vacuum Switch(es), Closed
:65	MID-Vacuum Switch, Closed

86674b18

Fig. 63 MCU system service codes — 6 and 8-cylinder engines

d. After four one-second initialization pulses appear, observe and record the voltmeter's pulses or the STAR tester's service code for vehicles **without** a knock sensor.

e. For vehicles equipped **with** a knock sensor, immediately after four initial pulses occur, simulate spark knock by placing a ³⁄₈ in. socket extension on the intake manifold, near the base of the knock sensor, and tapping lightly with a small hammer for approximately 15 seconds. Then, observe and record the voltmeter's pulses or the STAR tester's service code.

➡Within 90 seconds, the service codes are complete and the throttle kicker will retract, thereby decreasing rpm.

6. Turn the engine **OFF**. Disconnect all test equipment and restore all components to their pre-test configuration/condition.

EEC-IV System

GENERAL DESCRIPTION

One part of the Powertrain Control Module (PCM) is devoted to monitoring both input and output functions within the system. This ability forms the core of the self-diagnostic system. If a problem is detected within a circuit, the controller will recognize the fault, assign it an identification code, and store the code in a memory section. The stored code(s) may then be retrieved during diagnosis.

The EEC-IV system is capable of storing both ongoing "hard" and intermittent "soft" faults. As a result, it is possible to monitor irregularities which may not be immediately present.

While the EEC-IV system is capable of recognizing many internal faults, certain faults will not be recognized. Because the computer system reads only electrical signals, it cannot sense or react to mechanical or vacuum faults affecting engine operation. Some of these faults may affect another component which will set a code. For example, the PCM monitors the output signal to the fuel injectors, but cannot detect a partially clogged injector. As long as the output driver responds correctly, the computer will read the system as functioning correctly. However, the improper flow of fuel may result in a lean mixture. This would, in turn, be detected by the oxygen sensor and noticed as a constantly lean signal by the PCM. Once the signal falls outside the pre-programmed limits, the engine control assembly would notice the fault and set an identification code.

Additionally, the EEC-IV system employs adaptive fuel logic. This process is used to compensate for normal wear and variability within the fuel system. Once the engine enters steady-state operation, the engine control assembly watches the oxygen sensor signal for a bias or tendency to run slightly rich or lean. If such a bias is detected, the adaptive logic corrects the fuel delivery to bring the air/fuel mixture towards a 14.7:1 or "centered" ratio. This compensating shift is stored in a non-volatile memory which is retained by battery power even with the ignition switched **OFF**. The correction factor is then available the next time the vehicle is operated.

➡If the negative battery cable is disconnected for longer than 5 minutes, the adaptive fuel factor will be lost. After repair, it will be necessary to drive the car at least 10 miles to allow the processor to relearn the correct factors. If possible, the driving period should include steady-throttle open road driving. During the drive, the vehicle may exhibit driveability symptoms not noticed before. These symptoms should clear as the PCM computes the correction factor. The PCM will also store Code "19" indicating loss of power to the controller.

Failure Mode Effects Management (FMEM)

The engine controller assembly contains back-up programs which allow the engine to operate if a sensor signal is lost. If a sensor's input is seen to be out of range — either high or low — the FMEM program is used. The processor substitutes a fixed value for the missing sensor signal. The engine will continue to operate, although performance and driveability may be noticeably reduced. This function of the controller is sometimes referred to as the limp-in or fail-safe mode. If the missing sensor signal is restored, the FMEM system immediately returns the system to normal operation.

Hardware Limited Operation Strategy (HLOS)

This mode is only used if the microprocessor fails to operate, or if the fault is too extreme for the FMEM circuit to handle. In this mode, the processor has ceased all computation and control, and the entire system is run on fixed values. The vehicle may be operated, but performance and driveability will be greatly reduced. The fixed or default settings provide minimal calibration, allowing the vehicle to be carefully driven in for service.

TOOLS AND EQUIPMENT

Hand-Held Scan Tools

Although stored codes may be read using a suitable analog voltmeter, the use of a hand-held scan tool, such as Ford's Self-Test Automatic Readout (STAR) tester or the second generation SUPER STAR tester, or equivalent, is highly recommended. There are many manufacturers of such tools, but the purchaser must be certain that the tool is appropriate for the intended use.

Both the STAR and SUPER STAR testers are designed to communicate directly with the EEC-IV system and interpret the electrical signals. The scan tool allows any stored faults to be read from the engine controller memory. Use of the scan tool provides additional data during troubleshooting, but does not eliminate the use of the charts. The scan tool makes information collection easier, but the data must still be correctly interpreted by an operator familiar with the system.

Other Diagnostic Tools
▶ See Figure 64

The most commonly required electrical diagnostic tool is the digital multimeter, allowing voltage, ohms (resistance) and amperage to be read by one instrument. Many of the diagnostic charts require the use of a voltmeter or ohmmeter during diagnosis.

The multimeter must be a high impedance unit, with 10 megohms of impedance in the voltmeter. This type of meter will not place an additional load on the circuit it is testing; this is extremely important in low voltage circuits. The multimeter must be of high quality in all respects. It should be handled carefully and protected from impact or damage. Replace the batteries frequently in the unit.

Additionally, an analog (needle type) voltmeter may be used to read stored fault codes if the STAR tester is not available. The codes are transmitted as visible needle sweeps on the face of the instrument.

Although code retrieval does not require additional equipment, diagnostic procedures such as pinpoint testing will be easier with a "breakout box" (a device which connects into the EEC-IV harness and contains testing ports for the dozens of wires in the harness). Direct testing of the harness connectors at the terminals or by backprobing is not recommended; damage to the wiring and terminals is almost certain to occur.

Other necessary tools for testing/troubleshooting include a quality tachometer with inductive (clip-on) pickup, a fuel pressure gauge with system adapters and a vacuum gauge with an auxiliary source of vacuum.

DIAGNOSIS AND TESTING

Diagnosis of a driveability problem requires attention to detail and following the diagnostic procedures in the correct order. Resist the temptation to begin extensive testing before completing the preliminary diagnostic steps. The preliminary or visual inspection must be completed in detail before diagnosis begins. In many cases, this will shorten diagnostic time and often cure the problem without electronic testing.

Visual Inspection

This is possibly the most critical step of diagnosis. A detailed examination of all connectors, wiring and vacuum hoses can often lead to a repair without further diagnosis. Performance of this step relies on the skill of the person performing it; a careful inspector will check the undersides of hoses as well as the integrity of hard-to-reach hoses blocked by the air cleaner or other components. Wiring should be checked carefully for any sign of strain, burning, crimping or terminal pull-out from a connector.

You should always check connectors at components or in harnesses as required. Pushing them together will usually reveal a loose fit. Pay particular attention to ground circuits, making sure they are not loose or corroded. Remember to inspect connectors and hose fittings at components not mounted on the engine, such as the evaporative canister or relays mounted on the fender aprons. Any component or wiring in the vicinity of a fluid leak or spillage should be given extra attention during inspection.

Additionally, inspect maintenance items such as belt condition and tension, battery charge and condition, and the radiator cap carefully. Any of these simple items may affect the system enough to set a fault.

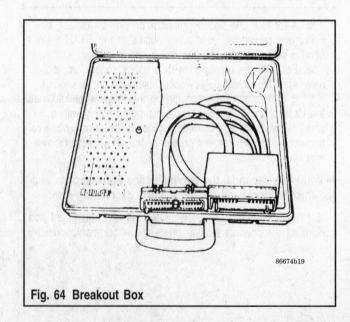

86674b19

Fig. 64 Breakout Box

Reading Codes

▶ See Figures 65 and 66

WITH A HAND-HELD SCAN TOOL

A hand-held scan tool, such as the STAR or SUPER STAR tester, may be used to retrieve stored fault codes. Simply connect the tester's service connectors to the vehicle's Self-Test connectors.

Follow the directions given later in this section under Quick Test Procedures for performing the KOEO and KOER tests. Be sure to release the tester's push button, if applicable, before beginning the Self-Test.

Digital codes, such as "23" will be output and displayed as numbers on the hand-held scan tool. (The codes may also be read using an analog voltmeter. For further details on this alternative method, please refer to the following portion of this section.)

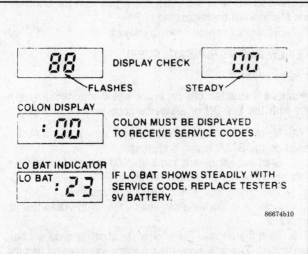

Fig. 65 STAR tester displays. Note that the colon (:) must be present before codes can be received

WITH AN ANALOG VOLTMETER

▶ See Figure 67

In the absence of a scan tool, an analog voltmeter may be used to retrieve stored fault codes. Set the meter range to read 0-15 volts DC. Connect the positive (+) lead of the meter to the positive battery terminal and connect the negative (-) lead of the meter to the self-test output pin of the diagnostic connector.

Follow the directions for performing the KOEO and KOER tests. To activate the tests, use a jumper wire to connect the signal return pin on the diagnostic connector to the self-test input connector. The self-test input line is the separate wire and connector with or near the diagnostic connector.

The codes will be transmitted as groups of needle sweeps, whose cadence corresponds to the codes' numerical representation. Please refer to the accompanying illustration for details on counting the needle sweeps in order to determine the transmitted code. Continuous Memory (intermittent fault) codes, if present, are separated from the KOEO codes by a 6-second delay, a single sweep and another 6-second delay.

SELF-TESTING (GENERATING STORED CODES)

Quick Test Procedures

The EEC-IV system may be interrogated for stored codes using the Quick Test Procedures. These tests will reveal "on-demand" faults immediately present during the test, as well as any intermittent or "continuous" codes set within the previous 20 warm-up cycles. If a code was set before a problem self-corrected (such as a momentarily loose connector), the code will be erased if the problem does not reoccur within 20 subsequent warm-up cycles.

The Quick Test procedure is divided into multiple sections, the most common of which are: Key On Engine Off (KOEO), Key On Engine Running (KOER), and Continuous Testing. Other tests may be performed, including Output State checking and, on SEFI engines, cylinder balance testing. These series of diagnostic procedures must be performed correctly if the

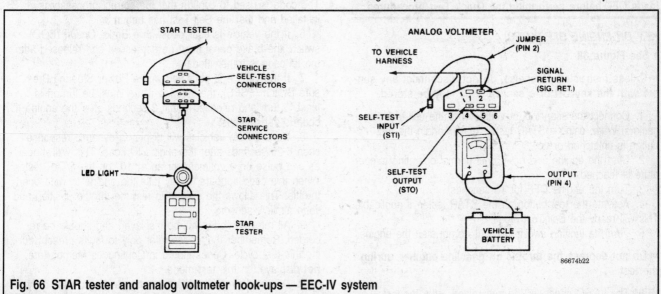

Fig. 66 STAR tester and analog voltmeter hook-ups — EEC-IV system

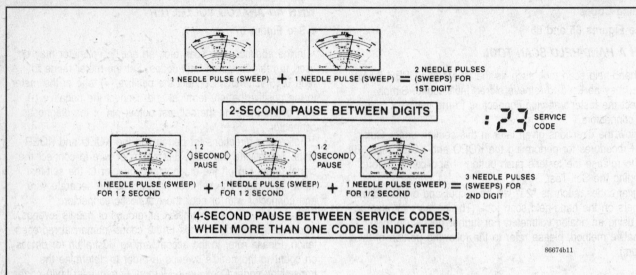

1 NEEDLE PULSE (SWEEP) + 1 NEEDLE PULSE (SWEEP) = 2 NEEDLE PULSES (SWEEPS) FOR 1ST DIGIT

2-SECOND PAUSE BETWEEN DIGITS

:23 SERVICE CODE

1 NEEDLE PULSE (SWEEP) FOR 1/2 SECOND + 1 NEEDLE PULSE (SWEEP) FOR 1/2 SECOND + 1 NEEDLE PULSE (SWEEP) FOR 1/2 SECOND = 3 NEEDLE PULSES (SWEEPS) FOR 2ND DIGIT

1/2 SECOND PAUSE   1/2 SECOND PAUSE

4-SECOND PAUSE BETWEEN SERVICE CODES, WHEN MORE THAN ONE CODE IS INDICATED

86674b11

Fig. 67 Code display patterns on an analog voltmeter

system is to run the internal Self-Test checks and provide accurate fault codes.

If the vehicle passes all three sections of the Quick Test, the EEC-IV system is all right and the vehicle's problem exists elsewhere. Once the Quick Test has been performed and all fault codes recorded, refer to the code charts found later in this section.

➡In all cases, code 11 is used to indicate PASS during testing. Note that the PASS code may appear, followed by other stored codes. These are codes from the Continuous Memory and may indicate intermittent faults, even though the system does not presently contain the fault. The PASS designation only indicates that the system passes all internal tests at the moment.

✳✳CAUTION

To prevent injury and/or property damage, always block the drive wheels, firmly apply the parking brake, place the transmission in PARK or NEUTRAL and turn all electrical loads OFF before performing the Quick Test procedures.

KEY ON ENGINE OFF (KOEO)

▶ See Figure 68

➡**Unless instructed otherwise, do not disconnect any sensor with the key ON or a service code may be stored.**

1. Connect the scan tool or voltmeter to the self-test connectors. When using a STAR tester, make certain the test button is unlatched or up.
2. Start the engine and run it until normal operating temperature is reached.
3. Turn the engine OFF for 10 seconds.
4. Activate the test button on the STAR tester, if applicable. This will ready the Self-Test mode.
5. Turn the ignition switch ON, but do not start the engine.

➡**Do not depress the throttle on gasoline engines during the test.**

6. The KOEO codes will be transmitted. After the last KOEO code, a single separator pulse will be transmitted. Six

to nine seconds after this pulse, the codes from the Continuous Memory will be transmitted.

7. Record all service codes displayed.

KEY ON ENGINE RUNNING (KOER)

▶ See Figure 69

➡**Unless instructed otherwise, do not disconnect any sensor with the key ON or a service code may be stored.**

1. Make certain the self-test button is released or de-activated on the STAR tester, if applicable.
2. Start the engine and run it at 2000 rpm for two minutes. This action warms up the oxygen sensor.
3. Turn the ignition switch OFF for 10 seconds.
4. Activate or latch the self-test button on the scan tool, if applicable.
5. Start the engine. The engine identification code will be transmitted. This is a single digit number representing half the number of cylinders in a gasoline engine. On the STAR tester, this number may appear with a zero (for example, 20 = 2). The code is used to confirm that the correct processor is installed and that the Self-Test has begun.
6. If the vehicle is equipped with a Brake On/Off (BOO) switch, the brake pedal must be depressed and released after the ID code is transmitted.
7. If the vehicle is equipped with a Power Steering Pressure Switch (PSPS), the steering wheel must be turned at least 1/2 turn and released within 2 seconds after the engine ID code is transmitted.
8. Certain Ford vehicles will display a dynamic response code 6-20 seconds after the engine ID code. This will appear as one pulse on a voltmeter or as a "10" on the STAR tester. When this code appears, briefly take the engine to wide open throttle. This allows the system to test the throttle position and vane air flow sensors.
9. All relevant codes will be displayed and should be recorded. Remember that codes refer only to faults present during this test cycle. Codes stored in Continuous Memory are **not** displayed in this test mode.
10. Do not depress the throttle during testing unless a dynamic response code is displayed.

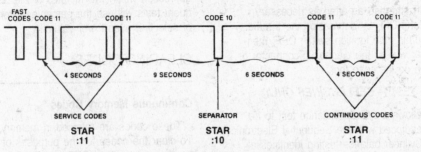

SELF-TEST OUTPUT CODE FORMAT
KEY ON — ENGINE OFF

DIGIT PULSES ARE 1/2 SECOND "ON" AND 1/2 SECOND "OFF"

86674b23

Fig. 68 Code transmission during KOEO test. Note that the Continuous Memory codes are transmitted after a pause, a separator code, and another pause.

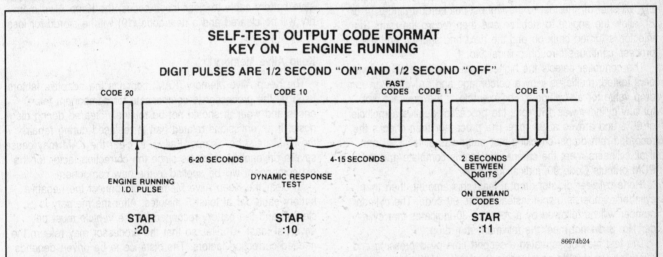

SELF-TEST OUTPUT CODE FORMAT
KEY ON — ENGINE RUNNING

DIGIT PULSES ARE 1/2 SECOND "ON" AND 1/2 SECOND "OFF"

86674b24

Fig. 69 Code transmission during KOER testing begins with the engine identification code, and may include a dynamic response code

CONTINUOUS MONITOR (WIGGLE TEST MODE)

Once entered, this mode allows the technician to attempt to recreate intermittent faults by wiggling or tapping components, wiring or connectors. The test may be performed during either KOEO or KOER procedures. The test requires the use of either an analog voltmeter or a hand-held scan tool.

1. To enter the Continuous Monitor mode during KOEO testing:

a. Turn the ignition switch **ON**.

b. Activate the test, wait 10 seconds, then deactivate and reactivate the test; the system will enter the continuous monitor mode.

c. Tap, move or wiggle the harness, component or connector suspected of causing the problem; if a fault is detected, the code will store in the memory. When the fault occurs, either the STAR tester will light a red indicator (and possibly beep) or the analog meter needle will sweep once.

2. To enter this mode in the KOER test:

a. Start the engine and run it at 2000 rpm for two minutes. This action warms up the oxygen sensor.

b. Turn the ignition switch **OFF** for 10 seconds.

c. Start the engine.

d. Activate the test, wait 10 seconds, then deactivate and reactivate the test; the system will enter the continuous monitor mode.

e. Tap, move or wiggle the harness, component or connector suspected of causing the problem; if a fault is detected, the code will store in the memory.

f. When the fault occurs, either the STAR tester will light a red indicator (and possibly beep) or the analog meter needle will sweep once.

OUTPUT STATE CHECK

This testing mode allows the operator to energize and de-energize most of the outputs controlled by the EEC-IV system. Many of the outputs may be checked at the component by listening for a click or feeling the item move or engage using a hand placed on the case. To enter this check:

1. Enter the KOEO test mode.

2. When all codes have been transmitted, depress the accelerator all the way to the floor and release it.

3. The output actuators are now all ON. Depressing the throttle pedal to the floor again switches all the actuator outputs OFF.

4. This test may be performed as often as necessary, switching between ON and OFF by depressing the throttle.

5. Exit the test by turning the ignition switch **OFF**, then disconnecting the jumper wire at the diagnostic connector or releasing the test button on the scan tool.

CYLINDER BALANCE TEST — SEFI ENGINES ONLY

The EEC-IV system allows a cylinder balance test to be performed on engines equipped with the Sequential Electronic Fuel Injection system. Cylinder balance testing identifies a weak or non-contributing cylinder.

Enter the cylinder balance test by depressing and releasing the throttle pedal within 2 minutes of the last code output in the KOER test. The idle speed will become fixed and engine rpm is recorded for later reference. The engine control assembly will shut off the fuel to the highest-numbered cylinder (4 or 8), allow the engine to stabilize and then record the rpm. The injector is turned back on and the next one shut off and the process continues through cylinder No. 1.

The controller selects the highest rpm drop from all the cylinders tested, multiplies it by a percentage and arrives at an rpm drop value for all cylinders. For example, if the greatest drop for any cylinder was 150 rpm, the processor applies a multiple of 65% and arrives at 98 rpm. The processor then checks the recorded rpm drops, checking that each was at least 98 rpm. If all cylinders meet the criteria, the test is complete and the PCM outputs Code 90, indicating PASS.

If one cylinder did not drop at least this amount, then that cylinder number is output instead of the 90 code. The cylinder number will be followed by a zero, so 30 indicates that cylinder No. 3 did not meet the minimum rpm drop.

The test may be repeated a second time by depressing and releasing the throttle pedal within 2 minutes of the last code output. For the second test, the controller uses a lower percentage (and thus a lower rpm) to determine the minimum acceptable rpm drop. Again, either Code 90 or the number of the weak cylinder will be output.

Performing a third test causes the PCM to select an even lower percentage and rpm drop. If a cylinder is shown as weak in the third test, it should be considered non-contributing. The tests may be repeated as often as needed if the throttle is depressed within two minutes of the last code output. Subsequent tests will use the percentage from the third test instead of selecting even lower values.

CLEARING CODES

Continuous Memory Codes

These codes are retained in memory for 20 warm-up cycles. To clear the codes for the purposes of testing or confirming repair, perform the KOEO test. When the fault codes begin to display, de-activate the test by either disconnecting the jumper wire (if using a voltmeter) or releasing the test button on the hand-held scanner. Stopping the test during code transmission will erase the Continuous Memory. Do not disconnect the negative battery cable to clear these codes; the Keep Alive memory will be cleared and a new code (19) will be stored for loss of PCM power.

Keep Alive Memory

The Keep Alive Memory (KAM) contains the adaptive factors used by the processor to compensate for component tolerances and wear. It should not be routinely cleared during diagnosis. If an emissions related part is replaced during repair, the KAM must be cleared. Failure to clear the KAM may cause severe driveability problems since the correction factor for the old component will be applied to the new component.

To clear the Keep Alive Memory, disconnect the negative battery cable for at least 5 minutes. After the memory is cleared and the battery reconnected, the vehicle must be driven at least 10 miles so that the processor may relearn the needed correction factors. The distance to be driven depends on the engine and vehicle, but all drives should include steady-throttle cruising on open roads. Certain driveability problems may be noted during the drive because the adaptive factors are not yet functioning.

ON-DEMAND SERVICE CODES

SERVICE CODE	EXPLANATION OF SERVICE CODE	POSSIBLE CAUSES OF CONCERN		POSSIBLE SYMPTOMS
12 KOER	Indicates the system is not capable of raising engine speed above curb idle.	Non-EEC:	— Engine running rough/missing. — Throttle linkage binding. — Improper vehicle prep. (e.g., warm-up).	— Rough idle or stalls due to lack of rpm increase with added loads (e.g., Power Steering lock or A/C "on").
		EEC:	— ISC motor/TKS system/ISC solenoid problems. — Wire harness problems. — ECA problems.	
13 KOER	Indicates that the engine did not return to a specified lower rpm prior to entering the "goose" test portion of Quick Test.	Non-EEC:	— Improper curb idle set. — Throttle/TVS linkage binding. — Improper throttle stop set. — Improper cruise control set.	— Idle speed concerns (may be accompanied by code 58).
		EEC:	— ISC motor/ISC solenoid problems. — Idle tracking switch problems. — Wire harness problems. — ECA problems.	
15 KOEO	Indicates an ECA failure.	EEC:	— ECA problems.	— Erratic operation or no start.
16 KOER	Indicates that the fuel system has been driven "lean" until the rpm drops, but the EGO sensor continues to indicate "rich."	EEC:	— Contaminated EGO sensor. — Wire harness problems. — ECA problems.	— System may correct "lean" inducing stumbles or hesitation.
17 KOER	Indicates that with thermactor air upstream the fuel system has been driven "lean" until the rpm drops, but the EGO sensor continues to indicate "rich" (5.0L CFI only)	EEC:	— Contaminated or disconnected EGO sensor. — Wire harness problems. — ECA problems.	— System may correct "rich" causing reduced MPG or black smoke.

21 KOEO	Indicates that the engine coolant temperature is out of range.	Non-EEC:	— Engine not up to operating temperature or, in the case of a no-start, test performed in cool ambient conditions.
			— Engine over operating temperature.
			  • Low coolant.
			  • Stuck thermostat.
			  • Cooling fan problems.
				— Reduced MPG.
				— Rough idle.
				— Improper idle speed.
				— Detonation.

		EEC:	— ECT sensor problems. — Wire harness problems. — ECA problems.	
21 KOER	Indicates that the engine coolant is not at normal operating temperature.	Non-EEC:	— Engine not warmed up. — Thermostat stuck open. — Low coolant level. — Coolant fan not operating. — Thermostat stuck closed. — Radiator blockage (internal or external). — Improper spark timing. — Fuel problems.	— Reduced MPG. — Rough idle. — Improper idle speed. — Detonation.
		EEC:	— ECT sensor problems. — Wire harness problems. — ECA problems.	

86674b25

Fig. 70 1983-85 Ford EEC-IV Vehicles 2-Digit On-Demand Service Codes

ON-DEMAND SERVICE CODES

SERVICE CODE	EXPLANATION OF SERVICE CODE		POSSIBLE CAUSES OF CONCERN	POSSIBLE SYMPTOMS
22 KOEO	Indicates that the MAP BP sensor is out of range. The sensor(s) should read atmospheric pressure.	Non-EEC:	— Unusually high atmospheric pressure. — Vacuum trapped at MAP sensor.	— No-start. — Stalls. — Detonation. — Reduced MPG. — Loss of power.
		EEC:	— MAP BP sensor problems. — Wire harness problems. — ECA problems.	

22 KOER	Indicates that the MAP BP sensor is not at normal vacuum levels for Quick Test. The MAP sensor should indicate engine manifold vacuum. The BP sensor should indicate atmospheric pressure.	Non-EEC:	— Base engine problems (MAP).
			  • Compression problems.
			  • Improper timing.
			  • Vacuum leaks.
			  • Excess EGR.
			— Vacuum line connected to BP sensor (BP).
				— Stalls.
				— Detonation.
				— Reduced MPG.
				— Loss of power.

		EEC:	— MAP BP sensor problems. — Wire harness problems. — ECA problems.	
23 KOEO	Indicates that the TP sensor is not at the proper closed throttle position. Failure may occur either above or below the proper closed throttle position.	Non-EEC:	— Improper base adjustment of curb set, ISC motor, TSP, TKS, or cruise control linkage.	— No-start (EFI/CFI) — Hesitation. — Stalls. — Low/high idle. — Poor performance. — Reduced MPG.
		EEC:	— TKS ISC motor problems. — Wire harness problems. — TP sensor problems. — ECA problems.	
23 KOER	Indicates that the TP sensor is not at the normal throttle position for Quick Test conditions.	Non-EEC:	Improper base adjustment of curb set, ISC motor, TSP, TKS, or cruise control linkage.	— Hesitation. — Stalls. — Low/high idle. — Poor performance. — Reduced MPG.
		EEC:	— TKS ISC motor problems. — Wire harness problems. — TP sensor problems. — ECA problems.	
24 KOEO	Indicates that the Air Charge Vane Air temperature is out of range.	Non-EEC:	— Vehicle testing performed in ambient temperature less than +50 deg. F. — Improper air cleaner duct/door operation.	— Poor idle. — Reduced MPG.
		EEC:	— ACT sensor problems. — Wire harness problems. — ECA problems.	
24 KOER	Indicates that the ACT VAT sensor is not at normal engine operating temperature.	Non-EEC:	— Improper operation of the air cleaner duct door. — Cooling system problems. — Base timing problems.	— Poor idle. — Reduced MPG.
		EEC:	— ACT VAT sensor problems. — Wire harness problems. — ECA problems.	
25 KOER	Indicates that knock was not sensed during the "goose" test.	Non-EEC:	— Base timing problems.	— Detonation. — Poor performance.
		EEC:	— Knock sensor problems. — Wire harness problems. — ECA problems.	

86674b26

Fig. 71 1983-858 Ford EEC-IV Vehicles 2-Digit On-Demand Service Codes (Continued)

ON-DEMAND SERVICE CODES

SERVICE CODE	EXPLANATION OF SERVICE CODE	POSSIBLE CAUSES OF CONCERN		POSSIBLE SYMPTOMS
26 KOEO	Indicates that the VAF meter is not in its closed position.	Non-EEC:	— Obstruction in VAF meter.	— No-start. — Stalls. — Runs rough. — Hesitates.
		EEC:	— VAF Meter problems — Wire harness problems — ECA problems	
26 KOER	Indicates that the VAF meter is not at the normal position for Quick Test conditions.	Non-EEC:	— Unmetered air leaks. — Improper idle speeds — Engine not at normal operating temperature.	— Stalls. — Runs rough. — Hesitates.
		EEC:	— VAF meter problems. — Wire harness problems. — ECA problems.	
31 KOEO KOER	Indicates that the EGR valve is not in its normal closed position.	Non-EEC:	— Sticking/damaged EGR valve. — Vacuum trapped at EGR valve.	— Stalls. — Runs rough. — Dies at idle. — Detonation.
		EEC:	— EGR solenoid problems. — EVP sensor problems. — Wire harness problems. — ECA problems.	
32 KOER	Indicates that the system is not able to open and maintain a specified EGR valve position.	Non-EEC:	— Stuck or damaged EGR valve. — Vacuum leaks.	— Detonation. — Poor performance.
		EEC:	— EGR solenoid problems. — EVP sensor problems. — Wire harness problems. — ECA problems.	
33 KOER	Indicates that the EGR valve has not returned to its normal closed position after the EGR test.	Non-EEC:	— Stuck or damaged EGR valve.	— Decel stall. — Runs rough.
		EEC:	— EGR solenoid problems. — EVP sensor problems.	
34 KOER	Indicates that, with engine rpm elevated and stabilized, a specified rpm drop did not occur when EGR was turned "on."	Non-EEC:	— Stuck or damaged EGR valve. — BVT/EGR problems. — Vacuum leaks. — Improper exhaust back-pressure	— Detonation.
		EEC:	— EGR solenoid problems. — Wire harness problems. — ECA problems.	
35 KOER	Indicates that the engine rpm is too low for the EGR test.	Non-EEC:	— Base engine problems.	— May run rough. — Lacks power.
		EEC:	— ISC problems.	
41* KOER	Indicates that the EGO sensor output voltage is always less than 0.5 volts ("lean") during the fuel test.	Non-EEC:	— Improper fuel delivery. — Carburetor/Throttle-Body injector problem. — Vacuum leaks. — Unmetered air. — Thermactor air is always upstream.	— Runs rough. — Stalls. — Hesitates. — Runs "lean". — May correct "rich" if sensor or harness related. • Spark plugs fouled. • Reduced MPG.
		EEC:	— EGO sensor problems. — Wire harness problems. — ECA problems.	

86674b27

Fig. 72 1983-85 Ford EEC-IV Vehicles 2-Digit On-Demand Service Codes (Continued)

ON-DEMAND SERVICE CODES

SERVICE CODE	EXPLANATION OF SERVICE CODE	POSSIBLE CAUSES OF CONCERN		POSSIBLE SYMPTOMS

42*
KOER
	Indicates that the EGO sensor output voltage is always greater than 0.5 volts ("rich") during the fuel test.	Non-EEC:	— Improper fuel delivery.
			— Carburetor/Throttle-Body injector problems.
			— Obstructed air intake.
			— Ignition system problems.
			— Cannister purge problems.
				— Runs rough.
				— Runs "rich."
				— Reduced MPG.
				— Spark plugs fouled.
				— May correct "lean" if sensor or harness related.
				  ● Hesitations.
				  ● Stalls.

		EEC:	— EGO sensor problems. — Wire harness problems. — ECA problems.	
43* KOER	Indicates that the EGO sensor has cooled down and may not have given the proper responses during Quick Test.	Non-EEC:	— Vehicle not properly prepared for test (Run at 2000 rpm for 2 minutes prior to test). — Engine below operating temperature.	— Usually no drive complaint.
44* KOER	Indicates that there is a thermactor problem.	Non-EEC:	— Air pump problems. — Thermactor valve problems.	— Usually no drive complaint.
		EEC:	— Thermactor solenoid problems. — Wire harness problems. — ECA problems.	
45* KOER	Indicates that thermactor air is always upstream during Quick Test.	Non-EEC:	— Air pump problems. — Thermactor valve problems.	— Catalyst over temperature.
		EEC:	— Thermactor solenoid problems. — Wire harness problems. — ECA problems.	
46* KOER	Indicates that the system is unable to hypass (vent to atmosphere) thermactor air.	Non-EEC:	— Air pump problems. — Thermactor valve problems.	— Catalyst over temperature.
		EEC:	— Thermactor solenoid problems. — Wire harness problems. — ECA problems.	

47*
KOER
	Indicates that, even though thermactor air is upstream and fuel control is max. "lean", the EGO sensor indicates "rich".	Non-EEC:	— Improper fuel delivery.
			— Carburetor/Throttle-Body injector problems.
			— Obstructed air intake.
			— Ignition system problems.
				— Runs "rich".
				— Runs rough.
				— Reduced MPG.
				— Spark plugs fouled.
				— May correct "lean" if sensor or harness related.
				  ● Hesitations
				  ● Stalls.

		EEC:	— EGO sensor problems. — Wire harness problems. — ECA problems.	

86674b28

Fig. 73 1983-85 Ford EEC-IV Vehicles 2-Digit On-Demand Service Codes (Continued)

ON-DEMAND SERVICE CODES

SERVICE CODE	EXPLANATION OF SERVICE CODE	POSSIBLE CAUSES OF CONCERN		POSSIBLE SYMPTOMS
48 KOER	Indicates that the system does not have proper side-to-side fuel control. (3.8L only.)	Non-EEC:	— Catalyst blockage. — Stuck injector. — Plugged injector.	— Stumbles. — Stalls. — Reduce MPG. — Black smoke.

		EEC:	— Wire harness problems.
			  • Injector connections reversed.
			  • EGO connections reversed.
			  • One injector disconnected.
			  • One EGO disconnected.
			— EGO sensor problems.
			— ECA problems.	

51 KOEO	Indicates that the ECT signal failed at the high end (approximately 5.0 volts). Failure mode indicates – 40 deg. F.	EEC:	— ECT sensor problems. — Wire harness problems. — ECA problems.	— Hard to start Hot. — Black smoke. — Reduced MPG.

53 KOEO	Indicates that the TP signal has failed at the high end (approximately 5.0 volts). Failure mode indicates WOT.	EEC:	— Wire harness problems.
			  • Open signal return circuit.
			  • TP signal shorted to VREF.
			— TP sensor problems.
			— ECA problems.
				— No start (EFI/CFI).
				— Poor part throttle performance.

54 KOEO	Indicates that the ACT signal has failed at the high end (approximately 5.0 volts). Failure mode indicates – 40 deg. F.	EEC:	— Wire harness problems.
			  • Vref open.
			  • ACT signal shorted to signal return.
			  • ACT signal open.
			— ACT sensor problems.
			— ECA problems.
				— Reduced MPG.
				— Black smoke.

56 KOEO	Indicates that the VAF signal has failed at the high end (approximately 5.0 volts). Failure mode indicates wide open throttle.	EEC:	— Wire harness problems. — VAF sensor problems. — ECA problems.	— Black smoke.
58 KOER	Indicates that the ITS is not in contact with the throttle lever with the ISC motor extended.	Non-EEC:	— Improper throttle plate stop adjustment. — Throttle linkage binding. — Cruise control misadjusted. — Improper ISC adjustment.	— Improper idle speeds. — Stalls.
		EEC:	— ITS problems. — Wire harness problems. — ECA problems.	
61 KOEO	Indicates that the ECT signal has failed at the low end (approximately 0.0 volts). Failure mode indicates + 240 deg. F.	EEC:	— ECT sensor problems. — Wire harness problems. — ECA problems.	— Hard start/no start (cold).

63 KOEO	Indicates that the TP signal has failed at the low end (approximately 0.0 volts). Failure mode indicates closed throttle.	EEC:	— Wire harness problems.
			  • Vref open.
			  • TP signal shorted to signal return.
			  • TP signal open.
			— TP sensor problems.
			— ECA problems.
				— Runs rough.
				— Stumbles.
				— Stalls.

86674b29

Fig. 74 1983-85 Ford EEC-IV Vehicles 2-Digit On-Demand Service Codes (Continued)

ON-DEMAND SERVICE CODES

SERVICE CODE	EXPLANATION OF SERVICE CODE	POSSIBLE CAUSES OF CONCERN		POSSIBLE SYMPTOMS
64 KOEO	Indicates that the ACT/VAT signal has failed at the low end (approximately 0.0 volts) Failure mode indicates +240 deg.	EEC:	— ACT/VAT sensor problems. — Wire harness problems. — ECA problems.	— Runs rough — Stumbles. — Stalls.
66 KOEO	Indicates that the VAF signal has failed at the low end (approximately 0.0 volts). Failure mode indicates closed throttle.	EEC:	— Wire harness problems. — VAF sensor problems. — ECA problems.	— Stumbles — Stalls.
67 KOEO	Indicates that the system is receiving an improper neutral/drive or A/C clutch status input.	Non-EEC: EEC:	— Vehicle in gear or A/C "on." — Neutral drive switch problems. — Wire harness problems. — ECA problems.	— Improper ISC. — Stalls.
68 KOEO	Indicates that the ITS is in contact with the throttle lever with the ISC motor retracted	Non-EEC: EEC:	— Improper ISC motor adjustment. — ITS problems. — Wire harness problems. — ECA problems.	— Improper idle speed control. — Stalls.
72 KOER	Indicates that the MAP sensor has not detected a sufficient manifold vacuum change during the "goose" test.	Non-EEC: EEC:	— Vacuum leaks. — Base engine problems. — Map sensor problems. — ECA problems.	— Stumbles. — Hesitations. — Stalls.
73 KOER	Indicates that the system has not detected a sufficient TP change during the "goose" test.	EEC:	— TP sensor stuck at WOT. — TP sensor not tracking throttle shaft — ECA problems.	— Stumbles. — Hesitations
76 KOER	Indicates that the system has not detected a sufficient VAF change during the "goose" test.	Non-EEC: EEC:	— Unmetered air entering engine. — VAF meter sticking. — ECA problems.	— Stumbles. — Hesitations.
77 KOER	Indicates that the operator did not do the "goose" test.	Non-EEC: EEC:	— Operator did not do a brief WOT. — ECA problems.	———————
81 KOEO	Indicates a TAD circuit fault. (For 2.8L only, code indicates a TAB circuit fault.)	EEC:	— Open/shorted TAD solenoid. — Wire harness problems. — ECA problems.	— Thermactor service code KOER.
82 KOEO	Indicates a TAB circuit fault. (For 2.8L only, code indicates a TAD circuit fault.)	EEC:	— Open/shorted TAB solenoid. — Wire harness problems. — ECA problems.	— Thermactor service code KOER.
83 KOEO	Indicates an EGRC circuit fault.	EEC:	— Open/shorted EGRC solenoid. — Wire harness problems. — ECA problems.	— No EGR control. — Detonation.
84 KOEO	Indicates an EGRV circuit fault.	EEC:	— Open/shorted EGRV solenoid. — Wire harness problems. — ECA problems.	— Improper EGR control. — Stalls. — Runs rough.
85 KOEO	Indicates a CANP circuit fault.	EEC:	— Open/shorted CANP valve. — Wire harness problems. — ECA problems.	— Customer complaints of gasoline odor.
86 KOEO	Indicates a WAC circuit fault.	EEC:	— Open/shorted WAC controller. — Wire harness problems. — ECA problems.	— No A/C operation. — No WOT-A/C cutoff.

86674b30

Fig. 75 1983-85 Ford EEC-IV Vehicles 2-Digit On-Demand Service Codes (Continued)

ON-DEMAND SERVICE CODES

SERVICE CODE	EXPLANATION OF SERVICE CODE	POSSIBLE CAUSES OF CONCERN		POSSIBLE SYMPTOMS
87 KOEO	Indicates a fuel pump relay circuit fault	EEC:	— Inertia switch problems. — Open short fuel pump relay. — Wire harness problems. — ECA problems.	— No start. — Pump runs with key in "off" position.
	or a TCP circuit fault (2.8L only).	EEC:	— TCP solenoid problems. — Wiring harness problems. — ECA problems.	— Poor cold start driveaway.
88 KOEO	Indicates a TKS circuit fault (5.0L CFI only)	EEC:	— Open shorted TKS solenoid. — Wire harness problems. — ECA problems.	— High idle speeds. — Stalls (low idle speeds).
	or a VVC circuit fault (2.8L only).	EEC:	— VVC relay problems. — Wiring harness problems. — ECA problems.	— Poor cold start driveaway. — Spark plug loading. — Reduced MPG. — Black smoke.
89 KOEO	Indicates an exhaust heat control circuit fault.	EEC:	— Open shorted EHC solenoid. — Wire harness problems. — ECA problems.	— Stumbles. — Hesitations cold.

91 KOER	Indicates that the right EGO sensor output voltage is always less than 0.5 volts ("lean") during the fuel test (3.8L only).	Non-EEC:
		
		EEC:
			— Improper fuel delivery.
			— Carburetor Throttle-Body injector problems.
			— Vacuum leaks.
			— Unmetered air.
			— Thermactor air is always upstream.
			— EGO sensor problems.
			— Wire harness problems.
			— ECA problems.
				— Runs rough.
				— Stalls.
				— Hesitates.
				— Runs "lean".
				— May correct "rich" if sensor or harness related
				  • Spark plugs fouled.
				  • Reduced MPG.

92 KOER	Indicates that the right EGO sensor output voltage is always greater than 0.5 volts ("rich") during the fuel test (3.8L only).	Non-EEC:
		
		EEC:
			— Improper fuel delivery.
			— Carburetor Throttle-Body injector problems.
			— Obstructed air intake.
			— Ignition system problems.
			— EGO sensor problems.
			— Wire harness problems.
			— ECA problems.
				— Runs rough.
				— Runs "rich".
				— Reduced MPG.
				— Spark plugs fouled.
				— May correct "lean" if sensor or harness related.
				  • Hesitations.
				  • Stalls.

93 KOER	Indicates that the right EGO sensor has cooled down and may not have given the proper responses during Quick Test (3.8L only).	Non-EEC:	— Vehicle not properly prepared for test (Run at 2000 rpm for 2 minutes prior to test). — Engine below operating temperature.	— Usually no drive complaint.
94 KOER	Indicates that there is a thermactor problem on the right bank (3.8L only).	Non-EEC: EEC:	— Air pump problems. — Thermactor valve problems. — Thermactor solenoid problems. — Wire harness problems. — ECA problems.	— Usually no drive complaint.
95 KOER	Indicates that the right bank thermactor air is always upstream during Quick Test (3.8L only).	Non-EEC: EEC:	— Air pump problems. — Thermactor valve problems. — Thermactor solenoid problems. — Wire harness problems. — ECA problems.	— Catalyst over temperature.

86674b31

Fig. 76 1983-85 Ford EEC-IV Vehicles 2-Digit On-Demand Service Codes (Continued)

ON-DEMAND SERVICE CODES

SERVICE CODE	EXPLANATION OF SERVICE CODE	POSSIBLE CAUSES OF CONCERN		POSSIBLE SYMPTOMS
96 KOER	Indicates that the system is unable to bypass (vent to atmosphere) thermactor air on the right bank (3 8L only).	Non-EEC:	— Air pump problems. — Thermactor valve problems.	— Catalyst over temperature.
		EEC:	— Thermactor solenoid problems. — Wire harness problems. — ECA problems.	
97 KOER	Indicates that, even though thermactor air is upstream and fuel control is max. "lean," the right EGO sensor indicates "rich" (3 8L only).	Non-EEC:	— Improper fuel delivery. — Carburetor/Throttle-Body injector problems. — Obstructed air intake. — Ignition system problems.	— Runs "rich." — Runs rough. — Reduced MPG. — Spark plugs fouled. — May correct "lean" if sensor or harness related. • Hesitations. • Stalls.
		EEC:	— EGO sensor problems. — Wire harness problems. — ECA problems.	

86674b32

Fig. 77 1983-85 Ford EEC-IV Vehicles 2-Digit On-Demand Service Codes (Continued)

CONTINUOUS CODES

SERVICE CODE	EXPLANATION OF SERVICE CODE	POSSIBLE CAUSES OF CONCERN		POSSIBLE SYMPTOMS
13 Cont.	Indicates that during recent operation, while in the normal operating mode an ISC command to extend the ISC motor shaft occurred without a corresponding TP sensor change.	Non-EEC:	— Throttle shaft binding. — Improper ISC adjustment.	— Improper idle speed. — Possible stalls.
		EEC:	— ISC motor problems. — TP sensor problems. — Wire harness problems. — ECA problems.	
14 Cont.	Indicates that erratic operation or intermittent loss of PIP information to the ECA has occurred during recent operation.	Non-EEC:	— Distributor pickup problems. — TFI module problems.	— Engine miss. — Surge. — Rough idle. — Stall.
		EEC:	— Wire harness problems. — ECA problems.	
15 Cont.	Indicates loss of Keep-Alive-Memory during recent operation.	EEC:	— Loss of Keep-Alive-Memory battery power. — ECA problems.	— No codes in memory.
18 Cont.	Indicates that during recent operation the ECA received a PIP signal input without receiving a corresponding tach signal input.	Non-EEC:	— Ignition coil problems. — TFI module problems. — Vehicle wire harness.	— No start. — Stalls. — Idles/runs rough.
		EEC:	— Wire harness problems. — ECA problems.	
21 Cont.	Indicates that during a single drive cycle the engine has reached normal operating temperature and then has cooled down.	Non-EEC:	— Thermostat failure. — Coolant loss.	— Reduced MPG. — Heater output loss.
		EEC:	— ECT sensor problems. — Wire harness problems. — ECA problems.	
22 Cont.	Indicates that a gross MAP/BP sensor signal error has occurred during recent operation.	Non-EEC:	Basic engine problems. • Compression problems. • Improper timing. • Vacuum leaks.	— Detonation. — Poor performance. — Reduced MPG. — Surge. — Stumbles.
		EEC:	— MAP/BP sensor problems. — Wire harness problems. — ECA problems.	

86674b33

Fig. 78 1983-85 Ford EEC-IV Vehicles 2-Digit Continuous Codes

CONTINUOUS CODES

SERVICE CODE	EXPLANATION OF SERVICE CODE	POSSIBLE CAUSES OF CONCERN		POSSIBLE SYMPTOMS
31 Cont.	Indicates that the EVP sensor signal has been off scale at the high or low end during recent operation.	Non-EEC: EEC:	— EGR valve sticks at wide open. — EGR over travel (normal condition on some applications, refer to diagnostics manual). — EVP sensor problems — Wire harness problems — ECA problems.	— Detonation. — Hard to start. — No start. — Runs rough. — Stalls. — Dies at idle.

53 Cont.	Indicates that the TP sensor signal has been off scale at the high end during recent operation.	EEC:	— Wire harness problems
			  • Open signal return.
			  • Signal short circuit to Vref
			— TP sensor problems.
			— ECA problems.
				— No start (CFI/EFI)
				— Detonation.
				— Stumbles.
				— Poor performance

54 Cont.	Indicates that the ACT/VAT sensor signal has been off scale at the high end during recent operation.	EEC:	— ACT/VAT sensor problems — Wire harness open circuit — ECA problems.	— Runs rough. — Black smoke. — Reduced MPG.
56 Cont.	Indicates that the VAF meter signal has been off scale at the high end during recent operation.	EEC:	— VAF sensor problems — Wire harness problems. — ECA problems	— No start. — Stumbles. — Stalls. — Runs only at WOT.
61 Cont.	Indicates that the ECT sensor signal has been off scale at the low end during recent operation.	EEC:	— ECT sensor problems — Wire harness shorted to ground. — ECA problems.	— Runs rough. — Stalls. — Erratic idle.

63 Cont.	Indicates that the TP sensor signal has been off scale at the low end during recent operation.	EEC:	— Wire harness problems
			  • Vref open
			  • Signal line open
			  • Signal shorted to sensor return.
			— TP sensor problems.
			— ECA problems.
				— Poor performance.
				— Stumbles.
				— Detonation.

64 Cont.	Indicates that the ACT/VAT sensor signal has been off scale at the low end during recent operation.	EEC:	— ACT/VAT sensor problems — Wire harness shorted to ground. — ECA problems.	— Runs rough. — Stalls. — Erratic idle.
65 Cont.	Indicates that during recent operation a charging system over-voltage condition (greater than 17.5 v) has occurred	Non-EEC: EEC:	— Voltage regulator problems — Alternator problems — Wire harness problems — ECA problems	— Lamp burnout. — Electronic component burnout (e.g. TFI, ECA. Radio, etc.)

66 Cont.	Indicates that the VAF meter signal has been off scale at the low end during recent operation.	EEC:	— Wire harness problems
			  • Vref circuit open.
			  • Signal circuit open.
			  • Signal circuit shorted to signal return.
			— VAF meter problems.
			— ECA problems
				— No start.
				— Stalls.
				— Lacks power.
				— Runs only at WOT.

86674b34

Fig. 79 1983-85 Ford EEC-IV Vehicles 2-Digit Continuous Codes (Continued)

VACUUM DIAGRAMS

Each vehicle is equipped with a decal containing emission control data specific to that vehicle and engine. The decal is typically located on the underside of the hood, but might instead be found on the fan shroud, the coil appearance cover or elsewhere. These specifications are critical to the effective servicing of the applicable system. In addition to the tune-up specifications and procedures, the emission control data decal includes a color-coded schematic of the engine vacuum system. The color coding on the schematic represents the actual color coding on the vacuum hoses, although there may be some exceptions.

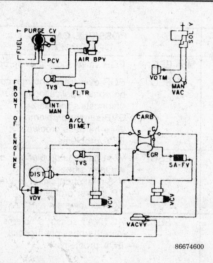

86674600

Fig. 80 Vacuum schematic — 1979 4-cylinder engine

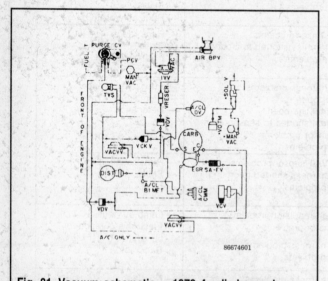

86674601

Fig. 81 Vacuum schematic — 1979 4-cylinder engine

Since this book covers approximately two hundred calibrations, all of which correspond to a specific vacuum diagram, it is not feasible to include a schematic of every vacuum system. In addition, mid-year production changes often result in different vacuum schematics from those which are published. For this reason, the best source for vacuum diagrams is the vehicle's emission control data decal. The following vacuum diagrams cover most, but not all, calibrations pertaining to the 1971-85 Mid-sized Ford vehicles. For ease of use, these diagrams are arranged by engine size within each model year.

If your exact calibration is not covered here, use a similar configuration as a guide or see your local dealer about purchasing a replacement sticker.

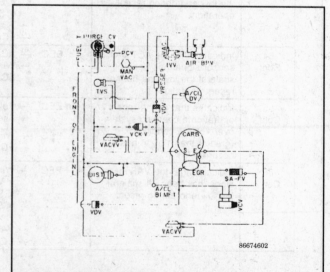

86674602

Fig. 82 Vacuum schematic — 1979 4-cylinder engine

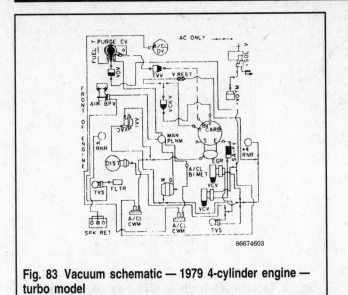

Fig. 83 Vacuum schematic — 1979 4-cylinder engine — turbo model

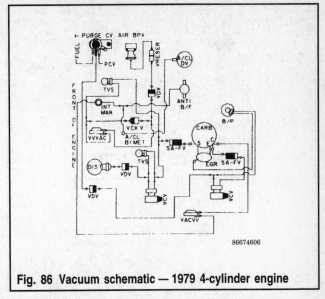

Fig. 86 Vacuum schematic — 1979 4-cylinder engine

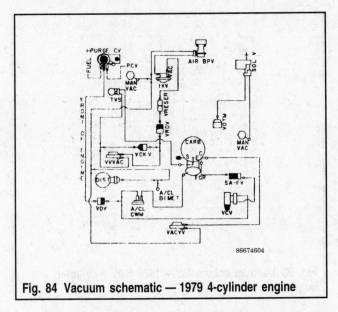

Fig. 84 Vacuum schematic — 1979 4-cylinder engine

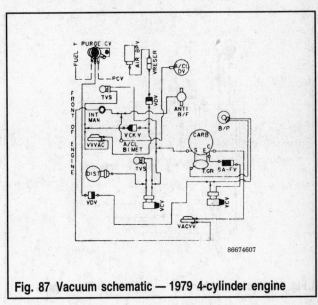

Fig. 87 Vacuum schematic — 1979 4-cylinder engine

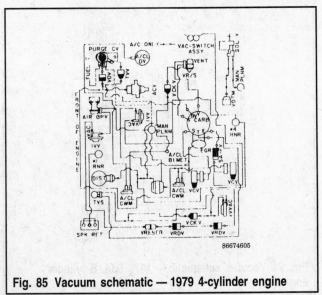

Fig. 85 Vacuum schematic — 1979 4-cylinder engine

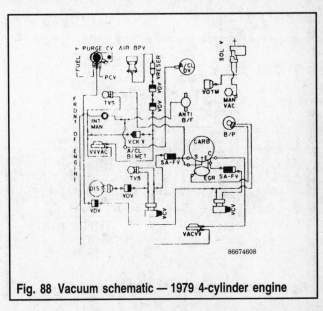

Fig. 88 Vacuum schematic — 1979 4-cylinder engine

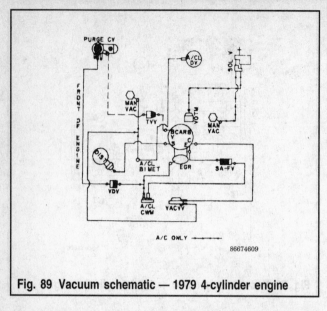

Fig. 89 Vacuum schematic — 1979 4-cylinder engine

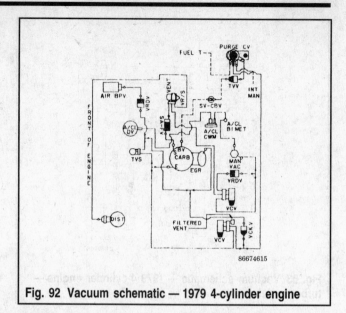

Fig. 92 Vacuum schematic — 1979 4-cylinder engine

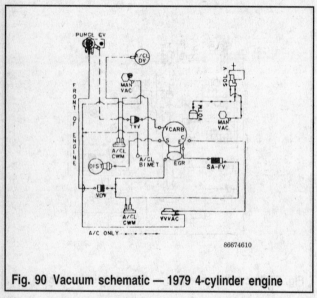

Fig. 90 Vacuum schematic — 1979 4-cylinder engine

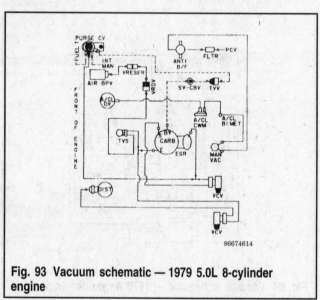

Fig. 93 Vacuum schematic — 1979 5.0L 8-cylinder engine

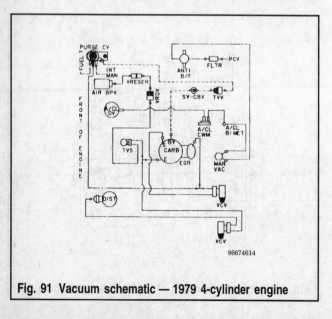

Fig. 91 Vacuum schematic — 1979 4-cylinder engine

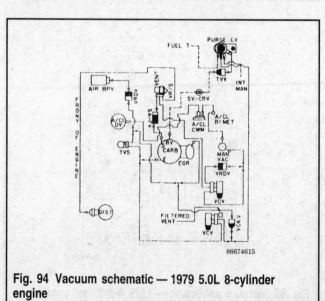

Fig. 94 Vacuum schematic — 1979 5.0L 8-cylinder engine

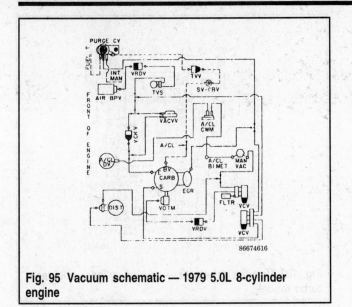

Fig. 95 Vacuum schematic — 1979 5.0L 8-cylinder engine

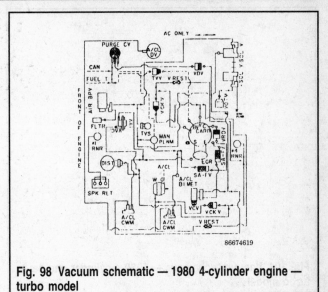

Fig. 98 Vacuum schematic — 1980 4-cylinder engine — turbo model

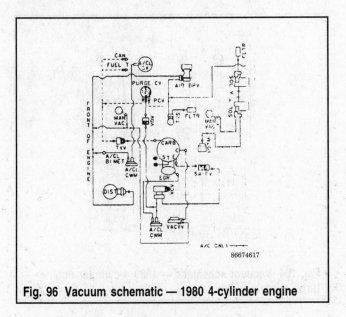

Fig. 96 Vacuum schematic — 1980 4-cylinder engine

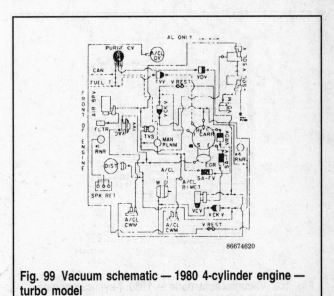

Fig. 99 Vacuum schematic — 1980 4-cylinder engine — turbo model

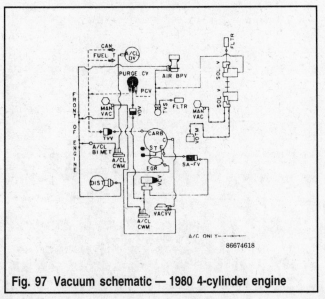

Fig. 97 Vacuum schematic — 1980 4-cylinder engine

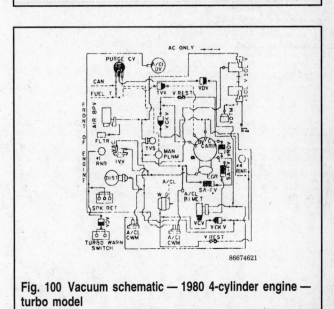

Fig. 100 Vacuum schematic — 1980 4-cylinder engine — turbo model

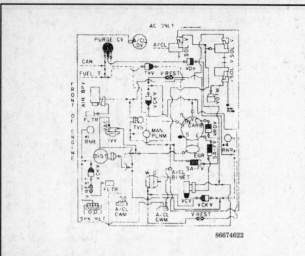

Fig. 101 Vacuum schematic — 1980 4-cylinder engine — turbo model

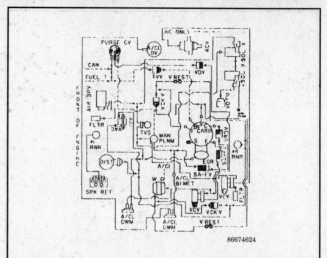

Fig. 103 Vacuum schematic — 1980 4-cylinder engine — turbo model

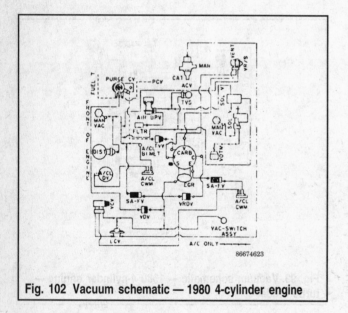

Fig. 102 Vacuum schematic — 1980 4-cylinder engine

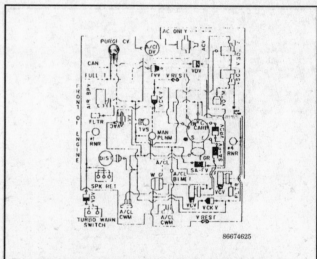

Fig. 104 Vacuum schematic — 1980 4-cylinder engine — turbo model

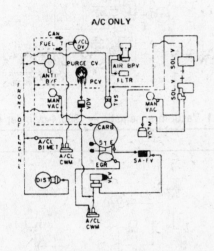

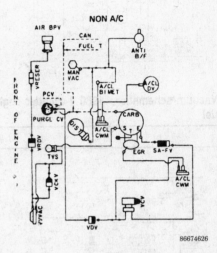

Fig. 105 Vacuum schematic — 1980 4-cylinder engine

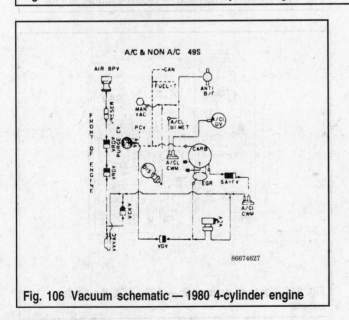

Fig. 106 Vacuum schematic — 1980 4-cylinder engine

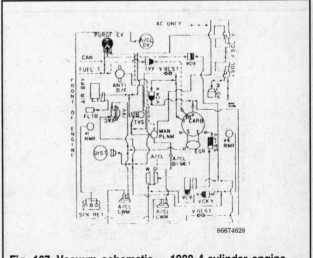

Fig. 107 Vacuum schematic — 1980 4-cylinder engine —
turbo model

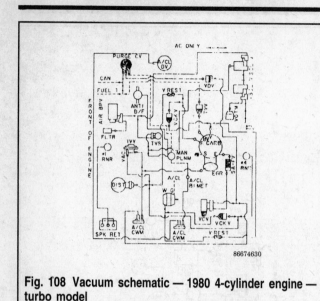

Fig. 108 Vacuum schematic — 1980 4-cylinder engine — turbo model

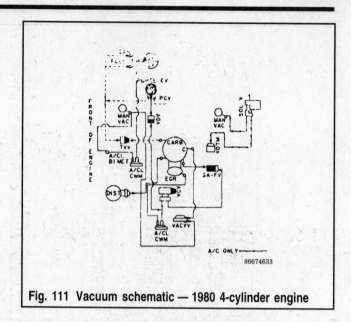

Fig. 111 Vacuum schematic — 1980 4-cylinder engine

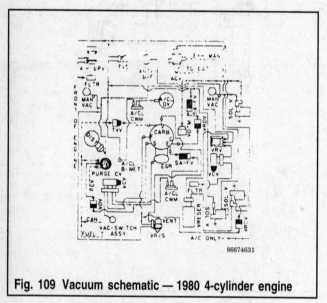

Fig. 109 Vacuum schematic — 1980 4-cylinder engine

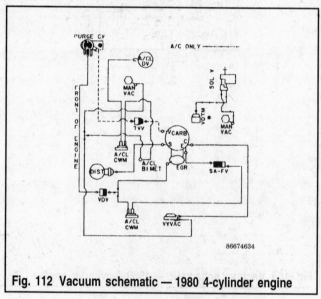

Fig. 112 Vacuum schematic — 1980 4-cylinder engine

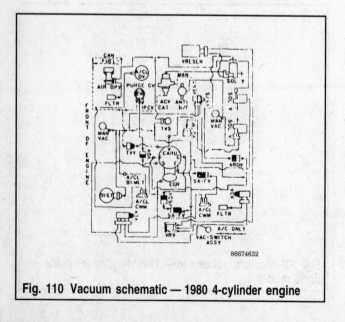

Fig. 110 Vacuum schematic — 1980 4-cylinder engine

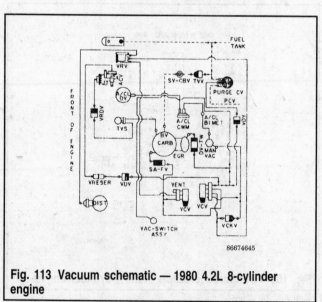

Fig. 113 Vacuum schematic — 1980 4.2L 8-cylinder engine

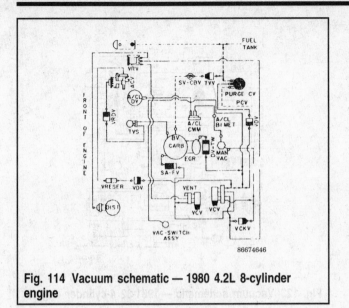

Fig. 114 Vacuum schematic — 1980 4.2L 8-cylinder engine

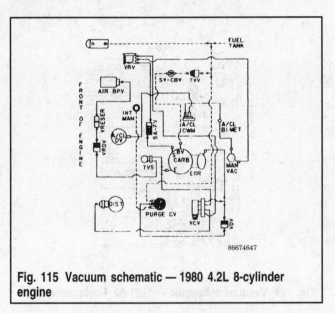

Fig. 115 Vacuum schematic — 1980 4.2L 8-cylinder engine

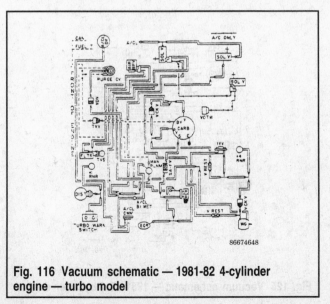

Fig. 116 Vacuum schematic — 1981-82 4-cylinder engine — turbo model

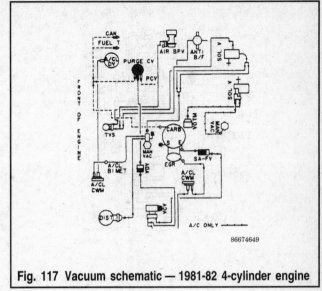

Fig. 117 Vacuum schematic — 1981-82 4-cylinder engine

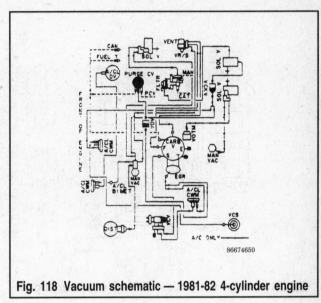

Fig. 118 Vacuum schematic — 1981-82 4-cylinder engine

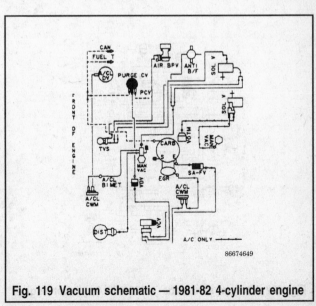

Fig. 119 Vacuum schematic — 1981-82 4-cylinder engine

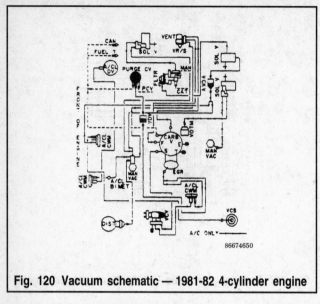

Fig. 120 Vacuum schematic — 1981-82 4-cylinder engine

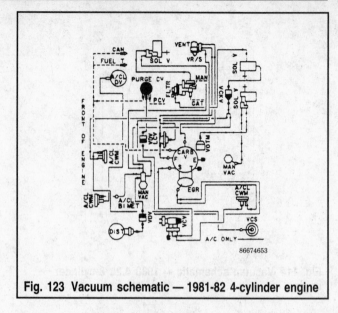

Fig. 123 Vacuum schematic — 1981-82 4-cylinder engine

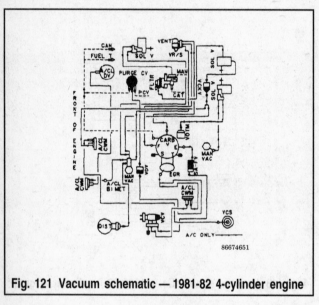

Fig. 121 Vacuum schematic — 1981-82 4-cylinder engine

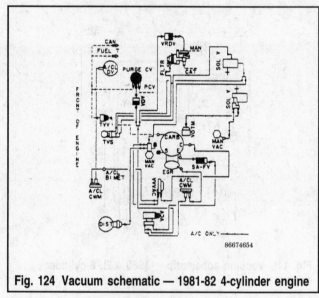

Fig. 124 Vacuum schematic — 1981-82 4-cylinder engine

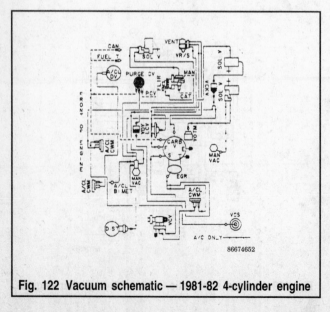

Fig. 122 Vacuum schematic — 1981-82 4-cylinder engine

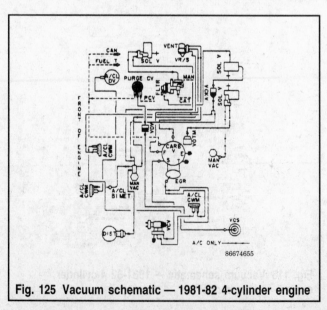

Fig. 125 Vacuum schematic — 1981-82 4-cylinder engine

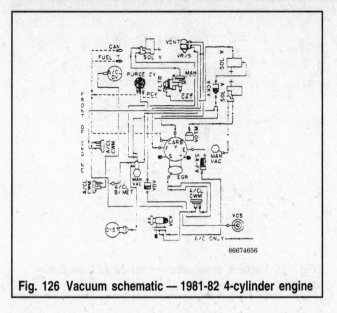

Fig. 126 Vacuum schematic — 1981-82 4-cylinder engine

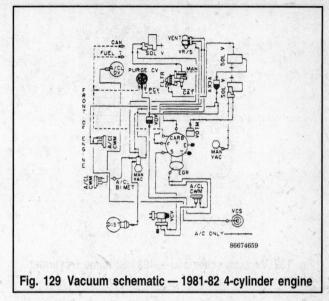

Fig. 129 Vacuum schematic — 1981-82 4-cylinder engine

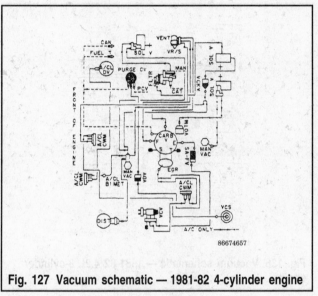

Fig. 127 Vacuum schematic — 1981-82 4-cylinder engine

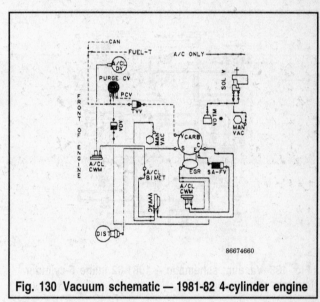

Fig. 130 Vacuum schematic — 1981-82 4-cylinder engine

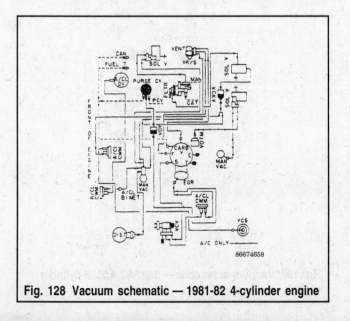

Fig. 128 Vacuum schematic — 1981-82 4-cylinder engine

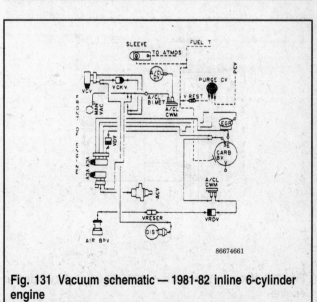

Fig. 131 Vacuum schematic — 1981-82 inline 6-cylinder engine

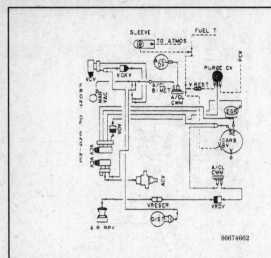

Fig. 132 Vacuum schematic — 1981-82 inline 6-cylinder engine

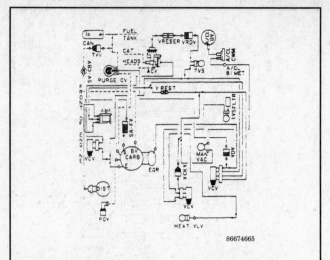

Fig. 135 Vacuum schematic — 1981-82 4.2L 8-cylinder engine

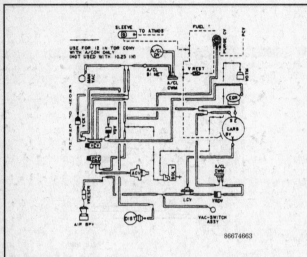

Fig. 133 Vacuum schematic — 1981-82 inline 6-cylinder engine

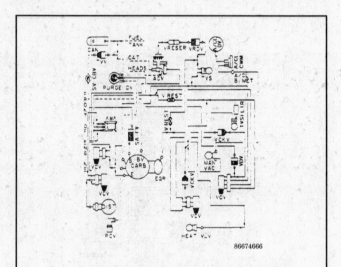

Fig. 136 Vacuum schematic — 1981-82 4.2L 8-cylinder engine

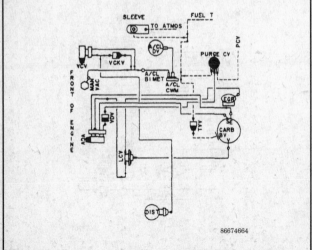

Fig. 134 Vacuum schematic — 1981-82 inline 6-cylinder engine

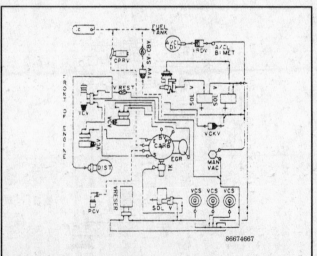

Fig. 137 Vacuum schematic — 1981-82 4.2L 8-cylinder engine

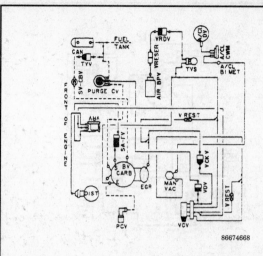

Fig. 138 Vacuum schematic — 1981-82 4.2L 8-cylinder engine

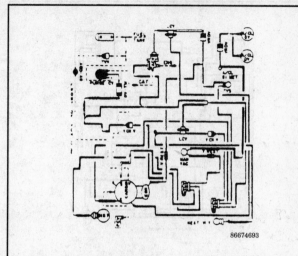

Fig. 141 Vacuum schematic — 1981-82 5.0L 8-cylinder engine

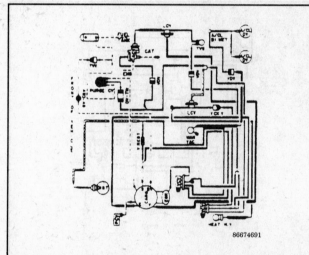

Fig. 139 Vacuum schematic — 1981-82 5.0L 8-cylinder engine

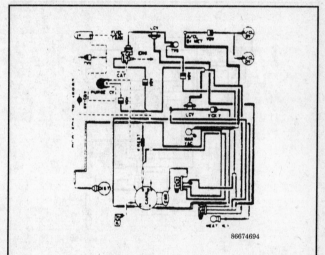

Fig. 142 Vacuum schematic — 1981-82 5.0L 8-cylinder engine

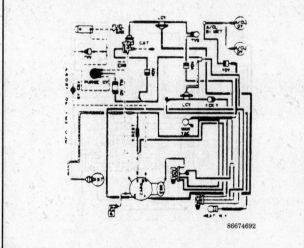

Fig. 140 Vacuum schematic — 1981-82 5.0L 8-cylinder engine

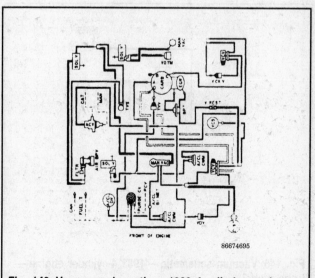

Fig. 143 Vacuum schematic — 1983 4-cylinder engine

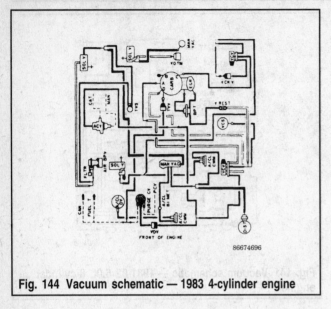

Fig. 144 Vacuum schematic — 1983 4-cylinder engine

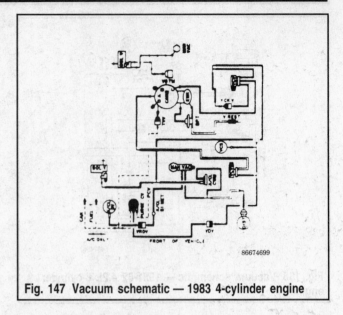

Fig. 147 Vacuum schematic — 1983 4-cylinder engine

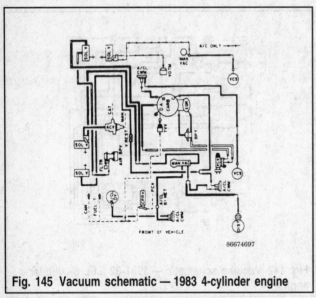

Fig. 145 Vacuum schematic — 1983 4-cylinder engine

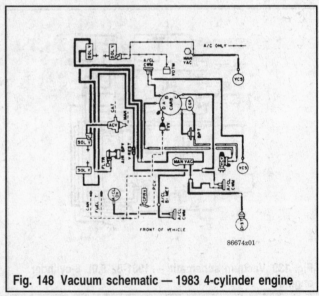

Fig. 148 Vacuum schematic — 1983 4-cylinder engine

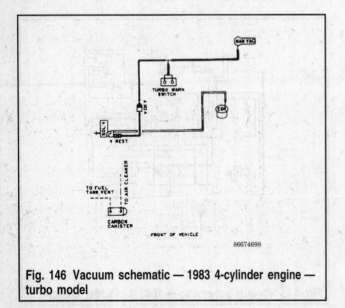

Fig. 146 Vacuum schematic — 1983 4-cylinder engine — turbo model

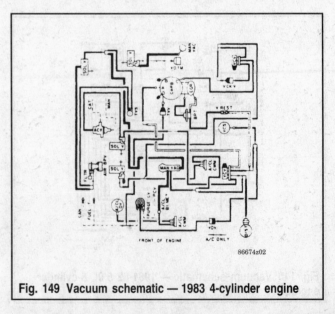

Fig. 149 Vacuum schematic — 1983 4-cylinder engine

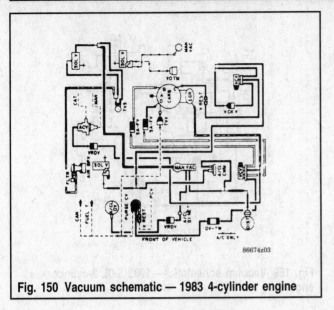

Fig. 150 Vacuum schematic — 1983 4-cylinder engine

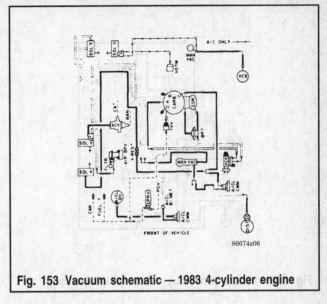

Fig. 153 Vacuum schematic — 1983 4-cylinder engine

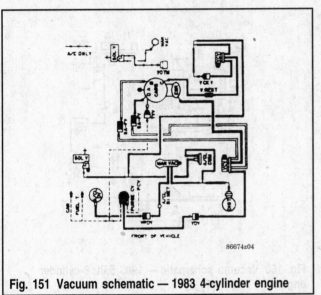

Fig. 151 Vacuum schematic — 1983 4-cylinder engine

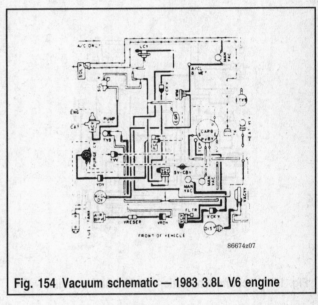

Fig. 154 Vacuum schematic — 1983 3.8L V6 engine

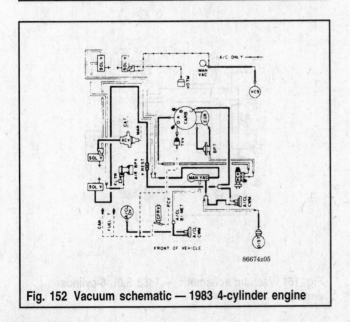

Fig. 152 Vacuum schematic — 1983 4-cylinder engine

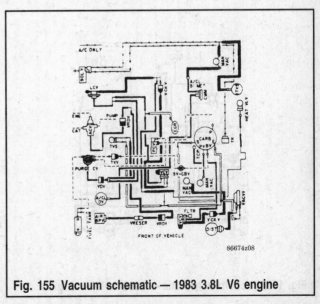

Fig. 155 Vacuum schematic — 1983 3.8L V6 engine

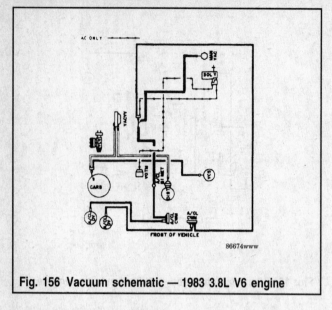

Fig. 156 Vacuum schematic — 1983 3.8L V6 engine

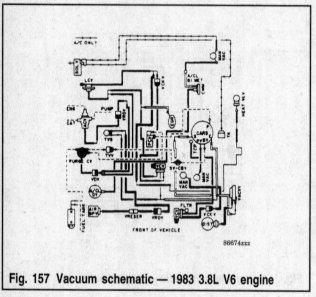

Fig. 157 Vacuum schematic — 1983 3.8L V6 engine

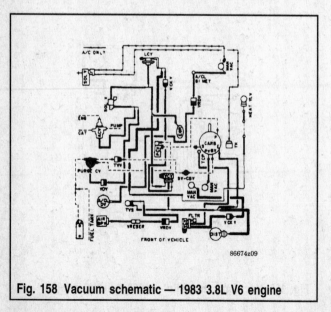

Fig. 158 Vacuum schematic — 1983 3.8L V6 engine

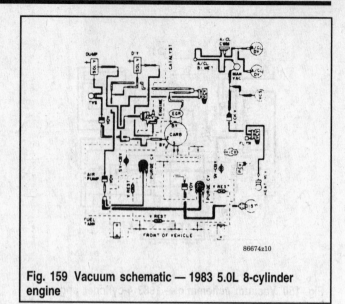

Fig. 159 Vacuum schematic — 1983 5.0L 8-cylinder engine

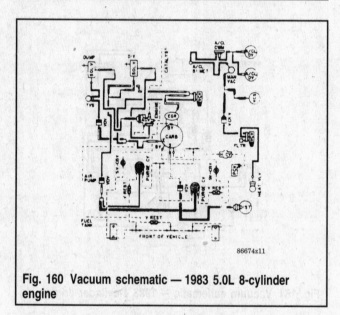

Fig. 160 Vacuum schematic — 1983 5.0L 8-cylinder engine

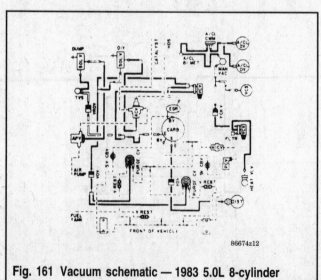

Fig. 161 Vacuum schematic — 1983 5.0L 8-cylinder engine

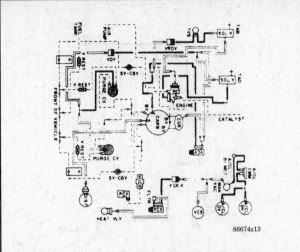

Fig. 162 Vacuum schematic — 1983 5.0L 8-cylinder engine

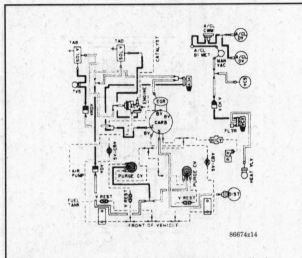

Fig. 163 Vacuum schematic — 1983 5.0L 8-cylinder engine

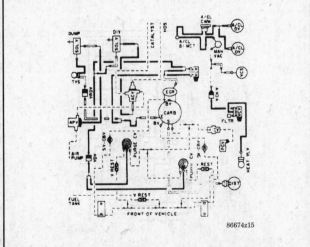

Fig. 164 Vacuum schematic — 1983 5.0L 8-cylinder engine

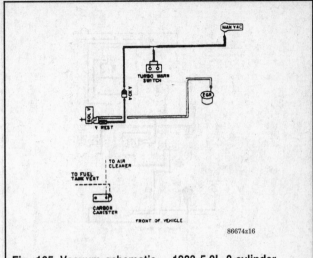

Fig. 165 Vacuum schematic — 1983 5.0L 8-cylinder engine

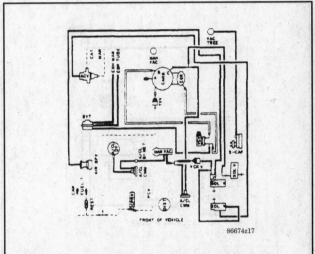

Fig. 166 Vacuum schematic — 1983 5.0L 8-cylinder engine

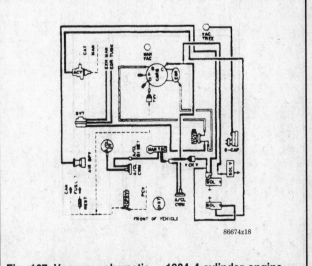

Fig. 167 Vacuum schematic — 1984 4-cylinder engine

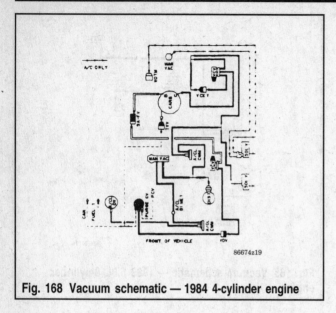

Fig. 168 Vacuum schematic — 1984 4-cylinder engine

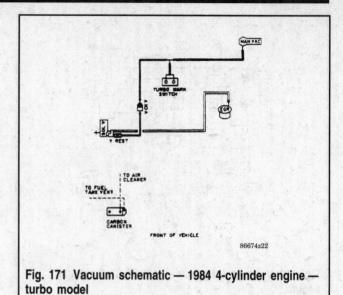

Fig. 171 Vacuum schematic — 1984 4-cylinder engine — turbo model

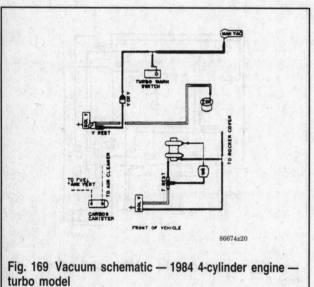

Fig. 169 Vacuum schematic — 1984 4-cylinder engine — turbo model

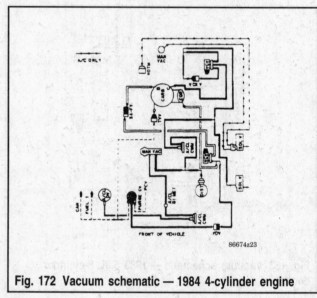

Fig. 172 Vacuum schematic — 1984 4-cylinder engine

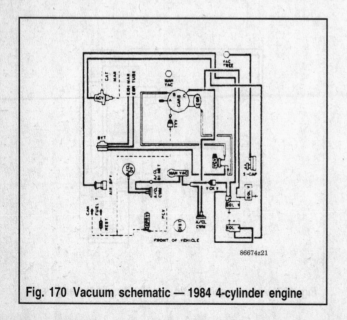

Fig. 170 Vacuum schematic — 1984 4-cylinder engine

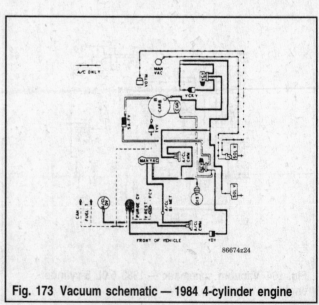

Fig. 173 Vacuum schematic — 1984 4-cylinder engine

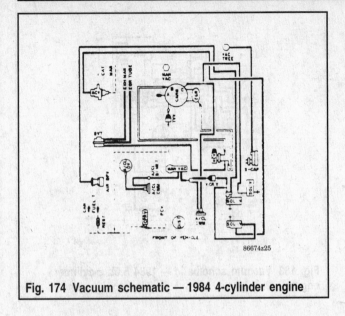

Fig. 174 Vacuum schematic — 1984 4-cylinder engine

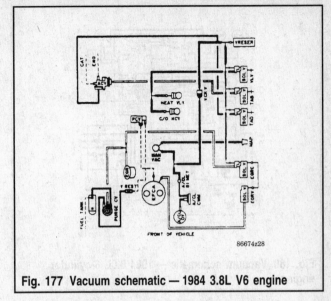

Fig. 177 Vacuum schematic — 1984 3.8L V6 engine

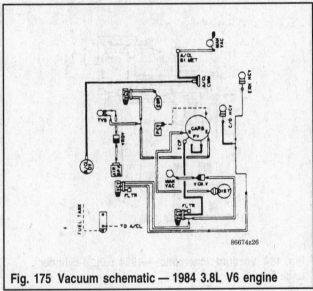

Fig. 175 Vacuum schematic — 1984 3.8L V6 engine

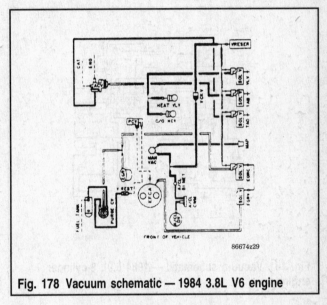

Fig. 178 Vacuum schematic — 1984 3.8L V6 engine

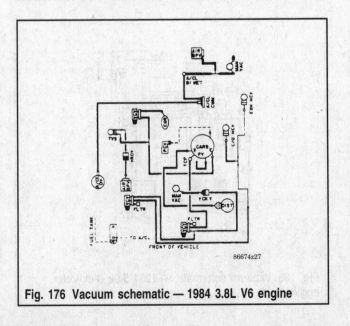

Fig. 176 Vacuum schematic — 1984 3.8L V6 engine

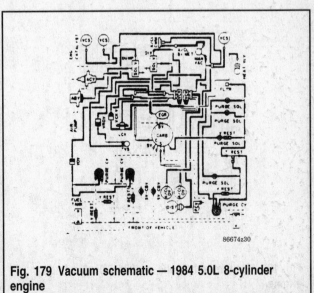

Fig. 179 Vacuum schematic — 1984 5.0L 8-cylinder engine

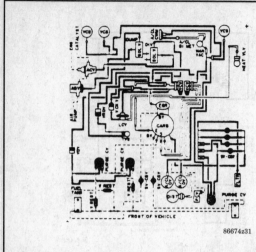

Fig. 180 Vacuum schematic — 1984 5.0L 8-cylinder engine

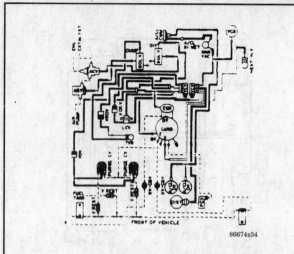

Fig. 183 Vacuum schematic — 1984 5.0L 8-cylinder engine

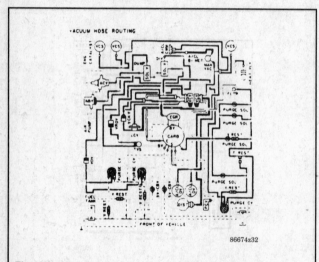

Fig. 181 Vacuum schematic — 1984 5.0L 8-cylinder engine

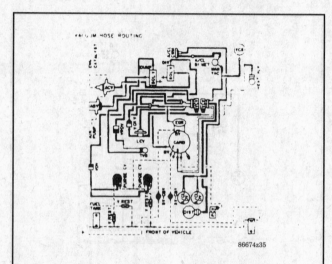

Fig. 184 Vacuum schematic — 1984 5.0L 8-cylinder engine

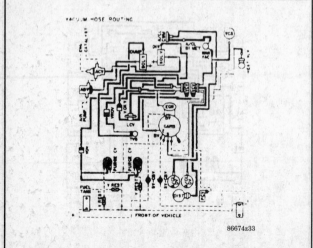

Fig. 182 Vacuum schematic — 1984 5.0L 8-cylinder engine

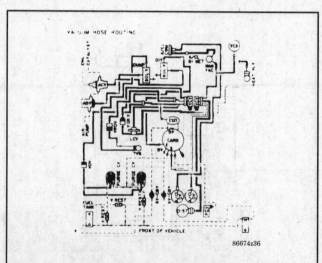

Fig. 185 Vacuum schematic — 1984 5.0L 8-cylinder engine

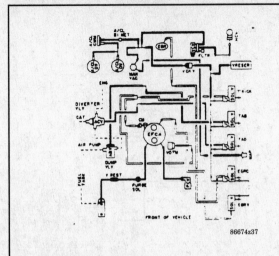

Fig. 186 Vacuum schematic — 1984 5.0L 8-cylinder engine

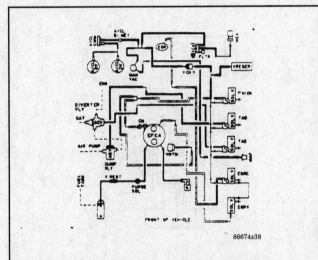

Fig. 187 Vacuum schematic — 1984 5.0L 8-cylinder engine

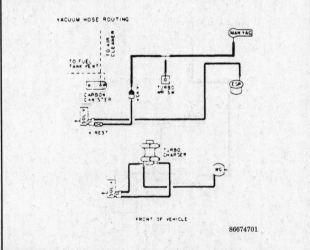

Fig. 188 Vacuum schematic — 1985 4-cylinder engine with turbo

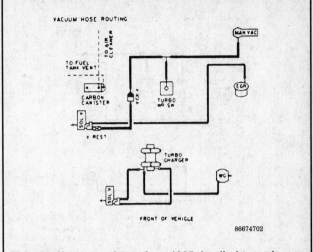

Fig. 189 Vacuum schematic — 1985 4-cylinder engine with turbo

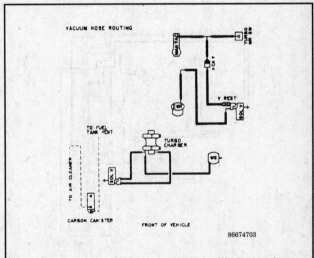

Fig. 190 Vacuum schematic — 1985 4-cylinder engine with turbo

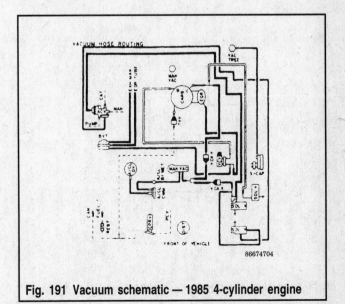

Fig. 191 Vacuum schematic — 1985 4-cylinder engine

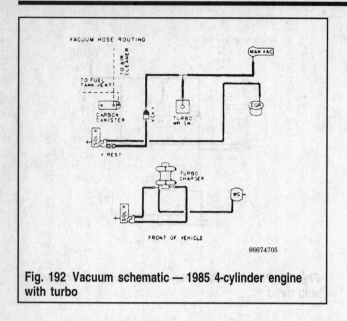

Fig. 192 Vacuum schematic — 1985 4-cylinder engine with turbo

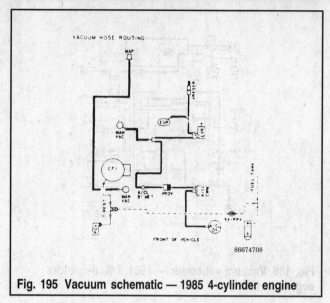

Fig. 195 Vacuum schematic — 1985 4-cylinder engine

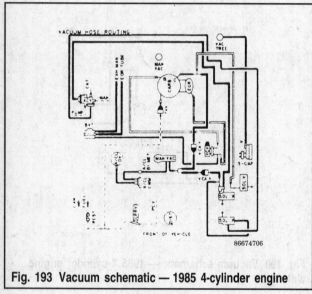

Fig. 193 Vacuum schematic — 1985 4-cylinder engine

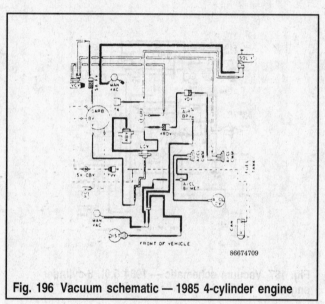

Fig. 196 Vacuum schematic — 1985 4-cylinder engine

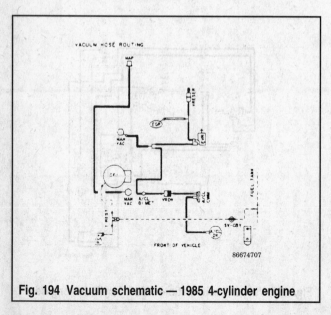

Fig. 194 Vacuum schematic — 1985 4-cylinder engine

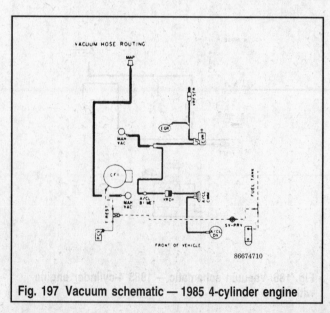

Fig. 197 Vacuum schematic — 1985 4-cylinder engine

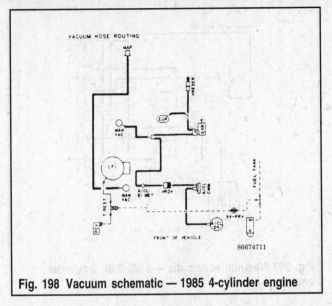

Fig. 198 Vacuum schematic — 1985 4-cylinder engine

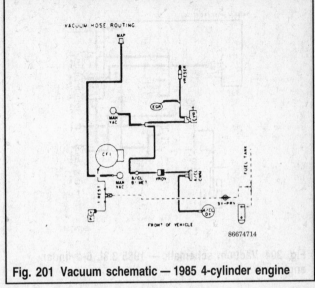

Fig. 201 Vacuum schematic — 1985 4-cylinder engine

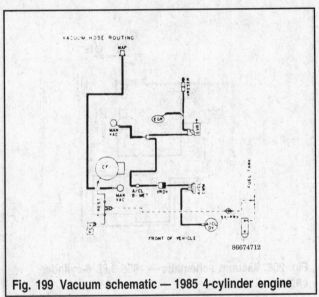

Fig. 199 Vacuum schematic — 1985 4-cylinder engine

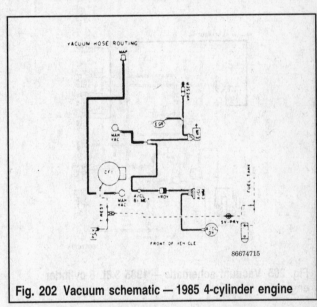

Fig. 202 Vacuum schematic — 1985 4-cylinder engine

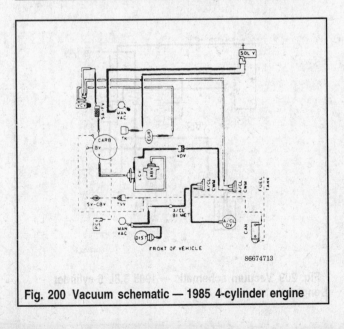

Fig. 200 Vacuum schematic — 1985 4-cylinder engine

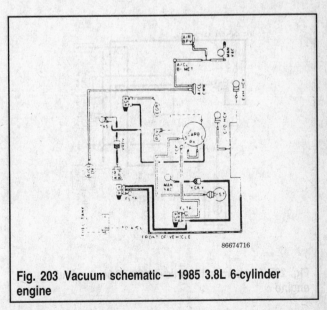

Fig. 203 Vacuum schematic — 1985 3.8L 6-cylinder engine

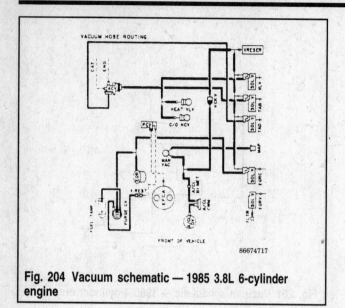

Fig. 204 Vacuum schematic — 1985 3.8L 6-cylinder engine

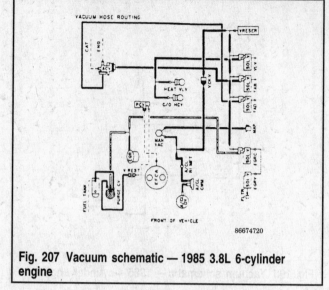

Fig. 207 Vacuum schematic — 1985 3.8L 6-cylinder engine

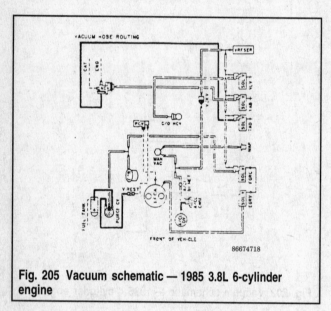

Fig. 205 Vacuum schematic — 1985 3.8L 6-cylinder engine

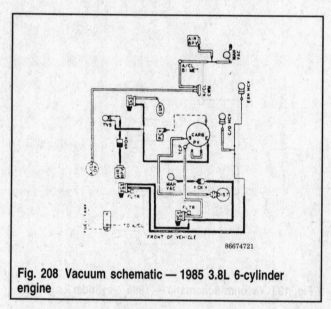

Fig. 208 Vacuum schematic — 1985 3.8L 6-cylinder engine

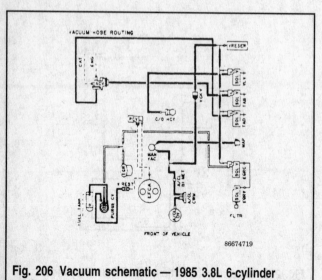

Fig. 206 Vacuum schematic — 1985 3.8L 6-cylinder engine

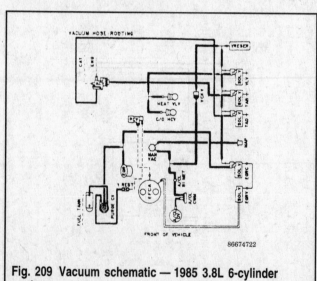

Fig. 209 Vacuum schematic — 1985 3.8L 6-cylinder engine

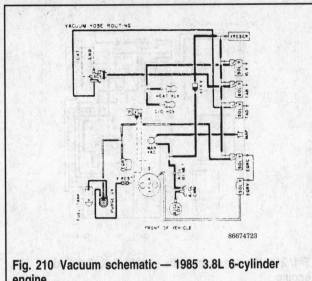

Fig. 210 Vacuum schematic — 1985 3.8L 6-cylinder engine

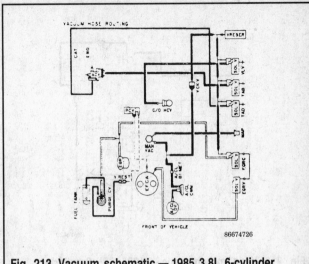

Fig. 213 Vacuum schematic — 1985 3.8L 6-cylinder engine

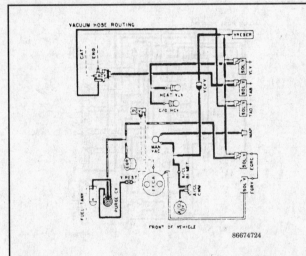

Fig. 211 Vacuum schematic — 1985 3.8L 6-cylinder engine

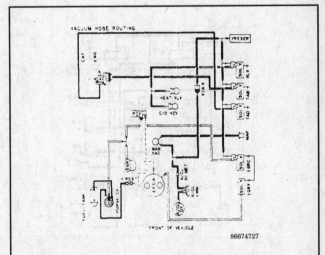

Fig. 214 Vacuum schematic — 1985 3.8L 6-cylinder engine

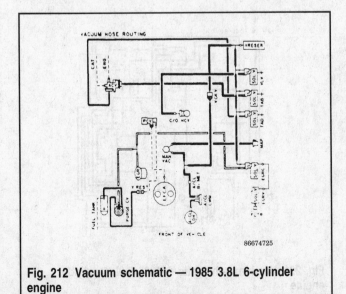

Fig. 212 Vacuum schematic — 1985 3.8L 6-cylinder engine

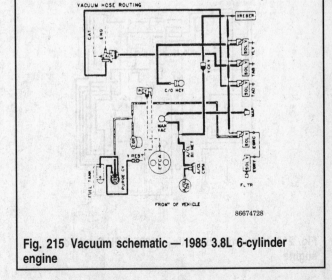

Fig. 215 Vacuum schematic — 1985 3.8L 6-cylinder engine

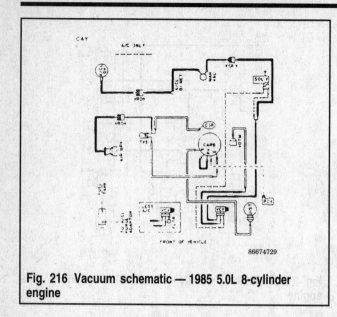

Fig. 216 Vacuum schematic — 1985 5.0L 8-cylinder engine

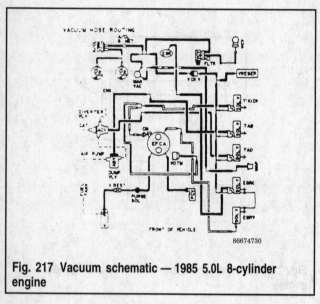

Fig. 217 Vacuum schematic — 1985 5.0L 8-cylinder engine

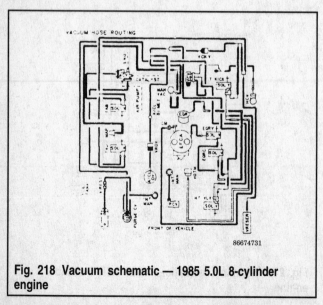

Fig. 218 Vacuum schematic — 1985 5.0L 8-cylinder engine

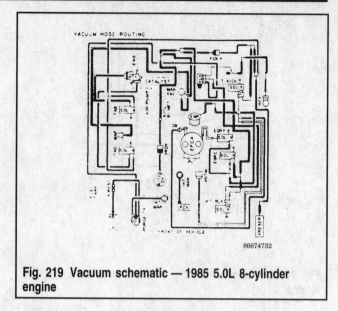

Fig. 219 Vacuum schematic — 1985 5.0L 8-cylinder engine

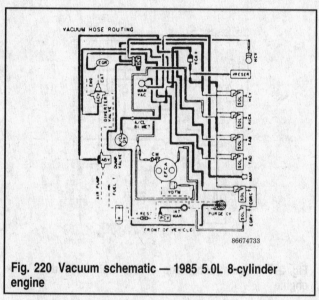

Fig. 220 Vacuum schematic — 1985 5.0L 8-cylinder engine

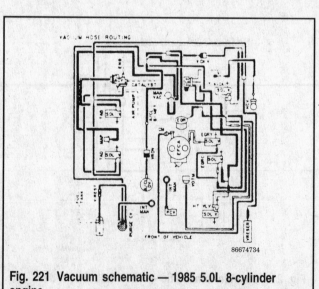

Fig. 221 Vacuum schematic — 1985 5.0L 8-cylinder engine

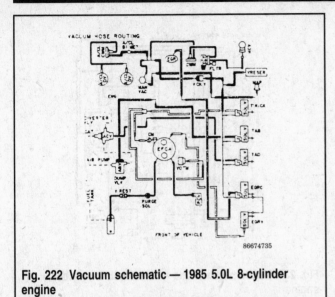

Fig. 222 Vacuum schematic — 1985 5.0L 8-cylinder engine

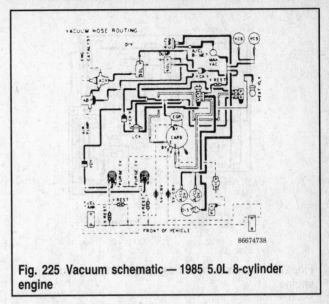

Fig. 225 Vacuum schematic — 1985 5.0L 8-cylinder engine

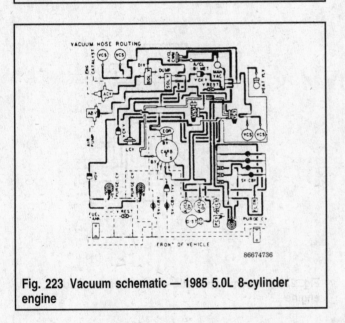

Fig. 223 Vacuum schematic — 1985 5.0L 8-cylinder engine

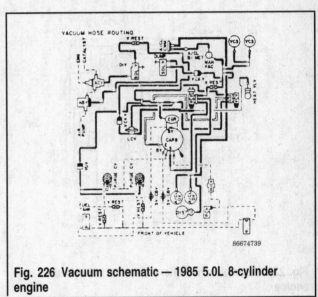

Fig. 226 Vacuum schematic — 1985 5.0L 8-cylinder engine

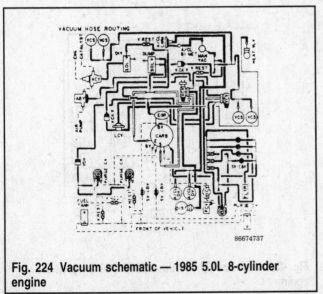

Fig. 224 Vacuum schematic — 1985 5.0L 8-cylinder engine

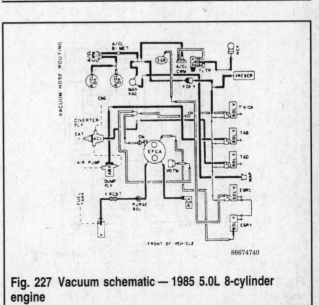

Fig. 227 Vacuum schematic — 1985 5.0L 8-cylinder engine

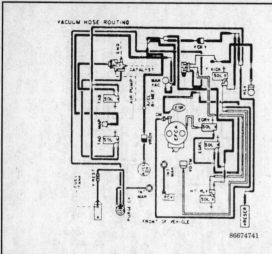

Fig. 228 Vacuum schematic — 1985 5.0L 8-cylinder engine

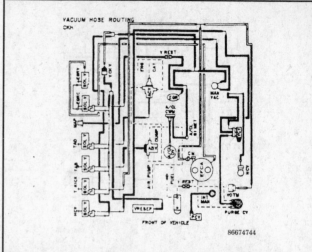

Fig. 231 Vacuum schematic — 1985 5.0L 8-cylinder engine

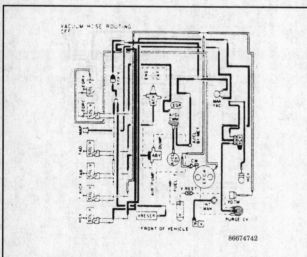

Fig. 229 Vacuum schematic — 1985 5.0L 8-cylinder engine

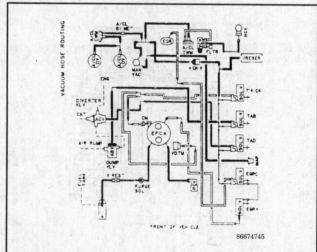

Fig. 232 Vacuum schematic — 1985 5.0L 8-cylinder engine

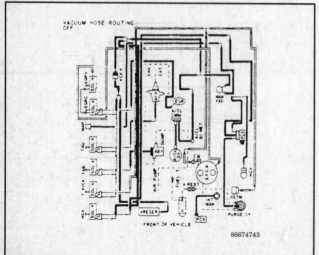

Fig. 230 Vacuum schematic — 1985 5.0L 8-cylinder engine

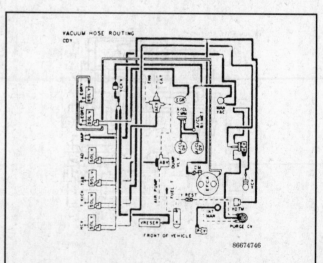

Fig. 233 Vacuum schematic — 1985 5.0L 8-cylinder engine

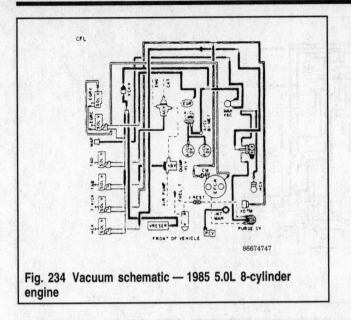

Fig. 234 Vacuum schematic — 1985 5.0L 8-cylinder engine

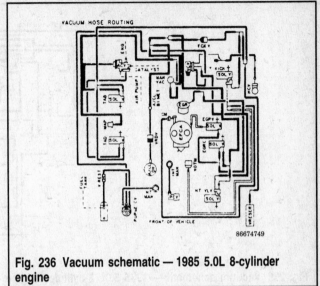

Fig. 236 Vacuum schematic — 1985 5.0L 8-cylinder engine

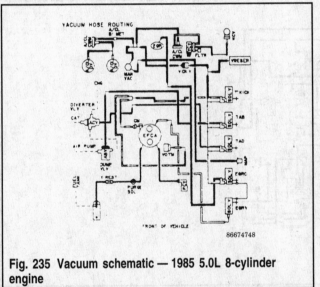

Fig. 235 Vacuum schematic — 1985 5.0L 8-cylinder engine

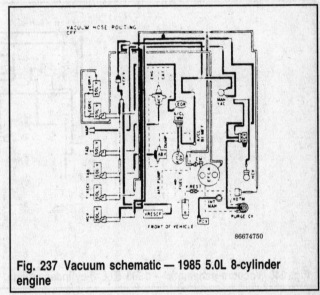

Fig. 237 Vacuum schematic — 1985 5.0L 8-cylinder engine

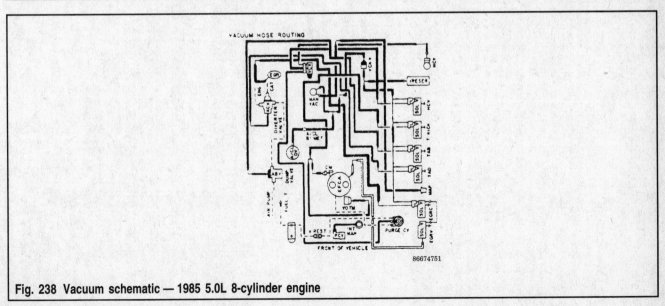

Fig. 238 Vacuum schematic — 1985 5.0L 8-cylinder engine

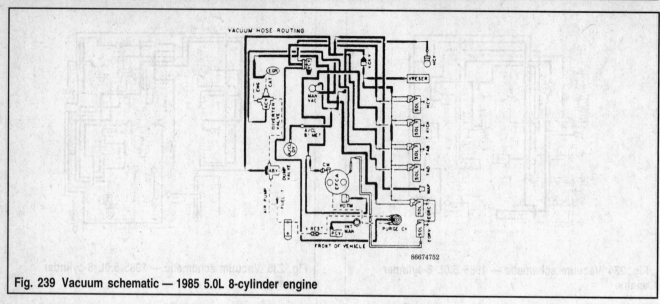

Fig. 239 Vacuum schematic — 1985 5.0L 8-cylinder engine

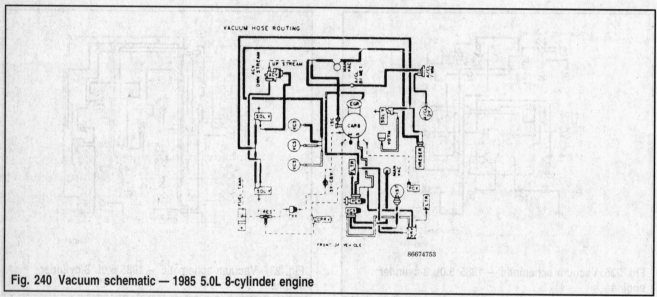

Fig. 240 Vacuum schematic — 1985 5.0L 8-cylinder engine

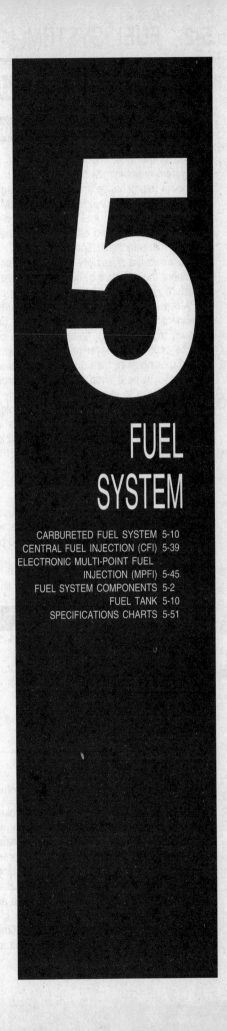

5

FUEL SYSTEM

FUEL SYSTEM COMPONENTS

Fuel System Service Precautions

Safety is the most important factor when performing not only fuel system maintenance but any type of maintenance. Failure to conduct maintenance and repairs in a safe manner may result in serious personal injury or death. Maintenance and testing of the vehicle's fuel system components can be accomplished safely and effectively by adhering to the following rules and guidelines.

• To avoid the possibility of fire and personal injury, always disconnect the negative battery cable unless the repair or test procedure requires that battery voltage be applied.

• Always relieve the fuel system pressure prior to disconnecting any fuel system component (injector, fuel rail, pressure regulator, etc.), fitting or fuel line connection. Exercise extreme caution whenever relieving fuel system pressure to avoid exposing skin, face and eyes to fuel spray.

• Always place a shop towel or cloth around the fitting or connection prior to loosening to absorb any excess fuel due to spillage. Ensure that all fuel spillage (should it occur) is quickly removed from engine surfaces. Ensure that all fuel soaked cloths or towels are deposited into a suitable waste container.

• Always keep a dry chemical (Class B) fire extinguisher near the work area.

• Do not allow fuel spray or fuel vapors to come into contact with a spark or open flame.

• Always use a backup wrench when loosening and tightening fuel line connection fittings. This will prevent unnecessary stress and torsion to fuel line piping. Always follow the proper tighten specifications.

• Always replace fuel fitting O-rings with new ones. Do not substitute fuel hose or equivalent where fuel pipe is installed.

Mechanical Fuel Pump

▶ See Figures 1 and 2

A single action mechanical fuel pump, driven by the camshaft, is used on all carbureted models except some 7.0L and 7.5L engines.

TESTING

▶ See Figure 3

➡No adjustments may be made to the fuel pump.

Incorrect fuel pump pressure and low volume (flow rate) are the two most likely fuel pump troubles that will affect engine performance. Low pressure will cause a lean mixture and fuel starvation at high speeds and excessive pressure will cause high fuel consumption and carburetor flooding.

To determine that the fuel pump is in satisfactory operating condition, test for both fuel pump pressure and fuel volume should be performed.

The tests are performed with the fuel pump installed and the engine idling at normal operating temperature.

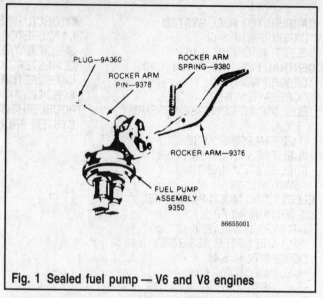

Fig. 1 Sealed fuel pump — V6 and V8 engines

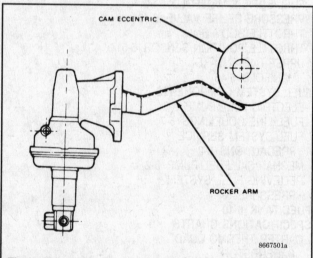

Fig. 2 The rocker arm on the fuel pump is driven by the camshaft

Before testing, make sure that the replaceable fuel filter has been changed at the proper mileage interval. If in doubt, install a new filter.

Pressure Test

1. Remove the air cleaner assembly.
2. Disconnect the fuel inlet line of the fuel filter at the carburetor. Place an absorbent cloth under the connection before removing the line to catch any fuel that might flow out of the line.
3. Connect a pressure gauge, a restrictor and a flexible hose between the fuel filter and the carburetor.
4. Position the flexible hose and the restrictor so that the fuel can be discharged into a suitable graduated container.
5. Before taking a pressure reading, operate the engine at idle and vent the system into the container by opening the hose restrictor momentarily.

6. Close the hose restrictor, allowing the pressure to stabilize and note the reading. The pressure should be 5 psi (34 kPa).

If the pump pressure is not 4-6 psi (27-41 kPa) and the fuel lines and filter are in satisfactory condition, the pump is defective and should be replaced.

If the pump pressure is within the proper range, perform the test for fuel volume.

Volume Test

1. Operate the engine at specified idle.
2. Open the hose restrictor and catch the fuel in the container while observing the time it takes to pump out 1 pint. It should take about 20 seconds. If not, check for proper fuel tank venting or a restriction in the fuel line leading from the fuel tank to the carburetor before replacing the fuel pump.

REMOVAL & INSTALLATION

◆ **See Figures 4, 5 and 6**

1. Disconnect the negative battery cable.
2. Loosen but do not remove the threaded fuel line connection(s) with a flare wrench.
3. Loosen the fuel pump mounting bolts 1-2 turns. If the fuel pump does not come loose from its mounting, the gasket is probably stuck; apply force with your hands to loosen the pump.
4. Rotate the crankshaft until the fuel pump eccentric is near its low position, reducing the tension on the fuel pump rocker arm. It should now be easier to remove and install the fuel pump.
5. Disconnect the fuel pump inlet, outlet and fuel vapor return line, if equipped.

❋❋CAUTION

The outlet line is pressurized. Wrap a rag around the line, release pressure slowly to contain spillage. Observe no smoking/no open flame precautions. Have a class B-C (dry powder) fire extinguisher within arm's reach at all times.

6. Remove the fuel pump mounting bolts and remove the fuel pump. Discard the old gasket.

To install:

➡**Prior to installation, check the rubber fuel lines and make sure they are not cracked, hardened or frayed. If replacement is necessary, use only rubber hose made for fuel line use.**

7. Clean all old gasket material from the pump mounting surface on the engine and from the fuel pump, if it is to be reused.
8. Apply a coat of oil resistant sealer to a new gasket.
9. Install the mounting bolts into the fuel pump and positioned the gasket. Install the pump on the engine. Turn the mounting bolts alternately and evenly tightening to 19-27 ft. lbs. (26-37 Nm).
10. Connect the fuel pump outlet line. If it is a threaded connection, start the fitting by hand to avoid crossthreading. Tighten the fitting to 15-18 ft. lbs. (20-24 Nm).
11. Connect the inlet line and fuel vapor return line, if equipped. Tighten the hose clamp(s).
12. Connect the negative battery cable, start the engine and check for leaks.
13. Stop the engine and check all fuel line connections for leaks. Check the fuel pump mounting pad for oil leaks.

Electric Fuel Pump

◆ **See Figure 7**

Two different electric fuel pump configurations were used on fuel injected models. One consists of a low pressure in-tank boost pump in conjunction with an external, frame-mounted high pressure pump. The low pressure pump is used to provide pressurized fuel to the inlet of the high pressure pump and helps prevent noise and heating problems. System pressure is controlled by a pressure regulator mounted on the engine.

The other configuration consists of an in-tank high pressure pump which does not utilize a boost pump.

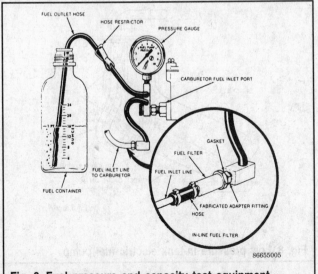

Fig. 3 Fuel pressure and capacity test equipment

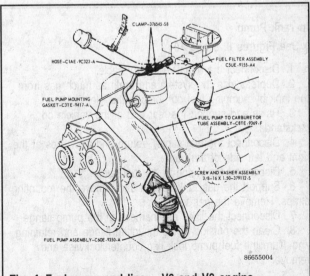

Fig. 4 Fuel pump and line — V6 and V8 engine

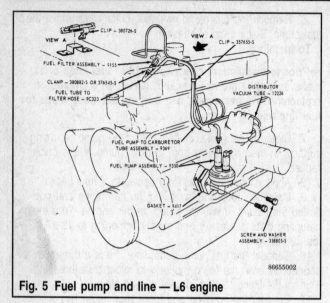

Fig. 5 Fuel pump and line — L6 engine

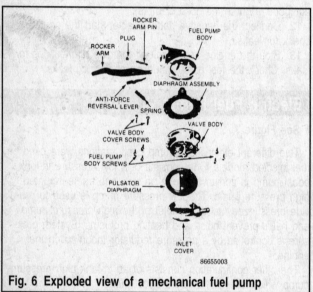

Fig. 6 Exploded view of a mechanical fuel pump

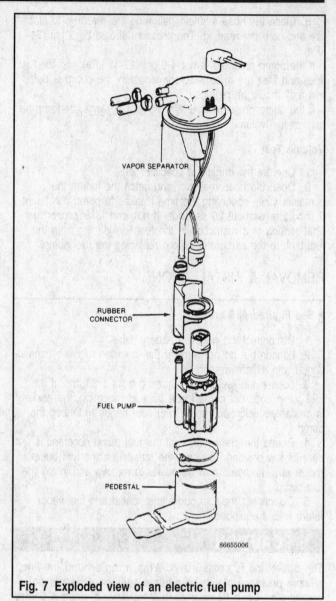

Fig. 7 Exploded view of an electric fuel pump

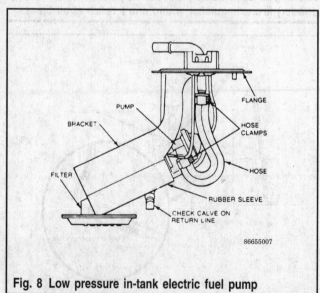

Fig. 8 Low pressure in-tank electric fuel pump

REMOVAL & INSTALLATION

In-Tank Pump

▶ **See Figures 8, 9 and 10**

1. Disconnect the negative battery cable.
2. Depressurize the system and drain as much gas from the tank by pumping fuel out through the filler neck.
3. Raise and support the rear end of the vehicle on jackstands.
4. Disconnect the fuel supply, return and vent lines at the right and left side of the frame.
5. Disconnect the wiring to the fuel pump.
6. Support the gas tank, loosen and remove the mounting straps. Remove the gas tank.
7. Disconnect the lines and harness at the pump flange.
8. Clean the outside of the mounting flange and retaining ring. Turn the fuel pump lock ring counterclockwise and remove.

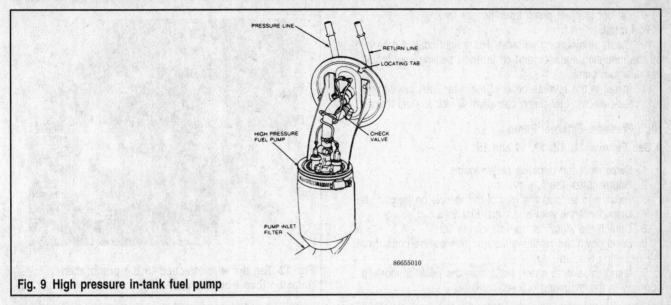

Fig. 9 High pressure in-tank fuel pump

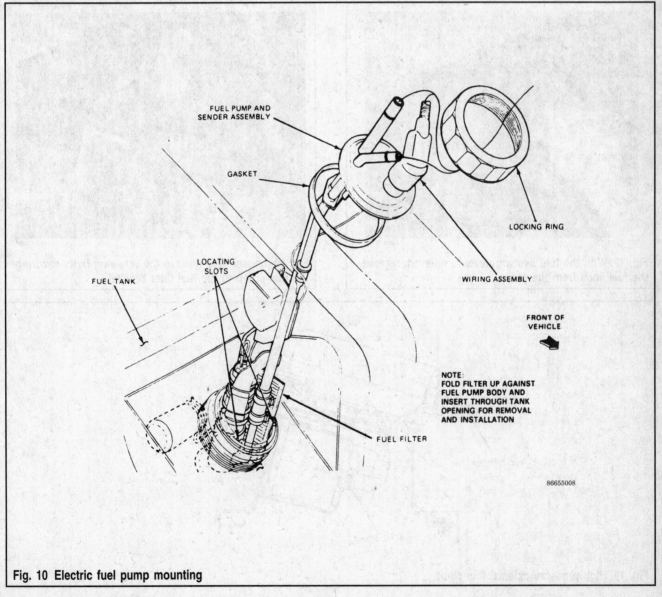

Fig. 10 Electric fuel pump mounting

9. Lift out the fuel pump from the gas tank.

To install:

10. Clean all mounting surfaces. Put a light coat of grease on the mounting surfaces and on the new sealing ring. Install the new fuel pump.

11. Install in the reverse order of removal. Start the vehicle and check electric fuel pump operation. Check for fuel leaks.

High Pressure External Pump

▶ **See Figures 11, 12, 13, 14 and 15**

1. Disconnect the negative battery cable.
2. Depressurize the fuel system.
3. Raise and support the rear of the vehicle on jackstands.
4. Disconnect the inlet and outlet fuel lines.
5. Detach the electrical harness connection.
6. Bend down the retaining tab and remove the pump from the mounting bracket ring.
7. Install in reverse order. Make sure the pump is indexed correctly in the mounting bracket insulator.

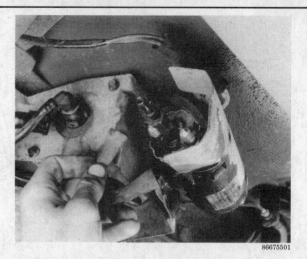

Fig. 13 Tag the wire attached to the pump, then unfasten then from the unit

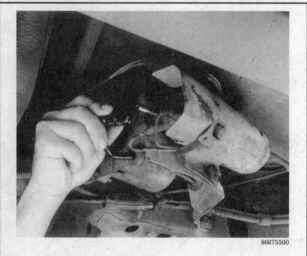

Fig. 12 With the fuel system pressure relieved, remove the fuel lines from the pump

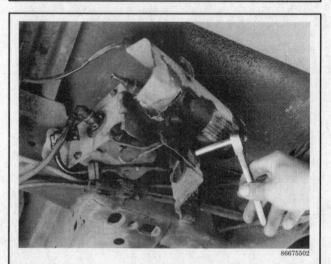

Fig. 14 Loosen and remove the retaining bolts securing the fuel pump to the fuel filter bracket

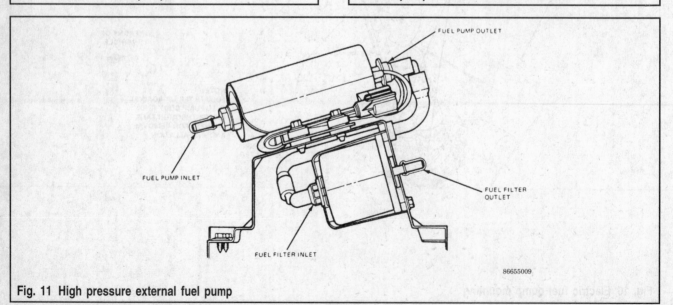

Fig. 11 High pressure external fuel pump

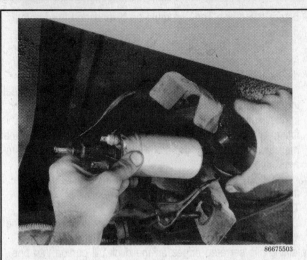

86675503

Fig. 15 Remove the fuel pump from the rubber sleeve and bracket

8. Start the vehicle and check electric fuel pump operation. Check for fuel leaks.

Relieving Fuel System Pressure

❈❈CAUTION

Fuel supply lines on fuel injected vehicles will remain pressurized for some time after the engine is shut off. Fuel pressure must be relieved before servicing the fuel system.

As a safety feature, all electronic fuel injected engines are equipped with a pressure relief valve. On the 4-cylinder engine with Multi Port Fuel Injection (MPFI), this valve is located in the flexible fuel supply tube approximately 12 in. (30cm) back from where it connects to the engine fuel rail, on the driver's side of the engine compartment. On V8 equipped engines with MPFI, the valve is located in the metal fuel line at the left front corner of the engine.

Before opening the fuel system on a fuel injected vehicle, relieve the fuel pressure as follows:

1. Disconnect the negative battery cable.
2. Remove the fuel tank cap to relieve the pressure in the fuel tank.
3. Remove the cap from the Schrader valve located on the fuel supply manifold.
4. Attach fuel pressure gauge T80L-9974-A or equivalent, to the Schrader valve and drain fuel through the drain tube into a suitable container.
5. After the fuel system pressure is relieved, remove the fuel pressure gauge and install the cap on the Schrader valve.

Fuel Line Couplings

REMOVAL & INSTALLATION

There are 3 types of fuel line couplings used on fuel injected models. Each requires a different procedure to disconnect and connect.

Hairpin Clip Push Connect Fitting
▶ See Figure 16

1. Inspect the visible portion of the fitting for dirt accumulation. If more than a light coating of dust is present, clean the fitting before disassembly.
2. Some adhesion between the seals in the fitting and the tubing will occur with time. To separate, twist the fitting on the tube, then push and pull the fitting until it moves freely on the tube.
3. Remove the hairpin clip from the fitting by first bending and breaking the shipping tab. Next, spread the 2 clip legs by hand about 1/8 in. (3mm) each to disengage the body and push the legs into the fitting. Lightly pull the triangular end of the clip and work it clear of the tube and fitting.

➡ Do not use hand tools to complete this operation.

4. Grasp the fitting and pull apart to remove the fitting from the tube.

❈❈WARNING

Be careful on 90° elbow connectors, as excessive side loading could break the connector body.

5. After disassembly, inspect and clean the tube end sealing surfaces. The tube end should be free of scratches and corrosion that could cause leaks. Inspect the inside of the fitting for any internal parts such as O-rings and spacers that may have been dislodged from the fitting. Replace any damaged connectors.

To connect:

6. Install a new connector if damage was found. Insert a new clip into any 2 adjacent openings with the triangular portion pointing away from the fitting opening. Install the clip until the legs of the clip are locked on the outside of the body. Piloting with an index finger is necessary.
7. Before installing the fitting on the tube, wipe the tube end with a clean cloth. Inspect the inside of the fitting to make sure it is free of dirt and/or obstructions.
8. Apply a light coating of engine oil to the tube end. Align the fitting and tube axially, then push the fitting onto the tube end. When the fitting is engaged, a definite click will be heard. Pull on the fitting to make sure it is fully engaged.

Duck Bill Clip or Steel Push Connect Fitting
▶ **See Figures 17, 18 and 19**

This fitting consists of a body, spacers, O-rings and a retaining clip. The retaining clip is referred to as a "duck bill" on these vehicles.

1. Inspect the visible internal portion of the fitting for dirt accumulation. If more than a light coating of dust is present, clean the fitting before disassembly.

2. Some adhesion between the seals in the fitting and the tubing will occur with time. To separate, twist the fitting on the tube, then push and pull the fitting until it moves freely on the tube.

3. Align the slot on the disassembly tool (T82L-9500-AH or equivalent), with either tab on the clip, 90°s from the slots on the side of the fitting and insert the tool. This disengages the duck bill retainer from the tube. Holding the tool and the tube with one hand, pull the fitting away from the tube.

4. Install disassembly tool T90T-9550-B (size 5/16 in.) or T90T-9550-C (size 3/8 in.) or equivalent, with either tab on the fuel line to be disconnected. Push the tool into the connector to release the internal locking fingers. Separate the fuel line from the connector and remove the tool.

➡**Use hands only. Only moderate effort is required if the tube has been properly disengaged.**

5. After disassembly, inspect and clean the tube end sealing surfaces. The tube end should be free of scratches and corrosion that could provide leak paths. Inspect the inside of the fitting for any internal parts such as O-rings and spacers that may have been dislodged from the fitting. Replace any damaged connectors.

6. Some fuel tubes have a secondary bead which aligns with the outer surface of the clip. These beads can make tool insertion difficult. If there is extreme difficulty, use the following disassembly method:

a. Using pliers with a jaw width of 0.2 in. (5mm) or less, align the jaws with the openings in the side of the fitting case and compress the portion of the retaining clip that engages the fitting case. This disengages the retaining clip from the case. Often, one side of the clip will disengage

before the other. The clip must be disengaged from both openings.

b. Pull the fitting off the tube by hand only. Only moderate effort is required if the retaining clip has been properly disengaged.

c. After disassembly, inspect and clean the tube end sealing surfaces. The tube end should be free of scratches and corrosion that could cause leaks. Inspect the inside of the fitting for any internal parts such as O-rings and spacers that may have been dislodged from the fitting. Replace any damaged connector.

d. The retaining clip will remain on the tube. Disengage the clip from the tube bead and remove.

To connect:

7. Install a new connector if damage was found. Install the new replacement clip into the body by inserting one of the retaining clip serrated edges on the duck bill portion into one side of the window openings. Push on the other side until the clip snaps into place.

8. Before installing the fitting on the tube, wipe the tube end with a clean cloth. Inspect the inside of the fitting to make sure it is free of dirt and/or obstructions.

9. Apply a light coating of engine oil to the tube end. Align the fitting and tube axially and push the fitting onto the tube end. When the fitting is engaged, a definite click will be heard. Pull on the fitting to make sure it is fully engaged.

Spring Lock Coupling
▶ **See Figure 20**

The spring lock coupling is a fuel line coupling held together by a garter spring inside a circular cage. When the coupling is connected together, the flared end of the female fitting slips behind the garter spring inside the cage of the male fitting. The garter spring and cage then prevent the flared end of the female fitting from pulling out of the cage. As an additional locking feature, a horseshoe shaped retaining clip is incorporated which improves the retaining reliability of the spring lock coupling. Refer to the illustration for disconnecting and connecting the fuel lines.

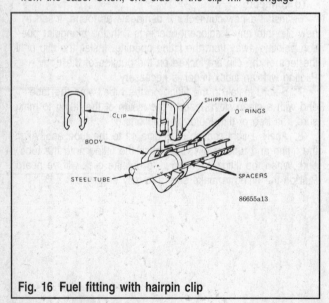

Fig. 16 Fuel fitting with hairpin clip

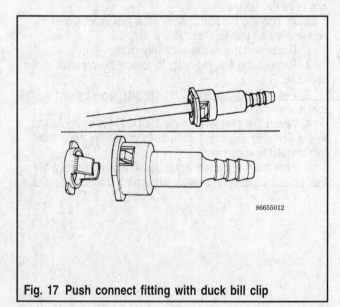

Fig. 17 Push connect fitting with duck bill clip

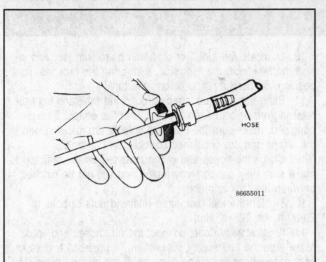

Fig. 18 Use a disassembly tool to remove the push connect fuel line

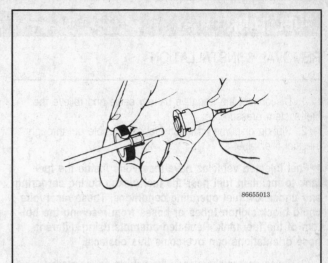

Fig. 19 With tool inserted into the fitting, the lines can be separated

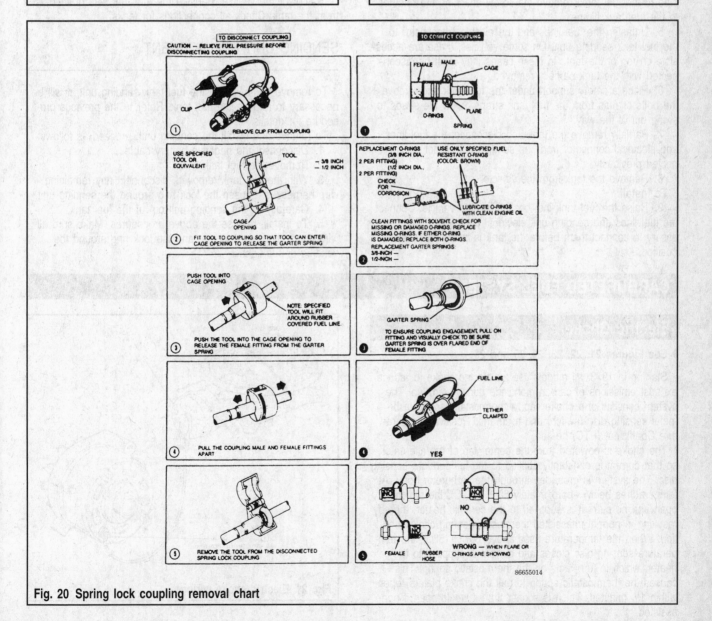

Fig. 20 Spring lock coupling removal chart

FUEL TANK

REMOVAL & INSTALLATION

1. Disconnect the negative battery cable and relieve the fuel system pressure.

2. Siphon or pump as much fuel as possible out through the fuel filler pipe.

➡Fuel injected vehicles have reservoirs inside the fuel tank to maintain fuel near the fuel pickup during cornering and under low fuel operating conditions. These reservoirs could block siphon tubes or hoses from reaching the bottom of the fuel tank. Repeated attempts using different hose orientations can overcome this obstacle.

3. Raise and safely support the vehicle on jackstands.

4. If equipped with a metal retainer that fastens the filler pipe to the fuel tank, remove the screw attaching the retainer to the fuel tank flange.

5. Unfasten the fuel lines and the electrical connector to the fuel tank sending unit. On some vehicles, these are accessible on top of the tank. In these cases they must be disconnected with the tank partially removed.

6. Place a safety support under the fuel tank and remove the bolts or nuts from the fuel tank straps. Allow the straps to swing out of the way.

7. Partially remove the tank and disconnect the fuel lines and electrical connector from the sending unit, if not disconnected previously.

8. Remove the tank from the vehicle.

To install:

9. Raise the fuel tank into position on the vehicle. Connect the fuel lines and sending unit electrical connector if it is necessary to connect them before the tank is in the final installed position.

10. Lubricate the fuel filler pipe with petroleum jelly and install the tank onto the filler pipe, then bring the tank into final position. Be careful not to deform the tank.

11. Bring the fuel tank straps around the tank and start the retaining nut or bolt. Align the tank with the straps. If equipped, make sure the fuel tank shields are installed with the straps and are positioned correctly on the tank.

12. Check the hoses and wiring mounted on the tank top to make sure they are correctly routed and will not be pinched between the tank and body.

13. Tighten the fuel tank strap retaining nuts or bolts to 20-30 ft. lbs. (28-40 Nm).

14. If not already done, connect the fuel hoses and lines. Make sure the fuel supply, fuel return, (if present,) and vapor vent connections are made correctly. If not already done, fasten the sending unit electrical connector.

15. Lower the vehicle. Replace the fuel that was drained from the tank. Check all connections for leaks.

SENDING UNIT REPLACEMENT

To remove and/or install the fuel tank sending unit, it will be necessary to remove the fuel tank. Refer to the previous procedure for details.

To remove and install the sending unit, proceed as follows:

1. Disconnect the negative battery cable.

2. Remove the fuel tank.

3. With the fuel tank removed, disconnect any remaining wire harnesses. Loosen the lock ring around the sending unit.

4. Carefully lift the sending unit out of the fuel tank.

5. To install, reverse the above procedures. Make sure all wire connections are secure, and the lock ring around the sending unit is tight.

CARBURETED FUEL SYSTEM

Electric Choke

▶ **See Figures 21, 22, 23, 24, 25 and 26**

Starting in 1973, all models use an electric choke to reduce exhaust emissions of carbon monoxide during warm-up. The system consists of a choke cap, a thermostatic spring, a bi-metal sensing disc (switch) and a ceramic Positive Temperature Coefficient (PTC) heater.

The choke is powered from the center tap of the alternator, so that current is constantly applied to the temperature sensing disc. The system is grounded through the carburetor body. At temperatures below approximately 60°F (15°C), the switch is open and no current is supplied to the ceramic heater, thereby resulting in normal unassisted thermostatic spring choking action. When the temperature rises above 60°F (15°C), the temperature sensing disc closes and current is supplied to the heater, which in turn, acts on the thermostatic spring. This causes the thermostatic spring to pull the choke plate(s) open within 1½ minutes, which is sooner than it would open if non-assisted.

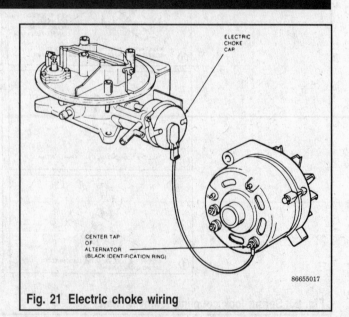

Fig. 21 Electric choke wiring

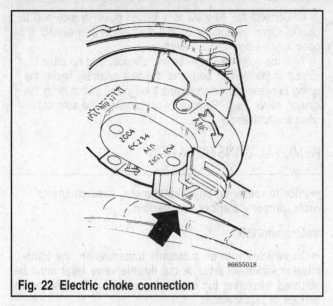

Fig. 22 Electric choke connection

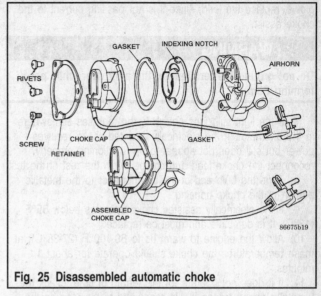

Fig. 25 Disassembled automatic choke

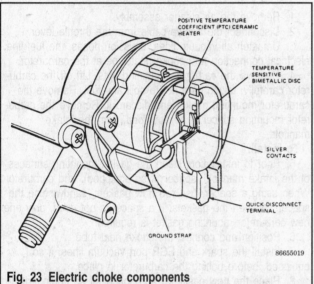

Fig. 23 Electric choke components

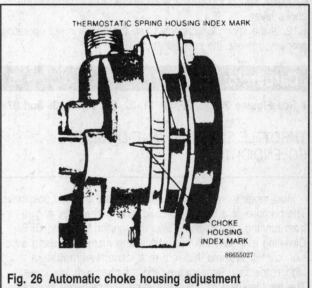

Fig. 26 Automatic choke housing adjustment

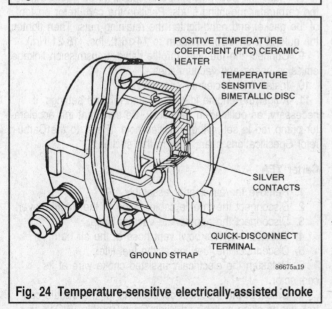

Fig. 24 Temperature-sensitive electrically-assisted choke

TESTING

1. Detach the electrical lead from the choke cap.

2. Use a jumper lead to connect the terminal on the choke cap and the wire terminal, so that the electrical circuit is still completed.

3. Start the engine.

4. Hook up a test light between the connector on the choke lead and ground.

5. The test light should glow. If it does not, current is not being supplied to the electrically assisted choke.

6. Connect the test light between the terminal on the alternator and the terminal on the choke cap. If the light now

glows, replace the lead, since it is not passing current to the choke assist.

7. If the light still does not glow, the fault lies somewhere in the alternator. If the electrically assisted choke receives power but still does not appear to be functioning properly, reconnect the choke lead and proceed with the rest of the test.

8. Tape the bulb end of the thermometer to the metallic portion of the choke housing.

9. If the electrically assisted choke operates below 55°F (13°C), it is defective and must be replaced.

10. Allow the engine to warm up to 80-100°F (27-38°C); at these temperatures the choke should operate for about 1½ minutes.

11. If it does not operate for this length of time, check the bimetallic spring to see if it is connected to the tang on the choke lever.

12. If the spring is connected and the choke is not operating properly, replace the cap assembly.

Carburetor

▶ **See Figures 27, 28, 29, 30, 31, 32, 33, 34, 35, 36 and 37**

THROTTLE SOLENOID (ANTI-DIESELING SOLENOID) TEST

Most models are equipped with a throttle solenoid positioner. The purpose of a throttle solenoid is to prevent the engine from running on (dieseling) after the ignition is turned **OFF**. Dieseling is a common occurrence with many cars using emission control systems that require a leaner fuel mixture, a higher operating temperature, and a higher curb idle speed. The throttle solenoid prevents run-on and dieseling by closing the throttle plate(s) after the key is switched to **OFF**, thereby shutting off the air and gas to the overheated combustion chamber.

1. Turn the ignition key **ON** and open the throttle. The solenoid plunger should extend (solenoid energize.)

2. Turn the ignition **OFF**. The plunger should retract, allowing the throttle to close.

➡**With the anti-dieseling solenoid de-energized, the carburetor idle speed adjusting screw must make contact with the throttle shaft to prevent the throttle plates from jamming in the throttle bore when the engine is turned OFF.**

3. If the solenoid is functioning properly and the engine is still dieseling, check for one of the following:
   a. High idle or engine shut off speed.
   b. Engine timing not set to specification.
   c. Binding throttle linkage.
   d. Too low an octane fuel being used.

4. Correct any of these problems as necessary.

5. If the solenoid fails to function as outlined, disconnect the solenoid leads. The solenoid should de-energize. If it does not, it is jammed and must be replaced.

6. Connect the solenoid to a 12 volt power source and to ground. Open the throttle so that the plunger can extend. If it does not, the solenoid is defective.

7. If the solenoid is functioning correctly and no other source of trouble can be found, the fault probably lies in the wiring between the solenoid and the ignition switch or in the ignition switch itself. Remember to reconnect the solenoid when finished testing.

REMOVAL & INSTALLATION

➡**Prior to removing any wire harness, vacuum line or cable, properly mark or tag the item.**

Motorcraft 2150

➡**On vehicles with an automatic transmission, the transmission kickdown lever or the throttle valve lever must be adjusted whenever the carburetor assembly is removed for service or replacement.**

1. Remove the air cleaner assembly.

2. Disconnect the throttle cable from the throttle lever.

3. Unfasten all vacuum lines, emission hoses, the fuel line, electrical connection and choke heat tube at the carburetor.

4. Remove the carburetor retaining nuts. Lift off the carburetor carefully, taking care not to spill any fuel. Remove the carburetor mounting gasket and discard it. Remove the carburetor mounting spacer, if so equipped, from the intake manifold.

To install:

5. Prior to installation, clean the gasket mounting surfaces of the intake manifold, spacer (if so equipped), and carburetor. When using a spacer, use two new gaskets, sandwiching the spacer between the gaskets. If a spacer is not used, only one new carburetor mounting gasket is required.

6. Position and connect the choke heat tube.

7. Install the spark and EGR port vacuum lines, if so equipped, before bolting the carburetor in place.

8. Place the new gasket(s) and spacer (if so equipped) on the carburetor mounting studs. Position the carburetor on top of the gasket and hand-tighten the retaining nuts. Then tighten the nuts in a crisscross pattern to 14-16 ft. lbs. (18-21 Nm).

9. Connect the fuel line, throttle cable, transmission linkage, emission hoses and vacuum lines.

10. Install the air cleaner assembly.

11. Adjust the engine idle speed and mixture settings, if necessary, as outlined in Section 2. Be sure that the accelerator pump rod is set in the specified hole. (Refer to the Carburetor Specifications chart, later in this section.)

Carter YFA

1. Remove the air cleaner assembly.

2. Disconnect the throttle cable or rod at the throttle lever.

3. Disconnect the appropriate vacuum lines.

4. Unfasten the fuel bowl vent hose at the air horn.

5. Disconnect the fuel line at the fuel filter.

6. Unfasten the electrically assisted choke wire at its connector.

7. Unfasten the electrical connections for the throttle control, idle tracking switch and Wide Open Throttle (WOT) air conditioning cut-off switch, if so equipped.

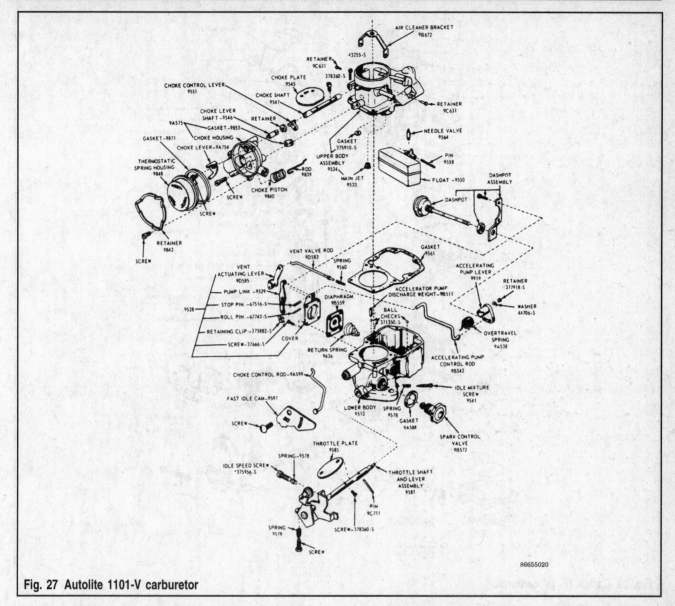

Fig. 27 Autolite 1101-V carburetor

8. On feedback model carburetors, disconnect the feedback solenoid, idle speed control motor and throttle position sensor wires.

9. Remove the carburetor retaining nuts. Lift off the carburetor carefully, taking care not to spill any fuel. Remove the carburetor mounting gasket and discard it. Remove the carburetor mounting spacer, if so equipped, from the intake manifold.

To install:

10. Prior to installation, clean the gasket mounting surfaces of the intake manifold, spacer (if so equipped), and carburetor. When using a spacer, use two new gaskets, sandwiching the spacer between the gaskets. If a spacer is not used, only one new carburetor mounting gasket is required.

11. Place the new gasket(s) and spacer (if so equipped) on the carburetor mounting studs. Position the carburetor on top of the gasket and hand-tighten the retaining nuts. Then tighten the nuts in a crisscross pattern to 12-15 ft. lbs. (16-19 Nm).

12. Connect the fuel line, throttle cable or rod, and the appropriate vacuum lines.

13. Connect the fuel bowl vent hose to the air horn.

14. Fasten the electrical connections for the throttle control, idle tracking switch and WOT air conditioning cut-off switch, if so equipped.

15. Connect the electrically assisted choke wire. On feedback model carburetors, connect the feedback solenoid, idle speed control motor and throttle position sensor wires.

16. Install the air cleaner assembly.

17. Check and adjust the engine idle speed settings, as outlined in Section 2.

Holley 5200 or 6500

1. Remove the air cleaner assembly.

2. Disconnect the throttle cable from the throttle lever.

3. Disconnect the canister bowl vent tube, bowl vent tube, vacuum throttle kicker tube (if so equipped), and feedback tube (model 6500 only).

4. Disconnect the distributor vacuum tube, Thermactor® dump valve vacuum tube, EGR vacuum tube and external choke pulldown vacuum tube (if so equipped).

5. Disconnect the fuel inlet line.

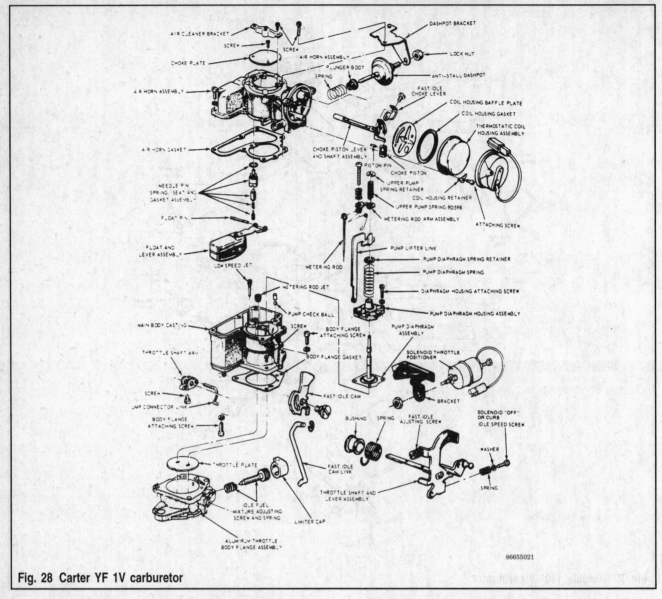

Fig. 28 Carter YF 1V carburetor

86655021

6. Unfasten the electric choke cap, bowl vent switch connector, throttle solenoid connector (if so equipped) and idle tracking switch connector.

7. Remove the carburetor retaining nuts. Lift off the carburetor carefully, taking care not to spill any fuel. Remove the carburetor mounting gasket and discard it. Remove the carburetor mounting spacer, if so equipped, from the intake manifold.

To install:

8. Prior to installation, clean the gasket mounting surfaces of the intake manifold, spacer (if so equipped), and carburetor. When using a spacer, use two new gaskets, sandwiching the spacer between the gaskets. If a spacer is not used, only one new carburetor mounting gasket is required.

9. Place the new gasket(s) and spacer (if so equipped) on the carburetor mounting studs. Position the carburetor on top of the gasket and hand-tighten the retaining nuts. Then tighten the nuts in a crisscross pattern to 10-14 ft. lbs. (13-18 Nm).

10. Connect the electric choke, bowl vent switch, throttle solenoid (if so equipped) and idle tracking switch.

11. Connect the canister bowl vent tube, bowl vent tube, vacuum throttle kicker tube (if so equipped), and feedback tube (model 6500 only).

12. Connect the distributor vacuum tube, Thermactor® dump valve vacuum tube, EGR vacuum tube and external choke pulldown vacuum tube (if so equipped).

13. Connect the fuel inlet line.

14. Connect the throttle cable at the throttle lever.

15. Install the air cleaner assembly.

16. Adjust the curb idle and fast idle speed settings, if necessary, as outlined in Section 2.

Holley 1946

1. Remove the air cleaner assembly.

2. Disconnect the throttle cable from the throttle lever.

3. Disconnect the distributor vacuum line, EGR vacuum line, venturi vacuum line and fuel line.

4. Disconnect the choke heat tube, if so equipped.

5. Unfasten the throttle solenoid positioner and choke cap at their electrical connections.

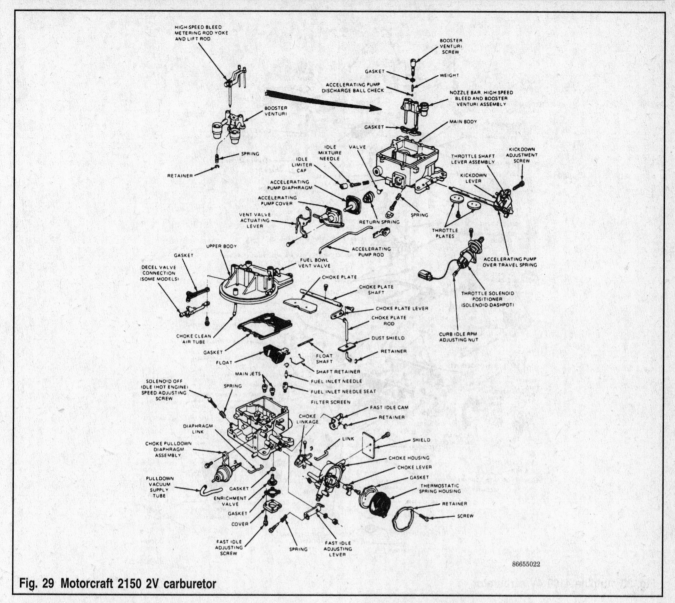

Fig. 29 Motorcraft 2150 2V carburetor

6. Remove the canister bowl vent electrical connector and the canister vent hose.

7. Remove the carburetor retaining nuts. Lift off the carburetor carefully, taking care not to spill any fuel. Remove the carburetor mounting gasket and discard it. Remove the carburetor mounting spacer, if so equipped, from the intake manifold.

To install:

8. Prior to installation, clean the gasket mounting surfaces of the intake manifold, spacer (if so equipped), and carburetor. When using a spacer, use two new gaskets, sandwiching the spacer between the gaskets. If a spacer is not used, only one new carburetor mounting gasket is required.

9. Place the new gasket(s) and spacer (if so equipped) on the carburetor mounting studs. Position the carburetor on top of the gasket and hand-tighten the retaining nuts. Then tighten the nuts in a crisscross pattern to 12-15 ft. lbs. (16-19 Nm).

10. Connect the fuel line, throttle cable, distributor vacuum line, EGR vacuum line, and venturi vacuum line.

11. Connect the canister vent hose and the canister bowl vent electrical connector.

12. Connect the choke heat tube, if so equipped.

13. Fasten the throttle solenoid positioner and choke cap at their electrical connections.

14. Install the air cleaner assembly.

15. Adjust the curb idle and fast idle speed settings, if necessary. (On 1979 models, also adjust the slow idle speed with the throttle solenoid positioner OFF.)

Holley 4180

1. Remove the air cleaner assembly.

2. Disconnect the throttle rod from the throttle lever.

3. Unfasten the distributor vacuum lines, PCV hose, fuel line and any electrical connections.

4. Disconnect the choke heat tube, if so equipped.

5. Remove the carburetor retaining nuts. Lift off the carburetor carefully, taking care not to spill any fuel. Remove the carburetor mounting gasket and discard it. Remove the carburetor mounting spacer from the intake manifold.

To install:

6. Prior to installation, clean the gasket mounting surfaces of the intake manifold, spacer and carburetor. When using a

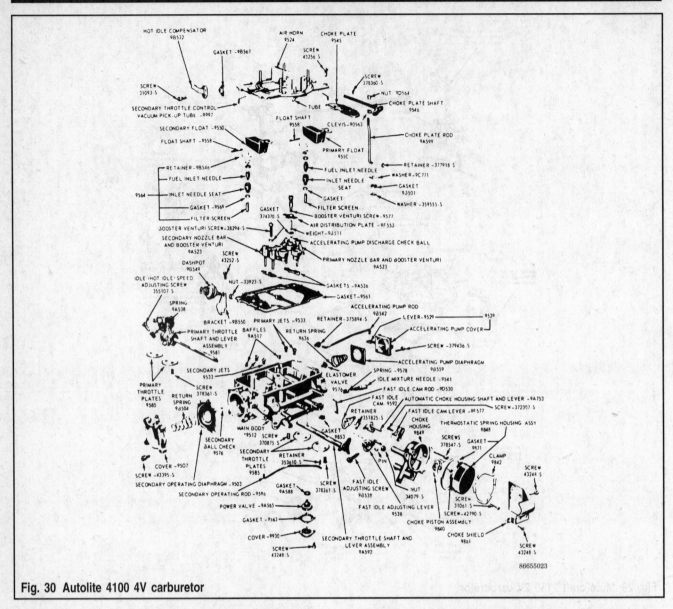

Fig. 30 Autolite 4100 4V carburetor

spacer, use two new gaskets, sandwiching the spacer between the gaskets.

7. Place the new gaskets and spacer on the carburetor mounting studs. Position the carburetor on top of the gasket and hand-tighten the retaining nuts. Then tighten the nuts in a crisscross pattern to 14-20 ft. lbs. (18-26 Nm).

8. Fasten the throttle rod, vacuum lines, PCV hose, fuel line and electrical connections.

9. Connect the choke heat tube, if so equipped.

10. Install the air cleaner assembly.

11. Check and adjust the idle speed settings, if necessary, as outlined in Section 2.

All Other Carburetors

➡**Prior to removing any wire harness, vacuum line or cable, properly mark or tag the item.**

1. Remove the air cleaner.

2. Disconnect the throttle cable or rod at the throttle lever. Unfasten the distributor vacuum line, exhaust gas recirculation line (1973 and later models), inline fuel filter, choke heat tube and the positive crankcase ventilation hose at the carburetor.

3. Unfasten the throttle solenoid (if so equipped) and electric choke assist (1973 and later models) at their connectors. Remove the wires to the carburetor on the 7200 VV.

4. Remove the carburetor retaining nuts. Lift off the carburetor carefully, taking care not to spill any fuel. Remove the carburetor mounting gasket and discard it. Remove the carburetor mounting spacer, if so equipped, from the intake manifold.

To install:

5. Prior to installation, clean the gasket mounting surfaces of the intake manifold, spacer, (if so equipped), and carburetor. When using a spacer, use two new gaskets, sandwiching the spacer between the gaskets. If a spacer is not used, only one new carburetor mounting gasket is required.

6. Place the new gasket(s) and spacer (if so equipped) on the carburetor mounting studs. Position the carburetor on top of the gasket and hand-tighten the retaining nuts. Then tighten the nuts in a crisscross pattern to 10-15 ft. lbs. (13-19 Nm).

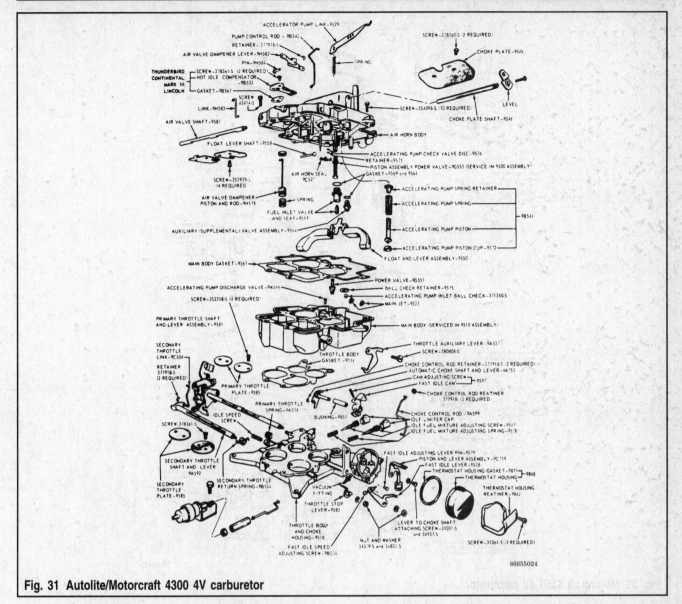

Fig. 31 Autolite/Motorcraft 4300 4V carburetor

7. Connect the throttle linkage, the distributor vacuum line, exhaust gas recirculation line (1973 and later models), inline fuel filter, choke heat tube, positive crankcase ventilation hose, throttle solenoid (if so equipped) and electric-choke assist (1973 and later models).

8. Adjust the curb idle speed, the idle fuel mixture and the accelerator pump stroke (Autolite/Motorcraft 2 and 4-barrel carburetors only).

OVERHAUL

Efficient carburetion depends on careful cleaning and inspection during overhaul, since dirt, gum, water, or varnish in or on the carburetor parts can be responsible for poor performance.

Overhaul your carburetor in a clean, dust free area. Carefully disassemble the carburetor, referring often to the exploded views. Keep all similar and look-alike parts segregated during the disassembly and cleaning to avoid accidental interchange during assembly. Make a note of all jet sizes.

When the carburetor is disassembled, wash all parts (except diaphragms, electric choke units, pump plunger, and any other plastic, leather, fiber, or rubber parts) in clean carburetor solvent. Do not leave parts in the solvent any longer than is necessary to sufficiently loosen the deposits. Excessive cleaning may remove the special finish from the float bowl and choke valve bodies, leaving these parts unfit for service. Rinse all parts in clean solvent and blow them dry with compressed air or allow them to air dry. Wipe clean all cork, plastic, leather, and fiber parts with a clean, lint-free cloth.

Blow out all passages and jets with compressed air and be sure that there are no restrictions or blockages. Never use wire of similar tools to clean jets, fuel passages, or air bleeds. Clean all jets and valves separately to avoid accidental interchange.

Check all parts for wear or damage. If wear or damage is found, replace the defective parts. Especially check the following:

1. Check the float needle and seat for wear. If wear is found, replace the complete assembly.

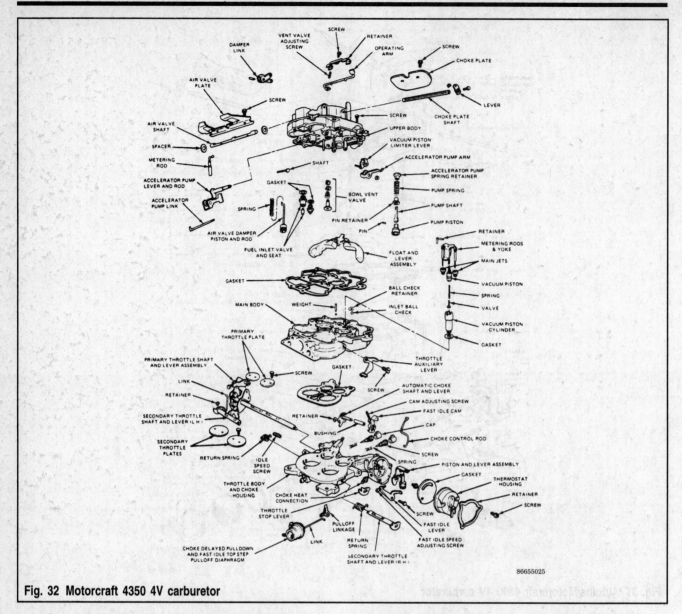

Fig. 32 Motorcraft 4350 4V carburetor

2. Check the float hinge pin for wear and the float(s) for dents or distortion. Replace the float if fuel has leaked into it.

3. Check the throttle and choke shaft bores for wear or an out-of-round condition. Damage or wear to the throttle arm, shaft, or shaft bore will often require replacement of the throttle body. These parts require a close tolerance of fit. Slight wear may allow air linkage, which could affect starting and idling.

➡Throttle shafts and bushings are not included in over-haul kits. They usually can be purchased separately.

4. Inspect the idle mixture adjusting needles for burrs or grooves. Any such condition requires replacement of the needle, since you will not be able to obtain a satisfactory idle.

5. Check the bowl cover for warped surfaces with a straightedge.

6. Closely inspect the valves and seats for wear and damage, replacing as necessary.

7. After the carburetor is assembled, check the choke valve for freedom of operation.

Carburetor overhaul kits are recommended for each overhaul. These kits contain all gaskets and new parts to replace those which deteriorate most rapidly. Failure to replace all parts supplied with the kit (especially gaskets) can result in poor performance later.

Some carburetor manufacturers supply overhaul kits of three basic types: minor repair; major repair; and gasket kits. Basically, they contain the following:

Minor Repair Kits:
- All gaskets
- Float needle valve
- Volume control screw
- All diaphragms
- Spring for the pump diaphragm

Major Repair Kits:
- All jets and gaskets
- All diaphragms
- Float needle valve
- Volume control screw
- Pump ball valve

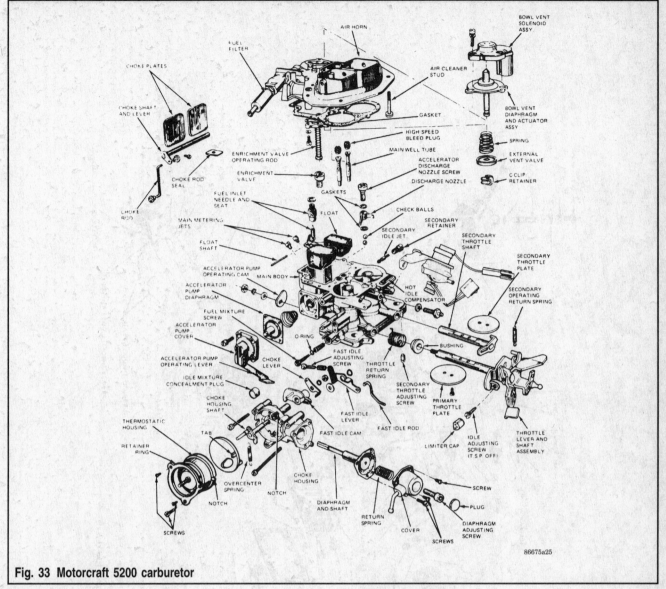

Fig. 33 Motorcraft 5200 carburetor

- Float
- Complete intermediate rod
- Intermediate pump lever
- Some cover hold-down screws and washers

Gasket Kits:
- All gaskets

After cleaning and checking all components, reassemble the carburetor, using new parts referring to the exploded view as needed. When reassembling, make sure that all screws and jets are tight in their seats, but do not overtighten as the tops will be distorted. Tighten all screws gradually, in rotation. Do not tighten needle valves into their seats; uneven jetting will result. Always use new gaskets. Be sure to adjust the float level when reassembling.

ADJUSTMENTS

Automatic Choke

1971-78 MODELS

Original equipment carburetors have adjustable choke caps. On a vehicle of this type, the reaction of the choke to engine temperature can be controlled by positioning and rotating the cap in relation to an index mark or reference point. In spite of their adjustability, these carburetors each have a preferred setting, as determined by the manufacturer. Most original equipment carburetors on 1980 and later vehicles utilize adjustment-limiting or non-adjustable choke caps. The inclusion of a locking/indexing plate or spacer with locating tabs eliminates the need for choke cap adjustment. Nevertheless, the removal and installation procedures for these non-adjustable choke caps are essentially the same as those for their adjustable counterparts. One significant difference is in the type of fastener used to retain the caps. Generally, regular slotted screws are used to retain adjustable choke caps, thereby permitting easy removal.

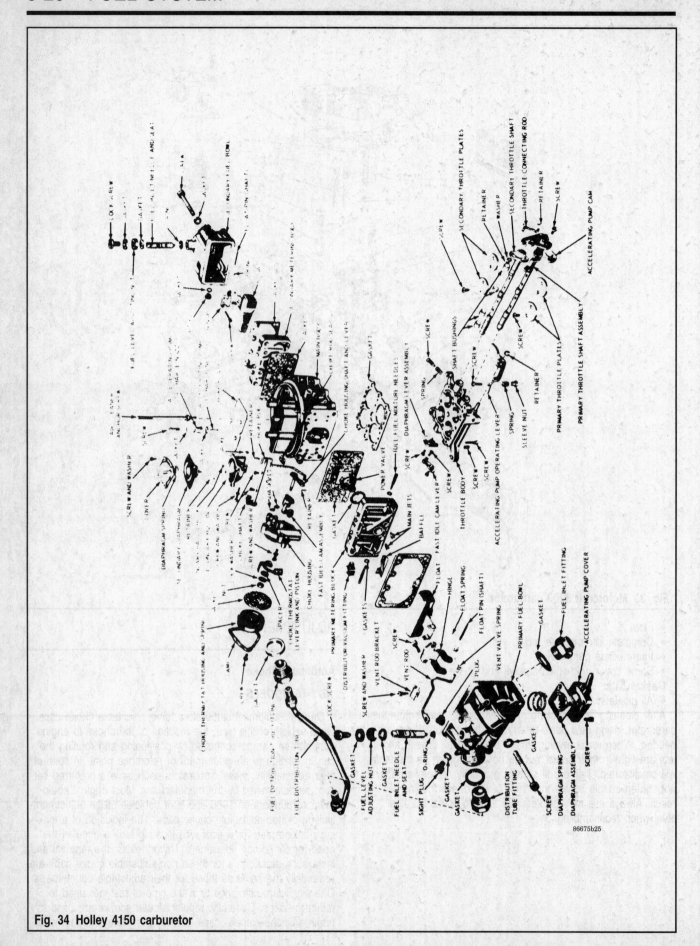

Fig. 34 Holley 4150 carburetor

86675b25

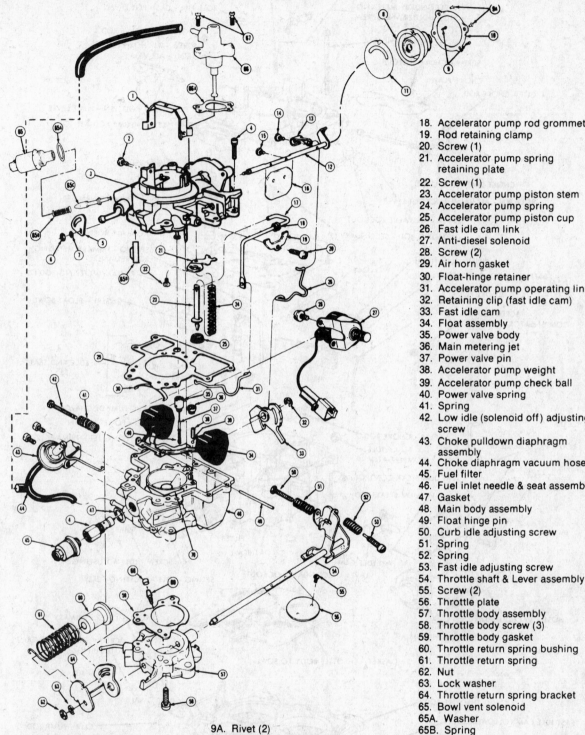

18. Accelerator pump rod grommet
19. Rod retaining clamp
20. Screw (1)
21. Accelerator pump spring retaining plate
22. Screw (1)
23. Accelerator pump piston stem
24. Accelerator pump spring
25. Accelerator pump piston cup
26. Fast idle cam link
27. Anti-diesel solenoid
28. Screw (2)
29. Air horn gasket
30. Float-hinge retainer
31. Accelerator pump operating link
32. Retaining clip (fast idle cam)
33. Fast idle cam
34. Float assembly
35. Power valve body
36. Main metering jet
37. Power valve pin
38. Accelerator pump weight
39. Accelerator pump check ball
40. Power valve spring
41. Spring
42. Low idle (solenoid off) adjusting screw
43. Choke pulldown diaphragm assembly
44. Choke diaphragm vacuum hose
45. Fuel filter
46. Fuel inlet needle & seat assembly
47. Gasket
48. Main body assembly
49. Float hinge pin
50. Curb idle adjusting screw
51. Spring
52. Spring
53. Fast idle adjusting screw
54. Throttle shaft & Lever assembly
55. Screw (2)
56. Throttle plate
57. Throttle body assembly
58. Throttle body screw (3)
59. Throttle body gasket
60. Throttle return spring bushing
61. Throttle return spring
62. Nut
63. Lock washer
64. Throttle return spring bracket
65. Bowl vent solenoid
65A. Washer
65B. Spring
65C. Pintle
65D. Seal
66. Power valve piston assembly
66A. Gasket
67. Screw (2)
68. Idle mixture
69. Concealment plug idle mixture needle
70. Fuel bowl filler

1. Air cleaner bracket (1)
2. Air cleaner bracket screw (2)
3. Air horn
4. Screw and washer (8)
5. Choke pulldown lever
6. Choke shaft nut
7. Lockwasher (1)
8. Choke bimetal assembly
9. Screw (2)

9A. Rivet (2)
10. Choke cover retainer
11. Choke thermostatic housing locating disc
12. Choke shaft and lever assembly
13. Choke control lever
14. Screw (1)
15. Screw (1)
16. Choke plate
17. Accelerator pump operating rod

Fig. 35 Holley 1946 carburetor

86675c25

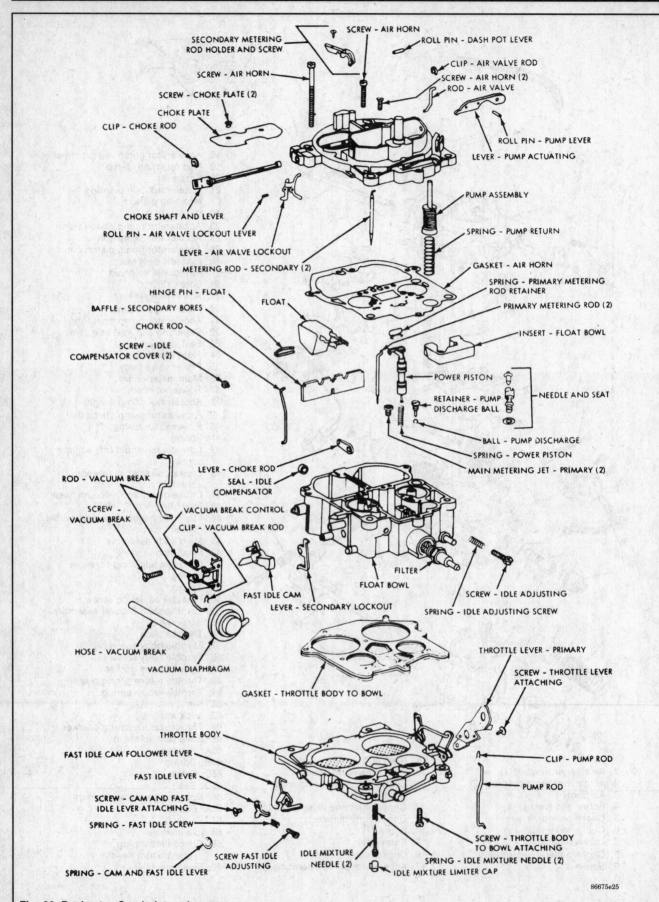

Fig. 36 Rochester Quadrajet carburetor

86675e25

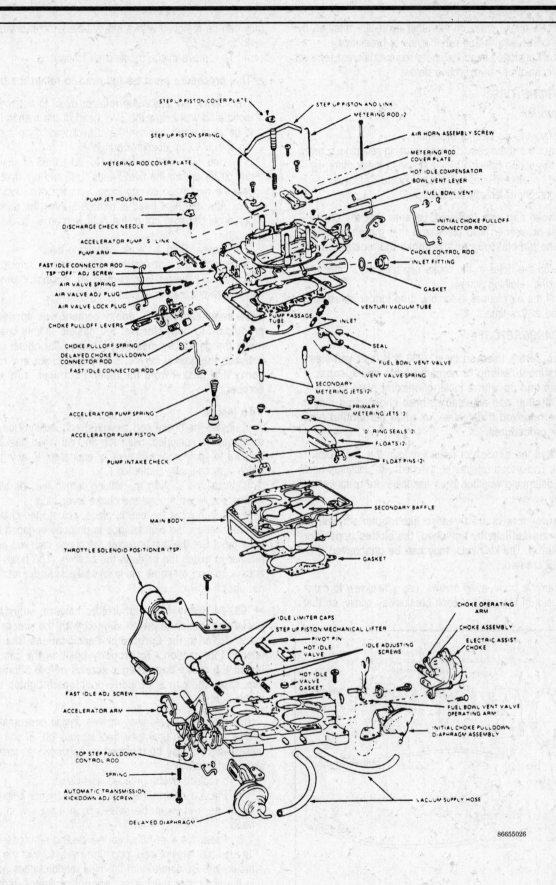

Fig. 37 Carter Thermo-Quad carburetor

Non-adjustable choke caps, on the other hand, are retained by a combination of screws and either rivets or break-away screws. Such unslotted-head fasteners require different removal tools and techniques, as described below.

1979 CARBURETORS

▶ **See Figure 38**

1. Remove the air cleaner assembly.
2. Loosen the thermostatic spring housing retaining screws.
3. Set the spring housing to the specified index mark, by rotating the housing. (Refer to the appropriate Carburetor Specifications chart, later in this section.)

➡**If the choke cap was removed, be sure that the choke cap gasket or spacer is in place and that the choke cap engages the bimetal loop on the choke thermostatic lever.**

4. Line up the holes in the choke cap retainer, if removed, and fasten the retaining screws.
5. Install the air cleaner assembly, if no further adjustments are required at this time.

1980-86 CARBURETORS

➡**The carburetors used on most 1980 and later vehicles have adjustment-limiting or non-adjustable choke caps which must line up with a locking/indexing plate or spacer. Although non-adjustable, these choke caps may have to be removed if defective, or when performing other carburetor procedures.**

1. Remove the air cleaner assembly from the carburetor.
2. If the choke cap retainer is fastened with unslotted-head fasteners, determine whether those fasteners are rivets or break-away screws.

➡**Break-away screws are threaded like regular screws, but once they are sufficiently tightened, the slotted upper portion breaks off. Unlike rivets, they can be unscrewed if a new slot is created.**

3. To remove break-away screws, use a hacksaw to carefully cut a slot in the head of each break-away screw, so that

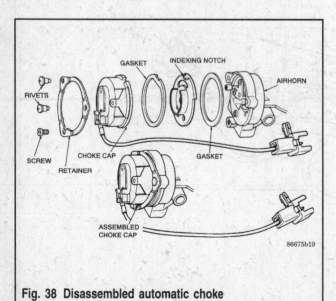

GASKET INDEXING NOTCH AIRHORN RIVETS SCREW CHOKE CAP RETAINER GASKET ASSEMBLED CHOKE CAP

86675b19

Fig. 38 Disassembled automatic choke

they can be removed with a straight-blade screwdriver. Proceed to Step 5.

4. To remove rivets, proceed as follows:

➡**This procedure must be followed to retain the hole size.**

a. Check the choke cap retainer rivets to determine if the mandrel is well below the rivet head. If the mandrel appears to be at or within the rivet head thickness, drive it down or out with a $^1/_{16}$ in. diameter punch.
b. Use a $^1/_8$ in. diameter or No. 30 (.1285 in. diameter) drill bit for drilling the rivet heads. Drill into the rivet head until the rivet head comes loose from the rivet body.
c. After the rivet head is removed, drive the remaining portion of the rivet out of the hole with an $^1/_8$ in. diameter punch.
d. Repeat Step 4 for the remaining rivet.
5. Remove the screw(s) with a proper size screwdriver.
6. Remove the retainer, choke cap, locking/indexing plate and/or gasket(s), as equipped.

➡**On some carburetors, epoxy cement was applied during production to both sides of the gasket. In this case, remove the gasket by inserting a sharp, flat chisel or knife between the gasket layers. Be sure to clean any remaining epoxy and gasket from the mating surfaces with a gasket scraper.**

To install:
7. Install the choke cap gasket(s) and locking/indexing plate or spacer, as equipped. (Replace any damaged gasket(s) and be sure to apply epoxy cement or equivalent to any gasket which was originally cemented.)
8. Install the choke cap, making certain that the bimetal loop is positioned around the choke lever tang.
9. While holding the cap in place, actuate the choke plate to make certain the bimetal loop is properly engaged with the lever tang. Set the retainer over the choke cap and orient the retainer to match the holes in the casting. (The holes are not equally spaced on some models.) Make sure the retainer is not upside down.

➡**1983-84 Holley 4180 carburetors have an adjustable choke cap, which must be aligned with the proper index mark. (Refer to the Carburetor Specifications Chart, found later in this section.) To properly position the cap, loosely install the choke cap retainer screws before aligning the cap. Once the cap is properly positioned, tighten the retainer screws.**

10. To replace break-away screws, install new break-away screws and tighten until their heads break off. (If you prefer, these fasteners may be replaced by conventional screws of the same installed size.)
11. To replace rivets, proceed as follows:
a. Place a rivet in the rivet gun and trigger it lightly to retain the rivet ($^1/_8$ in. diameter x $^1/_2$ in. long x $^1/_4$ in. diameter head).
b. Press the rivet fully into the casting after passing through the retainer and "pop" the rivet, so that the mandrel breaks off. Be careful that the rivet mandrel does not lodge in the carburetor mechanism when it separates from the rivet.
c. Repeat this step for the remaining rivet.

12. Install and tighten the remaining conventional screw(s).

13. Install the air cleaner assembly, if no further adjustments are required at this time.

Choke Plate Pulldown Clearance

AUTOLITE 1101

1. Remove the air cleaner assembly.

2. Remove the choke cover and thermostatic coil assembly. Block the throttle valve half open so that the fast idle screw does not contact the fast idle cam.

3. Bend a 0.036 in. (0.9mm) wire gauge at a 90° angle about 1/8 in. (3mm) from the end. Insert the bent end between the lower edge of the choke piston slot and the upper edge of the right hand slot in the choke housing.

4. Move the piston lever counterclockwise until the gauge fits snugly in the slot. Hold the gauge in place by exerting light pressure on the lever.

5. Insert a drill or gauge of the specified thickness (see Carburetor Specifications chart) between the lower edge of the choke plate and the air horn wall.

6. To adjust, carefully bend the choke piston link (in an S or Z-shaped bend) until the choke plate clearance is that of the drill gauge.

7. After adjustment, install the choke cover and adjust it.

8. Install the air cleaner.

CARTER YFA — PISTON TYPE

▶ See Figure 39

1. Remove the air cleaner assembly.

2. Remove the retainer, choke cap and gasket, as described previously in this section.

3. Bend a 0.026 in. diameter wire gauge at a 90° angle, approximately 1/8 in. (3mm) from one end. Insert the bent end of the gauge between the choke piston slot and the right hand slot in the choke housing. Rotate the choke piston lever counterclockwise until the gauge is shut in the piston slot.

4. Apply light pressure on the choke piston lever to hold the gauge in place. Then, measure the clearance between the lower edge of the choke plate and the carburetor bore using a drill bit with a diameter equal to the specified pulldown clearance. (Refer to the Carburetor Specifications chart, later in this section.)

5. Bend the choke piston lever to obtain the proper clearance. Be careful not to distort the piston link.

6. Install the gasket, choke cap and retainer.

7. Fasten the retainer screw(s) and apply new rivets, where necessary.

8. Install the air cleaner assembly, if no further adjustments are required at this time.

CARTER YFA — DIAPHRAGM-TYPE

▶ See Figure 40

1. Activate the pulldown motor by applying an external vacuum source.

2. Close the choke plate as far as possible without forcing it.

3. Using a drill bit of the specified size (as indicated in the Carburetor Specifications chart, later in this section), measure the clearance between the lower edge of the choke plate and the air horn wall.

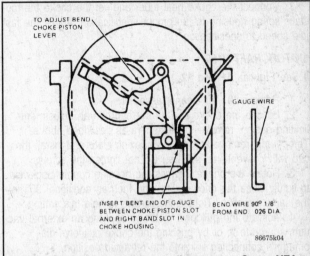

Fig. 39 Choke plate pulldown adjustment — Carter YFA carburetor with piston-type choke

4. If adjustment is necessary, bend the choke diaphragm link as required.

5. Reconnect the pulldown motor vacuum line.

MOTORCRAFT 2100

1. Remove the air cleaner.

2. With the engine at normal operating temperature, loosen the choke thermostatic spring housing retaining screws. Set the housing 90°s in the right direction.

3. Disconnect and remove the choke heat tube from the choke housing.

4. Turn the fast idle adjusting screw outward one full turn.

5. Start the engine. Use a drill of a diameter specified in the chart at the end of this section to check the clearance between the lower edge of the choke plate and the air horn wall.

6. To adjust the clearance, turn the diaphragm stop screw (located on the underside of the choke diaphragm housing). Turning clockwise will decrease the clearance; counterclockwise will increase it.

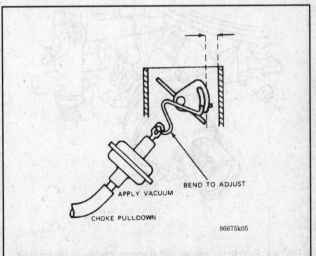

Fig. 40 Choke plate pulldown adjustment — Carter YFA carburetor with diaphragm-type choke

7. Connect the choke heat tube, and set the choke thermostatic spring housing to the proper specification. Adjust the fast idle speed to specification.

MOTORCRAFT 2150

▶ **See Figures 41 and 42**

1. Remove the air cleaner assembly.

2. Loosen the choke cap. (If the cap has an adjustment-limiting design, remove the fasteners as described above. Temporarily remove the locking/indexing plate and install the cap with conventional screws.) Do not tighten the screws.

3. Rotate the choke thermostatic housing counterclockwise to lightly close the choke plate, and then an additional 90° in the same direction. Tighten the screws to hold this setting.

4. Activate the pulldown motor by applying an external vacuum source to it, or by pushing the choke pulldown diaphragm's connecting link into the retracted position.

5. Using a drill bit of the specified diameter (as indicated in the Carburetor Specifications chart, later in this section), measure the clearance between the lower edge of the choke plate and the air horn wall.

6. Turn the adjusting screw on the pulldown motor clockwise to decrease the pulldown, or counterclockwise to increase it.

➡ **After each pulldown adjustment, it is necessary to check the fast idle cam setting. This procedure is covered later in this section.**

7. After the final adjustment, reset the choke housing cap to its proper position. (Be sure to replace the locking/indexing plate, if so equipped, and install new fasteners where necessary.)

8. If disconnected, reconnect the vacuum hose to the pulldown motor.

9. Install the air cleaner assembly, if no further adjustments are required at this time.

AUTOLITE/MOTORCRAFT 4300, 4350

1. Follow Steps 1-5 of the Autolite 1101 carburetor adjustment procedure.

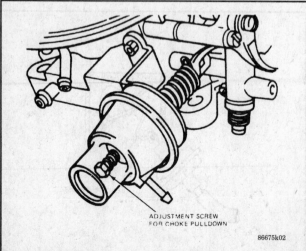

Fig. 41 Pulldown motor adjustment screw — Motorcraft 2150 carburetor

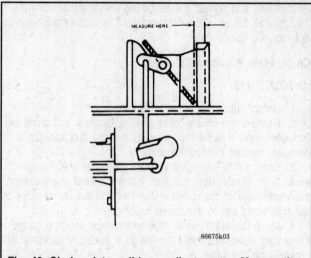

Fig. 42 Choke plate pulldown adjustment — Motorcraft 2150 carburetor

2. To adjust, loosen the hex head screw (left hand thread) on the choke plate shaft and pry the link away from the tapered shaft. Using a drill gauge 0.010 in. thinner than the specified clearance (to allow for tolerances in the linkage), insert the gauge between the lower edge of the choke plate and the air horn wall. Hold the choke plate against the gauge and maintain a light pressure in a counterclockwise direction on the choke lever. With the choke piston snug against the 0.036 in. wire gauge and the choke plate against the 0.010 in. smaller drill gauge, tighten the hex head screw (left hand thread) on the choke plate shaft. After tightening the hex head screw, make a final check using a drill gauge of the specified clearance between the choke plate and air horn.

3. After adjustment, install the choke cover and adjust.

4. Install the air cleaner.

1979 MOTORCRAFT 5200 OR 6500

1. Remove the retaining screws and ring retaining the choke thermostatic spring housing.

2. Remove the thermostatic spring housing and the electric choke heater.

3. Set the fast idle cam on the second step.

4. Attach a rubber band to the choke operating lever to take up any slack in the linkage.

5. Push the diaphragm stem against its stop with a screwdriver, and insert a drill bit of the specified diameter (as indicated in the Carburetor Specifications chart, later in this section), between the lower edge of the choke plate and the air horn wall.

6. Turn the diaphragm adjusting screw in or out to get the proper clearance.

7. Install the electric choke heater, thermostatic spring housing, retaining ring and attaching screws. (Be sure that the choke plate is in the fully closed position before installing the electric choke heater.)

8. Rotate the housing to the specified index mark and tighten the screws.

1980-81 MOTORCRAFT 5200 OR 6500

▶ **See Figures 43 and 44**

1. Remove the retainer, choke cap and locking/indexing plate as described earlier in this section.

2. Remove the plastic dust cover, if so equipped.

3. Set the fast idle adjusting screw on the high step of the fast idle cam.

4. Attach a rubber band, as illustrated, to remove slack from the choke linkage. Push the diaphragm stem against its stop with a screwdriver, and insert a drill bit of the specified diameter (as indicated in the Carburetor Specifications chart, later in this section,) between the lower edge of the choke plate and the air horn wall.

5. If the original choke pulldown diaphragm cover is still in place, and an adjustment is necessary, a service replacement kit will be required. This kit contains a new choke pulldown diaphragm cover, adjusting screw and a cup plug. Proceed as follows:

    a. Remove the three choke pulldown diaphragm cover retaining screws and the cover.

    b. Install a new cover and adjusting screw.

6. Turn the diaphragm adjusting screw clockwise to decrease, or counterclockwise to increase the clearance.

7. When the adjustment is complete, install a new cup plug in the choke pulldown adjustment access opening.

8. Remove the rubber band and install the plastic dust cover, if so equipped.

9. Install the locking and indexing plate, the choke cap and retainer. Be sure that the bimetal loop is properly engaged.

10. Fasten the retainer screw(s) and apply new rivets, where necessary.

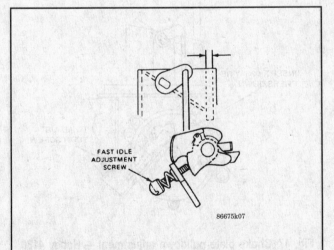

Fig. 43 Choke plate pulldown adjustment — Motorcraft 5200 or 6500 carburetor

FAST IDLE
ADJUSTMENT
SCREW

86675k07

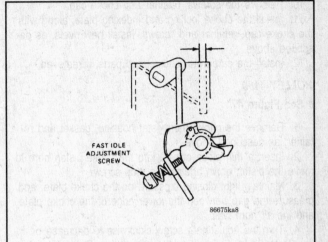

FAST IDLE
ADJUSTMENT
SCREW

86675ka8

Fig. 44 Fast idle cam setting — 1980-82 Motorcraft 5200 or 6500 carburetor

HOLLEY 1946

➡ **Early models of this carburetor can be adjusted, if necessary, without drilling or removing the carburetor. If the choke pulldown diaphragm's connecting link has a U-shaped bend, adjustments are simply made by bending the link.**

▶ **See Figures 45 and 46**

1. Remove the retainer and choke cap, as described above. (If the pulldown diaphragm's connecting link has a U-shaped bend, simply loosen the choke cap's retainer screws, and proceed to Step 4.)

2. Temporarily remove the choke locking and indexing plate.

3. Loosely reassemble the choke cap and retainer with the two screws.

4. Rotate the cap counterclockwise to lightly close the choke plate, and then an additional 90° in the same direction. Tighten the screws to hold this setting.

5. Activate the pulldown motor by applying an external vacuum source.

6. Using a drill bit of the specified diameter (as indicated in the Carburetor Specifications chart, later in this section), measure the clearance between the upper edge of the choke plate and the air horn wall.

➡ **The remaining steps only apply to those carburetors in which the pulldown diaphragm has a straight connecting link. For early models with a U-shaped link, bend the link until the specified clearance is achieved, then set the choke cap to the original setting and tighten the screws.**

7. If an adjustment is necessary, drill a $^3/_{32}$ in. diameter hole through the hardened steel plug at the base of the pulldown motor, and remove the plug with a tap. (It may be necessary to first remove the carburetor, in order to allow sufficient access. If so, follow the instructions later in this section.)

8. Repeat Steps 6 and 7, and turn the adjusting screw in or out as required until the adjustment is within specifications.

9. Install a new steel plug in the adjusting screw access hole.

10. Remove the screws, retainer and choke cap.

11. Install the choke locking and indexing plate, along with the choke cap, retainer and screws. Install new rivets, as described above.

12. Install the carburetor and related parts, if removed.

HOLLEY 4180

▶ See Figure 47

1. Remove the choke thermostat housing, gasket and retainer, as described above.

2. Insert a thin piece of wire into the choke piston bore to move the piston down against the stop screw.

3. Maintain light closing pressure on the choke plate, and measure the gap between the lower edge of the choke plate and the air horn wall.

4. Turn the adjustment screw clockwise to decrease or counterclockwise to increase the gap setting. Be sure to close the choke plate during adjustment, to avoid turning the screw into the side of the piston.

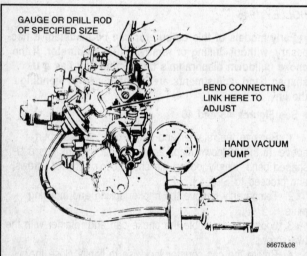

Fig. 45 Choke plate pulldown adjustment — Holley 1946 early-model carburetor

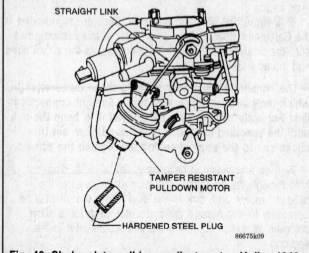

Fig. 46 Choke plate pulldown adjustment — Holley 1946 carburetor

5. Remove the wire and install the choke thermostat housing, gasket and retainer. Use new fasteners when replacing rivets or break-away screws.

Float Level

AUTOLITE 1101

▶ See Figure 48

1. Remove the carburetor air horn and gasket from the carburetor.

2. Measure the distance from the gasket surface of the air horn to the top of the float. If the measurement is not within the specified tolerance, bend the float arm tab as necessary to obtain the specified dimension. Be careful not to exert any pressure on the fuel inlet needle, as this will damage it and result in an improper fuel level within the float bowl.

3. Install the carburetor air horn to the main body of the carburetor, using a new gasket.

CARTER YFA

▶ See Figure 49

➡ The dry float fuel level adjustment is a final float or fuel level adjustment.

1. Remove the air cleaner assembly.

2. Disconnect the fuel inlet line at the filter, and the vacuum pulldown hose at the pulldown motor.

3. Unfasten the electric choke wire at the connector and at the clip on the throttle control bracket. Remove the throttle control bracket assembly from the main body. Remove the external bowl vent line.

4. Remove the wire clip retaining the link which joins the fast idle choke lever to the fast idle cam, and remove the link.

5. Remove the air horn attaching screws and carburetor identification tag. Remove the air horn and gasket.

6. Invert the air horn assembly and check the clearance from the top of the float to the surface of the air horn with a T-scale or float level gauge. The air horn should be held at eye level when gauging, and the float arm should be resting on the needle pin.

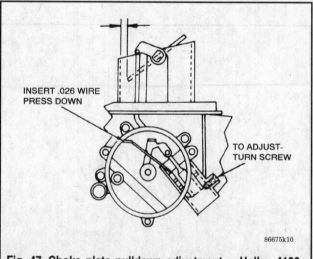

Fig. 47 Choke plate pulldown adjustment — Holley 4180 carburetor

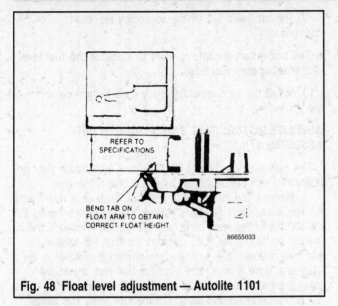

Fig. 48 Float level adjustment — Autolite 1101

7. Do not exert pressure on the needle valve when measuring or adjusting the float. Bend the float arm as necessary to adjust the float level to specifications.

✳✳CAUTION

Do not bend the tab at the end of the float arm, as it prevents the float from striking the bottom of the fuel bowl when empty and keeps the needle in place.

8. Install the air horn with a new gasket. Be sure to install the identification tag in its proper location and tighten the attaching screws to 27-37 inch lbs. (3-4 Nm).

9. Connect the external bowl vent line.

10. Install the throttle control bracket assembly on the main body.

11. Position the link and plastic bushing which join the fast idle cam to the fast idle choke lever, and retain them in place on the fast idle cam with the plastic bushing and wire clip. Make sure that the mechanical fuel bowl vent rod is engaged with the forked actuating lever, if so equipped.

12. Connect the fuel inlet line to the fuel filter, and the vacuum line to the pulldown motor.

13. Connect the electric choke wire, and clip the wire to the throttle control bracket.

14. Install the air cleaner assembly.

MOTORCRAFT 5200 OR 6500

1. Remove the bowl cover (air horn) attaching screws and lockwashers.

2. Remove the plastic retainer bushings from the choke rod and remove the air horn. Be sure that the gasket is not attached.

3. Turn the air horn upside down. With the float tang resting lightly on the spring loaded fuel inlet needle, measure the clearance between the edge of the float and the air horn.

4. To adjust the float level, bend the float tang. Make sure that both floats are adjusted equally.

5. Hold the air horn in its normal position to check and adjust the float drop, if necessary.

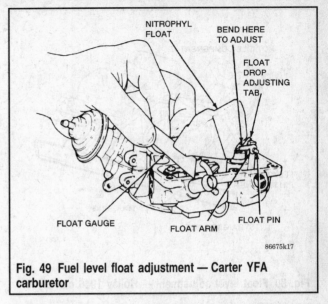

Fig. 49 Fuel level float adjustment — Carter YFA carburetor

6. Position the air horn and gasket on the main body, and install the attaching screws and lockwashers. Tighten the attaching screws to 20 inch lbs. (2 Nm).

7. Install the plastic retainer bushings on the choke rod.

HOLLEY 1946

▶ See Figure 50

➡**This setting of the float level adjustment must be done with the carburetor removed from the engine.**

1. Remove the air horn attaching screws and carburetor identification tag. Remove the air horn and gasket.

2. Place a finger over the hinge pin retainer and invert the main body. Catch the accelerator pump check ball and weight when they fall out.

3. Lay a ruler across the housing under the floats. The lowest point of the floats should be just touching the ruler for all except California models. For California models, the ruler should just contact the heel (raised step) of the floats.

4. Bend the float tangs to adjust. Once this adjustment is correct, turn the main body right side up and check the float alignment. The floats should move freely without touching the fuel bowl walls. If the floats are misaligned, straighten them by bending the float arms. Recheck the float level adjustment, and adjust if necessary.

5. Insert the accelerator pump check ball and weight.

6. Install the air horn with a new gasket, and fasten with the screws. Be sure to install the identification tag in its proper location.

HOLLEY 4180

To perform a preliminary dry float adjustment on both the primary and secondary fuel bowl assemblies, remove each fuel bowl and invert it, allowing the float to rest on the fuel inlet valve and seat assembly. The fuel inlet valve and seat can be rotated until the float is parallel with the fuel bowl floor (actually, the top of the fuel bowl chamber when inverted). Note that this is an initial dry float setting which must be rechecked

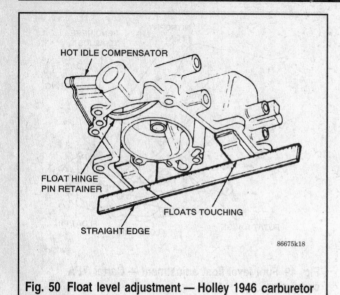

HOT IDLE COMPENSATOR

FLOAT HINGE
PIN RETAINER

FLOATS TOUCHING

STRAIGHT EDGE

86675k18

Fig. 50 Float level adjustment — Holley 1946 carburetor

with the carburetor assembled and on the engine to obtain the proper wet fuel level.

➡This carburetor has an externally adjustable needle and seat assembly which allows the fuel level to be checked and adjusted without removing the carburetor from the engine.

1. Run the engine with the vehicle resting on a level surface until the engine reaches normal operating temperature.
2. Remove the air cleaner assembly.
3. Place a suitable container or an absorbent cloth below the fuel level sight plug in the fuel bowl.
4. Run the engine at 1000 rpm for about 30 seconds to stabilize the fuel level.
5. Stop the engine and remove the sight plug and gasket on the primary float bowl. The fuel level in the bowl should be at the lower edge of the sight plug hole, plus or minus $1/16$ in. (1.5mm). If the level is too high, loosen one of the lower fuel bowl retaining screws and drain the fuel from the bowl.

✳✳CAUTION

Never loosen the lockscrew or nut, or attempt to adjust the fuel level with the sight plug removed or the engine running, since fuel will spray out, creating a fire hazard!

6. To adjust the fuel level, loosen the lockscrew on top of the fuel bowl just enough to allow the adjusting nut to be turned. Turn the adjusting nut about $1/2$ turn clockwise to lower the fuel level, or about $1/2$ turn counterclockwise to raise the fuel level. (By turning the adjusting nut $5/16$ of a turn, the fuel level will change $1/16$ in. (1.5mm) at the sight plug.) Tighten the lock screw and install the sight plug, using the old gasket.
7. Start the engine and allow the fuel level to stabilize again, by running the engine at 1000 rpm for about 30 seconds. Stop the engine and re-check the fuel level as outlined in Step 5.
8. Repeat the procedure in Step 6 until the fuel level is at the bottom of the sight plug hole. Install the sight plug using a new gasket.

9. Repeat Steps 5-8 for the secondary fuel bowl adjustment.

➡The secondary throttle is used to stabilize the fuel level in the secondary fuel bowl.

10. Install the air cleaner assembly if no further adjustments are necessary.

AUTOLITE/MOTORCRAFT 2100, 2150, 4100 (DRY ADJUSTMENT)

This preliminary setting of the float level adjustment must be performed with the carburetor removed from the engine.

1. Remove the air horn and see that the float is raised and the fuel inlet needle is seated. Check the distance between the top surface of the main body (with the gasket removed) and the top surface of the float. Depress the float tab to seat the fuel inlet needle. Take a measurement near the center of the float, at a point $1/8$ in. (3mm) from the free end. If you are using a prefabricated float gauge, place the gauge in the corner of the enlarged end section of the fuel bowl. The gauge should touch the float near the end, but not on the end radius.
2. If necessary, bend the tab on the end of the float to bring the setting within the specified limits.

AUTOLITE/MOTORCRAFT 2100, 2150, 4100 (WET ADJUSTMENT)

▶ See Figure 51

1. Bring the engine to its normal operating temperature. Park the car on as nearly level a surface as possible, and stop the engine.
2. Remove the air cleaner assembly from the carburetor.
3. Remove the air horn retaining screws and the carburetor identification tag. Leave the air horn and gasket in position on the carburetor main body. Start the engine, let it idle for several minutes. Rotate the air horn out of the way, and remove the gasket to provide access to the float assembly.
4. With the engine idling, use a standard depth scale to measure the vertical distance from the top machined surface of the carburetor main body to the level of the fuel in the fuel bowl. This measurement must be made at least $1/4$ in. (6mm) away from any vertical surface in order to assure an accurate reading.
5. Stop the engine before making any adjustment to the float level. Adjustment is accomplished by bending the float tab (which contacts the fuel inlet valve) up or down as required to raise or lower the fuel level. After making an adjustment, start the engine, and allow it to idle for several minutes before repeating the fuel level check. Repeat as necessary until the proper fuel level is attained.
6. Reinstall the air horn with a new gasket and secure it with the screws. Install the identification tag in its proper location.
7. Check the idle speed, mixture, and dashpot adjustments. Install the air cleaner assembly.

MOTORCRAFT 4300, 4350

▶ See Figures 52 and 53

1. Refer to the illustration for construction of a tool used in checking the parallel setting of the dual pontoons.
2. Install the gauge on the carburetor and set it to the specified height.

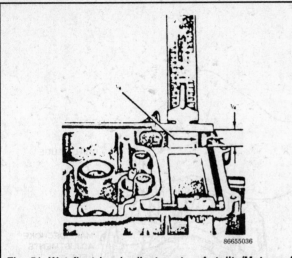

Fig. 51 Wet float level adjustment — Autolite/Motorcraft 2100, 2150, 4100

3. Check the clearance and alignment of the pontoons to the gauge. Both pontoons should just barely touch the gauge for the proper setting. Pontoons may be aligned if necessary by slightly twisting them.

4. To adjust the float level, bend the primary needle tab down to raise the float and up to lower it.

CARTER THERMO-QUAD

1. Taking note of their placement, disconnect all linkages and rods which connect the bowl cover to the carburetor body.

2. Remove the screws retaining the bowl cover.

3. Remove the bowl cover. Invert the bowl cover, taking care not to lose any of the small parts.

4. With the bowl cover inverted and the floats resting on the seated needle, measure the distance between the bowl cover (new gasket installed) to the bottom side of each float.

5. If not to specifications, bend the float lever.

➡ **Never allow the lip of the float to be pressed against the needle when adjusting the float height.**

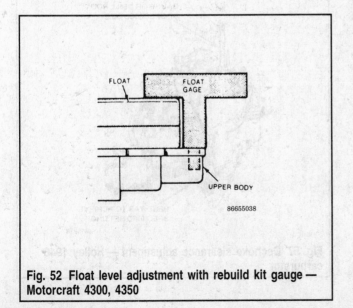

Fig. 52 Float level adjustment with rebuild kit gauge — Motorcraft 4300, 4350

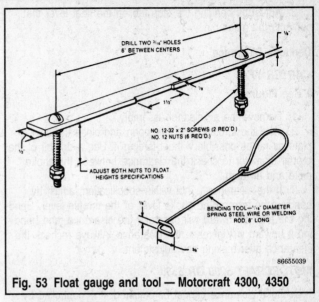

Fig. 53 Float gauge and tool — Motorcraft 4300, 4350

6. Install the bowl cover. Make sure that the float pin does not protrude past the edge of the bowl cover.

MOTORCRAFT 2700 VV AND 7200 VV

▶ **See Figure 54**

1. Remove and invert the upper part of the carburetor, with the gasket in place.

2. Measure the vertical distance between the carburetor body (outside the gasket) and the bottom of the float.

3. To adjust, bend the float operating lever that contacts the needle valve. Make sure that the float remains parallel to the gasket surface.

Float Drop

MOTORCRAFT 2700 VV AND 7200 VV

▶ **See Figure 55**

1. Remove and hold upright the upper part of the carburetor.

2. Measure the vertical distance between the carburetor body (outside the gasket) and the bottom of the float.

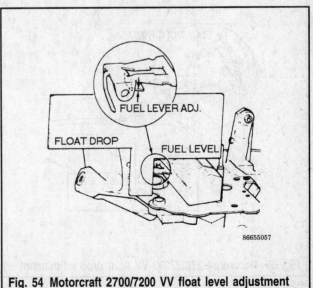

Fig. 54 Motorcraft 2700/7200 VV float level adjustment

3. Adjust by bending the stop tab on the float lever that contacts the hinge pin.

Dechoke Clearance

CARTER YFA

▶ See Figure 56

1. Remove the air cleaner assembly.
2. Hold the throttle plate fully open and close the choke plate as far as possible without forcing it. Use a drill bit of the proper diameter to check the clearance between the choke plate and air horn.
3. If the clearance is not within specification, adjust by bending the arm on the choke lever of the throttle lever. Bending the arm downward will decrease the clearance, and bending it upward will increase the clearance. Always recheck the clearance after making any adjustment.

MOTORCRAFT 5200 OR 6500

Dechoke clearance cannot be adjusted. It is controlled by the fast idle cam settings.

HOLLEY 1946

▶ See Figure 57

1. Remove the air cleaner assembly.
2. With the engine off, hold the throttle in the wide open position.
3. Insert a drill bit of the specified diameter (as indicated in the Carburetor Specifications chart, later in this section), between the upper edge of the choke plate and the air horn wall.
4. With a slight pressure against the choke shaft, a slight drag should be felt when the gauge is withdrawn.
5. To adjust, bend the unloader tab on the throttle lever.
6. Install the air cleaner assembly, if no further adjustments are required at this time.

HOLLEY 4180

1. Verify that the choke cap is set to the proper index mark, and adjust if necessary.
2. Hold the throttle in the wide open position.

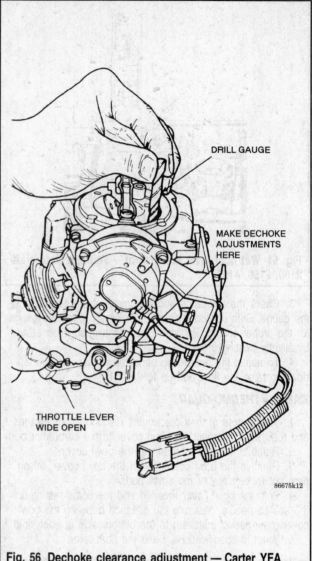

Fig. 56 Dechoke clearance adjustment — Carter YFA carburetor

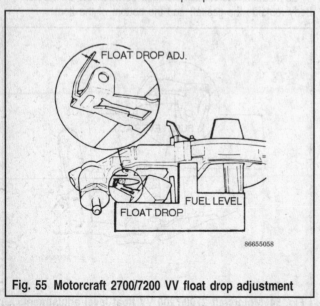

Fig. 55 Motorcraft 2700/7200 VV float drop adjustment

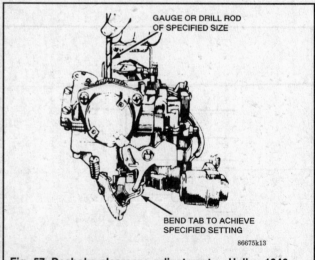

Fig. 57 Dechoke clearance adjustment — Holley 1946 carburetor

3. Apply light closing pressure on the choke plate and measure the gap between the lower edge of the choke plate and the air horn wall.

4. If adjustment is necessary, bend the pawl on the fast idle lever.

MOTORCRAFT 4300, 4350

1. Remove the air cleaner assembly.
2. Remove the automatic choke housing from the carburetor.
3. With the throttle plate wide-open and the choke plate closed as far as possible without forcing it, insert a drill gauge of the specified diameter between the choke plate and air horn.
4. To adjust, bend the arm on the choke trip lever. Bend downward to increase clearance and upward to decrease clearance. After adjusting, recheck the clearance.
5. Install the automatic choke housing, taking care to engage the thermostatic spring with the tang on the choke lever and shaft assembly.
6. Adjust the automatic choke setting. Install the air cleaner. Adjust the idle speed and dashpot, if so equipped.

Metering Rod

CARTER YFA

Remove the carburetor air horn and gasket from the carburetor. Unscrew the idle speed adjusting screw until the throttle plate is tightly closed in the throttle bore. Press downward on the end of the diaphragm shaft until the metering rod arm contacts the lifter link at the diaphragm stem. With the metering rod in this position, turn the rod adjustment screw until the metering rod just bottoms in the body casting. Turn the metering rod adjusting screw one additional turn in the clockwise direction. Install the carburetor air horn along with a new gasket.

MOTORCRAFT 2700 VV AND 7200 VV

▶ See Figure 58

➡A dial indicator and the stator cap are required for this adjustment.

1. Remove the choke coil cap, if equipped.
2. Attach a weight to the choke coil mechanism to seat the cold enrichment rod.
3. Install and zero a dial indicator with the tip placed on top of the enrichment rod. Raise and release the weight to verify zero on the dial indicator.
4. With the stator cap at the index position, the dial indicator should read the specified dimension. Turn the adjusting nut to correct it.
5. Install the choke cap at the correct setting.

Accelerator Pump Stroke

AUTOLITE/MOTORCRAFT 2100, 2150, 4100

▶ See Figure 59

The accelerating pump operating rod should be in the over-travel lever hole number listed in the Carburetor Specification chart, and in the inboard hole (hole closest to the pump plunger) in the accelerating pump link. If the pump stroke has

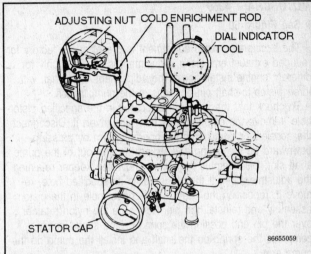

Fig. 58 Motorcraft 2700/7200 VV cold enrichment metering rod adjustment

been changed from the specified settings, use the following procedure to correct the stroke:

1. Release the operating rod from the retaining clip by pressing the tab end of the clip toward the rod while pressing the rod away from the clip until it disengages.
2. Position the clip over the specified hole (see Carburetor Specification chart) in the over-travel lever. Press the ends of the clip together and insert the operating rod through the clip and the over-travel lever. Release the clip to engage the rod.

AUTOLITE/MOTORCRAFT 4300

The pump stroke is preset at the factory to limit exhaust emissions. The additional holes in the operating arm are provided for different engine applications. The stroke should not be changed from the specified hole (see Carburetor Specifications chart).

The only adjustments possible are the pump stroke and pump stem height. To change the pump stroke, merely remove the pivot pin and reposition it in the specified hole. To adjust the pump stem height, bend the operating rod at the angles, taking care not to cause binds in the system.

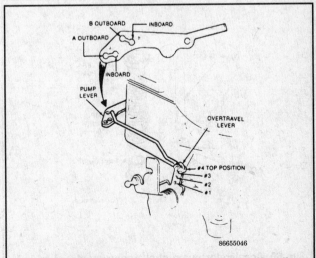

Fig. 59 Accelerator pump stroke adjustment — Autolite 2100, 2150, 4100

MOTORCRAFT 4350

▶ See Figure 60

The accelerator pump adjustment is preset at the factory for reduced exhaust emissions. Adjustment is provided only for different engine installations. The adjustment is internal, with three piston-to-shaft pin positions in the pump piston.

To check that the shaft pin is located in the specified piston hole, remove the carburetor air horn and invert it. Disconnect the accelerator pump from the operating arm by pressing downward on the spring and sliding the arm out of the pump shaft slot. Disassemble the spring and nylon keeper retaining the adjustment pin. If the pin is not in its specified hole, remove it, reposition the shaft to the correct hole in the piston assembly and reinstall the pin. Now slide the nylon retainer over the pin and position the spring on the shaft. Finally, compress the spring on the shaft and install the pump on the pump arm.

➡ **Under no circumstances should you adjust the stroke of the accelerator pump by turning the vacuum limiter lever adjusting nut. This adjustment is preset at the factory and modification could result in poor cold driveability.**

HOLLEY 1946

▶ See Figure 61

➡ **The accelerator pump stroke is pre-set at the factory and should not be adjusted in an effort to improve driveability. After disassembling the carburetor, be sure to return the accelerator pump operating link to its proper slot in the throttle return spring arm.**

1. Check the length of the accelerator pump operating link from its outside edge at the accelerator pump rod to its inside edge at the applicable slot. The measurement should be 2.140-2.160 in. (54-55mm) (1979-81) or 2.385-2.405 in. (60-61mm) (1982).

2. Adjust to the proper length, if necessary, by bending the loop in the operating link.

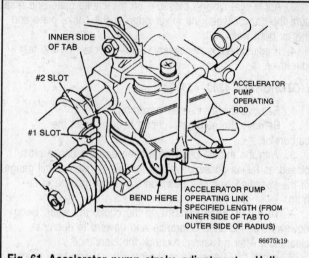

Fig. 61 Accelerator pump stroke adjustment — Holley 1946

Accelerating Pump Lever

HOLLEY 4180

1. Hold the primary throttle plates in the wide open position.

2. Using a feeler gauge, check the clearance between the accelerating pump operating lever adjustment screw head and the pump arm while depressing the pump arm with your finger.

3. To make an adjustment, loosen and hold the adjusting screw locknut and turn the adjusting screw inward to increase, or outward to decrease the adjustment. Keep in mind that a ½ turn will change the clearance by approximately 0.015 in. (0.381 mm). When the adjustment is complete, hold the adjusting screw stationary and tighten the locknut.

Throttle Positioner Clearance

ALL CARBURETORS

1. Check that the engine idle speed and mixture settings are correct and that the engine is at normal operating temperature.

2. Loosen the dashpot or solenoid locking nut.

3. With the throttle held closed, depress the plunger with a screwdriver blade and measure the clearance between the throttle lever and the plunger tip. If the clearance is not within specifications, turn the dashpot or solenoid until the proper clearance is obtained between the throttle lever and the plunger tip.

4. Tighten the locking nut and recheck the adjustment. Readjust if necessary.

Anti-Stall Dashpot

ALL MODELS

▶ See Figure 62

Make sure that the engine idle speed and mixture are correct and that the engine is at normal operating temperature. Loosen the anti-stall dashpot locknut (see accompanying illustration). With the throttle held closed, depress the plunger with a prytool and measure the clearance between the throttle lever and the plunger tip. If the clearance is not as specified in the

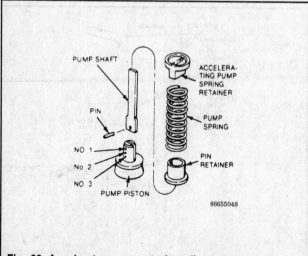

Fig. 60 Accelerator pump stroke adjustment — Motorcraft 4350

Carburetor Specification charts, turn the dashpot until the proper clearance is obtained between the throttle lever and the plunger tip. After tightening the locknut, recheck the adjustment.

Fast Idle Speed

EXCEPT MOTORCRAFT 2700 VV and 7200 VV

▶ See Figure 63

➡ **Be sure that the curb idle speed and idle mixture are set to specification before adjusting the fast idle speed.**

1. Remove the air cleaner assembly, if necessary.
2. Place the transmission in NEUTRAL or PARK and bring the engine to normal operating temperature.
3. Turn **OFF** the ignition. If so equipped, set the A/C selector to the **OFF** position.
4. Disconnect the vacuum hose at the EGR valve and plug the hose.
5. If so equipped, disconnect the wire to the electric Pump Valve Solenoid (PVS).
6. Place the fast idle adjusting screw on the specified step of the fast idle cam.
7. Connect a suitable tachometer.
8. Start the engine without touching the accelerator pedal.
9. Adjust the fast idle speed to specification by turning the adjusting screw.
10. Rev the engine momentarily to allow the engine to return to idle and turn off the ignition.
11. Disconnect and remove the tachometer.
12. Remove the plug from the EGR vacuum hose and reconnect the hose.
13. If so equipped, reconnect the wire to the electric PVS.
14. Install the air cleaner assembly, if no further adjustments are required at this time.

MOTORCRAFT 2700 VV AND 7200 VV

1. With the engine warmed up and idling, place the fast idle lever on the step specified on the engine compartment sticker or in the specifications chart. Disconnect and plug the EGR vacuum line.

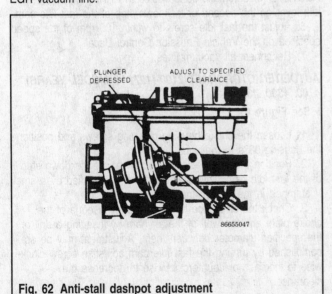

Fig. 62 Anti-stall dashpot adjustment

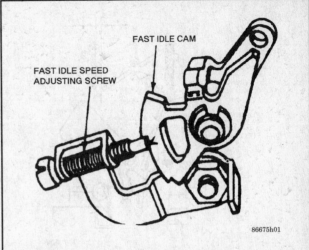

Fig. 63 Place the fast idle adjusting screw on the specified step of the fast idle cam before adjusting

2. Make sure the high speed cam positioner lever is disengaged.
3. Turn the fast idle speed screw to adjust to the specified speed.

Fast Idle Cam Index Setting

CARTER YFA

▶ See Figure 64

1. Position the fast idle screw on the second (kickdown) step of the fast idle cam, against the shoulder of the high step.
2. Apply light closing pressure on the choke plate.
3. Check the clearance between the lower edge of the choke plate and the air horn wall.
4. Adjust, if necessary, by bending the choke plate connecting rod.

1979 MOTORCRAFT 5200 OR 6500

▶ See Figure 65

1. Place the fast idle screw on the second (kickdown) step of the fast idle cam, against the shoulder of the top step.
2. Place a ⁵⁄₁₆ in. drill bit between the lower edge of the choke plate and the air horn wall. Apply light closing pressure on the choke plate to hold the drill bit in place.
3. Measure the clearance between the tang on the choke lever and the arm on the fast idle cam. This measurement should be 0.010 in. (0.25mm) maximum.
4. If the clearance is out of specification, bend the choke lever tang to adjust.

1980-82 MOTORCRAFT 5200 OR 6500

1. Place the fast idle screw on the second (kickdown) step of the fast idle cam, against the shoulder of the top step.
2. Apply light downward pressure on the choke lever tang and, using the proper size drill bit (as indicated in the Carburetor Specifications chart, later in this section), check the clearance between the lower edge of the choke plate and the air horn wall.

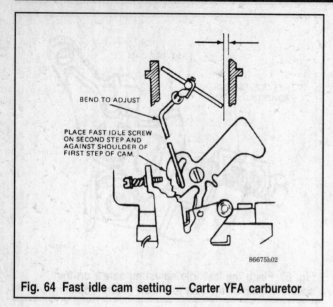

Fig. 64 Fast idle cam setting — Carter YFA carburetor

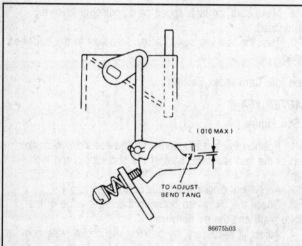

Fig. 65 Fast idle cam setting — 1979 Motorcraft 5200 or 6500 carburetor

3. If the clearance is out of specification, replace the choke lever. Do not attempt to bend the choke lever tang, since it is hardened.

HOLLEY 1946

▶ See Figure 66

1. Position the fast idle adjusting screw on the second (kickdown) step of the fast idle cam, against the shoulder of the top step.

2. Apply light closing pressure on the choke plate.

3. Check the fast idle cam setting by placing a drill bit of the specified size (as indicated in the Carburetor Specifications chart, later in this section), between the upper edge of the choke plate and the air horn wall.

4. If necessary, bend the fast idle cam link to adjust.

HOLLEY 4180

1. Remove the spark delay valve, if so equipped, from the Distributor vacuum advance line, and route the vacuum line directly to the advance side of the distributor.

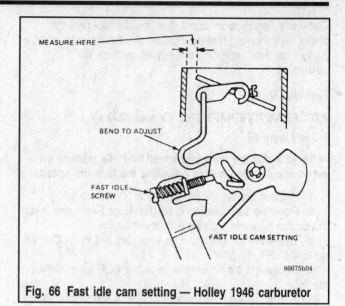

Fig. 66 Fast idle cam setting — Holley 1946 carburetor

2. Trace the Exhaust Gas Recirculation (EGR) signal vacuum line from the EGR valve to the carburetor and if there is EGR/PVS valve or temperature vacuum switch located in the vacuum line routing, disconnect the EGR vacuum line at the EGR valve and plug the line.

3. If not equipped with an EGR/PVS valve or temperature vacuum switch do not detach the EGR vacuum line.

4. Trace the purge valve vacuum line from the purge valve located on the canister, to the first point where the vacuum line can be detached from the underhood hose routing. Disconnect the vacuum line at that point, cap the open port, and plug the vacuum line.

✳✳WARNING

To prevent damage to the purge valve, do not disconnect the vacuum line at the purge valve.

5. With the engine running at normal operating temperature, the choke plate fully opened and the manual transmission in NEUTRAL (or automatic transmission in PARK), place the fast idle lever on the second or kickdown step of the fast idle cam.

6. Adjust the fast idle screw to within 100 rpm of the speed specified on the Vehicle Emission Control Decal.

7. Reconnect all vacuum lines.

AUTOLITE/MOTORCRAFT 2100 (1971-72 MODEL YEARS), 4100, 4300, 4350

▶ See Figure 67

1. Loosen the choke housing retaining screws and position the housing 90°s to the right.

2. Position the fast idle speed screw at the kickdown step of the fast idle cam. This kickdown step is identified by a small V stamped in the side of the casting.

3. Check the clearance between the lower edge of the choke plate and the wall of the air horn by inserting a drill of the specified diameter between them. Adjustment may be accomplished by turning the fast idle cam adjusting screw clockwise to increase or counterclockwise to decrease the clearance.

4. Set the choke housing to specifications, and adjust the anti-stall dashpot, idle speed, and mixture.

1973 AND LATER AUTOLITE/MOTORCRAFT 2100, 2150

1. Loosen the choke thermostatic spring housing retaining screws and rotate the housing 90°s in the rich direction.

2. Position the fast idle speed screw or lever on the high step of the cam.

3. Depress the choke pulldown diaphragm against the diaphragm stop screw thereby placing the choke in the pulldown position.

4. While holding the choke pulldown diaphragm depressed, slightly open the throttle and allow the fast idle cam to fall.

5. Close the throttle and check the position of the fast idle cam lever. When the fast idle cam is adjusted correctly, the screw should contact the V mark on the cam. Adjustment is accomplished by rotating the fast idle cam adjusting screw as needed.

MOTORCRAFT 2700 VV AND 7200 VV

▶ See Figure 68

A special tool is required for this job. Ford calls it a stator cap (#T77L-9848-A). It fits over the choke thermostatic lever when the choke cap is removed.

1. Remove the choke coil cap. On 1980 and later California models, the choke cap is riveted in place. The top rivets will have to be drilled out. The bottom rivet will have to be driven out from the rear. New rivets must be used upon installation.

2. Place the fast idle lever in the specified step of the fast idle cam (the highest step is first) with the high speed cam positioner retracted.

3. If the adjustment is being made with the carburetor removed, hold the throttle lightly closed with a rubber band.

4. Turn the stator cap clockwise until the lever contacts the fast idle cam adjusting screw.

5. Turn the fast idle cam adjusting screw until the index mark on the cap lines up with the specified mark on the casting.

6. Remove the stator cap. Install the choke coil cap and set it to the specified housing mark.

Control Vacuum

➡This procedure applies only to the Motorcraft 2700 VV and 7200 VV carburetors.

1977 MODELS

1. Make sure the idle speed is correct.

2. Using a 5/32 in. Allen wrench, turn the venturi valve diaphragm adjusting screw clockwise until the valve is firmly closed.

3. Connect a vacuum gauge to the vacuum tap on the venturi valve cover.

4. Idle the engine and use a 1/8 in. Allen wrench to turn the venturi bypass adjusting screw to the specified vacuum setting. You may have to correct the idle speed.

5. Turn the venturi valve diaphragm adjusting screw counterclockwise until the vacuum drops to the specified setting. You will have to work the throttle to get the vacuum to drop.

6. Reset the idle speed.

1980-82 MODELS

➡This procedure applies only to the Motorcraft 2700 VV and 7200 VV carburetors.

1. Remove the carburetor. Remove the venturi valve diaphragm plug with a center punch.

2. If the carburetor has a venturi valve bypass, remove it by unfastening the two cover retaining screw. Invert and remove the bypass screw plug from the cover with a drift. Install the cover.

3. Install the carburetor. Start the engine and allow it to reach normal operating temperature. Connect a vacuum gauge to the venturi valve cover. Set the idle speed to 500 rpm with the transmission in DRIVE.

4. Push and hold the venturi valve closed. Adjust the bypass screw to obtain a reading of 8 in. Hg (2 kPa) on the vacuum gauge. Make sure the idle speed remains constant. Open and close the throttle and check the idle speed.

5. With the engine idling, adjust the venturi valve diaphragm screw to obtain a reading of 6 in. Hg (1.5 kPa). Set the curb idle to specification. Install new venturi valve bypass and diaphragm plugs.

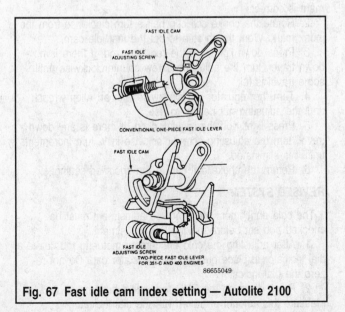

Fig. 67 Fast idle cam index setting — Autolite 2100

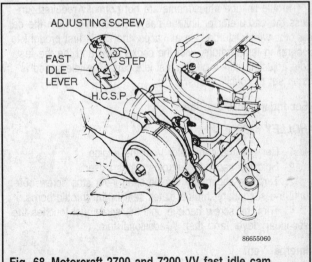

Fig. 68 Motorcraft 2700 and 7200 VV fast idle cam adjustment

Throttle Positioner Clearance

ALL CARBURETORS

1. Check that the engine idle speed and mixture settings are correct and that the engine is at normal operating temperature.
2. Loosen the dashpot or solenoid locking nut.
3. With the throttle held closed, depress the plunger with a screwdriver blade and measure the clearance between the throttle lever and the plunger tip. If the clearance is not within specifications, turn the dashpot or solenoid until the proper clearance is obtained between the throttle lever and the plunger tip.
4. Tighten the locking nut and recheck the adjustment. Re-adjust if necessary.

Vacuum Operated Throttle Modulator

HOLLEY 4180

1. Set the parking brake, put the transmission in PARK or NEUTRAL and run the engine up to operating temperature.
2. Turn off the air conditioning and heater controls.
3. Disconnect and plug the vacuum hoses at the air control valve and EGR valve and purge control valve.
4. Place the transmission in the position specified on the underhood decal.
5. If necessary, check and adjust the curb idle rpm.
6. Place the transmission in NEUTRAL or PARK and rev the engine. Place the transmission in the specified position according to the underhood decal and recheck the curb idle rpm. Readjust if necessary.
7. Connect an external vacuum source which provides a minimum of 10 in. (68 kPa) of vacuum to the Vacuum Operated Throttle Modulator (VOTM) kicker.
8. Place the transmission in the specified position.
9. Adjust the throttle kicker (VOTM) locknut if necessary to obtain the proper idle rpm.
10. Reconnect all vacuum hoses.

Throttle and Downshift Linkage

WITH MANUAL TRANSMISSION

Throttle linkage adjustments are not normally required, unless the carburetor or linkage has been removed from the car or otherwise disturbed. In all cases, the car is first brought to operating temperature, with the choke open and the the fast idle adjusting screw off the fast idle cam. The idle speed is then set to specifications.

Secondary Throttle Plate

HOLLEY 4180

1. Remove the carburetor from the engine.
2. Hold the secondary throttle plates closed.
3. Turn the secondary throttle shaft lever stop screw out until the secondary throttle plates seat in the throttle bores.
4. Turn the screw back in until the screw just touches the secondary lever, and then ¼ additional turn.

Internal Vent

➡ This procedure applies only to the Motorcraft 2700 VV and 7200 VV carburetors.

It is required whenever the idle speed adjustment is changed.
1. Make sure the idle speed is correct.
2. Place a 0.010 in. (0.25mm) feeler gauge between the accelerator pump stem and the operating link.
3. Turn the nylon adjusting nut until there is a slight drag.

Venturi Valve Limiter

➡ This procedure applies only to the Motorcraft 2700 VV and 7200 VV carburetors.

1. Remove the carburetor. Remove the venturi valve cover and the two rollers.
2. Use a center punch to loosen the expansion plug at the rear of the carburetor main body on the throttle side.
3. Use a suitable Allen wrench to remove the venturi valve wide open stop screw.
4. Hold the throttle wide-open.
5. Apply a light closing pressure on the venturi valve and check the gap between the valve and the air horn wall. To adjust, move the venturi valve to the wide-open position and insert an Allen wrench into the stop screw hole. Turn clockwise to increase the gap. Remove the wrench and check the gap again.
6. Install the wide open stop screw and turn it clockwise until it contacts the valve.
7. Push the venturi valve wide-open and check the gap. Turn the stop screw to bring the gap to specifications.
8. Reassemble the carburetor with a new expansion plug.

Control Vacuum Regulator (CVR)

➡ This procedure applies only to the Motorcraft 2700 VV and 7200 VV carburetors.

There are two systems used. The earlier system's CVR rod threads directly through the arm. The revised system, introduced in late 1977, has a ⅜ in. nylon hex adjusting nut on the CVR rod and a flange on the rod.

EARLY SYSTEM

1. Make sure that the cold enrichment metering rod adjustment is correct.
2. Rotate the choke coil cap half a turn clockwise from the index mark. Work the throttle to set the fast idle cam.
3. Press down lightly on the regulator rod. If there is no down travel, turn the adjusting screw counterclockwise until some travel is felt.
4. Turn the regulator rod clockwise with an Allen wrench until the adjusting nut begins to rise.
5. Press lightly on the regulator rod. If there is any down travel, turn the adjusting screw clockwise in ¼ turn increments until it is eliminated.
6. Return the choke coil cap to the specified setting.

REVISED SYSTEM

The cold enrichment metering rod adjustment must be checked and set before making this adjustment.
1. After adjusting the cold enrichment metering rod, leave a dial indicator in place but remove the stator cap. Do not re-zero the dial indicator.
2. Press down on the CVR rod until it bottoms on its seat. Measure this amount of travel with the dial indicator.

3. If the adjustment is incorrect, hold the ⅜ in. CVR adjusting nut with a box wrench to prevent it from turning. Use an ¹¹/₃₂ in. Allen wrench to turn the CVR rod. Turning counterclockwise will increase the travel, and vice-versa.

High Speed Cam Positioner

➡This procedure applies only to the Motorcraft 2700 VV and 7200 VV carburetors.

1. Place the high speed cam positioner in the specified cam step, counting the highest step as the first.
2. Place the fast idle lever in the corner of the positioner.
3. Hold the throttle firmly closed.
4. Remove the diaphragm cover. Adjust the diaphragm assembly clockwise until it lightly bottoms. Turn it counterclockwise ½-1½ turns until the vacuum port and diaphragm hole line up.
5. Install the cover.

CENTRAL FUEL INJECTION (CFI)

Description and Operation

▶ See Figures 69 and 70

Central Fuel Injection (CFI) is a throttle body injection system in which two fuel injectors are mounted in a common throttle body.

Fuel is supplied from the fuel tank by a high pressure, in-tank fuel pump. The fuel passes through a filter and is sent to the throttle body where a regulator keeps the fuel delivery pressure at a constant 39 psi (265 kPa). The two fuel injectors are mounted vertically above the throttle plates and are connected in line with the fuel pressure regulator. Excess fuel supplied by the pump, but not needed by the engine, is returned to the fuel tank by a steel fuel return line.

The fuel injection system is linked with and controlled by the Electronic Engine Control (EEC) system.

Fuel System Inertia Switch

▶ See Figure 71

In the event of a collision, the electrical contacts in the inertia switch open and the fuel pump automatically shuts off. The fuel pump will shut off even if the engine does not stop running. The engine, however, will stop a few seconds after the fuel pump stops. It is not possible to restart the engine until the inertia switch is manually reset. The switch is located in the luggage compartment on the left hinge support on pas-

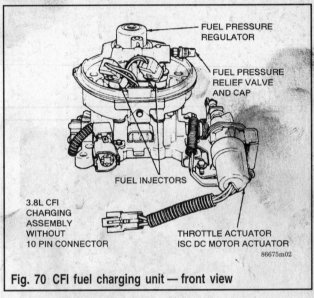
Fig. 70 CFI fuel charging unit — front view

senger vehicles or on the left side storage compartment on station wagon models. To reset, depress both buttons on the switch at the same time. Some applications have only one button on the switch assembly.

✳✳CAUTION

Do not reset the inertia switch until the complete fuel system has been inspected for leaks.

Fuel Charging Assembly

REMOVAL & INSTALLATION

▶ See Figures 72 and 73

1. Disconnect the negative battery cable. Remove the air cleaner.
2. Release the pressure from the fuel system.
3. Disconnect the throttle cable and transmission throttle valve lever.
4. Unfasten and label the fuel, vacuum and electrical connections. Use care to prevent combustion of spilled fuel.
5. Remove the fuel charging assembly retaining nuts then remove the fuel charging assembly.
6. Remove the mounting gasket from the intake manifold.
7. Installation is the reverse of removal. Tighten the fuel charging assembly nuts evenly to 120 inch lbs. (13 Nm).

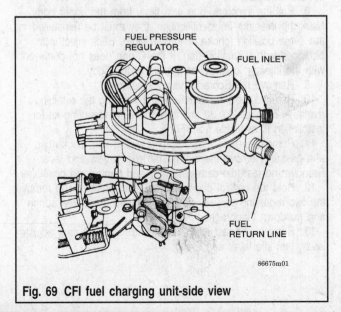
Fig. 69 CFI fuel charging unit-side view

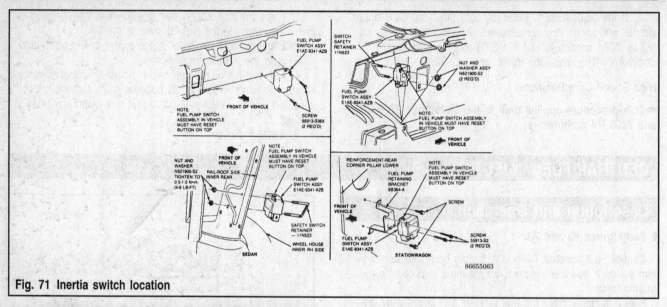

Fig. 71 Inertia switch location

Fig. 72 Remove the retaining nuts securing the fuel charging assembly to the intake manifold

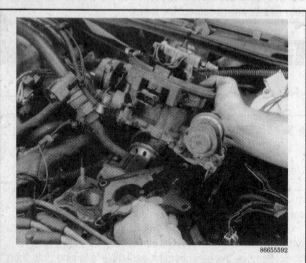

Fig. 73 Lift the assembly up and out of the engine compartment

DISASSEMBLY & ASSEMBLY

▶ **See Figure 74**

1. Remove the air cleaner mounting stud in order to separate the upper body from the throttle body.

2. Turn the fuel charging assembly (throttle body) over and remove the four screws from the bottom of the throttle body.

3. Separate the throttle body (lower half) from the main body (upper half).

4. Remove the gasket. If it is stuck and scraping is necessary, use only a plastic or wood scraper. Take care not to damage the gasket surfaces.

5. Remove the three pressure regulator mounting screws. Remove the pressure regulator.

6. Unfasten the electrical connectors at each injector by pulling outward on the connector and not on the wire. Loosen but do not remove the wiring harness retaining screw. Push in on the harness tabs to remove it from the upper body.

7. Remove the fuel injector retaining screw. Remove the injection retainer.

8. Pull the injectors, one at a time, from the upper body. Mark the injectors for identification, they must be reinstalled in the same position (choke or throttle side). Each injector is equipped with a small O-ring. If the O-ring does not come out with the injector, carefully pick it out of the body.

9. Remove the Schrader valve assembly.

10. Remove the thermostat cover by drilling the retaining rivets. A 1/8 in. or No. 30 drill is required. A mounting kit for installation is available from Ford.

11. Remove the thermostat cap retaining ring, choke cap and gasket. Remove the thermostat lever screw and lever. Remove the fast idle cam assembly and control rod positioner.

12. Hold the control diaphragm cover in position and remove the two mounting screws. Carefully remove the cover, spring and pulldown diaphragm.

13. Remove the fast idle retaining nut, fast idle cam adjuster lever, fast idle lever and E-clip.

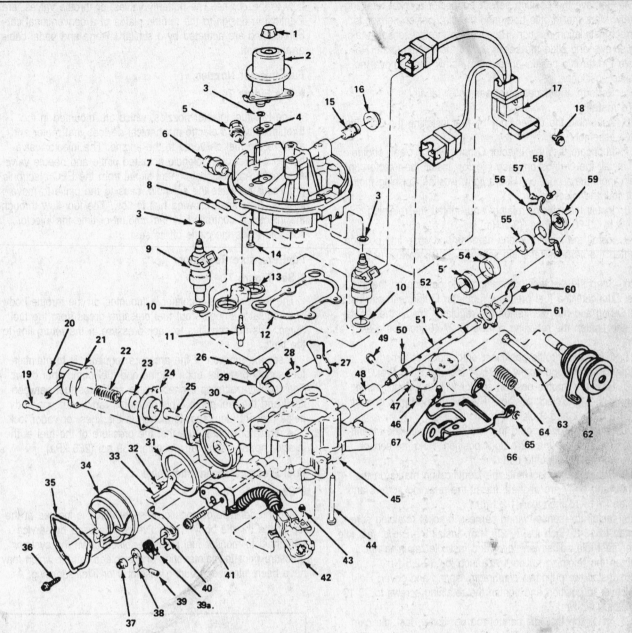

Fig. 74 Central fuel injection unit and components

Legend:

1. PLUG – FUEL PRESSURE REGULATOR ADJUSTING SCREW
2. REGULATOR ASSEMBLY – FUEL PRESSURE
3. SEAL – 5/16 x .070 "O" RING
4. GASKET – FUEL PRESSURE REGULATOR
5. CONNECTOR – 1/4 PIPE TO 1/2-20
6. CONNECTOR – 1/8 PIPE TO 9/16-16
7. BODY – FUEL CHARGING MAIN
8. PLUG – 1/16 x 27 HEADLESS HEX
9. INJECTOR ASSEMBLY – FUEL
10. SEAL – 5/8 x .103 "O" RING
11. SCREW – FUEL INJECTOR RETAINING
12. GASKET – FUEL CHARGING BODY
13. RETAINER – FUEL INJECTOR
14. SCREW M5.0 x 20.0 PAN HEAD
15. VALVE ASSEMBLY – DIAGNOSTIC VALVE
16. CAP – FUEL PRESSURE RELIEF VALVE
17. WIRING ASSEMBLY – FUEL CHARGING
18. SCREW – M3.5 x 1.27 x 12.7 PAN HEAD
19. SCREW & WASHER – M4 x 7.0 20.00
20. BALL – LEAD SHOT .26 .24 DIA.
21. COVER ASSEMBLY – CONTROL DIAPHRAGM
22. SPRING – CONTROL MODULATOR
23. RETAINER – PULLDOWN DIAPHRAGM
24. DIAPHRAGM – PULLDOWN CONTROL
25. ADJUSTER – PULLDOWN CONTROL
26. ROD – FAST IDLE CONTROL
27. CAM – FAST IDLE
28. SHAFT – CHOKE HOUSING
29. POSITIONER – FAST IDLE CONTROL ROD
30. BUSHING – CHOKE HOUSING
31. GASKET – THERMOSTAT HOUSING
32. SCREW & WASHER – M3.5 x 0.6 x 6 PAN HEAD
33. LEVER – CHOKE THERMOSTAT
34. HOUSING ASSEMBLY – THERMOSTAT
35. RETAINER – HOUSING ASSEMBLY
36. SCREW
37. NUT & WASHER ASSEMBLY – .7-6H HEX
38. LEVER – FAST IDLE CAM ADJUSTER
39. SCREW – NO. 10 - 32 x .50 SET SLOTTED HEAD
39a. FAST IDLE PICK-UP LEVER RETURN SPRING
40. LEVER – FAST IDLE
41. SCREW & WASHER – M4.07 x 22.0 PAN HEAD
42. THROTTLE POSITION SENSOR
43. SCREW – M4 x .7 x 14.0 HEX WASHER TAP
44. SCREW – M5 x .7 x 55.0
45. BODY – FUEL CHARGING – THROTTLE
46. SCREW – M3 x 0.5 x 7.4 HEX WASHER HEAD
47. PLATE – THROTTLE
48. BEARING – THROTTLE CONTROL LINKAGE
49. "E" RING – 7/32 RETAINING
50. PIN – SPRING COILED
51. SHAFT – THROTTLE
52. "C" RING – THROTTLE SHAFT BUSHING
53. BEARING – THROTTLE CONTROL LINKAGE
54. SPRING – THROTTLE RETURN
55. BUSHING – ACCELERATOR PUMP OVER TRAVEL SPRING
56. LEVER – TRANSMISSION LINKAGE
57. SCREW – M4 x 0.7 x 7.6
58. PIN – TRANSMISSION LINKAGE LEVER
59. SPACER – THROTTLE SHAFT
60. BALL – THROTTLE LEVER
61. LEVER – THROTTLE
62. POSITIONER ASSEMBLY – THROTTLE
63. SCREW – 1/4 - 28 x 2.53 HEX HEAD ADJUSTING
64. SPRING – THROTTLE POSITIONER RETAINING
65. "E" RING – RETAINING
66. BRACKET – THROTTLE POSITIONER
67. SCREW – M5 x 8 x 14.0 HEX WASHER TAP

86675mmm

14. Remove the position sensor connector bracket retaining screw. Mark the throttle body and throttle position sensor for correct installation position. Remove the throttle sensor retaining screws and slide the sensor off of the throttle shaft. Remove the throttle positioner retaining screw and remove the throttle positioner.

15. Perform any necessary cleaning or repair.

To install:

16. Assemble the upper body by first installing the Schrader valve assembly.

17. Lubricate the new injector O-rings with a clean engine oil. Install the O-rings on each injector. Install the injectors in their appropriate position. Use a light, twisting, pushing motion to install the injectors.

18. Install the injector retainer and tighten the retaining screw to 30-60 inch lbs. (3-7 Nm).

19. Install the injector wiring harness and snap into position. Tighten the harness retaining screw to 8-10 inch lbs. (0.9-1.1 Nm).

20. Snap the electrical connectors into position on the injectors. Lubricate the fuel pressure regulator O-ring with oil. Install the O-ring and new gasket on the regulator. Install the regulator and tighten the retaining screws to 27-40 inch lbs. (3-4 Nm).

21. Install the throttle positioner onto the throttle body. Tighten the retaining screw to 32-44 inch lbs. (3-5 Nm).

22. Hold the throttle position sensor with the identification mark in the 12 o'clock position. The two rotary tangs should be at 3 o'clock and 9 o'clock positions.

23. Slide the sensor onto the throttle shaft with the identification mark still in the 12 o'clock position. Hold the sensor firmly against the throttle body.

24. Rotate the sensor until the identification marks on the sensor and body are aligned. Install the retaining screws and tighten to 13-18 inch lbs. (1-2 Nm).

25. Install the sensor wiring harness bracket retaining screw, tighten to 18-22 inch lbs. (2-2.5 Nm). Install the E-clip, fast idle lever, fast idle adjustment lever and fast idle retaining nut. Tighten the retaining nut to 16-20 inch lbs. (2-2.5 Nm).

26. Install the pulldown diaphragm, spring and cover. Hold the cover in position and tighten the retaining screws to 13-19 inch lbs. (1-2 Nm).

27. Install the fast idle control rod positioner, fast idle cam and the thermostat lever. Tighten the retaining screw to 13-19 inch lbs. (1-2 Nm).

28. Install the thermostat gasket, bi-metal spring, cap and retaining ring. Install new rivets and snug them with the rivet gun. Do not break the rivets yet, loosely install so the thermostat cover can rotate. Index the thermostat and break rivets to tighten.

29. Install the gasket between the main body and the throttle body. Place the throttle body in position. Install the four retaining screws loosely. Install the air cleaner stud and tighten to 70-95 inch lbs. (8-11 Nm). Tighten the four retaining screws.

30. The rest of the assembly is in the reverse order of disassembly.

Butterfly Valves (Air Flow Control)

▶ See Figure 75

The two butterfly valves, which are mounted in a two-piece, die-cast aluminum housing called the throttle body, control air flow to the engine. The butterfly valves, or throttle valves, are identical in design to the throttle plates of a conventional carburetor and are actuated by a similar linkage and pedal cable arrangement.

Fuel Injector Nozzles

▶ See Figure 76

The two fuel injector nozzles, which are mounted in the throttle body, are electro-mechanical devices that meter and atomize the fuel delivered to the engine. The injector valve bodies consist of a solenoid actuated pintle and needle valve assembly. An electrical control signal from the EEC electronic processor activates the solenoid, causing the pintle to move inward off its seat, allowing fuel to flow. The fuel flow through the injector is controlled by the amount of time the injector solenoid holds the pintle off its seat.

Fuel Pressure Regulator

▶ See Figure 77

The fuel pressure regulator is mounted on the throttle body. The regulator smooths out fuel pressure drops from the fuel pump. It is not sensitive to back pressure in the return line to the tank.

A second function of the pressure regulator is to maintain fuel supply pressure upon engine and fuel pump shut down. The regulator acts as a check valve and traps fuel between itself and the fuel pump. This promotes rapid start ups and helps prevent fuel vapor formation in the lines, or vapor lock. The regulator makes sure that the pressure of the fuel at the injector nozzles stays at a constant 39 psi (265 kPa).

Fuel Pressure Diagnostic Valve

▶ See Figure 78

A Schrader-type diagnostic pressure valve is located at the top of the throttle body. This valve can be used by service personnel to monitor fuel pressure, bleed down the system pressure prior to maintenance and to bleed out air which may have been introduced during assembly or filter servicing. A

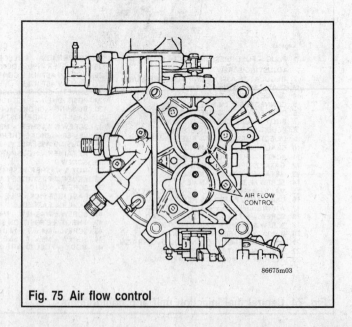

86675m03

Fig. 75 Air flow control

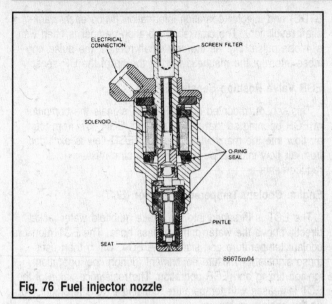

Fig. 76 Fuel injector nozzle

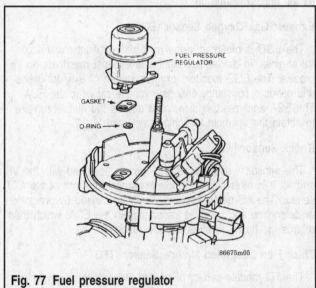

Fig. 77 Fuel pressure regulator

special Ford Tool (T80L-9974-A) is used to accomplish these procedures.

✳✳CAUTION

Under no circumstances should compressed air be forced into the fuel system using the diagnostic valve.

Cold Engine Speed Control (Throttle Stop Cam Positioner) — V8 engine

The cold engine speed control serves the same purpose as the fast idle speed device on a carbureted engine, which is to raise engine speed during cold engine idle. A throttle stop cam positioner is used on the V8 engine. The cam is positioned by a bimetal spring and an electric heating element. The cold engine speed control is attached to the throttle body. As the engine heats up, the fast idle cam on the cold engine speed control is gradually repositioned by the bimetal spring, heating element and EEC computer until normal idle speed is reached. The EEC computer automatically kicks down the fast idle cam

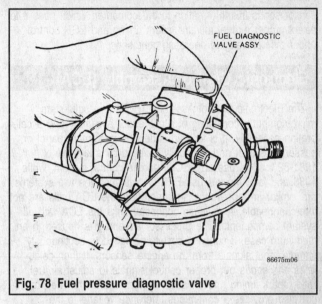

Fig. 78 Fuel pressure diagnostic valve

to a lower step (lower engine speed) by supplying vacuum to the automatic kickdown motor which physically moves the high speed cam a predetermined time after the engine starts.

Idle Speed Controller (ISC) DC Motor Actuator — V6 engine
▶ See Figure 79

The DC motor actuator controls idle speed by modulating the throttle lever. The resulting airflow regulation permits the desired engine rpm for warm engine operation, as well as the additional engine speed required during cold engine idle. An Idle Tracking Switch (ITS), integral to the DC motor, determines when the throttle lever has contacted the actuator, thereby signaling the need to control engine rpm. The DC motor extends or retracts a linear shaft through a gear reduction system. The motor direction is determined by the polarity of the applied voltage.

Throttle Position Sensor

This sensor is attached to the throttle body and is used to monitor changes in throttle plate position. The throttle position

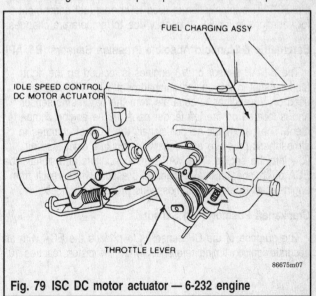

Fig. 79 ISC DC motor actuator — 6-232 engine

sensor sends this information to the computer, which uses it to select proper air/fuel mixture, spark timing and EGR control under different engine operating conditions.

Electronic Control Assembly (ECA)

The Electronic Control Assembly (ECA) is a solid-state micro-computer consisting of a processor assembly and a calibration assembly. It is located under the instrument panel or passenger's seat and is usually covered by a kick panel. 1981-82 models use an EEC-III engine control system, while 1983 and later models use EEC-IV. Although the two systems are similar in appearance and operation, the ECA units are not interchangeable. A multi-pin connector links the ECA with all system components. The processor assembly is housed in an aluminum case. It contains circuits designed to continuously sample input signals from the engine sensors. It then calculates and sends out proper control signals to adjust air/fuel ratio, spark timing and emission system operation. The processor also provides a continuous reference voltage to the B/MAP, EVP and TPS sensors. EEC-III reference voltage is 8-10 volts, while EEC-IV systems use a 5-volt reference signal. The calibration assembly is contained in a black plastic housing which plugs into the top of the processor assembly. It contains the memory and programming information used by the processor to determine optimum operating conditions. Different calibration information is used in different vehicle applications, such as California or Federal models. For this reason, careful identification of the engine, year, model and type of electronic control system is essential to insure correct component replacement.

ENGINE SENSORS

Air Charge Temperature Sensor (ACT)

The ACT is threaded into the intake manifold air runner. It is located behind the distributor on V6 engines and directly below the accelerator linkage on V8 engines. The ACT monitors air/fuel charge temperature and sends an appropriate signal to the ECA. This information is used to correct fuel enrichment for variations in intake air density due to temperature changes.

Barometric & Manifold Absolute Pressure Sensors (B/MAP)

The B/MAP sensor on V8 engines is located on the right fender panel in the engine compartment. The MAP sensor used on V6 engines is separate from the barometric sensor and is located on the left fender panel in the engine compartment. The barometric sensor signals the ECA of changes in atmospheric pressure and density to regulate calculated air flow into the engine. The MAP sensor monitors and signals the ECA of changes in intake manifold pressure which result from engine load, speed and atmospheric pressure changes.

Crankshaft Position (CP) Sensor

The purpose of the CP sensor is to provide the ECA with an accurate ignition timing reference (when the piston reaches 10°

BTDC) and injector operation information (twice each crankshaft revolution). The crankshaft vibration damper is fitted with a 4-lobe pulse ring. As the crankshaft rotates, the pulse ring lobes interrupt the magnetic field at the tip of the CP sensor.

EGR Valve Position Sensor (EVP)

This sensor, mounted on EGR valve, signals the computer of EGR opening so that it may subtract EGR flow from total air flow into the manifold. In this way, EGR flow is excluded from air flow information used to determine mixture requirements.

Engine Coolant Temperature Sensor (ECT)

The ECT is threaded into the intake manifold water jacket directly above the water pump bypass hose. The ECT monitors coolant temperature and signals the ECA, which then uses these signals for mixture enrichment (during cool operation), ignition timing and EGR operation. The resistance value of the ECT increases with temperature, causing a voltage signal drop as the engine warms up.

Exhaust Gas Oxygen Sensor (EGO)

The EGO is mounted in the right side exhaust manifold on V8 engines, in the left and right side exhaust manifolds on V6 models. The EGO monitors oxygen content of exhaust gases and sends a constantly changing voltage signal to the ECA. The ECA analyzes this signal and adjusts the air/fuel mixture to obtain the optimum (stoichiometric) ratio.

Knock Sensor (KS)

This sensor is used on various models equipped with the V6 engine. It is attached to the intake manifold in front of the ACT sensor. The KS detects engine vibrations caused by preignition or detonation and provides information to the ECA, which then retards the timing to eliminate detonation.

Thick Film Integrated Module Sensor (TFI)

The TFI module sensor plugs into the distributor just below the distributor cap and replaces the CP sensor on some engines. Its function is to provide the ECA with ignition timing information, similar to what the CP sensor provides.

Throttle Position Sensor (TPS)

The TPS is mounted on the right side of the throttle body, directly connected to the throttle shaft. The TPS senses the throttle movement and position, and transmits an appropriate electrical signal to the ECA. These signals are used by the ECA to adjust the air/fuel mixture, spark timing and EGR operation according to engine load at idle, part throttle, or full throttle. The TPS is nonadjustable.

CFI COMPONENT TESTING

➡**Diagnostic and test procedures on the EEC-III and EEC-IV electronic control systems require the use of special test equipment. Have these systems tested professionally.**

Before beginning any component testing, always check the following:

• Check the fuel and ignition systems to ensure that there is fuel and spark.

• Remove the air cleaner assembly and inspect all vacuum and pressure hoses for proper connection to fittings. Check for damaged or pinched hoses.

• Inspect all sub-system wiring harnesses for proper connections to the EGR solenoid valves, injectors, sensors, etc.

• Check for loose or detached connectors and broken or detached wires. Check that all terminals are seated firmly and are not corroded. Look for partially broken or frayed wires or any shorting between the wires.

• Inspect the sensors for physical damage. Inspect the vehicle electrical system. Check the battery for full charge and cable connections for tightness.

• Inspect the relay connector and make sure the ECA power relay is securely attached and making a good ground connection.

Solenoid and Sensor Resistance Tests

All CFI components must be disconnected from the circuit before testing the resistance with a suitable ohmmeter. Replace any component whose measured resistance does not agree with the specifications chart. Shorting the wiring harness across a solenoid valve can burn out the circuitry in the ECA that controls the solenoid valve actuator. Exercise caution when testing the solenoid valves to avoid accidental damage to the ECA.

Fuel Pressure Tests

The Schrader valve is located at the top of the fuel charging main body. This valve provides a convenient point to monitor fuel pressure, bleed down the system pressure prior to maintenance, and to bleed out air which may become trapped in the system during filter replacement. A pressure gauge with a adapter is required to perform pressure tests.

SYSTEM PRESSURE TEST

Testing fuel pressure requires the use of a special pressure gauge (T80L-9974-A or equivalent) that attaches to the pressure tap on the fuel charging assembly. Depressurize the fuel system before disconnecting any lines.

1. Disconnect the fuel return line at the throttle body and position the hose into a 1 quart (448 g) calibrated container. Connect a pressure gauge.

ELECTRONIC MULTI-POINT FUEL INJECTION (MPFI)

▶ **See Figures 80 and 81**

Description

The Electronic Fuel Injection (EFI) system is classified as a multi-point, pulse time, mass air flow (or speed density control) fuel injection system. Fuel is metered into the intake air stream

2. Unfasten the electrical connector at the fuel pump. The connector is located ahead of fuel tank (in-tank high pressure pump) or just forward of pump outlet (in-line high pressure pump). Connect an auxiliary wiring harness to the connector of the fuel pump. Energize the pump for 10 seconds by applying 12 volts to the auxiliary harness connector. Allow the fuel to drain into the calibrated container. Note the fuel volume and pressure gauge reading.

3. Correct fuel pressure should be 35-45 psi (241-310 kPa). Fuel volume should be 10 oz. (280 g) in 10 seconds (minimum) and fuel pressure should maintain a minimum of 30 psi (206 kPa) immediately after pump cut-off.

If the pressure condition is met, but the fuel flow is below specification, check for blocked filter(s) and fuel supply lines. After correcting the problem, repeat the test procedure. If the fuel flow is still inadequate, replace the high pressure pump. If the flow specification is met but the pressure is not, check for a worn or damaged pressure regulator valve on the throttle body. If both the pressure and fuel flow specifications are met, but the pressure drops excessively after de-energizing, check for a leaking injector valve(s) and/or pressure regulator valve. If the injector valves and pressure regulator valve are okay, replace the high pressure pump. If no pressure or flow is seen in the fuel system, check for blocked filters and fuel lines. If no trouble is found, replace the inline fuel pump, in-tank fuel pump and the fuel filter inside the tank.

FUEL INJECTOR PRESSURE TEST

1. Connect pressure gauge T80L-9974-A, or equivalent, to the fuel pressure test fitting. Unplug the coil connector from the ignition coil. Unfasten the electrical lead from one injector and pressurize the fuel system. Disable the fuel pump by disconnecting the inertia switch or the fuel pump relay and observe the pressure gauge reading.

2. Crank the engine for 2 seconds. Turn the ignition **OFF** and wait 5 seconds, then observe the pressure drop. If the pressure drop is 2-16 psi (14-110 kPa), the injector is operating properly. Reconnect the injector, activate the fuel pump, then repeat the procedure for other injector.

3. If the pressure drop is less than 2 psi (14 kPa) or more than 16 psi (110 kPa), switch the electrical connectors on the injectors and repeat the test. If the pressure drop is still incorrect, replace the suspected injector with one of the same color code, then reconnect both injectors properly and repeat the test.

in accordance with engine demand through four injectors mounted on a tuned intake manifold. In addition, a blow-through turbocharger system is utilized on 1984 — 85 4-cylinder engines to reduce fuel delivery time and increase power.

An on-board vehicle electronic engine control (EEC) computer accepts input from various engine sensors to compute the required fuel flow rate necessary to maintain a prescribed air/fuel ratio throughout the entire engine operational range.

The computer then outputs a command to the fuel injectors to meter the approximate quantity of fuel.

The EFI fuel delivery sub-system consists of a high pressure, chassis-mounted, electric fuel pump delivering fuel from the fuel tank through a 20 micron fuel filter to a fuel charging manifold assembly. The SEFI fuel delivery sub-system consists of a low pressure in-tank mounted fuel pump, a fuel filter/reservoir and a high pressure electric fuel pump delivering fuel from the fuel tank through a 20 micron fuel filter to a fuel charging manifold assembly.

The fuel charging manifold assembly incorporates electrically actuated fuel injectors directly above each of the engine's intake ports. The injectors, when energized, spray a metered quantity of fuel into the intake air stream.

A constant fuel pressure drop is maintained across the injector nozzles by a pressure regulator. The regulator is connected in series with the fuel injectors and positioned downstream from them. Excess fuel supplied by the pump, but not required by the engine, passes through the regulator and returns to the fuel tank through a fuel return line.

All EFI injectors are energized simultaneously, once every crankshaft revolution. The period of time that the injectors are energized (injector on-time or the pulse width) is controlled by the vehicle's Engine Electronic Control (EEC) computer, which responds to input from various engine sensors. In this manner, the EEC computer determines the required fuel flow rate, in order to maintain a prescribed air/fuel ratio throughout the entire engine operational range. In addition, on turbocharged models, air entering the engine is measured by a vane air flow meter, located between the air cleaner and the fuel charging manifold assembly. This air flow information is used in conjunction with input from the other engine sensors to compute the required fuel flow rate. The computer determines the needed injector pulse width and outputs a command to the injector to meter the exact quantity of fuel.

Fig. 80 MPFI system components

86655065

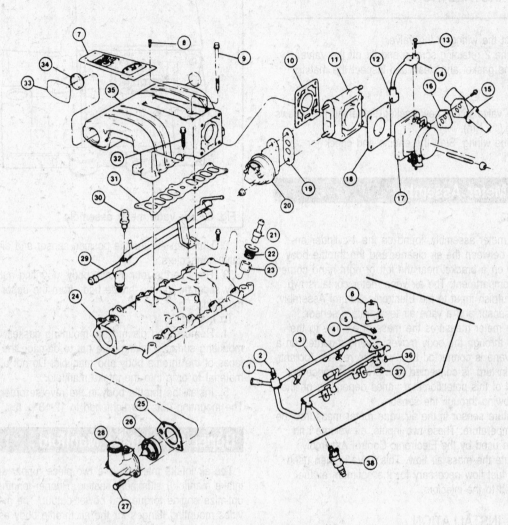

1. Schrader valve
2. Cap-Schrader valve
3. Fuel rail assy
4. Seal O-ring ⁵⁄₁₆-18 × 6.07 inch
5. Gasket, fuel pressure regulator
6. Fuel pressure regulator
7. Cover, upper manifold
8. Screw
9. Bolt ⁵⁄₁₆-18 × 6.07 inch
10. Gasket, EGR spacer
11. EGR spacer
12. Connector, tp sensor (pia tps)
13. Screw
14. Sensor, throttle position
15. Throttle air bypass valve
16. Gasket, throttle air bypass valve
17. Throttle body assy
18. Gasket, throttle body
19. Gasket, EGR valve
20. EGR valve assy
21. PCV valve assy
22. PCV grommet
23. Element, crankcase vent
24. Lower intake manifold
25. Gasket, thermostat housing
26. Thermostat
27. Bolt ⁵⁄₁₆-18 × 3.50 inch
28. Connector assy, engine coolant outlet
29. Tube, heater water supply and return
30. Sensor, EEC coolant temperature
31. Gasket, upper to lower manifold
32. Bolt ⁵⁄₁₆-18 × 1.62 inch
33. Cover, decorative end
34. Plug—cap 1.75 inch dia.
35. Upper intake manifold
36. Screw—socket head 5.0 × 0.8 × 1.0
37. Botl, att rail assy to lower manifold
38. Fuel injector

86655a70

Fig. 81 Exploded view of MPFI components

Air Bypass Valve

REMOVAL & INSTALLATION

1. Disconnect the wiring at the valve.
2. Remove the 2 retaining screws and lift off the valve.
3. Discard the gasket and clean and inspect the mating surfaces.

To install:

4. Install the valve with a new gasket, tightening the screws to 102 inch lbs. (11 Nm).
5. Connect the wiring. Start the engine and check for proper operation.

Air Vane Meter Assembly

▶ **See Figure 82**

The air vane meter assembly, found on the 4-cylinder engine, is located between the air cleaner and the throttle body and is mounted on a bracket near the left or right hand corner of the engine compartment. The air vane meter contains two sensors which furnish input to the Electronic Control Assembly: a vane airflow sensor and a vane air temperature sensor.

The air vane meter measures the mass of air flow to the engine. Air flow through the body moves a vane mounted on a pivot pin. This vane is connected to a variable resistor (potentiometer) which, in turn, is connected to a 5-volt reference voltage. The output of this potentiometer varies depending on the volume of air flowing through the sensor.

The temperature sensor in the air vane meter measures the incoming air temperature. These two inputs, air volume and temperature, are used by the Electronic Control Assembly (ECA) to compute the mass air flow. This valve is then used to compute the fuel flow necessary for the optimum air/fuel ratio which is fed to the injectors.

REMOVAL & INSTALLATION

1. Loosen the hose clamp which secures the engine air cleaner outlet hose to the vane meter assembly.
2. Remove air intake and outlet tube from the air cleaner.
3. Disengage four spring clamps and remove air cleaner front cover and air cleaner filter panel.
4. Remove the two screw and washer assemblies which secure the air meter to its bracket. Remove the air vane meter assembly.
5. Installation is the reverse of removal.

Throttle Body

REMOVAL & INSTALLATION

▶ **See Figures 83 and 84**

1. Disconnect the air intake hose.

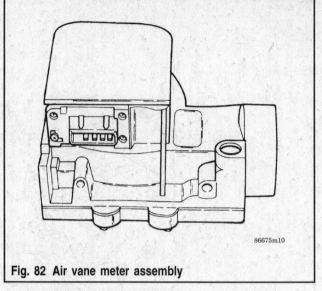

Fig. 82 Air vane meter assembly

2. Unfasten the throttle position sensor and air bypass valve connectors.
3. Remove the four throttle body mounting nuts and carefully separate the air throttle body from the upper intake manifold.

To install:

4. Remove and discard the mounting gasket. Clean all mounting surfaces taking care not to damage the gasket surfaces of the throttle body and manifold. Do not allow any material to drop into the intake manifold.
5. Install the throttle body in the reverse order of removal. The mounting nuts are tightened to 12-18 ft. lbs. (16-23 Nm).

Upper (Air) Intake Manifold

The air intake manifold is a two piece (upper and lower intake manifold) aluminum casting. Runner lengths are tuned to optimize engine torque and power output. The manifold provides mounting flanges for the air throttle body assembly, fuel supply manifold and accelerator control bracket and the EGR valve and supply tube. Vacuum taps are provided to support

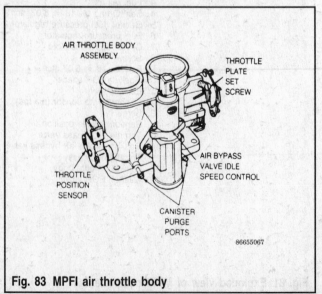

Fig. 83 MPFI air throttle body

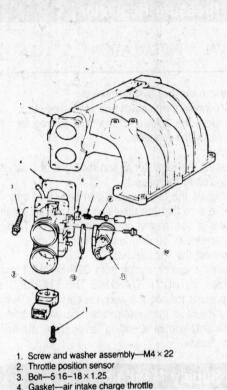

1. Screw and washer assembly—M4 × 22
2. Throttle position sensor
3. Bolt—5 16–18 × 1.25
4. Gasket—air intake charge throttle
5. Manifold—intake upper
6. Plug—throttle plate set screw locking
7. Spring—throttle plate set screw
8. Screw—10.32 × 1 50 hex head slotted
9. Cap—throttle plate set screw
10. Bolt—M6 × 20
11. Air bypass valve assembly
12. Gasket—air bypass

86655068

Fig. 84 Disassembled MPFI throttle body

various engine accessories. Pockets for the fuel injectors are machined to prevent both air and fuel leakage. The pockets, in which the injectors are mounted, are placed to direct the injector fuel spray immediately in front of each engine intake valve.

REMOVAL & INSTALLATION

1. Disconnect the air cleaner outlet tube from the air intake throttle body.
2. Unplug the throttle position sensor from the wiring harness.
3. Unplug the air by-pass valve connector.
4. Remove the three upper manifold retaining bolts.
5. Remove the upper manifold assembly.

6. Remove and discard the gasket from the lower manifold assembly.

❋❋WARNING

If scraping is necessary, be careful not to damage the gasket surfaces, or allow any material to drop into the lower manifold.

7. Installation is the reverse of removal. Tighten the upper intake manifold bolts 15-22 ft. lbs. (19-29 Nm). Use a new gasket between the manifolds.

Pressure Relief Valve

REMOVAL & INSTALLATION

▶ **See Figure 85**

1. If the fuel charging assembly is mounted on the engine, the fuel system must be depressurized.
2. Using an open end wrench or suitable deep well socket, remove the pressure relief valve from the injection manifold.
3. Installation is the reverse of removal. Torque the valve 48-84 inch lbs.

Fuel Injectors

REMOVAL & INSTALLATION

▶ **See Figures 86 and 87**

1. Relieve the fuel system pressure.
2. Disconnect the negative battery cable.
3. Remove the upper intake manifold.
4. Remove the fuel supply manifold.
5. Disconnect the wiring at the injectors.
6. Pull upward on the injector body while gently rocking it from side-to-side.

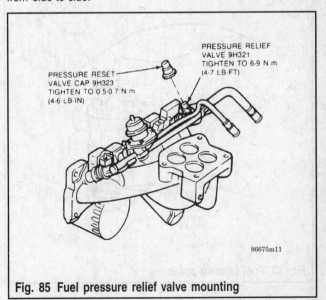

86675m11

Fig. 85 Fuel pressure relief valve mounting

To install:

7. Inspect the O-rings on the injector for any sign of leakage or damage. Replace any suspected O-rings.

8. Inspect the plastic cap at the top of each injector and replace it if any sign of deterioration is noticed.

9. Lubricate the O-rings with clean engine oil only.

10. Install the injectors by pushing them in with a gentle rocking motion.

11. Install the fuel supply manifold.

12. Connect the electrical wiring.

13. Install the upper intake manifold.

14. Turn the ignition switch from **OFF** to **ON** a at least half a dozen times, WITHOUT STARTING THE ENGINE, leaving it in the **ON** position for about 5 seconds each time. This will build up fuel pressure in the system. Start the engine and allow it to run at idle until normal operating temperature is reached. Check for leaks.

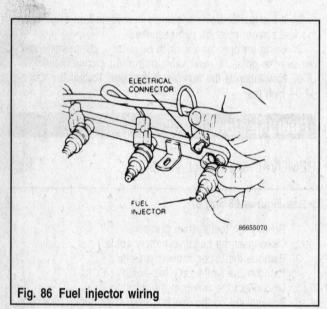

Fig. 86 Fuel injector wiring

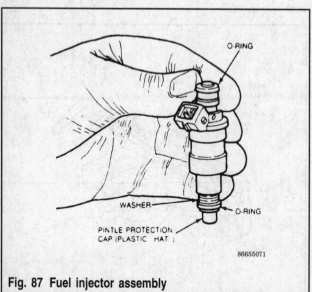

Fig. 87 Fuel injector assembly

Fuel Pressure Regulator

REMOVAL & INSTALLATION

1. Relieve the fuel system pressure.
2. Disconnect the vacuum line at the regulator.
3. Remove the 3 Allen screws from the regulator housing.
4. Remove the regulator.

To install:

5. Inspect the regulator O-ring for signs of deterioration or damage. Discard the gasket.

6. Lubricate the O-ring with clean engine oil only.

7. Make sure that the mounting surfaces are clean.

8. Using a new gasket, install the regulator. Tighten the retaining screws to 40 inch lbs. (4 Nm).

9. Connect the vacuum line.

10. Turn the ignition switch from **OFF** to **ON** at least half a dozen times, WITHOUT STARTING THE ENGINE, leaving it in the **ON** position for about 5 seconds each time. This will build up fuel pressure in the system. Start the engine and allow it to run at idle until normal operating temperature is reached. Check for leaks.

Fuel Supply Manifold

REMOVAL & INSTALLATION

1. Relieve the fuel system pressure.
2. Remove the upper manifold.
3. Disconnect the chassis fuel inlet and outlet lines at the fuel supply manifold using tool T81P-19623-G or G1 or equivalent.
4. Remove the 4 fuel supply manifold retaining bolts.
5. Carefully disengage the manifold from the injectors and lift it off.

To install:

6. Inspect all components for signs of damage. Make sure that the injector caps are clean.

➡ **When installing fuel rail assemblies with new or used injectors particular attention should be paid to proper seating of O-rings to ensure that no fuel leaks exist.**

7. Place the fuel supply manifold over the injectors and seat the injectors carefully in the manifold. Push fuel rail down to ensure all injector O-rings are fully seated in the fuel rail cups and intake manifold.

8. Install the 4 bolts and tighten them to 20 ft. lbs. (26 Nm).

9. Connect the fuel lines.

10. Install the upper manifold.

11. Turn the ignition switch from **OFF** to **ON** at least half a dozen times, WITHOUT STARTING THE ENGINE, leaving it in the **ON** position for about 5 seconds each time. This will build up fuel pressure in the system. Start the engine and allow it to run at idle until normal operating temperature is reached. Check for leaks.

Throttle Position Sensor

REMOVAL & INSTALLATION

1. Disconnect the wiring harness from the TPS.
2. Matchmark the sensor and throttle body for installation reference.
3. Remove the 2 retaining screws and remove the TPS.

To install:

4. The throttle position sensor must be reused. Install bushing wit outward.
5. Install the TPS on throttle shaft rotate assembly 10-20° counterclockwis
6. Install the 2 throttle position senso Tighten to 11-16 inch lbs. (1-2 Nm).
7. Cycle throttle lever to the wide-open t return without any interference.
8. Connect throttle position sensor to the w Start the engine and check system for proper op

Troubleshooting Basic Fuel System Problems

Problem	Cause	Solution
Engine cranks, but won't start (or is hard to start) when cold	· Empty fuel tank · Incorrect starting procedure · Defective fuel pump · No fuel in carburetor · Clogged fuel filter · Engine flooded · Defective choke	· Check for fuel in tank · Follow correct procedure · Check pump output · Check for fuel in the carburetor · Replace fuel filter · Wait 15 minutes; try again · Check choke plate
Engine cranks, but is hard to start (or does not start) when hot— (presence of fuel is assumed)	· Defective choke	· Check choke plate
Rough idle or engine runs rough	· Dirt or moisture in fuel · Clogged air filter · Faulty fuel pump	· Replace fuel filter · Replace air filter · Check fuel pump output
Engine stalls or hesitates on acceleration	· Dirt or moisture in the fuel · Dirty carburetor · Defective fuel pump · Incorrect float level, defective accelerator pump	· Replace fuel filter · Clean the carburetor · Check fuel pump output · Check carburetor
Poor gas mileage	· Clogged air filter · Dirty carburetor · Defective choke, faulty carburetor adjustment	· Replace air filter · Clean carburetor · Check carburetor
Engine is flooded (won't start accompanied by smell of raw fuel)	· Improperly adjusted choke or carburetor	· Wait 15 minutes and try again, without pumping gas pedal · If it won't start, check carburetor

86655400

Carter YFA Specifications

Year	Model ①	Float Level (in.)	Fast Idle Cam (in.)	Choke Plate Pulldown (in.)	Unloader (in.)	Dechoke (in.)	Choke
1983	E3ZE-LA	0.650	0.140	0.260	—	0.220	—
	E3ZE-MA	0.650	0.140	0.260	—	0.220	—
	E3ZE-TB	0.650	0.140	0.240	—	0.220	—
	E3ZE-UA	0.650	0.140	0.240	—	0.220	—
	E3ZE-VA	0.650	0.140	0.260	—	0.220	—
	E3ZE-YA	0.650	0.140	0.260	—	0.220	—
	E3ZE-NB	0.650	0.160	0.260	—	0.220	—
	E3ZE-PB	0.650	0.160	0.260	—	0.220	—
	E3ZE-ASA	0.650	0.160	0.260	—	0.220	—
	E3ZE-APA	0.650	0.140	0.240	—	0.220	—
	E3ZE-ARA	0.650	0.140	0.240	—	0.220	—
	E3ZE-ADA	0.650	0.140	0.260	—	0.220	—
	E3ZE-AEA	0.650	0.140	0.260	—	0.220	—
	E3ZE-ACA	0.650	0.140	0.260	—	0.220	—
	E3ZE-ATA	0.650	0.160	0.260	—	0.220	—
	E3ZE-ABA	0.650	0.140	0.260	—	0.220	—
	E3ZE-UB	0.650	0.140	0.240	—	0.220	—
	E3ZE-TC	0.650	0.140	0.240	—	0.220	—
1984—85	E4ZE-HC, DB	0.650	0.140	0.260	—	0.270	—
	E4ZE-MA, NA	0.650	0.140	0.240	—	0.270	—
	E4ZE-PA, RA	0.650	0.140	0.260	—	0.270	—
	E5ZE-CA	0.650	0.140	0.260	—	0.270	—
	E4ZE-PB, RB	0.650	0.140	0.240	—	0.270	—

① Model number located on the tag or casting

86675cca

Motorcraft 2100, 2150 Specifications

Year	(9510) * Carburetor Identification	Dry Float Level (in.)	Wet Float Level (in.)	Pump Setting Hole # ①	Choke Plate Pulldown (in.)	Fast Idle Cam Linkage Clearance (in.)	Fast Idle (rpm)	Dechoke (in.)	Choke Setting
1971	D1YF-DA	7/16	13/16	3	0.200	0.160	1500	0.060	Index
	D1MF-JA	7/16	13/16	3	0.190	0.160	1500	0.060	1 Rich
	D1MF-FA	7/16	13/16	3	0.200	0.160	1500	0.060	1 Rich
1972	D2AF-FB	7/16	13/16	3	0.140	0.130	1500	0.030	Index
	D2AF-GB	7/16	13/16	3	0.140	0.130	1500	0.030	Index
	D2AF-HA	7/16	13/16	2	0.150	0.130	1400	0.060	1 Rich
	D2GF-AA	7/16	13/16	2	0.150	0.130	1400	0.060	1 Rich
	D2GF-BA	7/16	13/16	2	0.150	0.130	1400	0.060	1 Rich
	D2MF-FB	7/16	13/16	4	0.180	0.150	1500	0.060	1 Rich
	D2OF-KA	7/16	13/16	2	0.150	0.130	1400	0.060	1 Rich
	D2OF-VB	7/16	13/16	3	0.190	0.160	1400	0.030	2 Rich
	D2WF-CA	7/16	13/16	3	0.190	0.160	1400	0.030	2 Rich
	D2ZF-FA	7/16	13/16	2	0.150	0.130	1400	0.060	1 Rich
	D2ZF-LA	7/16	13/16	3	0.240	0.210	1500	0.030	1 Rich
1973	D3AF-CE	7/16	13/16	3	②	②	1500	②	1 Rich
	D3AF-DC	7/16	13/16	3	②	②	1500	②	3 Rich
	D3GF-AF	7/16	13/16	2	②	②	1400	②	3 Rich
	D3GF-BB	7/16	13/16	2	②	②	1250	②	3 Rich
	D3ZF-EA	7/16	13/16	2	②	②	1400	②	1 Rich
	D3AF-KA	7/16	13/16	3	②	②	1500	②	3 Rich
	D3MF-AE	7/16	13/16	3	②	②	1500	②	3 Rich
	D3MF-BA	7/16	13/16	3	②	②	1500	②	3 Rich

86675ccc

Motorcraft 2100, 2150 Specifications (Cont.)

Year	(9510) * Carburetor Identification	Dry Float Level (in.)	Wet Float Level (in.)	Pump Setting Hole # ①	Choke Plate Pulldown (in.)	Fast Idle Cam Linkage Clearance (in.)	Fast Idle (rpm)	Dechoke (in.)	Choke Setting
1974	D4AE-DA	7/16	13/16	2	②	②	1500	②	1 Rich
	D4AE-EA	7/16	13/16	2	②	②	.1500	②	3 Rich
	D4AE-FA	7/16	13/16	3	②	②	1500	②	3 Rich
	D4AE-GA	7/16	13/16	3	②	②	1500	②	3 Rich
	D4DE-LA	7/16	13/16	2	②	②	1500	②	3 Rich
	D4DE-RB	7/16	13/16	2	②	②	1500	②	3 Rich
	D4OE-FA	7/16	13/16	2	②	②	1500	②	3 Rich
	D4AE-HB	7/16	13/16	3	②	②	1500	②	3 Rich
	D4DE-NB	7/16	13/16	2	②	②	1500	②	3 Rich
	D4DE-PA	7/16	13/16	2	②	②	1500	②	3 Rich
	D4OE-CA	7/16	13/16	2	②	②	1500	②	3 Rich
	D4ME-BA	7/16	13/16	3	②	②	1500	②	3 Rich
	D4ME-CA	7/16	13/16	3	②	②	1500	②	3 Rich
1975	D5ZE-AC	3/8	3/4	2	0.145	②	1500	②	2 Rich
	D5ZE-BC	3/8	3/4	2	0.145	②	1500	②	2 Rich
	D5ZE-CC	3/8	3/4	3	0.145	②	1500	②	2 Rich
	D5ZE-DC	3/8	3/4	2	0.145	②	1500	②	2 Rich
	D5DE-AA	7/16	13/16	2	0.140	②	1500	②	3 Rich
	D5DE-BA	7/16	13/16	2	0.140	②	1500	②	3 Rich
	D5DE-JA	7/16	13/16	2	0.140	②	1500	②	3 Rich
	D5ZE-JA	7/16	13/16	2	0.140	②	1500	②	3 Rich
	D5OE-AA	7/16	13/16	2	0.140	2	1500	②	3 Rich
	D5OE-DA	7/16	13/16	2	0.140	②	1500	②	3 Rich
	D5DE-HA	7/16	13/16	3	0.140	②	1500	②	3 Rich
	D5DE-UA	7/16	13/16	2	0.140	②	1500	②	3 Rich
	D5OE-BA	7/16	13/16	3	0.125	②	1500	②	3 Rich
	D5OE-CA	7/16	13/16	3	0.125	②	1500	②	3 Rich
	D5OE-GA	7/16	13/16	2	0.125	②	1500	②	3 Rich
	D5AE-AA	7/16	13/16	3	0.125	②	1500	②	3 Rich
	D5AE-EA	7/16	13/16	3	0.125	②	1500	②	3 Rich
	D5ME-BA	7/16	13/16	2	0.125	②	1500	②	3 Rich
	D5ME-FA	7/16	13/16	2	0.125	②	1500	②	3 Rich
1976–77	D5ZE-BE	3/8	3/4	2	0.105	②	1600 ③	②	3 Rich
	D6ZE-AA	3/8	3/4	2	0.100	②	1600 ③	②	3 Rich
	D6ZE-BA	3/8	3/4	2	0.100	②	1600 ③	②	3 Rich
	D6ZE-CA	13/32	3/4	2	0.110	②	1600 ③	②	3 Rich
	D6ZE-DA	3/8	3/4	3	0.110	②	1600 ③	②	3 Rich
	D5DE-AEA	7/16	13/16	2	0.160	②	2000 ④	②	3 Rich
	D5DE-AFA	7/16	13/16	2	0.160	②	2000 ④	②	3 Rich

Motorcraft 2100, 2150 Specifications (Cont.)

Year	(9510) * Carburetor Identification	Dry Float Level (in.)	Wet Float Level (in.)	Pump Setting Hole # ①	Choke Plate Pulldown (in.)	Fast Idle Cam Linkage Clearance (in.)	Fast Idle (rpm)	Dechoke (in.)	Choke Setting
	D5WE-FA	7/16	13/16	2	0.160	②	2000 ④	②	3 Rich
	D6ZE-JA	7/16	13/16	2	0.160	②	2000 ④	②	3 Rich
	D6OE-AA	7/16	13/16	3	0.160	②	2000 ④	②	3 Rich
	D6OE-BA	7/16	13/16	3	0.160	②	2000 ④	②	3 Rich
	D6OE-CA	7/16	13/16	3	0.160	②	2000 ④	②	3 Rich
	D6WE-AA	7/16	13/16	2	0.160	②	1350 ⑤	②	3 Rich
	D6WE-BA	7/16	13/16	2	0.160	②	1350 ⑤	②	3 Rich
	D6AE-HA	7/16	13/16	2	0.160	②	1350 ⑤	②	3 Rich
	D6ME-AA	7/16	13/16	2	0.160	②	1350 ⑤	②	3 Rich
1978	D84E-EA	7/16	13/16	2	0.110	⑥	⑦	—	3 Rich
	D8AE-JA	3/8	3/4	3	0.167	⑥	⑦	—	3 Rich
	D8BE-ACA	7/16	3/4	4	0.155	⑥	⑦	—	2 Rich
	D8BE-ADA	7/16	13/16	2	0.110	⑥	⑦	—	3 Rich
	D8BE-AEA	7/16	13/16	2	0.110	⑥	⑦	—	4 Rich
	D8BE-AFA	7/16	13/16	2	0.110	⑥	⑦	—	4 Rich
	D8BE-MB	3/8	13/16	3	0.122	⑥	⑦	—	Index
	D8DE-HA	19/32	13/16	3	0.157	⑥	⑦	—	Index
	D8KE-EA	19/32	13/16	2	0.135	⑥	⑦	—	3 Rich
	D8OE-BA	3/8	3/4	3	0.167	⑥	⑦	—	3 Rich
	D8OE-EA	19/32	13/16	2	0.136	⑥	⑦	—	Index
	D8OE-HA	7/16	13/16	3	0.180	⑥	⑦	—	2 Rich
	D8SE-CA	19/32	13/16	3	0.150	⑥	⑦	—	2 Rich
	D8ZE-TA	3/8	3/4	4	0.135	⑥	⑦	—	Index
	D8ZE-UA	3/8	3/4	4	0.135	⑥	⑦	—	Index
	D8WE-DA	7/16	13/16	4	0.143	⑥	⑦	—	1 Rich
	D8YE-AB	3/8	13/16	3	0.122	⑥	⑦	—	Index
	D8SE-DA, EA	7/16	13/16	3	0.147	⑥	⑦	—	3 Rich
	D8SE-FA, GA	3/8	13/16	3	0.147	⑥	⑦	—	3 Rich
1979	D9AE-AHA	7/16	13/16	3	0.147	⑥	⑦	0.250	3 Rich
	D9AE-AJA	7/16	13/16	3	0.147	⑥	⑦	0.250	3 Rich
	D9AE-ANB	7/16	13/16	3	0.129	⑥	⑦	—	1 Rich
	D9AE-APB	7/16	13/16	3	0.129	⑥	⑦	—	1 Rich
	D9AE-AVB	7/16	13/16	3	0.129	⑥	⑦	—	1 Rich
	D9AE-AYA	7/16	13/16	3	0.129	⑥	⑦	—	1 Rich
	D9AE-AYB	7/16	13/16	3	0.129	⑥	⑦	—	1 Rich
	D9AE-TB	7/16	13/16	3	0.129	⑥	⑦	—	2 Rich
	D9AE-UB	7/16	13/16	3	0.129	⑥	⑦	—	2 Rich
	D9BE-VB	7/16	13/16	3	0.153	⑥	⑦	0.250	2 Rich
	D9BE-YB	7/16	13/16	3	0.153	⑥	⑦	—	2 Rich

86675cce

Motorcraft 2100, 2150 Specifications (Cont.)

Year	(9510) * Carburetor Identification	Dry Float Level (in.)	Wet Float Level (in.)	Pump Setting Hole # ①	Choke Plate Pulldown (in.)	Fast Idle Cam Linkage Clearance (in.)	Fast Idle (rpm)	Dechoke (in.)	Choke Setting
1979	D9DE-NB	7/16	13/16	3	0.153	⑥	⑦	0.250	2 Rich
	D9DE-RA	7/16	13/16	2	0.125	⑥	⑦	0.115	3 Rich
	D9DE-RB	7/16	13/16	2	0.125	⑥	⑦	0.115	3 Rich
	D9DE-RD	7/16	13/16	2	0.125	⑥	⑦	—	3 Rich
	D9DE-SA	7/16	13/16	2	0.125	⑥	⑦	0.250	3 Rich
	D9DE-SC	7/16	13/16	2	0.125	⑥	⑦	—	3 Rich
	D9ME-BA	7/16	13/16	2	0.136	⑥	⑦	0.115	Index
	D9ME-CA	7/16	13/16	2	0.136	⑥	⑦	0.115	Index
	D9OE-CB	7/16	13/16	3	0.132	⑥	⑦	0.115	3 Rich
	D9OE-DB	7/16	13/16	3	0.132	⑥	⑦	—	3 Rich
	D9OE-EA	7/16	13/16	3	0.132	⑥	⑦	0.115	2 Rich
	D9OE-FA	7/16	13/16	3	0.132	⑥	⑦	0.115	2 Rich
	D9SE-GA	7/16	13/16	3	0.150	⑥	⑦	0.250	2 Rich
	D9VE-LC	7/16	13/16	3	0.145	⑥	⑦	0.250	3 Rich
	D9VE-SA	7/16	13/16	3	0.147	⑥	⑦	—	3 Rich
	D9VE-UB	7/16	13/16	3	0.155	⑥	⑦	0.250	3 Rich
	D9VE-VA	3/8	3/4	3	0.145	⑥	⑦	—	3 Rich
	D9VE-YB	3/8	3/4	2	0.145	⑥	⑦	0.250	3 Rich
	D9WE-CB	7/16	13/16	3	0.132	⑥	⑦	—	3 Rich
	D9WE-DB	7/16	13/16	3	0.132	⑥	⑦	—	3 Rich
	D9WE-EB	7/16	13/16	3	0.132	⑥	⑦	—	2 Rich
	D9WE-FB	7/16	13/16	3	0.132	⑥	⑦	—	2 Rich
	D9WE-JA	7/16	13/16	3	0.150	⑥	⑦	0.250	2 Rich
	D9WE-MB	7/16	13/16	3	0.132	⑥	⑦	—	1 Rich
	D9WE-NB	7/16	13/16	3	0.132	⑥	⑦	—	1 Rich
	D9YE-EA	7/16	13/16	3	0.118	⑥	⑦	0.115	1 Rich
	D9YE-FA	7/16	13/16	3	0.118	⑥	⑦	0.115	1 Rich
	D9YE-AB	7/16	13/16	3	0.118	⑥	⑦	0.115	Index
	D9YE-BB	7/16	13/16	3	0.118	⑥	⑦	0.115	Index
	D9YE-CA	7/16	13/16	2	0.118	⑥	⑦	0.115	Index
	D9YE-DA	7/16	13/16	2	0.118	⑥	⑦	0.115	Index
	D9ZE-AYA	7/16	13/16	3	0.138	⑥	⑦	0.115	Index
	D9ZE-BFB	7/16	13/16	2	0.125	⑥	⑦	—	3 Rich
	D9ZE-BGB	7/16	13/16	2	0.125	⑥	⑦	—	3 Rich
	D9ZE-BHB	7/16	13/16	2	0.125	⑥	⑦	0.250	3 Rich
	D9ZE-BJB	7/16	13/16	2	0.125	⑥	⑦	—	3 Rich
1980	EO4E-PA, RA	—	13/16	2	0.104	⑥	⑦	1/4	⑦
	EOBE-AUA	—	13/16	3	0.116	⑥	⑦	1/4	⑦
	EODE-SA, TA	—	13/16	2	0.104	⑥	⑦	1/4	⑦

86675ccf

Motorcraft 2100, 2150 Specifications (Cont.)

Year	(9510) * Carburetor Identification	Dry Float Level (in.)	Wet Float Level (in.)	Pump Setting Hole # ①	Choke Plate Pulldown (in.)	Fast Idle Cam Linkage Clearance (in.)	Fast Idle (rpm)	Dechoke (in.)	Choke Setting
	EOKE-CA, DA	—	13/16	3	0.116	⑥	⑦	¼	⑦
	EOKE-GA, HA	—	13/16	3	0.116	⑥	⑦	¼	⑦
	EOKE-JA, KA	—	13/16	3	0.116	⑥	⑦	¼	⑦
	D84E-TA, UA	—	13/16	2	0.125	⑥	⑦	¼	⑦
	EO4E-ADA, AEA	—	13/16	2	0.104	⑥	⑦	¼	⑦
	EO4E-CA	—	13/16	2	0.104	⑥	⑦	¼	⑦
	EO4E-EA, FA	—	13/16	2	0.104	⑥	⑦	¼	⑦
	EO4E-JA, KA	—	13/16	2	0.137	⑥	⑦	¼	⑦
	EO4E-SA, TA	—	13/16	2	0.104	⑥	⑦	¼	⑦
	EO4E-VA, YA	—	13/16	2	0.104	⑥	⑦	¼	⑦
	EODE-TA, VA	—	13/16	2	0.104	⑥	⑦	¼	⑦
	EOSE-GA, HA	—	13/16	2	0.104	⑥	⑦	¼	⑦
	EOSE-LA, MA	—	13/16	2	0.104	⑥	⑦	¼	⑦
	EOSE-NA	—	13/16	2	0.104	⑥	⑦	¼	⑦
	EOSE-PA	—	13/16	2	0.137	⑥	⑦	¼	⑦
	EOVE-FA	—	13/16	2	0.104	⑥	⑦	¼	⑦
	EOWE-BA, CA	—	13/16	2	0.137	⑥	⑦	¼	⑦
	D9AE-ANA, APA	—	13/16	3	0.129	⑥	⑦	¼	⑦
	D9AE-AVA, AYA	—	13/16	3	0.129	⑥	⑦	¼	⑦
	EOAE-AGA	—	13/16	3	0.159	⑥	⑦	¼	⑦
1981	EIKE-CA	7/16	0.810	3	0.124	⑥	⑦	0.250	⑦
	EIKE-EA	7/16	0.810	3	0.124	⑥	⑦	0.250	⑦
	EIKE-DA	7/16	0.810	3	0.124	⑥	⑦	0.250	⑦
	EIKE-FA	7/16	0.810	3	0.124	⑥	⑦	0.250	⑦
	EIWE-FA	7/16	0.810	2	0.120	⑥	⑦	0.250	⑦
	EIWE-EA	7/16	0.810	2	0.120	⑥	⑦	0.250	⑦
	EIWE-CA	7/16	0.810	2	0.120	⑥	⑦	0.250	⑦
	EIWE-DA	7/16	0.810	2	0.120	⑥	⑦	0.250	⑦
	EIAE-YA	7/16	0.810	3	0.124	⑥	⑦	0.250	⑦
	EIAE-ZA	7/16	0.810	3	0.124	⑥	⑦	0.250	⑦
	EIAE-ADA	7/16	0.810	3	0.124	⑥	⑦	0.250	⑦
	EIAE-AEA	7/16	0.810	3	0.124	⑥	⑦	0.250	⑦
	EIAE-TA	—	0.810	2	0.104	⑥	⑦	0.250	⑦
	EIAE-UA	—	0.810	2	0.104	⑥	⑦	0.250	⑦
1982	E2ZE-BAA	13/32	0.780	2	0.172	⑥	1400	0.250	⑧
	E2ZE-BBA	13/32	0.780	2	0.172	⑥	1400	0.250	⑧
	E3CE-LA	7/16	0.810	3	0.103	⑥	2200	0.250	⑧
	E3CE-MA	7/16	0.810	3	0.103	⑥	2200	0.250	⑧
	E3CE-JA	7/16	0.810	3	0.103	⑥	2200	0.250	⑧

86675ccg

Motorcraft 2100, 2150 Specifications (Cont.)

Year	(9510) * Carburetor Identification	Dry Float Level (in.)	Wet Float Level (in.)	Pump Setting Hole # ①	Choke Plate Pulldown (in.)	Fast Idle Cam Linkage Clearance (in.)	Fast Idle (rpm)	Dechoke (in.)	Choke Setting
1982	E3CE-KA	7/16	0.810	3	0.103	⑥	2200	0.250	⑧
	E3CE-NA	7/16	0.810	3	0.120	⑥	2100	0.250	⑧
	E3CE-PA	7/16	0.810	3	0.120	⑥	2100	0.250	⑧
1983	E3CE-AA	7/16	0.810	3	0.103	⑥	2200	0.250	⑧
	E3CE-BA	7/16	0.810	3	0.103	⑥	2200	0.250	⑧
	E3CE-GA	7/16	0.810	3	0.103	⑥	2200	0.250	⑧
	E3CE-HA	7/16	0.810	3	0.103	⑥	2200	0.250	⑧
	E3CE-EA	7/16	0.810	3	0.113	⑥	2100	0.250	⑧
	E3CE-FA	7/16	0.810	3	0.113	⑥	2100	0.250	⑧
	E3SE-ATA	7/16	0.810	3	0.113	⑥	2200	0.250	⑧
	E3SE-AUA	13/16	0.810	3	0.113	⑥	2200	0.250	⑧
	E3SE-ALA	7/16	0.810	3	0.107	⑥	2200	0.250	⑧
	E3SE-AMA	7/16	0.810	3	0.107	⑥	2200	0.250	⑧
	E3SE-BDA	7/16	0.810	3	0.107	⑥	2200	0.250	⑧
	E3SE-BEA	7/16	0.810	3	0.107	⑥	2200	0.250	⑧
	E3SE-ANA	7/16	0.810	3	0.101	⑥	2200	0.250	⑧
	E3SE-APA	7/16	0.810	3	0.101	⑥	2200	0.250	⑧
	E3SE-AJA	7/16	0.810	3	0.107	⑥	2200	0.250	⑧
	E3SE-BFA	7/16	0.810	3	0.107	⑥	2200	0.250	⑧
	E3SE-BGA	7/16	0.810	3	0.107	⑥	2200	0.250	⑧
	E3SE-EA	7/16	0.810	3	0.113	⑥	2200	0.250	⑧
	E3SE-FA	7/16	0.810	3	0.113	⑥	2200	0.250	⑧
	E3SE-LA	7/16	0.810	3	0.107	⑥	2200	0.250	⑧
	E3SE-MA	7/16	0.810	3	0.107	⑥	2200	0.250	⑧
	E3SE-JA	7/16	0.810	3	0.101	⑥	2200	0.250	⑧
	E3SE-KA	7/16	0.810	3	0.101	⑥	2200	0.250	⑧
	E3SE-NA	7/16	0.810	3	0.107	⑥	2200	0.250	⑧
	E3SE-PA	7/16	0.810	3	0.107	⑥	2200	0.250	⑧
	E3SE-GA	7/16	0.810	3	0.120	⑥	2100	0.250	⑧
	E3SE-HA	7/16	0.810	3	0.120	⑥	2100	0.250	⑧
	E3AE-TA	7/16	0.810	3	0.103	⑥	2200	0.250	⑧
	E3AE-ADA	7/16	0.810	3	0.103	⑥	2200	0.250	⑧
	E3AE-UA	7/16	0.810	3	0.103	⑥	2200	0.250	⑧
	E3AE-AEA	7/16	0.810	3	0.103	⑥	2200	0.250	⑧
	E3AE-TA	7/16	0.810	3	0.103	⑥	2200	0.250	⑧
	E3AE-UA	7/16	0.810	3	0.103	⑥	2200	0.250	⑧
	E3AE-RA	7/16	0.810	3	0.103	⑥	2200	0.250	⑧
	E3AE-SA	7/16	0.810	3	0.103	⑥	2200	0.250	⑧
	E3AE-EA	7/16	0.810	2	—	⑥	1550	0.250	⑧

86675cch

Motorcraft 2100, 2150 Specifications (Cont.)

Year	(9510) * Carburetor Identification	Dry Float Level (in.)	Wet Float Level (in.)	Pump Setting Hole # ①	Choke Plate Pulldown (in.)	Fast Idle Cam Linkage Clearance (in.)	Fast Idle (rpm)	Dechoke (in.)	Choke Setting
1984–85	E3EA-EA	7/16	0.810	2	—	⑥	1550	0.250	⑧
	E4CE-AA	7/16	0.810	3	0.103	⑥	2200	0.250	2NR
	E4CE-BA	7/16	0.810	3	0.103	⑥	2200	0.250	2NR
	E4SE-CA	7/16	0.810	3	0.103	⑥	2200	0.250	⑧
	E4SE-DA	7/16	0.810	3	0.103	⑥	2200	0.250	⑧
	E5AE-CA	7/16	0.810	2	—	⑥	1550	0.250	⑧

* Basic carburetor number for Ford products
① With link in inboard hole of pump lever
② Electric choke; see procedure in text
③ Figure given is for manual transmission; for automatics add 100 RPM.
④ Figure given is for 49 states Granada and Monarch; for Calif. Granada and Monarch and all Torino, Montego and Cougar models, figure is 1400 RPM.
⑤ Figure given is for 49 states model; Calif. specification is 1150 RPM.
⑥ Opposite V- notch
⑦ See underhood sticker
⑧ V-notch

86675cci

Carter Thermo-Quad Specifications

Year	Model ①	Float Setting (in.)	Secondary Throttle Linkage (in.)	Secondary Air Valve Opening (in.)	Secondary Air Valve Spring (turns)	Accelerator Pump (in.)	Choke Control Lever (in.)	Choke Unloader (in.)	Vacuum Kick (in.)	Fast Idle Speed (rpm)
1974	6488S	1	②	½	1¼	$^{31}/_{64}$	3⅛	.310	21	1800
	6452S	1	②	½	1¼	$^{35}/_{64}$	3⅜	.310	4	1900
	6453S	1	②	½	1¼	$^{31}/_{64}$	3⅜	.310	21	1900
	6454S	1	②	½	1¼	$^{31}/_{64}$	3⅜	.310	4	1900
	6455S	1	②	½	1¼	$^{31}/_{64}$	3⅜	.310	21	1900
	6489S	1	②	½	1¼	$^{31}/_{64}$	3⅜	.310	21	2000
	6496S	1	②	½	1¼	$^{31}/_{64}$	3⅜	.310	21	2000
	6456S	1	②	½	1¼	$^{31}/_{64}$	3⅜	.310	4	1700
	6457S	1	②	½	1¼	$^{31}/_{64}$	3⅜	.310	21	1800
	6459	1	②	½	1¼	$^{31}/_{64}$	3⅜	.310	21	1800
	6460S	1	②	½	1¼	$^{31}/_{64}$	3⅜	.310	21	1700
	6461S	1	②	½	1¼	$^{31}/_{64}$	3⅜	.310	21	1700
	6462S	1	②	½	1¼	$^{31}/_{64}$	3⅜	.310	21	1700
	6463S	1	②	½	1¼	$^{31}/_{64}$	3⅜	.310	21	1700

① Model numbers located on the tag or on the casting
② Adjust link so primary and secondary stops both contact at same time
NOTE: All choke settings are fixed

86675ccj

Motorcraft 4300, 4350 Specifications

Year	(9510)* Carburetor Identification ①	Dry Float Level (in.)	Pump Hole Setting	Choke Plate Pulldown (in.)	Fast Idle Cam Linkage (in.)	Fast Idle (rpm)	Dechoke (in.)	Choke Setting	Dashpot
1971	D1AF-MA	49/64	2	0.220	—	1350	—	Index	1/16
	D1OF-EA	13/16	2	0.180	0.160	1250	—	Index	—
	D1OF-AAA	13/16	2	0.200	0.180	1400	—	Index	—
	D1SF-AA	49/64	2	0.220	—	1350	—	Index	1/16
	D1VF-AA	49/64	2	0.220	0.170	1250	—	1 Rich	0.100
1972	D2AF-AA	49/64	1	0.220	0.200	1350	—	2 Rich	—
	D2AF-LA	49/64	1	0.215	0.190	1900	—	2 Rich	—
	D2SF-AA	49/64	1	0.220	0.200	1350	—	2 Rich	—
	D2SF-BA	49/64	1	0.220	0.200	1350	—	2 Rich	—
	D2VF-AA	49/64	1	0.230	0.200	1250	—	Index	—
	D2VF-BA	49/64	1	0.230	0.200	1250	—	Index	—
	D2ZF-AA	13/16	1	0.200	0.180	1200	—	Index	—
	D2ZF-BB	13/16	1	0.200	0.200	1200	—	Index	—
	D2ZF-DA	13/16	1	0.200	0.200	1200	—	Index	—
	D2ZF-GA	13/16	1	0.200	0.180	1200	—	Index	—
1973	D3VF-DA	0.76	1	0.210	0.190	1350	—	Index	—
	D3ZF-AC	0.82	1	0.180	0.180	1300	—	Index	—
	D3ZF-BC	0.82	1	0.170	0.170	1300	—	INR	—
	D3ZF-CD	0.82	1	0.180	0.180	1300	—	Index	—
	D3AF-HA	0.76	1	0.210	0.200	1350	—	Index	—
	D3AF-EB	0.88	1	0.200	0.200	1900	—	Index	—
1974	D4AE-AA	3/4	1	0.230	0.200	1900	—	Index	—
	D4AE-NA, D4VE-AB	3/4	1	0.220	0.200	1250	—	Index	—
	D4TE-ATA	13/16	1	0.220	0.180	1250	—	Index	—
	D4OE-AA	13/16	1	0.180	0.180	1800	—	Index	—
1975	D5VE-AD	15/16	1	②	0.160	1600	0.300	2 Rich	—
	D5VE-BA	15/16	1	②	0.160	1600	0.300	2 Rich	—
	D5AE-CA	31/32	1	②	0.160	1600	0.300	2 Rich	—
	D5AE-DA	31/32	1	②	0.160	1600	0.300	2 Rich	—
1976–77	D6AE-CA	1.00	2	0.140 ③	0.140	1350	0.30	2 Rich	—
	D6AE-FA	1.00	2	0.140 ③	0.140	1350	0.30	2 Rich	—
	D6AE-DA	1.00	2	0.160 ④	0.160	1350	0.30	2 Rich	—

*Basic carburetor number for Ford products.
① The identification tag is on the bowl cover.
② Initial—0.160 in.
  Delayed—0.190 in.
③ Initial Figure given; delayed—0.190
④ Initial Figure given; delayed—0.210

86675cck

Motorcraft Model 2700 VV Specifications

Year	Model	Float Level (in.)	Float Drop (in.)	Fast Idle Cam Setting (notches)	Cold Enrichment Metering Rod (in.)	Control Vacuum (in. H_2O)	Venturi Valve Limiter (in.)	Choke Cap Setting (notches)	Control Vacuum Regulator Setting (in.)
1977–78	All	1 3/64	1 15/32	1 Rich/3rd step	.125	5.0	61/64	Index	—
1979	D9ZE-LB	1 3/64	1 15/32	1 Rich/2nd step	.125	①	②	Index	.230
	D84E-KA	1 3/64	1 15/32	1 Rich/3rd step	.125	5.5	61/64	Index	—
1980	All	1 3/64	1 15/32	1 Rich/4th step	.125	③	④	⑤	.075
1981	EIAE-AAA	1.015–1.065	1.435–1.485	—	—	③	④	⑤	—

① Venturi Air Bypass 6.8–7.3
   Venturi Valve Diaphragm 4.6–5.1
② Limiter Setting .38–.42
   Limiter Stop Setting .73–.77

③ See text
④ Opening gap: 0.99–1.01
   Closing gap: 0.94–0.98
⑤ See underhood decal

86675ccl

Motorcraft Model 7200 VV Specifications

Year	Model	Float Level (in.)	Float Drop (in.)	Fast Idle Cam Setting (notches)	Cold Enrichment Metering Rod (in.)	Control Vacuum (in. H$_2$O)	Venturi Valve Limiter (in.)	Choke Cap Setting (notches)
1979	D9AE-ACA	1³⁄₆₄	1¹⁵⁄₃₂	1 Rich/3rd step	.125	7.5	.73–.77 [1]	Index
	D9ME-AA	1³⁄₆₄	1¹⁵⁄₃₂	1 Rich/3rd step	.125	7.5	.73–.77 [1]	Index
1980	All	1³⁄₆₄	1¹⁵⁄₃₂	1 Rich/3rd step	.125	[2]	[3]	[4]
1981	D9AE-AZA	1.015–1.065	1.435–1.485	1 Rich/3rd step	.125	[2]	[5]	Index
	E1AE-LA	1.015–1.065	1.435–1.485	0.360/2nd step	[7]	[2]	[6]	INR
	E1AE-SA	1.015–1.065	1.435–1.485	0.360/2nd step	[7]	[2]	[6]	INR
	E1VE-AA	1.015–1.065	1.435–1.485	0.360/2nd step	[7]	[2]	[3]	Index
1982	E2AE-LB	1.010–1.070	1.430–1.490	0.360/2nd step	[8]	[2]	[9]	Index
	E2DE-NA	1.010–1.070	1.430–1.490	0.360/2nd step	[8]	[2]	[9]	Index
	E2AE-LC	1.010–1.070	1.430–1.490	0.360/2nd step	[8]	[2]	[9]	Index
	E25E-FA	1.010–1.070	1.430–1.490	0.360/2nd step	[8]	[2]	[9]	Index
	E25E-GB	1.010–1.070	1.430–1.490	0.360/2nd step	[8]	[2]	[9]	Index
	E2SE-GA	1.010–1.070	1.430–1.490	0.360/2nd step	[8]	[2]	[9]	Index
	E2AE-RA	1.010–1.070	1.430–1.490	0.360/2nd step	[10]	[2]	[9]	Index
	E1AE-ACA	1.010–1.070	1.430–1.490	0.360/2nd step	[10]	[2]	[9]	Index
	E2SE-DB	1.010–1.070	1.430–1.490	0.360/2nd step	[11]	[2]	[9]	Index
	E2SE-DA	1.010–1.070	1.430–1.490	0.360/2nd step	[11]	[2]	[9]	Index
	E1AE-SA	1.010–1.070	1.430–1.490	0.360/2nd step	[12]	[2]	[13]	1 Rich
	E2AE-MA	1.010–1.070	1.430–1.490	0.360/2nd step	[12]	[2]	[13]	1 Rich
	E2AE-MB	1.010–1.070	1.430–1.490	0.360/2nd step	[12]	[2]	[13]	1 Rich
	E2AE-TA	1.010–1.070	1.430–1.490	0.360/2nd step	[12]	[2]	[13]	Index
	E2AE-TB	1.010–1.070	1.430–1.490	0.360/2nd step	[12]	[2]	[13]	Index
	E25E-AC	1.010–1.070	1.430–1.490	0.360/2nd step	[11]	[2]	[9]	Index
	E1AE-AGA	1.010–1.070	1.430–1.490	0.360/2nd step	[12]	[2]	[9]	Index
	E2AE-NA	1.010–1.070	1.430–1.490	0.360/2nd step	[12]	[2]	[9]	Index
1983–84	E2AE-NA	1.010–1.070	1.430–1.490	0.360/2nd step	[12]	[2]	[9]	Index
	E2AE-AJA	1.010–1.070	1.430–1.490	0.360/2nd step	[12]	[2]	[9]	Index
	E2AE-APA	1.010–1.070	1.430–1.490	0.360/2nd step	[12]	[2]	[9]	Index
	E2AE-AJA	1.010–1.070	1.430–1.490	0.360/2nd step	[12]	[2]	[9]	Index
	E2AE-APA	1.010–1.070	1.430–1.490	0.360/2nd step	[12]	[2]	[9]	Index

[1] Limiter Stop Setting: .99–1.01
[2] See text
[3] Opening gap: 0.99–1.01
   Closing gap: 0.39–0.41
[4] See underhood decal
[5] Maximum opening: 99/1.01
   Wide open on throttle: .94/.98
[6] Maximum opening: .99/1.01
   Wide open on throttle: .74/.76
[7] 0°F—0.490 @ starting position
   75°F—0.475 @ starting position
[8] 0°F—0.525 @ starting position
   75°F—0.445 @ starting position
[9] Maximum opening: .99/1.01
   Wide open on throttle: .39/.41
[10] 0°F—0.490 @ starting position
   75°F—0.445 @ starting position
[11] 0°F—0.525 @ starting position
   75°F—0.475 @ starting position
[12] 0°F—0.490 @ starting position
   75°F—0.460 @ starting position
[13] Maximum opening: .99/1.01
   Wide open on throttle: .74/.76

Rochester Quadrajet Specifications

Year	Carburetor Identification ①	Float Level (in.)	Air Valve Spring	Pump Rod (in.)	Vacuum Break (in.)	Secondary Opening (in.)	Choke Rod (in.)	Choke Unloader (in.)	Fast Idle Speed (rpm)
1971	DOOF-A	11/32	0.030	5/16	0.140	—	0.130	0.300	1800 ②
	DOOF-E	11/32	0.030	5/16	0.190	—	0.166	0.300	2000 ②

① The carburetor identification tag is located at the rear of the carburetor on one of the air horn screws.
② Second step of cam.

86675ccn

Holly 4150C Specifications

Year	Carb. Part No. ①	Float Level (Dry) (in.)	Accelerator Pump Lever Adjustment (in.)	Choke Setting (in.)	Choke Unloader Clearance (in.)	Fast Idle On Car (rpm)	Choke Vacuum Break (in.)
1971	R4800-A	②	0.015	1.320 ③	0.350	2200	0.350
	R4801-A	②	0.015	1.320 ③	0.350	2200	0.350
	R4802-A	②	0.015	1.320 ③	0.350	2200	0.350
	R4803-A	②	0.015	1.320 ③	0.350	2200	0.350

① Located on tag attached to carburetor, or on the casting or choke plate
② The fuel level is adjusted to the lower edge of the sight plug hole on the Holley 4150C carburetor.
③ Bottom of throttle body to center of hole in operating lever

86675ccp

Model 1946

Year	Part Number	Float Level (in.)	Choke Pulldown (in.)	Dechoke (in.)	Fast Idle Cam (in.)	Accelerator Pump Stroke Slot
1981	EIBE-AFA	.69	.113	.150	.082	#2
	EIBE-AKA	.69	.113	.150	.082	#2
	EOBE-CA	.69	.100	.150	.070	#2
	EOBE-AA	.69	.100	.150	.070	#2
1982	EIBE-AGA	.69	.120	.150	.086	#2
	E2BE-CA	.69	.110	.150	.078	#2
	E2BE-BA	.69	.110	.150	.078	#2
	E2BE-JA	.69	.110	.150	.078	#2
	E2BE-HA	.69	.110	.150	.078	#2
	E2BE-TA	.69	.110	.150	.078	#2
	E2BE-SA	.69	.110	.150	.078	#2
1983	E2BE-CA	.69	.110	.150	.078	#2
	E2BE-BA	.69	.110	.150	.078	#2
	E2BE-TA	.69	.110	.150	.078	#2
	E2BE-SA	.69	.110	.150	.078	#2
	E3SE-CA	.69	.105	.150	.078	#2
	E3SE-DA	.69	.105	.150	.078	#2
	E3SE-AA	.69	.095	.150	.078	#2
	E3SE-BA	.69	.095	.150	.078	#2

86675ccq

Motocraft (Holley) Model 5200 Specifications

Year	(9510)* Carburetor Identification ①	Dry Float Level (in.)	Pump Hole Setting	Choke Plate Pulldown (in.)	Fast Idle Cam Linkage (in.)	Fast Idle (rpm)	Dechoke (in.)	Choke Setting
1981	EIZE-YA	.41–.51	2	0.200	.080	②	0.200	②
	EOEE-RB	.41–.51	2	0.200	.080	②	0.200	②
	EIZE-VA	.41–.51	2	0.200	.080	②	0.200	②
	D9EE-ANA	.41–.51	2	0.240	0.720	②	0.200	②
	D9EE-APA	.41–.51	2	0.240	0.120	②	0.200	②

*Basic carburetor number
① Figure given is for all manual transmissions; for automatic trans. the figures are: (49 states) 2000 RPM; (Calif.) 1800 RPM.
② See underhood decal

86675cco

Ford Electronic Fuel Injection Troubleshooting

Symptom	Possible Problem Areas
Surging, backfire, misfire, runs rough	1. EEC distributor rotor registry 2. EGR solenoid(s) defective 3. Distributor, cap, body, rotor, ignition wires, plugs, coil defective 4. Pulse ring behind vibration damper misaligned or damaged 5. Spark plug fouling
Stalls on deceleration	1. EGR solenoid(s) or valve defective 2. EEC distributor rotor registry
Stalls at idle	1. Idle speed wrong 2. Throttle kicker not working
Hesitates on acceleration	1. Acceleration enrichment system defective 2. Fuel pump ballast bypass relay not working
Fuel pump noisy	1. Fuel pump ballast bypass relay not working
Engine won't start	1. Fuel pump power relay defective, no spark, EGR system defective, no or low fuel pressure 2. Crankshaft position sensor not seated, clearance wrong, defective 3. Pulse ring behind vibration damper misaligned, sensor tabs damaged 4. Power and ground wires open or shorted, poor electrical connections 5. Inertia switch tripped
Engine starts and stalls or runs rough	1. Fuel pump ballast wire defective 2. Manifold absolute pressure (MAP) sensor circuit not working 3. Low fuel pressure 4. EGR system problem 5. Microprocessor and calibration assembly faulty
Starts hard when cold	1. Cranking signal circuit faulty

86655402

CFI Resistance Specifications

Component	Resistance (Ohms)
Air Charge Temp (ACT)	
1981–83	1700–60,000
1984	1100–58,000
Coolant (ECT) Sensor	
1981–83	1100–8000
1984 — Engine Off	1300–7700
1984 — Engine On	1500–4500
Crank Position Sensor	100–640
FGB	30–70
EGR Vent Solenoid	30–70
Fuel Pump Relay	50–100
Throttle Kicker Solenoid	50–100
Throttle Position Sensor	
1981–83 Closed Throttle	3000–5000
1984 Closed Throttle	550–1100
Wide Open Throttle	More than 2100
TAB Solenoid	50–100
TAD Solenoid	50–100

86655401

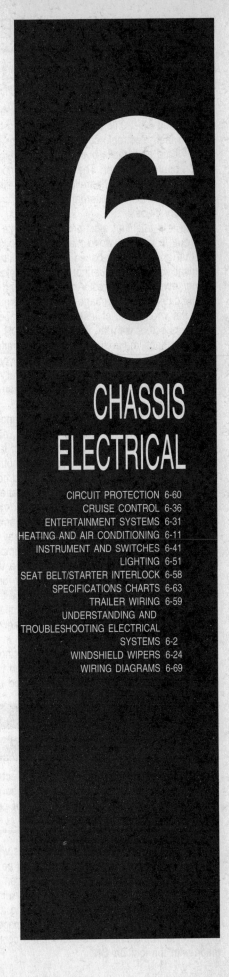

6

CHASSIS
ELECTRICAL

UNDERSTANDING AND TROUBLESHOOTING ELECTRICAL SYSTEMS

Over the years import and domestic manufacturers have incorporated electronic control systems into their production lines. In fact, electronic control systems are so prevalent that all new cars and trucks built today are equipped with at least one on-board computer. These electronic components (with no moving parts) should theoretically last the life of the vehicle, provided that nothing external happens to damage the circuits or memory chips.

While it is true that electronic components should never wear out, in the real world malfunctions do occur. It is also true that any computer-based system is extremely sensitive to electrical voltages and cannot tolerate careless or haphazard testing/service procedures. An inexperienced individual can literally cause major damage looking for a minor problem by using the wrong kind of test equipment or connecting test leads/connectors with the ignition switch **ON**. When selecting test equipment, make sure the manufacturer's instructions state that the tester is compatible with whatever type of system is being serviced. Read all instructions carefully and double check all test points before installing probes or making any test connections.

The following section outlines basic diagnosis techniques for dealing with automotive electrical systems. Along with a general explanation of the various types of test equipment available to aid in servicing modern automotive systems, basic repair techniques for wiring harnesses and connectors are also given. Read the basic information before attempting any repairs or testing. This will provide the background of information necessary to avoid the most common and obvious mistakes that can cost both time and money. Although the replacement and testing procedures are simple in themselves, the systems are not, and unless one has a thorough understanding of all components and their function within a particular system, the logical test sequence these systems demand cannot be followed. Minor malfunctions can make a big difference, so it is important to know how each component affects the operation of the overall system in order to find the ultimate cause of a problem without replacing good components unnecessarily. It is not enough to use the correct test equipment; the test equipment must be used correctly.

Safety Precautions

✳✳CAUTION

Whenever working on or around any electrical or electronic systems, always observe these general precautions to prevent the possibility of personal injury or damage to electronic components.

• Never install or remove battery cables with the key **ON** or the engine running. Jumper cables should be connected with the key **OFF** to avoid power surges that can damage electronic control units. Engines equipped with computer controlled systems should avoid both giving and getting jump starts due to the possibility of serious damage to components from arcing in the engine compartment if connections are made with the ignition **ON**.

• Always remove the battery cables before charging the battery. Never use a high output charger on an installed battery or attempt to use any type of "hot shot" (24 volt) starting aid.

• Exercise care when inserting test probes into connectors to insure good contact without damaging the connector or spreading the pins. Always probe connectors from the rear (wire) side, NOT the pin side, to avoid accidental shorting of terminals during test procedures.

• Never remove or attach wiring harness connectors with the ignition switch **ON**, especially to an electronic control unit.

• Do not drop any components during service procedures and never apply 12 volts directly to any component (like a solenoid or relay) unless instructed specifically to do so. Some component electrical windings are designed to safely handle only 4 or 5 volts and can be destroyed in seconds if 12 volts are applied directly to the connector.

• Remove the electronic control unit if the vehicle is to be placed in an environment where temperatures exceed approximately 176°F (80°C), such as a paint spray booth or when arc/gas welding near the control unit location.

Understanding Basic Electricity

Understanding the basic theory of electricity makes electrical troubleshooting much easier. Several gauges are used in electrical troubleshooting to see inside the circuit being tested. Without a basic understanding, it will be difficult to understand testing procedures.

THE WATER ANALOGY

Electricity is the flow of electrons — hypothetical particles thought to constitute the basic stuff of electricity. Many people have been taught electrical theory using an analogy with water. In a comparison with water flowing in a pipe, the electrons would be the water. As the flow of water can be measured, the flow of electricity can be measured. The unit of measurement is amperes, frequently abbreviated amps. An ammeter will measure the actual amount of current flowing in the circuit.

Just as the water pressure is measured in units such as pounds per square inch, electrical pressure is measured in volts. When a voltmeter's two probes are placed on two live portions of an electrical circuit with different electrical pressures, current will flow through the voltmeter and produce a reading which indicates the difference in electrical pressure between the two parts of the circuit.

While increasing the voltage in a circuit will increase the flow of current, the actual flow depends not only on voltage, but on the resistance of the circuit. The standard unit for measuring circuit resistance is an ohm, measured by an ohmmeter. The ohmmeter is somewhat similar to an ammeter, but incorporates its own source of power so that a standard voltage is always present.

CIRCUITS

An actual electric circuit consists of four basic parts. These are: the power source, such as a generator or battery; a hot wire, which conducts the electricity under a relatively high voltage to the component supplied by the circuit; the load, such as a lamp, motor, resistor or relay coil; and the ground wire, which carries the current back to the source under very low voltage. In such a circuit the bulk of the resistance exists between the point where the hot wire is connected to the load, and the point where the load is grounded. In an automobile, the vehicle's frame or body, which is made of steel, is used as a part of the ground circuit for many of the electrical devices.

Remember that, in electrical testing, the voltmeter is connected in parallel with the circuit being tested (without disconnecting any wires) and measures the difference in voltage between the locations of the two probes; that the ammeter is connected in series with the load (the circuit is separated at one point and the ammeter inserted so it becomes a part of the circuit); and the ohmmeter is self-powered, so that all the power in the circuit should be off and the portion of the circuit to be measured contacted at either end by one of the probes of the meter.

For any electrical system to operate, it must make a complete circuit. This simply means that the power flow from the battery must make a complete circle. When an electrical component is operating, power flows from the battery to the component, passes through the component causing it to perform it to function (such as lighting a light bulb) and then returns to the battery through the ground of the circuit. This ground is usually (but not always) the metal part of the vehicle on which the electrical component is mounted.

Perhaps the easiest way to visualize this is to think of connecting a light bulb with two wires attached to it to your vehicle's battery. The battery in your car has two posts (negative and positive). If one of the two wires attached to the light bulb was attached to the negative post of the battery and the other wire was attached to the positive post of the battery, you would have a complete circuit. Current from the battery would flow out one post, through the wire attached to it and then to the light bulb, where it would pass through causing it to light. It would then leave the light bulb, travel through the other wire, and return to the other post of the battery.

AUTOMOTIVE CIRCUITS

The normal automotive circuit differs from this simple example in two ways. First, instead of having a return wire from the bulb to the battery, the light bulb return the current to the battery through the chassis of the vehicle. Since the negative battery cable is attached to the chassis and the chassis is made of electrically conductive metal, the chassis of the vehicle can serve as a ground wire to complete the circuit. Secondly, most automotive circuits contain switches to turn components on and off.

Some electrical components which require a large amount of current to operate also have a relay in their circuit. Since these circuits carry a large amount of current, the thickness of the wire in the circuit (gauge size) is also greater. If this large wire were connected from the component to the control switch on the instrument panel, and then back to the component, a voltage drop would occur in the circuit. To prevent this potential drop in voltage, an electromagnetic switch (relay) is used. The large wires in the circuit are connected from the car battery to one side of the relay, and from the opposite side of the relay to the component. The relay is normally open, preventing current from passing through the circuit. An additional, smaller wire is connected from the relay to the control switch for the circuit. When the control switch is turned on, it grounds the smaller wire from the relay and completes the circuit.

SHORT CIRCUITS

If you were to disconnect the light bulb (from the previous example of a light-bulb being connected to the battery by two wires) from the wires and touch the two wires together (please take our word for this; don't try it), the result will be a shower of sparks. A similar thing happens (on a smaller scale) when the power supply wire to a component or the electrical component itself becomes grounded before the normal ground connection for the circuit. To prevent damage to the system, the fuse for the circuit blows to interrupt the circuit — protecting the components from damage. Because grounding a wire from a power source makes a complete circuit — less the required component to use the power — the phenomenon is called a short circuit. The most common causes of short circuits are: the rubber insulation on a wire breaking or rubbing through to expose the current carrying core of the wire to a metal part of the car, or a shorted switch.

Some electrical systems on the car are protected by a circuit breaker which is, basically, a self-repairing fuse. When either of the described events takes place in a system which is protected by a circuit breaker, the circuit breaker opens the circuit the same way a fuse does. However, when either the short is removed from the circuit or the surge subsides, the circuit breaker resets itself and does not have to be replaced as a fuse does.

Troubleshooting

When diagnosing a specific problem, organized troubleshooting is a must. The complexity of a modern automobile demands that you approach any problem in a logical, organized manner. There are certain troubleshooting techniques that are standard:

1. Establish when the problem occurs. Does the problem appear only under certain conditions? Were there any noises, odors, or other unusual symptoms?

2. Isolate the problem area. To do this, make some simple tests and observations; then eliminate the systems that are working properly. Check for obvious problems such as broken wires, dirty connections or split/disconnected vacuum hoses. Always check the obvious before assuming something complicated is the cause.

3. Test for problems systematically to determine the cause once the problem area is isolated. Are all the components functioning properly? Is there power going to electrical switches and motors? Is there vacuum at vacuum switches and/or actuators? Is there a mechanical problem such as bent linkage

or loose mounting screws? Performing careful, systematic checks will often turn up most causes on the first inspection without wasting time checking components that have little or no relationship to the problem.

4. Test all repairs after the work is done to make sure that the problem is fixed. Some causes can be traced to more than one component, so a careful verification of repair work is important in order to pick up additional malfunctions that may cause a problem to reappear or a different problem to arise. A blown fuse, for example, is a simple problem that may require more than another fuse to repair. If you don't look for a problem that caused a fuse to blow, a shorted wire (for example) may go undetected.

Experience has shown that most problems tend to be the result of a fairly simple and obvious cause, such as loose or corroded connectors or air leaks in the intake system. This makes careful inspection of components during testing essential to quick and accurate troubleshooting.

BASIC TROUBLESHOOTING THEORY

Electrical problems generally fall into one of three areas:
• The component that is not functioning is not receiving current.
• The component itself is not functioning.
• The component is not properly grounded.
Problems that fall into the first category are by far the most complicated. It is the current supply system to the component which contains all the switches, relay, fuses, etc.

The electrical system can be checked with a test light and a jumper wire. A test light is a device that looks like a pointed screwdriver with a wire attached to it. It has a light bulb in its handle. A jumper wire is a piece of insulated wire with an alligator clip attached to each end.

If a light bulb is not working, you must follow a systematic plan to determine which of the three causes is the villain.

1. Turn on the switch that controls the inoperable bulb.
2. Disconnect the power supply wire from the bulb.
3. Attach the ground wire to the test light to a good metal ground.
4. Touch the probe end of the test light to the end of the power supply wire that was disconnected from the bulb. If the bulb is receiving current, the test light will go on.

➡ **If the bulb is one which works only when the ignition key is turned on (turn signal), make sure the key is turned on.**

If the test light does not go on, then the problem is in the circuit between the battery and the bulb. As mentioned before, this includes all the switches, fuses, and relays in the system. Turn to a wiring diagram and find the bulb on the diagram. Follow the wire that runs back to the battery. The problem is an open circuit between the battery and the bulb. If the fuse is blown and, when replaced, immediately blows again, there is a short circuit in the system which must be located and repaired. If there is a switch in the system, bypass it with a jumper wire. This is done by connecting one end of the jumper wire to the power supply wire into the switch and the other end of the jumper wire to the wire coming out of the switch. If the test light illuminates with the jumper wire installed, the switch or whatever was bypassed is defective.

➡ **Never substitute the jumper wire for the bulb, as the bulb is the component required to use the power from the power source.**

5. If the bulb in the test light goes on, then the current is getting to the bulb that is not working in the car. This eliminates the first of the three possible causes. Connect the power supply wire and connect a jumper wire from the bulb to a good metal ground. Do this with the switch which controls the bulb works with jumper wire installed, then it has a bad ground. This is usually caused by the metal area on which the bulb mounts to the car being coated with some type of foreign matter.

6. If neither test located the source of the trouble, then the light bulb itself is defective.

The above test procedure can be applied to any of the components of the chassis electrical system by substituting the component that is not working for the light bulb. Remember that for any electrical system to work, all connections must be clean and tight.

➡ **A new upper speedometer cable was released during the 1982 model year. This cable offers improved lubrication, grease retention, and noise suppression however, this cable should not be used on any models older than 1981. This cable can be identified by a longer ferrule at the speedometer end.**

TEST EQUIPMENT

➡ **Pinpointing the exact cause of trouble in an electrical system can sometimes only be accomplished by the use of special test equipment. The following describes different types of commonly used test equipment and explains how to use them in diagnosis. In addition to the information covered below, the tool manufacturer's instructions booklet (provided with the tester) should be read and clearly understood before attempting any test procedures.**

Jumper Wires

Jumper wires are simple, yet extremely valuable, pieces of test equipment. They are basically test wires which are used to bypass sections of a circuit. The simplest type of jumper wire is a length of multi-strand wire with an alligator clip at each end. Jumper wires are usually fabricated from lengths of standard automotive wire and whatever type of connector (alligator clip, spade connector or pin connector) that is required for the particular vehicle being tested. The well equipped tool box will have several different styles of jumper wires in several different lengths. Some jumper wires are made with three or more terminals coming from a common splice for special purpose testing. In cramped, hard-to-reach areas it is advisable to have insulated boots over the jumper wire terminals in order to prevent accidental grounding, sparks, and possible fire, especially when testing fuel system components.

Jumper wires are used primarily to locate open electrical circuits, on either the ground (-) side of the circuit or on the hot (+) side. If an electrical component fails to operate, connect the jumper wire between the component and a good ground. If the component operates only with the jumper installed, the ground circuit is open. If the ground circuit is good, but the component does not operate, the circuit between the power feed and component may be open. By moving the jumper wire successively back from the lamp toward the power source, you can isolate the area of the circuit where the open is located. When the component stops functioning, or the power is cut off, the open is in the segment of wire between the jumper and the point previously tested.

You can sometimes connect the jumper wire directly from the battery to the hot terminal of the component, but first make sure the component uses 12 volts in operation. Some electrical components, such as fuel injectors, are designed to operate on about 4 volts and running 12 volts directly to the injector terminals can cause damage.

By inserting an in-line fuse holder between a set of test leads, a fused jumper wire can be used for bypassing open circuits. Use a 5 amp fuse to provide protection against voltage spikes. When in doubt, use a voltmeter to check the voltage input to the component and measure how much voltage is normally being applied.

✴✴CAUTION

Never use jumpers made from wire that is of lighter gauge than that which is used in the circuit under test. If the jumper wire is of too small a gauge, it may overheat and possibly melt. Never use jumpers to bypass high resistance loads in a circuit. Bypassing resistances, in effect, creates a short circuit. This may, in turn, cause damage and fire. Jumper wires should only be used to bypass lengths of wire.

Unpowered Test Lights

The 12 volt test light is used to check circuits and components while electrical current is flowing through them. It is used for voltage and ground tests. Twelve volt test lights come in different styles but all have three main parts; a ground clip, a probe, and a light. The most commonly used 12 volt test lights have pick-type probes. To use a 12 volt test light, connect the ground clip to a good ground and probe wherever necessary with the pick. The pick should be sharp so that it can be probed into tight spaces.

✴✴CAUTION

Do not use a test light to probe electronic ignition spark plug or coil wires. Never use a pick-type test light to probe wiring on computer controlled systems unless specifically instructed to do so. Any wire insulation that is pierced by the test light probe should be taped and sealed with silicone after testing.

Like the jumper wire, the 12 volt test light is used to isolate opens in circuits. But, whereas the jumper wire is used to bypass the open to operate the load, the 12 volt test light is used to locate the presence of voltage in a circuit. If the test light glows, you know that there is power up to that point; if the 12 volt test light does not glow when its probe is inserted into the wire or connector, you know that there is an open circuit (no power). Move the test light in successive steps back

toward the power source until the light in the handle does glow. When it glows, the open is between the probe and point which was probed previously.

➡**The test light does not detect that 12 volts (or any particular amount of voltage) is present; it only detects that some voltage is present. It is advisable before using the test light to touch its terminals across the battery posts to make sure the light is operating properly.**

Self-Powered Test Lights

The self-powered test light usually contains a 1.5 volt penlight battery. One type of self-powered test light is similar in design to the 12 volt unit. This type has both the battery and the light in the handle, along with a pick-type probe tip. The second type has the light toward the open tip, so that the light illuminates the contact point. The self-powered test light is a dual purpose piece of test equipment. It can be used to test for either open or short circuits when power is isolated from the circuit (continuity test). A powered test light should not be used on any computer controlled system or component unless specifically instructed to do so. Many engine sensors can be destroyed by even this small amount of voltage applied directly to the terminals.

Voltmeters

A voltmeter is used to measure voltage at any point in a circuit, or to measure the voltage drop across any part of a circuit. It can also be used to check continuity in a wire or circuit by indicating current flow from one end to the other. Analog voltmeters usually have various scales on the meter dial and a selector switch to allow the selection of different voltages. The voltmeter has a positive and a negative lead. To avoid damage to the meter, always connect the negative lead to the negative (-) side of the circuit (to ground or nearest the ground side of the circuit) and connect the positive lead to the positive (+) side of the circuit (to the power source or the nearest power source). Note that the negative voltmeter lead will always be black and that the positive voltmeter will always be some color other than black (usually red).

Depending on how the voltmeter is connected into the circuit, it has several uses. A voltmeter can be connected either in parallel or in series with a circuit and it has a very high resistance to current flow. When connected in parallel, only a small amount of current will flow through the voltmeter current path; the rest will flow through the normal circuit current path and the circuit will work normally. When the voltmeter is connected in series with a circuit, only a small amount of current can flow through the circuit. The circuit will not work properly, but the voltmeter reading will show if the circuit is complete or not.

Ohmmeters

The ohmmeter is designed to read resistance (which is measured in ohms or Ω) in a circuit or component. Although there are several different styles of ohmmeters, all analog meters will usually have a selector switch which permits the measurement of different ranges of resistance (usually the selector switch allows the multiplication of the meter reading by 10, 100, 1000, and 10,000). A calibration knob allows the meter to be set at zero for accurate measurement. Since all ohmmeters are powered by an internal battery, the ohmmeter can be used as a self-powered test light. When the ohmmeter is connected, current from the ohmmeter flows through the circuit or component being tested. Since the ohmmeter's internal resistance and voltage are known values, the amount of current flow through the meter depends on the resistance of the circuit or component being tested.

The ohmmeter can be used to perform a continuity test for opens or shorts (either by observation of the meter needle or as a self-powered test light), and to read actual resistance in a circuit. It should be noted that the ohmmeter is used to check the resistance of a component or wire while there is no voltage applied to the circuit. Current flow from an outside voltage source (such as the vehicle battery) can damage the ohmmeter, so the circuit or component should be isolated from the vehicle electrical system before any testing is done. Since the ohmmeter uses its own voltage source, either lead can be connected to any test point.

➡When checking diodes or other solid state components, the ohmmeter leads can only be connected one way in order to measure current flow in a single direction. Make sure the positive (+) and negative (-) terminal connections are as described in the test procedures to verify the one-way diode operation.

In using the meter for making continuity checks, do not be concerned with the actual resistance readings. Zero resistance, or any ohm reading, indicates continuity in the circuit. Infinite resistance indicates an open in the circuit. A high resistance reading where there should be none indicates a problem in the circuit. Checks for short circuits are made in the same manner as checks for open circuits except that the circuit must be isolated from both power and normal ground. Infinite resistance indicates no continuity to ground, while zero resistance indicates a dead short to ground.

Ammeters

An ammeter measures the amount of current flowing through a circuit in units called amperes or amps. Amperes are units of electron flow which indicate how fast the electrons are flowing through the circuit. Since Ohms Law dictates that current flow in a circuit is equal to the circuit voltage divided by the total circuit resistance, increasing voltage also increases the current level (amps). Likewise, any decrease in resistance will increase the amount of amps in a circuit. At normal operating voltage, most circuits have a characteristic amount of amperes, called "current draw" which can be measured using an ammeter. By referring to a specified current draw rating, measuring the amperes, and comparing the two values, one can determine what is happening within the circuit to aid in diagnosis. An open circuit, for example, will not allow any current to flow so the ammeter reading will be zero. More current flows through a heavily loaded circuit or when the charging system is operating.

An ammeter is always connected in series with the circuit being tested. All of the current that normally flows through the circuit must also flow through the ammeter; if there is any other path for the current to follow, the ammeter reading will not be accurate. The ammeter itself has very little resistance to current flow and therefore will not affect the circuit, but it will measure current draw only when the circuit is closed and

electricity is flowing. Excessive current draw can blow fuses and drain the battery, while a reduced current draw can cause motors to run slowly, lights to dim and other components to not operate properly. The ammeter can help diagnose these conditions by locating the cause of the high or low reading.

Multimeters

Different combinations of test meters can be built into a single unit designed for specific tests. Some of the more common combination test devices are known as Volt/Amp testers, Tach/Dwell meters, or Digital Multimeters. The Volt/Amp tester is used for charging system, starting system or battery tests and consists of a voltmeter, an ammeter and a variable resistance carbon pile. The voltmeter will usually have at least two ranges for use with 6, 12 and/or 24 volt systems. The ammeter also has more than one range for testing various levels of battery loads and starter current draw. The carbon pile can be adjusted to offer different amounts of resistance. The Volt/Amp tester has heavy leads to carry large amounts of current and many later models have an inductive ammeter pickup that clamps around the wire to simplify test connections. On some models, the ammeter also has a zero-center scale to allow testing of charging and starting systems without switching leads or polarity. A digital multimeter is a voltmeter, ammeter and ohmmeter combined in an instrument which gives a digital readout. These are often used when testing solid state circuits because of their high input impedance (usually 10 megohms or more).

The tach/dwell meter that combines a tachometer and a dwell (cam angle) meter is a specialized kind of voltmeter. The tachometer scale is marked to show engine speed in rpm and the dwell scale is marked to show degrees of distributor shaft rotation. In most electronic ignition systems, dwell is determined by the control unit, but the dwell meter can also be used to check the duty cycle (operation) of some electronic engine control systems. Some tach/dwell meters are powered by an internal battery, while others take their power from the vehicle battery in use. The battery powered testers usually require calibration (much like an ohmmeter) before testing.

TESTING

Open Circuits

To use the self-powered test light or a multimeter to check for open circuits, first isolate the circuit from the vehicle's 12 volt power source by disconnecting the battery or wiring harness connector. Connect the test light or ohmmeter ground clip to a good ground and probe sections of the circuit sequentially with the test light. (start from either end of the circuit). If the light is out/or there is infinite resistance, the open is between the probe and the circuit ground. If the light is on/or the meter shows continuity, the open is between the probe and end of the circuit toward the power source.

Short Circuits

By isolating the circuit both from power and from ground, and using a self-powered test light or multimeter, you can check for shorts to ground in the circuit. Isolate the circuit from power and ground. Connect the test light or ohmmeter ground clip to a good ground and probe any easy-to-reach test point in the circuit. If the light comes on or there is continuity, there is a short somewhere in the circuit. To isolate the short, probe a test point at either end of the isolated circuit (the light should be on/there should be continuity). Leave the test light probe engaged and open connectors, switches, remove parts, etc., sequentially, until the light goes out/continuity is broken. When the light goes out, the short is between the last circuit component opened and the previous circuit opened.

➡The battery in the test light and does not provide much current. A weak battery may not provide enough power to illuminate the test light even when a complete circuit is made (especially if there are high resistances in the circuit). Always make sure that the test battery is strong. To check the battery, briefly touch the ground clip to the probe; if the light glows brightly the battery is strong enough for testing. Never use a self-powered test light to perform checks for opens or shorts when power is applied to the electrical system under test. The 12 volt vehicle power will quickly burn out the light bulb in the test light.

Available Voltage Measurement

Set the voltmeter selector switch to the 20V position and connect the meter negative lead to the negative post of the battery. Connect the positive meter lead to the positive post of the battery and turn the ignition switch **ON** to provide a load. Read the voltage on the meter or digital display. A well charged battery should register over 12 volts. If the meter reads below 11.5 volts, the battery power may be insufficient to operate the electrical system properly. This test determines voltage available from the battery and should be the first step in any electrical trouble diagnosis procedure. Many electrical problems, especially on computer controlled systems, can be caused by a low state of charge in the battery. Excessive corrosion at the battery cable terminals can cause a poor contact that will prevent proper charging and full battery current flow.

Normal battery voltage is 12 volts when fully charged. When the battery is supplying current to one or more circuits it is said to be "under load." When everything is off the electrical system is under a "no-load" condition. A fully charged battery may show about 12.5 volts at no load; will drop to 12 volts under medium load; and will drop even lower under heavy load. If the battery is partially discharged the voltage decrease under heavy load may be excessive, even though the battery shows 12 volts or more at no load. When allowed to discharge further, the battery's available voltage under load will decrease more severely. For this reason, it is important that the battery be fully charged during all testing procedures to avoid errors in diagnosis and incorrect test results.

Voltage Drop

When current flows through a resistance, the voltage beyond the resistance is reduced (the larger the current, the greater the reduction in voltage). When no current is flowing, there is no voltage drop because there is no current flow. All points in the circuit which are connected to the power source are at the same voltage as the power source. The total voltage drop always equals the total source voltage. In a long circuit with

many connectors, a series of small, unwanted voltage drops due to corrosion at the connectors can add up to a total loss of voltage which impairs the operation of the normal loads in the circuit. The maximum allowable voltage drop under load is critical, especially if there is more than one high resistance problem in a circuit because all voltage drops are cumulative. A small drop is normal due to the resistance of the conductors.

INDIRECT COMPUTATION OF VOLTAGE DROPS

1. Set the voltmeter selector switch to the 20 volt position.
2. Connect the meter negative lead to a good ground.
3. While operating the circuit, probe all loads in the circuit with the positive meter lead and observe the voltage readings. A drop should be noticed after the first load. But, there should be little or no voltage drop before the first load.

DIRECT MEASUREMENT OF VOLTAGE DROPS

1. Set the voltmeter switch to the 20 volt position.
2. Connect the voltmeter negative lead to the ground side of the load to be measured.
3. Connect the positive lead to the positive side of the resistance or load to be measured.
4. Read the voltage drop directly on the 20 volt scale.

Too high a voltage indicates too high a resistance. If, for example, a blower motor runs too slowly, you can determine if perhaps there is too high a resistance in the resistor pack. By taking voltage drop readings in all parts of the circuit, you can isolate the problem. Too low a voltage drop indicates too low a resistance. Take the blower motor for example again. If a blower motor runs too fast in the MED and/or LOW position, the problem might be isolated in the resistor pack by taking voltage drop readings in all parts of the circuit to locate a possibly shorted resistor.

HIGH RESISTANCE TESTING

1. Set the voltmeter selector switch to the 4 volt position.
2. Connect the voltmeter positive lead to the positive post of the battery.
3. Turn on the headlights and heater blower to provide a load.
4. Probe various points in the circuit with the negative voltmeter lead.
5. Read the voltage drop on the 4 volt scale. Some average maximum allowable voltage drops are:
   - FUSE PANEL: 0.7 volts
   - IGNITION SWITCH: 0.5 volts
   - HEADLIGHT SWITCH: 0.7 volts
   - IGNITION COIL (+): 0.5 volts
   - ANY OTHER LOAD: 1.3 volts

➡Voltage drops are all measured while a load is operating; without current flow, there will be no voltage drop.

Resistance Measurement

The batteries in an ohmmeter will weaken with age and temperature, so the ohmmeter must be calibrated or "zeroed before taking measurements. To zero the meter, place the selector switch in its lowest range and touch the two ohmmeter leads together. Turn the calibration knob until the meter needle is exactly on zero.

➥All analog (needle) type ohmmeters must be zeroed before use, but some digital ohmmeter models are automatically calibrated when the switch is turned on. Self-calibrating digital ohmmeters do not have an adjusting knob, but its a good idea to check for a zero readout before use by touching the leads together. All computer controlled systems require the use of a digital ohmmeter with at least 10 megohms impedance for testing. Before any test procedures are attempted, make sure the ohmmeter used is compatible with the electrical system or damage to the on-board computer could result.

To measure resistance, first isolate the circuit from the vehicle power source by disconnecting the battery cables or the harness connector. Make sure the key is **OFF** when disconnecting any components or the battery. Where necessary, also isolate at least one side of the circuit to be checked in order to avoid reading parallel resistances. Parallel circuit resistances will always give a lower reading than the actual resistance of either of the branches. When measuring the resistance of parallel circuits, the total resistance will always be lower than the smallest resistance in the circuit. Connect the meter leads to both sides of the circuit (wire or component) and read the actual measured ohms on the meter scale. Make sure the selector switch is set to the proper ohm scale for the circuit being tested to avoid misreading the ohmmeter test value.

✳✳WARNING

Never use an ohmmeter with power applied to the circuit. Like the self-powered test light, the ohmmeter is designed to operate on its own power supply. The normal 12 volt automotive electrical system current could damage the meter!

Wiring Harnesses

▶ See Figure 1

The average automobile contains about ½ mile of wiring, with hundreds of individual connections. To protect the many wires from damage and to keep them from becoming a confusing tangle, they are organized into bundles, enclosed in plastic or taped together and called wiring harnesses. Different harnesses serve different parts of the vehicle. Individual wires are color coded to help trace them through a harness where sections are hidden from view.

Automotive wiring or circuit conductors can be in any one of three forms:

1. Single strand wire
2. Multi-strand wire
3. Printed circuitry

Single strand wire has a solid metal core and is usually used inside such components as alternators, motors, relays and other devices. Multi-strand wire has a core made of many small strands of wire twisted together into a single conductor. Most of the wiring in an automotive electrical system is made up of multi-strand wire, either as a single conductor or grouped together in a harness. All wiring is color coded on the

insulator, either as a solid color or as a colored wire with an identification stripe. A printed circuit is a thin film of copper or other conductor that is printed on an insulator backing. Occasionally, a printed circuit is sandwiched between two sheets of plastic for more protection and flexibility. A complete printed circuit, consisting of conductors, insulating material and connectors for lamps or other components is called a printed circuit board. Printed circuitry is used in place of individual wires or harnesses in places where space is limited, such as behind instrument panels.

Since automotive electrical systems are very sensitive to changes in resistance, the selection of properly sized wires is critical when systems are repaired. A loose or corroded connection or a replacement wire that is too small for the circuit will add extra resistance and an additional voltage drop to the circuit. A ten percent voltage drop can result in slow or erratic motor operation, for example, even though the circuit is complete. The wire gauge number is an expression of the cross-section area of the conductor. The most common system for expressing wire size is the American Wire Gauge (AWG) system.

Gauge numbers are assigned to conductors of various cross-section areas. As gauge number increases, area decreases and the conductor becomes smaller. A 5 gauge conductor is smaller than a 1 gauge conductor and a 10 gauge is smaller than a 5 gauge. As the cross-section area of a conductor decreases, resistance increases and so does the gauge number. A conductor with a higher gauge number will carry less current than a conductor with a lower gauge number.

➥Gauge wire size refers to the size of the conductor, not the size of the complete wire. It is possible to have two wires of the same gauge with different diameters because one may have thicker insulation than the other.

12 volt automotive electrical systems generally use 10, 12, 14, 16 and 18 gauge wire. Main power distribution circuits and larger accessories usually use 10 and 12 gauge wire. Battery cables are usually 4 or 6 gauge, although 1 and 2 gauge wires are occasionally used. Wire length must also be considered when making repairs to a circuit. As conductor length increases, so does resistance. An 18 gauge wire, for example,

86656499

Fig. 1 This exposed wire could quickly corrode and break or short itself on a nearby piece of metal. It should be repaired immediately

can carry a 10 amp load for 10 feet without excessive voltage drop; however if a 15 foot wire is required for the same 10 amp load, it must be a 16 gauge wire.

An electrical schematic shows the electrical current paths when a circuit is operating properly. It is essential to understand how a circuit works before trying to figure out why it doesn't. Schematics break the entire electrical system down into individual circuits and show only one particular circuit. In a schematic, no attempt is made to represent wiring and components as they physically appear on the vehicle; switches and other components are shown as simply as possible. Face views of harness connectors show the cavity or terminal locations in all multi-pin connectors to help locate test points.

If you need to backprobe a connector while it is on the component, the order of the terminals must be mentally reversed. The wire color code can help in this situation, as well as a keyway, lock tab or other reference mark.

WIRING REPAIR

Soldering is a quick, efficient method of joining metals permanently. Everyone who has the occasion to make wiring repairs should know how to solder. Electrical connections that are soldered are far less likely to come apart and will conduct electricity much better than connections that are only "pig-tailed" together. The most popular (and preferred) method of soldering is with an electrical soldering gun. Soldering irons are available in many sizes and wattage ratings. Irons with higher wattage ratings deliver higher temperatures and recover lost heat faster. A small soldering iron rated for no more than 50 watts is recommended, especially on electrical systems where excess heat can damage the components being soldered.

There are three ingredients necessary for successful soldering; proper flux, good solder and sufficient heat. A soldering flux is necessary to clean the metal of tarnish, prepare it for soldering and to enable the solder to spread into tiny crevices. When soldering, always use a rosin core solder which is non-corrosive and will not attract moisture once the job is finished. Other types of flux (acid core) will leave a residue that will attract moisture and cause the wires to corrode. Tin is a unique metal with a low melting point. In a molten state, it dissolves and alloys easily with many metals. Solder is made by mixing tin with lead. The most common proportions are 40/60, 50/50 and 60/40, with the percentage of tin listed first. Low priced solders usually contain less tin, making them very difficult for a beginner to use because more heat is required to melt the solder. A common solder is 40/60 which is well suited for all-around general use, but 60/40 melts easier and is preferred for electrical work.

Soldering Techniques

Successful soldering requires that the metals to be joined be heated to a temperature that will melt the solder, usually 360-460°F (182-238°C). Contrary to popular belief, the purpose of the soldering iron is not to melt the solder itself, but to heat the parts being soldered to a temperature high enough to melt the solder when it is touched to the work. Melting flux-cored solder on the soldering iron will usually destroy the effectiveness of the flux.

➡ **Soldering tips are made of copper for good heat conductivity, but must be "tinned" regularly for quick transference of heat to the project and to prevent the solder from sticking to the iron. To "tin" the iron, simply heat it and touch the flux-cored solder to the tip; the solder will flow over the hot tip. Wipe the excess off with a clean rag, but be careful as the iron will be hot.**

After some use, the tip may become pitted. If so, simply dress the tip smooth with a smooth file and "tin" the tip again. Flux-cored solder will remove oxides but rust, bits of insulation and oil or grease must be removed with a wire brush or emery cloth. For maximum strength in soldered parts, the joint must start off clean and tight. Weak joints will result in gaps too wide for the solder to bridge.

If a separate soldering flux is used, it should be brushed or swabbed on only those areas that are to be soldered. Most solders contain a core of flux and separate fluxing is unnecessary. Hold the work to be soldered firmly. It is best to solder on a wooden board, because a metal vise will only rob the piece to be soldered of heat and make it difficult to melt the solder. Hold the soldering tip with the broadest face against the work to be soldered. Apply solder under the tip close to the work, using enough solder to give a heavy film between the iron and the piece being soldered, while moving slowly and making sure the solder melts properly. Keep the work level or the solder will run to the lowest part and favor the thicker parts, because these require more heat to melt the solder. If the soldering tip overheats (the solder coating on the face of the tip burns up), it should be retinned. Once the soldering is completed, let the soldered joint stand until cool. Tape and seal all soldered wire splices after the repair has cooled.

Wire Harness Connectors

Most connectors in the engine compartment or that are otherwise exposed to the elements are protected against moisture and dirt which could create oxidation and deposits on the terminals.

These special connectors are weather-proof. All repairs require the use of a special terminal and the tool required to service it. This tool is used to remove the pin and sleeve terminals. If removal is attempted with an ordinary pick, there is a good chance that the terminal will be bent or deformed. Unlike standard blade type terminals, these weather-proof terminals cannot be straightened once they are bent. Make certain that the connectors are properly seated and all of the sealing rings are in place when connecting leads. On some models, a hinge-type flap provides a backup or secondary locking feature for the terminals. Most secondary locks are used to improve connector reliability by retaining the terminals if the small terminal lock tangs are not positioned properly.

Molded-on connectors require complete replacement of the connection. This means splicing a new connector assembly into the harness. All splices should be soldered to insure proper contact. Use care when probing the connections or replacing terminals in them as it is possible to short between opposite terminals. If this happens to the wrong terminal pair, it is possible to damage certain components. Always use jumper wires between connectors for circuit checking and never probe through weatherproof seals.

Open circuits are often difficult to locate by sight because corrosion or terminal misalignment are hidden by the connectors. Merely wiggling a connector on a sensor or in the wiring harness may correct the open circuit condition. This should always be considered when an open circuit or a failed sensor is indicated. Intermittent problems may also be caused by oxidized or loose connections. When using a circuit tester for diagnosis, always probe connections from the wire side. Be careful not to damage sealed connectors with test probes.

All wiring harnesses should be replaced with identical parts, using the same gauge wire and connectors. When signal wires are spliced into a harness, use wire with high temperature insulation only. It is seldom necessary to replace a complete harness. If replacement is necessary, pay close attention to insure proper harness routing. Secure the harness with suitable plastic wire clamps to prevent vibrations from causing the harness to wear in spots or contact any hot components.

➡️**Weatherproof connectors cannot be replaced with standard connectors. Instructions are provided with replacement connector and terminal packages. Some wire harnesses have mounting indicators (usually pieces of colored tape) to mark where the harness is to be secured.**

In making wiring repairs, its important that you always replace damaged wires with wiring of the same gauge as the wire being replaced. The heavier the wire, the smaller the gauge number. Wires are color-coded to aid in identification and whenever possible the same color coded wire should be used for replacement. A wire stripping and crimping tool is necessary to install solderless terminal connectors. Test all crimps by pulling on the wires; it should not be possible to pull the wires out of a good crimp.

Wires which are open, exposed or otherwise damaged are repaired by simple splicing. Where possible, if the wiring harness is accessible and the damaged place in the wire can be located, it is best to open the harness and check for all possible damage. In an inaccessible harness, the wire must be bypassed with a new insert, usually taped to the outside of the old harness.

When replacing fusible links, be sure to use fusible link wire, NOT ordinary automotive wire. Make sure the fusible segment is of the same gauge and construction as the one being replaced and double the stripped end when crimping the terminal connector for a good contact. The melted (open) fusible link segment of the wiring harness should be cut off as close to the harness as possible, then a new segment spliced in as described. In the case of a damaged fusible link that feeds two harness wires, the harness connections should be replaced with two fusible link wires so that each circuit will have its own separate protection.

➡️**Most of the problems caused in the wiring harness are due to bad ground connections. Always check all vehicle ground connections for corrosion or looseness before performing any power feed checks to eliminate the chance of a bad ground affecting the circuit.**

Hard-Shell Connectors

Unlike molded connectors, the terminal contacts in hard-shell connectors can be replaced. Weatherproof hard-shell connectors with the leads molded into the shell have non-replaceable terminal ends. Replacement usually involves the use of a special terminal removal tool that depresses the locking tangs (barbs) on the connector terminal and allows the connector to be removed from the rear of the shell. The connector shell should be replaced if it shows any evidence of burning, melting, cracks, or breaks. Replace individual terminals that are burnt, corroded, distorted or loose.

➡️**The insulation crimp must be tight to prevent the insulation from sliding back on the wire when the wire is pulled. The insulation must be visibly compressed under the crimp tabs, and the ends of the crimp should be turned in for a firm grip on the insulation.**

The wire crimp must be made with all wire strands inside the crimp. The terminal must be fully compressed on the wire strands with the ends of the crimp tabs turned in to make a firm grip on the wire. Check all connections with an ohmmeter to insure a good contact. There should be no measurable resistance between the wire and the terminal when connected.

Add-On Electrical Equipment

The electrical system in your vehicle is designed to perform under reasonable operating conditions without interference between components. Before any additional electrical equipment is installed, it is recommended that you consult your dealer or a reputable repair facility that is familiar with the vehicle and its systems.

If the vehicle is equipped with mobile radio equipment and/or mobile telephone, it may have an effect upon the operation of the ECM. Radio Frequency Interference (RFI) from the communications system can be picked up by the vehicle's wiring harnesses and conducted into the ECM, giving it the wrong messages at the wrong time. Although well shielded against RFI, the ECM should be further protected by taking the following measures:

• Install the antenna as far as possible from the ECM. For instance, if the ECM is located behind the center console area, then the antenna should be mounted at the rear of the vehicle.

• Keep the antenna wiring a minimum of eight inches away from any wiring running to the ECM and from the ECM itself. NEVER wind the antenna wire around any other wiring.

• Mount the equipment as far from the ECM as possible. Be very careful during installation not to drill through any wires or short a wire harness with a mounting screw.

• Insure that the electrical feed wire(s) to the equipment are properly and tightly connected. Loose connectors can cause interference.

• Make certain that the equipment is properly grounded to the vehicle. Poor grounding can damage expensive equipment.

HEATING AND AIR CONDITIONING

Blower Motor

REMOVAL & INSTALLATION

Except Air Conditioned Vehicles

▶ See Figures 2, 3 and 4

➡The right side ventilator assembly must be removed for access to the blower motor and wheel.

1. Open the glove box door and remove the straps attached to the door. With the straps removed, unfasten the retaining screws securing the door to the hinge. If equipped with a liner, remove it now.
2. Remove the retaining screw from the right register duct mounting bracket.
3. Remove the screws holding the control cable lever assembly to the instrument panel.
4. Remove the plastic rivets securing the grille to the floor outlet, and remove the grille.
5. Remove the right register duct and register assembly:
   a. Remove the register duct bracket retaining screw on the lower edge of the instrument panel, and disengage the duct from the opening and then remove them through the glove box opening.
   b. Insert a thin blade under the retaining tab and pry the tab toward the louvers until retaining tab pivot clears the hole in the register opening. Pull the register assembly end out from the housing only enough to prevent the pivot from going back into the pivot hole. Pry the other retaining tab loose and remove the register assembly from the opening.
6. Remove the retaining screws securing the ventilator assembly to the blower housing. The upper right screw can be reached with a long extension through the register opening; the upper left screw can be reached through the glove box opening. The other two screws are on the bottom of the assembly.
7. Slide the assembly to the right, then down and out from under the instrument panel.
8. Remove the motor lead wire connector from the register and push it back through the hole in the case. Remove the right side cowl trim panel for access, and remove the ground terminal lug retaining screw.
9. Remove the hub clamp spring from the motor shaft and remove the blower wheel.
10. Remove the blower motor bolts from the housing and remove the motor.
11. Service as required and reinstall in the reverse order of removal.

Air Conditioned Vehicles

✳✳WARNING

Removal of the heater/air conditioner (evaporator) housing requires evacuation and recovery of the air conditioner refrigerant using a proper recovery/recycling station. This

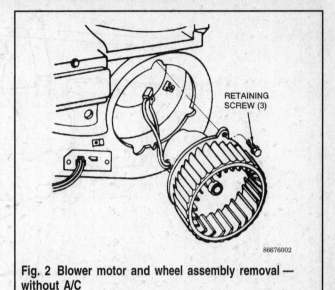

Fig. 2 Blower motor and wheel assembly removal — without A/C

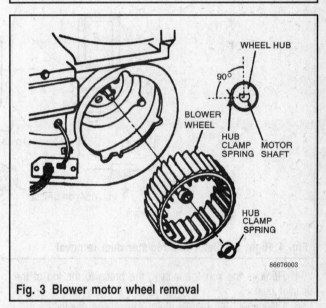

Fig. 3 Blower motor wheel removal

operation requires a thorough familiarity with automotive refrigerant systems. Failure to follow proper safety precautions may cause personal injury. If you are not familiar with these systems, it is recommended that discharging and charging of the A/C system be performed by an experienced professional mechanic. For discharging, recovery, evacuating and charging procedures, see Section 1.

▶ See Figures 5, 6, 7, 8, 9, 10, 11, 12, 13, 14, 15, 16, 17 and 18

➡The air inlet duct and blower housing assembly must be removed for access to the blower motor.

1. Remove the glove box liner and door assembly.
2. Disconnect the hose from the vacuum motor.
3. Remove the instrument panel lower right side to cowl attaching bolt.

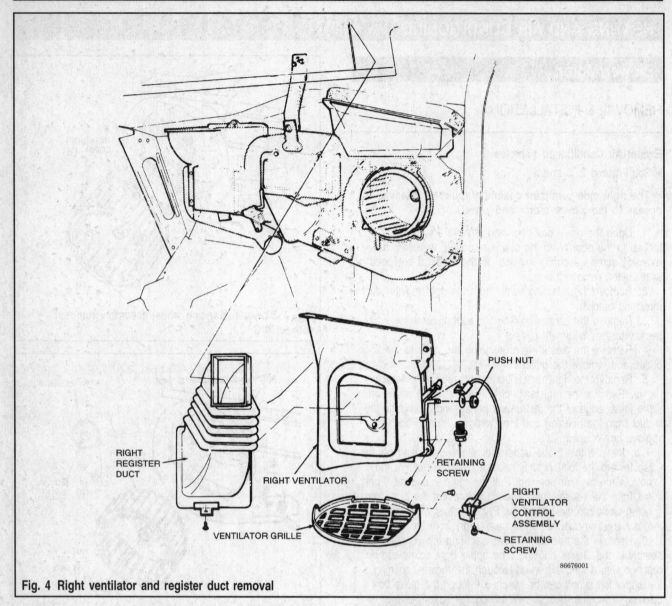

RIGHT REGISTER DUCT

RIGHT VENTILATOR

VENTILATOR GRILLE

PUSH NUT

RETAINING SCREW

RIGHT VENTILATOR CONTROL ASSEMBLY

RETAINING SCREW

86676001

Fig. 4 Right ventilator and register duct removal

4. Remove the screw attaching the brace to the top of the air inlet duct.

5. Disconnect the blower motor wire at the electrical connector.

6. Remove the housing lower support bracket to case nut.

7. Remove the side cowl trim panel and remove the ground wire screw.

8. Remove the screw attaching the top of the air inlet duct to the evaporator case.

9. Move the air inlet duct and housing assembly down and away from the evaporator case.

10. Remove the four blower motor mounting plate screws then remove the blower motor and wheel as an assembly from the housing. Do not remove the mounting plate from the motor.

11. Service as required and reinstall in the reverse order of removal. Tape the blower motor power lead to the air inlet duct to keep the wire away from the blower outlet during installation.

86676500

Fig. 5 Remove the clip which secures the glove box retaining strap

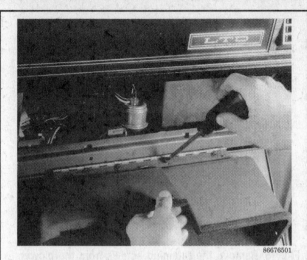

Fig. 6 Loosen and remove the screws from the glove box hinge

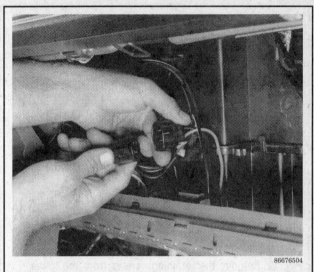

Fig. 9 Unclip the blower motor wire harness

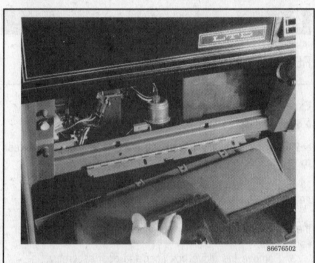

Fig. 7 With the screws removed, withdraw the glove box and place aside

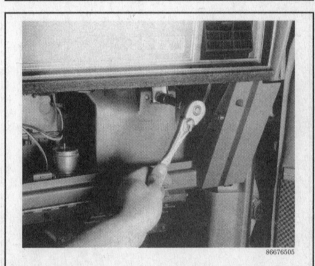

Fig. 10 Remove the retaining screw securing the blower case

Fig. 8 Remove the vacuum line from the top of the vacuum motor

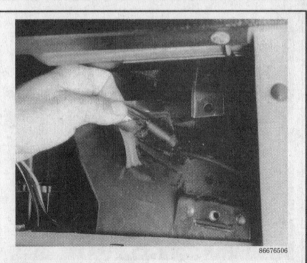

Fig. 11 Unfasten the tape or tar paper over the vent cable placed on top of the blower case

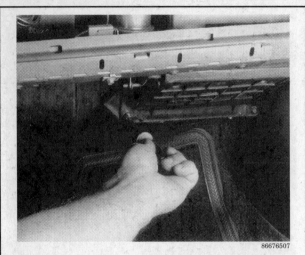

Fig. 12 Remove the retaining screws from the lower portion of the blower case

Fig. 13 Using a suitable prytool, separate the blower case from the vent duct

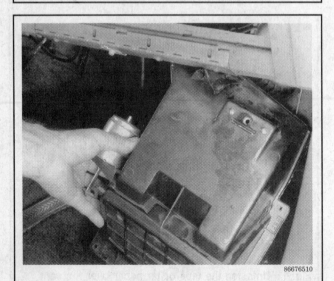

Fig. 14 Lower the blower case

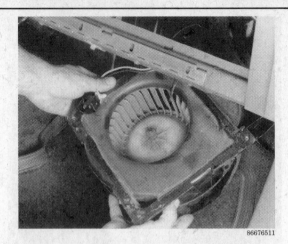

Fig. 15 Remove the retaining screws from the blower case and separate the halves to reveal the blower motor

Heater Core

REMOVAL & INSTALLATION

Except Air Conditioned Vehicles
▶ See Figures 19 and 20

➡It is not necessary to remove the heater case for access to the heater core.

1. Drain enough coolant from the radiator to drain the heater core.
2. Loosen the heater hose clamps on the engine side of the firewall and disconnect the heater hoses. Cap the heater core tubes.
3. Remove the glove box liner and door assembly.
4. Remove the instrument panel-to-cowl brace retaining screws and remove the brace.
5. Move the temperature lever to WARM.
6. Remove the heater core cover screws. Remove the cover through the glove box.
7. Loosen the heater case mounting nuts on the engine side of the firewall.
8. Push the heater core tubes and seals toward the interior of the car to loosen the core.
9. Remove the heater core through the glove box opening.
10. Service as required and reinstall in the reverse order of removal.

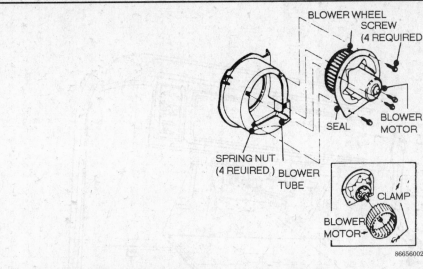

Fig. 16 Blower motor and wheel assembly — models with A/C

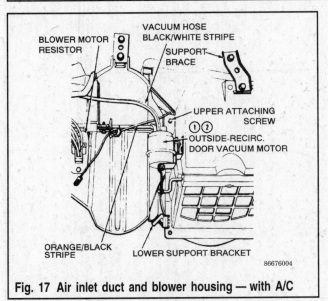

Fig. 17 Air inlet duct and blower housing — with A/C

Fig. 19 Loosen the clamps on the heater core coolant hoses

Air Conditioned Vehicles
▶ See Figures 21, 22, 23 and 24

✲✲WARNING

Removal of the heater/air conditioner (evaporator) housing requires evacuation and recovery of the air conditioner refrigerant using a proper recovery/recycling station. This operation requires a thorough familiarity with automotive refrigerant systems. Failure to follow proper safety precautions may cause personal injury. If you are not familiar with these systems, it is recommended that discharging and charging of the A/C system be performed by an experienced professional mechanic. For discharging, recovery, evacuating and charging procedures, see Section 1.

➡The instrument panel must be removed for access to the heater core.

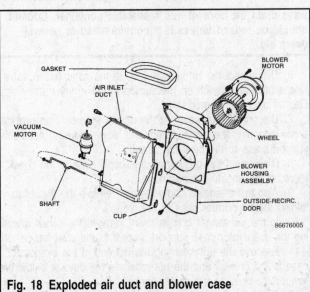

Fig. 18 Exploded air duct and blower case

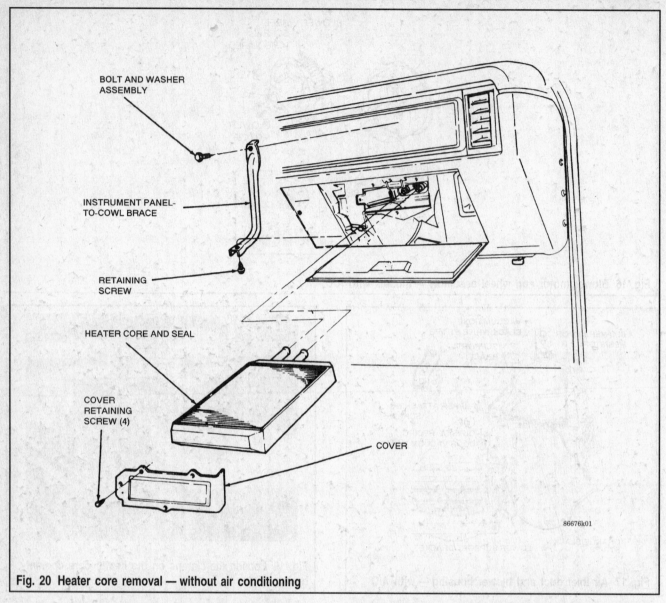

BOLT AND WASHER
ASSEMBLY

INSTRUMENT PANEL-
TO-COWL BRACE

RETAINING
SCREW

HEATER CORE AND SEAL

COVER
RETAINING
SCREW (4)

COVER

86676k01

Fig. 20 Heater core removal — without air conditioning

1. Using an approved refrigerant recovery/recycling station which meets SAE standards, discharge the system at the service access port on the underside of the combination valve.

2. Disconnect the negative battery cable.

3. Remove the instrument panel pad:

a. Remove the screws attaching the instrument cluster trim panel to the pad.

b. Remove the screw attaching the pad to the panel at each defroster opening.

c. Remove the screws attaching the edge of the pad to the panel.

4. Remove the instrument panel and lay it on the front seat.

5. Drain the cooling system and disconnect the heater hoses at the core tubes.

✳✳CAUTION

When draining coolant, keep in mind that cats and dogs are attracted to ethylene glycol antifreeze, and could drink any that is left in an uncovered container or in puddles on the ground. This will prove fatal in sufficient quantity. Al-ways drain the coolant into a sealable container. Coolant should be reused unless it is contaminated or several years old.

6. Disconnect the refrigerant lines at the combination valve. Use a back-up wrench on the suction throttling valve manifold. Cap all openings immediately!

7. Disconnect the wiring at the blower resistor. Remove the screw attaching the air inlet duct and blower housing assembly support brace to the cowl top panel.

8. Disconnect the black vacuum supply hose at the check valve, in the engine compartment.

9. Also in the engine compartment, remove the 2 nuts retaining the evaporator case to the firewall.

10. In the passenger compartment, remove the screw attaching the evaporator case support bracket to the cowl top panel.

11. Remove the nut retaining the left end of the evaporator case to the firewall and the nut retaining the bracket below the evaporator case, to the dash panel.

12. Carefully pull the case away from the firewall and remove the case from the car.

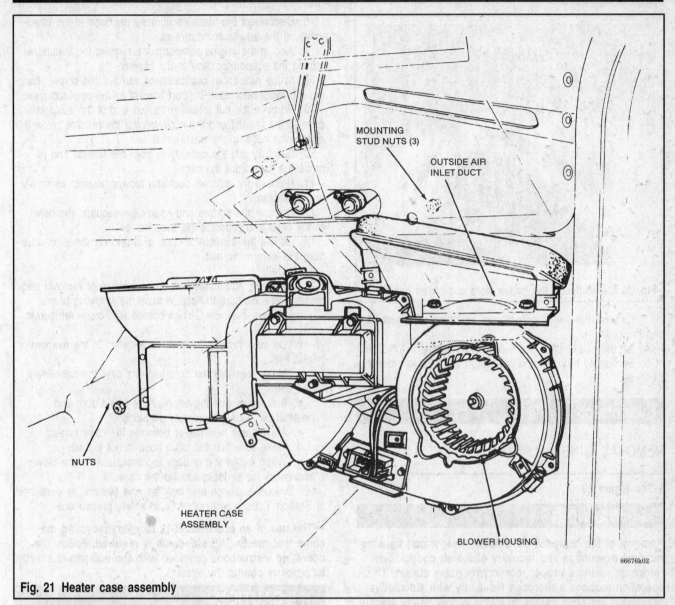

Fig. 21 Heater case assembly

Labels on Fig. 21:
- MOUNTING STUD NUTS (3)
- OUTSIDE AIR INLET DUCT
- NUTS
- HEATER CASE ASSEMBLY
- BLOWER HOUSING

86676k02

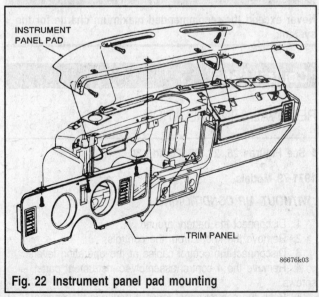

Fig. 22 Instrument panel pad mounting

Labels on Fig. 22:
- INSTRUMENT PANEL PAD
- TRIM PANEL

86676k03

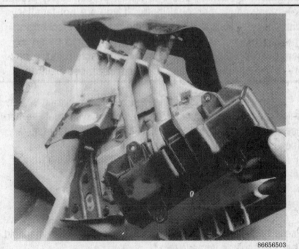

Fig. 23 Remove the case cover to expose the heater core

86656503

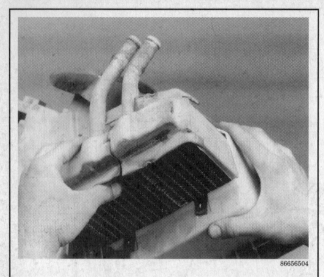

86656504

Fig. 24 Carefully lift the heater core out of the case

13. Remove the heater core access cover retaining screws and the cover.

14. Lift the heater core and seals from the evaporator case.

15. Service as required and reinstall in the reverse order of removal.

Evaporator

REMOVAL & INSTALLATION

▶ See Figure 25

✳✳WARNING

Removal of the heater/air conditioner (evaporator) housing requires evacuation and recovery of the air conditioner refrigerant using a proper recovery/recycling station. This operation requires a thorough familiarity with automotive refrigerant systems. Failure to follow proper safety precautions may cause personal injury. If you are not familiar with these systems, it is recommended that discharging and charging of the A/C system be performed by an experienced professional mechanic. For discharging, recovery, evacuating and charging procedures, see Section 1.

1. Using an approved refrigerant recovery/recycling station which meets SAE standards, discharge the system at the service access port on the underside of the combination valve. See Section 1 of this manual.

2. Remove the instrument panel and lay it on the front seat.

3. Drain the cooling system and disconnect the heater hoses at the core tubes.

4. Disconnect the refrigerant lines at the combination valve. Use a back-up wrench on the suction throttling valve manifold. Cap all openings immediately!

5. Disconnect the wiring at the blower resistor. Remove the screw attaching the air inlet duct and blower housing assembly support brace to the cowl top panel.

6. Disconnect the black vacuum supply hose at the check valve, in the engine compartment.

7. Also in the engine compartment, remove the 2 nuts retaining the evaporator case to the firewall.

8. In the passenger compartment, remove the screw attaching the evaporator case support bracket to the cowl top panel.

9. Remove the nut retaining the left end of the evaporator case to the firewall and the nut retaining the bracket below the evaporator case, to the dash panel.

10. Carefully pull the case away from the firewall and remove the case from the car.

11. Remove the air inlet duct and blower housing assembly from the case.

12. Remove the screws and snap-clips securing the halves of the case and separate the case halves.

13. Lift out the evaporator core, seal and combination valve from the lower case half.

To install:

14. Assembly and installation is the reverse of removal and disassembly. Be sure to keep in mind the following points:

   a. Always use new O-rings coated with clean refrigerant oil.

   b. Be sure that the restrictor is installed in the evaporator inlet line.

   c. Make sure that the core seal fits over the case lower half edge.

   d. Make sure that the temperature blend door and heat/defrost door are properly positioned.

   e. Always use new sealer between the case halves.

   f. Make sure that the drain hose is not kinked.

   g. When everything is back together, turn on the blower and check for air leaks around the case.

15. Evacuate, charge and leak test the system, as described in Section 1. Be sure to observe all safety precautions.

➡The use of an approved R-12 recovery/recycling machine that meets SAE standards is required. Follow the operating instructions provided with the equipment exactly to properly charge the system.

✳✳CAUTION

Never exceed the recommended maximum charge for the system.

Control Panel

REMOVAL & INSTALLATION

▶ See Figures 26, 27, 28, 29 and 30

1971-79 Models

WITHOUT AIR CONDITIONING

1. Disconnect the battery ground.

2. Remove the knobs from the controls.

3. Disconnect the control cables at the operating levers.

4. Remove the 4 control assembly-to-instrument panel screws.

5. Push the control panel forward (towards the engine).

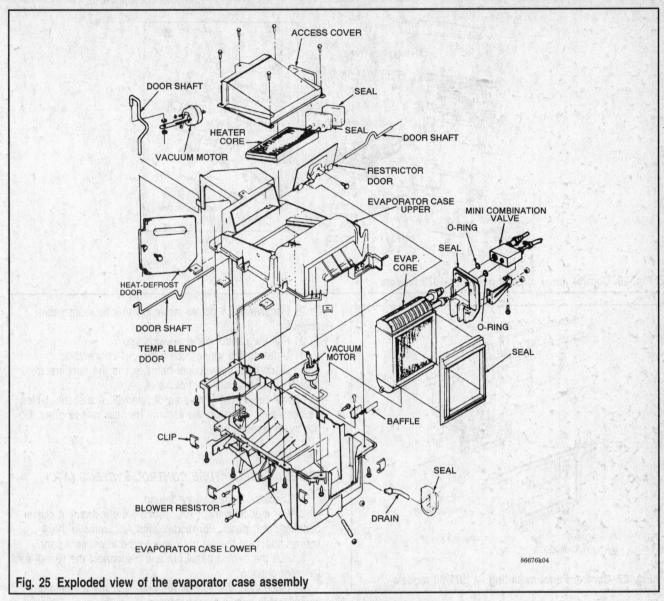

Fig. 25 Exploded view of the evaporator case assembly

6. Disconnect the wiring (mark location for correct installation) from the panel connectors.

7. Lower the control panel and remove it.

8. Installation is the reverse of removal. Adjust the cables as necessary.

WITH AIR CONDITIONING

1. Disconnect the battery ground.

2. Remove the control knobs.

3. Remove the 2 lower control assembly attaching screws.

4. Remove the 2 upper attaching screws.

5. Disconnect the temperature control cable at the control head.

6. Disconnect the vacuum harness at the vacuum selector valve.

7. Disconnect the wiring at the blower switch.

8. Push the panel forward and remove it from the instrument panel.

9. Installation is the reverse of removal. Adjust the cables as necessary.

1980-81 Models

➡This procedure applies for both vehicles with and without air conditioning.

1. Disconnect the battery ground.

2. Remove the 4 control assembly-to-instrument panel screws.

3. Pull the control panel towards you.

4. Unplug the wiring from the panel connectors.

5. Disconnect the vacuum harness and the temperature control cable from the control panel.

6. Installation is the reverse of removal. Adjust the cables as necessary. Push on the vacuum harness retaining nut, Do not try to screw it on!

1982-83 Models

➡This procedure applies for both vehicles with and without air conditioning.

1. Disconnect the battery ground.

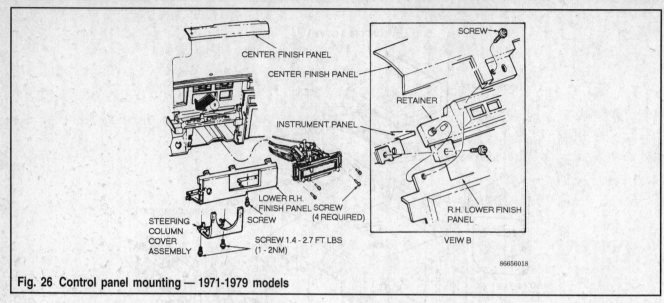

Fig. 26 Control panel mounting — 1971-1979 models

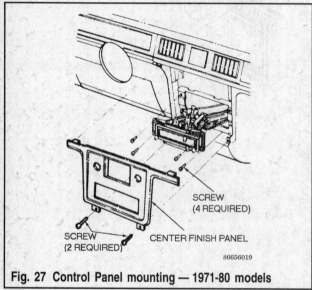

Fig. 27 Control Panel mounting — 1971-80 models

2. Remove the 4 control assembly-to-instrument panel screws.

3. Pull the control panel towards you.

4. Unfasten the wiring from the panel connectors.

5. Disconnect the vacuum harness and the temperature control cable from the control panel.

6. Installation is the reverse of removal. Adjust the cables as necessary. Push on the vacuum harness retaining nut, Do not try to screw it on!

1984 Models

EXCEPT TEMPERATURE CONTROL SYSTEMS (ATC)

1. Disconnect the battery ground.

2. For models without A/C, remove the instrument cluster opening finish panel. For models with A/C, remove the 4 screws attaching the control panel to the instrument panel.

3. Pull the control panel out and disconnect the wiring from the control panel.

4. Disconnect the vacuum harness and the temperature control cable from the control panel.

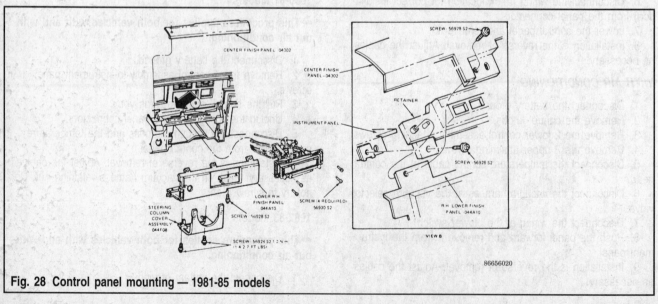

Fig. 28 Control panel mounting — 1981-85 models

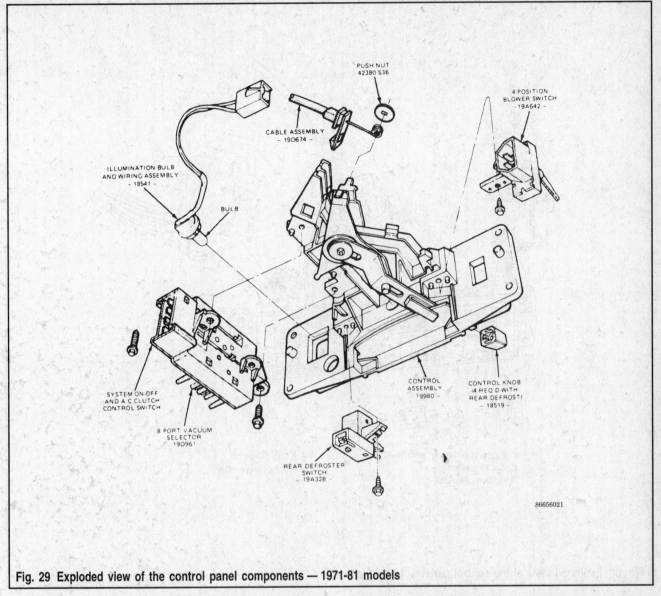

Fig. 29 Exploded view of the control panel components — 1971-81 models

5. Installation is the reverse of removal. Remember that the vacuum harness nut is a pushnut. It does not screw on.

WITH AUTOMATIC TEMPERATURE CONTROL (ATC) SYSTEMS

1. Disconnect the battery ground.
2. Remove the radio knobs.
3. Open the ashtray and remove the 2 screws attaching the center finish panel to the instrument panel at the ashtray opening.
4. Pull the lower edge of the center finish panel away from the instrument panel and disengage the upper tabs of the finish panel from the instrument panel.
5. Remove the 4 screws attaching the control panel to the instrument panel.
6. Pull the control panel towards you about 1½ in. (38mm). Insert a screwdriver and remove the control panel harness connector locator from the hole in the instrument panel.
7. Pull the control panel from the instrument panel and unfasten the wire connectors from the control panel.

8. Disconnect the vacuum harness and temperature control cable from the control panel. Discard the pushnuts.
9. Installation is the reverse of removal. If the lamp wires become disconnected during the panel removal, put the clips back on the controls before installing the panel.

1985 Models

➡This procedure applies for both vehicles with and without air conditioning.

1. Disconnect the battery ground cable.
2. Pull the knobs from the radio control shafts.
3. Open the ashtray and remove the 2 screws that attach the center finish panel to the instrument panel.
4. Pull the lower edge of the center finish panel away from the instrument panel and disengage the tabs of the finish panel from the instrument panel.
5. Remove the 4 control panel attaching screws.
6. Carefully pull the control panel away from the instrument panel and disconnect the wires and hoses.

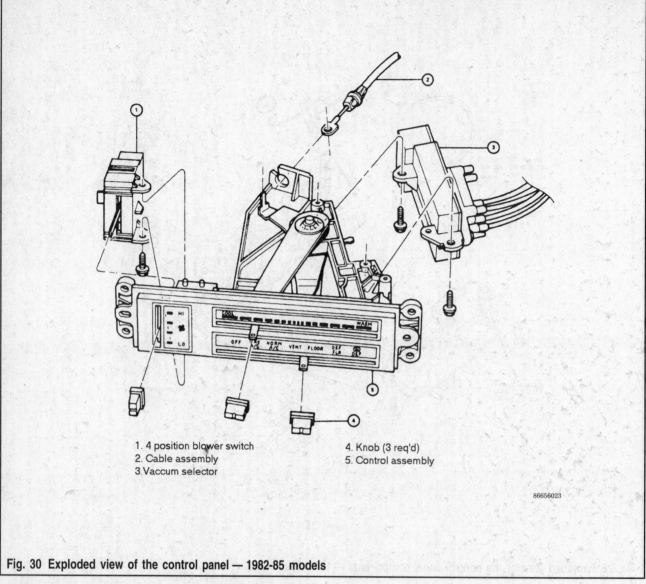

1. 4 position blower switch
2. Cable assembly
3. Vaccum selector

4. Knob (3 req'd)
5. Control assembly

86656023

Fig. 30 Exploded view of the control panel — 1982-85 models

7. Installation is the reverse of removal procedure. Check system for proper operation.

Control Cables

REMOVAL & INSTALLATION

▶ See Figure 31

1971-72 Models

1. Disconnect the negative battery cable.
2. Press the glove compartment door stops inward and allow the door to hang by the hinge.
3. Remove the control panel from the instrument panel.
4. Disconnect the cable housing from the control assembly and disengage the cable from the temperature control lever.
5. Working through the glove compartment opening, disconnect the cable from the plenum temperature blend door crank arm and cable mounting bracket.

6. Note the cable routing and remove the cable from the vehicle.

To install:

7. Make sure the self-adjusting clip is at least 1 in. (25mm) from the end loop of the control cable.
8. Route the cable behind the instrument panel and connect the control cable to the mounting bracket on the plenum.
9. Install the self-adjusting clip on the temperature blend door crank arm.
10. Connect the other end of the cable to the temperature lever arm on the control assembly. Snap the cable housing into place at the control assembly.
11. Install the control panel in the instrument panel.
12. Return the glove compartment door to the normal position and connect the negative battery cable.
13. Check the system for proper operation.

1972-85 Models

▶ See Figures 32 and 33

1. Using the control cable disconnect tool T83P-18532-AH or equivalent, detach the control cable bullet connector from

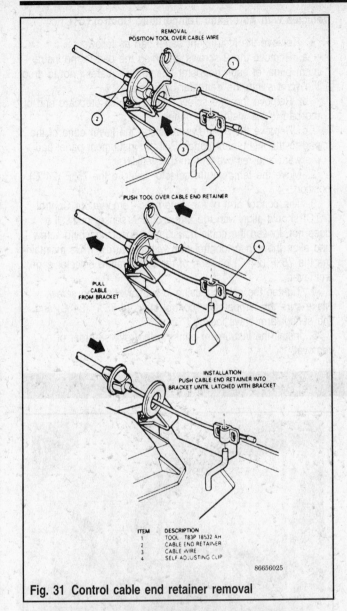

ITEM | DESCRIPTION
1 | TOOL T83P 18532 AH
2 | CABLE END RETAINER
3 | CABLE WIRE
4 | SELF-ADJUSTING CLIP

86656025

Fig. 31 Control cable end retainer removal

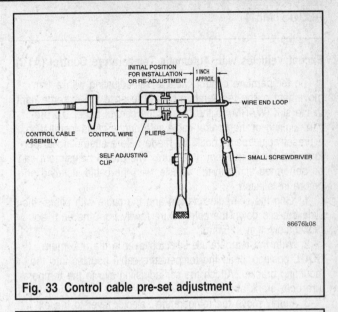

86676k08

Fig. 33 Control cable pre-set adjustment

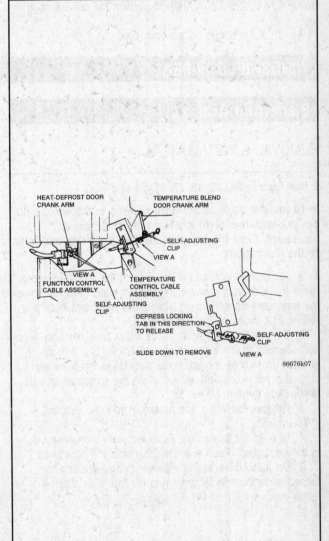

86676k07

Fig. 32 Function and temperature control cable removal

the applicable heater case cable housing mounting bracket (function cable — white; temperature cable — black).

2. Slide the self-adjusting cable attaching clip off the end of the crank arm.

3. Remove the control panel assembly and disengage the cable(s).

To install:

4. Connect the cable(s) to the control panel assembly and install.

5. Slide the self-adjusting cable attaching clip over the end of the heater case's door crank arm until it seats on the tab stop.

6. Insert the control cable bullet connector into the cable bracket hole until the locking tabs are fully engaged.

7. Adjust the control cable(s).

ADJUSTMENT

Except Vehicles with Automatic Temperature Control (ATC)

The temperature control cable is self-adjusting with a firm movement of the temperature control lever to the extreme right of the slot (**WARM**) in the face of the control panel. To prevent kinking of the control cable wire during cable installation, a preset adjustment should be made before attempting to perform the self-adjustment procedure. The preset adjustment can be performed either in the vehicle, with the cable installed or before installation.

1. Grip the self-adjusting clip and the cable with pliers, then slide the clip down the control wire (away from the end) approximately 1 in. (25mm).
2. With the temperature selector lever in the maximum **COOL** position, snap the temperature cable housing into the mounting bracket. Attach the self-adjusting clip to the temperature door crank arm.
3. Firmly move the temperature selector lever to the extreme right of the slot (**WARM**) to position the self-adjusting clip.
4. Check for proper control operation.

Vehicles with Automatic Temperature Control (ATC)

1. Remove the instrument panel pad as follows:
   a. Remove the 2 screws attaching the pad to the instrument panel at each defroster opening. Be careful not to drop the screws into the defroster openings.
   b. Remove the one screw attaching each outboard end of the pad to the instrument panel.
   c. Remove the 5 screws attaching the lower edge of the pad to the instrument panel. Pull the instrument panel pad rearward and remove it from the vehicle.
2. Move the temperature selector lever to the 75°F (24°C) position.
3. The control arm of the Automatic Temperature Control (ATC) should align with the arrow on the sensor body. If it does not, loosen the cable housing-to-sensor attaching screw and align the sensor control arm with the arrow while maintaining the 75°F (24°C) position of the temperature selector control lever.
4. Tighten the cable housing-to-sensor attaching screw. Make sure the temperature control stays at 75°F (24°C) and the sensor arm stays locked.
5. Install the instrument panel in the reverse order of removal.

WINDSHIELD WIPERS

Blade And Arm

REMOVAL & INSTALLATION

▶ See Figures 34, 35, 36, 37, 38, 39 and 40

➡To prevent glass and/or paint damage to the vehicle do not pry arm from pivot location with metal tool or equivalent. Read the complete service procedure and refer to the illustrations.

1. Raise the blade end of the arm off the windshield and move the slide latch away from the pivot shaft. This will unlock the wiper arm from the shaft. Rotate the wiper arm back and forth until it slides off the pivot shaft.
2. Some late model driver's side wiper arms have an extra arm attached to the wiper linkage assembly. This arm is smaller. To remove the additional arm, follow the previous step. this will expose the tab on which the additional arm is fitted. Slide the arm off the tab.
3. Remove the wiper arm assembly from the vehicle.

To install:

4. Line up the key on the wiper arm with the keyway slot in the pivot shaft. Push arm assembly onto the pivot shaft.
5. On those driver's side wipers with an extra arm attached, slide the smaller arm on to the tab, then attach the larger arm.

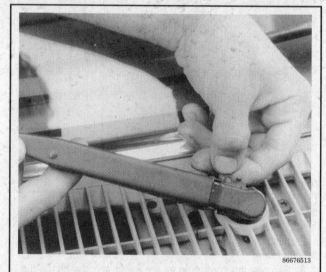

86676513

Fig. 34 Loosen the tab on the side of the wiper arm

6. Hold the main arm head onto the pivot shaft while raising the blade end of the wiper arm and push the slide latch into the lock under the pivot shaft. Then, lower the blade assembly to the windshield.

➡If the wiper blade does not touch the windshield, the slide latch is not completely in place. For procedures on replacement of wiper blades and elements refer to the necessary illustrations.

Fig. 35 With the wiper arm removed, check the splines or keyway on the arm and linkage

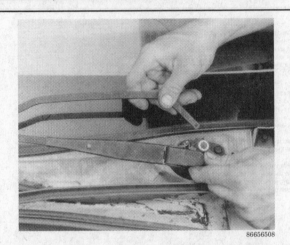

Fig. 36 To remove some late model driver's side wiper arms, the main arm must first be removed, then the smaller arm can be lifted off

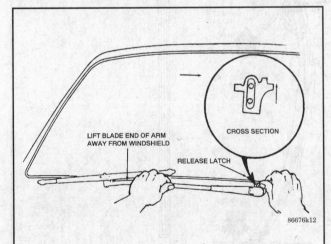

LIFT BLADE END OF ARM AWAY FROM WINDSHIELD

CROSS SECTION

RELEASE LATCH

86676k12

Fig. 37 Installation of the wiper arm and blade to the pivot shaft

Rear Window Wiper Blade and Arm

REMOVAL & INSTALLATION

1. Raise the blade end of the arm off the rear window. Move the slide latch away from the pivot shaft, and hold the blade end of the arm off the glass at the same time.
2. Pull the wiper arm off of the pivot shaft.
To install:
3. Be sure that the pivot shaft is in the **PARK** position and that the blade assembly is positioned properly. The distance between the blade saddle centerline and the lower weatherstrip or moulding should be 1-2.5 inches. (25-63mm).
4. Push the arm over the pivot shaft and hold it while raising the blade end of the wiper arm. Push the latch into the lock under the pivot shaft.
5. Lower the blade to the rear window. (If the blade does not touch the window, the slide latch is not completely in place. If this occurs, repeat the previous step.)

Wiper Motor

REMOVAL & INSTALLATION

▶ **See Figures 41, 42, 43, 44, 45 and 46**

➡**Use care when handling the motor to avoid damaging the ceramic magnets. Do not strike or tap the motor with a hammer or other object.**

1. Disconnect the negative battery cable.
2. Remove the right hand wiper arm and blade assembly.
3. Remove the cowl top grille attaching screws and grille. If washer nozzles are attached to the grille, remove the washer hoses at the end of each nozzle.
4. Remove the retaining clip and disconnect the linkage drive arm from the motor crank pin.
5. Unfasten the wiper motor's wiring connector.
6. Remove the wiper motor's three attaching screws and remove the motor.
To install:
7. Install the motor and the three attaching screws. Tighten to 60-85 inch lbs (7-8 Nm).
8. Fasten the wiper motor's wiring connector.
9. Connect the linkage drive arm to the motor crank pin and install the retaining clip.
10. Install the cowl top grille and attaching screws.
11. Install the wiper arm and blade assembly. Ensure that the motor is in **PARK** and that the distance between the blade saddle centerline and the weatherstrip or moulding is 2-3 inches (58-89mm).
12. Connect the negative battery cable.

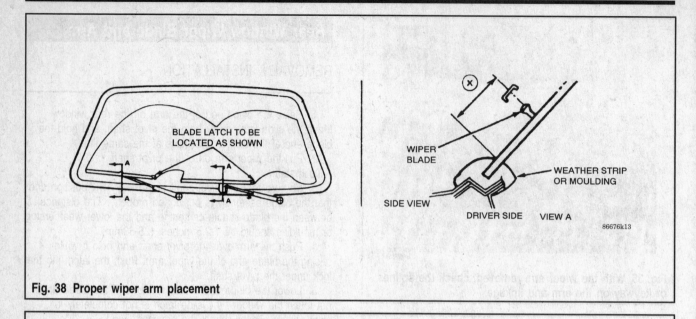

BLADE LATCH TO BE LOCATED AS SHOWN

A ← A
A ← A

WIPER BLADE

WEATHER STRIP OR MOULDING

SIDE VIEW

DRIVER SIDE   VIEW A

86676k13

Fig. 38 Proper wiper arm placement

BLADE REPLACEMENT

1. Cycle arm and blade assembly to a position on the windshield where removal of blade assembly can be performed without difficulty. Turn ignition key off at desired position.
2. To remove blade assembly from wiper arm, pull up on spring lock and pull blade assembly from pin (View A). Be sure spring lock is not pulled excessively or it will become distorted.
3. To install, push the blade assembly onto the pin so that the spring lock engages the pin (View A). Be sure the blade assembly is securely attached to pin.

ELEMENT REPLACEMENT

1. In the plastic backing strip which is part of the rubber blade assembly, there is an 11.11mm (7/16 inch) long notch located approximately one inch from either end. Locate either notch.
2. Place the frame of the wiper blade assembly on a firm surface with either notched end of the backing strip visible.
3. Grasp the frame portion of the wiper blade assembly and push down until the blade assembly is tightly bowed.
4. With the blade assembly in the bowed position, grasp the tip of the backing strip firmly, pulling up and twisting C.C.W. at the same time. The backing strip will then snap out of the retaining tab on the end of the frame.
5. Lift the wiper blade assembly from the surface and slide the backing strip down the frame until the notch lines up with the next retaining tab, twist slightly, and the backing strip will snap out. Continue this operation with the remaining tabs until the blade element is completely detached from the frame.
6. To install blade element, reverse the above procedure, making sure all six (6) tabs are locked to the backing strip before installing blade to wiper arm.

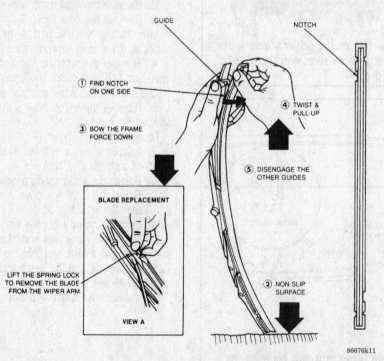

GUIDE

NOTCH

① FIND NOTCH ON ONE SIDE

③ BOW THE FRAME FORCE DOWN

④ TWIST & PULL-UP

⑤ DISENGAGE THE OTHER GUIDES

② NON SLIP SURFACE

BLADE REPLACEMENT

LIFT THE SPRING LOCK TO REMOVE THE BLADE FROM THE WIPER ARM

VIEW A

86676k11

Fig. 39 Tridon wiper blade replacement

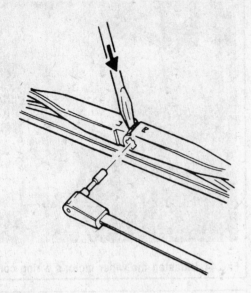

BLADE REPLACEMENT

1. CYCLE ARM AND BLADE ASSEMBLY TO UP POSITION-ON THE WINDSHIELD WHERE REMOVAL OF BLADE ASSEMBLY CAN BE PERFORMED WITHOUT DIFFICULTY. TURN IGNITION KEY OFF AT DESIRED POSITION.

2. TO REMOVE BLADE ASSEMBLY, INSERT SCREWDRIVER IN SLOT, PUSH DOWN ON SPRING LOCK AND PULL BLADE ASSEMBLY FROM PIN (VIEW A)

3. TO INSTALL, PUSH THE BLADE ASSEMBLY ON THE PIN SO THAT THE SPRING LOCK ENGAGES THE PIN (VIEW A). BE SURE THE BLADE ASSEMBLY IS SECURELY ATTACHED TO PIN.

VIEW A

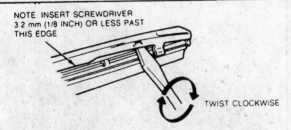

NOTE INSERT SCREWDRIVER 3.2 mm (1/8 INCH) OR LESS PAST THIS EDGE

TWIST CLOCKWISE

ELEMENT REPLACEMENT

1. INSERT SCREWDRIVER BETWEEN THE EDGE OF THE SUPER STRUCTURE AND THE BLADE BACKING DRIP (VIEW B) TWIST SCREWDRIVER SLOWLY UNTIL ELEMENT CLEARS ONE SIDE OF THE SUPER STRUCTURE CLAW

2. SLIDE THE ELEMENT INTO THE SUPER STRUCTURE CLAWS.

VIEW B

4. INSERT ELEMENT INTO ONE SIDE OF THE END CLAWS (VIEW D) AND WITH A ROCKING MOTION PUSH ELEMENT UPWARD UNTIL IT SNAPS IN (VIEW E)

VIEW D

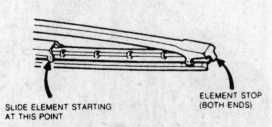

SLIDE ELEMENT STARTING AT THIS POINT

ELEMENT STOP (BOTH ENDS)

3. SLIDE THE ELEMENT INTO THE SUPER STRUCTURE CLAWS, STARTING WITH SECOND SET FROM EITHER END (VIEW C) AND CONTINUE TO SLIDE THE BLADE ELEMENT INTO ALL THE SUPER STRUCTURE CLAWS TO THE ELEMENT STOP (VIEW C)

VIEW C

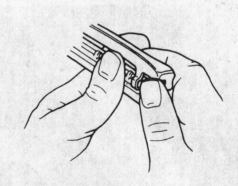

VIEW E

86676k10

Fig. 40 Trico wiper blade replacement

Fig. 41 The cowl top grille is retained by screws

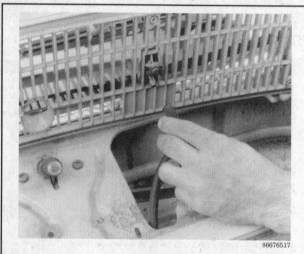

Fig. 42 Remove any washer nozzles hose(s) attached to the grille

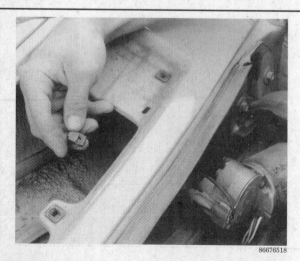

Fig. 43 Remove the retaining clip and disconnect the linkage drive arm from the motor crank pin

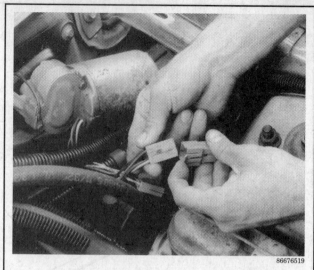

Fig. 44 Unfasten the wiper motor's wiring connector

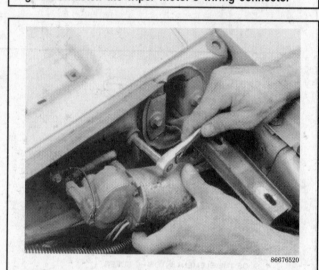

Fig. 45 Loosen and remove the wiper motor retaining screws

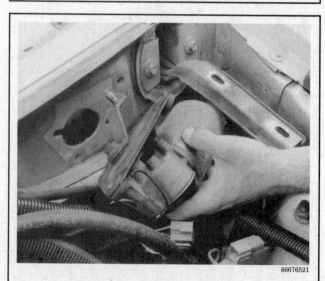

Fig. 46 Lift the wiper motor from the mounting hole

Rear Wiper Motor and Linkage

REMOVAL & INSTALLATION

1. Turn the ignition switch **OFF**.
2. Remove the wiper arm and blade assembly from the pivot shaft, as described earlier in this section.
3. Remove the pivot shaft nut and spacers.
4. Open the hatch and remove the inner trim panel.
5. Disconnect the wiper motor wiring.
6. Remove the motor and bracket attaching screws and remove the motor, bracket and linkage assembly.
7. Installation is the reverse of removal.

Wiper Linkage

REMOVAL & INSTALLATION

▶ See Figure 47

➡The pivot shaft and linkage assemblies are connected together with non-removable plastic ball joints. The left-hand shaft, right-hand pivot shafts and linkage are serviced as one unit.

1. Disconnect the negative battery cable.
2. Remove both wiper arm assemblies.
3. Remove the cowl top grille attaching screws and grille.
4. Remove the wiper linkage retainer clip and disconnect the linkage drive arm from the motor crankpin.
5. Remove the two screws retaining the right-hand pivot shaft to the cowl.
6. Remove the large nut, washer and spacer from the left-hand pivot shaft.
7. Remove the linkage and pivot shaft assembly from the cowl.

To install:

8. Position and attach the linkage along with the pivot shaft assembly to the cowl using the proper fasteners. Tighten the screws to 60-85 inch lbs. (7-10 Nm) and the nut to 70-110 inch lbs. (8-12 Nm). Be sure to include the washer and spacer on the left-hand pivot shaft.
9. Connect the linkage drive arm to the motor crankpin and secure with the retainer clip.
10. Attach the cowl top grille with its retaining screws.
11. Replace both wiper arm assemblies. Be sure that the motor is in the **PARK** position. Install both wiper arm assemblies to provide the proper distance between the blade saddle centerline and the weatherstrip or moulding.
12. Connect the negative battery cable.

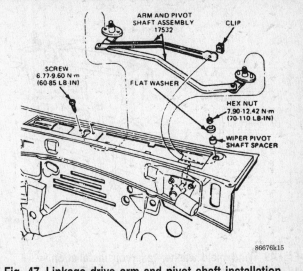

Fig. 47 Linkage drive arm and pivot shaft installation

Windshield Washer Fluid Reservoir

REMOVAL & INSTALLATION

▶ See Figures 48 and 49

1. Disconnect the wiring at the pump motor. Use a small prytool to unlock the connector tabs.
2. Disconnect the supply hose. (Since this will permit the reservoir to drain, you might want to cap the fitting.)
3. Remove the reservoir attaching screws or nuts and lift the assembly from the vehicle's fender apron.

To install:

4. Position the reservoir/pump assembly and secure with the retaining screws or nuts.
5. Fasten the supply hose and engage the electrical connector.
6. Fill the reservoir and operate the washer system.

➡It is unadvisable to operate the window washer pump without first filling the reservoir. Dry-running will damage the motor.

Windshield Washer Motor

REMOVAL & INSTALLATION

▶ See Figures 50 and 51

1. Remove the reservoir, as described above.
2. Pry out the motor retaining ring using a small prytool.
3. Using pliers, grip one edge of the electrical connector ring, then pull the motor, seal and impeller from the reservoir.

➡If the seal and impeller come apart from the motor, it can all be re-assembled.

To install:

4. Take the time to clean out the reservoir before installing the motor.

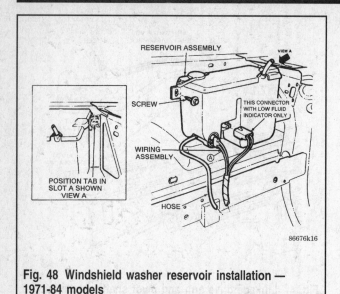

Fig. 48 Windshield washer reservoir installation —
1971-84 models

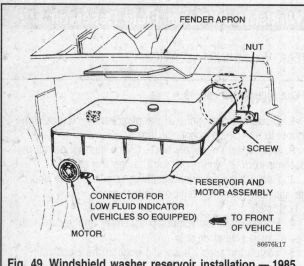

Fig. 49 Windshield washer reservoir installation — 1985
models

5. Coat the seal with a dry lubricant, such as powdered graphite or spray Teflon®. This will aid assembly.

6. Align the small projection on the motor end cap with the slot in the reservoir and install the motor so that the seal seats against the bottom of the motor cavity.

7. Press the retaining ring into position. A 1-inch, 12-point socket or a smooth 1-inch piece of plastic tubing will do nicely as an installation tool.

8. Install the reservoir and connect the wiring.

9. Fill the reservoir and operate the washer system.

➡It is unadvisable to operate the window washer pump without first filling the reservoir. Dry-running will damage the motor.

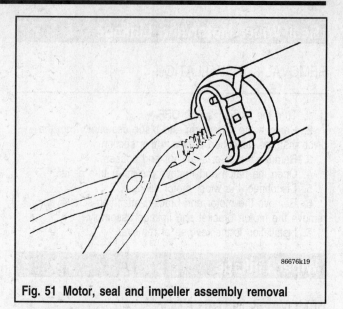

Fig. 51 Motor, seal and impeller assembly removal

Rear Window Washer Reservoir

REMOVAL & INSTALLATION

◆ See Figure 52

1. Remove the left-hand quarter trim panel, if equipped.

2. Unfasten the electrical connector and reservoir supply hose. (Since this will permit the reservoir to drain, you might want to cap the fitting.)

3. Remove the reservoir retaining screws and remove the reservoir from the vehicle.

To install:

4. Position the reservoir/pump assembly and secure with the retaining screws.

5. Connect the supply hose and the electrical connector.

6. Install the left-hand quarter trim panel.

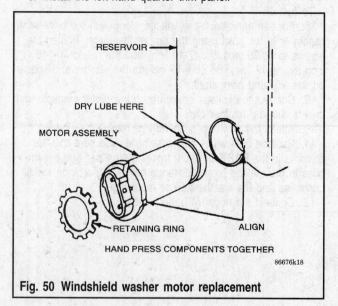

Fig. 50 Windshield washer motor replacement

7. Fill the reservoir and operate the washer system.

➡It is unadvisable to operate the window washer pump without first filling the reservoir. Dry-running will damage the motor.

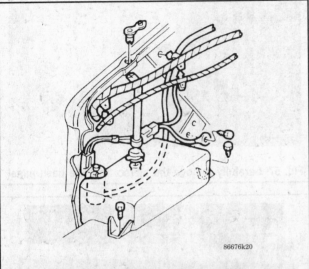

Fig. 52 Rear window washer reservoir and pump

ENTERTAINMENT SYSTEMS

Stereo

REMOVAL & INSTALLATION

▶ See Figures 53, 54, 55, 56, 57, 58 and 59

➡Refer to the necessary illustration as a guide for this repair. Although the dash panel may vary from year to year, the basic procedure will remain the same.

Conventional and Premium Sound Systems

As originally offered on the 1971-85 vehicles, the premium sound system had either four or six speakers and was available with both conventional stereo and electronically tuned radios. The premium sound system's unique wiring provides separate lines to the speakers, which are powered at all times by a premium sound amplifier.

1. Disconnect the negative battery cable.
2. Remove the radio control knobs.
3. Remove the ash receptacle and bracket, to provide sufficient clearance for removal of the radio trim plate.
4. Remove the trim panel surrounding the radio by removing the retaining screw as at the base of the panel.
5. With the trim panel removed, unfasten the mounting screws securing the radio bracket to the dash panel.
6. Slide the mounting bracket and radio out of the dash panel.
7. Unfasten the wire harnesses and antenna cable from the rear of the radio. If helpful, mark the harnesses.

Rear Window Washer Motor

REMOVAL & INSTALLATION

1. Remove the rear window washer reservoir, as described in this section.
2. Using a small prytool to remove the motor assembly. Remove the screen and the seal.
3. Flush the reservoir and clean any foreign material from the motor cavity or the reservoir.
To install:
4. Lubricate the outside of the seal with a dry lubricant (such as powdered graphite) to prevent the seal from sticking during reassembly.
5. Insert the screen in the seal, and insert the seal all the way down in the cavity.
6. Align the motor in the cavity on the reservoir, and insert the motor in the seal using hand pressure only.
7. Install the rear window washer reservoir, as described above.
8. Fill the reservoir and operate the washer system.

➡It is unadvisable to operate the window washer pump without first filling the reservoir. Dry-running will damage the motor.

8. On vehicles equipped with premium sound, remove the radio support attaching nut, ground cable and bracket from the radio.
9. To install, reverse the removal procedure. After connecting the battery cable, check the radio for proper operation and reset the memory buttons, if applicable.

Electronic Stereo Systems

1. Disconnect the negative battery cable.
2. Remove the center instrument trim panel.

Fig. 53 Remove the control knobs from the unit, if equipped — 1984 model shown (all models similar)

Fig. 54 Remove the trim screws between the ashtray and stereo. This is required on all 1971-85 models

Fig. 55 With the screws removed, the panel can be lifted out, some you may need a small prytool to free the upper clips

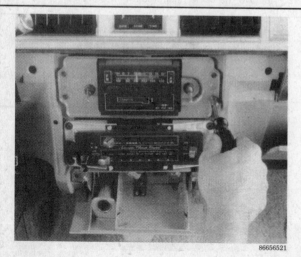

Fig. 56 Remove the retaining screws around the mounting plate

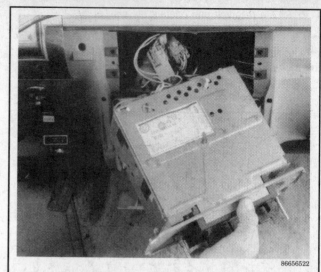

Fig. 57 Carefully remove the stereo from the dash panel

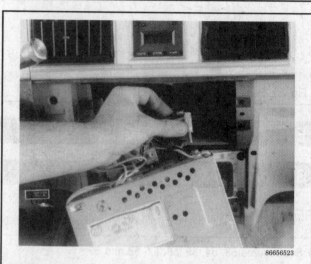

Fig. 58 Unplug all the wire connectors. Do not forget the antenna

3. Remove the four screws retaining the radio and mounting bracket to the instrument panel.

4. Push the radio to the front and raise the rear of the radio slightly so that the rear support bracket clears the clip in the instrument panel. Slowly pull the radio out of the instrument panel.

5. Unfasten the wiring connectors and antenna cable.

6. If installing a new radio, remove the rear support bracket from the radio by removing the rear nut.

7. To install, reverse the removal procedure. After connecting the battery cable, check the radio for proper operation and reset the memory buttons, if applicable.

To install:

8. Fasten the wiring connectors and antenna cable to the radio.

9. Slide the radio into the console, ensuring that the rear bracket is engaged on the upper support rail.

10. Connect the negative battery cable. Check the radio for proper operation and reset the memory buttons.

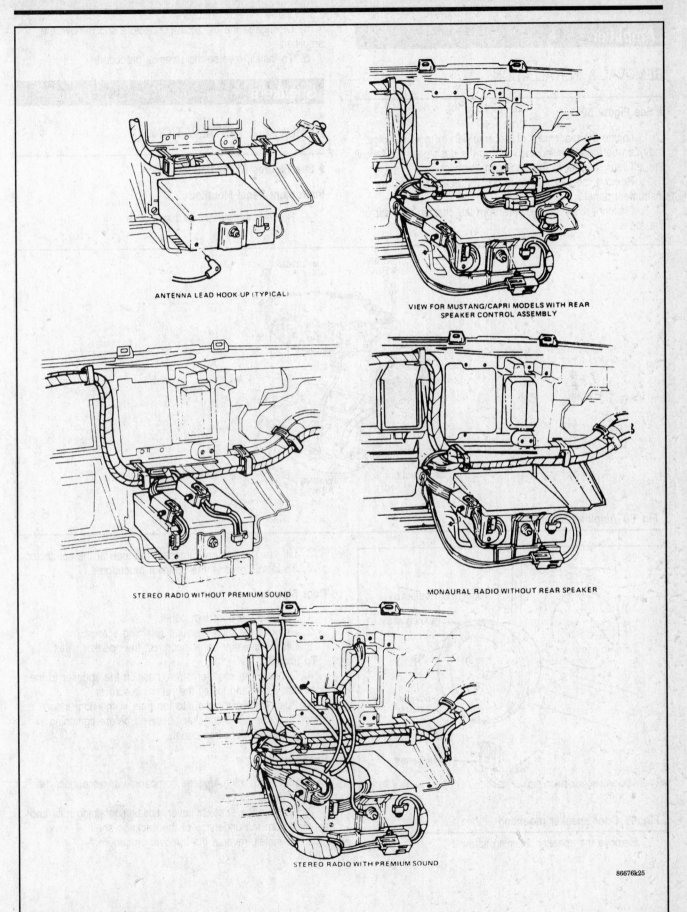

ANTENNA LEAD HOOK UP (TYPICAL)

VIEW FOR MUSTANG/CAPRI MODELS WITH REAR
SPEAKER CONTROL ASSEMBLY

STEREO RADIO WITHOUT PREMIUM SOUND

MONAURAL RADIO WITHOUT REAR SPEAKER

STEREO RADIO WITH PREMIUM SOUND

86676k25

Fig. 59 Radio system wiring

Amplifier

REMOVAL & INSTALLATION

▶ **See Figure 60**

1. Locate the placement of the amplifier. In most vehicles, they can be found behind the radio in the dash panel or below the left rear speaker in the trunk compartment.
2. Remove the two screws attaching the amplifier to the instrument panel.
3. Disconnect the ground wire from the stud on the rear of the radio.

4. Disengage the electrical connectors and remove the amplifier.
5. To install, reverse the removal procedure.

Speakers

REMOVAL & INSTALLATION

▶ **See Figures 61, 62 and 63**

Instrument Panel Mounted

1. Remove the instrument panel pad.

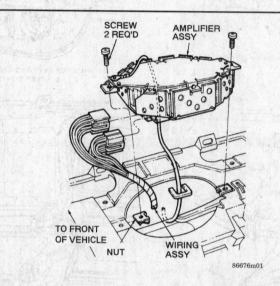

Fig. 60 Amplifier mounting

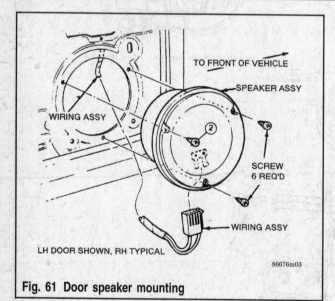

Fig. 61 Door speaker mounting

2. Remove the speaker retaining screws.

3. Lift the speaker and unfasten the lead at the connector.
4. To install, reverse the removal procedure.

Door Mounted

1. Remove the door trim panel.
2. Remove the three speaker retaining screws.
3. Lift the speaker and disconnect the speaker wires.
   To install:
4. Connect the speaker wires, position the speaker to the door side panel and install the retaining screws.
5. Push the locator clip into the hole in the door inner panel, and check the speaker operation before tightening.
6. Install the door trim panel.

Rear Mounted

1. From within the luggage compartment, disconnect the speaker wiring.
2. Remove the speaker cover, speaker retaining nuts and speaker from the underside of the package shelf.
3. To install, reverse the removal procedure.

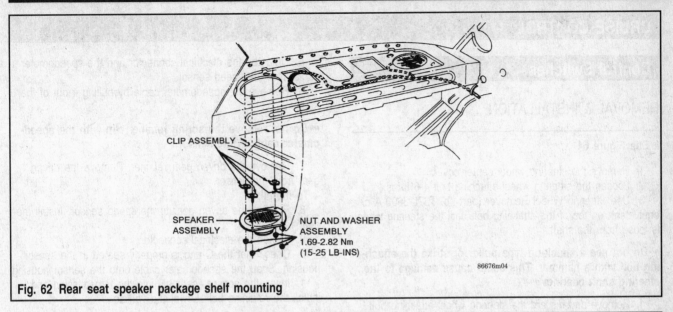

CLIP ASSEMBLY

SPEAKER
ASSEMBLY

NUT AND WASHER
ASSEMBLY
1.69-2.82 Nm
(15-25 LB-INS)

86676m04

Fig. 62 Rear seat speaker package shelf mounting

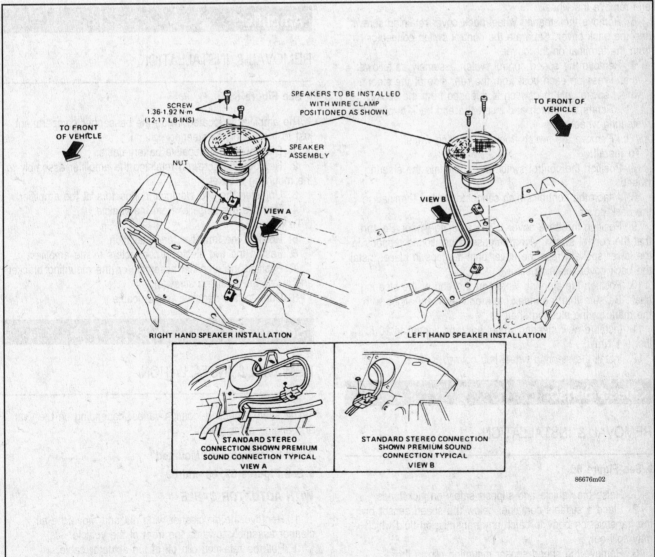

SCREW
1.36-1.92 N·m
(12-17 LB-INS)

SPEAKERS TO BE INSTALLED
WITH WIRE CLAMP
POSITIONED AS SHOWN

TO FRONT
OF VEHICLE

TO FRONT
OF VEHICLE

SPEAKER
ASSEMBLY

NUT

VIEW A

VIEW B

RIGHT HAND SPEAKER INSTALLATION

LEFT HAND SPEAKER INSTALLATION

STANDARD STEREO
CONNECTION SHOWN PREMIUM
SOUND CONNECTION TYPICAL
VIEW A

STANDARD STEREO CONNECTION
SHOWN PREMIUM SOUND
CONNECTION TYPICAL
VIEW B

86676m02

Fig. 63 Front stereo dash mounted speaker

CRUISE CONTROL

Control Switches

REMOVAL & INSTALLATION

▶ See Figure 64

1. Remove the steering wheel center cover.
2. Loosen the steering wheel attaching bolt 4-6 turns.
3. Use Steering Wheel Remover (part no. T67L-3600-A or equivalent) on top of the attaching bolt until the steering wheel is loose from the shaft.

➡**Do not use a knock-off type puller or strike the attaching bolt with a hammer. This could cause damage to the steering shaft bearing.**

4. Remove and discard the steering wheel attaching bolt and remove the wheel.
5. Remove the steering wheel back cover retaining screws and the back cover. Separate the control switch connector from the terminal on the cover.
6. Remove the speed control switch assembly as follows:
   a. Press on each post from the rear side of the steering wheel spoke until the switch is released from the spoke.
   b. Rotate the switch and insert the end back through the steering wheel.
   c. Remove the switch from the steering wheel.
   To install:
7. Position the control switch assembly into the steering wheel.
8. Attach the control switch connector to the terminal on the back cover.
9. Position the back cover to the steering wheel. Be sure that the control switch wiring harness is positioned properly in the lower spoke. Press the cover until it snaps in place. Install the back cover retaining screws.
10. Position the steering wheel on the end of the steering shaft. Be sure that the index mark on the wheel aligns with the mark on the steering shaft.
11. Install a new steering wheel bolt and tighten to 30 ft. lbs. (41 Nm).
12. Install the steering wheel hub cover.

Speed Sensor

REMOVAL & INSTALLATION

▶ See Figure 65

1. Raise the vehicle and support safely on jackstands.
2. Place a suitable container below the speed sensor on the transmission body to catch any transmission fluid which may spill out.
3. Remove the speed sensor mounting clip to the transmission.
4. Remove the sensor and the driven gear from the transmission.

5. Unfasten the electrical connector and the speedometer cable from the speed sensor.
6. Remove the speedometer cable by pulling it out of the sensor.

➡**Do not remove the spring retainer clip with the speedometer cable in the sensor.**

7. Remove the driven gear retainer. Remove the driven gear from the sensor.
   To install:
8. Position the driven gear to the speed sensor. Install the gear retainer.
9. Fasten the electrical connector.
10. Check that the O-ring is properly seated in the sensor housing. Snap the speedometer cable onto the sensor housing.
11. Insert the sensor assembly into the transmission and install the retaining bolt. Lower the vehicle.

Amplifier

REMOVAL & INSTALLATION

▶ See Figure 66

The amplifier is located inside the passenger compartment, just to the left of the steering column.

1. Disconnect the negative battery cable.
2. Remove the screw(s) retaining the amplifier assembly to the mounting bracket.
3. Unfasten the two electrical connectors at the amplifier.
4. Remove the amplifier from the vehicle.
   To install:
5. Position the amplifier for installation.
6. Fasten the two electrical connectors to the amplifier.
7. Position the amplifier assembly on the mounting bracket and install the retaining screw(s).
8. Connect the negative battery cable.

Servo

REMOVAL & INSTALLATION

The servo mounting location varies, depending on the year and engine combination.

Engine Compartment Mounted
▶ See Figures 67, 68 and 69

WITH ACTUATOR CABLE

1. Remove the air cleaner wing nut and move the air cleaner assembly towards the front of the vehicle.
2. Pull the retaining clip off of the actuator cable.
3. Disconnect the speed control actuator cable from the accelerator cable.

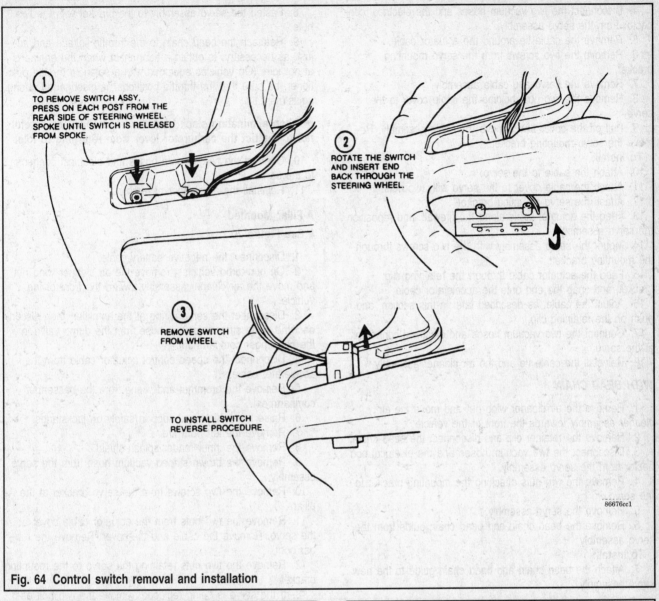

① TO REMOVE SWITCH ASSY, PRESS ON EACH POST FROM THE REAR SIDE OF STEERING WHEEL SPOKE UNTIL SWITCH IS RELEASED FROM SPOKE.

② ROTATE THE SWITCH AND INSERT END BACK THROUGH THE STEERING WHEEL.

③ REMOVE SWITCH FROM WHEEL.

TO INSTALL SWITCH REVERSE PROCEDURE.

86676cc1

Fig. 64 Control switch removal and installation

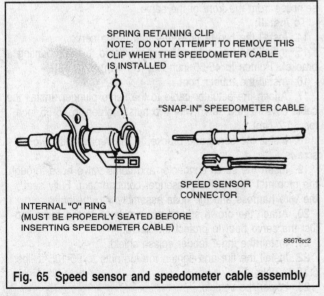

SPRING RETAINING CLIP
NOTE: DO NOT ATTEMPT TO REMOVE THIS CLIP WHEN THE SPEEDOMETER CABLE IS INSTALLED

"SNAP-IN" SPEEDOMETER CABLE

SPEED SENSOR CONNECTOR

INTERNAL "O" RING
(MUST BE PROPERLY SEATED BEFORE INSERTING SPEEDOMETER CABLE)

86676cc2

Fig. 65 Speed sensor and speedometer cable assembly

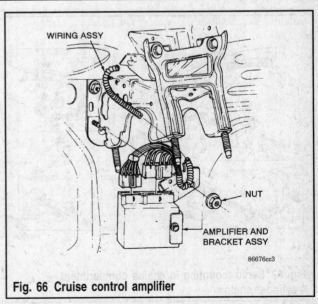

WIRING ASSY

NUT

AMPLIFIER AND BRACKET ASSY

86676cc3

Fig. 66 Cruise control amplifier

4. Disconnect the two vacuum hoses and the electrical connector from the servo assembly.

5. Remove the cable tie around the actuator cable.

6. Remove the two screws from the servo mounting bracket.

7. Remove the servo and cable assembly.

8. Remove the two nuts holding the cable cover to the servo.

9. Pull off the cover and remove the cable assembly. Remove the servo mounting bracket.

To install:

10. Attach the cable to the servo.

11. Attach the cable cover to the servo with two nuts.

12. Attach the servo mounting bracket.

13. Feed the actuator cable along the firewall, and reposition the servo assembly.

14. Mount the servo assembly with the two screws through the mounting bracket.

15. Feed the actuator cable through the retaining clip bracket, and snap the end onto the accelerator cable.

16. Adjust the cable, as described later in this section, and push on the retaining clip.

17. Connect the two vacuum hoses and electrical connector at the servo.

18. Reinstall the cable tie and the air cleaner assembly.

WITH BEAD CHAIN

1. Remove the air cleaner wing nut and move the air cleaner assembly towards the front of the vehicle.

2. Remove the retainer clip and disconnect the bead chain.

3. Disconnect the two vacuum hoses and the electrical connector from the servo assembly.

4. Remove the two nuts attaching the mounting bracket to the servo.

5. Remove the servo assembly.

6. Remove the bead chain and bead chain guide from the servo assembly.

To install:

7. Attach the bead chain and bead chain guide to the new servo assembly.

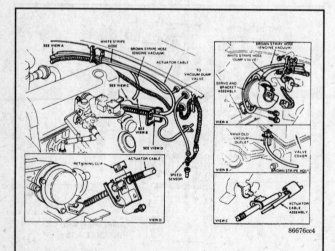

Fig. 67 Servo mounting in engine compartment — 4-cylinder engine

8. Fasten the servo assembly to the bracket with the two nuts.

9. Reattach the bead chain to the throttle linkage and adjust, as necessary, to obtain a tight chain when the engine is at hot idle. (On vehicles equipped with a solenoid throttle positioner, be sure that the throttle positioner is disengaged during adjustment.)

➡ **When eliminating slack from the bead chain, be careful not to restrict the carburetor lever from returning to idle.**

10. Connect the two vacuum hoses and electrical connector to the servo.

11. Reinstall the air cleaner assembly.

A-Pillar Mounted
▶ **See Figure 70**

1. Disconnect the negative battery cable.

2. On non-turbo vehicles, remove the air cleaner wing nut and move the air cleaner assembly toward the front of the vehicle.

3. Disconnect the servo wiring at the amplifier, then disconnect the white striped vacuum hose from the dump valve in the passenger compartment.

4. Disconnect the speed control actuator cable from the accelerator cable.

5. Remove the grommet and wiring from the passenger compartment.

6. Raise the vehicle and support safely on jackstands.

7. Remove the left front tire.

8. Remove the inner fender splash shield.

9. Remove the brown striped vacuum hose from the servo assembly.

10. Remove the two screws from the servo bracket at the A-pillar.

11. Remove the two nuts from the actuator cable cover at the servo. Remove the cable and the cover. Remove the rubber boot.

12. Remove the two nuts retaining the servo to the mounting bracket.

13. If the servo is being replaced, remove the two bolt assemblies from the front of the servo.

To install:

14. Install the two bolts to the front of the servo.

15. Install the two nuts retaining the servo to the mounting bracket. Tighten to 45-65 inch lbs. (5-7 Nm).

16. Install the rubber boot.

17. Attach the actuator cable to the servo plunger. Install the cable cover to the servo with two nuts. Tighten to 45-65 inch lbs. (5-7 Nm).

18. Install the servo and bracket to the A-pillar with two screws.

19. Insert the servo connector and dump valve hose through the grommet hole in the passenger compartment. Fully seat the wire harness and the hose assembly into the hole.

20. Attach the brown striped vacuum hose to the servo. Adjust the servo boot to protect the servo.

21. Install the inner fender splash shield.

22. Install the tire and tighten the lug nuts to 85-105 ft. lbs. (115-142 Nm).

23. Lower the vehicle.

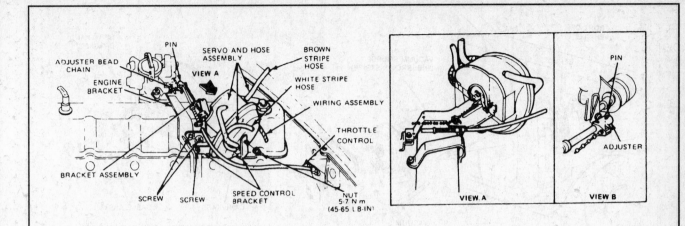

Fig. 68 Servo mounting in engine compartment — L6 engine

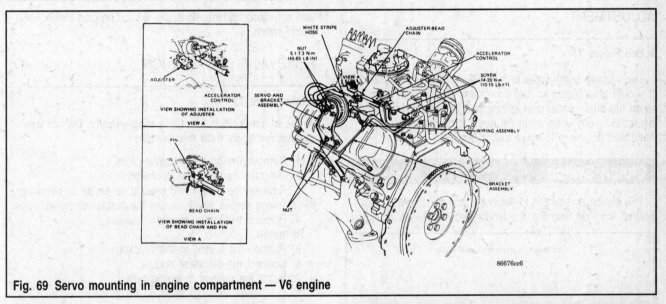

Fig. 69 Servo mounting in engine compartment — V6 engine

24. Connect the servo wiring at the amplifier in the passenger compartment.

25. Attach the servo vacuum hose with the white stripe to the dump valve in the passenger compartment.

26. Connect the speed control actuator cable to the speedometer cable. Connect the negative battery cable.

27. On non-turbo vehicles, reposition the air cleaner assembly and tighten the wing nut.

ACTUATOR CABLE LINKAGE ADJUSTMENT

1. Remove the cable retaining clip.

2. Push the cable through the adjuster until a slight tension is felt.

3. Insert the cable retaining clip and snap into place.

Vacuum Dump Valve

REMOVAL & INSTALLATION

1. Remove the vacuum hose from the valve.

2. Remove the valve from the bracket by removing the clip, if equipped, or rotating the valve back and forth and carefully lifting out of the bracket assembly.

To install:

3. Install the valve to the bracket by pushing the valve in. Install the retaining clip if equipped.

4. Connect the vacuum hose.

5. Adjust the valve, as described.

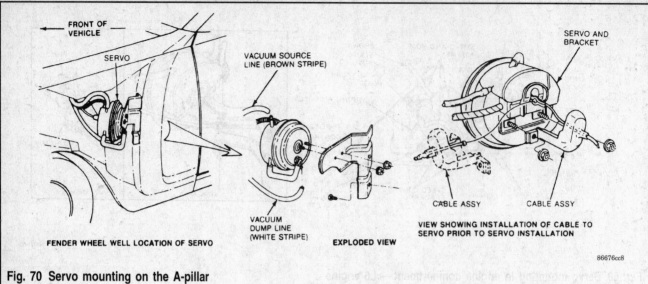

Fig. 70 Servo mounting on the A-pillar

ADJUSTMENT

▶ **See Figure 71**

The vacuum dump valve is movable in its mounting bracket. It should be adjusted so that it is closed (no vacuum leak) when the brake pedal is in its normal released position (not depressed), and open when the pedal is depressed. Use a hand vacuum pump to make this adjustment.

Clutch Switch

This switch is mounted to the brake and clutch pedal support on the side near the accelerator pedal. Vehicles equipped with automatic transmissions use a shorting plug instead of a clutch switch.

REMOVAL & INSTALLATION

▶ **See Figure 72**

➡ **The clutch switch functions magnetically. Do not use magnetized tools near this switch.**

1. Remove the bracket mounting nuts.
2. Unfasten the electrical connector.
3. Remove the switch and bracket assembly by removing the retaining screws which secure the bracket to the vehicle.
4. Remove the switch from the bracket.

To install:

5. Position the switch on the bracket.
6. Connect the electrical lead.
7. Install the bracket mounting nuts.

ADJUSTMENT

➡ **The clutch switch functions magnetically. Do not use magnetized tools near this switch.**

1. Prop the clutch pedal in the full-up position, with the pawl fully released from the sector.
2. Loosen the switch retaining screw.
3. Slide the switch forward toward the clutch pedal until the switch plunger cap is 0.030 in. (0.76mm) from contacting the switch housing. Then, tighten the retaining screw.
4. Remove the prop from the clutch pedal and test drive for clutch switch cancellation of cruise control.

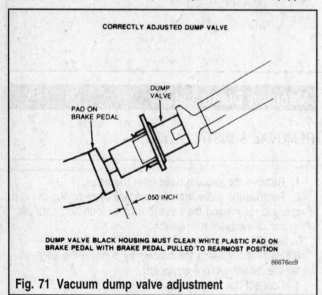

Fig. 71 Vacuum dump valve adjustment

INSTRUMENT AND SWITCHES

Instrument Cluster

REMOVAL & INSTALLATION

▶ See Figures 73, 74, 75, 76, 77, 78, 79, 80, 81, 82, 83, 84, 85 and 86

➡Although the models and interior trim levels may vary greatly from year-to-year, the removal and installation procedures are basically the same.

1971-79 Models

1. Disconnect negative battery cable.
2. Remove the right and left windshield moldings.
3. Remove the dash panel above the instrument cluster by removing the screws on the driver's and passenger's side of the panel, as well as above the instrument cluster itself. Remove the panel from the vehicle and place aside.
4. Remove the panel below the steering column by unfastening the screws at each corner.
5. Remove the cluster trim panel around the instruments by removing the retaining screws and then using a small prytool to slide the panel out.
6. Remove the screw attaching the transmission selector lever indicator cable to the column.
7. Remove the instrument cluster retaining screws and lift the cluster from the instrument panel.
8. Disconnect the speedometer cable and the wire plugs to the printed circuit. Tag each harness for easier installation.
9. Reverse the above procedure to install, taking care to ensure that the selector pointer is aligned.

1980-85 Models

NON-ELECTRIC CLUSTER

1. Disconnect the negative battery cable.

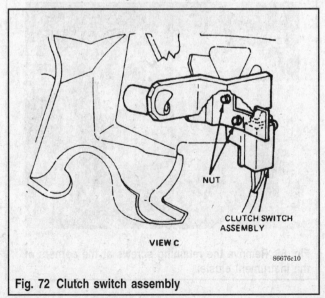

Fig. 72 Clutch switch assembly

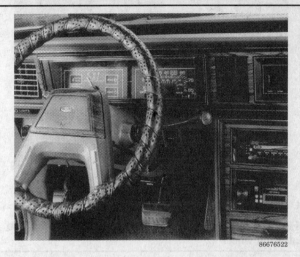

Fig. 73 This instrument cluster may look difficult to remove, but it just takes a little time and patience

Fig. 74 Remove the steering wheel horn pad

2. Disconnect the speedometer cable.
3. Remove the instrument cluster trim cover attaching screws and the lower two steering column cover attaching screws. Remove the trim covers.
4. Remove the lower half of the steering column shroud.
5. Remove the screw attaching the transmission selector indicator bracket to the steering column. Unfasten the cable loop from the retainer on the shift lever. Remove the column bracket.
6. Remove the cluster attaching screws. Disconnect the cluster feed plug and remove the cluster.
7. Reverse the procedure for installation. Be sure to lubricate the speedometer drive head. Adjust the selector indicator if necessary.

ELECTRIC CLUSTER

1. Disconnect negative battery cable.

Fig. 75 Unfasten the horn button wire harness from the steering wheel

Fig. 76 Remove the retaining bolt

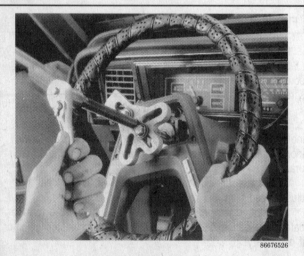

Fig. 77 Use a steering wheel puller to remove the steering wheel from the column

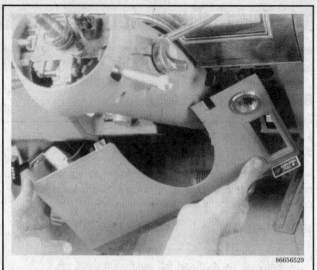

Fig. 78 Remove the panel below the steering column

Fig. 79 Unfasten the screws at the lower portion of the cluster cover, then lift the cover away

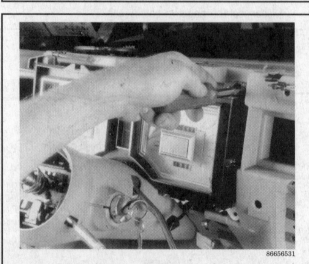

Fig. 80 Remove the retaining screws at the corners of the instrument cluster

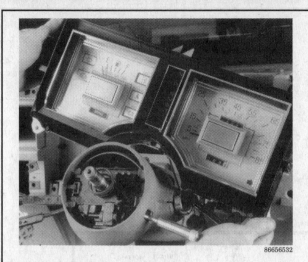

86656532

Fig. 81 Unfasten the speedometer cable and other wire harnesses from the rear of the instrument cluster

2. Remove the steering column trim cover and lower instrument panel trim cover. Remove the keyboard trim panel and the trim panel on the left of the column.

3. Remove the instrument cluster trim cover screw and remove the trim panel.

4. Remove the instrument cluster mounting screws and pull the cluster forward. Disconnect the feed plugs and the ground wire from the back of the cluster. Disconnect the speedometer cable.

5. Remove the screw attaching the transmission indicator cable bracket to the steering column. Unfasten the cable loop from the retainer. Remove the bracket.

6. Unfasten the plastic clamp from around the steering column. Remove the cluster.

To install:

7. Apply a small amount of silicone lubricant into the drive hole of the speedometer head.

8. Connect the feed plugs and the ground wire to the cluster. Install the speedometer cable. Attach the instrument cluster to the instrument panel.

9. Install the plastic indicator cable clamp around the steering column and engage the clamp locator pin in the column tube.

10. Place the transmission selector in the DRIVE position. Install the mounting screw into the retainer but do not tighten.

11. Rotate the plastic cable clamp until the indicator flag covers both location dots. Tighten the retainer screw.

12. Move the selector through all positions. Readjust, if necessary.

13. The rest of the installation is in the reverse order of removal.

Speedometer Cable

REMOVAL & INSTALLATION

▶ See Figures 87, 88 and 89

Core and Casing

1. Disconnect the negative battery cable.

2. If necessary, remove the dash panel and/or instrument cluster to access the speedometer cable and case.

3. Reach up behind the speedometer and depress the flat, quick-disconnect tab, while pulling back on the cable.

4. Push the cable and grommet through the opening in the floorpan or dash panel.

5. Raise and safely support the car on jackstands and disengage the cable from all retaining clips.

6. Remove the speedometer cable mounting bolt and clip at the transmission, then pull the cable from the transmission.

➡ **On vehicles equipped with cruise control, remove the speedometer cable by pulling it out of the speed sensor. Do not attempt to remove the spring retainer clip with the cable attached to the sensor.**

7. Remove the speedometer cable from the vehicle.

To install:

8. Insert the new speedometer cable through the O-ring and into the speedometer driven gear. On vehicles equipped with cruise control, insert the cable into the speed sensor.

9. Attach the speedometer cable mounting bolt and clip at the transmission.

10. Engage the cable in the retaining clips and route it through the opening in the floorpan or dash panel. Be careful to observe the proper routing, particularly in relation to other cables. Push the grommet in place.

11. Lower the vehicle and remove the jackstands.

12. Apply a $3/16$ in. (4.76mm) diameter ball of Silicone Damping Grease (part no. D7AZ-19A331-A or equivalent) in the drive hole of the speedometer head.

13. Push connect the speedometer cable to the speedometer head. Install the instrument cluster or any dash panels which were removed.

14. Connect the negative battery cable.

Oil Pressure Gauge

REMOVAL & INSTALLATION

1. Disconnect the negative battery cable.

2. Remove the instrument cluster from the dash.

3. Remove the screws which attach the lens and mask assembly to the cluster backplate. Remove the mask and lens assembly.

4. Remove the two retaining nuts and the oil pressure gauge.

To install:

5. Position the oil pressure gauge to the cluster backplate and install the two retaining nuts.

6. Position the lens and mask assembly to the cluster backplate, then install the retaining screws.

7. Install the instrument cluster, as described above.

8. Connect the negative battery cable and check the oil pressure gauge operation.

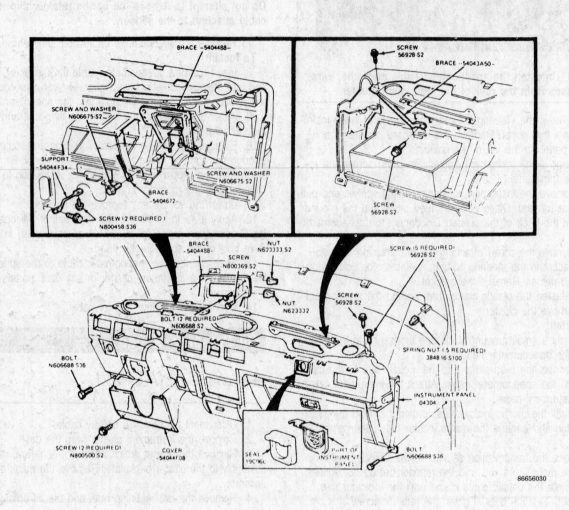

Fig. 82 Exploded view of a 1971-79 Ford dash panel

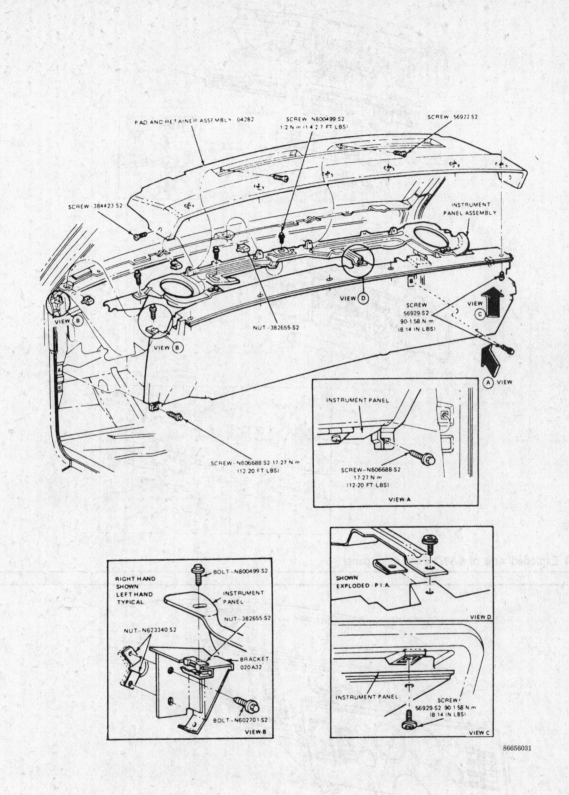

PAD AND RETAINER ASSEMBLY 04282

SCREW N800499 S2
1 2 N m (1 4 2 7 FT LBS)

SCREW 56922 S2

SCREW 384423 S2

INSTRUMENT
PANEL ASSEMBLY

VIEW D

VIEW B

VIEW B

NUT 382655 S2

VIEW C

SCREW
56929 S2
90 1 58 N m
(8 14 IN LBS)

A VIEW

SCREW N606688 S2 17 27 N m
(12 20 FT LBS)

INSTRUMENT PANEL

INSTRUMENT PANEL

SCREW N606688 S2
17 27 N m
(12 20 FT LBS)

VIEW A

RIGHT HAND
SHOWN
LEFT HAND
TYPICAL

BOLT N800499 S2

INSTRUMENT
PANEL

NUT 382655 S2

NUT N623340 S2

BRACKET
020 A32

BOLT N602701 S2

VIEW B

SHOWN
EXPLODED P I A

VIEW D

INSTRUMENT PANEL

SCREW
56929 S2 90 1 58 N m
(8 14 IN LBS)

VIEW C

86656031

Fig. 83 Exploded view of a 1976 Ford dash panel

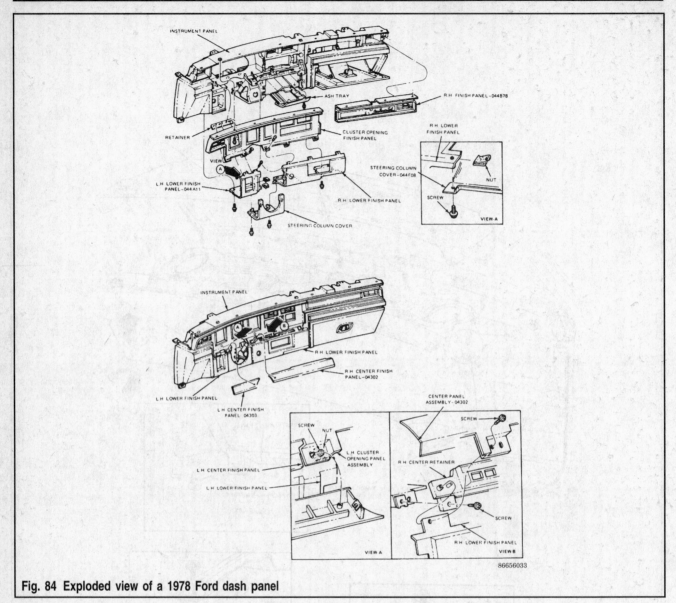

Fig. 84 Exploded view of a 1978 Ford dash panel

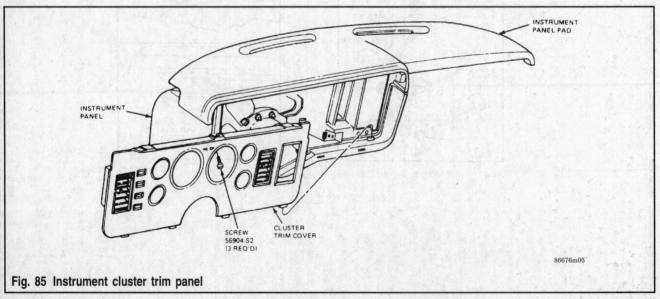

Fig. 85 Instrument cluster trim panel

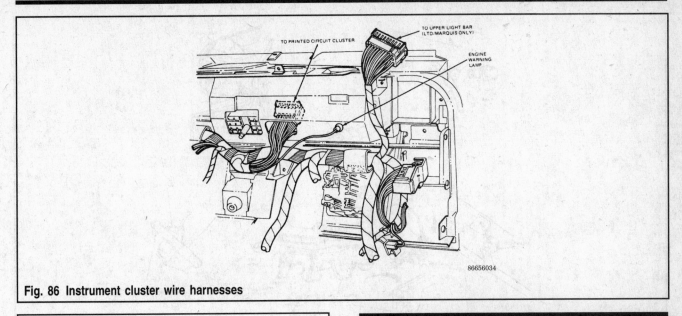

Fig. 86 Instrument cluster wire harnesses

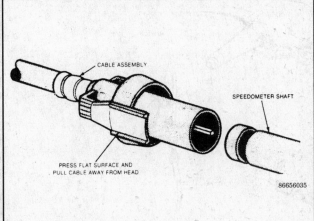

Fig. 87 Speedometer cable quick-disconnect. Notice the tab fitting

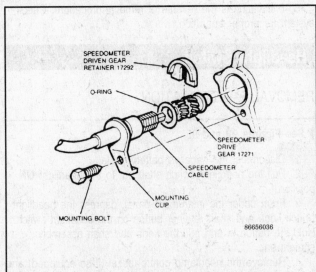

Fig. 88 Speedometer cable-to-transmission mounting

Fuel Gauge

REMOVAL & INSTALLATION

1. Disconnect the negative battery cable.
2. Remove the instrument cluster from the dash.
3. From the front side of the cluster, remove the retaining screws, then separate the cluster mask and lens assembly from the backplate. (These screws also retain the cluster lens to the mask.)
4. Remove the two fuel gauge retaining nuts from the rear side of the cluster. Withdraw the gauge from the front side of the backplate.
   To install:
5. Position the gauge to the cluster backplate and install the two retaining nuts from the rear side.
6. Position the mask and lens assembly to the cluster backplate and install the retaining screws.
7. Install the cluster assembly.
8. Connect the negative battery cable and check the gauge operation.

Temperature Gauge

REMOVAL & INSTALLATION

1. Disconnect the negative battery cable.
2. Remove the instrument cluster, as described earlier in this section.
3. Remove the screws that retain the mask and lens to the cluster backplate, then remove the mask and lens.
4. Remove the two temperature gauge retaining nuts and remove the gauge.
   To install:
5. Position the gauge to the cluster backplate and install the two retaining nuts.

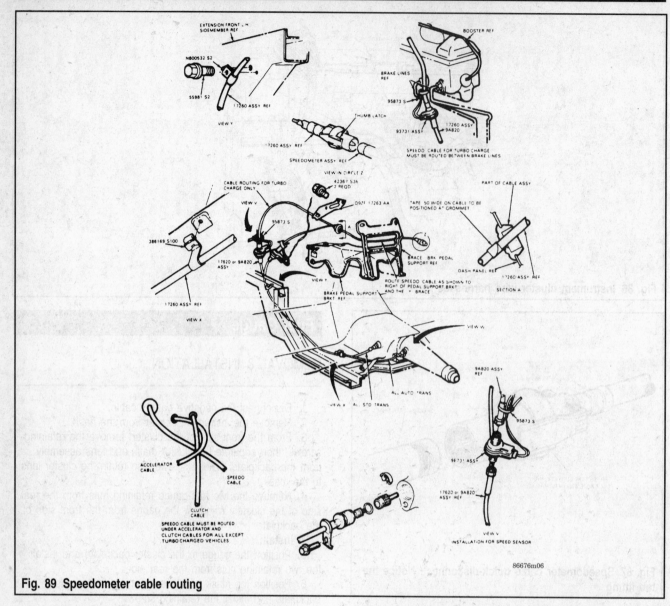

Fig. 89 Speedometer cable routing

6. Position the mask and lens assembly to the cluster backplate, then install the retaining screws.

7. Install the cluster assembly.

8. Connect the negative battery cable and check gauge operation.

Windshield Wiper Switch

REMOVAL & INSTALLATION

▶ See Figures 90 and 91

➡ On some vehicles, the wiper switch is a component of the "Combination Switch." In this event, refer to the necessary service procedure in Section 8.

1. Disconnect the battery ground.
2. Remove the steering column cover halves.
3. Remove the 2 wiper switch retaining screws.
4. Unplug the electrical connection at the rear of the switch.

5. Installation is the reverse of removal procedure. Check system for proper operation.

Headlight Switch

REMOVAL & INSTALLATION

▶ See Figures 92 and 93

1. Disconnect the negative battery cable.
2. Pull the headlight switch shaft out to the headlight **ON** position.
3. From under the instrument panel, depress the headlight switch knob and shaft retainer button on the headlight switch. Hold the button in and pull the knob and shaft assembly straight out.
4. Remove the headlamp control bezel (if so equipped) and remove the locknut.
5. From under the instrument panel, move the switch toward the front of the vehicle while tilting it downward.

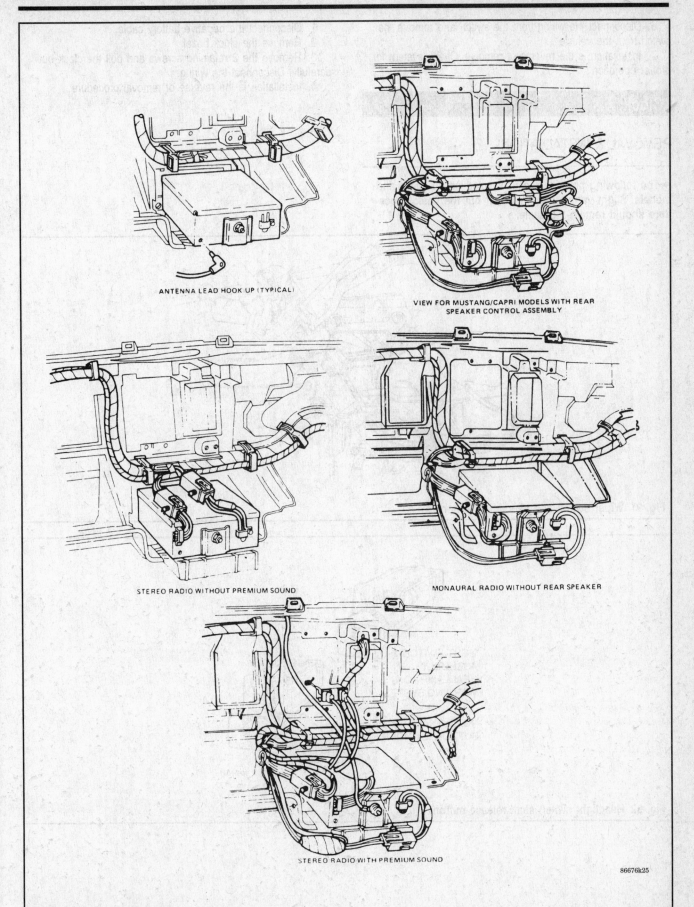

ANTENNA LEAD HOOK UP (TYPICAL)

VIEW FOR MUSTANG/CAPRI MODELS WITH REAR
SPEAKER CONTROL ASSEMBLY

STEREO RADIO WITHOUT PREMIUM SOUND

MONAURAL RADIO WITHOUT REAR SPEAKER

STEREO RADIO WITH PREMIUM SOUND

86676k25

Fig. 90 Interval wiper switch

6. Disconnect the wiring from the switch and remove the switch from the vehicle.

7. Installation is the reverse of removal. Check system for proper operation.

Clock

REMOVAL & INSTALLATION

➡The following procedure can be used on all years and models. Slight variations may occur but the basic procedure should remain the same.

1. Disconnect the negative battery cable.
2. Remove the clock bezel.
3. Remove the 3 retaining screws and pull the clock out carefully. Disconnect the wiring.
4. Installation is the reverse of removal procedure.

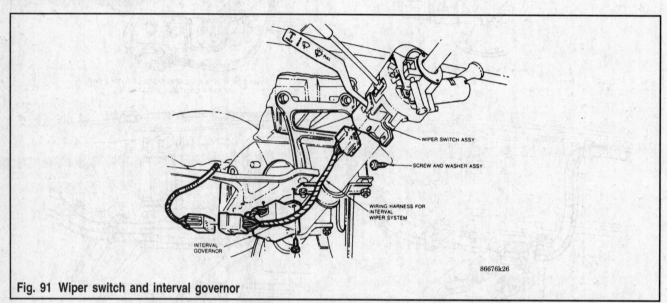

Fig. 91 Wiper switch and interval governor

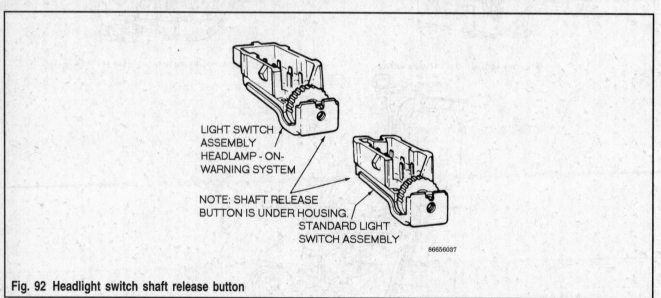

Fig. 92 Headlight switch shaft release button

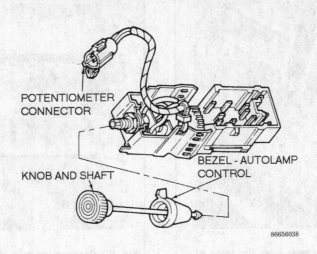

Fig. 93 Headlight switch assembly

LIGHTING

Headlights

REMOVAL & INSTALLATION

▶ See Figures 94, 95, 96, 97, 98, 99 and 100

1. Disconnect the negative battery cable.
2. Remove the headlight trim ring mounting screws and then the trim ring assembly.

➡When removing a headlight, identify the headlight retaining ring screws as well the headlight adjustment screws. The slightest turn of the adjustment screws will mis-align the light, requiring adjustment. If the headlight is rectangular, there are four screws attached to the ring for each light. If the headlight is round, there are three screws attached to the ring on each light. Each light has two adjustment screws. The retaining ring screws are usually shorter than the adjustment screws. Also, the retaining ring flange can be followed by eye around or under the ring screws; while the adjustment screws are completely independent of the ring.

3. Remove the screws that hold the headlight retaining ring to the headlight base, and remove the retainer.
4. Pull the headlight forward and disconnect the wire plug. Remove the headlight.

To install:

5. Attach a new headlight to the wiring plug.
6. Position the light into the base and attach the retainer ring.
7. Reinstall the headlight trim ring.
8. Connect the negative battery cable.

Fig. 94 Remove the screws from the side of the headlight trim ring

Hi-Mount Stop Lamp

REMOVAL & INSTALLATION

Models Except Station Wagon

▶ See Figure 101

1. Remove the screw covers from each side of the lamp.
2. Remove the screws from the retainer.
3. Pull the lamp up and forward to detach it from the retainer brackets.
4. On the bottom of the lamp body, pull the wire assembly locator from the lamp body.
5. From the bottom of the lamp, remove the bulb and socket by turning it counterclockwise.
6. Installation is the reverse of removal.

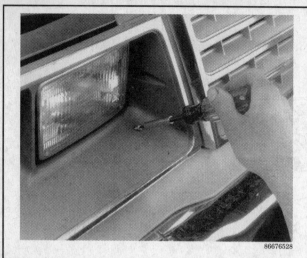

Fig. 95 Remove the retaining screws from the front of the headlight trim ring

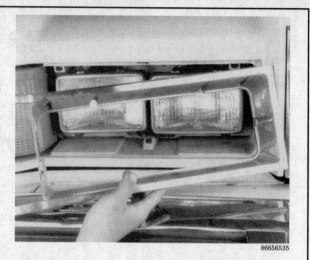

Fig. 97 Remove the trim ring from around the headlight assembly

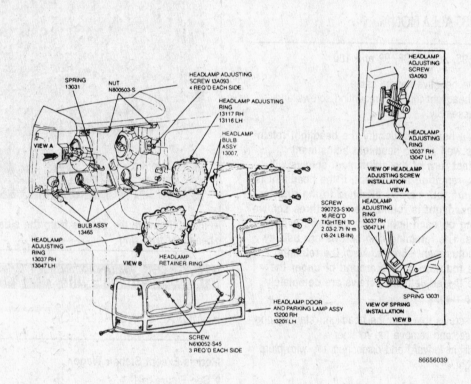

Fig. 96 Exploded view of headlamps, brackets and alignment springs

Fig. 98 Remove the screws from around the headlight retaining ring. Do not get these screws confused with the headlight alignment screws

Fig. 99 Separate the headlight from the retaining ring

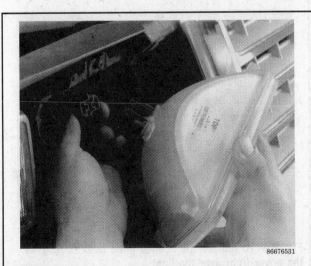

Fig. 100 Unplug the headlight from the harness at the rear of the unit

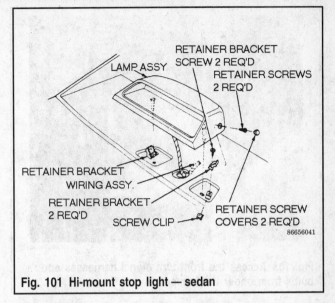

Fig. 101 Hi-mount stop light — sedan

Station Wagon

▶ **See Figure 102**

1. Remove the 2 screws from the lamp.
2. Pull the lamp rearward and remove it from the tailgate moulding.
3. Disengage the wiring harness strain relief clip by pulling it straight out of the lamp.
4. Remove the bulb and socket by turning it gently while pulling it out of the lamp.
5. Installation is the reverse of removal.

Parking, Side Marker and Rear Lamps

▶ **See Figures 103, 104, 105, 106, 107, 108, 109, 110, 111 and 112**

These bulbs are accessed by removing the lamp assembly and twisting the bulb socket ½ turn.

In some cases, the bulb socket may be accessed by reaching behind the lamp or sheetmetal, without removing the lamp assembly. Refer to the illustrations.

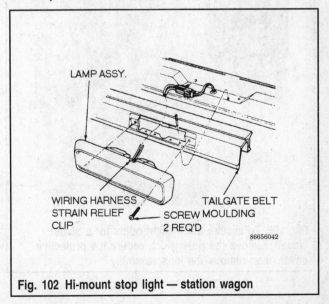

Fig. 102 Hi-mount stop light — station wagon

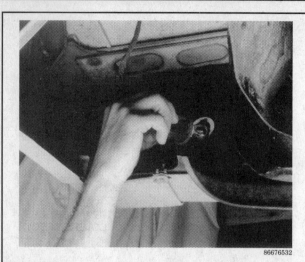

Fig. 103 Access the front turn signal harnesses and bulbs from under the bumper

Fig. 106 On all other vehicles, the sockets are more accessible

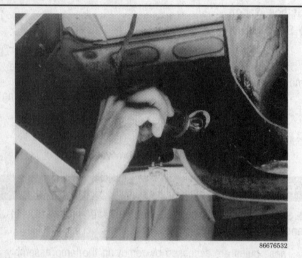

Fig. 104 To remove the bulb, twist and slide bulb out of the socket

Fig. 107 Twist the socket out, then push and twist the bulb out

Fig. 105 To access the taillight bulbs for a station wagon, remove the nuts which secure the protective cover, then remove the lens assembly

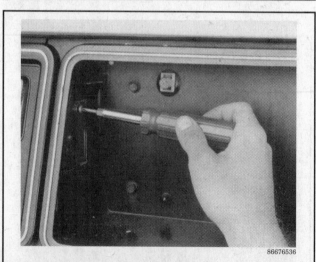

Fig. 108 To replace the licence plate bulb(s), remove the cover from over the light

Fig. 109 Slide the light out to access the bulb and socket

Fig. 110 Separate the cover from the light

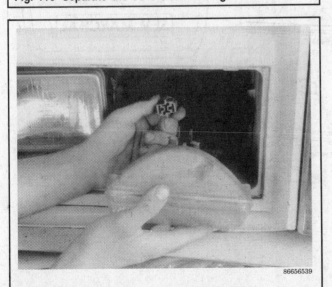

Fig. 111 Pull the bulb from the light socket

Fog Lights

REMOVAL & INSTALLATION

Fog Lamp Bulb
▶ See Figure 113

1. Remove the two screws that retain the lens assembly to the lamp housing.
2. Remove the lens and body assembly from the lamp housing, then turn it access the rear of the lamp body.
3. Release the bulb socket retainer from its locking tabs.
4. Remove the bulb and socket assembly from the lamp body, then pull the bulb directly out of the socket.

✳✳WARNING

Do not touch the new halogen bulb with bare hands. This will cause contamination of the quartz, which may result in early failure of the lamp. Do not remove the protective plastic sleeve until the lamp is inserted into the socket. If you inadvertently touch the quartz, clean it prior to installation.

To install:

5. Insert the new bulb into the socket, and the socket into the lamp body. Attach the bulb socket retainer.
6. Position the lens and body assembly right side up (as indicated on the lens) into the lamp housing.
7. Secure the lens assembly to the lamp housing with the two screws and test the lamp for proper operation.

AIMING

▶ See Figure 114

If necessary, turn the adjusting nut on each fog lamp until the beams fall within the range indicated by the accompanying illustration.

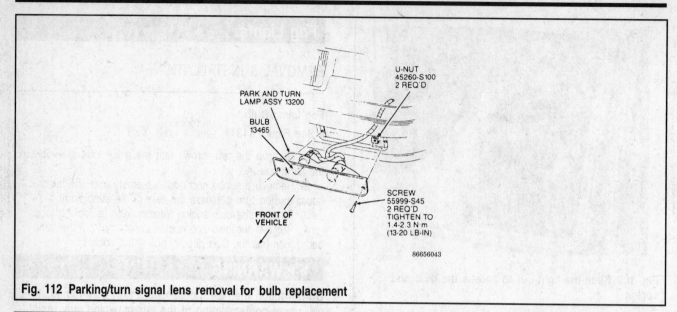

Fig. 112 Parking/turn signal lens removal for bulb replacement

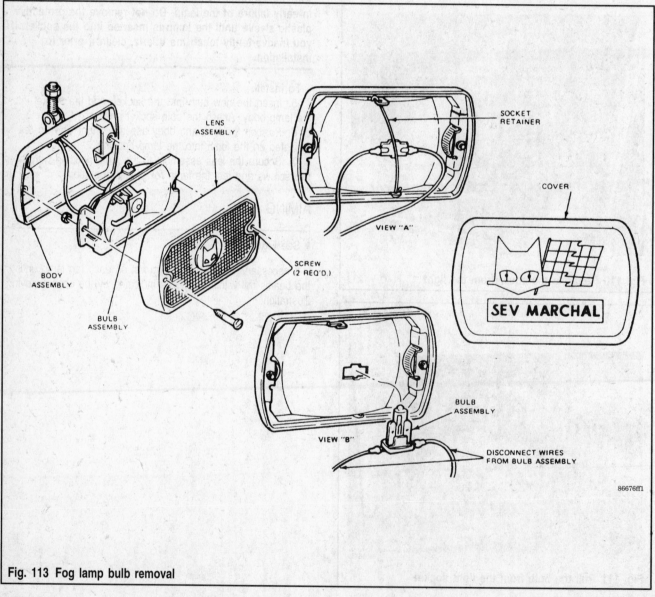

Fig. 113 Fog lamp bulb removal

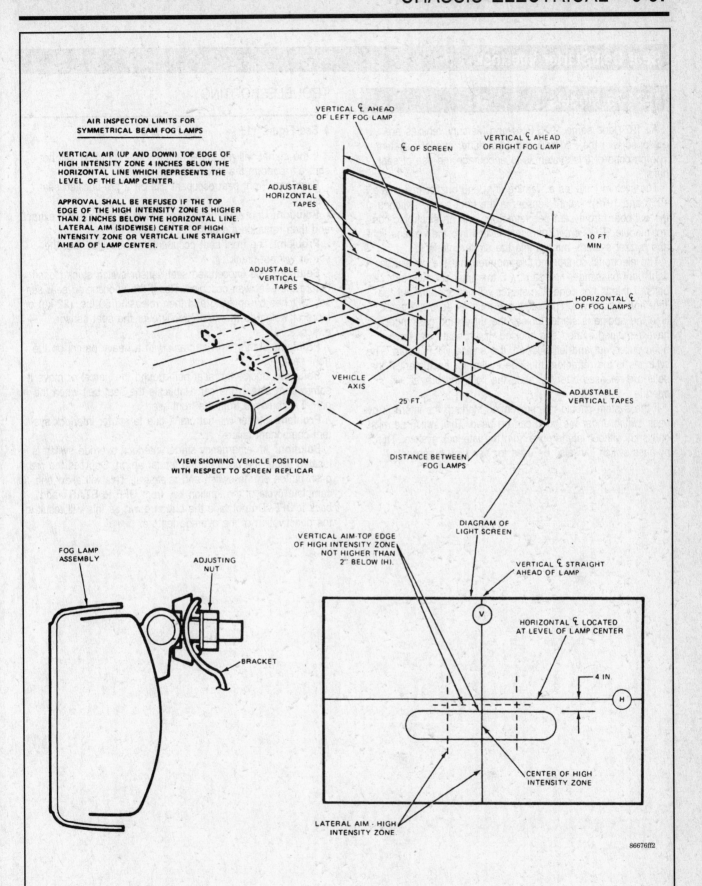

Fig. 114 Fog lamp aiming

Seat Belt/Starter Interlock

1974-75 Models

All 1974 and some 1975 Ford and Mercury vehicles are equipped with the Federally required starter interlock system. The purpose of this system is to encourage the use of seat belts.

The system includes a warning light and buzzer (as in late 1972 and 1973), weight sensors in the front seats, switches in the out-board front seat belt retractors, and an electronic control module. The center front seat is tied into the warning light and buzzer system, but not into the starter interlock.

The electronic control module requires that the driver and right front passenger first sit down, then pull out their seat belts. If this is not done, the starter will not operate, but the light and buzzer will. The sequence must be followed each time the engine is started unless the driver and passenger have remained seated and buckled. If the seat belts have been pulled out and left buckled, the engine will not start. The switches in the retractors must be cycled for each start. If the belts are released after the start, the light and buzzer will operate.

If the system should fail, preventing starting, the interlock by-pass switch under the hood can be used. This switch permits one start without interference from the interlock system. This by-pass switch can also be used for servicing purposes.

TROUBLESHOOTING

▶ **See Figure 115**

If the starter will not crank or the warning buzzer will not shut off, perform the following checks:

Problem: Front seat occupant sits on a pre-buckled seat belt.

Solution: Unbuckle the pre-buckled belt, fully retract, extract, and then rebuckle the belt.

Problem: The front seat occupants are buckled, but the starter will not crank.

Solution: The unoccupied seat sensor switch stuck closed before the seat was occupied. Reset the unoccupied seat sensor switches by applying and then releasing 50 lbs. (22 kg) or more of weight to the seat directly over the seat sensor switches.

Problem: Starter will not crank with a heavy parcel on the front seat.

Solution: Buckle the seat belt around the parcel or move it somewhere else in the car. Unbuckle the seat belt when the parcel is removed from the front seat.

Problem: Starter will not crank due to starter interlock system component failure.

Solution: An emergency starter interlock override switch is located under the hood on the fender apron. Depress the red push button on the switch and release it. This will allow one complete cycle of the ignition key from **OFF** to **START** and back it **OFF**. Do not tape the button down as this will result in the deactivation of the override feature.

TRAILER WIRING

Wiring the car for towing is fairly easy. There are a number of good wiring kits available and these should be used, rather than trying to design your own. All trailers will need brake lights and turn signals as well as tail lights and side marker lights. Most states require extra marker lights for overly wide trailers. Also, most states have recently required back-up lights for trailers, and most manufacturers have been building trailers with back-up lights for several years.

Additionally, some Class I, most Class II and just about all Class III trailers will have electric brakes. Add to this number an accessories wire, to operate trailer internal equipment or to charge the trailer's battery, and you can have as many as seven wires in the harness.

Determine the equipment on your trailer and buy the wiring kit necessary. The kit will contain all the wires needed, plus a plug adapter set which includes the female plug, mounted on the bumper or hitch, and the male plug, wired into, or plugged into the trailer harness.

When installing the kit, follow the manufacturer's instructions. The color coding of the wires should be standard throughout the industry.

One point to note, some domestic vehicles, and most imported vehicles, have separate turn signals. On most domestic vehicles, the brake lights and rear turn signals operate with the same bulb. For those vehicles with separate turn signals, you can purchase an isolation unit so that the brake lights won't blink whenever the turn signals are operated, or, you can go to your local electronics supply house and buy four diodes to wire in series with the brake and turn signal bulbs. Diodes will isolate the brake and turn signals. The choice is yours. The isolation units are simple and quick to install, but far more expensive than the diodes. The diodes, however, require more work to install properly, since they require cutting each bulb's wire and soldering the diode in place.

One final point, the best kits are those with a spring loaded cover on the vehicle mounted socket. This cover prevents dirt

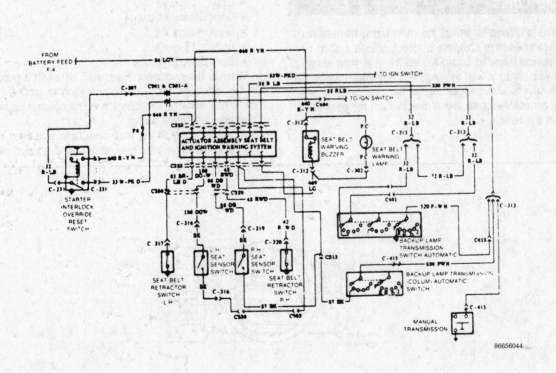

Fig. 115 Seat belt/starter interlock system circuit — 1974-75

and moisture from corroding the terminals. Never let the vehicle socket hang loosely. Always mount it securely to the bumper or hitch.

CIRCUIT PROTECTION

Fuses

All vehicles are equipped with a fuse panel located on the left side of the lower instrument panel.

REPLACEMENT

▶ **See Figures 116, 117, 118 and 119**

1. Locate the fuse panel, if necessary and remove the cover.
2. Look through the clear side of the fuse in question, to see if the metal wire inside is separated. If the wire is separated, the fuse is blown and must be replaced.
3. Remove the fuse by pulling it from its cavity; no special tools are required.
4. Replace the blown fuse using only one with the proper amp rating for that particular circuit. Push the fuse straight in until the fuse seats fully in the cavity.

Fusible Links

Fuse links are used to protect the main wiring harness and selected branches from complete burn-out, should a short circuit or electrical overload occur. A fuse link is a short length of insulated wire, integral with the engine compartment wiring harness. It is several wire gauges smaller than the circuit it protects and generally located in-line directly from the positive terminal of the battery.

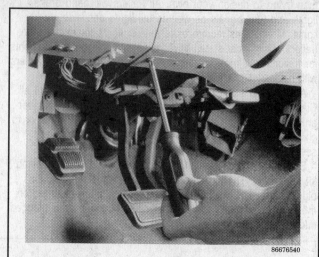

86676540

Fig. 117 Remove the retaining screws securing the panel below the steering column

Production fuse links are color coded as follows:
- Gray: 12 gauge
- Dark Green: 14 gauge
- Black: 16 gauge
- Brown: 18 gauge
- Dark Blue: 20 gauge

When a heavy current flows, such as when a booster battery is connected incorrectly or when a short to ground occurs in the wiring harness, the fuse link burns out and protects the alternator and other wiring.

A burned out fuse link may have bare wire ends protruding from the insulation, or it may have only expanded or bubbled

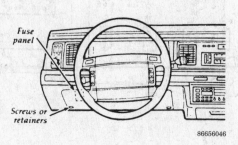

Fuse
panel

Screws or
retainers

86656046

Fig. 116 A standard fuse box located below the steering column

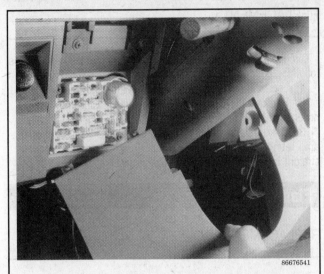

Fig. 118 Unclip the panel from the instrument dash

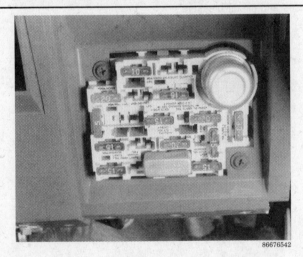

Fig. 119 With the panel removed, the fuse block is clearly visible

insulation with illegible identification. When it is hard to determine if the fuse link is burned out, perform the continuity test:

1. Make sure the battery is okay, then turn on the headlights or other accessories. If the headlights or accessories do not work, the fuse link is probably burned out.

2. If equipped with more than one fuse link, use a voltmeter to test each link with accessories turned **ON** and **OFF**. No voltage indicates that the fuse link is probably burned out.

3. To test the fuse link that protects the alternator, make sure the battery is okay, then check with a voltmeter for voltage at the **BAT** terminal of the alternator. No voltage indicates that the fuse link is probably burned out.

REPLACEMENT

When replacing a fuse link, always make sure the replacement fuse link is a duplicate of the one removed with respect to gauge, length and insulation. Original equipment and original equipment specification replacement fuse links have insulation that is flame proof. Do not fabricate a fuse link from ordinary wire because the insulation may not be flame proof.

If a circuit protected by a fuse link becomes inoperative, inspect for a blown fuse link. If the fuse link wire insulation is burned or opened, disconnect the feed as close as possible behind the splice in the harness. If the damaged fuse link is between 2 splices (weld points in the harness), cut out the damaged portion as close as possible to the weld points.

Replace the fuse link as follows:

1. To service a 2-link group when only one link has blown and the other link is not damaged, proceed as follows:

a. Disconnect the negative battery cable.

b. Cut out the blown fusible link (2 places).

c. Position the correct eyelet type service fusible link with the bare end to the correct size wire connector and crimp to the wire ends.

d. Heat the splice insulation until the tubing shrinks and adhesive flows from each end of the connector.

e. Connect the negative battery cable.

2. To service a fuse link in a multi-feed or single circuit, proceed as follows:

a. Disconnect the negative battery cable.

b. Determine which circuit is damaged, its location and the cause of the open fuse link. If the damaged fuse link is one of 3 fed by a common number 10 or 12 gauge feed wire, determine the specific affected circuit.

c. Cut the damaged fuse link from the wiring harness and discard. If the fuse link is one of 3 circuits fed by a single feed wire, cut it out of the harness at each splice end and discard.

d. Obtain the proper fuse link and butt connectors for attaching the fuse link to the harness.

e. Strip 5/16in. (8mm) of insulation from the wire ends and insert into the proper size wire connector. Crimp and heat the splice insulation until the tubing shrinks and adhesive flows from each end of the connector.

f. To replace a fuse link on a single circuit in a harness, cut out the damaged portion. Strip approximately 1/2 in. (13mm) of insulation from the 2 wire ends and attach the correct size fuse link to each wire end with the proper gauge wire connectors. Crimp and heat the splice insulation until the tubing shrinks and adhesive flows from each end of the connector.

g. Connect the negative battery cable.

3. To service a fuse link with an eyelet terminal on one end, such as the charging circuit, proceed as follows:

a. Disconnect the negative battery cable.

b. Cut off the fuse link behind the weld, strip approximately 1/2 in. (13mm) of insulation from the cut end, and attach the appropriate new eyelet fuse link to the cut stripped wire with the proper size connector.

c. Crimp and heat the splice insulation until the tubing shrinks and adhesive flows from each end of the connector.

d. Connect the negative battery cable.

➡**Do not mistake a resistor wire for a fuse link. The resistor wire is generally longer and has print stating "Resistor — do not cut or splice." When attaching a No. 16, 18 or 20 gauge fuse link to a heavy gauge wire, always double the stripped wire end of the fuse link before inserting and crimping it into the wire connector for positive wire retention.**

Circuit Breakers

Circuit breakers are used on certain electrical components requiring high amperage. The advantage of the circuit breaker is its ability to open and close the electrical circuit as the load demands, rather than the necessity of a part replacement. The following circuit breakers are used:

Windshield Wiper Circuit — one 8.25 amp circuit breaker located on the fuse panel.

Power Windows — one or two 20 amp circuit breaker located on the fuse panel.

Power Windows and Tailgate Power Window Switch — one 20 amp circuit breaker located on the fuse panel.

Power Windows and Trunk Lid Release — one 20 amp circuit breaker located on the fuse panel.

Headlight and High Beam — one 22 amp circuit breaker incorporated in the lighting switch.

Power Seats and Door Locks — one 30 amp circuit breaker located on the fuse panel.

REPLACEMENT

Circuit breakers that are fuse panel mounted are replaced as follows:

1. Locate the fuse panel and remove the cover, if equipped

2. Remove the circuit breaker by pulling it from its cavity; no special tools are required.

3. Only replace circuit breakers using one with the proper amp rating for that particular circuit. Push the circuit breaker straight in until it seats fully in the cavity.

Flashers

REPLACEMENT

The turn signal and emergency flashers are attached to the fuse panel. They are replaced in the same manner as the fuses and circuit breakers.

REMOVE EXISTING VINYL TUBE SHIELDING
REINSTALL OVER FUSE LINK BEFORE CRIMPING
FUSE LINK TO WIRE ENDS

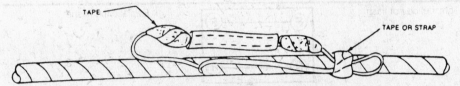

TYPICAL REPAIR USING THE SPECIAL #17 GA. (9.00" LONG YELLOW) FUSE LINK REQUIRED FOR THE AIR/COND
CIRCUITS (2) #687E and #261A LOCATED IN THE ENGINE COMPARTMENT

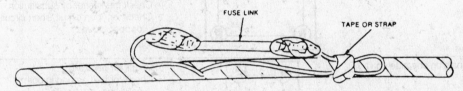

TYPICAL REPAIR FOR ANY IN-LINE FUSE LINK USING THE SPECIFIED GAUGE FUSE LINK FOR THE SPECIFIC CIRCUIT

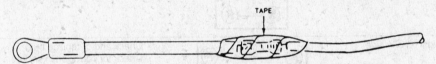

TYPICAL REPAIR USING THE EYELET TERMINAL FUSE LINK OF THE SPECIFIED GAUGE FOR ATTACHMENT TO A CIRCUIT WIRE END

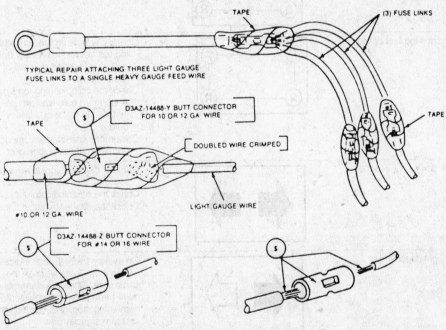

TYPICAL REPAIR ATTACHING THREE LIGHT GAUGE
FUSE LINKS TO A SINGLE HEAVY GAUGE FEED WIRE

FUSIBLE LINK REPAIR PROCEDURE

86656128

Troubleshooting Basic Turn Signal and Flasher Problems

Most problems in the turn signals or flasher system, can be reduced to defective flashers or bulbs, which are easily replaced. Occasionally, problems in the turn signals are traced to the switch in the steering column, which will require professional service.

F = Front   R = Rear   • = Lights off   ○ = Lights on

Problem		Solution
Turn signals light, but do not flash		• Replace the flasher
No turn signals light on either side		• Check the fuse. Replace if defective. • Check the flasher by substitution • Check for open circuit, short circuit or poor ground
Both turn signals on one side don't work		• Check for bad bulbs • Check for bad ground in both housings
One turn signal light on one side doesn't work		• Check and/or replace bulb • Check for corrosion in socket. Clean contacts. • Check for poor ground at socket
Turn signal flashes too fast or too slow		• Check any bulb on the side flashing too fast. A heavy-duty bulb is probably installed in place of a regular bulb. • Check the bulb flashing too slow. A standard bulb was probably installed in place of a heavy-duty bulb. • Check for loose connections or corrosion at the bulb socket
Indicator lights don't work in either direction		• Check if the turn signals are working • Check the dash indicator lights • Check the flasher by substitution
One indicator light doesn't light		• On systems with 1 dash indicator: See if the lights work on the same side. Often the filaments have been reversed in systems combining stoplights with taillights and turn signals. Check the flasher by substitution • On systems with 2 indicators: Check the bulbs on the same side Check the indicator light bulb Check the flasher by substitution

86656201

Troubleshooting Basic Dash Gauge Problems

Problem	Cause	Solution
Coolant Temperature Gauge		
Gauge reads erratically or not at all	• Loose or dirty connections • Defective sending unit	• Clean/tighten connections • Bi-metal gauge: remove the wire from the sending unit. Ground the wire for an instant. If the gauge registers, replace the sending unit.
	• Defective gauge	• Magnetic gauge: disconnect the wire at the sending unit. With ignition ON gauge should register COLD. Ground the wire; gauge should register HOT.
Ammeter Gauge—Turn Headlights ON (do not start engine). Note reaction		
Ammeter shows charge Ammeter shows discharge Ammeter does not move	• Connections reversed on gauge • Ammeter is OK • Loose connections or faulty wiring • Defective gauge	• Reinstall connections • Nothing • Check/correct wiring • Replace gauge
Oil Pressure Gauge		
Gauge does not register or is inaccurate	• On mechanical gauge, Bourdon tube may be bent or kinked	• Check tube for kinks or bends preventing oil from reaching the gauge
	• Low oil pressure	• Remove sending unit. Idle the engine briefly. If no oil flows from sending unit hole, problem is in engine.
	• Defective gauge	• Remove the wire from the sending unit and ground it for an instant with the ignition ON. A good gauge will go to the top of the scale.
	• Defective wiring	• Check the wiring to the gauge. If it's OK and the gauge doesn't register when grounded, replace the gauge.
	• Defective sending unit	• If the wiring is OK and the gauge functions when grounded, replace the sending unit
All Gauges		
All gauges do not operate	• Blown fuse • Defective instrument regulator	• Replace fuse • Replace instrument voltage regulator
All gauges read low or erratically	• Defective or dirty instrument voltage regulator	• Clean contacts or replace
All gauges pegged	• Loss of ground between instrument voltage regulator and car • Defective instrument regulator	• Check ground • Replace regulator
Warning Lights		
Light(s) do not come on when ignition is ON, but engine is not started	• Defective bulb • Defective wire	• Replace bulb • Check wire from light to sending unit
	• Defective sending unit	• Disconnect the wire from the sending unit and ground it. Replace the sending unit if the light comes on with the ignition ON.
Light comes on with engine running	• Problem in individual system • Defective sending unit	• Check system • Check sending unit (see above)

86656202

Troubleshooting Basic Lighting Problems

Problem	Cause	Solution
Lights		
One or more lights don't work, but others do	• Defective bulb(s) • Blown fuse(s) • Dirty fuse clips or light sockets • Poor ground circuit	• Replace bulb(s) • Replace fuse(s) • Clean connections • Run ground wire from light socket housing to car frame
Lights burn out quickly	• Incorrect voltage regulator setting or defective regulator • Poor battery/alternator connections	• Replace voltage regulator • Check battery/alternator connections
Lights go dim	• Low/discharged battery • Alternator not charging • Corroded sockets or connections • Low voltage output	• Check battery • Check drive belt tension; repair or replace alternator • Clean bulb and socket contacts and connections • Replace voltage regulator
Lights flicker	• Loose connection • Poor ground • Circuit breaker operating (short circuit)	• Tighten all connections • Run ground wire from light housing to car frame • Check connections and look for bare wires
Lights "flare"—Some flare is normal on acceleration—if excessive, see "Lights Burn Out Quickly"	• High voltage setting	• Replace voltage regulator
Lights glare—approaching drivers are blinded	• Lights adjusted too high • Rear springs or shocks sagging • Rear tires soft	• Have headlights aimed • Check rear springs/shocks • Check/correct rear tire pressure
Turn Signals		
Turn signals don't work in either direction	• Blown fuse • Defective flasher • Loose connection	• Replace fuse • Replace flasher • Check/tighten all connections
Right (or left) turn signal only won't work	• Bulb burned out • Right (or left) indicator bulb burned out • Short circuit	• Replace bulb • Check/replace indicator bulb • Check/repair wiring
Flasher rate too slow or too fast	• Incorrect wattage bulb • Incorrect flasher	• Flasher bulb • Replace flasher (use a variable load flasher if you pull a trailer)
Indicator lights do not flash (burn steadily)	• Burned out bulb • Defective flasher	• Replace bulb • Replace flasher
Indicator lights do not light at all	• Burned out indicator bulb • Defective flasher	• Replace indicator bulb • Replace flasher

86656203

Troubleshooting Basic Windshield Wiper Problems

Problem	Cause	Solution
Electric Wipers		
Wipers do not operate— Wiper motor heats up or hums	• Internal motor defect • Bent or damaged linkage • Arms improperly installed on linking pivots	• Replace motor • Repair or replace linkage • Position linkage in park and reinstall wiper arms
Wipers do not operate— No current to motor	• Fuse or circuit breaker blown • Loose, open or broken wiring • Defective switch • Defective or corroded terminals • No ground circuit for motor or switch	• Replace fuse or circuit breaker • Repair wiring and connections • Replace switch • Replace or clean terminals • Repair ground circuits
Wipers do not operate— Motor runs	• Linkage disconnected or broken	• Connect wiper linkage or replace broken linkage
Vacuum Wipers		
Wipers do not operate	• Control switch or cable inoperative • Loss of engine vacuum to wiper motor (broken hoses, low engine vacuum, defective vacuum/fuel pump) • Linkage broken or disconnected • Defective wiper motor	• Repair or replace switch or cable • Check vacuum lines, engine vacuum and fuel pump • Repair linkage • Replace wiper motor
Wipers stop on engine acceleration	• Leaking vacuum hoses • Dry windshield • Oversize wiper blades • Defective vacuum/fuel pump	• Repair or replace hoses • Wet windshield with washers • Replace with proper size wiper blades • Replace pump

86656204

Troubleshooting the Heater

Problem	Cause	Solution
Blower motor will not turn at any speed	· Blown fuse · Loose connection · Defective ground · Faulty switch · Faulty motor · Faulty resistor	· Replace fuse · Inspect and tighten · Clean and tighten · Replace switch · Replace motor · Replace resistor
Blower motor turns at one speed only	· Faulty switch · Faulty resistor	· Replace switch · Replace resistor
Blower motor turns but does not circulate air	· Intake blocked · Fan not secured to the motor shaft	· Clean intake · Tighten security
Heater will not heat	· Coolant does not reach proper temperature · Heater core blocked internally · Heater core air-bound · Blend-air door not in proper position	· Check and replace thermostat if necessary · Flush or replace core if necessary · Purge air from core · Adjust cable
Heater will not defrost	· Control cable adjustment incorrect · Defroster hose damaged	· Adjust control cable · Replace defroster hose

86656200

WIRING DIAGRAMS

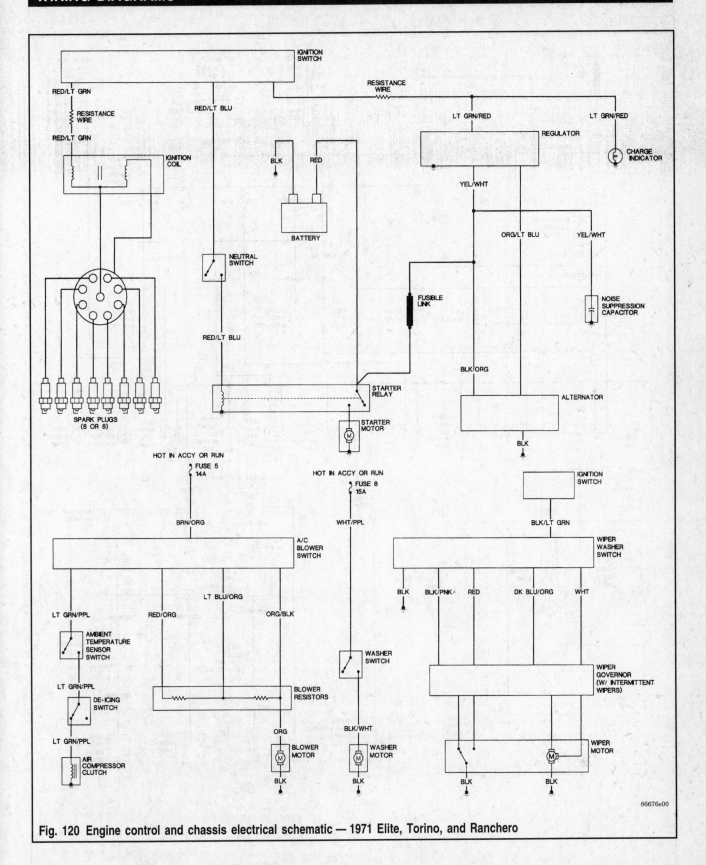

Fig. 120 Engine control and chassis electrical schematic — 1971 Elite, Torino, and Ranchero

86676e00

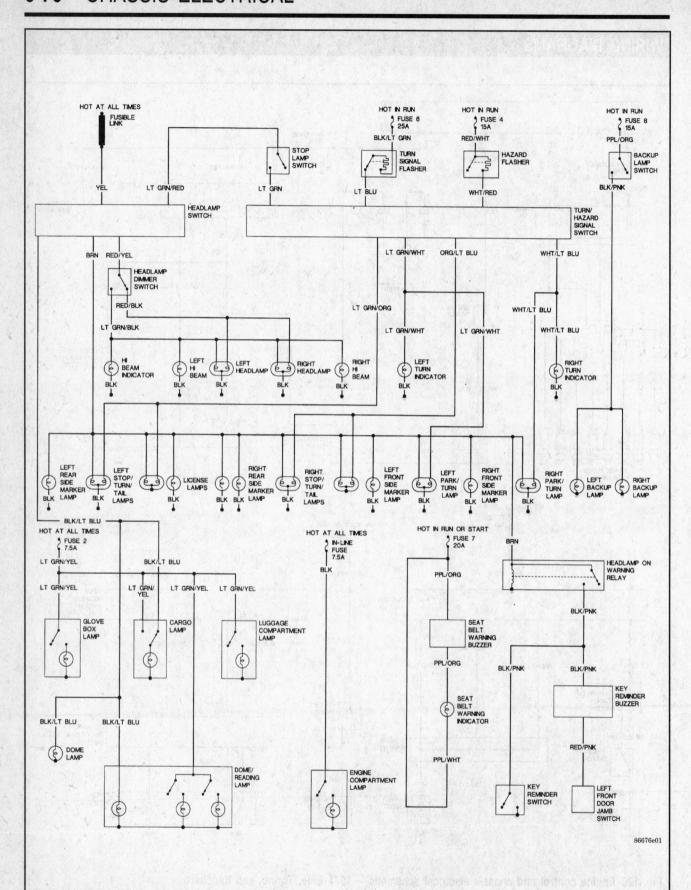

Fig. 121 Chassis electrical schematic continued — 1971 Elite, Torino and Ranchero

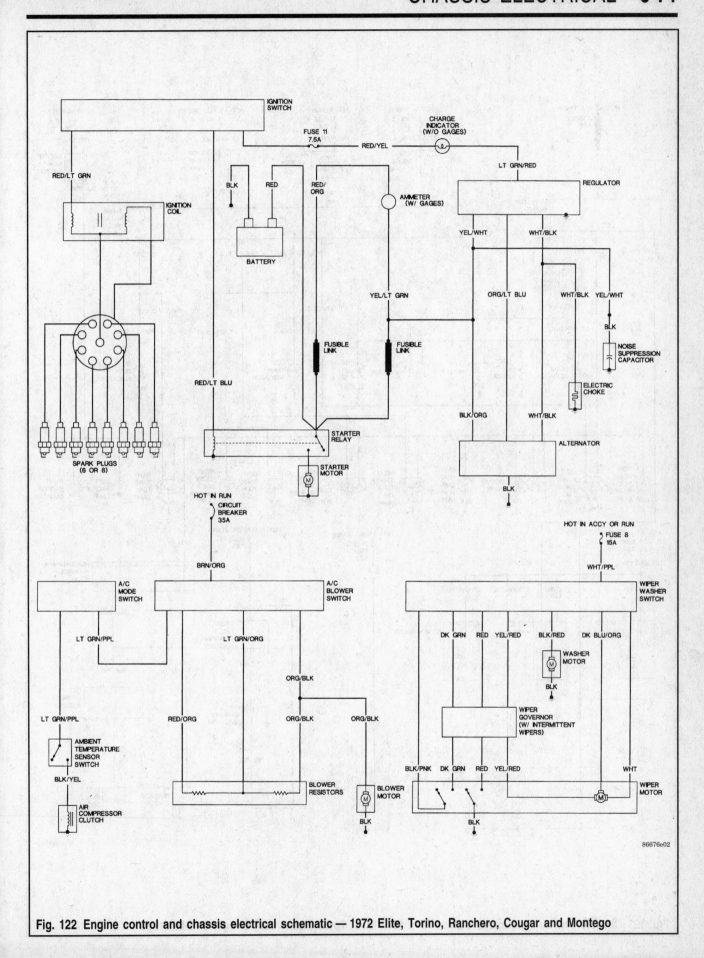

Fig. 122 Engine control and chassis electrical schematic — 1972 Elite, Torino, Ranchero, Cougar and Montego

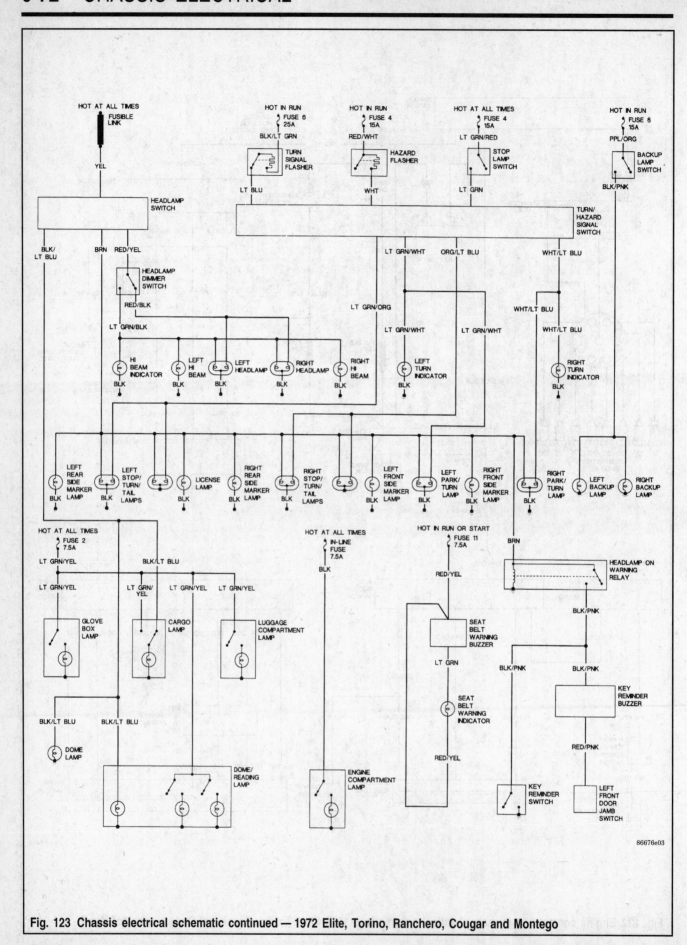

Fig. 123 Chassis electrical schematic continued — 1972 Elite, Torino, Ranchero, Cougar and Montego

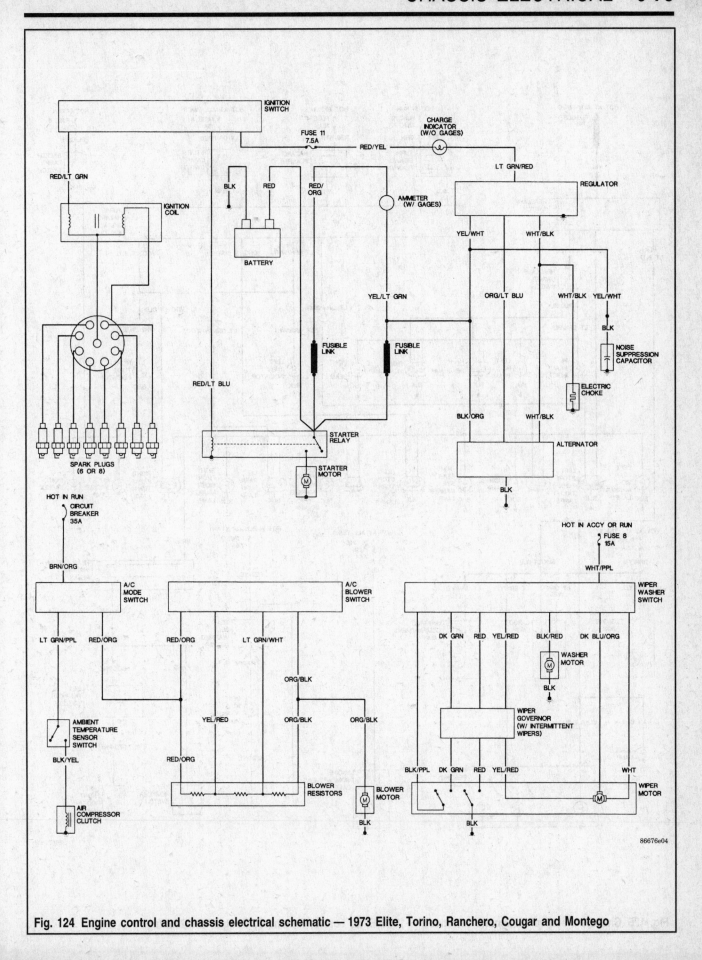

Fig. 124 Engine control and chassis electrical schematic — 1973 Elite, Torino, Ranchero, Cougar and Montego

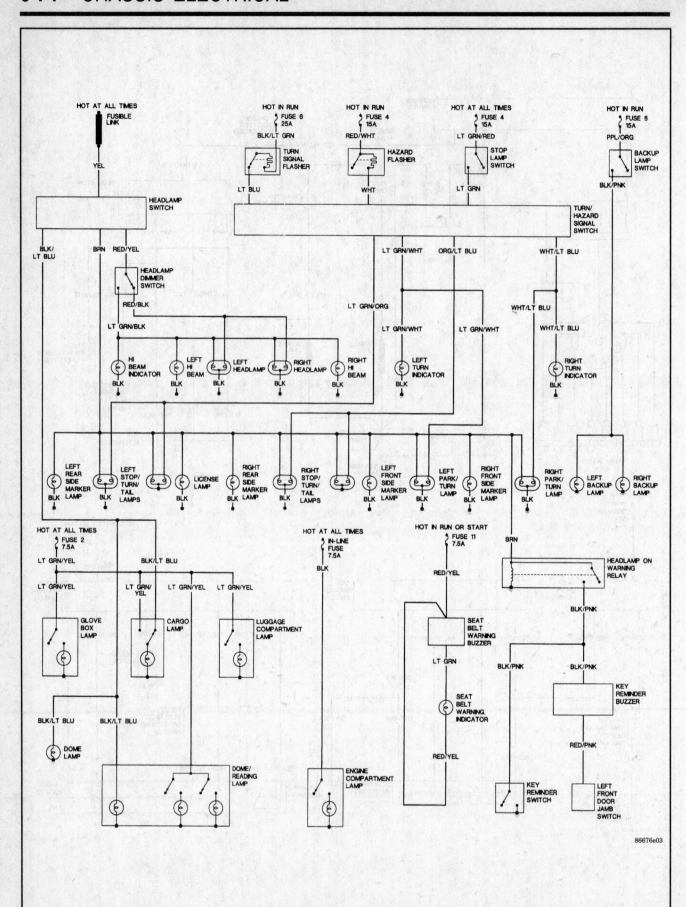

Fig. 125 Chassis electrical schematic continued — 1973 Elite, Torino, Ranchero, Cougar and Montego

86676e03

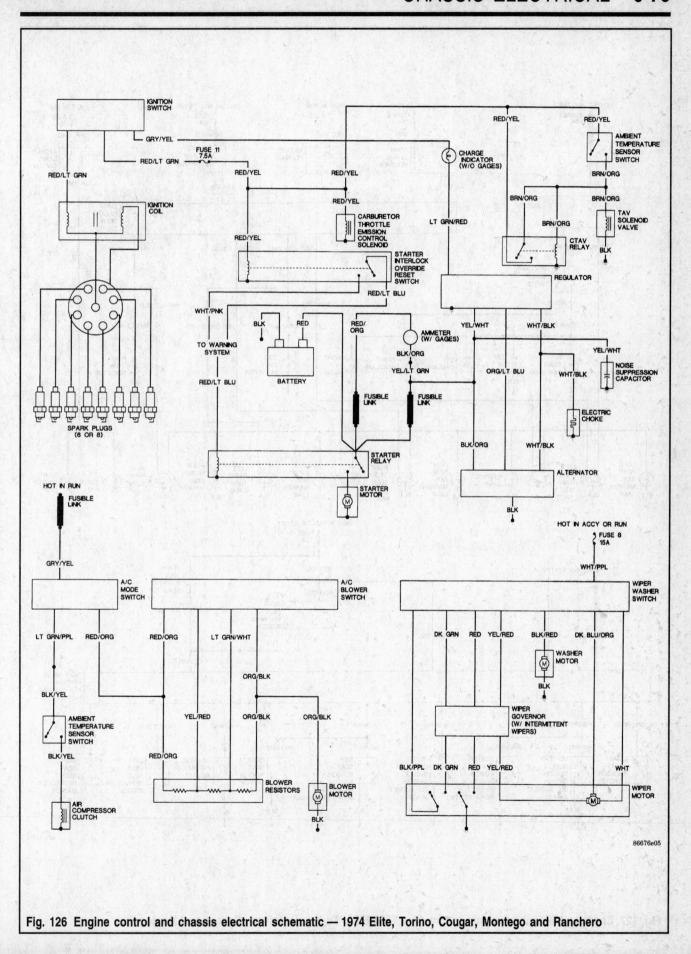

Fig. 126 Engine control and chassis electrical schematic — 1974 Elite, Torino, Cougar, Montego and Ranchero

86676e05

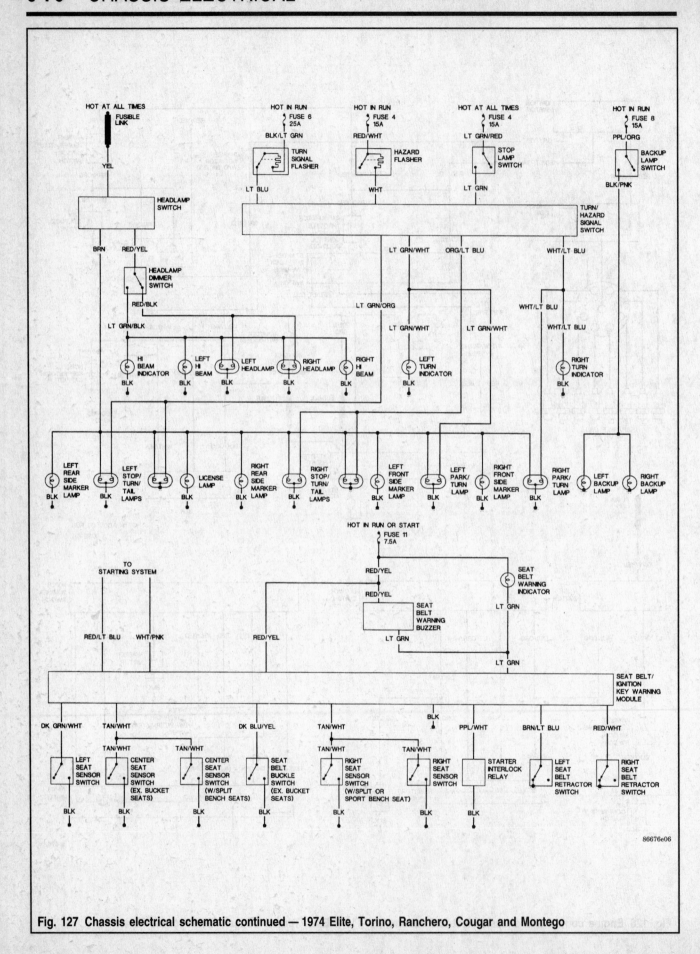

Fig. 127 Chassis electrical schematic continued — 1974 Elite, Torino, Ranchero, Cougar and Montego

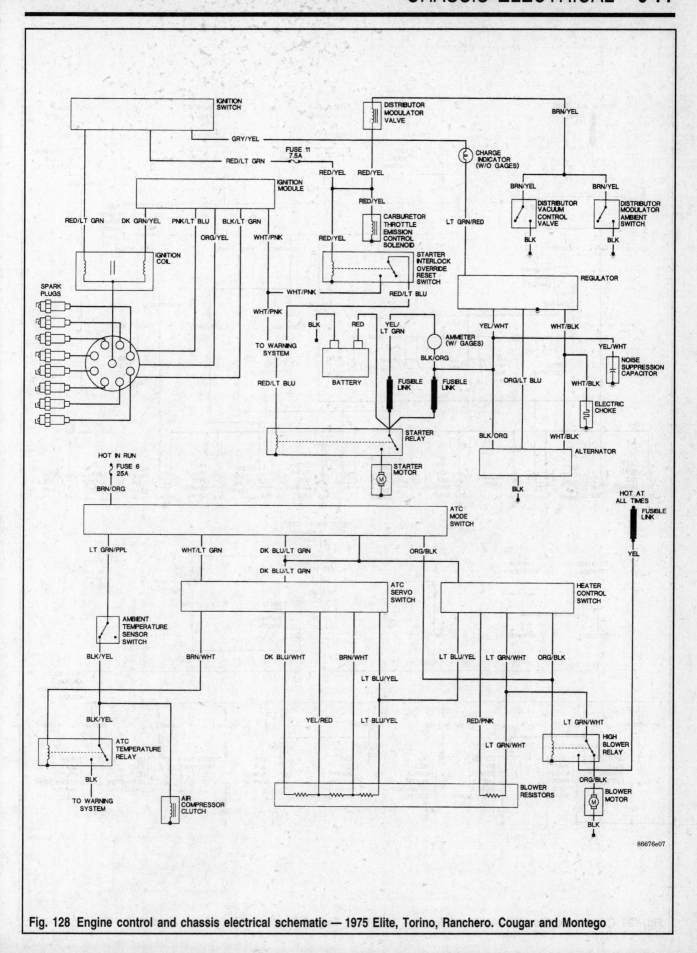

Fig. 128 Engine control and chassis electrical schematic — 1975 Elite, Torino, Ranchero. Cougar and Montego

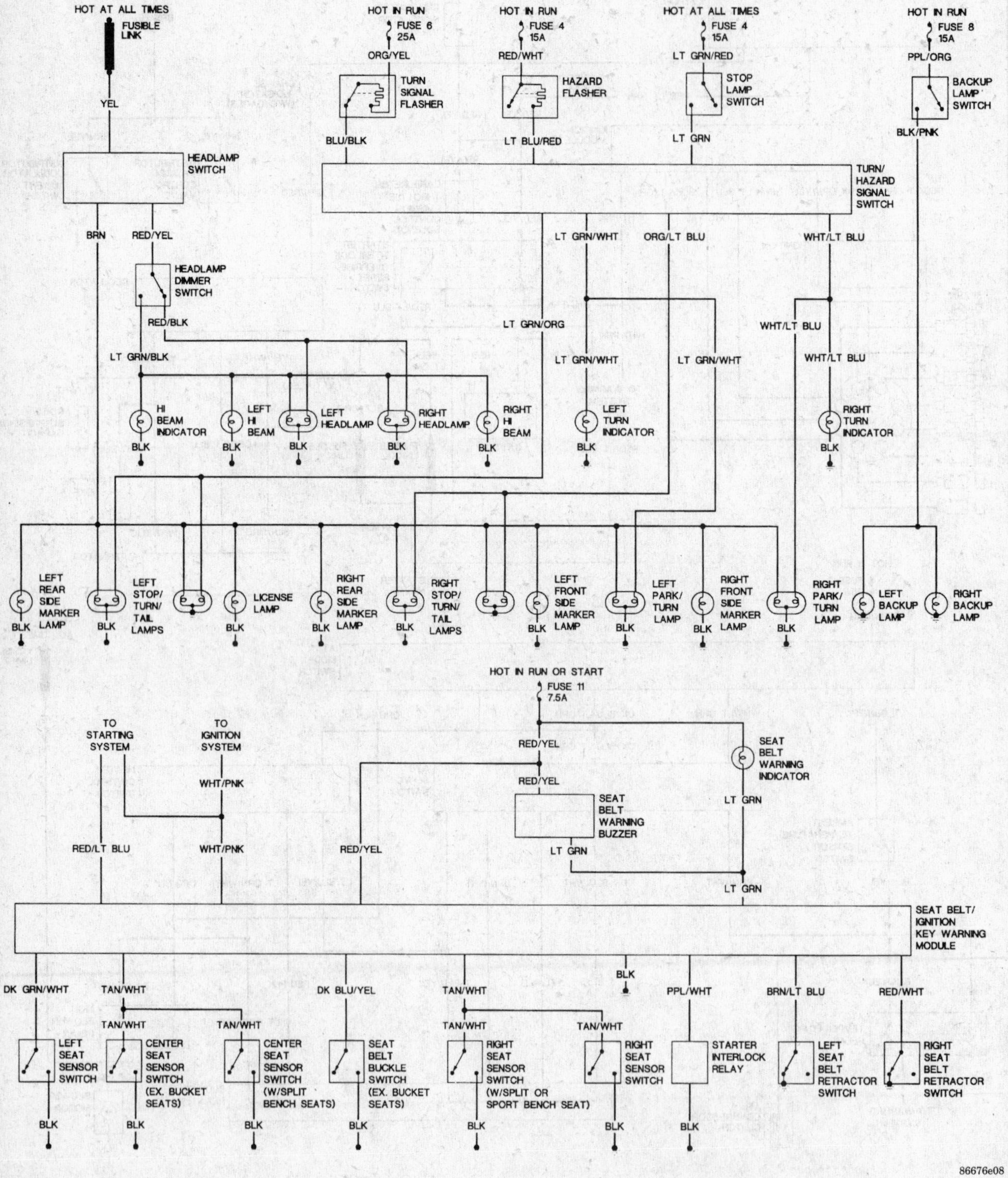

Fig. 129 Chassis electrical schematic continued — 1975 Elite, Torino, Ranchero, Cougar and Montego

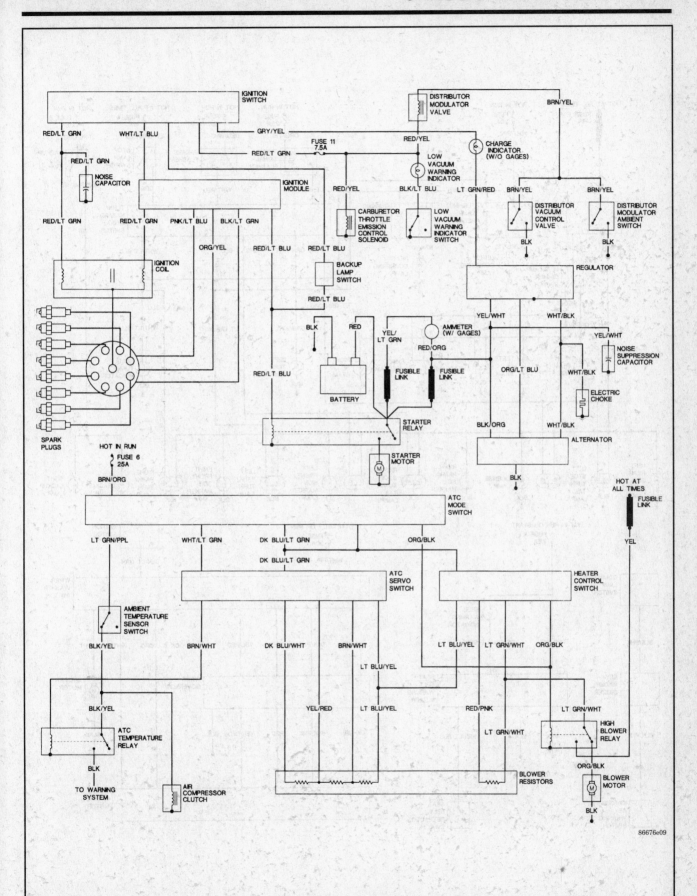

Fig. 130 Engine control and chassis electrical schematic — 1976 Elite, Torino, Ranchero, Cougar, Thunderbird and Montego

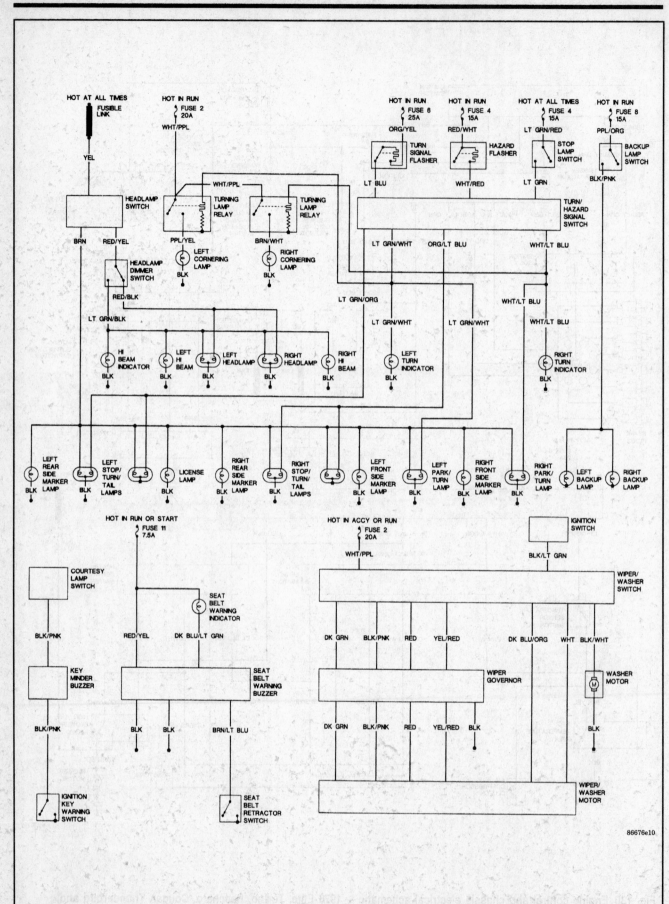

Fig. 131 Chassis electrical schematic continued — 1976 Elite, Torino, Ranchero, Cougar, Thunderbird and Montego

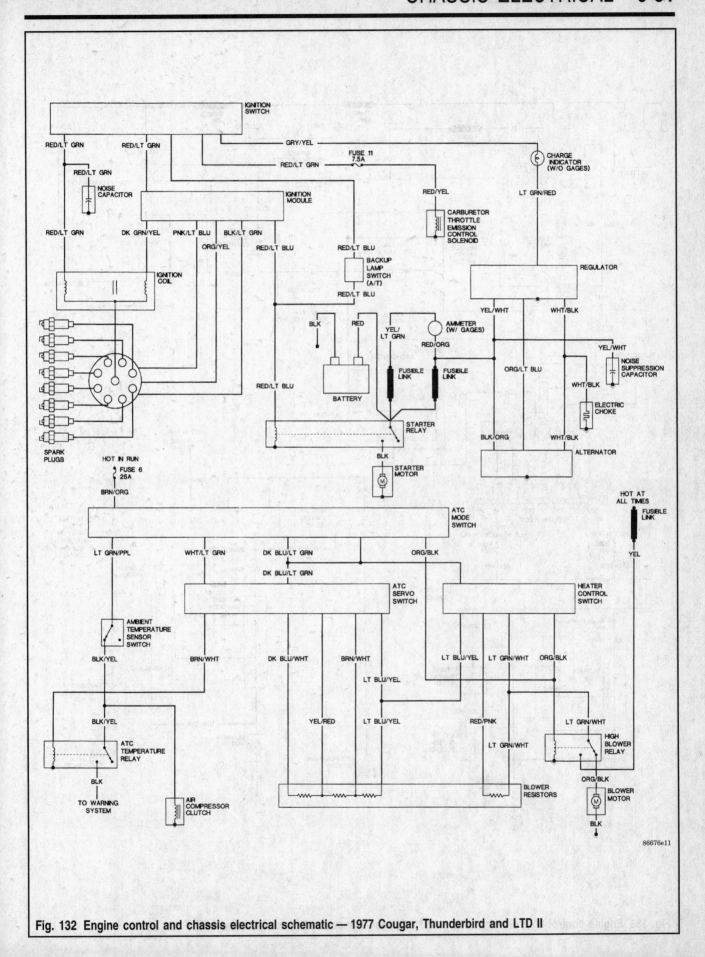

Fig. 132 Engine control and chassis electrical schematic — 1977 Cougar, Thunderbird and LTD II

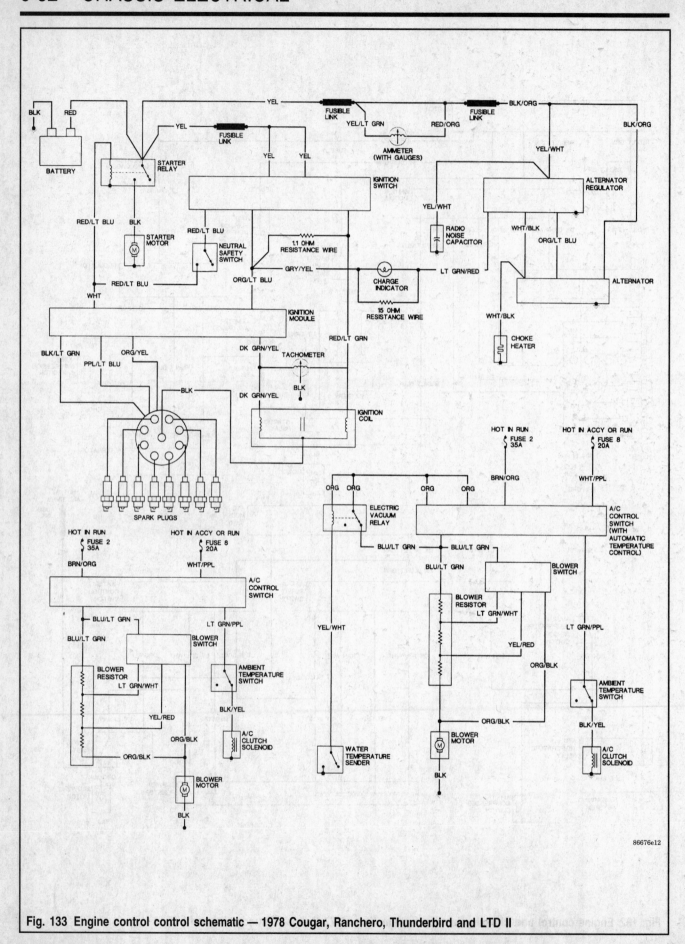

Fig. 133 Engine control control schematic — 1978 Cougar, Ranchero, Thunderbird and LTD II

86676e12

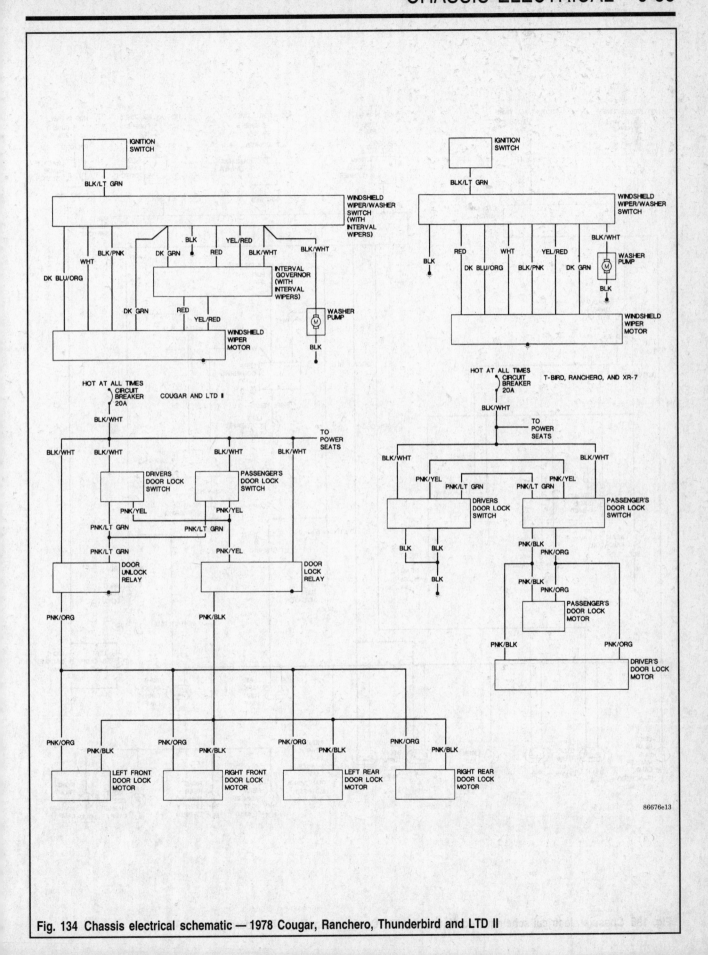

Fig. 134 Chassis electrical schematic — 1978 Cougar, Ranchero, Thunderbird and LTD II

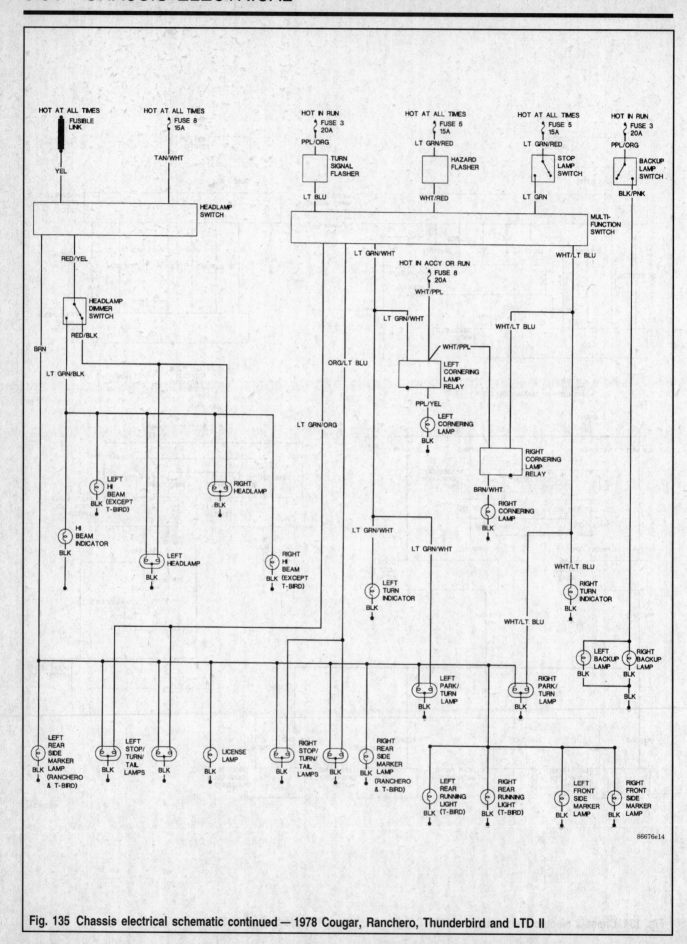

Fig. 135 Chassis electrical schematic continued — 1978 Cougar, Ranchero, Thunderbird and LTD II

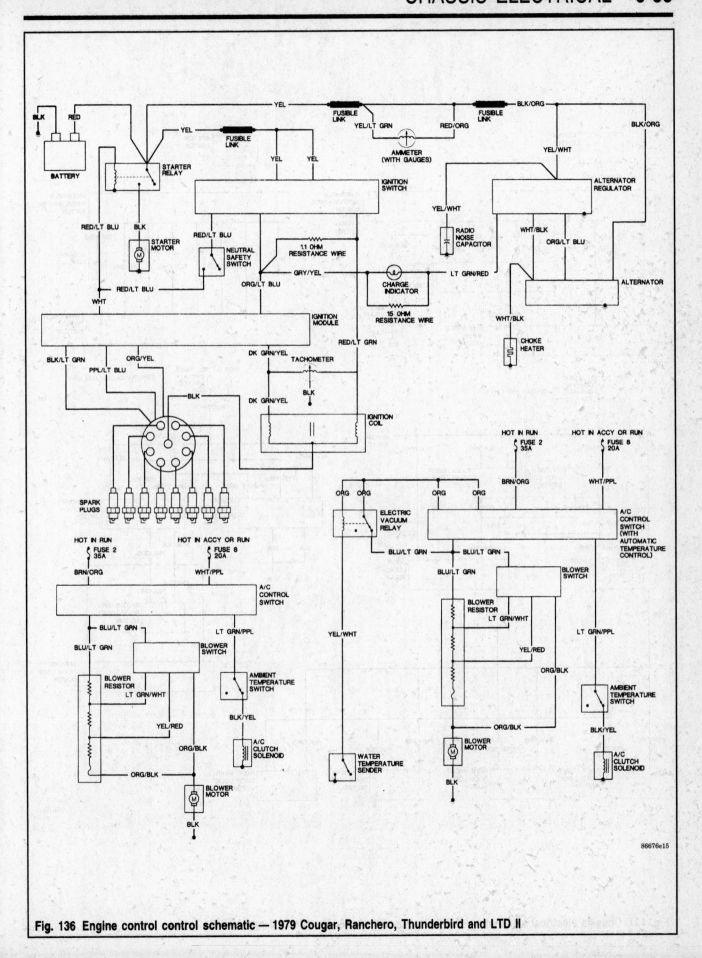

Fig. 136 Engine control control schematic — 1979 Cougar, Ranchero, Thunderbird and LTD II

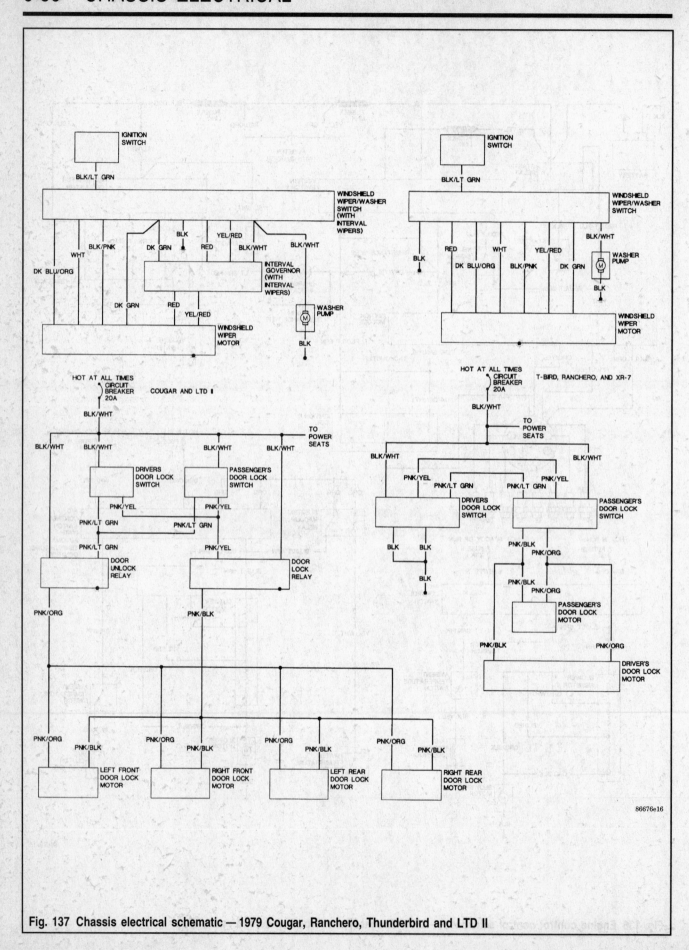

Fig. 137 Chassis electrical schematic — 1979 Cougar, Ranchero, Thunderbird and LTD II

86676e16

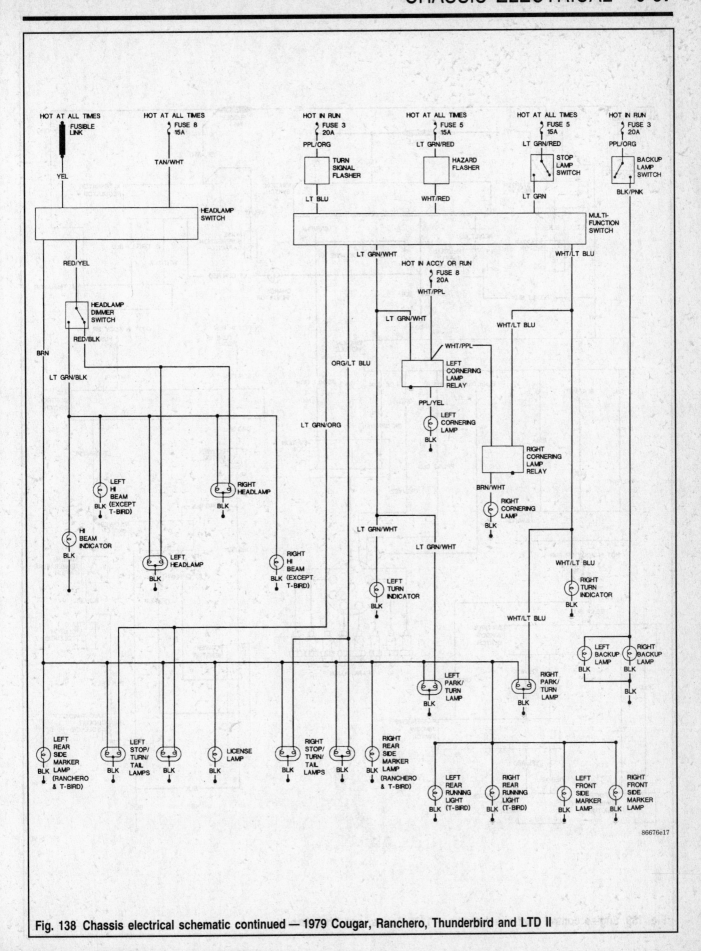

Fig. 138 Chassis electrical schematic continued — 1979 Cougar, Ranchero, Thunderbird and LTD II

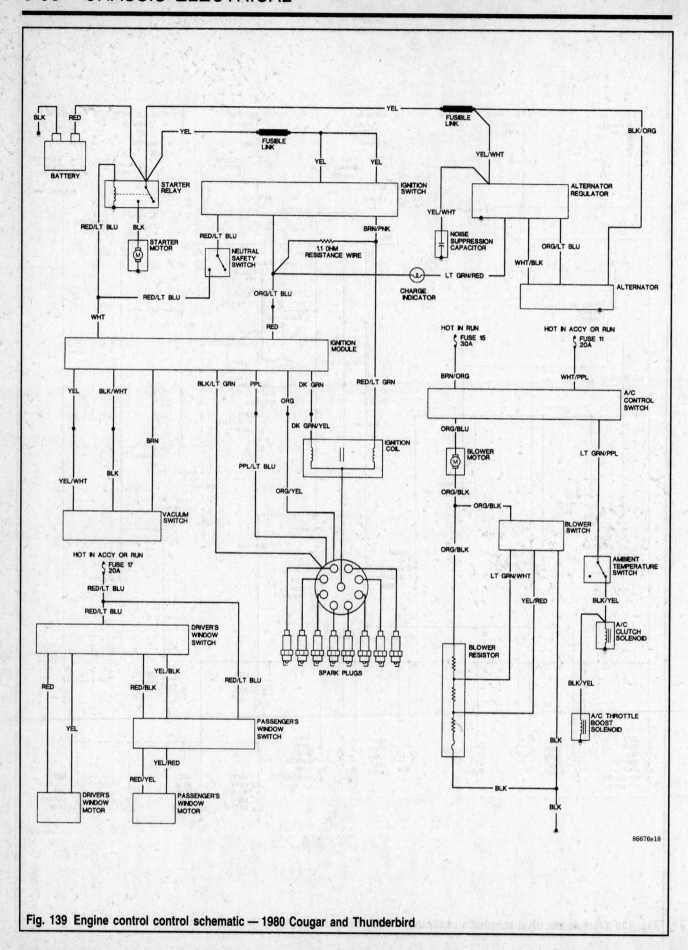

Fig. 139 Engine control control schematic — 1980 Cougar and Thunderbird

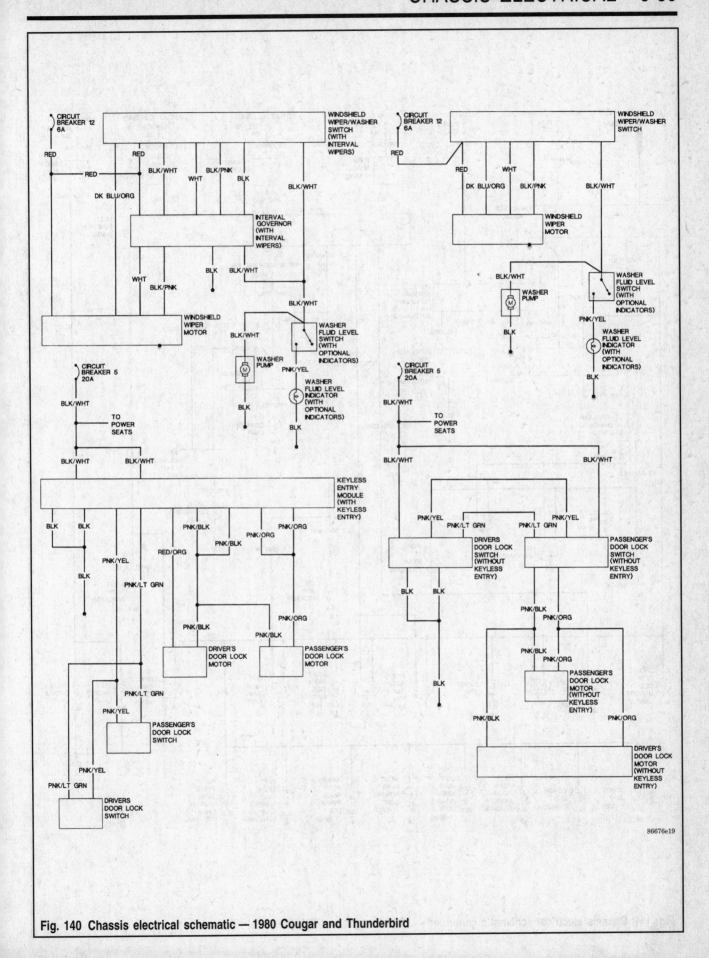

Fig. 140 Chassis electrical schematic — 1980 Cougar and Thunderbird

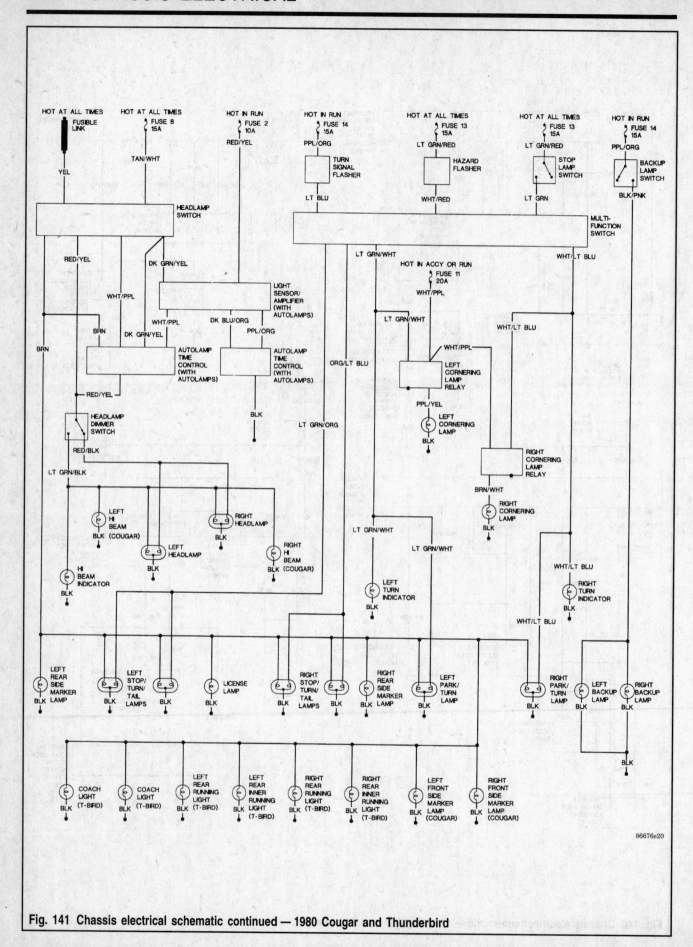

Fig. 141 Chassis electrical schematic continued — 1980 Cougar and Thunderbird

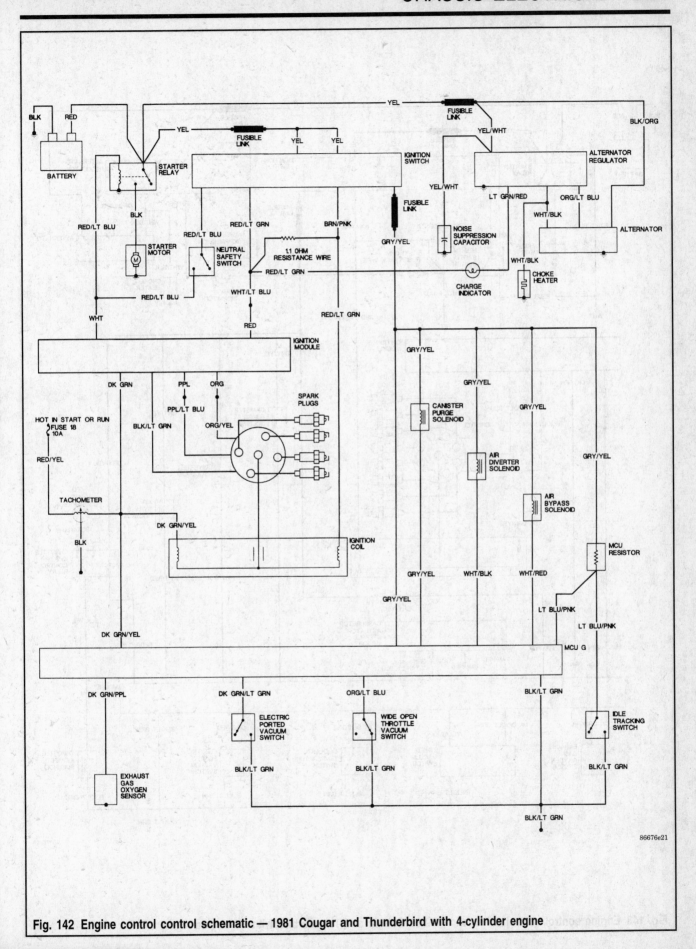

Fig. 142 Engine control control schematic — 1981 Cougar and Thunderbird with 4-cylinder engine

86676e21

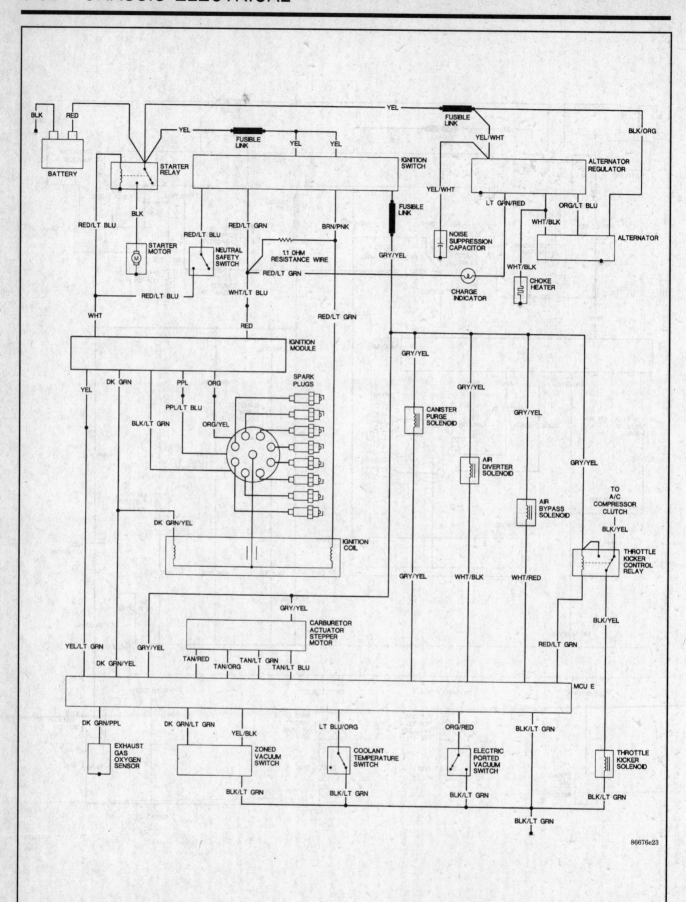

Fig. 143 Engine control control schematic — 1981 Cougar and Thunderbird with V8 engine

86676e23

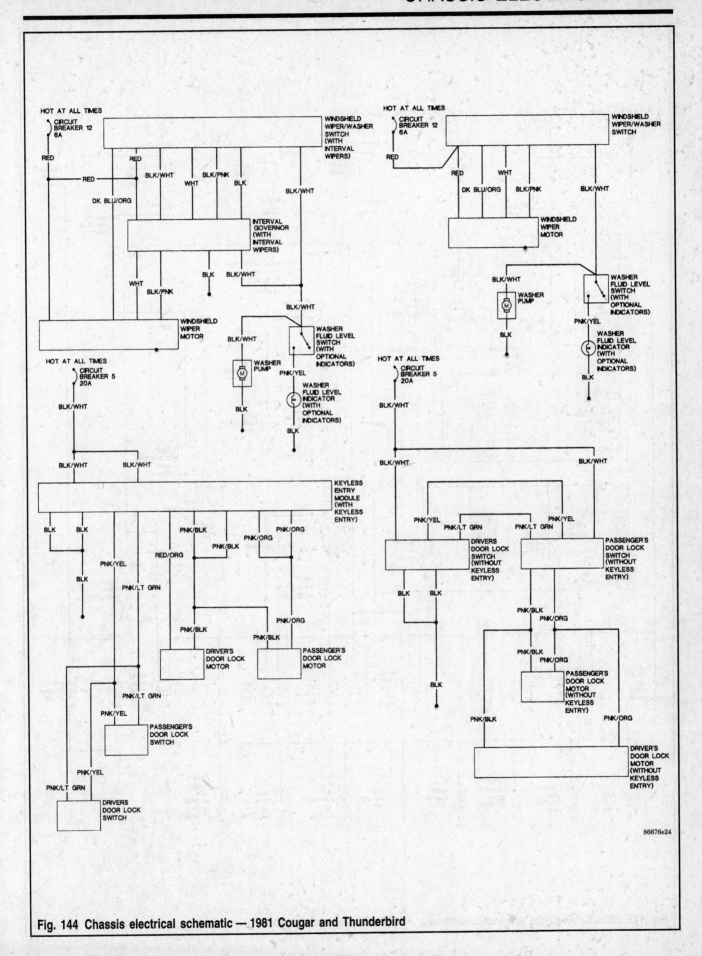

Fig. 144 Chassis electrical schematic — 1981 Cougar and Thunderbird

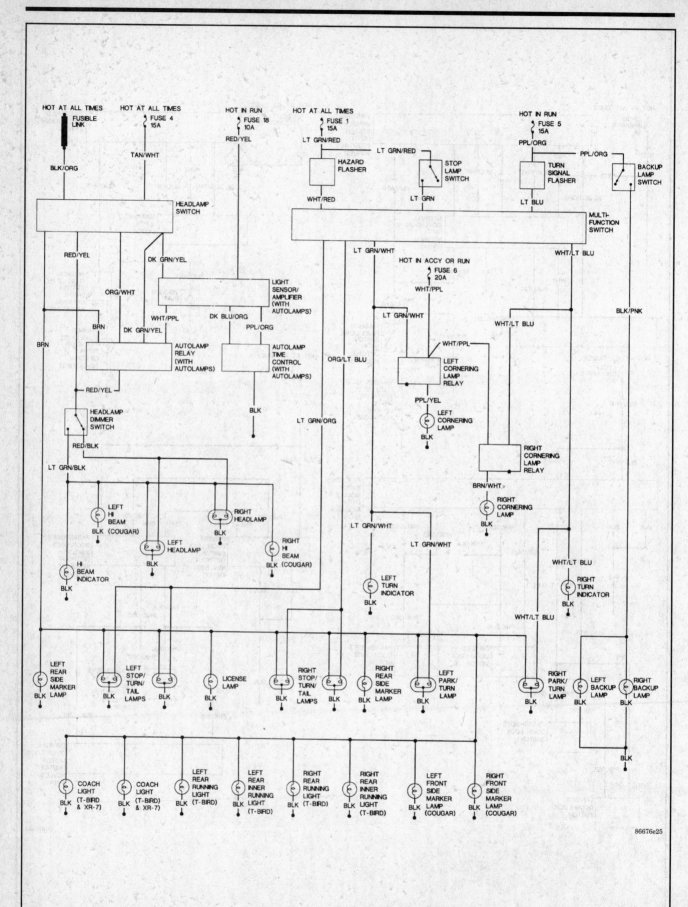

Fig. 145 Chassis electrical schematic continued — 1981 Cougar and Thunderbird

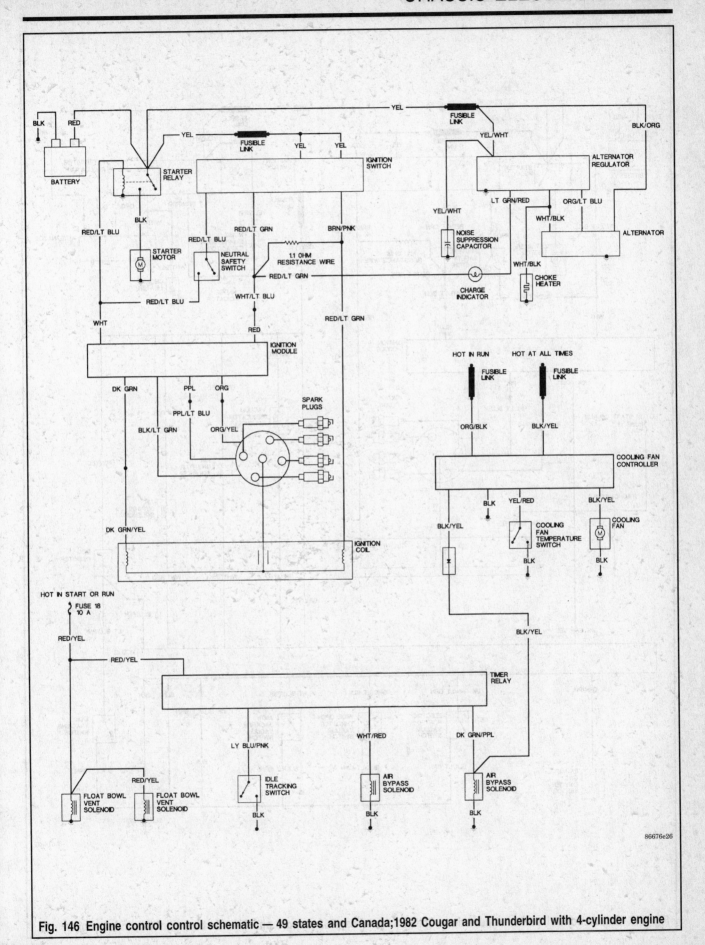

Fig. 146 Engine control control schematic — 49 states and Canada;1982 Cougar and Thunderbird with 4-cylinder engine

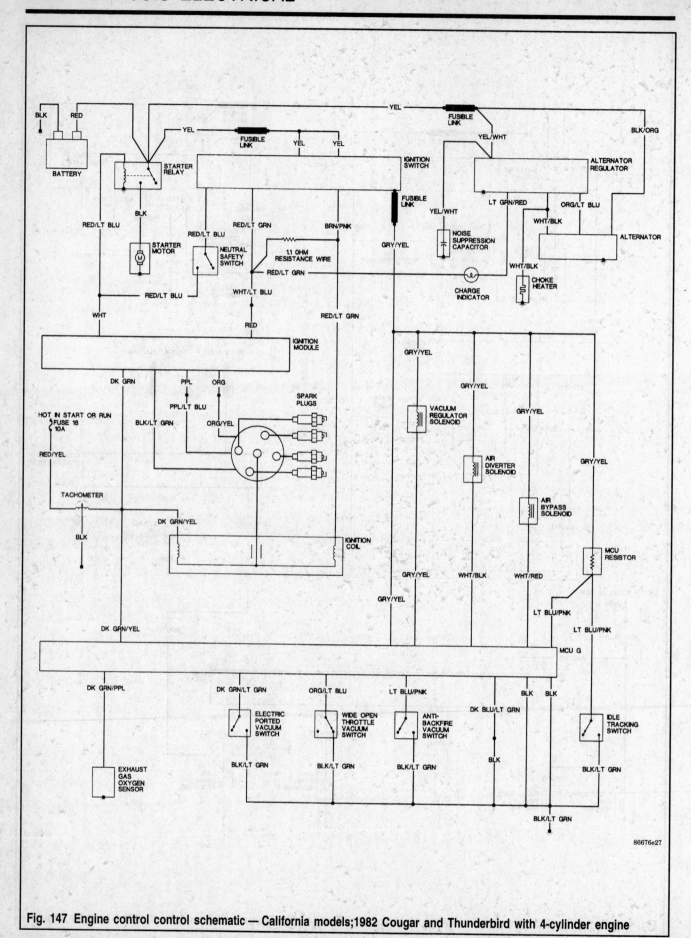

Fig. 147 Engine control control schematic — California models;1982 Cougar and Thunderbird with 4-cylinder engine

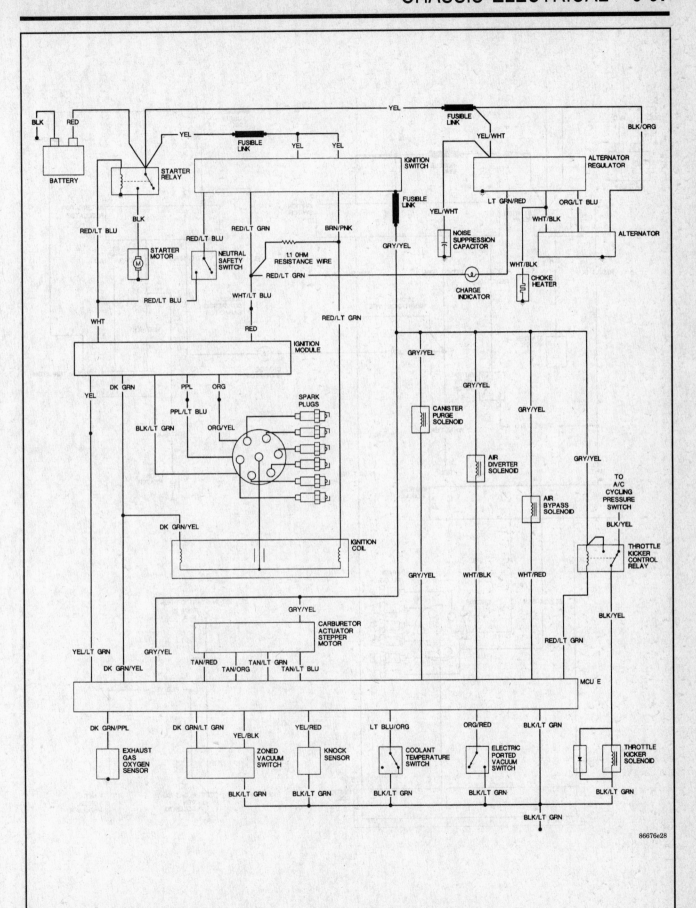

Fig. 148 Engine control control schematic — 1982 Cougar and Thunderbird with V6 engine

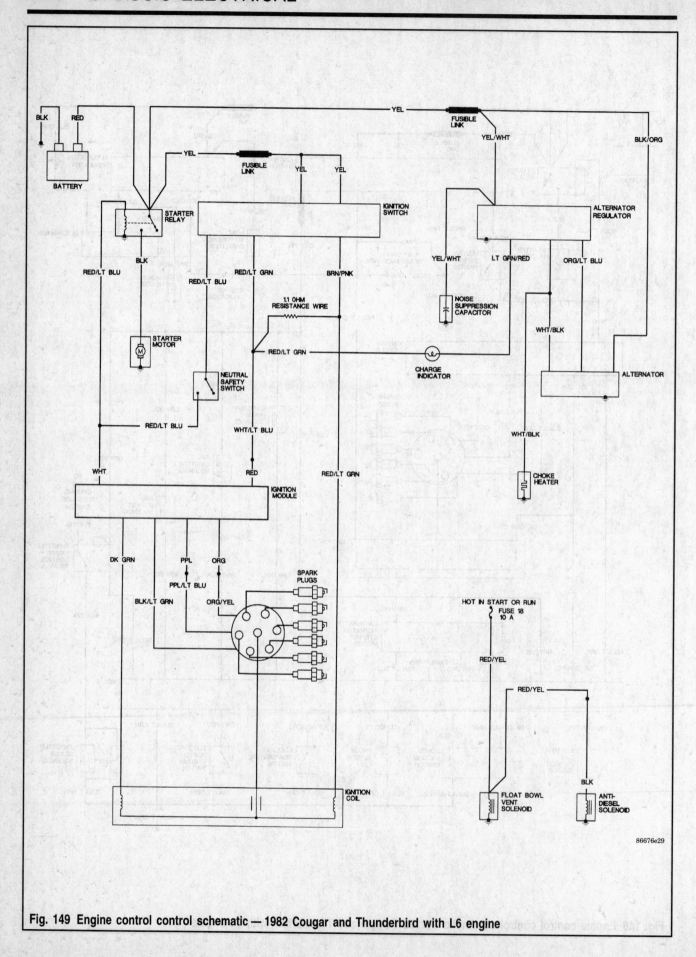

Fig. 149 Engine control control schematic — 1982 Cougar and Thunderbird with L6 engine

86676e29

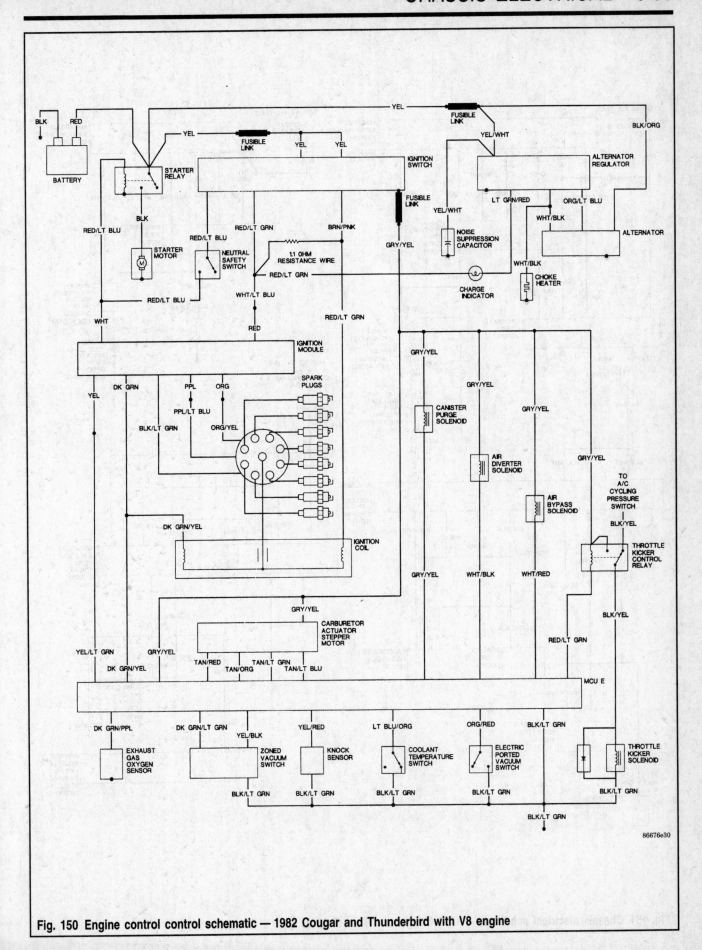

Fig. 150 Engine control control schematic — 1982 Cougar and Thunderbird with V8 engine

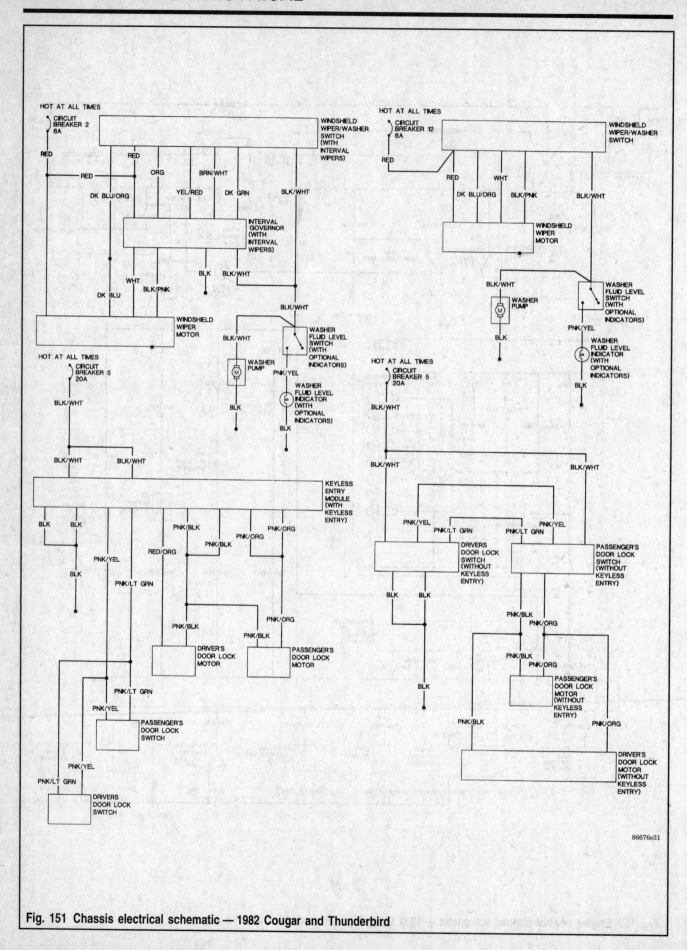

Fig. 151 Chassis electrical schematic — 1982 Cougar and Thunderbird

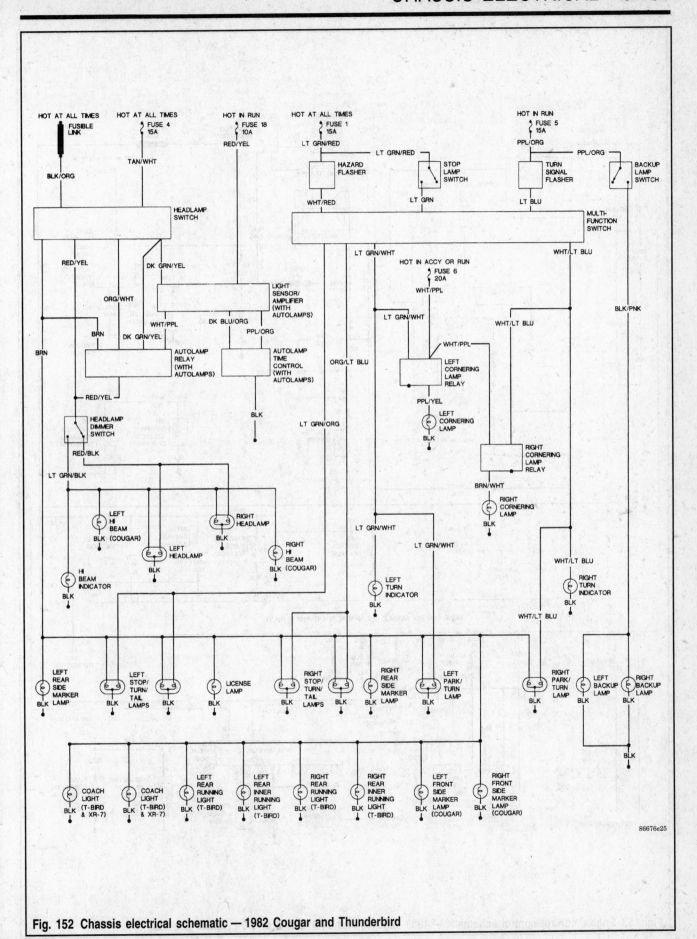

Fig. 152 Chassis electrical schematic — 1982 Cougar and Thunderbird

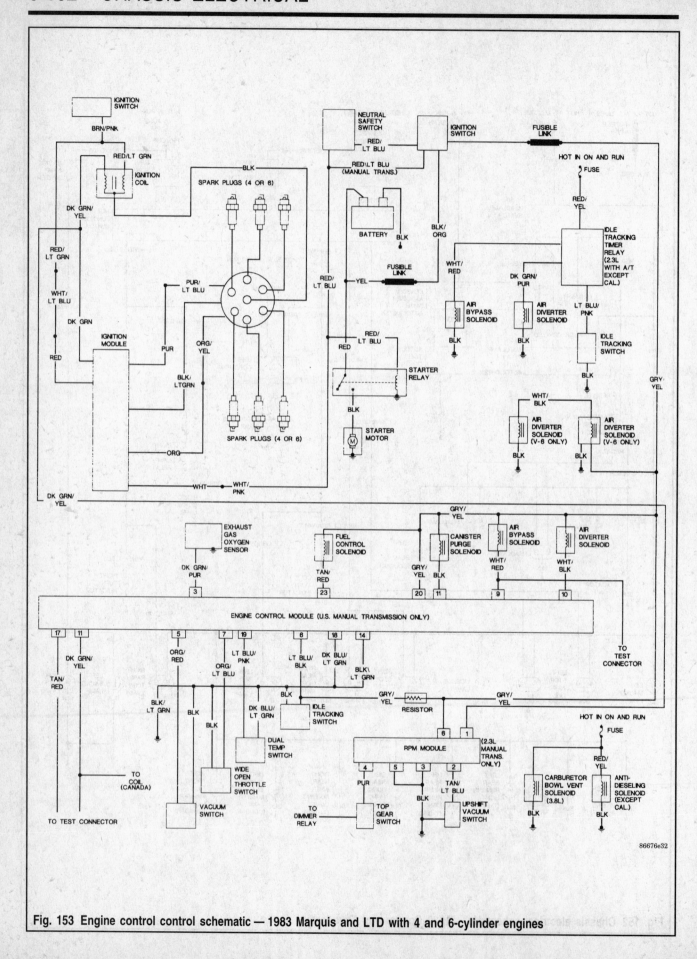

Fig. 153 Engine control control schematic — 1983 Marquis and LTD with 4 and 6-cylinder engines

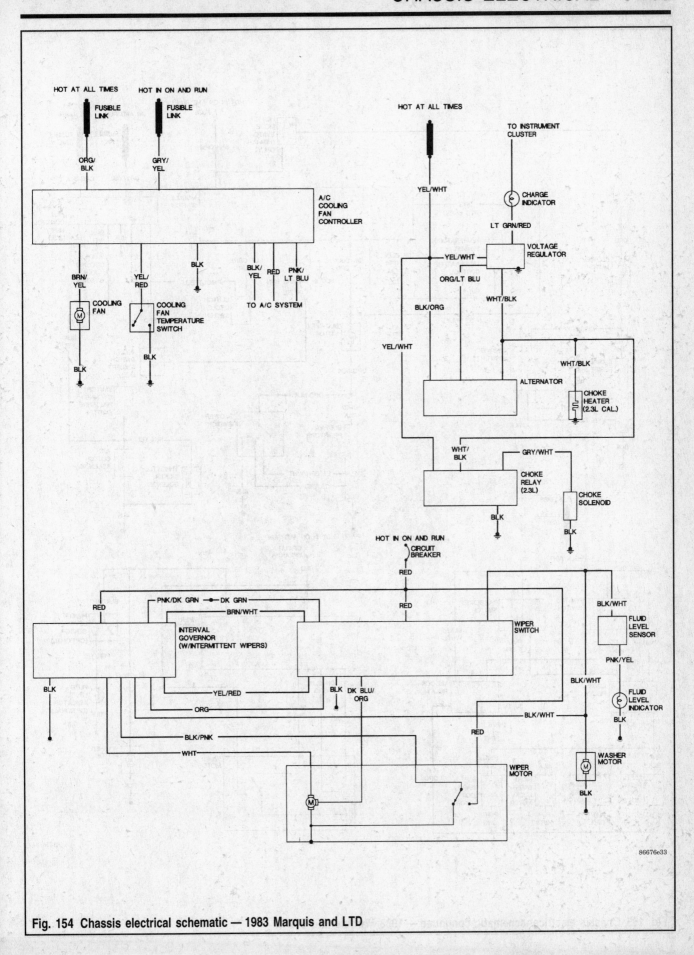

Fig. 154 Chassis electrical schematic — 1983 Marquis and LTD

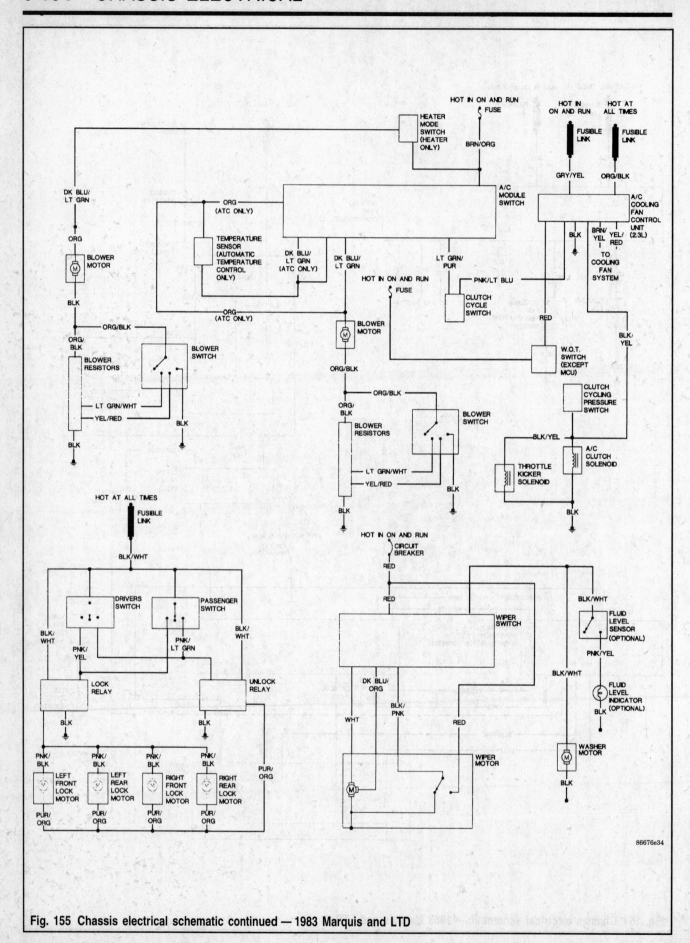

Fig. 155 Chassis electrical schematic continued — 1983 Marquis and LTD

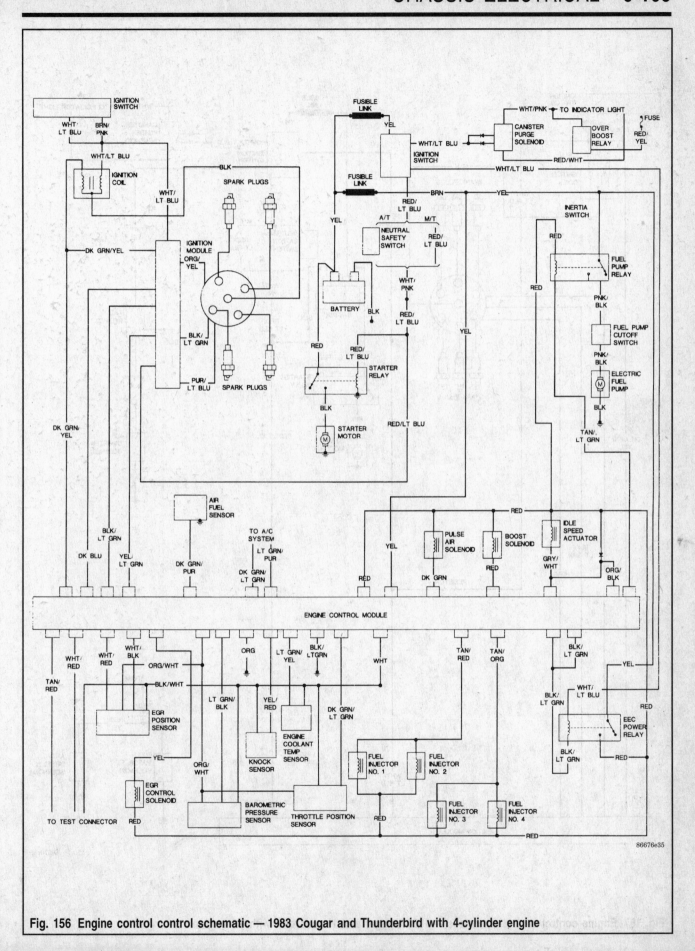

Fig. 156 Engine control control schematic — 1983 Cougar and Thunderbird with 4-cylinder engine

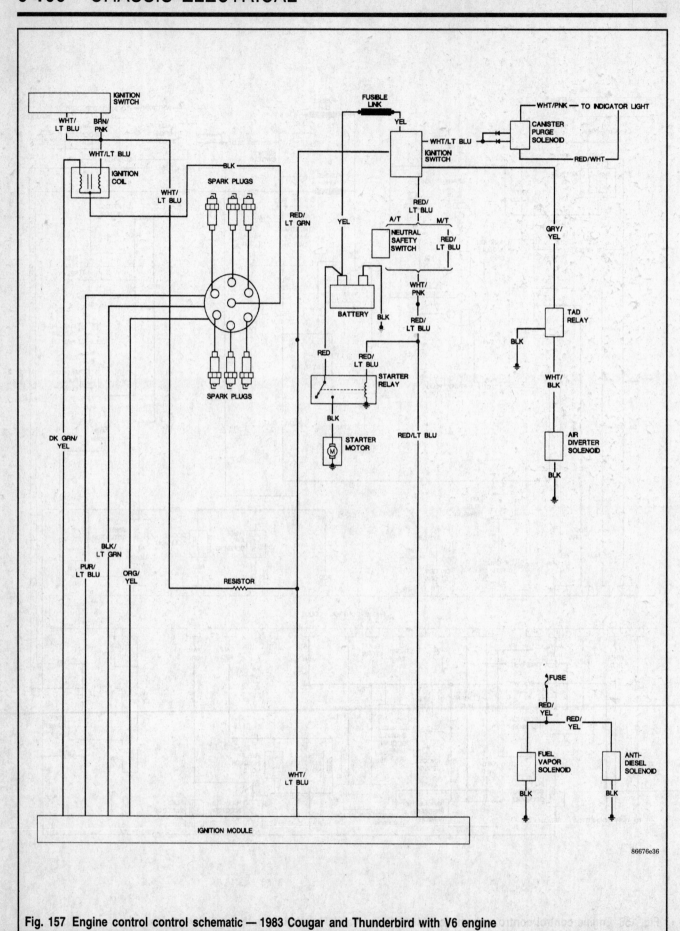

Fig. 157 Engine control control schematic — 1983 Cougar and Thunderbird with V6 engine

86676e36

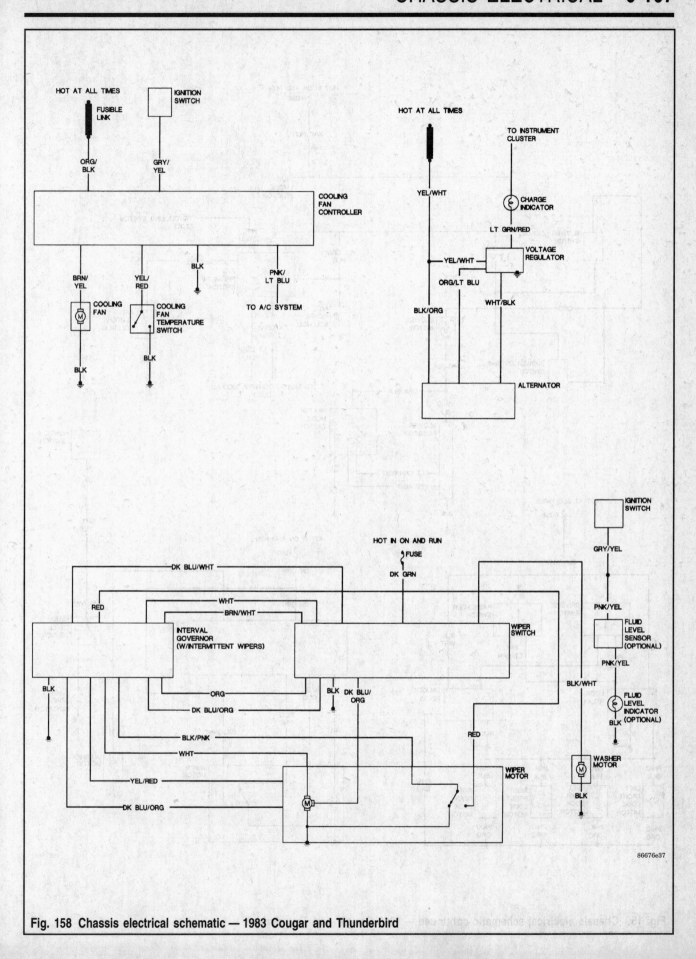

Fig. 158 Chassis electrical schematic — 1983 Cougar and Thunderbird

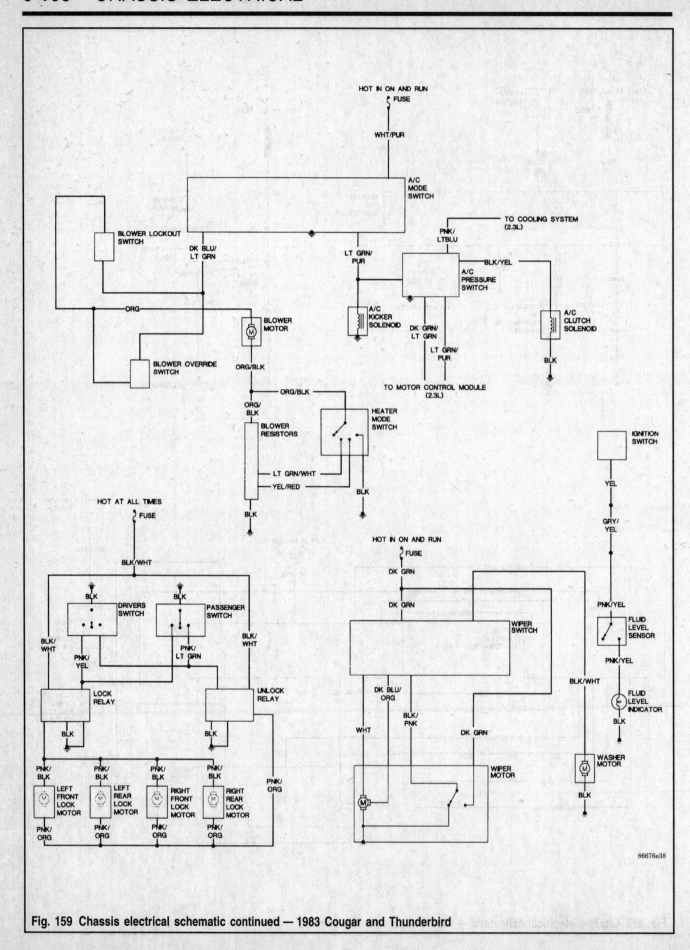

Fig. 159 Chassis electrical schematic continued — 1983 Cougar and Thunderbird

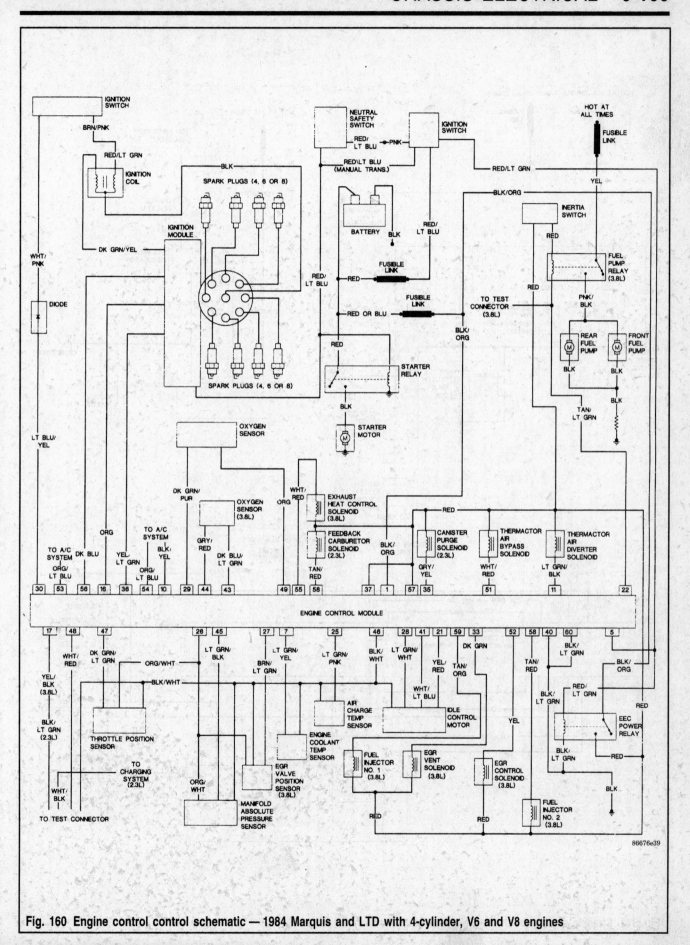

Fig. 160 Engine control control schematic — 1984 Marquis and LTD with 4-cylinder, V6 and V8 engines

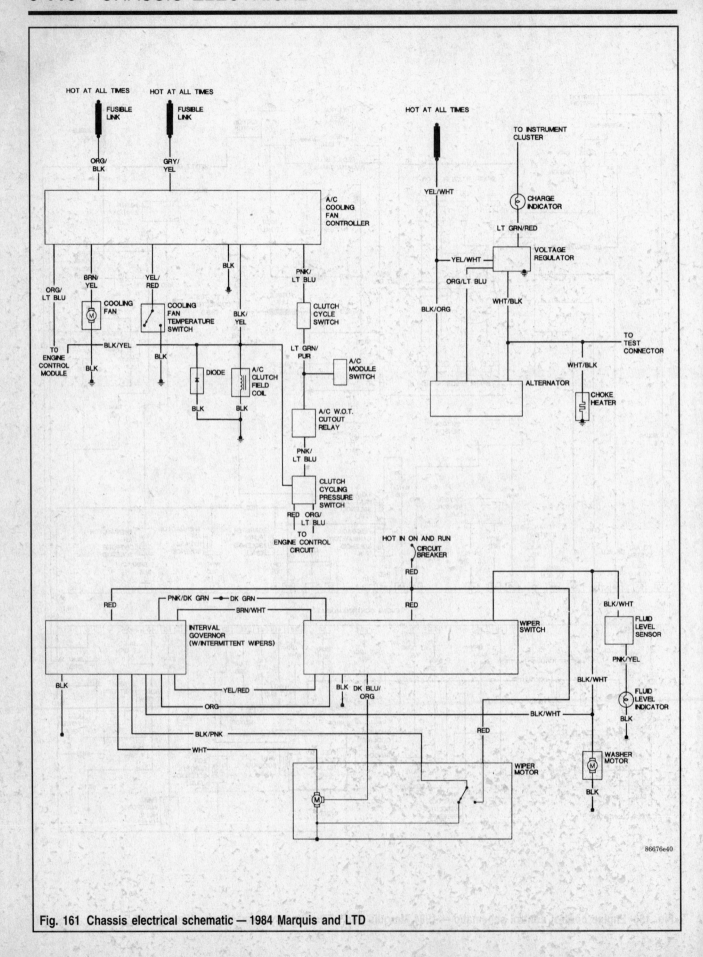

Fig. 161 Chassis electrical schematic — 1984 Marquis and LTD

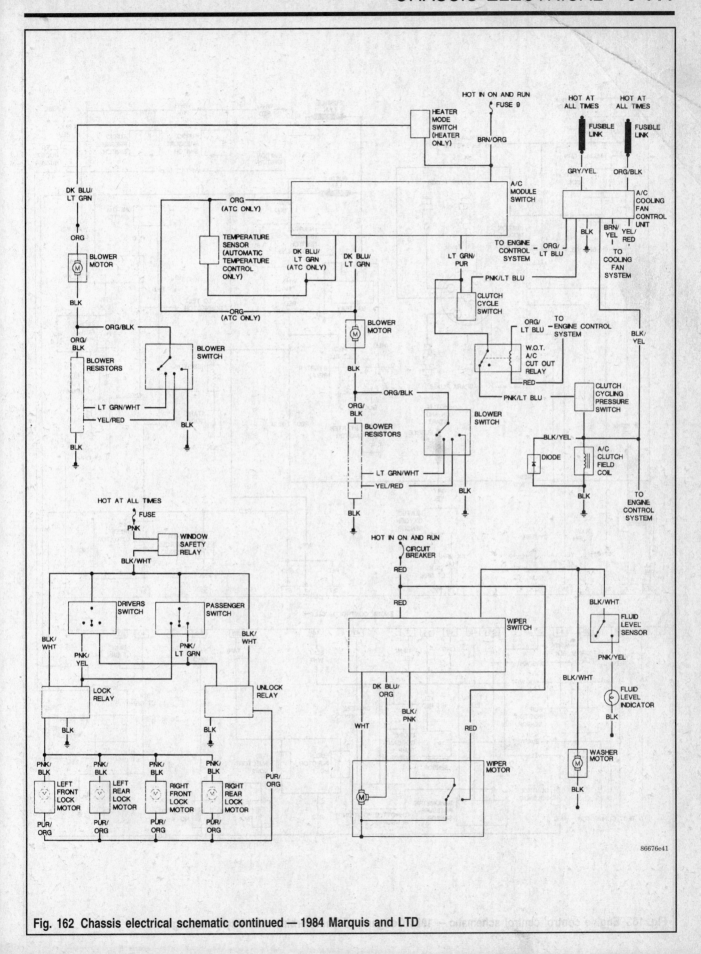

Fig. 162 Chassis electrical schematic continued — 1984 Marquis and LTD

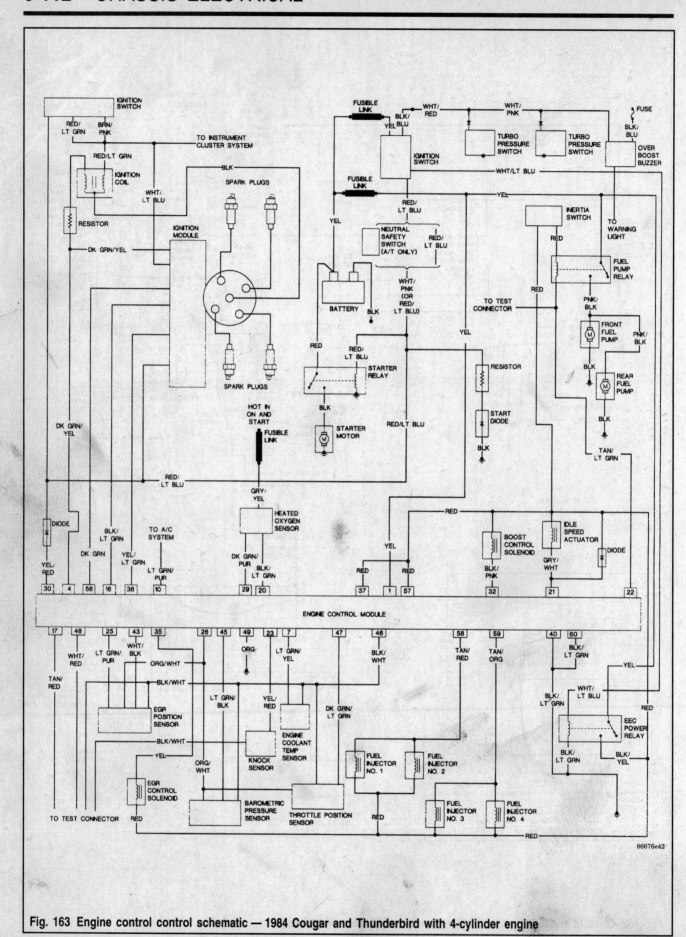

Fig. 163 Engine control control schematic — 1984 Cougar and Thunderbird with 4-cylinder engine

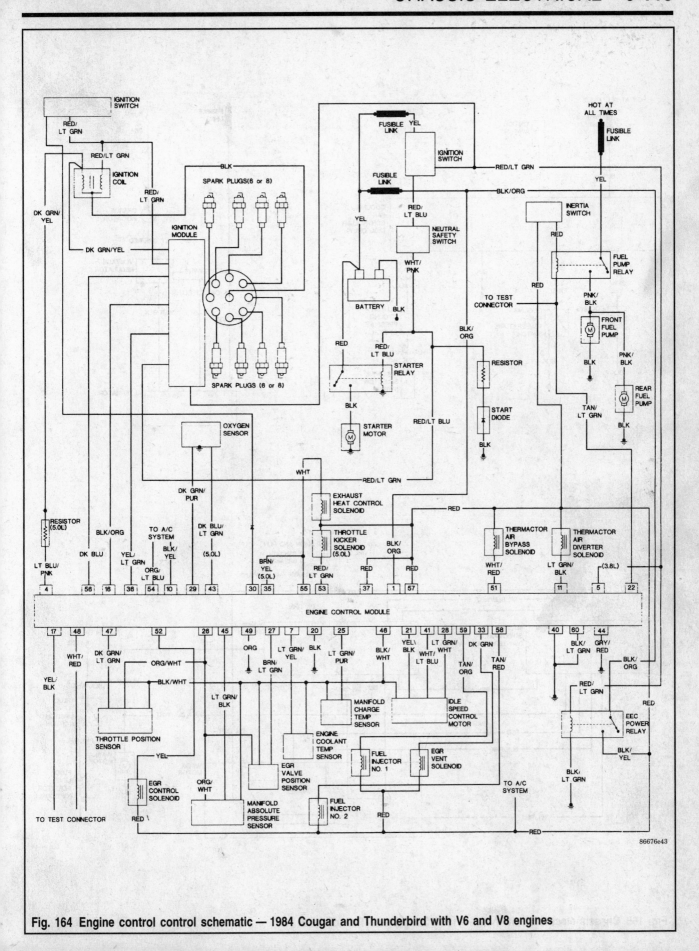

Fig. 164 Engine control control schematic — 1984 Cougar and Thunderbird with V6 and V8 engines

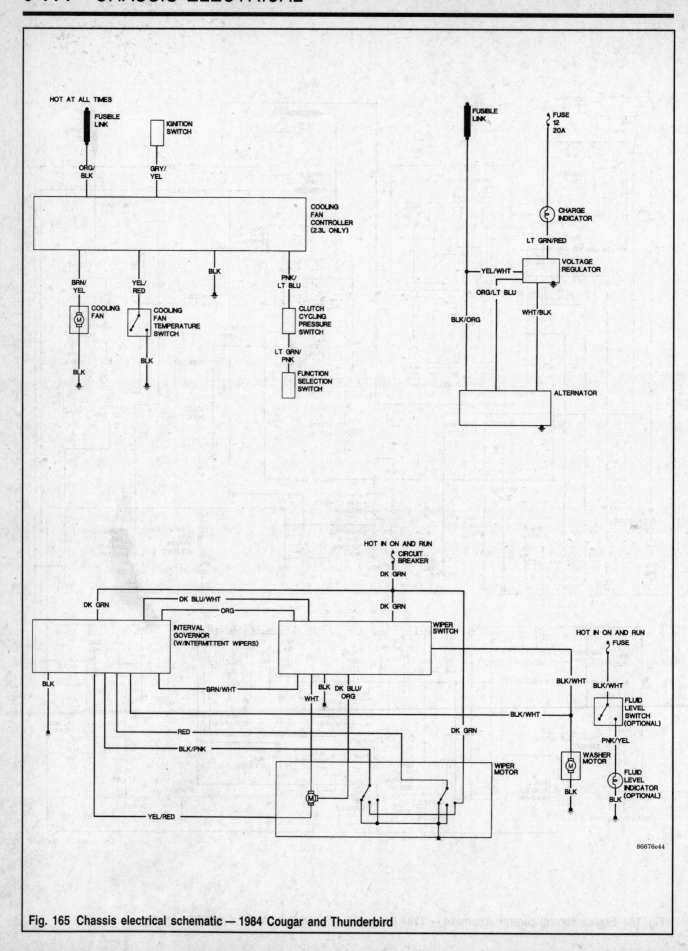

Fig. 165 Chassis electrical schematic — 1984 Cougar and Thunderbird

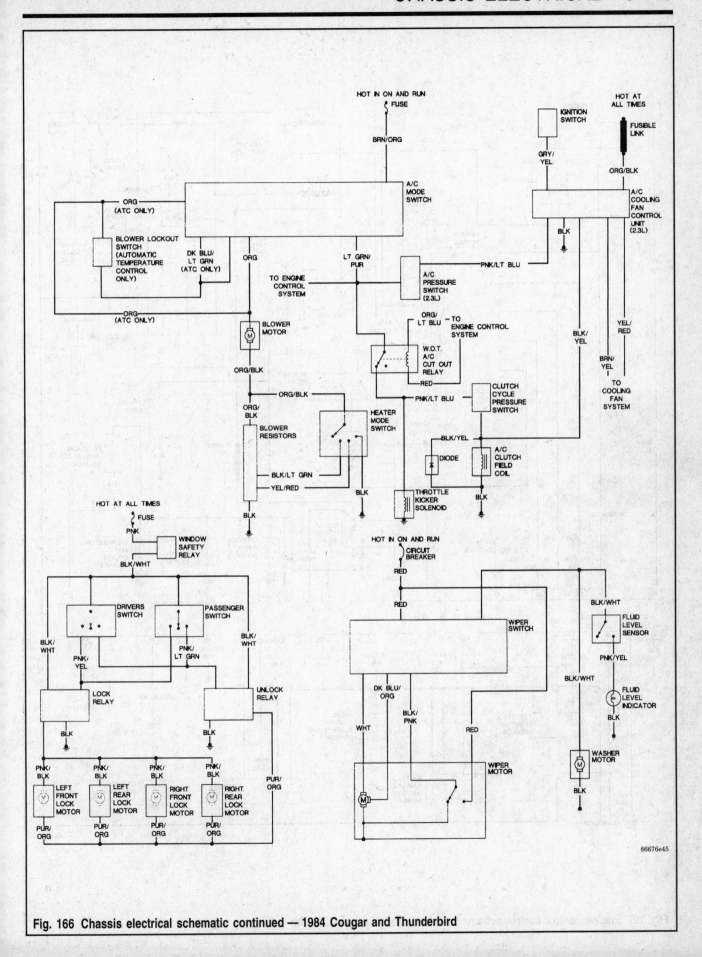

Fig. 166 Chassis electrical schematic continued — 1984 Cougar and Thunderbird

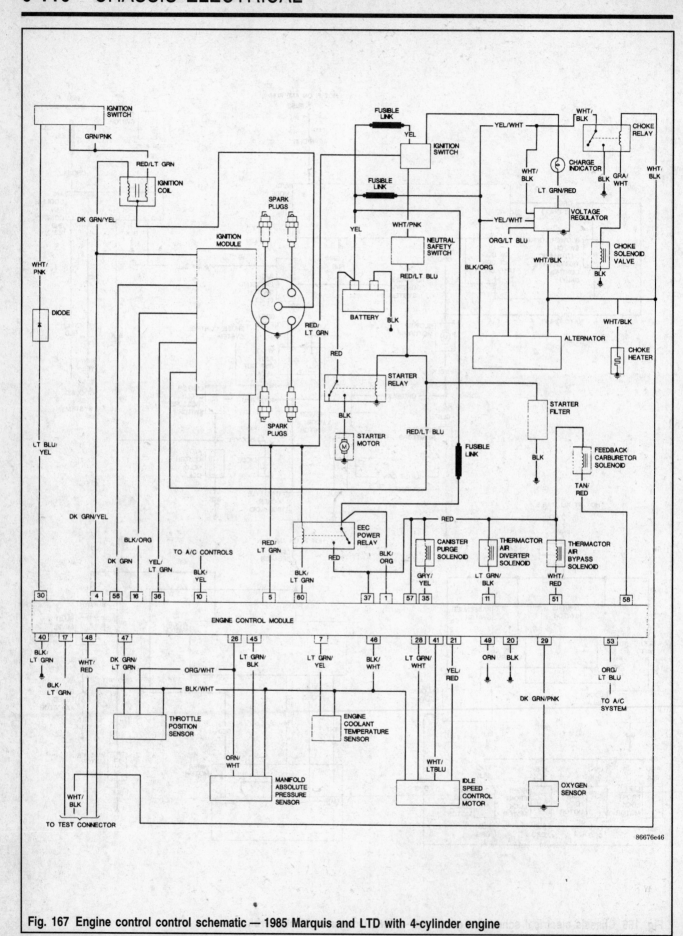

Fig. 167 Engine control control schematic — 1985 Marquis and LTD with 4-cylinder engine

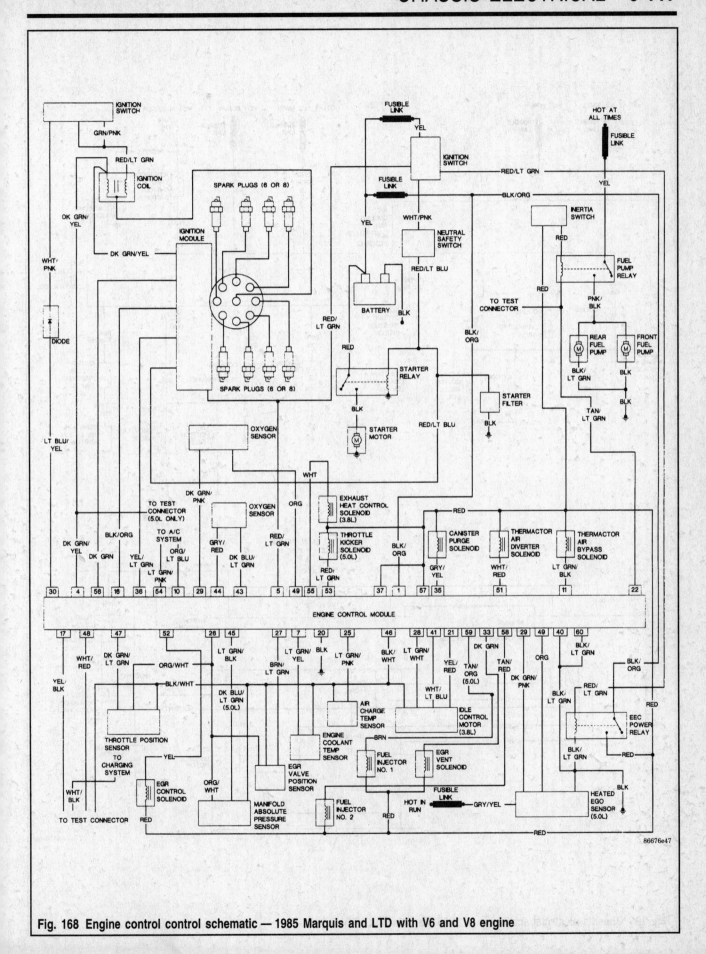

Fig. 168 Engine control control schematic — 1985 Marquis and LTD with V6 and V8 engine

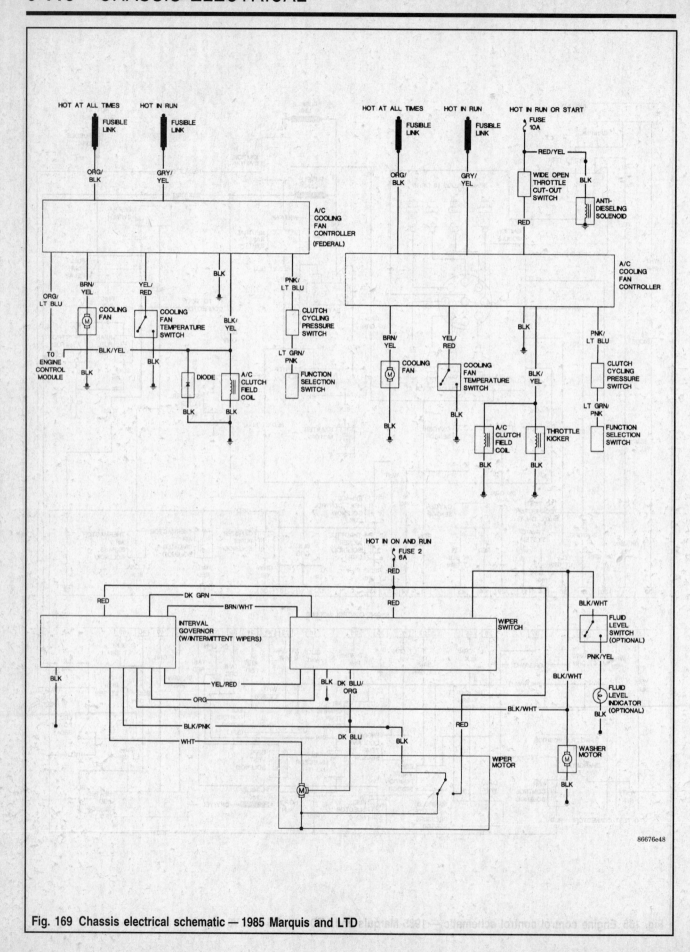

Fig. 169 Chassis electrical schematic — 1985 Marquis and LTD

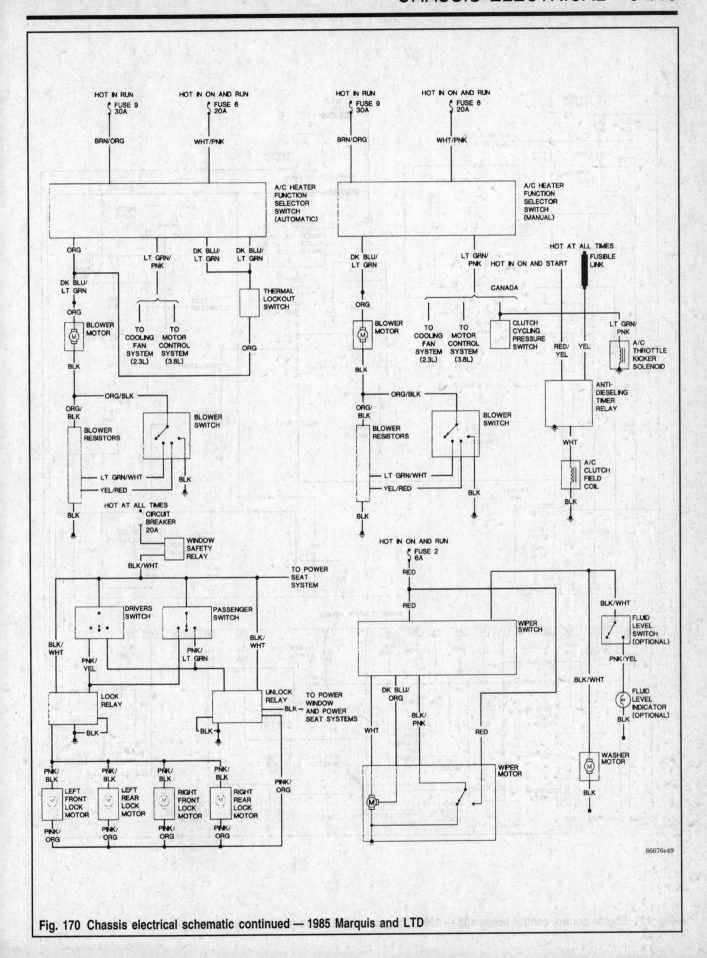

Fig. 170 Chassis electrical schematic continued — 1985 Marquis and LTD

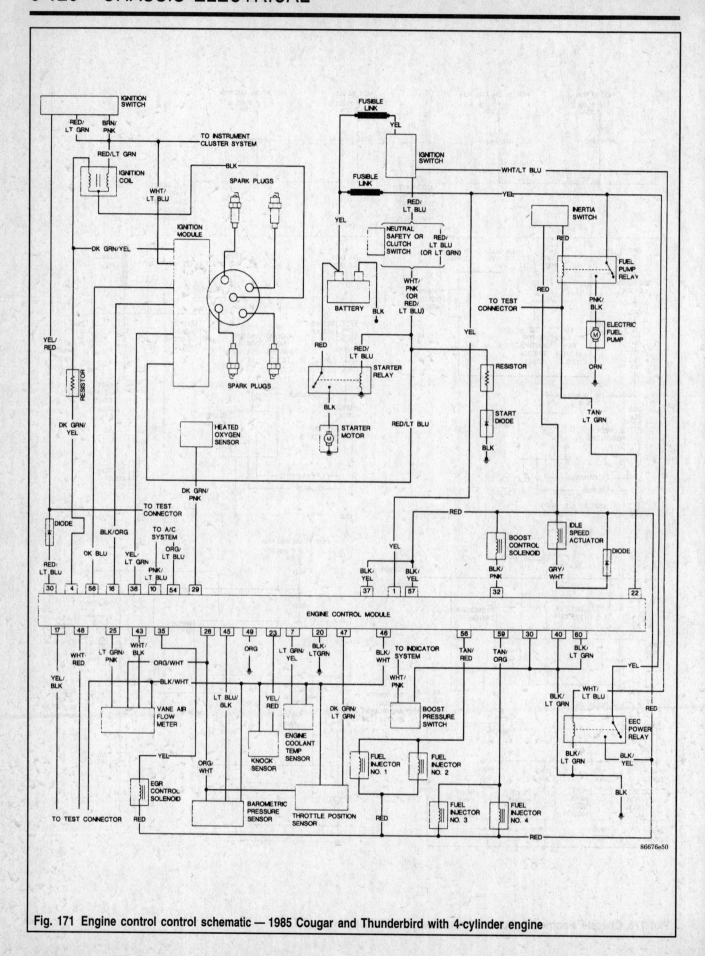

Fig. 171 Engine control control schematic — 1985 Cougar and Thunderbird with 4-cylinder engine

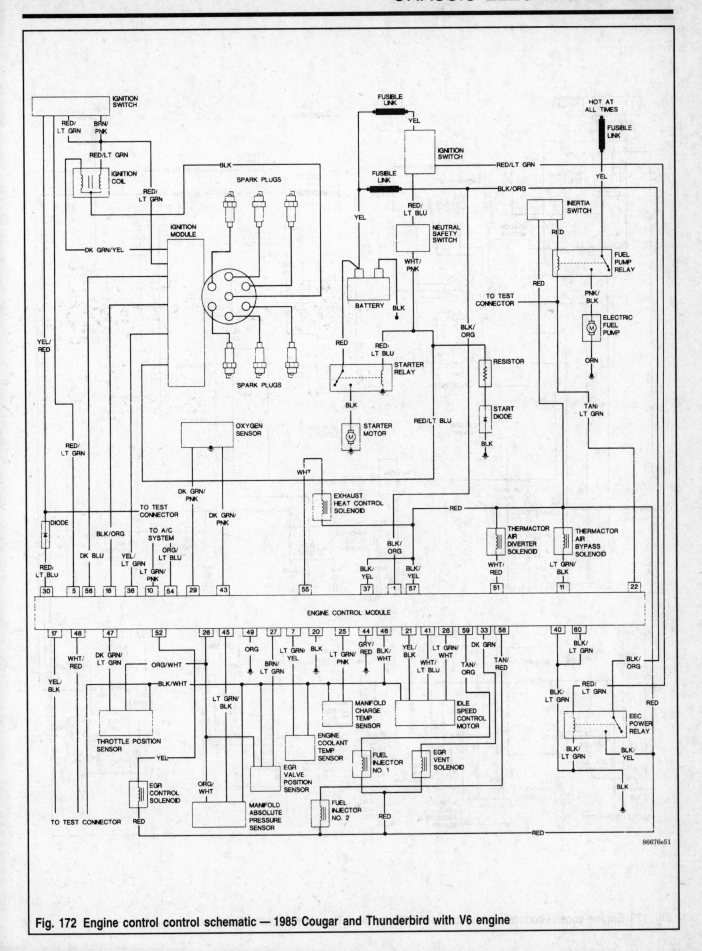

Fig. 172 Engine control control schematic — 1985 Cougar and Thunderbird with V6 engine

86676e51

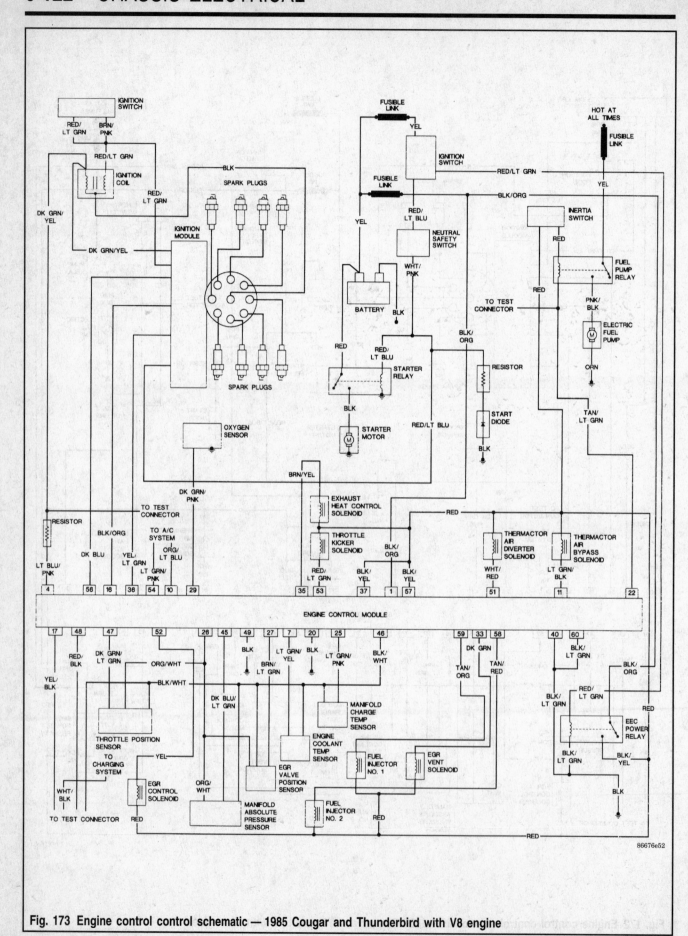

Fig. 173 Engine control control schematic — 1985 Cougar and Thunderbird with V8 engine

86676e52

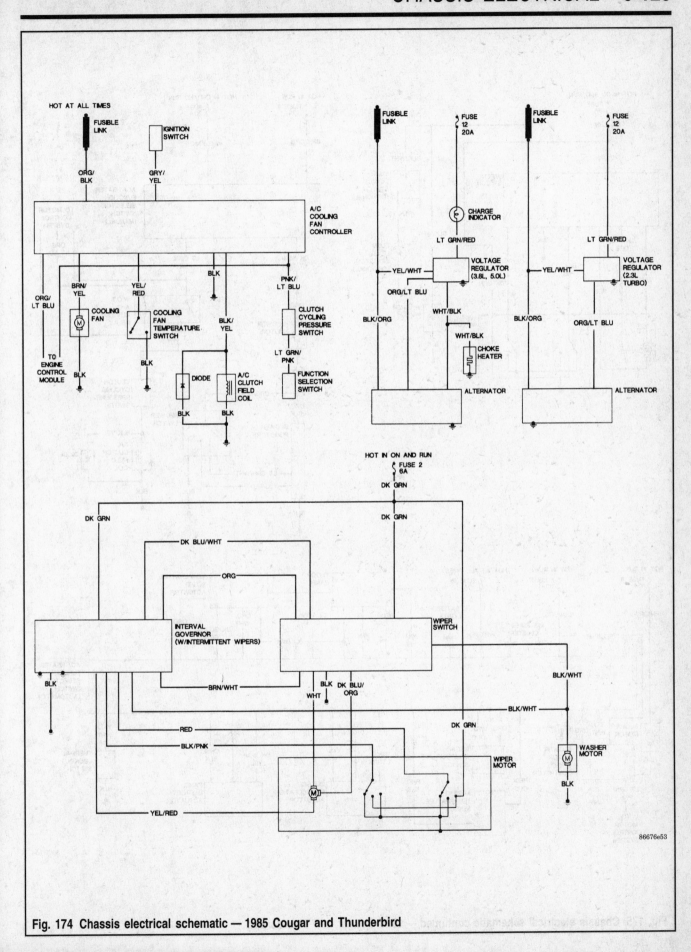

Fig. 174 Chassis electrical schematic — 1985 Cougar and Thunderbird

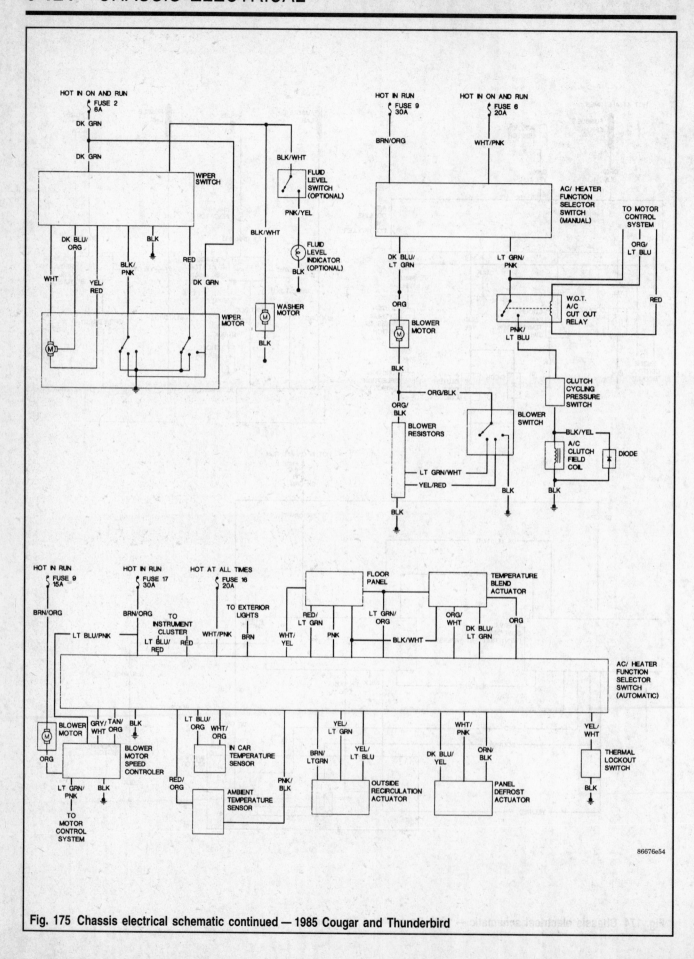

Fig. 175 Chassis electrical schematic continued — 1985 Cougar and Thunderbird

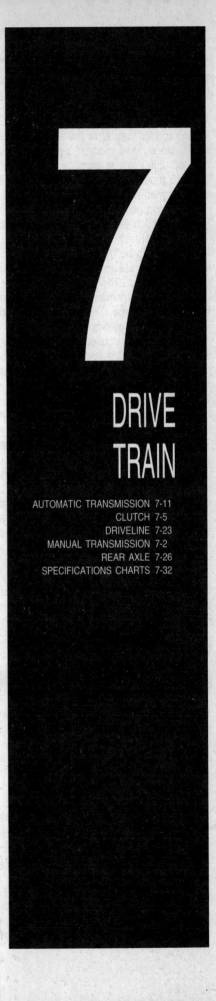

7

DRIVE
TRAIN

MANUAL TRANSMISSION

Because of the way an internal combustion engine breathes, it can produce torque, or twisting force, only within a narrow speed range. Most modern, overhead valve engines must turn at about 2500 rpm to produce their peak torque. By 4500 rpm they are producing so little torque that continued increases in engine speed produce no power increases.

The torque peak on overhead camshaft engines is, generally, much higher, but much narrower.

The manual transmission and clutch are employed to vary the relationship between engine speed and the speed of the wheels so that adequate engine power can be produced under all circumstances. The clutch allows engine torque to be applied to the transmission input shaft gradually, due to mechanical slippage. The car can, consequently, be started smoothly from a full stop.

The transmission changes the ratio between the rotating speeds of the engine and the wheels by the use of gears. 4-speed or 5-speed transmissions are most common. The lower gears allow full engine power to be applied to the rear wheels during acceleration at low speeds.

The transmission contains a mainshaft which passes all the way through the transmission, from the clutch to the driveshaft. This shaft is separated at one point, so that front and rear portions can turn at different speeds.

Power is transmitted by a countershaft in the lower gears and reverse. The gears of the countershaft mesh with gears on the mainshaft, allowing power to be carried from one to the other. All the countershaft gears are integral with that shaft, while several of the mainshaft gears can either rotate independently of the shaft or be locked to it. Shifting from one gear to the next causes one of the gears to be freed from rotating with the shaft and locks another to it. Gears are locked and unlocked by internal dog clutches which slide between the center of the gear and the shaft. The forward gears usually employ synchronizers; friction members which smoothly bring gear and shaft to the same speed before the toothed dog clutches are engaged.

Identification

Several manual transmissions were available over the years. In order to properly identify a particular application, obtain the transmission code from the Vehicle Certification Label and refer to the following list:

2 — Five speed overdrive
4 — Four speed (TREMEC)
5 — Four speed overdrive (1979 only)
5 — Five speed overdrive RAP model (1980-83)
5 — Five speed overdrive (Borg Warner model T5OD) (1984-85)
6 — Four speed (Borg Warner model RAD) (1979-82)
7 — Four speed ET model (1979-85)
7 — Four speed overdrive RUG model (1980-83)

For example, if your transmission code on your Vehicle Certification Label is 2, then the vehicle was originally equipped with a five speed overdrive transmission.

Adjustments

LINKAGE

▶ See Figure 1

3-Speed

1. Place the gearshift lever in the NEUTRAL position.
2. Loosen the two gearshift adjustment nuts on the shift linkage.
3. Insert a 3/16 in. (4.7mm) diameter pin through the 1st and REVERSE lever, the 2nd and 3rd gear shift lever, and the two holes in the lower casing. The pin can be fabricated from 3/16 in. rod bent to an L- shape. The extension that is to be inserted into the levers should be 1 in. (25mm) in length from the elbow.
4. Manipulate the levers so that the alignment tool will move freely through the alignment holes.
5. Tighten the two gearshift rod adjustment nuts.
6. Remove the tool and check linkage operation.

4-Speed

1. Place the gearshift lever in NEUTRAL position, then raise car on a hoist.
2. Insert a 1/4 in. (6mm) diameter rod into the alignment holes of the shift levers.
3. If the holes are not in exact alignment, check for bent connecting rods or loose lever locknuts at the rod ends. Make replacements or repairs, then adjust as follows.
4. Loosen the three rod-to-lever retaining locknuts and move the levers until the 1/4 in. (6mm) gauge rod will enter the alignment holes. Be sure that the transmission shift levers are in NEUTRAL, and the REVERSE shifter lever is in the NEUTRAL detent.
5. Install shift rods and tighten locknuts to 18-23 ft. lbs. (24-31 Nm).

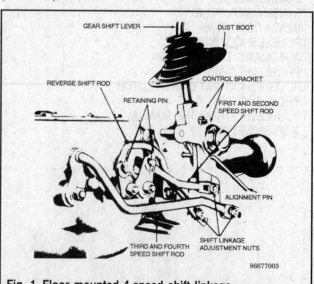

86677003

Fig. 1 Floor mounted 4-speed shift linkage

6. Remove the ¼ in. (6mm) gauge rod.
7. Operate the shift levers to assure correct shifting.
8. Lower the car and road test.

TRANSMISSION LOCK ROD

Some models with floor or console mounted shifters with manual transmissions incorporate a transmission lock rod which prevents the shifter from being moved from the Reverse position when the ignition lock is in the **OFF** position. The lock rod connects the shift tube in the steering column to the transmission reverse lever. The lock rod cannot be properly adjusted until the manual linkage adjustment is correct.

1. With the transmission selector lever in the NEUTRAL position, loosen the lock rod adjustment nut on the transmission REVERSE lever.

2. Insert a 0.180 in. diameter rod (No. 15 drill bit) in the gauge pin hole located in the six o'clock position on the steering column socket casting, directly below the ignition lock.

3. Manipulate the lever until the casting will not move with the pin inserted.

Shift Lever

REMOVAL & INSTALLATION

▶ See Figure 2

1. Place the gear shift lever in the Neutral position.

2. If applicable, remove the attaching screws at the rear of the coin tray and lift to release from the front hold down notch on the boot retainer. Lift the tray over the gear shift lever boot.

3. If equipped with a console tray assembly, use a putty knife to pry up the rear of the cover plate behind the gear shift selector, and remove the screw securing the tray assembly to the rear bracket. Push the tray assembly forward to disengage from the front bracket, and remove the tray assembly.

4. If equipped with a floor console (rather than a console tray assembly), pry up the front of the cover plate, then slide the plate forward and lift over the gear shift lever boot. Remove the screws securing the finish panel to the console and remove the finish panel.

5. Remove the capscrews attaching the boot to the floor pan and move the boot upward, out of the way.

6. Remove the lever attaching bolts.

7. Remove the lever and boot assembly from the extension housing.

8. Remove the gearshift knob and locknut and slide the boot off the lever.

9. Installation is the reverse of removal.

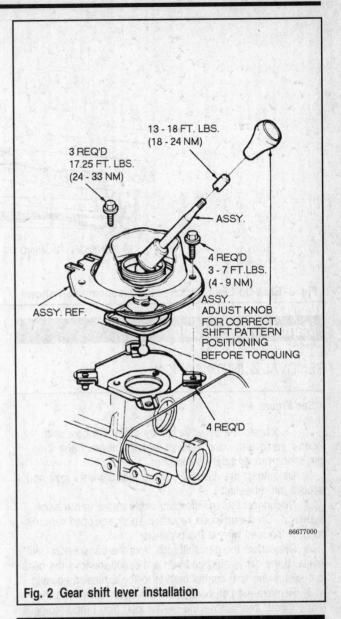

Fig. 2 Gear shift lever installation

13 - 18 FT. LBS.
(18 - 24 NM)

3 REQ'D
17.25 FT. LBS.
(24 - 33 NM)

ASSY.

4 REQ'D
3 - 7 FT.LBS.
(4 - 9 NM)

ASSY. REF.

ASSY.
ADJUST KNOB
FOR CORRECT
SHIFT PATTERN
POSITIONING
BEFORE TORQUING

4 REQ'D

86677000

Back-Up Light switch

REMOVAL & INSTALLATION

▶ See Figure 3

➡ **It is possible that a small amount of transmission fluid may leak out while removing and installing the back-up switch. Therefore before removing the switch, place a suitable container below the switch to catch any fluid which may spill out.**

1. Place the shift lever in NEUTRAL.
2. Raise and support the car on jackstands.
3. Unplug the electrical connector at the switch.
4. Unscrew the switch from the transmission extension housing.
5. Screw the new switch into place and tighten it to 60 inch lbs. (7 Nm).
6. Connect the wiring.

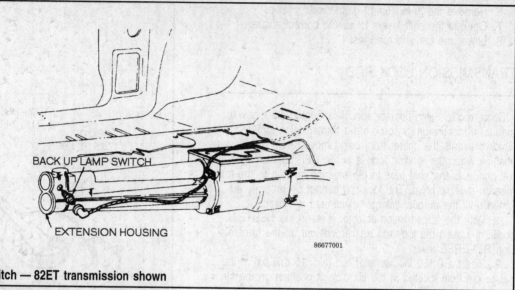

BACK UP LAMP SWITCH

EXTENSION HOUSING

86677001

Fig. 3 Back-Up Light Switch — 82ET transmission shown

Manual Transmission

REMOVAL & INSTALLATION

▶ See Figure 4

1. Disconnect the negative battery cable. On floor shift models, remove the boot retainer and shift lever. Raise the car, taking proper safety precautions.

2. Disconnect the driveshaft at the rear universal joint and remove the driveshaft.

3. Disconnect the speedometer cable at the transmission extension. On transmission regulated spark equipped cars, disconnect the lead wire at the connector.

4. Disconnect the gearshift rods from the transmission shift levers. If the car is equipped with a 4-speed, remove the bolts that secure the shift control bracket to the extension housing.

5. Remove the bolt holding the extension housing to the rear support, and remove the muffler inlet pipe bracket-to-housing bolt.

6. Remove the two rear support bracket insulator nuts from the underside of the crossmember. Remove the crossmember.

7. Place a jack (equipped with a protective piece of wood) under the rear of the engine oil pan. Raise the engine slightly.

8. Remove the transmission-to-flywheel housing bolts.

➡On 7.0L engines, the upper left hand transmission attaching bolt is a seal bolt. Carefully note its position so that it may be reinstalled in its original position.

9. Slide the transmission back and out of the car.
To install:

10. Start the transmission extension housing up and over the rear support. After moving the transmission back just far enough for the pilot shaft to clear the clutch housing, move it upward into position onto the transmission guide studs.

11. Slide the transmission forward and into place against the flywheel housing.

12. Remove the guide studs and tighten the transmission to flywheel bolts to 37-42 ft. lbs. (48-55 Nm).

13. Position the crossmember to the frame and install the attaching bolts. Slowly lower the engine onto the crossmember.

14. Install the insulator-to-crossmember nuts. Tighten the nuts to 30-50 ft. lbs. (39-65 Nm).

15. Connect the gear shaft rods and the speedometer cable. On cars with transmission regulated spark, connect the lead wires at the plug connector. On floor shift models, install the shift lever and boot.

16. Connect the driveshaft.

17. Check the fluid level and add if needed. Road test the vehicle, checking for proper operation.

CLUTCH

▶ **See Figures 4, 5 and 6**

The purpose of the clutch is to disconnect and connect engine power from the transmission. A car at rest requires a lot of engine torque to get all that weight moving. An internal combustion engine does not develop a high starting torque (unlike steam engines), so it must be allowed to operate without any load until it builds up enough torque to move the car. Torque increases with engine rpm. The clutch allows the engine to build up torque by physically disconnecting the engine from the transmission, relieving the engine of any load or resistance. The transfer of engine power to the transmission (the load) must be smooth and gradual; if it weren't, drive line components would wear out or break quickly. This gradual power transfer is made possible by gradually releasing the clutch pedal. The clutch disc and pressure plate are the connecting link between the engine and transmission. When the clutch pedal is released, the disc and plate contact each other (clutch engagement), physically joining the engine and trans-

mission. When the pedal is pushed in, the disc and plate separate (the clutch is disengaged), disconnecting the engine from the transmission.

The clutch assembly consists of the flywheel, the clutch disc, the clutch pressure plate, the throwout bearing and fork, the actuating linkage and the pedal. The flywheel and clutch pressure plate (driving members) are connected to the engine crankshaft and rotate with it. The clutch disc is located between the flywheel and pressure plate, and splined to the transmission shaft. A driving member is one that is attached to the engine and transfers engine power to a driven member (clutch disc) on the transmission shaft. A driving member (pressure plate) rotates (drives) a driven member (clutch disc) on contact and, in so doing, turns the transmission shaft. There is a circular diaphragm spring within the pressure plate cover (transmission side). In a relaxed state (when the clutch pedal is fully released), this spring is convex; that is, it is dished outward toward the transmission. Pushing in the clutch

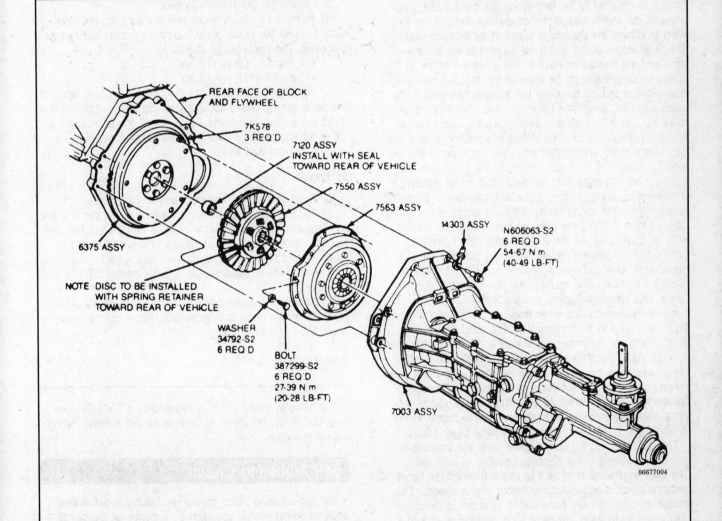

REAR FACE OF BLOCK
AND FLYWHEEL

7K578
3 REQ'D

7120 ASSY
INSTALL WITH SEAL
TOWARD REAR OF VEHICLE

7550 ASSY

7563 ASSY

14303 ASSY

N606063-S2
6 REQ D
54-67 N m
(40-49 LB-FT)

6375 ASSY

NOTE DISC TO BE INSTALLED
WITH SPRING RETAINER
TOWARD REAR OF VEHICLE

WASHER
34792-S2
6 REQ D

BOLT
387299-S2
6 REQ'D
27-39 N m
(20-28 LB-FT)

7003 ASSY

86677004

Fig. 4 Manual transmission and clutch assembly

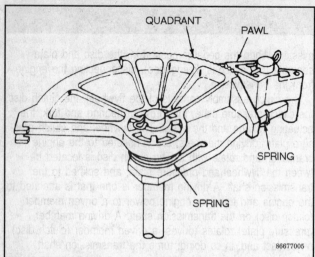

Fig. 5 Clutch components — 1971-73 manual transmission

pedal actuates an attached linkage rod. Connected to the other end of this rod is the throwout bearing fork. The throwout bearing is attached to the fork. When the clutch pedal is depressed, the clutch linkage pushes the fork and bearing forward to contact the diaphragm spring of the pressure plate. The outer edges of the spring are secured to the pressure plate and are pivoted on rings so that when the center of the spring is compressed by the throwout bearing, the outer edges bow outward and, by so doing, pull the pressure plate in the same direction, away from the clutch disc. This action separates the disc from the plate, disengaging the clutch and allowing the transmission to be shifted into another gear. A coil type clutch return spring attached to the clutch pedal arm permits full release of the pedal. Releasing the pedal pulls the throwout bearing away from the diaphragm spring resulting in a reversal of spring position. As bearing pressure is gradually released from the spring center, the outer edges of the spring bow outward, pushing the pressure plate into closer contact with the clutch disc. As the disc and plate move closer together, friction between the two increases and slippage is reduced until, when full spring pressure is applied (by fully releasing the pedal), The speed of the disc and plate are the same. This stops all slipping, creating a direct connection between the plate and disc which results in the transfer of power from the engine to the transmission. The clutch disc is now rotating with the pressure plate at engine speed and, because it is splined to the transmission shaft, the shaft now turns at the same engine speed. As mentioned earlier, the clutch pedal return spring permits full release of the pedal and reduces linkage slack due to wear. As the linkage wears, clutch free-pedal travel will increase and free-travel will decrease as the clutch wears. Free-travel is actually throwout bearing lash.

The diaphragm spring type clutches used are available in two different designs: flat diaphragm springs or bent spring. The bent fingers are bent back to create a centrifugal boost ensuring quick re-engagement at higher engine speeds. This design enables pressure plate load to increase as the clutch disc wears and makes low pedal effort possible even with a heavy duty clutch. The throwout bearing used with the bent finger design is 1¼ in. (31.8mm) long and is shorter than the bearing used with the flat finger design. These bearings are

not interchangeable. If the longer bearing is used with the bent finger clutch, free-pedal travel will not exist. This results in clutch slippage and rapid wear.

The transmission varies the gear ratio between the engine and rear wheels. It can be shifted to change engine speed as driving conditions and loads change. The transmission allows disengaging and reversing power from the engine to the wheels.

Adjustment

PEDAL FREE TRAVEL

➡ Vehicles produced until 1980 require a clutch pedal height adjustment. Vehicles produced in 1981 and later are equipped with self-adjusting clutch assemblies.

Except L6 Engine

1. Raise and support the front end on jackstands.
2. Remove the dust shield.
3. Loosen the clutch cable locknut.
4. To raise the clutch pedal, turn the adjusting nut clockwise; to lower the clutch pedal, turn the adjusting nut counterclockwise. The pedal height should be:
   - 4-cylinder: 5.3 in. (13cm)
   - 8-cylinder: 6.5 in. (16cm)
5. Tighten the locknut. When the pedal is properly adjusted, the pedal can be raised about 2¾ in. (8cm) on vehicles with a 4-cylinder engine, and about 1½ in. (4cm) on vehicles with a V6 or V8 engine, before reaching the pedal stop.
6. Install the dust shield.

L6 Engine

1. Raise and support the front end on jackstands.
2. Pull the clutch cable toward the front of the car until the adjusting nut can be rotated. In order to free the nut from the rubber insulator, it may be necessary to block the clutch release forward so the clutch is partially disengaged.
3. Rotate the adjusting nut to obtain a pedal height of 5.3 in. (13cm).
4. Depress the pedal a few times and recheck the adjustment. When the pedal is properly adjusted, it can be raised about 2¾ in. (8cm) to reach the pedal stop.

FREE-PLAY

The free-play in the clutch is adjusted by a built-in mechanism that allows the clutch controls to be self-adjusted during normal operation.

Self-Adjusting Clutch

The self-adjusting clutch control mechanism is automatically adjusted during normal operation by a device on the clutch pedal. The system consists of a spring-loaded gear quadrant, a spring-loaded pawl, and a clutch cable which is spring-loaded to preload the clutch release lever bearing to compensate for movement of the release lever, as the clutch disc

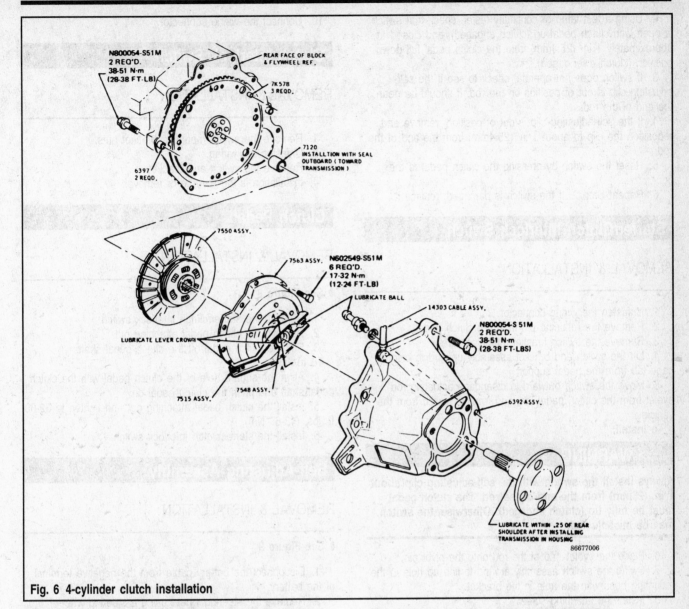

Fig. 6 4-cylinder clutch installation

wears. The spring-loaded pawl, located at the top of the clutch pedal, engages the gear quadrant when the clutch pedal is depressed, and pulls the cable through its continuously adjusted stroke. Clutch cable adjustments are not required because of this feature.

INSPECTION

The self-adjusting feature should be checked every 5000 miles (8000 km). This is accomplished by insuring that the clutch pedal travels to the top of its upward position. Grasp the clutch pedal with your hand or put your foot under the clutch pedal, pull up on the pedal until it stops. Very little effort is required, usually about 10 lbs. (4 kg.) During the application of upward pressure, a click may be heard, which means an adjustment was necessary and has been accomplished.

STARTER/CLUTCH INTERLOCK SWITCH

The starter/clutch switch is designed to prevent starting the engine unless the clutch pedal is fully depressed. The switch is connected between the ignition switch and the starter motor relay coil and maintains an open circuit with the clutch pedal up (clutch engaged).

The switch is designed to self-adjust automatically the first time the clutch pedal is pressed to the floor. The self-adjuster consists of a two-piece clip snapped together over a serrated rod. When the plunger or rod is extended, the clip bottoms out on the switch body and allows the rod to ratchet over the serrations to a position determined by the clutch pedal travel limit. In this way, the switch is set to close the starter circuit when the clutch is pressed all the way to the floor (clutch disengaged).

Testing Continuity
▶ **See Figure 7**

1. Unfasten the in-line wiring connector at jumper harness.

2. Using a test lamp or continuity tester, check that switch is open with clutch pedal up (clutch engaged), and closed at approximately 1 in. (25.4mm) from the clutch pedal full down position (clutch disengaged).

3. If switch does not operate, check to see if the self-adjusting clip is out of position on the rod. It should be near the end of the rod.

4. If the self-adjusting clip is out of position, remove and reposition the clip to about 1 in. (25.4mm) from the end of the rod.

5. Reset the switch by pressing the clutch pedal to the floor.

6. Repeat Step 2. If the switch is damaged, replace it.

Starter/Clutch Interlock Switch

REMOVAL & INSTALLATION

1. Unfasten the wiring connector.
2. Remove the retaining pin from the clutch pedal.
3. Remove the switch bracket attaching screw.
4. Lift the switch and bracket assembly upward to disengage tab from the pedal support.
5. Move the switch outward to disengage actuating rod eyelet from the clutch pedal pin, and remove switch from the vehicle.
To install:

✳✳WARNING

Always install the switch with the self-adjusting clip about 1 in. (25mm) from the end of the rod. The clutch pedal must be fully up (clutch engaged). Otherwise, the switch may be misadjusted.

6. Place the eyelet end of the rod onto the pivot pin.
7. Swing the switch assembly around to line up hole in the mounting boss with the hole in the bracket.
8. Install the attaching screw.
9. Replace the retaining pin in the pivot pin.

10. Connect the wiring connector.

Clutch Interlock Switch

REMOVAL & INSTALLATION

1. Remove the switch mounting bracket nuts.
2. Unfasten the wiring.
3. Remove the switch and bracket.
4. Installation is the reverse of removal.

Clutch Pedal

REMOVAL & INSTALLATION

▶ See Figure 8

1. Remove the starter/clutch interlock switch.
2. Remove the clutch pedal attaching nut.
3. Pull the clutch pedal off the clutch pedal shaft.
To install:
4. Align the square hole of the clutch pedal with the clutch pedal shaft and push the clutch pedal on.
5. Install the clutch pedal attaching nut and tighten to 32-50 ft. lbs. (43-67 Nm).
6. Install the starter/clutch interlock switch.

Self-Adjusting Assembly

REMOVAL & INSTALLATION

▶ See Figure 9

1. Disconnect the battery cable from the negative terminal of the battery.
2. Remove the steering wheel using a steering wheel puller, Tool T67L-3600-A or equivalent.

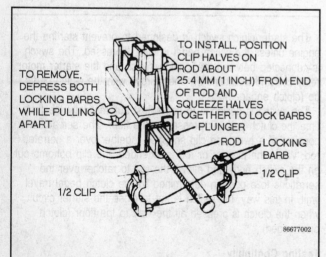

TO REMOVE, DEPRESS BOTH LOCKING BARBS WHILE PULLING APART

TO INSTALL, POSITION CLIP HALVES ON ROD ABOUT 25.4 MM (1 INCH) FROM END OF ROD AND SQUEEZE HALVES TOGETHER TO LOCK BARBS

PLUNGER
ROD
LOCKING BARB
1/2 CLIP
1/2 CLIP

86677002

Fig. 7 Starter/clutch interlock switch self-adjuster clip installation

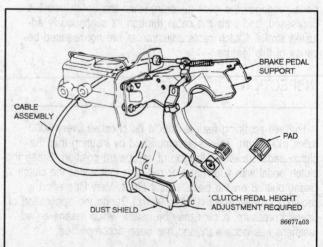

BRAKE PEDAL SUPPORT
CABLE ASSEMBLY
PAD
DUST SHIELD
CLUTCH PEDAL HEIGHT ADJUSTMENT REQUIRED

86677a03

Fig. 8 Clutch pedal and cable assembly — 1971-80 models

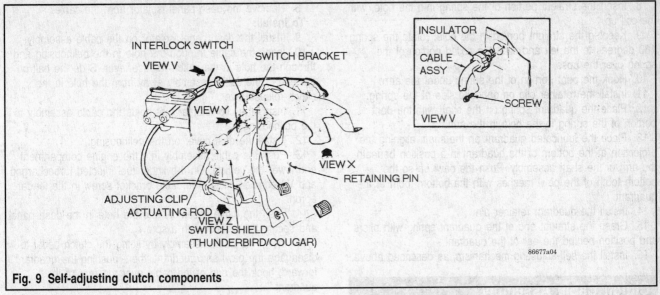

Fig. 9 Self-adjusting clutch components

Labels within figure:
INTERLOCK SWITCH
VIEW V
SWITCH BRACKET
INSULATOR
CABLE ASSY
SCREW
VIEW V
VIEW Y
VIEW X
RETAINING PIN
ADJUSTING CLIP/
ACTUATING ROD
VIEW Z
SWITCH SHIELD
(THUNDERBIRD/COUGAR)
86677a04

3. Remove the lower dash panel section to the left of the steering column.

4. Remove the shrouds from the steering column.

5. Disconnect the brake lamp switch and the master cylinder pushrod from the brake pedal.

6. Rotate the clutch quadrant forward and unhook the clutch cable from the quadrant. Allow the quadrant to slowly swing rearward.

7. Remove the bolt holding the brake pedal support bracket lateral brace to the left side of the vehicle.

8. Unfasten all electrical connectors from the steering column.

9. Remove the 4 nuts that hold the steering column to the brake pedal support bracket and lower the steering column to the floor.

10. Remove the 4 booster nuts that hold the brake pedal support bracket to the dash panel.

11. Remove the bolt that holds the brake pedal support bracket to the underside of the instrument panel, and remove the brake pedal support bracket assembly from the vehicle.

12. Remove the clutch pedal shaft nut and the clutch pedal, as outlined above.

13. Slide the self-adjusting mechanism out of the brake pedal support bracket.

14. Examine the self-adjusting mechanism shaft bushings on either side of the brake pedal support bracket, and replace if worn.

To install:

15. Lubricate the self-adjusting mechanism shaft with motor oil and install the mechanism into the brake pedal support bracket.

16. Position the quadrant towards the top of the vehicle. Align the flats on the shaft with the flats in the clutch pedal assembly, and install the retaining nuts. Tighten to 32-50 ft. lbs. (43-67 Nm).

17. Position the brake pedal support bracket assembly beneath the instrument panel, aligning the four holes with the studs in the dash panel. Install the four nuts loosely.

18. Install the bolt through the support bracket and into the instrument panel. Tighten to 13-25 ft. lbs. (18-34 Nm).

19. Tighten the four booster nuts that hold the brake pedal support bracket to the dash panel to 13-25 ft. lbs. (18-34 Nm).

20. Connect the brake lamp switch and the master cylinder pushrod to the brake pedal.

21. Attach the clutch cable to the quadrant.

22. Position the steering column onto the four studs in the support bracket and start the four nuts.

23. Connect the steering column electrical connectors.

24. Install the steering column shrouds.

25. Install the brake pedal support lateral brace.

26. Tighten the steering column attaching nuts to 20-37 ft. lbs. (27-50 Nm).

27. Install the lower dash panel section.

28. Install the steering wheel.

29. Connect the battery cable to the negative terminal on the battery.

30. Check the steering column for proper operation.

31. Depress the clutch pedal several times to adjust the cable.

Quadrant and Pawl

REMOVAL & INSTALLATION

▶ See Figure 10

1. Remove the self-adjusting mechanism, as described above.

2. Remove the two hairpin clips that hold the pawl and quadrant on the shaft assembly.

3. Remove the quadrant and quadrant spring.

4. Remove the pawl spring.

5. Remove the pawl.

To install:

6. Lubricate the pawl and quadrant pivot shafts with M1C75B or equivalent grease.

7. Install the pawl. Position the teeth of the pawl toward the long shaft, and the spring hole at the end of the arm. Do not position the spring hole beneath the arm.

8. Insert the straight portion of the spring into the hole, with the coil up.

9. Keeping the straight portion in the hole, rotate the spring 180 degrees to the left and slide the coiled portion of the spring over the boss.

10. Hook the bent portion of the spring under the arm.

11. Install the retainer clip on opposite side of the spring.

12. Place the quadrant spring on the shaft with the bent portion of the spring in the hole in the arm.

13. Place the lubricated quadrant on the shaft, aligning the projection at the bottom of the quadrant in a position beneath the arm of the shaft assembly. Push the pawl up so the bottom tooth of the pawl meshes with the bottom tooth of the quadrant.

14. Install the quadrant retainer pin.

15. Grasp the straight end of the quadrant spring with pliers and position behind the ear of the quadrant.

16. Install the self-adjusting mechanism, as described above.

Clutch Cable Assembly

REMOVAL & INSTALLATION

1. Lift the clutch pedal to its upwardmost position to disengage the pawl and quadrant. Push the quadrant forward, unhook the cable from the quadrant and allow it to slowly swing rearward.

2. Open the hood and remove the screw that holds the cable assembly isolator to the dash panel.

3. Pull the cable through the dash panel and into the engine compartment. On 4-cylinder fuel injected turbocharged and V8 engines, remove the cable bracket screw from the fender apron.

4. Raise the vehicle and safely support on jackstands.

5. Remove the dust cover from the bellhousing.

6. Remove the clip retainer holding the cable assembly to the bellhousing.

7. Slide the ball on the end of the cable assembly through the hole in the clutch release lever and remove the cable.

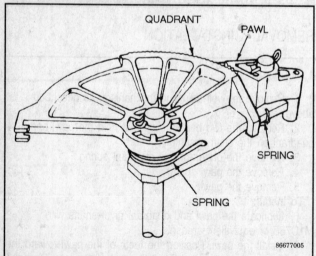

Fig. 10 The quadrant and pawl are part of the self-adjusting clutch mechanism

8. Remove the dash panel isolator from the cable.

To install:

9. Install the dash panel isolator on the cable assembly.

10. Insert the cable through the hole in the bellhousing and through the hole in the clutch release lever. Slide the ball on the end of the cable assembly away from the hole in the clutch release lever.

11. Install the clip retainer that holds the cable assembly to the bellhousing.

12. Install the dust cover on the bellhousing.

13. Push the cable assembly into the engine compartment and lower the vehicle. On 4-cylinder fuel injected turbocharged and V8 engines, install the cable bracket screw in the fender apron.

14. Push the cable assembly into the hole in the dash panel and secure the isolator with a screw.

15. Install the cable assembly by lifting the clutch pedal to disengage the pawl and quadrant, then, pushing the quadrant forward, hook the end of the cable over the rear of the quadrant.

16. Depress the clutch pedal several times to adjust the cable.

Clutch Disc

REMOVAL & INSTALLATION

▶ See Figures 11, 12 and 13

❋❋CAUTION

The clutch driven disc may contain asbestos, which has been determined to be a cancer causing agent. Never clean clutch surfaces with compressed air! Avoid inhaling any dust from any clutch surface! When cleaning clutch surfaces, use a commercially available brake cleaning fluid.

1. Remove the transmission.

2. Mark the cover and flywheel to facilitate reassembly in the same position. Loosen the 6 pressure plate cover attaching bolts evenly to release the spring pressure.

3. Remove the six attaching bolts while holding the pressure plate cover. Remove the pressure plate and clutch disc.

➡**Do not depress the clutch pedal while the transmission is removed.**

4. Before installing the clutch, clean the flywheel surface. Inspect the flywheel and pressure plate for wear, scoring, or burn marks (blue color). Light scoring and wear may be cleaned up with emery paper; heavy wear may require refacing of the flywheel or replacement of the damaged parts.

To install:

5. Attach the clutch disc and pressure plate assembly to the flywheel. The 3 dowel pins on the flywheel, if so equipped, must be properly aligned. Damaged pins must be replaced. Avoid touching the clutch plate surface. Tighten the bolts finger-tight.

6. Align the clutch disc with the pilot bushing. Tighten the cover bolts EVENLY in steps to 12-14 ft. lbs. (16-19 Nm).

Engine	Disc Diameter (in.)
240 Six	9.5
302 V8	10.0
240, 302 Heavy-Duty	11.0
351, 390, 400 V8	11.0
429 V8	11.5

86657010

Fig. 11 Clutch disc diameter varies with engine size

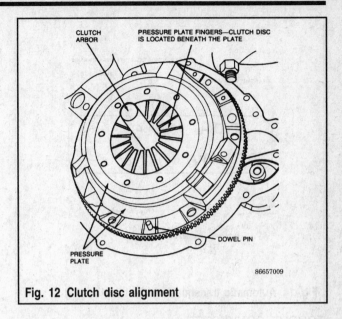

86657009

Fig. 12 Clutch disc alignment

7. Lightly lubricate the release lever fulcrum ends.

8. Install the release lever in the flywheel housing and install the dust shield.

9. Apply very little lubricant on the release bearing retainer journal. Fill the groove in release bearing hub with grease. Clean all excess grease from the inside bore of the hub to prevent clutch disc contamination. Attach the release bearing and hub on the release lever.

10. Install the transmission. Road test the vehicle for proper operation.

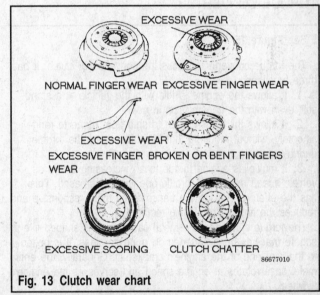

86677010

Fig. 13 Clutch wear chart

AUTOMATIC TRANSMISSION

Understanding Automatic Transmissions

The automatic transmission allows engine torque and power to be transmitted to the rear wheels within a narrow range of engine operating speeds. The transmission will allow the engine to turn fast enough to produce plenty of power and torque at very low speeds, while keeping it at a sensible rpm at high vehicle speeds. The transmission performs this job entirely without driver assistance. The transmission uses a light fluid as the medium for the transmission of power. This fluid also works in the operation of various hydraulic control circuits and as a lubricant. Because the transmission fluid performs all of these three functions, trouble within the unit can easily travel from one part to another. For this reason, and because of the complexity and unusual operating principles of the transmission, a very sound understanding of the basic principles of operation will simplify troubleshooting.

Identification

▶ See Figure 14

Several automatic transmissions were available over the years. In order to properly identify a particular application, obtain the transmission code from the Vehicle Certification Label and refer to the following list:

C — C5 automatic
T — AOD (automatic overdrive)
V — C3 automatic
W — C4 automatic

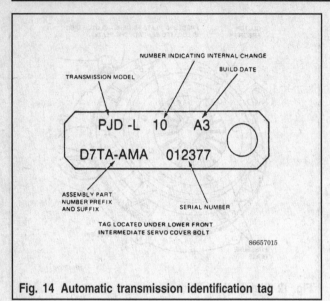

Fig. 14 Automatic transmission identification tag

TORQUE CONVERTER

▶ See Figure 15

The torque converter replaces the conventional clutch. It has three functions:

1. It allows the engine to idle with the vehicle at a standstill, even with the transmission in gear.

2. It allows the transmission to shift from range to range smoothly, without requiring that the driver close the throttle during the shift.

3. It multiplies engine torque to an increasing extent as vehicle speed drops and throttle opening is increased. This has the effect of making the transmission more responsive and reduces the amount of shifting required.

The torque converter is a metal case which is shaped like a sphere that has been flattened on opposite sides. It is bolted to the rear end of the engine's crankshaft. Generally, the entire metal case rotates at engine speed and serves as the engine's flywheel.

The case contains three sets of blades. One set is attached directly to the case. This set forms the torus or pump. Another set is directly connected to the output shaft, and forms the turbine. The third set is mounted on a hub which, in turn, is mounted on a stationary shaft through a one-way clutch. This third set is known as the stator.

A pump, which is driven by the converter hub at engine speed, keeps the torque converter full of transmission fluid at all times. Fluid flows continuously through the unit to provide cooling.

Under low speed acceleration, the torque converter functions as follows:

The torus is turning faster than the turbine. It picks up fluid at the center of the converter and, through centrifugal force, slings it outward. Since the outer edge of the converter moves faster than the portions at the center, the fluid picks up speed.

The fluid then enters the outer edge of the turbine blades. It then travels back toward the center of the converter case along the turbine blades. In impinging upon the turbine blades, the fluid loses the energy picked up in the torus.

If the fluid were now to immediately be returned directly into the torus, both halves of the converter would have to turn at approximately the same speed at all times, and torque input and output would both be the same.

In flowing through the torus and turbine, the fluid picks up two types of flow, or flow in two separate directions. It flows through the turbine blades, and it spins with the engine. The stator, whose blades are stationary when the vehicle is being accelerated at low speeds, converts one type of flow into another. Instead of allowing the fluid to flow straight back into the torus, the stator's curved blades turn the fluid almost 90° toward the direction of rotation of the engine. Thus the fluid does not flow as fast toward the torus, but is already spinning when the torus picks it up. This has the effect of allowing the torus to turn much faster than the turbine. This difference in speed may be compared to the difference in speed between the smaller and larger gears in any gear train. The result is that engine power output is higher, and engine torque is multiplied.

As the speed of the turbine increases, the fluid spins faster and faster in the direction of engine rotation. As a result, the ability of the stator to redirect the fluid flow is reduced. Under cruising conditions, the stator is eventually forced to rotate on its one-way clutch in the direction of engine rotation. Under these conditions, the torque converter begins to behave almost like a solid shaft, with the torus and turbine speeds being almost equal.

PLANETARY GEARBOX

▶ See Figures 16, 17, 18 and 19

The ability of the torque converter to multiply engine torque is limited. Also, the unit tends to be more efficient when the turbine is rotating at relatively high speeds. Therefore, a planetary gearbox is used to carry the power output of the turbine to the driveshaft.

Planetary gears function very similarly to conventional transmission gears. However, their construction is different in that three elements make up one gear system, and, in that all three elements are different from one another. The three ele-

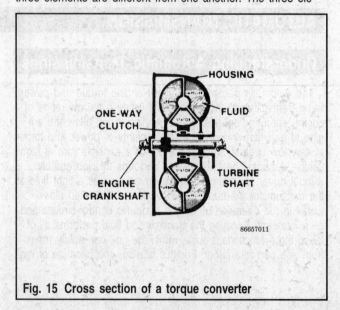

Fig. 15 Cross section of a torque converter

ments are: an outer gear that is shaped like a hoop, with teeth cut into the inner surface; a sun gear, mounted on a shaft and located at the very center of the outer gear; and a set of three planet gears, held by pins in a ring-like planet carrier, meshing with both the sun gear and the outer gear. Either the outer gear or the sun gear may be held stationary, providing more than one possible torque multiplication factor for each set of gears. Also, if all three gears are forced to rotate at the same speed, the gear set forms, in effect, a solid shaft.

Most modern automatics use the planetary gears to provide either a single reduction ratio of about 1.8:1, or two reduction gears: a low of about 2.5:1, and an intermediate of about 1.5:1. Bands and clutches are used to hold various portions of the gear sets to the transmission case or to the shaft on which they are mounted. Shifting is accomplished, then, by changing the portion of each planetary gear set which is held to the transmission case or to the shaft.

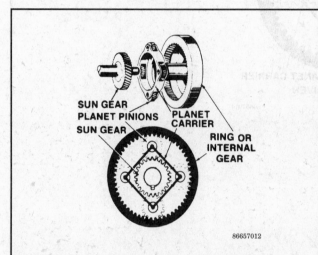

86657012

Fig. 16 Planetary gears are similar to manual transmission gears but are composed of three parts

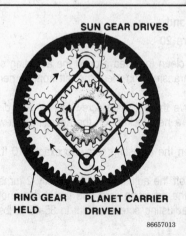

86657013

Fig. 17 Planetary gears in the maximum reduction (low) range. The ring gear is held and a lower gear ration is obtained

SERVOS AND ACCUMULATORS

▶ **See Figure 19**

The servos are hydraulic pistons and cylinders. Hydraulic fluid enters the cylinder, under pressure, and forces the piston to move to engage the band or clutches.

The accumulators are used to cushion the engagement of the servos. The transmission fluid must pass through the accumulator on the way to the servo. The accumulator housing contains a thin piston which is sprung away from the discharge passage of the accumulator. When fluid passes through the accumulator on the way to the servo, it must move the piston against spring pressure, and this action smooths out the action of the servo.

THE HYDRAULIC CONTROL SYSTEM

The hydraulic pressure used to operate the servos comes from the main transmission oil pump. This fluid is channeled to the various servos through the shift valves. There is generally a manual shift valve which is operated by the transmission selector lever and an automatic shift valve for each automatic upshift the transmission provides: i.e., 2-speed automatics have a low/high shift valve, while 3-speeds have a 1-2 valve, and a 2-3 valve.

There are two pressures which effect the operation of these valves. One is the governor pressure which is affected by vehicle speed. The other is the modulator pressure which is affected by intake manifold vacuum or throttle position. Governor pressure rises with an increase in vehicle speed, and modulator pressure rises as the throttle is opened wider. By responding to these two pressures, the shift valves cause the upshift points to be delayed with increased throttle opening to make the best use of the engine's power output.

Most transmissions also make use of an auxiliary circuit for downshifting. This circuit may be actuated by the throttle linkage or the vacuum line which actuates the modulator, or by a cable or solenoid. It applies pressure to a special downshift surface on the shift valve or valves.

The transmission modulator also governs the line pressure, used to actuate the servos. In this way, the clutches and bands will be actuated with a force matching the torque output of the engine.

Fluid Pan

For automatic transmission fluid pan removal and installation, refer to the service procedure in Section 1.

Adjustments

BANDS

➡**No external adjustments are possible on AOD transmissions.**

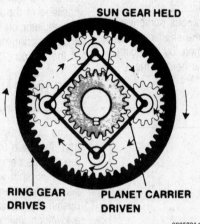

SUN GEAR HELD

RING GEAR DRIVES

PLANET CARRIER DRIVEN

86657014

Fig. 18 Planetary gears in the minimum reduction (drive) range. The ring gear is allowed to revolve, providing a higher gear ratio

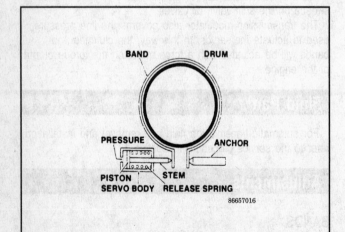

BAND   DRUM

PRESSURE   ANCHOR

PISTON   STEM
SERVO BODY   RELEASE SPRING

86657016

Fig. 19 Servos, operated by pressure, are used to apply or release the bands, to either hold the ring gear or allow the ring gear to rotate

C3 Front Band
▶ See Figure 20

1. Wipe clean the area around the adjusting screw on the side of the transmission, near the left front corner of the transmission.

2. Remove the adjusting screw locknut and discard it.

3. Install a new locknut on the adjusting screw but do not tighten it.

4. Tighten the adjusting screw to exactly 10 ft. lbs. (14 Nm).

5. Back off the adjusting screw exactly 2 turns.

6. Hold the adjusting screw so that it does not turn and tighten the adjusting screw locknut to 35-45 ft. lbs. (47-61 Nm).

C4 and C5 Intermediate Band
▶ See Figure 21

1. Clean all the dirt from the adjusting screw and remove and discard the locknut.

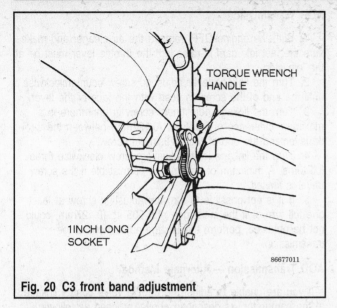

Fig. 20 C3 front band adjustment

2. Install a new locknut on the adjusting screw using a torque wrench, tighten the adjusting screw to 10 ft. lbs. (14 Nm).

3. Back off the adjusting screw exactly 1¾ turns for the C4 and 4¼ turns for the C5.

4. Hold the adjusting screw steady and tighten the locknut to 35 ft. lbs. (47 Nm).

C4 and C5 Low-Reverse Band

▶ See Figure 22

1. Clean all dirt from around the band adjusting screw, and remove and discard the locknut.

2. Install a new locknut of the adjusting screw. Using a torque wrench, tighten the adjusting screw to 10 ft. lbs. (14 Nm).

3. Back off the adjusting screw exactly three full turns.

4. Hold the adjusting screw steady and tighten the locknut to 35 ft. lbs. (47 Nm).

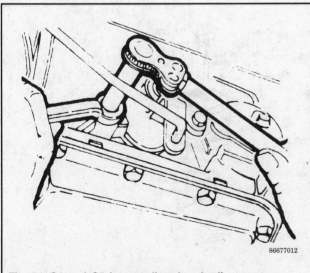

Fig. 21 C4 and C5 intermediate band adjustment

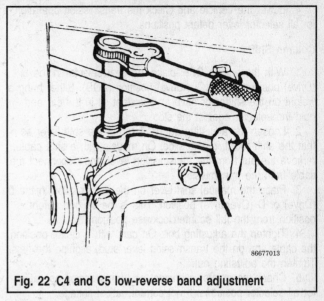

Fig. 22 C4 and C5 low-reverse band adjustment

SHIFT LINKAGE

Floor or Console Shift

SOLID LINK TYPE

▶ See Figure 23

1. Place the transmission shift lever in the DRIVE position (OVERDRIVE for the A4LD transmission), against the rearward DRIVE (or OVERDRIVE) stop.

➡ The shift lever should be held against the rearward DRIVE (OVERDRIVE) stop when the linkage is adjusted.

2. Raise the vehicle and loosen the manual lever shift rod retaining nut. Move the transmission manual lever to the DRIVE (OVERDRIVE) position.

➡ DRIVE is the second detent from the rear of the transmission; OVERDRIVE is the third detent from the full counterclockwise position.

3. With the transmission shift lever and manual lever in position, tighten the attaching nut to 10-15 ft. lbs. (14-20 Nm); on the A4LD transmission, tighten the nut to 10-20 ft. lbs. (14-27 Nm).

4. Lower the vehicle and check the transmission operation for all selector lever detent positions.

CABLE TYPE

1. Place the transmission shift lever in the DRIVE position, against the rearward DRIVE stop.

➡ The shift lever should be held against the rearward DRIVE stop when the linkage is adjusted.

2. Raise the vehicle and loosen the manual lever shift rod retaining nut. Move the transmission manual lever to the DRIVE position. DRIVE is the third detent from the rear of the transmission (or second detent from the full counterclockwise position).

3. With the transmission shift lever and manual lever in position, tighten the attaching nut to 10-20 ft. lbs. (14-19 Nm).

4. Lower the vehicle and check the transmission operation for all selector lever detent positions.

Column Shift

1. With the engine **OFF**, place the gear selector in the D (Drive) position, or D (Overdrive) position (AOD). Either hang a weight on the shifter or have an assistant sit in the car and hold the selector against the stop.

2. Loosen the adjusting nut or clamp at the shift lever so that the shift rod if free to slide. On models with a shift cable, remove the nut from the transmission lever and disconnect the cable from the transmission.

3. Place the manual shift lever on the transmission in the D (Drive) or D (Overdrive) position. This is the second detent position from the full counterclockwise position.

4. Tighten the adjusting bolt. On cars with a cable, position the cable end on the transmission lever stud, aligning the flats. Tighten the adjusting nut.

5. Check the pointer alignment and transmission operation for all selector positions. If not correct, adjust linkage.

DOWNSHIFT (THROTTLE) LINKAGE

All Models Except AOD Transmission

1. With the engine **OFF**, disconnect the throttle and downshift return springs, if equipped.

2. Hold the carburetor throttle lever in the wide open position against the stop.

3. Hold the transmission downshift linkage in the full downshift position against the internal stop.

4. Turn the adjustment screw on the carburetor downshift lever to obtain 0.010-0.080 in. (0.254-2.032mm) clearance between the screw tip and the throttle shaft lever tab.

5. Release the transmission and carburetor to their normal free positions. Install the throttle and downshift return springs, if removed.

AOD Transmission

1. With the engine **OFF**, remove the air cleaner and make sure the fast idle cam is released; the throttle lever must be at the idle stop.

2. Turn the linkage lever adjusting screw counterclockwise until the end of the screw is flush with the face of the lever.

3. Turn the linkage adjustment screw in until there is a maximum clearance of 0.005 in. (0.127mm) between the throttle lever and the end of the adjustment screw.

4. Turn the linkage lever adjusting screw clockwise three full turns. A minimum of one turn is permissible if the screw travel is limited.

5. If it is not possible to turn the adjusting screw at least one full turn or if the initial gap of 0.005 in. (0.127mm) could not be obtained, perform the linkage adjustment at the transmission.

AOD Transmission — Alternate Method

If you are unable to adjust the throttle valve control linkage at the carburetor, as described above, proceed as follows.

1. At the transmission, loosen the 8mm bolt on the throttle (TV) control rod sliding trunnion block. Make sure the trunnion block slides freely on the control rod.

2. Push up on the lower end of the TV control rod to insure that the carburetor linkage lever is held against the throttle lever. When the pressure is released, the control rod must stay in position.

3. Force the TV control lever on the transmission against its internal stop. While maintaining pressure tighten the trunnion block bolt. Make sure the throttle lever is at the idle stop.

AOD IDLE SPEED

Whenever it is necessary to adjust the idle speed by more than 50 rpm either above or below the factory specifications, the adjustment screw on the linkage lever at the carburetor should used. 1½ turns either way will change the idle speed by 50-100 rpm; 2½ turns either way will change the idle speed by 100-150 rpm.

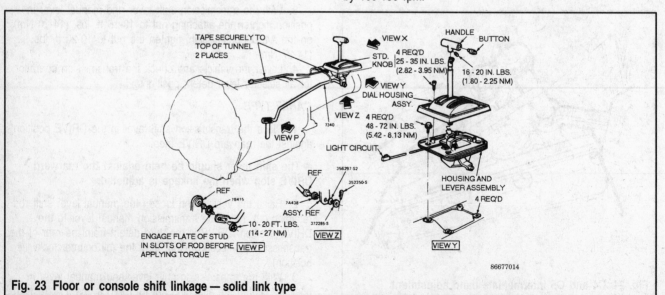

Fig. 23 Floor or console shift linkage — solid link type

After making any idle speed adjustments, make sure the linkage lever and throttle lever are in contact with the throttle lever at its idle stop and verify that the shift lever is in N (neutral).

Neutral Safety Switch

REMOVAL & INSTALLATION

▶ See Figures 24 and 25

➡The neutral safety switch on C3, AOD and A4LD transmissions is non-adjustable.

1971-80 Floor Mounted Shifter

1. Place the shift lever in NEUTRAL.
2. Raise and support the car on jackstands.
3. Remove the nut that secures the shift rod to the transmission manual lever. Make sure that the rod is free on the selector lever grommet.
4. Remove the shift lever handle.
5. Remove the shift lever selector housing.
6. Unfasten the dial light.
7. Disconnect the back-up/neutral start switch wires and selector indicator light wires at the instrument panel.
8. Remove the selector lever housing.
9. Remove the selector pointer shield.
10. Remove the 2 neutral start/back-up light switch screws and remove the switch. Push the harness plug inward and remove the switch and harness.
To install:
11. Before installing the new switch, be sure that the selector lever is against the neutral detent stop and the actuator lever is properly aligned in the neutral position.
12. Position the harness and switch in the housing. Install the two screws loosely.
13. Put the selector lever in PARK and hold it against the forward stop.
14. Move the switch to the end of its rearward travel.

15. Hold the switch in this position and tighten the two attaching screws.
16. The remainder of installation is the reverse of removal. Check the operation of the switch.

1981-84 Transmissions w/Floor Mounted Shifter

1. Raise and support the front end on jackstands.
2. Remove the downshift linkage rod from the transmission downshift lever.
3. Apply penetrating oil to the downshift lever shaft and nut. Remove the transmission downshift outer lever retaining nut and lever.
4. Remove the 2 switch attaching screws.
5. Unplug the connector and remove the switch.
To install:
6. Position the new switch on the transmission and install the bolts loosely.
7. Place the transmission lever in NEUTRAL, rotate the switch until the hole in the switch aligns with the depression in the case and insert a No. 43 drill bit through the hole and into

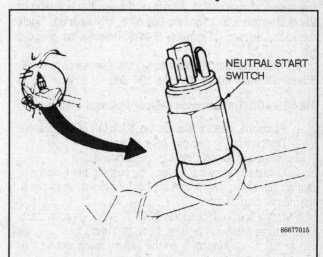

NEUTRAL START SWITCH

86677015

Fig. 25 Neutral safety switch used on C3, AOD and A4LD transmissions

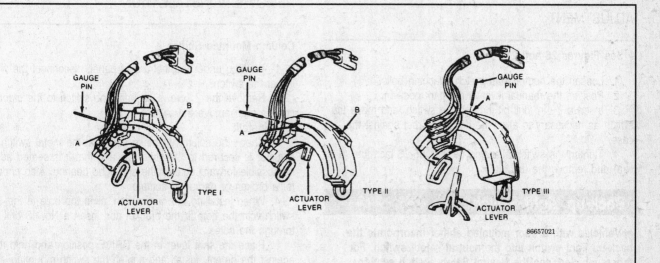

GAUGE PIN

GAUGE PIN

GAUGE PIN

A

B

A

B

A

ACTUATOR LEVER

ACTUATOR LEVER

ACTUATOR LEVER

TYPE I

TYPE II

TYPE III

86657021

Fig. 24 Column mounted neutral safety switch

the depression. Make sure the drill bit is fully inserted. Tighten the switch bolts to 60 inch lbs. (7 Nm). Remove the gauge pin.

8. The remainder of installation is the reverse of removal. Torque the shaft nut to 20 ft. lbs. (27 Nm).

1985 C5 Transmission w/Floor Mounted Shifter

1. Raise and support the front end on jackstands.
2. Remove the downshift linkage rod from the transmission downshift lever.
3. Apply penetrating oil to the downshift lever shaft and nut. Remove the transmission downshift outer lever retaining nut and lever.
4. Remove the 2 switch attaching screws.
5. Unplug the connector and remove the switch.

To install:
6. Position the new switch on the transmission and install the bolts loosely.
7. Place the transmission lever in NEUTRAL, rotate the switch until the hole in the switch aligns with the depression in the case and insert a No. 43 drill bit through the hole and into the depression. Make sure the drill bit is fully inserted. Tighten the switch bolts to 60 inch lbs. (7 Nm). Remove the gauge pin.
8. The remainder of installation is the reverse of removal. Torque the shaft nut to 20 ft. lbs. (27 Nm).

1984-85 AOD Transmission w/Floor Mounted Shifter

1. Place the selector lever in the MANUAL LOW position.
2. Disconnect the negative battery cable.
3. Raise and support the car on jackstands.
4. Unfasten the switch harness by pushing the harness straight up off the switch with a long screwdriver underneath the rubber plug section.
5. Using special tool socket T74P-77247-A, or equivalent, on a ratchet extension at least 9½ in. (241mm) long, unscrew the switch. Once the tool is on the switch, reach around the rear of the transmission over the extension housing.
6. Installation is the reverse of removal. Use a new O-ring, and torque the switch to 8-11 ft. lbs. (11-15 Nm).

ADJUSTMENT

▶ **See Figures 26 and 27**

1. Loosen the neutral start switch attaching bolts.
2. Position the manual lever in the park position.
3. Insert a ³/₃₂ in. drill bit through the switch, and move the switch as necessary to allow the drill bit to rest against the case.
4. Tighten the switch attaching bolts to 55-75 inch lbs. (6-8 Nm) and remove the drill bit.

Back-up Light Switch

➡ **Vehicles with a floor mounted shifter incorporate the back-up light switch into the neutral safety switch. For those vehicles, see the Neutral Safety Switch section, above.**

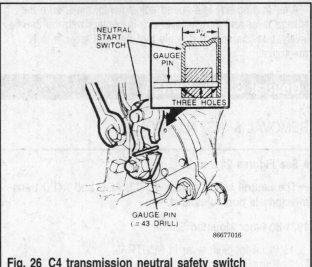

Fig. 26 C4 transmission neutral safety switch adjustment

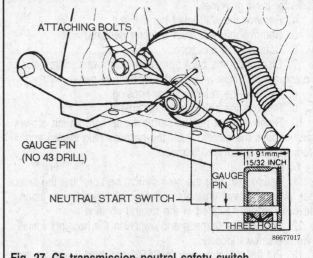

Fig. 27 C5 transmission neutral safety switch adjustment

REMOVAL & INSTALLATION

Column Mounted Shifter

1. Working under the instrument panel, disconnect the wiring at the switch.
2. Remove the 2 screws securing the switch to the steering column and remove the switch.

To install:
3. Check the column to make sure that the metal switch actuator is secured to the shift tube and that it is seated as far as possible forward against the shift tube bearing. Also check for a broken or damaged actuator.
4. When installing the new switch, align the hole in the switch with the hole in the bracket and insert a No. 43 drill bit through the holes.
5. Place the shift lever in the DRIVE position and hold it against the detent. Install and tighten the switch mounting screws.
6. Remove the drill bit and connect the wires.

Transmission

REMOVAL & INSTALLATION

C3 Transmission

1. Raise and safely support the vehicle.
2. Place a drain pan under the transmission fluid pan. Starting at the rear of the pan and working toward the front, loosen the attaching bolts and allow the fluid to drain. Then remove all of the pan attaching bolts except two at the front, to allow the fluid to further drain. After all the fluid has drained, install two bolts on the rear side of the pan to temporarily hold it in place.
3. Remove the converter drain plug access cover and adapter plate bolts from the lower end of the converter housing.
4. Remove the four flywheel-to-converter attaching nuts. Crank the engine to turn the converter to gain access to the nuts, using a wrench on the crankshaft pulley attaching bolt. On belt driven overhead camshaft engines, never turn the engine backwards.
5. Crank the engine until the converter drain plug is accessible and remove the plug. Place a drain pan under the converter to catch the fluid. After all the fluid has been drained from the converter, reinstall the plug and tighten to specification.
6. Remove the driveshaft and install the extension housing seal replacer tool in the extension housing.
7. Remove the speedometer cable from the extension housing.
8. Disconnect the shift rod at the transmission manual lever. Disconnect the downshift rod at the transmission downshift lever.
9. Remove the starter-to-converter housing attaching bolts and position the starter out of the way.
10. Unfasten the neutral start switch wires from the switch.
11. Remove the vacuum line from the transmission vacuum unit.
12. Position a transmission jack under the transmission and raise it slightly.
13. Remove the engine rear support-to-crossmember nut.
14. Remove the crossmember-to-frame side support attaching bolts and remove the crossmember.
15. Remove the inlet pipe steady rest from the inlet pipe and rear engine support; then disconnect the muffler inlet pipe at the exhaust manifold and secure it.
16. Lower the jack under the transmission and allow the transmission to hang.
17. Position a jack to the front of the engine and raise the engine to gain access to the two upper converter housing-to-engine attaching bolts.
18. Disconnect the oil cooler lines at the transmission. Plug all openings to keep out dirt.
19. Remove the lower converter housing-to-engine attaching bolts.
20. Remove the transmission filter tube.
21. Secure the transmission to the jack with a safety chain.

22. Remove the two upper converter housing-to-engine attaching bolts. Move the transmission to the rear and down to remove it from under the vehicle.

To install:

23. Tighten the converter drain plug to 20-30 ft. lbs. (27-40 Nm) if not previously done.
24. Position the converter to the transmission making sure the converter hub is fully engaged in the pump gear. The dimension given in the illustration is for guidance only. It does not indicate engagement.
25. With the converter properly installed, place the transmission on the jack and secure with safety chain.
26. Rotate the converter so the drive studs and drain plug are in alignment with their holes in the flywheel.
27. With the transmission mounted on a transmission jack, move the converter and transmission assembly forward into position being careful not to damage the flywheel and the converter pilot. During this move, to avoid damage, do not allow the transmission to get into a nosed down position as this will cause the converter to move forward and disengage from the pump gear. The converter must rest squarely against the flywheel. This indicates that the converter pilot is not binding in the engine crankshaft.
28. Install the two upper converter housing-to-engine attaching bolts and tighten to 28-38 ft. lbs. (38-51 Nm).
29. Remove the safety chain from the transmission.
30. Insert the filler tube in the stub tube and secure it to the cylinder block with the attaching bolt. Tighten the bolt to 28-38 ft. lbs. (38-51 Nm). If the stub tube is loosened or dislodged, it should be replaced.
31. Install the oil cooler lines in the retaining clip at the cylinder block. Connect the lines to the transmission case.
32. Remove the jack supporting the front of the engine.
33. Position the muffler inlet pipe support bracket to the converter housing and install the four lower converter housing-to-engine attaching bolts. Tighten the bolts to 28-38 ft. lbs. (38-51 Nm).
34. Raise the transmission. Position the crossmember to the frame side supports and install the attaching bolts. Tighten the bolts to 30-40 ft. lbs.
35. Lower the transmission and install the rear engine support-to-crossmember nut. Tighten the nut to 30-40 ft. lbs. (41-54 Nm).
36. Remove the transmission jack.
37. Install the vacuum hose on the transmission vacuum unit. Install the vacuum line into the retaining clip.
38. Connect the neutral start switch plug to the switch.
39. Install the starter and tighten the attaching bolts.
40. Install the four flywheel-to-converter attaching nuts.
41. Install the converter drain plug access cover and adaptor plate bolts. Tighten the bolts to 15-20 ft. lbs. (20-27 Nm).
42. Connect the muffler inlet pipe to the exhaust manifold.
43. Connect the transmission shift rod to the manual lever.
44. Connect the downshift rod to the downshift lever.
45. Connect the speedometer cable to the extension housing.
46. Install the driveshaft. Tighten the companion flange U-bolt attaching nuts to 30 ft. lbs. (40 Nm).
47. Adjust the manual and downshift linkage as required.
48. Lower the vehicle. Fill the transmission to the proper level with the recommended fluid. Pour in 5 quarts of fluid, then run the engine and add fluid as required.

49. Check the transmission, converter assembly and oil cooler lines for leaks.

C4 Transmission

1. Disconnect the negative battery cable. Raise and safely support the vehicle on jackstands.

2. Place a drain pan under the transmission fluid pan. Remove the fluid filler tube and pan. After the fluid has drained, install two bolts on the rear side of the pan to temporarily hold it in place.

3. Remove the converter drain plug access cover from the lower end of the converter housing.

4. Remove the converter-to-flywheel attaching nuts. Place a wrench on the crankshaft pulley attaching bolt to turn the converter to gain access to the nuts.

5. With the wrench on the crankshaft pulley attaching bolt, turn the converter to gain access to the converter drain plug. Remove the plug. Place a drain pan under the converter to catch the fluid. After the fluid has been drained from the converter, reinstall the plug.

6. Remove the driveshaft and insert a shop towel into the extension housing to prevent fluid from leaking out.

7. Remove the vacuum line hose from the transmission vacuum unit. Disconnect the vacuum line from the retaining clip. Disconnect the Transmission Regulated Spark (TRS) switch wire at the transmission, if so equipped.

8. Remove the engine support-to-crossmember bolts or nuts.

9. Remove the speedometer cable from the extension housing.

10. Disconnect the oil cooler lines from the transmission case.

11. Disconnect the selector rod or cable at the transmission manual lever. Disconnect the downshift rod at the transmission downshift lever.

12. On console and floor shift vehicles, disconnect the column lock rod at the transmission, if equipped.

13. Disconnect the starter cable. Remove the starter attaching bolts and remove the starter from the converter housing.

14. Position a transmission jack to support the transmission and secure the transmission to the jack with a safety chain.

15. Remove the crossmember attaching bolts and lower the crossmember.

16. Remove the five converter housing-to-engine attaching bolts. Lower the transmission and remove it from under the vehicle.

To install:

17. Tighten the converter drain plug to 20-30 ft. lbs. (26-39 Nm).

18. Position the converter to the transmission making sure the converter drive flats are fully engaged in the pump gear.

19. With the converter properly installed, place the transmission on the jack. Secure the transmission to the jack with a safety chain.

20. Rotate the converter so that the studs and drain plug are in alignment with their holes in the flywheel.

21. With the transmission mounted on a transmission jack, move the converter and transmission assembly forward into position, using care not to damage the flywheel and the converter pilot. The converter must rest squarely against the fly-wheel. This indicates that the converter pilot is not binding in the engine crankshaft.

22. Install the five converter housing-to-engine attaching bolts. Tighten the bolts to 23-28 ft. lbs. (30-36 Nm). Remove the safety chain from the transmission.

23. Position the crossmember and install the attaching bolts. Tighten the bolts to 40-50 ft. lbs. (52-65 Nm).

24. Lower the transmission and install the engine support to crossmember bolts or nuts. Tighten the bolts or nuts to 30-40 ft. lbs. (39-52 Nm).

25. Install the flywheel to the converter attaching nuts. Tighten the nuts to 23-28 ft. lbs. (30-36 Nm).

26. Remove the transmission jack. Install the fluid filler tube in the transmission case or pan. Secure the tube to the cylinder head with the attaching bolt. Install the vacuum hose on the transmission vacuum unit. Install the vacuum line retaining clip. Connect the Transmission Regulated Spark (TRS) switch wires to the switch, if equipped.

27. Connect the fluid cooling lines to the transmission case.

28. Connect the downshift rod to the downshift lever.

29. Connect the selector rod or cable to the transmission manual lever. Connect the column lock rod on console and floor shift vehicles, if equipped.

30. Connect the speedometer cable to the extension housing.

31. Install the converter housing cover and tighten the attaching bolts to 12-16 ft. lbs. (16-21 Nm).

32. Install the starter and tighten the attaching bolts to 25-30 ft. lbs. (32-39 Nm). Connect the starter cable.

33. Install the driveshaft. Tighten the companion flange U-bolts attaching nuts to 25-30 ft. lbs. (32-39 Nm).

34. Lower the vehicle. Fill the transmission to the proper level with fluid. Adjust the manual and downshift linkage as necessary. Road test the vehicle for proper shift pattern.

C5 Transmission

1. Open the hood and install protective covers on the fenders.

2. Disconnect the battery negative cable.

3. On models equipped with a V6 engine, remove the air cleaner assembly.

4. Remove the fan shroud attaching bolts and position the shroud back over the fan.

5. On models equipped with a V6 engine, loosen the clamp and disconnect the Thermactor® air injection hose at the catalytic converter check valve. The check valve is located on the right side of the engine compartment near the dash panel.

6. On models equipped with a V6 engine, remove the two transmission-to-engine attaching bolts located at the top of the transmission bell housing. These bolts are accessible from the engine compartment.

7. Raise and safely support the vehicle.

8. Remove the driveshaft.

9. Unfasten the muffler inlet pipe from the catalytic converter outlet pipe. Support the muffler/pipe assembly by wiring it to a convenient underbody bracket.

10. Remove the nuts attaching the exhaust pipe(s) to the exhaust manifold(s).

11. Pull back on the catalytic converter to release the converter hangers from the mounting bracket.

12. Remove the speedometer clamps bolt and pull the speedometer out of the extension housing.

13. Separate the neutral start switch harness connector.

14. Disconnect the kickdown rod at the transmission lever.

15. Disconnect the shift linkage at the linkage bellcrank. On vehicles equipped with floor mounted shift, remove the shift cable routing bracket attaching bolts and disconnect the cable at the transmission lever.

16. Remove the converter dust shield.

17. Remove the torque converter to drive plate attaching nuts. To gain access to the converter nuts, turn the crankshaft and drive plate using a ratchet handle and socket on the crankshaft pulley attaching bolt.

18. Remove the starter attaching bolts.

19. Loosen the nuts attaching the rear support to the No. 3 crossmember.

20. Position a transmission jack under the transmission oil pan. Secure the transmission to the jack with a safety chain.

21. Remove the through bolts attaching the No. 3 crossmember to the body brackets.

22. Lower the transmission enough to allow access to the cooler line fittings. Disconnect the cooler lines.

23. On models with the V6, remove the (4) remaining transmission-to-engine attaching bolts (2 on each side). On all models, remove the (6) transmission-to-engine attaching bolts.

24. Pull the transmission back to disengage the converter studs from the drive plate. Lower the transmission out of the vehicle.

To install:

25. Raise the transmission into the vehicle. As the transmission is being slowly raised into position, rotate the torque converter until the studs and drain plug are aligned with the holes in the drive plate.

26. Move the converter/transmission assembly forward against the back of the engine. Make sure the converter studs engage the drive plate and that the transmission dowels on the back of the engine engage the bolts holes in the bellhousing.

27. On models equipped with a V6 engine, install four transmission-to-engine attaching bolts (2 on each side). On all other models, install the (6) transmission-to-engine attaching bolts. Tighten the attaching bolts to 40-50 ft. lbs. (54-67 Nm).

28. Connect the cooler lines.

29. Raise the transmission and install the No. 3 crossmember through bolts. Tighten the attaching nuts to 20-30 ft. lbs. (27-40 Nm).

30. Remove the safety chain and transmission jack.

31. Tighten the rear support attaching nuts to 30-50 ft. lbs. (41-67 Nm).

32. Position the starter and install the attaching bolts.

33. Install the torque converter-to-drive plate attaching nuts. Tighten the attaching nuts to 20-30 ft. lbs. (27-40 Nm).

34. Position the dust shield and on vehicles with a column mounted shift, position the linkage bellcrank bracket. Install the attaching bolts and tighten to 12-16 ft. lbs. (16-21 Nm).

35. Connect the shift linkage to the linkage bellcrank. On vehicles equipped with a floor mounted shift, connect the cable to the shift lever and install the routing bracket attaching bolt.

36. Connect the kickdown rod to the transmission lever.

37. Connect the neutral start switch harness.

38. Install the speedometer and the clamp bolt. Tighten the clamp bolt to 35-54 inch lbs. (4-6 Nm).

39. Install the catalytic converts using new seal(s) at the pipe(s) to exhaust manifold connection(s).

40. Install the pipe(s) to exhaust manifold attaching nuts. Do not tighten the attaching nuts.

41. Remove the wire supporting the muffler/pipe assembly and connect the pipe to the converter outlet. Do not tighten the attaching nuts.

42. Align the exhaust system and tighten the manifold and converter outlet attaching nuts.

43. Install the driveshaft.

44. Check and adjust the shift linkage, if necessary.

45. Lower the vehicle.

46. On models equipped with a V6 engine, install the two transmission-to-engine attaching bolts located at the top of the transmission bellhousing.

47. On models equipped with a V6 engine, connect the Thermactor® air injection hose to the converter check valve.

48. Position the fan shroud and install the attaching bolts.

49. On models equipped with a V6 engine, install the air cleaner assembly.

50. Connect the battery negative cable.

51. Start the engine. Make sure the engine cranks only when the selector lever is positioned in the NEUTRAL or PARK detent.

52. Fill the transmission with type H fluid.

53. Raise the vehicle and inspect for fluid leaks.

C6 Transmission

1. Disconnect the negative battery cable. Working from the engine compartment, remove the two bolts retaining the fan shroud to the radiator.

2. Raise and safely support the vehicle on jackstands

3. Place a drain pan under the transmission fluid pan. Starting at the rear of the pan and working toward the front, loosen the attaching bolts and allow the fluid to drain. Finally remove all of the pan attaching bolts except two at the front, to allow the fluid to further drain. After the fluid has drained, install two bolts on the rear side of the pan to temporarily hold it in place.

4. Remove the converter drain plug access cover and adapter plate bolts from the lower end of the converter housing.

5. Remove the converter-to-flywheel attaching nuts.

6. Disconnect the driveshaft from the rear axle and slide the shaft rearward from the transmission. Install the seal installation tool in the extension housing to prevent fluid leakage. A shop towel could also be used here.

7. Disconnect the speedometer cable from the extension housing.

8. Disconnect the downshift rod from the transmission downshift lever.

9. Disconnect the shift cable form the manual lever at the transmission.

10. Remove the two bolts that secure the shift cable bracket to the converter housing and position the cable and bracket out of the way.

11. Remove the starter motor attaching bolts and position the starter out of the way.

12. Disconnect the rubber hose from the vacuum diaphragm at the rear of the transmission. Remove the vacuum tube from the retaining clip at the transmission. Disconnect the Transmis-

sion Regulated Spark (TRS) switch wire at the transmission, if equipped.

13. Disconnect the muffler inlet pipe at the exhaust manifolds and allow the pipe to hang.

14. Remove the crossmember-to-frame side support bolts and nuts. Remove the nuts securing the rear engine supports to the crossmember. Position a jack under the transmission and raise it slightly. Remove the bolts securing the rear engine support to the extension housing and remove the crossmember and rear supports from the vehicle.

15. Loosen the parking brake adjusting nut at the equalizer and remove the cable from the idler hook attaching to the floor pan.

16. Lower the transmission, then disconnect the oil cooler lines from the transmission case.

17. Secure the transmission to the jack with a chain.

18. Remove the six bolts that attach the converter housing to the cylinder block.

19. Remove the bolt that secures the transmission filler tube to the cylinder block. Lift the filler tube and dipstick from the transmission.

20. Move the transmission away from the cylinder block.

21. Carefully lower the transmission and remove it from under the vehicle.

22. Remove the converter and mount the transmission in a holding fixture.

To install:

23. Tighten the converter drain plug to 14-28 ft. lbs. (18-36 Nm).

24. Position the converter to the transmission making sure the converter drive flats are fully engaged in the pump gear.

25. With the converter properly installed, place the transmission on the jack. Secure the transmission to the jack with the safety chain.

26. Rotate the converter so that the studs and drain plug are in alignment with their holes in the flywheel.

27. With the transmission mounted on a transmission jack, move the converter and transmission assembly forward into position using care not to damage the flywheel and converter pilot. The converter must rest squarely against the flywheel. This indicates that the converter pilot is not binding in the engine crankshaft.

28. Install a new O-ring on the lower end of the transmission filler tube. Insert the tube in the transmission case and secure the tube to the engine with the attaching bolts.

29. Install the converter housing-to-engine attaching bolts. Tighten the bolts to 40-50 ft. lbs. (52-65 Nm). Remove the safety chain from the transmission.

30. Connect the oil cooler lines to the transmission case.

31. Raise the transmission.

32. Position the parking brake cable in the idler hook and tighten the adjusting nut at the equalizer.

33. Place the rear engine supports on the crossmember and position the crossmember on the frame side supports.

34. Secure the engine rear supports to the extension housing with the attaching bolts. Tighten the bolts and nuts to 35-40 ft. lbs. (45-52 Nm).

35. Remove the transmission jack from under the vehicle and install the crossmember-to-frame side support bolts and nuts. Tighten the bolts to 35-40 ft. lbs. (45-52 Nm).

36. Install and tighten the engine rear support-to-crossmember attaching nuts.

37. Connect the muffler inlet pipe to the exhaust manifolds.

38. Connect the vacuum line to the vacuum diaphragm making sure that the metal tube is secured in the retaining clip. Connect the Transmission Regulated Spark (TRS) switch wire to the switch, if equipped.

39. Position the starter motor to the converter housing and secure it with the attaching bolts.

40. Install the torque converter-to-flywheel attaching nuts and tighten them to 20-30 ft. lbs. (26-39 Nm).

41. Position the shift cable bracket to the converter housing and install the two attaching bolts.

42. Connect the shift cable to the manual lever at the transmission.

43. Connect the downshift rod to the lever on the transmission.

44. Connect the speedometer cable to the extension housing.

45. Install the driveshaft.

46. Install the converter drain plug access cover and adapter plate bolts. Tighten the bolts to 12-16 ft. lbs. (16-21 Nm).

47. Adjust the manual and downshift linkage as required.

48. Lower the vehicle.

49. Working from the engine compartment, position the fan shroud to the radiator and secure with the two attaching bolts.

50. Fill the transmission to the proper level.

51. Check the transmission, converter assembly and oil cooler lines for leaks. Road test the vehicle for proper shift pattern.

Automatic Overdrive (AOD) Transmission

1. Raise and safely support the vehicle.

2. Place the drain pan under the transmission fluid pan. Starting at the rear of the pan and working toward the front, loosen the attaching bolts and allow the fluid to drain. Finally, remove all of the pan attaching bolts except two at the front, to allow the fluid to further drain. With the fluid drained, install two bolts on the rear side of the pan to temporarily hold it in place.

3. Remove the converter drain plug access cover from the lower end of the converter housing.

4. Remove the converter-to-flywheel attaching nuts. place a wrench on the crankshaft pulley attaching bolt to turn the converter to gain access to the nuts.

5. Place a drain pan under the converter to catch the fluid. With the wrench on the crankshaft pulley attaching bolts, turn the converter to gain access to the converter drain plug and remove the plug. After the fluid has been drained, reinstall the plug.

6. Disconnect the driveshaft from the rear axle and slide shaft rearward from the transmission. Install a seal installation tool in the extension housing to prevent fluid leakage.

7. Disconnect the cable from the terminal on the starter motor. Remove the three attaching bolts and remove the starter motor. Disconnect the neutral start switch wires at the plug connector.

8. Remove the rear mount-to-crossmember attaching bolts and the two crossmember-to-frame attaching bolts.

9. Remove the two engine rear support-to-extension housing attaching bolts.

10. Unfasten the TV linkage rod from the transmission TV lever. Disconnect the manual rod from the transmission manual lever at the transmission.

11. Remove the two bolts securing the bellcrank bracket to the converter housing.

12. Raise the transmission with a transmission jack to provide clearance to remove the crossmember. Remove the rear mount from the crossmember and remove the crossmember from the side supports.

13. Lower the transmission to gain access to the oil cooler lines.

14. Disconnect each oil line from the fittings on the transmission.

15. Disconnect the speedometer cable from the extension housing.

16. Remove the bolt that secures the transmission fluid filler tube to the cylinder block. Lift the filler tube and the dipstick from the transmission.

17. Secure the transmission to the jack with the chain.

18. Remove the converter housing-to-cylinder block attaching bolts.

19. Carefully move the transmission and converter assembly away from the engine and, at the same time, lower the jack to clear the underside of the vehicle.

20. Remove the converter and mount the transmission in a holding fixture.

To install:

21. Tighten the converter drain plug to 20-28 ft. lbs. (27-38 Nm).

22. Position the converter on the transmission, making sure the converter drive flats are fully engaged in the pump gear by rotating the converter.

23. With the converter properly installed, place the transmission on the jack. Secure the transmission to the jack with a chain.

24. Rotate the converter until the studs and drain plug are in alignment with the holes in the flywheel.

➡**Be sure to lubricate the pilot bushing.**

25. Align the yellow balancing marks on converter and flywheel on models with the V8 engine.

26. Move the converter and transmission assembly forward into position, using care not to damage the flywheel and the converter pilot. The converter must rest squarely against the flywheel. This indicates that the converter pilot is not binding in the engine crankshaft.

27. Install and tighten the converter housing-to-engine attaching bolts to 40-50 ft. lbs. (54-67 Nm). Make sure that the vacuum tube retaining clips are properly positioned.

28. Remove the safety chain from around the transmission.

29. Install a new O-ring on the lower end of the transmission filler tube. Insert the tube in the transmission case and secure the tube to the engine with the attaching bolts.

30. Connect the speedometer cable to the extension housing.

31. Connect the oil cooler lines to the right side of the transmission case.

32. Position the crossmember on the side supports. Position the rear mount on the crossmember and install the attaching bolt and nut.

33. Secure the engine rear support to the extension housing and tighten the bolts to 35-40 ft. lbs. (47-54 Nm).

34. Lower the transmission and remove the jack.

35. Secure the crossmember to the side supports with the attaching bolts and tighten them to 35-40 ft. lbs. (47-54 Nm).

36. Position the bellcrank to the converter housing and install the two attaching bolts.

37. Connect the TV linkage rod to the transmission TV lever. Connect the manual linkage rod to the manual lever at the transmission.

38. Secure the converter-to-flywheel attaching nuts and tighten them to 20-30 ft. lbs. (27-40 Nm).

39. Install the converter housing access cover and secure it with the attaching bolts.

40. Secure the starter motor in place with the attaching bolts. Connect the cable to the terminal on the starter. Connect the neutral start switch wires at the plug connector.

41. Connect the driveshaft to the rear axle.

42. Adjust the shift linkage as required.

43. Adjust throttle linkage.

44. Lower the vehicle.

45. Fill the transmission to the correct level with Dexron®II or Mercon® fluid. Start the engine and shift the transmission to all ranges, then recheck the fluid level.

DRIVELINE

Driveshaft and U-Joints

▶ **See Figure 28**

The driveshaft is the means by which the power from the engine and transmission is transferred to the differential and rear axles, and finally to the rear wheels. It incorporates two universal joints, one at each end, and a slip yoke at the front end of the assembly, which fits into the back of the transmission.

REMOVAL

1. Matchmark the relationship of the rear driveshaft yoke and the drive pinion flange of the axle. If the original yellow alignment marks are visible, there is no need for new marks. The purpose of this marking is to facilitate installation of the assembly in its exact original position, thereby maintaining proper driveshaft balance.

2. Remove the four bolts or U-clamps which hold the rear universal joint to the pinion flange. Wrap tape around the loose bearing caps in order to prevent them from falling off the spider.

3. Pull the driveshaft toward the rear of the vehicle until the slip yoke clears the transmission housing and the seal. Plug

the hole at the rear of the transmission housing or place a container under the opening to catch any fluid which might leak.

UNIVERSAL JOINT OVERHAUL

▶ **See Figures 29, 30 and 31**

1. Position the driveshaft assembly in a sturdy vise.
2. Remove the snaprings which retain the bearings in the slip yoke (front only) and in the driveshaft (front and rear).
3. Using a large vise or an arbor press and a socket smaller than the bearing cap on one side and a socket larger than the bearing cap on the other side, drive one of the bearings in toward the center of the universal joint, which will force the opposite bearing out.
4. As each bearing is forced far enough out of the universal joint assembly, grip it with a pair of pliers, and pull it from the driveshaft yoke. Drive the spider in the opposite direction in order to make the opposite bearing accessible, and pull it

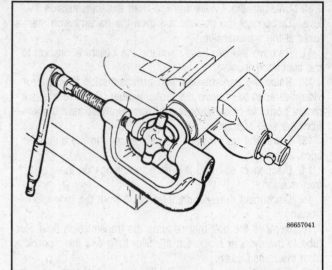

86657041

Fig. 29 Remove the bearing from the universal joint

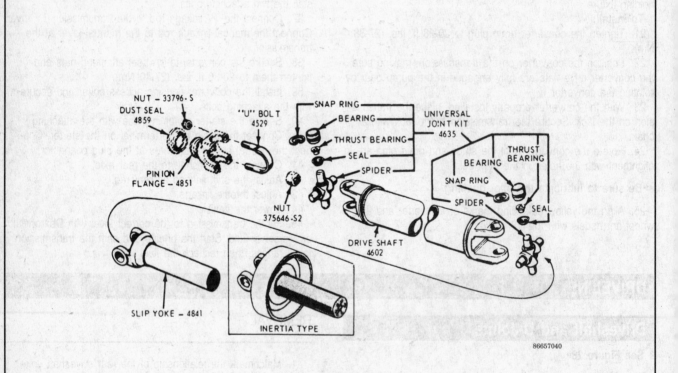

86657040

Fig. 28 Exploded view — driveshaft and U-joint

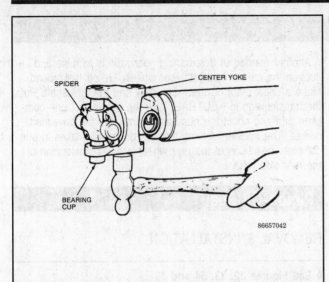

Fig. 30 Remove the universal joint from the center yoke

free with a pair of pliers. Use this procedure to remove all the bearings from both universal joints.

5. After removing the bearings, lift the spider from the yoke.

6. Thoroughly clean all dirt and foreign matter from the yokes on both ends of the driveshaft.

➡When installing new bearings in the yokes, it is advisable to use an arbor press. However, if this tool is not available, the bearings should be driven into position with extreme care, as a heavy jolt on the needle bearings can easily damage or mis-align the bearing.

To assemble:

7. Start a new bearing into the yoke at the rear of the driveshaft.

8. Position a new spider in the rear yoke and press the new bearing ¼ in. (6mm) below the outer surface of the yoke.

9. With the bearing in position, install a new snapring.

10. Start a new bearing into the opposite side of the yoke.

11. Press the bearing until the opposite bearing, which you have just installed, contacts the inner surface of the snapring.

12. Install a new snapring on the second bearing. It may be necessary to grind the surface of this second snapring.

13. Reposition the driveshaft in the vise, so that the front universal joint is accessible.

14. Install the new bearings, new spider, and new snaprings in the same manner as you did for the rear universal joint.

15. Position the slip yoke on the spider. Install new bearings, nylon thrust bearings, and snaprings.

16. Check both reassembled joints for freedom of movement. If misalignment of any part is causing a bind, a sharp rap on the side of the yoke with a brass hammer should seat the bearing needle and provide the desired freedom of movement. Care should be exercised to firmly support the shaft end during this operation, as well as to prevent blows to the bearings themselves. Under no circumstances should the driveshaft be installed in a car if there is any binding in the universal joints.

DRIVESHAFT INSTALLATION

1. Carefully inspect the rubber seal on the output shaft and the seal in end of the transmission extension housing. Replace them if they are damaged.

2. Examine the lugs on the axle pinion flange and replace the flange if the lugs are shaved or distorted.

3. Coat the yoke spline with special purpose lubricant. The Ford part number for this lubricant is B8A-1589-A.

4. Remove the plug from the rear of the transmission housing.

5. Insert the yoke into the transmission housing and onto the transmission output shaft. Make sure that the yoke assembly does not bottom on the output shaft with excessive force.

6. Locate the marks which you made on the rear driveshaft yoke and the pinion flange prior to removal of the driveshaft assembly. Install the driveshaft assembly with the marks properly aligned.

7. Install the U-bolts and nuts or bolts which attach the universal joint to the pinion flange finger-tight.

8. Tighten the U-bolts nuts evenly in steps to 8-15 ft. lbs. (10-19 Nm). Flange bolts are tightened to 70-95 ft. lbs. (91-123 Nm).

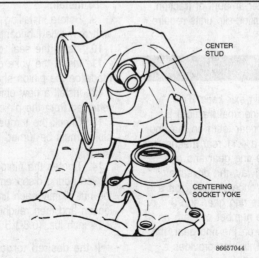

Fig. 31 Removal of the center yoke section

REAR AXLE

Understanding Drive Axles

The drive axle is a special type of transmission that reduces the speed of the drive from the engine and transmission and divides the power to the wheels. Power enters the axle from the driveshaft via the companion flange. The flange is mounted on the drive pinion shaft. The drive pinion shaft and gear which carry the power into the differential turn at engine speed. The gear on the end of the pinion shaft drives a large ring gear the axis of rotation of which is 90° away from the of the pinion. The pinion and gear reduce the gear ratio of the axle, and change the direction of rotation to turn the axle shafts which drive both wheels. The axle gear ratio is found by dividing the number of pinion gear teeth into the number of ring gear teeth.

The ring gear drives the differential case. The case provides the two mounting points for the ends of a pinion shaft on which are mounted two pinion gears. The pinion gears drive the two side gears, one of which is located on the inner end of each axle shaft.

By driving the axle shafts through the arrangement, the differential allows the outer drive wheel to turn faster than the inner drive wheel in a turn.

The main drive pinion and the side bearings, which bear the weight of the differential case, are shimmed to provide proper bearing preload, and to position the pinion and ring gears properly.

➡The proper adjustment of the relationship of the ring and pinion gears is critical. It should be attempted only by those with the proper equipment and experience.

Limited-slip differentials include clutches which tend to link each axle shaft to the differential case. Clutches may be engaged either by spring action or by pressure produced by the torque on the axles during a turn. During turning on a dry pavement, the effects of the clutches are overcome, and each wheel turns at the required speed. When slippage occurs at either wheel, however, the clutches will transmit some of the power to the wheel which has the greater amount of traction. Because of the presence of clutches, limited-slip units require a special lubricant.

Determining Axle Ratio

The drive axle is said to have a certain axle ratio. This number (usually a whole number and a decimal fraction) is actually a comparison of the number of gear teeth on the ring gear and the pinion gear. For example, a 4.11 rear means that theoretically, there are 4.11 teeth on the ring gear and one tooth on the pinion gear or, put another way, the driveshaft must turn 4.11 times to turn the wheels once. Actually, on a 4.11 rear, there might be 37 teeth on the ring gear and 9 teeth on the pinion gear. By dividing the number of teeth on the pinion gear into the number of teeth on the ring gear, the numerical axle ratio (4.11) is obtained. This also provides a good method of ascertaining exactly what axle ratio one is dealing with.

Another method of determining gear ratio is to raise and support the car so that both rear wheels are off the ground. Make a chalk mark on the rear wheel and the driveshaft. Put the transmission in NEUTRAL. Turn the rear wheel one complete turn and count the number of turns that the driveshaft makes. The number of turns that the driveshaft makes in one complete revolution of the rear wheel is an approximation of the rear axle ratio.

Pinion Oil Seal

REMOVAL & INSTALLATION

▶ See Figures 32, 33, 34 and 35

➡The following procedure can be used on all years and models. Slight variations may occur but the basic procedure should cover all years and models. Special tools and mechanical skill are needed for this job.

1. Raise and support the vehicle. Remove the rear wheels and brake drums, or calipers.
2. Mark the driveshaft and yoke for reassembly and disconnect the driveshaft from the rear yoke.
3. With a socket on the pinion nut and an inch lb. torque wrench, rotate the drive pinion several revolutions. Check and record the torque required to turn the drive pinion.
4. Remove the pinion nut. Use a flange holding tool to hold the flange while removing the pinion nut. Discard the pinion nut.
5. Mark the yoke and the drive pinion shaft for reassembly reference.
6. Remove the rear yoke with a puller.
7. Inspect the seal surface of the yoke and replace it with a new one if the seal surface is pitted, grooved, or otherwise damaged.
8. Remove the pinion oil seal using tools 1175-AC and T50T-100A or equivalent.

To install:
9. Before installing the new seal, coat the lip of the seal with rear axle lubricant.
10. Install the seal, driving it into place with a seal driver.
11. Install the yoke on the pinion shaft. Align the marks made on the pinion shaft and yoke during disassembly.
12. Install a new pinion nut. Tighten the nut until end-play is removed from the pinion bearing. Do not overtighten.
13. Check the torque required to turn the drive pinion. The pinion must be turned several revolutions to obtain an accurate reading.
14. Tighten the pinion nut to obtain the torque reading observed during disassembly (Step 3) plus 5 inch lbs. Tighten the nut slightly each time, to avoid overtightening. Do not loosen and then retighten the nut. Pinion preload should be 8-14 inch lbs. (0.8-1.5 Nm).

➡If the desired torque is exceeded a new collapsible pinion spacer sleeve must be installed and the pinion gear preload reset.

15. Install the driveshaft, aligning the index marks made during disassembly. Install the rear brake drums, or calipers, and wheels.

Axle Shaft and Bearing

➡️Both integral and removable carrier type axles are used. The axle type and ratio are stamped on a plate attached to a rear housing cover bolt. Axle types also indicate whether the axle shafts are retained by C-locks. To properly identify a C-lock axle, drain the lubricant, remove the rear cover and look for the C-lock on the end of the axle shaft in the differential side gear bore. If the axle has no cover (solid housing) it is not a C-lock. Always refer to the axle tag code and ratio when ordering parts.

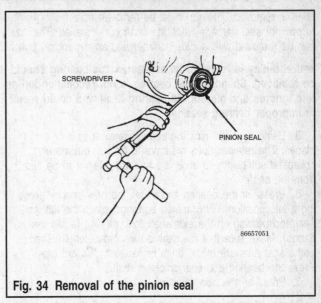

Fig. 34 Removal of the pinion seal

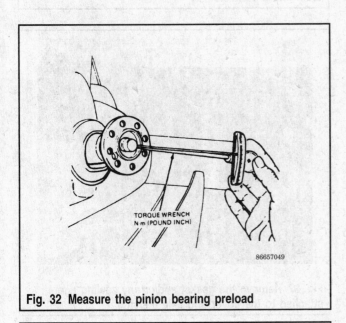

Fig. 32 Measure the pinion bearing preload

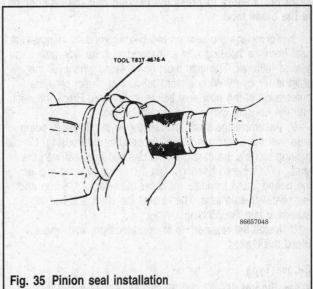

Fig. 35 Pinion seal installation

REMOVAL & INSTALLATION

➡️Bearings must be pressed on and off the shaft with an arbor press. Unless you have access to one, it is inadvisable to attempt any repair work on the axle shaft bearing assemblies.

Flange Type

1. Remove the wheel, tire, and brake drum. With disc brakes, remove the caliper, retainer, nuts and rotor. New anchor plate bolts will be needed for reassembly.
2. Remove the nuts securing the retainer plate in the backing plate, or axle shaft retainer bolts from the housing. Disconnect the brake line with drum brakes.
3. Remove the retainer and install nuts, finger-tight, to prevent the brake backing plate from being dislodged.
4. Pull out the axle shaft and bearing assembly, using a slide hammer. On models with a tapered roller bearing, the tapered cup will normally remain in the axle housing when the

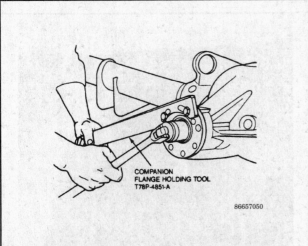

Fig. 33 Remove the companion flange from the rear axle assembly

shaft is removed. The cup must be removed from the housing to prevent seal damage when the shaft is reinstalled. The cup can be removed with a slide hammer and an expanding puller.

➡If end-play is found to be excessive, the bearing should be replaced. Shimming the bearing is not recommended as this ignores end-play of the bearing itself and could result in improper bearing seating.

5. Using a chisel, nick the bearing retainer in 3 or 4 places. The retainer does not have to be cut, but merely collapsed sufficiently to allow the bearing retainer to be slid from the shaft.

6. Press off the bearing and install the new one by pressing it into position. With tapered bearings, place the lubricated seal and bearing on the axle shaft (cup rib ring facing the flange). Make sure that the seal is the correct length. Disc brake seal rims are black, drum brake seal rims are grey. Press the bearing and seal onto the shaft.

7. Press on the new retainer.

➡Do not attempt to press the bearing and the retainer on at the same time.

8. To replace the seal on ball bearing models, remove the seal from the housing with an expanding cone type puller and a slide hammer. The seal must be replaced whenever the shaft is removed. Wipe a small amount of sealer onto the outer edge of the new seal before installation. Press the seal into the housing with a seal installation tool.

9. Assemble the shaft and bearing in the housing, being sure that the bearing is seated properly in the housing. On ball bearing models, be careful not to damage the seal with the shaft. With tapered bearings, first install the tapered cup on the bearing, and lubricate the outer diameter of the cup and the seal with axle lube. Then install the shaft and bearing assembly into the housing.

10. Install the retainer, drum or rotor/caliper and wheel. Bleed the brakes.

C-Lock Type

▶ **See Figures 36, 37, 38, 39, 40, 41, 42, 43 and 44**

1. Lift and safely support the rear of the car on jackstands.
2. Remove the wheels from the brake drums.
3. Place a drain pan under the housing and drain the lubricant by loosening the housing cover.
4. Remove the locks securing the brake drums to the axle shaft flanges and remove the drums.
5. Remove the housing cover and gasket, if used.
6. Position jackstands under the rear frame member and lower the axle housing. This is done to give easy access to the inside of the differential.
7. Working through the opening in the differential case, remove the side gear pinion shaft lockbolt and the side gear pinion shaft.
8. Push the axle shafts inward and remove the C-locks from the inner end of the axle shafts. Temporarily insert the shaft and lockbolt to retain the differential gears in position.
9. Remove the axle shafts with a slide hammer. Be sure the seal is not damaged by the splines on the axle shaft.

Fig. 36 Remove the cover plate, and allow the fluid to drain into a container

Fig. 37 Remove the gasket and/or any sealing agent attached to the cover and axle housing

Fig. 38 Use a ratchet and socket to loosen the retaining bolt . . .

Fig. 39 . . . then remove the bolt

Fig. 40 Remove the retaining pin

Fig. 41 Remove the C-clip securing the axle shafts together . . .

Fig. 42 . . . then slide the axle shaft out

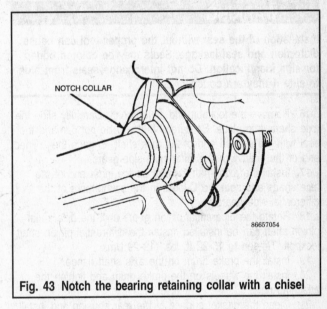

NOTCH COLLAR

Fig. 43 Notch the bearing retaining collar with a chisel

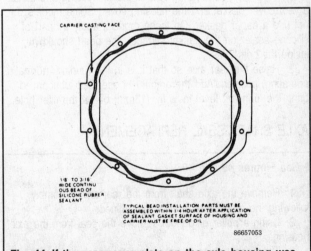

CARRIER CASTING FACE

1/8 TO 3/16 WIDE CONTINUOUS BEAD OF SILICONE RUBBER SEALANT

TYPICAL BEAD INSTALLATION PARTS MUST BE ASSEMBLED WITHIN 1/4 HOUR AFTER APPLICATION OF SEALANT GASKET SURFACE OF HOUSING AND CARRIER MUST BE FREE OF OIL

Fig. 44 If the rear cover plate on the axle housing was installed using sealant only, apply new sealant using this pattern

10. Remove the bearing and oil seal from the housing. Both the seal and bearing can be removed with a slide hammer. Two types of bearings are used on some axles, one requiring a press fit and the other a loose fit. A loose fitting bearing does not necessarily indicate excessive wear.

11. Inspect the axle shaft housing and axle shafts for burrs or other irregularities. Replace any worn or damaged parts. A light yellow color on the bearing journal of the axle shaft is normal, and does not require replacement of the axle shaft. Slight pitting and wear is also normal.

To install:

12. Lightly coat the wheel bearing rollers with axle lubricant. Install the bearings in the axle housing until the bearing seats firmly against the shoulder.

13. Wipe all lubricant from the oil seal bore, before installing the seal.

14. Inspect the original seals for wear. If necessary, these may be replace with new seals, which are prepacked with lubricant and do not require soaking.

15. Install the oil seal.

✳✳WARNING

Installation of the seal without the proper tool can cause distortion and seal leakage. Seals may be colored coded for side identification. Do not interchange seals from side to side if they are coded.

16. Remove the lockbolt and pinion shaft. Carefully slide the axle shafts into place. Be careful that you do not damage the seal with the splined end of the axle shaft. Engage the splined end of the shaft with the differential side gears.

17. Install the axle shaft C-locks on the inner end of the axle shafts and seat the C-locks in the counterbore of the differential side gears.

18. Rotate the differential pinion gears until the differential pinion shaft can be installed. Install the differential pinion shaft lockbolt. Tighten to 15-22 ft. lbs. (19-29 Nm).

19. Install the brake drum on the axle shaft flange.

20. Install the wheels on the brake drum and tighten the attaching nuts.

21. Clean the gasket surface of the rear housing and install a new cover gasket and the housing cover. Some models do not use a paper gasket. On these models, apply a bead of silicone sealer on the gasket surface. The bead should run inside the bolt holes.

22. Raise the rear axle so that it is in the running (normal operating) position. Add the amount of specified lubricant to bring the lubricant level to ½ in. (13mm) below the filler hole.

AXLE SHAFT SEAL REPLACEMENT

▶ See Figures 45 and 46

1. Remove the axle shaft from the rear axle assembly, following the procedures previously outlined.

2. Using a puller or prytool, remove the seal from the axle housing.

3. Thoroughly clean the recess in the rear axle housing from which the seal was removed.

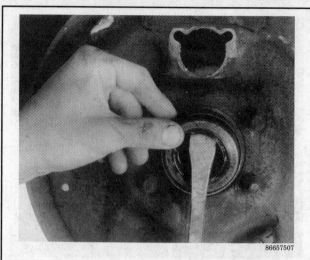

Fig. 45 With the axle shaft removed, pry the outer seal out

To install:

4. Position a new seal on the housing and drive it into place with a seal installation tool. If this tool is not available, a wood block may be substituted.

➡**Although the right and left end seals are usually identical, there are many different types of seals which have been used on rear axle assembles. It is advisable to have one of the old seals with you when you are purchasing new ones.**

5. When the seal is properly installed, install the axle shaft assembly.

Axle Housing

REMOVAL & INSTALLATION

1. Raise the vehicle and support it on jackstands placed under the frame.

Fig. 46 Install a new seal using a proper sized driver

2. Remove the rear wheels.

3. Place an indexing mark on the rear yoke and driveshaft, and disconnect the shaft.

4. Disconnect the shock absorbers from the axle tubes. Disconnect the stabilizer bar at the axle bracket, on vehicles so equipped.

5. Unfasten the brake hose from the tee fitting on the axle housing. Disconnect the brake lines at the clips on the housing. Disconnect the vent tube at the axle.

6. Disconnect the parking brake cable at the frame mounting.

7. Support the rear axle with a jack.

8. Disconnect the lower control arms at the axle and swing them down out of the way.

9. Disconnect the upper control arms at the axle and swing them up out of the way.

10. Lower the axle slightly, remove the coil springs and insulators.

11. Lower the axle housing.

To install:

12. Raise the axle into position and connect the lower arms. Don't tighten the bolts yet.

13. Lower the axle slightly and install the coil springs and insulators.

14. Raise the axle and connect the upper control arms. Don't tighten the bolts yet.

15. Connect the parking brake cable at the frame mounting.

16. Connect the brake hose at the tee fitting on the axle housing.

17. Connect the vent tube at the axle. Apply thread locking compound to the threads.

18. Connect the stabilizer bar at the axle bracket, on vehicles so equipped.

19. Connect the shock absorbers from the axle tubes. Always use a new locknut when installing.

20. Connect the driveshaft.

21. Install the rear wheels.

22. Lower the vehicle.

23. Once the car is back on its wheels, observe the following torques:

Removable carrier axles:

- Lower control arm bolts — 100 ft. lbs. (130 Nm)
- Lower shock absorber nuts — 85 ft. lbs. (110 Nm)
- Upper control arm bolts — 120 ft. lbs. (156 Nm)

Integral carrier axles:

- Lower arm bolts — 100 ft. lbs. (130 Nm)
- Lower shock absorber nuts — 55 ft. lbs. (71 Nm)
- Upper arm bolts — 100 ft. lbs. (130 Nm)

➡**Bleed and adjust the brakes accordingly.**

Troubleshooting the Manual Transmission

Problem	Cause	Solution
Transmission shifts hard	• Clutch adjustment incorrect • Clutch linkage or cable binding • Shift rail binding	• Adjust clutch • Lubricate or repair as necessary • Check for mispositioned selector arm roll pin, loose cover bolts, worn shift rail bores, worn shift rail, distorted oil seal, or extension housing not aligned with case. Repair as necessary.
	• Internal bind in transmission caused by shift forks, selector plates, or synchronizer assemblies	• Remove, dissemble and inspect transmission. Replace worn or damaged components as necessary.
	• Clutch housing misalignment	• Check runout at rear face of clutch housing
	• Incorrect lubricant	• Drain and refill transmission
	• Block rings and/or cone seats worn	• Blocking ring to gear clutch tooth face clearance must be 0.030 inch or greater. If clearance is correct it may still be necessary to inspect blocking rings and cone seats for excessive wear. Repair as necessary.
Gear clash when shifting from one gear to another	• Clutch adjustment incorrect • Clutch linkage or cable binding • Clutch housing misalignment	• Adjust clutch • Lubricate or repair as necessary • Check runout at rear of clutch housing
	• Lubricant level low or incorrect lubricant	• Drain and refill transmission and check for lubricant leaks if level was low. Repair as necessary.
	• Gearshift components, or synchronizer assemblies worn or damaged	• Remove, disassemble and inspect transmission. Replace worn or damaged components as necessary.
Transmission noisy	• Lubricant level low or incorrect lubricant	• Drain and refill transmission. If lubricant level was low, check for leaks and repair as necessary.
	• Clutch housing-to-engine, or transmission-to-clutch housing bolts loose	• Check and correct bolt torque as necessary
	• Dirt, chips, foreign material in transmission	• Drain, flush, and refill transmission
	• Gearshift mechanism, transmission gears, or bearing components worn or damaged	• Remove, disassemble and inspect transmission. Replace worn or damaged components as necessary.
	• Clutch housing misalignment	• Check runout at rear face of clutch housing
Jumps out of gear	• Clutch housing misalignment	• Check runout at rear face of clutch housing
	• Gearshift lever loose	• Check lever for worn fork. Tighten loose attaching bolts.
	• Offset lever nylon insert worn or lever attaching nut loose	• Remove gearshift lever and check for loose offset lever nut or worn insert. Repair or replace as necessary.
	• Gearshift mechanism, shift forks, selector plates, interlock plate, selector arm, shift rail, detent plugs, springs or shift cover worn or damaged	• Remove, disassemble and inspect transmission cover assembly. Replace worn or damaged components as necessary.
	• Clutch shaft or roller bearings worn or damaged	• Replace clutch shaft or roller bearings as necessary

86657100

Troubleshooting the Manual Transmission (cont.)

Problem	Cause	Solution
Jumps out of gear (cont.)	• Gear teeth worn or tapered, synchronizer assemblies worn or damaged, excessive end play caused by worn thrust washers or output shaft gears • Pilot bushing worn	• Remove, disassemble, and inspect transmission. Replace worn or damaged components as necessary. • Replace pilot bushing
Will not shift into one gear	• Gearshift selector plates, interlock plate, or selector arm, worn, damaged, or incorrectly assembled • Shift rail detent plunger worn, spring broken, or plug loose • Gearshift lever worn or damaged • Synchronizer sleeves or hubs, damaged or worn	• Remove, disassemble, and inspect transmission cover assembly. Repair or replace components as necessary. • Tighten plug or replace worn or damaged components as necessary • Replace gearshift lever • Remove, disassemble and inspect transmission. Replace worn or damaged components.
Locked in one gear—cannot be shifted out	• Shift rail(s) worn or broken, shifter fork bent, setscrew loose, center detent plug missing or worn • Broken gear teeth on countershaft gear, clutch shaft, or reverse idler gear Gearshift lever broken or worn, shift mechanism in cover incorrectly assembled or broken, worn damaged gear train components	• Inspect and replace worn or damaged parts • Inspect and replace damaged part • Disassemble transmission. Replace damaged parts or assemble correctly.
Transfer case difficult to shift or will not shift into desired range	• Vehicle speed too great to permit shifting • If vehicle was operated for extended period in 4H mode on dry paved surface, driveline torque load may cause difficult shifting • Transfer case external shift linkage binding • Insufficient or incorrect lubricant • Internal components binding, worn, or damaged	• Stop vehicle and shift into desired range. Or reduce speed to 3–4 km/h (2–3 mph) before attempting to shift. • Stop vehicle, shift transmission to neutral, shift transfer case to 2H mode and operate vehicle in 2H on dry paved surfaces • Lubricate or repair or replace linkage, or tighten loose components as necessary • Drain and refill to edge of fill hole with SAE 85W-90 gear lubricant only • Disassemble unit and replace worn or damaged components as necessary
Transfer case noisy in all drive modes	• Insufficient or incorrect lubricant	• Drain and refill to edge of fill hole with SAE 85W-90 gear lubricant only. Check for leaks and repair if necessary. Note: If unit is still noisy after drain and refill, disassembly and inspection may be required to locate source of noise.
Noisy in—or jumps out of four wheel drive low range	• Transfer case not completely engaged in 4L position • Shift linkage loose or binding • Shift fork cracked, inserts worn, or fork is binding on shift rail	• Stop vehicle, shift transfer case in Neutral, then shift back into 4L position • Tighten, lubricate, or repair linkage as necessary • Disassemble unit and repair as necessary
Lubricant leaking from output shaft seals or from vent	• Transfer case overfilled • Vent closed or restricted	• Drain to correct level • Clear or replace vent if necessary

86657101

Troubleshooting the Manual Transmission(cont.)

Problem	Cause	Solution
Lubricant leaking from output shaft seals or from vent (cont.)	• Output shaft seals damaged or installed incorrectly	• Replace seals. Be sure seal lip faces interior of case when installed. Also be sure yoke seal surfaces are not scored or nicked. Remove scores, nicks with fine sandpaper or replace yoke(s) if necessary.
Abnormal tire wear	• Extended operation on dry hard surface (paved) roads in 4H range	• Operate in 2H on hard surface (paved) roads

86657102

Troubleshooting Basic Clutch Problems

Problem	Cause
Excessive clutch noise	Throwout bearing noises are more audible at the lower end of pedal travel. The usual causes are: • Riding the clutch • Too little pedal free-play • Lack of bearing lubrication A bad clutch shaft pilot bearing will make a high pitched squeal, when the clutch is disengaged and the transmission is in gear or within the first 2″ of pedal travel. The bearing must be replaced. Noise from the clutch linkage is a clicking or snapping that can be heard or felt as the pedal is moved completely up or down. This usually requires lubrication. Transmitted engine noises are amplified by the clutch housing and heard in the passenger compartment. They are usually the result of insufficient pedal free-play and can be changed by manipulating the clutch pedal.
Clutch slips (the car does not move as it should when the clutch is engaged)	This is usually most noticeable when pulling away from a standing start. A severe test is to start the engine, apply the brakes, shift into high gear and SLOWLY release the clutch pedal. A healthy clutch will stall the engine. If it slips it may be due to: • A worn pressure plate or clutch plate • Oil soaked clutch plate • Insufficient pedal free-play
Clutch drags or fails to release	The clutch disc and some transmission gears spin briefly after clutch disengagement. Under normal conditions in average temperatures, 3 seconds is maximum spin-time. Failure to release properly can be caused by: • Too light transmission lubricant or low lubricant level • Improperly adjusted clutch linkage
Low clutch life	Low clutch life is usually a result of poor driving habits or heavy duty use. Riding the clutch, pulling heavy loads, holding the car on a grade with the clutch instead of the brakes and rapid clutch engagement all contribute to low clutch life.

86657103

Self-Adjusting Clutch Diagnosis

Condition	Possible Source	Action
Clutch does not disengage.	Pawl binding due to entrapped sound absorber	Remove contamination and free up pawl.
Clutch gears clash while shifting.	Pawl does not fully engage due to missing or weak pawl spring	Install new spring (pawl).
Pedal makes racheting noise while traveling to floor.	Teeth stripped on pawl or quadrant	Replace worn components.
Pedal travels to floor with no effort or noise.	Pawl does not engage quadrant due to missing spring	Install new spring (pawl).
Excessive pedal effort over 20 kg (45 lbs).*	Damaged or worn cable	Inspect cable. Replace if kinked or crushed.
	Clutch cable excessive wear	Disconnect cable from release lever. Check for smooth operation or binding. Replace if operation is erratic.
	Clutch pedal binding	Disconnect cable from release lever. Check for free pedal movement. Free up as required.
	Clutch release lever binding	Inspect and service as required.
	Clutch disc worn or pressure plate damaged	Service as required
Vehicle will not start with clutch pedal fully depressed.	Clutch interlock switch improperly adjusted.	Reposition self-adjusting clip or rod on press and release clutch pedal.
	Clutch interlock switch damaged.	Perform continuity test. Replace switch if necessary.
	Starter, wiring or battery damaged.	Refer to Section 28-02 and/or Section 31-02.

*NOTE: In the event of a sheared teeth condition on the pawl or quadrant, the pedal efforts are to be evaluated after installation of new components. If the pedal efforts are in excess of 45 lbs., the clutch disc, pressure plate or clutch cable may require replacement.

86677ccc

Troubleshooting Basic Automatic Transmission Problems

Problem	Cause	Solution
Fluid leakage	• Defective pan gasket	• Replace gasket or tighten pan bolts
	• Loose filler tube	• Tighten tube nut
	• Loose extension housing to transmission case	• Tighten bolts
	• Converter housing area leakage	• Have transmission checked professionally
Fluid flows out the oil filler tube	• High fluid level	• Check and correct fluid level
	• Breather vent clogged	• Open breather vent
	• Clogged oil filter or screen	• Replace filter or clean screen (change fluid also)
	• Internal fluid leakage	• Have transmission checked professionally
Transmission overheats (this is usually accompanied by a strong burned odor to the fluid)	• Low fluid level	• Check and correct fluid level
	• Fluid cooler lines clogged	• Drain and refill transmission. If this doesn't cure the problem, have cooler lines cleared or replaced.
	• Heavy pulling or hauling with insufficient cooling	• Install a transmission oil cooler
	• Faulty oil pump, internal slippage	• Have transmission checked professionally
Buzzing or whining noise	• Low fluid level	• Check and correct fluid level
	• Defective torque converter, scored gears	• Have transmission checked professionally
No forward or reverse gears or slippage in one or more gears	• Low fluid level	• Check and correct fluid level
	• Defective vacuum or linkage controls, internal clutch or band failure	• Have unit checked professionally
Delayed or erratic shift	• Low fluid level	• Check and correct fluid level
	• Broken vacuum lines	• Repair or replace lines
	• Internal malfunction	• Have transmission checked professionally

86657104

Lockup Torque Converter Service Diagnosis

Problem	Cause	Solution

No lockup	· Faulty oil pump
	· Sticking governor valve
	· Valve body malfunction
	   (a) Stuck switch valve
	   (b) Stuck lockup valve
	   (c) Stuck fail-safe valve
	· Failed locking clutch
	· Leaking turbine hub seal
	· Faulty input shaft or seal ring
		· Replace oil pump
		· Repair or replace as necessary
		· Repair or replace valve body or its internal components as necessary
		
		· Replace torque converter
		· Replace torque converter
		· Repair or replace as necessary

Will not unlock	· Sticking governor valve
	· Valve body malfunction
	   (a) Stuck switch valve
	   (b) Stuck lockup valve
	   (c) Stuck fail-safe valve
		· Repair or replace as necessary
		· Repair or replace valve body or its internal components as necessary

Stays locked up at too low a speed in direct	· Sticking governor valve
	· Valve body malfunction
	   (a) Stuck switch valve
	   (b) Stuck lockup valve
	   (c) Stuck fail-safe valve
		· Repair or replace as necessary
		· Repair or replace valve body or its internal components as necessary

Locks up or drags in low or second	· Faulty oil pump
	· Valve body malfunction
	   (a) Stuck switch valve
	   (b) Stuck fail-safe valve
		· Replace oil pump
		· Repair or replace valve body or its internal components as necessary

Vibration when revved in neutral Overheating: oil blows out of dip stick tube or pump seal	· Torque converter out of balance · Plugged cooler, cooler lines or fittings · Stuck switch valve	· Replace torque converter · Flush or replace cooler and flush lines and fittings · Repair switch valve in valve body or replace valve body
Shudder after lockup engagement	· Faulty oil pump · Plugged cooler, cooler lines or fittings · Valve body malfunction · Faulty torque converter · Fail locking clutch · Exhaust system strikes underbody · Engine needs tune-up · Throttle linkage misadjusted	· Replace oil pump · Flush or replace cooler and flush lines and fittings · Repair or replace valve body or its internal components as necessary · Replace torque converter · Replace torque converter · Align exhaust system · Tune engine · Adjust throttle linkage

86677ccd

Transmission Fluid Indications

The appearance and odor of the transmission fluid can give valuable clues to the overall condition of the transmission. Always note the appearance of the fluid when you check the fluid level or change the fluid. Rub a small amount of fluid between your fingers to feel for grit and smell the fluid on the dipstick.

If the fluid appears:	It indicates:
Clear and red colored	• Normal operation
Discolored (extremely dark red or brownish) or smells burned	• Band or clutch pack failure, usually caused by an overheated transmission. Hauling very heavy loads with insufficient power or failure to change the fluid, often result in overheating. Do not confuse this appearance with newer fluids that have a darker red color and a strong odor (though not a burned odor).
Foamy or aerated (light in color and full of bubbles)	• The level is too high (gear train is churning oil) • An internal air leak (air is mixing with the fluid). Have the transmission checked professionally.
Solid residue in the fluid	• Defective bands, clutch pack or bearings. Bits of band material or metal abrasives are clinging to the dipstick. Have the transmission checked professionally.
Varnish coating on the dipstick	• The transmission fluid is overheating

86677ccf

8

SUSPENSION AND STEERING

WHEELS

Wheel and Tire Assembly

✱✱CAUTION

Some aftermarket wheels may not be compatible with these vehicles. The use of incompatible wheels may result in equipment failure and possible personal injury! Use only approved wheels!

REMOVAL & INSTALLATION

1. Remove any hubcaps or protective covers over the tire retaining hardware.
2. Loosen each lugnut ½ turn.
3. Raise and safely support the vehicle on jackstands.
4. Remove the lugnuts from the wheel, then remove the wheel and tire assembly.

For detailed wheel removal and installation procedures, see Section 1.

INSPECTION

Replace any wheel that is bent, dented or heavily rusted, has air leaks (aluminum wheels can, in some instances, be repaired), elongated bolt holes, or has excessive lateral or radial runout. Wheels with excessive lateral or radial runout can cause a high-speed vehicle vibration.

The replacement wheels must be of the same load capacity, diameter, width, offset and mounting configuration as the original equipment wheels. Improper wheels may affect wheel and bearing life, ground and tire clearance, or speedometer and odometer calibrations.

Wheel Lug Studs

REPLACEMENT

Lug studs may be removed by using either an arbor press, a heavy duty C-clamp or a hammer and driver. Although the press method is preferred, either method may be used.

Front Wheels

1. Remove the wheel.
2. Remove the hub/rotor or assembly, as described in Section 9.
3. If using a press to remove the stud, proceed as follows:
    a. Place the hub/rotor assembly in a press, supported by the hub surface. Never rest the assembly on the rotor!
    b. Press the stud from the hub.
    c. Position the new stud in the hub and align the serrations. Make sure it is square and press it into place.

4. If you are using a heavy duty C-clamp, proceed as follows:
    a. Support the hub/rotor assembly on a flat, hard surface, resting the assembly on the hub. Never rest the assembly on the rotor!
    b. Using a large C-clamp and socket placed over the stud, tighten the C-clamp to remove the stud from the drum or rotor.
    c. Coat the serrated part of the stud with liquid soap and place it in the hole. Align the serrations.
    d. Place 3 or 4 flat washers on the outer end of the stud and thread a lug nut on the stud with the flat side against the washers. Tighten the lug nut until the stud is drawn all the way in, then remove the nut.

✱✱WARNING

Do not use an impact wrench!

5. If you decide to use a hammer and driver to remove the stud, proceed as follows:
    a. Support the hub/rotor assembly on a flat, hard surface, resting the assembly on the hub. Never rest the assembly on the rotor!
    b. Position a driver, such as a drift or broad punch, on the outer end of the stud and drive it from the hub.
    c. Turn the assembly over, coat the serrations of the new stud with liquid soap, position the stud in the hole, aligning the serrations, then, using the drift and hammer, drive it into place until fully seated.
6. Reinstall the hub/rotor assembly, as described in Section 9.
7. Install the wheel and tighten the lug nuts to 80-105 ft. lbs. (108-142 Nm).

Rear Wheels

1. Remove the wheel.
2. Remove the drum or rotor from the axle shaft or hub studs. (For rotor removal and installation, please refer to Section 9.)
3. Using a large C-clamp and socket, press the stud from the drum or rotor.
4. Coat the serrated part of the stud with liquid soap and place it in the hole. Align the serrations.
5. Place 3 or 4 flat washers on the outer end of the stud and thread a lug nut on the stud with the flat side against the washers. Tighten the lug nut until the stud is drawn all the way in, then remove the nut.

✱✱WARNING

Do not use an impact wrench!

6. Install the drum or rotor.
7. Install the wheel and tighten the lug nuts to 80-105 ft. lbs. (108-142 Nm).

FRONT SUSPENSION

▶ **See Figures 1, 2, 3 and 4**

Each front wheel rotates on a spindle. The spindle's upper and lower ends attach to the upper and lower ball joints which mount to an upper and lower arm respectively. Through 1978 the upper arm pivots on a bushing and shaft assembly bolted to the frame. The lower arm pivots on a crossmember bolt. The coil spring is seated between the lower arm and the top of the spring housing on the underside of the upper arm. A shock absorber is bolted to the lower arm at the bottom and the top of the spring housing. For 1979, the front suspension was redesigned. The arm and strut assembly has been re-placed by a new lower A-arm. The upper ball joint incorporates a new low friction design, and the lower ball joint has a built-in wear indicator. A front stabilizer bar is standard.

➡**All suspension fasteners are important in that they could affect the performance of vital parts and systems, and/or could result in major service expense. Any part must be replaced with one of the same part number or with an exact equivalent. Do not use a replacement part of lesser quality or substitute design. Torque values must be used as specified during assembly to ensure proper retention.**

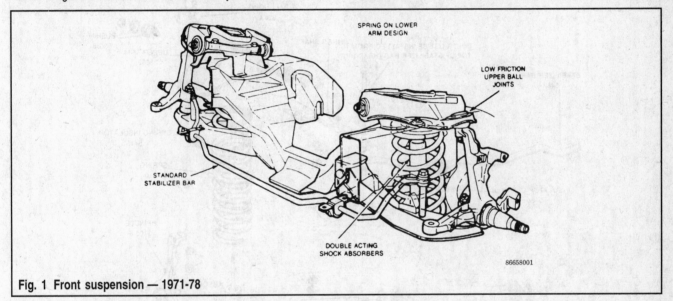

Fig. 1 Front suspension — 1971-78

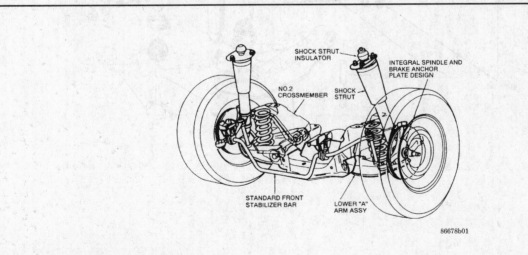

Fig. 2 Front suspension — 1979-1985

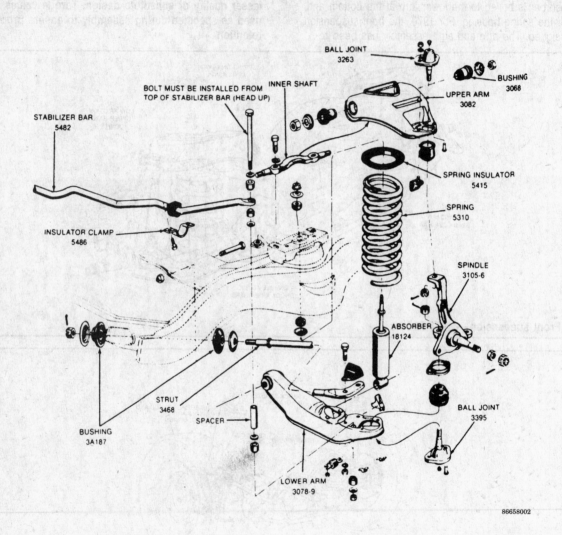

BALL JOINT
3263

BUSHING
3068

UPPER ARM
3082

BOLT MUST BE INSTALLED FROM
TOP OF STABILIZER BAR (HEAD UP)

INNER SHAFT

STABILIZER BAR
5482

SPRING INSULATOR
5415

SPRING
5310

INSULATOR CLAMP
5486

SPINDLE
3105-6

ABSORBER
18124

STRUT
3468

SPACER

BALL JOINT
3395

BUSHING
3A187

LOWER ARM
3078-9

86658002

Fig. 3 Exploded view of the front suspension — 1971-78

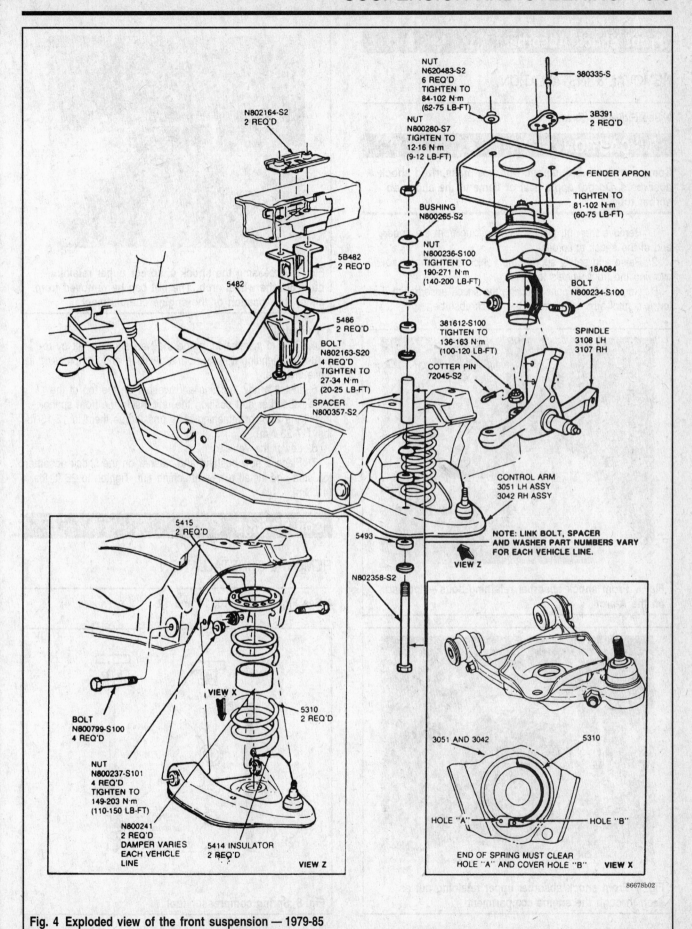

Fig. 4 Exploded view of the front suspension — 1979-85

Front Shock Absorber

REMOVAL & INSTALLATION

▶ See Figures 5, 6 and 7

✳✳CAUTION

Some vehicles are equipped with gas-pressurized shock absorbers. Do not apply heat or flame to the shock absorber tube.

1. Remove the nut, washer and bushing from the upper end of the shock absorber.
2. Raise and safely support the vehicle by the frame rails allowing the front wheels to hang.
3. Remove the 2 bolts securing the shock absorber to the lower control arm and remove the shock absorber.

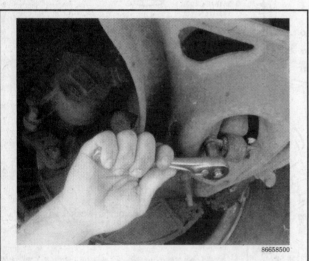

Fig. 5 Front shock absorber retaining bolts — located on the A-arm

Fig. 6 Front shock absorber upper retaining nut as seen through the engine compartment

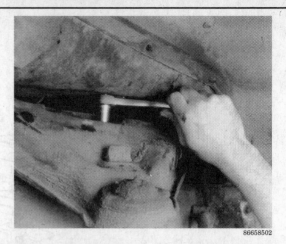

Fig. 7 Accessing the shock absorber upper retaining nut from the wheel arch. The nut can be removed from either this location or the engine compartment

To install:

4. Prior to installation, purge the new shock of air by repeatedly extending it in its normal position and compressing it while inverted.
5. Install a new bushing and washer on the top of the shock absorber and position the unit inside the front spring. Install the 2 lower attaching bolts and torque them to 13-16 ft. lbs. (17-23 Nm).
6. Lower the vehicle.
7. Place a new bushing and washer on the shock absorber top stud and install a new attaching nut. Tighten to 26 ft. lbs. (41 Nm).

Coil Springs

REMOVAL & INSTALLATION

▶ See Figures 8, 9, 10, 11 and 12

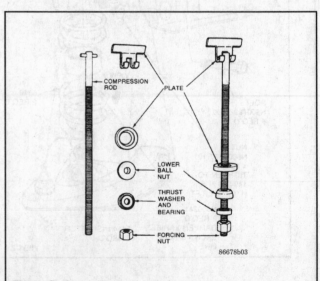

Fig. 8 Spring compressor tool

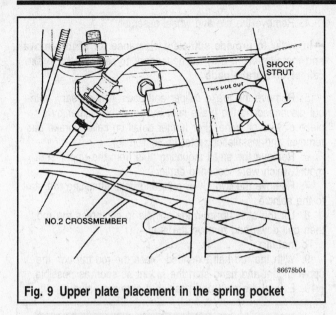

Fig. 9 Upper plate placement in the spring pocket

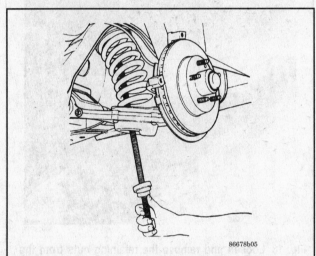

Fig. 10 Spring compressor tool inserted through the control arm

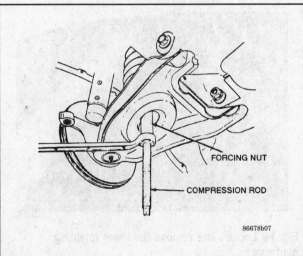

Fig. 11 Begin tightening the tool to compress the spring

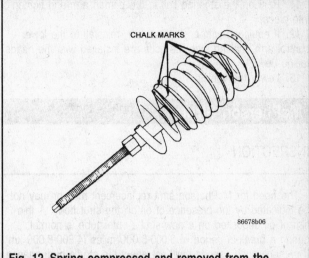

Fig. 12 Spring compressed and removed from the vehicle

➡All suspension fasteners are important in that they could affect the performance of vital parts and systems, and/or could result in major service expense. Any part must be replaced with one of the same part number or with an exact equivalent. Do not use a replacement part of lesser quality or substitute design. Torque values must be used as specified during assembly to ensure proper retention.

1. Raise and safely support the vehicle. Remove the wheel and tire assembly.

2. Disconnect the stabilizer bar link from the lower arm, if equipped.

3. Remove the shock absorber. Remove the steering link from the pitman arm.

4. Using spring compressor tool D78P-5310-A or equivalent, compress the spring.

✳✳CAUTION

Use extreme care whenever working around coil springs. Because of their design and installation, coil springs can exert a high degree of force which could cause injury. Always use the correct tools whenever removing or installing coil springs.

5. Mark the position of the upper and lower coil ends on the spring seats.

6. Remove the 2 lower arm pivot bolts, disengage the lower arm from the frame crossmember and remove the spring.

7. Loosen the forcing nut to relieve the spring tension and remove the tools from the spring.

To install:

8. Assemble the spring in the compressor. Position the spring in its seat and align the coil ends with the marks made earlier. Slowly allow the spring to expand into place.

9. Remove the spring compressor.

10. Install the shock absorber into place, securing with the hardware. Tighten the attaching bolts to 13-16 ft. lbs (17-23 Nm).

11. Position the steering link to the pitman arm and tighten into place.

12. If equipped with a stabilizer bar, reinstall to the lower control arm, making sure the bolts are installed with the heads facing up.

13. Lower the vehicle.

McPherson Struts

INSPECTION

The need for McPherson strut replacement may or may not be indicated by the presence of oil on the strut body. A thin film of oil deposited on a new strut's outer tube is normal during a break-in period of 3,000-5,000 miles (4,800-8,000 km). If present, such seepage will not affect the strut's performance and will normally cease after the initial wetting of the strut body and seal break-in period. However, when oil leakage occurs beyond this period, or causes a constantly wet condition on the entire strut body (and possibly, the lower control arm) strut replacement is indicated.

➡**McPherson struts are non-serviceable, and must be replaced as a unit. Although Ford deems it unnecessary to replace both struts if only one is defective, we suggest that you consider replacing struts in pairs, particularly after several years of service or extended mileage.**

REMOVAL & INSTALLATION

▶ **See Figures 13, 14 and 15**

1. Place the ignition key in the **UNLOCKED** position to permit free movement of the front wheels.

2. Working from the engine compartment, remove the large nut that attaches the strut to the upper mount. A large prytool inserted into the slot will hold the strut rod stationary while removing the nut. Loosen the smaller strut retaining nuts (usually 3), but do not remove them at this time.

✳✳WARNING

The vehicle should not be driven while the nut is removed, so make sure the car is in position for lifting purposes.

3. Raise the front of the vehicle by the lower control arms, then place safety stands under the frame jacking pads, rearward of the wheels, but DO NOT remove the floor jack from the control arm.

✳✳CAUTION

The floor jack must support the control arm at all times during this procedure to keep the coil spring from dislodging and releasing suddenly. This could cause severe personal injury. If available, install a safety chain or spring compressor in order to assure the spring cannot release.

4. Remove the tire and wheel assembly.

➡**In order to provide sufficient clearance for strut removal and installation, it may be necessary to remove the brake caliper and brake pads.**

5. Remove the brake caliper and pads, if necessary, without disconnecting the brake line. Suspend the caliper by a piece of wire or twine. (For further detail on caliper/brake pad removal and installation, refer to Section 9.)

6. Remove the small mounting nuts from the upper strut mount which were loosened earlier.

7. Remove the two lower nuts and bolts attaching the strut to the spindle.

8. Lift the strut up from the spindle to compress the rod, then pull down and remove the strut.

To install:

9. With the rod half extended, place the rod through the upper mount and hand start the mount as soon as possible.

10. Extend the strut and position it onto the spindle.

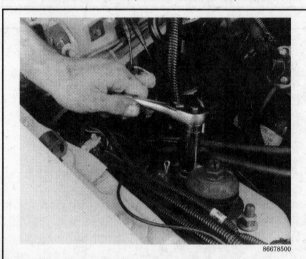

86678500

Fig. 13 Loosen and remove the retaining nuts from the sides of the strut assembly

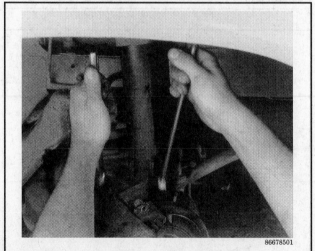

86678501

Fig. 14 Loosen and remove the lower retaining hardware

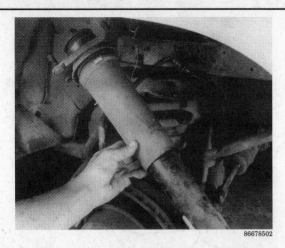

86678502

Fig. 15 Separate the strut assembly from the steering knuckle, then lower the strut down to complete the removal

11. Install the two lower mounting bolts and hand start the nuts.

12. Loosely install the small upper mounting nuts.

➡**Position a large prytool tool in the slot to hold the strut rod stationary while the nut is being tightened.**

13. Remove the suspension load from the lower control arm by lowering the jack, and tighten the lower mounting nuts to 150 ft. lbs. (203 Nm).

14. Raise the suspension control arm and tighten the nut that attaches the strut to the upper body mount to 60-75 ft. lbs. (81-102 Nm). This can be done from inside the engine compartment. Tighten the small upper mounting nuts which were loosely installed earlier.

15. If applicable, remove the wire or twine and install the brake caliper and pads.

16. Install the tire and wheel assembly.

17. Remove the safety stands and lower the vehicle.

18. Check and adjust the front wheel alignment, if necessary.

Upper Control Arm

REMOVAL & INSTALLATION

1971-78 Models

1. Raise and safely support the vehicle on jackstands positioned on the frame just behind the lower arm. Remove the wheel and tire assembly.

2. As a protective measure, compress the coil spring slightly using a spring compressor.

3. Remove the cotter pin from the upper ball joint stud nut. Loosen the nut a few turns but do not remove.

4. Install ball joint press T57P-3006-B or equivalent, between the upper and lower ball joint studs with the adapter screw on top.

➡**This tool should be seated firmly against the ends of both studs, not against the nuts or lower stud cotter pin.**

5. With a wrench, turn the adapter screw until the tool places the stud under compression. Tap the spindle near the upper stud with a hammer to loosen the stud in the spindle.

➡**Do not loosen the stud from the spindle with tool pressure only. Do not contact the boot seal with the hammer.**

6. Remove the tool from between the ball joint studs and place a floor jack under the lower arm.

7. Remove the upper arm attaching bolts and the upper arm.

To install:

8. Transfer the rebound bumper from the old arm to the new arm, or replace the bumper if worn or damaged.

9. Position the upper arm shaft to the frame bracket. Install the 2 attaching bolts and washers. Tighten to 100-140 ft. lbs. (136-190 Nm).

10. Connect the upper ball joint stud to the spindle and install the attaching nut. Tighten the nut to 60-90 ft. lbs. (81-122 Nm). Continue to tighten the nut until the slot for the cotter pin is aligned. Install a new cotter pin.

11. Install the wheel and tire assembly and lower the vehicle. Have the front end alignment checked.

1979-85 Models

1. Raise and safely support the vehicle on safety stands positioned on the frame just behind the lower arm.

2. Scribe position marks around the caster and camber cams for ease of realignment. Use either a centerpunch or screwdriver to scratch marks, or paint to draw the marks.

3. As a protective measure, compress the coil spring slightly using a spring compressor.

4. Remove the wheel and tire assembly and position a floor jack under the lower arm.

5. Remove the retaining nut from the upper ball joint stud to spindle pinch bolt. Tap the pinch bolt to remove from the spindle.

6. Using a suitable prytool, spread the slot to allow the ball joint stud to release out of the spindle.

7. Remove the upper arm retaining bolts and the upper arm.

To install:

8. Transfer the rebound bumper from the old arm to the new arm, or replace the bumper if worn or damaged.

9. Use reference marks from the camber and caster cams as initial settings.

10. Position the upper arm shaft to the frame bracket. Install the 2 retaining bolts and washers. Position the arm in the center of the slot adjustment range and tighten to 100-140 ft. lbs. (130-182 Nm).

11. Connect the upper ball joint stud to the spindle and install the retaining pinch bolt and nut. Tighten the nut to 67 ft. lbs. (92 Nm).

12. Install the wheel and tire assembly and lower the vehicle. Have the front end alignment checked.

CONTROL ARM BUSHING REPLACEMENT

▶ **See Figures 16, 17 and 18**

1. Remove the upper control arm from the vehicle.

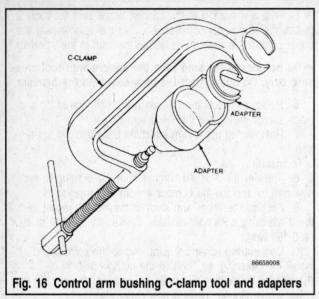

Fig. 16 Control arm bushing C-clamp tool and adapters

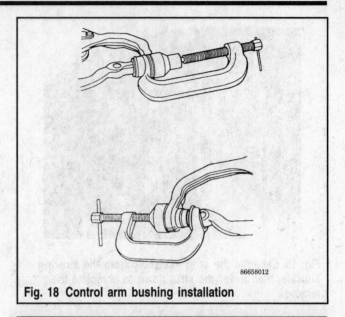

Fig. 18 Control arm bushing installation

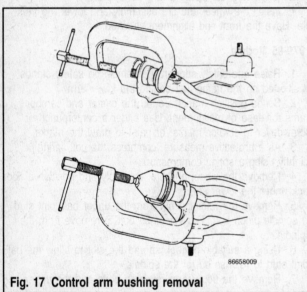

Fig. 17 Control arm bushing removal

2. Remove the nuts and washers from both ends of the control arm shaft. Discard the nuts.

3. Press the bushings from the control arm and shaft using C-clamp tool T74P-3044-A1 or equivalent, and its adapters.

4. Position the shaft and new bushings to the upper control arm. Use the C-clamp tool and adapters to press the new bushings into place.

5. Make sure the control arm shaft is positioned so the serrated side contacts the frame.

6. Install an inner washer, rear bushing only, and 2 outer washers with new nuts on each end of the shaft. Tighten the nuts to 85-100 ft. lbs. (115-136 Nm).

Lower Control Arm

REMOVAL & INSTALLATION

1. Raise the front of the vehicle and position safety stands on the frame behind the lower control arms. Remove the wheel and tire assembly.

2. If equipped with front disc brakes, remove the brake caliper and suspend with a length of wire; do not let the caliper hang by the brake hose. Remove the brake rotor and dust shield.

3. If equipped with front drum brakes, remove the brake line from the rear of the wheel cylinder.

4. Remove the jounce bumper; inspect and save for installation if in good condition. Remove the shock absorber.

5. Disconnect the stabilizer link from the lower arm, if equipped.

6. Disconnect the steering center link from the pitman arm.

7. Remove the cotter pin and loosen the lower ball joint stud nut 1-2 turns.

➡ **Do not remove the nut at this time.**

8. Install a suitable ball joint press tool to place the ball joint stud under compression. With the stud under compression, tap the spindle sharply with a hammer to loosen the stud in the spindle. Remove the ball joint press tool.

9. Tap the spindle boss sharply to relieve the stud pressure. Tap the spindle sharply, near the lower stud, with a hammer to loosen the stud in the spindle.

10. Place a floor jack under the lower arm and remove the coil spring.

11. Remove the ball joint nut and remove the lower control arm.

To install:

12. Position the arm assembly ball joint stud into the spindle and install the nut. Tighten to 80-120 ft. lbs. (108-163 Nm). Continue to tighten until the slot for the cotter pin is aligned. Install a new cotter pin.

13. Position the coil spring into the upper spring pocket and raise the lower arm, aligning the holes in the arm with the holes in the crossmember. Install the bolts and nuts with the washer installed on the front bushing. Do not tighten at this time.

➡**Make sure the pigtail of the lower coil of the spring is in the proper location of the seat on the lower arm, between the 2 holes.**

14. Remove the spring compressor tool.
15. Connect the steering center link at the pitman arm and install the nut. Tighten to 44-46 ft. lbs. (59-63 Nm). Continue to tighten until the slot for the cotter pin is aligned. Install a new cotter pin.
16. Install the shock absorber and the jounce bumper.
17. Install the dust shield, rotor and caliper, if equipped with front disc brakes.
18. Install the brake line and bleed the entire brake system, if equipped with front drum brakes.
19. If equipped, position the stabilizer link to the lower control arm and install the link, bushing and retaining nut. Tighten to 9-15 ft. lbs. (12-20 Nm).
20. Tighten the lower control arm-to-crossmember bolts to 109-140 ft. lbs. (148-190 Nm).
21. Have the front end alignment checked.

CONTROL ARM BUSHING REPLACEMENT

The control arm bushings are integral with the lower control arm. If the bushings are defective, the entire lower control arm must be replaced.

Upper Ball Joint

INSPECTION

▶ **See Figure 19**

1. Raise the vehicle and place floor jacks beneath the lower control arms.
2. Make sure the front wheel bearings are properly adjusted.
3. Inspect the lower ball joint. Replace the lower control arm assembly, if required.
4. Have an assistant grasp the bottom of the tire and move the wheel in and out.
5. As the wheel is being moved, observe the upper control arm where the spindle attaches to it. Any movement between the upper part of the spindle and the upper control arm indicates a bad ball joint which must be replaced.

REMOVAL & INSTALLATION

➡**Ford Motor Company recommends replacement of the upper control arm and ball joint as an assembly. However, aftermarket replacement parts are available, which can be installed using the following procedure.**

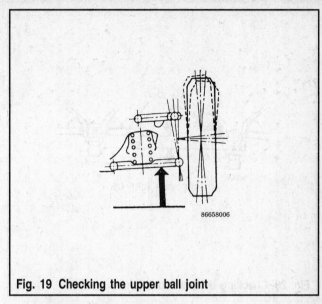

86658006

Fig. 19 Checking the upper ball joint

1. Raise the vehicle and support on frame points so the front wheels fall to their full down position. Remove the wheel and tire assembly.
2. Drill a 1/8 in. hole completely through each ball joint attaching rivet.
3. Using a large chisel, cut off the head of each rivet and drive them from the arm.
4. Place a jack under the lower arm and raise to compress the coil spring.
5. Remove the cotter pin and attaching nut from the ball joint stud.
6. Using a ball joint removal tool, loosen the ball joint stud from the spindle and remove the ball joint from the arm.
   To install:
7. Clean all metal burrs from the arm and install the new ball joint, using the service part nuts and bolts to attach the ball joint.
8. Install the ball joint stud into the spindle. Tighten the ball joint-to-upper spindle nut to 60-90 ft. lbs. (81-122 Nm). Continue to tighten until the slot for the cotter pin is aligned. Install a new cotter pin.
9. Install the wheel and tire assembly and lower the vehicle. Have the front end alignment checked.

Lower Ball Joint

INSPECTION

▶ **See Figures 20 and 21**

1. Support the vehicle in normal driving position with ball joints loaded. This is most easily done with the front of the vehicle supported on ramps.
2. Wipe the grease fitting and ball joint cover checking surface clean.
3. The checking surface should project outside the cover. The checking surface is the round boss into which the grease fitting is threaded. If the checking surface is inside the cover, replace the lower control arm assembly.

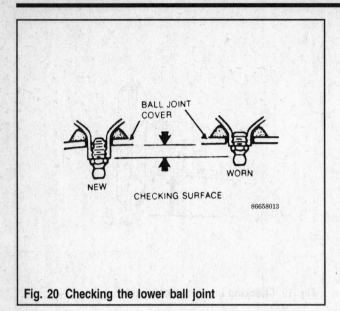

Fig. 20 Checking the lower ball joint

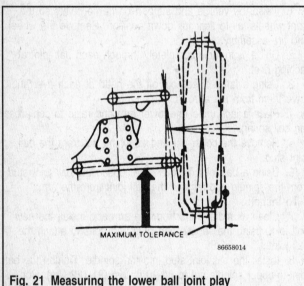

Fig. 21 Measuring the lower ball joint play

REMOVAL & INSTALLATION

The ball joint is an integral part of the lower control arm. If the ball joint is defective, the entire lower control arm must be replaced.

Stabilizer Bar

REMOVAL & INSTALLATION

▶ See Figure 22

1. Raise the front of the vehicle and support the frame using jackstands. Use a hydraulic jack under the control arms to compress the coil spring. Do not compress the spring too much or you will raise the vehicle off the jackstand.

2. Remove the link nuts and disconnect the stabilizer bar from the links.

3. Remove the retaining nuts from the pinch bolts at the spindles. Spread the slots in the spindles with a prytool to e the ball studs. Be careful not to damage the ball joint stud seal.

4. Remove the stabilizer bar brackets from the frame and remove the stabilizer bar. If worn, cut the insulators from the stabilizer bar.

5. Unfasten the retaining nuts from the studs at the end of the bar. Use removal tool 3290-D or equivalent to separate the links from the ends of the stabilizer bar.

To install:

6. Coat the necessary parts of the stabilizer bar with petroleum jelly. Slide new insulators onto the stabilizer bar.

7. Install the ball joint links into the ends of the bar with the retaining nuts. Tighten to 30-40 ft. lbs. (40-55 Nm).

8. Attach the ends of the stabilizer bar to the lower control arm with new nuts and links. Tighten the nuts to 9-15 ft. lbs. (12-20 Nm). Install the insulator brackets and tighten the bolts to 14-26 ft. lbs. (19-35 Nm).

9. Position the bar under the vehicle and engage the upper ball joint links to the spindles. Install the insulator brackets with the retaining nuts. Tighten the pinch bolts and nuts at the spindles to 30-40 ft. lbs. (40-55 Nm) Tighten the bracket-to-frame nuts to 44-59 ft. lbs. (59-81 Nm).

Knuckle and Spindle

REMOVAL & INSTALLATION

1971-78 Models

1. Raise the front of the vehicle and position safety stands on the frame behind the lower control arms. Remove the wheel and tire assembly.

2. As a protective measure, use a spring compressor and compress the coil spring slightly.

3. If equipped with front disc brakes, remove the brake caliper and suspend with a length of wire; do not let the caliper hang by the brake hose. Remove the brake rotor and dust shield.

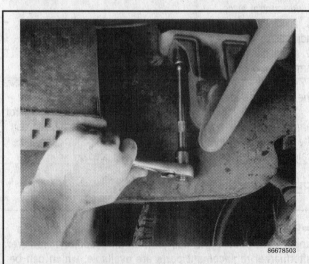

Fig. 22 Loosen and remove the retaining bolts securing the sway bar to the vehicle body

4. If equipped with front drum brakes, disconnect the brake line from the rear of the wheel cylinder.

5. Disconnect the tie rod end from the spindle using removal tool 3290-D or equivalent.

6. Remove and discard the cotter pins from both ball joint studs and loosen the stud nuts 1-2 turns. Do not remove the nuts at this time.

7. Place a floor jack under the spring/control arm and lift the assembly slightly.

8. Position a suitable ball joint press tool between the upper and lower ball joint studs. Turn the tool with a wrench until the tool places the studs under compression.

9. Using a hammer, sharply hit the spindle near the studs to loosen the studs from the spindle.

10. Raise the jack more to further support the lower control arm. Remove the upper and lower ball joint stud nuts and remove the spindle.

11. Do not lower the floor jack.

To install:

12. Position the spindle on the stabilizer bar upper ball joint stud. Install the pinch bolt and loosely install the nut.

13. Position the spindle on the lower ball joint stud and install the stud nut. Tighten the nut to 80-119 ft. lbs. (108-162 Nm). Continue to tighten the nut until a slot for the cotter pin is aligned. Install a new cotter pin.

14. Raise the lower arm and guide the upper ball joint stud into the spindle.

15. Install the upper ball joint stud nut and tighten to 60-90 ft. lbs. (81-122 Nm). Continue to tighten the nut until a slot for the cotter pin is aligned. Install a new cotter pin.

16. Connect the tie rod end to the spindle. Install the nut and tighten to 43-46 ft. lbs. (59-63 Nm). Continue to tighten the nut until the slot for the cotter pin is aligned and install a new cotter pin.

17. If equipped with front disc brakes, install the brake dust shield, caliper and rotor.

18. If equipped with front drum brakes, connect the brake line to the wheel cylinder, and bleed the entire brake system.

19. Lower the floor jack to relieve pressure from the control arm assembly. Remove the spring compressor from the coil spring.

20. Install the wheel and tire assembly and lower the vehicle.

21. Have the the front end alignment checked.

1979-85 Models

1. Raise and support the front end on jackstands positioned under the frame.

2. Remove the wheels.

3. As a protective measure, use a spring compressor to compress the coil springs slightly.

4. Remove the calipers and suspend them out of the way.

5. Remove the hub and rotor assemblies.

6. Remove the rotor dust shields.

7. Unbolt the stabilizer links from the control arms.

8. Using a separator, disconnect the tie rod ends from the spindle.

9. Remove the cotter pin and loosen the ball joint stud nut a few turns. Do not remove it at this time!

10. Place a floor jack under the spring/control arm and lift the assembly slightly.

11. Using a hammer, tap the spindle boss sharply to relieve stud pressure.

12. While supporting the lower control arm with the floor jack, compress the coil spring further, using the spring compressor, then remove the stud nut.

13. Remove the two bolts and nuts attaching the spindle to the shock strut. Compress the shock strut until working clearance is obtained.

14. Remove the spindle.

To install:

15. Place the spindle on the ball joint stud, and install the stud nut, but do not tighten it yet.

16. Lower the shock strut until the attaching holes are aligned with the holes in the spindle. Install two new bolts and nuts.

17. Tighten the ball joint stud nut to 100-120 ft. lbs. (136-163 Nm) and install the cotter pin.

18. Torque the shock strut-to-spindle attaching nuts to 150-180 ft. lbs. (203-244 Nm).

19. Lower the floor jack.

20. Install the stabilizer links. Torque the nuts to 9-12 ft. lbs. (12-16 Nm).

21. Remove the spring compressor from the coil spring.

22. Attach the tie rod ends and torque the nuts to 35-47 ft. lbs. (47-64 Nm).

23. The remainder of installation is the reverse of removal. Have the alignment checked after the work is completed.

Front Wheel Bearings

Please refer to Section 1 for the procedure on removal, packing and installation of the front wheel bearings.

ADJUSTMENT

1. Raise and safely support the front of the vehicle.

2. Remove the wheel cover and grease cap.

3. Remove the cotter pin and nut retainer.

4. Loosen the adjusting nut 3 turns, then rock the wheel back and forth a few times to release the brake pads from the rotor.

5. While rotating the wheel and hub assembly, tighten the adjusting nut to 17-25 ft. lbs. (23-34 Nm), to seat the bearings.

6. Back off the adjusting nut ½ turn, then retighten to 10-15 inch lbs. (1.1-1.7 Nm).

7. Install the nut retainer and a new cotter pin. Check the wheel rotation. If it is noisy or rough, the bearings either need to be cleaned and repacked or replaced. After adjustment is completed, install the grease cap and wheel cover.

8. Lower the vehicle. Before driving the vehicle, pump the brake pedal several times to restore normal brake pedal travel.

Front End Alignment

➡Because of the delicate nature of alignment as well as the need for special tools, it is recommended that a professional perform all alignment procedures.

CASTER

Caster is the forward or rearward tilt of the top of the front wheel spindle. If the top of the spindle tilts to the rear, caster is positive. If the top of the spindle tilts to the front, caster is negative.

Caster adjustment is made using special tools that are inserted into holes in the frame. The upper control arm shaft retaining bolts are then loosened and the tools are used to act on the control arm shaft to make the caster adjustment.

CAMBER

Camber is the amount the centerline of the wheel is tilted inward or outward from the true vertical. If a wheel tilts out-ward away from the vehicle, camber is positive. If the top of a wheel tilts inward toward the vehicle, camber is negative.

Camber adjustment is made using the same tools described under caster.

TOE-IN

With the front wheels in the straight-ahead position, measure the distance between the extreme front and also between the extreme rear of both front wheels. The difference between the 2 distances is the toe-in or toe-out. Toe is only adjusted after the caster and camber is checked and adjusted.

Toe-in adjustment is made by turning the threaded sleeves connecting the inner and outer tie rod ends. Toe should be checked with the engine running, so the power steering control valve will be in the center (neutral) position, if equipped, and the steering wheel locked in place with a steering wheel holder.

REAR SUSPENSION

▶ **See Figures 23 and 24**

The rear axle is attached to the vehicle frame by control arms mounted to the lower portion of the axle. Two coil springs are connected between the rear axle and the frame on 1971-82 models and between the control arms and frame on 1983-85 models. Ride control is provided by 2 shock absorbers mounted independantly to the frame and axle.

In addition, some vehicles are equipped with a stabilizer bar to control side roll.

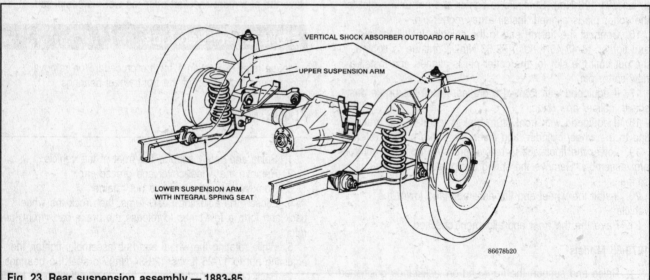

VERTICAL SHOCK ABSORBER OUTBOARD OF RAILS

UPPER SUSPENSION ARM

LOWER SUSPENSION ARM WITH INTEGRAL SPRING SEAT

86678b20

Fig. 23 Rear suspension assembly — 1883-85

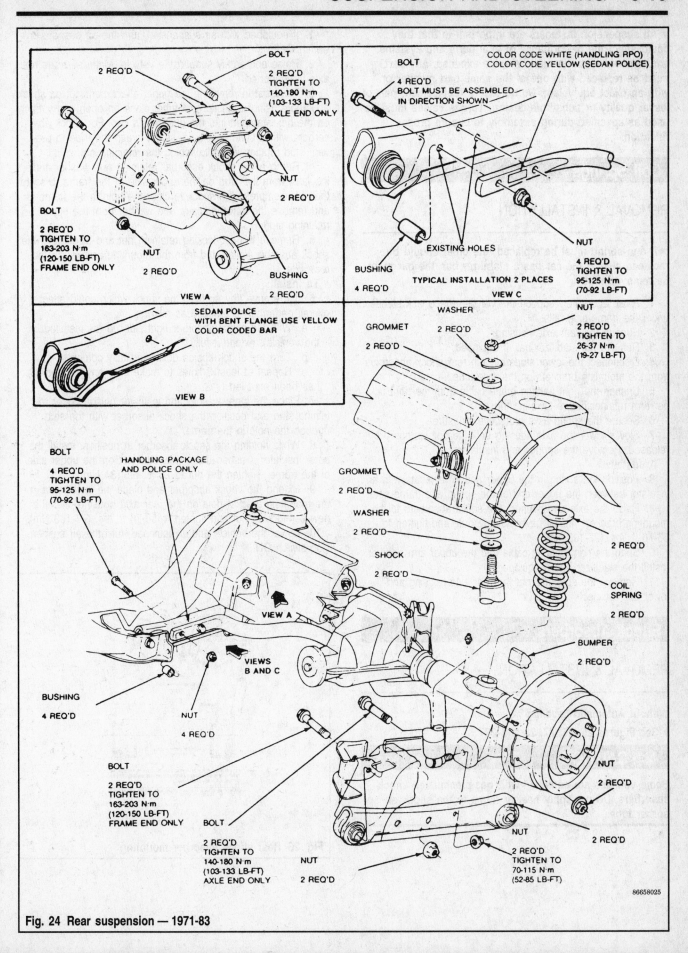

Fig. 24 Rear suspension — 1971-83

86658025

➡All suspension fasteners are important in that they could affect the performance of vital parts and systems, and/or could result in major service expense. Any part must be replaced with one of the same part number or with an exact equivalent. Do not use a replacement part of lesser quality or substitute design. Torque values must be used as specified during assembly to ensure proper retention.

Coil Springs

REMOVAL & INSTALLATION

➡If one spring must be replaced, the other should be replaced also. If the car has a stabilizer bar, the bar must be removed first.

1. Raise and safely support the vehicle. Place jack stands under the frame side rails.
2. Support the rear axle housing.
3. Remove the stabilizer bar, if equipped.
4. Disconnect the lower studs of both rear shock absorbers from the mounting brackets on the axle tube.
5. Unsnap the right parking brake cable from the right upper arm retainer before lowering the axle.
6. Secure the spring as a protective measure
7. Slowly lower the axle housing until the coil springs are released. Remove the springs and insulators.

To install:

8. Position the spring in the upper and lower seats with an insulator between the upper end of the spring and frame seat.
9. Raise the axle and connect the shock absorbers to the mounting brackets. Install new retaining nuts and tighten to 56-76 ft. lbs. (77-103 Nm).
10. Snap the right parking cable into the upper arm retainer. Install the stabilizer bar, if equipped.
11. Remove the support from the rear axle housing and lower the vehicle.

Shock Absorbers

REMOVAL & INSTALLATION

Without Automatic Leveling

▶ See Figures 25, 26, 27, 28 and 29

✳✳CAUTION

Some vehicles are equipped with gas-pressurized shock absorbers. Do not apply heat or flame to the shock absorber tube.

1. If equipped with air suspension, turn the air suspension switch **OFF**.
2. Raise and safely support the vehicle. Make sure the rear axle is supported.
3. To assist in removing the upper attachment nut on shock absorbers using a plastic dust tube, place an open end wrench on the hex stamped into the dust tube's cap. For shock absorbers with a steel dust tube, simply grasp the tube to prevent stud rotation when loosening the retaining nut.
4. Remove the shock absorber retaining nut, washer and insulator from the stud on the upper side of the frame. Discard the nut. Compress the shock to clear the hole in the frame and remove the inner insulator and washer from the upper retaining stud.
5. Remove the self-locking retaining nut and disconnect the shock absorber lower stud from the mounting bracket on the rear axle.

To install:

6. To remove any air from the shock which could effect overall performance proceed as follows:
   a. With the shock absorber right side up (as installed in the vehicle), extend it fully.
   b. Turn the shock upside down and fully compress it.
   c. Repeat at least 3 times to make sure any trapped air has been expelled.
7. Place the inner washer and insulator on the upper retaining stud and position the shock absorber with the stud through the hole in the frame.
8. While holding the shock absorber in position, install the outer insulator, washer and a new stud nut on the upper side of the frame. Tighten the nut to 25 ft. lbs. (34 Nm).
9. Extend the shock absorber and place the lower stud in the mounting bracket hole on the rear axle housing. Install a new self-locking nut and tighten to 56-76 ft. lbs. (77-103 Nm).
10. Lower the vehicle and, if equipped, turn the air suspension switch **ON**.

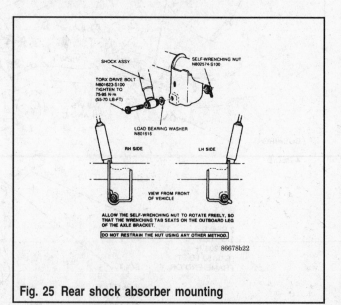

Fig. 25 Rear shock absorber mounting

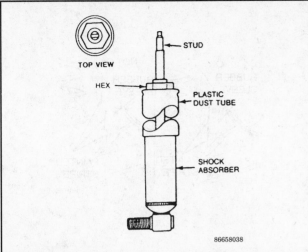

Fig. 26 Rear shock absorber — except with automatic leveling suspension

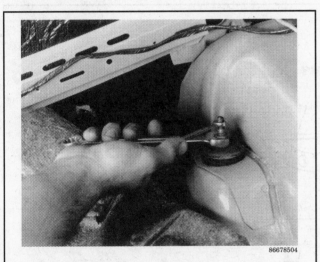

Fig. 27 Loosen and remove the retaining nuts securing the shock to the vehicle body

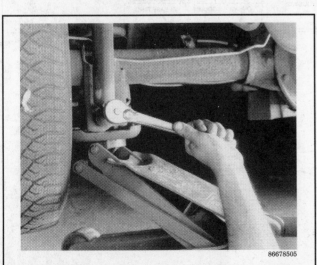

Fig. 28 The shock absorber lower retaining bolts are accessed from under the car

Fig. 29 With the hardware unfastened, the shock can be lowered and removed

With Automatic Leveling

▶ **See Figures 30, 31 and 32**

1. Make sure the ignition switch is in the **OFF** position.
2. Disconnect the height sensor connector link before allowing the rear axle to hang free.
3. Raise and safely support the vehicle so the suspension arms hang free. The rear shock absorbers will vent air through the compressor and a hissing noise will be heard. When the noise stops, the air lines can be disconnected. A residual pressure of 8-24 psi (55-165 kPa) will remain in the air lines.
4. Disconnect the air line by pushing in on the retainer ring(s) and pulling the line(s) out.
5. Remove the top retaining nut, washer and bushing.
6. Remove the bottom retaining nut and washer. Remove the shock absorber.

To install:

7. Position the shock absorber and install the bottom retaining washer and nut. Tighten to 52-85 ft. lbs. (70-115 Nm).
8. Install the top bushing, washer and retaining nut. Tighten to 14-26 ft. lbs. (19-35 Nm).

➡Check the rubber sleeve on the shock absorber to be sure it is not wrapped up. To assist in identifying wrap-up during installation, a white stripe is on the rubber sleeve and on the shock absorber body. The stripes should align. To correct a wrap-up condition, loosen the upper shock retaining nut and turn the shock to align the stripes. Retighten the retaining nut.

9. Connect the air line to the shock absorber by pushing in on the retainer ring and installing the air line.
10. Connect the height sensor connecting link and lower the vehicle.

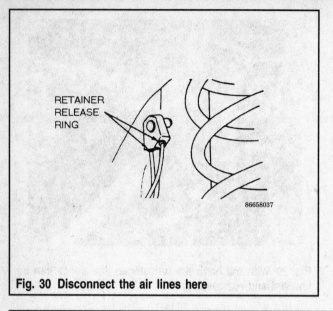

RETAINER
RELEASE
RING

86658037

Fig. 30 Disconnect the air lines here

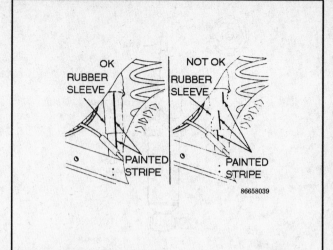

OK
RUBBER
SLEEVE

NOT OK
RUBBER
SLEEVE

PAINTED
STRIPE

PAINTED
STRIPE

86658039

Fig. 31 Make sure the rubber sleeve on the air shock absorber is not wrapped up

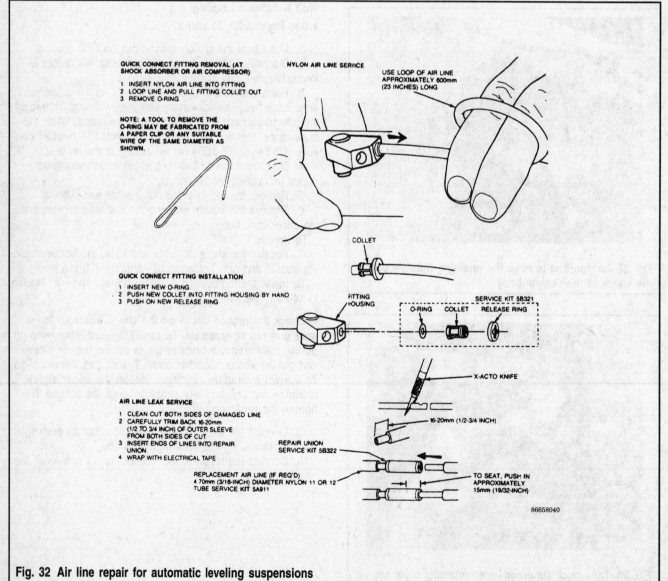

QUICK CONNECT FITTING REMOVAL (AT
SHOCK ABSORBER OR AIR COMPRESSOR)

1 INSERT NYLON AIR LINE INTO FITTING
2 LOOP LINE AND PULL FITTING COLLET OUT
3 REMOVE O-RING

NOTE: A TOOL TO REMOVE THE
O-RING MAY BE FABRICATED FROM
A PAPER CLIP OR ANY SUITABLE
WIRE OF THE SAME DIAMETER AS
SHOWN.

NYLON AIR LINE SERVICE

USE LOOP OF AIR LINE
APPROXIMATELY 600mm
(23 INCHES) LONG

COLLET

QUICK CONNECT FITTING INSTALLATION

1 INSERT NEW O-RING
2 PUSH NEW COLLET INTO FITTING HOUSING BY HAND
3 PUSH ON NEW RELEASE RING

FITTING
HOUSING

SERVICE KIT 5B321

O-RING   COLLET   RELEASE RING

X-ACTO KNIFE

16-20mm (1/2-3/4 INCH)

AIR LINE LEAK SERVICE

1 CLEAN CUT BOTH SIDES OF DAMAGED LINE
2 CAREFULLY TRIM BACK 16-20mm
   (1/2 TO 3/4 INCH) OF OUTER SLEEVE
   FROM BOTH SIDES OF CUT
3 INSERT ENDS OF LINES INTO REPAIR
   UNION
4 WRAP WITH ELECTRICAL TAPE

REPAIR UNION
SERVICE KIT 5B322

REPLACEMENT AIR LINE (IF REQ'D)
4 70mm (3/16-INCH) DIAMETER NYLON 11 OR 12
TUBE SERVICE KIT 5A911

TO SEAT, PUSH IN
APPROXIMATELY
15mm (19/32-INCH)

86658040

Fig. 32 Air line repair for automatic leveling suspensions

INSPECTING

Bounce Test

Each shock absorber can be tested by bouncing the corner of the vehicle until maximum up and down movement is obtained. Let go of the vehicle. It should stop bouncing in 1-2 bounces. If not, the shock absorber should be inspected for damage and possibly replaced.

Shock Absorber Mounting

Check the shock absorber mountings for worn or defective grommets, loose mounting nuts, interference or missing bump stops. If no apparent defects are noted, continue testing.

Fluid Leaks

Disconnect each shock absorber lower mount and pull down on the unit until it is fully extended. Inspect for leaks in the seal area. Shock absorber fluid is very thin and has a characteristic odor and dark brown color. Do not confuse the glossy paint on some shock absorbers with leaking fluid. A slight trace of fluid is a normal condition; shock absorbers are designed to seep a certain amount of fluid past the seals for lubrication. If you are in doubt as to whether the fluid is coming from the shock absorber itself or from some other source, wipe the seal area clean and manually operate the shock absorber, using the following procedure. Fluid will appear if the unit is leaking.

➡️**It may be necessary to fabricate a holding fixture for certain types of shock absorbers.**

1. Grip the lower end of the shock absorber. Pull down (rebound stroke) and then push up (compression stroke). Compare the rebound resistance of both shock absorbers and compare the compression resistance. Usually, any shock absorber showing a noticeable difference will be the one at fault.

2. If the shock absorber has internal noises, extend it fully, then exert an extra pull. If a small additional movement is felt, this usually means a loose piston, and the shock absorber should be replaced. Other noises which indicate the need for replacement are a squeal after a full stroke in both directions, a clicking noise on fast reverse, and a lag at reversal near mid-stroke.

Control Arms

REMOVAL & INSTALLATION

Upper Control Arm

➡️**If one upper control arm requires replacement, also replace the upper control arm on the other side of the vehicle. Remove and install one at a time to prevent the axle from rolling or slipping sideways. If both upper control arms and both lower control arms are to be removed at the same time, remove both coil or air springs, as detailed in this section.**

1. If equipped with an air suspension, make sure the switch is in the **OFF** position.
2. Raise the vehicle and support the frame side rails with jack stands.
3. Support the rear axle under the differential pinion nose as well as under the axle.
4. Unsnap the parking brake cable from the upper arm retainer. If equipped, disconnect the height sensor from the ball stud on the left upper control arm.
5. Remove and discard the nuts and bolts retaining the upper arm to the axle housing and frame. Remove the arm from the vehicle.
   To install:
6. Hold the upper arm in place on the front arm bracket and install a new retaining bolt and self-locking nut. Do not tighten at this time.
7. Secure the upper arm to the axle housing with new retaining bolts and nuts. The bolts must be pointed toward the front of the vehicle.
8. Raise the suspension with a jack until the upper arm rear pivot hole is in position with the hole in the axle bushing. Install a new pivot bolt and nut with the nut facing inboard.
9. Tighten the upper arm-to-axle pivot bolts to 103-132 ft. lbs. (140-180 Nm) and upper arm-to-frame pivot bolts to 119-149 ft. lbs. (162-203 Nm).
10. Snap the parking brake cable into the upper arm retainer. Connect the height sensor to the ball stud on the left upper arm, if equipped.
11. Remove the supports from the frame and axle and lower the vehicle. If equipped, turn the air suspension switch **ON**.

Lower Control Arm

➡️**If one lower control arm requires replacement, also replace the lower control arm on the other side of the vehicle. If both upper control arms and both lower control arms are to be removed at the same time, remove both coil or air springs, as detailed in this section.**

1. Mark the rear shock absorber tube position in relation to the protective sleeve, with the vehicle on a level surface and in the normal ride height position.
2. If equipped with air suspension, make sure the switch is in the **OFF** position.
3. Raise and safely support the vehicle on jackstands.
4. Remove the stabilizer bar, if equipped.
5. Support the axle with jack stands under the differential pinion nose as well as under the axle.
6. Remove and discard the lower arm pivot bolts and nuts and remove the lower arm.
   To install:
7. Position the lower arm to the frame bracket and axle. Install new bolts and nuts with the nuts facing outboard.
8. Raise the axle to the normal ride height position, compressing the shock absorbers to the marks made during the removal procedure. Tighten the lower arm-to-axle pivot bolt to 103-132 ft. lbs. (140-180 Nm) and lower arm-to-frame pivot bolt to 119-149 ft. lbs. (162-203 Nm).
9. Install the stabilizer bar, if equipped.
10. Remove the jack stands and lower the vehicle. If equipped, turn the air suspension switch **ON**.

Stabilizer Bar

REMOVAL & INSTALLATION

▶ See Figure 33

1. If equipped, turn the air suspension switch **OFF**.

2. Raise the vehicle and support the frame side rails with jack stands. Allow the axle housing to hang with the shock absorbers fully extended.

3. Remove the bolts, nuts and spacers retaining the stabilizer bar to the lower control arms and remove the stabilizer bar. Discard the bolts and nuts.

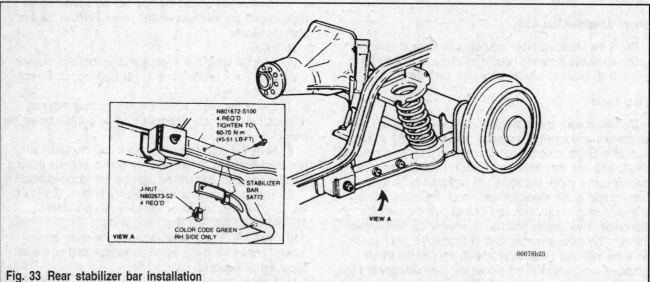

N801672-S100
4 REQ'D
TIGHTEN TO
60-70 N·m
(45-51 LB-FT)

J-NUT
N802673-S2
4 REQ'D

STABILIZER
BAR
5A772

COLOR CODE GREEN
RH SIDE ONLY

VIEW A

VIEW A

86678b23

Fig. 33 Rear stabilizer bar installation

To install:

4. Align the 4 holes in the stabilizer bar with the holes in the lower control arms. Install the color coded end of the bar on the right side of the vehicle. Install 4 new bolts and nuts and the existing spacers. Tighten to 70-92 ft. lbs. (95-125 Nm).

5. Remove the jack stands and lower the vehicle. If equipped, turn the air suspension switch **ON**.

STEERING

Steering Wheel

REMOVAL & INSTALLATION

▶ See Figures 34, 35, 36 and 37

1. Disconnect the negative battery cable.
2. Remove the horn pad and cover assembly. A small prytool can be used here. Unplug the horn electrical connector.
3. Unplug the cruise control switch electrical connector, if equipped.
4. Scribe a mark on the bolt, column shaft and steering wheel for alignment.

5. Remove and discard the steering wheel bolt. Remove the steering wheel using a suitable puller.

➡**Do not use a knock-off type steering wheel puller or strike the retaining bolt with a hammer. This could cause damage to the steering shaft bearing.**

To install:

6. Align the index marks on the steering wheel and shaft and install the steering wheel.
7. Install a new steering wheel retaining bolt and tighten to 30-35 ft. lbs. (41-47 Nm).
8. Connect the cruise control electrical connector, if equipped.
9. Connect the horn electrical connector and install the horn pad and cover.
10. Connect the negative battery cable.

Fig. 34 Remove the steering wheel pad using a small prytool if needed

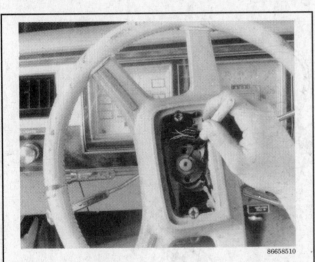

Fig. 35 Scribe marks on the steering wheel nut, column shaft and steering wheel

Fig. 36 Use a suitable ratchet and socket to loosen and remove the retaining nut

Fig. 37 Install a steering wheel puller, and remove the wheel from the column

Turn Signal/Combination Switch

REMOVAL & INSTALLATION

▶ See Figures 38, 39, 40, 41, 42, 43 and 44

1971-78 Models

1. Disconnect the negative battery cable.
2. Remove the steering wheel as previously outlined.
3. Unscrew the turn signal lever from the side of the column. Remove the emergency flasher retainer and knob, if so equipped.
4. Locate and remove the finish cover on the steering column and disconnect the wiring connector plugs.
5. On all 1971 and models with a tilt steering column it is necessary to separate the wires from the connector plug in order to remove the switch and wires. First note the location and color code of each wire, prior to removal. Remove the plastic cover from the wiring harness. Attach a piece of heavy cord to the switch wires to pull them down through the column during installation.
6. Remove the retaining clips and screws from the turn signal switch and lift the switch and wire assembly from the top of the column.

To install:

7. Tape the ends of the new switch wires together and transfer the pull cord to these wires.
8. Pull the wires down through the column with the cord and attach the new switch to the column hub.
9. If the switch wires were separated from the connector plug, press the wires into their proper location. Connect the wiring connector plugs and install the finish cover on the column.
10. Install the turn signal lever. Install the emergency flasher retainer and knob, if so equipped.
11. Install the steering wheel as outlined in this section.
12. Connect the negative battery cable and test the operation of the turn signals, horn, emergency flashers, and speed control, if equipped.

1979-85 Models

1. Disconnect the negative battery cable. On standard steering columns, remove the upper extension shroud (below the steering wheel) by unsnapping the shroud from the retaining clip. On tilt columns, remove the trim shroud by removing the five self-tapping screws.

2. Use a pulling and twisting motion, while pulling straight out, to remove the turn signal switch lever.

3. Peel back the piece of foam rubber from around the switch.

4. Disconnect the two switch electrical connectors.

5. Remove the two self-tapping screws which secure the switch to the lock cylinder housing, and disengage the switch from the housing.

To install:

6. Align the switch mounting holes with the corresponding holes in the lock cylinder housing. Install the two screws.

7. Position the foam back into place.

8. Align the key on the turn signal lever with the keyway in the switch and push the lever into place.

9. Install the two electrical connectors.

10. Install the trim shrouds.

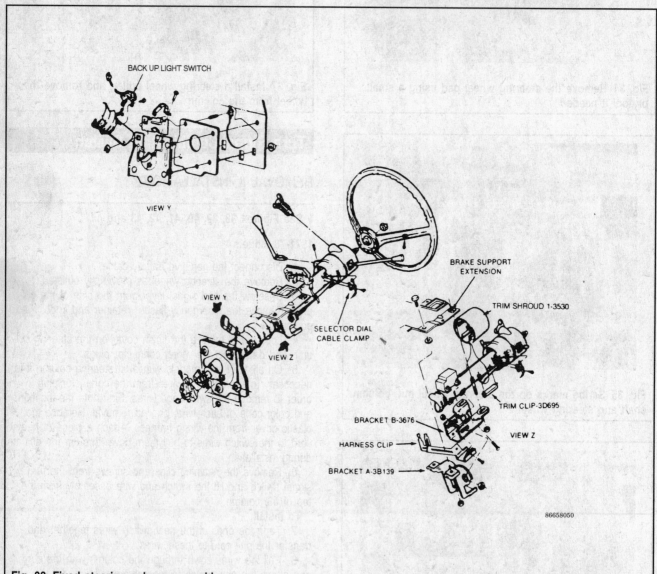

Fig. 38 Fixed steering column assembly

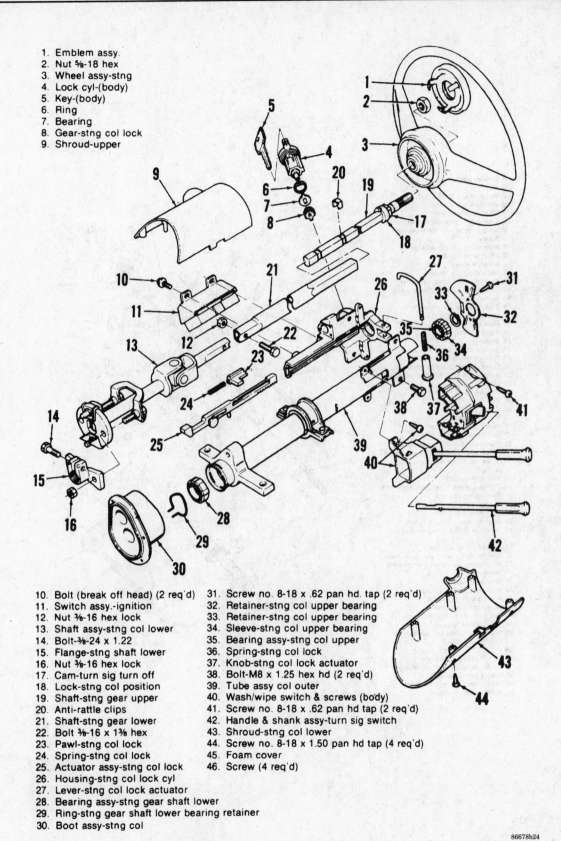

1. Emblem assy.
2. Nut ⅝-18 hex
3. Wheel assy-stng
4. Lock cyl-(body)
5. Key-(body)
6. Ring
7. Bearing
8. Gear-stng col lock
9. Shroud-upper

10. Bolt (break off head) (2 req'd)
11. Switch assy.-ignition
12. Nut ⅜-16 hex lock
13. Shaft assy-stng col lower
14. Bolt-⅜-24 x 1.22
15. Flange-stng shaft lower
16. Nut ⅜-16 hex lock
17. Cam-turn sig turn off
18. Lock-stng col position
19. Shaft-stng gear upper
20. Anti-rattle clips
21. Shaft-stng gear lower
22. Bolt ⅜-16 x 1⅜ hex
23. Pawl-stng col lock
24. Spring-stng col lock
25. Actuator assy-stng col lock
26. Housing-stng col lock cyl
27. Lever-stng col lock actuator
28. Bearing assy-stng gear shaft lower
29. Ring-stng gear shaft lower bearing retainer
30. Boot assy-stng col

31. Screw no. 8-18 x .62 pan hd. tap (2 req'd)
32. Retainer-stng col upper bearing
33. Retainer-stng col upper bearing
34. Sleeve-stng col upper bearing
35. Bearing assy-stng col upper
36. Spring-stng col lock
37. Knob-stng col lock actuator
38. Bolt-M8 x 1.25 hex hd (2 req'd)
39. Tube assy col outer
40. Wash/wipe switch & screws (body)
41. Screw no. 8-18 x .62 pan hd tap (2 req'd)
42. Handle & shank assy-turn sig switch
43. Shroud-stng col lower
44. Screw no. 8-18 x 1.50 pan hd tap (4 req'd)
45. Foam cover
46. Screw (4 req'd)

86678b24

Fig. 39 Exploded view of fixed steering column assembly

1 Emblem assy.
2 Bolt
3 Wheel assy. - strng.
4 Handle & shank assy.
   tilt strng. wheel lever
5 Extension - strng. col. shroud
6 Spring - strng. col. upper bearing
7 Screw
8 Plate strng. col. clip retainer
9 Lever strng. col. link
10 Ring 3/4 retaining type
11 Clip - strng. col. shroud
12 Bearing assy. - strng. col. upper
13 Pin 4mm x 25.6 straight roune end
14 Release lever
15 Spring - strng. col. release lever
16 Pin - 4mm x 5.75
17 Pivot pin
18 Flange casting
19 Bumpers
20 Bearing assy. - strng. col. upper
21 Position spring
22 Cover - strng. col. lock actuator
23 Screw no. 8-18 x .62 pan head tapping
24 Lock cyl. (body)
25 Ring 24 x 1.07 retainer type
26 Bearing
27 Gear - strng. col. lock
28 Shroud - upper
29 Housing - strng. col lock cyl.
30 Bolt (break off head) (2 req'd.)
31 Wash/wipe switch & screws (body)
32 Foam cover - turn signal & w/w switch
33 Screw no. 8-18 x .62 pan head tap
   (2 req'd)
34 Turn signal switch
35 Handle & shank assy. - turn sig. switch
36 Pawl - strng. col. lock
37 Spring - strng. col. lock
38 Tube assy. col. outer
39 Actuator assy. - strng. col. lock
40 Screw no. 8-18 x 1.50 pan head tap
   (5 req'd)
41 Shroud - strng. col. lower
42 Bearing assy. - strng. gear shaft lower
43 Ring - strng. gear shaft lower bearing
   retainer
44 Boot assy. - strng. col.
45 Shaft assy. - strng. col. upper
46 Anti-rattle clips (2 req'd)
47 Shaft - strng. gear lower
48 Bolt 7/16 - 14 x 1.50 hex
49 Nut 7/16 - 14 hex lock
50 Shaft assy. - strng. col. lower
51 Bolt 3/8 - 24 x 1.22
52 Nut 3/8 - 16 hex lock
53 Flange - strng. shaft lower
54 Lever - strng. col. lock actuator
55 Spring - strng. col. lock
56 Knob - strng. col. lock actuator
57 Screw - strng. wheel

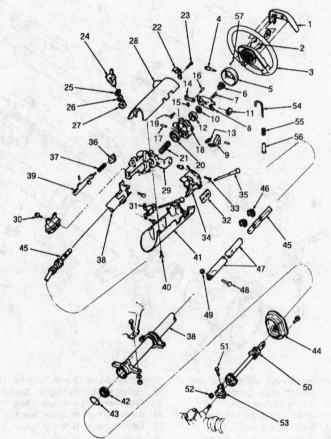
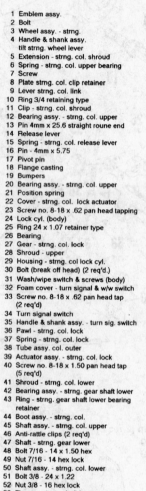

86678b25

Fig. 40 Tilt steering column components

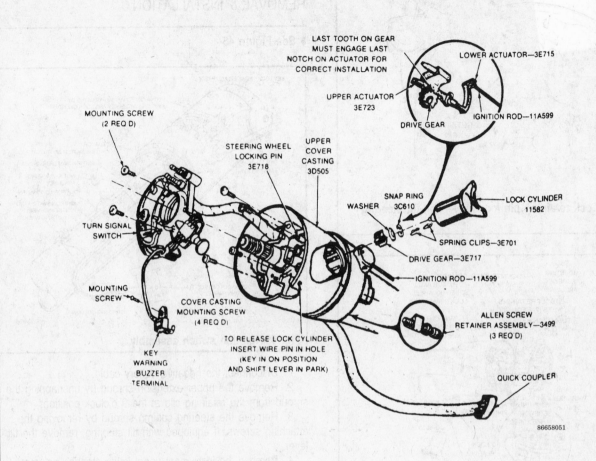

Fig. 41 Exploded view of tilt steering column upper components

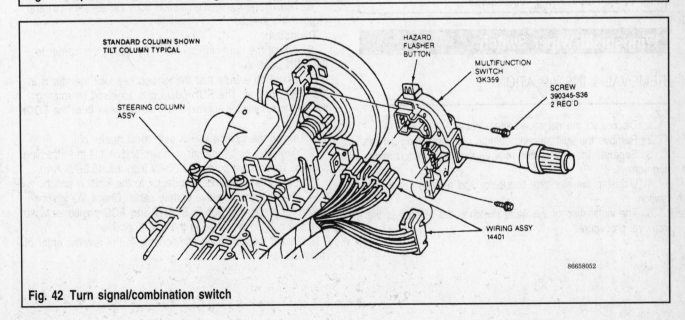

Fig. 42 Turn signal/combination switch

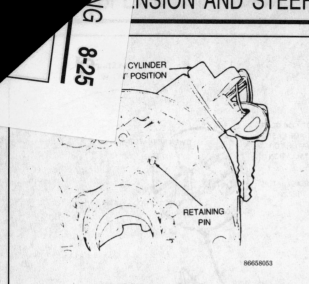

Fig. 43 Lock retaining pin location — non-tilt steering systems

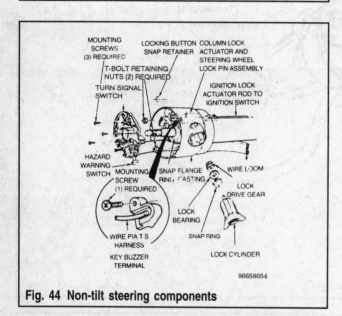

Fig. 44 Non-tilt steering components

Windshield Wiper Switch

REMOVAL & INSTALLATION

1. Disconnect the negative battery cable.
2. Remove the split steering column cover retaining screws.
3. Separate the halves and remove the wiper switch retaining screws.
4. Unfasten the electrical connector and remove the wiper switch.
5. The installation of the wiper switch is the reverse of the removal procedure.

Ignition Switch

REMOVAL & INSTALLATION

▶ **See Figure 45**

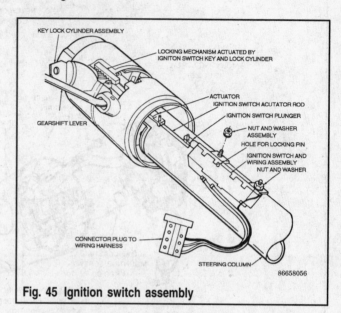

Fig. 45 Ignition switch assembly

1. Disconnect the negative battery cable.
2. Remove the upper extension shroud by unsnapping the shroud from the retaining clip at the 9 o'clock position.
3. Remove the steering column shroud by removing the attaching screws. If equipped with tilt steering, remove the tilt lever.
4. Remove the instrument panel lower steering column cover.
5. Unfasten the electrical connector from the ignition switch.
6. Rotate the ignition key lock cylinder to the **RUN** position.
7. Remove the 2 screws attaching the ignition switch.
8. Disengage the ignition switch from the actuator pin and remove the switch.

To install:

9. Adjust the new ignition switch by sliding the carrier to the **RUN** position.
10. Check to ensure that the ignition key lock cylinder is in the **RUN** position. The **RUN** position is achieved by rotating the key lock cylinder approximately 90 degrees from the **LOCK** position.
11. Install the ignition switch onto the actuator pin.
12. Align the switch mounting holes and install the attaching screws. Tighten the screws to 50-69 inch lbs. (5.6-7.9 Nm).
13. Plug in the electrical connector to the ignition switch.
14. Connect the negative battery cable. Check the ignition switch for proper function in **START** and **ACC** positions. Make sure the column is locked in the **LOCK** position.
15. Install the remaining components in the reverse order of removal.

Ignition Lock Cylinder

REMOVAL & INSTALLATION

Functional Lock
▶ See Figure 46

The following procedure is for vehicles with functioning lock cylinders. Ignition keys are available for these vehicles from the dealer or local locksmith if the key number is known. In some areas, locksmiths are able to make a key from the lock cylinder itself, although this is a fairly expensive task.

To remove the lock cylinder, proceed as follows:
1. Disconnect the negative battery cable.
2. Remove the trim shroud halves by removing the attaching screws. Remove the electrical connector from the key warning switch.

3. Turn the ignition to the **RUN** position.
4. Place a ⅛ in. diameter wire pin or small drift punch in the hole in the casting surrounding the lock cylinder and depress the retaining pin while pulling out on the lock cylinder to remove it from the column housing.

To install:
5. To install the lock cylinder, turn it to the **RUN** position and depress the retaining pin. Insert the lock cylinder into its housing in the lock cylinder casting.
6. Make sure the cylinder is fully seated and aligned in the interlocking washer before turning the key to the **OFF** position. This action will permit the cylinder retaining pin to extend into the hole in the lock cylinder housing.
7. Using the ignition key, rotate the cylinder to ensure the correct mechanical operation in all positions.
8. Check for proper start in **P** or **N**. Also make sure the start circuit cannot be actuated in **D** or **R** positions and that the column is locked in the **LOCK** position.
9. Connect the key warning buzzer electrical connector and install the trim shrouds, if required.

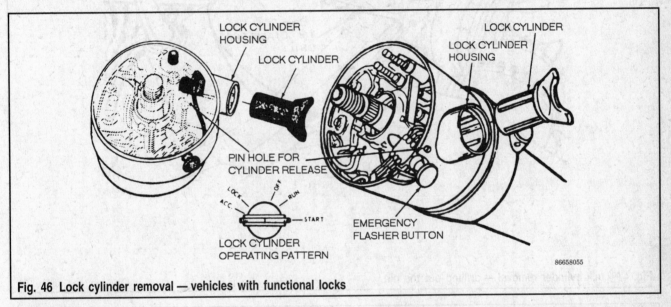

Fig. 46 Lock cylinder removal — vehicles with functional locks

Non-Functional Lock
▶ See Figures 47 and 48

The following procedure is for vehicles with non-functioning locks. On these vehicles, the lock cylinder cannot be rotated due to a lost or broken key, the key number is not known, or the lock cylinder cap is damaged and/or broken, preventing the lock cylinder from rotating.
1. Disconnect the negative battery cable.
2. Remove the steering wheel; refer to the procedure in this section.
3. Remove the trim shroud halves by removing the attaching screws. Remove the electrical connector from the key warning switch.
4. Drill out the retaining pin using a ⅛ in. (3mm) diameter drill, being careful not to drill deeper than ½ in. (13mm). Position a chisel at the base of the ignition lock cylinder. Strike the chisel with sharp blows, using a hammer, to break the cap away from the lock cylinder.

5. Drill approximately 1¾ in. (4cm) down the middle of the ignition key slot, using a ⅜ in. (9mm) diameter drill bit, until the lock cylinder breaks loose from the base of the lock cylinder. Remove the lock cylinder and drill shavings from the lock cylinder housing.
6. Remove the snapring or retainer, washer and steering column lock gear. Thoroughly clean all drill shavings and other foreign materials from the casting.
7. Inspect the lock cylinder housing for damage and replace, as necessary.

To install:
8. Install the ignition lock cylinder and check for smooth operation.
9. Unfasten the electrical connector to the key warning switch and install the trim shrouds, if necessary.
10. Install the steering wheel and connect the negative battery cable.

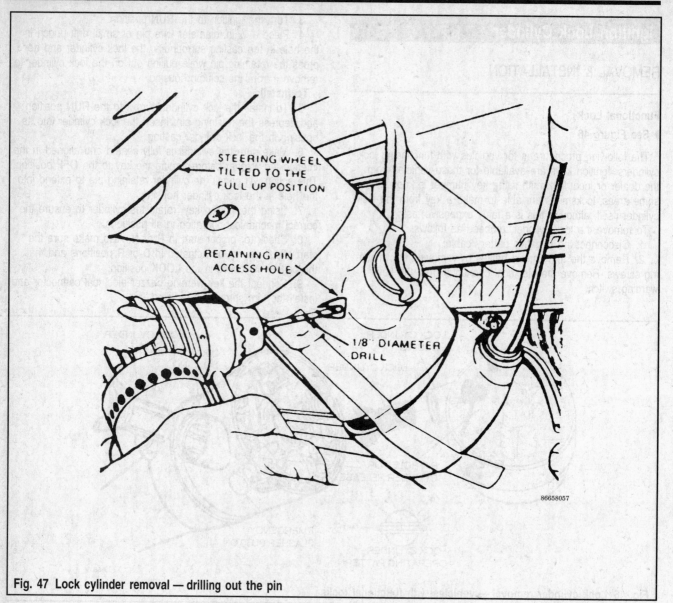

STEERING WHEEL
TILTED TO THE
FULL UP POSITION

RETAINING PIN
ACCESS HOLE

1/8" DIAMETER
DRILL

86658057

Fig. 47 Lock cylinder removal — drilling out the pin

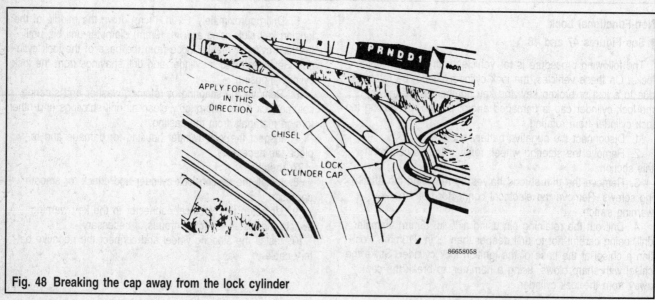

PRNDD1

APPLY FORCE
IN THIS
DIRECTION

CHISEL

LOCK
CYLINDER CAP

86658058

Fig. 48 Breaking the cap away from the lock cylinder

Steering Column

REMOVAL & INSTALLATION

▶ See Figure 49

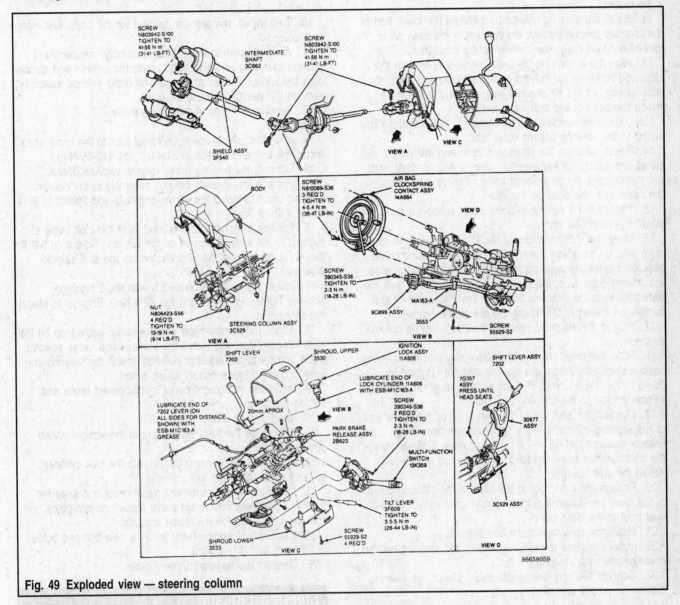

Fig. 49 Exploded view — steering column

1971-78 Models

1. Disconnect the negative battery cable.
2. Remove the bolt attaching the steering column shaft to the lower steering shaft assembly. Disengage the U-joint stub shaft from the column shaft by collapsing the intermediate shaft assembly. Disconnect the transmission shift rod from the transmission control selector lever, at the bottom of the shift tube.
3. Remove the shift linkage grommet and replace with new, using shift linkage insulator tool T67P-7341-A or equivalent.
4. Remove the steering column trim shrouds.
5. Remove the steering column cover and hood release mechanism directly under the column.

6. Unfasten the electrical connectors to the steering column switches.
7. Loosen the 4 nuts holding the column to the brake pedal support, allowing the column to be lowered enough for access to the shift indicator lever and cable assembly.

➡**Be careful not to lower the column too far, so the plastic lever or cable is not damaged due to the weight of the column.**

8. Reach between the steering column and instrument panel and gently lift the transmission range indicator cable off the cleat on the transmission range indicator lever. Remove

the transmission range indicator cable clamp from the steering column tube.

9. Remove the 4 screws that attach the dust boot to the dash panel.

10. Remove the 4 attaching nuts securing the column to the brake pedal support. Lower the column to clear the 4 mounting bolts and pull the column out.

To install:

11. Install the steering column by inserting the lower end of the steering column through the opening in the dash panel. Be careful not to damage the column during installation.

12. Align the 4 bolts on the brake pedal support with the mounting holes on the column collar and bracket. Attach the nuts loosely, so the column will hang with a clearance between the column and instrument panel.

13. Loosely assemble the transmission range indicator cable clamp to the steering column outer tube.

14. Reach between the steering column and instrument panel and attach the transmission range indicator cable onto the transmission range indicator lever by slipping the loop on the cable over the cleat on the lever.

15. Tighten the 4 column-to-brake pedal support nuts to 20-37 ft. lbs. (27-50 Nm).

16. Move the shift selector into the **D** position against the drive stop on the insert plate. Rotate the transmission range indicator bracket, located approximately midpoint on the steering column outer tube, clockwise or counterclockwise until the transmission range indicator pointer in the instrument cluster centers on the letter **D**. Tighten the nut on the bracket.

17. Plug in the electrical connectors to the steering column switches.

18. Slide the lower steering shaft assembly into the steering column shaft and attach with the bolt and nut. Tighten to 35-45 ft. lbs. (48-61 Nm). The stone shield must be removed to gain access to the coupling insulator.

19. Connect the shift rod to the shift lever on the lower end of the steering column in the engine compartment using linkage insulator tool T67P-7341-A or equivalent. Make sure the grommet has been replaced before the rod is installed. Adjust the shift linkage.

20. Engage the dust boot at the base of the steering column to the dash panel opening. Install the 4 screws that attach the dust boot to the dash panel.

21. Install the steering column trim shrouds.

22. Install the hood release mechanism and steering column cover beneath the steering column.

23. Connect the negative battery cable. Check the steering column for proper operation.

1979-85 Models

1. Make sure the front wheels are in the straight-ahead position.

2. Remove the steering wheel as described in this section.

3. Remove the right and left lower moldings from the instrument panel.

4. Unscrew the tilt lever from the column.

5. Remove the 2 instrument panel reinforcement brace bolts and remove the reinforcement.

6. Remove the steering column to parking brake control shake brace. Disconnect the transmission range selector cable from the actuator housing by removing the screw.

7. Remove the 2 combination switch retaining screws and set the combination switch aside.

8. Remove the pinch bolt from the steering column to extension shaft. Compress the extension shaft toward the engine and separate it from the column U-joint.

9. Disconnect the shift cable from the selector lever pivot. Remove the shift cable and bracket from the lower column mounting.

10. If equipped, remove the harness for the brake shift interlock solenoid.

11. While supporting the column assembly, remove the 4 column assembly retaining nuts. Lower the column and disconnect the vacuum hoses at the parking brake release switch or remove the vacuum release assembly.

12. Remove the column from the vehicle.

To install:

13. Align the column lower universal joint to the lower shaft. Install the bolt and tighten to 31-41 ft. lbs. (40-56 Nm).

14. Connect the parking brake release vacuum hoses.

15. Position the steering column assembly to the column support bracket. Install the 4 retaining nuts and tighten to 9-14 ft. lbs. (13-19 Nm).

16. Position the shift cable bracket, with the shift cable attached, to the lower 2 screws of the column. Tighten to 5-8 ft. lbs. (7-11 Nm). Snap the shift cable onto the shift selector pivot ball.

17. Install the combination switch with the 2 retaining screws. Tighten to 18-26 inch lbs. (2-3 Nm). Engage all electrical connectors.

18. Attach the transmission range selector cable loop on the shift selector hook and install the transmission range selector cable bracket to the actuator housing. Install the steering column to parking brake control shake brace.

19. Install the instrument panel reinforcement brace and tighten the bolts.

20. Install the tilt lever.

21. Make sure the front wheels are in the straight-ahead position.

22. Install the key warning buzzer into the lock cylinder housing and secure the lock cylinder.

23. Install the lower instrument panel cover and snap the right and left lower instrument panel mouldings into place. Install the upper and lower column shrouds.

24. Install the steering wheel. Install a new bolt and tighten to 23-33 ft. lbs. (31-48 Nm).

25. Connect the negative battery cable.

Steering Linkage

▶ See Figure 50

REMOVAL & INSTALLATION

Pitman Arm

▶ See Figure 51

1. Position the front wheels in the straight-ahead position. Raise and safely support the vehicle.

2. Remove and discard the cotter pin from the castellated nut that attaches the center link to the pitman arm. Remove the castellated nut.

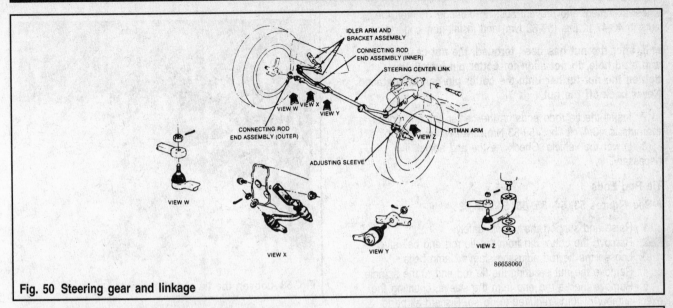

Fig. 50 Steering gear and linkage

3. Disconnect the center link from the pitman arm using removal tool 3290-D or equivalent.

4. Remove the pitman arm retaining nut and lockwasher

5. Make sure the front wheel are in the straight-ahead position. Remove the pitman arm from the steering gear sector shaft using pitman arm puller T64P-3590-F or equivalent.

To install:

6. With the front wheels in the straight-ahead position, place the pitman arm, pointing it rearward, on the sector shaft. Align the blind tooth on the pitman arm with the blind tooth on the steering gear sector shaft.

7. Install the nut and lockwasher and tighten to 233-250 ft. lbs. (316-338 Nm).

8. Install the center link on the pitman arm and install the castellated nut. Tighten the nut to 43-47 ft. lbs. (59-63 Nm) and install a new cotter pin.

➡ If, after the nut has been torqued, the nut castellations and stud hole do not align for cotter pin installation, tighten the nut further until the cotter pin can be installed. Never back off the nut.

Idler Arm

1. Raise and safely support the vehicle.

2. Remove the cotter pin, nut and washer retaining the center link to the idler arm. Discard the cotter pin.

3. Remove the center link from the idler arm.

4. Remove the bolts and nuts securing the idler arm to the frame and remove the idler arm.

To install:

5. Install the idler arm to the frame with the bolts and nuts. Tighten to 85-97 ft. lbs. (115-132 Nm).

6. Place the idler arm and front wheels in the straight-ahead position to maintain steering wheel alignment and prevent bushing damage.

7. Install the center link nut and washer and tighten to 43-47 ft. lbs. (59-63 Nm). Install a new cotter pin.

➡ If, after the nut has been torqued, the nut castellations and stud hole do not align for cotter pin installation, tighten the nut further until the cotter pin can be installed. Never back off the nut.

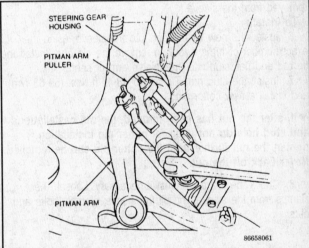

Fig. 51 Removing the pitman arm from the steering gear sector shaft

Center Link

▶ See Figure 52

1. Raise and safely support the vehicle.

2. Remove the cotter pins and nuts that attach the inner tie rod ends to the center link. Discard the cotter pins.

3. Disconnect the inner tie rod ends from the center link using removal tool 3290-D or equivalent.

4. Remove the cotter pin and nut that retains the pitman arm to the center link. Disconnect the pitman arm from the center link using removal tool 3290-D or equivalent.

5. Remove the cotter pin and nut retaining the idler arm to the center link and remove the center link. Discard the cotter pin.

To install:

6. Position the center link to the pitman arm and idler arm and loosely install the nuts. Place the idler arm and front wheels in the straight-ahead position to maintain steering

wheel alignment and prevent bushing damage. Tighten the nuts to 43-47 ft. lbs. (59-63 Nm) and install new cotter pins.

➡If, after the nut has been torqued, the nut castellations and stud hole do not align for cotter pin installation, tighten the nut further until the cotter pin can be installed. Never back off the nut.

7. Install the tie rode ends on the center link and tighten the nuts to 43-47 ft. lbs. (59-63 Nm). Install new cotter pins.

8. Lower the vehicle. Check the toe and adjust, if necessary.

Tie Rod Ends

▶ See Figures 53, 54, 55, 56, 57 and 58

1. Raise and support the vehicle safely.
2. Remove the cotter pin from the tie rod end ball stud.
3. Loosen the tie rod adjusting sleeve clamp bolts.
4. Remove the nut securing the tie rod end to the spindle.
5. Remove the tie rod end from the sleeve, counting the exact number of turns required to do so. Discard all parts removed from the sleeve.

To install:

6. Install the new tie rod end into the sleeve, using the exact number of turns it took to remove the old one. Install the tie rod end ball stud into the spindle arm or center link.

7. Install the stud nut. Tighten to 43-47 ft. lbs. (59-63 Nm) and install a new cotter pin.

➡If, after the nut has been torqued, the nut castellations and stud hole do not align for cotter pin installation, tighten the nut further until the cotter pin can be installed. Never back off the nut.

8. Check the toe and adjust if necessary. Loosen the clamps from the sleeve and oil the sleeve, clamps, bolts and nuts.

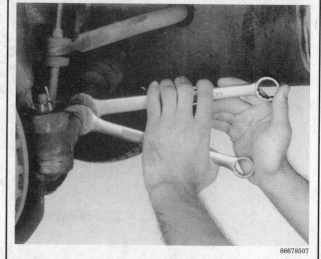
Fig. 53 Loosen the tie rod clamp nuts

Fig. 54 Remove the cotter pin from the tie rod stud

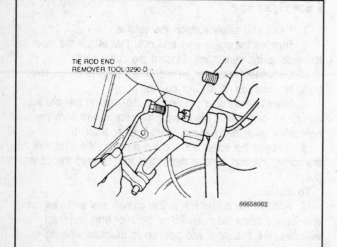
Fig. 52 Remove the tie rod end from the center link

Fig. 55 Loosen the nut on the tie rod shaft. Do not remove the nut, only loosen it

Fig. 56 Separate the tie rod from the spindle using a suitable tie rod puller

Fig. 57 Unthread the tie rod end from the shaft. Remember the number of turns it took to remove the tie rod

Fig. 58 With the tie rod removed, check the shaft to make sure the threads are in good condition

Manual Rack and Pinion Steering Gear

▶ See Figure 59

ADJUSTMENTS

The manual rack and pinion gear provides two means of service adjustment. The gear must be removed from the vehicle to perform both adjustments.

Support Yoke-to-Rack

▶ See Figure 60

1. Clean the exterior of the steering gear thoroughly and mount the gear by installing two long bolts and washers through the mounting boss bushings and attaching to a bench mounted holding fixture, tool T57L-500-B, or equivalent.
2. Remove the yoke cover, gasket, shims, and yoke spring.
3. Clean the cover and housing flange areas thoroughly.
4. Reinstall the yoke and cover, omitting the gasket, shims, and the spring.
5. Tighten the cover bolts lightly until the cover just touches the yoke.
6. Measure the gap between the cover and the housing flange. With the gasket, add selected shims to give a combined pack thickness 0.005-0.006 inches (0.13-0.15mm) greater than the measured gap.
7. Remove the cover.
8. Assemble the gasket next to the housing flange, then the selected shims, spring, and cover.
9. Install the cover bolts, sealing the threads with ESW-M46-132A or equivalent, and tighten.
10. Check to see that the gear operates smoothly without binding or slack.

Pinion Bearing Preload

▶ See Figure 61

1. Clean the exterior of the steering gear thoroughly and place the gear in the bench mounted holding fixture as outlined under Support Yoke-to-Rack Adjustment.
2. Loosen the bolts of the yoke cover to relieve spring pressure on the rack.
3. Remove the pinion cover and gasket. Clean the cover flange area thoroughly.
4. Remove the spacer and shims.
5. Install a new gasket, and fit shims between the upper bearing and the spacer until the top of the spacer is flush with the gasket. Check with a straightedge, using light pressure.
6. Add one shim, 0.0025-0.0050 in. (0.0635-0.1270mm) to the pack in order to preload the bearings. The spacer must be assembled next to the pinion cover.
7. Install the cover and bolts.

REMOVAL & INSTALLATION

1. Disconnect the negative battery cable.
2. Remove the one bolt retaining the flexible coupling to the input shaft.

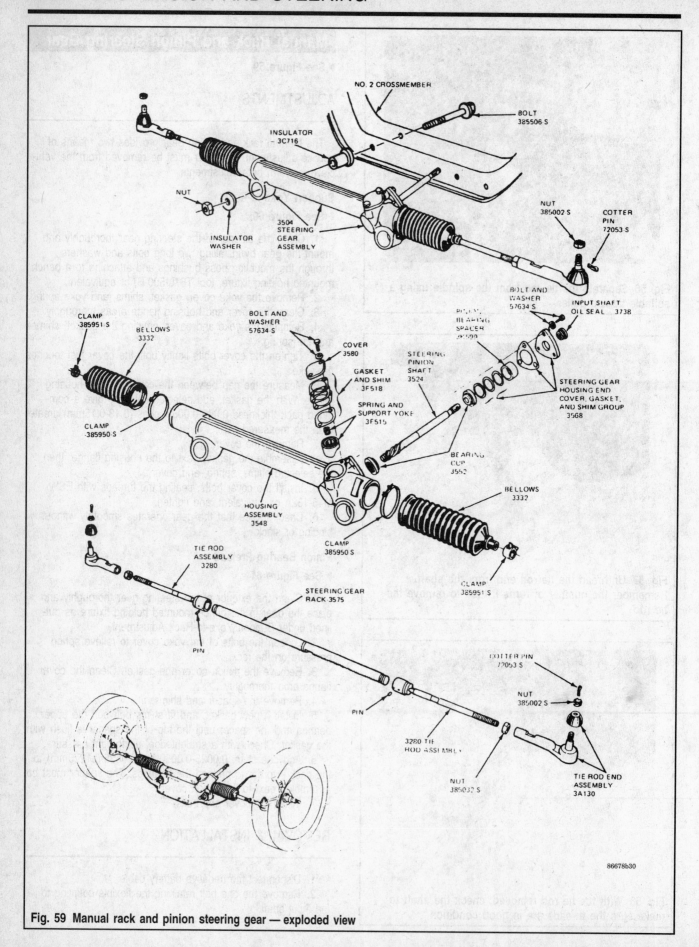

Fig. 59 Manual rack and pinion steering gear — exploded view

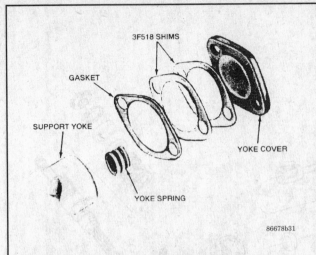

Fig. 60 Support yoke arrangement from rack and pinion housing assembly

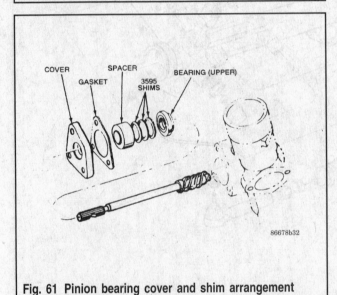

Fig. 61 Pinion bearing cover and shim arrangement

3. Leave the ignition key in the **ON** position, and raise the vehicle on a hoist.

4. Remove the two tie rod end retaining cotter pins and nuts. Separate the studs from the spindle arms, using the ball joint separator tool. Do not use a hammer or similar tool as this may damage spindle arms or rod studs.

5. Support the steering gear, and remove the two nuts, insulator washers, and bolts retaining the steering gear to the No. 2 crossmember.

6. Remove the steering gear assembly from the vehicle.

To install:

7. Insert the input shaft into the flexible coupling, aligning the flats, and position the steering gear to the No. 2 crossmember. Install the two bolts and tighten them to 90-100 ft. lbs. (122-136 Nm).

8. Connect the tie rod ends to the spindle arms, and install the two retaining nuts. Tighten the nuts to 35-47 ft. lbs. (47-64 Nm) and install the two cotter pins.

9. Lower the vehicle, and install the one bolt retaining the flexible coupling to the input shaft. Tighten the bolt to 20-37 ft. lbs. (27-50 Nm).

10. Turn the ignition key to the **OFF** position

11. Connect the negative battery cable.

12. Check the toe, and reset if necessary.

Power Rack and Pinion Steering Gear

▶ See Figure 62

ADJUSTMENTS

The power rack and pinion gear provides for only one service adjustment. This adjustment can be performed with the gear in or out of the vehicle.

Rack Yoke Plug Preload

▶ See Figures 63 and 64

IN VEHICLE

1. Position the steering wheel in a straight ahead position.

2. Clean the exterior of the steering gear in the area of the yoke plug thoroughly.

3. Loosen the yoke plug locknut with a pinion housing yoke locknut wrench, tool T78P-3504-H or equivalent. Back off at least one-quarter turn.

4. Loosen yoke plug with a 3/4 in. socket wrench.

5. With the steering gear still at the center of travel, tighten the yoke plug to 45-50 inch lbs. (5-5.6 Nm). Clean the threads of the yoke plug prior to tightening to prevent a false reading.

6. Back off the yoke plug approximately 1/8 turn (44 degrees minimum to 54 degrees maximum).

7. Place tool T78P-3504-H or equivalent on the yoke plug locknut. While holding the yoke plug, tighten the locknut to 44-66 ft. lbs. (60-89 Nm). Do not allow the yoke plug to move while tightening or the preload will be affected. Recheck input shaft torque after tightening the locknut.

OUT OF VEHICLE

1. Clean the exterior of the steering gear thoroughly.

2. Install two long bolts and washers through the bushing, and attach to the bench mounted holding fixture, Tool T57L-500-B or equivalent.

3. Do not remove the external pressure lines, unless they are leaking or damaged. If these lines are removed, they must be replaced with new lines.

4. Drain the power steering fluid by rotating the input shaft lock-to-lock twice using a pinion shaft torque adjuster, tool T74P-3504-R, or equivalent. Cover ports on the valve housing with shop cloth while draining the gear.

5. Insert an inch lb. torque wrench with a maximum capacity of 30-60 inch lbs. (3.4-6.8 Nm) into the pinion shaft torque adjuster. Position the adapter and wrench on the input shaft splines.

6. Loosen the yoke plug locknut with pinion housing yoke locknut wrench, tool T78P-3504-H or equivalent.

7. Loosen the yoke plug with a 3/4 in. socket wrench.

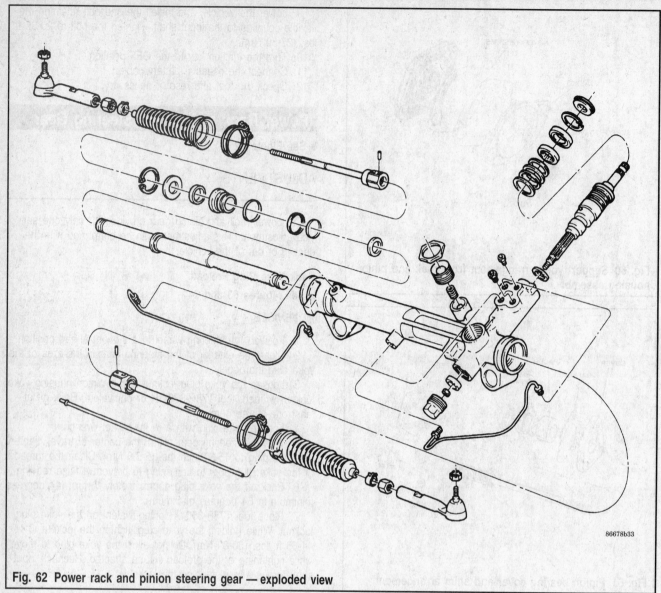

Fig. 62 Power rack and pinion steering gear — exploded view

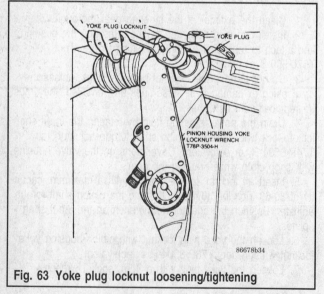

Fig. 63 Yoke plug locknut loosening/tightening

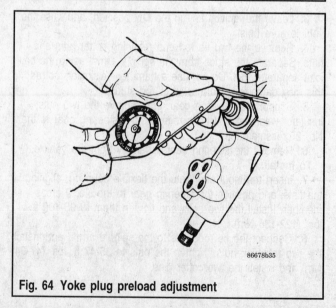

Fig. 64 Yoke plug preload adjustment

8. With the rack at the center of travel, tighten the yoke plug to 45-50 inch lbs. (5-5.6 Nm). Clean the threads of the yoke plug prior to tightening, to prevent a false reading.

9. Back off the yoke plug approximately ⅛ turn (44 degrees minimum to 54 degrees maximum) until the torque required to initiate and sustain rotation of the input shaft is 7-18 inch lbs. (0.8-2.0 Nm).

10. Place Tool T78P-3504-H or equivalent on the yoke plug locknut. While holding the yoke plug, tighten the locknut to 44-66 ft. lbs. (60-90 Nm). Do not allow the yoke plug to move while tightening or the preload will be affected. Recheck input shaft torque after tightening the locknut.

11. If the external pressure lines were removed, they must be replaced with new service lines. Remove the plastic or copper seals from the housing ports prior to installation of new lines.

REMOVAL & INSTALLATION

▶ **See Figures 65, 66, 67, 68, 69, 70, 71 and 72**

1. Disconnect the negative battery cable. Leave the ignition key in the **ON** position.

2. Raise and safely support the vehicle. Position a drain pan to catch fluid from the power steering lines.

3. Remove the one bolt retaining the flexible coupling to the input shaft.

4. Remove the two tie rod end retaining cotter pins and nuts. Separate the studs from the spindle arms, using TOOL-3290-C or an equivalent puller.

5. Support the steering gear, and remove the two nuts, insulator, washers, and bolts retaining the steering gear to the No. 2 crossmember. Lower the gear slightly to permit access to the pressure and return line fittings.

6. Disconnect the pressure and return lines from the steering gear valve housing. Plug the lines and parts in the valve housing to prevent the entry of dirt.

7. Remove the steering gear assembly from the vehicle.

To install:

8. Support and position the steering gear, so that the pressure and return line fittings can be connected to the valve housing. Tighten the fittings to 10-15 ft. lbs. (14-20 Nm). The design allows the hoses to swivel when tightened properly. Do not attempt to eliminate looseness by overtightening, since this can cause damage to the fittings.

➡**The rubber insulators must be pushed completely inside the gear housing before the installation of the gear housing on the No. 2 crossmember.**

9. No gap is allowed between the insulator and the face of the gear boss. A rubber lubricant should be used to facilitate proper installation of the insulators in the gear housing. Insert the input shaft into the flexible coupling, and position the steering gear to the No. 2 crossmember. Install the two bolts, insulator washers, and nuts. Tighten the two nuts to 80-100 ft. lbs. (108-136 Nm) for 1979-84 cars, 90-100 ft. lbs. (122-136 Nm) for 1985 cars, or 30-40 ft. lbs. (41-54 Nm) for 1986-88 cars.

10. Install the one bolt retaining the flexible coupling to the input shaft. Tighten the bolt to 20-30 ft. lbs. (27-41 Nm).

11. Connect the tie rod ends to the spindle arms and install the two retaining nuts. Tighten the nuts to 35-47 ft. lbs. (47-64 Nm), then tighten the nuts to their nearest cotter pin castellation, and install two new cotter pins.

12. Remove the drain pan and lower the vehicle.

13. Turn the ignition key to the **OFF** position.

14. Connect the negative battery cable.

15. Remove the ignition coil wire.

16. Fill the power steering pump reservoir.

17. Engage the starter, and cycle the steering wheel to distribute the fluid. Check the fluid level and add as required.

18. Install the coil wire, start the engine, and cycle the steering wheel. Check for fluid leaks.

19. If the tie rod ends were loosened, check and adjust the wheel alignment, as required.

86678508

Fig. 65 Remove the cotter pins from each tie rod stud

86678509

Fig. 66 Loosen and remove the retainer nuts from both tie rod ends

Fig. 67 Separate the tie rods from each knuckle using a suitable tie rod remover

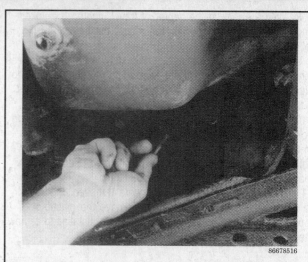

Fig. 70 Remove the nut and bolt and separate the pieces

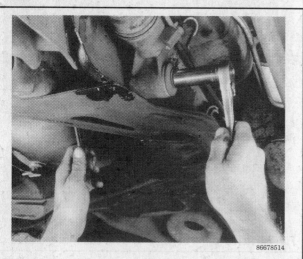

Fig. 68 Loosen the bolts which secure the steering rack to the vehicle body

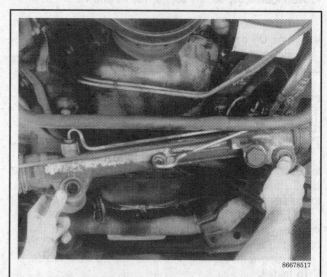

Fig. 71 Lower the steering rack from the vehicle

Fig. 69 Loosen the nut and bolt connecting the steering column to the rack assembly

Fig. 72 Remove the bushings from the steering rack and inspect. If excessively worn replace with new

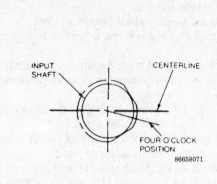

Fig. 73 During installation, position the steering gear input shaft as shown

Steering Rack Boots

REMOVAL & INSTALLATION

▶ See Figures 74, 75 and 76

➡This procedure applies to manual steering as well as power equipped steering racks

1. Remove the tie rod from the steering knuckle. Refer to the tie rod procedure in this section.
2. Remove the tie rod end and clamp nut from the tie rod shaft.
3. Using a pair of pliers or other suitable tool, remove the clamp from the outer portion of the boot.
4. Loosen and remove the clamp from the inner portion of the boot.
5. Slide the boot off the tie rod shaft.
6. Reverse the procedure to install the boot.

Fig. 74 Remove the clamp from the outer section of the steering boot

Fig. 75 Remove the inner clamp from the boot

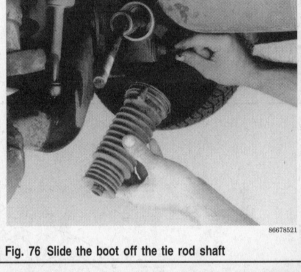

Fig. 76 Slide the boot off the tie rod shaft

Power Steering Pump

REMOVAL & INSTALLATION

▶ See Figure 77

1. Drain the fluid from the pump reservoir by disconnecting the fluid return hose at the pump. Disconnect the pressure hose from the pump.
2. Remove the mounting bolts from the front of the pump.
3. Move the pump inward to loosen the belt tension and remove the belt from the pulley. Remove the pump from the car.

To install:

4. Position the pump on the mounting bracket and loosely install the mounting bolts and nuts. Put the drive belt over the pulley and move the pump outward against the belt until the proper belt tension is obtained. Do not pry against the pump body. Measure the belt tension with a belt tension gauge for

the proper adjustment. Only in cases where a belt tension gauge is not available should the belt deflection method be used.

5. Tighten the mounting bolts and nuts.
6. Connect the hoses, then refill the reservoir.
7. Properly bleed the power steering pump system.

SYSTEM BLEEDING

1. Disconnect the ignition coil, then raise and support the front wheels off the floor.
2. Fill the power steering fluid reservoir.
3. Crank the engine with the starter and add fluid until the level remains constant.

✴✴WARNING

Do not crank the engine for periods of more than 15 seconds at a time. After cranking, allow a minute for the starter to cool. Failure to heed this may cause starter damage from overheating.

4. While cranking the engine, rotate the steering wheel from lock-to-lock.

➡**The front wheels must be off the floor during lock-to-lock rotation of the steering wheel.**

5. Check the fluid level and add fluid, if necessary.

6. Connect the ignition coil wire. Start the engine and allow it to run for several minutes.
7. Rotate the steering wheel from lock-to-lock.
8. Shut off the engine and check the fluid level. Add fluid, if necessary.
9. If air is still present in the system, purge the system of air using a power steering pump air evacuator assembly, as follows:

a. Make sure the power steering pump reservoir is filled to the COLD FULL mark on the dipstick.

b. Tightly insert the rubber stopper of the air evacuator assembly into the pump reservoir fill neck.

c. Apply 15 in. Hg (50.65 kpa) maximum vacuum to the pump reservoir for a minimum of 3 minutes with the engine idling. As air purges from the system, vacuum will fall off. Maintain adequate vacuum with the vacuum source.

d. Release the vacuum and remove the vacuum source. Fill the reservoir to the COLD FULL mark.

e. With the engine idling, apply 15 in. Hg (50.65 kpa) vacuum to the pump reservoir. Slowly cycle the steering wheel from lock-to-lock every 30 seconds for approximately 5 minutes. Do not hold the steering wheel on the stops while cycling. Maintain adequate vacuum with the vacuum source as the air purges.

f. Release the vacuum and remove the vacuum source. Fill the reservoir to the COLD FULL mark.

g. Start the engine and cycle the steering wheel. Check for oil leaks at all connections. In severe cases of aeration, it may be necessary to repeat Steps 9b-9f.

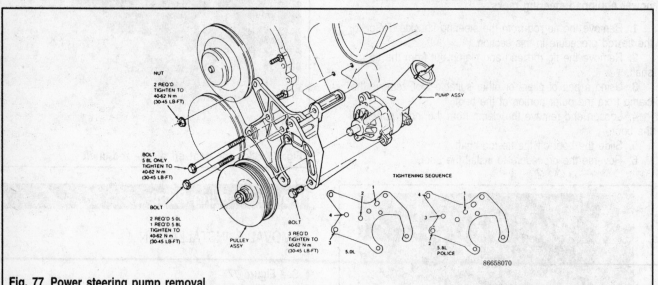

Fig. 77 Power steering pump removal

Troubleshooting the Steering Column

Problem	Cause	Solution
Will not lock	• Lockbolt spring broken or defective	• Replace lock bolt spring
High effort (required to turn ignition key and lock cylinder)	• Lock cylinder defective • Ignition switch defective • Rack preload spring broken or deformed • Burr on lock sector, lock rack, housing, support or remote rod coupling • Bent sector shaft • Defective lock rack • Remote rod bent, deformed • Ignition switch mounting bracket bent • Distorted coupling slot in lock rack (tilt column)	• Replace lock cylinder • Replace ignition switch • Replace preload spring • Remove burr • Replace shaft • Replace lock rack • Replace rod • Straighten or replace • Replace lock rack
Will stick in "start"	• Remote rod deformed • Ignition switch mounting bracket bent	• Straighten or replace • Straighten or replace
Key cannot be removed in "off-lock"	• Ignition switch is not adjusted correctly • Defective lock cylinder	• Adjust switch • Replace lock cylinder
Lock cylinder can be removed without depressing retainer	• Lock cylinder with defective retainer • Burr over retainer slot in housing cover or on cylinder retainer	• Replace lock cylinder • Remove burr
High effort on lock cylinder between "off" and "off-lock"	• Distorted lock rack • Burr on tang of shift gate (automatic column) • Gearshift linkage not adjusted	• Replace lock rack • Remove burr • Adjust linkage
Noise in column	• One click when in "off-lock" position and the steering wheel is moved (all except automatic column) • Coupling bolts not tightened • Lack of grease on bearings or bearing surfaces • Upper shaft bearing worn or broken • Lower shaft bearing worn or broken • Column not correctly aligned • Coupling pulled apart • Broken coupling lower joint • Steering shaft snap ring not seated • Shroud loose on shift bowl. Housing loose on jacket—will be noticed with ignition in "off-lock" and when torque is applied to steering wheel.	• Normal—lock bolt is seating • Tighten pinch bolts • Lubricate with chassis grease • Replace bearing assembly • Replace bearing. Check shaft and replace if scored. • Align column • Replace coupling • Repair or replace joint and align column • Replace ring. Check for proper seating in groove. • Position shroud over lugs on shift bowl. Tighten mounting screws.
High steering shaft effort	• Column misaligned • Defective upper or lower bearing • Tight steering shaft universal joint • Flash on I.D. of shift tube at plastic joint (tilt column only) • Upper or lower bearing seized	• Align column • Replace as required • Repair or replace • Replace shift tube • Replace bearings
Lash in mounted column assembly	• Column mounting bracket bolts loose • Broken weld nuts on column jacket • Column capsule bracket sheared	• Tighten bolts • Replace column jacket • Replace bracket assembly

Troubleshooting the Steering Column (cont.)

Problem	Cause	Solution
Lash in mounted column assembly (cont.)	• Column bracket to column jacket mounting bolts loose	• Tighten to specified torque
	• Loose lock shoes in housing (tilt column only)	• Replace shoes
	• Loose pivot pins (tilt column only)	• Replace pivot pins and support
	• Loose lock shoe pin (tilt column only)	• Replace pin and housing
	• Loose support screws (tilt column only)	• Tighten screws
Housing loose (tilt column only)	• Excessive clearance between holes in support or housing and pivot pin diameters	• Replace pivot pins and support
	• Housing support-screws loose	• Tighten screws
Steering wheel loose—every other tilt position (tilt column only)	• Loose fit between lock shoe and lock shoe pivot pin	• Replace lock shoes and pivot pin
Steering column not locking in any tilt position (tilt column only)	• Lock shoe seized on pivot pin	• Replace lock shoes and pin
	• Lock shoe grooves have burrs or are filled with foreign material	• Clean or replace lock shoes
	• Lock shoe springs weak or broken	• Replace springs
Noise when tilting column (tilt column only)	• Upper tilt bumpers worn	• Replace tilt bumper
	• Tilt spring rubbing in housing	• Lubricate with chassis grease
One click when in "off-lock" position and the steering wheel is moved	• Seating of lock bolt	• None. Click is normal characteristic sound produced by lock bolt as it seats.
High shift effort (automatic and tilt column only)	• Column not correctly aligned	• Align column
	• Lower bearing not aligned correctly	• Assemble correctly
	• Lack of grease on seal or lower bearing areas	• Lubricate with chassis grease
Improper transmission shifting— automatic and tilt column only	• Sheared shift tube joint	• Replace shift tube
	• Improper transmission gearshift linkage adjustment	• Adjust linkage
	• Loose lower shift lever	• Replace shift tube

86658302

Troubleshooting the Turn Signal Switch

Problem	Cause	Solution
Turn signal will not cancel	• Loose switch mounting screws • Switch or anchor bosses broken • Broken, missing or out of position detent, or cancelling spring	• Tighten screws • Replace switch • Reposition springs or replace switch as required
Turn signal difficult to operate	• Turn signal lever loose • Switch yoke broken or distorted • Loose or misplaced springs • Foreign parts and/or materials in switch • Switch mounted loosely	• Tighten mounting screws • Replace switch • Reposition springs or replace switch • Remove foreign parts and/or material • Tighten mounting screws
Turn signal will not indicate lane change	• Broken lane change pressure pad or spring hanger • Broken, missing or misplaced lane change spring • Jammed wires	• Replace switch • Replace or reposition as required • Loosen mounting screws, reposition wires and retighten screws
Turn signal will not stay in turn position	• Foreign material or loose parts impeding movement of switch yoke • Defective switch	• Remove material and/or parts • Replace switch
Hazard switch cannot be pulled out	• Foreign material between hazard support cancelling leg and yoke	• Remove foreign material. No foreign material impeding function of hazard switch—replace turn signal switch.
No turn signal lights	• Inoperative turn signal flasher • Defective or blown fuse • Loose chassis to column harness connector • Disconnect column to chassis connector. Connect new switch to chassis and operate switch by hand. If vehicle lights now operate normally, signal switch is inoperative • If vehicle lights do not operate, check chassis wiring for opens, grounds, etc.	• Replace turn signal flasher • Replace fuse • Connect securely • Replace signal switch • Repair chassis wiring as required
Instrument panel turn indicator lights on but not flashing	• Burned out or damaged front or rear turn signal bulb • If vehicle lights do not operate, check light sockets for high resistance connections, the chassis wiring for opens, grounds, etc. • Inoperative flasher • Loose chassis to column harness connection • Inoperative turn signal switch • To determine if turn signal switch is defective, substitute new switch into circuit and operate switch by hand. If the vehicle's lights operate normally, signal switch is inoperative.	• Replace bulb • Repair chassis wiring as required • Replace flasher • Connect securely • Replace turn signal switch • Replace turn signal switch
Stop light not on when turn indicated	• Loose column to chassis connection • Disconnect column to chassis connector. Connect new switch into system without removing old.	• Connect securely • Replace signal switch

86658303

Troubleshooting the Turn Signal Switch (cont.)

Problem	Cause	Solution
Stop light not on when turn indicated (cont.)	Operate switch by hand. If brake lights work with switch in the turn position, signal switch is defective.	
	• If brake lights do not work, check connector to stop light sockets for grounds, opens, etc.	• Repair connector to stop light circuits using service manual as guide
Turn indicator panel lights not flashing	• Burned out bulbs • High resistance to ground at bulb socket • Opens, ground in wiring harness from front turn signal bulb socket to indicator lights	• Replace bulbs • Replace socket • Locate and repair as required
Turn signal lights flash very slowly	• High resistance ground at light sockets • Incorrect capacity turn signal flasher or bulb • If flashing rate is still extremely slow, check chassis wiring harness from the connector to light sockets for high resistance • Loose chassis to column harness connection • Disconnect column to chassis connector. Connect new switch into system without removing old. Operate switch by hand. If flashing occurs at normal rate, the signal switch is defective.	• Repair high resistance grounds at light sockets • Replace turn signal flasher or bulb • Locate and repair as required • Connect securely • Replace turn signal switch
Hazard signal lights will not flash— turn signal functions normally	• Blow fuse • Inoperative hazard warning flasher • Loose chassis-to-column harness connection • Disconnect column to chassis connector. Connect new switch into system without removing old. Depress the hazard warning lights. If they now work normally, turn signal switch is defective. • If lights do not flash, check wiring harness "K" lead for open between hazard flasher and connector. If open, fuse block is defective	• Replace fuse • Replace hazard warning flasher in fuse panel • Conect securely • Replace turn signal switch • Repair or replace brown wire or connector as required

86658304

Troubleshooting the Power Steering Gear

Problem	Cause	Solution
Hissing noise in steering gear	• There is some noise in all power steering systems. One of the most common is a hissing sound most evident at standstill parking. There is no relationship between this noise and performance of the steering. Hiss may be expected when steering wheel is at end of travel or when slowly turning at standstill.	• Slight hiss is normal and in no way affects steering. Do not replace valve unless hiss is extremely objectionable. A replacement valve will also exhibit slight noise and is not always a cure. Investigate clearance around flexible coupling rivets. Be sure steering shaft and gear are aligned so flexible coupling rotates in a flat plane and is not distorted as shaft rotates. Any metal-to-metal contacts through flexible coupling will transmit valve hiss into passenger compartment through the steering column.
Rattle or chuckle noise in steering gear	• Gear loose on frame • Steering linkage looseness • Pressure hose touching other parts of car • Loose pitman shaft over center adjustment **NOTE:** A slight rattle may occur on turns because of increased clearance off the "high point." This is normal and clearance must not be reduced below specified limits to eliminate this slight rattle. • Loose pitman arm	• Check gear-to-frame mounting screws. Tighten screws to 88 N·m (65 foot pounds) torque. • Check linkage pivot points for wear. Replace if necessary. • Adjust hose position. Do not bend tubing by hand. • Adjust to specifications • Tighten pitman arm nut to specifications
Squawk noise in steering gear when turning or recovering from a turn	• Damper O-ring on valve spool cut	• Replace damper O-ring
Poor return of steering wheel to center	• Tires not properly inflated • Lack of lubrication in linkage and ball joints • Lower coupling flange rubbing against steering gear adjuster plug • Steering gear to column misalignment • Improper front wheel alignment • Steering linkage binding • Ball joints binding • Steering wheel rubbing against housing • Tight or frozen steering shaft bearings • Sticking or plugged valve spool • Steering gear adjustments over specifications • Kink in return hose	• Inflate to specified pressure • Lube linkage and ball joints • Loosen pinch bolt and assemble properly • Align steering column • Check and adjust as necessary • Replace pivots • Replace ball joints • Align housing • Replace bearings • Remove and clean or replace valve • Check adjustment with gear out of car. Adjust as required. • Replace hose
Car leads to one side or the other (keep in mind road condition and wind. Test car in both directions on flat road)	• Front end misaligned • Unbalanced steering gear valve **NOTE:** If this is cause, steering effort will be very light in direction of lead and normal or heavier in opposite direction	• Adjust to specifications • Replace valve

Troubleshooting the Power Steering Gear (cont.)

Problem	Cause	Solution
Momentary increase in effort when turning wheel fast to right or left	• Low oil level • Pump belt slipping • High internal leakage	• Add power steering fluid as required • Tighten or replace belt • Check pump pressure. (See pressure test)
Steering wheel surges or jerks when turning with engine running especially during parking	• Low oil level • Loose pump belt • Steering linkage hitting engine oil pan at full turn • Insufficient pump pressure • Pump flow control valve sticking	• Fill as required • Adjust tension to specification • Correct clearance • Check pump pressure. (See pressure test). Replace relief valve if defective. • Inspect for varnish or damage, replace if necessary
Excessive wheel kickback or loose steering	• Air in system • Steering gear loose on frame • Steering linkage joints worn enough to be loose • Worn poppet valve • Loose thrust bearing preload adjustment • Excessive overcenter lash	• Add oil to pump reservoir and bleed by operating steering. Check hose connectors for proper torque and adjust as required. • Tighten attaching screws to specified torque • Replace loose pivots • Replace poppet valve • Adjust to specification with gear out of vehicle • Adjust to specification with gear out of car
Hard steering or lack of assist	• Loose pump belt • Low oil level **NOTE:** Low oil level will also result in excessive pump noise • Steering gear to column misalignment • Lower coupling flange rubbing against steering gear adjuster plug • Tires not properly inflated	• Adjust belt tension to specification • Fill to proper level. If excessively low, check all lines and joints for evidence of external leakage. Tighten loose connectors. • Align steering column • Loosen pinch bolt and assemble properly • Inflate to recommended pressure
Foamy milky power steering fluid, low fluid level and possible low pressure	• Air in the fluid, and loss of fluid due to internal pump leakage causing overflow	• Check for leak and correct. Bleed system. Extremely cold temperatures will cause system aeration should the oil level be low. If oil level is correct and pump still foams, remove pump from vehicle and separate reservoir from housing. Check welsh plug and housing for cracks. If plug is loose or housing is cracked, replace housing.
Low pressure due to steering pump	• Flow control valve stuck or inoperative • Pressure plate not flat against cam ring	• Remove burrs or dirt or replace. Flush system. • Correct
Low pressure due to steering gear	• Pressure loss in cylinder due to worn piston ring or badly worn housing bore • Leakage at valve rings, valve body-to-worm seal	• Remove gear from car for disassembly and inspection of ring and housing bore • Remove gear from car for disassembly and replace seals

86658307

Troubleshooting the Power Steering Pump

Problem	Cause	Solution
Chirp noise in steering pump	• Loose belt	• Adjust belt tension to specification
Belt squeal (particularly noticeable at full wheel travel and stand still parking)	• Loose belt	• Adjust belt tension to specification
Growl noise in steering pump	• Excessive back pressure in hoses or steering gear caused by restriction	• Locate restriction and correct. Replace part if necessary.
Growl noise in steering pump (particularly noticeable at stand still parking)	• Scored pressure plates, thrust plate or rotor • Extreme wear of cam ring	• Replace parts and flush system • Replace parts
Groan noise in steering pump	• Low oil level • Air in the oil. Poor pressure hose connection.	• Fill reservoir to proper level • Tighten connector to specified torque. Bleed system by operating steering from right to left—full turn.
Rattle noise in steering pump	• Vanes not installed properly • Vanes sticking in rotor slots	• Install properly • Free up by removing burrs, varnish, or dirt
Swish noise in steering pump	• Defective flow control valve	• Replace part
Whine noise in steering pump	• Pump shaft bearing scored	• Replace housing and shaft. Flush system.
Hard steering or lack of assist	• Loose pump belt • Low oil level in reservoir **NOTE:** Low oil level will also result in excessive pump noise • Steering gear to column misalignment • Lower coupling flange rubbing against steering gear adjuster plug • Tires not properly inflated	• Adjust belt tension to specification • Fill to proper level. If excessively low, check all lines and joints for evidence of external leakage. Tighten loose connectors. • Align steering column • Loosen pinch bolt and assemble properly • Inflate to recommended pressure
Foaming milky power steering fluid, low fluid level and possible low pressure	• Air in the fluid, and loss of fluid due to internal pump leakage causing overflow	• Check for leaks and correct. Bleed system. Extremely cold temperatures will cause system aeriation should the oil level be low. If oil level is correct and pump still foams, remove pump from vehicle and separate reservoir from body. Check welsh plug and body for cracks. If plug is loose or body is cracked, replace body.
Low pump pressure	• Flow control valve stuck or inoperative • Pressure plate not flat against cam ring	• Remove burrs or dirt or replace. Flush system. • Correct
Momentary increase in effort when turning wheel fast to right or left	• Low oil level in pump • Pump belt slipping • High internal leakage	• Add power steering fluid as required • Tighten or replace belt • Check pump pressure. (See pressure test)
Steering wheel surges or jerks when turning with engine running especially during parking	• Low oil level • Loose pump belt • Steering linkage hitting engine oil pan at full turn • Insufficient pump pressure	• Fill as required • Adjust tension to specification • Correct clearance • Check pump pressure. (See pressure test). Replace flow control valve if defective.

86658308

Troubleshooting the Power Steering Pump (cont.)

Problem	Cause	Solution
Steering wheel surges or jerks when turning with engine running especially during parking (cont.)	• Sticking flow control valve	• Inspect for varnish or damage, replace if necessary
Excessive wheel kickback or loose steering	• Air in system	• Add oil to pump reservoir and bleed by operating steering. Check hose connectors for proper torque and adjust as required.
Low pump pressure	• Extreme wear of cam ring • Scored pressure plate, thrust plate, or rotor • Vanes not installed properly • Vanes sticking in rotor slots • Cracked or broken thrust or pressure plate	• Replace parts. Flush system. • Replace parts. Flush system. • Install properly • Freeup by removing burrs, varnish, or dirt • Replace part

86658309

Wheel Alignment Specifications

Year	Model	Caster Range (deg)	Caster Pref Setting	Camber Range (deg)	Camber Pref Setting	Toe-in (in.)	Steering Axis Inclination (deg)	Wheel Pivot Ratio Inner (deg)	Wheel Pivot Ratio Outer (deg)
'71	All	1¼N to ¼N	¾N	½N to 1P	¼P	⅛ to ⅜	7⅔	20	①
'72–'73	All	1¼N to 2¾P	¾P	¼N to 1¾P	¾P	1/16 to 7/16	7⅔	20	17¾
'74	All	½P to 3½P	2P	Left ⅜N to 1⅝P Right ⅞N to 1⅛P	½P ⅛P	0 to ⅜	9	20	18⁷/₆₄
'75–'79	All	3¼P to 4¾P	4P	Left ¼N to 1¼P Right ½N to 1P	½P ¼P	0 to ⅜	9	20	18¹/₁₀
'78–'80	Versailles	1¼N to ¼P	½N	½N to 1P	¼P	0 to ¼	6¾	20	②
'80–'82	Thunderbird, XR-7	⅛P to 1⅞P	1P	½N to 1¼P	⅜P	1/16 to 5/16	15⅓	20	19.77
'80–'82	Cougar	⅛P to 1⅞P	1P	5/16N to 1³/16P	7/16P	1/16 to 5/16	15¼	20	19.84
'82	Continental	1¾N to 2¼P	1¼P	½N to 1¼P	⅜P	0 to ¼	15¼	20	19.84
'83–'85	Thunderbird Cougar XR-7	½P to 2P	1¼P	½N to 1P	¼P	1/16 to 5/16	—	20	19.73
'83–'85	LTD, Marquis (Sedan)	1⅛P to 2⅛P	1⅛P	5/16N to 1³/16P	7/16	1/16 to 5/16	—	20	19.84
'83–'85	LTD, Marquis (Station Wagon)	⅛N to 1⅞P	⅞P	¼N to 1¼P	½P	1/16 to 5/16	—	20	19.84
'82–'83	Continental	⅜P to 2⅛P	1¼P	½N to 1¼P	⅜P	0 to ¼	—	20	19.13

① Manual steering—17° 19'; power steering—17° 49'
N Negative
P Positive

86678xxz

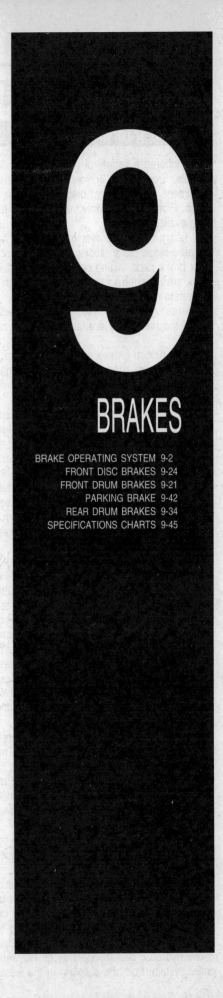

9

BRAKES

BRAKE OPERATING SYSTEM

General Information

Ford offered a variety of brake systems on their 1971-85 vehicles. From 1971-72, front drum brakes were standard equipment, although front disc brakes were available as an option. From 1973-85, only front disc and rear drum brakes were available.

The front disc brake system consists of hydraulically actuated single-piston sliding caliper assemblies with inner and outer brake pads, acting on ventilated cast iron rotors. The rotors are attached to the front hubs, which are attached to and rotate on the front spindles.

The rear disc brake system is similar in design to the front, except the rear rotors are mounted to the rear axle shaft flanges.

The rear drum brakes use internal, hydraulically actuated, expanding brake shoes that are applied against a rotating cast iron brake drum. The brake drum is mounted to the rear axle shaft flange.

The pedal actuated brake hydraulic system consists of the power brake booster, master cylinder, pressure control valve and brake lines and hoses. On many later model vehicles the dual hydraulic system was split front to rear. Both front brakes comprise one circuit and both rear brakes the other circuit.

Hydraulic systems are used to actuate the brakes of all automobiles. The system transports the power required to force the frictional surfaces of the braking system together from the pedal to the individual brake units at each wheel. A hydraulic system is used for two reasons.

First, fluid under pressure can be carried to all parts of an automobile by small pipes and flexible hoses without taking up a significant amount of room or posing routing problems.

Second, a great mechanical advantage can be given to the brake pedal end of the system, and the foot pressure required to actuate the brakes can be reduced by making the surface area of the master cylinder pistons smaller than that of any of the pistons in the wheel cylinders or calipers.

The master cylinder consists of a fluid reservoir and a double cylinder and piston assembly. Double type master cylinders are designed to separate the front and rear braking systems hydraulically in case of a leak.

Steel lines carry the brake fluid to a point on the vehicle's frame near each of the vehicle's wheels. The fluid is then carried to the calipers and wheel cylinders by flexible tubes in order to allow for suspension and steering movements.

In drum brake systems, each wheel cylinder contains two pistons, one at either end, which push outward in opposite directions.

In disc brake systems, the cylinders are part of the calipers. One cylinder in each caliper is used to force the brake pads against the disc.

All pistons employ some type of seal, usually made of rubber, to minimize fluid leakage. A rubber dust boot seals the outer end of the cylinder against dust and dirt. The boot fits around the outer end of the piston on disc brake calipers, and around the brake actuating rod on wheel cylinders.

The hydraulic system operates as follows: When at rest, the entire system, from the piston(s) in the master cylinder to those in the wheel cylinders or calipers, is full of brake fluid. Upon application of the brake pedal, fluid trapped in front of the master cylinder piston(s) is forced through the lines to the wheel cylinders. Here, it forces the pistons outward, in the case of drum brakes, and inward toward the disc, in the case of disc brakes. The motion of the pistons is opposed by return springs mounted outside the cylinders in drum brakes, and by spring seals, in disc brakes.

Upon release of the brake pedal, a spring located inside the master cylinder immediately returns the master cylinder pistons to the normal position. The pistons contain check valves and the master cylinder has compensating ports drilled in it. These are uncovered as the pistons reach their normal position. The piston check valves allow fluid to flow toward the wheel cylinders or calipers as the pistons withdraw. Then, as the return springs force the brake pads or shoes into the released position, the excess fluid reservoir through the compensating ports. It is during the time the pedal is in the released position that any fluid that has leaked out of the system will be replaced through the compensating ports.

Dual circuit master cylinders employ two pistons, located one behind the other, in the same cylinder. The primary piston is actuated directly by mechanical linkage from the brake pedal through the power booster. The secondary piston is actuated by fluid trapped between the two pistons. If a leak develops in front of the secondary piston, it moves forward until it bottoms against the front of the master cylinder, and the fluid trapped between the pistons will operate the rear brakes. If the rear brakes develop a leak, the primary piston will move forward until direct contact with the secondary piston takes place, and it will force the secondary piston to actuate the front brakes. In either case, the brake pedal moves farther when the brakes are applied, and less braking power is available.

All dual circuit systems use a switch to warn the driver when only half of the brake system is operational. This switch is located in a valve body which is mounted on the firewall or the frame below the master cylinder. A hydraulic piston receives pressure from both circuits, each circuit's pressure being applied to one end of the piston. When the pressures are in balance, the piston remains stationary. When one circuit has a leak, however, the greater pressure in that circuit during application of the brakes will push the piston to one side, closing the switch and activating the brake warning light.

In disc brake systems, this valve body also contains a metering valve and, in some cases, a proportioning valve. The metering valve keeps pressure from traveling to the disc brakes on the front wheels until the brake shoes on the rear wheels have contacted the drums, ensuring that the front brakes will never be used alone. The proportioning valve controls the pressure to the rear brakes to lessen the chance of rear wheel lock-up during very hard braking.

Warning lights may be tested by depressing the brake pedal and holding it while opening one of the wheel cylinder bleeder screws. If this does not cause the light to go on, substitute a new lamp, make continuity checks and, finally, replace the switch as necessary.

The hydraulic system may be checked for leaks by applying pressure to the pedal gradually and steadily. If the pedal sinks very slowly to the floor, the system has a leak. This is not to be confused with a springy or spongy feel due to the compression of air within the lines. If the system leaks, there will be a gradual change in the position of the pedal with a constant pressure.

Check for leaks along all lines and at wheel cylinders. If no external leaks are apparent, the problem is inside the master cylinder.

BASIC OPERATING PRINCIPLES

Disc Brakes

Instead of the traditional expanding brakes that press outward against a circular drum, disc brake systems utilize a disc (rotor) with brake pads positioned on either side of it. Braking effect is achieved in a manner similar to the way you would squeeze a spinning phonograph record between your fingers. The disc (rotor) is a casting with cooling fins between the two braking surfaces. This enables air to circulate between the braking surfaces making them less sensitive to heat buildup and more resistant to fade. Dirt and water do not affect braking action since contaminants are thrown off by the centrifugal action of the rotor or scraped off the by the pads. Also, the equal clamping action of the two brake pads tends to ensure uniform, straight line stops. Disc brakes are inherently self-adjusting.

There are three general types of disc brake:
- A fixed caliper
- A floating caliper
- A sliding caliper

A fixed caliper design uses two pistons mounted on either side of the rotor (in each side of the caliper). The caliper is mounted rigidly and does not move.

The sliding and floating designs are quite similar. In fact, these two types are often lumped together. In both designs, the pad on the inside of the rotor is moved into contact with the rotor by hydraulic force. The caliper, which is not held in a fixed position, moves slightly, bringing the outside pad into contact with the rotor. There are various methods of attaching floating calipers. Some pivot at the bottom or top, and some slide on mounting bolts. In any event, the end result is the same.

Drum Brakes

Drum brakes employ two brake shoes mounted on a stationary backing plate. These shoes are positioned inside a circular drum which rotates with the wheel assembly. The shoes are held in place by springs. This allows them to slide toward the drums (when they are applied) while keeping the linings and drums in alignment. The shoes are actuated by a wheel cylinder which is mounted at the top of the backing plate. When the brakes are applied, hydraulic pressure forces the wheel cylinder's actuating links outward. Since these links bear directly against the top of the brake shoes, the tops of the shoes are then forced against the inner side of the drum. This action forces the bottoms of the two shoes to contact the brake drum by rotating the entire assembly slightly (known as servo action). When pressure within the wheel cylinder is relaxed, return springs pull the shoes back away from the drum.

Most modern drum brakes are designed to self-adjust during application when the vehicle is moving in reverse. This motion causes both shoes to rotate very slightly with the drum, rocking an adjusting lever, thereby causing rotation of the adjusting screw.

Adjustment

❋❋WARNING

Because brake fluid can remove automotive paint, use extreme care when bleeding the brake system, or performing any other procedure which requires the use or handling of brake fluid.

DRUM BRAKES

▶ See Figures 1, 2, 3 and 4

➡Drum brakes installed in Ford and Mercury vehicles are self-adjusting. All that is normally required to adjust the brakes is to apply them moderately hard several times while carefully backing the car in reverse. However, if this action proves unsatisfactory, or if it proves necessary to readjust the brakes after replacing the linings or removing the drum, the following procedure may be used.

1. Raise the car and safely support it with jackstands.
2. Remove the rubber plug from the adjusting slot on the backing plate.
3. Insert a brake adjusting spoon or equivalent into the slot and engage the lowest possible tooth on the starwheel. Move the end of the brake spoon downward to move the starwheel upward and expand the adjusting screw. Repeat this operation until the brakes lock the wheel.
4. Insert a small prytool or piece of firm wire (coat hanger wire) into the adjusting slot and push the automatic adjuster lever out and free of the starwheel on the adjusting screw.
5. Holding the adjusting lever out of the way, engage the topmost tooth possible on the starwheel with a brake adjusting spoon. Move the end of the adjusting spoon upward to move the adjusting screw starwheel downward and contract the adjusting screw. Back off the adjusting screw starwheel until the wheel spins freely with the minimum of drag. Keep track of the number of turns the starwheel is backed off.
6. Repeat this operation for the other side. When backing off the brakes on the other side, the adjusting lever must be backed off the same number of turns to prevent side-to-side brake pull.
7. When the brakes are correctly adjusted, lower the vehicle and road test. Make several stops, while backing the car, to equalize all of the wheels.
8. Check the brake fluid in the master cylinder assembly. Add if necessary.

PARKING BRAKE

▶ See Figures 5 and 6

The parking brake should be checked for proper operation every 2 years or 30,000 miles (48,309 km) and adjusted when-

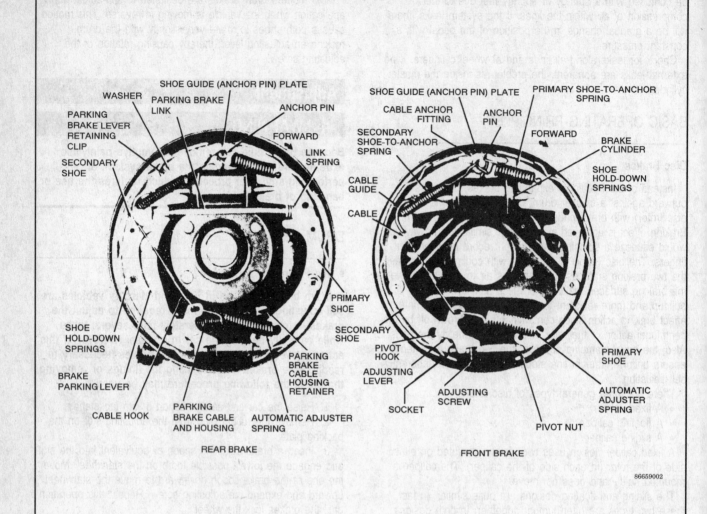

SHOE GUIDE (ANCHOR PIN) PLATE

WASHER

PARKING BRAKE
LINK

ANCHOR PIN

PARKING
BRAKE LEVER
RETAINING
CLIP

FORWARD

SECONDARY
SHOE

LINK
SPRING

SHOE
HOLD-DOWN
SPRINGS

BRAKE
PARKING LEVER

PRIMARY
SHOE

CABLE HOOK

PARKING
BRAKE CABLE
AND HOUSING

PARKING
BRAKE
CABLE
HOUSING
RETAINER

AUTOMATIC ADJUSTER
SPRING

REAR BRAKE

SHOE GUIDE (ANCHOR PIN) PLATE

CABLE ANCHOR
FITTING

ANCHOR
PIN

PRIMARY SHOE-TO-ANCHOR
SPRING

SECONDARY
SHOE-TO-ANCHOR
SPRING

FORWARD

BRAKE
CYLINDER

CABLE
GUIDE

SHOE
HOLD-DOWN
SPRINGS

CABLE

SECONDARY
SHOE

PIVOT
HOOK

ADJUSTING
LEVER

SOCKET

ADJUSTING
SCREW

PIVOT NUT

PRIMARY
SHOE

AUTOMATIC
ADJUSTER
SPRING

FRONT BRAKE

86659002

Fig. 1 Self-adjusting drum brake system

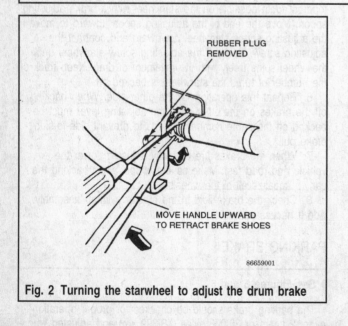

RUBBER PLUG
REMOVED

MOVE HANDLE UPWARD
TO RETRACT BRAKE SHOES

86659001

Fig. 2 Turning the starwheel to adjust the drum brake

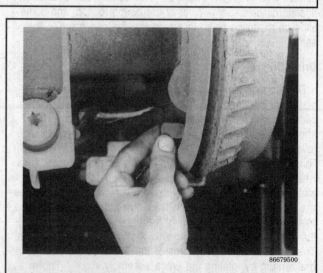

86679500

Fig. 3 Remove the rubber plug from the rear of the drum brake assemble

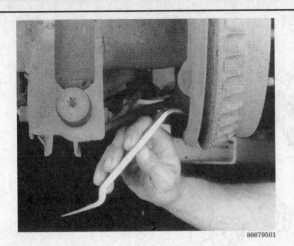

Fig. 4 With the brake spoon inserted into the adjustment slot, push the spoon up or down to adjust the drum brake

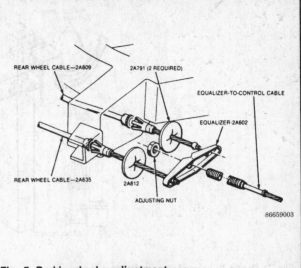

Fig. 5 Parking brake adjustment

ever there is slack in the cables. A cable with too much slack will not hold a vehicle on an incline which presents a serious safety hazard. Usually, a rear brake adjustment will restore parking brake efficiency, but if the cables appear loose or stretched when the parking brake is released, adjust as necessary.

The procedure for adjusting the parking brake on all pedal actuated systems is as follows:

1. Fully release the parking brake.
2. Depress the parking brake pedal one notch from its normal released position. On vacuum release brakes, the first notch is approximately 2 in. (51mm) of travel.
3. Taking proper safety precautions, raise the car and place the transmission in NEUTRAL.
4. Loosen the equalizer locknut and turn the adjusting nut forward against the equalizer until moderate drag is felt when turning the rear wheels. Tighten the locknut.
5. Release the parking brake, making sure that the brake shoes return to the fully released position.
6. Lower the car and apply the parking brake. Under normal conditions, the third through fifth notches will hold the car if the brake is adjusted properly.

Brake Light Switch

REMOVAL & INSTALLATION

1971-79 Models
▶ See Figure 7

1. Unplug the wiring harness at the switch.
2. Remove the hairpin clip from the stud and slide the switch and washers off of the pedal.
3. Installation is the reverse of removal. Check operation of brake light switch.

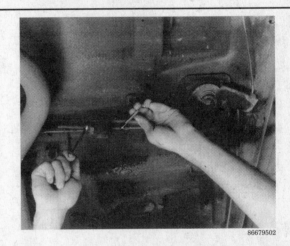

Fig. 6 Hold the bracket firmly while adjusting the cable. If excessively rusty, spray penetrant on the piece before adjusting

1980-85 Models
▶ See Figures 8 and 9

1. Disconnect the negative battery cable.
2. Raise the locking tab and unplug the wiring harness at the switch.
3. Remove the hairpin clip from the stud and slide the switch up and down, remove the switch and washers off of the pedal.

➡It is not necessary to remove the pushrod from the stud.

4. Installation is the reverse of removal. Position the U-shaped side nearest the pedal and directly over/under the pin. Slide the switch up and down trapping the pushrod and bushing between the switch sideplates.
5. Depress the brake pedal to make sure the brake light is functioning correctly.

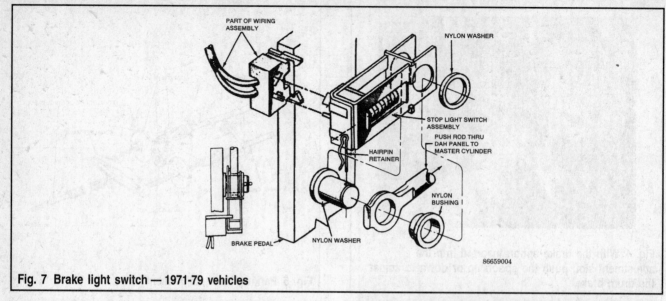

Fig. 7 Brake light switch — 1971-79 vehicles

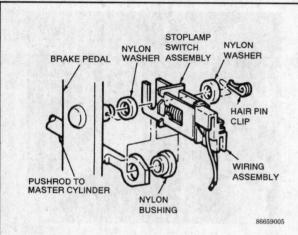

Fig. 8 Brake light switch — 1980-83 vehicles with non-power brakes

Brake Pedal

REMOVAL & INSTALLATION

1. Disconnect the negative battery cable.

2. Disconnect the brake light switch electrical harness from the switch.

3. Loosen the booster retaining nuts approximately ¼ in. (6.35mm) at the pedal support. Remove the pushrod retainer and nylon washer. Slide the brake light switch outboard along the brake pedal pin just far enough for the outer hole of the switch frame to clear the pin. Remove the switch by sliding it downward. Remove the black brake light switch bushing from the pushrod.

4. Slide the pushrod and nylon washer, if equipped, off the pedal pin.

5. Unfasten the locknut then remove the pivot bolt, brake pedal, pivot spacer and bushings from the pedal support.

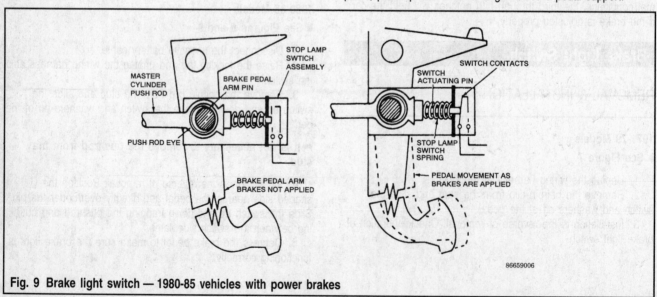

Fig. 9 Brake light switch — 1980-85 vehicles with power brakes

To install:

6. Apply a light coating of SAE 10W-40 engine oil to the bushings. Locate the bushings and pivot spacer in the brake pedal hub.

7. Position the brake pedal assembly in the pedal support and install the pivot bolt. Install the locknut and tighten to 10-20 ft. lbs. (14-27 Nm).

8. Install the inner nylon washer, if equipped, the master cylinder pushrod and the black brake light switch bushing on the brake pedal pin. Position the brake light switch so it straddles the pushrod with the slot on the pedal pin and the switch outer frame hole just clearing the pin. Slide the switch upward onto the pin and pushrod. Slide the assembly inboard toward the brake pedal arm. Install the outer nylon washer and the pushrod retainer. Lock the retainer securely.

9. Tighten the booster retaining nuts to 21 ft. lbs. (29 Nm).

10. Fasten the brake light switch electrical connector and connect the negative battery cable.

11. Test all components before driving the vehicle.

Master Cylinder

REMOVAL & INSTALLATION

Non-Power System

▶ **See Figure 10**

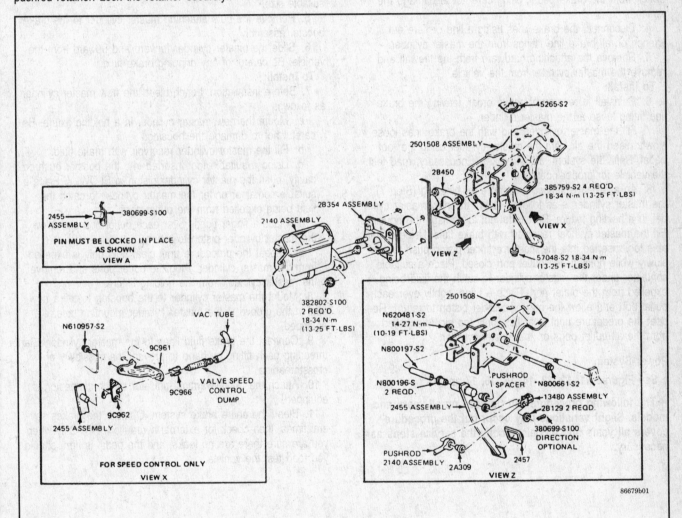

Fig. 10 Exploded view of master cylinder and pedal assembly — non-power system

✳✳WARNING

Because brake fluid can remove automotive paint, use extreme care when bleeding the brake system, or performing any other procedure which requires the use or handling of brake fluid.

1. Using a turkey baster or other device, remove as much brake fluid as possible from the reservoir.

2. Disconnect the negative battery cable. Working under the dash, disconnect the master cylinder pushrod from the brake pedal. The pushrod cannot be removed from the master cylinder.

3. Disconnect the stop light switch wires and remove the switch from the brake pedal, using care not to damage the switch.

4. Disconnect the brake lines using a line or flare nut wrench on all brake line fittings from the master cylinder.

5. Remove the attaching hardware from the firewall and remove the master cylinder from the vehicle.

   To install:

6. Reinstall in reverse of above order, leaving the brake line fitting loose at the master cylinder.

7. Fill the master cylinder, and with the brake lines loose, slowly bleed the air from the master cylinder using the foot pedal. Refill the system, adjust brakes if necessary, road test the vehicle for proper operation.

8. An alternative service procedure for bleeding (Step 7) the master cylinder is as follows. Mount the new master cylinder in a holding fixture. Be careful not to damage the housing. Fill the master cylinder reservoir with brake fluid. Using a suitable tool inserted into the master cylinder piston push tool in slowly while holding one outlet port closed. Place a suitable container under the master cylinder to catch the fluid being expelled from the outlet port. Place a finger tightly over each outlet port and allow the master cylinder piston to return. Repeat the procedure until clear fluid only (no air) is expelled from the all outlet ports on the master cylinder.

Power System

▶ **See Figures 11, 12, 13, 14, 15, 16, 17 and 18**

➡The following procedure can be used on all years and models. Slight variations may occur but the procedure covers all years and models. Modify the service steps as necessary.

1. Disconnect the negative battery cable.

2. Using a turkey baster or other suitable device, remove as much brake fluid from the reservoir as possible.

✳✳WARNING

Because brake fluid can remove automotive paint, use extreme care when bleeding the brake system, or any other procedure which requires the use or handling of brake fluid.

3. If equipped with a warning switch, disconnect the wire harness attached.

4. Remove the brake lines from the primary and secondary outlet ports of the master cylinder. Use a flare wrench of a suitable size.

5. Remove the nuts attaching master cylinder to the brake booster assembly.

6. Slide the master cylinder forward and upward from the vehicle. Be careful of any dripping brake fluid.

   To install:

7. Before installation, bench bleed the new master cylinder as follows:

   a. Mount the new master cylinder in a holding fixture. Be careful not to damage the housing.

   b. Fill the master cylinder reservoir with brake fluid.

   c. Using a suitable tool inserted into the booster pushrod cavity, push the master cylinder piston in SLOWLY. Place a suitable container under the master cylinder to catch the fluid being expelled from the outlet ports.

   d. Place a finger tightly over each outlet port and allow the master cylinder piston to return.

   e. Repeat the procedure until clear fluid only is expelled from the master cylinder. Plug the outlet ports and remove the master cylinder from the holding fixture.

8. Mount the master cylinder to the booster. Install a new seal in the groove in the master cylinder mounting face, if equipped.

9. Connect the brake fluid lines to the master cylinder. Start threading each fitting by hand to prevent the possibility of crossthreading.

10. Attach the brake warning indicator switch connector, if equipped.

11. Bleed the entire brake system. Operate the brakes several times, then check for external hydraulic leaks. Only when you are sure there are no leaks, and the pedal is firm, should you road test the vehicle.

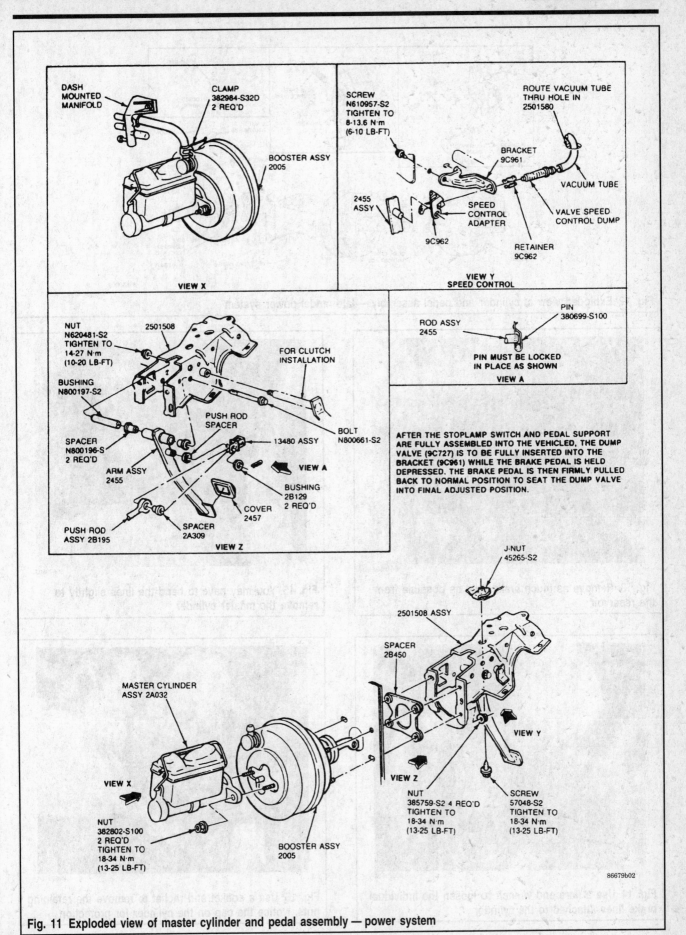

VIEW X

DASH MOUNTED MANIFOLD

CLAMP 382984-S32D 2 REQ'D

BOOSTER ASSY 2005

VIEW Y SPEED CONTROL

SCREW N610957-S2 TIGHTEN TO 8-13.6 N·m (6-10 LB-FT)

ROUTE VACUUM TUBE THRU HOLE IN 2501580

BRACKET 9C961

VACUUM TUBE

2455 ASSY

SPEED CONTROL ADAPTER

9C962

VALVE SPEED CONTROL DUMP

RETAINER 9C962

NUT N620481-S2 TIGHTEN TO 14-27 N·m (10-20 LB-FT)

2501508

FOR CLUTCH INSTALLATION

BUSHING N800197-S2

SPACER N800196-S 2 REQ'D

ARM ASSY 2455

PUSH ROD SPACER

13480 ASSY

BOLT N800661-S2

VIEW A

BUSHING 2B129 2 REQ'D

PUSH ROD ASSY 2B195

SPACER 2A309

COVER 2457

VIEW Z

VIEW A

PIN 380699-S100

ROD ASSY 2455

PIN MUST BE LOCKED IN PLACE AS SHOWN

AFTER THE STOPLAMP SWITCH AND PEDAL SUPPORT ARE FULLY ASSEMBLED INTO THE VEHICLED, THE DUMP VALVE (9C727) IS TO BE FULLY INSERTED INTO THE BRACKET (9C961) WHILE THE BRAKE PEDAL IS HELD DEPRESSED. THE BRAKE PEDAL IS THEN FIRMLY PULLED BACK TO NORMAL POSITION TO SEAT THE DUMP VALVE INTO FINAL ADJUSTED POSITION.

J-NUT 45265-S2

2501508 ASSY

SPACER 2B450

MASTER CYLINDER ASSY 2A032

VIEW X

VIEW Y

VIEW Z

NUT 382802-S100 2 REQ'D TIGHTEN TO 18-34 N·m (13-25 LB-FT)

BOOSTER ASSY 2005

NUT 385759-S2 4 REQ'D TIGHTEN TO 18-34 N·m (13-25 LB-FT)

SCREW 57048-S2 TIGHTEN TO 18-34 N·m (13-25 LB-FT)

86679b02

Fig. 11 Exploded view of master cylinder and pedal assembly — power system

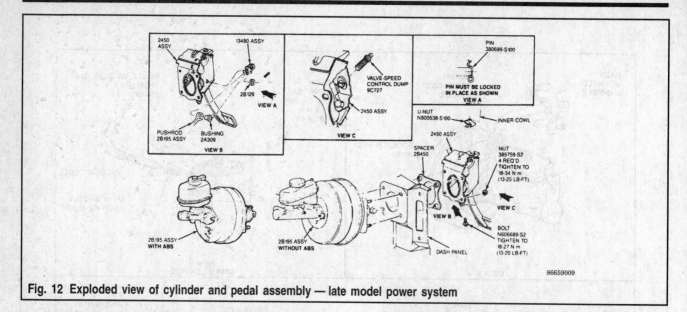

Fig. 12 Exploded view of cylinder and pedal assembly — late model power system

Fig. 13 Remove as much brake fluid as possible from the reservoir

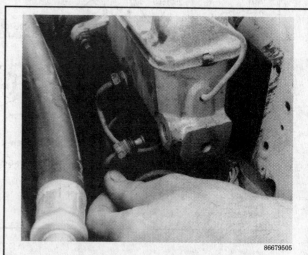

Fig. 15 You may have to bend the lines slightly to remove the master cylinder

Fig. 14 Use a flare end wrench to loosen the individual brake lines attached to the cylinder

Fig. 16 Use a socket and rachet to remove the retaining nuts. Notice the cap on the cylinder for protection

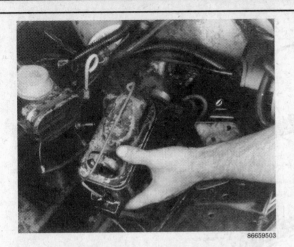

Fig. 17 With the cap on the cylinder to prevent unwanted spillage, remove the master cylinder from the engine compartment

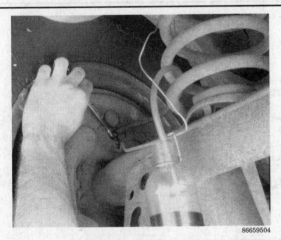

Fig. 18 With the cylinder installed, and the reservoir filled, bleed each wheel. Start from the rear and work forward

OVERHAUL

▶ See Figures 19, 20, 21, 22, 23, 24, 25, 26, 27, 28 and 29

➡Use this service procedure and exploded view illustrations as a guide for overhaul of the master cylinder assembly. If in doubt about overhaul condition or service procedure replace the complete assembly with a new master cylinder assembly.

❋❋WARNING

Because brake fluid can remove automotive paint, use extreme care when bleeding the brake system, or any other procedure which requires the use or handling of brake fluid.

1. Remove the cylinder from the car and drain the brake fluid.
2. Mount the cylinder in a vise. Clean around the end of the cylinder. Using a snapring pliers, remove the ring and seal from the hub.
3. If equipped, remove the stopscrew from the bottom of the front reservoir.
4. Remove the piston assembly from the bore.
5. Clean all the metal parts in brake fluid and discard the rubber parts.
6. Inspect the bore for damage or wear, and check the pistons for damage and proper clearance in the bore. If worn, replace the parts or the entire assembly.

➡Some late model vehicles are equipped with aluminum master cylinders. DO NOT HONE! If the bore is pitted or scored deeply, the master cylinder assembly must be replaced.

7. If the bore is only slightly scored or pitted it may be honed. Always use hones that are in good condition. Completely clean the cylinder with brake fluid when the honing is completed. If any evidence of contamination exist in the master cylinder, the entire hydraulic system should be flushed and refilled with clean brake fluid. Blow out the passages with compressed air.

➡The rebuilding kit may contain secondary and primary piston assemblies instead of just rubber seals. In this case, seal installation is not required.

8. Install new secondary seals in the two grooves in the flat end of the front piston. The lips of the seals will be facing away from each other.
9. Install a new primary seal and the seal protector on the opposite end of the front piston with the lips of the seal facing outward.
10. Coat the seals with brake fluid. Install the spring on the front piston with the spring retainer in the primary seal.
11. Insert the piston assembly, spring end first, into the bore and use a wooden rod to seat it properly.
12. Coat the rear piston seals with brake fluid and install it into the piston grooves with the lips facing the spring end.
13. Assemble the spring onto the piston and install the assembly into the bore spring first. When correctly positioned, install the snapring.
14. If equipped with a stopscrew, hold the piston train at the bottom of the bore and install the stopscrew.
15. Install a new seal on the hub. Bench-bleed the cylinder or install and bleed the cylinder on the car.

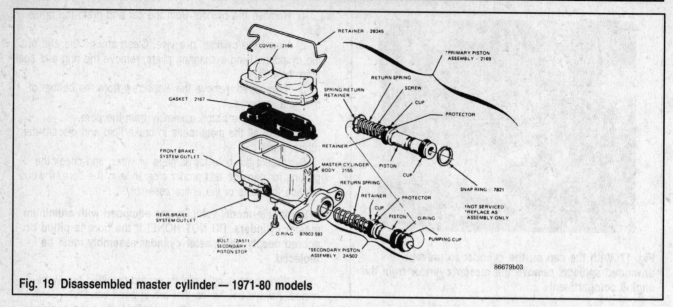

Fig. 19 Disassembled master cylinder — 1971-80 models

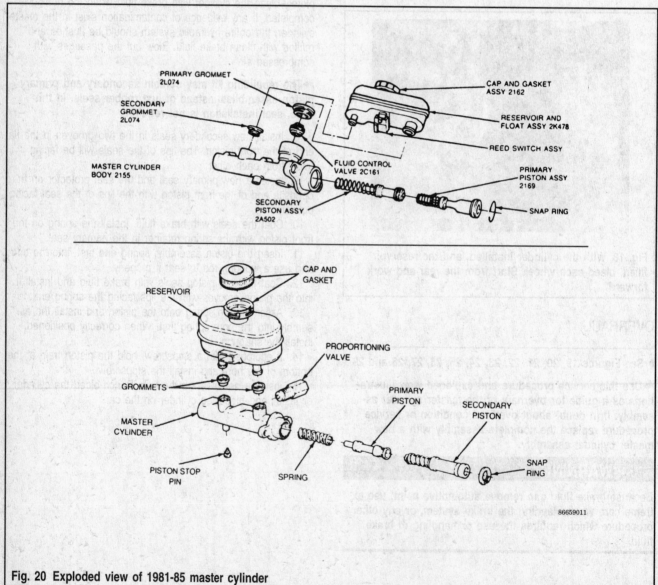

Fig. 20 Exploded view of 1981-85 master cylinder

Fig. 21 Clean around the snapring with a rag or other clean instrument

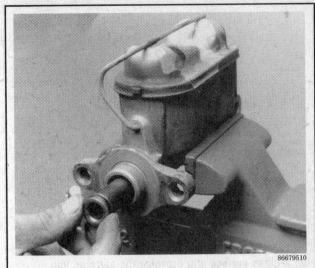

Fig. 24 Remove the primary (rear) piston assembly . . .

Fig. 22 Remove the snapring using a suitable pair of snapring pliers

Fig. 25 . . . then remove the secondary (front) piston assembly

Fig. 23 If the snapring is difficult to remove, press on the piston with a rounded punch. This will ease the removal of the snapring and prevent the pistons from ejecting out of the cylinder bore

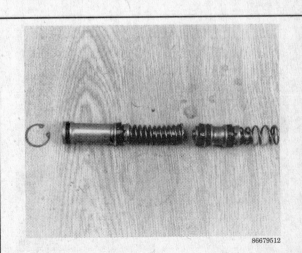

Fig. 26 Note that the front and rear pistons and springs are of different lengths. Do not mix these parts because they are not interchangeable

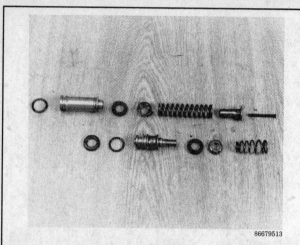

Fig. 27 When you disassemble the pistons, perform the on a clean surface and organize the parts as you disassemble

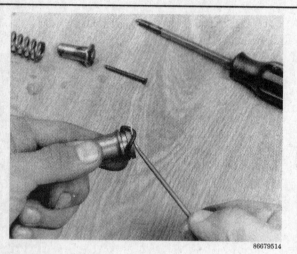

Fig. 28 To remove the O-ring seal, use a pick tool to pull the O-ring off the piston

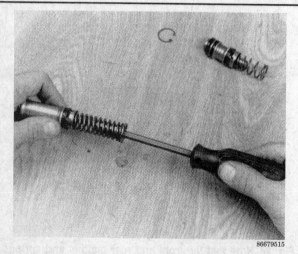

Fig. 29 When you secure the spring to the piston, make sure the spring is facing in the correct direction

Power Brake Booster

▶ See Figure 30

Power brakes operate just as non-power brake systems except in the actuation of the master cylinder pistons. On systems other than Hydro-Boost, a vacuum diaphragm is located on the front of the master cylinder; this device assists the driver in applying the brakes, reducing both the effort and travel he must put into moving the brake pedal.

The vacuum diaphragm housing is connected to the intake manifold by a vacuum hose. A check valve is placed at the point where the hose enters the diaphragm housing, so that during periods of low manifold vacuum, brake assist vacuum will not be lost.

Depressing the brake pedal closes off the vacuum source and allows atmospheric pressure to enter on one side of the diaphragm. This causes the master cylinder piston(s) to move and apply the brakes. When the brake pedal is released, vacuum is applied to both sides of the diaphragm, and return springs return the diaphragm and master cylinder pistons to the released position. If the vacuum fails, the brake pedal rod will butt against the end of the master cylinder actuating rod, and direct mechanical application will occur as the pedal is depressed.

TESTING

The hydraulic and mechanical problems that apply to conventional brake systems also apply to power brakes, and should be checked for if the tests below do not reveal the problem.

System Vacuum Leak

1. Operate the engine at idle without touching the brake pedal for at least one minute.
2. Turn off the engine, and wait one minute.
3. Test for the presence of assist vacuum by depressing the brake pedal and releasing it several times. Light application will produce less and less pedal travel, if vacuum was present. If there is no vacuum, air is leaking into the system somewhere.

Proper System Operation

1. Pump the brake pedal (with engine off) until the supply vacuum is entirely gone.
2. Put a light, steady pressure on the pedal.
3. Start the engine, and operate it at idle. If the system is operating, the brake pedal should fall toward the floor if constant pressure is maintained on the pedal.
4. Power brake systems may be tested for hydraulic leaks just as ordinary systems are tested.

Most mid-sized models have been equipped with power brakes. On all drum brake equipped car, as well as those equipped with a disc front/drum rear brake configuration, the power assist has been supplied by a manifold vacuum-operated servo, located between the master cylinder and the firewall.

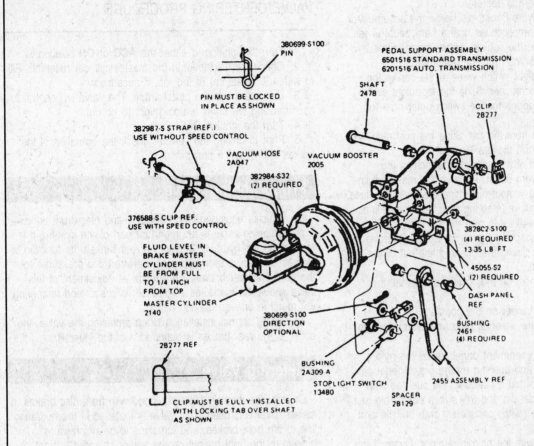

380699-S100 PIN

PIN MUST BE LOCKED IN PLACE AS SHOWN

382987-S STRAP (REF.) USE WITHOUT SPEED CONTROL

VACUUM HOSE 2A047

376588-S CLIP REF. USE WITH SPEED CONTROL

FLUID LEVEL IN BRAKE MASTER CYLINDER MUST BE FROM FULL TO 1/4 INCH FROM TOP

MASTER CYLINDER 2140

2B277 REF

CLIP MUST BE FULLY INSTALLED WITH LOCKING TAB OVER SHAFT AS SHOWN

VACUUM BOOSTER 2005

382984-S32 (2) REQUIRED

PEDAL SUPPORT ASSEMBLY 6501516 STANDARD TRANSMISSION 6201516 AUTO. TRANSMISSION

SHAFT 2478

CLIP 2B277

3828C2-S100 (4) REQUIRED 13-35 LB-FT

45055-S2 (2) REQUIRED

DASH PANEL REF

BUSHING 2461 (4) REQUIRED

380699-S100 DIRECTION OPTIONAL

BUSHING 2A309-A

STOPLIGHT SWITCH 13480

SPACER 2B129

2455 ASSEMBLY REF

86659008

Fig. 30 Exploded view of master cylinder and pedal assembly — power system

REMOVAL & INSTALLATION

Vacuum Booster

➡The following procedure can be used on all years and models. Slight variations may occur but the basic procedure should cover all years and models.

1. Disconnect the negative battery cable.
2. Disconnect the manifold vacuum hose from the booster check valve.
3. Disconnect the brake lines from the master cylinder, remove the master cylinder-to-booster retaining nuts and remove the master cylinder.

➡On some vehicles, it may be possible to remove the master cylinder and move it aside without disconnecting the brake lines. If you do this, be careful not to kink the brake lines.

4. Working inside the vehicle below the instrument panel, remove the stop light switch connector. Remove the switch retaining pin and slide the switch off the brake pedal pin just far enough for the outer arm to clear the pin, then remove the switch. Be careful not to damage the switch.

5. Remove the booster-to-dash panel attaching nuts. If necessary, remove the cowl top intrusion bolt.
6. Slide the booster pushrod, washers and bushing off the brake pedal pin. Remove the booster assembly.
7. Installation is the reverse of the removal procedure. Tighten the booster-to-dash panel attaching nuts and the master cylinder attaching nuts to 13-25 ft. lbs. (18-34 Nm). If the brake lines were disconnected, bleed the brake system. Refer to the necessary service procedures in this section.

Hydro-Boost Hydraulic Booster

◗ See Figure 31

The Hydro-Boost assembly contains a valve which controls pump pressure while braking, a lever to control the position of the valve, and a boost piston to provide the force to operate a conventional master cylinder attached to the front of the booster. The Hydro-Boost also has a reserve system, designed to store sufficient pressurized fluid to provide at least 2 brake applications in the event of insufficient fluid flow from the power steering pump. The brakes can also be applied unassisted if the reserve system is depleted.

Before removing the Hydro-Boost, discharge the accumulator by making several brake applications until a hard pedal is felt.

1. Working from inside the vehicle, below the instrument panel, disconnect the pushrod from the brake pedal.

2. Unfasten the stop light switch wires at the connector.

3. Remove the hairpin retainer. Slide the stop light switch off the brake pedal far enough for the switch outer hole to clear the pin.

4. Remove the switch from the pin. Slide the pushrod, nylon washers and bushing off the brake pedal pin.

5. Open the hood and remove the nuts attaching the master cylinder to the Hydro-Boost. Remove the master cylinder. Secure it to one side without disturbing the hydraulic lines.

6. Disconnect the pressure, steering gear and return lines from the booster. Plug the lines to prevent the entry of dirt.

7. Remove the nuts attaching the Hydro-Boost. Remove the booster from the firewall, sliding the pushrod link out of the engine side of the firewall.

8. Install the Hydro-Boost on the firewall and install the attaching nuts.

9. Install the master cylinder on the booster.

10. Connect the pressure, steering gear and return lines to the booster.

11. Working below the instrument panel, install the nylon washer, booster pushrod and bushing on the brake pedal pin.

12. Install the switch so that it straddles the pushrod with the switch slot on the pedal pin and the switch outer hole just clearing the pin. Slide the switch completely onto the pin and install the nylon washer.

13. Attach these parts with the hairpin retainer. Connect the stop light switch wires and install the wires in the retaining clip.

14. Remove the coil high tension wire so that the engine will not start. Fill the power steering pump and engage the starter. Apply the brakes with a pumping action. Do not turn the steering wheel until air has been bled from the booster.

15. Check the fluid level and add as required. Start the engine and apply the brakes, checking for leaks. Cycle the steering wheel.

16. If a whine-type noise is heard, suspect fluid aeration. Bleed the system.

Pressure Differential Warning Valve

▶ **See Figures 32 and 33**

Since the introduction of the tandem master cylinders to the hydraulic brake system, a pressure differential warning signal has been added. This signal consists of a warning light on the dashboard activated by a differential pressure switch located below the master cylinder. The signal indicates a hydraulic pressure differential between the front and rear brakes of 80-150 psi (280-495 kPa), and should warn the driver that a hydraulic failure has occurred.

After repairing and bleeding any part of the hydraulic system, the warning light may remain on due to the pressure differential valve remaining in the off-center position. To centralize the valve, a pressure difference must be created in the

opposite branch of the hydraulic system that was repaired or bled last.

VALVE CENTERING PROCEDURE

1. Turn the ignition to either the **ACC** or **ON** position.

2. Check the fluid level in the master cylinder reservoir. Fill to within 1/4 in. (6mm) of the top, if necessary.

3. Depress the brake pedal firmly. The valve will centralize itself causing the brake warning light to go out.

4. Turn the ignition **OFF**.

5. Prior to driving the vehicle, check the operation of the brakes and obtain a firm pedal.

Proportioning Valve

On vehicles equipped with front disc and rear drum brakes, a proportioning valve is an important part of the system. It is installed in the hydraulic line to the rear brakes. Its function is to maintain the correct proportion between line pressures to the front and rear brakes. No attempt at adjustment of this valve should be made, as adjustment is preset and tampering will result in uneven braking action.

To assure correct installation when replacing the valve, the outlet to the rear brakes is stamped with the letter R.

Metering Valve

On vehicles through 1980 equipped with front disc brakes, a metering valve is used. This valve is installed in the hydraulic line to the front brakes, and functions to delay pressure buildup to the front brakes on application. It reduces front brake pressure until rear brake pressure builds up adequately to overcome the rear brake shoe return springs. In this way, disc brake pad life is extended because it prevents the front disc brakes from carrying all or most of the braking load at low operating line pressures.

The metering valve can be checked very simply. With the car stopped, gently apply the brakes. At about 1 in. (25mm) of travel, a very small change in pedal effort (like a small bump) will be felt if the valve is operating properly. Metering valves are not serviceable and must be replaced if defective.

Brake Hoses

INSPECTION

Check the flexible brake hoses that connect the steel tubing to each wheel cylinder. Replace the hose if it shows any signs of softening, cracking, or other damage. When installing a new front brake hose, position the hose to avoid contact with other chassis parts. Place a new copper gasket over the hose fitting and thread the hose assembly into the front wheel cylinder. A new rear brake hose must be positioned clear of the exhaust pipe or shock absorber. Thread the hose into the rear brake tube connector. When installing either a new front or rear brake hose, engage the opposite end of the hose to the

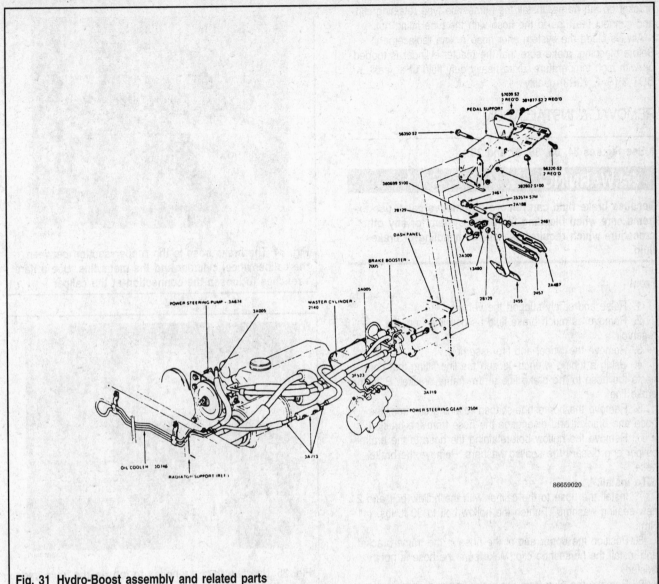

Fig. 31 Hydro-Boost assembly and related parts

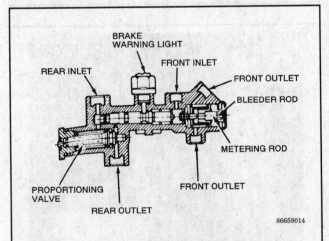

Fig. 32 3-way brake control valve housing a metering, pressure differential and proportioning valve in one unit — 1980-82 vehicles

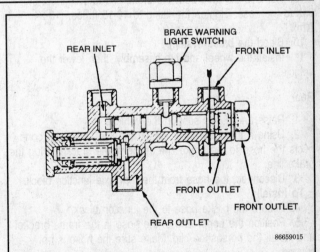

Fig. 33 2-way brake control valve housing a pressure differential and proportioning valve in one unit — 1980-85 vehicles

bracket on the frame. Install the horseshoe type retaining clip and connect the tube to the hose with the tube fitting nut.

Always bleed the system after hose or line replacement. Before bleeding, make sure that the master cylinder is topped up with high temperature, extra heavy duty fluid of at least DOT 3 (SAE 70R3) quality.

REMOVAL & INSTALLATION

▶ See Figures 34, 35, 36, 37 and 38

❊❊WARNING

Because brake fluid can remove automotive paint, use extreme care when bleeding the brake system, or any other procedure which requires the use or handling of brake fluid.

Front

1. Raise and safely support the vehicle.
2. Remove as much brake fluid as possible from the reservoir.
3. Remove the wheel and tire assembly.
4. Using a tubing wrench, loosen the line fitting that connects the hose to the brake line at the frame bracket. Plug the brake line.
5. Remove the horseshoe-shaped retaining clip from the hose and bracket and disengage the hose from the bracket.
6. Remove the hollow bolt retaining the hose to the brake caliper and discard the sealing washers. Remove the brake hose.

To install:

7. Install the hose to the caliper with the hollow bolt and 2 new sealing washers. Tighten the hollow bolt to 30 ft. lbs. (41 Nm).
8. Position the upper end of the hose in the frame bracket and install the horseshoe clip. Make sure the hose is not twisted.
9. Remove the plug from the brake line and connect the line to the hose. Tighten the fitting to 10-18 ft. lbs. (13-24 Nm).
10. Bleed the brake system.
11. Install the wheel and tire assembly, then lower the vehicle.

Rear

1. Raise and safely support the vehicle.
2. Using a tubing wrench, loosen the line fitting that connects the hose to the brake line at the frame bracket. Plug the brake line.
3. Disconnect the hose from the rear axle junction block.

To install:

4. Secure the brake hose to the junction block.
5. Position the upper end of the hose in the frame bracket and install the horseshoe clip. Make sure the hose is not twisted.
6. Remove the plug from the brake line and connect the line to the hose. Tighten the fitting to 10-18 ft. lbs. (13-24 Nm).
7. Bleed the brake system and lower the vehicle.

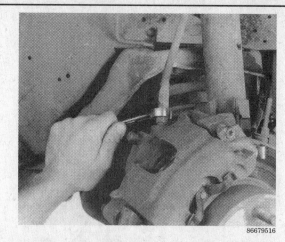

Fig. 34 The brake hose is the rubber section between the caliper/wheel cylinder and the metal line. Use a flare wrenches to loosen the connection at the caliper

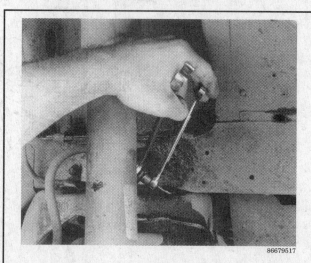

Fig. 35 Use two flare wrenches to loosen the hose and brake line

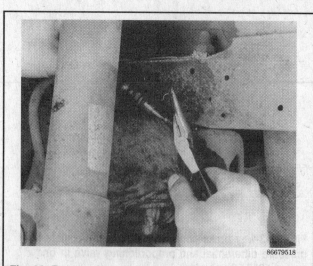

Fig. 36 Remove the clip securing the brake hose to the brake line bracket

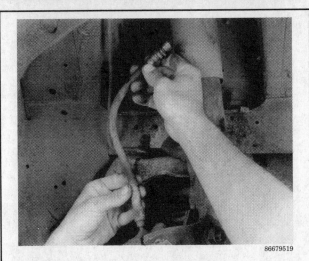

Fig. 37 Finish unscrewing the brake hose, then remove from the vehicle

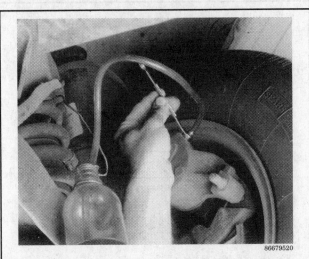

Fig. 38 After the hose is installed, bleed the entire brake system

Brake Lines

INSPECTION

The hydraulic brake lines and brake linings are to be inspected at the recommended intervals in the maintenance schedule. Follow the steel tubing from the master cylinder to the flexible hose fitting at each wheel. If a section of the tubing is found to be damaged, replace the entire section with tubing of the same type (steel, not copper), size, shape, and length. When installing a new section of brake tubing, flush clean brake fluid or denatured alcohol through to remove any dirt or foreign material from the line. Be sure to flare both ends to provide sound, leak-proof connections. When bending the tubing to fit the underbody contours, be careful not to kink or crack the line. Torque all hydraulic connections to 10-15 ft. lbs.

REMOVAL & INSTALLATION

◆ See Figure 39

❋❋WARNING

Because brake fluid can remove automotive paint, use extreme care when bleeding the brake system, or performing any other procedure which requires the use or handling of brake fluid.

1. Raise and safely support the vehicle.
2. Remove the necessary components to gain access to the brake line.
3. Disconnect the brake line fittings at each end of the line. Use 2 flare or open ended wrenches.
4. Disconnect the line from any retaining clips and remove the line from the vehicle.
   To install:
5. Try to obtain a replacement line that is the same length as the line that was removed. If the line is longer, you will have to cut it and flare the end.

➡**Use only brake line tubing approved for automotive use.**

6. Use a suitable tubing bender to make the necessary bends in the line. Work slowly and carefully; try to make the bends look as close as possible to those on the line being replaced.

➡**When bending the brake line, be careful not to kink or crack the line. If the brake line becomes kinked or cracked, it must be replaced.**

7. Before installing the brake line, flush it with brake cleaner to remove any dirt or foreign material.
8. Install the line into the vehicle. Be sure to attach the line to the retaining clips, as necessary. Make sure the replacement brake line does not contact any components that could rub the line and cause a leak.
9. Connect the brake line fittings and tighten to 10-18 ft. lbs. (13-24 Nm).
10. Bleed the brake system.
11. Install any removed components and lower the vehicle.

BRAKE LINE FLARING

◆ See Figures 40 and 41

Use only brake line tubing approved for automotive use; never use copper tubing. Whenever possible, try to work with brake lines that are already cut to the length needed. These lines are available at most auto parts stores and have machine made flares, the quality of which is hard to duplicate with most of the available inexpensive flaring kits.

When the brakes are applied, there is a great amount of pressure developed in the hydraulic system. An improperly formed flare can leak with resultant loss of stopping power. If you have never formed a double-flare, take time to familiarize yourself with the flaring kit; practice forming double-flares on scrap tubing until you are satisfied with the results.

Fig. 39 Use a flare wrench to carefully loosen the connections at the different ends of the brake line. Remember, brake line tubing is made from soft metal, so extreme care is needed required when working on these parts

The following procedure applies to most commercially available double-flaring kits. If these instructions differ in any way from those in your kit, follow the instructions in the kit.

1. Cut the brake line to the necessary length using a tubing cutter.

2. Square the end of the tube with a file and chamfer the edges.

3. Insert the tube into the proper size hole in the bar until the end of the tube sticks out the thickness of the single flare adapter. Tighten the bar wing nuts tightly so the tube cannot move.

4. Place the single flare adapter into the tube and slide the bar into the yoke.

5. Position the yoke screw over the single flare adapter and tighten it until the bar is locked in the yoke. Continue tightening the yoke screw until the adapter bottoms on the bar. This should form the single flare.

➡ Make sure the tube is not forced out of the hole in the bar during the single flare operation. If it is, the single flare will not be formed properly and the procedure must be repeated from Step 1.

6. Loosen the yoke screw and remove the single flare adapter.

7. Position the yoke screw over the tube and tighten until the taper contacts the single flare and the bar is locked in the yoke. Continue tightening to form the double flare.

➡ Make sure the tube is not forced out of the hole in the bar during the double flare operation. If it is, the double flare will not be formed properly and the procedure must be repeated from Step 1.

8. Loosen the screw and remove the bar from the yoke. Remove the tube from the bar.

9. Check the flare for cracks or uneven flaring. If the flare is not perfect, cut it off and begin again at Step 1.

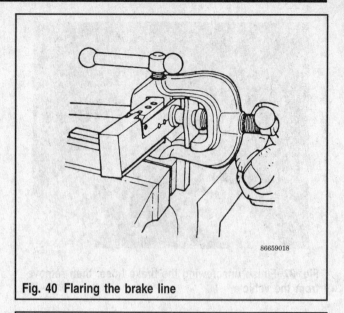

Fig. 40 Flaring the brake line

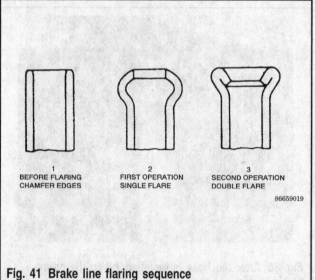

1 BEFORE FLARING CHAMFER EDGES

2 FIRST OPERATION SINGLE FLARE

3 SECOND OPERATION DOUBLE FLARE

Fig. 41 Brake line flaring sequence

Bleeding Brake System

▶ See Figures 42 and 43

✳✳WARNING

Because brake fluid can remove automotive paint, use extreme care when bleeding the brake system, or any other procedure which requires the use or handling of brake fluid.

1. Clean all dirt from the master cylinder filler cap.

2. If the master cylinder is known or suspected to have air in the bore, it must be bled before any of the wheel cylinders or calipers are bled. This can be done as follows:

a. Position a shop towel under the primary (rear) outlet fitting and loosen the fitting approximately ¾ turn.

b. Have an assistant depress the brake pedal slowly through its full travel.

c. Close the outlet fitting and let the pedal return slowly to the fully released position. Wait 5 seconds, then repeat the operation until all the air bubbles disappear.

3. Repeat Step 2 with the secondary (front) outlet fitting.

➡On some vehicles, the master cylinder is equipped with a bleeder fitting. In these cases, the master cylinder can be bled in the same manner as a caliper or wheel cylinder.

4. Continue to bleed the brake system by removing the rubber dust cap from the wheel cylinder bleeder fitting or caliper fitting at the right-hand rear of the vehicle. Place a suitable flare or box wrench on the bleeder fitting and attach a rubber drain tube to the fitting. The end of the tube should fit snugly around the bleeder fitting. Submerge the other end of the tube in a container partially filled with clean brake fluid and loosen the fitting ¾ turn.

5. Have an assistant push the brake pedal down slowly through its full travel. Close the bleeder fitting and allow the

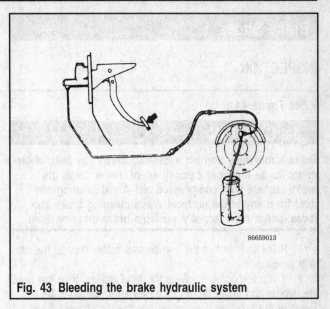

86659013

Fig. 43 Bleeding the brake hydraulic system

pedal to slowly return to its full release position. Wait 5 seconds and repeat the procedure until no bubbles appear at the submerged end of the bleeder tube. Secure the bleeder fitting and remove the bleeder tube. Install the rubber dust cap on the bleeder fitting.

6. Repeat the procedure in Steps 4 and 5 in the following sequence: left rear, right front, left front. Refill the master cylinder reservoir after each wheel cylinder or caliper has been bled and install the master cylinder cover and gasket. When brake bleeding is completed, the fluid level should be filled to the maximum level indicated on the reservoir.

➡Never reuse brake fluid that has been drained from the hydraulic system or has been allowed to stand in an open container for an extended period of time.

7. Always make sure the disc brake pistons are returned to their normal positions by depressing the brake pedal several times until normal pedal travel is established. If the pedal feels spongy, repeat the bleeding procedure.

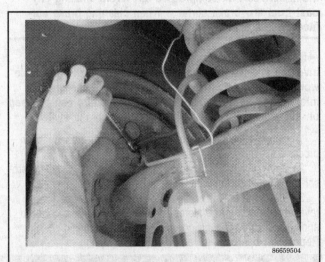

86659504

Fig. 42 Use the correct size flare or box wrench to loosen the bleeder fitting

FRONT DRUM BRAKES

✳✳CAUTION

Brake shoes may contain asbestos, which has been determined to be a cancer causing agent. Never clean the brake surface with compressed air! Avoid inhaling any dust from any brake surface! When cleaning brake surfaces, use a commercially available brake cleaning fluid.

Drum brakes on all Ford and Mercury vehicles employ single anchor, internal-expanding, and self-adjusting brake assemblies. The automatic adjuster continuously maintains correct operating clearance between the linings and the drums by adjusting the brake in small increments in direct proportion to

lining wear. When applying the brakes while backing up, the linings tend to follow the rotating drum counterclockwise, thus forcing the upper end of the primary shoe against the anchor pin. simultaneously, the wheel cylinder pushes the upper end of the secondary shoe and cable guide outward, away from the anchor pin. This movement of the secondary shoe causes the cable to pull the adjusting lever upward and against the end of the tooth on the adjusting screw starwheel. As lining wear increases, the upward travel of the adjusting lever also increases. When the linings have worn sufficiently to allow the lever to move upward far enough, it passes over the end of the tooth and engages it. Upon release of the brakes, the adjusting spring pulls the adjuster lever downward, turning the starwheel and expanding the brakes.

Brake Shoes

INSPECTION

▶ See Figure 44

> ❋❋**CAUTION**
>
> **Brake shoes may contain asbestos, which has been determined to be a cancer causing agent. Never clean the brake surface with compressed air! Avoid inhaling any dust from any brake surface! When cleaning brake surfaces, use a commercially available brake cleaning fluid.**

1. Raise the front of the vehicle and safely support the car with jackstands.

2. If you are going to check the front brakes, then the front tire, wheel and brake drum can be removed as assembly. Remove the hub cap, then either pry the dust cover off the spindle with a small prybar or pull it off with a pair of pliers. Remove the cotter pin from the spindle. Slide the nut lock off the adjusting nut, then loosen the adjusting nut until it reaches the end of the spindle. Do not remove the adjusting nut yet. Grab the tire/wheel and pull it toward yourself, then push it back into position. This will free the outer wheel bearing from the drum hub. Remove the adjusting nut, then remove the hub/drum tire assembly. Store outer bearing and race in a clean place. If the brakes are adjusted too tightly to remove the drum, see Step 3. If you can remove the drum, proceed to Step 4.

3. If the brakes are too tight to remove the drum, get under the car (make sure that your have jack stands under the car to support it) and remove the rubber plug from the bottom of the brake backing plate. Shine a flashlight into the slot in the plate. You will see the top of the adjusting screw starwheel and the adjusting lever for the automatic brake adjusting mechanism. To back off on the adjusting screw, you must first insert a small thin prybar or a piece of firm wire (such as coat hanger wire) into the adjusting slot and push the adjusting lever away from the adjusting screw. Then, insert a brake adjusting spoon into the slot and engage the top of the starwheel. Lift up on the bottom of the adjusting spoon to force the adjusting screw starwheel downward. Repeat this operation until the brake drum is free of the brake shoes and can be pulled off.

4. Clean the brake shoes and the inside of the brake drum. There must be at least $\frac{1}{16}$ in. (1.6mm) of brake lining above the heads of the brake shoe attaching rivets. The lining should not be cracked or contaminated with grease or brake fluid. If there is grease or brake fluid on the lining, it must be replaced and the source of the leak must be found and corrected. Brake fluid on the lining means leaking wheel cylinders. Grease on the brake lining means a leaking grease seal. If the lining is slightly glazed but otherwise in good condition, it can be cleaned up with medium sandpaper. Lift up the bottom of the wheel cylinder boots and inspect the ends of the wheel cylinders. A small amount of fluid in the end of the cylinders should be considered normal. If fluid runs out of the cylinder when the boots are lifted, the wheel cylinder must be rebuilt or

replaced. Examine the inside of the brake drum; it should have a smooth, dull finish. If excessive brake shoe wear caused grooves to wear in the drum it must be machined or replaced. If the inside of the drum is slightly glazed, but otherwise good, it can be cleaned up with medium sandpaper.

5. If no repairs are required, install the drum and wheel. If the brake adjustment was changed to remove the drum, adjust the brakes until the drum will just fit over the brakes. After the wheel is installed it will be necessary to complete the adjustment. See Brake Adjustment in this section.

REMOVAL & INSTALLATION

> ❋❋**CAUTION**
>
> **Brake shoes may contain asbestos, which has been determined to be a cancer causing agent. Never clean the brake surface with compressed air! Avoid inhaling any dust from any brake surface! When cleaning brake surfaces, use a commercially available brake cleaning fluid.**

➡**If you are not thoroughly familiar with the procedures involved in brake replacement, disassemble and assemble work only one side at a time, leaving the other wheel intact as a reference. The following procedure can be used on all years and models with front drum brake system.**

1. Remove the brake drum as described in the inspection procedure.

2. Spray the entire brake shoe friction surface with an aerosol brake cleaner to control the brake dust.

3. Place the hollow end of a brake spring service tool (available at auto parts stores) on the brake shoe anchor pin and twist it to disengage one of the brake retracting springs. Repeat this operation to remove the other spring.

> ❋❋**CAUTION**
>
> **Be careful the springs do not slip off the tool during removal, as they could cause personal injury.**

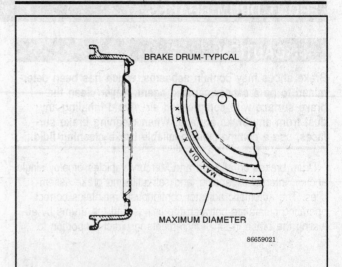

BRAKE DRUM-TYPICAL

MAXIMUM DIAMETER

86659021

Fig. 44 The maximum inside diameter will be stamped on the outside of each brake drum

4. Reach behind the brake backing plate and place a finger on the end of one of the brake hold-down spring mounting pins. Using a pair of pliers, grasp the washer on the top of the hold-down spring which corresponds to the pin that you are holding. Push down on the pliers and turn them 90° to align the slot in the washer with the head on the spring mounting pin. Remove the spring and washer and repeat this operation on the hold-down spring on the other brake shoe.

5. Place the top of a prytool on the top of the brake adjusting screw and move the brake adjusting lever. When there is enough slack in the automatic adjuster cable, disconnect the loop on the top of the cable from the anchor. Grasp the top of each brake shoe and move it outward to disengage it from the wheel cylinder. When the brake shoes are clear, lift them from the backing plate. Twist the shoes slightly and the automatic adjuster assembly will disassemble itself. Check all brake hardware springs etc. and replace as necessary.

To install:

6. Apply a light coating of high-temperature grease to the brake shoe contact points on the backing plate. Position the primary brake shoe (short shoe-front of vehicle) on the front of the backing plate and install the hold-down spring and washer over the mounting pin. Install the secondary shoe (long shoe-rear of vehicle) on the rear of the backing plate.

7. Install the automatic adjuster cable loop end on the anchor pin. Make sure that the crimped side of the loop faces the backing plate.

8. Install the return spring in the primary brake shoe and, using the tapered end of a brake spring service tool, slide the top of the spring onto the anchor pin.

✳✳CAUTION

Be careful to make sure that the spring does not slip off the tool during installation, as it could cause injury.

9. Install the automatic adjuster cable guide in the secondary brake shoe, making sure that the flared hole in the cable guide is inside the hole in the brake shoe. Fit the cable into the groove in the top of the cable guide.

10. Install the secondary shoe return spring through the hole in the cable guide and the brake shoe. Using the brake spring tool, slide the top of the spring onto the anchor pin.

11. Clean the threads on the adjusting screw and apply a light coating of high temperature grease to the threads. Screw the adjuster closed, then open it ½ turn.

12. Install the adjusting screw between the brake shoes with the starwheel nearest to the secondary shoe. Make sure that the starwheel is in a position that is accessible from the adjusting slot in the backing plate.

13. Install the short hooked end of the automatic adjuster spring in the proper hole in the primary brake shoe.

14. Connect the hooked end of the automatic adjuster cable and the free end of the automatic adjuster spring in the slot in the top of the automatic adjuster lever.

15. Pull the automatic adjuster lever (the lever will pull the cable and spring with it) downward and to the left and engage the pivot hook of the lever in the hole in the secondary brake shoe.

16. Check the entire brake assembly to make sure that everything is installed properly. Make sure that the shoes engage the wheel cylinder properly and are flush on the anchor pin.

Make sure that the automatic adjuster cable is flush on the anchor pin and in the slot on the back of the cable guide. Make sure that the adjusting lever rests on the adjusting screw starwheel. Pull upward on the adjusting cable until the adjusting lever is free of the starwheel, then release the cable. The adjusting lever should snap back into place on the adjusting screw starwheel and turn the wheel one tooth.

17. Expand the brake adjusting screw until the brake drum will just fit over the brake shoes.

18. Install the wheel and hub/drum (wheel bearing and locknut), then adjust the wheel bearings. Adjust the brakes and check the brake fluid.

Wheel Cylinders

REMOVAL & INSTALLATION

✳✳CAUTION

Brake shoes may contain asbestos, which has been determined to be a cancer causing agent. Never clean the brake surface with compressed air! Avoid inhaling any dust from any brake surface! When cleaning brake surfaces, use a commercially available brake cleaning fluid.

1. Remove the brake shoes.

2. Loosen the brake line on the rear of the cylinder but do not pull the line away from the cylinder or it may bend.

3. Remove the bolts and lockwashers which attach the wheel cylinder to the backing plate and remove the cylinder.

To install:

4. Position the new wheel cylinder on the backing plate and install the cylinder attaching bolts and lockwashers.

5. Attach the metal brake line.

6. Install the brakes. Bleed and adjust the brake system.

OVERHAUL

▶ See Figure 45

Since the travel of the pistons in the wheel cylinder changes when new brake shoes are installed, it is possible for previously good wheel cylinders to start leaking after new brakes are installed. Therefore, to save yourself the expense of having to replace new brakes which become saturated with brake fluid and the aggravation of having to take everything apart again, it is strongly recommended that wheel cylinders be rebuilt every time new brake shoes are installed. This is especially true on high mileage cars.

1. Remove the brakes.

2. Remove the wheel cylinder from the vehicle and place on a clean well lighted table.

3. Remove the boots from the ends of the wheel cylinders.

4. Push one piston toward the center of the cylinder to force the opposite piston and cup out of the other end of the cylinder. Reach in the open end of the cylinder and push the spring, cup, and piston out of the cylinder.

5. Remove the bleeder screw from the rear of the cylinder on the back of the backing plate.

6. Inspect the inside of the wheel cylinder. If it is scored in any way, the cylinder must be honed with a wheel cylinder hone or fine emery paper, and finished with crocus cloth if emery paper is used. If the inside of the cylinder is excessively worn, the cylinder will have to be replaced, as only 0.003 in. (0.076mm) of material can be removed from the cylinder walls. When honing or cleaning the wheel cylinders, keep a small amount of brake fluid in the cylinder to serve as a lubricant.

7. Clean any foreign matter from the pistons. The side of the pistons must be smooth for the wheel cylinders to operate properly.

8. Clean the cylinder bore with alcohol and a lint-free rag. Pull the rag through the bore several times to remove all foreign matter and dry the cylinder.

9. Install the bleeder screw and the return spring in the cylinder.

10. Coat new cylinder cups with new brake fluid and install them in the cylinder. Make sure that they are square in the bore or they will leak.

11. Install the pistons in the cylinder after coating them with new brake fluid.

12. Coat the insides of the boots with new brake fluid and install them in the cylinder. Install the brakes.

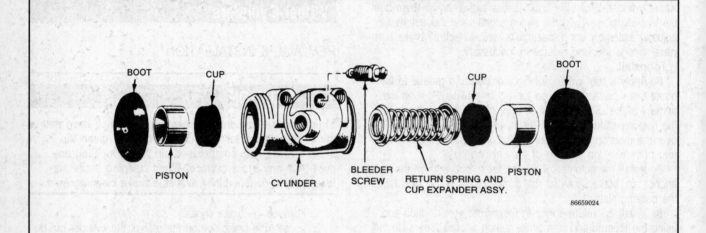

Fig. 45 A disassembled wheel cylinder

FRONT DISC BRAKES

▶ **See Figures 46 and 47**

Floating caliper front disc brakes were available on all models starting in the late 1960's. Starting in 1973, sliding caliper front discs were made standard equipment with vacuum power assist.

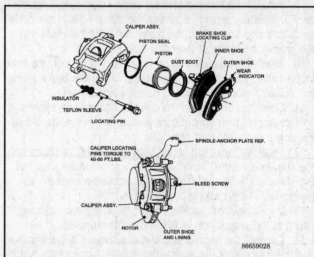

Fig. 46 An example of a sliding front disc brake assembly

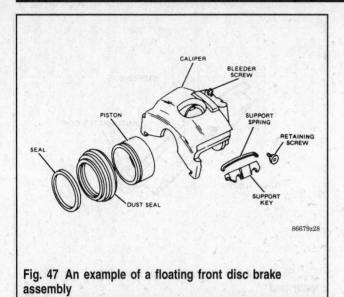

Fig. 47 An example of a floating front disc brake assembly

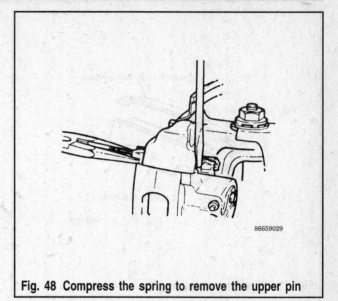

Fig. 48 Compress the spring to remove the upper pin

Brake Pads

REMOVAL & INSTALLATION

Single Piston Floating Caliper Disc Brakes

1973-79 MODELS

▶ See Figures 48, 49, 50, 51, 52, 53, 54, 55, 56, 57 and 58

1. Remove approximately ⅔ of the fluid from the rear reservoir of the tandem master cylinder. Raise and support the vehicle, taking proper safety precautions.
2. Remove the wheel and tire assembly.

✳✳CAUTION

Brake pads may contain asbestos, which has been determined to be a cancer causing agent. Never clean the brake surfaces with compressed air! Avoid inhaling any dust from any brake surface! When cleaning brake surfaces, use a commercially available brake cleaning fluid.

3. Remove the key retaining screw from the caliper retaining key.
4. Slide the retaining key and support spring either inward or outward from the anchor plate. To remove the key and spring, a hammer and drift may be used, taking care not to damage the key in the process.
5. Lift the caliper assembly away from the anchor plate by pushing the caliper downward against the anchor plate and rotating the upper end upward out of the anchor plate. Be careful not to stretch or twist the flexible brake hose.
6. Remove the inner shoe and lining assembly from the anchor plate. The inner shoe anti-rattle clip may become displaced at this time and should be repositioned on the anchor plate. Lightly tap on the outer shoe and lining assembly to free it from the caliper.

To install:

7. Clean the caliper, anchor plate, and disc assemblies, and inspect them for brake fluid leakage, excessive wear or

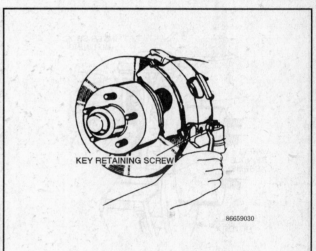

Fig. 49 If equipped, remove the retaining screw, then compress the spring and remove the lower pin

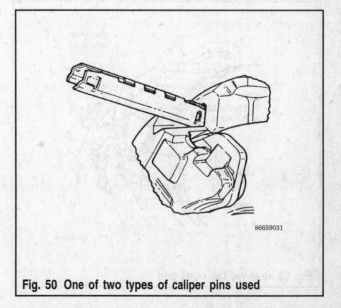

Fig. 50 One of two types of caliper pins used

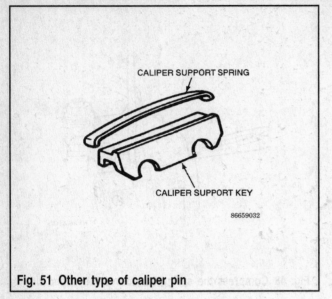

Fig. 51 Other type of caliper pin

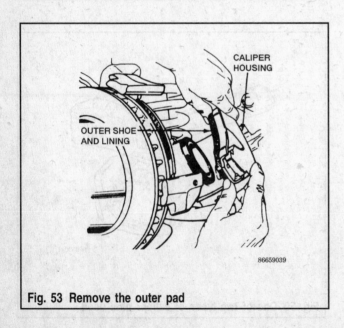

Fig. 52 Remove the inner pad

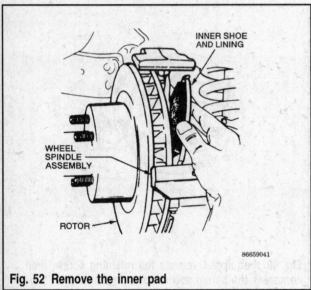

Fig. 53 Remove the outer pad

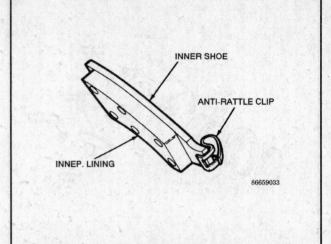

Fig. 54 Install the anti-rattle clip, if equipped, on the inner pad

signs of damage. Replace the pads if either of them are worn to within 1/32 in. (0.8mm) of the rivet heads.

8. To install new pads, use a 4 in. (10cm) C-clamp and a block of wood 1 in. (25mm) and approximately 3/4 in. (19mm) thick to seat the caliper hydraulic piston in its bore. This must be done in order to provide clearance for the caliper to fit over the rotor when new linings are installed.

9. At this point, the anti-rattle clip should be in its place on the lower inner brake shoe support of the anchor plate with the pigtail of the clip toward the inside of the anchor plate. Position the inner brake shoe and lining assembly on the anchor plate with the pad toward the disc.

10. Install the outer brake shoe with the lower flange ends against the caliper leg abutments and the brake shoe upper flanges over the shoulders on the caliper legs. The shoe is installed correctly when its flanges fit snugly against the machined surfaces of the shoulders.

11. Remove the C-clamps used to seat the caliper piston in its bore. The piston will remain seated.

12. Position the caliper housing lower V-groove on the anchor place lower abutment surface.

13. Pivot the caliper housing upward toward the disc until the outer edge of the piston dust boot is about 1/4 in. (6mm) from the upper edge of the inboard pad.

14. In order to prevent pinching of the dust boot between the piston and the inboard pad during installation of the caliper, place a clean piece of thin cardboard between the inboard pad and the lower half of the piston dust boot.

15. Rotate the caliper housing toward the disc until a slight resistance is felt. At this point, pull the cardboard downward toward the disc centerline while rotating the caliper over the disc. Then remove the cardboard and complete the rotation of the caliper down over the disc

16. Slide the caliper up against the upper abutment surfaces of the anchor plate and center the caliper over the lower anchor plate abutment.

17. Position the caliper support spring and key in the key slot and slide them into the opening between the lower end of the caliper and the lower anchor plate abutment until the key semicircular slot is centered over the retaining screw threaded hole in the anchor plate.

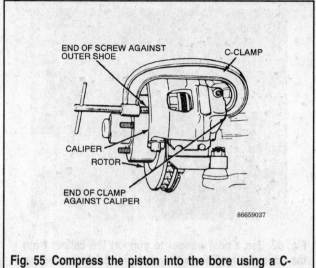

Fig. 55 Compress the piston into the bore using a C-clamp

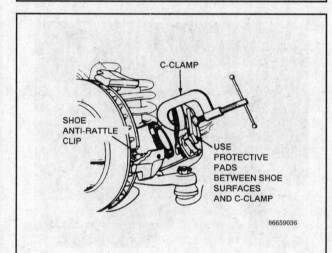

Fig. 56 A C-clamp can be helpful in installing the outer pad

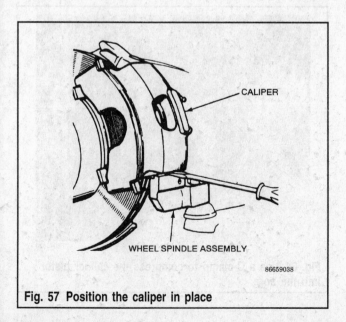

Fig. 57 Position the caliper in place

Fig. 58 Use a plastic tipped hammer to position the pin in place

18. Install the key retaining screw and tighten to 12-16 ft. lbs. (16-22 Nm).

19. Check the fluid level in the master cylinder and fill as necessary. Install the reservoir cover. Depress the brake pedal several times to properly seat the caliper and pads. Check for leakage around the caliper and pads. Check for leakage around the caliper and flexible brake hose.

20. Install the wheel and tire assembly and tighten the nuts to 70-115 ft. lbs. (94-154 Nm). Install the wheel cover.

21. Adjust the rear brakes and lower the car. Make sure that you obtain a firm brake pedal and then road test the car for proper brake operation.

Sliding Caliper Disc Brakes

1980-85 Models

▶ See Figures 59, 60, 61, 62, 63, 64 and 65

1. Raise the vehicle, and safely support with jackstands. Remove the front wheels.

2. Remove the lockwires from the two mounting bolts. Remove the mounting bolts and lift the caliper away from the disc. Support the caliper with a coat hanger or other piece of wire.

3. Remove the retaining clips with a suitable prytool and slide the outboard pad and retaining pins out of the caliper. Remove the inboard pad.

4. Use a C-clamp or other suitable tool to compress the caliper piston back into the caliper bore.

To install:

5. Slide the new inboard pad into the caliper so that the tabs are between the retaining clips and anchor plate and the backing plate lies flush against the piston.

6. Insert the inboard pad retaining pins into the outboard pad and position them in the caliper.

➡Stabilizer, insulator, pad clips, and pins should always be replaced when the disc pads are replaced.

7. Hold the retaining pins in place (one at a time) with a short drift pin or dowel and install the retaining clips.

8. Slide the caliper assembly over the disc and align the mounting bolt holes.

Fig. 59 Loosen the mounting bolts securing the caliper to the carrier. Some use a standard type socket for removal, while others use a Torx®

Fig. 60 Once the bolts are loosened, remove them and check for worn threads or other damage

Fig. 61 Slide the caliper off the rotor

Fig. 62 Use a coat hanger to support the caliper from the control arm. This will prevent the brake hose from being stretched

Fig. 63 Unclip the outer brake pad from the caliper assembly

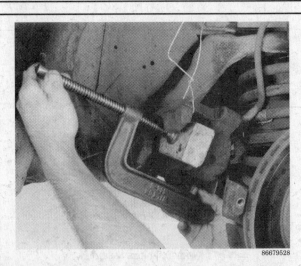

Fig. 64 Use a C-clamp to compress the caliper piston into the bore

Fig. 65 Remove the inner brake pad

9. Install the lower bolt finger-tight. Install the upper bolt and tighten. Secure the lower bolt. Safety-wire both bolts. The torque specifications are: Upper anchor plate mounting bolt 125 ft. lbs. (169 Nm) and lower anchor plate mounting bolt 105 ft. lbs. (142 Nm). The caliper mounting bolts 25-35 ft. lbs. (34-47 Nm).

➡Do not deviate from this procedure. The alignment of the anchor plate depends on the proper sequence of bolt installation.

10. Check the brake fluid level and pump and brake pedal to seat the lining against the disc. Adjust the rear brakes if necessary. Replace the wheels and road-test the vehicle.

INSPECTION

1. Raise the vehicle until the wheel and tire clear the floor. Place safety stands under the vehicle.
2. Remove the wheel cover.
3. Remove the wheel and tire from the hub and disc.

✳✳CAUTION

Brake shoes contain asbestos, which has been determined to be a cancer causing agent. Never clean the brake surfaces with compressed air! Avoid inhaling any dust from any brake surface! When cleaning brake surfaces, use a commercially available brake cleaning fluid.

4. Remove the brake pads as described above and visually inspect the shoe and lining assemblies. If the lining material has worn to a thickness of 0.125 in. (3.175mm) or less, or if the lining is contaminated with brake fluid, replace all pad assemblies on **both** front wheels. Make all thickness measurements across the thinnest section of the pad assembly. A slight taper on a used lining should be considered normal.
5. Reinstall or replace the brake pads and caliper assemblies, as described above.

➡When installing new brake linings, replace the pads at both front wheels to avoid uneven braking.

6. Refill the master cylinder, if necessary.
7. Install the wheel and tire assembly and tighten the wheel lug nuts.
8. Install the wheel cover and lower the vehicle.

Brake Caliper

INSPECTION

1. Raise the vehicle until the wheel and tire clear the floor. Place safety stands under the vehicle.
2. Remove the wheel cover.
3. Remove the wheel and tire from the hub and disc.

✳✳CAUTION

Brake shoes contain asbestos, which has been determined to be a cancer causing agent. Never clean the brake surfaces with compressed air! Avoid inhaling any dust from any brake surface! When cleaning brake surfaces, use a commercially available brake cleaning fluid.

4. Visually check the caliper for signs of leakage. If leakage is evident, the caliper should be overhauled or replaced.
5. Install the wheel and tire assembly and tighten the wheel lug nuts. Install the wheel cover.
6. Remove the safety stands and lower the vehicle.

REMOVAL & INSTALLATION

◗ See Figure 66

1. Raise and safely support the vehicle. Remove the front wheel and tire assembly.
2. Loosen the brake line fitting that connects the brake hose to the brake line at the frame bracket. Plug the brake line. Remove the retaining clip from the hose and bracket and disengage the hose from the bracket.
3. Remove the hollow bolt attaching the brake hose to the caliper and remove the brake hose. Discard the sealing washers.
4. Remove the caliper locating pins and remove the caliper. If removing both calipers, mark the right and left sides so they may be reinstalled correctly.
   To install:
5. Install the caliper over the rotor with the outer brake pad against the rotor's braking surface. This prevents pinching the piston boot between the inner brake pad and the piston.
6. Lubricate the locating pins and the inside of the locating pin insulators with silicone dielectric grease. Install the caliper locating pins and thread them into the spindle/anchor plate assembly by hand.
7. Tighten the caliper locating pins to 45-65 ft. lbs. (61-88 Nm).
8. Install new sealing washers on each side of the brake hose fitting outlet and install the hollow bolt, through the hose fitting and into the caliper. Tighten the bolt to 30 ft. lbs. (41 Nm).

Fig. 66 Before removing the caliper, loosen the brake hose fitting on the caliper

Fig. 67 If the rubber sleeves on the caliper need replacing, use a suitable pair of pliers to remove them

Fig. 68 When removing the sleeves, make sure you remove the entire portion

9. Position the other end of the brake hose in the bracket and install the retaining clip. Make sure the hose is not twisted.

10. Remove the plug from the brake line, connect the brake line to the brake hose and tighten the fitting nut to 10-18 ft. lbs. (13-24 Nm).

11. Bleed the brake system, install the wheel and tire assembly and lower the vehicle.

12. Apply the brake pedal several times before moving the vehicle, to position the brake pads.

13. Road test the vehicle.

OVERHAUL

▶ See Figures 67, 68, 69, 70, 71, 72, 73, 74 and 75

Disassembly

1. Remove the front disc brake caliper from the vehicle and place it on a bench.

2. Remove the brake pads from the caliper.

3. Place a piece of wood between the caliper piston and the caliper bridge to cushion the piston's impact. Using an air nozzle, apply air pressure to the caliper fluid port to blow the piston out of its bore. If the piston is seized and cannot be forced from the caliper, tap lightly around the piston while applying air pressure.

❊❊CAUTION

Apply only enough air pressure to ease the piston out of the caliper. Excessive pressure can force the piston out of the caliper bore with enough force to cause personal injury. Never attempt to catch the piston by hand as it comes out of the bore.

❊❊WARNING

Do not use a screwdriver or prybar to pry the piston out of the bore; damage to the piston may result.

4. Remove the dust boot from the caliper.

5. Remove and discard the rubber piston seal from the caliper bore.

Cleaning and Inspection

1. Clean all metal parts with isopropyl alcohol, then clean out and dry the grooves and passageways with compressed air. Make sure the caliper bore and component parts are thoroughly clean.

2. Check the caliper bore and piston for damage or excessive wear. Replace the piston if it is pitted or scored, or on Police vehicles if the chrome plating is worn off. The piston should also be replaced if it does not meet the requirements.

Assembly

1. Apply a film of clean brake fluid to a new caliper piston seal and install it in the caliper bore. Make sure the seal is firmly seated in the groove and not twisted.

2. Install a new dust boot by setting the flange squarely in the outer groove of the caliper bore.

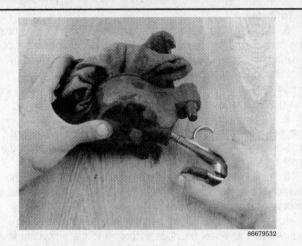

Fig. 69 With the caliper removed, use a rag or block of wood and compressed air to force the piston out. Keep your hands away from the piston

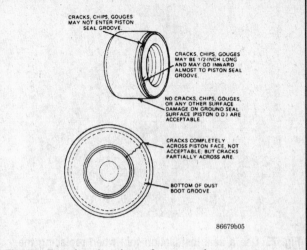

Fig. 72 Examine the piston for excessive wear or damage

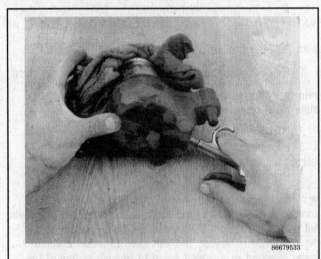

Fig. 70 Use compressed air until the piston is fully extended from the caliper bore

Fig. 73 Remove the dust boot

Fig. 71 Piston and caliper separated

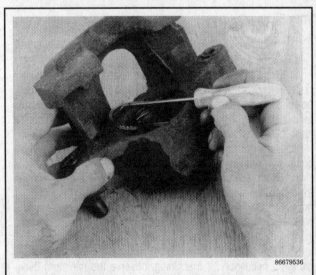

Fig. 74 Use a pick tool to remove the inner seal

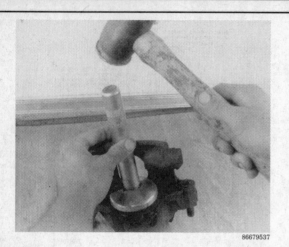

Fig. 75 Use a seal installation tool when replacing the dust boot. Do not hammer on the plastic piston or it will most likely break

3. Coat the piston with brake fluid. Using a C-clamp and a wood block, install the piston into the caliper bore. Make sure the piston is not cocked. Spread the dust boot over the piston as it is installed.

✳✳WARNING

Never apply the C-clamp directly to the caliper piston; damage to the piston may result.

4. Seat the dust boot in the piston groove. Make sure the dust boot is tight in the boot groove on the piston.
5. Install the disc brake pads and install the caliper on the vehicle.

Brake Disc (Rotor)

REMOVAL & INSTALLATION

With Sliding Caliper
▶ See Figure 76

1. Raise and safely support the vehicle.
2. Remove the wheel and tire assembly.
3. Remove the caliper from the spindle and rotor, but do not disconnect the brake hose. Suspend the caliper inside the fender housing with a length of wire. Do not let the caliper hang by the brake hose.
4. Remove the grease cap from the hub and remove the cotter pin, nut retainer and adjusting nut.
5. Grasp the hub/rotor assembly and pull it out far enough to loosen the washer and outer wheel bearing. Push the hub/rotor assembly back onto the spindle, then remove the washer and outer wheel bearing.
6. Remove the hub/rotor assembly from the spindle.
7. Inspect the rotor for scoring and wear. Replace or machine as necessary. If machining, observe the minimum thickness specification.

To install:

8. If the rotor is being replaced, remove the protective coating from the new rotor with brake cleaner. Pack a new set of bearings with high-temperature wheel bearing grease and install the inner roller bearing in the inner cup. Pack grease lightly between the lips of a new seal and install the seal, using a seal installer.
9. If the original rotor is being installed, make sure the grease in the hub is clean and adequate, the inner bearing and grease seal are lubricated and in good condition, and the rotor braking surfaces are clean.
10. Install the hub/rotor assembly on the spindle. Keep the assembly centered on the spindle to prevent damage to the grease seal or spindle threads.
11. Install the outer wheel bearing, washer and adjusting nut. Adjust the wheel bearings according to the procedure in this section, then install the nut retainer, cotter pin and grease cap.
12. Install the caliper and the wheel and tire assembly. Lower the vehicle.
13. Apply the brake pedal several times before moving the vehicle, to position the brake pads.

With Floating Caliper

1. Raise the front of the car and support it with jackstands.

➡ **In order to remove the rotor, the caliper and anchor plate must be removed from the car.**

2. Remove the front wheel(s).
3. Loosen, but do not remove, the upper anchor plate attaching bolt with a suitable rachet and socket.
4. Remove the lower anchor plate attaching bolt.

➡ **When the caliper is removed from the car it must be wired out of the way of the rotor. Also, the brake pads will fall out of the caliper if they are not held in place when the caliper is removed. You will have to insert a small piece of wood or a folded piece of heavy cardboard between the shoes to hold them in place. Have a piece of wire and a piece of wood handy before you start the next step.**

Fig. 76 Front brake rotor removed

5. Hold the caliper in place and remove the upper anchor plate attaching bolt.

6. Slide the caliper and anchor plate assembly off the rotor, inserting the block of wood between the brake pads as they become visible above the rotor.

7. When the anchor plate is clear of the rotor, wire it out of the way.

8. Remove the dust cap from the rotor hub by either prying it off with a small prytool or pulling it off with a pair of slip-lock pliers.

9. Remove the cotter pin and nut lock from the spindle.

10. Loosen the bearing adjusting nut until it is at the end of the spindle.

11. Grasp the rotor with a rag and pull it outward, push it inward.

12. Remove the adjusting nut and the outer bearing.

13. Remove the rotor from the spindle.

To install:

14. Pack the inside of the rotor hub with a moderate amount of grease, between the bearing cups. Do not overload the hub with grease.

15. Apply a small amount of grease to the spindle.

16. Coat the lip of a new grease seal with a small amount of grease and position it on the rotor.

17. Position the rotor on the spindle

18. Install the outer bearing and washer on the spindle, inside the rotor hub.

19. Install the bearing adjusting nut and tighten it to 17-25 inch lbs. (2-3 Nm) while spinning the rotor. This will seat the bearing.

20. Back off the adjusting nut one half turn.

21. Tighten the adjusting nut to 10-15 inch lbs. (1.1-1.7 Nm).

22. Install the nut lock on the adjusting nut so two of the slots align with the holes in the spindle.

23. Install a new cotter pin and bend the ends back so that they will not interfere with the dust cap.

24. Install the dust cap.

25. Install the anchor plate assembly and caliper. The torque specifications are: Upper anchor plate mounting bolt 125 ft. lbs. (169 Nm) and lower anchor plate mounting bolt 105 ft. lbs. (142 Nm). The caliper mounting bolts 25-35 ft. lbs. (34-47).

26. Install the front tires.

INSPECTION

1. Raise the vehicle until the wheel and tire clear the floor. Place safety stands under the vehicle.

2. Remove the wheel cover.

3. Remove the wheel and tire from the hub and disc.

❄❄CAUTION

Brake shoes contain asbestos, which has been determined to be a cancer causing agent. Never clean the brake surfaces with compressed air! Avoid inhaling any dust from any brake surface! When cleaning brake surfaces, use a commercially available brake cleaning fluid.

4. Tighten the wheel bearing adjusting nut to eliminate end-play. Check to make sure the disc can still be rotated. Use a

micrometer and measure the thickness of the rotor in several places. Rotor thickness should not vary more than 0.0008 in (0.02mm) between different places on the rotor. Refer to the specifications chart at the end of this section to determine allowable thickness for the rotor.

5. Hand spin the disc and visually check. If the disc appears to be out of round or if it wobbles, it needs to be machined or replaced. When complete, loosen the wheel bearing adjusting nut and retighten to specifications, in order to prevent bearing damage.

6. Visually check the disc for scoring. Minor scores can be removed with fine emery cloth. If it is excessively scored, it must be machined or replaced.

7. Install the wheel and tire assembly and tighten the wheel lug nuts.

8. Install the wheel cover. Remove the safety stands and lower the vehicle.

Caliper Splash Shield

REMOVAL & INSTALLATION

▶ See Figures 77, 78, 79 and 80

1. Remove the caliper and rotor as outlined earlier in this section.

➡**The brake hose does not need to be removed from the caliper. Securely hang the caliper assembly from the control arm using a coat hanger.**

2. Loosen and remove the retaining bolts securing the shield to the knuckle assembly.

3. Slide the shield off the spindle.

4. Remove and discard the plastic washer between the shield and the knuckle assembly.

5. Reverse to install. Replace the plastic washer with a new washer. Tighten the retaining bolts securely.

Fig. 77 Caliper splash shield ready for removal

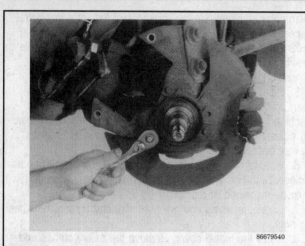

Fig. 78 Loosen the retaining bolts. Some may be excessively rusty, therefore you might want to spray the bolts with penetrating oil

Fig. 80 Remove and discard the plastic washer between the shield and knuckle assembly

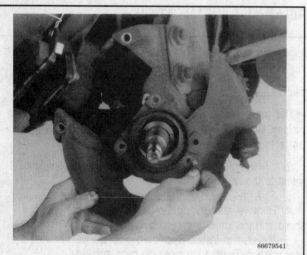

Fig. 79 Remove the bolts and slide the shield off the spindle

REAR DRUM BRAKES

✳✳CAUTION

Brake shoes may contain asbestos, which has been determined to be a cancer causing agent. Never clean the brake surfaces with compressed air! Avoid inhaling any dust from any brake surface! When cleaning brake surfaces, use a commercially available brake cleaning fluid.

Basic Operating Principles

Drum brakes on all Ford and Mercury cars employ hydraulically actuated, internally expanding brake shoes. Correct operating clearance between the shoe linings and drums is maintained by a self-adjusting assembly, which moves in small increments, in direct proportion to lining wear. When applying the brakes while backing up, the linings tend to follow the rotating drum counterclockwise, thus forcing the upper end of the primary shoe against the anchor pin. Simultaneously, the wheel cylinder pushes the upper end of the secondary shoe and cable guide outward, away from the anchor pin. This movement of the secondary shoe causes the cable to pull the adjusting lever upward and against the end of the tooth on the adjusting screw star wheel. As lining wear increases, the upward travel of the adjusting lever also increases. When the linings have worn sufficiently to allow the lever to move upward far enough, it passes over the end of the tooth and engages it. Upon release of the brakes, the adjusting spring pulls the adjuster lever downward, turning the star wheel and expanding the brakes.

Brake Drum

REMOVAL & INSTALLATION

▶ See Figures 81, 82, 83, 84 and 85

1. Raise and safely support the vehicle.
2. Remove the wheel and tire assembly.
3. Remove the drum retaining nuts, if equipped, and remove the brake drum.

➡If the drum will not come off, pry the rubber plug from the backing plate. Insert a narrow rod through the hole in the backing plate and disengage the adjusting lever from the adjusting screw. While holding the adjustment lever away from the screw, back off the adjusting screw with a brake adjusting tool. Be careful not damage the notches in the adjusting screw or the self-adjusting mechanism will not function properly.

4. Inspect the brake drum for scoring and wear. Replace or machine as necessary. If machining, observe the maximum diameter specification.

To install:

5. If a new drum is being installed, remove the protective coating from the drum using brake cleaner. Sand the drum lightly and wipe with a cloth soaked in denatured alcohol.
6. Adjust the brake shoes according to the procedure in this Section.
7. Install the brake drum and the wheel and tire assembly.
8. Lower the vehicle.

INSPECTION

Clean all grease, brake fluid and other contaminants from the brake drum using brake cleaner. Visually check the drum for scoring, cracks or other damage.

Measure the diameter of the drum using a suitable micrometer. Measure the diameter at various points around the circumference of the drum and at the bottom of the deepest groove,

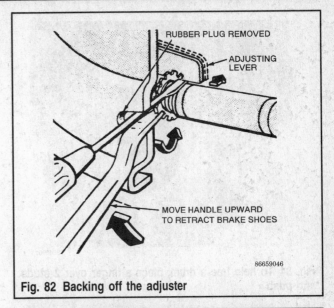

Fig. 82 Backing off the adjuster

Fig. 83 A rear brake drum assembly

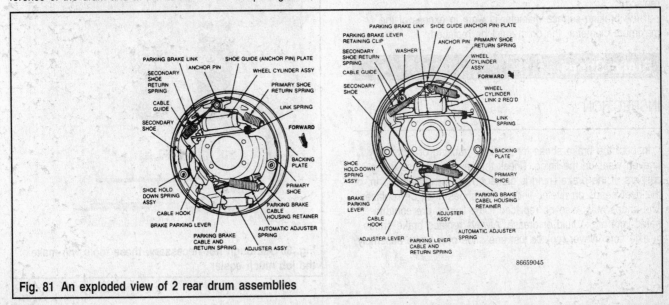

Fig. 81 An exploded view of 2 rear drum assemblies

Fig. 84 To help free a drum, place a finger over 2 studs and push

Fig. 85 Lift the drum away from the brake assembly

to determine if the drum can be machined or must be replaced.

If the braking surface diameter is worn in excess of the maximum diameter, the drum must be replaced.

Brake Shoes

INSPECTION

Inspect the brake shoes for peeling, cracking or extremely uneven wear on the lining. Check the lining thickness using calipers. If the brake lining is damaged or worn within $\frac{1}{32}$ in. of the rivet heads on riveted linings, the shoes must be replaced. The shoes must also be replaced if the linings are contaminated with brake fluid or grease. Always replace brake shoes in axle sets. Never replace just one shoe of a brake assembly.

Check the condition of the brake shoes, brake springs and drums for signs of overheating. If the drums have a slight blue coloring, indicating overheating, the brake springs should be replaced. Overheated springs lose their tension and could allow the new shoes to drag and wear prematurely, if not replaced.

REMOVAL & INSTALLATION

▶ **See Figures 86, 87, 88, 89, 90, 91, 92, 93, 94, 95, 96, 97, 98, 99, 100 and 101**

1. Raise and safely support the vehicle. Remove the rear wheel and tire assemblies. Remove the brake drum.
2. Remove the shoe-to-anchor springs and unhook the cable eye from the anchor pin. Remove the anchor pin plate.
3. Remove the shoe hold-down springs, shoes, adjusting screw, pivot nut, socket and automatic adjustment parts.
4. Remove the parking brake link, spring and retainer. Disconnect the parking brake cable from the parking brake lever.
5. After removing the rear brake secondary shoe, disassemble the parking brake lever from the shoe by removing the retaining clip and spring washer.

To install:

6. Before installing the rear brake shoes, assemble the parking brake lever to the secondary shoe and secure it with the spring washer and retaining clip.
7. Apply a light coating of caliper slide grease at the points where the brake shoes contact the backing plate. Be careful not to get any lubricant on the brake linings.
8. Position the brake shoes on the backing plate. The primary shoe with the short lining faces the front of the vehicle, the secondary shoe with the long lining, to the rear. Secure the assembly with the hold-down springs. Install the parking brake link, spring and retainer. Back off the parking brake adjustment, then connect the parking brake cable to the parking brake lever.
9. Install the anchor pin plate on the anchor pin. Place the cable eye over the anchor pin with the crimped side toward the drum. Install the primary shoe-to-anchor spring.

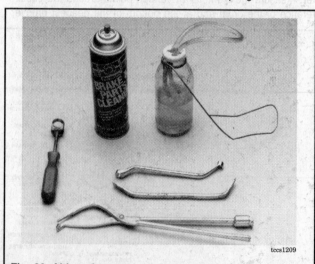

Fig. 86 Although not necessary, these tools will make the job much easier

Fig. 87 Spray the entire brake assembly with a brake cleaning solution to control dust. Be sure to wear a mask, since the dust may contain asbestos

Fig. 88 Use a brake spring tool to remove the shoe-to-anchor spring

Fig. 89 Remember the direction of the spring

Fig. 90 Remove the other upper spring

Fig. 91 Remove the brake shoe anchor spring

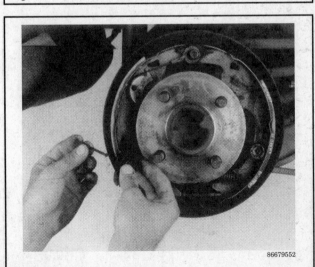

Fig. 92 Slide the anchor pin out from the rear of the drum assembly

Fig. 93 Pry up on the adjuster cable bracket at the base of the assembly and free the cable from the central perch

Fig. 96 Remove the remaining anchor hardware

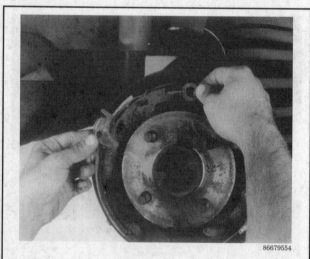

Fig. 94 The adjuster cable can be removed from the anchor points

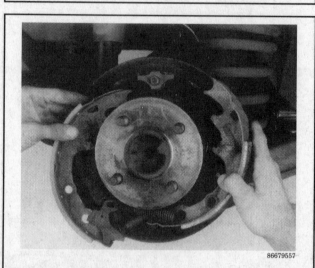

Fig. 97 Separate the two shoes and remove them from the drum housing

Fig. 95 Inspect the cable for signs of excessive wear and replace if needed

Fig. 98 Pry up on the emergency brake cable bracket. . .

Fig. 99 Unclip the bracket from the brake shoe

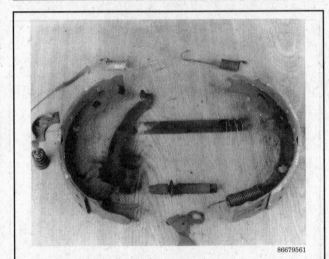

Fig. 100 Lay all the parts out on a clean surface. this will help during the reinstallation process

Fig. 101 Before you reassemble the drum assembly, apply grease to each of the brake shoe contact point on the drum backing plate

10. Install the cable guide on the secondary shoe web with the flanged hole fitted into the hole in the secondary shoe web. Thread the cable around the cable guide groove.

➡ **The cable must be positioned in the groove and not between the guide and the shoe web.**

11. Install the secondary shoe-to-anchor spring. Make sure the cable eye is not cocked or binding on the anchor pin when installed. All parts should be flat on the anchor pin.

12. Apply a thin coat of lubricant to the threads and the socket end of the adjusting screw. Turn the adjusting screw into the adjusting pivot nut to the limit of the threads, then back off ½ turn.

➡ **Make sure the socket end of the adjusting screw is stamped with an R or L, indicating the right or left side of the vehicle. The adjusting screw assemblies must be installed on the correct side for proper brake shoe adjustment.**

13. Place the adjusting socket on the screw and install the assembly between the shoe ends with the adjusting screw toothed wheel nearest the secondary shoe.

14. Hook the cable hook into the hole in the adjusting lever. The adjusting levers are stamped with an **R** or **L** to indicate their installation on the right or left side.

15. Position the hooked end of the adjuster spring completely into the large hole in the primary shoe web. Connect the loop end of the spring to the adjuster lever hole.

16. Pull the adjuster lever, cable and automatic adjuster spring down and toward the rear, engaging the pivot hook in the large hole of the secondary shoe web.

17. After installation, check the action of the adjuster by pulling the cable between the cable guide and the adjuster lever toward the secondary shoe web, far enough to lift the lever past a tooth on the adjusting screw wheel. The lever should snap into position behind the next tooth, and the release of the cable should cause the adjuster spring to return the lever to its original position. This return action of the lever will turn the adjusting screw one tooth.

18. If pulling the cable does not produce the action described in Step 17, or if the lever action is sluggish instead of positive and sharp, check the position of the lever on the adjusting screw toothed wheel.

19. With the brake in a vertical position (anchor at the top), the lever should contact the adjusting wheel ³/₁₆ in. above the centerline of the screw. If the contact point is below this centerline, the lever will not lock on the teeth in the adjusting screw wheel, and the screw will not be turned.

20. Adjust the brake shoes as explained in this Section, then proceed as follows to determine the cause of this condition:

   a. Make sure that the upper or anchor pin end of the cable is pulled toward the cable guide as far as possible and that the end fitting is pointing toward the cable guide.

   b. Check the cable end fittings. The cable should completely fill or extend slightly beyond the crimped section of the fittings. If it does not meet this specification, possible damage is indicated and the cable assembly should be replaced.

   c. Check the cable length. Measure from the inside edge of the hook to the far edge of the anchor hole. The cable length is 11 in. (28cm).

d. Check the cable guide for damage. The cable groove should be parallel to the shoe web, and the body of the guide should lie flat against the web. Replace the guide if it shows damage.

e. Check the pivot hook on the lever. The hook surfaces should be square with the body of the lever for proper pivoting. Replace the lever if the hook shows damage.

f. Make sure that the adjusting screw socket is properly seated in the notch in the shoe web.

21. Make sure the upper ends of the brake shoes are seated against the anchor pin and the shoes are centered on the backing plate. If they are not seated, back off the parking brake system adjustment to obtain 0.005-0.025 in. (0.127-0.635mm) play after overcoming the load of the parking brake link spring.

➡**Whenever the brake shoes are removed, the parking brake cable adjustment should be checked.**

22. Make sure the brake shoes are properly adjusted, then install the brake drum and wheel and tire assemblies and lower the vehicle.

23. Apply the brakes several times while backing up the vehicle. After each stop, the vehicle must be moved forward.

24. Check brake operation by making several stops from varying forward speeds.

Wheel Cylinders

INSPECTION

Carefully pull the lower edges of the wheel cylinder boots away from the cylinders to see if the interior of the cylinder is wet with brake fluid. Excessive fluid at this point indicates leakage past the piston cups and a need for wheel cylinder replacement.

➡**A slight amount of fluid is nearly always present and acts as a lubricant for the piston.**

REMOVAL & INSTALLATION

▶ **See Figures 102, 103, 104, 105, 106, 107, 108, 109 and 110**

1. Raise and safely support the vehicle.
2. Remove the wheel and tire assembly and the brake drum.
3. Remove the brake shoe assembly.
4. Disconnect the brake line from the wheel cylinder at the backing plate. The line will separate from the wheel cylinder when the wheel cylinder is removed from the backing plate.
5. Remove the wheel cylinder attaching bolts and remove the wheel cylinder.

➡**Be careful to prevent brake fluid from contacting the brake shoe linings or they must be replaced.**

To install:
6. Wipe the end of the brake line to remove any foreign matter before making connections.

7. Position the wheel cylinder on the backing plate and finger-tighten the brake line to the wheel cylinder.
8. Install the wheel cylinder attaching bolts and tighten to 10-20 ft. lbs. (14-28 Nm).
9. Tighten the brake line fitting nut to 10-18 ft. lbs. (13-24 Nm).
10. Install the links in the ends of the wheel cylinder and install the brake shoe assembly.
11. Adjust the brakes and install the brake drum. Bleed the brake system.
12. Install the wheel and tire assembly and lower the vehicle.

Brake Backing Plate

REMOVAL & INSTALLATION

1. Raise and safely support the vehicle.

Fig. 102 Use a ratchet and socket to remove the wheel cylinder. The bolts are accessed from the rear of the backing plate — front view

Fig. 103 Removing the wheel cylinder — side view

Fig. 104 With the brake line unfastened and the bolts removed, the wheel cylinder can be taken out of the backing plate

86679563

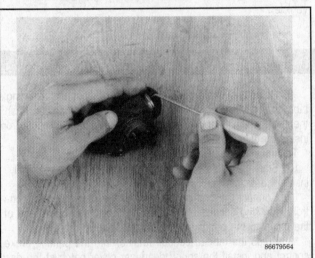

Fig. 105 Use a pick to remove the hood over each end of the wheel cylinder

86679564

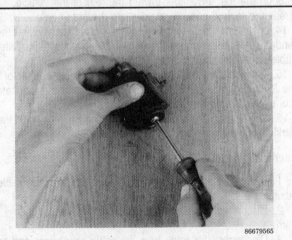

Fig. 106 Use a suitable tool to apply force on one piston, causing the piston and spring assembly to slide out of the bore

86679565

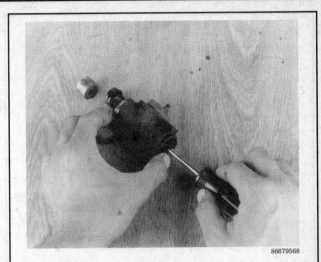

Fig. 107 Forcing the piston and spring assembly out of the bore

86679568

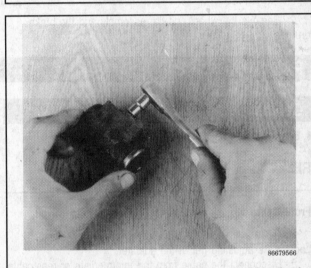

Fig. 108 Use a ratchet and socket to remove the wheel cylinder bleeder valve

86679566

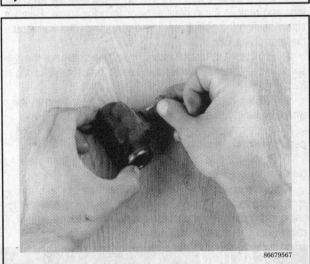

Fig. 109 Check the bleeder valve threads and replace if needed

86679567

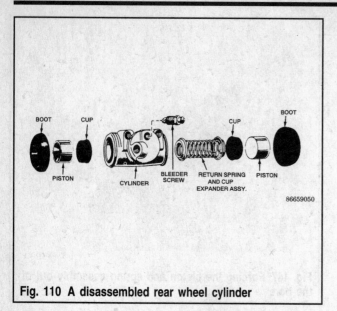

Fig. 110 A disassembled rear wheel cylinder

2. Remove the wheel and tire assembly and the brake drum.

3. Disconnect the brake line from the wheel cylinder.

4. Remove the brake shoe assembly and the wheel cylinder.

5. Compress the prongs on the parking brake cable retainer, so they can pass through the hole in the brake backing plate. Pull the cable through the backing plate hole.

6. Remove the axle shaft. Refer to the procedure in Section 7.

7. Remove the backing plate.

To install:

8. Install the backing plate and tighten the bolts to 20-39 ft. lbs. (28-54 Nm).

9. Install the axle shaft.

10. Insert the parking brake cable through the backing plate hole until the retainer prongs expand. The prongs must be securely locked in place.

11. Install the wheel cylinder and the brake shoe assembly.

12. Adjust the brake shoes and install the brake drum. Bleed the brake system.

13. Install the wheel and tire assembly and lower the vehicle.

PARKING BRAKE

Cables

▶ See Figure 111

REMOVAL & INSTALLATION

Front Cable

1. Raise and safely support the vehicle on jackstands. Loosen the adjusting nut at the adjuster.

2. Disconnect the cable from the intermediate or rear cable connector located along the left side frame rail.

3. Use a suitable box end wrench to depress the retaining tabs and remove the conduit retainer from the frame. Remove screw holding the plastic inner fender apron to the frame, at the rear of the fender panel.

4. Pull back the fender apron. If equipped, remove the spring clip retainer that holds the parking brake cable to the frame.

5. Pull the cable through the frame and let it hang in the wheel housing. Lower the vehicle.

6. Inside the passenger compartment, remove the sound deadener cover from the cable at the dash panel.

7. Remove the spring retainer and cable end from the clevis at the parking brake control.

8. Pull the cable until the parking brake control take up spring tang is at full clockwise position. Retain the reel spring using a piece of wire or suitable fixture and disconnect the cable from the take up reel.

✳✳CAUTION

Keep fingers away from the reel mechanism while the fabricated tool is in place.

9. Using a suitable box end wrench, depress the retaining tabs and remove the conduit from the control assembly. Push the cable down through the dash panel and remove cable from inside the wheel housing.

To install:

10. Start the cable through the opening in the dash panel inside the passenger compartment.

11. Connect the end of the cable to the parking brake control clevis and secure it with a spring clip. Connect the end of the cable to the parking brake control take up reel.

12. Press the tabbed conduit retainer into the parking brake control and install the sound deadener cover patch at the dash panel.

13. Raise and safely support the vehicle. Insert the cable through the frame member toward the rear of the vehicle. Press the tabbed conduit retainer into the frame hole.

14. Install the cable-to-frame spring clip retainer behind the fender apron and connect the front cable to the intermediate cable connector on the left side frame rail.

15. Connect the control cable to the rear cable connector on the left side frame rail and use pliers to remove the fabricated tool used to retain the take up reel.

16. Lower the vehicle. Adjust the parking brake. Check the parking brake operation.

Intermediate Cable

1. Raise and safely support the vehicle. Loosen the cable adjusting nut.

2. Disconnect the parking brake release spring at the frame.

3. Disconnect the cable from the cable connectors and remove it from the vehicle.

To install:

4. Attach the intermediate cable to the front and rear cable connectors. Make sure the rearward end of the cable goes

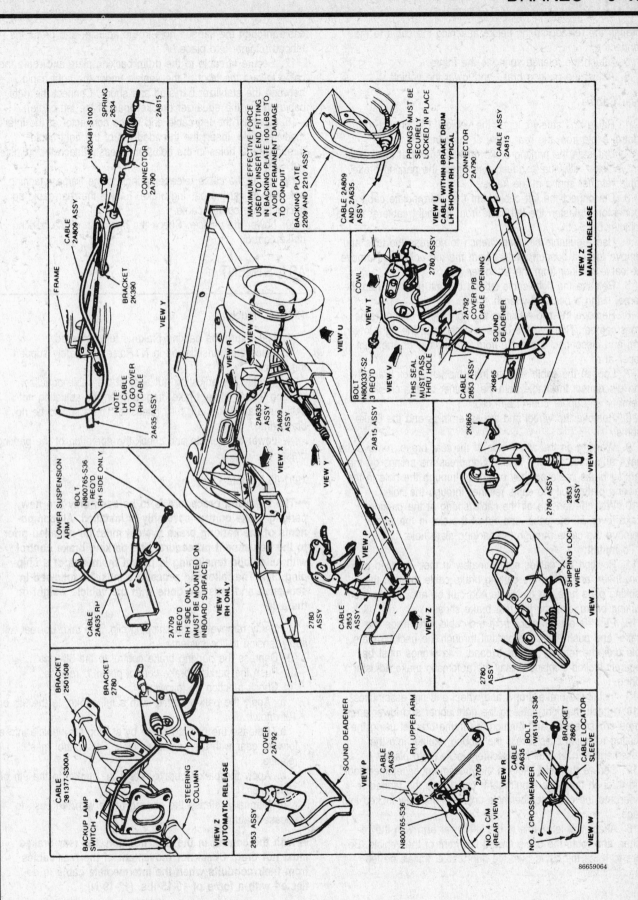

Fig. 111 Parking brake cable routing — 1971-85 vehicles

86659064

through the release spring before attaching the cable to the connector.

5. Attach the release spring to the frame.

6. Adjust the parking brake and lower the vehicle.

Rear Cables

1. Raise and safely support the vehicle. Disconnect the control cable from the rear cable at the connector.

2. Unfasten the parking brake release spring at the frame. On vehicles with dual exhaust, disconnect the parking brake cable retainer spring at the frame.

3. Disconnect the left cable from the intermediate cable connector. Unfasten the left cable from the right cable at the adjuster bracket.

4. Use a suitable box end wrench to depress the tabs and remove the left conduit retainer from the rod adjuster. Remove the cable retainer from the left lower arm.

5. Release the right cable tabbed conduit retainer from the frame, using a box end wrench.

6. Remove the clip retaining the right cable to the frame crossmember. Remove the cable retainer from the right lower arm and disconnect the cable from the retainer on the right upper arm.

7. Loosen the cable retainer from the left shock bracket and disconnect the cable from the retainer on the cross-member and upper control arm clip.

8. Remove the wheel and tire assemblies and the brake drums.

9. Working on the wheel side of the rear brake, remove the brake automatic adjuster spring. Compress the prongs on the parking brake cable so they can pass through the hole in the backing plate. Pull the cable retainer through the hole.

10. With the tension off the cable spring at the parking brake lever, lift the cable end out of the slot in the lever. Remove the cable through the backing plate hole.

To install:

11. Position the cables approximately in their installed position. Insert enough of the parking brake cable through the backing plate hole, so the cable end can be attached to the parking brake lever on the rear brake shoe.

12. Pull the excess slack from the cable wire inside the brake, and push the cable conduit through the backing plate hole until the retainer prongs expand. The prongs must be securely locked in place. Install the automatic brake adjuster spring.

13. Install the brake drums and wheel and tire assemblies.

14. Attach the right cable to the right upper and lower arms, frame crossmember and through the frame bracket using the existing retaining clips. Press the tabbed retainer into the crossmember hole until it is securely locked into place.

15. Secure the right cable to the crossmember retainer hook and through the upper control arm clip. Press the tabbed retainer into the crossmember hole until it is securely locked into place.

16. Attach the left cable to the left lower arm with the retainer, and route the cable toward the front of the vehicle. Be sure to route the cable over the right cable. Install the left

cable through the flanged hole in the adjuster and press the tabbed retainer into place.

17. Secure fit cable to the drum backing plate and route the cable toward the front of the vehicle under the right cable between the stabilizer bar stud and shock. Connect the right cable end to the equalizer bracket (part of the left cable).

18. Connect the left cable end to the connector at the intermediate cable. Insert the threaded rod of the right cable through the 2 holes in the adjuster. Loosely attach the adjuster nut.

19. Install the cable release springs to the frame attaching hole and adjust the parking brake. Fasten the rear cable connector to the control cable.

20. Lower the vehicle. Check the operation of the parking brake control.

ADJUSTMENT

1971-80 Models

1. Make sure the parking brake is fully released.

2. Place the transmission in **N**. Raise and safely support the vehicle.

3. Tighten the adjusting nut against the cable equalizer, causing a rear wheel brake drag. Loosen the adjusting nut until the rear brakes are fully released. There should be no brake drag.

4. Lower the vehicle and check the operation of the parking brake.

1981-85 Models

➡ The following procedure is to be used only if a new parking brake control assembly is installed. All components of the parking brake system must be installed prior to the adjustment procedure. The parking brake control with automatic tensioning is preset by means of a shipping clip. The following procedure must be followed in sequence and must be done with the vehicle weight on the axle.

1. Verify removal of the shipping clip. The take up reel will apply tension to the system.

2. Depress the parking brake control to the 8th notch.

3. Push the parking brake control pedal to release.

4. Check function as follows:

   a. Apply the parking brake with a full stroke, to the 9th or 10th notch.

   b. Release the parking brake by shifting the vehicle into a forward gear with the engine running. The control must release.

   c. Apply the parking brake with a full stroke, to the 9th or 10th notch.

   d. Manually release the parking brake with the push to release feature.

➡ With the control in the OFF position, the rear brakes must not drag. Check for movement of the rear cables from their conduits when the intermediate cable is deflected with a force of 10-15 lbs. (13-19 N).

Troubleshooting the Brake System

Problem	Cause	Solution
Low brake pedal (excessive pedal travel required for braking action.)	• Excessive clearance between rear linings and drums caused by inoperative automatic adjusters	• Make 10 to 15 alternate forward and reverse brake stops to adjust brakes. If brake pedal does not come up, repair or replace adjuster parts as necessary.
	• Worn rear brakelining	• Inspect and replace lining if worn beyond minimum thickness specification
	• Bent, distorted brakeshoes, front or rear	• Replace brakeshoes in axle sets
	• Air in hydraulic system	• Remove air from system. Refer to Brake Bleeding.
Low brake pedal (pedal may go to floor with steady pressure applied.)	• Fluid leak in hydraulic system	• Fill master cylinder to fill line; have helper apply brakes and check calipers, wheel cylinders, differential valve tubes, hoses and fittings for leaks. Repair or replace as necessary.
	• Air in hydraulic system	• Remove air from system. Refer to Brake Bleeding.
	• Incorrect or non-recommended brake fluid (fluid evaporates at below normal temp).	• Flush hydraulic system with clean brake fluid. Refill with correct-type fluid.
	• Master cylinder piston seals worn, or master cylinder bore is scored, worn or corroded	• Repair or replace master cylinder
Low brake pedal (pedal goes to floor on first application—o.k. on subsequent applications.)	• Disc brake pads sticking on abutment surfaces of anchor plate. Caused by a build-up of dirt, rust, or corrosion on abutment surfaces	• Clean abutment surfaces
Fading brake pedal (pedal height decreases with steady pressure applied.)	• Fluid leak in hydraulic system	• Fill master cylinder reservoirs to fill mark, have helper apply brakes, check calipers, wheel cylinders, differential valve, tubes, hoses, and fittings for fluid leaks. Repair or replace parts as necessary.
	• Master cylinder piston seals worn, or master cylinder bore is scored, worn or corroded	• Repair or replace master cylinder
Decreasing brake pedal travel (pedal travel required for braking action decreases and may be accompanied by a hard pedal.)	• Caliper or wheel cylinder pistons sticking or seized	• Repair or replace the calipers, or wheel cylinders
	• Master cylinder compensator ports blocked (preventing fluid return to reservoirs) or pistons sticking or seized in master cylinder bore	• Repair or replace the master cylinder
	• Power brake unit binding internally	• Test unit according to the following procedure: (a) Shift transmission into neutral and start engine (b) Increase engine speed to 1500 rpm, close throttle and fully depress brake pedal (c) Slow release brake pedal and stop engine (d) Have helper remove vacuum check valve and hose from power unit. Observe for backward movement of brake pedal. (e) If the pedal moves backward, the power unit has an internal bind—replace power unit

86659777

Troubleshooting the Brake System (cont.)

Problem	Cause	Solution
Spongy brake pedal (pedal has abnormally soft, springy, spongy feel when depressed.)	• Air in hydraulic system	• Remove air from system. Refer to Brake Bleeding.
	• Brakeshoes bent or distorted	• Replace brakeshoes
	• Brakelining not yet seated with drums and rotors	• Burnish brakes
	• Rear drum brakes not properly adjusted	• Adjust brakes
Hard brake pedal (excessive pedal pressure required to stop vehicle. May be accompanied by brake fade.)	• Loose or leaking power brake unit vacuum hose	• Tighten connections or replace leaking hose
	• Incorrect or poor quality brakelining	• Replace with lining in axle sets
	• Bent, broken, distorted brakeshoes	• Replace brakeshoes
	• Calipers binding or dragging on mounting pins. Rear brakeshoes dragging on support plate.	• Replace mounting pins and bushings. Clean rust or burrs from rear brake support plate ledges and lubricate ledges with molydisulfide grease. **NOTE:** If ledges are deeply grooved or scored, do not attempt to sand or grind them smooth—replace support plate.
	• Caliper, wheel cylinder, or master cylinder pistons sticking or seized	• Repair or replace parts as necessary
	• Power brake unit vacuum check valve malfunction	• Test valve according to the following procedure: (a) Start engine, increase engine speed to 1500 rpm, close throttle and immediately stop engine (b) Wait at least 90 seconds then depress brake pedal (c) If brakes are not vacuum assisted for 2 or more applications, check valve is faulty
	• Power brake unit has internal bind	• Test unit according to the following procedure: (a) With engine stopped, apply brakes several times to exhaust all vacuum in system (b) Shift transmission into neutral, depress brake pedal and start engine (c) If pedal height decreases with foot pressure and less pressure is required to hold pedal in applied position, power unit vacuum system is operating normally. Test power unit. If power unit exhibits a bind condition, replace the power unit.
	• Master cylinder compensator ports (at bottom of reservoirs) blocked by dirt, scale, rust, or have small burrs (blocked ports prevent fluid return to reservoirs).	• Repair or replace master cylinder **CAUTION:** Do not attempt to clean blocked ports with wire, pencils, or similar implements. Use compressed air only.
	• Brake hoses, tubes, fittings clogged or restricted	• Use compressed air to check or unclog parts. Replace any damaged parts.
	• Brake fluid contaminated with improper fluids (motor oil, transmission fluid, causing rubber components to swell and stick in bores	• Replace all rubber components, combination valve and hoses. Flush entire brake system with DOT 3 brake fluid or equivalent.
	• Low engine vacuum	• Adjust or repair engine

Troubleshooting the Brake System (cont.)

Problem	Cause	Solution
Grabbing brakes (severe reaction to brake pedal pressure.)	• Brakelining(s) contaminated by grease or brake fluid	• Determine and correct cause of contamination and replace brakeshoes in axle sets
	• Parking brake cables incorrectly adjusted or seized	• Adjust cables. Replace seized cables.
	• Incorrect brakelining or lining loose on brakeshoes	• Replace brakeshoes in axle sets
	• Caliper anchor plate bolts loose	• Tighten bolts
	• Rear brakeshoes binding on support plate ledges	• Clean and lubricate ledges. Replace support plate(s) if ledges are deeply grooved. Do not attempt to smooth ledges by grinding.
	• Incorrect or missing power brake reaction disc	• Install correct disc
	• Rear brake support plates loose	• Tighten mounting bolts
Dragging brakes (slow or incomplete release of brakes)	• Brake pedal binding at pivot	• Loosen and lubricate
	• Power brake unit has internal bind	• Inspect for internal bind. Replace unit if internal bind exists.
	• Parking brake cables incorrrectly adjusted or seized	• Adjust cables. Replace seized cables.
	• Rear brakeshoe return springs weak or broken	• Replace return springs. Replace brakeshoe if necessary in axle sets.
	• Automatic adjusters malfunctioning	• Repair or replace adjuster parts as required
	• Caliper, wheel cylinder or master cylinder pistons sticking or seized	• Repair or replace parts as necessary
	• Master cylinder compensating ports blocked (fluid does not return to reservoirs).	• Use compressed air to clear ports. Do not use wire, pencils, or similar objects to open blocked ports.
Vehicle moves to one side when brakes are applied	• Incorrect front tire pressure	• Inflate to recommended cold (reduced load) inflation pressure
	• Worn or damaged wheel bearings	• Replace worn or damaged bearings
	• Brakelining on one side contaminated	• Determine and correct cause of contamination and replace brakelining in axle sets
	• Brakeshoes on one side bent, distorted, or lining loose on shoe	• Replace brakeshoes in axle sets
	• Support plate bent or loose on one side	• Tighten or replace support plate
	• Brakelining not yet seated with drums or rotors	• Burnish brakelining
	• Caliper anchor plate loose on one side	• Tighten anchor plate bolts
	• Caliper piston sticking or seized	• Repair or replace caliper
	• Brakelinings water soaked	• Drive vehicle with brakes lightly applied to dry linings
	• Loose suspension component attaching or mounting bolts	• Tighten suspension bolts. Replace worn suspension components.
	• Brake combination valve failure	• Replace combination valve
Chatter or shudder when brakes are applied (pedal pulsation and roughness may also occur.)	• Brakeshoes distorted, bent, contaminated, or worn	• Replace brakeshoes in axle sets
	• Caliper anchor plate or support plate loose	• Tighten mounting bolts
	• Excessive thickness variation of rotor(s)	• Refinish or replace rotors in axle sets
Noisy brakes (squealing, clicking, scraping sound when brakes are applied.)	• Bent, broken, distorted brakeshoes	• Replace brakeshoes in axle sets
	• Excessive rust on outer edge of rotor braking surface	• Remove rust

86659779

Troubleshooting the Brake System (cont.)

Problem	Cause	Solution
Noisy brakes (squealing, clicking, scraping sound when brakes are applied.) (cont.)	• Brakelining worn out—shoes contacting drum of rotor	• Replace brakeshoes and lining in axle sets. Refinish or replace drums or rotors.
	• Broken or loose holdown or return springs	• Replace parts as necessary
	• Rough or dry drum brake support plate ledges	• Lubricate support plate ledges
	• Cracked, grooved, or scored rotor(s) or drum(s)	• Replace rotor(s) or drum(s). Replace brakeshoes and lining in axle sets if necessary.
	• Incorrect brakelining and/or shoes (front or rear).	• Install specified shoe and lining assemblies
Pulsating brake pedal	• Out of round drums or excessive lateral runout in disc brake rotor(s)	• Refinish or replace drums, re-index rotors or replace

86659780

BRAKE SPECIFICATIONS
All measurements in inches unless noted

Year	Model	Lug Nut Torque (ft. lbs.)	Master Cylinder Bore	Brake Disc			Brake Drum Diameter		
				Original Thickness	Minimum Thickness	Maximum Runout	Original Inside Diameter	Maximum Machine Diameter	Minimum Lining Thickness
1971	All	70-155	0.938 [1]	1.180	1.120	0.007	10.00 [2]	10.06	0.030
1972	All	70-115	1.000	1.180	1.120	0.003	10.00	10.06	0.030
1973	All	70-115	1.000	1.180	1.120	0.003	10.00	10.06	0.030
1974	All	70-115	1.000	1.180	1.120	0.003	10.00	10.06	0.030
1975	All	70-115	1.000	1.180	1.120	0.003	10.00	10.06	0.030
1976	All	70-115	1.000	1.030	0.972	0.003	11.03	11.09	0.030
1977	All	70-115	1.000	1.030	0.972	0.003	11.03	11.09	0.030
1978	All	70-115	1.000	1.030	0.972	0.003	11.03	11.09	0.030
1979	All	70-115	1.000	1.030	0.972	0.003	11.03 [4]	11.09 [5]	0.030
1980	All	80-105	0.875 [3]	1.030	0.972	0.003	11.03 [6]	11.09 [7]	0.030
1981	All	80-105	0.875 [3]	1.030	0.972	0.003	11.03 [6]	11.09 [7]	0.030
1982	All	80-105	0.875 [3]	1.030	0.972	0.003	11.03 [6]	11.09 [7]	0.030
1983	All	80-105	0.875 [3]	1.030	0.972	0.003	11.03 [6]	11.09 [7]	0.030
1984	All	80-105	0.875 [3]	1.030	0.972	0.003	11.03 [6]	11.09 [7]	0.030
1985	All	80-105	0.875 [3]	1.030	0.972	0.003	11.03 [6]	11.09 [7]	0.030

NOTES: 1 With disc: 0.938
           With drum brake: 1.000
     2 Front or rear drum
     3 With power brakes: 0.750
     4 11.0 brakes available
     5 With 11.0 brakes: 11.090
     6 9.0 brakes available
     7 With 9.0 brakes: 9.060

86679zzz

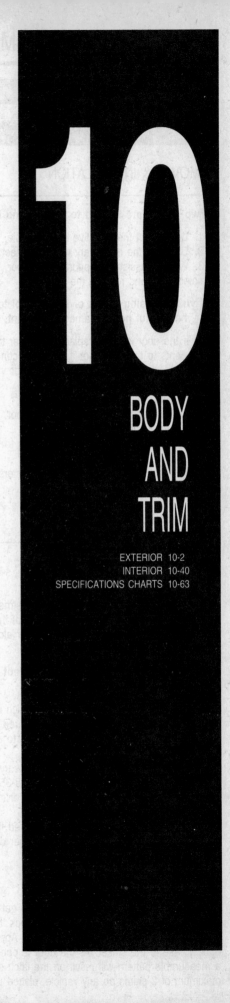

10

**BODY
AND
TRIM**

EXTERIOR

Doors

REMOVAL & INSTALLATION

➡ Two people are needed to remove and install the doors.

1. Disconnect the negative battery cable.
2. Unfasten the necessary wiring connectors.
3. With an assistant supporting the door, remove the hinge retaining bolts and remove the door.

➡ If you are using a jack or similar tool to support the door, be careful not to damage the paint.

4. If the door is to be replaced, transfer the following components to the new door if in usable condition: trim panel, watershield, outside mouldings, clips, window regulators and door latch components.

To install:

5. With an assistant positioning the door, install and partially tighten the hinge bolts.
6. Align the door and tighten the bolts to 19-25 ft. lbs. (25-35 Nm).
7. Fasten the necessary wiring connectors and connect the negative battery cable.

ADJUSTMENT

Door Hinges

▶ See Figure 1

The door hinges provide sufficient adjustment to correct most door misalignment conditions. The holes of the hinge and/or the hinge attaching points are enlarged or elongated to provide for hinge and door alignment.

➡ Do not cover up a poor door alignment with a latch striker adjustment.

1. Refer to the figure to determine which hinge bolts must be loosened to move the door in the desired direction.
2. Loosen the hinge bolts just enough to permit movement of the door with a padded prytool.
3. Move the door the estimated necessary distance, then tighten the hinge bolts to 19-25 ft. lbs. (25-35 Nm). Check the door fit to make sure there is no binding or interference with the adjacent panel.
4. Repeat the operation until the desired fit is obtained. Check the striker plate alignment for proper door closing.

Door Latch Striker

▶ See Figures 2 and 3

The latch striker should be shimmed to get the clearance between the striker and the latch. To check this clearance, clean the latch jaws and the striker area. Apply a thin layer of dark grease to the striker. As the door is opened and closed, a measurable pattern will result on the latch striker. Use a maximum of 2 shims on any vehicle, placed under the striker.

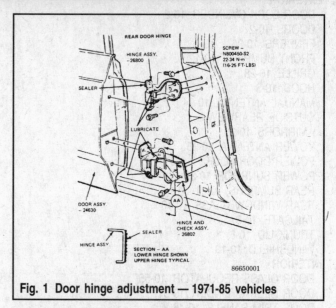

Fig. 1 Door hinge adjustment — 1971-85 vehicles

Use Torx® drive bit set D79P-2100-T or equivalent, to loosen and tighten the latch striker to 25-32 ft. lbs. (35-45 Nm).

Door Lock Cylinder

REMOVAL & INSTALLATION

➡ The key code is stamped on the driver's door lock cylinder to aid in replacing lost keys.

1. Remove the trim panel and watershield.
2. Disconnect the lock control-to-door lock cylinder rod from the lock cylinder arm.
3. Remove the door lock cylinder retainer and slide the cylinder from the door. If a new lock cylinder is being installed transfer the arm to the new cylinder.
4. Installation is the reverse of removal.

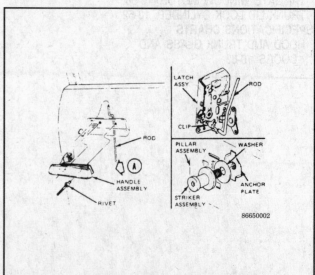

Fig. 2 Door latch installation — 1971-85 vehicles

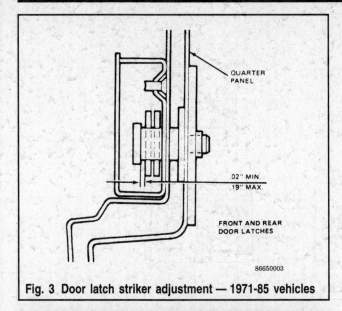

Fig. 3 Door latch striker adjustment — 1971-85 vehicles

Power Door Locks

REMOVAL & INSTALLATION

▶ **See Figures 4, 5, 6, 7 and 8**

Actuator Motor

1. Disconnect the negative battery cable.
2. Remove the door trim panel and watershield.
3. Disconnect the actuator motor link from the door latch.
4. Remove the pop rivet attaching the actuator motor to the door.
5. Disconnect the wiring at the connector.
6. Remove the actuator motor.
7. Installation is the reverse of removal. Be careful to avoid twisting the actuator boot. Make sure that the actuator is tight against the inner panel when installing the pop rivet.

Hood

REMOVAL & INSTALLATION

▶ **See Figure 9**

1. Open and support the hood. Mark the position of the hood hinges on the hood.
2. Protect the body with covers over the fenders to prevent damage to the paint.
3. Scribe marks around the outside of each hinge with a marker pen to use as alignment marks during installation.
4. With the help of an assistant, remove the 2 bolts attaching each hinge to the hood, being careful not to let the hood slip when the bolts are removed.
5. Remove the hood from the vehicle.

To install:

6. With the help of an assistant, position the hood on its hinges and install the attaching bolts. Remove the body covers.
7. Adjust the hood for an even fit between the fenders and a flush fit with the front of the fenders.
8. Adjust the hood latch, if necessary.

ALIGNMENT

Hood

The hood can be adjusted fore-and-aft and side-to-side by loosening the hood-to-hinge retaining bolts and repositioning the hood. To raise or lower the hood, loosen the hinge-to-fender reinforcement retaining bolts and raise or lower the hinge as necessary.

Latch

▶ **See Figure 10**

➡ Before adjusting the hood latch mechanism, make sure the hood is properly aligned.

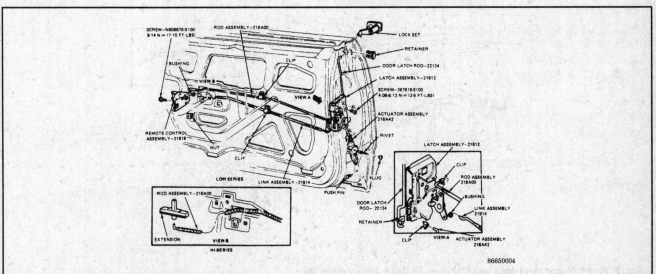

Fig. 4 Power door lock assembly — 1971-80 2-door vehicles

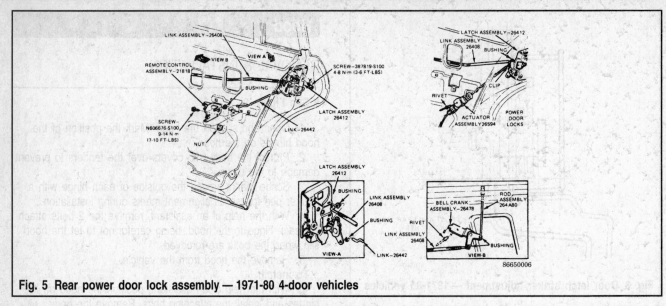

Fig. 5 Rear power door lock assembly — 1971-80 4-door vehicles

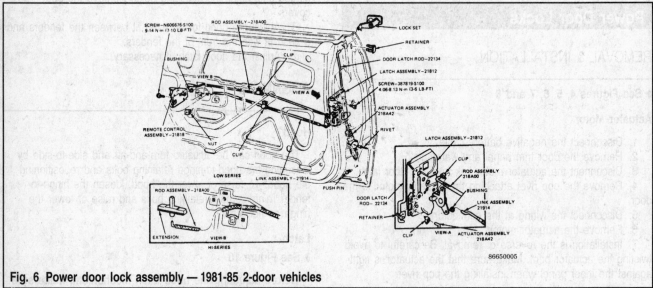

Fig. 6 Power door lock assembly — 1981-85 2-door vehicles

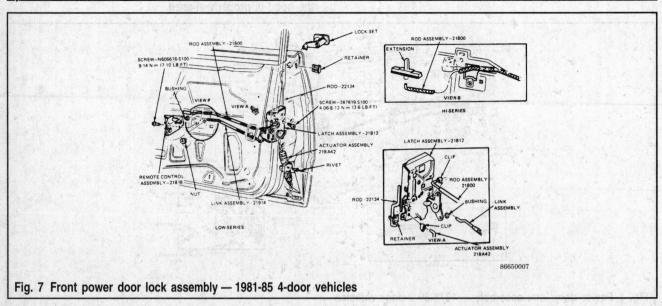

Fig. 7 Front power door lock assembly — 1981-85 4-door vehicles

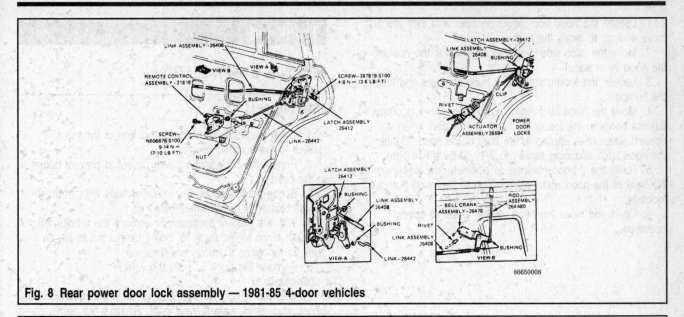

Fig. 8 Rear power door lock assembly — 1981-85 4-door vehicles

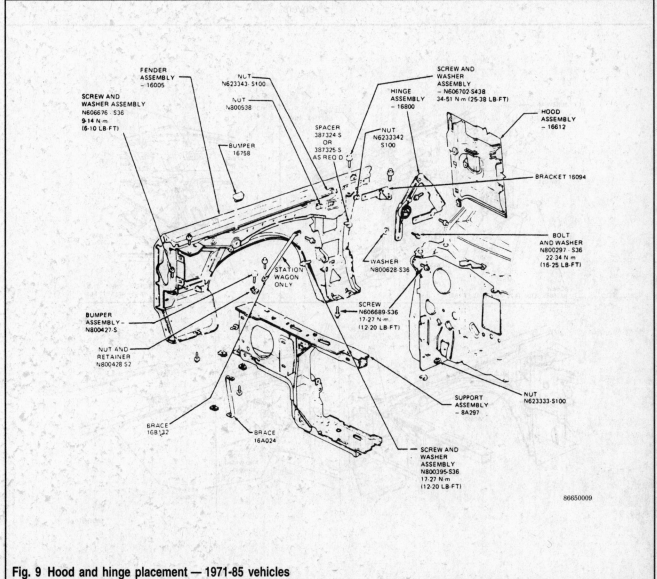

Fig. 9 Hood and hinge placement — 1971-85 vehicles

1. Loosen the hood latch attaching bolts until they are just loose enough to move the latch.

2. Move the latch side-to-side to align it with the opening in the hood inner panel.

3. Loosen the locknuts on the 2 hood bumpers and lower the bumpers.

4. Move the hood latch up or down as required to obtain a flush fit between the top of the hood and fenders when an upward pressure is applied to the front of the hood. Tighten the hood latch attaching screws to 7-10 ft. lbs. (9-14 Nm).

5. Raise the 2 hood bumpers to eliminate any looseness at the front of the hood when closed. Tighten the hood bumper locknuts.

6. Open and close the hood several times, to check operation.

Trunk Lid

REMOVAL & INSTALLATION

▶ See Figure 11

1. Open the trunk lid. Mark the position of the trunk lid relative to the trunk lid hinges.

2. Protect the body fenders with covers to prevent damage to the paint.

3. Scribe marks around the retaining bolts with a marker pen as reference points when installing.

4. With the help of an assistant, remove the 2 bolts attaching each hinge to the trunk lid, being careful not to let the trunk lid slip when the bolts are removed.

5. Remove the trunk lid from the vehicle.

To install:

6. With the help of an assistant, position the trunk lid on its hinges and install the attaching bolts. Remove the body covers.

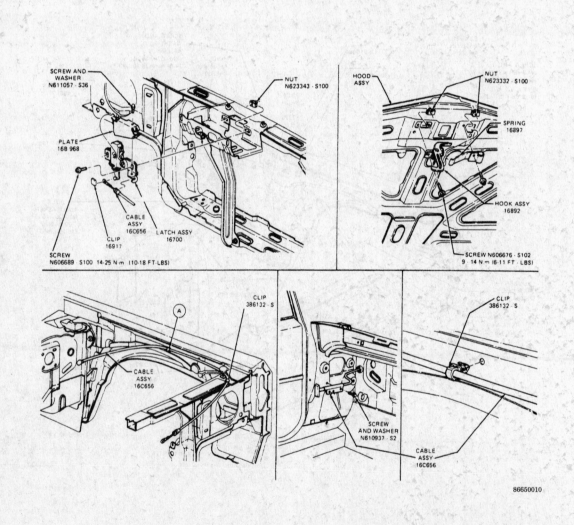

Fig. 10 Hood hinge, latch and cable — 1971-85 vehicles

7. Adjust the trunk lid's position in the trunk lid opening.
8. Adjust the trunk lid latch and/or striker, if necessary.

ALIGNMENT

Trunk Lid Alignment

The trunk lid can be shifted fore-and-aft by loosening the hinge-to-trunk lid retaining screws. The up and down adjustment is made by loosening the hinge-to-trunk lid retaining screws and raising or lowering the trunk lid.

The trunk lid should be adjusted for an even and parallel fit with the trunk lid opening. The trunk lid should also be adjusted up and down for a flush fit with the surrounding panels. Be careful not to damage the trunk lid or surrounding body panels.

Trunk Lid Latch/Striker

➡The latch assembly is fixed and not adjustable on all vehicles. Any latch adjustment must be made at the striker.

Before adjusting the striker, open and close the trunk lid to double-check the striker alignment. Remove the scuff plate striker covering, if equipped, before attempting any striker adjustment.

Loosen the 2 screw and washer assemblies and adjust the striker by moving up and down or from side-to-side as necessary. Tighten the screw and washer assemblies to 7-10 ft. lbs. (9-14 Nm).

➡Do not try to correct a poor trunk lid alignment with a latch striker adjustment.

TRUNK LID TORSION BAR LOADING ADJUSTMENT

▶ **See Figures 12, 13, 14 and 15**

❊❊CAUTION

Always wear safety glasses when performing this service procedure.

1. Open the luggage compartment deck lid and note the pop-up distance of the deck lid. The deck lid should have finger clearance. If not, the torsion bar tension should be increased. If the deck lid pops open with more than necessary force, the torsion bar tension should be decreased.

❊❊CAUTION

The torsion bar is under great tension! Be careful when adjusting, as it can spring out of control with considerable force if not handled properly!

2. Support the deck lid in the fully open position before adjusting the torsion bar.
3. To adjust a torsion bar, use a suitable tool designed to safely perform the adjustment. Then move the torsion bar end to another position (notch) to increase or decrease the tension. Refer to the tool illustration.
4. Adjust one torsion bar and check the adjustment before adjusting the other torsion bar.
5. After torsion bar adjustment, the difference of the position of the torsion bar ends, between the right and left side, must not be more than one slot.

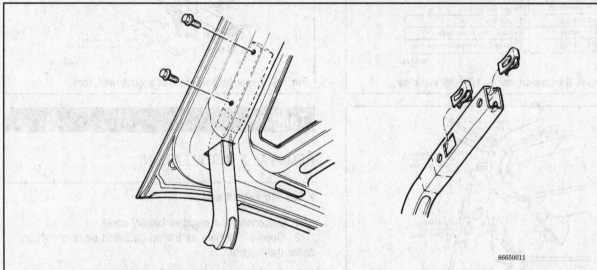

Fig. 11 Trunk lid installation — 1971-85 vehicles

86650011

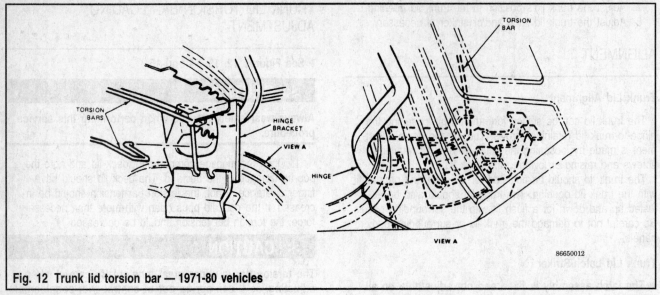

Fig. 12 Trunk lid torsion bar — 1971-80 vehicles

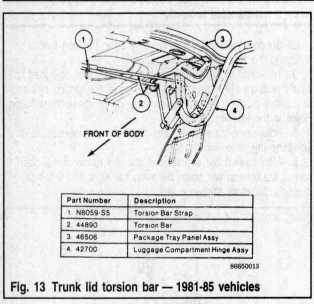

Part Number	Description
1. N8059-S5	Torsion Bar Strap
2. 44890	Torsion Bar
3. 46506	Package Tray Panel Assy
4. 42700	Luggage Compartment Hinge Assy

Fig. 13 Trunk lid torsion bar — 1981-85 vehicles

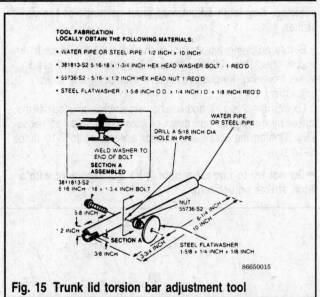

Fig. 15 Trunk lid torsion bar adjustment tool

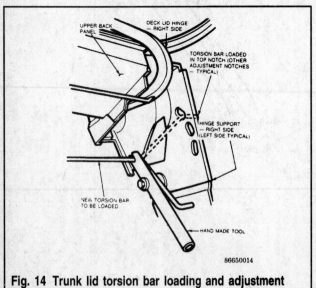

Fig. 14 Trunk lid torsion bar loading and adjustment

Tailgate

REMOVAL & INSTALLATION

▶ **See Figures 16 and 17**

    1. Disconnect the negative battery cable.
    2. Open the tailgate as a drop gate and place a support under the tailgate.

➡**Be careful not to damage the paint.**

    3. Remove the tailgate inside trim panel and access cover.
    4. Remove the torsion bar retainer bracket.

✳✳CAUTION

Be careful when working with the torsion bar. The bar is under tension in the installed position.

5. Raise the tailgate glass and latch the upper tailgate latch by hand. Make sure the glass is supported.

6. Remove the wiring harness from the tailgate.

7. Mark the location of the hinge to the tailgate and remove the nuts attaching the hinge to the tailgate.

8. Actuate the outside handle to disengage the lower latch and remove the tailgate.

9. Installation is the reverse of the removal procedure.

ALIGNMENT

Upper Latch-to-Lower Latch Link

▶ See Figure 18

Place the tailgate latches in the closed (latched) position. Disconnect the upper latch-to-lower latch link from the lower latch. Adjust the upper latch-to-lower latch link to engage with the lower latch (no load on the link).

To check the adjustment, the upper latch must not close when the lower latch is in the open position. The upper and lower latches must open at approximately the same time when the outside handle is operated.

Upper Hinge and Latch Release Link

Remove the tailgate inside trim panel and access cover. Disengage the upper hinge release link from the lock release control assembly. Position the adjuster on the upper hinge release link to engage the lever on the lock release control assembly with no load on the link. Assemble the link to the control assembly.

Check the adjustment as follows:

1. The power window regulator, if equipped, must not operate when the latch release control is in the released position.

2. The inside release handle must not operate when the window is down and the upper latch is locked by either the key or the inside push button.

Tailgate Striker

Fore-and-aft and up and down adjustment of the strikers is accomplished by means of square holes in the pillar, backed

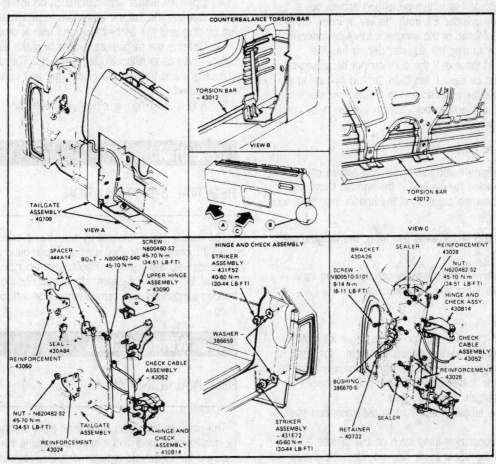

Fig. 16 Tailgate assembly — 1971-85 vehicles

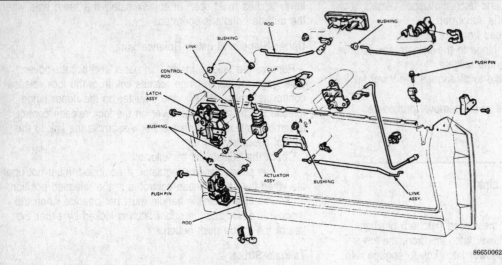

Fig. 17 Exploded view of tailgate latch, linkage and acutator

by floating tapping plates. Lateral adjustment is accomplished by adding or removing shims.

Upper Key Cylinder to Latch Link

Remove the tailgate inside trim panel and access cover. Disengage the key cylinder link from the key cylinder. If the door cannot be unlocked or the window cannot be lowered, shorten the rod by turning the adjuster deeper into the threaded portion of the rod. If the door cannot be locked or the window cannot be raised, lengthen the rod by turning the adjuster. Assemble the adjusted link to the key cylinder lever.

The door must lock and unlock and the window must open and close when properly adjusted.

Outside Handle to Latch Link

Remove the tailgate inside trim panel and access cover. Disengage the outside handle link at the handle. Close the upper latch. Position the adjuster on the handle lever with no load on the link.

➡If the release rod is adjusted too long, the tailgate will not lock.

Adjustment is correct if the tailgate can be opened as a door, and the door locks and unlocks properly.

Testing

Visually inspect the lever position to the upper left-hand hinge on the tailgate to determine whether or not the lever is fully seated in the correct design position. If the lever is only partially seated, the following adjustment must be made:
1. Open the tailgate as a drop gate.
2. Remove the tailgate inside handle assembly and trim panel.
3. Close the upper right-hand latch on the tailgate.
4. Disconnect the upper hinge link rod retainer clip from the lock release control assembly.
5. With the upper hinge release link rod in the normal position, turn the adjuster on the threaded end of the rod so that it can be aligned and easily inserted into the lock release control assembly lever.
6. Lock the retainer clip assembly over the threaded rod and loosely install the inside handle.
7. Open the upper right-hand latch on the tailgate.
8. Operate the tailgate as a gate to make sure the gate is not binding and the latches lock and unlock properly.
9. Operate the tailgate as a door to make sure that it opens and closes without disengagement. The door must lock and unlock and the window must open and close when properly adjusted.
10. Adjust the hinge or striker, as necessary. Install the trim panel.

Windshield

REMOVAL & INSTALLATION

The windshield is retained by a urethane adhesive. Several special tools and a special urethane compound are required for windshield replacement. Replacement bonding must meet Federal Motor Vehicle Safety standards. For these reasons, bonded windshield replacement should be left to a professional shop.

Rear Window Glass

REMOVAL & INSTALLATION

The rear window glass is retained by a urethane adhesive. Several special tools and a special urethane compound are required for windshield replacement. Replacement bonding must meet Federal Motor Vehicle Safety standards. For these reasons, bonded windshield replacement should be left to a professional shop.

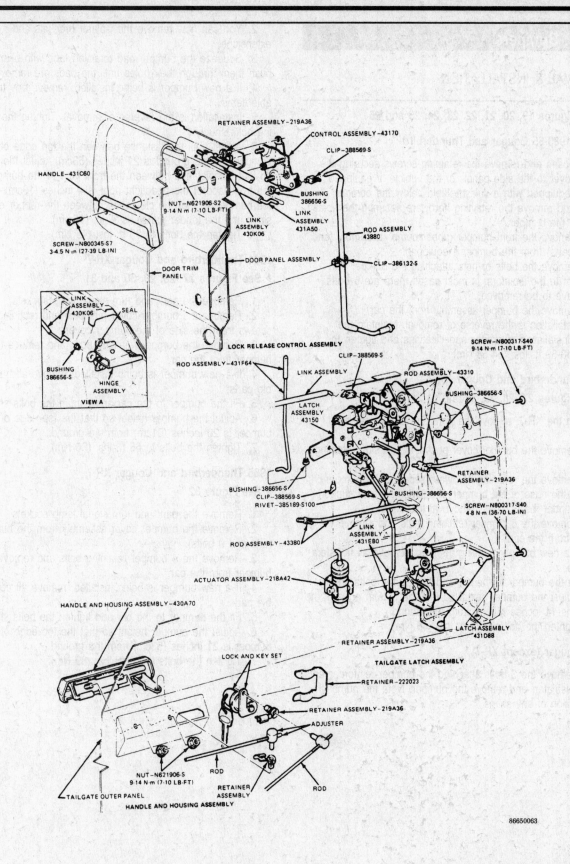

RETAINER ASSEMBLY-219A36

CONTROL ASSEMBLY-43170

CLIP-388569-S

HANDLE-431C60

BUSHING 386656-S

NUT-N621906-S2
9-14 N·m (7-10 LB·FT)

LINK ASSEMBLY 430K06

LINK ASSEMBLY 431A50

ROD ASSEMBLY 43880

SCREW-N800345-S7
3-4.5 N·m (27-39 LB·IN)

DOOR TRIM PANEL

DOOR PANEL ASSEMBLY

CLIP-386132-S

LOCK RELEASE CONTROL ASSEMBLY

LINK ASSEMBLY-430K06

SEAL

BUSHING 386656-S

HINGE ASSEMBLY

VIEW A

ROD ASSEMBLY-431F64

LINK ASSEMBLY

CLIP-388569-S

ROD ASSEMBLY-43310

BUSHING-386656-S

SCREW-N800317-S40
9-14 N·m (7-10 LB·FT)

LATCH ASSEMBLY 43150

RETAINER ASSEMBLY-219A36

BUSHING-386656-S
CLIP-388569-S
RIVET-385189-S100

BUSHING-386656-S

SCREW-N800317-S40
4-8 N·m (36-70 LB·IN)

ROD ASSEMBLY-43380

LINK ASSEMBLY 431EB0

ACTUATOR ASSEMBLY-218A42

LATCH ASSEMBLY 431D88

RETAINER ASSEMBLY-219A36

TAILGATE LATCH ASSEMBLY

HANDLE AND HOUSING ASSEMBLY-430A70

LOCK AND KEY SET

RETAINER-222023

RETAINER ASSEMBLY-219A36

ADJUSTER

NUT-N621906-S
9-14 N·m (7-10 LB·FT)

ROD

RETAINER ASSEMBLY

ROD

TAILGATE OUTER PANEL

HANDLE AND HOUSING ASSEMBLY

86650063

Fig. 18 Tailgate upper latch-to-lower latch link adjustment

Front Bumpers

REMOVAL & INSTALLATION

◆ **See Figures 19, 20, 21, 22, 23, 24, 25 and 26**

Except 1983-85 Cougar and Thunderbird

1. Loosen and remove the retaining screws securing the plastic cover to the side panels of the vehicle, if equipped.
2. If equipped with a splash shield below the bumper, loosen and remove the retaining hardware securing the splash shield to the bumper.
3. Remove the front bumper rubber bump assembly (and related parts) from the bumper if equipped.
4. Remove the bolts or nuts attaching the bumper reinforcement to the isolators. In most cases there are 6 bolts which have to be removed.
5. Remove the bumper assembly from the car.
6. Installation is the reverse of removal. Maintain the bumper installation clearance specifications and tighten the nuts to 40-50 ft. lbs. (54-68 Nm).

1983 Thunderbird and Cougar XR-7

◆ **See Figures 27, 28, 29, 30 and 31**

1. On the XR-7, remove the park and turn signal lamp sockets.
2. Remove the bumper cover pushpins and side retaining screws.
3. Remove the retaining hardware securing the bumper cover at the base of the bumper. If equipped with a support bracket under the bumper, remove at this time.
4. Remove the 8 bumper retaining bolts and remove the bumper from the car.
5. If a new bumper is being installed, remove all transferable parts.
6. Fit the bumper to the car and tighten the bolts snugly.
7. Adjust the bumper height so that the bottom edge of the bumper is 14 inches (36cm) from the ground.
8. Tighten the bolts to 35 ft. lbs. (45 Nm).

1983 Cougar (except XR-7)

1. Remove the 3 bolts attaching the bumper reinforcement to each isolator, and remove the bumper. Note the number and position of any shims.

2. You can now remove the isolator brackets and rubber extensions.
3. Squeeze the bumper pad retaining tabs with pliers and push them through their holes until the pads are removed.
4. If a new bumper is being installed, remove any transferable items.
5. Installation is the reverse of removal. Tighten the mounting bolts snugly.
6. Adjust until the distance between the top edge of the bumper and the ground is 21 inches (53cm). Adjust the bumper so that the distance between the front face of the bumper and the front face of the headlight door is 4 inches (10cm). Adjust the bumper so that the clearance between the rubber extensions and the fender panels is ⅝ in. (16mm).
7. Tighten the bolts to 35 ft. lbs. (45 Nm).

1984 Thunderbird and Cougar XR-7

◆ **See Figures 27, 28, 29, 30 and 31**

1. Remove the park and turn signal lamp sockets.
2. Remove the bumper cover pushpins and retaining screws from the side of the bumper cover.
3. Remove the bumper retaining bolts and remove the bumper from the car.
4. If a new bumper is being installed, remove all transferable parts.
5. Fit the bumper to the car and tighten the bolts snugly.
6. Adjust the bumper height so that the top edge of the bumper is 20 inches (51cm) from the ground.
7. Tighten the bolts to 66 ft. lbs. (86 Nm).

1985 Thunderbird and Cougar XR-7

◆ **See Figure 32**

1. Remove the park and turn signal lamp sockets.
2. Remove the bumper cover assembly from the bumper (6 nuts and 9 bolts).
3. Remove the 4 bumper retaining bolts and remove the bumper from the car.
4. If a new bumper is being installed, remove all transferable parts.
5. Fit the bumper to the car and tighten the bolts snugly.
6. Adjust the bumper height so that the top edge of the bumper is 21 inches (53cm) from the ground.
7. Tighten the bolts to 66 ft. lbs. (89 Nm).

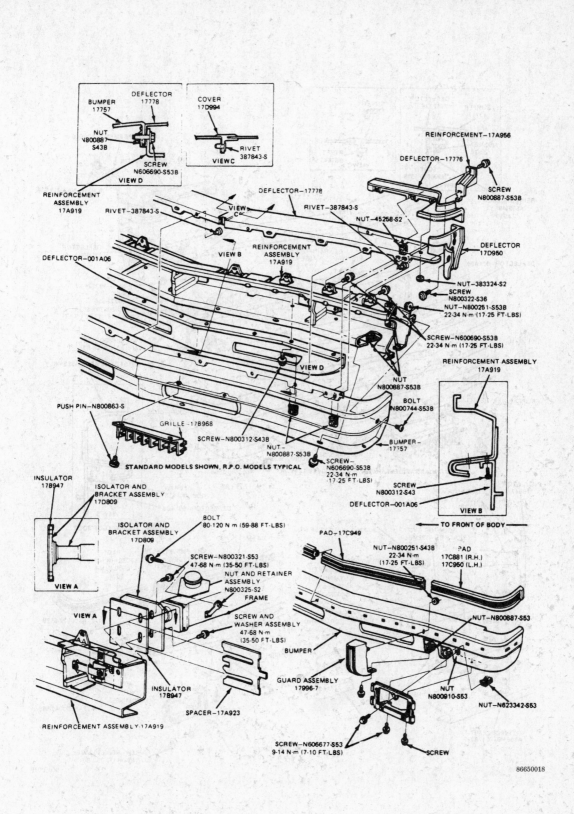

Fig. 19 Front bumper assembly — 1971-80 vehicles

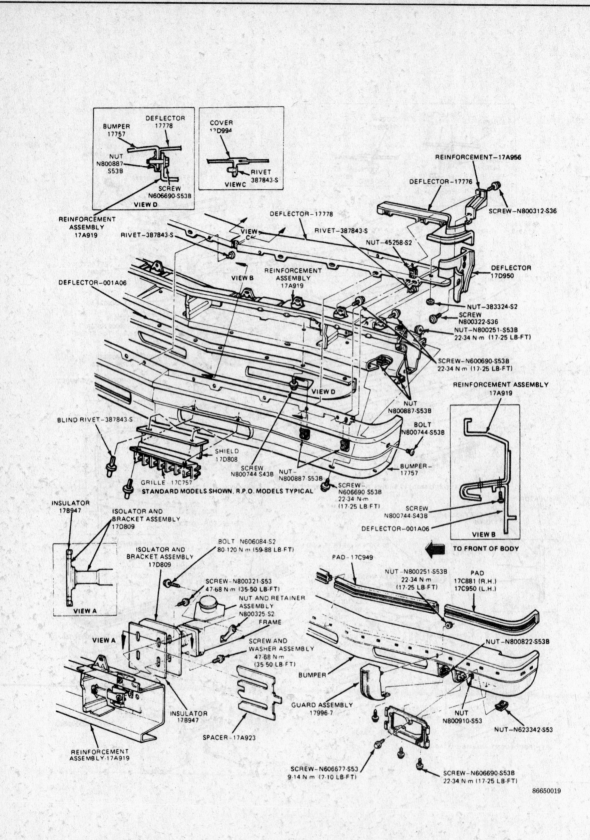

Fig. 20 Ford front bumper assembly — 1981-82 vehicles

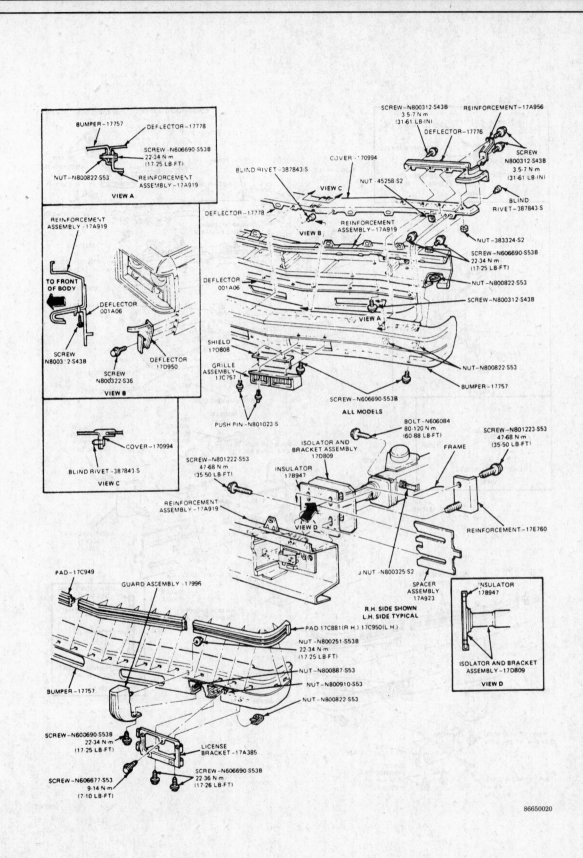

Fig. 21 Mercury front bumper assembly — 1981-82 vehicles

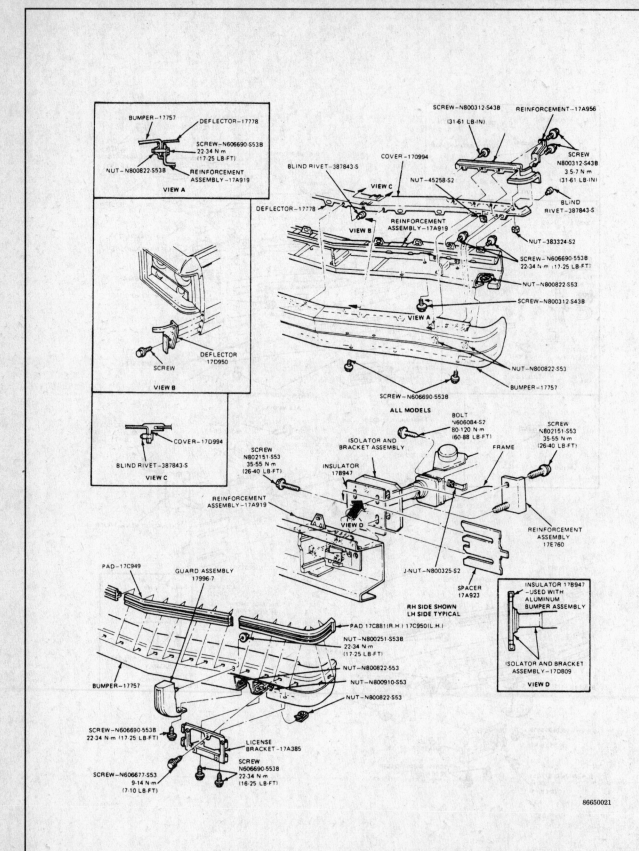

Fig. 22 Front bumper assembly — 1983-84 vehicles

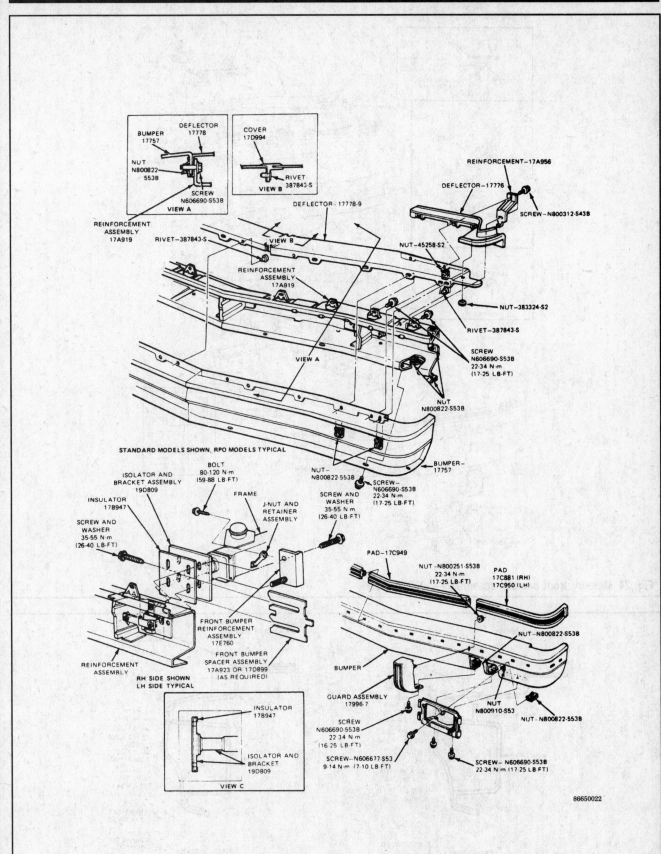

Fig. 23 Ford front bumper assembly — 1985 vehicles

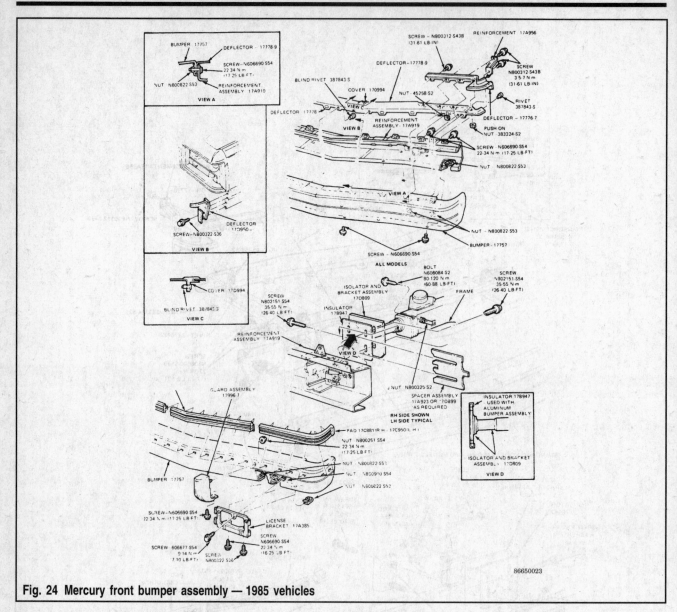

Fig. 24 Mercury front bumper assembly — 1985 vehicles

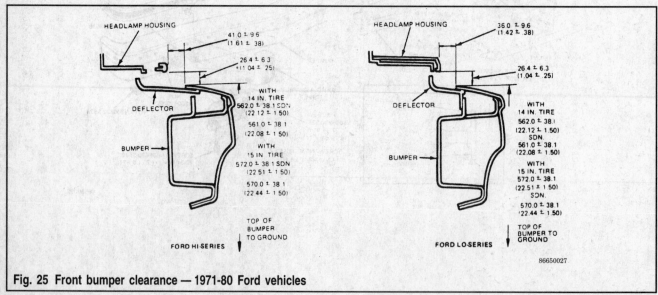

Fig. 25 Front bumper clearance — 1971-80 Ford vehicles

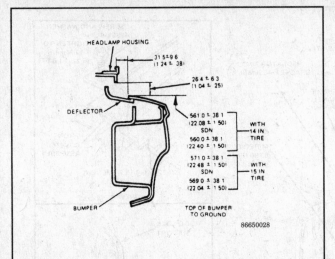

Fig. 26 Front bumper clearance — 1983-84 Mercury vehicles

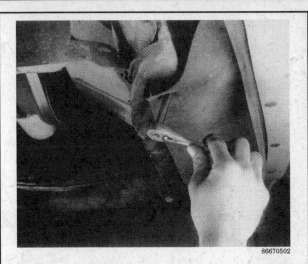

Fig. 29 Remove the screws securing the splash shield to the lower body panel

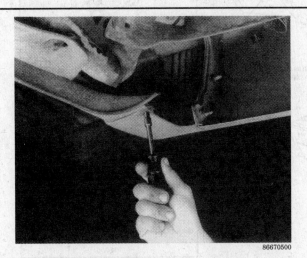

Fig. 27 Remove the retaining screws securing the base of the bumper cover assembly to the vehicle

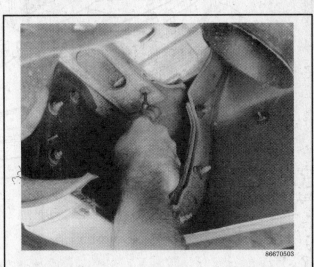

Fig. 30 Unfasten the screws attaching the support bracket to the top of the bumper

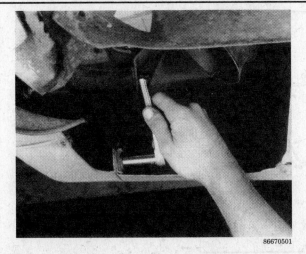

Fig. 28 Make sure you get the ones hidden in out of the way places

Fig. 31 Loosen the retaining bolts securing the bumper assembly to the isolator

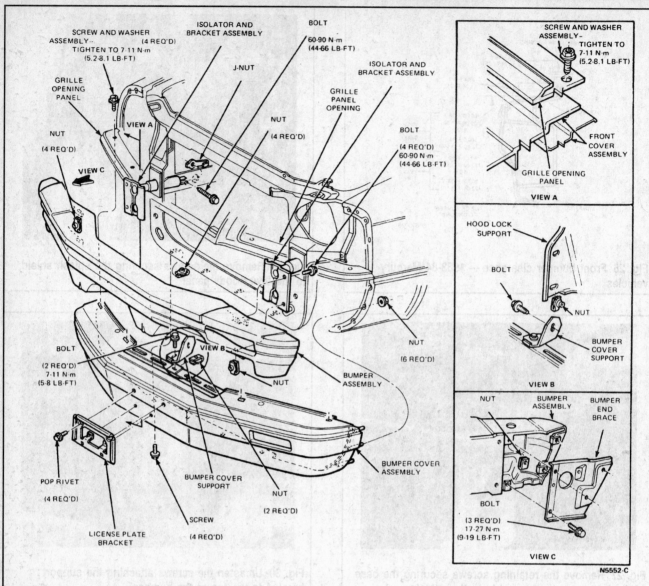

FIG. 2 Bumper, Front—Installation

Labels in figure:
- SCREW AND WASHER ASSEMBLY— (4 REQ'D) TIGHTEN TO 7-11 N·m (5.2-8.1 LB-FT)
- GRILLE OPENING PANEL
- NUT (4 REQ'D)
- VIEW A
- VIEW C
- ISOLATOR AND BRACKET ASSEMBLY
- J-NUT
- NUT (4 REQ'D)
- BOLT 60-90 N·m (44-66 LB-FT)
- ISOLATOR AND BRACKET ASSEMBLY
- GRILLE PANEL OPENING
- BOLT (4 REQ'D) 60-90 N·m (44-66 LB-FT)
- NUT (6 REQ'D)
- BUMPER ASSEMBLY
- BUMPER COVER ASSEMBLY
- VIEW B
- NUT
- BOLT (2 REQ'D) 7-11 N·m (5-8 LB-FT)
- POP RIVET (4 REQ'D)
- LICENSE PLATE BRACKET
- BUMPER COVER SUPPORT
- SCREW (4 REQ'D)
- NUT (2 REQ'D)

VIEW A:
- SCREW AND WASHER ASSEMBLY— TIGHTEN TO 7-11 N·m (5.2-8.1 LB-FT)
- FRONT COVER ASSEMBLY
- GRILLE OPENING PANEL

VIEW B:
- HOOD LOCK SUPPORT
- BOLT
- NUT
- BUMPER COVER SUPPORT

VIEW C:
- NUT
- BUMPER ASSEMBLY
- BUMPER END BRACE
- BOLT (3 REQ'D) 17-27 N·m (9-19 LB-FT)

N5552-C

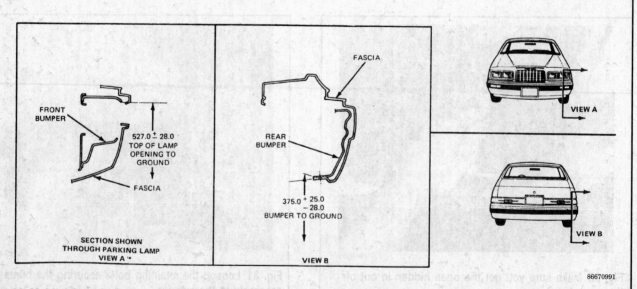

View A:
- FRONT BUMPER
- 527.0 ± 28.0 TOP OF LAMP OPENING TO GROUND
- FASCIA
- SECTION SHOWN THROUGH PARKING LAMP VIEW A

View B:
- FASCIA
- REAR BUMPER
- 375.0 +25.0 -28.0 BUMPER TO GROUND
- VIEW B

- VIEW A
- VIEW B

86670991

Fig. 32 Molded front bumper assembly — 1985 models

Rear Bumpers

REMOVAL & INSTALLATION

▶ **See Figures 33, 34, 35, 36, 37, 38, 39 and 40**

Except 1983-85 Cougar and Thunderbird

1. Remove the rear bumper cover assembly (and related parts) from the bumper if equipped.

2. Remove the bolts or nuts attaching the bumper reinforcement to the isolators. In most applications, there are 6 bolts to remove.

3. Remove the bumper assembly from the car.

4. Installation is the reverse of removal. Tighten the nuts to 40-50 ft. lbs. (54-68 Nm).

5. Check the bumper installation clearance specifications in the accompanying illustrations if necessary.

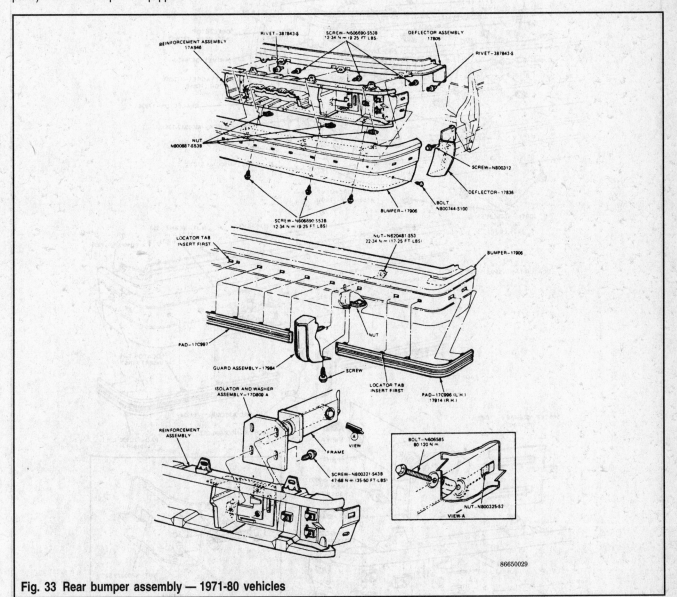

86650029

Fig. 33 Rear bumper assembly — 1971-80 vehicles

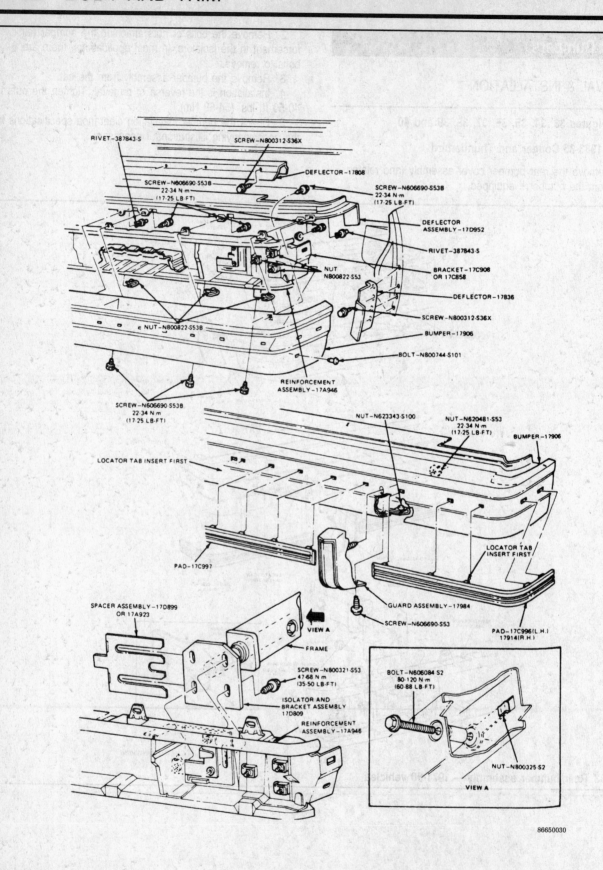

Fig. 34 Rear bumper assembly — 1981-83 vehicles

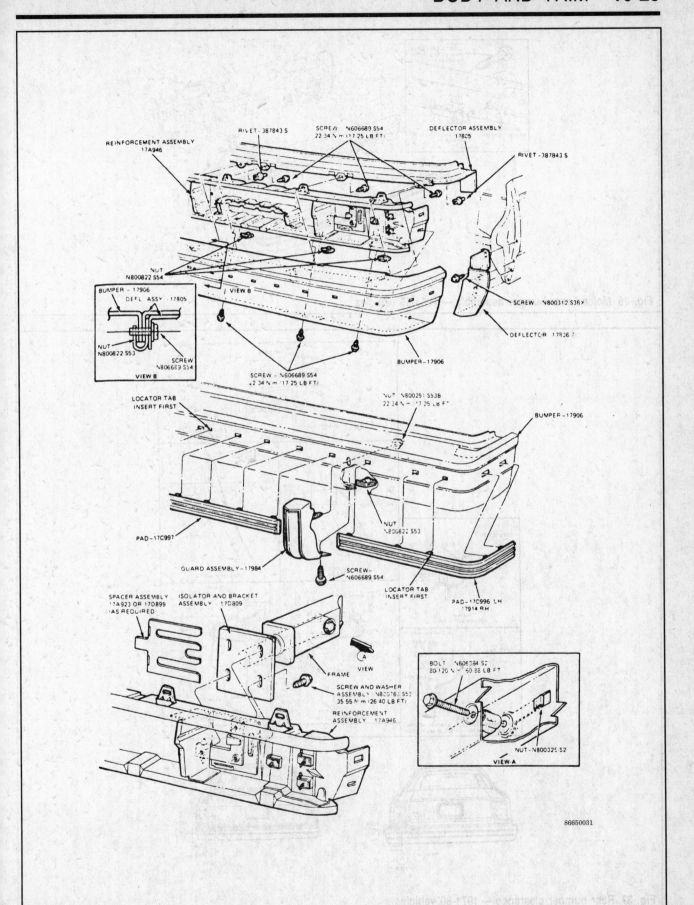

Fig. 35 Rear bumper assembly — 1984-85 vehicles

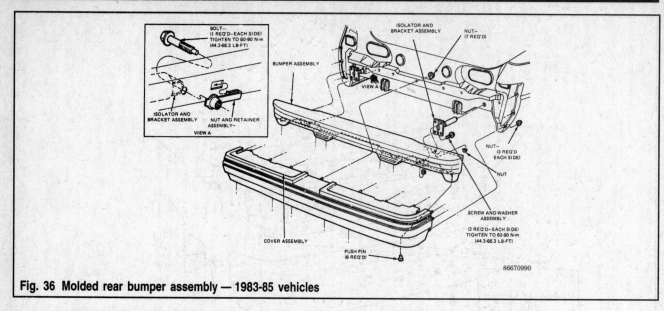

Fig. 36 Molded rear bumper assembly — 1983-85 vehicles

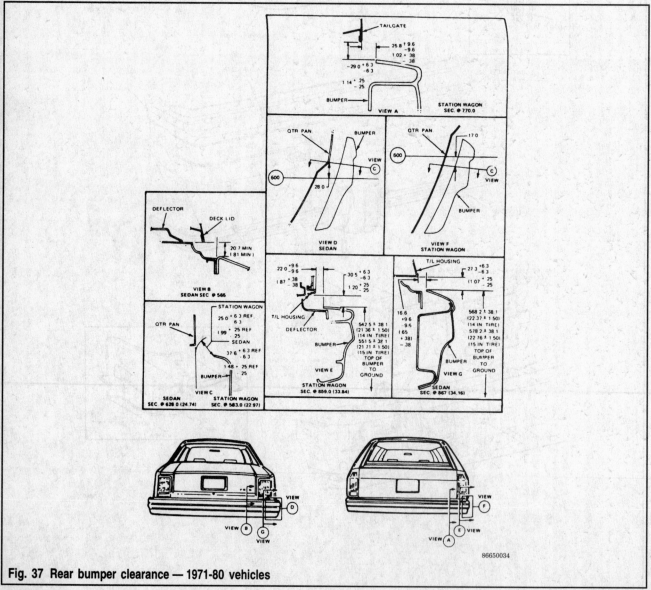

Fig. 37 Rear bumper clearance — 1971-80 vehicles

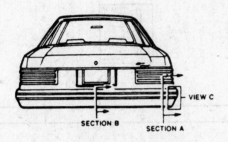

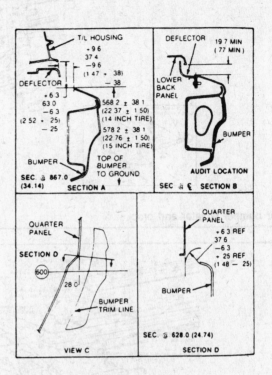

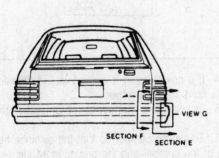

METRIC DIMENSIONS SHOWN FIRST.
ENGLISH DIMENSIONS IN PARENTHESES

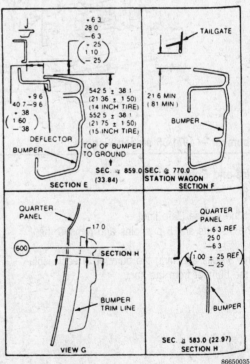

86650035

Fig. 38 Rear bumper clearance — 1981-85 vehicles

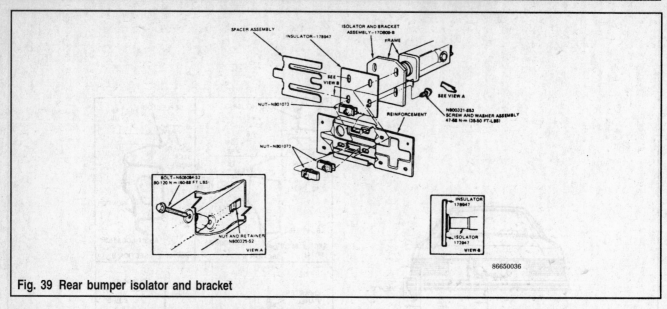

Fig. 39 Rear bumper isolator and bracket

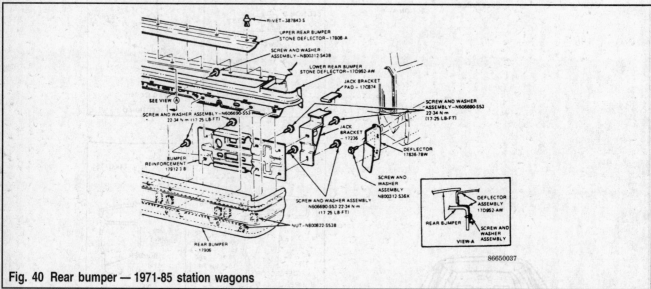

Fig. 40 Rear bumper — 1971-85 station wagons

1983 Thunderbird and Cougar XR-7

▶ See Figure 41

1. Disconnect the license plate light.
2. Remove the 12 nuts and 8 pushpins and remove the bumper cover.
3. Remove the 3 bolts attaching the bumper to each isolator and remove the bumper from the car.

4. If a new bumper is being installed, transfer any good parts from the old bumper.
5. Installation is the reverse of removal. Tighten the bolts snugly.
6. Adjust the bumper so that the distance between the bottom of the bumper and the ground is 14 inches (35cm).
7. Tighten the bolts to 35 ft. lbs.

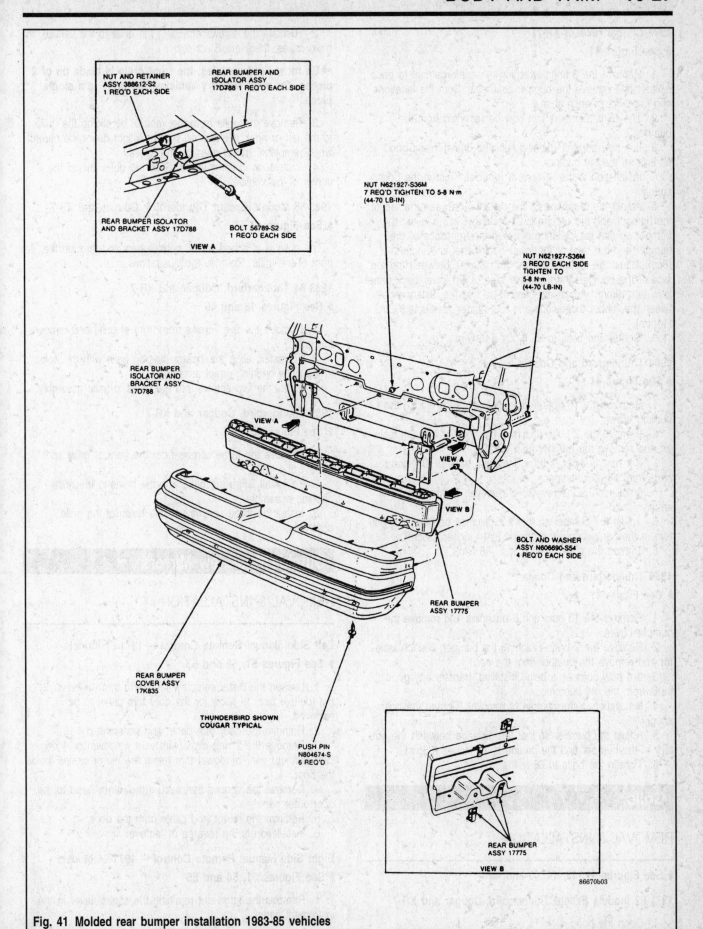

NUT AND RETAINER
ASSY 388612-S2
1 REQ'D EACH SIDE

REAR BUMPER AND
ISOLATOR ASSY
17D788 1 REQ'D EACH SIDE

REAR BUMPER ISOLATOR
AND BRACKET ASSY 17D788

BOLT 56789-S2
1 REQ'D EACH SIDE

VIEW A

NUT N621927-S36M
7 REQ'D TIGHTEN TO 5-8 N·m
(44-70 LB-IN)

NUT N621927-S36M
3 REQ'D EACH SIDE
TIGHTEN TO
5-8 N·m
(44-70 LB-IN)

REAR BUMPER
ISOLATOR AND
BRACKET ASSY
17D788

VIEW A

VIEW A

VIEW B

BOLT AND WASHER
ASSY N606690-S54
4 REQ'D EACH SIDE

REAR BUMPER
ASSY 17775

REAR BUMPER
COVER ASSY
17K835

THUNDERBIRD SHOWN
COUGAR TYPICAL

PUSH PIN
N804674-S
6 REQ'D

REAR BUMPER
ASSY 17775

VIEW B

86670b03

Fig. 41 Molded rear bumper installation 1983-85 vehicles

1983 Cougar (except XR-7)

▶ **See Figure 41**

1. Remove the 3 bolts attaching the reinforcement to each isolator and remove the bumper assembly. Note the locations and numbers of each shim.

2. The reinforcements can now be removed from the bumper.

3. If a new bumper is being installed, transfer any good parts from the old bumper.

4. Installation is the reverse of removal. Tighten the bolts snugly.

5. Adjust the bumper until the distance between the top of the bumper and the ground is 21 inches (53cm). Adjust the bumper so that the distance between the front face of the bumper and the face of the lower back panel is 3 inches (8cm). Adjust the bumper so that the distance between the top face of the bumper and the lower face of the lower back panel is ¾ in. (19mm). Adjust the bumper so that the distance between the rubber extensions and the quarter panels is 9/16 in. (14mm).

6. Tighten the bolts to 35 ft. lbs. (45 Nm).

1984 Thunderbird and Cougar

▶ **See Figure 41**

1. Remove the 13 nuts and 6 pushpins and remove the bumper cover.

2. Remove the 2 bolts attaching the bumper to each isolator and remove the bumper from the car.

3. If a new bumper is being installed, transfer any good parts from the old bumper.

4. Installation is the reverse of removal. Tighten the bolts snugly.

5. Adjust the bumper so that the distance between the bottom of the bumper and the ground is 14 inches (35cm).

6. Tighten the bolts to 66 ft. lbs. (86 Nm).

1985 Thunderbird and Cougar

▶ **See Figure 41**

1. Remove the 13 nuts and 6 pushpins and remove the bumper cover.

2. Remove the 2 bolts attaching the bumper to each isolator and remove the bumper from the car.

3. If a new bumper is being installed, transfer any good parts from the old bumper.

4. Installation is the reverse of removal. Tighten the bolts snugly.

5. Adjust the bumper so that the distance between the bottom of the bumper and the ground is 14 inches (35cm).

6. Tighten the bolts to 66 ft. lbs.

Grille

REMOVAL & INSTALLATION

▶ **See Figures 42, 43, 44, 45 and 46**

1971-82 models Except Thunderbird, Cougar and XR-7

1. Open the hood.

2. Remove the screws attaching the grille to the vehicle. In most cases, there are 6 screws.

➡ **On most Ford vehicles, the front grille is made up of 2 pieces. On most Mercury vehicles, the grille is a single piece.**

3. Remove the grille from the vehicle, by sliding the grille to the left or right. If equipped with headlight doors, be careful when removing, not to damage the doors.

4. Installation is the reverse. Slide the grille toward the center of the vehicle.

1983-85 Models Except Thunderbird, Cougar and XR-7

▶ **See Figure 47**

The grille is attached with 6 screws removed through the front of the grille. Refer to the illustrations.

1983-84 Thunderbird, Cougar and XR-7

▶ **See Figures 48 and 49**

1. Remove the five screws from front of grille and remove the grille.

2. To install, align the locator pins on grille with the holes in the grille opening panel assembly.

3. Install the five screws into the holes in grille assembly.

1985 Thunderbird, Cougar and XR-7

▶ **See Figure 50**

1. Remove the three screws from the front of grille and remove the grille.

2. To install, align the grille with the holes in the grille opening assembly.

3. Install the three screws into the holes of the grille assembly.

Outside Rearview Mirrors

REMOVAL & INSTALLATION

Left Side Manual Remote Control — 1971-84 Models

▶ **See Figures 51, 52 and 53**

1. Loosen the bezel setscrew (standard trim) or retaining nut (deluxe trim) to allow for the door trim panel to be removed.

2. Remove the door trim panel and watershield.

3. Remove the 2 ring clips (with vent windows) or 4 ring clips (without vent windows) that retain the mirror cables inside the door.

4. Remove the screws that secure the mirror head to the door outer panel.

5. Remove the mirror and cable from the door.

6. Installation is the reverse of removal.

Right Side Manual Remote Control — 1971-84 Models

▶ **See Figures 51, 54 and 55**

1. Remove the large nut retaining the control lever in the instrument panel.

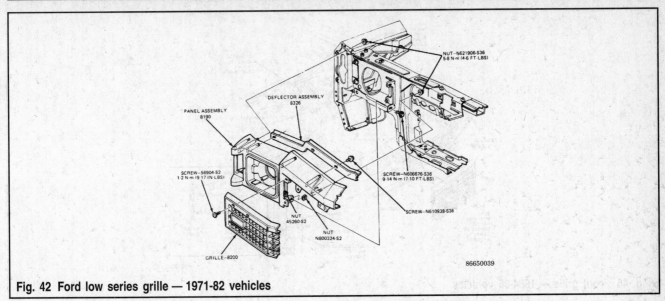

Fig. 42 Ford low series grille — 1971-82 vehicles

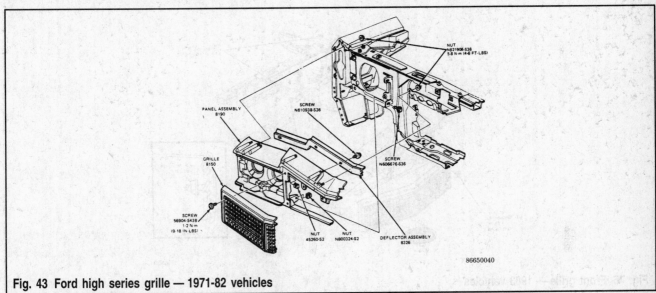

Fig. 43 Ford high series grille — 1971-82 vehicles

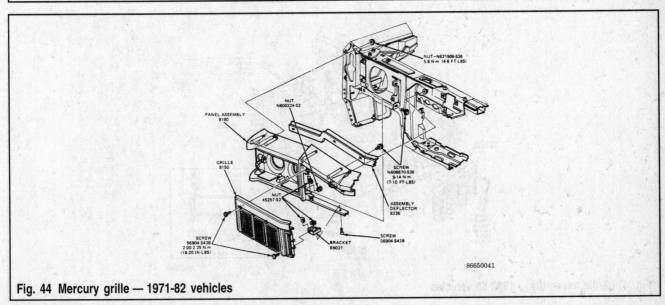

Fig. 44 Mercury grille — 1971-82 vehicles

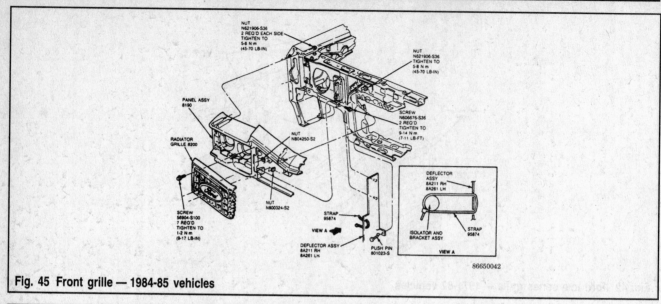

Fig. 45 Front grille — 1984-85 vehicles

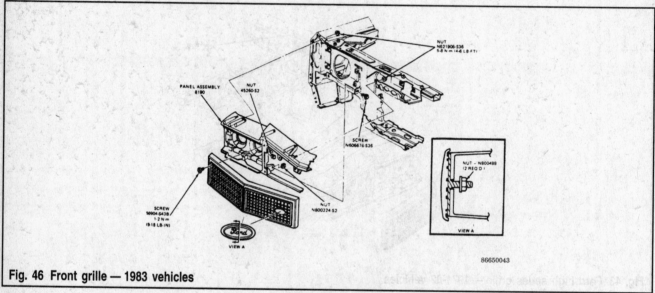

Fig. 46 Front grille — 1983 vehicles

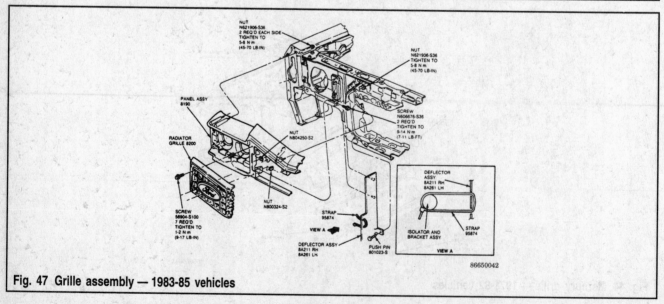

Fig. 47 Grille assembly — 1983-85 vehicles

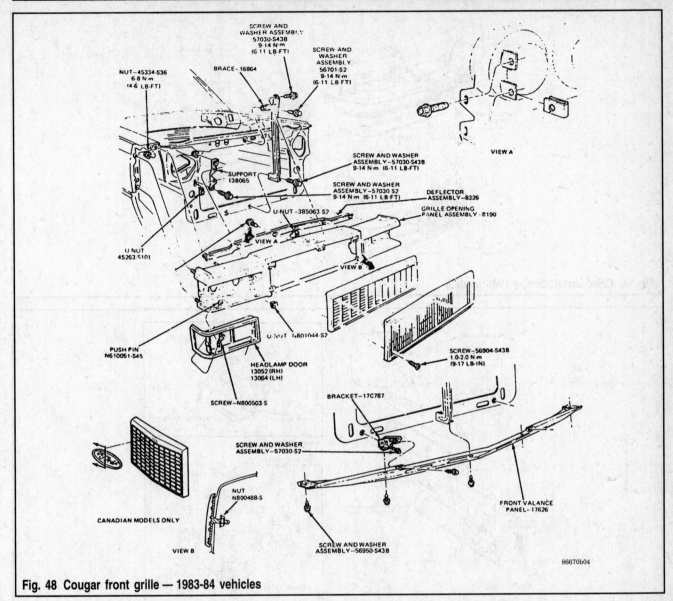

Fig. 48 Cougar front grille — 1983-84 vehicles

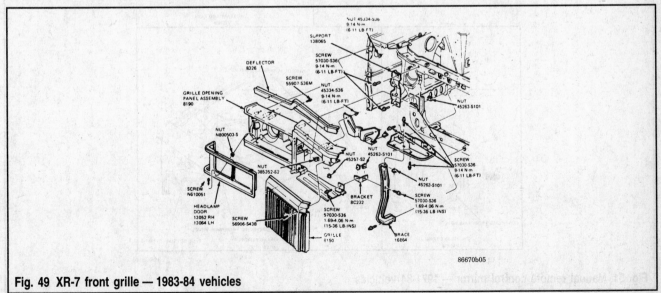

Fig. 49 XR-7 front grille — 1983-84 vehicles

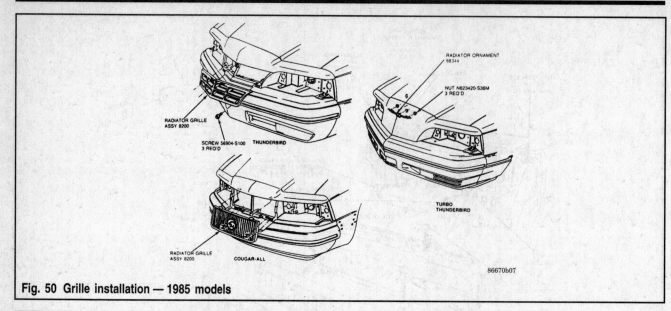

Fig. 50 Grille installation — 1985 models

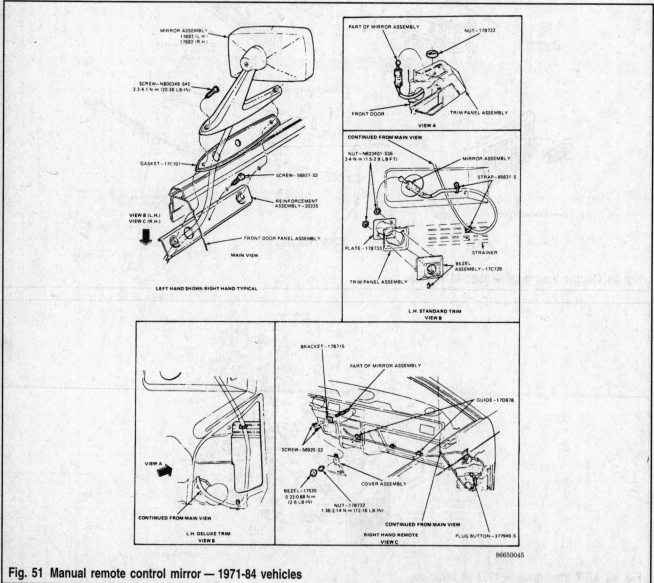

Fig. 51 Manual remote control mirror — 1971-84 vehicles

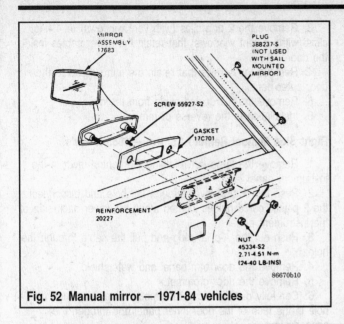

Fig. 52 Manual mirror — 1971-84 vehicles

2. Push the control lever through the hole and disconnect the 3 plastic cable guides located along the lower back side of the instrument panel.

3. Push out the A-pillar plug and pull the cable through the hole.

4. Remove the door trim panel and watershield.

5. Remove the door grommet.

6. Carefully pull the cable and rubber plug(s) through the hole in the face of the door inner panel and through the support strap.

7. Remove the 2 screws that retain the mirror head assembly to the door outer panel.

8. Carefully remove the mirror and cable.

9. Installation is the reverse of removal.

Left Side Manual Remote Control — 1985 Models

1. Loosen the bezel setscrew (standard trim) or retaining nut (deluxe trim) to allow for the door trim panel to be removed.

2. Remove the door trim panel and watershield.

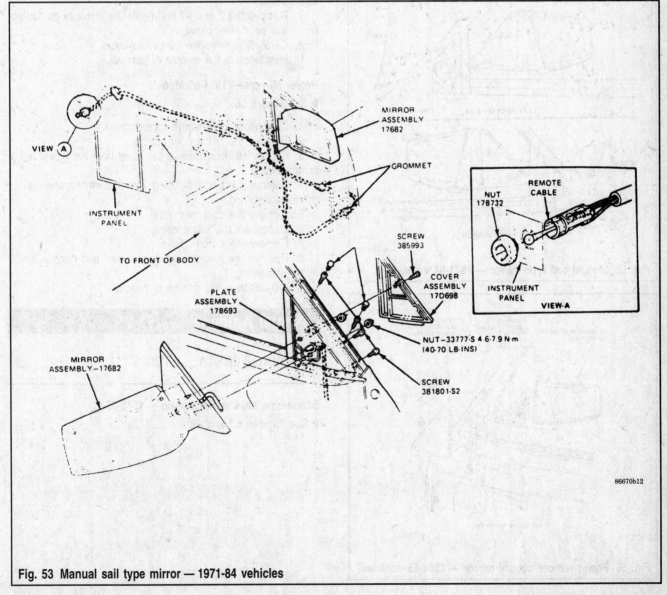

Fig. 53 Manual sail type mirror — 1971-84 vehicles

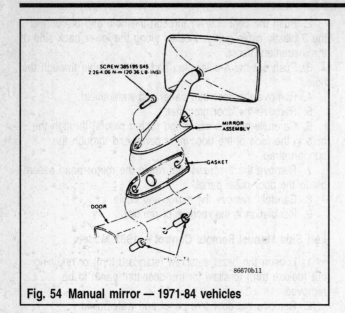

Fig. 54 Manual mirror — 1971-84 vehicles

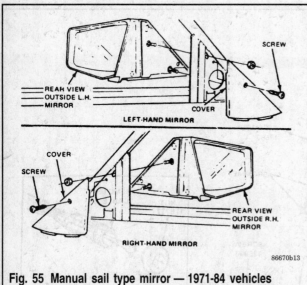

Fig. 55 Manual sail type mirror — 1971-84 vehicles

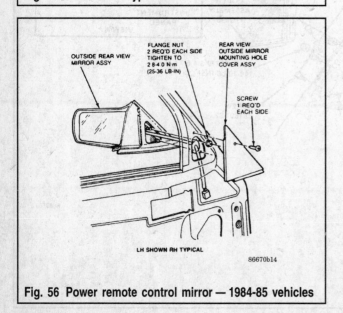

Fig. 56 Power remote control mirror — 1984-85 vehicles

3. Remove the 2 ring clips (with vent windows) or 4 ring clips (without vent windows) that retain the mirror cables inside the door.

4. Remove the screws that retain the mirror head to the door outer panel.

5. Remove the mirror and cable from the door.

6. Installation is the reverse of removal.

Right Side Manual Remote Control — 1985 Models

1. Remove the large nut retaining the control lever in the instrument panel.

2. Push the control lever through the hole and disconnect the 3 plastic cable guides located along the lower back side of the instrument panel.

3. Push out the A-pillar plug and pull the cable through the hole.

4. Remove the door trim panel and watershield.

5. Remove the door grommet.

6. Carefully pull the cable and rubber plug(s) through the hole in the face of the door inner panel and through the support strap.

7. Remove the 2 screws that retain the mirror head assembly to the door outer panel.

8. Carefully remove the mirror and cable.

9. Installation is the reverse of removal.

Power Mirrors — 1984-85 Models
▶ See Figure 56

1. Disconnect the negative battery cable.

2. Remove the inside door handle.

3. On the left door, remove the bezel from the power mirror control switch.

4. Remove the switch housing from the armrest and disconnect the wiring.

5. Remove the door trim panel.

6. Disconnect the mirror wiring.

7. Remove the wiring guides.

8. Remove the 2 mirror retaining screws and remove the mirror and wiring.

9. Installation is the reverse of removal.

Manual Antenna

REMOVAL & INSTALLATION

Screw-type antenna and cable — 1971-85
▶ See Figures 57 and 58

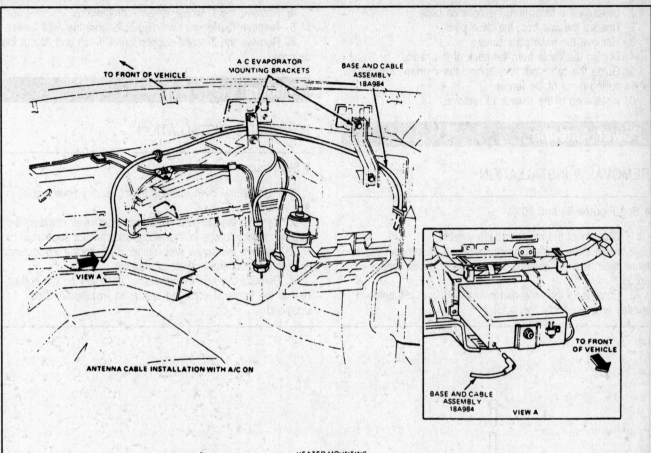

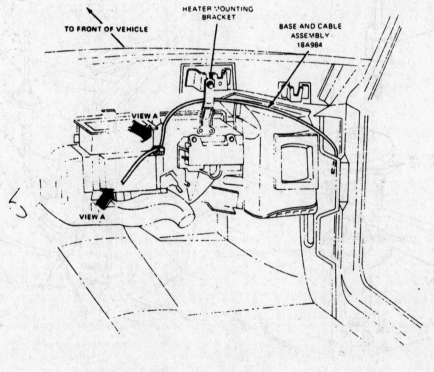

Fig. 57 Antenna wiring through instrument panel with and without A/C — 1971-85 models

1. Unscrew the mast from the antenna base.
2. Unsnap the cap from the base plate.
3. Remove the base plate screws.
4. Unplug the cable from the back of the radio.
5. Guide the cable out from behind the instrument panel while pulling it out of the fender.
6. Installation is the reverse of removal.

Power Antenna

REMOVAL & INSTALLATION

▶ See Figures 59 and 60

1. Disconnect the negative battery cable.
2. From inside the engine compartment, disconnect the antenna lead from the antenna, near the right plastic fender apron.
3. Disconnect the antenna motor wiring from the antenna overlay wire assembly connector.

4. Remove the antenna nut and chrome trim.
5. Remove the fender attaching bolts from the right fender.
6. Remove the antenna support bracket bolt and lift out the antenna.

Fenders

REMOVAL & INSTALLATION

▶ See Figure 61

1. Remove the grille opening panel, as described earlier in this section.
2. Remove the screw and washer assemblies retaining the radiator support brace to the fender and radiator support.
3. Remove the screw and washer retaining the fender and rear upper mounting bracket to the body.
4. Remove the screw and washer assembly on the bottom rear of the fender. Retain the spacer for installation, if so equipped.

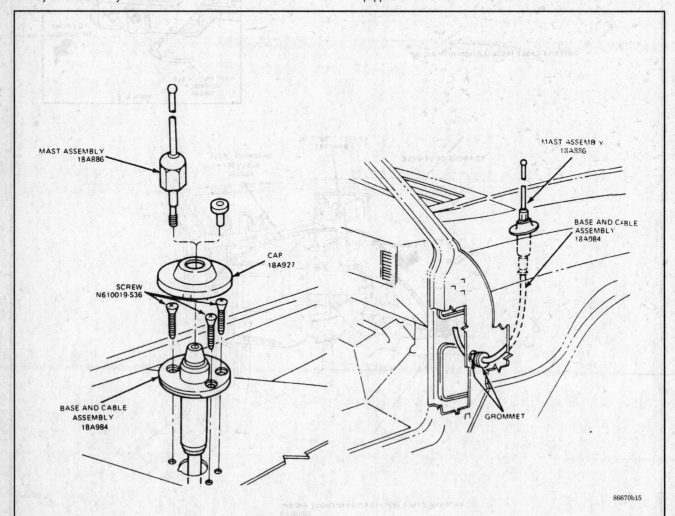

Fig. 58 Manual antenna mast removal and installation

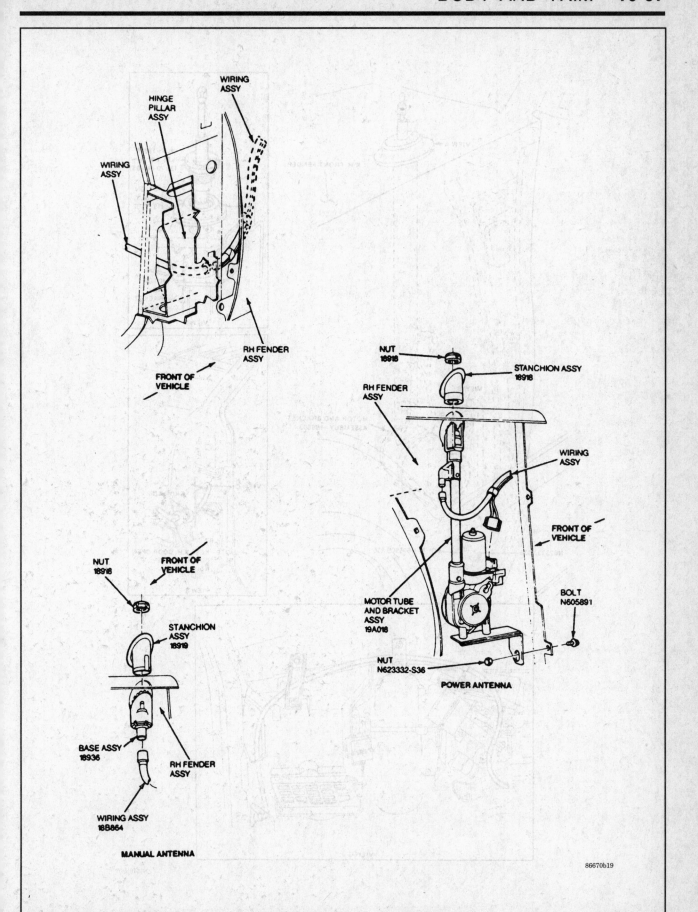

WIRING ASSY

HINGE PILLAR ASSY

WIRING ASSY

RH FENDER ASSY

FRONT OF VEHICLE

NUT 18918

STANCHION ASSY 18918

RH FENDER ASSY

WIRING ASSY

FRONT OF VEHICLE

MOTOR TUBE AND BRACKET ASSY 19A018

BOLT N605891

NUT N623332-S36

POWER ANTENNA

NUT 18918

FRONT OF VEHICLE

STANCHION ASSY 18919

BASE ASSY 18936

RH FENDER ASSY

WIRING ASSY 18B864

MANUAL ANTENNA

86670b19

Fig. 59 Clamp-type power antenna cable installation and routing — front fender mount

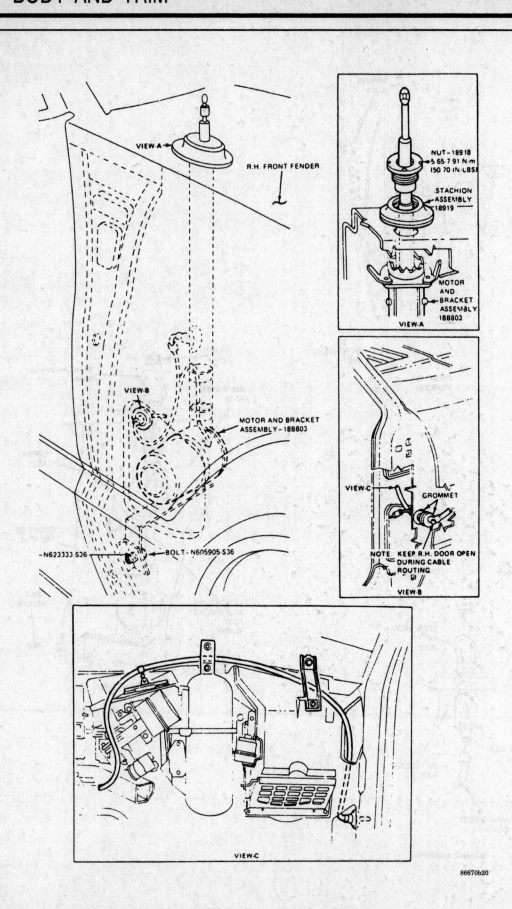

Fig. 60 Power antenna installation on Thunderbird and XR-7 — 1983-85 models

5. Remove the push pins retaining the splash shield to the body.

6. Remove the screw and washer assemblies along the bottom of the fender, and the screws in the wheel opening, which retain the splash shield to the fender. Separate the splash shield from the fender.

7. Remove the screw and washer assemblies from the top of the fender, retaining the fender to the body.

8. Remove the fender from the vehicle.

9. Remove the push pins which retain the splash shield sound insulator to the fender.

10. Installation is the reverse of the removal procedure.

Power Sunroof

REMOVAL & INSTALLATION

1. Open the glass panel approximately half way.

2. Unsnap the halo from the glass panel assembly.

3. Raise the glass panel to the vent position.

4. Slide the halo fully rearward.

5. Remove the six glass panel retaining screws.

6. From outside the vehicle, remove the glass panel.

To install:

7. Operate the moon roof system to lower the glass lifter arms approximately one quarter of the way. This relieves tension on the cables, enabling lifter arms to move for easier glass positioning and for installation of the glass panel retaining screws.

8. Position the sliding glass panel. Install the six retaining screws. Finger tighten the center screws and tighten the remaining screws to 18-35 inch lbs. (2-4 Nm).

9. Lower the glass panel from the vented position to slightly below the roof panel sheet metal surface, then raise it to the closed position, but do not allow the glass panel to slide rearward.

10. Check and adjust the glass panel to 1mm low at the front and flush to 1mm high at the rear.

11. Tighten all the retaining screws.

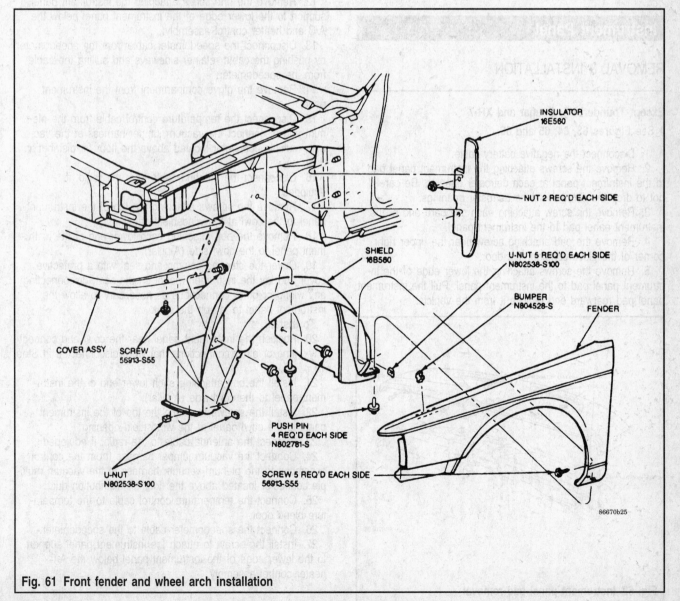

Fig. 61 Front fender and wheel arch installation

12. Slide the halo forward. Open the moon roof approximately one quarter of the way and install the halo to the glass panel.

INTERIOR

Instrument Panel Pad

REMOVAL & INSTALLATION

▶ See Figure 62

1. Remove the instrument cluster and finish panel retaining screws.
2. Unfasten the instrument panel pad retaining screws in front, or on the ends of the panel.
3. Remove the instrument panel pad retaining screws in the top defroster openings, and remove the pad.
4. Installation is the reverse of removal.

Instrument Panel

REMOVAL & INSTALLATION

Except Thunderbird, Cougar and XR-7
▶ See Figures 63, 64, 65 and 66

1. Disconnect the negative battery cable.
2. Remove the screws attaching the instrument panel pad to the instrument panel at each defroster opening. Be careful not to drop the screws into the defroster openings.
3. Remove the screw attaching each outboard end of the instrument panel pad to the instrument panel.
4. Remove the pad attaching screw near the upper right corner of the glove compartment door.
5. Remove the screws attaching the lower edge of the instrument panel pad to the instrument panel. Pull the instrument panel pad rearward and remove it from the vehicle.

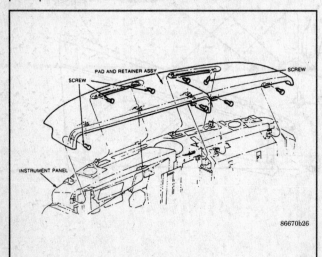

Fig. 62 Instrument panel pad removal

6. Remove the screws attaching the steering column opening cover to the instrument panel and remove the cover.
7. Loosen the right and left front door sill plate screws, then remove the right and left cowl side trim panels.
8. Disconnect the wiring harnesses from the steering column at the multiple connectors.
9. Disconnect the transmission selector indicator from the steering column.
10. Remove the nuts and washers attaching the steering column to the instrument panel brace and lay the steering column down on the seat.
11. Remove the screw attaching the lower flange brace to the lower flange of the instrument panel just to the right of the steering column opening.
12. Remove the one screw attaching the instrument panel support to the lower edge of the instrument panel below the A/C and heater control assembly.
13. Disconnect the speedometer cable from the speedometer by pushing the cable retainer sideways and pulling the cable from the speedometer.
14. Remove the glove compartment from the instrument panel.
15. Disconnect the temperature control cable from the plenum and disconnect the vacuum jumper harness at the vacuum multiple connector located above the floor air distribution duct.
16. Disconnect the antenna cable from the radio, if equipped.
17. Remove the screws attaching the top of the instrument panel to the cowl at the windshield opening.
18. Remove the bolt attaching each lower end of the instrument panel to the cowl side (A-pillar).
19. Cover the steering column and seat with a protective cover and lay the instrument panel on the seat, disconnecting any wiring or other connections as necessary to allow the instrument panel to lay on the seat.

To install:

20. Position the instrument panel near the cowl and connect any wiring or other connections that were disconnected in Step 19.
21. Install the bolt attaching each lower end of the instrument panel to the cowl side (A-pillar).
22. Install the screws to attach the top of the instrument panel to the cowl panel at the windshield opening.
23. Connect the antenna cable to the radio, if equipped.
24. Connect the vacuum jumper harness (from the control assembly) to the plenum vacuum harness at the vacuum multiple connector located above the floor air distribution duct.
25. Connect the temperature control cable to the temperature blend door.
26. Connect the speedometer cable to the speedometer.
27. Install the screw to attach the instrument panel support to the lower edge of the instrument panel below the A/C-heater control assembly.

28. Install one screw to attach the lower flange brace to the lower flange of the instrument panel just to the right of the steering column opening.

29. Install the glove compartment and check the arms.

30. Install the right and left cowl side trim panels and tighten the door sill plate attaching screws.

31. Position the steering column to the instrument panel brace and install the retaining nuts and washers.

32. Connect the transmission indicator to the steering column.

33. Connect the wire harnesses to the steering column at the multiple connectors. Install the steering column opening cover.

34. Position the instrument panel pad to the instrument panel and install the screws along the lower edge of the pad.

35. Install the screw to attach each outboard end of the pad to the instrument panel.

36. Install the pad attaching screw near the upper right corner of the glove compartment door.

37. Install the instrument panel pad attaching screws at each defroster opening. Be careful not to drop the screws into the defroster opening.

38. Connect the negative battery cable. Check operation of all instruments, lights, controls and the A/C-heater system.

Thunderbird, Cougar and XR-7

▶ See Figures 67 and 68

➡Removal and installation of the instrument panel is best accomplished by two people.

1. Disconnect the negative battery cable.

2. In the engine compartment, disconnect all main wiring harness-to-instrument panel connectors.

3. Remove the rubber grommet from the firewall and feed all the wiring into the passenger compartment.

4. Remove the headlamp/fog lamp switch and disconnect the wiring.

5. Remove the steering column extension shroud.

6. Remove the steering column cover.

7. Remove the 6 steering column nuts (2 retaining the hood release mechanism and 4 retaining the steering column

to the lower brake pedal support). Lower the steering column to the floor.

8. Remove the floor console.

9. Snap out the defroster grille.

10. Remove the screws from the speaker covers and snap them out.

11. Remove the 4 screws retaining the steering column reinforcement opening.

12. Remove the right and left side cowl panels.

13. Remove the cowl side retaining bolts.

14. Open the glove compartment door and bend the bin tabs inward. Let the door assembly drop.

15. Remove the brake pedal support nut.

16. Remove the 5 cowl top screw attachments.

17. Gently pull the instrument panel away from the cowl. Disconnect the air conditioning controls and wire connectors.

To install:

18. Connect the air conditioning controls and wire connectors, then position the instrument panel in the car.

19. Install the 5 cowl top screw attachments.

20. Install the brake pedal support nut.

21. Assemble the glove compartment.

22. Install the cowl side retaining bolts.

23. Install the right and left side cowl panels.

24. Install the 4 screws retaining the steering column reinforcement opening.

25. Install the the speaker covers.

26. Install the defroster grille.

27. Install the floor console.

28. Install the steering column.

29. Install the steering column cover.

30. Install the steering column extension shroud.

31. Attach the electrical connector(s) and install the headlamp/fog lamp switch.

32. Install the wiring and rubber grommet in the firewall.

33. In the engine compartment, connect all main wiring harness-to-instrument panel connectors.

34. Connect the negative battery cable.

Floor Console

REMOVAL & INSTALLATION

Except Thunderbird, Cougar and XR-7

1. Pull up the gear shift lever opening plate at the front and remove from catch.

2. Push the gear shift lever opening plate forward and remove.

3. Remove two screws securing the console finish panel to the console assembly. Remove the finish panel.

4. Remove the front ash receptacle.

5. Remove two screws under the ash receptacle, securing the console assembly to the floorpan.

6. Open the console storage compartment door and remove four screws securing the console to the floorpan.

7. Disconnect all console electrical connectors.

8. Remove the console assembly.

9. Installation is the reverse of the removal procedure.

86650502

Fig. 63 An example of a mid-size Ford dashboard and instrument panel

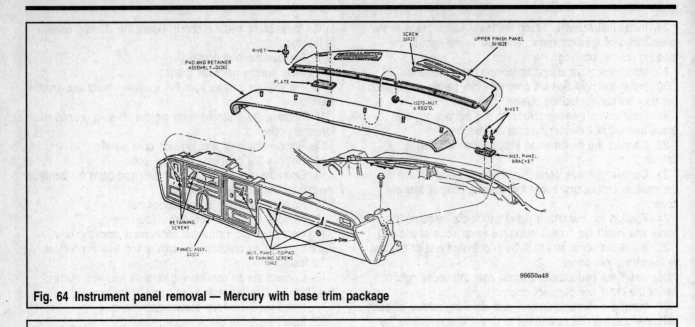

Fig. 64 Instrument panel removal — Mercury with base trim package

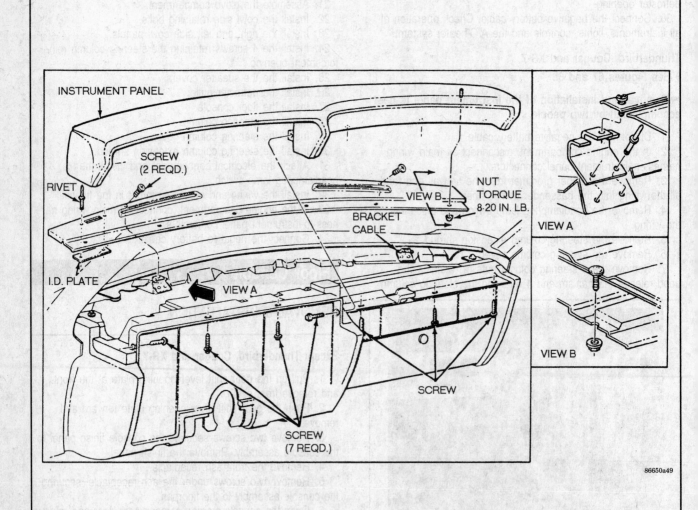

Fig. 65 Instrument panel removal — Ford with base trim package

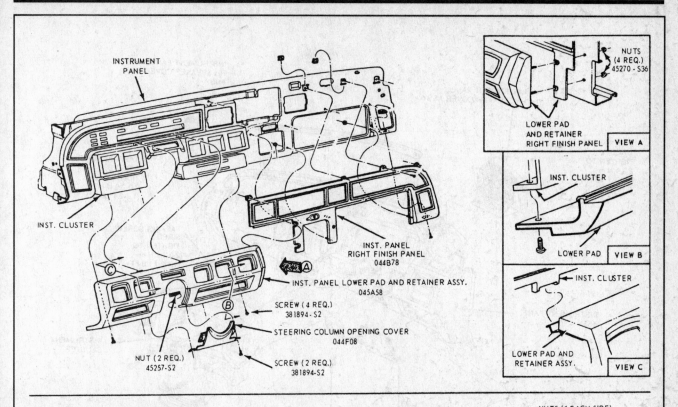

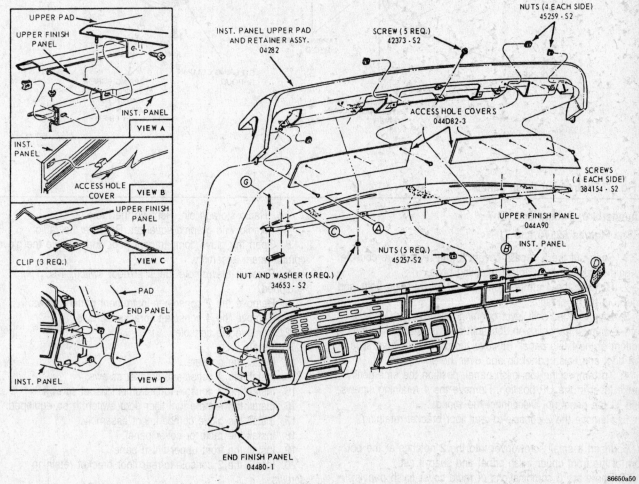

Fig. 66 Instrument panel removal — vehicles with deluxe trim package

86650a50

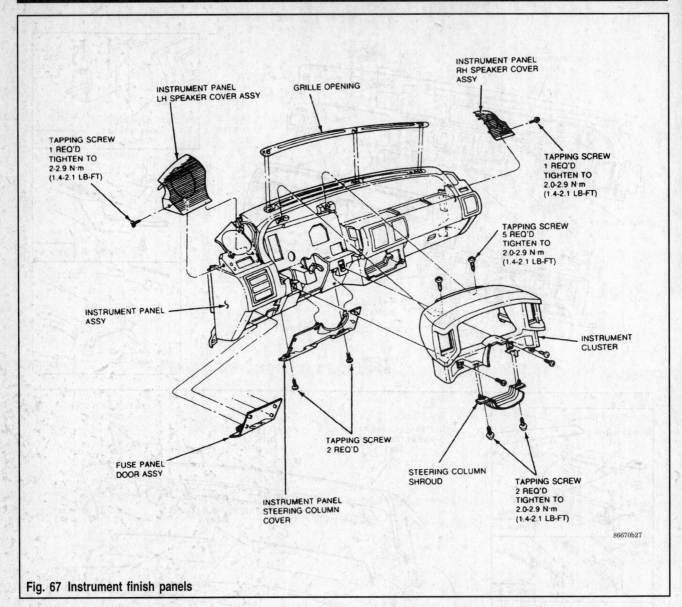

TAPPING SCREW
1 REQ'D
TIGHTEN TO
2-2.9 N·m
(1.4-2.1 LB-FT)

INSTRUMENT PANEL
LH SPEAKER COVER ASSY

GRILLE OPENING

INSTRUMENT PANEL
RH SPEAKER COVER
ASSY

TAPPING SCREW
1 REQ'D
TIGHTEN TO
2.0-2.9 N·m
(1.4-2.1 LB-FT)

TAPPING SCREW
5 REQ'D
TIGHTEN TO
2.0-2.9 N·m
(1.4-2.1 LB-FT)

INSTRUMENT PANEL
ASSY

INSTRUMENT
CLUSTER

FUSE PANEL
DOOR ASSY

INSTRUMENT PANEL
STEERING COLUMN
COVER

TAPPING SCREW
2 REQ'D

STEERING COLUMN
SHROUD

TAPPING SCREW
2 REQ'D
TIGHTEN TO
2.0-2.9 N·m
(1.4-2.1 LB-FT)

86670b27

Fig. 67 Instrument finish panels

Thunderbird, Cougar and XR-7

▶ **See Figures 69, 70 and 71**

1. Snap out the 2 access covers at the rear of the console to gain access to the armrest retaining bolts.

2. Remove the 4 armrest-to-floor bracket retaining bolts and snap out the armrest.

3. Snap out the shift lever opening finish panel. On cars with a manual transmission, the shift boot is attached to the bottom of the finish panel. Remove the shift knob, then slide the boot and finish panel up and over the shift lever.

4. To remove the top finish panel, position the emergency brake lever in the UP position. Remove the 4 retaining screws and lift the panel up. Disconnect the wiring.

5. Remove the 2 console-to-rear floor bracket retaining screws.

6. Insert a small screwdriver into the 2 notches at the bottom of the front upper finish panel and snap it out.

7. There are 3 combinations of radio cover finish panels:

   a. Radio opening cover plate with storage bin. Pry the finish cover out of the console.

   b. Radio storage bin. Remove the radio.

   c. Radio with graphic equalizer. Remove the radio.

8. Open the glove compartment door and remove the glove compartment assembly.

9. Remove the remote fuel filler door switch, if so equipped.

10. Remove the 2 console-to-instrument panel screws.

11. Remove the 4 console-to-bracket screws.

12. Remove the console.

To install:

13. Install the console.

14. Install the 4 console-to-bracket screws.

15. Install the 2 console-to-instrument panel screws.

16. Install the remote fuel filler door switch, if so equipped.

17. Install the glove compartment assembly.

18. Install the radio or cover panel.

19. Install the front upper finish panel.

20. Install the 2 console-to-rear floor bracket retaining screws.

21. Install the top finish panel. Connect the wiring.

22. Install the shift lever opening finish panel.

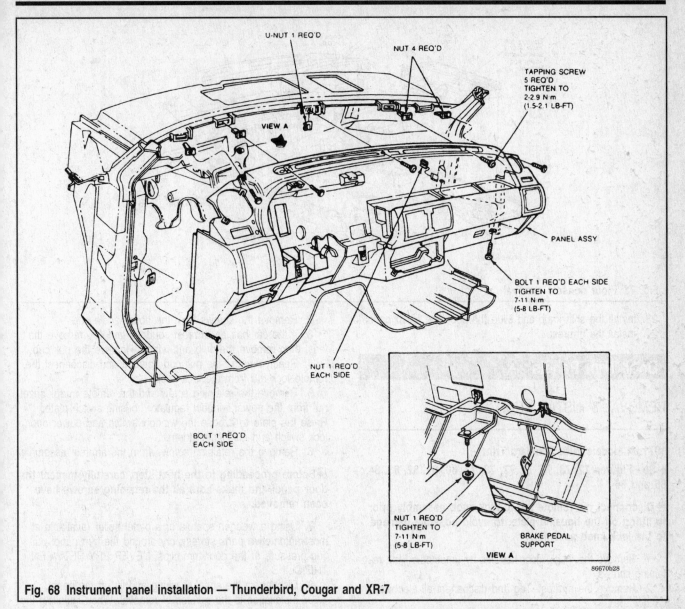

U-NUT 1 REQ'D

NUT 4 REQ'D

TAPPING SCREW
5 REQ'D
TIGHTEN TO
2-2.9 N·m
(1.5-2.1 LB-FT)

VIEW A

PANEL ASSY

BOLT 1 REQ'D EACH SIDE
TIGHTEN TO
7-11 N·m
(5-8 LB-FT)

NUT 1 REQ'D
EACH SIDE

BOLT 1 REQ'D
EACH SIDE

NUT 1 REQ'D
TIGHTEN TO
7-11 N·m
(5-8 LB-FT)

BRAKE PEDAL
SUPPORT

VIEW A

86670b28

Fig. 68 Instrument panel installation — Thunderbird, Cougar and XR-7

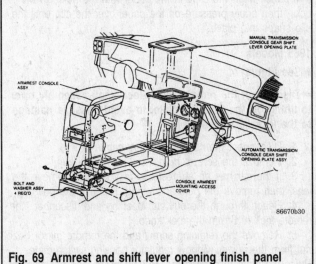

MANUAL TRANSMISSION
CONSOLE GEAR SHIFT
LEVER OPENING PLATE

ARMREST CONSOLE
ASSY

AUTOMATIC TRANSMISSION
CONSOLE GEAR SHIFT
OPENING PLATE ASSY

CONSOLE ARMREST
MOUNTING ACCESS
COVER

BOLT AND
WASHER ASSY
4 REQ'D

86670b30

Fig. 69 Armrest and shift lever opening finish panel removal

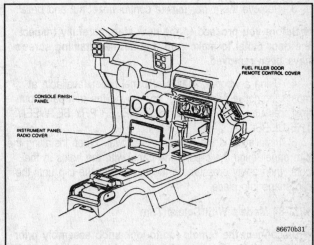

FUEL FILLER DOOR
REMOTE CONTROL COVER

CONSOLE FINISH
PANEL

INSTRUMENT PANEL
RADIO COVER

86670b31

Fig. 70 Upper finish panel and radio cover finish panel removal

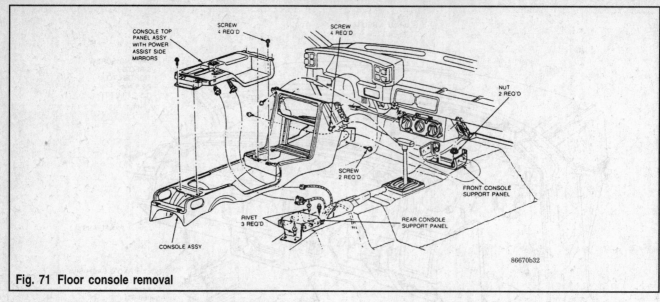

Fig. 71 Floor console removal

23. Install the shift knob and slide the boot and finish panel.
24. Install the armrest.

Door Trim Panels

REMOVAL & INSTALLATION

1971-84 Models With Standard Trim

▶ See Figures 72, 73, 75, 76, 77, 78, 79, 80, 81, 82, 83, 84, 85 and 86

➡Disconnect the remote rod-to-lock knob assembly prior to lifting off the housing plate, to avoid possible damage to the lock knob assembly.

1. Remove the inside door handles by unfastening the retaining screws.
2. Remove the armrest. Tag and disconnect all electrical connectors.
3. Remove the mirror remote control bezel nut and bezel.

➡Before you proceed to the next step, carefully inspect the door panel to make sure that all the retaining screws have been removed.

4. Using a wooden spatula or panel puller (available at most automotive parts stores), pry around the trim panel putting pressure at the door trim clips. NEVER PRY BETWEEN THE CLIPS.
5. Installation is the reverse of removal. When installing the trim panel, align the clips in the panel with the holes in the door, then apply pressure on the panel over the clip until the clip snaps into place.

1971-84 Models With Deluxe Trim

➡Disconnect the remote rod-to-lock knob assembly prior to lifting off the housing plate, to avoid possible damage to the lock knob assembly.

1. Disconnect the negative battery cable.

2. Remove the screws from the door handle cup.
3. If the car has an armrest courtesy lamp(s), remove the lens, then remove the bulb and wiring. Remove the pull cup.
4. Reach through the pull cup opening and disconnect the remote lock rod from the lock knob.
5. Remove the retaining screw and the remote mirror bezel nut from the power window regulator housing switch plate. Raise the plate to expose the window switch and power door lock switch and disconnect them.
6. Remove the retaining screws from the armrest assembly.

➡Before proceeding to the next step, carefully inspect the door panel and make sure all the retaining screws have been removed.

7. Using a wooden spatula or a panel puller (available at most automotive parts stores), pry around the trim panel putting pressure at the door trim clips. NEVER PRY BETWEEN THE CLIPS.
8. Disconnect the speaker wiring and lift off the panel.
9. Installation is the reverse of removal. When installing the trim panel, align the clips in the panel with the holes in the door, then apply pressure on the panel over the clip until the clip snaps into place.

1985 Models

▶ See Figure 74

➡Disconnect the remote rod-to-lock knob assembly prior to lifting off the housing plate, to avoid possible damage to the lock knob assembly.

1. Disconnect the negative battery cable.
2. Remove the screws from the door handle cup.
3. If the car has an armrest courtesy lamp(s), remove the lens, then remove the bulb and wiring. Remove the pull cup.
4. Reach through the pull cup opening and disconnect the remote lock rod from the lock knob.
5. Remove the retaining screw and the remote mirror bezel nut from the power window regulator housing switch plate. Raise the plate to expose the window switch and power door lock switch and disconnect them.

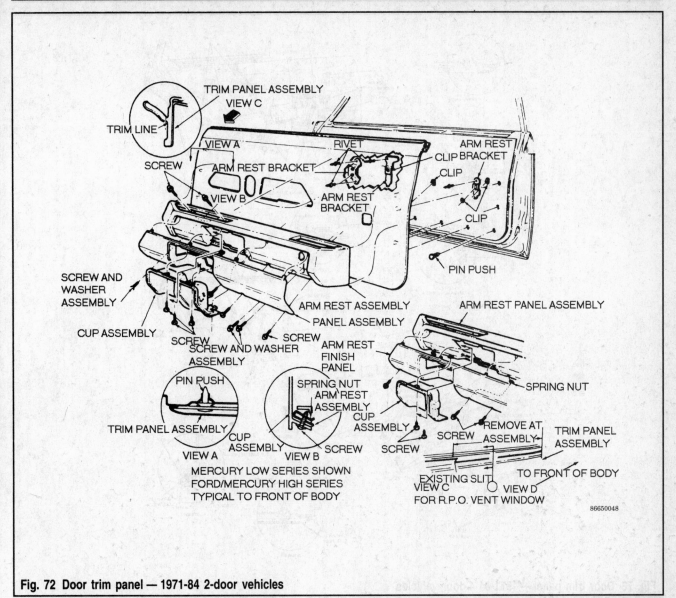

Fig. 72 Door trim panel — 1971-84 2-door vehicles

6. Remove the retaining screws from the armrest assembly.

➡**Before proceeding to the next step, inspect the door panel carefully to make sure all the retaining screws have been removed.**

7. Using a wooden spatula or a panel puller (available at most automotive parts stores), pry around the trim panel putting pressure at the door trim clips. Never pry between the clips.

8. Disconnect the speaker wiring and lift off the panel.

9. Installation is the reverse of removal. When installing the trim panel, align the clips in the panel with the holes in the door, then apply pressure on the panel over the clip until the clip snaps into place.

Rear Trim Panels

REMOVAL & INSTALLATION

Except Station Wagons

1. Open the luggage compartment door, and unplug the trunk light harness if equipped.

2. Remove the scuff plate from around the latch assembly.

3. Remove the trim panel attaching screws.

4. Remove the trim panel, by carefully prying up around the edges of the panel to unfasten the retaining clips.

To install:

5. Position the trim panel in the vehicle. Lightly tap on the edges of the trim panel to set the retaining clips into their securing holes.

6. Install the doorsill scuff plate.

7. Reconnect the interior light harness, if equipped.

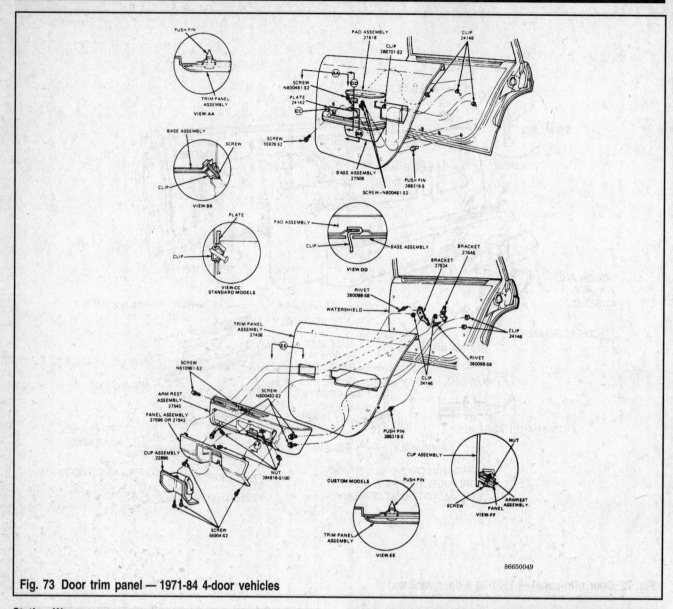

Fig. 73 Door trim panel — 1971-84 4-door vehicles

Station Wagons

1. Open rear compartment door, and unplug the trunk light harness if equipped.

2. Remove the scuff plate from around the latch assembly, by removing the retaining screws.

3. Remove the trim panel attaching screws.

4. Remove the seat belt retractors from the vertical pillars of the vehicle.

5. Remove the trim panel, by carefully prying up around the edges of the panel to unfasten the retaining clips.

To install:

6. Position the trim panel in the vehicle. Lightly tap on the edges of the trim panel to set the retaining clips into their securing holes.

7. Install the trim panel retaining screws.

8. Install the seat belt retractors to the vehicle pillars, making sure the retaining bolts are secure.

9. Install the doorsill scuff plate.

10. Reconnect the interior light harness, if equipped.

Headliner

REMOVAL & INSTALLATION

1. Remove the sun visors, retainer clips and bracket assemblies.

2. Remove the assist handle assemblies, if so equipped, and the coat hooks.

3. Remove the upper screws and loosen the lower screws retaining the windshield side garnish mouldings.

4. Remove the remaining screw securing the windshield upper garnish moulding and remove the moulding.

5. Remove the roof side rail mouldings.

6. Remove the upper screw and loosen the lower screws retaining the center body pillar inside finish panel to the body side assembly.

7. Remove the upper screw and loosen the lower screws retaining the rear window side garnish mouldings to the body assembly.

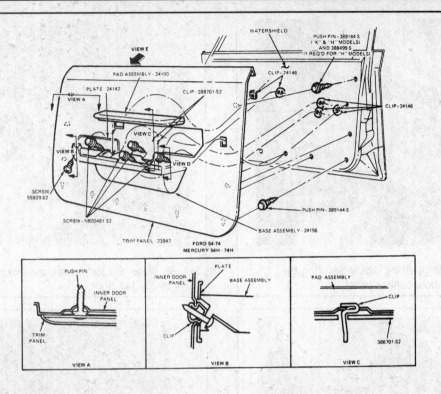

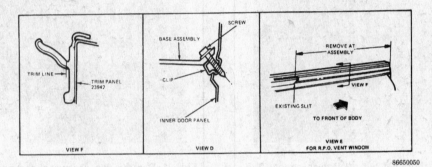

Fig. 74 Door trim panel — 1985 vehicles

Fig. 75 Remove the retaining screw securing the trim plate around the door handle

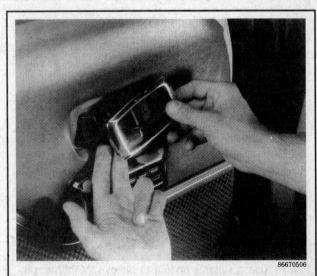

Fig. 76 Lift the handle to remove the trim plate

Fig. 77 Unfasten the retaining screw securing the power lock and window control panel

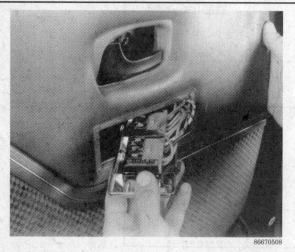

Fig. 78 Pull the control panel out enough to access the wire harnesses at the rear

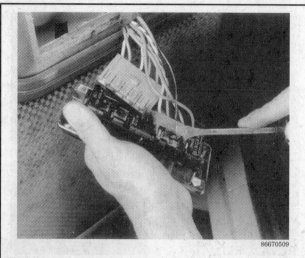

Fig. 79 Use a suitable prytool to remove the harnesses from the connector

Fig. 80 When the harnesses are disconnected, tuck them inside the door panel

Fig. 81 Remove the screws at the base of the door panel

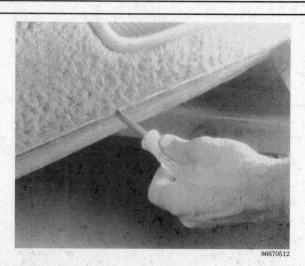

Fig. 82 Do not forget the screw in the middle of the panel

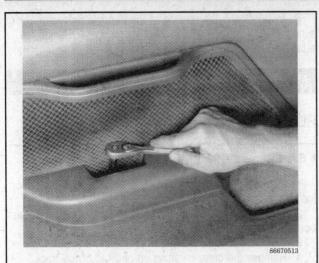

Fig. 83 Remove the screw securing the armrest to the door

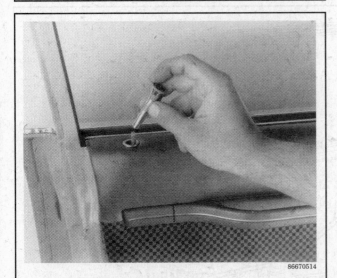

Fig. 84 Unscrew the lock knob

Fig. 85 Use a panel puller or other suitable tool to remove the door panel. Do not pull on the panel

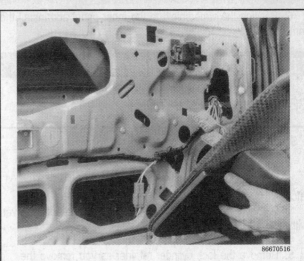

Fig. 86 When removing the panel, make sure none of the wire harnesses get caught on the panel

8. Remove the remaining screw securing the back window upper garnish moulding and remove the moulding.

9. Remove the dome lamp.

10. Shift the roof trim panel all the way to one side, allowing it to be removed, and bend the opposite side flap inward to remove.

11. On 2-door vehicles, remove the headliner through the passenger door; on station wagons, remove it through the hatch opening.

To install:

12. If a new headliner is being installed, unpack the roof trim panel, lay it out on a flat surface and break score (contour) the ends.

13. Position the headliner assembly in the vehicle and secure it to the roof panel with the push pins first.

14. To complete installation, reverse steps 1-9.

Door Lock Cylinder

REMOVAL & INSTALLATION

◆ See Figure 87

➥The key code is stamped on the driver's door lock cylinder to aid in replacing lost keys. If a lock cylinder needs to be replaced, it is advisable to replace the ignition lock cylinder and other door lock cylinder as a set; otherwise, two different keys will be required.

1. Remove the door trim panel and watershield.

2. Disconnect the lock control-to-door lock cylinder rod from the lock cylinder arm.

3. Remove the door lock cylinder retainer and slide the cylinder from the door. If a new lock cylinder is being installed, transfer the arm to the new cylinder.

To install:

4. Position the lock cylinder in the door and install the lock cylinder retainer.

5. Connect the lock control-to-door lock cylinder rod at the lock cylinder, and secure the retainer.

6. Position the watershield to the inner panel and install the trim panel.

Trunk Lid Lock Cylinder

REMOVAL & INSTALLATION

▶ **See Figure 88**

1. Open the trunk lid.
2. Unfasten the latch retaining screws and remove the latch.
3. Remove the lock cylinder retainer by drilling out the rivet with a ¼ in. (6mm) drill.
4. Remove the lock support and bracket.
5. Remove the lock cylinder retainer as you remove the lock cylinder and extension.

6. Installation is the reverse of the removal procedure. Use a new rivet or replace with a sheet metal screw. Torque the retaining screws 6-10 ft. lbs. (8-13 Nm).

Manual Door Glass

REMOVAL & INSTALLATION

▶ **See Figures 89, 90, 91, 92 and 93**

1. Remove the door trim panel and watershield. On 2-door models, loosen the glass belt stabilizers.
2. Raise the glass sufficiently enough to access the 3 glass bracket rivets and support it in that position.
3. Drill out the rivets using a ¼ in. (6mm) drill bit.
4. Remove the glass by lifting up and out of the track.
5. Installation is the reverse of removal. Replace the rivets with new ¼ in. nuts, bolts and lockwashers.

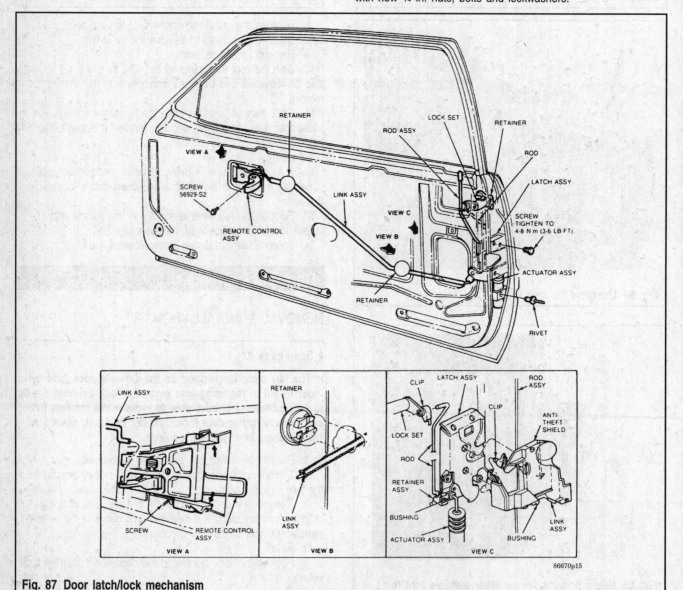

86670p15

Fig. 87 Door latch/lock mechanism

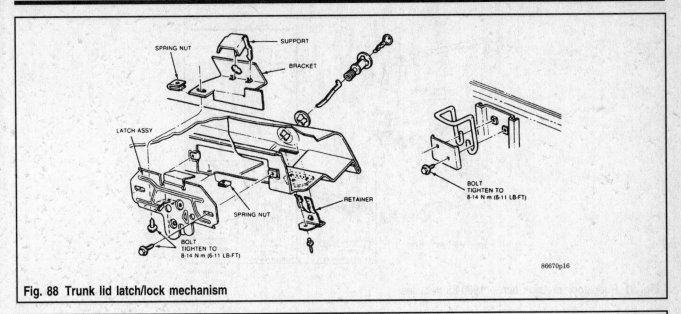

Fig. 88 Trunk lid latch/lock mechanism

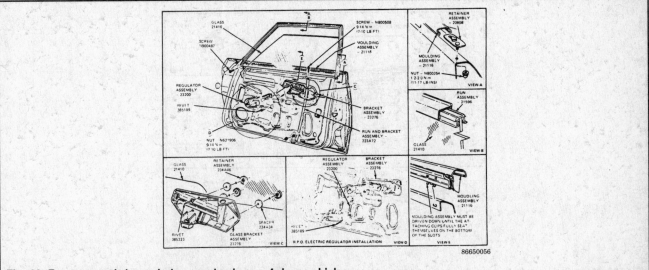

Fig. 89 Front manual door window mechanism — 4-door vehicles

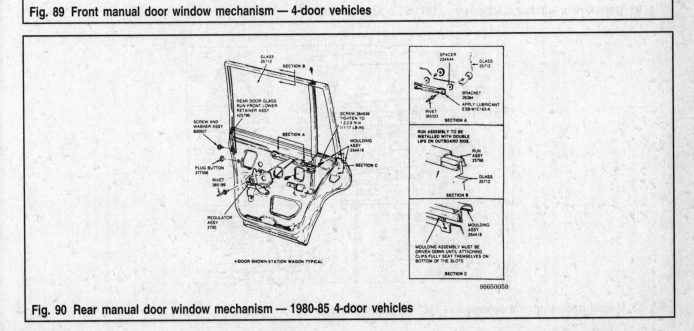

Fig. 90 Rear manual door window mechanism — 1980-85 4-door vehicles

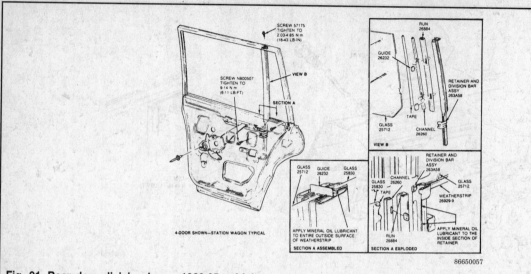

Fig. 91 Rear door division bar — 1980-85 vehicles

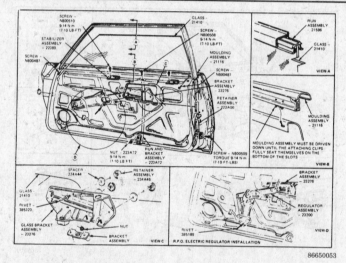

Fig. 92 Manual door window mechanism — 1971-80 2-door vehicles

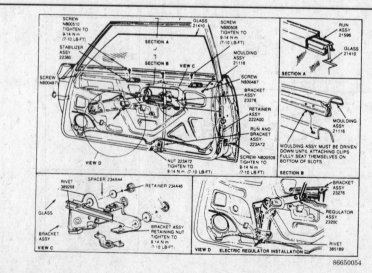

Fig. 93 Manual door window mechanism — 1981-85 2-door vehicles

Door Glass Regulator

REMOVAL & INSTALLATION

1. Remove the door trim panel and watershield. On 2-door models, loosen the glass belt stabilizers.
2. Raise the glass sufficiently enough to access the 3 glass bracket rivets and support it in that position.
3. Drill out the rivets using a ¼ in. (6mm) drill bit.
4. Disengage the regulator slide arm from the glass C-channel and remove the regulator from the door.
5. Installation is the reverse of removal. Replace the rivets with new ¼ in. nuts, bolts and lockwashers.

Front Door Electric Window Motor

REMOVAL & INSTALLATION

▶ See Figure 94

1. Raise the window to the full up position.
2. Disconnect the battery ground.
3. Remove the door trim panel and watershield.
4. Disconnect the power window motor wiring.
5. Drill 3-½ in. (13mm) holes in the door to expose the motor attaching bolts. Refer to the illustrations.
6. With the bolts exposed, use the suitable tool(s) to remove the bolts.
7. Push the motor outward to disengage the motor and drive assembly from the regulator gear. Unplug the wire harness from the motor assembly.
8. Remove the motor from the door.
9. Install the new motor and tighten the bolts to 50-85 inch lbs. (5.6-9.5 Nm). The new motor kit will have plugs to fill the drilled holes.
10. Connect the wiring and install the watershield and trim panel.

Rear Door Electric Window Motor

REMOVAL & INSTALLATION

▶ See Figure 95

1. Raise the window to the full up position.
2. Disconnect the negative battery cable.
3. Remove the door trim panel and watershield.
4. Disconnect the power window motor wiring.
5. Drill out a ½ in. (13mm) hole at each of the 3 dimples provided to gain access to the mounting bolts. Refer to the illustration.

❋❋CAUTION

Prior to removing the mounting bolts, make sure that the regulator arm is in a fixed position to prevent the counterbalance arm from suddenly unwinding!

6. Remove the bolts using the appropriate tools.
7. Remove the wire connector from the motor assembly.
8. Push the motor outward to disengage the motor and drive assembly from the regulator gear.
9. Remove the motor from the door.
10. Install the new motor, tightening the bolts to 50-85 inch lbs. (5.6-9.5 Nm) The new motor kit will have plugs to fill the drilled holes.
11. Connect the wiring and install the watershield and trim panel.

Tailgate Glass

REMOVAL & INSTALLATION

▶ See Figures 96 and 97

1. Remove the tailgate trim panel and watershield.
2. Remove the inner panel lower access cover.

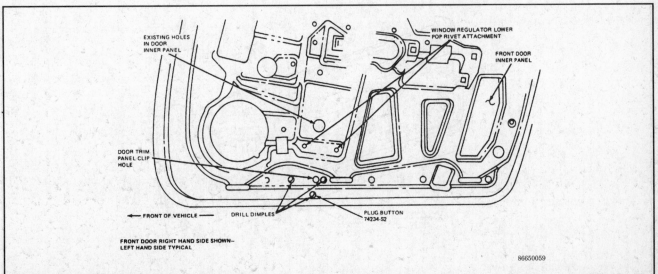

Fig. 94 Front door power window motor removal

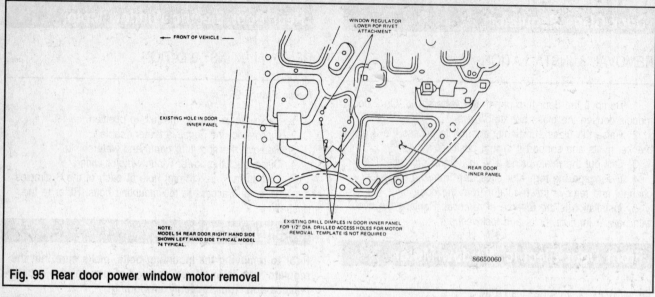

Fig. 95 Rear door power window motor removal

3. Drop the tailgate to the down position and raise the glass until the glass brackets are accessible.

4. Disconnect the negative battery terminal.

5. Drill out the glass bracket rivets with a ¼ in. (6mm) drill bit.

6. Disconnect the wiring from the window glass defroster grid.

7. Slide the glass from the door.

8. Installation is the reverse of removal. Use ¼ bolts, nuts and lockwashers in place of the rivets. Tighten the bolts to 36-60 inch lbs. (4.0-7.0 Nm).

Tailgate Window Motor

REMOVAL & INSTALLATION

▶ **See Figure 97**

1. Remove the tailgate trim panel and watershield.
2. Remove the inner panel lower access cover.

3. Disconnect the negative battery cable.

4. Disconnect the wiring at the motor.

5. Remove the covers to access the motor mounting bolts and remove the bolts.

6. Installation is the reverse of removal. Tighten the bolts to 50-85 inch lbs. (5.6 -9.5 Nm).

Inside Rear View Mirror

REPLACEMENT

▶ **See Figure 98**

1. Loosen the mirror assembly-to-mounting bracket setscrew.

2. Remove the mirror assembly by sliding it upward and away from the mounting bracket.

3. If the bracket vinyl pad remains on the windshield, apply low heat from an electric heat gun until the vinyl softens. Peel the vinyl off the windshield and discard.

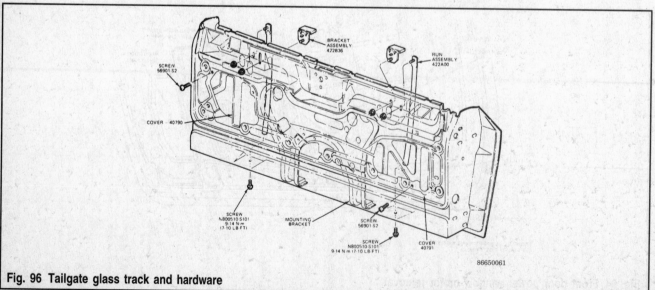

Fig. 96 Tailgate glass track and hardware

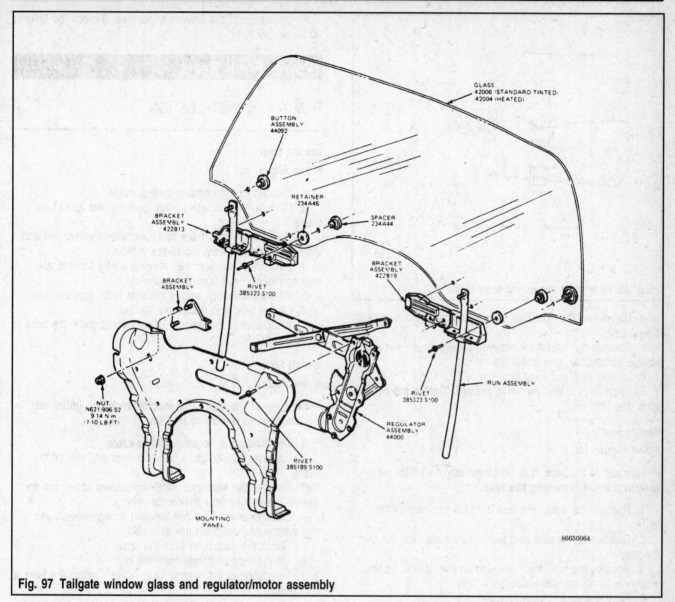

Fig. 97 Tailgate window glass and regulator/motor assembly

To install:

4. Make sure the glass, bracket and adhesive kit (Rear View Mirror Repair Kit D9AZ-19554-B or equivalent) are at a temperature of at least 65-75° F (18-24° C).

5. Locate and mark the mirror mounting bracket location on the outside surface of the windshield with a wax pencil.

6. Thoroughly clean the bonding surfaces of the glass and the bracket to remove the old adhesive. Use a mild abrasive cleaner on the glass and fine sandpaper on the bracket to lightly roughen the surface. Wipe clean with the alcohol-moistened cloth.

7. Crush the accelerator vial (part of Rear View Mirror Repair Kit D9AZ-19554-B or equivalent), and apply the accelerator to the bonding surface of the bracket and windshield. Let it dry for three minutes.

8. Apply two drops of adhesive (part of Rear View Mirror Repair Kit D9AZ-19554-B or equivalent) to the mounting surface of the bracket. Using a clean toothpick or wooden match, quickly spread the adhesive evenly over the mounting surface of the bracket.

9. Quickly position the mounting bracket on the windshield. The ³/₈ in. (10mm) circular depression in the bracket must be toward the inside of the passenger compartment. Press the bracket firmly against the windshield for one minute.

10. Allow the bond to set for five minutes. Remove any excess bonding material from the windshield with an alcohol dampened cloth.

11. Attach the mirror to the mounting bracket and tighten the setscrew to 10-20 inch lbs. (1-2 Nm).

Manual Front Seats

REMOVAL & INSTALLATION

Bucket Seat
▶ **See Figure 99**

1. Remove the insulators from the front and rear of the tracks.

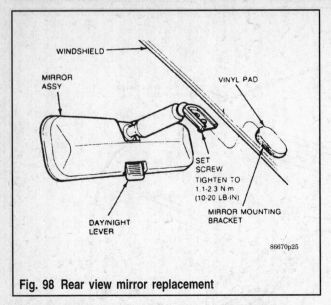

Fig. 98 Rear view mirror replacement

2. Disconnect the seat beat warning harness from the seat, if equipped.

3. Remove the seat track retaining screws and/or nut and washer assemblies from inside the vehicle.

4. Lift the seat and track from the car.

5. Installation is the reverse of removal. Tighten the bolts to 20 ft. lbs. (27 Nm).

Bench Seat

▶ See Figure 100

➡Because of the size, it is recommended to utilize an assistant when removing this unit.

1. Remove the insulators from the front and rear of the tracks.

2. Disconnect the seat beat warning harness from the seat, if equipped.

3. Remove the seat track retaining screws and/or nut and washer assemblies from inside the vehicle.

4. Lift the seat and track from the car.

5. Installation is the reverse of removal. Tighten the bolts to 20 ft. lbs. (27 Nm).

Power Front Seats

REMOVAL & INSTALLATION

Bucket Seat

▶ See Figure 101

1. Disconnect the negative battery cable.

2. Remove the insulators from the front and rear of the tracks.

3. Remove the seat track retaining screws and/or nut and washer assemblies from inside the vehicle.

4. Disconnect the seat belt warning wiring harness and seat control harness from the assembly.

5. Where necessary, unbolt the seat belts from the floor.

6. Lift the seat and track from the car.

7. Installation is the reverse of removal. Tighten the bolts to 20 ft. lbs. (27 Nm).

Bench Seat

▶ See Figure 102

➡Because of the size, it is recommended to utilize an assistant when removing this unit.

1. Disconnect the negative battery cable.

2. Remove the insulators from the front and rear of the tracks.

3. Remove the seat track retaining screws and/or nut and washer assemblies from inside the vehicle.

4. Disconnect the seat belt warning wiring harness and seat control harness from the assembly.

5. Unbolt the seat belts from the floor.

6. Lift the seat and track from the car.

7. Installation is the reverse of removal. Tighten the bolts to 20 ft. lbs. (27 Nm).

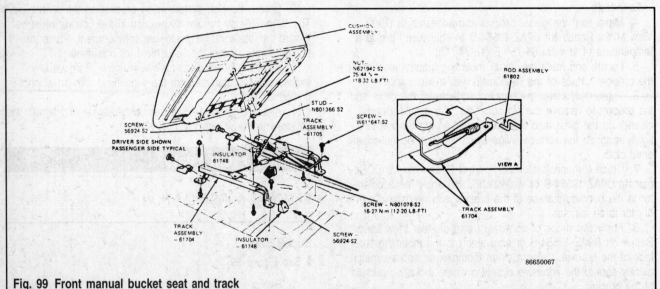

Fig. 99 Front manual bucket seat and track

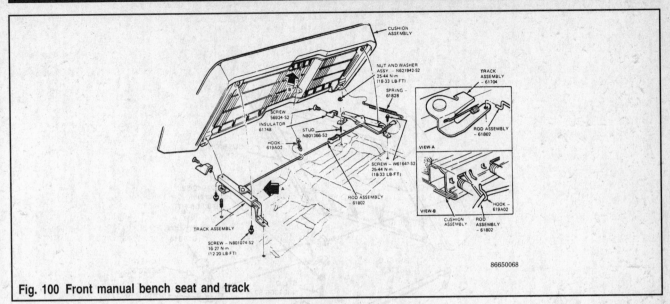

Fig. 100 Front manual bench seat and track

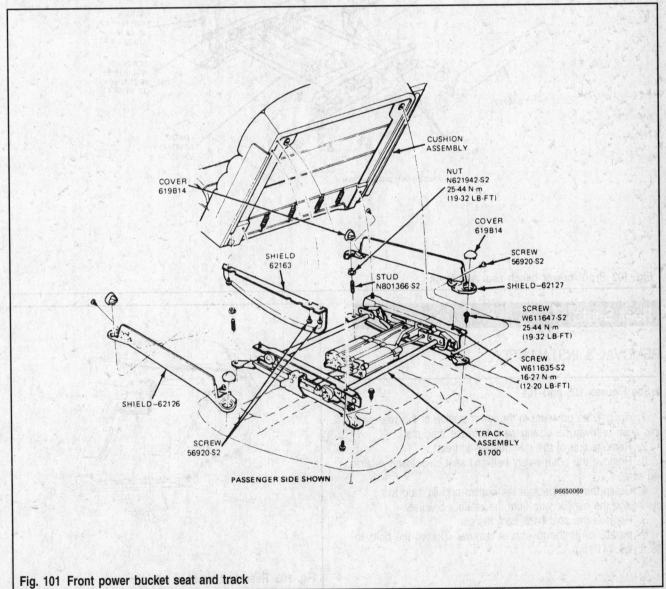

Fig. 101 Front power bucket seat and track

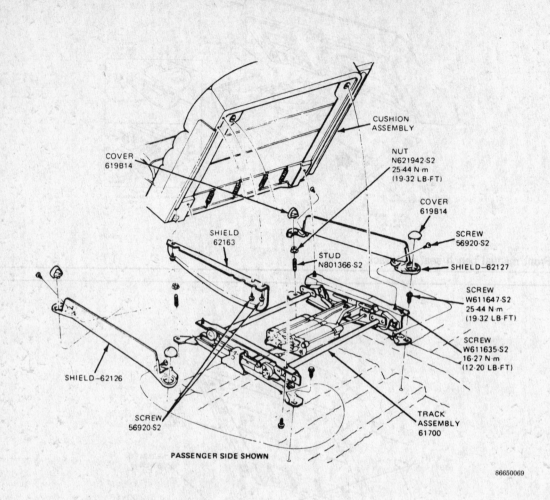

COVER
619B14

CUSHION
ASSEMBLY

NUT
N621942-S2
25-44 N·m
(19-32 LB·FT)

COVER
619B14

SCREW
56920-S2

SHIELD
62163

STUD
N801366-S2

SHIELD-62127

SCREW
W611647-S2
25-44 N·m
(19-32 LB·FT)

SCREW
W611635-S2
16-27 N·m
(12-20 LB·FT)

SHIELD-62126

SCREW
56920-S2

TRACK
ASSEMBLY
61700

PASSENGER SIDE SHOWN

86650069

Fig. 102 Front power bench seat and track

Rear Seats

REMOVAL & INSTALLATION

▶ **See Figures 103 and 104**

1. Apply knee pressure to the lower portion of the rear seat and push rearward to disengage it from the brackets.
2. Remove one of the rear quarter armrests.
3. Remove the outer safety belt and seat back lower retaining screws.
4. Grasp the seat back at the bottom and lift it up to disengage the hanger wire from the retainer brackets.
5. Remove the seat back from the car.
6. Installation is the reverse of removal. Tighten the bolts to 30 ft. lbs. (41 Nm).

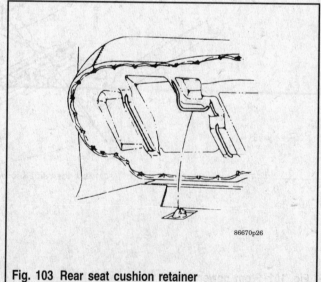

86670p26

Fig. 103 Rear seat cushion retainer

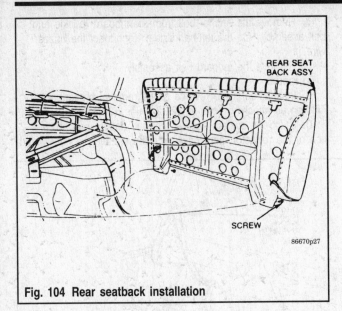

Fig. 104 Rear seatback installation

Fold-Down Rear Seats

▶ See Figure 105

REMOVAL & INSTALLATION

Auxiliary Seat Back and Cushion

1. Remove the 2 lower retaining screws securing the seat back to the floor.
2. Lift up and disengage the upper clips of the rear seat back from the top of the folding floor.
3. Disengage the seat cushion latch and remove the seat cushion from the car.
4. Installation is the reverse of removal.

Second Seat Back

1. Remove the 3 screws attaching the seat back to the seat back floor panel.
2. Pull the bottom of the seat forward and lift the seat off the floor panel.
3. Installation is the reverse of removal.

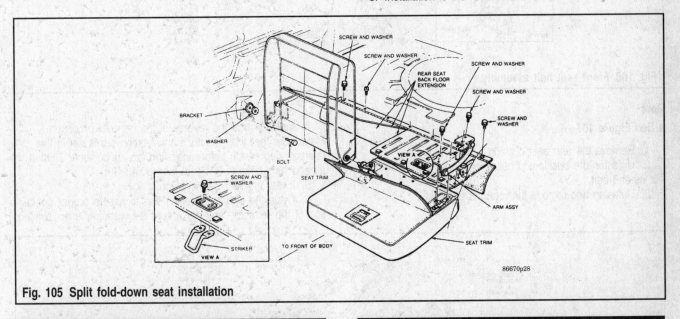

Fig. 105 Split fold-down seat installation

Power Seat Motor

REMOVAL & INSTALLATION

1. Disconnect the negative battery cable.
2. Remove the seat(s) from the vehicle.
3. Remove the 3 motor assembly mounting bolts.
4. Remove the clamps from the drive cables, open the wire retaining straps and remove the motor assembly and cables from the seat tracks.
5. Installation is the reverse of removal. Tighten the bolts to 20 ft. lbs. (27 Nm).

Seat Belt Systems

REMOVAL & INSTALLATION

➡Seat belt bolt bit T77L-2100-A, or equivalent, should be used for removal and installation of seat belt systems.

Front

▶ See Figure 106

1. Remove the seat belt anchor-to-sill bolt and rubber washer.
2. Slip a finger behind the D-ring cover, and push the bottom of the cover toward the center of the vehicle to dislodge. Lift up to remove the cover and expose the attaching bolt.

3. Remove the rear seat lower cushion and rear seat back cushions.

4. Remove the quarter trim panel, and feed the seat belt through the slot in the panel.

5. Remove the bezel from the plunger, and twist the plunger 90 degrees to unlock.

6. Remove the retractor mounting bolt and the outboard belt assembly.

7. Remove the anchor bolt from the inboard (buckle end) belt assembly. On the left-hand side, disconnect the buzzer wire.

8. Remove the inboard belt assembly.

To install:

9. Installation is the reverse of the removal procedure. Tighten all attaching bolts to 22-32 ft. lbs. (30-43 Nm).

10. Cycle the system several times to assure proper operation of the retractor, and make sure the webbing is not twisted.

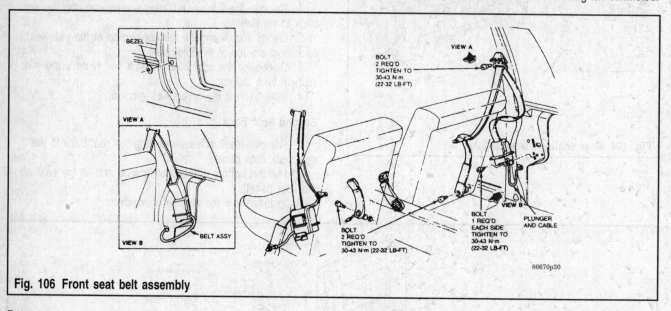

Fig. 106 Front seat belt assembly

Rear

♦ **See Figure 107**

1. Remove the rear seat cushion.

2. Unfasten the buckle-end belt anchor and remove the buckle-end belt.

3. Unfasten and remove the retractor assembly.

To install:

4. Installation is the reverse of the removal procedure. Make sure that the retractor's anti-rotation tab is set in the floorpan depression before installing the anchor bolt. Tighten all attaching bolts to 22-32 ft. lbs. (30-43 Nm).

5. Install the rear seat cushion.

6. Cycle the system several times to assure proper operation of the retractor, and make sure the webbing is not twisted.

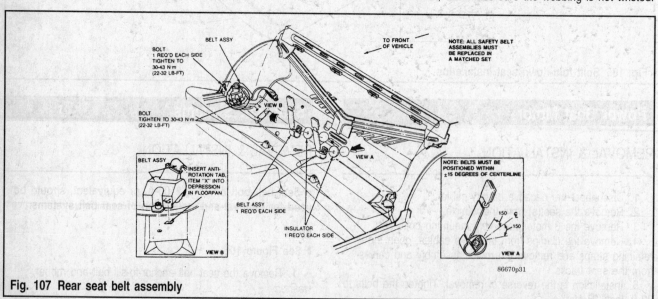

Fig. 107 Rear seat belt assembly

Hood, Trunk Lid, Hatch Lid, Glass and Doors

Problem	Possible Cause	Correction
HOOD/TRUNK/HATCH LID		
Improper closure.	• Striker and latch not properly aligned.	• Adjust the alignment.
Difficulty locking and unlocking.	• Striker and latch not properly aligned.	• Adjust the alignment.
Uneven clearance with body panels.	• Incorrectly installed hood or trunk lid.	• Adjust the alignment.
WINDOW/WINDSHIELD GLASS		
Water leak through windshield	• Defective seal.	• Fill sealant
	• Defective body flange.	• Correct.
Water leak through door window glass.	• Incorrect window glass installation.	• Adjust position.
	• Gap at upper window frame.	• Adjust position.
Water leak through quarter window.	• Defective seal.	• Replace seal.
	• Defective body flange.	• Correct.
Water leak through rear window.	• Defective seal.	• Replace seal.
	• Defective body flange.	• Correct.
FRONT/REAR DOORS		
Door window malfunction.	• Incorrect window glass installation.	• Adjust position.
	• Damaged or faulty regulator.	• Correct or replace.
Water leak through door edge.	• Cracked or faulty weatherstrip.	• Replace.
Water leak from door center.	• Drain hole clogged.	• Remove foreign objects.
	• Inadequate waterproof skeet contact or damage.	• Correct or replace.
Door hard to open.	• Incorrect latch or striker adjustment.	• Adjust.
Door does not open or close completely.	• Incorrect door installation.	• Adjust position.
	• Defective door check strap.	• Correct or replace.
	• Door check strap and hinge require grease.	• Apply grease.
Uneven gap between door and body.	• Incorrect door installation.	• Adjust position.
Wind noise around door.	• Improperly installed weatherstrip.	• Repair or replace.
	• Improper clearance between door glass and door weatherstrip.	• Adjust.
	• Deformed door.	• Repair or replace.

86670yzy

AIR/FUEL RATIO: The ratio of air-to-gasoline by weight in the fuel mixture drawn into the engine.

AIR INJECTION: One method of reducing harmful exhaust emissions by injecting air into each of the exhaust ports of an engine. The fresh air entering the hot exhaust manifold causes any remaining fuel to be burned before it can exit the tailpipe.

ALTERNATOR: A device used for converting mechanical energy into electrical energy.

AMMETER: An instrument, calibrated in amperes, used to measure the flow of an electrical current in a circuit. Ammeters are always connected in series with the circuit being tested.

AMPERE: The rate of flow of electrical current present when one volt of electrical pressure is applied against one ohm of electrical resistance.

ANALOG COMPUTER: Any microprocessor that uses similar (analogous) electrical signals to make its calculations.

ARMATURE: A laminated, soft iron core wrapped by a wire that converts electrical energy to mechanical energy as in a motor or relay. When rotated in a magnetic field, it changes mechanical energy into electrical energy as in a generator.

ATMOSPHERIC PRESSURE: The pressure on the Earth's surface caused by the weight of the air in the atmosphere. At sea level, this pressure is 14.7 psi at 32°F (101 kPa at 0°C).

ATOMIZATION: The breaking down of a liquid into a fine mist that can be suspended in air.

AXIAL PLAY: Movement parallel to a shaft or bearing bore.

BACKFIRE: The sudden combustion of gases in the intake or exhaust system that results in a loud explosion.

BACKLASH: The clearance or play between two parts, such as meshed gears.

BACKPRESSURE: Restrictions in the exhaust system that slow the exit of exhaust gases from the combustion chamber.

BAKELITE: A heat resistant, plastic insulator material commonly used in printed circuit boards and transistorized components.

BALL BEARING: A bearing made up of hardened inner and outer races between which hardened steel balls roll.

BALLAST RESISTOR: A resistor in the primary ignition circuit that lowers voltage after the engine is started to reduce wear on ignition components.

BEARING: A friction reducing, supportive device usually located between a stationary part and a moving part.

BIMETAL TEMPERATURE SENSOR: Any sensor or switch made of two dissimilar types of metal that bend when heated or cooled due to the different expansion rates of the alloys. These types of sensors usually function as an on/off switch.

BLOWBY: Combustion gases, composed of water vapor and unburned fuel, that leak past the piston rings into the crankcase during normal engine operation. These gases are removed by the PCV system to prevent the buildup of harmful acids in the crankcase.

BRAKE PAD: A brake shoe and lining assembly used with disc brakes.

BRAKE SHOE: The backing for the brake lining. The term is, however, usually applied to the assembly of the brake backing and lining.

BUSHING: A liner, usually removable, for a bearing; an anti-friction liner used in place of a bearing.

CALIPER: A hydraulically activated device in a disc brake system, which is mounted straddling the brake rotor (disc). The caliper contains at least one piston and two brake pads. Hydraulic pressure on the piston(s) forces the pads against the rotor.

CAMSHAFT: A shaft in the engine on which are the lobes (cams) which operate the valves. The camshaft is driven by the crankshaft, via a belt, chain or gears, at one half the crankshaft speed.

CAPACITOR: A device which stores an electrical charge.

CARBON MONOXIDE (CO): A colorless, odorless gas given off as a normal byproduct of combustion. It is poisonous and extremely dangerous in confined areas, building up slowly to toxic levels without warning if adequate ventilation is not available.

CARBURETOR: A device, usually mounted on the intake manifold of an engine, which mixes the air and fuel in the proper proportion to allow even combustion.

CATALYTIC CONVERTER: A device installed in the exhaust system, like a muffler, that converts harmful byproducts of combustion into carbon dioxide and water vapor by means of a heat-producing chemical reaction.

CENTRIFUGAL ADVANCE: A mechanical method of advancing the spark timing by using flyweights in the distributor that react to centrifugal force generated by the distributor shaft rotation.

CHECK VALVE: Any one-way valve installed to permit the flow of air, fuel or vacuum in one direction only.

CHOKE: A device, usually a moveable valve, placed in the intake path of a carburetor to restrict the flow of air.

CIRCUIT: Any unbroken path through which an electrical current can flow. Also used to describe fuel flow in some instances.

CIRCUIT BREAKER: A switch which protects an electrical circuit from overload by opening the circuit when the current flow exceeds a predetermined level. Some circuit breakers must be reset manually, while most reset automatically.

COIL (IGNITION): A transformer in the ignition circuit which steps up the voltage provided to the spark plugs.

COMBINATION MANIFOLD: An assembly which includes both the intake and exhaust manifolds in one casting.

COMBINATION VALVE: A device used in some fuel systems that routes fuel vapors to a charcoal storage canister instead of venting them into the atmosphere. The valve relieves fuel tank pressure and allows fresh air into the tank as the fuel level drops to prevent a vapor lock situation.

COMPRESSION RATIO: The comparison of the total volume of the cylinder and combustion chamber with the piston at BDC and the piston at TDC.

CONDENSER: 1. An electrical device which acts to store an electrical charge, preventing voltage surges. 2. A radiator-like device in the air conditioning system in which refrigerant gas condenses into a liquid, giving off heat.

CONDUCTOR: Any material through which an electrical current can be transmitted easily.

CONTINUITY: Continuous or complete circuit. Can be checked with an ohmmeter.

COUNTERSHAFT: An intermediate shaft which is rotated by a mainshaft and transmits, in turn, that rotation to a working part.

CRANKCASE: The lower part of an engine in which the crankshaft and related parts operate.

CRANKSHAFT: The main driving shaft of an engine which receives reciprocating motion from the pistons and converts it to rotary motion.

CYLINDER: In an engine, the round hole in the engine block in which the piston(s) ride.

CYLINDER BLOCK: The main structural member of an engine in which is found the cylinders, crankshaft and other principal parts.

CYLINDER HEAD: The detachable portion of the engine, usually fastened to the top of the cylinder block and containing all or most of the combustion chambers. On overhead valve engines, it contains the valves and their operating parts. On overhead cam engines, it contains the camshaft as well.

DEAD CENTER: The extreme top or bottom of the piston stroke.

DETONATION: An unwanted explosion of the air/fuel mixture in the combustion chamber caused by excess heat and compression, advanced timing, or an overly lean mixture. Also referred to as "ping".

DIAPHRAGM: A thin, flexible wall separating two cavities, such as in a vacuum advance unit.

DIESELING: A condition in which hot spots in the combustion chamber cause the engine to run on after the key is turned off.

DIFFERENTIAL: A geared assembly which allows the transmission of motion between drive axles, giving one axle the ability to turn faster than the other.

DIODE: An electrical device that will allow current to flow in one direction only.

DISC BRAKE: A hydraulic braking assembly consisting of a brake disc, or rotor, mounted on an axle, and a caliper assembly containing, usually two brake pads which are activated by hydraulic pressure. The pads are forced against the sides of the disc, creating friction which slows the vehicle.

DISTRIBUTOR: A mechanically driven device on an engine which is responsible for electrically firing the spark plug at a predetermined point of the piston stroke.

DOWEL PIN: A pin, inserted in mating holes in two different parts allowing those parts to maintain a fixed relationship.

DRUM BRAKE: A braking system which consists of two brake shoes and one or two wheel cylinders, mounted on a fixed backing plate, and a brake drum, mounted on an axle, which revolves around the assembly.

DWELL: The rate, measured in degrees of shaft rotation, at which an electrical circuit cycles on and off.

ELECTRONIC CONTROL UNIT (ECU): Ignition module, module, amplifier or igniter. See Module for definition.

ELECTRONIC IGNITION: A system in which the timing and firing of the spark plugs is controlled by an electronic control unit, usually called a module. These systems have no points or condenser.

END-PLAY: The measured amount of axial movement in a shaft.

ENGINE: A device that converts heat into mechanical energy.

EXHAUST MANIFOLD: A set of cast passages or pipes which conduct exhaust gases from the engine.

FEELER GAUGE: A blade, usually metal, of precisely predetermined thickness, used to measure the clearance between two parts.

FIRING ORDER: The order in which combustion occurs in the cylinders of an engine. Also the order in which spark is distributed to the plugs by the distributor.

FLOODING: The presence of too much fuel in the intake manifold and combustion chamber which prevents the air/fuel mixture from firing, thereby causing a no-start situation.

FLYWHEEL: A disc shaped part bolted to the rear end of the crankshaft. Around the outer perimeter is affixed the ring gear. The starter drive engages the ring gear, turning the flywheel, which rotates the crankshaft, imparting the initial starting motion to the engine.

FOOT POUND (ft. lbs. or sometimes, ft.lb.): The amount of energy or work needed to raise an item weighing one pound, a distance of one foot.

FUSE: A protective device in a circuit which prevents circuit overload by breaking the circuit when a specific amperage is present. The device is constructed around a strip or wire of a lower amperage rating than the circuit it is designed to protect. When an amperage higher than that stamped on the fuse is present in the circuit, the strip or wire melts, opening the circuit.

GEAR RATIO: The ratio between the number of teeth on meshing gears.

GENERATOR: A device which converts mechanical energy into electrical energy.

HEAT RANGE: The measure of a spark plug's ability to dissipate heat from its firing end. The higher the heat range, the hotter the plug fires.

HUB: The center part of a wheel or gear.

HYDROCARBON (HC): Any chemical compound made up of hydrogen and carbon. A major pollutant formed by the engine as a byproduct of combustion.

HYDROMETER: An instrument used to measure the specific gravity of a solution.

INCH POUND (inch lbs.; sometimes in.lb. or in. lbs.): One twelfth of a foot pound.

INDUCTION: A means of transferring electrical energy in the form of a magnetic field. Principle used in the ignition coil to increase voltage.

INJECTOR: A device which receives metered fuel under relatively low pressure and is activated to inject the fuel into the engine under relatively high pressure at a predetermined time.

INPUT SHAFT: The shaft to which torque is applied, usually carrying the driving gear or gears.

INTAKE MANIFOLD: A casting of passages or pipes used to conduct air or a fuel/air mixture to the cylinders.

JOURNAL: The bearing surface within which a shaft operates.

KEY: A small block usually fitted in a notch between a shaft and a hub to prevent slippage of the two parts.

MANIFOLD: A casting of passages or set of pipes which connect the cylinders to an inlet or outlet source.

MANIFOLD VACUUM: Low pressure in an engine intake manifold formed just below the throttle plates. Manifold vacuum is highest at idle and drops under acceleration.

MASTER CYLINDER: The primary fluid pressurizing device in a hydraulic system. In automotive use, it is found in brake and hydraulic clutch systems and is pedal activated, either directly or, in a power brake system, through the power booster.

MODULE: Electronic control unit, amplifier or igniter of solid state or integrated design which controls the current flow in the ignition primary circuit based on input from the pick-up coil. When the module opens the primary circuit, high secondary voltage is induced in the coil.

NEEDLE BEARING: A bearing which consists of a number (usually a large number) of long, thin rollers.

OHM:(Ω) The unit used to measure the resistance of conductor-to-electrical flow. One ohm is the amount of resistance that limits current flow to one ampere in a circuit with one volt of pressure.

OHMMETER: An instrument used for measuring the resistance, in ohms, in an electrical circuit.

OUTPUT SHAFT: The shaft which transmits torque from a device, such as a transmission.

OVERDRIVE: A gear assembly which produces more shaft revolutions than that transmitted to it.

OVERHEAD CAMSHAFT (OHC): An engine configuration in which the camshaft is mounted on top of the cylinder head and operates the valve either directly or by means of rocker arms.

OVERHEAD VALVE (OHV): An engine configuration in which all of the valves are located in the cylinder head and the camshaft is located in the cylinder block. The camshaft operates the valves via lifters and pushrods.

OXIDES OF NITROGEN (NOx): Chemical compounds of nitrogen produced as a byproduct of combustion. They combine with hydrocarbons to produce smog.

OXYGEN SENSOR: Used with the feedback system to sense the presence of oxygen in the exhaust gas and signal the computer which can reference the voltage signal to an air/fuel ratio.

PINION: The smaller of two meshing gears.

PISTON RING: An open-ended ring which fits into a groove on the outer diameter of the piston. Its chief function is to form a seal between the piston and cylinder wall. Most automotive pistons have three rings: two for compression sealing; one for oil sealing.

PRELOAD: A predetermined load placed on a bearing during assembly or by adjustment.

PRIMARY CIRCUIT: The low voltage side of the ignition system which consists of the ignition switch, ballast resistor or resistance wire, bypass, coil, electronic control unit and pick-up coil as well as the connecting wires and harnesses.

PRESS FIT: The mating of two parts under pressure, due to the inner diameter of one being smaller than the outer diameter of the other, or vice versa; an interference fit.

RACE: The surface on the inner or outer ring of a bearing on which the balls, needles or rollers move.

REGULATOR: A device which maintains the amperage and/or voltage levels of a circuit at predetermined values.

RELAY: A switch which automatically opens and/or closes a circuit.

RESISTANCE: The opposition to the flow of current through a circuit or electrical device, and is measured in ohms. Resistance is equal to the voltage divided by the amperage.

RESISTOR: A device, usually made of wire, which offers a preset amount of resistance in an electrical circuit.

RING GEAR: The name given to a ring-shaped gear attached to a differential case, or affixed to a flywheel or as part of a planetary gear set.

ROLLER BEARING: A bearing made up of hardened inner and outer races between which hardened steel rollers move.

ROTOR: 1. The disc-shaped part of a disc brake assembly, upon which the brake pads bear; also called, brake disc. 2. The device mounted atop the distributor shaft, which passes current to the distributor cap tower contacts.

SECONDARY CIRCUIT: The high voltage side of the ignition system, usually above 20,000 volts. The secondary includes the ignition coil, coil wire, distributor cap and rotor, spark plug wires and spark plugs.

SENDING UNIT: A mechanical, electrical, hydraulic or electromagnetic device which transmits information to a gauge.

SENSOR: Any device designed to measure engine operating conditions or ambient pressures and temperatures. Usually electronic in nature and designed to send a voltage signal to an on-board computer, some sensors may operate as a simple on/off switch or they may provide a variable voltage signal (like a potentiometer) as conditions or measured parameters change.

SHIM: Spacers of precise, predetermined thickness used between parts to establish a proper working relationship.

SLAVE CYLINDER: In automotive use, a device in the hydraulic clutch system which is activated by hydraulic force, disengaging the clutch.

SOLENOID: A coil used to produce a magnetic field, the effect of which is to produce work.

SPARK PLUG: A device screwed into the combustion chamber of a spark ignition engine. The basic construction is a conductive core inside of a ceramic insulator, mounted in an outer conductive base. An electrical charge from the spark plug wire travels along the conductive core and jumps a preset air gap to a grounding point or points at the end of the conductive base. The resultant spark ignites the fuel/air mixture in the combustion chamber.

SPLINES: Ridges machined or cast onto the outer diameter of a shaft or inner diameter of a bore to enable parts to mate without rotation.

TACHOMETER: A device used to measure the rotary speed of an engine, shaft, gear, etc., usually in rotations per minute.

THERMOSTAT: A valve, located in the cooling system of an engine, which is closed when cold and opens gradually in response to engine heating, controlling the temperature of the coolant and rate of coolant flow.

TOP DEAD CENTER (TDC): The point at which the piston reaches the top of its travel on the compression stroke.

TORQUE: The twisting force applied to an object.

TORQUE CONVERTER: A turbine used to transmit power from a driving member to a driven member via hydraulic action, providing changes in drive ratio and torque. In automotive use, it links the driveplate at the rear of the engine to the automatic transmission.

TRANSDUCER: A device used to change a force into an electrical signal.

TRANSISTOR: A semi-conductor component which can be actuated by a small voltage to perform an electrical switching function.

TUNE-UP: A regular maintenance function, usually associated with the replacement and adjustment of parts and components in the electrical and fuel systems of a vehicle for the purpose of attaining optimum performance.

TURBOCHARGER: An exhaust driven pump which compresses intake air and forces it into the combustion chambers at higher than atmospheric pressures. The increased air pressure allows more fuel to be burned and results in increased horsepower being produced.

VACUUM ADVANCE: A device which advances the ignition timing in response to increased engine vacuum.

VACUUM GAUGE: An instrument used to measure the presence of vacuum in a chamber.

VALVE: A device which control the pressure, direction of flow or rate of flow of a liquid or gas.

VALVE CLEARANCE: The measured gap between the end of the valve stem and the rocker arm, cam lobe or follower that activates the valve.

VISCOSITY: The rating of a liquid's internal resistance to flow.

VOLTMETER: An instrument used for measuring electrical force in units called volts. Voltmeters are always connected parallel with the circuit being tested.

WHEEL CYLINDER: Found in the automotive drum brake assembly, it is a device, actuated by hydraulic pressure, which, through internal pistons, pushes the brake shoes outward against the drums.

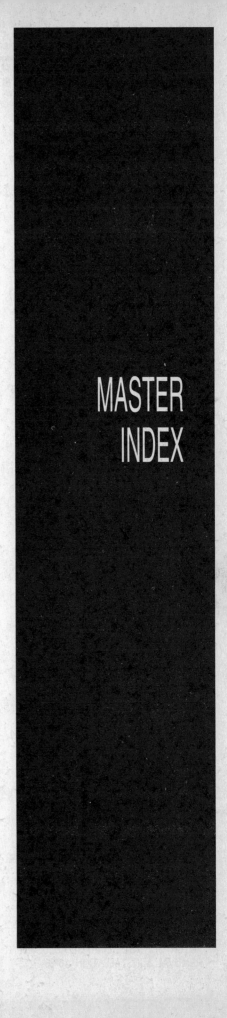

MASTER INDEX